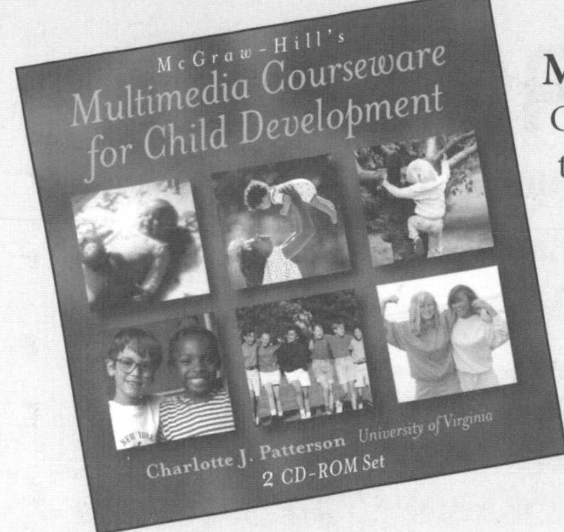

Multimedia Courseware for Child Development

Created by Charlotte J. Patterson of the University of Virginia, this 2 CD set is sure to enhance a student's journey through the child development course.

ISBN: 0-07-254580-1

This set is also available packaged with *Human Development* Ninth Edition.

Designed for student use, these interactive, video-based 2 CD-ROM sets bring the central phenomena and classic experiments in developmental psychology to life.

- Includes relevant video footage of classic and contemporary experiments, detailed viewing guides, challenging preview, follow-up exercises and interactive feedback, graphics, graduated developmental charts, a variety of hands-on projects, related websites, and navigation aids.

- Programmed in a modular format, the content focuses on integrating digital media to better explain physical, cognitive, social, and emotional development. Multimedia Courseware for Child Development deals with childhood and adolescence, while Multimedia Courseware for Adult Development deals with early, middle, and late adulthood.

Multimedia Courseware for Adult Development

Created by Carolyn Johnson of The Pennsylvania State University, this 2 CD set is sure to bring the study of adult development to life for your students.

ISBN: 0-07-251761-1

This set is also available packaged with *Human Development* Ninth Edition.

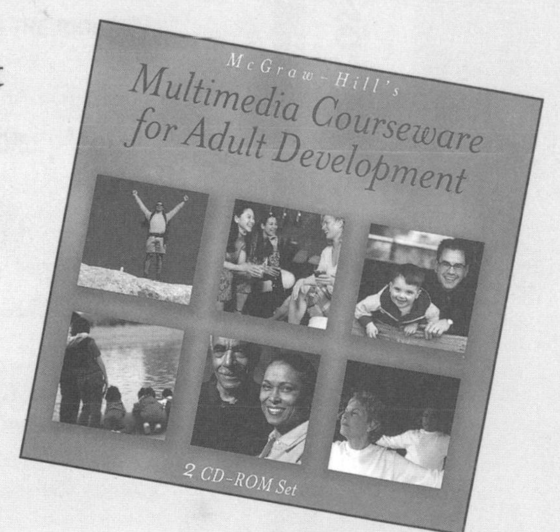

To find out more, please contact your McGraw-Hill representative, or visit us on the web at www.mhhe.com.

Human Development

9th Edition

Diane E. Papalia

Sally Wendkos Olds

Ruth Duskin Feldman

in consultation with

Dana Gross

Boston Burr Ridge, IL Dubuque, IA Madison, WI New York San Francisco St. Louis
Bangkok Bogotá Caracas Kuala Lumpur Lisbon London Madrid Mexico City
Milan Montreal New Delhi Santiago Seoul Singapore Sydney Taipei Toronto

HUMAN DEVELOPMENT, NINTH EDITION

Published by McGraw-Hill, a business unit of The McGraw-Hill Companies, Inc., 1221 Avenue of the Americas, New York, NY 10020.

Some ancillaries, including electronic and print components, may not be available to customers outside the United States.

This book is printed on acid-free paper.

International 2 3 4 5 6 7 8 9 0 VNH/VNH 0 9 8 7 6 5 4 3
Domestic 2 3 4 5 6 7 8 9 0 VNH/VNH 0 9 8 7 6 5 4 3

ISBN 0-07-282030-6
ISBN 0-07- 121501-8 (ISE)

Vice president and editor-in-chief: *Thalia Dorwick*
Publisher: *Stephen D. Rutter*
Senior sponsoring editor: *Rebecca H. Hope*
Developmental editor: *Sienne Patch*
Marketing manager: *Melissa Caughlin*
Project manager: *Richard H. Hecker*
Production supervisor: *Enboge Chong*
Media technology producer: *Ginger Bunn*
Manager, Design: *Laurie Entringer*
Cover/interior designer: *Maureen McCutcheon*
Art editor: *Jen DeVere*
Senior photo research coordinator: *Nora Agbayani*
Photo research: *Toni Michaels/PhotoFind, L.L.C.*
Senior supplement producer: *David A. Welsh*
Compositor: *The GTS Companies*/York, PA Campus
Typeface: 10.5/13 Minion
Printer: *Von Hoffmann Press*

The credits section for this book begins on page A-1 and is considered an extension of the copyright page.

Library of Congress Cataloging-in-Publication Data

Papalia, Diane E.
Human development / Diane Papalia, Sally Wendkos Olds, Ruth Duskin Feldman.-- 9th ed.
p. cm.
Includes bibliographical references and index.
ISBN 0-07-282030-6 (alk. paper) -- ISBN 0-07-121501-8 (ISE)
1. Developmental psychology. 2. Developmental psychobiology. I. Olds, Sally Wendkos. II. Feldman, Ruth Duskin. III. Title.

BF713.P35 2003
155--dc21

2003042019

INTERNATIONAL EDITION ISBN 0-07-121501-8

www.mhhe.com

About the Authors

As a professor, **Diane E. Papalia** taught thousands of undergraduates at the University of Wisconsin-Madison. She received her bachelor's degree, majoring in psychology, from Vassar College and both her master's degree in child development and family relations and her Ph.D. in life-span developmental psychology from West Virginia University. She has published numerous articles in such professional journals as *Human Development, International Journal of Aging and Human Development, Sex Roles, Journal of Experimental Child Psychology,* and *Journal of Gerontology.* Most of these papers have dealt with her major research focus, cognitive development from childhood through old age. She is especially interested in intelligence in old age and factors that contribute to the maintenance of intellectual functioning in late adulthood. She is a Fellow in the Gerontological Society of America. She is the coauthor of *A Child's World,* now in its ninth edition, with Sally Wendkos Olds and Ruth Duskin Feldman; of *Adult Development and Aging,* now in its second edition, with Harvey L. Sterns, Ruth Duskin Feldman, and Cameron J. Camp; of *Psychology* with Sally Wendkos Olds; and of *Child Development: A Topical Approach* with Dana Gross and Ruth Duskin Feldman.

Sally Wendkos Olds is an award-winning professional writer who has written more than 200 articles in leading magazines and is the author or coauthor of seven books addressed to general readers, in addition to the three textbooks she has coauthored with Dr. Papalia. Her newest book, *A Balcony in Nepal: Glimpses of a Himalayan Village,* describes her encounters with the people and way of life in a remote hill village in eastern Nepal. The updated and expanded third edition of her classic book *The Complete Book of Breastfeeding* was published in 1999. She is also the author of *The Working Parents' Survival Guide* and *The Eternal Garden: Seasons of Our Sexuality* and the coauthor of *Raising a Hyperactive Child* (winner of the Family Service Association of America National Media Award) and *Helping Your Child Find Values to Live By.* She has spoken widely on the topics of her books and articles to both professional and lay audiences, in person and on television and radio. She received her bachelor's degree from the University of Pennsylvania, where she majored in English literature and minored in psychology. She was elected to Phi Beta Kappa and was graduated summa cum laude.

Ruth Duskin Feldman is an award-winning writer and educator. With Diane E. Papalia and Sally Wendkos Olds, she coauthored the fourth, seventh, and eighth editions of *Human Development* and the eighth and ninth editions of *A Child's World.* She also is coauthor of *Adult Development and Aging* and of *Child Development: A Topical Approach.* A former teacher, she has developed educational materials for all levels from elementary school through college and has prepared ancillaries to accompany the Papalia-Olds books. She is author or coauthor of four books addressed to general readers, including *Whatever Happened to the Quiz Kids? Perils and Profits of Growing Up Gifted,* republished in 2000 by iUniverse. She has written for numerous newspapers and magazines, has lectured extensively, and has made national and local media appearances throughout the United States on education and gifted children. She received her bachelor's degree from Northwestern University, where she was graduated with highest distinction and was elected to Phi Beta Kappa.

To all those who have had an impact
on our own development—
our families and friends and teachers
who have nurtured us, challenged us,
taught us by their example,
provided support and companionship,
and been there for us over the years.

Dana Gross, chief consultant to this edition, is an associate professor of psychology at St. Olaf College. She received her bachelor's degree, majoring in psychology, from Smith College and her Ph.D. in child psychology from the Institute of Child Development at the University of Minnesota. Her broad teaching and research interests include perception, language, cognition, and social cognition, as well as cross-cultural child development. She has published articles in such professional journals as *Child Development, Cognitive Development, Educational Gerontology,* and the *International Journal of Behavioral Development* and has presented her work at numerous conferences. She has also published chapters in edited books, including *Developing Theories of Mind* and *Play & Culture Studies* (Vol. 5). In addition to membership in several national professional societies, Dr. Gross serves on the Governing Council of the Minnesota Psychological Association and is a founding member of its Division of Academic Psychology. Dr. Gross has prepared instructor's manuals and test banks for several McGraw-Hill textbooks and served as chief consultant on the previous edition of *Human Development* and the eighth and ninth editions of *A Child's World.* She is coauthor, with Dr. Papalia and Ruth Duskin Feldman, of *Child Development: A Topical Approach.*

Contents in Brief

Contents

Chapter 4 Physical Development During the First Three Years

Chapter 5 Cognitive Development During the First Three Years

Chapter 6 Psychosocial Development During the First Three Years

PART 3
Early Childhood

PART 4
Middle Childhood

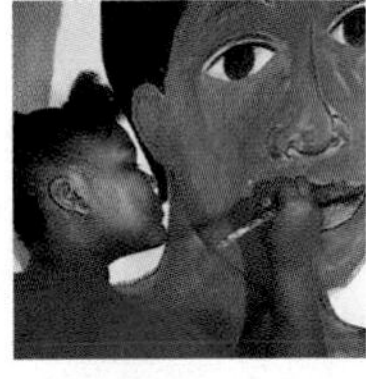

PART 6
Young Adulthood

Chapter 13
Physical and Cognitive Development in Young Adulthood

Chapter 14
Psychosocial Development in Young Adulthood

PART 7
Middle Adulthood

Chapter 15
Physical and Cognitive Development in Middle Adulthood

PART 9
The End of Life

Preface

In the previous, eighth edition, of *Human Development* we completely revamped the entire book—its design, content, and pedagogical features. In this ninth edition we have built on the innovations of the last edition, updating, consolidating, and fine-tuning. At the same time, we have sought to retain the engaging qualities of tone, style, and substance that have contributed to this book's popularity over the years.

Our Aims for This Edition

The primary aims of this ninth edition are the same as those of the first eight: to emphasize the continuity of development throughout the life span; to highlight the interrelationships among the physical, cognitive, and psychosocial realms of development; and to integrate theoretical, research-related, and practical concerns.

A special goal for this edition has been to *enhance coverage of the adult years* while *reducing overall length.* We have striven to make each chapter as concise and readable as possible, while still doing justice to the vast scope and significance of current theoretical and research work.

The Ninth Edition: What's New?

Organizational Changes

There are two major approaches to the study of human development: the *chronological approach* (describing all aspects of development at each period of life) and the *topical approach* (focusing on one aspect of development at a time). For this book we have chosen the *chronological* approach, which provides a sense of the multifaceted sweep of human development, as we get to know first the developing person-to-be in the womb, then the infant and toddler, then the young child, the schoolchild, the adolescent, the young adult, the adult at midlife, and the person in late adulthood.

In line with our chronological approach, we have divided this book into nine parts. After Part One, which introduces the study of human development, Parts Two through Eight discuss physical, cognitive, and psychosocial development during each of the periods of the life span, concluding with Part Nine, the end of life.

In this edition, we have given special consideration to the *opening and concluding sections.* To make sure that students pay proper attention to important concepts formerly covered in a prologue, we have integrated this material into appropriate sections of Chapter 1. And we have extended our coverage of death and bereavement, from an epilogue to a full chapter.

New Pedagogical Features

In addition to the engaging biographical *"Focus"* vignettes that begin each chapter (see the Visual Walk-Through following this preface), we now end each chapter with a *"Refocus" feature.* This series of interpretive questions encourages students to think back over major chapter themes and their application to the famous person described in the opening vignette. We have also replaced a few of the vignettes with more contemporary or more appropriate subjects.

In the unique *Learning System* introduced in the eighth edition, we have changed the periodic marginal "Consider this . . ." feature to "What's Your View?" The new title more sharply challenges students to think critically or to apply what they have learned. Also, *marginal definitions* of key terms have been shortened and simplified, where necessary, for ease of retention.

Content Changes

Because we believe that all parts of life are important, challenging, and full of opportunities for growth and change, we provide evenhanded treatment of all periods of the life span, taking care not to overemphasize some and slight others. In line with the growing recognition of human development as a rigorous scientific enterprise, we have *broadened the research base* of each chapter, especially the chapters on adulthood, more extensively than ever before, taking special pains to draw on the most recent information available. We have added many tables and figures and have updated statistics throughout.

This edition continues to expand our *cultural* and *historical* coverage, reflecting the diversity of the population in the United States and around the world and how cultures change across time. Our photo illustrations show an ever greater commitment to depicting this diversity.

Among the important topics given new or greatly revised or expanded coverage, chapter by chapter, are the following:

Chapter 1

- New section on historical contexts of development
- Revised section on the science of human development, including methodological advances
- Expansion of six principles of Baltes's life-span developmental approach, placed at end of chapter for emphasis and summation

Chapter 2

- Revised explanation of mechanistic and organismic models
- Revised discussion of Bandura's social learning (social cognitive) theory
- Ethological approach now discussed as part of broader evolutionary/sociobiological perspective
- Expanded discussion of cognitive neuroscience perspective
- Inclusion of qualitative research methods

Chapter 3

- Revised discussions of genetic imprinting, the nonshared environment, and autism, including Asperger's syndrome
- Updated discussion of prenatal environmental influences
- New Digging Deeper box on fetal welfare versus mothers' rights

Chapter 4

- Revised discussions of cesarean sections, low birthweight, infant mortality, sudden infant death syndrome, and infant feeding

Chapter 5

- Updated discussions of HOME (Home Observation for Measurement of the Environment) and infant information processing

Chapter 6

- New "Focus" vignette on the anthropologist Mary Catherine Bateson
- Revised and expanded material on emotions, including nonorganic failure to thrive
- Inclusion of Rothbart's Infant Behavior Questionnaire and Children's Behavior Questionnaire for measuring temperament
- Expanded discussion of the father's role, including factors contributing to "responsible fathering"
- Revised information on infant attachment
- New information on implications of infants' reactions to the "still-face" procedure
- New discussion of the "I-self" and "me-self"
- New information on effects of child care from the NICHD Early Child Care Research Network

Chapter 7

- Revised material on nutrition and obesity
- Updated information on the relationship between socioeconomic status and health
- Revised and updated information on causality, theory of mind, and Early Head Start

Chapter 8

- New "Focus" vignette on the writer Isabel Allende
- Updated material on cultural factors in parenting styles
- New Digging Deeper box on the case against corporal punishment

Chapter 9

- New "Focus" vignette on the polar explorer Ann Bancroft
- Updated information on obesity and asthma
- New Practically Speaking box on the homework debate
- Material on methods of teaching reading moved from box to text

Chapter 10

- New information on effects of joint custody, relational aggression, and sibling relationships in various cultures
- Revised discussion of bullies and of living with gay and lesbian parents
- Revised discussion of stress, including children's reactions to the September 11 terrorist attacks

Chapter 11

- New information on pubertal development and how family relations may affect it
- Updated information on nutrition, obesity, body image, eating disorders, and drug use
- New section on teenage suicide plus new Practically Speaking box on suicide prevention
- New section on implications of adolescents' time use
- Updated information on high school dropouts
- New Window on the World box on "pubilect" (teenage dialect)
- Material on working part time moved from box to text

Chapter 12

- Revised discussion of adolescent sexuality, with updated statistics
- Revised discussion of sex education, including abstinence programs
- Updated statistics on sexually transmitted diseases
- Revised information on adjustment to parental divorce, including the role of genetic factors

Chapter 13

- Updated health statistics
- New section on genetic influences on health
- Revised material on lifestyle factors and health

- Updated information on sexually transmitted diseases, assisted reproduction (moved from box to text), and college and work experiences
- New Practically Speaking box on sleep deprivation

Chapter 14

- Updated information on sexual attitudes and behaviors, marital and nonmarital lifestyles, and becoming parents

Chapter 15

- Updated material on health and influences on it
- Updated discussion of hormone replacement theory and phytoestrogens
- New material on breast cancer and hysterectomy
- Revised material on stress, including New Yorkers' reactions to the September 11 terrorist attacks

Chapter 16

- Revised information on parents' relationships with grown children, including the "cluttered nest"
- Critique of the presumed prevalence of the "sandwich generation"

Chapter 17

- Updated information on the aging population and on life expectancy, including regional, ethnic, and gender differences; material on centenarians moved from box to text
- Updated research findings on effects of dietary restriction on life extension
- Updated information on health status, influences on health, and health-threatening conditions, including Alzheimer's disease
- New Digging Deeper box: "Do 'Anti-Aging' Remedies Work?"

Chapter 18

- Updated material on religion and well-being in late adulthood
- Updated discussions of trends in late-life work, retirement, and living arrangements

Chapter 19

- New "Focus" vignette on Louisa May Alcott
- Expanded coverage of all topics
- New section on mourning a miscarriage
- New Digging Deeper box on "ambiguous loss"
- New Window on the World box on organ donation

Supplementary Materials

Human Development, ninth edition, is accompanied by a complete learning and teaching package, keyed into the Learning System. Each component of this package has been thoroughly revised and expanded to include important new course material.

For the Instructor

Instructor's Manual

Saundra K. Ciccarelli, Gulf Coast Community College

Designed specifically for the ninth edition, this manual contains materials and resources for the instructor's use in teaching topics from each of the nineteen chapters of the text. Each chapter in the *Instructor's Manual* begins with the Total Teaching Package Outline, a table that coordinates subject matter within the chapter with the various features in the manual, including the Guideposts for Study, lecture suggestions, classroom activities and demonstrations, film and video suggestions, and web resources. Also included is a detailed Chapter Outline with key terms and definitions as stated in the text; Guideposts for Study, which are also in the main text, as well as in the test bank and study guide; lecture openers; critical thinking exercises; essay questions and answers; activities; and ideas for independent study. Updated audio/visual resources, suggested readings, and web resources are also included. New to this edition of the *Instructor's Manual* are activities that are specifically geared to education majors and future nurses and health care workers. Also new to this edition is a section of observation, lab, and interview projects, which relate to each chapter's content. The *Instructor's Manual* is available on the instructor's side of the Online Learning Center (*http://www.mhhe.com/papaliah9*) and on the Instructor's Resource CD-ROM. It is also available in hard copy on request from your local McGraw-Hill representative.

Test Bank

Barbara Lane Radigan, Community College of Allegheny County

This comprehensive test bank includes a wide range of multiple-choice, fill-in-the-blank, critical thinking, and essay questions. Each chapter has approximately 100–125 test questions per chapter. Questions are organized around the Guideposts for Study, as presented in the main text. Each item is designated as factual, conceptual, or applied, and includes the answer, the appropriate Guidepost designation, the page in the main text where the information is located, and the question's level of difficulty.

The test bank is available in both printed and computerized format. The computerized test bank is available on the Instructor's Resource CD-ROM (IRCD), and is compatible with both Macintosh and Windows platforms. The program provides an editing feature that enables instructors to integrate their own questions, scramble items, and modify questions, as well as offering the instructor the option of implanting the following features unique to this program: Online Testing Program, Internet Testing, and Grade Management.

Instructor's Resource CD-ROM

This CD-ROM offers instructors the opportunity to customize McGraw-Hill materials to prepare for and create their lecture presentations. Among the resources included on the CD-ROM are the instructor's manual; the test bank in computerized, Word, and Rich Text formats; PowerPoint slides; as well as a link to the Online Learning Center, interactive exercises, and other useful features.

Visual Asset Database

Jasna Jovanovic, University of Illinois Urbana-Champaign

McGraw-Hill's Visual Assets Database is a password-protected online database of hundreds of multimedia resources for use in classroom presentations, including original video clips, audio clips, photographs, and illustrations—all designed to bring to life concepts in developmental psychology. In addition to offering ready-made multimedia presentations for every stage of the lifespan, the VAD's search engine and unique "My Modules" program allows instructors to select from the database's resources to create their own customized presentations, or "modules." These customized presentations are saved in an instructor's folder on the McGraw-Hill site, and the presentation is then run directly from the VAD to the Internet-equipped classroom.

Annual Editions: Human Development (03/04)

Karen L. Freiberg, University of Maryland

This annually updated reader is a compilation of carefully selected articles from magazines, newspapers, and journals. This title is supported by Dushkin Online, a student website that provides study support and tools and links to related sites. An *Instructor's Manual* and *Using Annual Editions in the Classroom* are available as support materials for instructors.

Sources: Notable Selections in Human Development (2/e)

Rhett Diessner and Jacquelyne K. Tiegs, Lewis Clark State College

This book includes more than forty book excerpts, classic articles, and research studies that have shaped the study of human development and our contemporary understanding of it. Students of human development will appreciate the broad range of coverage and the accessibility of the material within this volume. An accompanying *Instructor's Manual* is also available.

Online Learning Center

http://www.mhhe.com/papaliah9

This extensive website, designed specifically to accompany *Human Development*, offers a variety of resources for both instructors and students. The password-protected instructor side of the site includes the *Instructor's Manual*, PowerPoint slides, links to professional resources, and interactive activities. The Online Learning Center also includes PowerWeb. PowerWeb is a password-protected website that includes current articles, weekly updates with assessment, informative and timely world news, web links, interactive exercises, and much more.

For the Student

Study Guide

Saundra K. Ciccarelli, Gulf Coast Community College

This comprehensive study guide is organized by chapter and integrates the Guideposts for Study found in the main text. It is designed to help students make the most of their time when reviewing the material in the text and studying for exams. The study guide includes a variety of self-tests, including true/false, multiple-choice, and essay questions.

Online Learning Center

http://www.mhhe.com/papaliah9

This extensive website, designed to accompany *Human Development,* offers a wide variety of resources for both instructors and students. The student side of the website includes the Guideposts for Study, chapter outlines, and a variety of self-quizzes. The site also includes a glossary of the key terms in the book, a list of helpful and informative websites related to topics highlighted in the text, an Internet guide, a guide to doing electronic research, and a study skills primer. The Online Learning Center also includes PowerWeb. PowerWeb is a password-protected website that includes current articles, weekly updates with assessment, informative and timely world news, web links, interactive exercises, and much more. A PowerWeb access card is free with each copy of the text.

Multimedia Courseware for Child Development

Charlotte J. Patterson, University of Virginia

This interactive CD-ROM covers central phenomena and classic experiments in the field of child development. Included are hours of video footage of classic and contemporary experiments, detailed viewing guides, challenging follow-up and interactive feedback, graduated developmental charts, a variety of hands-on projects, and related websites and navigation aids.

Multimedia Courseware for Adult Development

Carolyn Johnson, Pennsylvania State University

This interactive CD-ROM showcases video clips central to phenomena in adult development. The CD-ROM includes hours of video footage of classic and contemporary experiments, detailed viewing guides, challenging follow-up and interactive feedback, graphics, graduated developmental charges, a variety of hands-on projects, and related websites and navigation aids.

Acknowledgments

Once again, Dana Gross, Ph.D., associate professor of psychology at St. Olaf College in Northfield, Minnesota, has served as consultant for this edition, helping us keep up with the latest findings in a rapidly expanding field. Dr. Gross not only uncovered many new references, but also participated in the planning of this revision and read and commented on the manuscript. She also prepared the links to relevant websites for material related to boxes in each chapter, to be found on the Online Learning Center. Her current classroom experience provides a valuable perspective on the needs of students today. In addition, as a parent of two young children, she rounds out an author team that consists of the parent of an adolescent and two grandparents whose children are now young and middle-aged adults. (Detailed information about Dr. Gross's career can be found on the dedication page.)

We would like to express our gratitude to the many friends and colleagues who, through their work and their interest, helped us clarify our thinking about human development. We are especially grateful for the valuable help given by those who reviewed the eighth edition of *Human Development* and the manuscript drafts of this ninth edition, whose evaluations and suggestions helped greatly in the preparation of this new edition. These reviewers, who are affiliated with both two- and four-year institutions are as follows:

Gary L. Allen,
University of South Carolina

Margarita Azmitia,
University of California–Santa Cruz

Daniel E. Bontempo,
The Pennsylvania State University

Yiwei Chen,
Bowling Green State University

Jennie Dilworth,
Georgia Southern University

Raymond E. Eilenstine,
Southeastern Community College

Beverly A. Farrow,
Marshall University

Lynn Haller,
Morehead State University

Sarah Huyvaert,
Eastern Michigan University

Francene Kaplan,
Cypress Community College

Rosalyn M. King,
Northern Virginia Community College

Jerry A. Martin,
University of North Florida

Pamela S. Maykut,
Viterbo University

Jim Hail,
McLennan Community College

Rosemary Rosser,
University of Arizona–Tucson

Jill Schultz,
Frederick Community College

Kaia Skaggs,
Eastern Michigan University

Marilynn Thomas,
Prince George's Community College

Stephen A. Truhon,
Winston-Salem State University

Lori Werdenschlag,
Lyndon State College

We appreciate the strong support we have had from our publisher through the years. We would like to express special thanks to Rebecca Hope, our sponsoring editor; Sienne Patch, developmental editor; Rick Hecker, project manager; Laurie McGee, copy editor; Dave Welsh, supplement producer; Maggie Barbieri, print supplement manager; and our research assistant, Leilani Gjellstad Endicott. Toni Michaels used her sensitivity, her interest, and her good eye to find outstanding photographs. Maureen McCutcheon produced a strikingly new and attractive book design.

As always, we welcome and appreciate comments from readers, which help us continue to improve *Human Development.*

Diane E. Papalia
Sally Wendkos Olds
Ruth Duskin Feldman

Visual Walk-Through

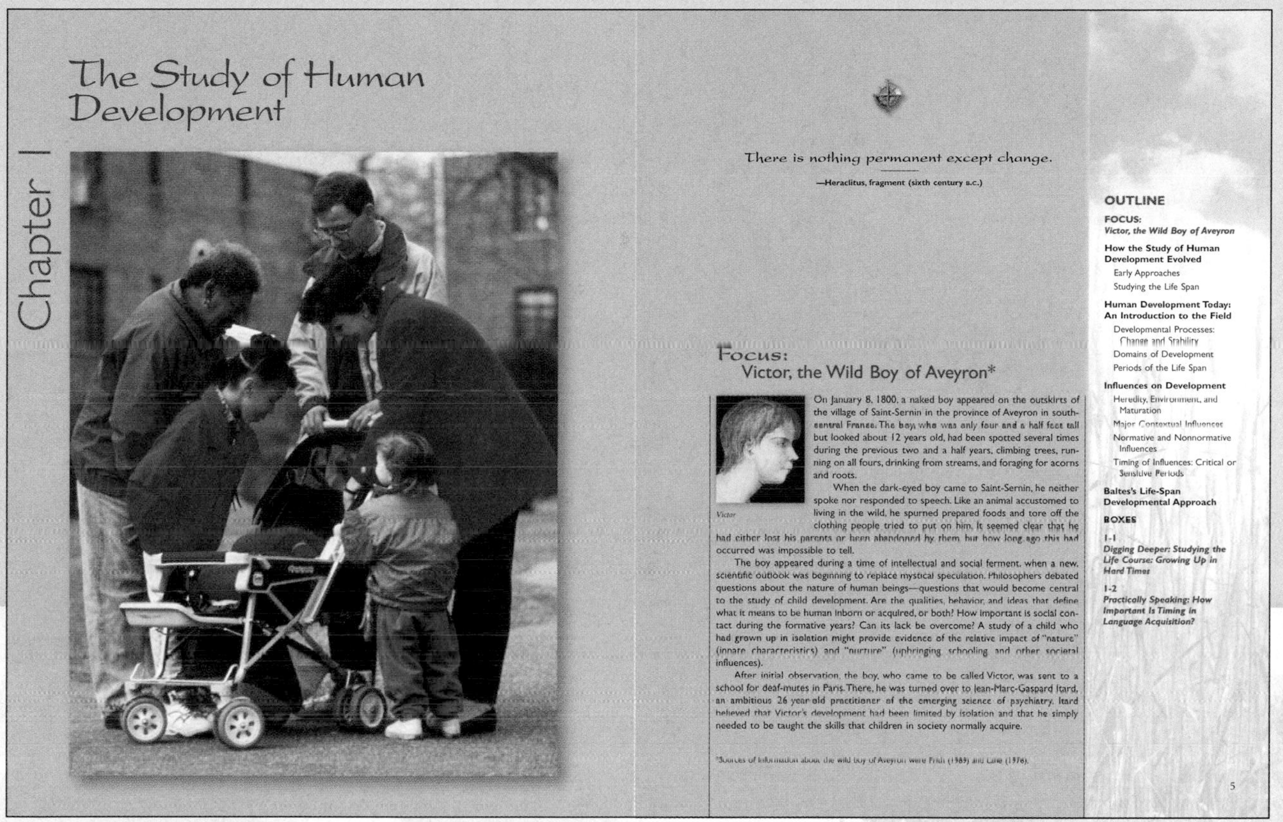

The Study of Human Development

Chapter 1

There is nothing permanent except change.

—Heraclitus, fragment (sixth century B.C.)

OUTLINE

FOCUS:
Victor, the Wild Boy of Aveyron

How the Study of Human Development Evolved
Early Approaches
Studying the Life Span

Human Development Today: An Introduction to the Field
Developmental Processes: Change and Stability
Domains of Development
Periods of the Life Span

Influences on Development
Heredity, Environment, and Maturation
Major Contextual Influences
Normative and Nonnormative Influences
Timing of Influences: Critical or Sensitive Periods

Baltes's Life-Span Developmental Approach

BOXES

1-1
Digging Deeper: Studying the Life Course: Growing Up in Hard Times

1-2
Practically Speaking: How Important Is Timing in Language Acquisition?

Focus:
Victor, the Wild Boy of Aveyron*

Victor

On January 8, 1800, a naked boy appeared on the outskirts of the village of Saint-Sernin in the province of Aveyron in south-central France. The boy, who was only four and a half feet tall but looked about 12 years old, had been spotted several times during the previous two and a half years, climbing trees, running on all fours, drinking from streams, and foraging for acorns and roots.

When the dark-eyed boy came to Saint-Sernin, he neither spoke nor responded to speech. Like an animal accustomed to living in the wild, he spurned prepared foods and tore off the clothing people tried to put on him. It seemed clear that he had either lost his parents or been abandoned by them, but how long ago this had occurred was impossible to tell.

The boy appeared during a time of intellectual and social ferment, when a new, scientific outlook was beginning to replace mystical speculation. Philosophers debated questions about the nature of human beings—questions that would become central to the study of child development. Are the qualities, behavior, and ideas that define what it means to be human inborn or acquired, or both? How important is social contact during the formative years? Can its lack be overcome? A study of a child who had grown up in isolation might provide evidence of the relative impact of "nature" (innate characteristics) and "nurture" (upbringing, schooling, and other societal influences).

After initial observation, the boy, who came to be called Victor, was sent to a school for deaf-mutes in Paris. There, he was turned over to Jean-Marc-Gaspard Itard, an ambitious 26 year old practitioner of the emerging science of psychiatry. Itard believed that Victor's development had been limited by isolation and that he simply needed to be taught the skills that children in society normally acquire.

*Sources of information about the wild boy of Aveyron were Frith (1989) and Lane (1976).

5

A special goal for this edition, like the previous one, has been to increase its pedagogical value. The single-column format has made it possible to introduce a comprehensive, unified Learning System, which will help students focus their reading and review and retain what they learn.

As always, we seek to make the study of human development come alive by telling illustrative stories about actual incidents in the lives of real people. In this edition, each chapter opens with a fascinating biographical vignette from a period in the life of a well-known person (such as Elvis Presley, Isabel Allende, Anne Frank, Jackie Robinson, John Glenn, and Mahatma Gandhi) or a classic case (such as the Wild Boy of Aveyron and Charles Darwin's diary of his son's first year). The subjects of these vignettes are people of diverse national and ethnic origins, whose experiences dramatize important themes in the chapter. We believe students will enjoy and identify with these stories, which lead directly into the body of the chapter, are woven into its fabric, and are revisited in the new Refocus feature at the end of each chapter. These vignettes, along with the shorter true anecdotes that appear throughout the book—some of them about the author's own children and grandchildren—underline the fact that there is no "average" or "typical" human being, that each person is an individual with a unique personality and a unique set of life circumstances. They are reminders that whenever we talk about human development, we talk about real people in a real world.

Learning System

The Learning System forms the conceptual framework of each chapter and is carried through all text supplements. It has the following four parts.

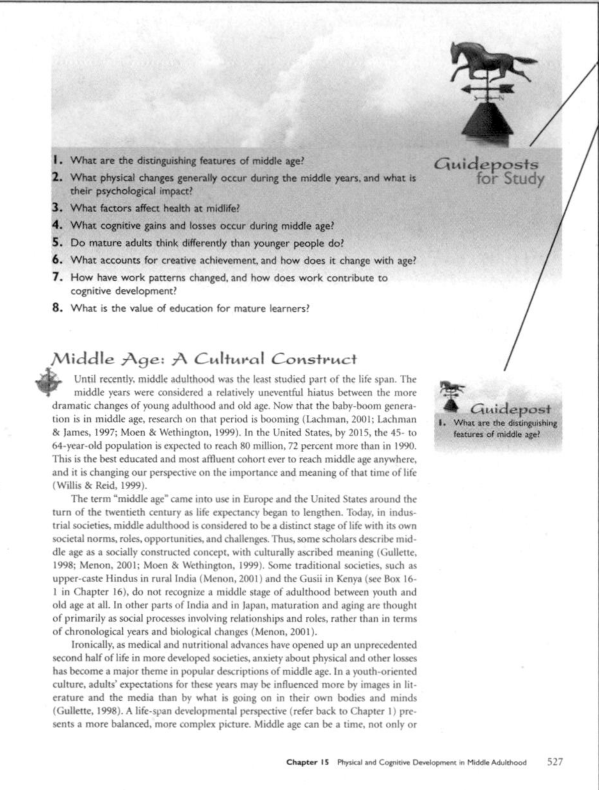

1. What are the distinguishing features of middle age?
2. What physical changes generally occur during the middle years, and what is their psychological impact?
3. What factors affect health at midlife?
4. What cognitive gains and losses occur during middle age?
5. Do mature adults think differently than younger people do?
6. What accounts for creative achievement, and how does it change with age?
7. How have work patterns changed, and how does work contribute to cognitive development?
8. What is the value of education for mature learners?

Middle Age: A Cultural Construct

Guidepost
1. What are the distinguishing features of middle age?

Until recently, middle adulthood was the least studied part of the life span. The middle years were considered a relatively uneventful hiatus between the more dramatic changes of young adulthood and old age. Now that the baby-boom generation is in middle age, research on that period is booming (Lachman, 2001; Lachman & James, 1997; Moen & Wethington, 1999). In the United States, by 2015, the 45- to 64-year-old population is expected to reach 80 million, 72 percent more than in 1990. This is the best educated and most affluent cohort ever to reach middle age anywhere, and it is changing our perspective on the importance and meaning of that time of life (Willis & Reid, 1999).

The term "middle age" came into use in Europe and the United States around the turn of the twentieth century as life expectancy began to lengthen. Today, in industrial societies, middle adulthood is considered to be a distinct stage of life with its own societal norms, roles, opportunities, and challenges. Thus, some scholars describe middle age as a socially constructed concept, with culturally ascribed meaning (Gullette, 1998; Menon, 2001; Moen & Wethington, 1999). Some traditional societies, such as upper-caste Hindus in rural India (Menon, 2001) and the Gusii in Kenya (see Box 16-1 in Chapter 16), do not recognize a middle stage of adulthood between youth and old age at all. In other parts of India and in Japan, maturation and aging are thought of primarily as social processes involving relationships and roles, rather than in terms of chronological years and biological changes (Menon, 2001).

Ironically, as medical and nutritional advances have opened up an unprecedented second half of life in more developed societies, anxiety about physical and other losses has become a major theme in popular descriptions of middle age. In a youth-oriented culture, adults' expectations for these years may be influenced more by images in literature and the media than by what is going on in their own bodies and minds (Gullette, 1998). A life-span developmental perspective (refer back to Chapter 1) presents a more balanced, more complex picture. Middle age can be a time, not only or

Chapter 15 Physical and Cognitive Development in Middle Adulthood 527

Guideposts for Study

These topical questions, similar to Learning Objectives, are first posted near the beginning of each chapter to capture students' interest and motivate them to look for answers as they read. The questions are broad enough to form a coherent outline of each chapter's content, but specific enough to invite careful study. Each Guidepost is repeated in the margin at the beginning of the section that deals with the topic in question and is repeated in the Chapter Summary to facilitate study.

Checkpoints

These more detailed marginal questions, placed at or near the end of major sections of text, enable students to test their understanding of what they have read. Students should be encouraged to stop and review any section for which they cannot answer one or more Checkpoints.

sports are important but that she is not athletic, she will lose self-esteem no matter how much praise she gets from others.

Children who are socially withdrawn or isolated may be overly concerned about their performance in social situations. They may attribute rejection to their own personality deficiencies, which they believe they are helpless to change. Rather than trying new ways to gain approval, they repeat unsuccessful strategies or just give up. (This is similar to the "helpless pattern" in younger children, described in Chapter 8.) Children with high self-esteem, by contrast, tend to attribute failure to factors outside themselves or to the need to try harder. If initially unsuccessful, they persevere, trying new strategies until they find one that works (Erdley et al., 1997).

Checkpoint

Can you . . .

- ✔ Discuss how the self-concept develops in middle childhood?
- ✔ Compare Erikson's and Harter's findings about sources of self-esteem?
- ✔ Describe how the "helpless pattern" can affect children's reactions to social rejection?

Emotional Growth

As children grow older, they are more aware of their own and other people's feelings. They can better regulate their emotional expression in social situations, and they can respond to others' emotional distress (Saarni et al., 1998).

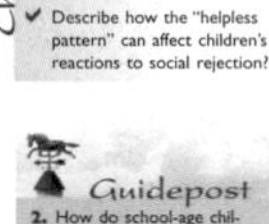

Guidepost
2. How do school-age children show emotional growth?

By age 7 or 8, shame and pride, which depend on awareness of the implications of their actions and on what kind of socialization children have received, affect their opinion of themselves (Harter, 1993, 1996). Increasingly, children can verbalize conflicting emotions (see Table 10-1). As Lisa says, "Most of the boys at school are pretty yukky. I don't feel that way about my little brother Jason, although he does get on my nerves. I love him but at the same time, he also does things that make me mad. But I control my temper, I'd be ashamed of myself if I didn't" (Harter, 1996, p. 208).

Children become more empathic and more inclined to prosocial behavior in middle childhood. Prosocial behavior is a sign of positive adjustment. Prosocial children tend to act appropriately in social situations, to be relatively free from negative emotion, and to cope with problems constructively (Eisenberg, Fabes, & Murphy, 1996).

Control of negative emotions is an aspect of emotional growth. Children learn what makes them angry, fearful, or sad and how other people react to a display of these

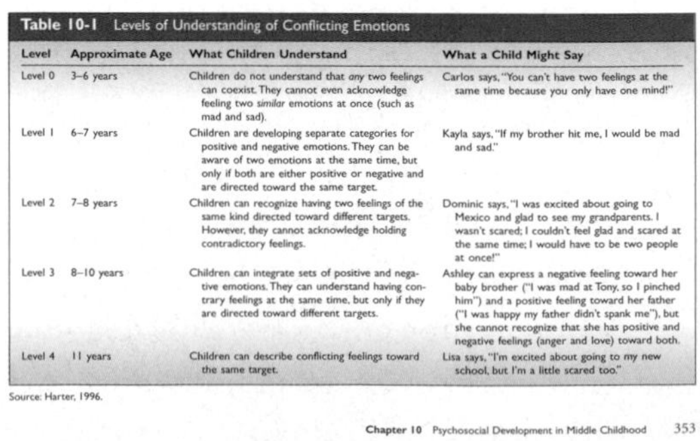

Table 10-1 Levels of Understanding of Conflicting Emotions

Level	Approximate Age	What Children Understand	What a Child Might Say
Level 0	3–6 years	Children do not understand that *any* two feelings can coexist. They cannot even acknowledge feeling two *similar* emotions at once (such as mad and sad).	Carlos says, "You can't have two feelings at the same time because you only have one mind!"
Level 1	6–7 years	Children are developing separate categories for positive and negative emotions. They can be aware of two emotions at the same time, but only if both are either positive or negative and are directed toward the same target.	Kayla says, "If my brother hit me, I would be mad and sad."
Level 2	7–8 years	Children can recognize having two feelings of the same kind directed toward different targets. However, they cannot acknowledge holding contradictory feelings.	Dominic says, "I was excited about going to Mexico and glad to see my grandparents. I wasn't scared; I couldn't feel glad and scared at the same time; I would have to be two people at once!"
Level 3	8–10 years	Children can integrate sets of positive and negative emotions. They can understand having contrary feelings at the same time, but only if they are directed toward different targets.	Ashley can express a negative feeling toward her baby brother ("I was mad at Tony, so I pinched him") and a positive feeling toward her father ("I was happy my father didn't spank me"), but she cannot recognize that she has positive and negative feelings (anger and love) toward both.
Level 4	11 years	Children can describe conflicting feelings toward the same target.	Lisa says, "I'm excited about going to my new school, but I'm a little scared too."

Source: Harter, 1996.

Chapter 10 Psychosocial Development in Middle Childhood 353

In *surrogate motherhood,* a fertile woman is impregnated by the prospective father, usually by artificial insemination. She carries the baby to term and gives the child to the father and his mate. Surrogate motherhood is in legal limbo; courts in most states view surrogacy contracts as unenforceable, and some states have either banned the practice or placed strict conditions on it. The American Academy of Pediatrics (AAP) Committee on Bioethics (1992) recommends that surrogacy be considered a tentative preconception adoption agreement in which the surrogate is the sole decision maker before the birth. The AAP committee also recommends a prebirth agreement on the period of time in which the surrogate may assert her parental rights.

Perhaps the most objectionable aspect of surrogacy, aside from the possibility of forcing the surrogate to relinquish the baby, is the payment of money. The creation of a "breeder class" of poor and disadvantaged women who carry the babies of the well-to-do strikes many people as wrong. Similar concerns have been raised about payment for donor eggs. Exploitation of the would-be parents is an issue, too (Gabriel, 1996).

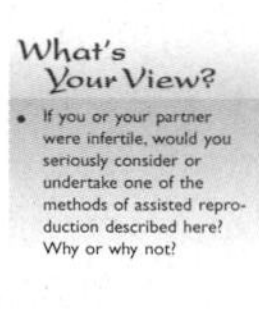

What's Your View?

- If you or your partner were infertile, would you seriously consider or undertake one of the methods of assisted reproduction described here? Why or why not?

How do children conceived by artificial means turn out? Among babies born in Western Australia between 1993 and 1997, those conceived by IVF or ICSI were twice as likely to show major birth defects during the first year as infants conceived naturally (Hansen, Kurinczuk, Bower, & Webb, 2002). It is not known whether these increased risks are due to the fertility procedures themselves or to characteristics connected with infertility. There is no evidence of adverse cognitive effects from IVF, other than those associated with the increased risk of premature or multiple births (Saunders, Spensley, Munro, & Halasz, 1996). Socially and emotionally, artificially conceived children tend to be well adjusted. Two longitudinal studies—one of 34 children conceived by IVF (but genetically related to both parents) and the other of 37 children conceived by DI—found little or no difference in socioemotional development at age 12 between these children and naturally conceived or adopted children (Golombok, MacCallum, & Goodman, 2001; Golombok, MacCallum, Goodman, & Rutter, 2002).

Checkpoint

Can you . . .

- ✔ Discuss ways to control the spread of STDs?
- ✔ Identify several causes of male and female infertility?
- ✔ Describe several means of assisted reproduction, and discuss issues they raise?

One thing seems certain: as long as there are people who want children but are unable to conceive or bear them, human ingenuity and technology will come up with ways to satisfy their need.

COGNITIVE DEVELOPMENT

Perspectives on Adult Cognition

Guidepost

3. What is distinctive about adult thought and intelligence?

Common sense tells us that adults think differently from children or adolescents. They hold different kinds of conversations, understand more complicated material, and use their broader experience to solve practical problems. Is common sense correct? Developmental theorists and researchers have studied adult cognition from a variety of perspectives. Some investigators, such as K. Warner Schaie, take a stage approach, seeking to identify what is distinctive about the way adults think, as Piaget did for children's thinking. Other investigators, such as Robert Sternberg, focus on types or aspects of intelligence, overlooked by psychometric tests, that tend to come to the fore in adulthood. One current theory highlights the role of emotion in intelligent behavior.

Beyond Piaget: The Shift to Postformal Thought

Although Piaget described the stage of formal operations as the pinnacle of cognitive achievement, some developmental scientists maintain that changes in cognition extend beyond that stage. According to Piaget's critics, formal reasoning is not the only, and perhaps not even the most important, capability of mature thought (Moshman, 1998). Research and theoretical work since the 1970s suggest that mature thinking may

472 **Part 6** Young Adulthood

What's Your View?

These periodic marginal questions challenge students to interpret, apply, or critically evaluate information presented in the text.

Summary and Key Terms

As in previous editions, the Chapter Summaries are organized by the major topics in the chapter. In this edition, the Guidepost questions appear under the appropriate major topics. Each Guidepost is followed by a series of brief statements restating the most important points that fall under it, thus creating a self-testing question-answer format. Students should be encouraged to try to answer each Guidepost question before reading the summary material that follows. Key Terms are now listed under each Guidepost summary with the pages on which their definitions can be found.

SUMMARY AND KEY TERMS

The Search for Identity

Guidepost **1.** How do adolescents form an identity?

- A central concern during adolescence is the search for identity, which has occupational, sexual, and values components. Erik Erikson described the psychosocial conflict of adolescence as *identity versus identity confusion.* The "virtue" that should arise from this crisis is *fidelity.*
- James Marcia, in research based on Erikson's theory, described four identity statuses with differing combinations of crisis and commitment: identity achievement, foreclosure, moratorium, and identity diffusion.
- Researchers differ on whether girls and boys take different paths to identity formation. Although some research suggests that girls' self-esteem tends to fall in adolescence, later research does not support that finding.
- Ethnicity is an important part of identity. Minority adolescents seem to go through stages of ethnic identity development much like Marcia's identity statuses.

identity *(425)*
identity versus identity confusion *(425)*
identity statuses *(427)*
crisis *(427)*
commitment *(427)*
identity achievement *(427)*
foreclosure *(428)*
moratorium *(428)*
identity diffusion *(428)*

Sexuality

Guidepost **2.** What determines sexual orientation?

- Sexual orientation appears to be influenced by an interaction of biological and environmental factors and may be at least partly genetic.

sexual orientation *(430)*

Guidepost **3.** What sexual practices are common among adolescents, and what leads some teenagers to engage in risky sexual behavior?

- Sexual behaviors are more liberal than in the past. Teenage sexual activity involves risks of pregnancy and sexually transmitted disease. Adolescents at greatest risk are those who begin sexual activity early, have multiple partners, do not use contraceptives, and are ill-informed about sex.
- Regular condom use is the best safeguard for sexually active teens.
- Comprehensive sex education programs delay sexual initiation and encourage contraceptive use. Abstinence-only programs have not been effective.
- Many teenagers get misleading information about sexuality from the media.

sexually transmitted diseases (STDs) *(433)*

Guidepost **4.** How common are sexually transmitted diseases and teenage pregnancy, and what are their usual outcomes?

- Rates of sexually transmitted diseases (STDs) in the United States are among the highest in the industrialized world; one in three cases occurs in adolescents. STDs can be transmitted by oral sex as well as intercourse. They are more likely to develop undetected in girls than in boys.
- Teenage pregnancy and birthrates in the United States have declined but are still highest in the industrialized world. Most of the pregnancies are unintended, and most of the births are to unmarried mothers.
- Teenage childbearing often has negative outcomes. Teenage mothers and their families tend to suffer ill health and financial hardship, and the children often suffer from ineffective parenting.

Relationships with Family, Peers, and Adult Society

Guidepost **5.** How typical is "adolescent rebellion"?

- Although relationships between adolescents and their parents are not always smooth, full-scale adolescent rebellion is unusual.

adolescent rebellion *(440)*

Guidepost **6.** How do adolescents relate to parents, siblings, and peers?

- Adolescents in the United States, who have a large amount of discretionary time, spend an increasing amount of it with peers, but relationships with parents continue to be close and influential, especially among some ethnic minorities.
- Family interactions change during the teenage years. There is more intimacy, but also more conflict over issues of autonomy. Conflict with parents tends to be most frequent during early adolescence and most intense during mid-adolescence. Authoritative parenting is associated with the most positive outcomes.
- Effects of divorce and single parenting on adolescents' development depend on the way they affect family atmosphere. Genetic factors may affect the way young adolescents adapt to divorce.
- Effects of maternal employment depend on such factors as the presence or absence of the other parent, how closely parents monitor adolescents' activity, and the mother's workload. A mother's working may help shape attitudes toward gender roles.
- Economic stress affects relationships in both single-parent and two-parent families.
- Relationships with siblings tend to become more equal and more distant during adolescence.
- The peer group can have both positive and negative influences. Adolescents who are rejected by peers tend to have the greatest adjustment problems.
- Friendships, especially among girls, become more intimate and supportive in adolescence.

Guidepost **7.** What are the root causes of antisocial behavior and juvenile delinquency, and what can be done to reduce these and other risks of adolescence?

- Chronic delinquency is associated with multiple interacting risk factors, including ineffective parenting, school failure, peer influence, neighborhood influences, and low socioeconomic status. Programs that attack such risk factors from an early age have had success.

Chapter 12 Psychosocial Development in Adolescence 453

Other Special Features in This Edition

This edition includes three kinds of boxed material.

"Digging Deeper" Boxes

These boxes explore in depth important, cutting-edge, or controversial research-related issues mentioned more briefly in the text. Some of these include new or significantly expanded or updated discussions of fetal welfare versus mothers' rights, the case against corporal punishment, anti-aging remedies, and ambiguous loss.

BOX 3-2

Digging Deeper
Fetal Welfare versus Mothers' Rights

A Wisconsin woman persists in using cocaine while pregnant. A juvenile court orders her unborn child placed in protective custody by forcing the expectant mother into inpatient treatment. The Wisconsin Supreme Court later holds that she was wrongfully detained (Lewin, 1997).

A South Carolina hospital routinely tests the urine of pregnant women suspected to be using illegal drugs and reports the evidence to police. Ten women sue the hospital after being arrested. They argue that the urine tests constitute an unconstitutional search of their persons (Greenhouse, 2000b).

In Chicago, Cook County officials try to force a mother to have a cesarean delivery that doctors say is needed to protect her fetus. Before the dispute can be resolved in court, the woman gives birth normally—to a healthy boy ("Woman Delivers," 1993).

In all these cases, the issue is the conflict between protection of a fetus and a woman's right to privacy or to make her own decisions about her body. It is tempting to require a pregnant woman to adopt practices that will ensure her baby's health, or to stop or punish her if she doesn't. But what about her personal freedom? Can civil rights be abrogated for the protection of the unborn?

The argument about the right to choose abortion, which rests on similar grounds, is far from settled. But the examples just given deal with a different aspect of the problem. What can or should society do about a woman who does *not* choose abortion, but instead goes on carrying her baby while engaging in behavior destructive to it, or refuses tests or treatment that medical providers consider essential to its welfare?

Ingesting Harmful Substances Does a woman have the right to knowingly ingest a substance, such as alcohol or another drug, which can permanently damage her unborn child, as Abel Dorris's birth mother did? Some advocates for fetal rights think it should be against the law for pregnant women to smoke or use alcohol, even though these activities are legal for other adults. Other experts argue that incarceration for substance abuse is unworkable and self-defeating. They say that expectant mothers who have a drinking or drug problem need education and treatment, not prosecution (Marwick, 1997, 1998).

Since 1985 at least 240 women in thirty-five states have been prosecuted for using illegal drugs or alcohol during pregnancy, even though no state legislature has criminalized such activity (Nelson & Marshall, 1998). Most of the cases were dismissed or the convictions overturned ("States Look," 1998; Terry, 1996), but one South Carolina woman received an eight-year prison sentence for criminal child neglect for using crack cocaine during her pregnancy. The U.S. Supreme Court declined to hear an appeal ("Condon Pleased," 1997; "Supreme Court Ruling," 1998). In 1998, South Dakota and Wisconsin adopted laws permitting pregnant women who abuse alcohol or drugs to be involuntarily confined or committed to treatment programs, and similar legislation was pending in several other states ("States Look," 1998).

The wind may be starting to shift, however. In March 2001, the U.S. Supreme Court invalidated the South Carolina hospital's urine testing policy. Criticism of the

Women addicted to heroin or to opiates such as morphine and codeine are likely to bear premature babies who will be addicted to the same drugs. Prenatally exposed newborns are restless and irritable and often have tremors, convulsions, fever, vomiting, and breathing difficulties (Cobrinick, Hood, & Chused, 1959; Henly & Fitch, 1966; Ostrea & Chavez, 1979). They cry often, are less alert and less responsive than other babies (Strauss, Lessen-Firestone, Starr, & Ostrea, 1975), and tend to show acute withdrawal symptoms and sleep disturbances during the neonatal period, requiring prompt treatment (O'Brien & Jeffery, 2002; Wagner, Katikaneni, Cox, & Ryan, 1998).

At 1 year, these infants are likely to show somewhat slowed psychomotor development (Bunikowski et al., 1998). In early childhood they weigh less than average, are shorter, are less well adjusted, and score lower on tests of perceptual and learning abilities (G. Wilson, McCreary, Kean, & Baxter, 1979). These children tend not to do well in school, to be unusually anxious in social situations, and to have trouble making friends (Householder, Hatcher, Burns, & Chasnoff, 1982).

96 **Part 2** Beginnings

"Window on the World" Boxes

This boxed feature offers focused glimpses of human development in societies other than our own (in addition to the cultural coverage in the main body of the text). These boxes highlight the fact that people grow up, live, and thrive in many different kinds of cultures, under many different influences. Among the new, significantly updated, or expanded topics are teenage dialect and organ donation.

BOX 11-2

Window on the World

Pubilect: The Dialect of Adolescence

"That guy's hot!"
"She's fine!"
"Chill!"
"Let's bounce!"

Adolescents' conversation is mainly about the people and events in their everyday world (Labov, 1992). They use slang (nonstandard speech) to label people ("dork" or "loser"), to pronounce positive or negative judgments ("That's cool!" or "What a beast!"), and to describe alcohol or drug-related activity ("She's wasted" or "He's blazed").

The Canadian linguist Marcel Danesi (1994)* argues that adolescent speech is more than just slang (which, of course, adults can use, too). Instead, it constitutes a dialect of its own: *pubilect*, "the social dialect of puberty" (p. 97).

Pubilect is more than an occasional colorful expression. It is the primary mode of verbal communication among teenagers, by which they differentiate themselves from adults. As they approach puberty, youngsters absorb this dialect from slightly older peers. Like any other linguistic code, pubilect serves to strengthen group identity and to shut outsiders (adults) out. Teenage vocabulary is characterized by rapid change. Although some of its terms have entered common discourse, adolescents keep inventing new ones all the time.

Analysis of recorded samples of adolescent conversation reveals several key features of pubilect. First, it is an *emotive* code. Through exaggerated tone, slow and deliberate delivery, prolonged stress, accompanying gestures, and vulgar interjections, it draws attention to feelings and attitudes ("Yeah, riiight!" "Well, duuuh!"). Such emotive utterances seem to constitute about 65 percent of adolescent speech. The use of fillers, such as the word *like*, as well as the typical pattern of narrative intonation, in which each phrase or sentence seems to end with a question mark, reflects unconscious uncertainty and serves to draw the listener into the speaker's state of mind.

A second feature of pubilect is its *connotative* function. Teenagers coin descriptive words (or extend the meaning of existing words) to convey their view of their world and the people in it—often, in highly metaphorical ways. A person does not need a dictionary to figure out the meanings of such expressions as "space cadet" and "ditz." Such terms provide a ready lexicon for quick, automatic value judgments about others.

In the United States, there is not just a single youth culture, but many subcultures. Vocabulary may differ by gender, ethnicity, age, geographical region, neighborhood (city, suburban, or rural) and type of school (public or private) (Labov, 1992). Also, pubilect is *clique-coded:* it varies from one clique to another. "Druggies" and "jocks" engage in different kinds of activities, which form the main subjects of their conversation. This talk, in turn, cements bonds within the clique. Males use verbal dueling to assert power. Contenders for leadership trade insults and clever retorts in an effort to symbolically gain the upper hand in front of the group.

A study of teenage speech patterns in Naples, Italy, suggests that similar features may emerge "in any culture where teenagerhood constitutes a distinct social category" (Danesi, 1994, p. 123). Neapolitan teenagers use "mmmm" much as U.S. teenagers use "like": "Devo, mmmm, dire che, mmmm, non capisco, mmmm, . . ." ("I have, mmmm, to say that, mmmm, I don't understand, mmmm, . . ."). Exaggerated tone and rising intonation at the ends of phrases are also common. The Italian young people have terms roughly equivalent to the English "cool" (*togo*), "loser" (*grasta*), and "dork" or "nerd" (*secchione*). Other investigators report that adolescents in Milan, Bologna, and other northern Italian cities speak "the language of rock and roll." This cultural borrowing—the result of wide dissemination of English-language television channels, such as MTV—may well be creating a "symbolic universe" for teenagers around the world (Danesi, 1994, p. 123).

What's Your View?

Can you remember "pubilect" expressions from your own adolescence? When and why did you use such expressions? What was their effect on others your age? On adults?

Check It Out:

For more information on this topic, go to http://www.mhhe.com/papaliah9, where you will find a link to a website called "American Slanguages."

*Unless otherwise referenced, the source of this discussion is Danesi, 1994.

2. *Argumentativeness:* Adolescents are constantly looking for opportunities to try out—and show off—their newfound formal reasoning abilities. They often become argumentative as they marshal facts and logic to build a case for, say, staying out late.
3. *Indecisiveness:* Adolescents can keep many alternatives in mind at the same time, but because of their inexperience, they lack effective strategies for choosing among

406 **Part 5** Adolescence

Practically Speaking

Sleep Deprivation

BOX 13-1

If you have ever experienced jet lag—fatigue due to rapid time change during a cross-country or overseas flight—you know how it feels to have your *circadian rhythms* disrupted. Circadian rhythms are daily cycles of physiological and behavioral changes (such as falling asleep and waking up) that are linked to the cycles of light and dark in nature. These rhythmic cycles are governed by a biological clock in the brain, which may be genetically based. They go on even in the absence of natural external cues—for example, in a windowless room that is kept constantly light or constantly dark (Vitaterna, Takahashi, & Turek, 2001).

Human beings can override their circadian rhythms by choosing when and how long they will sleep (for example, by setting an alarm clock). Normally, when the light-dark cycle changes (as in daylight savings time or travel across time zones), the internal clock will adjust. But when the sleep-wake cycle is seriously and chronically out of phase with circadian rhythms, health, safety, and productivity may suffer (Vitaterna et al., 2001).

Adverse health effects may include gastrointestinal and cardiovascular problems, altered hormonal functioning, and depression (Monk, 2000; Vitaterna et al., 2001). In a large-scale poll by the National Sleep Foundation (2001), respondents said they were more likely to make mistakes, to become impatient or aggravated when waiting, or to get upset with their children or others when they had not had enough sleep the night before. Sleep deprivation can be lethal on the road; drowsy drivers cause an estimated 3.6 percent of all fatal crashes (Peters et al., 1994). Sleep deprivation may even lead to premature aging. In one study, 36 hours of sleep deprivation in young adults produced effects on the prefrontal cortex—a part of the brain heavily involved in working memory and verbal fluency—similar to those found in non-sleep-deprived 60-year-olds (Harrison, Horne, & Rothwell, 2000).

Many young adults, especially those who work abnormal hours, go without adequate sleep. Night shift workers may find it difficult to fall asleep in the daytime, when it is light out and family activities are going on (Monk, 2000). Furthermore, not everyone has the same pattern of circadian rhythms. Some people call themselves "morning people" or "evening people" because they are more alert at one time or the other. Chronobiologists—scientists who study circadian rhythms—call such people "larks" and "owls." If work or school schedules force an "owl" to get up early every morning or a "lark" to regularly burn the midnight oil, trouble can ensue (McEnany & Lee, 2000).

Adequate sleep improves learning of complex motor skills (Walker, Brakefield, Morgan, Hobson, & Stickgold, 2002) and consolidates previous learning. Even a short nap can prevent burnout—oversaturation of the brain's perceptual processing systems (Mednick et al., 2002). Sleep deprivation tends to impair verbal learning (Horne, 2000), some aspects of memory (Harrison & Horne, 2000b), and speech articulation (Harrison & Horne, 1997), and to increase distractibility (Blagrove, Alexander, & Horne, 1995). Impairment seems to be selective, mainly affecting dull, monotonous tasks. Complex tasks that involve decisions tend to call forth greater motivation and effort to make up for lost sleep (Horne, 2000). However, high-level decision making can be impaired, especially in emergency situations that require innovation, flexibility, avoidance of distraction, realistic risk assessment, metamemory, and communication skills (Harrison & Horne, 2000a).

Brain imaging studies show how compensatory changes in the brain can help maintain initial cognitive performance after short-term loss of sleep. In an experiment on 13 healthy young adults, the prefrontal cortex was more responsive during verbal memory tasks after 35 sleepless hours than after normal sleep. In addition, while sleep-deprived participants showed reduced verbal recall, activation of the parietal lobes, not normally involved in verbal tasks, tended to lessen the impairment (Drummond et al., 2000). However, chronic sleep deprivation (less than six hours a night for three or more nights) can seriously worsen cognitive performance even when a person is not aware of it (Van Dongen, Maislin, Mullington, & Dinges, 2003).

What's Your View?

Do the findings about sleep deprivation and circadian rhythms suggest desirable changes in the workplace?

Check It Out:

For more information on this topic, go to http://www.mhhe.com/papaliah9, where you'll find links to information on sleep and sleep deprivation.

Nutrition and Cholesterol The saying "You are what you eat" sums up the importance of nutrition for physical and mental health. What people eat affects how they look, how they feel, and how likely they are to get sick.

Eating habits play an important part in heart disease—which, as Arthur Ashe's story shows, is not necessarily limited to later life. People who eat a variety of fruits and vegetables, especially those rich in carotenoids (such as carrots, sweet potatoes,

Chapter 13 Physical and Cognitive Development in Young Adulthood 461

"Practically Speaking" Boxes

These boxes build bridges between academic study and everyday life by showing ways to apply research findings on various aspects of human development. Among the new, expanded, or substantially updated topics are the homework debate, suicide prevention, and sleep deprivation.

We also provide a number of other new and/or enhanced teaching and learning aids:

Part Overviews

At the beginning of each part, an overview introduces the period of life discussed in the chapters that follow.

Linkups to look for

The part overviews include bulleted lists that point to examples of the interaction of physical, cognitive, and psychosocial aspects of development.

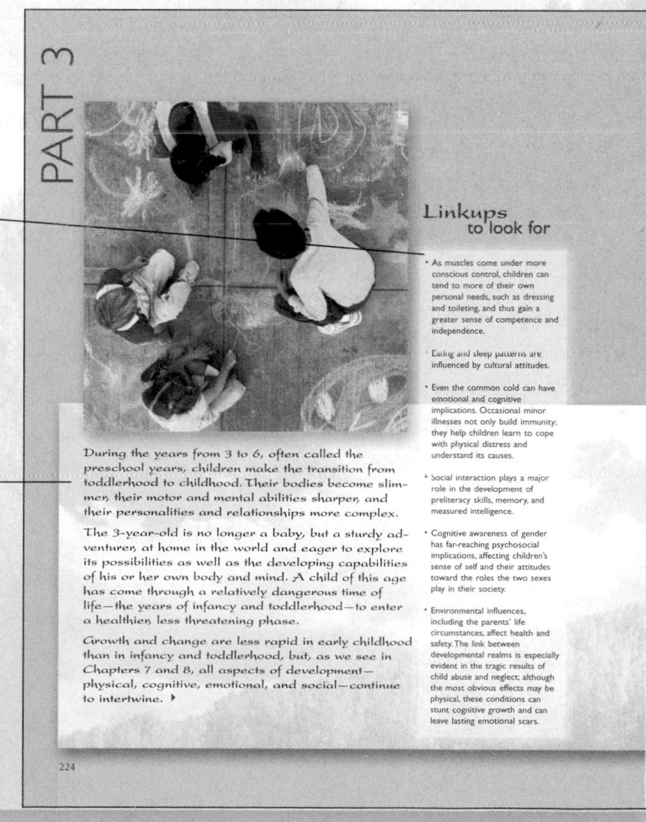

PART 3

During the years from 3 to 6, often called the preschool years, children make the transition from toddlerhood to childhood. Their bodies become slimmer, their motor and mental abilities sharper, and their personalities and relationships more complex.

The 3-year-old is no longer a baby, but a sturdy adventurer, at home in the world and eager to explore its possibilities as well as the developing capabilities of his or her own body and mind. A child of this age has come through a relatively dangerous time of life—the years of infancy and toddlerhood—to enter a healthier, less threatening phase.

Growth and change are less rapid in early childhood than in infancy and toddlerhood, but, as we see in Chapters 7 and 8, all aspects of development—physical, cognitive, emotional, and social—continue to intertwine.

Linkups to look for

- As muscles come under more conscious control, children can tend to more of their own personal needs, such as dressing and toileting, and thus gain a greater sense of competence and independence.
- Eating and sleep patterns are influenced by cultural attitudes.
- Even the common cold can have emotional and cognitive implications. Occasional minor illnesses not only build immunity; they help children learn to cope with physical distress and understand its causes.
- Social interaction plays a major role in the development of preliteracy skills, memory, and measured intelligence.
- Cognitive awareness of gender has far-reaching psychosocial implications, affecting children's sense of self and their attitudes toward the roles the two sexes play in their society.
- Environmental influences, including the parents' life circumstances, affect health and safety. The link between developmental realms is especially evident in the tragic results of child abuse and neglect; although the most obvious effects may be physical, these conditions can stunt cognitive growth and can leave lasting emotional scars.

224

Part Preview Tables

These tables, visually keyed to each chapter of the text, preview the main features of each period of development. The contents of the part preview tables are coordinated with Table 1-1 in Chapter 1, which summarizes major developments of each period of the life span.

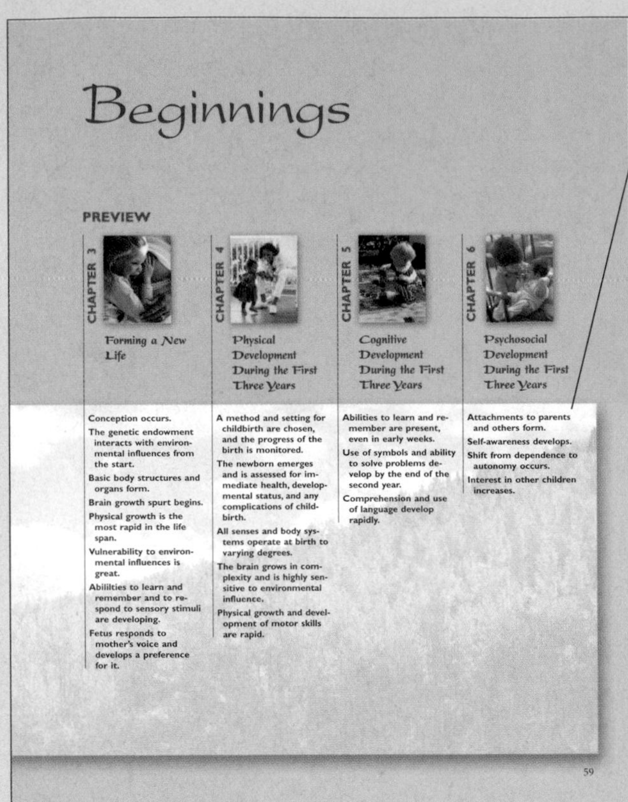

Beginnings

PREVIEW

CHAPTER 3	CHAPTER 4	CHAPTER 5	CHAPTER 6
Forming a New Life	Physical Development During the First Three Years	Cognitive Development During the First Three Years	Psychosocial Development During the First Three Years
Conception occurs. The genetic endowment interacts with environmental influences from the start. Basic body structures and organs form. Brain growth spurt begins. Physical growth is the most rapid in the life span. Vulnerability to environmental influences is great. Abililties to learn and remember and to respond to sensory stimuli are developing. Fetus responds to mother's voice and develops a preference for it.	A method and setting for childbirth are chosen, and the progress of the birth is monitored. The newborn emerges and is assessed for immediate health, developmental status, and any complications of childbirth. All senses and body systems operate at birth to varying degrees. The brain grows in complexity and is highly sensitive to environmental influence. Physical growth and development of motor skills are rapid.	Abilities to learn and remember are present, even in early weeks. Use of symbols and ability to solve problems develop by the end of the second year. Comprehension and use of language develop rapidly.	Attachments to parents and others form. Self-awareness develops. Shift from dependence to autonomy occurs. Interest in other children increases.

59

Chapter-Opening Outlines

At the beginning of each chapter, an outline previews the major topics included in the chapter.

Chapter-Opening Vignettes

Biographical vignettes from the lives of well-known people illustrate chapter themes.

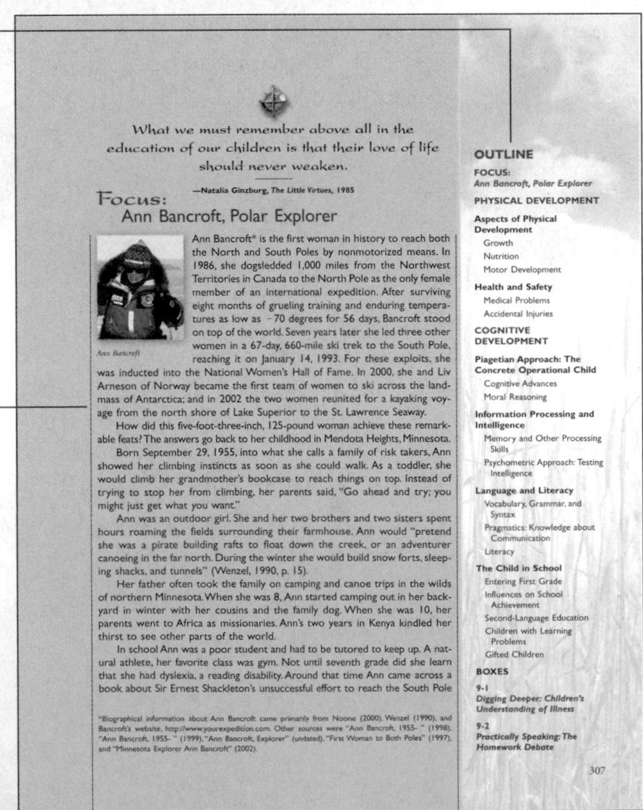

What we must remember above all in the education of our children is that their love of life should never weaken.

—Natalia Ginzburg, *The Little Virtues*, 1985

Focus: Ann Bancroft, Polar Explorer

Ann Bancroft

Ann Bancroft* is the first woman in history to reach both the North and South Poles by nonmotorized means. In 1986, she dogsledded 1,000 miles from the Northwest Territories in Canada to the North Pole as the only female member of an international expedition. After surviving eight months of grueling training and enduring temperatures as low as −70 degrees for 56 days, Bancroft stood on top of the world. Seven years later she led three other women in a 67-day, 660-mile ski trek to the South Pole, reaching it on January 14, 1993. For these exploits, she was inducted into the National Women's Hall of Fame. In 2000, she and Liv Arneson of Norway became the first team of women to ski across the landmass of Antarctica; and in 2002 the two women reunited for a kayaking voyage from the north shore of Lake Superior to the St. Lawrence Seaway.

How did this five-foot-three-inch, 125-pound woman achieve these remarkable feats? The answers go back to her childhood in Mendota Heights, Minnesota.

Born September 29, 1955, into what she calls a family of risk takers, Ann showed her climbing instincts as soon as she could walk. As a toddler, she would climb her grandmother's bookcase to reach things on top. Instead of trying to stop her from climbing, her parents said, "Go ahead and try; you might just get what you want."

Ann was an outdoor girl. She and her two brothers and two sisters spent hours roaming the fields surrounding their farmhouse. Ann would "pretend she was a pirate building rafts to float down the creek, or an adventurer canoeing in the far north. During the winter she would build snow forts, sleeping shacks, and tunnels" (Wenzel, 1990, p. 15).

Her father often took the family on camping and canoe trips in the wilds of northern Minnesota. When she was 8, Ann started camping out in her backyard in winter with her cousins and the family dog. When she was 10, her parents went to Africa as missionaries. Ann's two years in Kenya kindled her thirst to see other parts of the world.

In school Ann was a poor student and had to be tutored to keep up. A natural athlete, her favorite class was gym. Not until seventh grade did she learn that she had dyslexia, a reading disability. Around that time Ann came across a book about Sir Ernest Shackleton's unsuccessful effort to reach the South Pole

*Biographical information about Ann Bancroft came primarily from Noone (2000), Wenzel (1990), and Bancroft's website, http://www.yourexpedition.com. Other sources were "Ann Bancroft, 1955- " (1998), "Ann Bancroft, 1955- " (1999), "Ann Bancroft, Explorer" (undated), "First Woman to Both Poles" (1997), and "Minnesota Explorer Ann Bancroft" (2002).

307

Chapter Overviews

Near the beginning of each chapter, a brief overview of topics to be covered leads the reader smoothly from the opening vignette into the body of the chapter.

Space travel is a challenge even for the youngest and most physically fit adults. Not everyone can be an astronaut; candidates have to pass stringent physical and mental tests. Because of his age, Glenn was held to even tougher physical standards. An avid weight lifter and power walker, he was in superb physical condition. He passed the examinations with flying colors and then spent nearly 500 hours in training.

It was a clear, cloudless October day when, after two suspenseful delays, the shuttle *Discovery* lifted off with what the countdown commentator called "a crew of six astronaut heroes and one American legend." Three hours and ten minutes later, 342 miles above Hawaii, a beaming Glenn repeated his own historic words broadcast thirty-six years before: "Zero G, and I feel fine." On November 7, *Discovery* touched down at Cape Canaveral, and John Glenn, though weak and wobbly, walked out of the shuttle on his own two feet. Within four days he had fully recovered his balance and was completely back to normal.

Glenn's achievement proved that, at 77, he still had "the right stuff." His heroic exploit captured public imagination around the world. As Stephen J. Cutler, president of the Gerontological Society of America, put it, ". . . it's hard to imagine a better demonstration of the capabilities of older persons and of the productive contributions they can make" (1998, p. 1).

John Glenn epitomizes a new view of aging, challenging the formerly pervasive picture of old age as a time of inevitable physical and mental decline. On the whole, people today are living longer and better than at any time in history. In the United States, older adults as a group are healthier, more numerous, and younger at heart than ever before. With improved health habits and medical care, it is becoming harder to draw the line between the end of middle adulthood and the beginning of late adulthood. Many 70-year-olds act, think, and feel much as 50-year-olds did a decade or two ago.

Of course, not all older adults are models of vigor and zest. Indeed, Glenn's achievement is impressive precisely because it is unusual. As we will see in this chapter and the next, older adults vary greatly in health, education, income, occupation, and living arrangements. Like people of all ages, they are individuals with differing needs, desires, abilities, lifestyles, and cultural backgrounds.

In this chapter we begin by sketching demographic trends among today's older population. We look at the increasing length and quality of life in late adulthood and at theories and research on causes of biological aging. We examine physical changes and health. We then turn to cognitive development: changes in intelligence and memory, the emergence of wisdom, and the prevalence of continuing education in late life. In Chapter 18, we look at adjustment to aging and at changes in lifestyles and relationships. What emerges is a picture not of "the elderly" but of individual human beings—some needy and frail, but most of them independent, healthy, and involved.

After you have read and studied this chapter, you should be able to answer each of the following Guidepost questions. Look for them again in the margins, where they point to important concepts throughout the chapter. To check your understanding of these Guideposts, review the end-of-chapter summary. Checkpoints located at periodic spots throughout the chapter will help you verify your understanding of what you have read.

606 **Part 8** Late Adulthood

Key Terms

Whenever an important new term is introduced in the text, it is highlighted in boldface and defined, both in the text and, sometimes more formally, in the end-of-book glossary. Key terms and their definitions appear in the margins near the place where they are introduced in the text, and all key terms are listed in the Chapter Summaries and subject index.

perhaps because they lack the appropriate vocabulary or do not realize what information the other person needs (Plumert, Pick, Marks, Kintsch, & Wegesin, 1994).

Judgments about cause and effect also improve during middle childhood. When 5- to 12-year-olds were asked to predict how levers and balance scales would perform with varying numbers and weights of objects placed at varying distances from the center, the older children gave more correct answers than the younger children (Amsel, Goodman, Savoie, & Clark, 1996).

Categorization The ability to categorize helps children think logically. Categorization now includes such sophisticated abilities as *seriation, transitive inference,* and *class inclusion.* Children show that they understand **seriation** when they can arrange objects in a series according to one or more dimensions, such as weight (lightest to heaviest) or color (lightest to darkest). By 7 or 8, children can grasp the relationships among a group of sticks on sight and arrange them in order of size (Piaget, 1952).

seriation Ability to order items along a dimension.

Transitive inference is the ability to recognize a relationship between two objects by knowing the relationship between each of them and a third object. Catherine is shown three sticks: a yellow one, a green one, and a blue one. She is shown that the yellow stick is longer than the green one, and the green one is longer than the blue. Without physically comparing the yellow and blue sticks, she knows that the yellow one is longer than the blue one (Chapman & Lindenberger, 1988; Piaget & Inhelder, 1967).

transitive inference Understanding of the relationship between two objects by knowing the relationship of each to a third object.

Class inclusion is the ability to see the relationship between a whole and its parts. If preoperational children are shown a bunch of ten flowers—seven roses and three carnations—and are asked whether there are more roses or more flowers, they are likely to say there are more roses, because they are comparing the roses with the carnations rather than with the whole bunch. Not until the stage of concrete operations do children come to realize that roses are a subclass of flowers and that, therefore, there cannot be more roses than flowers (Flavell, 1963).

class inclusion Understanding of the relationship between a whole and its parts.

Inductive and Deductive Reasoning According to Piaget, children in the stage of concrete operations use **inductive reasoning.** Starting with observations about particular members of a class of people, animals, objects, or events, they then draw general conclusions about the class as a whole. ("My dog barks. So does Terry's dog and Melissa's dog. So it looks as if all dogs bark.") Inductive conclusions must be tentative because it is always possible to come across new information (a dog that does not bark) that does not support the conclusion.

inductive reasoning Type of logical reasoning that moves from particular observations about members of a class to a general conclusion about that class.

Deductive reasoning, which Piaget believed does not develop until adolescence, starts with a general statement (premise) about a class and applies it to particular members of the class. If the premise is true of the whole class, and the reasoning is sound, then the conclusion must be true: "All dogs bark. Spot is a dog. Spot barks."

deductive reasoning Type of logical reasoning that moves from a general premise about a class to a conclusion about a particular member or members of the class.

Researchers gave 16 inductive and deductive problems to 16 kindergartners, 17 second-graders, 16 fourth-graders, and 17 sixth-graders. The problems were designed so as *not* to call upon knowledge of the real world. For example, one deductive problem was: "All poggops wear blue boots. Tombor is a poggop. Does Tombor wear blue boots?" The corresponding inductive problem was: "Tombor is a poggop. Tombor wears blue boots. Do all poggops wear blue boots?" Contrary to Piagetian theory, second-graders (but not kindergartners) were able to correctly answer both kinds of problems, to see the difference between them, and to explain their responses, and they (appropriately) expressed more confidence in their deductive answers than in their inductive ones (Galotti, Komatsu, & Voelz, 1997).

What's Your View?

- How can parents and teachers help children improve their reasoning ability?

Conservation In solving various types of conservation problems, children in the stage of concrete operations can work out the answers in their heads; they do not have to measure or weigh the objects.

318 **Part 4** Middle Childhood

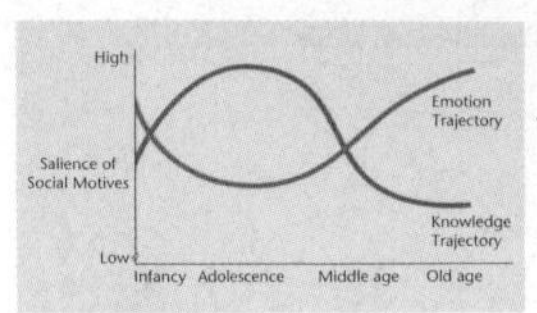

Figure 16-1
How motives for social contact change across the life span. According to socioemotional selectivity theory, infants seek social contact primarily for emotional comfort. In adolescence and young adulthood, people tend to be most interested in seeking information from others. From middle age on, emotional needs increasingly predominate. (Source: Carstensen, Gross, & Fung, 1997. Copyright 1997 by Springer Publishing Company. Reprinted with permission.)

main goals: (1) it is a source of information; (2) it helps people develop and maintain a sense of self; and (3) it is a source of pleasure and comfort, or emotional well-being. In infancy, the third goal, the need for emotional support, is paramount. From childhood through young adulthood, information-seeking comes to the fore. As young people strive to learn about their society and their place in it, strangers may well be the best sources of knowledge. By middle age, although information-seeking remains important (Fung, Carstensen, & Lang, 2001), the original, emotion-regulating function of social contacts begins to reassert itself. In other words, middle-aged people increasingly seek out others who make them feel good (see Figure 16-1). In research testing the theory, middle-aged and older adults placed greater emphasis than young adults on emotional affinity in choosing hypothetical social partners (Carstensen et al., 1999).

What's Your View?

- Does either the social convoy model or socioemotional selectivity theory fit your own experience and observations?

Relationships and Quality of Life

Most middle-aged and older adults are optimistic about the quality of their lives as they age, according to a mail survey of 1,384 adults ages 45 and older (NFO Research, Inc., 1999). Although they consider satisfying sexual relationships important to that quality of life, social relationships are even more important. About nine out of ten men and women say a good relationship with a spouse or partner is important to their quality of life, and so are close ties to friends and family.

As in young adulthood, relationships seem to be good for physical as well as mental health. In a longitudinal study of 32,624 healthy U.S. men between ages 42 and 77, socially isolated men—those who were not married, had fewer than six friends and relatives, and did not belong to religious or community groups—were more likely to die of cardiovascular disease, accidents, or suicide during the next four years than men with larger social networks (Kawachi et al., 1996).

On the other hand, midlife relationships also present demands that can be stressful and restrictive. These demands, and their psychological repercussions, tend to fall most heavily on women. A sense of responsibility and concern for others may impair a woman's well-being when problems or misfortunes beset her mate, children, parents, friends, or coworkers. This "vicarious stress" may help explain why middle-aged women are especially susceptible to depression and other mental health problems and why they tend to be unhappier with their marriages than men (Antonucci & Akiyama, 1997; Thomas, 1997).

This couple, glowing with health and enjoyment, seem to typify the connection between relationships and quality of life.

Chapter 16 Psychosocial Development in Middle Adulthood 583

Art Program

Many points in the text are underscored pictorially through carefully selected drawings, graphs, and photographs. The illustration program includes new figures and many full-color photographs.

New Feature to This Edition

Refocus

New to this edition, this series of interpretive questions encourages students to think back over major chapter themes and their application to the famous person described in the chapter opening vignette.

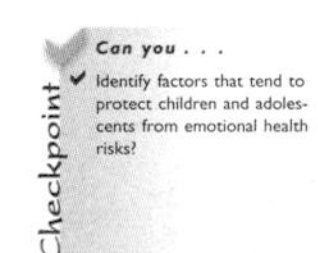

Checkpoint

Can you . . .

- Identify factors that tend to protect children and adolescents from emotional health risks?

negative childhood experiences do not necessarily determine the outcome of a person's life and that many children have the strength to navigate through the most difficult passages.

Refocus

- What do you think were major sources of self-esteem for Marian Anderson as a child? Would you estimate her self-esteem as high or low?
- How would you describe the family atmosphere in Anderson's home? Was her upbringing authoritarian, authoritative, or permissive?
- How did poverty, and the need for her mother to work outside the home, affect Anderson?
- How did Anderson's experience living in an extended-family household affect her?
- Was Anderson's choice of her first friend consistent with what you have learned in this chapter about children's choice of friends?
- Can you point to examples of resilience in Marian Anderson's childhood and adult life? What do you think accounted for her resilience?

Adolescence, too, is a stressful, risk-filled time—more so than middle childhood. Yet most adolescents develop the skills and competence to deal with the challenges they face, as we'll see in Chapters 11 and 12.

SUMMARY AND KEY TERMS

The Developing Self

Guidepost **1.** How do school-age children develop a realistic self-concept, and what contributes to self-esteem?

- The self-concept becomes more realistic during middle childhood, when, according to neo-Piagetian theory, children form representational systems.
- According to Erikson, the chief source of self-esteem is children's view of their productive competence. This "virtue" develops through resolution of the conflict of industry versus inferiority. According to Susan Harter's research, however, self-esteem arises primarily from self-evaluation and social support.

representational systems *(351)*
industry versus inferiority *(352)*

Guidepost **2.** How do school-age children show emotional growth?

- School-age children have internalized shame and pride and can better understand and control negative emotions.
- Empathy and prosocial behavior increase.
- Emotional growth is affected by parents' reactions to displays of negative emotions.

The Child in the Family

Guidepost **3.** How do parent-child relationships change in middle childhood?

- School-age children spend less time with, and are less close to, parents than before; but relationships with parents continue to be important. Culture influences family relationships and roles.
- Development of coregulation may affect the way a family handles conflicts and discipline.

coregulation *(355)*

Guidepost **4.** What are the effects of parents' work and of poverty on family atmosphere?

- The most important influence of the family environment on children's development comes from the atmosphere in the home.
- The impact of mothers' employment depends on many factors concerning the child, the mother's work and her feelings about it; whether she has a supportive mate; the family's socioeconomic status; and the kind of care the child receives.
- Homes with employed mothers tend to be more structured and more egalitarian than homes with at-home mothers. Maternal employment has a positive influence on school achievement in low-income families, but boys in middle-class families tend to do less well.

380 **Part 4** Middle Childhood

Human Development

PART I

Part 1 of this book is a guide map to the field of human development. It traces routes that investigators have followed in the quest for information about what makes children grow up the way they do, presents guideposts for studying how people continue to develop, points out the main directions students of development follow today, and poses questions about the best way to reach the destination: knowledge.

In Chapter 1, we describe how the study of human development has evolved and introduce its goals and basic concepts. We look at the many influences that help make each person a unique individual.

In Chapter 2, we introduce some of the most prominent theories about human development—theories that will come up in more detail later in this book. We explain how developmental scientists study people, what research methods they use, and what ethical standards govern their work. ▸

About Human Development

PREVIEW

CHAPTER 1

The Study of Human Development

- The scientific study of human development has evolved from studies of children to studies of the full life span.
- The study of human development seeks to describe, explain, predict, and modify behavior.
- Developmental scientists study change and stability in the physical, cognitive, and psychosocial domains.
- Development is subject to internal and external influences.
- Important contextual influences on development include family, neighborhood, socioeconomic status, culture, race/ethnicity, and history.

CHAPTER 2

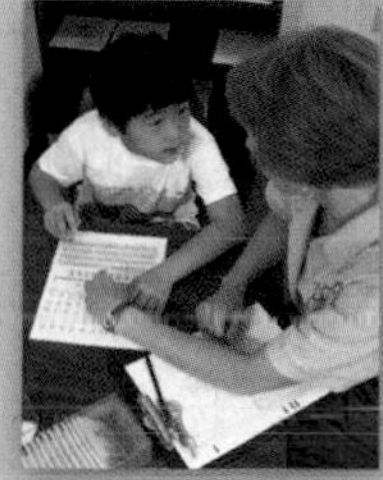

Theory and Research

- Theoretical perspectives on human development differ on three key issues: the relative importance of heredity and environment, whether development is active or passive, and whether it is continuous or occurs in stages.
- Major theoretical perspectives are psychoanalytic, learning, cognitive, evolutionary/sociobiological, and contextual. Various theories of development are influenced by these perspectives.
- Basic methods of data collection include self-reports, tests, and observation. Basic research designs may be qualitative or quantitative; they include case studies, ethnographic studies, correlational studies, and experiments.
- To study development, people may be followed over a period of time to see how they change, or people of different ages may be compared to see how they differ.

Chapter 1

The Study of Human Development

There is nothing permanent except change.

—Heraclitus, fragment (sixth century B.C.)

Focus: Victor, the Wild Boy of Aveyron*

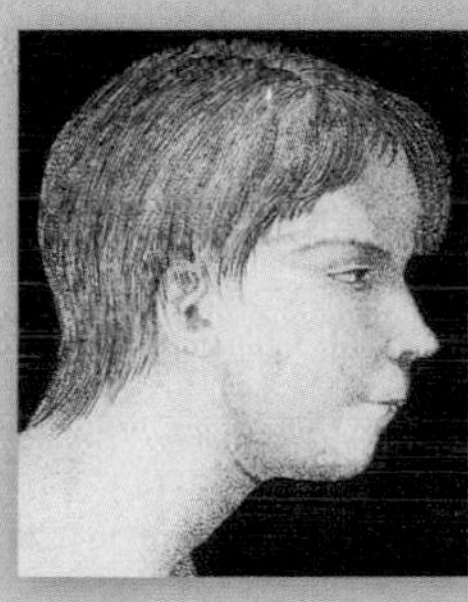

Victor

On January 8, 1800, a naked boy appeared on the outskirts of the village of Saint-Sernin in the province of Aveyron in south-central France. The boy, who was only four and a half feet tall but looked about 12 years old, had been spotted several times during the previous two and a half years, climbing trees, running on all fours, drinking from streams, and foraging for acorns and roots.

When the dark-eyed boy came to Saint-Sernin, he neither spoke nor responded to speech. Like an animal accustomed to living in the wild, he spurned prepared foods and tore off the clothing people tried to put on him. It seemed clear that he had either lost his parents or been abandoned by them, but how long ago this had occurred was impossible to tell.

The boy appeared during a time of intellectual and social ferment, when a new, scientific outlook was beginning to replace mystical speculation. Philosophers debated questions about the nature of human beings—questions that would become central to the study of child development. Are the qualities, behavior, and ideas that define what it means to be human inborn or acquired, or both? How important is social contact during the formative years? Can its lack be overcome? A study of a child who had grown up in isolation might provide evidence of the relative impact of "nature" (innate characteristics) and "nurture" (upbringing, schooling, and other societal influences).

After initial observation, the boy, who came to be called Victor, was sent to a school for deaf-mutes in Paris. There, he was turned over to Jean-Marc-Gaspard Itard, an ambitious 26-year-old practitioner of the emerging science of psychiatry. Itard believed that Victor's development had been limited by isolation and that he simply needed to be taught the skills that children in society normally acquire.

*Sources of information about the wild boy of Aveyron were Frith (1989) and Lane (1976).

OUTLINE

BOXES

Itard took Victor into his home and, during the next five years, gradually "tamed" him. Itard first awakened his pupil's ability to discriminate sensory experience through hot baths and dry rubs. He then moved on to painstaking, step-by-step training of emotional responses and instruction in moral and social behavior, language, and thought. The methods Itard used—based on principles of imitation, conditioning, and behavioral modification, all of which we discuss in Chapter 2—were far ahead of their time, and he invented many teaching devices used today.

But the education of Victor was not an unqualified success. The boy did make remarkable progress: he learned the names of many objects and could read and write simple sentences; he could express desires, obey commands, and exchange ideas. He showed affection, especially for Itard's housekeeper, Madame Guérin, as well as such emotions as pride, shame, remorse, and the desire to please. However, aside from uttering some vowel and consonant sounds, he never learned to speak. Furthermore, he remained focused on his own wants and needs and never seemed to lose his yearning "for the freedom of the open country and his indifference to most of the pleasures of social life" (Lane, 1976, p. 160). When the study ended, Victor—no longer able to fend for himself, as he had done in the wild—went to live with Madame Guérin until his death in his early forties in 1828.

Why did Victor fail to fulfill Itard's hopes for him? The boy may have been a victim of brain damage, autism (a brain disorder involving lack of social responsiveness), or severe early maltreatment. Itard's instructional methods, advanced as they were, may have been inadequate. Itard himself came to believe that the effects of long isolation could not be fully overcome, and that Victor may have been too old, especially for language learning.

Although Victor's story does not yield definitive answers to the questions Itard set out to explore, it is important because it was one of the first systematic attempts to study human development. Since Victor's time we have learned much about how people develop, but developmental scientists are still investigating such fundamental questions as the relative importance of inheritance and experience, and how they work together. Victor's story dramatizes the challenges and complexities of the scientific study of human development—the study on which you are about to embark.

In this introductory chapter, we describe how the field of human development has itself developed. We present the goals and basic concepts of the field today. We identify aspects of development and show how they interrelate. We summarize major developments during each period of life. We look at influences on development and the contexts in which it occurs.

After you have studied this chapter, you should be able to answer each of the following Guidepost questions. Look for them again in the margins, where they point to important concepts throughout the chapter. To check your understanding of these Guideposts, review the end-of-chapter summary. Checkpoints located at periodic spots throughout the chapter will help you verify your understanding of what you have read.

1. What is human development, and how has its study evolved?
2. What are the four goals of the scientific study of human development, and what do developmental scientists study?
3. What are three major domains and eight periods of human development?
4. What kinds of influences make one person different from another?
5. What are the six principles of the life-span developmental approach?

Guideposts for Study

How the Study of Human Development Evolved

From the moment of conception, human beings undergo processes of development. The field of **human development** is the scientific study of those processes. Developmental scientists—professionals who study human development—are interested in the ways in which people change throughout life, as well as in characteristics that remain fairly stable.

The formal study of human development is a relatively new field of scientific inquiry. Since the early nineteenth century, when Itard studied Victor, efforts to understand children's development have gradually expanded to include the whole life span.

Guidepost

1. What is human development, and how has its study evolved?

human development Scientific study of processes of change and stability throughout the human life span.

Early Approaches

Early forerunners of the scientific study of development were *baby biographies,* journals kept to record the early development of a child. One early journal, published in 1787 in Germany, contained Dietrich Tiedemann's (1897/1787) observations of his son's sensory, motor, language, and cognitive behavior during the first 2½ years. Typical of the speculative nature of such observations was Tiedemann's erroneous conclusion, after watching the infant suck more on a cloth tied around something sweet than on a nurse's finger, that sucking appeared to be "not instinctive, but acquired" (Murchison & Langer, 1927, p. 206).

It was Charles Darwin, originator of the theory of evolution, who first emphasized the *developmental* nature of infant behavior. In 1877 Darwin published notes on his son Doddy's sensory, cognitive, and emotional development during his first twelve months. Darwin's journal gave "baby biographies" scientific respectability; about thirty more were published during the next three decades (Dennis, 1936).

By the end of the nineteenth century, several important trends in the western world were preparing the way for the scientific study of development. Scientists had unlocked the mystery of conception and (as in the case of the wild boy of Aveyron) were arguing about the relative importance of "nature" and "nurture" (inborn characteristics and experiential influences). The discovery of germs and immunization made it possible for many more children to survive infancy. Laws protecting children from long workdays let them spend more time in school, and parents and teachers became more concerned with identifying and meeting children's developmental needs. The new science of psychology taught that people could understand themselves by learning what had influenced them as children. Still, this new discipline had far to go. For example, adolescence was not considered a separate period of development until the early twentieth century, when G. Stanley Hall, a pioneer in child study, published a popular (though unscientific) book called *Adolescence* (1904/1916).

Hall also was one of the first psychologists to become interested in aging. In 1922, at age 78, he published *Senescence: The Last Half of Life.* Six years later, Stanford University opened the first major scientific research unit devoted to aging. But not until a generation later did the study of aging blossom. Since the late 1930s a number of important long-term studies discussed in the second half of this book, such as those of K. Warner Schaie, George Vaillant, Daniel Levinson, and Ravenna Helson, have focused on intelligence and personality development in adulthood and old age.

Studying the Life Span

life-span development Concept of development as a lifelong process, which can be studied scientifically.

Today most developmental scientists recognize that development goes on throughout life. This concept of a lifelong process of development that can be studied scientifically is known as **life-span development.**

Life-span studies in the United States grew out of research designed to follow children through adulthood. The Stanford Studies of Gifted Children (begun in 1921 under the direction of Lewis M. Terman) trace the development of people (now in old age) who were identified as unusually intelligent in childhood. Other major studies that began around 1930—the Fels Research Institute Study, the Berkeley Growth and Guidance Studies, and the Oakland (Adolescent) Growth Study—have given us much information on long-term development.

Because human beings are complex, the study of life-span development is *interdisciplinary,* drawing on many fields, or disciplines. These include psychology, psychiatry, sociology, anthropology, biology, genetics (the study of inherited characteristics), family science (the study of family processes), education, history, philosophy, and medicine. This book reports on classic and current research in all these fields.

Checkpoint

Can you . . .

- ✔ Trace highlights in the evolution of the study of human development?
- ✔ Name at least six disciplines involved in the study of human development.

Human Development Today: An Introduction to the Field

Guidepost

2. What are the four goals of the scientific study of human development, and what do developmental scientists study?

As the field of human development became a scientific discipline, its goals evolved to include *description, explanation, prediction,* and *modification* of behavior. These four goals work together, as we can see by looking at language development. For example, to *describe* when most normal children say their first word or how large their vocabulary typically is at a certain age, developmental scientists observe large groups of children and establish norms, or averages, for behavior at various ages. They then attempt to *explain* what causes or influences the observed behavior—for example, how children acquire and learn to use language, and why a child like Victor, who may have lacked early exposure to language, did not learn to speak. This knowledge may make it possible to *predict* what language ability at a given age can tell about later behavior—for example, about the likelihood that a child with delayed language development might still be taught to speak. Finally, awareness of how language develops may be used to *modify* behavior, as Itard attempted to do in tutoring Victor.

The scientific study of human development is an ever-evolving endeavor. The questions that developmental scientists seek to answer, the methods they use, and the explanations they propose are not the same today as they were even twenty-five years ago. These shifts reflect progress in understanding, as new investigations build on or challenge earlier ones. They also reflect advances in technology and changes in cultural attitudes.

Sensitive instruments that measure eye movements, heart rate, blood pressure, muscle tension, and the like are turning up intriguing connections between biological functions and infant visual attentiveness and childhood intelligence. Cameras, videocassette recorders, and computers allow investigators to scan infants' facial expressions for early signs of emotions and to analyze how mothers and babies communicate. Advances in neuroscience and brain imaging now make it possible to probe the mysteries of temperament, to pinpoint the sources of logical thought, and to compare a normally aging brain with the brain of a person with dementia.

Increasingly, research findings have direct application to child rearing, education, health, and social policy. For example, learning about childhood memory has helped determine the weight to be given children's courtroom testimony. Identifying factors that increase the risks of antisocial behavior has suggested ways to prevent it. Understanding how children think about death has enabled professionals to help them deal with bereavement. An understanding of adult development, too, has practical implications. It can help people deal with life's transitions: a woman returning to work after maternity leave, a person making a career change or about to retire, a widow or widower dealing with loss, someone coping with a terminal illness.

Checkpoint

Can you . . .

- ✔ Name four goals of the scientific study of human development?
- ✔ Give examples of practical applications of research on human development?

Developmental Processes: Change and Stability

Developmental scientists are interested in two kinds of developmental change: *quantitative* and *qualitative.* **Quantitative change** is a change in number or amount, such as growth in height, weight, vocabulary, aggressive behavior, or frequency of communication. **Qualitative change** is a change in kind, structure, or organization. It is marked by the emergence of new phenomena that cannot easily be anticipated on the basis of earlier functioning, such as the change from an embryo to a baby, or from a nonverbal child to one who understands words and can communicate verbally.

quantitative change Change in number or amount, such as in height, weight, or size of vocabulary.

qualitative change Change in kind, structure, or organization, such as the change from nonverbal to verbal communication.

Developmental scientists also are interested in the underlying *stability,* or constancy, of personality and behavior. For example, about 10 to 15 percent of children are consistently shy, and another 10 to 15 percent are very bold. Although various influences can modify these traits somewhat, they seem to persist to a moderate degree, especially in children at one extreme or the other (see Chapter 3). Broad dimensions of personality, such as conscientiousness and openness to new experience, seem to stabilize before or during young adulthood (see Chapter 14).

Which characteristics are most likely to endure? Which are likely to change, and why? These are among the basic questions that the study of human development seeks to answer. They are questions we address repeatedly throughout this book.

Domains of Development

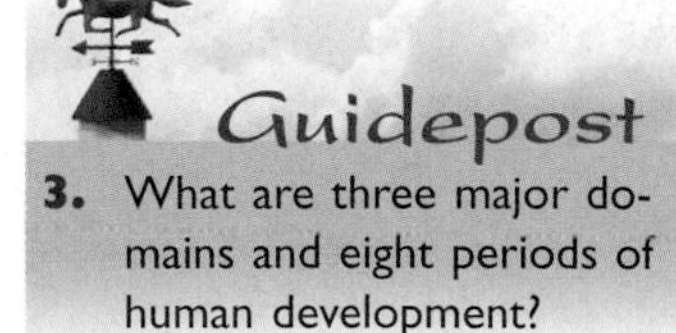

3. What are three major domains and eight periods of human development?

Change and stability occur in various *domains,* or dimensions, of the self. Developmental scientists talk separately about *physical development, cognitive development,* and *psychosocial development.* Actually, though, these domains are intertwined. Throughout life, each affects the others, and each domain is important throughout life.

Growth of the body and brain, sensory capacities, motor skills, and health are part of **physical development** and may influence other domains of development. For example, a child with frequent ear infections may develop language more slowly than a child without this problem. During puberty, dramatic physical and hormonal changes affect the developing sense of self. And, in some older adults, physical changes in the brain may lead to intellectual and personality deterioration.

physical development Growth of body and brain and change or stability in sensory capacities, motor skills, and health.

Change and stability in mental abilities, such as learning, attention, memory, language, thinking, reasoning, and creativity constitute **cognitive development.** Cognitive advances are closely related to physical and emotional growth. The ability to speak depends on the physical development of the mouth and brain. A child who has

cognitive development Change or stability in mental abilities, such as learning, attention, memory, language, thinking, reasoning, and creativity.

These children examining snails on a sand table illustrate the interrelationship of domains of development: sensory perception, cognitive learning, and emotional and social interaction.

difficulty expressing herself in words may evoke negative reactions in others, influencing her popularity and sense of self-worth.

psychosocial development Change and stability in emotions, personality, and social relationships.

Change and stability in emotions, personality, and social relationships together constitute **psychosocial development,** and this can affect cognitive and physical functioning. For example, anxiety about taking a test can impair performance. Social support can help people cope with the potentially negative effects of stress on physical and mental health. As we report in Chapter 18, researchers even have identified possible links between personality and length of life. Conversely, physical and cognitive capacities contribute greatly to self-esteem and can affect social acceptance and choice of occupation.

Although we look separately at physical, cognitive, and psychosocial development, a person is more than a bundle of isolated parts. Development is a unified process. Throughout the text, we highlight links among the three major domains of development.

Periods of the Life Span

social construction Concept about the nature of reality, based on societally shared perceptions or assumptions.

The concept of a division of the life span into periods is a **social construction:** an idea about the nature of reality that is widely accepted by members of a society at a particular time, on the basis of shared subjective perceptions or assumptions. In reality, days flow into years without any demarcation except one that people impose. There is no objectively definable moment when a child becomes an adult, or a young person becomes old.

The concept of childhood can be viewed as a social construction. Some controversial evidence suggests that children in earlier times were regarded and treated much like small adults (Ariès, 1962; Elkind, 1986; Pollock, 1983). Even now, in many developing countries, children labor alongside their elders, doing the same kinds of work for equally long hours.

What's Your View?

- Why do you think various societies divide the periods of development differently?

In industrial societies, as we have mentioned, the concept of adolescence as a period of development is quite recent. In some preindustrial societies, such as the Chippewa Indians, it does not exist: a child at puberty becomes what we would call an adult and remains so until becoming a grandparent. Similarly, as we report in Chapter 16, there are other societies, such as the Gusii of Kenya, that have no concept of middle age.

In this book, we follow a sequence of eight periods generally accepted in western industrial societies. After describing the crucial changes that occur in the first period, before birth, we trace all three domains of development through infancy and toddlerhood, early childhood, middle childhood, adolescence, young adulthood, middle adulthood, and late adulthood (see Table 1-1 on pages 12–13). For space reasons, for each period after infancy and toddlerhood (when change is most dramatic), we have combined physical and cognitive development into a single chapter.

The age divisions shown in Table 1-1 are approximate and somewhat arbitrary. This is especially true of adulthood, when there are no clear-cut social or physical landmarks, such as starting school or entering puberty, to signal a shift from one period to another. Also, individual differences exist in the way people deal with the characteristic events and issues of each period. One toddler may be toilet trained by 18 months; another, not until 3 years. One adult may eagerly anticipate retirement while another may dread it. Despite these differences, however, developmental scientists suggest that certain basic developmental needs must be met and certain developmental tasks mastered during each period for normal development to occur.

Infants, for example, depend on adults to meet their basic needs for food, clothing, and shelter, as well as for human contact and affection. They form attachments to parents or caregivers, who also become attached to them. With the development of speech and the ability to move about on their own, toddlers become more self-reliant; they need to assert their autonomy but also need parents to help them keep their impulses in check. During early childhood, children develop more self-control and more interest in other children. Control over behavior gradually shifts from parent to child during middle childhood, when the peer group becomes increasingly important. A main task of adolescence is the search for identity—personal, sexual, and occupational. As adolescents become physically mature, they deal with sometimes conflicting needs and emotions as they prepare to separate from the security of the parental nest.

The developmental tasks of young adulthood include the establishment of independent lifestyles, occupations, and, usually, families. During middle adulthood, most people need to deal with some decline in physical capabilities. At the same time, many middle-aged people find excitement and challenge in life changes—launching new careers and adult children—while some face the need to care for elderly parents. In late adulthood, people cope with losses in their faculties, the loss of loved ones, and preparations for death. If they retire, they must deal with the loss of work-based relationships but may get increased pleasure out of friendships, family, and volunteer work and the opportunity to explore previously neglected interests. Many older people become more introspective, searching out the meaning of their lives.

Checkpoint

Can you . . .

- ✔ Distinguish between quantitative and qualitative development and give an example of each?
- ✔ Identify three domains of development?
- ✔ Name eight periods of human development (as defined in this book) and list several key issues or events of each period?

Influences on Development

Students of development are interested in universal processes of development, but they also want to know about **individual differences,** both in influences on development and in its outcome. People differ in sex, height, weight, and body build; in constitutional factors such as health and energy level; in intelligence; and in personality characteristics and emotional reactions. The contexts of their lives and lifestyles differ, too: the homes, communities, and societies they live in, the relationships they have, the kinds of schools they go to (or whether they go to school at all), and how they spend their free time.

Guidepost

4. What kinds of influences make one person different from another?

individual differences Differences in characteristics, influences, or developmental outcomes.

Why does one person turn out unlike any other? Because development is complex, and the factors that affect it cannot always be measured precisely—or even discovered—scientists cannot answer that question fully. However, they have learned much about what people need to develop normally, how they react to the many influences upon and within them, and how they can best fulfill their potential.

Table 1-1 Typical Major Developments in Eight Periods of the Life Span

Age Period	Physical Developments	Cognitive Developments	Psychosocial Developments
Prenatal Period (conception to birth)	Conception occurs. The genetic endowment interacts with environmental influences from the start. Basic body structures and organs form. Brain growth spurt begins. Physical growth is the most rapid in the life span. Vulnerability to environmental influences is great.	Abilities to learn and remember, and to respond to sensory stimuli, are developing.	Fetus responds to mother's voice and develops a preference for it.
Infancy and Toddlerhood (birth to age 3)	All senses and body systems operate at birth to varying degrees. The brain grows in complexity and is highly sensitive to environmental influence. Physical growth and development of motor skills are rapid.	Abilities to learn and remember are present, even in early weeks. Use of symbols and ability to solve problems develop by end of second year. Comprehension and use of language develop rapidly.	Attachments to parents and others form. Self-awareness develops. Shift from dependence to autonomy occurs. Interest in other children increases.
Early Childhood (3 to 6 years)	Growth is steady; appearance becomes more slender and proportions more adultlike. Appetite diminishes, and sleep problems are common. Handedness appears; fine and gross motor skills and strength improve.	Thinking is somewhat egocentric, but understanding of other people's perspectives grows. Cognitive immaturity leads to some illogical ideas about the world. Memory and language improve. Intelligence becomes more predictable. Attending preschool is common, kindergarden more so.	Self-concept and understanding of emotions grow; self-esteem is global. Independence, initiative, self-control, and self-care increase. Gender identity develops. Play becomes more imaginative, more elaborate, and more social. Altruism, aggression, and fearfulness are common. Family is still focus of social life, but other children become more important.
Middle Childhood (6 to 11 years)	Growth slows. Strength and athletic skills improve. Respiratory illnesses are common, but health is generally better than at any other time in life span.	Egocentrism diminishes. Children begin to think logically but concretely. Memory and language skills increase. Cognitive gains permit children to benefit from formal schooling. Some children show special educational needs and strengths.	Self-concept becomes more complex, affecting self-esteem. Coregulation reflects gradual shift in control from parents to child. Peers assume central importance.

Heredity, Environment, and Maturation

heredity Inborn characteristics inherited from the biological parents at conception.

environment Totality of nonhereditary, or experiential, influences on development.

maturation Unfolding of a natural sequence of physical and behavioral changes, including readiness to master new abilities.

Some influences on development originate primarily with **heredity:** the genetic endowment inherited from a person's biological parents at conception. Other influences come largely from the inner and outer **environment:** the world outside the self beginning in the womb, and the learning that comes from experience. Individual differences increase as people grow older. Many typical changes of infancy and early childhood seem to be tied to **maturation** of the body and brain—the unfolding of a natural sequence of physical changes and behavior patterns, including readiness to master new abilities such as walking and talking. As children grow into adolescents and then into adults, differences in innate characteristics and life experience play a greater role.

Even in processes that all people go through, rates and timing of development vary. Throughout this book, we talk about certain *milestones,* or landmarks of development: average ages for the occurrence of certain events, such as the first word, the first step, the first menstruation or "wet dream," the development of logical thought,

Age Period	Physical Developments	Cognitive Developments	Psychosocial Developments
Adolescence (11 to about 20 years)	Physical growth and other changes are rapid and profound. Reproductive maturity occurs. Major health risks arise from behavioral issues, such as eating disorders and drug abuse.	Ability to think abstractly and use scientific reasoning develops. Immature thinking persists in some attitudes and behaviors. Education focuses on preparation for college or vocation.	Search for identity, including sexual identity, becomes central. Relationships with parents are generally good. Peer groups help develop and test self-concept but also may exert an antisocial influence.
Young Adulthood (20 to 40 years)	Physical condition peaks, then declines slightly. Lifestyle choices influence health.	Cognitive abilities and moral judgments assume more complexity. Educational and career choices are made.	Personality traits and styles become relatively stable, but changes in personality may be influenced by life stages and events. Decisions are made about intimate relationships and personal lifestyles. Most people marry, and most become parents.
Middle Adulthood (40 to 65 years)	Some deterioration of sensory abilities, health, stamina, and prowess may take place. Women experience menopause.	Most basic mental abilities peak; expertise and practical problem-solving skills are high. Creative output may decline but improve in quality. For some, career success and earning powers peak; for others, burnout or career change may occur.	Sense of identity continues to develop; stressful midlife transition may occur. Double responsibilities of caring for children and elderly parents may cause stress. Launching of children leaves empty nest.
Late Adulthood (65 years and over)	Most people are healthy and active, although health and physical abilities decline somewhat. Slowing of reaction time affects some aspects of functioning.	Most people are mentally alert. Although intelligence and memory may deteriorate in some areas, most people find ways to compensate.	Retirement from workforce may offer new options for use of time. People need to cope with personal losses and impending death. Relationships with family and close friends can provide important support. Search for meaning in life assumes central importance.

and menopause. But these ages are *merely* averages. Only when deviation from the average is extreme should we consider development exceptionally advanced or delayed.

In trying to understand the similarities and differences in development, then, we need to look at the *inherited* characteristics that give each person a special start in life. We also need to consider the many *environmental*, or experiential, factors that affect people, especially such major contexts as family, neighborhood, socioeconomic status, ethnicity, and culture. We need to look at influences that affect many or most people at a certain age or a certain time in history, and also at those that affect only certain individuals. Finally, we need to look at how timing can affect the impact of certain influences.

Major Contextual Influences

Human beings are social beings. Right from the start, they develop within a social and historical context. A child born in the United States today is likely to have very different experiences from a child born in colonial America, and also from a child born in Morocco or Greenland or Afghanistan. For an infant, the immediate context normally

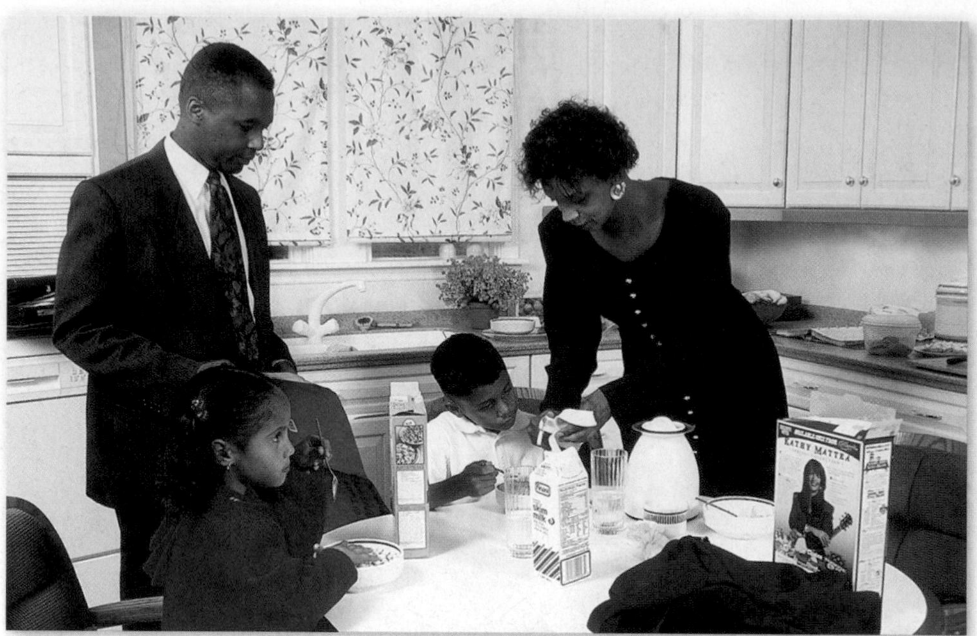

In today's nuclear family, unlike the typical U.S. family of 150 years ago, both parents are likely to work outside the home. Families are smaller than in the past, and children spend more of their time in school.

is the family, but the family in turn is subject to the wider and ever-changing influences of neighborhood, community, and society.

Family *Families* take diverse forms in different times and places. Their attributes have changed greatly during the past 150 years or so.

nuclear family Kinship and household unit made up of one or two parents and their natural, adopted, or stepchildren.

The **nuclear family** is a two-generational kinship, economic, and household unit consisting of one or two parents and their biological, adopted, or stepchildren. Historically, the two-parent nuclear family has been the dominant family unit in the United States and other western societies. Parents and children typically worked side by side on the family farm. Large families provided many hands to share the work, and children's activities and education revolved around the priorities of agricultural production. By the mid–twentieth century, most U.S. families had moved off the farm. Families were smaller, men were away at work for much of the day, and children spent much of their time in school (Hernandez, 1997).

During the past fifty years, change has accelerated. Today both parents are likely to work outside the home. A child is likely to receive a considerable amount of care from relatives or nonrelatives. If a couple are divorced, their children may live with one or the other parent or may move back and forth between their homes. The household may include a stepparent and stepsiblings, or a parent's live-in partner. There are increasing numbers of single and childless adults, unmarried parents, and gay and lesbian households (Hernandez, 1997; Teachman, Tedrow, & Crowder, 2000).

extended family Kinship network of parents, children, and other relatives, sometimes living together in an *extended-family household.*

In many societies, such as those of Asia, Africa, and Latin America, and among families in the United States that originated from those countries, the **extended family**—a multigenerational kinship network of grandparents, aunts, uncles, cousins, and more distant relatives—is the traditional pattern of societal organization. Many or most people live in *extended-family households,* where they have daily contact with kin. Social roles tend to be flexible: adults often share breadwinning, and children are given responsibility for younger brothers and sisters (Aaron, Parker, Ortega, & Calhoun, 1999; Harrison, Wilson, Pine, Chan, & Buriel, 1990; Levitt, Guacci-Franco, & Levitt, 1993; Perey, 1994; Smith, 1997).

Today the extended-family household is becoming less typical in developing countries, due to industrialization and migration to urban centers (N. M. Brown, 1990; Gorman, 1993), particularly among groups that have achieved upward mobility (Peterson, 1993). At the same time, with the aging of the population, multigenerational family bonds are becoming increasingly important in western societies (Bengtson, 2001).

Socioeconomic Status and Neighborhood **Socioeconomic status (SES)** combines several related factors, including income, education, and occupation. Throughout this book, we describe many studies that relate SES to developmental processes (such as differences in mothers' verbal interaction with their children) and to developmental outcomes (such as health and cognitive performance; see Table 1-2). It is generally not SES itself that affects these outcomes, but factors associated with SES, such as the kinds of homes and neighborhoods people live in and the quality of nutrition, medical care, supervision, schooling, and other opportunities available to them. Poor children, for example, are more likely than other children to have emotional or behavioral problems, and their cognitive potential and school performance suffer even more (Brooks-Gunn, Britto, & Brady, 1998; Brooks-Gunn & Duncan, 1997; Duncan & Brooks-Gunn, 1997; McLoyd, 1998). The harm done by poverty may be indirect, through its impact on parents' emotional state and parenting practices and on the home environment they create. (In Chapter 10 we'll look more closely at indirect effects of poverty.)

socioeconomic status (SES) Combination of economic and social factors describing an individual or family, including income, education, and occupation.

SES limits a family's choice of where to live. Researchers study how the composition of a neighborhood affects development. So far, the most powerful aspects seem to be average neighborhood *income* and *human capital*—the presence of educated, employed adults who can build the community's economic base and provide models of what a young person can hope to achieve (Brooks-Gunn, Duncan, Leventhal, & Aber, 1997; Leventhal & Brooks-Gunn, 2000). Threats to children's well-being multiply if several **risk factors**—conditions that increase the likelihood of a negative outcome—coexist. Living in a poor neighborhood with large numbers of people who are unemployed makes it less likely that effective social support will be available (Black & Krishnakumar, 1998).

risk factors Conditions that increase the likelihood of a negative developmental outcome.

Table 1-2 Poverty Hurts Children

Outcomes	Low-Income Children's Higher Risk
Health	
Death in infancy	1.6 times more likely
Premature birth (under 37 weeks)	1.8 times more likely
Low birthweight	1.9 times more likely
Inadequate prenatal care	2.8 times more likely
No regular source of health care	2.7 times more likely
Family had too little food sometime in the last 4 months	8 times more likely
Education	
Math scores at ages 7 to 8	5 test points lower
Reading scores at ages 7 to 8	4 test points lower
Repeated a grade	2.0 times more likely
Expelled from school	3.4 times more likely
Being a dropout at ages 16 to 24	3.5 times more likely
Finishing a four-year college	1/2 as likely

Source: Children's Defense Fund (2002b).

culture A society's or group's total way of life, including customs, traditions, beliefs, values, language, and physical products—all learned behavior passed on from parents to children.

ethnic group Group united by ancestry, race, religion, language, and/or national origins, which contribute to a sense of shared identity.

Culture and Race/Ethnicity **Culture** refers to a society's or group's total way of life, including customs, traditions, beliefs, values, language, and physical products, from tools to artworks—all of the learned behavior passed on from parents to children. Culture is constantly changing, often through contact with other cultures. For example, when Europeans arrived on American shores, they soon learned from the native Indians how to grow corn. And today American music is popular around the world.

Some cultures have variant *subcultures,* associated with certain groups, usually ethnic groups, within a society. An **ethnic group** consists of people united by ancestry, religion, language, and/or national origins, which contribute to a sense of shared identity and shared attitudes, beliefs, and values. Most ethnic groups trace their roots to a country of origin, where they or their forebears had a common culture that continues to influence their way of life. The term *race,* historically viewed as a biological category, is now considered a social one, similar to ethnicity (American Academy of Pediatrics Committee on Pediatric Research, 2000).

The United States has always been a nation of immigrants and ethnic groups. The European-descended "majority" actually consists of many distinct ethnic groups—German, Belgian, Irish, French, Italian, and so forth. There also is diversity within other minority groups. Cubans, Puerto Ricans, and Mexican Americans—all Hispanic Americans—have different histories and cultures. Similarly, African Americans from the rural South differ from those of Caribbean ancestry. Asian Americans, too, hail from a variety of countries with distinct cultures, from modern, industrial Japan to the remote mountains of Nepal, where many people still practice their ancient way of life.

In large, multiethnic societies such as the United States, immigrant groups adapt to the dominant culture by learning the language and customs needed to get along while trying to preserve some of their own cultural practices and values. These cultural patterns may influence the composition of the household, its economic and social resources, the way its members act toward one another, the foods they eat, the games children play, the way they learn, and how well they do in school. Families that have experienced racial or ethnic discrimination often have parenting goals and practices that are different from those of families that have not encountered prejudice. They must teach their children to adapt, not only to mainstream U.S. culture, but to their particular cultural heritage and to the oppression that may confront them (Bradley, Corwyn, McAdoo, & Coll, 2001).

What's Your View?

- How might you be different if you had grown up in a culture other than your own?

Although researchers today are paying much more attention to ethnic and cultural differences than in the past, it is difficult, if not impossible, to present a truly comprehensive picture of these differences. Many studies reported in this book are limited to the dominant group within a culture, and others compare only two groups, such as white Americans and African Americans. When multiple groups *are* studied, often only one or two are noticeably different and therefore worth noting. Even cross-cultural studies cannot capture all of the variations within and among cultures.

The Historical Context At one time developmental scientists paid little attention to the historical context—the time in which people grow up. Then, as the early longitudinal studies of childhood extended into the adult years, investigators began to focus on how particular experiences, tied to time and place, affect the course of people's lives. The Terman sample, for example, reached adulthood in the 1930s, during the Great Depression; the Oakland sample, during World War II; and the Berkeley sample around 1950, the postwar boom period. What did it mean to be a child in each of these periods? To be an adolescent? To become an adult? The answers differ in important ways (Modell, 1989; see Box 1-1). Today, as we discuss in the next section, attention to the historical context is part and parcel of the study of development.

Checkpoint

Can you . . .

- ✔ Explain why individual differences tend to increase with age?
- ✔ Give examples of the influences of family and neighborhood composition, socioeconomic status, culture, race/ethnicity, and historical context?

Digging Deeper

BOX 1–1

Studying the Life Course: Growing Up in Hard Times

Our awareness of the need to look at the life course in its social and historical context is indebted in part to Glen H. Elder, Jr. In 1962, Elder arrived on the campus of the University of California at Berkeley to work on the Oakland Growth Study, a longitudinal study of social and emotional development in 167 urban young people born around 1920, about half of them from middle-class homes. The study had begun at the outset of the Great Depression of the 1930s, when the youngsters, who had spent their childhoods in the boom years of the Roaring '20s, were entering adolescence. Elder observed how societal disruption can alter family processes, and through them, children's development (Elder, 1974).

As economic stress changed parents' lives, it changed children's lives, too. Deprived families reassigned economic roles. Fathers, preoccupied with job losses and irritable about their loss of status within the family, sometimes drank heavily. Mothers got outside jobs and took on more parental authority. Parents argued more. Adolescent children tended to show developmental difficulties.

Still, for boys, particularly, the long-term effects of the ordeal were not entirely negative. Boys who got jobs to help out became more independent and were better able to escape the stressful family atmosphere than girls, who helped at home. As adults, these boys were strongly work oriented but also valued family activities and cultivated dependability in their children.

Elder noted that effects of a major economic crisis depend on a child's stage of development. The children in the Oakland sample were already teenagers during the 1930s. They could draw on their own emotional, cognitive, and economic resources. A child born in 1929 would have been entirely dependent on the family. On the other hand, the parents of the Oakland children, being older, may have been less resilient in dealing with the loss of a job, and their emotional vulnerability may well have affected the tone of family life and their treatment of their children.

Fifty years after the Great Depression, in the early 1980s, a precipitous drop in the value of midwestern agricultural land pushed many farm families into debt or off the land. This Farm Crisis gave Elder the opportunity to replicate his earlier research, this time in a rural setting and with a different cohort. In 1989, he and his colleagues (Conger & Elder, 1994; Conger et al., 1993) interviewed 451 Iowa farm and small-town families with children of various ages. The researchers also videotaped family interactions.

As in the depression-era study, many of these rural parents, under pressure of economic hardship, developed

Glen Elder's studies of children growing up during the Great Depression showed how a major sociohistorical event can affect children's current and future development.

emotional problems. Depressed parents were more likely to fight with each other and to mistreat or withdraw from their children. The children, in turn, tended to lose self-confidence, to be unpopular, and to do poorly in school. But there was a cohort difference: whereas in the 1980s this pattern of parental behavior fit both mothers and fathers, in the 1930s it was less true of mothers, whose economic role before the collapse had been more marginal (Conger & Elder, 1994; Conger et al., 1993; Elder, 1998). Elder's work, like other studies of the life course, gives researchers a window into processes of development and their links with socioecoconomic change. The Farm Crisis study continues, with the families being reinterviewed yearly. Eventually it may enable us to see long-term effects of early hardship on the later lives of people who experienced it at different ages and in varying family situations.

Source: Bruer, J. T. (2001). A Critical and Sensitive Period Primer. In D. B. Bailey, J. T. Bruer, F. J. Symons, & J. W. Lichtman (Eds.), *Critical thinking about critical periods; A series from the National Center for Early Development and Learning* (pp. 289–292). Baltimore, MD: Paul Brooks Publishing.

What's Your View?

Can you think of a major cultural event within your lifetime that shaped the lives of families and children? How would you go about studying its effects?

Check It Out:

For more information on this topic, go to www.mhhe.com/papaliah9, where you'll find a link to a website containing oral histories from the Great Depression.

Normative and Nonnormative Influences

As we have pointed out, development has many roots. To understand similarities and differences in development, we must look at influences that impinge on many or most people and at those that touch only certain individuals. We also need to consider influences of time and place (Baltes, Reese, & Lipsitt, 1980).

normative Characteristic of an event that occurs in a similar way for most people in a group.

cohort Group of people growing up at about the same time.

A **normative** event or influence is experienced in a similar way by most people in a group. *Normative age-graded influences* are highly similar for people in a particular *age group.* They include biological events (such as puberty and menopause) and social events (such as entry into formal education, marriage, parenthood, and retirement). The timing of biological events is fairly predictable, within a normal range. (People don't experience puberty at age 35 or menopause at 12.) The timing of social events is more flexible and varies in different times and places. For example, children in western industrial societies generally begin formal education around age 5 or 6, but in some developing countries schooling begins much later, if at all.

Widespread use of computers is a normative history-graded influence on children's development, which did not exist in earlier generations.

Normative history-graded influences are common to a particular **cohort:** a group of people born around the same time, such as during the Great Depression (refer back to Box 1-1). Depending on when and where they live, entire generations may feel the impact of periods of economic prosperity, recessions, wars, famines, natural disasters, or nuclear explosions and of such cultural and technological developments as the changing roles of women and the impact of television and computers. In the year after Hurricane Hugo hit South Carolina in 1989, marriage, birthrates, and divorce rates increased in the areas declared disaster areas in comparison with other parts of the state. Apparently, then, a life-threatening, nonnormative event can motivate people to make life-changing decisions (Cohan & Cole, 2002).

nonnormative Characteristic of an unusual event that happens to a particular person, or a typical event that happens at an unusual time of life.

Nonnormative influences are unusual events that have a major impact on individual lives. They are either typical events that happen at an atypical time of life (such as marriage in the early teens, or the death of a parent when a child is young) or atypical events (such as having a birth defect or being exposed to terrorist attacks). They can also, of course, be happy events (such as winning a scholarship). People often help create their own nonnormative life events—say, by applying for a challenging new job or taking up a risky hobby such as skydiving—and thus participate actively in their own development. (Normative and nonnormative events are further discussed in Chapter 14.)

Timing of Influences: Critical or Sensitive Periods

imprinting Instinctive form of learning in which, during a critical period in early development, a young animal forms an attachment to the first moving object it sees, usually the mother.

In a well-known study, Konrad Lorenz (1957), an Austrian zoologist, waddled, honked, and flapped his arms—and got newborn ducklings to follow him as they would the mother duck. Lorenz showed that newly hatched ducklings will instinctively follow the first moving object they see, whether or not it is a member of their own species. This phenomenon is called **imprinting,** and Lorenz believed that it is automatic and irreversible. Usually, this instinctive bond is with the mother; but if

Newly hatched ducklings will follow and become attached to the first moving object they see, as the ethologist Konrad Lorenz showed. He called this behavior imprinting.

the natural course of events is disturbed, other attachments (like the one to Lorenz)—or none at all—can form. Imprinting, said Lorenz, is the result of a *predisposition toward learning:* the readiness of an organism's nervous system to acquire certain information during a brief *critical period* in early life.

A **critical period** is a specific time when a given event, or its absence, has a specific impact on development. Critical periods are not absolutely fixed; if ducklings' rearing conditions are varied to slow their growth, the usual critical period for imprinting can be lengthened. The window of opportunity and its effects may even be reversed, some scientists now suggest, but may never completely shut (Bruer, 2001).

critical period Specific time when a given event, or its absence, has a specific impact on development.

Do human beings experience critical periods, as ducklings do? One example occurs during gestation. As we point out in Chapter 3, if a woman receives X rays, takes certain drugs, or contracts certain diseases at certain times during pregnancy, the fetus may show specific ill effects, depending on the nature of the "shock" and on its timing. Critical periods also occur early in childhood. A child deprived of certain kinds of experience during a critical period is likely to show permanent stunting of physical development. For example, if a muscle problem interfering with the ability to focus both eyes on the same object is not corrected early in life, the brain mechanisms necessary for binocular depth perception probably will not develop (Bushnell & Boudreau, 1993).

The concept of critical periods is controversial. Because many aspects of human development, even in the biological domain, show plasticity, or modifiability of performance, it is often more useful to think about **sensitive periods** in development, when a person is especially responsive to certain kinds of experiences (Bruer, 2001). Box 1-2 on pages 20–21 discusses how the concepts of critical and sensitive periods apply to language development.

sensitive periods Times in development when a person is particularly responsive to certain kinds of experiences.

Baltes's Life-Span Developmental Approach

Paul B. Baltes and his colleagues (1987; Baltes, Lindenberger, & Staudinger, 1998; Staudinger & Bluck, 2001) have identified six key principles of the life-span developmental approach, which sum up many of the concepts discussed in this chapter. Together these principles serve as a widely accepted conceptual framework for the study of life-span development:

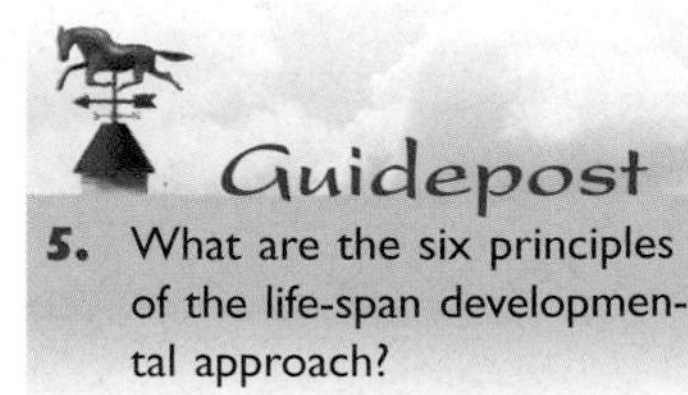

Guidepost

5. What are the six principles of the life-span developmental approach?

1. *Development is lifelong.* Development is a lifelong process of change in the ability to adapt to the situations one selects, or in which one finds oneself. Each period of the life span is affected by what happened before and will affect what is to come. Each period has its own unique characteristics and value; none is more or less important than any other. Although it was once widely believed

BOX 1-2

Practically Speaking
How Important Is Timing in Language Acquisition?

In 1970, a 13½-year-old girl called Genie (not her real name) was discovered in a suburb of Los Angeles (Curtiss, 1977; Fromkin, Krashen, Curtiss, Rigler, & Rigler, 1974; Pines, 1981; Rymer, 1993). She had been confined for nearly twelve years to a small room in her parents' home, tied to a potty chair and cut off from normal human contact. She weighed only 59 pounds, could not straighten her arms or legs, could not chew, had no bladder or bowel control, and did not speak. She recognized only her own name and the word *sorry*.

Only three years before, Eric Lenneberg (1967, 1969) had proposed that there is a critical period for language acquisition, beginning in early infancy and ending around puberty. Lenneberg argued that it would be difficult, if not impossible, for a child who had not yet acquired language to do so after that age.

The discovery of Genie offered the opportunity for a test of Lenneberg's hypothesis. Could Genie be taught to speak, or was it too late? The National Institutes of Mental Health (NIMH) funded a study, and a series of researchers took over Genie's care and gave her intensive testing and language training.

Genie's progress during the next few years (before the NIMH withdrew funding and her mother regained custody and cut her off from contact with the professionals who had been teaching her) both challenges and supports the idea of a critical period for language acquisition. Genie did learn some simple words and could string them together into primitive, but rule-governed, sentences. She also learned the fundamentals of sign language. But she never used language normally, and "her speech remained, for the most part, like a somewhat garbled telegram" (Pines, 1981, p. 29). When her mother, unable to care for her, turned her over to a series of abusive foster homes, she regressed into total silence.

What explains Genie's initial progress and her inability to sustain it? The fact that she was just beginning to show signs of puberty at age 13½ may indicate that she was still in the critical period, though near its end. The fact that she apparently had learned a few words before being locked up at the age of 20 months may mean that her language-learning mechanisms may have been triggered early in the critical period, allowing later learning to occur. On the other hand, the fact that she was so abused and

that development stops at adolescence, we now know that even very old people can grow. The experience of dying can be a final attempt to come to terms with one's life—in short, to develop.

2. *Development involves both gain and loss.* Development is multidimensional and multidirectional. It occurs along multiple interacting dimensions—biological, psychological, and social—each of which may develop at varying rates. Development also proceeds in more than one direction. As people gain in one area, they may lose in another, and at the same time. Children grow mostly in one direction—up—both in size and in abilities. Then the balance gradually shifts. Adolescents typically gain in physical abilities but lose their facility in learning language. Some abilities, such as vocabulary, typically continue to increase throughout most of adulthood; others, such as the ability to solve unfamiliar problems, may diminish; and some new attributes, such as expertise, may develop in midlife. People seek to maximize gains and to minimize losses by learning to manage or compensate for them.
3. *Relative influences of biology and culture shift over the life span.* The process of development is influenced by both biology and culture, and the balance between these influences changes over time. Biological influences, such as

Practically Speaking

BOX 1-2

—continued

neglected may have retarded her so much—emotionally, socially, and cognitively—that, like Victor, the wild boy of Aveyron, she cannot be considered a true test of the critical period (Curtiss, 1977).

Case studies like those of Genie and Victor dramatize the *difficulty* of acquiring language after the early years of life, but, because there are too many complicating factors, they do not permit conclusive judgments about whether such acquisition is *possible*. Recent brain imaging research has found that even if the parts of the brain best suited to language processing are damaged early in childhood, nearly normal language development can continue as other parts of the brain take over (Boatman et al., 1999; Hertz-Pannier et al., 2002; M. H. Johnson, 1998). In fact, shifts in brain organization and utilization occur throughout the course of normal language learning (M. H. Johnson, 1998; Neville & Bavelier, 1998). Neuroscientists also have observed different patterns of brain activity during language processing in people who learned American Sign Language (ASL) as a native language and those who learned it as a second language, after puberty (Newman, Bavelier, Corina, Jezzard, & Neville, 2002). It is possible to learn a second language, signed or spoken, even in adulthood, but typically not as easily or as well as in early childhood (Newport, 1991).

Because of the brain's plasticity, some researchers consider the prepubertal years a *sensitive*, rather than *critical*, period for learning language (Newport, Bavelier, & Neville, 2001; Schumann, 1997). But if either a critical or a sensitive period for language learning exists, what explains it? Do the brain's mechanisms for acquiring language decay as the brain matures? That would seem strange, since other cognitive abilities improve. An alternative hypothesis is that this very increase in cognitive sophistication interferes with an adolescent's or adult's ability to learn a language. Young children acquire language in small chunks that can be readily digested. Older learners, when they first begin learning a language, tend to absorb a great deal at once and then may have trouble analyzing and interpreting it (Newport, 1991).

What's Your View?

Do you see any ethical problems in the studies of Genie and Victor? Is the knowledge gained from such studies worth any possible damage to the individuals involved? (Keep this question, and your answer, in mind when you read the section on ethics of research in Chapter 2.)

Check It Out:

OLC

For more information on this topic, go to www.mhhe.com/papaliah9, where you'll find a link to a website developed by Professor Robert Beard, of the Linguistics Program at Bucknell University.

sensory acuity and muscular strength and coordination, become weaker as a person gets older, but cultural supports, such as education, relationships, and technologically age-friendly environments, may help compensate (see Box 17-2 in Chapter 17).

4. *Development involves a changing allocation of resources.* Nobody can do everything. Individuals choose to "invest" their resources of time, energy, talent, money, and social support in varying ways. Resources may be used for growth (for example, learning to play an instrument or improving one's skill), maintenance or recovery (practicing to maintain or regain proficiency), and dealing with loss when maintenance and recovery are not possible. The allocation of resources to these three functions changes throughout life as the total available pool of resources decreases. In childhood and young adulthood, the bulk of resources typically goes to growth; in old age, to regulation of loss. In midlife, the allocation is more evenly balanced among the three functions.
5. *Development is modifiable.* Throughout life, development shows plasticity. Many abilities, such as memory, strength, and endurance, can be significantly improved with training and practice, even late in life. However, as Itard learned, even in children the potential for change has limits. One of the tasks of devel-

Checkpoint

Can you . . .

- ✔ Give examples of normative age-graded, normative history-graded, and nonnormative influences? (Include some normative history-graded influences that impacted different generations.)
- ✔ Contrast critical and sensitive periods and give examples?
- ✔ Summarize the six principles of Baltes's life-span developmental approach?

opmental research is to discover to what extent particular kinds of development can be modified at various ages.

6. *Development is influenced by the historical and cultural context.* Each person develops within multiple contexts—circumstances or conditions defined in part by biology, in part by time and place. In addition to age-graded and nonnormative influences, human beings (as we have noted) influence, and are influenced by, their historical-cultural context. As we discuss throughout this book, developmental scientists have found significant cohort differences in intellectual functioning, in women's midlife emotional development, and in the flexibility of personality in old age.

Refocus

How does the story of Victor, the Wild Boy of Aveyron, illustrate the following chapter themes?

- How the study of human development has become more scientific
- The interrelationship of domains of development
- The influences of heredity, environment, and maturation
- The importance of contextual and historical influences
- The roles of nonnormative influences and critical or sensitive periods

Now that you have had a brief introduction to the field of human development and some of its basic concepts, it's time to look more closely at the issues developmental scientists think about and how they do their work. In Chapter 2, we discuss some influential theories of how development takes place and the methods investigators commonly use to study it.

SUMMARY AND KEY TERMS

How the Study of Human Development Evolved

Guidepost 1. What is human development, and how has its study evolved?

- Human development is the scientific study of processes of change and stability.
- The scientific study of human development began with studies of childhood during the nineteenth century. Adolescence was not considered a separate phase of development until the twentieth century, when scientific interest in aging also began.
- As researchers became interested in following development through adulthood, life-span development became a field of study.

human development *(7)*

life-span development *(8)*

Human Development Today: An Introduction to the Field

Guidepost 2. What are the four goals of the scientific study of human development, and what do developmental scientists study?

- The study of human development seeks to describe, explain, predict, and modify development.
- Ways of studying human development are still evolving, making use of advanced technologies.
- Developmental research has important applications.
- Developmental scientists study developmental change, both quantitative and qualitative, as well as stability of personality and behavior.

quantitative change *(9)*

qualitative change *(9)*

Guidepost 3. What are three major domains and eight periods of human development?

- The three major domains of development are physical, cognitive, and psychosocial. Each affects the others.
- The concept of periods of development is a social construction. In this book, the life span is divided into eight periods: the prenatal period, infancy and toddlerhood, early childhood, middle childhood, adolescence, young adulthood, middle adulthood, and late adulthood. In each period, people have characteristic developmental needs and tasks.

physical development *(9)*
cognitive development *(9)*
psychosocial development *(10)*
social construction *(10)*

Influences on Development

Guidepost 4. What kinds of influences make one person different from another?

- Influences on development come from both heredity and environment. Many typical changes during childhood are related to maturation. Individual differences increase with age.
- In some societies, the nuclear family predominates; in others, the extended family.
- Socioeconomic status (SES) affects developmental processes and outcomes through the quality of home and neighborhood environments, of nutrition, medical care, supervision, and schooling. The most powerful neighborhood influences seem to be neighborhood income and human capital. Multiple risk factors increase the likelihood of poor outcomes.
- Other important environmental influences stem from ethnicity, culture, and historical context. In large multiethnic societies, immigrant groups may adapt to the dominant culture while preserving aspects of their own.
- Influences may be normative (age-graded or history-graded) or nonnormative.
- There is evidence of critical or sensitive periods for certain kinds of early development.

individual differences *(11)*
heredity *(12)*
environment *(12)*
maturation *(12)*
nuclear family *(14)*
extended family *(14)*
socioeconomic status (SES) *(15)*
risk factors *(15)*
culture *(16)*
ethnic group *(16)*
normative *(18)*
cohort *(18)*
nonnormative *(18)*
imprinting *(18)*
critical period *(19)*
sensitive periods *(19)*

Baltes's Life-Span Developmental Approach

Guidepost 5. What are the six principles of the life-span developmental approach?

- The six principles of Baltes's life-span developmental approach are: (1) development is lifelong, (2) development involves both gain and loss, (3) the relative influences of biology and culture shift over the life span, (4) development involves a changing allocation of resources, (5) development is modifiable; and (6) development is influenced by the historical and cultural context.

Chapter 2

Theory and Research

There is one thing even more vital to science than intelligent methods; and that is, the sincere desire to find out the truth, whatever it may be.

—Charles Sanders Peirce, *Collected Papers*, vol. 5

OUTLINE

Focus: Margaret Mead, Pioneer in Cross-Cultural Research

Margaret Mead

Margaret Mead (1901–1978) was a world famous American anthropologist. In the 1920s, at a time when it was rare for a woman to expose herself to the rigors of fieldwork with remote, preliterate peoples, Mead spent nine months on the South Pacific island of Samoa, studying girls' adjustment to adolescence. Her best-selling first book, *Coming of Age in Samoa* (1928), challenged accepted views about the inevitability of adolescent rebellion.

An itinerant childhood built around her parents' academic pursuits prepared Mead for a life of roving research. In New Jersey, her mother, who was working on her doctoral thesis in sociology, took Margaret along on interviews with recent Italian immigrants—the child's first exposure to fieldwork. Her father, a professor at the University of Pennsylvania's Wharton business school, taught her respect for facts and "the importance of thinking clearly" (Mead, 1972, p. 40). He stressed the link between theory and application—as Margaret did when, years later, she applied her theories of child rearing to her daughter. Margaret's grandmother, a former schoolteacher, sent her out in the woods to collect and analyze mint specimens. "I was not well drilled in geography or spelling," Mead wrote in her memoir *Blackberry Winter* (1972, p. 47). "But I learned to observe the world around me and to note what I saw."

Margaret took copious notes on the development of her younger brother and two younger sisters. Her curiosity about why one child in a family behaved so differently from another led to her later interest in temperamental variations within a culture.

How cultures define male and female roles was another research focus. Margaret saw her mother and her grandmother as educated women who had managed to have husbands, children, and professional careers; and she expected to do the same. She was dismayed when, at the outset of her career, the distinguished anthropologist Edward Sapir told her she "would do better to stay at home and have children than to go off to the South Seas to study adolescent girls" (Mead, 1972, p. 11).

Margaret's choice of anthropology as a career was consistent with her homebred respect for the value of all human beings and their cultures. Recalling her father's insistence that the only thing worth doing is to add to the store of knowledge, she saw an urgent need to document once-isolated cultures now "vanishing before the onslaught of modern civilization" (Mead, 1972, p. 137).

"I went to Samoa—as, later, I went to the other societies on which I have worked—to find out more about human beings, human beings like ourselves in everything except their culture," she wrote. "Through the accidents of history, these cultures had developed so differently from ours that knowledge of them could shed a kind of light upon us, upon our potentialities and our limitations" (Mead, 1972, p. 293). The ongoing quest to illuminate those "potentialities and limitations" is the business of theorists and researchers in human development.

Margaret Mead's life was all of a piece. The young girl who filled notebooks with observations about her siblings became the scientist who traveled to distant lands and studied cultures very different from her own.

Mead's story underlines several important points about the study of human development. First, the study of people is not dry, abstract, or esoteric. It deals with the substance of real life.

Second, a cross-cultural perspective can reveal which patterns of behavior, if any, are universal and which are not. Most studies of human development have been done in western, developed societies, using white, middle-class participants. Today developmental scientists are increasingly conscious of the need to expand the research base, as Mead and her colleagues sought to do.

Third, theory and research are two sides of the same coin. As Mead reflected on her own experiences and observed the behavior of others, she constantly formed tentative explanations to be tested by later research.

Fourth, although the goal of science is to obtain verifiable knowledge through open-minded, impartial investigation, observations about human behavior are products of very human individuals whose inquiries and interpretations may be influenced by their own background, values, and experiences. As Mead's daughter, Mary Catherine Bateson (1984), herself an anthropologist, noted in response to methodological criticism of Mead's early work in Samoa, a scientific observer is like a lens, which may introduce some distortion into what is observed. This is why scientists have others check their results. In striving for greater objectivity, investigators must scrutinize how they and their colleagues conduct their work, the assumptions on which it is based, and how they arrive at their conclusions. And in studying the results of research, it is important to keep these potential biases in mind.

In the first part of this chapter, we present major issues and theoretical perspectives that underlie much research in human development. In the remainder of the chapter, we look at how researchers gather and assess information, so that you will be better able to judge whether their conclusions rest on solid ground.

After you have studied this chapter, you should be able to answer each of the following Guidepost questions. Look for them again in the margins, where they point to important concepts throughout the chapter. To check your understanding of these Guideposts, review the end-of-chapter summary. Checkpoints located at periodic spots throughout the chapter will help you verify your understanding of what you have read.

Guideposts for Study

1. What purposes do theories serve?
2. What are three basic theoretical issues on which developmental scientists differ?
3. What are five theoretical perspectives on human development, and what are some theories representative of each?
4. How do developmental scientists study people, and what are the advantages and disadvantages of each research method?
5. What ethical problems may arise in research on humans?

Basic Theoretical Issues

As we noted in Chapter 1, the goals of the study of human development are to describe, explain, predict, and modify human behavior. In keeping with these goals, developmental scientists have come up with theories about why people develop as they do. A **theory** is a set of logically related concepts or statements, which seeks to describe and explain development and to predict what kinds of behavior might occur under certain conditions. Theories organize data, the information gathered by research, and are a rich source of **hypotheses**—tentative explanations or predictions that can be tested by further research.

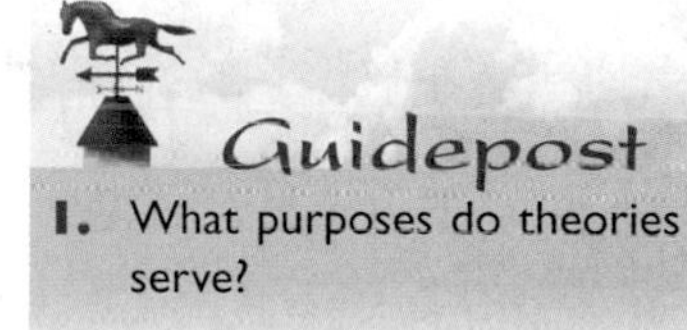

Guidepost

1. What purposes do theories serve?

theory Coherent set of logically related concepts that seeks to organize, explain, and predict data.

hypotheses Possible explanations for phenomena, used to predict the outcome of research.

Theories are dynamic—they change to incorporate new findings. Sometimes research supports a hypothesis and the theory on which it was based. At other times, as with Mead's findings challenging the inevitability of adolescent rebellion, scientists must modify their theories to account for unexpected data. Research findings often suggest additional questions and hypotheses to be examined and provide direction for dealing with practical issues.

The way theorists explain development depends in part on the way they view three basic issues: (1) the relative weight given to heredity and environment; (2) whether people are active or passive in their own development; and (3) whether development is continuous or occurs in stages.

Issue 1: Which Is More Important—Heredity or Environment?

Which has more impact on development: heredity or environment? This issue has aroused intense debate. Theorists have differed in the relative importance they give to *nature* (the inborn traits and characteristics inherited from the biological parents) and *nurture* (environmental influences, both before and after birth, including influences of family, peers, schools, neighborhoods, society, and culture).

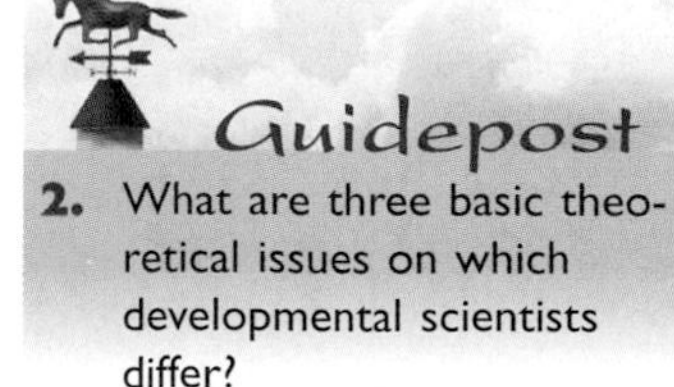

Guidepost

2. What are three basic theoretical issues on which developmental scientists differ?

How much is inherited? How much is environmentally influenced? These questions matter. If parents believe that intelligence can be strongly influenced by experience, they may make special efforts to talk to and read to their children and offer them

Does golf champion Tiger Woods owe his prowess to inborn talent or to his father's tough training? Most developmental scientists today would say, "Both."

playthings that help them learn. If parents believe that intelligence is inborn and unchangeable, they may be less likely to make such efforts.

Today, scientists have found ways to measure more precisely the roles of heredity and environment in the development of specific traits within a population. When we look at a particular person, however, research with regard to almost all characteristics points to a blend of inheritance and experience. Thus, even though intelligence has a strong hereditary component, parental stimulation, education, peer influence, and other variables also affect it. While there still is considerable dispute about the relative importance of nature and nurture, many contemporary theorists and researchers are more interested in finding ways to explain how they work together.

Issue 2: Is Development Active or Passive?

Are people active or passive in their own development? This controversy goes back to the eighteenth century, when the English philosopher John Locke held that a young child is a *tabula rasa*—a "blank slate"—on which society "writes." In contrast, the French philosopher Jean Jacques Rousseau believed that children are born "noble savages" who would develop according to their own positive natural tendencies unless corrupted by a repressive society. We now know that both views are too simplistic. Children have their own internal drives and needs, as well as hereditary endowments, that influence development; but children also are social animals, who cannot achieve optimal development in isolation.

The debate over Locke's and Rousseau's philosophies led to two contrasting models, or images, of development: *mechanistic* and *organismic.* Locke's view was the forerunner of the **mechanistic model** of development. In this model, people are like machines that react to environmental input (Pepper, 1942, 1961). If we know enough about how the human "machine" is put together and about the internal and external forces acting on it, we can predict what the person will do. Mechanistic research seeks to identify and isolate the factors that make people behave—or react—as they do. For example, in seeking to explain why some college students drink too much alcohol, a mechanistic theorist might look for environmental influences such as advertising and whether the person's friends drink to excess.

mechanistic model Model that views development as a passive, predictable response to stimuli.

Rousseau was the precursor of the **organismic model** of development. This model sees people as active, growing organisms that set their own development in motion (Pepper, 1942, 1961). They initiate events; they do not just react. The impetus for change is internal. Environmental influences do not cause development, though they can speed or slow it. Human behavior is an organic whole; it cannot be predicted by breaking it down into simple responses to environmental stimulation, as the mechanistic model suggests. An organismic theorist, in studying why some students drink too much, would be likely to look at what kinds of situations they choose to participate in, and with whom. Do they choose friends who like to party, or who are more studious?

organismic model Model that views development as internally initiated by an active organism, and as occurring in a sequence of qualitatively different stages.

Issue 3: Is Development Continuous, or Does It Occur in Stages?

The mechanistic and organismic models also differ on the third issue: Is development continuous, or does it occur in stages?

Mechanistic theorists see development as continuous, like walking or crawling up a ramp. These theorists describe development as always governed by the same processes, allowing prediction of earlier behaviors from later ones. Mechanistic theorists focus on *quantitative* change: for example, changes in the frequency with which a response is made, rather than changes in the kind of response.

Organismic theorists emphasize *qualitative* change (Looft, 1973). They see development as occurring in a series of distinct stages, like stair steps. At each stage, people cope with different kinds of problems and develop different kinds of abilities. Each stage builds on the previous one and prepares the way for the next.

An Emerging Consensus

As the study of human development has evolved, the mechanistic and organismic models have shifted in influence and support (Parke, Ornstein, Rieser, & Zahn-Waxler, 1994). Most of the early pioneers in the field, including Sigmund Freud, Erik Erikson, and Jean Piaget, favored organismic, or stage, approaches. However, the mechanistic view gained support during the 1960s with the popularity of learning theories derived from the work of John B. Watson. (We discuss all these theorists in the next section.)

Today the pendulum has swung back part way. Quasi-organismic approaches centered on the biological bases of behavior are on the rise; but instead of looking for broad stages, there is an effort to discover what specific kinds of behavior show continuity or lack of continuity and what processes are involved in each.

Just as a consensus is emerging about how heredity and environment work together, many developmentalists are coming to a more balanced view of active versus passive development. There is wide agreement that influence is *bidirectional:* children change their world even as it changes them. A baby girl born with a cheerful disposition is likely to get positive responses from adults, which strengthen her trust that her smiles will be rewarded and motivate her to smile more. A manager who offers constructive criticism and emotional support to subordinates is likely to elicit their openness and trust, as well as greater effort to produce. These positive responses, in turn, are likely to encourage her to keep using this managerial style.

Checkpoint

Can you . . .

- ✔ State three basic issues regarding the nature of human development?
- ✔ Contrast the mechanistic and organismic models of development?

Theoretical Perspectives

Despite the growing consensus on the basic issues just discussed, many investigators view development from differing theoretical perspectives. Theories generally fall within these broad perspectives, each of which emphasizes different kinds of developmental processes. These perspectives influence the questions researchers ask, the methods they use, and the ways they interpret data. Therefore, to evaluate and interpret research, it is important to recognize the theoretical perspective on which it is based.

Guidepost

3. What are five theoretical perspectives on human development, and what are some theories representative of each?

Five major perspectives (summarized in Table 2-1 on pages 30–31) underlie much influential theory and research on human development: (1) *psychoanalytic* (which focuses on unconscious emotions and drives); (2) *learning* (which studies observable behavior); (3) *cognitive* (which analyzes thought processes); (4) *evolutionary/sociobiological* (which considers evolutionary and biological underpinnings of behavior); and (5) *contextual* (which emphasizes the impact of the historical, social, and cultural context). Here is a general overview of the assumptions, central focus, and methods of each of these perspectives and some leading theorists within each perspective, who will be referred to throughout this book.

Perspective 1: Psychoanalytic

The **psychoanalytic perspective** views development as shaped by unconscious forces that motivate human behavior. Sigmund Freud (1856–1939), a Viennese physician, developed *psychoanalysis,* a therapeutic approach aimed at giving patients insight into unconscious emotional conflicts. Other theorists and practitioners, including Erik H. Erikson, have expanded and modified the psychoanalytic perspective.

psychoanalytic perspective View of development as shaped by unconscious forces.

Table 2-1 Five Perspectives on Human Development

Perspective	Important Theories	Basic Beliefs
Psychoanalytic	Freud's psychosexual theory	Behavior is controlled by powerful unconscious urges.
	Erikson's psychosocial theory	Personality is influenced by society and develops through a series of crises, or critical alternatives.
Learning	Behaviorism, or traditional learning theory (Pavlov, Skinner, Watson)	People are responders; the environment controls behavior.
	Social learning, or social cognitive, theory (Bandura)	People learn in a social context by observing and imitating models. Person is an active contributor to learning.
Cognitive	Piaget's cognitive-stage theory	Qualitative changes in thought occur between infancy and adolescence. Person is active initiator of development.
	Information-processing theory	Human beings are processors of symbols.
Evolutionary/ Sociobiological	Bowlby's and Ainsworth's attachment theory	Human beings have the adaptive mechanisms to survive; critical or sensitive periods are stressed; biological and evolutionary bases for behavior and predisposition toward learning are important.
Contextual	Bronfenbrenner's bioecological theory	Development occurs through interaction between a developing person and five surrounding, interlocking contextual systems of influences, from microsystem to chronosystem.
	Vygotsky's sociocultural theory	Sociocultural context is central to development.

psychosexual development In Freudian theory, an unvarying sequence of stages of personality development during infancy, childhood, and adolescence, in which gratification shifts from the mouth to the anus and then to the genitals.

Sigmund Freud: Psychosexual Development Freud (1953, 1964a, 1964b) believed that people are born with biological drives that must be redirected so as to live in society. He proposed that personality is formed in childhood, as children deal with unconscious conflicts between these inborn urges and the requirements of civilized life. These conflicts occur in an unvarying sequence of five maturationally based stages of **psychosexual development** (see Table 2-2 on page 32), in which sexual or sensual pleasure shifts from one body zone to another—from the mouth to the anus and then to the genitals. At each stage, the behavior that is the chief source of gratification (or frustration) changes—from feeding to elimination and eventually to sexual activity.

Freud considered the first three stages—those of the first few years of life—crucial. He suggested that if children receive too little or too much gratification in any of these stages, they are at risk of *fixation*—an arrest in development that can show up in adult personality. For example, babies whose needs are not met during the *oral stage,* when feeding is the main source of sensual pleasure, may grow up to become nail-biters or smokers or to develop "bitingly" critical personalities. A person who, as a toddler, had too-strict toilet training may be fixated at the *anal stage,* when the chief source of pleasure was moving the bowels. Such a person may have a "constipated" personality: obsessively clean and neat or rigidly tied to schedules and routines. Or the person may be defiantly messy.

According to Freud, a key event in psychosexual development occurs in the *phallic stage* of early childhood. Boys develop sexual attachment to their mothers and girls to their fathers, and they have aggressive urges toward the same-sex parent, whom they regard as a rival. Children eventually resolve their anxiety over these feelings by identifying with the same-sex parent and move into the *latency stage* of middle childhood, a period of sexual calm. They become socialized, develop skills, and learn about

Technique Used	Stage-Oriented	Causal Emphasis	Active or Passive Individual
Clinical observation	Yes	Innate factors modified by experience	Passive
Clinical observation	Yes	Interaction of innate and experiential factors	Active
Rigorous scientific (experimental) procedures	No	Experience	Passive
Rigorous scientific (experimental) procedures	No	Experienced modified by innate factors	Active and passive
Flexible interviews; meticulous observation	Yes	Interaction of innate and experiential factors	Active
Laboratory research; technological monitoring of physiologic responses	No	Interaction of innate and experiential factors	Active and passive
Naturalistic and laboratory observation	No	Interaction of innate and experiential factors	Active or passive (theorists vary)
Naturalistic observation and analysis	No	Interaction of innate and experiential factors	Active
Cross-cultural research; observation of child interacting with more competent person	No	Experience	Active

themselves and society. The *genital stage,* the final one, lasts throughout adulthood. The sexual urges repressed during latency now resurface to flow in socially approved channels, which Freud defined as heterosexual relations with persons outside the family of origin.

Freud proposed three hypothetical parts of the personality: the *id,* the *ego,* and the *superego.* Newborns are governed by the *id,* which operates under the *pleasure principle*—the drive to seek immediate satisfaction of its needs and desires. When gratification is delayed, as it is when infants have to wait to be fed, they begin to see themselves as separate from the outside world. The *ego,* which represents reason, develops gradually during the first year or so of life and operates under the *reality principle.* The ego's aim is to find realistic ways to gratify the id. The *superego* develops during early childhood. It includes the conscience and incorporates socially approved "shoulds" and "should nots" into the child's own value system. If its standards are not met, a child may feel guilty and anxious. The ego acts as a mediator between the impulses of the id and the demands of the superego.

The Viennese physician Sigmund Freud developed an original, influential, and controversial theory of psychosexual development in childhood, based on his adult patients' recollections. His daughter, Anna, shown here with her father, followed in his professional footsteps and constructed her own theories of personality development.

Freud's theory made historic contributions, and several of his central themes have been validated by research, though others have not (Emde, 1992; Westen, 1998). Freud made us aware of the importance of unconscious thoughts, feelings, and motivations; the role of childhood experiences in forming personality; the ambivalence of emotional responses, especially to parents; and ways in which early relationships affect later ones. Freud also opened our eyes to the presence from birth of sexual urges. Although many psychoanalysts today reject his narrow emphasis on sexual and aggressive drives, his psychoanalytic method greatly influenced modern-day psychotherapy.

We need to remember that Freud's theory grew out of his place in history and in society. Freud based his theories about normal development, not on a population of

Table 2-2 Developmental Stages According to Various Theories

Psychosexual Stages (Freud)	Psychosocial Stages (Erikson)	Cognitive Stages (Piaget)
Oral (birth to 12–18 months). Baby's chief source of pleasure involves mouth-oriented activities (sucking and feeding).	*Basic trust versus mistrust (birth to 12–18 months).* Baby develops sense of whether world is a good and safe place. Virtue: hope.	*Sensorlmotor (birth to 2 years).* Infant gradually becomes able to organize activities in relation to the environment through sensory and motor activity.
Anal (12–18 months to 3 years). Child derives sensual gratification from withholding and expelling feces. Zone of gratification is anal region, and toilet training is important activity.	*Autonomy versus shame and doubt (12–18 months to 3 years).* Child develops a balance of independence and self-sufficiency over shame and doubt. Virtue: will.	*Preoperational (2 to 7 years).* Child develops a representational system and uses symbols to represent people, places, and events. Language and imaginative play are important manifestations of this stage. Thinking is still not logical.
Phallic (3 to 6 years). Child becomes attached to parent of the other sex and later identifies with same-sex parent. Superego develops. Zone of gratification shifts to genital region.	*Initiative versus guilt (3 to 6 years).* Child develops initiative when trying out new activities and is not overwhelmed by guilt. Virtue: purpose.	
Latency (6 years to puberty). Time of relative calm between more turbulent stages.	*Industry versus inferiority (6 years to puberty).* Child must learn skills of the culture or face feelings of incompetence. Virtue: skill.	*Concrete operations (7 to 11 years).* Child can solve problems logically if they are focused on the here and now, but cannot think abstractly.
Genital (puberty through adulthood). Reemergence of sexual impulses of phallic stage, channeled into mature adult sexuality.	*Identity versus identity confusion (puberty to young adulthood).* Adolescent must determine own sense of self ("Who am I?") or experience confusion about roles. Virtue: fidelity.	*Formal operations (11 years through adulthood).* Person can think abstractly, deal with hypothetical situations, and think about possibilities.
	Intimacy versus isolation (young adulthood). Person seeks to make commitments to others; if unsuccessful, may suffer from isolation and self-absorption. Virtue: love.	
	Generativity versus stagnation (middle adulthood). Mature adult is concerned with establishing and guiding the next generation or else feels personal impoverishment. Virtue: care.	
	Ego integrity versus despair (late adulthood). Elderly person achieves acceptance of own life, allowing acceptance of death, or else despairs over inability to relive life. Virtue: wisdom.	

Note: All ages are approximate.

average children, but on a clientele of upper-middle-class adults, mostly women, in therapy. His concentration on the importance of sexual feelings and of early experience does not take into account other, and later, influences on personality—including the influences of society and culture, which many heirs to the Freudian tradition, notably Erikson, stress.

Erik Erikson: Psychosocial Development Erik Erikson (1902–1994), a German-born psychoanalyst who originally was part of Freud's circle in Vienna, modified and extended Freudian theory by emphasizing the influence of society on the developing personality. Erikson was a pioneer in a life-span perspective. Whereas Freud maintained that early childhood experiences permanently shape personality, Erikson contended that ego development is lifelong. He applied his own theory to well-known public figures, writing psychosocial biographies or "psychohistories" of Martin Luther and Mahatma Gandhi.

The psychoanalyst Erik H. Erikson departed from Freudian theory in emphasizing societal, rather than chiefly biological, influences on personality. Erikson described development as proceeding through eight turning points throughout the life span.

Erikson's (1950, 1982; Erikson, Erikson, & Kivnick, 1986) theory of **psychosocial development** covers eight stages across the life span (refer to Table 2-2), which we will discuss in the appropriate chapters. Each stage involves what Erikson originally called a "crisis" in personality—a major psychosocial theme that is particularly important at that time and will remain an issue to some degree throughout the rest of life.* These issues, which emerge according to a maturational timetable, must be satisfactorily resolved for healthy ego development.

psychosocial development In Erikson's eight-stage theory, the socially and culturally influenced process of development of the ego, or self.

Each stage requires the balancing of a positive tendency and a corresponding negative one. Although the positive quality should predominate, some degree of the negative is needed as well. The critical theme of infancy, for example, is *basic trust versus basic mistrust.* People need to trust the world and the people in it, but they also need to learn some mistrust to protect themselves from danger. The successful outcome of each stage is the development of a particular "virtue," or strength—in this case, the "virtue" of *hope.* Erikson's last stage, in late adulthood, is *ego integrity versus despair.* In this stage one must come to terms with the way one has lived one's life, or succumb to despair over the inability to live it over. The "virtue" of this stage is *wisdom.*

Erikson's theory has held up better than Freud's, especially in its emphasis on the importance of social and cultural influences and on development beyond adolescence. However, some of Erikson's concepts (like Freud's) do not lend themselves to rigorous testing.

Checkpoint

Can you . . .

- ✔ Identify the chief focus of the psychoanalytic perspective?
- ✔ Name Freud's five stages of development and three parts of the personality?
- ✔ Tell two ways in which Erikson's theory differs from Freud's?

Perspective 2: Learning

Whereas psychoanalysts are concerned with unconscious forces, proponents of the **learning perspective** are concerned with observable behaviors. These theorists maintain that development results from *learning,* a long-lasting change in behavior based on experience, or adaptation to the environment. Learning theorists are concerned with finding out the objective laws that govern changes in observable behavior and apply equally to all age groups. They see development as continuous (not in stages) and emphasize quantitative change.

learning perspective View of development that holds that changes in behavior result from experience, or adaptation to the environment.

Learning theorists have helped to make the study of human development more scientific. Their terms are defined precisely, and their theories can be tested in the laboratory. By stressing environmental influences, they help explain cultural differences in behavior. Two important learning theories are *behaviorism* and *social learning theory.*

Behaviorism

Behaviorism is a mechanistic theory, which describes observed behavior as a predictable response to experience. Although biology sets limits on what people do, behaviorists view the environment as much more influential. They hold that human beings at all ages learn about the world the same way other organisms do: by reacting to conditions, or aspects of their environment, that they find pleasing, painful, or threatening. Behaviorists look for events that determine whether or not a particular behavior will be repeated. Behavioral research focuses on *associative learning,* in which a mental link is formed between two events. Two kinds of associative learning are *classical conditioning* and *operant conditioning.*

behaviorism Learning theory that emphasizes the predictable role of environment in causing observable behavior.

Classical Conditioning

The Russian physiologist Ivan Pavlov (1849–1936) devised experiments in which dogs learned to salivate at the sound of a bell that rang at feeding time. These experiments were the foundation for **classical conditioning,** in which a response (salivation) to a stimulus (the bell) is evoked after repeated association with a stimulus that automatically elicits it (food).

classical conditioning Learning based on association of a stimulus that does not ordinarily elicit a response with another stimulus that does elicit the response.

The American behaviorist John B. Watson (1878–1958) applied stimulus-response theories to children, claiming that he could mold any infant in any way he chose. In

*Erikson later dropped the term "crisis" and referred instead to conflicting or competing tendencies.

What's Your View?

- In an experiment with classical conditioning, what standards would you suggest to safeguard participants' rights?

one of the earliest and most famous demonstrations of classical conditioning in human beings (Watson & Rayner, 1920), Watson set out to teach an 11-month-old baby known as "Little Albert" to fear furry white objects.

In this study, Albert was exposed to a loud noise just as he was about to stroke a furry white rat. The noise frightened him, and he began to cry. After repeated pairings of the rat with the loud noise, Watson reported, Albert whimpered with fear whenever he saw the rat. This study suggested that a baby could be conditioned to fear things he had not been afraid of before. However, as we will discuss at the end of this chapter, such research would be considered unethical today.

Classical conditioning is a natural form of learning that occurs even without intervention. By learning what events go together, children can anticipate what is going to happen, and this knowledge makes their world a more orderly, predictable place.

Operant Conditioning Baby Terrell lies peacefully in his crib. When he happens to smile, his mother goes over to the crib and plays with him. Later his father does the same thing. As this sequence is repeated, Terrell learns that his behavior (smiling) can produce a desirable consequence (loving attention from a parent); and so he keeps smiling to attract his parents' attention. An originally accidental behavior (smiling) has become a conditioned response.

operant conditioning Learning based on reinforcement or punishment.

This kind of learning is called **operant conditioning** because the individual learns from the consequences of "operating" on the environment. Unlike classical conditioning, operant conditioning involves voluntary behavior, such as Terrell's smiling.

The American psychologist B. F. Skinner (1904–1990), who formulated the principles of operant conditioning, worked primarily with rats and pigeons, but Skinner (1938) maintained that the same principles apply to human beings. He found that an organism will tend to repeat a response that has been reinforced and will suppress a response that has been punished. **Reinforcement** is a consequence of behavior that increases the likelihood that the behavior will be repeated; in Terrell's case, his parents' attention reinforces his smiling. **Punishment** is a consequence of behavior that *decreases* the likelihood of repetition. If Terrell's parents frowned when he smiled, he would be less likely to smile again. Whether a consequence is reinforcing or punishing depends on the person. What is reinforcing for one person may be punishing for another. For example, for a child who likes being alone, being sent to his or her room could be reinforcing rather than punishing.

reinforcement In operant conditioning, a stimulus that encourages repetition of a desired behavior.

punishment In operant conditioning, a stimulus that discourages repetition of a behavior.

Reinforcement can be either positive or negative. *Positive reinforcement* consists of *giving* a reward, such as food, gold stars, a bonus, or praise—or playing with a baby. *Negative reinforcement* consists of *taking away* something the individual does not like (known as an *aversive event*), such as a loud raspy noise. Negative reinforcement is sometimes confused with punishment. However, they are different. Punishment *suppresses* a behavior by *bringing on* an aversive event (such as spanking a child or giving an electric shock to an animal), or by *withdrawing* a positive event (such as watching television). Negative reinforcement *encourages* repetition of a behavior by *removing* an aversive event. When a toddler in the process of toilet training tells his parents he has soiled his diaper, the removal of the smelly, sticky diaper may encourage the child to signal again the next time he has an "accident."

Reinforcement is most effective when it immediately follows a behavior. If a response is no longer reinforced, it will eventually be *extinguished,* that is, return to its original (baseline) level. If, after a while, no one plays with Terrell when he smiles, he may not stop smiling but will smile far less than if his smiles still brought reinforcement.

Behavior modification, or behavior therapy, is the use of conditioning to gradually change behavior. It can cut down on the frequency of a child's temper tantrums and increase acceptable substitute behaviors. It is effective among children with special needs, such as autism, and among persons with eating disorders.

Social Learning (Social Cognitive) Theory The American psychologist Albert Bandura (b. 1925) developed many of the principles of **social learning theory.** Whereas behaviorists see the environment, acting upon the person, as the chief impetus for development, social learning or social cognitive theorists (Bandura, 1977, 1989) believe that the impetus for development comes from the person.

social learning theory Theory that behaviors are learned by observing and imitating models. Also called *social cognitive theory.*

Classic social learning theory maintains that people learn appropriate social behavior chiefly by observing and imitating models—that is, by watching other people. This process is called *modeling,* or **observational learning.** People initiate or advance their own learning by choosing models to imitate—say, a parent or a popular sports hero. Imitation of models is the most important element in how children learn a language, deal with aggression, develop a moral sense, and learn gender-appropriate behaviors. However, observational learning can occur even if the child does not imitate the observed behavior.

observational learning Learning through watching the behavior of others.

The specific behavior people imitate depends on what they perceive as valued in their culture. If all the teachers in Carlos's school are women, he probably will not copy their behavior, which he may consider "unmanly." However, if he meets a male teacher he likes, he may change his mind about the value of teachers as models. *Applied behavior analysis,* a combination of conditioning and modeling, can be used to help eliminate undesirable behaviors and encourage socially desirable ones.

Bandura's (1989) newest version of social learning theory is called *social cognitive theory.* The evolution from one name to the other reflects Bandura's increasing emphasis on cognitive responses to perceptions as central to development. Cognitive processes are at work as people observe models, learn "chunks" of behavior, and mentally put the chunks together into complex new behavior patterns. Rita, for example, imitates the toes-out walk of her dance teacher but models her dance steps after those of Carmen, a slightly more advanced student. Even so, she develops her own style of dancing by putting her observations together into a new pattern.

Through feedback on their behavior, children gradually form standards for judging their own actions and become more selective in choosing models who exemplify those standards. They also begin to develop a sense of *self-efficacy,* or confidence that they have the characteristics they need to succeed.

Checkpoint

Can you . . .

- ✔ Identify the chief concerns, strengths, and weaknesses of the learning perspective?
- ✔ Tell how classical conditioning and operant conditioning differ?
- ✔ Distinguish among positive reinforcement, negative reinforcement, and punishment?
- ✔ Compare behaviorism and social learning (or social cognitive) theory?

Perspective 3: Cognitive

The **cognitive perspective** focuses on thought processes and the behavior that reflects those processes. This perspective encompasses both organismic and mechanistically influenced theories. It includes the cognitive-stage theory of Piaget, the newer information-processing approach, and neo-Piagetian theories, which combine elements of both. It also includes contemporary efforts to apply findings of brain research to the understanding of cognitive processes. (Vygotsky's theory, which deals largely with the social contexts of cognition, will be discussed under the contextual perspective.)

cognitive perspective View that thought processes are central to development.

Jean Piaget's Cognitive-Stage Theory Much of what we know about how children think is due to the Swiss theoretician Jean Piaget (1896–1980). Piaget's theory was the forerunner of today's "cognitive revolution" with its emphasis on mental processes. Piaget took an organismic perspective, viewing cognitive development as the product of children's efforts to understand and act on their world.

Piaget's *clinical method* combined observation with flexible questioning. To find out how children think, Piaget followed up their answers with more questions. In this way he discovered that a typical 4-year-old believed that pennies or flowers were more numerous when arranged in a line than when heaped or piled up. From his observations of his own and other children, Piaget created a comprehensive theory of cognitive development.

Piaget believed that cognitive development begins with an inborn ability to adapt to the environment. By rooting for a nipple, feeling a pebble, or exploring the boundaries of a room, young children develop a more accurate picture of their surroundings and greater competence in dealing with them.

Piaget described cognitive development as occurring in four qualitatively different stages (listed in Table 2-2 and discussed in detail in later chapters), which represent universal patterns of development. At each stage a child's mind develops a new way of operating. From infancy through adolescence, mental operations evolve from learning based on simple sensory and motor activity to logical, abstract thought. Cognitive growth occurs through three interrelated processes: *organization, adaptation,* and *equilibration.*

organization Piaget's term for integration of knowledge into systems.

schemes Piaget's term for organized patterns of behavior used in different situations.

adaptation Piaget's term for adjustment to new information about the environment.

assimilation Piaget's term for incorporation of new information into an existing cognitive structure.

accommodation Piaget's term for changes in a cognitive structure to include new information.

equilibration Piaget's term for the tendency to seek a stable balance among cognitive elements.

Organization is the tendency to create increasingly complex cognitive structures: systems of knowledge or ways of thinking that incorporate more and more accurate images of reality. These structures, called **schemes,** are organized patterns of behavior that a person uses to think about and act in a situation. As children acquire more information, their schemes become more and more complex. An infant has a simple scheme for sucking, but soon develops varied schemes for how to suck at the breast, a bottle, or a thumb. At first schemes for looking and grasping operate independently. Later, infants integrate these separate schemes into a single scheme that allows them to look at an object while holding it.

Adaptation is Piaget's term for how children handle new information in light of what they already know. Adaptation involves two steps: (1) **assimilation,** taking in new information and incorporating it into existing cognitive structures, and (2) **accommodation,** changing one's cognitive structures to include the new information. **Equilibration**—a constant striving for a stable balance, or equilibrium—dictates the shift from assimilation to accommodation. When children cannot handle new experiences within their existing cognitive structures, and thus experience disequilibrium, they organize new mental patterns that integrate the new experience, thus restoring a more comfortable state of equilibrium. A breast- or bottle-fed baby who begins to suck on the spout of a "sippy" cup is showing assimilation—using an old scheme to deal with a new situation. When the infant discovers that sipping from a cup requires different tongue and mouth movements from those used to suck on a breast or bottle, she accommodates by modifying the old scheme. She has adapted her original sucking scheme to deal with a new experience: the cup. Thus, assimilation and accommodation work together to produce equilibrium and cognitive growth.

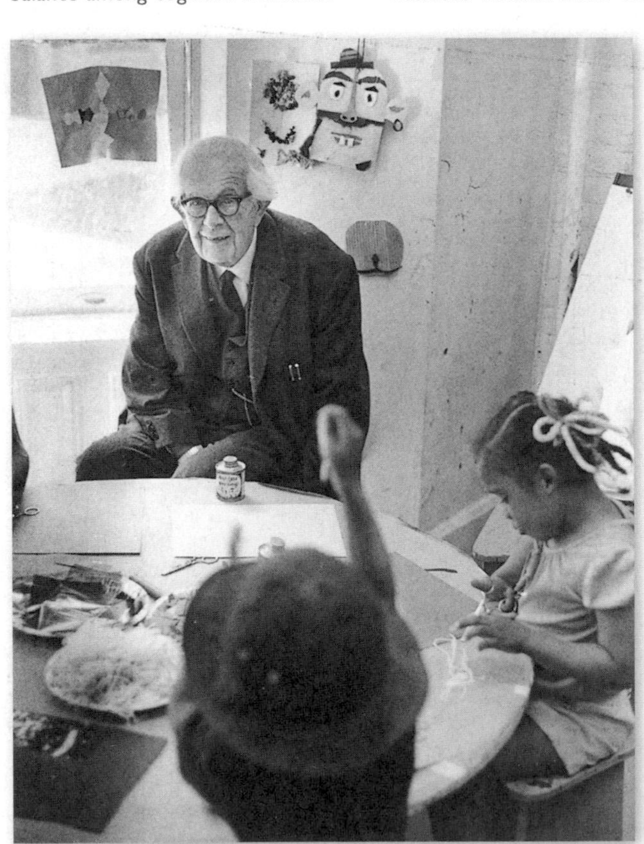

The Swiss psychologist Jean Piaget studied children's cognitive development by observing and talking with them in many settings, asking questions to find out how their minds worked.

Piaget's observations have yielded much information and some surprising insights. Who, for example, would have thought that most children younger than 7 do not realize that a ball of clay that has been rolled into a "worm" before their eyes still contains the same amount of clay? Or that an infant might think that a person who has moved out of sight may no longer exist? Piaget has shown us that children's minds are not miniature adult minds. Knowing how children think makes it easier for parents and teachers to understand them and teach them.

Yet Piaget seems to have seriously underestimated the abilities of infants and young children. Some contemporary psychologists question his distinct stages, pointing instead to evidence that cognitive development is more gradual and continuous (Flavell, 1992). Research beginning in the late 1960s has challenged Piaget's idea that thinking develops in a single, universal progression of stages leading to formal thought. Instead, children's cognitive processes seem closely tied to specific content (what they are thinking *about*), as well as to the context of a problem and the kinds of information and thought a culture considers important (Case & Okamoto, 1996). Finally, research on adults suggests that Piaget's focus on formal logic as the climax of cognitive development is too narrow. It does not account for the emergence of such mature abilities as practical problem solving, wisdom, and the capacity to deal with ambiguous situations and competing truths.

The Information-Processing Approach The newer **information-processing approach** attempts to explain cognitive development by analyzing the processes involved in perceiving and handling information. It is not a single theory but a framework, or set of assumptions, that underlies a wide range of theories and research.

information-processing approach Approach to the study of cognitive development by observing and analyzing the mental processes involved in perceiving and handling information.

The information-processing approach has practical applications. It enables researchers to estimate an infant's later intelligence from the efficiency of sensory perception and processing. It enables parents and teachers to help children learn by making them more aware of their own mental processes, and of strategies to enhance them. And psychologists can use information-processing models to test, diagnose, and treat learning problems (R. M. Thomas, 1996; Williams, 2001).

Computer-Based Models Some information-processing theorists compare the brain to a computer. Sensory impressions go in; behavior comes out. But what happens in between? How does the brain take sensation and perception, say, of an unfamiliar face, and use it to recognize that face again?

Information-processing researchers *infer* what goes on between a stimulus and a response. For example, they may ask a person to recall a list of words and then observe any difference in performance if the person repeats the list over and over before being asked to recall the words. Through such studies, some information-processing researchers have developed *computational models* or flow charts analyzing the specific steps people go through in gathering, storing, retrieving, and using information.

Despite the use of the "passive" computer model, information-processing theorists, like Piaget, see people as active thinkers about their world. Unlike Piaget, they generally do not propose stages of development. They view development as continuous and note age-related increases in the speed, complexity, and efficiency of mental processing and in the amount and variety of material that can be stored in memory.

Checkpoint

Can you . . .

- ✔ Contrast Piaget's assumptions and methods with those of classical learning theory?
- ✔ List three interrelated principles that bring about cognitive growth, according to Piaget, and give an example of each?
- ✔ Describe what information-processing researchers do, and tell three ways in which such research can be applied?
- ✔ Give an example of how neo-Piagetian theory draws from both Piaget and the information-processing approach?

Neo-Piagetian Theories During the 1980s, in response to criticisms of Piaget's theory, neo-Piagetian developmental psychologists began to integrate some elements of his theory with the information-processing approach. Instead of describing a single, general system of increasingly logical mental operations, neo-Piagetians focus on *specific* concepts, strategies, and skills, such as number concepts and comparisons of "more" and "less." They believe that children develop cognitively by becoming more efficient at processing information.

Because of its emphasis on efficiency of processing, the neo-Piagetian approach helps account for individual differences in cognitive ability and for uneven development in various domains. Currently a number of French and Swiss researchers are exploring the multiple processes and individual pathways of development that Piaget, for the most part, treated merely as variations on a general pattern (Larivée, Normandeau, & Parent, 2000).

The Cognitive Neuroscience Approach For most of the history of psychology, theorists and researchers studied cognitive processes apart from the physical structures of the brain in which these processes occur. Now that sophisticated instruments

cognitive neuroscience approach Approach to the study of cognitive development that links brain processes with cognitive ones.

make it possible to see the brain in action, adherents of the **cognitive neuroscience approach** argue that an accurate understanding of cognitive (and emotional) functioning must be linked to what happens in the brain (Gazzaniga, 2000; Humphreys, 2002; Posner & DiGirolamo, 2000). *Developmental* cognitive neuroscience may explain how cognitive growth occurs as the brain interacts with the environment (Johnson, 1999, 2001). It also may help us understand why some people do not develop normally and why adults age (Posner & DiGirolamo, 2000).

Brain research supports important aspects of information-processing models, such as the existence of separate physical structures to handle conscious and unconscious processing (Schacter, 1999; Yingling, 2001). It is giving scientists insight into why certain common memory failures, such as absentmindedness and difficulty accessing information in memory, occur (Schacter, 1999). Neurological research also may be able to shed light on such issues as whether intelligence is general or specialized and what influences a young child's readiness for formal learning (Byrnes & Fox, 1998).

social cognitive neuroscience An emerging interdisciplinary field that draws on cognitive neuroscience, information processing, and social psychology.

Social cognitive neuroscience is an emerging interdisciplinary field that bridges brain, mind, and behavior, bringing together data from cognitive neuroscience, social psychology, and the information-processing approach. Social cognitive neuroscientists use brain imaging and studies of people with brain injuries to figure out how neural pathways control such processes as memory and attention that in turn influence attitudes and emotions (Azar, 2002; Ochsner & Lieberman, 2001).

Checkpoint

Can you . . .

✔ Explain how brain research contributes to the understanding of cognitive processes and social behaviors and attitudes?

Ultimately, by shedding light on what neural and cognitive processes best explain particular social behaviors, social cognitive neuroscience may help to sift through competing theoretical explanations (Azar, 2002a; Ochsner & Lieberman, 2001). On a practical level, researchers can use tests of memory, attention, and language performance to figure out what brain systems are involved in such disorders as schizophrenia, anxiety, phobias, and obsessive-compulsive disorder (Ochsner & Lieberman, 2001).

Perspective 4: Evolutionary/Sociobiological

The *evolutionary/sociobiological perspective* is strongly influenced by Darwin's theory of evolution. According to Darwin, all animal species have developed through the related processes of *survival of the fittest* and *natural selection.* Individuals with traits better adapted to their environments survive; those less adapted do not. Through reproduction, more adaptive characteristics are passed on to future generations, while less adaptive characteristics die out. As environments change, some characteristics become more or less adaptive than before; this accounts for the emergence and extinction of species such as dinosaurs.

ethology Study of distinctive adaptive behaviors of species of animals that have evolved to increase survival of the species.

Ethology is the study of the distinctive behaviors of species of animals that have adaptive or survival value. Ethologists suggest that, for each species, certain innate behaviors have evolved to increase the odds of survival. One example, studied by Konrad Lorenz (refer back to Chapter 1), is newborn ducklings' instinct to follow their mother. Other examples are squirrels' burying of nuts in the fall and spiders' spinning of webs. Ethologists do comparative research to identify which behaviors are universal and which are specific to a particular species or are modified by culture. They do this by observing animals, usually in their natural surroundings. In the 1950s, the British psychologist John Bowlby applied ethological principles to human development. He saw infants' attachment to a caregiver as a behavior that evolved to promote the infant's survival.

sociobiological perspective View of development that focuses on biological bases of social behavior.

Ethology is now identified with the **sociobiological perspective** proposed by E. O. Wilson (1975), which focuses on biological bases of social behavior. It looks beyond an individual's immediate behavior to its function in promoting the survival of the group or species. Sociobiologists have studied such topics as reproductive patterns, altruism, parenting, and mating behavior. Besides ethology, the sociobiological perspective draws on the findings of several other scientific disciplines, including anthropology, ecology, genetics, and evolutionary psychology.

Evolutionary psychology applies the Darwinian principles of natural selection and survival of the fittest to individual behavior. According to this theory, people unconsciously strive not only for personal survival, but also to perpetuate their own genetic legacy. The result for the species is the development of mechanisms that have evolved to solve problems. For example, there is evidence that "morning sickness" and sudden aversion to certain foods, common during pregnancy, may actually be a mechanism for protecting the fetus from toxic substances during its most vulnerable period of development (Bjorklund & Pellegrini, 2000, 2002). However, such "evolved mechanisms" are not as universal or automatic as the innate mechanisms found in animals. Evolutionary psychology studies how biology and environment interact to produce behavior and development (Bjorklund & Pellegrini, 2000, 2002).

evolutionary psychology Application of Darwinian principles of natural selection and survival of the fittest to individual behavior.

Evolutionary *developmental* psychologists seek to identify behaviors that are adaptive at different ages (see Box 2-1 on pages 40–41). For example, an infant needs to stay close to the mother, but for an older child independent exploration is important.

Checkpoint

Can you . . .

- ✔ Tell how Darwin's theory of evolution underlies ethology and the sociobiological perspective?
- ✔ Explain how Darwin's principles of natural selection and survival of the fittest apply to evolutionary psychology?

Perspective 5: Contextual

According to the **contextual perspective,** development can be understood only in its social context. Contextualists see the individual, not as a separate entity interacting with the environment, but as an inseparable part of it.

contextual perspective View of development that sees the individual as inseparable from the social context.

Urie Bronfenbrenner's Bioecological Theory The American psychologist Urie Bronfenbrenner's (1979, 1986, 1994; Bronfenbrenner & Morris, 1998) currently influential **bioecological theory** describes the range of interacting influences that affect a developing person. Every biological organism develops within the context of ecological systems that support or stifle its growth. Just as we need to understand the ecology of the ocean or the forest if we wish to understand the development of a fish or a tree, we need to understand the ecology of the human environment if we wish to understand how people develop.

bioecological theory Bronfenbrenner's approach to understanding processes and contexts of development.

According to Bronfenbrenner, development occurs through increasingly complex processes of interaction between a developing person and the immediate, everyday environment—processes that are affected by more remote contexts of which the individual may not even be aware. To understand these processes, we must study the multiple contexts in which they occur. These begin with the home, classroom, workplace, and neighborhood; connect outward to societal institutions, such as educational and transportation systems; and finally encompass cultural and historical patterns that affect the family, the school, and virtually everything else in a person's life. By highlighting the interrelated contexts of, and influences on, development, Bronfenbrenner's theory provides a key to understanding the processes that underlie such diverse phenomena as academic achievement and antisocial behavior.

Bronfenbrenner identifies five interlocking contextual systems, from the most intimate to the broadest: the *microsystem, mesosystem, exosystem, macrosystem,* and *chronosystem* (see Figure 2-1 on page 42). Although we separate the various levels of influence for purposes of illustration, in reality they continually interact.

A **microsystem** is a pattern of activities, roles, and relationships within a setting, such as the home, school, workplace, or neighborhood, in which a person functions on a firsthand, day-to-day basis. It is through the microsystem that more distant influences, such as social institutions and cultural values, reach the developing person.

microsystem Bronfenbrenner's term for a setting in which a child interacts with others on an everyday, face-to-face basis.

BOX 2–1

Digging Deeper
The Adaptive Value of Immaturity

In comparison with other animals, human beings take a long time to grow up. For example, chimpanzees reach reproductive maturity in about eight years, rhesus monkeys in about four years, and lemurs in only two years or so. Human beings, by contrast, do not mature physically until the early teenage years and, at least in modern industrialized societies, typically reach cognitive and psychosocial maturity even later.

From the point of view of Darwinian evolutionary theory, this prolonged period of immaturity is essential to the survival and well-being of the species. Human beings, more than any other animal, live by their intelligence. Human communities and cultures are highly complex, and there is much to learn in order to "know the ropes." A long childhood serves as essential preparation for adulthood.

Some aspects of immaturity serve immediate adaptive purposes. For example, some primitive reflexes, such as rooting for the nipple, are protective for newborns and disappear when no longer needed. The development of the human brain, despite its rapid prenatal growth, is much less complete at birth than that of the brains of other primates; if the fetus's brain attained full human size before birth, its head would be too big to go through the birth canal. Instead, the human brain continues to grow throughout childhood, eventually far surpassing the brains of our simian cousins in the capacities for language and thought.

The human brain's slower development gives it greater flexibility, or *plasticity,* as not all connections are "hardwired" at an early age. "This behavioral and cognitive flexibility is perhaps the human species's greatest adaptive advantage" (Bjorklund, 1997, p. 157).

The extended period of immaturity and dependency during infancy and childhood allows children to spend much

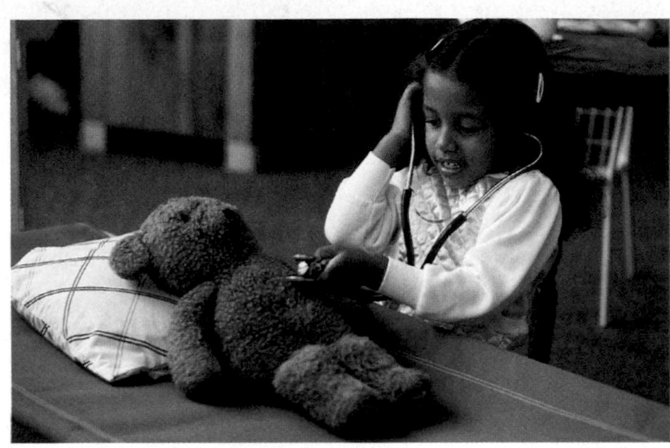

From an evolutionary perspective, the prolonged period of immaturity known as childhood *permits human beings to develop adaptive skills. One important way this happens is through "pretend" play. This girl playing "doctor" with her teddy bear is developing her imagination and experimenting with social roles.*

A microsystem involves personal, face-to-face relationships; and bidirectional influences flow back and forth. How, for example, does a new baby affect the parents' lives? How do their feelings and attitudes affect the baby? How does an employer's treatment of employees affect their productivity, and how does their productivity affect the employer's treatment of them?

mesosystem Bronfenbrenner's term for linkages between two or more microsystems.

A **mesosystem** is the interaction of two or more microsystems that contain the developing person. It may include linkages between home and school (such as parent-teacher conferences) or between the family and the peer group. Attention to mesosystems can alert us to differences in the ways the same person acts in different settings. For example, a child who can satisfactorily complete a school assignment at home may become tongue-tied when asked a question about the assignment in class.

exosystem Bronfenbrenner's term for linkages between two or more settings, one of which does not contain the child.

An **exosystem,** like a mesosystem, consists of linkages between two or more settings; but in an exosystem, unlike a mesosystem, at least one of these settings—such as parents' workplaces and parents' social networks—does *not* contain the developing person and thus affects him or her only indirectly. A woman whose employer encourages breast-feeding by providing pumping and milk storage facilities may be more likely to continue nursing her baby.

Digging Deeper

BOX 2-1

—*continued*

of their time in play; and, as Piaget maintained, it is largely through play that cognitive development occurs. Play also enables children to develop motor skills and experiment with social roles. It is a vehicle for creative imagination and intellectual curiosity, the hallmarks of the human spirit.

Research on animals suggests that the immaturity of early sensory and motor functioning may protect infants from overstimulation. By limiting the amount of information they have to deal with, it may help them make sense of their world and focus on experiences essential to survival, such as feeding and attachment to the mother. Later, infants' limited memory capacity may simplify the processing of linguistic sounds and thus facilitate early language learning.

Limitations on young children's thought also may have adaptive value. For example, Piaget observed that young children are *egocentric;* they tend to see things from their own point of view. This tendency toward egocentrism may actually help children learn. In one study (Ratner & Foley, 1997), 5-year-olds took turns with an adult in placing furniture in a dollhouse. In a control group, the adult had already placed half of the items, and the children were then asked to place the other half. When questioned afterward, the children who had taken turns with the adult remembered more about the task and were better able to repeat it. It may be that an "I did it!" bias helps young children's recall by avoiding the need to distinguish between their own actions and the actions of others. Young children also tend to be unrealistic in assessing their own abilities, believing they can do more than they actually can. This immature self-judgment can encourage children to try new things by reducing their fear of failure.

All in all, evolutionary theory and research suggest that immaturity is not necessarily equivalent to deficiency, and that some attributes of infancy and childhood have persisted because they are appropriate to the tasks of a particular time of life.

Source: Bjorklund, 1997; Bjorklund & Pellegrini, 2000, 2002.

What's Your View?

Can you think of additional examples of the adaptive value of immaturity? Can you think of ways in which immaturity may *not* be adaptive?

Check It Out:

For more information on this topic, go to www.mhhe.com/papaliah9, where you will find a link to the Brazelton Institute at Harvard Medical School. This site includes a link to the Brazelton Scale, which measures what newborns can do to adapt to their world.

The **macrosystem** consists of overall cultural patterns, like those Margaret Mead studied: dominant values, beliefs, customs, and economic and social systems of a culture or subculture, which filter down in countless ways to individuals' daily lives. For example, whether a child grows up in a nuclear or extended-family household is strongly influenced by a culture's macrosystem. We can see a more subtle macrosystem influence in the individualistic values stressed in the United States, as contrasted with the predominant value of group harmony in Chinese culture.

macrosystem Bronfenbrenner's term for a society's overall cultural patterns.

The **chronosystem** adds the dimension of time: the degree of stability or change in a child's world. This can include changes in family composition, place of residence, or parents' employment, as well as larger events such as wars, economic cycles, and waves of migration. Changes in family patterns (such as the increase in working mothers in western industrial societies and the decline of the extended-family household in developing countries) are chronosystem factors.

chronosystem Bronfenbrenner's term for effects of time on other developmental systems.

According to Bronfenbrenner, a person is not merely an outcome of development, but a shaper of it. People affect their own development through their biological and psychological characteristics, talents and skills, disabilities, and temperament.

Figure 2-1
Bronfenbrenner's bioecological theory. Concentric circles show five levels of environmental influence, from the most intimate environment (innermost circle) to the broadest—all within the dimension of time. The circles form a set of nested influences, like egg-shaped boxes that fit inside one another, encasing the developing person. The figure shows what we would see if we sliced the nested "boxes" across the middle and looked inside. Keep in mind that the boundaries between the "boxes" are fluid, and the "boxes" are interconnected. (*Source:* Adapted from Cole & Cole, 1989.)

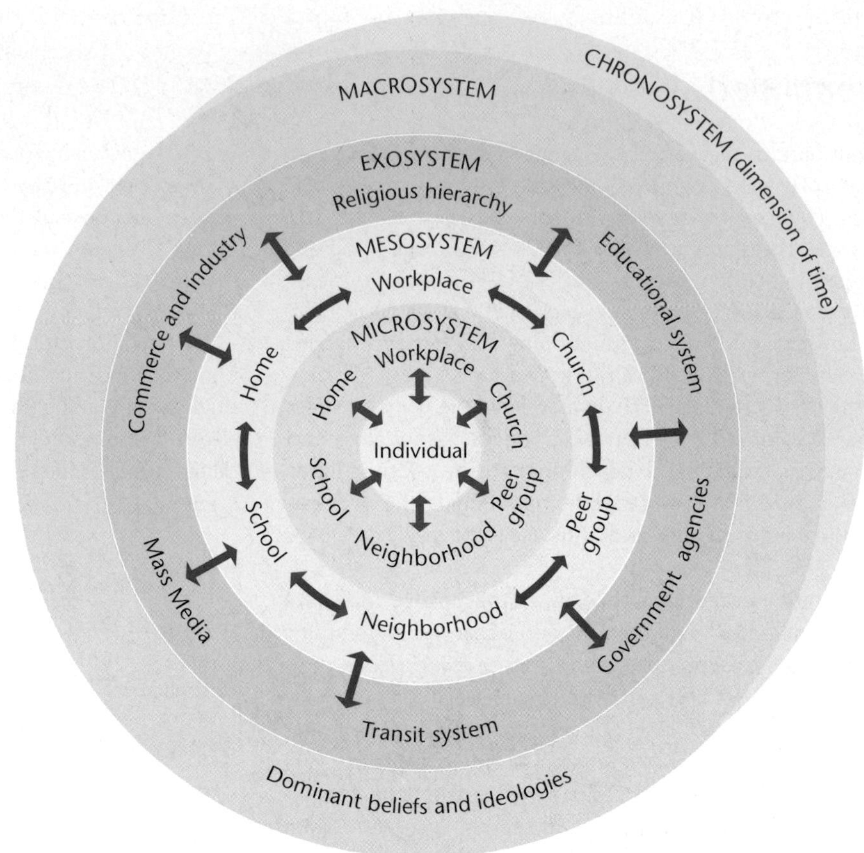

sociocultural theory
Vygotsky's theory of how contextual factors affect children's development.

zone of proximal development (ZPD)
Vygotsky's term for the difference between what a child can do alone and with help.

According to the Russian psychologist Lev Semenovich Vygotsky, children learn through social interaction.

Lev Vygotsky's Sociocultural Theory The Russian psychologist Lev Semenovich Vygotsky (1896–1934) was a prominent proponent of the contextual perspective, particularly as it applies to children's cognitive development. In contrast with Bronfenbrenner, who sees contextual systems as centered around the individual person, Vygotsky's central focus is the social, cultural, and historical complex of which a child is a part. To understand cognitive development, he maintained, one must look to the social processes from which a child's thinking is derived.

Vygotsky's (1978) **sociocultural theory,** like Piaget's theory of cognitive development, stresses children's active engagement with their environment. But whereas Piaget described the solo mind taking in and interpreting information about the world, Vygotsky saw cognitive growth as a *collaborative* process. Children, said Vygotsky, learn through social interaction. They acquire cognitive skills as part of their induction into a way of life. Shared activities help children to internalize their society's ways of thinking and behaving and to make those ways their own.

According to Vygotsky, adults (or more advanced peers) must help direct and organize a child's learning before the child can master and internalize it. This guidance is most effective in helping children cross the **zone of proximal development (ZPD),** the gap between what they are already able to do and what they are not quite ready to accomplish by themselves. (*Proximal* means "nearby.") Children in the ZPD for a particular task can almost, but not quite, perform the task on their own. With the right kind of guidance, however, they can do it successfully. In the course of the collaboration, responsibility for directing and monitoring learning gradually shifts to the child.

When an adult teaches a child to float, the adult first supports the child in the water and then lets go gradually as the child's body relaxes into a horizontal position. When the child seems ready, the adult withdraws all but one finger and finally lets the child float freely. Some followers of Vygotsky (Wood, 1980; Wood, Bruner, & Ross, 1976) have applied the metaphor of scaffolds—the temporary platforms on which construction workers stand—to this way of teaching. **Scaffolding,** then, is the temporary support that parents, teachers, or others give a child to do a task until the child can do it alone.

scaffolding Temporary support to help a child master a task.

Vygotsky's theory has important implications for education and for cognitive testing. Tests based on the ZPD, which focus on a child's potential, provide a valuable alternative to standard intelligence tests that assess what the child has already learned; and many children may benefit from the sort of expert guidance Vygotsky prescribes.

A major contribution of the contextual perspective has been its emphasis on the social component in development. Research attention has shifted from the individual to larger, interactional units—parent and child, sibling and sibling, the entire family, the neighborhood, and broader societal institutions. The contextual perspective also reminds us that the development of children in one culture or one group within a culture (such as white, middle-class Americans) may not be an appropriate norm for children in other societies or cultural groups.

Checkpoint

Can you . . .

- ✔ Identify the chief assumptions of the contextual perspective?
- ✔ Differentiate Bronfenbrenner's five systems of contextual influence?
- ✔ Tell how Vygotsky's theory applies to educational teaching and testing?

How Theory and Research Work Together

No one theory of human development is universally accepted, and no one theoretical perspective explains all facets of development. Lacking a widely accepted "grand" theory (such as those of Freud and Piaget), the trend today is toward smaller "minitheories" aimed at explaining specific phenomena, such as how poverty influences family relations. At the same time, there is increasing theoretical and research exploration of the interplay among the physical, cognitive, and psychosocial domains. There also is growing awareness of the importance of historical change and of the need to explore cultural diversity.

Theories of human development often grow out of, and are tested by, research. Thus research questions and methods tend to reflect the researcher's theoretical orientation. For example, in trying to understand how a child develops a sense of right and wrong, a behaviorist would examine the way parents respond to the child's behavior: what kinds of behavior they punish or praise. A social learning theorist would focus on imitation of moral examples, possibly in stories or in movies. An information-processing researcher might do a task analysis to identify the steps a child goes through in determining the range of moral options available and then in deciding which option to pursue.

What's Your View?

- Which of the theoretical perspectives would be most useful for (a) a mother trying to get her child to say "please," (b) a teacher interested in stimulating critical thinking, (c) a researcher studying siblings' imitation of one another?

With this vital connection between theory and research in mind, let's look at the methods developmental researchers use.

Research Methods

Guidepost

4. How do developmental scientists study people, and what are the advantages and disadvantages of each research method?

Two key issues at the outset of a scientific investigation are how the participants will be chosen and how the data will be collected. These decisions often depend on what questions the researcher wants to answer. All these issues play a part in a research design, or plan.

Researchers in human development work within two methodological traditions: *quantitative* and *qualitative.* **Quantitative research** deals with "hard," objectively measurable data; for example, how much fear or anxiety patients feel before surgery, as measured by standardized tests, physiological changes, or statistical analysis. Behaviorists generally use quantitative research. **Qualitative research** deals with "soft" data about the nature or quality of participants' subjective experiences, feelings, or beliefs—for instance, how patients describe their emotions before surgery (Morse & Field, 1995), or, as with Margaret Mead's research, how girls in the South Sea islands describe their experience of puberty. Piaget's clinical method is another example of qualitative research.

quantitative research Research that focuses on "hard" data and numerical or statistical measures.

qualitative research Research that focuses on "soft" data, such as subjective experiences, feelings, or beliefs.

scientific method System of established principles and processes of scientific inquiry.

Quantitative research is based on the **scientific method,** an overall process that generally characterizes scientific inquiry in any field. Careful use of the scientific method enables researchers to come to sound conclusions about human development. The usual steps in the method are

- *identifying a problem* to be studied, often on the basis of a theory or of previous research.
- *formulating hypotheses* to be tested by research.
- *collecting data.*
- *analyzing the data* to determine whether or not they support the hypothesis.
- *disseminating findings* so that other observers can check, learn from, analyze, repeat, and build on the results.

Qualitative research takes a more open-ended, exploratory route. Instead of generating hypotheses from previous research, qualitative researchers gather data and then examine it to see what hypotheses or theories may emerge. Qualitative research is highly interpretive; it cannot yield general conclusions, but it can be a rich source of insights into individuals' attitudes and behavior.

The selection of quantitative or qualitative methods depends on a number of factors: the topic for study, how much is already known about it, the researcher's expertise and theoretical orientation, and the setting. Quantitative research is often done in laboratory settings, where controlled conditions can produce replicable (repeatable) results. Qualitative research is most appropriate in everyday social settings, for investigating topics about which little is currently known. Qualitative research can be extremely time-consuming and expensive.

Investigators may combine the two methods. Often qualitative research yields findings that point the way to quantitative research. For example, patients' descriptions of their experience may suggest means of reducing stress before surgery, which can then be tested and compared for effectiveness (Morse & Field, 1995).

Checkpoint

Can you . . .

- ✔ Compare quantitative and qualitative research, and give an example of each?
- ✔ Summarize the five steps in the scientific method and tell why each is important?

Sampling

In qualitative research, samples tend to be small and need not be random. Participants in this kind of research may be chosen for their ability to communicate the nature of their experience—say, what it feels like to go through surgery—or because they have undergone a particular type of surgery. Sampling is a more complex issue for quantitative research.

sample Group of participants chosen to represent the entire population under study.

To be sure that the results of their research are true generally and not just for specific participants, quantitative researchers need to control who gets into the study. Because studying an entire *population* (a group to whom the findings may apply) is usually too costly and time-consuming, investigators select a **sample,** a smaller group within the population. The sample should adequately represent the target population—that is, it should show relevant characteristics in the same proportions as in the entire population. Otherwise the results cannot properly be *generalized,* or applied to the population as a whole. To judge how generalizable the findings are likely to be, we need to compare the characteristics of the people in the sample with the population as a whole.

Often researchers seek to achieve representativeness through *random selection,* in which each person in a population has an equal and independent chance of being chosen. If we wanted to study the effects of an educational program, one way to select a random sample would be to put all the names of participating children into a large bowl, stir it, and then draw out a certain number of names. A random sample, especially a large one, is likely to represent the population well.

To find out how the September 11 terrorist attacks affected the mental health of Manhattan residents, researchers reached 1,008 households by random digit dialing and conducted telephone interviews with the adult in the household whose birthday was most recent. In the interviews, which were conducted within two months after the attacks, 9.7 percent of the sample reported current symptoms of depression, and 7.5 percent appeared to suffer from post-traumatic stress disorder (PTSD). Among adults living near the World Trade Center, 20 percent reported symptoms of PTSD. The researchers then generalized the findings to estimate the extent of those disorders among the population of Manhattan (Galea et al., 2002).

Unfortunately, a random sample of a large population is often difficult to obtain. Instead, many studies use samples selected for convenience or accessibility (for example, children born in a particular hospital or patients in a nursing home). The findings of such studies may not apply to the population as a whole.

Forms of Data Collection

Common ways of gathering data (see Table 2-3) include self-reports (verbal reports by study participants), tests and other behavioral measures, and observation. Researchers may use one or more of these data collection techniques in any research design. Qualitative research tends to depend heavily on interviews and on observation in natural settings, whereas quantitative research makes use of more structured methods. A current trend is toward increased use of self-reports and observation in combination with more objective measures.

Self-Reports: Diaries, Interviews, Questionnaires The simplest form of self-report is a *diary* or log. Adolescents may be asked, for example, to record what they eat each day, or the times when they feel depressed. In studying young children, *parental self-reports*—diaries, journals, interviews, or questionnaires—are commonly used, often together with other methods, such as videotaping or recording.

In a face-to-face or telephone *interview,* researchers ask questions about attitudes, opinions, or behavior. In a *structured* interview (such as the one used in the study of reactions to September 11, described in the preceding "Sampling" section), each participant is asked the same set of questions. An *open-ended* interview, more often used in qualitative research, is more flexible; the interviewer can vary the topics and order of questions and can ask follow-up questions based on the responses. To reach more

Table 2-3 Characteristics of Major Methods of Data Collection

Type	Main Characteristics	Advantages	Disadvantages
Self-report: diary, interview, or questionnaire	Participants are asked about some aspect of their lives; questioning may be highly structured or more flexible.	Can provide firsthand information about a person's life, attitudes, or opinions.	Participant may not remember information accurately or may distort responses in a socially desirable way; how question is asked or by whom may affect answer.
Behavioral measures	Participants are tested on abilities, skills, knowledge, competencies, or physical responses.	Provides objectively measurable information; avoids subjective distortions.	Cannot measure attitudes or other nonbehavioral phenomena; results may be affected by extraneous factors.
Naturalistic observation	People are observed in their normal setting, with no attempt to manipulate behavior.	Provides good description of behavior; does not subject people to unnatural settings that may distort behavior.	Lack of control; observer bias.
Laboratory observation	Participants are observed in the laboratory, with no attempt to manipulate behavior.	Provides good descriptions; greater control than naturalistic observation, since all participants are observed under same conditions.	Observer bias; controlled situation can be artificial.

people and protect their privacy, researchers sometimes distribute a printed *questionnaire,* which participants fill out and return.

By questioning a large number of people, investigators get a broad picture—at least of what the respondents *say* they believe or do or did. However, people willing to participate in interviews or fill out questionnaires tend to be unrepresentative of the population as a whole. Furthermore, heavy reliance on self-reports may be unwise, since people may not have thought about what they feel and think, or honestly may not know. Some people forget when and how events actually took place, and others consciously or unconsciously distort their replies to fit what is considered socially desirable.

How a question is asked, and by whom, can affect the answer. When researchers at the National Institute on Drug Abuse reworded a question about alcohol use to indicate that a "drink" meant "more than a few sips," the percentage of teenagers who reported drinking alcohol dropped significantly (National Institute on Drug Abuse, 1996). When questioned about risky or socially disapproved behavior, such as sexual habits and drug use, respondents may be more candid in responding to a computerized survey than to a paper-and-pencil one (Turner et al., 1998).

Behavioral and Performance Measures In quantitative research, investigators often use more objective measures instead of, or in addition to, self-reports. A behavioral or performance measure *shows* something about a person rather than asking the person or someone else (such as a parent or friend) to *tell* about it. Tests and other behavioral and neuropsychological measures, including mechanical and electronic devices, may be used to assess abilities, skills, knowledge, competencies, or physiological responses, such as heart rate and brain activity. Although these measures are less subjective than self-reports, such factors as fatigue and self-confidence can affect results.

Some tests, such as intelligence tests, compare performance with that of other test-takers. Such tests can be meaningful and useful only if they are both *valid* (that is, the tests measure the abilities they claim to measure) and *reliable* (that is, the results are reasonably consistent from one time to another). To avoid bias, tests must be *standardized,* that is, given and scored by the same methods and criteria for all test-takers.

When measuring a characteristic such as intelligence, it is important to define exactly what is to be measured in such a way that other researchers will understand and can comment about the results. For this purpose, researchers use **operational definitions**—definitions stated solely in terms of the operations or procedures used to produce or measure a phenomenon. Intelligence, for example, can be defined as the ability to achieve a certain score on a test covering logical relationships, memory, and vocabulary recognition. Some people may disagree with this definition, but no one can resonably claim that it is not clear.

operational definitions Definitions stated solely in terms of the operations or procedures used to produce or measure a phenomenon.

Naturalistic and Laboratory Observation Observation can take two forms: *naturalistic observation* and *laboratory observation.* In **naturalistic observation,** common in qualitative research, researchers look at people in real-life settings. The researchers do not try to alter behavior or the environment; they simply record what they see. In **laboratory observation,** researchers observe and record behavior in a controlled situation, such as a laboratory. By observing all participants under the same conditions, investigators can more clearly identify differences in behavior not attributable to the environment.

naturalistic observation Research method in which behavior is studied in natural settings without intervention or manipulation.

laboratory observation Research method in which all participants are observed under the same controlled conditions.

Both kinds of observation can provide valuable descriptions of behavior, but they have limitations. For one, they do not explain *why* people behave as they do, though they may suggest interpretations. Then, too, an observer's presence can alter behavior. When people know they are being watched, they may act differently. Finally, there is a risk of *observer bias:* the researcher's tendency to interpret data to fit expectations, or to emphasize some aspects and minimize others.

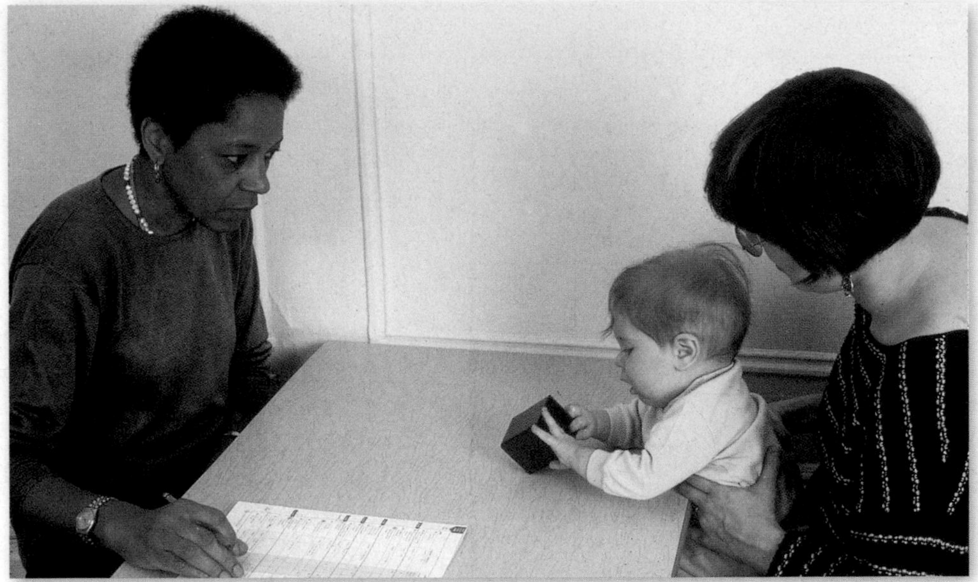

A child under laboratory observation may or may not behave the same way as in a naturalistic setting, such as at home or at school, but both kinds of observation can provide valuable information.

Checkpoint

Can you . . .

- ✔ Explain the purpose of random selection and tell how it can be achieved?
- ✔ Compare the advantages and disadvantages of various forms of data collection?

During the 1960s, laboratory observation was used most commonly so as to achieve more rigorous control. Now such technological devices as portable videotape recorders and computers enable researchers to analyze moment-by-moment changes in behavior—for example, in interaction between spouses (Gottman & Notarius, 2000)—making naturalistic observation more accurate and objective than it would otherwise be.

Basic Research Designs

A research design is a plan for conducting a scientific investigation: what questions are to be answered, how participants are to be selected, how data are to be collected and interpreted, and how valid conclusions can be drawn. Four of the basic designs used in developmental research are case studies, ethnographic studies, correlational studies, and experiments. The first two are generally qualitative, the last two quantitative. Each design has advantages and drawbacks, and each is appropriate for certain kinds of research problems (see Table 2-4 on page 48).

case study Study of an individual.

Case Studies A **case study** is a study of an individual, such as Victor, the wild boy of Aveyron (discussed in the Focus of Chapter 1). A number of theories, most notably Freud's, have grown out of clinical case studies, which include careful observation and interpretation of what patients say and do. Case studies also may use behavioral or neuropsychological measures and biographical, autobiographical, or documentary materials.

Case studies offer useful, in-depth information. They can explore sources of behavior and can test treatments. They also can suggest further research. Another advantage is flexibility: the researcher is free to explore avenues of inquiry that arise during the course of the study. However, case studies have shortcomings. From studying Victor, for instance, we learn much about the development of a single child, but not how the information applies to children in general. Furthermore, case studies cannot explain behavior with certainty, because there is no way to test their conclusions. Even though it seems reasonable that Victor's severely deprived environment caused or contributed to his language deficiency, it is impossible to know how he would have developed with a normal upbringing.

Table 2-4 Basic Research Designs

Type	Main Characteristics	Advantages	Disadvantages
Case study	Study of single individual in depth.	Flexibility; provides detailed picture of one person's behavior and development; can generate hypotheses.	May not generalize to others; conclusions not directly testable; cannot establish cause and effect.
Ethnographic study	In-depth study of a culture or subculture.	Can help overcome culturally-based biases in theory and research; can test universality of developmental phenomena.	Subject to observer bias.
Correlational study	Attempt to find positive or negative relationship between variables.	Allows prediction of one variable on basis of another; can suggest hypotheses about causal relationships.	Cannot establish cause and effect.
Experiment	Controlled procedure in which an experimenter controls the independent variable to determine its effect on the dependent variable; may be conducted in the laboratory or field.	Establishes cause-and-effect relationships; highly controlled procedure that can be repeated by another investigator. Degree of control is greatest in the laboratory experiment.	Findings, especially when derived from laboratory experiments, may not generalize to situations outside the laboratory.

ethnographic study In-depth study of a culture, which uses a combination of methods including participant observation.

participant observation Research method in which the observer lives with the people or participates in the activity being observed.

Ethnographic Studies An **ethnographic study** seeks to describe the pattern of relationships, customs, beliefs, technology, arts, and traditions that make up a society's way of life. Ethnographic research can be qualitative, quantitative, or both. It uses a combination of methods, including **participant observation.** Participant observation is a form of naturalistic observation in which researchers live or participate in the societies or groups they observe, as Margaret Mead (1928, 1930, 1935) did, often for long periods of time; thus, their findings are especially open to observer bias.

Despite later disputes over Mead's sampling methods and her findings on adolescence (D. Freeman, 1983; L. D. Holmes, 1987), the anthropologist Robert LeVine wrote, "Mead's basic message to the child development field remains as valid today as in 1930: To understand how children grow up under varied environmental conditions, one must be willing to go to where those conditions already exist, to examine them with respect and in detail, and to change one's assumptions in the face of new observations" (LeVine et al., 1994, p. 9).

Ethnographic research can help overcome cultural biases in theory and research (see Box 2-2). Ethnography demonstrates the error of assuming that principles developed from research in western cultures are universally applicable.

correlational study Research design intended to discover whether a statistical relationship between variables exists.

Correlational Studies A **correlational study** is an attempt to find a *correlation,* or statistical relationship, between *variables,* phenomena that change or vary among people or can be varied for purposes of research. Correlations are expressed in terms of direction (positive or negative) and magnitude (degree). Two variables that are related *positively* increase or decrease together. A positive, or direct, correlation between televised violence and aggressiveness would exist if children who watched more violent television hit, bit, or kicked more than children who watched less violent television. Two variables have a *negative,* or inverse, correlation if, as one increases, the other decreases. Studies show a negative correlation between amount of schooling and the risk of developing dementia (mental deterioration) due to Alzheimer's disease in old age. In other words, the less education, the more dementia (Katzman, 1993).

Correlations are reported as numbers ranging from -1.0 (a perfect negative relationship) to $+1.0$ (a perfect positive relationship). Perfect correlations are rare. The closer a correlation comes to $+1.0$ or -1.0, the stronger the relationship, either positive or negative. A correlation of zero means that the variables have no relationship.

Window on the World

BOX 2-2

Purposes of Cross-Cultural Research

When David, an American child, was asked to identify the missing detail in a picture of a face with no mouth, he said, "The mouth." But Ari, an Asian immigrant child in Israel, said that the *body* was missing. Since art in his culture does not present a head as a complete picture, he thought the absence of a body was more important than the omission of "a mere detail like the mouth" (Anastasi, 1988, p. 360).

By looking at different cultural groups, researchers can learn in what ways development is universal and in what ways it is culturally determined. For example, children everywhere learn to speak in the same sequence, advancing from cooing and babbling to single words and then to simple combinations of words. The words vary from culture to culture, but around the world toddlers put them together to form sentences similar in structure. Such findings suggest that the capacity for learning language is universal and inborn.

On the other hand, culture can exert a surprisingly large influence on early motor development. African babies, whose parents often prop them in a sitting position and bounce them on their feet, tend to sit and walk earlier than U.S. babies (Rogoff & Morelli, 1989).

The society in which children grow up influences the skills they learn. In the United States, children learn to read, write, and, increasingly, to operate computers. In rural Nepal, they learn how to drive water buffalo and find their way along mountain paths.

One important reason to conduct research among different cultural groups is to recognize biases in traditional western theories and research that often go unquestioned until they are shown to be a product of cultural influences. "Working with people from a quite different background can make one aware of aspects of human activity that are not noticeable until they are missing or differently arranged, as with the fish who reputedly is unaware of water until removed from it" (Rogoff & Morelli, 1989, p. 343).

Since so much research in human development has focused on western industrialized societies, many people have defined typical development in these societies as the norm, or standard of behavior. Measuring against this "norm" leads to narrow—and often, wrong—ideas about development. Pushed to its extreme, this belief can cause the development of people in other ethnic and cultural groups to be seen as deviant (Rogoff & Morelli, 1989).

In this book we discuss several influential theories developed from research in western societies that do not hold up when tested on people from other cultures—theories about gender roles, abstract thinking, moral reasoning, and a number of other aspects of human development. Throughout this book, we consistently look at people in cultures and subcultures other than the dominant one in the United States to show how closely development is tied to society and culture and to add to our understanding of normal development in many settings.

What's Your View?

Can you think of a situation in which you made an incorrect assumption about a person because you were unfamiliar with her or his cultural background?

Check It Out:

For more information on this topic, go to www.mhhe.com/papaliah9, where you will find a link to the website for the Department of Psychology at the University of Santa Cruz. This site includes information about faculty members who conduct cross-cultural research in human development.

Correlations allow us to predict one variable on the basis of another. If, for example, we found a positive correlation between watching televised violence and fighting, we would predict that children who watch violent shows are more likely to get into fights. The greater the magnitude of the correlation between two variables, the greater the ability to predict one from the other.

Although strong correlations may suggest possible causes, these possible cause-and-effect relations need to be examined very critically. We cannot be sure from a positive correlation between televised violence and aggressiveness that watching televised violence *causes* aggressive play; we can conclude only that the two variables are related. It is possible that the causation goes the other way: aggressive play may lead children to watch more violent programs. Or a third variable—perhaps an inborn predisposition toward aggressiveness, or living in a more violent envionment—may cause a child both to watch violent programs and to act aggressively. Similarly, we cannot be sure that schooling protects against dementia; it may be that another variable, such as socioeconomic status, might explain both lower levels of schooling and higher levels of dementia. The only way to show with certainty that one variable causes another is through an experiment—something that, in studying human beings, is not always possible for practical or ethical reasons.

experiment Rigorously controlled, replicable procedure in which the researcher manipulates variables to assess the effect of one on the other.

Experiments An **experiment** is a controlled procedure in which the experimenter manipulates variables to learn how one affects another. Scientific experiments must be conducted and reported in such a way that another experimenter can *replicate* them, that is, repeat them in exactly the same way with different participants to verify the results and conclusions.

experimental group In an experiment, the group receiving the treatment under study.

control group In an experiment, a group of people, similar to those in the experimental group, who do not receive the treatment whose effects are to be measured.

Groups and Variables A common way to conduct an experiment is to divide the participants into two kinds of groups. An **experimental group** is composed of people who are to be exposed to the experimental manipulation or *treatment*—the phenomenon the researcher wants to study. Afterward, the effect of the treatment will be measured one or more times to find out what changes, if any, it caused. A **control group** is composed of people who are similar to the experimental group but do not receive the treatment, or receive a different treatment. An experiment may include one or more of each type of group. Or, if the experimenter wants to compare the effects of different treatments (say, of two methods of teaching), the overall sample may be divided into *treatment groups,* each of which receives one of the treatments under study.

One team of researchers (Whitehurst et al., 1988) wanted to find out what effect *dialogic reading,* a special method of reading picture books to very young children, might have on their language and vocabulary skills. The researchers compared two groups of middle-class children ages 21 to 35 months. In the *experimental group,* the parents adopted the new read-aloud method (the treatment), which consisted of encouraging children's active participation and giving frequent, age-based feedback. In the *control group,* parents simply read aloud as they usually did. After 1 month, the children in the experimental group were 8.5 months ahead of the control group in level of speech and 6 months ahead in vocabulary; 9 months later, the experimental group were still 6 months ahead of the controls. It is fair to conclude, then, that this read-aloud method improved the children's language and vocabulary skills.

independent variable In an experiment, the condition over which the experimenter has direct control.

dependent variable In an experiment, the condition that may or may not change as a result of changes in the independent variable.

In this experiment, the type of reading approach was the *independent variable,* and the children's language skills were the *dependent variable.* An **independent variable** is something over which the experimenter has direct control. A **dependent variable** is something that may or may not change as a result of changes in the independent variable; in other words, it *depends* on the independent variable. In an experiment, a researcher manipulates the independent variable to see how changes in it will affect the dependent variable.

Random Assignment If an experiment finds a significant difference in the performance of the experimental and control groups, how do we know that the cause was the independent variable, in other words that the conclusion is valid? For example, in the read-aloud experiment, how can we be sure that the reading method and not some other factor (such as intelligence) caused the difference in language development of the two groups? The best way to control for effects of such extraneous factors is *random assignment:* assigning the participants to groups in such a way that each person has an equal chance of being placed in any group.

If assignment is random and the sample is large enough, differences in such factors as age, sex, race, IQ, and socioeconomic status will be evenly distributed so that the groups initially are as alike as possible in every respect except for the variable to be tested. Otherwise, unintended differences between the groups might *confound,* or contaminate, the results, and any conclusions drawn from the experiment would have to be viewed with suspicion. Also, during the course of the experiment, the experimenter must make sure that everything except the independent variable is held constant. For example, in the read-aloud study, parents of the experimental and control groups must spend the same amount of time reading to their children. In that way, the experimenter can be sure that any differences between the reading skills of the two groups are due to the reading method, and not some other factor.

When participants in an experiment are randomly assigned to treatment groups, the experimenter can be fairly confident that a causal relationship has (or has not) been established. However, random assignment with regard to some variables, such as age, gender, and race, is not always possible: we cannot assign Terry to be 5 years old and Brett to be 10, or one to be a boy and the other a girl, or one to be black and the other white. When studying such a variable—for example, whether boys or girls are stronger in certain abilities—researchers can strengthen the validity of their conclusions by randomly selecting participants and by trying to make sure that they are statistically equivalent in other ways that might make a difference in the study.

Laboratory, Field, and Natural Experiments The control necessary for establishing cause and effect is most easily achieved in *laboratory experiments.* In a laboratory experiment the participants are brought to a special place where they experience conditions manipulated by the experimenter. The experimenter records the participants' reactions to these conditions, perhaps comparing them with their own or other participants' behavior under different conditions.

However, not all experiments can be readily done in the laboratory. A *field experiment* is a controlled study conducted in an everyday setting, such as home or school. The experiment in which parents tried out a new way of reading aloud was a field experiment.

Laboratory and field experiments differ in two important respects. One is the *degree of control* exerted by the experimenter; the other is the degree to which findings can be *generalized* beyond the study situation. Laboratory experiments can be more rigidly controlled and thus easier to replicate. However, the results may be less

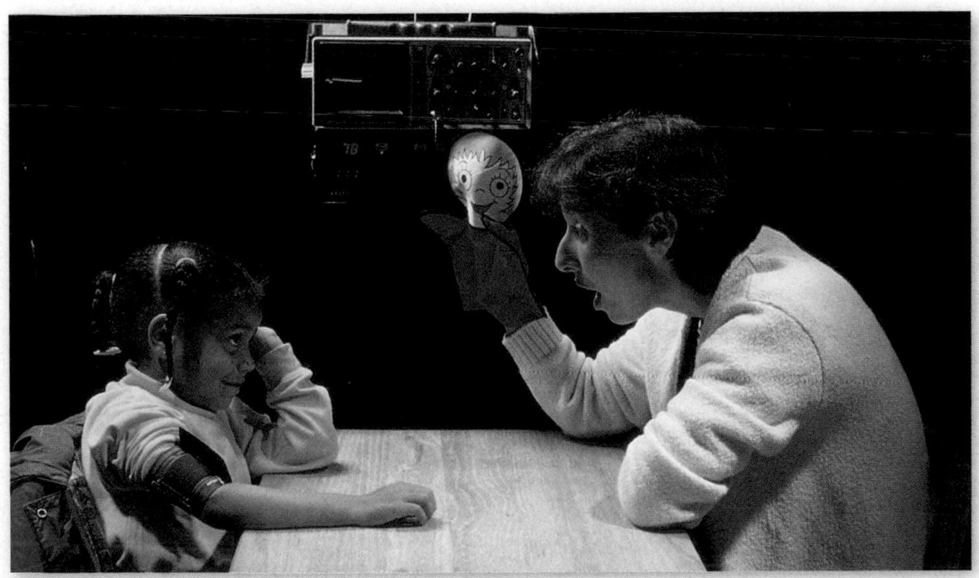

Experiments use strictly controlled procedures that manipulate variables to determine how one affects another. To study emotional resiliency, this research project at the University of California at San Francisco monitors the heart rate and blood pressure of young children as they explain their feelings in response to a hand puppet's happy or angry face.

generalizable to real life. Because of the artificiality of the situation, participants may not act as they normally would. For example, if children who watch violent television shows in the laboratory become more aggressive in that setting, we cannot be sure that children who watch a lot of violent shows at home hit their little brothers or sisters more often than children who watch fewer such shows.

Checkpoint

Can you . . .

- Compare the uses and drawbacks of case studies, ethnographic studies, correlational studies, and experiments?
- Explain why only a controlled experiment can establish causal relationships?
- Distinguish among laboratory, field, and natural experiments, and tell what kinds of research seem most suitable to each?

When, for practical or ethical reasons, it is impossible to conduct a true experiment, a *natural experiment* may provide a way of studying certain events. A natural experiment compares people who have been accidentally "assigned" to separate groups by circumstances of life—one group who were exposed, say, to famine or AIDS or a birth defect or superior education, and another group who were not. A natural experiment, despite its name, is actually a correlational study, since controlled manipulation of variables and random assignment to treatment groups are not possible.

Experiments have important advantages over other research designs: the ability to establish cause-and-effect relationships and to permit replication. However, experiments can be too artificial and too narrowly focused. In recent decades, therefore, many researchers have concentrated less on laboratory experimentation or have supplemented it with a wider array of methods.

Developmental Research Designs

The two most common research strategies used to study development are *longitudinal* and *cross-sectional* studies (see Figure 2-2). Longitudinal studies reveal how people change or stay the same as they grow older; cross-sectional studies show similarities and differences among age groups. Because each of these designs has drawbacks, researchers also have devised *sequential* designs. To directly observe change, *microgenetic studies* can be used.

longitudinal study Study designed to assess changes in a sample over time.

Longitudinal, Cross-Sectional, and Sequential Studies In a **longitudinal study,** researchers study the same person or persons more than once, sometimes years apart and sometimes over decades. They may measure a single characteristic, such as vocabulary size, height, or aggressiveness, or they may look at several aspects of development to find relationships among them. The Oakland (Adolescent) Growth Study (refer back to Chapter 1) initially was designed to assess social and emotional development from the preteens through the senior high school years; ultimately, many of the participants were followed into old age. The study found that participants who as teenagers showed

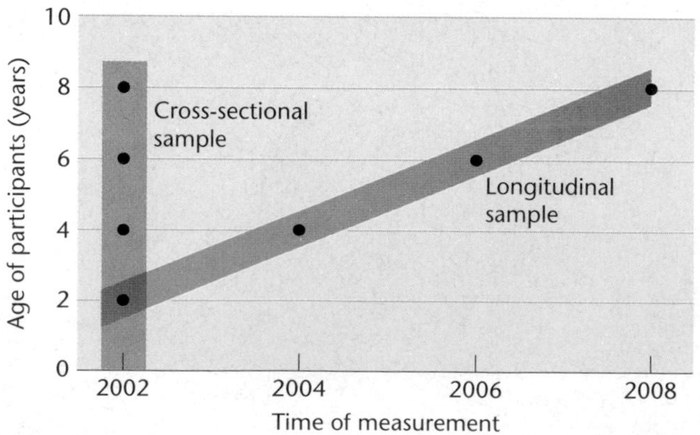

Figure 2-2

Developmental research designs. In this *cross-sectional* study, groups of 2-, 4-, 6-, and 8-year-olds were tested in 2002 to obtain data about age differences. In the *longitudinal* study, a sample of children were first measured in 2002, when they were 2 years old; follow-up testing is done when the children are 4, 6, and 8, to measure age-related changes in performance. (Note: Dots indicate times of measurement.)

self-confidence, intellectual commitment, and dependable effectiveness made good choices in adolescence and also in early adulthood, which often led to promising opportunities (scholarships, good jobs, and competent spouses). Less competent teenagers made poorer early decisions and tended to lead crisis-ridden lives (Clausen, 1993).

In a **cross-sectional study,** people of different ages are assessed at one time. In one cross-sectional study, researchers asked 3-, 4-, 6-, and 7-year-olds about what a pensive-looking woman was doing, or about the state of someone's mind. There was a striking increase with age in children's awareness of mental activity (J. H. Flavell, Green, & Flavell, 1995). These findings strongly suggest that as children become older, their understanding of mental processes improves. However, we cannot draw such a conclusion with certainty. We don't know whether the 7-year-olds' awareness of mental activity when they were 3 years old was the same as that of the current 3-year-olds in the study. The only way to see whether change occurs with age is to conduct a longitudinal study of a particular person or group.

cross-sectional study Study design in which people of different ages are assessed on one occasion.

Both cross-sectional and longitudinal designs have strengths and weaknesses (see Table 2-5). Longitudinal research, by repeatedly studying the same people, can track individual patterns of continuity and change. It avoids confounding developmental effects with effects of cohort membership (the differing experiences of people born, for example, before and after the advent of the Internet). However, a longitudinal study done on one cohort may not apply to another. (The results of a study of people born in the 1920s, such as the Oakland Growth Study, may not apply to people born in the 1990s.) Furthermore, longitudinal studies generally are more time consuming and expensive than cross-sectional studies. Another problem is attrition: participants may die, move away, or drop out. Also, longitudinal samples tend to be biased; those who stay with the study tend to have above average intelligence and socioeconomic status. Finally, results can be affected by repeated testing: participants may do better in later tests because of familiarity with test procedures.

Some longitudinal studies are *retrospective* (backward-looking). For example, a group of adolescents may be measured for some variable, such as antisocial behavior. Their parents are then asked about a hypothetically related variable, such as the disciplinary techniques they used when the children were young. Retrospective research enables researchers to draw correlations immediately, without waiting years to see, for example, how children who are spanked or not spanked turn out. However, this research has drawbacks: faulty memories of respondents and, perhaps, failure to identify other factors that may have played a part in the behavior being studied. For these reasons, whenever possible researchers try to do *prospective* (forward-looking) studies.

Advantages of cross-sectional research include speed and economy; data can be gathered fairly quickly from large numbers of people. And, since participants are

Table 2-5 Longitudinal, Cross-Sectional, and Sequential Research: Pros and Cons

Type of Study	Procedure	Advantages	Disadvantages
Longitudinal	Data are collected on same person or persons over a period of time	Can show age-related change or continuity; avoids confounding age with cohort effects	Time-consuming, expensive; problems of attrition, bias in sample, and effects of repeated testing; results may be valid only for cohort tested or sample studied
Cross-sectional	Data are collected on people of different ages at the same time	Can show similarities and differences among age groups; speedy, economical; no problem of attrition or repeated testing	Cannot establish age effects; masks individual differences; can be confounded by cohort effects
Sequential	Data are collected on successive cross-sectional or longitudinal samples	Can avoid drawbacks of both cross-sectional and longitudinal designs	Requires large amount of time and effort and the analysis of very complex data

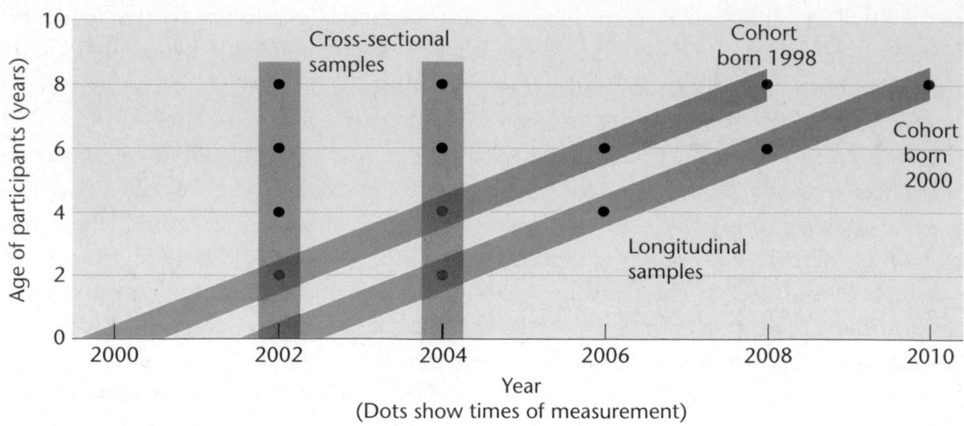

Figure 2-3
A sequential design. Two successive cross-sectional groups of 2-, 4-, 6-, and 8-year-olds were tested in 2002 and 2004. Also, a longitudinal study of a sample of children first measured in 2002, when they were 2 years old, is followed by a similar longitudinal study of another group of children who were 2 years old in 2004.

assessed only once, there is no problem of attrition or repeated testing. A drawback of cross-sectional studies is that they overlook individual differences by focusing on group averages. Their major disadvantage, however, is that cohort differences may affect the results. Cross-sectional studies are sometimes interpreted as yielding information about developmental changes, but this interpretation may be misleading. Thus, although cross-sectional studies still dominate the field—no doubt because they are so much easier to do—the proportion of research devoted to longitudinal studies, especially short-term ones, is increasing (Parke et al., 1994).

sequential study Study design that combines cross-sectional and longitudinal techniques.

The **sequential study**—a sequence of cross-sectional and/or longitudinal studies—is a complex strategy designed to overcome the drawbacks of longitudinal and cross-sectional research. Researchers may assess a cross-sectional sample on two or more occasions (that is, in sequence) to find out how members of each age cohort have changed. This procedure permits researchers to separate age-related changes from cohort effects. Another sequential design consists of a sequence of overlapping longitudinal studies, running concurrently but starting one after another. This design allows researchers to compare individual differences as well as developmental change. A combination of cross-sectional and longitudinal sequences (as shown in Figure 2-3) can provide a more complete picture of development than would be possible with longitudinal or cross-sectional research alone. The major drawbacks of sequential studies involve time, effort, and complexity. Sequential designs require large numbers of participants and the collection and analysis of huge amounts of data over a period of years. Interpreting their findings and conclusions can demand a high degree of sophistication.

microgenetic study Study design that allows researchers to directly observe change by repeated testing over a short time.

Microgenetic Studies Developmentalists rarely can observe change directly in everyday life because it usually happens so slowly. But what if the process could be compressed into a very short time frame? A **microgenetic study** does just that, by repeatedly exposing participants to a stimulus for change, or opportunity for learning, over a short period of time, enabling researchers to see and analyze the processes by which change occurs. Vygotsky, for example, used what he called "microgenesis experiments" in which he manipulated conditions to see how much children's performance could be improved over a short period of time.

Checkpoint

Can you . . .

- ✔ List advantages and disadvantages of longitudinal, cross-sectional, and sequential research?
- ✔ Explain how microgenetic studies are done and what they can reveal?

In one series of experiments using operant conditioning (Rovee-Collier & Boller, 1995; see Chapter 5), infants as young as 2 months old learned to kick to set in motion a brightly colored mobile to which one leg was attached—if the infants were exposed to a similar situation repeatedly within a few days or weeks. Building on this work,

Esther Thelen (1994) tied 3-month-olds' left and right legs together with soft elastic fabric. Would they learn to kick with both legs at once to activate the mobile? The infants' movements were videotaped, and the frequency and speed of kicks, using one or both legs, were then analyzed with the help of a computer. The results showed that the infants gradually switched to kicking with both legs when it proved more effective, and observers were able to chart exactly how and when this change occurred.

Ethics of Research

Should research that might harm its participants ever be undertaken? How can we balance the possible benefits against the risk of mental, emotional, or physical injury to individuals?

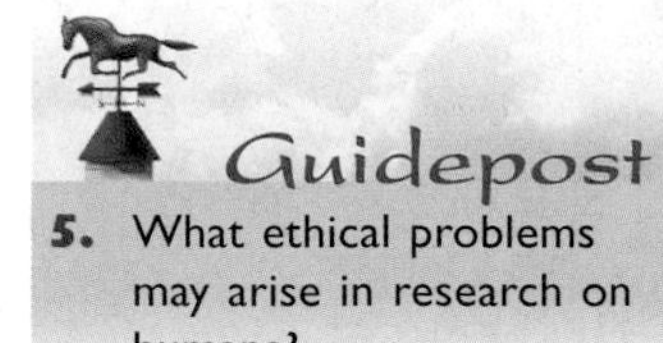

5. What ethical problems may arise in research on humans?

Objections to the study of "Little Albert" (described earlier in this chapter), as well as several other early studies, gave rise to today's more stringent ethical standards. Federally mandated committees at colleges, universities, and other institutions review proposed research from an ethical standpoint. Guidelines of the American Psychological Association (1992) and the Society for Research in Child Development (1996) cover such issues as *informed consent, avoidance of deception,* protection of participants from *harm and loss of dignity,* guarantees of *privacy and confidentiality,* the *right to decline or withdraw* from an experiment at any time, and the responsibility of investigators to *correct any undesirable effects.*

Still, ethical dilemmas sometimes exist. Different kinds of research may entail different ethical issues. For example, a study in which a new drug is being tested or compared with an established treatment is much riskier than an observational study of children playing together in a laboratory setting with their parents present.

Let's look more closely at a few of the ethical considerations that can present problems.

Right to Informed Consent Informed consent exists when participants voluntarily agree to be in a study, are competent to give consent, are fully aware of the risks as well as the potential benefits, and are not being exploited. The National Commission for the Protection of Human Subjects of Biomedical and Behavioral Research (1978) recommends that children age 7 or over be asked to give their own consent to take part in research and that children's objections should be overruled only if the research promises direct benefit to the child, as in the use of a new experimental drug.

However, some ethicists argue that young children cannot give meaningful, voluntary *consent,* since they cannot fully understand what is involved; they can merely *assent,* that is, agree to participate. The usual procedure, therefore, when children under 18 are involved, is to ask the parents or legal guardians, and sometimes school personnel, to give consent.

Some studies rely on participants who may be especially vulnerable. For example, studies that seek the causes and treatments for Alzheimer's disease need participants whose mental status may preclude their being fully or even partially aware of what is involved. What if a person gives consent and later forgets having done so? Current practice, to be on the safe side, is to ask both participants and caregivers for consent.

Avoidance of Deception Can informed consent exist if participants are deceived about the nature or purpose of a study, or about the procedures they will be subjected to? Suppose that children are told they are trying out a new game when they are actually being tested on their reactions to success or failure? Experiments like these, which cannot be carried out without deception, have been done—and they have added significantly to our knowledge, but at the cost of the participants' right to know what they were getting involved in.

What's Your View?

- What steps should be taken to protect children and other vulnerable persons from harm due to involvement in research?

Ethical guidelines call for withholding information *only* when it is essential to the study; and then, investigators should avoid methods that could cause pain, anxiety, or harm. Participants should be debriefed afterward to let them know the true nature of the study and why deception was necessary and to make sure they have not suffered as a result.

Right to Privacy and Confidentiality Is it ethical to use one-way mirrors and hidden cameras to observe people without their knowledge? How can we protect the confidentiality of personal information that participants may reveal in interviews or questionnaires?

What if, during the course of research, an investigator notices that a child or adult seems to have a learning disability or some other treatable condition? Is the researcher obliged to share such information with the participant, or with parents or guardians, or to recommend services that may help, when sharing the information might contaminate the research findings? Such a decision should not be made lightly, since sharing information of uncertain validity may create damaging misconceptions about a child. On the other hand, researchers need to know, and inform participants of, their legal responsibility to report abuse or neglect or any other illegal activity of which they become aware.

Checkpoint

Can you . . .

- ✔ Discuss three rights of research participants?
- ✔ Give examples of ethical dilemmas in research on human beings?

Refocus

- Based on the information given about Margaret Mead, what position do you think she might have taken on the issue of the relative influences of heredity and environment?
- Does Mead seem to fit within any of the five theoretical perspectives described in this chapter?
- What research methods described in the chapter did she use? What advantages and disadvantages existed because her research was done in the field, rather than in a laboratory?
- What ethical issues might be relevant to cross-cultural research such as Mead's?

Our final word in these introductory chapters is that this entire book is far from the final word. While we have tried to incorporate the most important and the most up-to-date information about how people develop, developmental scientists are constantly learning more. As you read this book, you are certain to come up with your own questions. By thinking about them, and perhaps eventually conducting research to find answers, it is possible that you yourself, now just embarking on the study of human development, will someday add to our knowledge about the interesting species to which we all belong.

SUMMARY AND KEY TERMS

Basic Theoretical Issues

Guidepost 1. What purposes do theories serve?

- A theory is used to explain data and generate hypotheses that can be tested by research.

theory *(27)*

hypotheses *(27)*

Guidepost 2. What are three basic theoretical issues on which developmental scientists differ?

- Developmental theories differ on three basic issues: the relative importance of heredity and environment, the active or passive character of development, and the existence of stages of development.
- Some theorists subscribe to a mechanistic model of development; others to an organismic model.

mechanistic model *(28)*

organismic model *(28)*

Theoretical Perspectives

Guidepost 3. What are five theoretical perspectives on human development, and what are some theories representative of each?

- The psychoanalytic perspective sees development as motivated by unconscious emotional drives or conflicts. Leading examples are Freud's and Erikson's theories.

  psychoanalytic perspective *(29)*
  psychosexual development *(30)*
  psychosocial development *(33)*

- The learning perspective views development as a result of learning based on experience. Leading examples are Watson's and Skinner's behaviorism and Bandura's social learning theory.

  learning perspective *(33)*
  behaviorism *(33)*
  classical conditioning *(33)*
  operant conditioning *(34)*
  reinforcement *(34)*
  punishment *(34)*
  social learning theory *(35)*
  observational learning *(35)*

- The cognitive perspective is concerned with thought processes. Leading examples are Piaget's cognitive-stage theory, the information-processing approach, and the cognitive neuroscience approach.

  cognitive perspective *(35)*
  organization *(36)*
  schemes *(36)*
  adaptation *(36)*
  assimilation *(36)*
  accommodation *(36)*
  equilibration *(36)*
  information-processing approach *(37)*
  cognitive neuroscience approach *(38)*
  social cognitive neuroscience *(38)*

- The evolutionary/sociobiological perspective focuses on the adaptiveness, or survival value, of behavior. It includes a number of disciplines, such as ethology and evolutionary psychology. Developmental evolutionary psychologists seek to identify behaviors that are especially adaptive at particular ages.

  ethology *(38)*
  sociobiological perspective *(38)*
  evolutionary psychology *(39)*

- The contextual perspective focuses on interaction between the individual and the social context. Leading examples are Bronfenbrenner's and Vygotsky's theories.

  contextual perspective *(39)*
  bioecological theory *(39)*
  microsystem *(39)*
  mesosystem *(40)*
  exosystem *(40)*
  macrosystem *(41)*
  chronosystem *(41)*
  sociocultural theory *(42)*
  zone of proximal development (ZPD) *(42)*
  scaffolding *(43)*

Research Methods

Guidepost 4. How do developmental scientists study people, and what are the advantages and disadvantages of each research method?

- Research can be either quantitative or qualitative, or both.
- To arrive at sound conclusions, quantitative researchers use the scientific method.
- Random selection of a research sample can ensure generalizability.
- Three forms of data collection are self-reports (diaries, interviews, and questionnaires); behavioral and performance measures; and observation.

  quantitative research *(43)*
  qualitative research *(43)*
  scientific method *(44)*
  sample *(44)*
  operational definitions *(46)*
  naturalistic observation *(46)*
  laboratory observation *(46)*

- Two basic qualitative designs used in developmental research are the case study and the ethnographic study. Cross-cultural research can indicate whether certain aspects of development are universal or culturally influenced.
- Two quantitative designs are the correlational study and experiment. Only experiments can firmly establish causal relationships.
- Experiments must be rigorously controlled so as to be valid and replicable. Random assignment of participants can ensure validity.
- Laboratory experiments are easiest to control and replicate, but findings of field experiments may be more generalizable beyond the study situation. Natural experiments may be useful in situations in which true experiments would be impractical or unethical.
- The two most common designs used to study age-related development are longitudinal and cross-sectional. Cross-sectional studies compare age groups; longitudinal studies describe continuity or change in the same participants. The sequential study is intended to overcome the weaknesses of the other two designs.
- A microgenetic study allows direct observation of change over a short period of time.

  case study *(47)*
  ethnographic study *(48)*
  participant observation *(48)*
  correlational study *(48)*
  experiment *(50)*
  experimental group *(50)*
  control group *(50)*
  independent variable *(50)*
  dependent variable *(50)*
  longitudinal study *(52)*
  cross-sectional study *(53)*
  sequential study *(54)*
  microgenetic study *(54)*

Guidepost 5. What ethical problems may arise in research?

- Ethical issues in research include the rights of participants to informed consent, avoidance of deception, protection from harm and loss of dignity, and guarantees of privacy and confidentiality.

PART 2

From the moment of conception to the moment of death, human beings undergo complex processes of development. The changes that occur during the earliest periods of the life span are broader and faster-paced than any a person will ever experience again.

Because human beings are whole persons, all aspects of development are interconnected, even in the womb. As we look at prenatal development in Chapter 3, at physical development of infants and toddlers in Chapter 4, at their cognitive development in Chapter 5, and at their psychosocial development in Chapter 6, we will see, right from the beginning, how these aspects of development are linked. ▸

Linkups to look for

- The physical growth of the brain before and after birth makes possible a great burst of cognitive and emotional development. Fetuses whose ears and brains have developed enough to hear sounds from the outside world seem to retain a memory of these sounds after birth.
- An infant's earliest smiles arise from central nervous system activity and may reflect nothing more than a pleasant physiological state, such as drowsiness and a full stomach. As the infant becomes cognitively aware of the warm responses of caregivers, and as vision becomes sharp enough to recognize a familiar face, the infant's smiles become more emotionally expressive and more socially directed.
- Infants learn through their physical movements where their bodies end and everything else begins. As they drop toys, splash water, and hurl sand, their minds grasp how their bodies can change their world, and their sense of self begins to flourish.
- Without the vocal structures and motor coordination to form sounds, babies would not be able to speak. Physical gestures precede and often accompany early attempts to form words. The acquisition of language dramatically advances cognitive understanding and social communication.

Beginnings

PREVIEW

CHAPTER 3

Forming a New Life

Conception occurs.

The genetic endowment interacts with environmental influences from the start.

Basic body structures and organs form.

Brain growth spurt begins.

Physical growth is the most rapid in the life span.

Vulnerability to environmental influences is great.

Abililties to learn and remember and to respond to sensory stimuli are developing.

Fetus responds to mother's voice and develops a preference for it.

CHAPTER 4

Physical Development During the First Three Years

A method and setting for childbirth are chosen, and the progress of the birth is monitored.

The newborn emerges and is assessed for immediate health, developmental status, and any complications of childbirth.

All senses and body systems operate at birth to varying degrees.

The brain grows in complexity and is highly sensitive to environmental influence.

Physical growth and development of motor skills are rapid.

CHAPTER 5

Cognitive Development During the First Three Years

Abilities to learn and remember are present, even in early weeks.

Use of symbols and ability to solve problems develop by the end of the second year.

Comprehension and use of language develop rapidly.

CHAPTER 6

Psychosocial Development During the First Three Years

Attachments to parents and others form.

Self-awareness develops.

Shift from dependence to autonomy occurs.

Interest in other children increases.

Chapter 3

Forming a New Life

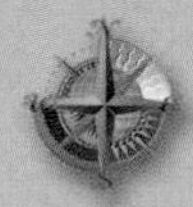

If I could have watched you grow
as a magical mother might,
if I could have seen through my magical
transparent belly,
there would have been such ripening within. . . .

—**Anne Sexton, 1966**

OUTLINE

Focus: Abel Dorris and Fetal Alcohol Syndrome

Abel Dorris

Fetal alcohol syndrome (FAS), a cluster of abnormalities shown by children whose mothers drank during pregnancy, is a leading cause of mental retardation. But in 1971, when the writer Michael Dorris adopted a 3-year-old Sioux boy whose mother had been a heavy drinker, the facts about FAS were not widely publicized or scientifically investigated, though the syndrome had been observed for centuries. Not until eleven years later, as Dorris relates in *The Broken Cord* (1989), did he discover the source of his adopted son's developmental problems.

The boy, named Abel ("Adam" in the book), had been born almost seven weeks premature, with low birthweight, and had been abused and malnourished before being removed to a foster home. His mother had died at 35 of alcohol poisoning. His father had been beaten to death in an alley after a string of arrests. The boy was small for his age, was not toilet trained, and could speak only about twenty words. Although he had been diagnosed as mildly retarded, Dorris was certain that with a positive environment the boy would catch up.

Abel did not catch up. When he turned 4, he was still in diapers and weighed only 27 pounds. He had trouble remembering names of playmates. His activity level was unusually high, and the circumference of his skull was unusually small. He suffered severe, unexplained seizures.

As the months went by, Abel had trouble learning to count, identifing primary colors, and tying his shoes. Before entering school, he was labeled "learning disabled." His IQ was, and remained, in the mid-60s. Thanks to the efforts of a devoted first-grade teacher, Abel did learn to read and write, but his comprehension was low. When the boy finished elementary school in 1983, he "still could not add, subtract, count money, or consistently identify the town, state, country, or planet of his residence" (Dorris, 1989, pp. 127–128).

By then, Michael Dorris had solved the puzzle of what was wrong with his son. As an associate professor of Native American studies at Dartmouth College, he was acquainted with the cultural pressures that make drinking prevalent among American Indians. In 1982, the year before Abel's graduation, Michael visited a treatment center for chemically dependent teenagers at a Sioux reservation in South Dakota. There he was astonished to see three boys who "could have been [Abel's] twin brothers" (Dorris, 1989, p. 137). They not only looked like Abel but acted like him.

Fetal alcohol syndrome had been identified during the 1970s, while Abel was growing up. Once alcohol enters a fetus's bloodstream, it remains there in high concentrations for long periods of time, causing brain damage and harming other body organs. There is no cure. As one medical expert wrote, "for the fetus the hangover may last a lifetime" (Enloe, 1980, p.15).

For the family, too, the effects of FAS can be devastating. The years of constant attempts first to restore Abel to normality and then to come to terms with the damage irrevocably done in the womb may well have been a factor in the later problems in Michael Dorris's marriage to the writer Louise Erdrich, which culminated in divorce proceedings, and in his suicide in 1997 at age 52. According to Erdrich, Dorris suffered from extreme depression, possibly exacerbated by the difficulties he faced as a father (L. Erdrich, personal communication, March 1, 2000).

As for Abel Dorris, at the age of 20 he had entered a vocational training program and had moved into a supervised home, taking along his collections of stuffed animals, paper dolls, newspaper cartoons, family photographs, and old birthday cards. At 23, five years before his father's death, he was hit by a car and killed (Lyman, 1997).

The story of Abel Dorris is a devastating reminder of the awesome responsibility prospective parents have for the development of the new life they have set in motion. First comes the hereditary endowment they provide. Then come environmental influences—starting with the mother's body. In addition to what the mother does and what happens to her, there are other environmental influences, from those that affect the father's sperm to the technological, social, and cultural environment, which may affect the kind of care a woman gets in the months before giving birth.

In this chapter, we describe how conception normally occurs, how the mechanisms of heredity operate, and how the biological inheritance interacts with environmental influences within and outside the womb. We trace the course of prenatal development, describe influences upon it, and report on ways to monitor and intervene in it.

After you have studied this chapter, you should be able to answer each of the following Guidepost questions. Look for them again in the margins, where they point to important concepts throughout the chapter. To check your understanding of these Guideposts, review the end-of-chapter summary. Checkpoints located at periodic spots throughout the chapter will help you verify your understanding of what you have read.

1. How does conception normally occur?
2. What causes multiple births?
3. How does heredity operate in determining sex and transmitting normal and abnormal traits?
4. How do scientists study the relative influences of heredity and environment, and how do heredity and environment work together?
5. What roles do heredity and environment play in physical health, intelligence, and personality?
6. What are the three stages of prenatal development, and what happens during each stage?
7. What can fetuses do?
8. What environmental influences can affect prenatal development?
9. What techniques can assess a fetus's health and well-being, and what is the importance of prenatal care?

Guideposts for Study

Conceiving New Life

Most adults, and even most children in developed countries, have a reasonably accurate idea of where babies come from. Yet only a generation or two ago, many parents told their children that a stork had brought them. The folk belief that children came from wells, springs, or rocks was common in north and central Europe as late as the beginning of the twentieth century. Conception was believed to be influenced by cosmic forces. A baby conceived under a new moon would be a boy; during the moon's last quarter, a girl (Gélis, 1991).

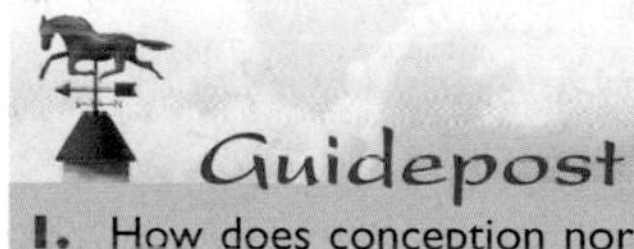

Guidepost

1. How does conception normally occur?

During the seventeenth and eighteenth centuries, a debate raged between two schools of biological thought. The *animalculists* (so named because the male sperm were then called *animalcules*) claimed that fully formed "little people" were contained in the heads of sperm, ready to grow when deposited in the nurturing environment of the womb. The *ovists,* inspired by the influential work of the English physician William Harvey, held an opposite but equally incorrect view: that a female's ovaries contained tiny, already formed humans whose growth was activated by the male's sperm. Finally, in the late eighteenth century, the German-born anatomist Kaspar Friedrich Wolff demonstrated that embryos are not preformed in either parent and that both contribute equally to the formation of a new being.

Although scientists have now found a way to **clone** (make a genetic copy of) a human embryo, and this has value for therapeutic research purposes (Cibelli, Lanza, & West, 2002), ethical and religious concerns about the dignity of individual human life make it unlikely—at least in the near future—that cloning will become a common means of reproduction. Until that happens, virtually every person's beginning will continue to be a split-second event when a single sperm from the biological father joins an ovum from the biological mother. As we will see, which sperm meets which ovum has tremendous implications for the new person.

clone *(verb)* To make a genetic copy of an individual; *(noun)* a genetic copy of an individual.

How Fertilization Takes Place

Fertilization, or conception, is the process by which sperm and ovum—the male and female *gametes,* or sex cells—combine to create a single cell called a **zygote,** which

fertilization Union of sperm and ovum fuse to produce a zygote; also called *conception.*

zygote One-celled organism resulting from fertilization.

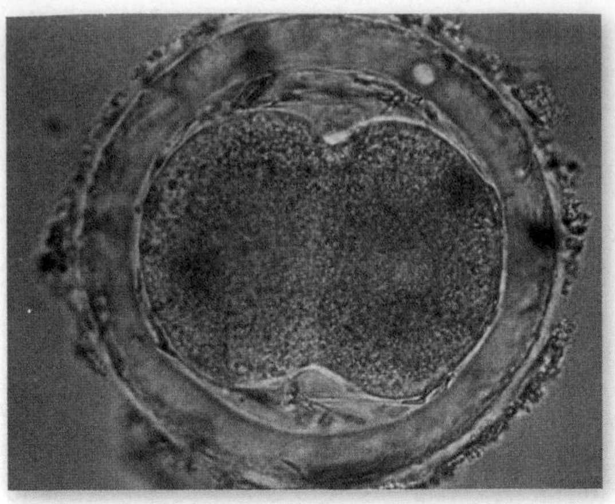

Fertilization takes place when a sperm cell unites with an ovum to form a single new cell. The fertilized ovum shown here has begun to grow by cell division. It will eventually differentiate into 800 billion or more cells with specialized functions.

then duplicates itself again and again by cell division to become a baby. At birth, a girl has all the ova (plural of ovum) she will ever have—about 400,000. These immature ova are in her two ovaries (see Figure 3-1a), each ovum in its own small sac, or *follicle.* In a sexually mature woman, *ovulation*—rupture of a mature follicle in either ovary and expulsion of its ovum—occurs about once every 28 days until menopause. The ovum is swept along through the fallopian tube by tiny hair cells, called *cilia,* toward the uterus, or womb. Fertilization normally occurs during the brief time the ovum is passing through the fallopian tube.

Sperm are produced in the testicles (testes), or reproductive glands, of a mature male (refer to Figure 3-1b) at a rate of several hundred million a day and are ejaculated in the semen at sexual climax. They enter the vagina and try to swim through the *cervix* (the opening of the uterus) and into the fallopian tubes, but only a tiny fraction make it that far.

Fertilization is most likely if intercourse occurs on the day of ovulation or during the five days before (Wilcox, Weinberg, & Baird, 1995). If fertilization does not occur, the ovum and any sperm cells in the woman's body die. The sperm are absorbed by the woman's white blood cells, and the ovum passes through the uterus and exits through the vagina. (In Chapter 13, we'll discuss techniques of artificially assisted reproduction often used when one or both prospective parents are infertile.)

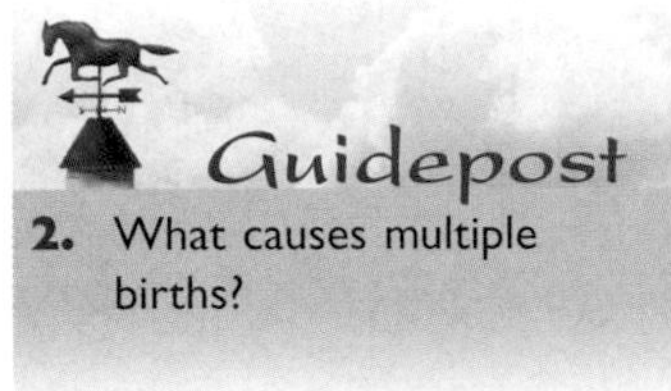

2. What causes multiple births?

dizygotic (two-egg) twins Twins conceived by the union of two different ova (or a single ovum that has split) with two sperm cells; also called *fraternal twins.*

monozygotic (one-egg) twins Twins resulting from the division of a single zygote after fertilization; also called *identical twins.*

What Causes Multiple Births?

Multiple births occur in two ways. Most commonly, the mother's body releases two ova within a short time (or sometimes, perhaps, a single unfertilized ovum splits) and then both are fertilized. The resulting babies are **dizygotic (two-egg) twins,** commonly called *fraternal twins.* The second way is for a single *fertilized* ovum to split into two. The babies that result from this cell division are **monozygotic (one-egg) twins,** commonly called *identical twins.* Triplets, quadruplets, and other multiple births can result from either of these processes or a combination of both.

Monozygotic twins have the same hereditary makeup and are the same sex, but—in part because of differences in prenatal as well as postnatal experience—they differ

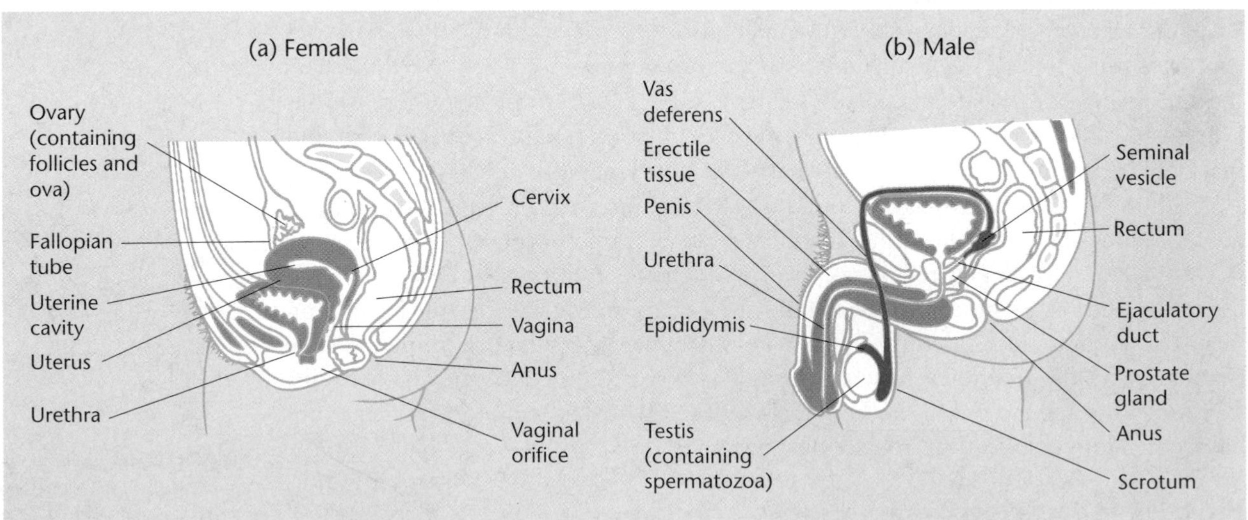

Figure 3-1
Human reproductive systems.

in some respects. They may not be identical in **temperament** (disposition, or style of approaching and reacting to situations). In some physical characteristics, such as hair whorls, dental patterns, and handedness, they may be mirror images of each other; one may be left-handed and the other right-handed. Dizygotic twins, who are created from different sperm cells and usually from different ova, are no more alike in hereditary makeup than any other siblings and may be the same sex or different sexes.

temperament Characteristic disposition, or style of approaching and reacting to situations.

Monozygotic twins—about one-third of all twins—seem to be the result of an "accident" of prenatal development; their incidence is about the same in all ethnic groups. Dizygotic twins are most common among African Americans, white northern Europeans, and east Indians and are least common among other Asians (Behrman, 1992). These differences may be due to hormonal tendencies that may make women of some ethnic groups more likely to release more than one ovum at the same time.

The incidence of multiple births in the United States has grown rapidly. Between 1980 and 2000, live twin births increased by 74 percent from 68,339 to 118,916, representing 2.9 percent of total births. The number of triplets and larger multiples more than quintupled from 1,337 to 7,325, 1.9 percent of all births (Martin, Hamilton, Ventura, Menacker, & Park, 2002).

The rise in multiple births is due in part to a trend toward delayed childbearing, since such births are more common among older women. Another important factor is the increased use of fertility drugs, which spur ovulation, and of such techniques as in vitro fertilization. These trends are of concern, since multiple births generally are more likely to be high-risk births (Martin, Hamilton, et al., 2002).

Checkpoint

Can you . . .

- ✔ Explain how and when fertilization normally takes place?
- ✔ Distinguish between monozygotic and dizygotic twins, and tell how each comes about?

Mechanisms of Heredity

The science of genetics is the study of *heredity*—the inborn factors, inherited from the biological parents, that affect development. When ovum and sperm unite, they endow the baby-to-be with a genetic makeup that influences a wide range of characteristics from color of eyes and hair to health, intellect, and personality.

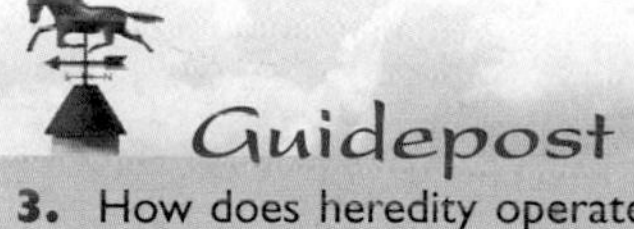

Guidepost

3. How does heredity operate in determining sex and transmitting normal and abnormal traits?

The Genetic Code

The basis of heredity is a chemical called **deoxyribonucleic acid (DNA),** which contains all the inherited material passed from biological parents to children. DNA carries the biochemical instructions that direct the formation of each cell in the body and tell the cells how to make the proteins that enable them to carry out specific body functions.

deoxyribonucleic acid (DNA) Chemical that carries inherited instructions for the formation and function of body cells.

The structure of DNA resembles a long, spiraling ladder made of four chemical units called *bases* (see Figure 3-2 on page 66). The bases—adenine, thymine, cytosine, and guanine—are known by their initials: A, T, C, and G. They pair up in four combinations—AT, TA, CG, and GC—and coil around each other. The sequence of 3 billion base pairs constitutes the **genetic code,** which determines all inherited characteristics.

Within each cell nucleus are **chromosomes,** coils of DNA that contain smaller segments called **genes,** the functional units of heredity. Each gene is a small unit of DNA, located in a definite position on its chromosome, and each gene contains the "instructions" for building a specific protein. A typical gene contains thousands of base pairs.

The complete sequence of genes in the human body constitutes the **human genome.** The genome specifies the order in which genes are expressed, or activated. In 2001, two teams of scientists completed the mapping of the human genome, which is estimated to contain between 30,000 and 40,000 genes, far fewer than the 80,000 to 100,000 previously estimated (McKusick, 2001). Most human genes seem to be similar to those of other animals; all but 300 human genes have counterparts in mice (Wade, 2001).

Every cell in the normal human body except the sex cells has 23 pairs of chromosomes—46 in all. Through a type of cell division called *meiosis,* each sex cell, or gamete (sperm or ovum), ends up with only 23 chromosomes—one from each pair.

genetic code Sequence of base pairs within DNA, which determine inherited characteristics.

chromosomes Coils of DNA that carry the genes.

genes Small segments of DNA located in definite positions on particular chromosomes.

human genome Complete sequence or mapping of genes in the human body and their locations.

Figure 3-2
DNA: The genetic code. (*Source:* Ritter, 1999).

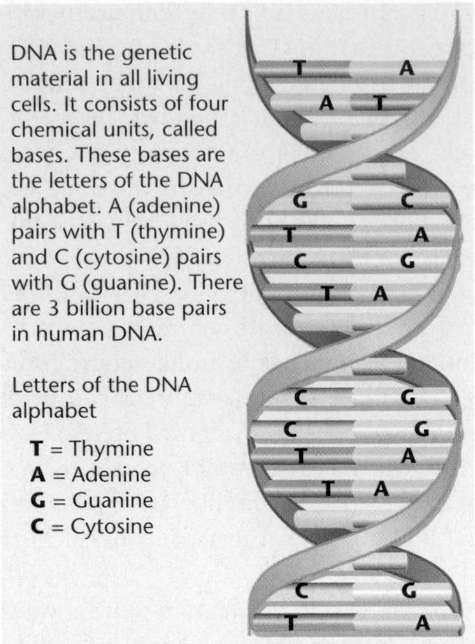

Thus, when sperm and ovum fuse at conception, they produce a zygote with 46 chromosomes, 23 from the father and 23 from the mother.

At conception, then, the single-celled zygote has all the biological information needed to guide its development into a human baby. This happens through *mitosis,* a process by which the cells divide in half over and over again. When a cell divides, the DNA spirals replicate themselves, so that each newly formed cell has the same DNA structure as all the others. Thus, each cell division creates a duplicate of the original cell, with the same hereditary information. When development is normal, each cell (except the gametes) continues to have 46 chromosomes identical to those in the original zygote. As the cells divide and the child grows and develops, the cells differentiate, specializing in a variety of complex bodily functions.

Genes do not do their work automatically. They spring into action when conditions call for the information they can provide. Genetic action that triggers growth of body and brain is often regulated by hormonal levels, which are affected by such environmental conditions as nutrition and stress. Thus, from the start, heredity and environment are interrelated (Brown, 1999).

What Determines Sex?

In many villages in Nepal, it is common for a man whose wife has borne no male babies to take a second wife. In some societies, a woman's failure to produce sons is justification for divorce. The irony in the beliefs about conception underlying these customs in male-dominated societies is that it is the father's sperm that determines a child's sex.

autosomes The 22 pairs of chromosomes not related to sexual expression.

sex chromosomes Pair of chromosomes that determines sex: XX in the normal female, XY in the normal male.

At the moment of conception, the 23 chromosomes from the sperm and the 23 from the mother's ovum form 23 pairs. Twenty-two pairs are **autosomes,** chromosomes that are not related to sexual expression. The twenty-third pair are **sex chromosomes**—one from the father and one from the mother—that govern the baby's sex.

Sex chromosomes are either *X chromosomes* or *Y chromosomes.* The sex chromosome of every ovum is an X chromosome, but the sperm may contain either an X or a Y chromosome. The Y chromosome contains the gene for maleness, called the SRY gene. When an ovum (X) is fertilized by an X-carrying sperm, the zygote formed is XX, a female. When an ovum (X) is fertilized by a Y-carrying sperm, the resulting zygote is XY, a male (see Figure 3-3).

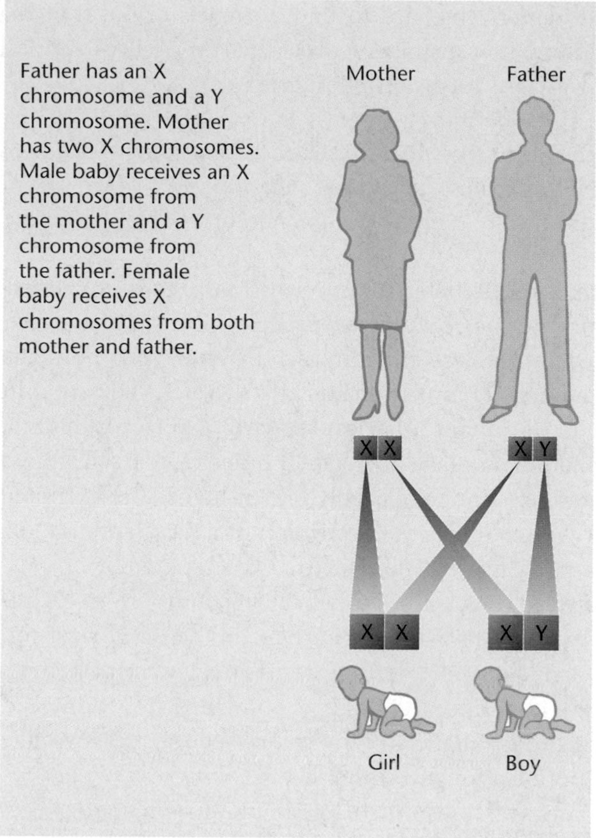

Father has an X chromosome and a Y chromosome. Mother has two X chromosomes. Male baby receives an X chromosome from the mother and a Y chromosome from the father. Female baby receives X chromosomes from both mother and father.

Mother Father

XX XY

XX XY

Girl Boy

Figure 3-3
Determination of sex. Since all babies receive an X chromosome from the mother, sex is determined by whether an X or Y chromosome is received from the father.

Initially, the embryo's rudimentary reproductive system is no different in males than in females. About six to eight weeks after conception, male embryos normally start producing the male hormone testosterone. Exposure to steady, high levels of testosterone results in the development of a male body with male sexual organs.

Until recently, then, it was assumed that femaleness is a genetic "default setting," which will be operative unless a gene for maleness and a resulting exposure to male hormones overrides it. Now, however, it appears that the development of female characteristics is controlled by a signaling molecule called *Wnt-4,* a mutation of which can "masculinize" a genetically female fetus (Vainio, Heikkiia, Kispert, Chin, & McMahon, 1999). Thus, sexual differentiation appears to be a more complex process than was previously thought.

Checkpoint

Can you . . .

- ✔ Explain why no two people, other than monozygotic twins, have the same genetic heritage?
- ✔ Explain why it is the sperm that determines a baby's sex?

Patterns of Genetic Transmission

During the 1860s, Gregor Mendel, an Austrian monk, laid the foundation for our understanding of patterns of inheritance. He cross-bred pea plants that produced only yellow seeds with pea plants that produced only green seeds. The resulting hybrid plants produced only yellow seeds, meaning, he said, that yellow was *dominant* over green. Yet when he bred the yellow-seeded hybrids with each other, only 75 percent of their offspring had yellow seeds, and the other 25 percent had green seeds. This showed that a hereditary characteristic (in this case, the color green) can be *recessive,* that is, carried by an organism that does not express, or show, it.

Mendel also tried breeding for two traits at once. Crossing pea plants that produced round yellow seeds with plants that produced wrinkled green seeds, he found that color and shape were independent of each other. Mendel thus showed that hereditary traits are transmitted separately.

Today we know that the genetic picture in humans is far more complex than Mendel imagined. Most human traits fall along a continuous spectrum (for example, from light skin to dark). It is hard to find a single normal trait that people inherit through simple dominant transmission other than the ability to curl the tongue lengthwise. Let's look at various forms of inheritance.

Dominant and Recessive Inheritance Can you curl your tongue? If so, you inherited this ability through *dominant inheritance.* If your parents can curl their tongues but you cannot, *recessive inheritance* occurred. How do these two types of inheritance work?

alleles Paired genes (alike or different) that affect a trait.

homozygous Possessing two identical alleles for a trait.

heterozygous Possessing differing alleles for a trait.

dominant inheritance Pattern of inheritance in which, when a child receives contradictory alleles, only the dominant one is expressed.

recessive inheritance Pattern of inheritance in which a child receives identical recessive alleles, resulting in expression of a nondominant trait.

Genes that can produce alternative expressions of a characteristic (such as ability or inability to curl the tongue) are called **alleles.** Every person receives a pair of alleles for a given characteristic, one from each parent. When both alleles are the same, the person is **homozygous** for the characteristic; when they are different, the person is **heterozygous.** In **dominant inheritance,** when a person is heterozygous for a particular trait, the dominant allele governs. In other words, when an offspring receives two contradictory alleles for a trait, only one of them, the dominant one, will be expressed. **Recessive inheritance,** the expression of a recessive trait, occurs only when a person receives two recessive alleles, one from each parent.

If you inherited one allele for tongue-curling ability from each parent (see Figure 3-4), you are homozygous for tongue curling and can curl your tongue. If, say, your mother passed on an allele for the ability and your father passed on an allele lacking it, you are heterozygous. Since the ability is dominant (D) and its lack is recessive (d), you, again, can curl your tongue. But if you received the recessive allele from both parents, you would not be a tongue-curler.

Some traits are not transmitted by simple dominant or recessive inheritance. *Codominance* occurs when neither of two alleles is dominant, and the resulting trait reflects the influence of both. For example, the blood type AB is a combination of alleles for types A and B.

polygenic inheritance Pattern of inheritance in which multiple genes affect a complex trait.

Most traits result from **polygenic inheritance,** the interaction of several genes. Skin color is the result of three or more sets of genes on three different chromosomes.

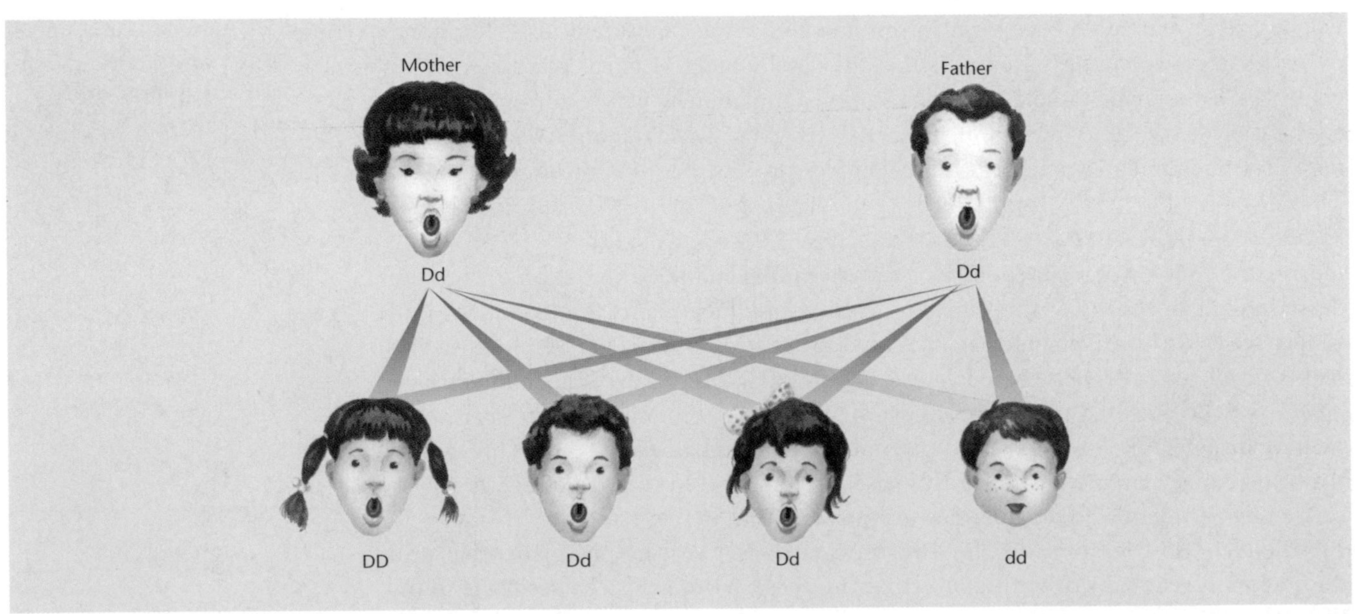

Figure 3-4
Dominant and recessive inheritance. Because of dominant inheritance, the same observable phenotype (in this case, the ability to curl the tongue lengthwise) can result from two different genotypes (DD and Dd). A phenotype expressing a recessive characteristic (such as inability to curl the tongue) must have a homozygous genotype (dd).

These genes work together to produce different amounts of brown pigment, resulting in hundreds of shades of skin. Intelligence may be affected by fifty or more genes. Indeed, whereas there are more than a thousand rare genes that individually determine abnormal traits, there is no known single gene that, by itself, significantly accounts for individual differences in any complex normal behavior. Instead, such behaviors are likely to be influenced by many genes with small but sometimes identifiable effects. Furthermore, there may be an average of twelve different versions, or variants, of each gene, each with varying influences (Stephens et al., 2001).

Researchers in *molecular genetics* have begun to identify specific genes that contribute to particular behavioral traits, such as reading disabilities (Plomin, 2001). The locations and relative effect sizes of contributing genes, called *quantitative trait loci (QTL),* can be determined by comparing the frequency of a certain allele in large samples of unrelated people who do and do not show a trait or disorder. The larger the sample size, the smaller the effect size that can be detected (McGuffin, Riley, & Plomin, 2001; Plomin, 1995; Plomin & DeFries, 1999).

Multifactorial transmission, a combination of genetic and environmental factors, plays a role in the expression of most traits. Let's see how this happens.

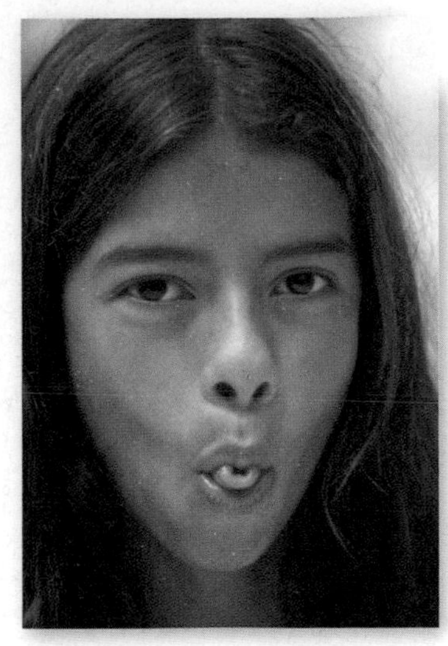

The ability to curl the tongue lengthwise, as this girl is doing, is unusual in that it is inherited through simple dominant transmission. Most normal traits are influenced by multiple genes, often in combination with environmental factors.

multifactorial transmission Combination of genetic and environ-mental factors to produce certain complex traits.

phenotype Observable characteristics of a person.

genotype Genetic makeup of a person, containing both expressed and unexpressed characteristics.

Genotypes and Phenotypes: Multifactorial Transmission If you can curl your tongue, that ability is part of your **phenotype,** the observable characteristics through which your **genotype,** or underlying genetic makeup, is expressed. Except for monozygotic twins, no two people have the same genotype. The phenotype is the product of the genotype and any relevant environmental influences. The difference between genotype and phenotype helps explain why a clone can never be an exact duplicate of another human being.

As Figure 3-4 shows, the same phenotypical characteristic may arise from different genotypes: either a homozygous combination of two dominant alleles or a heterozygous combination of one dominant allele and one recessive allele. If you are heterozygous for tongue curling, and you and a mate who is also heterozygous for the trait have four children, the statistical probability is that one child will be homozygous for the ability, one will be homozygous lacking it, and the other two will be heterozygous. Thus, three of your children will have phenotypes that include tongue curling (they will be able to curl their tongues), but this ability will arise from two different genotypical patterns (homozygous and heterozygous).

Tongue curling has a strong genetic base, but for most traits, experience modifies the expression of the genotype. Let's say that Steven has inherited musical talent. If he takes music lessons and practices regularly, he may delight his family with his performances. If his family likes and encourages classical music, he may play Bach preludes; if the other children on his block influence him to prefer popular music, he may eventually form a rock group. However, if from early childhood he is not encouraged and not motivated to play music, and if he has no access to a musical instrument or to music lessons, his genotype for musical ability may not be expressed (or may be expressed to a lesser extent) in his phenotype. Some physical characteristics (including height and weight) and most psychological characteristics (such as intelligence and personality traits, as well as musical ability) are products of multifactorial transmission.

Later in this chapter we discuss in more detail how environmental influences work together with the genetic endowment to influence development.

Checkpoint

Can you . . .

- ✔ Tell how dominant inheritance, recessive inheritance, and codominance work, and why most normal traits are not the products of simple dominant or recessive transmission?

Genetic and Chromosomal Abnormalities

Babies born with serious birth defects are at high risk of dying at or shortly after birth or during infancy or childhood (Skjaerven, Wilcox, & Lie, 1999). Although most birth disorders are fairly rare (see Table 3-1 on page 70), they accounted for 20.5 percent of

Table 3-1 Some Birth Defects

Problem	Characteristics of Condition	Who Is at Risk	What Can Be Done
Alpha$_1$ antitrypsin deficiency	Enzyme deficiency that can lead to cirrhosis of the liver in early infancy and emphysema and degenerative lung disease in middle age.	1 in 1,000 white births	No treatment.
Alpha thalassemia	Severe anemia that reduces ability of the blood to carry oxygen; nearly all affected infants are stillborn or die soon after birth.	Primarily families of Malaysian, African, and Southeast Asian descent.	Frequent blood transfusions.
Beta thalassemia (Cooley's anemia)	Severe anemia resulting in weakness, fatigue, and frequent illness; usually fatal in adolescence or young adulthood.	Primarily families of Mediterranean descent	Frequent blood transfusions.
Cystic fibrosis	Body makes too much mucus, which collects in the lung and digestive tract; children do not grow normally and usually do not live beyond age 30; the most common inherited *lethal* defect among white people.	1 in 2,000 white births	Daily physical therapy to loosen mucus; antibiotics for lung infections; enzymes to improve digestion; gene therapy (in experimental stage).
Duchenne muscular dystrophy	Fatal disease usually found in males, marked by muscle weakness; minor mental retardation is common; respiratory failure and death usually occur in young adulthood.	1 in 3,000 to 5,000 male births	No treatment.
Hemophilia	Excessive bleeding, usually affecting males rather than females; in its most severe form, can lead to crippling arthritis in adulthood.	1 in 10,000 families with a history of hemophilia	Frequent transfusions of blood with clotting factors.
Neural-tube defects:			
Anencephaly	Absence of brain tissues; infants are stillborn or die soon after birth.	1 in 1,000	No treatment.
Spina bifida	Incompletely closed spinal canal, resulting in muscle weakness or paralysis and loss of bladder and bowel control; often accompanied by hydrocephalus, an accumulation of spinal fluid in the brain, which can lead to mental retardation.	1 in 1,000	Surgery to close spinal canal prevents further injury; shunt placed in brain drains excess fluid and prevents mental retardation.
Phenylketonuria (PKU)	Metabolic disorder resulting in mental retardation.	1 in 15,000 births	Special diet begun in first few weeks of life can offset mental retardation.
Polycystic kidney disease	*Infantile form;* enlarged kidneys, leading to respiratory problems and congestive heart failure. *Adult form;* kidney pain, kidney stones, and hypertension resulting in chronic kidney failure.	1 in 1,000	Kidney transplants.
Sickle-cell anemia	Deformed, fragile red blood cells that can clog the blood vessels, depriving the body of oxygen; symptoms include severe pain, stunted growth, frequent infections, leg ulcers, gallstones, susceptibility to pneumonia, and stroke.	1 in 500 African Americans	Painkillers, transfusions for anemia and to prevent stroke, antibiotics for infections.
Tay-Sachs disease	Degenerative disease of the brain and nerve cells, resulting in death before age 5.	Historically found mainly in eastern European Jews	No treatment.

Source: Adapted from AAP Committee on Genetics, 1996; NIH Consensus Development Panel, 2001; Tisdale, 1988, pp 68–69.

infant deaths in the United States in 2000 (Anderson, 2002). Most of the serious malformations involve the circulatory or central nervous systems.

Because many defects are hereditary, affected people risk passing them on to their children. This increased risk may be one reason that men and women with birth defects are less likely than others to have children (Lie, Wilcox, & Skjaerven, 2001; Skjaerven et al., 1999).

It is in genetic defects and diseases that we see most clearly the operation of dominant and recessive transmission, and also of a variation, *sex-linked inheritance.* Some defects are due to abnormalities in genes or chromosomes, which may result from **mutations:** permanent alterations in genetic material that may produce harmful characteristics. Mutations can occur spontaneously or can be induced by environmental hazards, such as radiation. It has been estimated that the human species undergoes at least 1.6 harmful mutations per person in each generation (Crow, 1999; Eyre-Walker & Keightley, 1999, Keightley & Eyre-Walker, 2001).

mutations Permanent alterations in genes or chromosomes that may produce harmful characteristics.

Many disorders arise when an inherited predisposition (an abnormal variant of a normal gene) interacts with an environmental factor, either before or after birth. Spina bifida (incomplete closure of the vertebral canal) and cleft palate (a fissure in the roof of the mouth) probably result from multifactorial transmission (Botto, Moore, Khoury, & Erickson, 1999). Attention deficit disorder with hyperactivity (ADHD) is one of a number of behavioral disorders thought to be transmitted multifactorially (Price, Simonoff, Waldman, Asherson, & Plomin, 2001).

Not all genetic or chromosomal abnormalities show up at birth. Symptoms of Tay-Sachs disease (a fatal degenerative disease of the central nervous system that at one time occurred mostly among Jews of eastern European ancestry) and sickle-cell anemia (a blood disorder most common among African Americans) may not appear until at least 6 months of age; cystic fibrosis (a condition, especially common in children of northern European descent, in which excess mucus accumulates in the lungs and digestive tract), not until age 4; and glaucoma (a disease in which fluid pressure builds up in the eye) and Huntington's disease (a progressive degeneration of the nervous system) usually not until middle age.

Defects Transmitted by Dominant or Recessive Inheritance As Mendel discovered, characteristics can be passed on from parent to child by dominant or recessive inheritance. Most of the time, normal genes are dominant over those carrying abnormal traits, but sometimes the gene for an abnormal trait is dominant. When one parent has a dominant abnormal gene and one recessive normal gene and the other parent has two recessive normal genes, each of their children has a 50-50 chance of inheriting the dominant abnormal gene. Among the 1,800 disorders known to be transmitted by dominant inheritance are achondroplasia (a type of dwarfism) and Huntington's disease.

Recessive defects are expressed only if a child receives the same recessive gene from each biological parent. Some defects transmitted recessively, such as Tay-Sachs disease and sickle-cell anemia, which interferes with the transport of oxygen in the blood, are more common among certain ethnic groups, which, through inbreeding (marriage and reproduction within the group) have passed down recessive characteristics (see Table 3-2 on page 72).

Defects transmitted by recessive inheritance are more likely to be lethal at an early age than those transmitted by dominant inheritance. If a dominantly transmitted defect killed before the age of reproduction, it could not be passed on to the next generation and therefore would soon disappear. A recessive defect can be transmitted by carriers who do not have the disorder and thus may live to reproduce.

Some traits are only partly dominant or partly recessive. In **incomplete dominance** a trait is not fully expressed. For example, people with only one sickle-cell allele

incomplete dominance Partial expression of a trait.

Table 3-2 Chances of Genetic Disorders for Various Ethnic Groups

If You Are	The Chance Is About	That
African American	1 in 12	You are a carrier of sickle-cell anemia.
	7 in 10	You will have milk intolerance as an adult.
African American and male	1 in 10	You have a hereditary predisposition to develop hemolytic anemia after taking sulfa or other drugs.
African American and female	1 in 50	You have a hereditary predisposition to develop hemolytic anemia after taking sulfa or other drugs.
White	1 in 25	You are a carrier of cystic fibrosis.
	1 in 80	You are a carrier of phenylketonuria (PKU).
Jewish (Ashkenazic)	1 in 30	You are a carrier of Tay-Sachs disease.
	1 in 100	You are a carrier of familial dysautonomia.
Italian American or Greek American	1 in 10	You are a carrier of beta thalassemia.
Armenian or Jewish (Sephardic)	1 in 45	You are a carrier of familial Mediterranean fever.
Afrikaner (white South African)	1 in 330	You have porphyria.
Asian	almost 100%	You will have milk intolerance as an adult.

Source: Adapted from Milunsky, 1992, p. 122.

and one normal allele do not have sickle-cell anemia but do show some manifestations of the condition, such as shortness of breath at high altitudes.

sex-linked inheritance Pattern of inheritance in which certain characteristics carried on the X chromosome inherited from the mother are transmitted differently to her male and female offspring.

Defects Transmitted by Sex-Linked Inheritance In **sex-linked inheritance** (see Figure 3-5) certain recessive disorders linked to genes on the sex chromosomes show up differently in male and female children. Red-green color blindness is one of these sex-linked conditions. Another is hemophilia, a disorder in which blood does not clot when it should.

Sex-linked recessive traits are carried on one of the X chromosomes of an unaffected mother. The mother is a *carrier;* she does not have the disorder but can pass on the gene for it to her children. Sex-linked disorders almost always appear only in male children; in females, a normal dominant gene on the X chromosome from the father generally overrides the defective gene on the X chromosome from the mother. Boys are more vulnerable to these disorders because there is no opposite dominant gene on the shorter Y chromosome from the father to override a defect on the X chromosome from the mother.

Occasionally, however, a female does inherit a sex-linked condition. For example, if her father is a hemophiliac and her mother happens to be a carrier for the disorder, the daughter has a 50 percent chance of receiving the abnormal X chromosome from each parent and having the disease.

Genome (Genetic) Imprinting Through *genome,* or *genetic, imprinting,* some genes seem to be temporarily imprinted, or chemically altered, in either the mother or the father. These genes, when transmitted to offspring, have different effects than do counterpart genes from the other parent. Genome imprinting may explain why the child of a diabetic father, but not of a diabetic mother, is likely to develop diabetes, and why the opposite is true for asthma (Day, 1993). Imprinting also may explain why children who inherit Huntington's disease from their fathers are far more likely to be

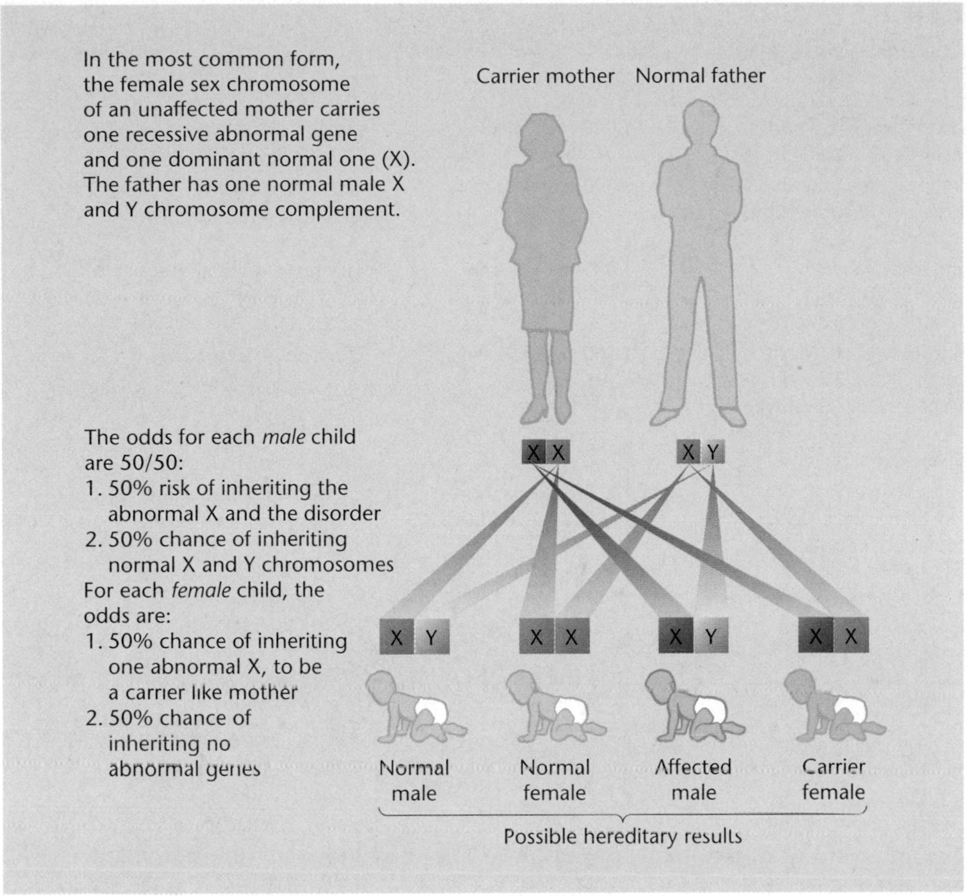

In the most common form, the female sex chromosome of an unaffected mother carries one recessive abnormal gene and one dominant normal one (X). The father has one normal male X and Y chromosome complement.

Carrier mother Normal father

X X X Y

The odds for each *male* child are 50/50:
1. 50% risk of inheriting the abnormal X and the disorder
2. 50% chance of inheriting normal X and Y chromosomes

For each *female* child, the odds are:
1. 50% chance of inheriting one abnormal X, to be a carrier like mother
2. 50% chance of inheriting no abnormal genes

X Y X X X Y X X

Normal male · Normal female · Affected male · Carrier female

Possible hereditary results

Figure 3-5
Sex-linked inheritance.

affected at an early age than children who inherit the Huntington's gene from their mothers (Sapienza, 1990) and why (as we report later in this chapter) children who receive a certain allele from the mother are more likely to have autism than those who receive that allele from the father (Ingram et al., 2000).

A particularly dramatic example appeared among 80 girls and young women with Turner syndrome (discussed in the next section), in which an X chromosome is missing. Those who had received their single X chromosome from their fathers were better adjusted socially and had stronger verbal and cognitive skills than those who had received the X chromosome from their mothers. This suggests that social competence is influenced by an imprinted gene or genes on the X chromosome, which is "turned off" when that chromosome comes from the mother (Skuse et al., 1997).

Checkpoint

Can you . . .

✔ Compare the operation of dominant inheritance, recessive inheritance, incomplete dominance, sex-linked inheritance, and genome imprinting in transmission of birth defects?

Chromosomal Abnormalities About 1 in every 156 children born in western countries is estimated to have a chromosomal abnormality (Milunsky, 1992). Some of these abnormalities are inherited; others result from accidents during prenatal development and are not likely to recur in the same family.

Some chromosomal disorders, such as Klinefelter syndrome, are caused by an extra sex chromosome (shown by the pattern XXY). Others, such as Turner syndrome, result from a missing sex chromosome (XO). Characteristics of the most common sex chromosome disorders are shown in Table 3-3 on page 74.

Other chromosomal abnormalities occur in the autosomes. **Down syndrome,** the most common of these, is responsible for about one-third of all cases of moderate-to-severe mental retardation. The condition, also called *trisomy-21,* is usually caused by an extra twenty-first chromosome or the translocation of part of the twenty-first

Down syndrome Chromosomal disorder characterized by moderate-to-severe mental retardation and by such physical signs as a downward-sloping skin fold at the inner corners of the eyes.

Table 3-3 Sex Chromosome Abnormalities

Pattern/Name	Characteristics*	Incidence	Treatment
XYY	Male; tall stature; tendency to low IQ, especially verbal.	1 in 1,000 male births	No special treatment
XXX (triple X)	Female, normal appearance, menstrual irregularities, learning disorders, mental retardation.	1 in 1,000 female births	Special education
XXY (Kleinfelter)	Male, sterility, underdeveloped secondary sex characteristics, small testes, learning disorders.	1 in 1,000 male births	Hormone therapy, special education
XO (Turner)	Female, short stature, webbed neck, impaired spatial abilities, no menstruation, infertility, underdeveloped sex organs, incomplete development of secondary sex characteristics.	1 in 1,500 to 2,500 female births	Hormone therapy, special education
Fragile X	Minor-to-severe mental retardation; symptoms, which are more severe in males, include delayed speech and motor development, speech impairments, and hyperactivity; the most common *inherited* form of mental retardation.	1 in 1,200 male births; 1 in 2,000 female births	Educational and behavioral therapies when needed

*Not every affected person has every characteristic.

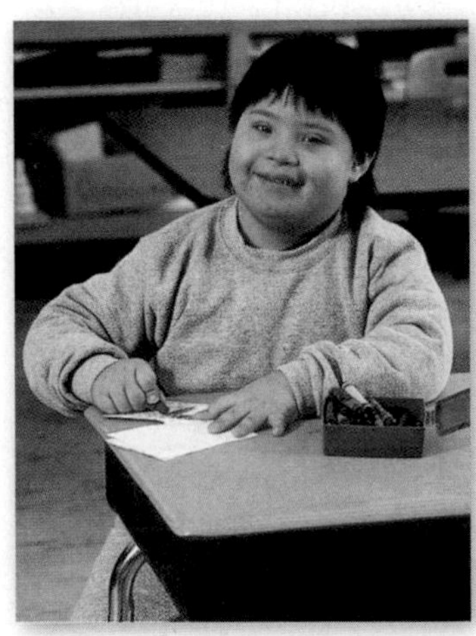

This boy shows the chief identifying characteristic of Down syndrome: a downward sloping skinfold at the inner corner of the eye. Although Down syndrome is a major cause of mental retardation, children with this chromosomal abnormality have a good chance of living productive lives.

genetic counseling Clinical service that advises couples of their probable risk of having children with hereditary defects.

chromosome onto another chromosome. The most obvious physical characteristic associated with the disorder is a downward-sloping skin fold at the inner corners of the eyes.

About 1 in every 700 babies born alive has Down syndrome (Hayes & Batshaw, 1993). The risk is greatest with older parents; when the mother is under age 35, the disorder is more likely to be hereditary. The extra chromosome seems to come from the mother's ovum in 95 percent of cases (Antonarakis & Down Syndrome Collaborative Group, 1991); the other 5 percent of cases seem to be related to the father.

The prognosis for children with Down syndrome is brighter than was once thought. As adults, many live in small group homes and support themselves; they tend to do well in structured job situations. More than 70 percent of people with Down syndrome live into their sixties, but they are at special risk of developing Alzheimer's disease (Hayes & Batshaw, 1993).

Genetic Counseling and Testing

Genetic counseling can help prospective parents assess their risk of bearing children with genetic or chromosomal defects. People who have already had a child with a genetic defect, who have a family history of hereditary illness, who suffer from conditions known or suspected to be inherited, or who come from ethnic groups at higher-than-average risk of passing on genes for certain diseases can get information about their likelihood of producing affected children.

A genetic counselor takes a family history and gives the prospective parents and any biological children physical examinations. Laboratory investigations of blood, skin, urine, or fingerprints may be performed. Chromosomes from body tissues may be analyzed and photographed, and the photographs enlarged and arranged according to size and structure on a chart called a *karyotype.* This chart can show chromosomal abnormalities and can indicate whether a person who appears normal might transmit genetic defects to a child (see Figure 3-6). The counselor tries to help clients under-

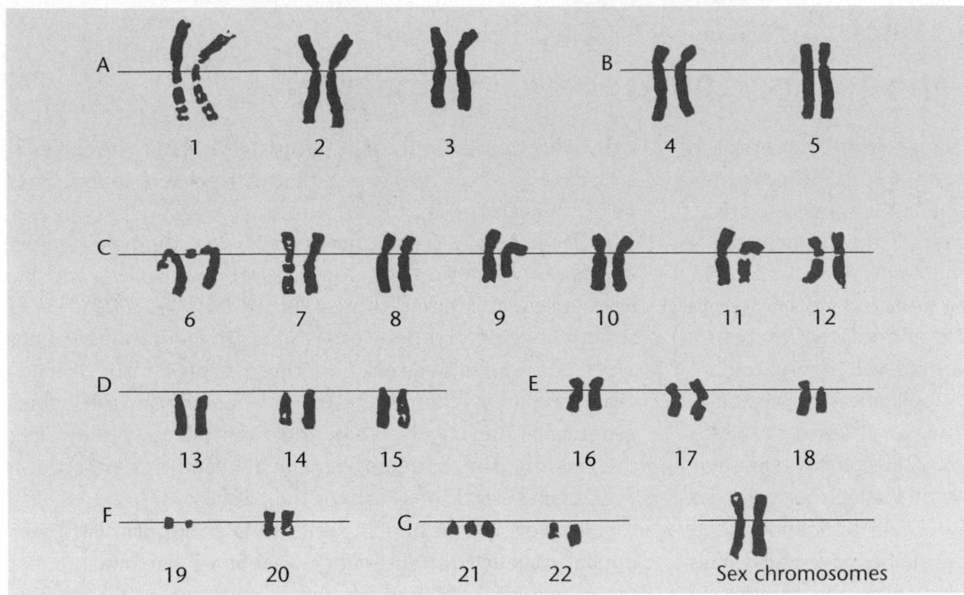

Figure 3-6
A karyotype is a photograph that shows the chromosomes when they are separated and aligned for cell division. We know that this is a karyotype of a person with Down syndrome, because there are three chromosomes instead of the usual two on chromosome 21. Since pair 23 consists of two X's, we know that this is the karyotype of a female. (*Source:* Babu & Hirschhorn, 1992; March of Dimes, 1987.)

stand the mathematical risk of a particular condition, explains its implications, and presents information about alternative courses of action.

Geneticists have made great contributions to avoidance of birth defects. For example, since so many Jewish couples have been tested for Tay-Sachs genes, the disease has been virtually eliminated among that population (Kolata, 2003). Similarly, screening and counseling of women of childbearing age from Mediterranean countries, where beta thalassemia (refer back to Table 3-1) is common, has brought a decline in births of affected babies and greater knowledge of the risks of being a carrier (Cao, Saba, Galanello, & Rosatelli, 1997).

Today, researchers are rapidly identifying genes that contribute to many serious diseases and disorders, as well as those that influence normal traits. Their work is likely to lead to widespread genetic testing to reveal genetic profiles—a prospect that involves dangers as well as benefits (see Box 3-1 on page 76).

Checkpoint

Can you . . .

- ✔ Tell three ways in which chromosomal disorders occur?
- ✔ Explain the purposes of genetic counseling?

Nature and Nurture: Influences of Heredity and Environment

While certain rare physical disorders are virtually 100 percent inherited, phenotypes for most complex normal traits, such as those having to do with health, intelligence, and personality are subject to a complex array of hereditary and environmental forces. Let's see how scientists study and explain the influences of heredity and environment and how these two forces work together.

Guidepost

4. How do scientists study the relative influences of heredity and environment, and how do heredity and environment work together?

Studying Heredity and Environment

One approach to the study of heredity and environment is quantitative: it seeks to measure *how much* heredity and environment influence particular traits. This is the traditional goal of the science of **behavioral genetics.**

behavioral genetics Quantita-tive study of relative hereditary and environmental influences.

Measuring Heritability **Heritability** is a statistical estimate of how great a contribution heredity makes toward individual differences in a specific observed trait at a certain time *within a given population.* Heritability does *not* refer to the relative influence of heredity and environment in a particular individual; those influences may

heritability Statistical estimate of contribution of heredity to individual differences in a specific trait within a given population.

BOX 3-1 Practically Speaking

Genetic Testing and Genetic Engineering

The Human Genome Project, under the joint leadership of the National Institutes of Health and the U.S. Department of Energy, in cooperation with Celera Genomics, a private firm in Rockville, Maryland, has mapped the order of DNA base pairs in all the genes in the human body. The mapping of the human genome has led to a new field of science: *genomics,* the study of the functions and interactions of the various genes in the genome. Genomics will have untold implications for *medical genetics,* the application of genetic information to therapeutic purposes (McKusick, 2001; Patenaude, Guttmacher, & Collins, 2002). As efforts shift from finding genes to understanding how they affect behavior (behavioral genomics), scientists will be able to identify genes that cause, trigger, or increase susceptibility to particular disorders (Plomin & Crabbe, 2000) and to screen at-risk population groups (Khoury, McCabe, & McCabe, 2003).

The genetic information gained from such research could increase our ability to predict, prevent, control, treat, and cure disease—even to pinpoint specific drug treatments to specific individuals (McGuffin et al., 2001; McKusick, 2001; Patenaude et al., 2002; Rutter, 2002; Subramanian, Adams, Venter, & Broder 2001). Already, genetic screening of newborns is saving lives and preventing mental retardation by permitting identification and treatment of infants with such disorders as sickle-cell anemia and phenylketonuria (PKU) (Holtzman, Murphy, Watson, & Barr, 1997; Khoury et al., 2003). Genetic screening for breast cancer probably would identify 88 percent of all high-risk persons, significantly more than are identified by currently used risk factors (Pharaoh et al., 2002). Genetic information can help people decide whether to have children and with whom, and it can help people with family histories of a disease to know the worst that is likely to happen (Post, 1994; Wiggins et al., 1992).

Gene therapy (repairing or replacing abnormal genes) is already an option for some genetic disorders and has been tried *in utero* (Flake et al., 1996). In 2000, French researchers reversed severe combined immunodeficiency, a serious immune disease, in three babies from 1 to 11 months old by taking bone marrow cells from the babies, genetically altering the cells, and then injecting them into the babies. The patients remained healthy as much as a year later (Cavazanna-Calvo et al., 2000).

However, such human gene transfer experiments raise ethical concerns about safety, benefit to participants, and the difficulty of obtaining meaningful informed consent (Sugarman, 1999). Gene therapy carries serious risks: an 18-year-old died after being given an experimental infusion of gene-altered viruses intended to treat a liver disorder (Stolberg, 2000). A group of scientists, ethicists, lawyers, and theologians concluded that gene therapy can damage reproductive cells and that it cannot yet be safely performed on human beings (Chapman & Frankel, 2000).

Genetic testing itself involves ethical and political issues involving privacy and fair use of genetic information (Jeffords & Daschle, 2001; Patenaude et al., 2002). Although medical data are supposed to be confidential, it is almost impossible to keep such information private. Parents, children, and siblings may have a legitimate claim to information about a patient that may affect them (Plomin & Rutter, 1998; Rennie, 1994), but what about employers and insurance companies?

What's Your View?

- In what ways are you more like your mother and in what ways like your father? How are you similar and dissimilar to your siblings? Which differences would you guess come chiefly from heredity and which from environment? Can you see possible effects of both?

be virtually impossible to separate. Nor does heritability tell us how traits develop. It merely indicates the statistical extent to which genes contribute to a trait.

Heritability is expressed as a number ranging from 0.0 to 1.0; the greater the number, the greater the heritability of a trait, with 1.0 meaning that genes are 100 percent responsible for individual differences in the trait. Since heritability cannot be measured directly, researchers in behavioral genetics rely chiefly on three types of correlational research: family, adoption, and twin studies.

Such studies are based on the assumption that immediate family members are more genetically similar than more distant relatives, monozygotic twins are more genetically similar than dizygotic twins, and adopted children are genetically more like their biological families than their adoptive families. Thus, if heredity is an important influence on a particular trait, siblings should be more alike than cousins with regard to that trait, monozygotic twins should be more alike than dizygotic twins, and adopted children should be more like their biological parents than their adoptive parents. By the same token, if a shared environment exerts an important influence on a trait, persons who live together should be more similar than persons who do *not* live together.

Practically Speaking

BOX 3-1

—continued

A major concern is *genetic determinism:* the misconception that a person with a gene for a disease is bound to get the disease. All genetic testing can tell us is the *likelihood* that a person will get a disease. Most diseases involve a complex combination of genes or depend in part on lifestyle or other environmental factors (Plomin & Rutter, 1998; Rutter, 2002). Job and insurance discrimination on the basis of genetic information has occurred—even though tests may be imprecise and unreliable and people deemed at risk of a disease may never develop it (Khoury et al., 2003; Lapham, Kozma, & Weiss, 1996). Federal and state antidiscrimination laws provide some protection, but it is not consistent or comprehensive. Policies protecting confidentiality of research also are needed (Jeffords & Daschle, 2001).

The psychological impact of test results is another concern (Patenaude et al., 2002). Predictions are imperfect; a false positive result may cause needless anxiety, while a false negative result may lull a person into complacency. And what if a genetic condition is incurable? Is there any point in knowing you have the gene for a potentially debilitating condition if you cannot do anything about it? A panel of experts has recommended against genetic testing for diseases for which there is no known cure (Institute of Medicine [IOM], 1993).

Specific issues have to do with testing of children. Should a child be tested to benefit a sibling or someone else? How will a child be affected by learning that he or she is likely to develop a disease twenty, thirty, or fifty years later? The American Academy of Pediatrics Committee on Bioethics (2001) recommends against genetic testing of children for conditions that cannot be treated in childhood.

Particularly chilling is the prospect that genetic testing could be misused to justify sterilization of people with "undesirable" genes, or abortion of a normal fetus with the "wrong" genetic makeup (Plomin & Rutter, 1998). Gene therapy has the potential for similar abuse. Should it be used to make a short child taller, or a chubby child thinner? To improve an unborn baby's appearance or intelligence? The path from therapeutic correction of defects to genetic engineering for cosmetic or functional purposes may well be a slippery slope (Anderson, 1998), leading to a society in which some parents could afford to provide the "best" genes for their children while others could not (Rifkin, 1998).

Within the next fifteen years, genetic testing and gene therapy "will almost certainly revolutionize the practice of medicine" (Anderson, 1998, p. 30). It is not yet clear whether the benefits of these new biotechnologies will outweigh the risks.

What's Your View?

Would you want to know that you had a gene predisposing you to lung cancer? To Alzheimer's disease? Would you want your child to be tested for these genes?

Check It Out:

For more information on this topic, go to www.mhhe.com/papaliah9. Here you will find a link to a page on the Human Genome Project information website entitled "Medicine and the New Genetics."

Family studies go beyond noting similarities in traits among family members. Researchers measure the *degree* to which biological relatives share certain traits and whether the closeness of the familial relationship is associated with the degree of similarity. If the correlation is strong, the researchers infer a genetic influence. However, family studies cannot rule out environmental influences on a trait. A family study alone cannot tell us whether obese children of obese parents inherited the tendency or whether they are fat because their diet is like that of their parents. For that reason, researchers do adoption studies, which can separate the effects of heredity from those of a shared environment.

Adoption studies look at similarities between adopted children and their adoptive families and also between adopted children and their biological families. When adopted children are more like their biological parents and siblings in a particular trait (say, obesity), we see the influence of heredity. When they resemble their adoptive families more, we see the influence of environment.

Studies of twins compare pairs of monozygotic twins and same-sex dizygotic twins. (Same-sex twins are used so as to avoid any confounding effects of gender.) Monozygotic twins are twice as genetically similar, on average, as dizygotic twins, who

Monozygotic twins separated at birth are sought after by researchers who want to study the impact of genes on personality. These twins, adopted by different families and not reunited till age 31, both became firefighters. Was this a coincidence, or did it reflect the influence of heredity?

concordant Term describing twins who share the same trait or disorder.

are no more genetically similar than other same-sex siblings. When monozygotic twins are more **concordant** (that is, have a statistically greater tendency to show the same trait) than dizygotic twins, we see the likely effects of heredity. Concordance rates, which may range from 0.0 to 1.0, estimate the probability that a pair of twins in a sample will be concordant for that trait.

When monozygotic twins show higher concordance for a trait than do dizygotic twins, the likelihood of a genetic factor can be studied further through adoption studies. Studies of monozygotic twins separated in infancy and reared apart have found strong resemblances between the twins. Twin and adoption studies support a moderate to high hereditary basis for many normal and abnormal characteristics (McGuffin et al., 2001).

Critics of behavioral genetics claim that its assumptions and methods tend to maximize the importance of hereditary effects and minimize environmental ones. Also, there are great variations in the findings, depending on the source of the data. For example, twin studies generally come up with higher heritability estimates than adoption studies do. This wide variability, critics say, "means that no firm conclusions can be drawn about the relative strength of these influences on development" (Collins, Maccoby, Steinberg, Hetherington, & Bornstein, 2000, p. 221).

Even behavioral geneticists recognize that the effects of genetic influences, especially on behavioral traits, are rarely inevitable: even in a trait strongly influenced by heredity, the environment can have substantial impact (Rutter, 2002), as much as 50 percent. In fact, environmental interventions sometimes can overcome genetically "determined" conditions. A special diet begun soon after birth often can prevent mental retardation in children with the genetic disease phenylketonuria (PKU) (Plomin & DeFries, 1999; refer back to Table 3-1). As we'll see in the next section, current studies based in part on behavioral genetics are throwing more light on the complex relationship between heredity and environment.

Effects of the Prenatal Environment One largely neglected environmental influence is what happens in the womb. Two newer types of twin studies—*co-twin control* and *chorion control* studies—allow researchers to look at the nature and timing of nongenetic influences in utero (Phelps, Davis, & Schartz, 1997). *Co-twin control stud-*

ies compare the prenatal (or postnatal) development and experiences of one monozygotic twin with those of the other, who serves as a one-person "control group." *Chorion control studies* focus on prenatal influences by comparing two types of monozygotic twins: (1) *monochorionic* twins, who developed within the same fluid-filled sac and thus had a similar prenatal environment, and (2) *dichorionic* twins, who grew within separate sacs, as about one-third of monozygotic twins, like all dizygotic twins, do.

Monochorionic twins normally share blood and have similar hormonal levels, which affect brain development. They also share exposure to any infectious agents that come from the mother's body. Because dichorionic twins are attached to different parts of the uterine wall, one twin may be better nourished than the other and better protected against infection. Twin studies that do not take account of these factors may either underestimate or overestimate genetic influences. Monochorionic twins tend to be more concordant than dichorionic twins in IQ, certain personality patterns, and cholesterol levels.

Checkpoint

Can you . . .

- ✔ State the basic assumption underlying studies of behavioral genetics and how it applies to family studies, twin studies, and adoption studies?
- ✔ Cite criticisms of the behavioral genetics approach?
- ✔ Identify two types of twin studies that focus on environmental influences in the womb?

How Heredity and Environment Work Together

Today, as research in cognitive neuroscience and molecular biology increasingly underlines the complexity of development, many developmental scientists have come to regard a solely quantitative approach to the study of heredity and environment as simplistic (Collins et al., 2000). They see these two forces as fundamentally intertwined and inseparable. Instead of looking at genes and experience as operating directly on an organism, they see both as part of a complex *developmental system* (Gottlieb, 1991). From conception on, throughout life, a combination of constitutional factors (related to biological and psychological makeup), and social, economic, and cultural factors help shape development. The more advantageous these circumstances and the experiences to which they give rise, the greater is the likelihood of optimum development (Horowitz, 2000).

Let's consider several ways in which inheritance and experience work together.

Reaction Range and Canalization Many characteristics vary, within limits, under varying hereditary or environmental conditions. The concepts of *reaction range* and *canalization* can help us visualize how this happens.

Reaction range refers to a range of potential expressions of a hereditary trait. Body size, for example, depends largely on biological processes, which are genetically regulated. Even so, a range of sizes is possible, depending on environmental opportunities and constraints and a person's own behavior. In societies in which nutrition has dramatically improved, an entire generation has grown up to tower over the generation before. The better-fed children share their parents' genes but have responded to a healthier world. Once a society's average diet becomes adequate for more than one generation, however, children tend to grow to heights similar to their parents'. Ultimately, height has genetic limits: we don't see people who are only a foot tall, or any who are 10 feet tall.

reaction range Potential variability, depending on environmental conditions, in the expression of a hereditary trait.

Heredity can influence whether a reaction range is wide or narrow. For example, a child born with a defect producing mild retardation is more able to respond to a favorable environment than a child born with more severe limitations. Likewise, a child with greater native intelligence is likely to benefit more from an enriched home and school environment than a child with normal ability (see Figure 3-7 on page 80).

Instead of a reaction range, advocates of a developmental system model prefer to talk about a *norm of reaction*. While recognizing that heredity does set some limits, they argue that, because development is so complex, these limits are unknowable and their effects unpredictable (Gottlieb, 1991).

The metaphor of **canalization** illustrates how heredity restricts the range of development for some traits. After a heavy storm, the rainwater that has fallen on a

canalization Limitation on variance of expression of certain inherited characteristics.

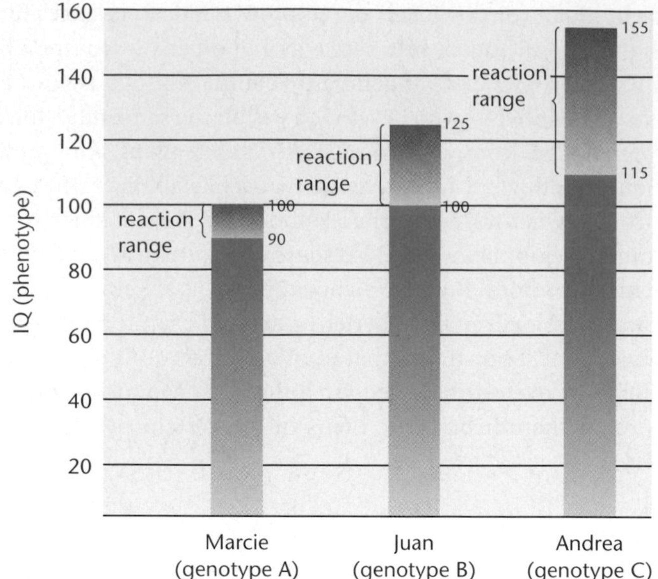

Figure 3-7
Intelligence and reaction range. Children with different genotypes for intelligence will show varying reaction ranges when exposed to a restricted (blue portion of bar) or enriched (entire bar) environment.

pavement has to go somewhere. If the street has potholes, the water will fill them. If deep canals have been dug along the edges of the street, the water will flow into the canals instead. Some human characteristics, such as eye color, are so strongly programmed by the genes that they are said to be highly canalized: there is little opportunity for variance in their expression.

Certain behaviors also develop along genetically "dug" channels; it takes an extreme change in environment to alter their course. Behaviors that depend largely on maturation seem to appear when a child is ready. Normal babies follow a typical sequence of motor development: crawling, walking, and running, in that order, at certain approximate ages. Still, this development is not completely canalized; experience can affect its pace and timing.

Cognition and personality are more subject to variations in experience: the kinds of families children grow up in, the schools they attend, and the people they encounter. Consider language. Before children can talk, they must reach a certain level of neurological and muscular maturation. No 6-month-old could speak this sentence, no matter how enriched the infant's home life might be. Still, environment plays a large part in language development. If parents encourage babies' first sounds by talking back to them, children are likely to start to speak earlier than if their early vocalizing is ignored.

Recently scientists have begun to recognize that a usual or typical *experience,* too, can dig canals, or channels for development (Gottlieb, 1991). For example, infants who hear only the sounds peculiar to their native language soon lose the ability to perceive sounds characteristic of other languages (see Chapter 5). Throughout this book you will find many examples of how socioeconomic status, neighborhood conditions, and educational opportunity can powerfully shape developmental outcomes, from the pace and complexity of language development to the likelihood of early sexual activity and antisocial behavior.

genotype-environment interaction The portion of phenotypic variation that results from the reactions of genetically different individuals to similar environmental conditions.

Genotype-Environment Interaction **Genotype-environment interaction** usually refers to the effects of similar environmental conditions on genetically different individuals. To take a familiar example, many people are exposed to pollen and dust, but people with a genetic predisposition are more likely to develop allergic reactions. But interactions can work the other way as well: genetically similar children often develop differently depending on their home environment (Collins et al., 2000). As we discuss in

Chapter 6, a child born with a "difficult" temperament may develop adjustment problems in one family and thrive in another, depending largely on parental handling. Thus certain outcomes depend on the interaction of hereditary and environmental factors, not on just one or the other.

Genotype-Environment Correlation The environment often reflects or reinforces genetic differences. That is, certain genetic and environmental influences tend to act in the same direction. This is called **genotype-environment correlation,** or *genotype-environment covariance,* and it works in three ways to strengthen the phenotypic expression of a genotypic tendency (Bergeman & Plomin, 1989; Scarr, 1992; Scarr & McCartney, 1983):

genotype-environment correlation Tendency of certain genetic and environmental influences to reinforce each other; may be passive, reactive (evocative), or active. Also called *genotype-environment covariance.*

- *Passive correlations:* Parents, who provide the genes that predispose a child toward a trait, also tend to provide an environment that encourages the development of that trait. For example, a musical parent is likely to create a home environment in which music is heard regularly, to give a child music lessons, and to take the child to musical events. If the child inherited the parent's musical talent, the child's musicality will reflect a combination of genetic and environmental influences. This type of correlation is called *passive* because the child does not control it; it is most applicable to young children, whose parents, the source of their genetic legacy, also have a great deal of control over their early experiences.
- *Reactive, or evocative, correlations:* Children with differing genetic makeups evoke different responses from adults. Parents who are *not* musically inclined may make a special effort to provide musical experiences to a child who shows interest and ability in musicthat they might not otherwise provide. This response, in turn, strengthens the child's genetic inclination toward music.
- *Active correlations:* As children get older and have more freedom to choose their own activities and environments, they actively select or create experiences consistent with their genetic tendencies. A child with a talent for music will probably seek out musical friends, take music classes, and go to concerts if such opportunities are available. A shy child is likely to spend more time in solitary pursuits than an outgoing youngster. This tendency to seek out environments compatible with one's genotype is called **niche-picking;** it helps explain why identical twins reared apart tend to be quite similar.

niche-picking Tendency of a person, especially after early childhood, to seek out environments compatible with his or her genotype.

Musical ability is one of many characteristics passed on from parents to children through a combination of genetic and environmental influences. This father playing the guitar with his daughter may be more motivated to do so because she shows interest and ability in music. In turn, the enjoyable experience with her father is likely to strengthen the little girl's natural inclination toward music.

What Makes Siblings Different? The Nonshared Environment Although two children in the same family may bear a striking physical resemblance, siblings can be very different in intellect and especially in personality (Plomin, 1989). One reason may be genetic or temperamental differences, which lead children to need different kinds of stimulation or to respond differently to a similar home environment. A child with a high IQ may be more stimulated by a roomful of books and puzzles than a child with a markedly lower IQ—an example of genotype-environment interaction. One child may be more affected by family discord than another (Rutter, 2002). In addition, studies in behavioral genetics suggest that many of the experiences that strongly affect development are different for different children in a family (McGuffin et al., 2001; Plomin & Daniels, 1987; Plomin & DeFries, 1999).

nonshared environmental effects The unique environment in which each child grows up, consisting of distinctive influences or influences that affect one child differently than another.

These **nonshared environmental effects** result from the unique environment in which each child in a family grows up. Children in a family have a shared environment, but they also, even if they are twins, have experiences that are not shared by their brothers and sisters. Parents and siblings may treat each child differently. Certain events, such as illnesses and accidents, and experiences outside the home (for example, with teachers and peers) affect one child and not another. Indeed, some behavioral geneticists have claimed that heredity accounts for most of the similarity between siblings and the nonshared environment accounts for most of the difference (McClearn et al., 1997; Plomin, 1996; Plomin & Daniels, 1987; Plomin & DeFries, 1999; Plomin, Owen, & McGuffin, 1994). However, methodological challenges and additional empirical evidence point to the more moderate conclusion that nonshared environmental effects do not greatly outweigh shared ones; rather, there seems to be a balance between the two (Rutter, 2002).

Genotype-environment correlations may play an important role in the nonshared environment. Children's genetic differences may lead parents and siblings to react to them differently and treat them differently, and genes may influence how children perceive and respond to that treatment, and what its outcome will be. Children also mold their own environments by the choices they make—what they do and with whom—and their genetic makeup influences these choices. A child who has inherited artistic talent may spend a great deal of time creating "masterpieces" in solitude, while a sibling who is athletically inclined spends more time playing ball with others. Thus, not only will the children's abilities (in, say, painting or soccer) develop differently, but their social lives will be different as well. These differences tend to be accentuated as children grow older and have more experiences outside the family (Bergeman & Plomin, 1989; Bouchard, 1994; Plomin, 1990, 1996; Plomin et al., 1994; Scarr, 1992; Scarr & McCartney, 1983).

Checkpoint

Can you . . .

- ✔ Explain and give at least one example of reaction range, canalization, genotype-environment interaction, and genotype-environment correlation?
- ✔ List three kinds of influences that contribute to nonshared environmental effects?
- ✔ Cite criticisms of behavioral, genetics research?

Critics of behavioral genetics research say that these studies give short shrift to the influence of parenting (Collins et al., 2000; Rutter, 2002). Some critics point to the narrow range of families sampled in some studies and to a lack of direct observation of family life. Instead, they look to longitudinal studies of effects of parenting practices and direct interventions that seem to foster effective parenting. Such studies offer evidence that parental influence contributes greatly to developmental outcomes, independent of hereditary effects or bidirectional processes. At the same time, this research points to "the interrelated effects of parenting, nonfamilial influences, and the role of the broader context in which families live" (Collins et al., 2000, p. 228).

The old nature-nurture puzzle is far from resolved; we know now that the problem is more complex than previously thought. A variety of research designs can continue to augment and refine our understanding of the forces affecting development.

Some Characteristics Influenced by Heredity and Environment

Keeping in mind the complexity of unraveling the influences of heredity and environment, let's look at what is known about their roles in producing certain characteristics.

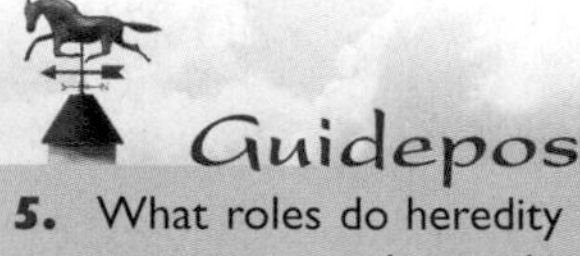

Guidepost

5. What roles do heredity and environment play in physical health, intelligence, and personality?

Physical and Physiological Traits Not only do monozygotic twins generally look alike, they are also more concordant than dizygotic twins in their risk for such medical disorders as hypertension (high blood pressure), heart disease, stroke, rheumatoid arthritis, peptic ulcers, and epilepsy (Brass, Isaacsohn, Merikangas, & Robinette, 1992; Plomin et al., 1994). Life span, too, seems to be influenced by the genes (Sorensen, Nielsen, Andersen, & Teasdale, 1988).

Obesity, or extreme overweight, is a multifactorial condition. Twin studies, adoption studies, and other research suggest that as much as 80 percent of the risk of obesity is genetic (Leibel, 1997). In genetic mapping, as many as 200 genes and other genetic markers have been linked with obesity so far (Pérusse, Chagnon, Weisnagel, & Bouchard, 1999). However, the kind and amount of food eaten in a particular home or in a particular social or ethnic group, and the amount of exercise that is encouraged, can increase or decrease the likelihood that a person will become obese. The rapid rise in the prevalence of obesity in western countries seems to result from the interaction of a genetic predisposition with inadequate exercise (Leibel, 1997; see Chapter 9).

Intelligence and School Achievement Heredity exerts a strong influence on general intelligence and also on specific abilities (McClearn et al., 1997; Plomin et al., 1994; Plomin & DeFries, 1999). Still, experience counts, too; an enriched or impoverished environment can substantially affect the development and expression of innate ability (Neisser et al., 1996). This seems to be an example of QTL: many genes, each with its own small effect, combine to establish a range of possible reactions to a range of possible experiences (Scarr, 1997a; Weinberg, 1989; refer back to Figure 3-7).

Evidence of the role of heredity in intelligence has emerged from adoption and twin studies. Adopted children's IQs are consistently closer to the IQs of their biological mothers than to those of their adoptive parents and siblings, and monozygotic twins are more alike in intelligence than dizygotic twins. This is also true of performance on elementary school achievement tests and on National Merit Scholarship examinations given to high school students. The studies yield a consistent estimate of heritability: 50 to 60 percent for verbal abilities and 50 percent for spatial abilities, meaning that genetic differences explain at least half of the observed variation among members of a population. The close correlation between verbal and spatial abilities suggests a genetic link among the components of intelligence (Plomin & DeFries, 1999).

Furthermore, the genetic influence increases with age. The family environment seems to have more influence on younger children, whereas adolescents are more apt to find their own niche by actively selecting environments compatible with their hereditary abilities and related interests (McClearn et al., 1997; McGue, 1997; McGue, Bouchard, Iacono, & Lykken, 1993; Plomin & DeFries, 1999).

The main environmental influences on intelligence, then, seem to occur early in life (McGue, 1997). In fact, an analysis of 212 studies (Devlin, Daniels, & Roeder, 1997) points to the impact of the earliest environment: the womb. According to this analysis, the prenatal environment may account for 20 percent of the similarity in IQ between twins and 5 percent of the similarity in nontwin siblings (who occupy the same womb at different times), bringing heritability of IQ below 50 percent. Thus the influence of genes on intelligence may be weaker, and the influence of the prenatal environment stronger, than was previously thought, underlining the importance of a healthy prenatal environment.

Personality Certain aspects of personality appear to be inherited, at least in part. Analyses of five major groupings of traits—extraversion, neuroticism (a group of traits involving anxiety), conscientiousness, agreeableness, and openness to experience—suggest a heritability of about 40 percent. Setting aside variances attributable to measurement error brings heritability closer to 66 percent for these trait groupings (Bouchard, 1994).

Temperament (discussed in detail in Chapter 6) appears to be largely inborn and is often consistent over the years, though it may respond to special experiences or parental handling (A. Thomas & Chess, 1984; A. Thomas, Chess, & Birch, 1968). An observational study of 100 pairs of 7-year-old siblings (half of them adoptive siblings and half siblings by birth) found significant genetic influences on activity, sociability,

What's Your View?

- What practical difference does it make whether a trait such as obesity, intelligence, or shyness is influenced more by heredity or by environment, since heritability can be measured only for a population, not for an individual?

and emotionality (Schmitz, Saudino, Plomin, Fulker, & DeFries, 1996). A large body of research (also discussed in Chapter 6) suggests that shyness and its opposite, boldness, are largely inborn and tend to stay with a person throughout life.

Although the research discussed so far provides strong evidence of genetic influences on personality, this evidence is indirect. Now scientists have begun to identify genes directly linked with specific personality traits. One of these genes has been found to play a part in neuroticism, which may contribute to depression. An estimated 10 to 15 other genes also may be involved in anxiety (Lesch et al., 1996). Future work in molecular genetics and brain physiology is likely to further illuminate the inheritance of personality traits (Bouchard & Loehlin, 2001).

Psychopathology There is evidence for a strong hereditary influence on such conditions as schizophrenia, autism, alcoholism, and depression. All tend to run in families and to show greater concordance between monozygotic twins than between dizygotic twins. However, heredity alone does not produce such disorders; an inherited tendency can be triggered by environmental factors. For example, researchers have linked a gene or genes on chromosome 1 to vulnerability to alcoholism or depression, or both, depending on circumstances (Nurnberger, 2001). (Alcoholism and depression are discussed later in this book.)

schizophrenia Mental disorder marked by loss of contact with reality; symptoms include hallucinations and delusions.

Schizophrenia, a disorder characterized by loss of contact with reality and by such symptoms as hallucinations and delusions, has a strong genetic component (Tuulio-Henriksson et al., 2002; Vaswani & Kapur, 2001). The risk of schizophrenia is ten times as great among siblings and offspring of schizophrenics as among the general population; and twin and adoption studies suggest that this increased risk comes from shared genes, not shared environments. The estimated genetic contribution is between 63 and 85 percent (McGuffin, Owen, & Farmer, 1995). Brain imaging may be useful in the search for genetic bases for schizophrenia and other psychiatric disorders (Morihisa, 2001).

However, since not all monozygotic twins are concordant for the illness, its cause cannot be purely genetic. Co-twin studies suggest that a prenatal viral infection, carried in the blood shared by monochorionic twins, may play a part (Phelps et al., 1997). In a study of the incidence of schizophrenia among all persons born in Denmark between 1935 and 1978, people born in urban areas were more likely to be schizophrenic than those born in rural areas, perhaps because of greater likelihood of birth complications and of exposure to infections during pregnancy and childhood (Mortenson et al., 1999). Among 87,907 babies born in Jerusalem between 1964 and 1976, the risk of the disorder was four times as high when the father was 50 years old or more than when the father was younger than 25 (Malaspina et al., 2001). And a study of 7,086 persons born in Helsinki, Finland, between 1924 and 1993 found indications that fetal undernutrition increases the risk of schizophrenia (Wahlbeck, Forsen, Osmond, Barker, & Eriksson, 2001).

A postmortem examination of the brains of schizophrenics suggests that the disorder may originate in a lack of a chemical called *reelin.* Reelin helps to correctly position and align nerve cells in the developing brain (Impagnatiello et al., 1998). A defective gene for reelin may result in misplacement of nerve cells, and this may create a predisposition, or vulnerability, to schizophrenia.

autism Pervasive developmental disorder of the brain, characterized by lack of normal social interaction, impaired communication and imagination, and a highly restricted range of abilities and interests.

Autism, a severe disorder of brain functioning, is characterized by lack of normal social interaction, impaired communication and imagination, and a highly restricted range of activities and interests. It usually appears within the first 3 years and continues to varying degrees throughout life (AAP Committee on Children with Disabilities, 2001; National Institute of Neurological Disorders and Stroke, 1999; Rapin, 1997; Rodier, 2000). Four out of five autistic children are boys (Yeargin-Allsopp et al., 2003).

An autistic child tends to avoid eye contact, even with a parent. However, these children often can learn basic social skills through behavior therapy.

An autistic baby may fail to notice the emotional signals of others (Sigman, Kasari, Kwon, & Yirmiya, 1992) and may refuse to cuddle or make eye contact. An autistic child may speak in a singsong voice, paying little or no attention to the listener. Severely autistic children often show repetitive behaviors, such as spinning, rocking, hand-flapping, and head-banging, and are obsessed with certain subjects, rituals, or routines (National Institute of Neurological Disorders and Stroke, 1999). About three out of four autistic children are mentally retarded (American Psychiatric Association, 1994), but they often do well on tests of manipulative or visual-spatial skill and may perform unusual mental feats, such as memorizing entire train schedules.

Autism is one of a group of *autistic spectrum disorders (ASD)* ranging from mild to severe, which may be more common than previously thought. Recent estimates are that about 6 children in 1,000 have one of these disorders (Fombonne, 2003; Yeargin-Allsopp et al., 2003). The most common is *Asperger's disorder,* which affects about 1 in 500 children. Children with Asperger's disorder usually have normal or even high verbal intelligence, are curious, and do good schoolwork; but they have limited, fixed interests, repetitive speech and behavior, and difficulty understanding social and emotional cues ("Autism—Part I," 2001). The increased number of children now diagnosed with ASDs may be due in part to improved diagnostic standards and heightened public awareness, as well as a broader definition of these disorders (AAP Committee on Children with Disabilities, 2001; Fombonne, 2003; Hyman, Rodier, & Davidson, 2001; Yeargin-Allsopp et al., 2003).

Autism runs in families and seems to have a strong genetic basis (Bailey, Le Couteur, Gottesman, & Bolton, 1995; National Institute of Neurological Disorders and

Stroke, 1999; Rodier, 2000; Szatmari, 1999; Trottier et al., 1999). Monozygotic twins are more concordant for autism than dizygotic twins. Several different genes may be involved in cases of varying symptoms and severity (Cook et al., 1997; Szatmari, 1999). One, recently identified, is a gene called *HOXA1,* which is involved in the development of the brain stem, the most primitive part of the brain, during the first few weeks of fetal growth (Rodier, 2000). A variant of HOXA1, especially when inherited from the mother, may predispose an infant to autism (Ingram et al., 2000).

Environmental factors, such as exposure to certain viruses or chemicals, may trigger an inherited tendency toward autism (National Institute of Neurological Disorders and Stroke, 1999; Rodier, 2000; Trottier et al., 1999). Certain complications of pregnancy, such as uterine bleeding, vaginal infection, and use of contraceptives during conception seem to be associated with a higher incidence of autism (Juul-Dam, Townsend, & Courchesne, 2001). A possible factor is major stress during the twenty-fourth to twenty-eighth weeks of pregnancy, which may deform the developing brain (Beversdorf et al., 2001). The claim that the rise in autism rates is related to administration of the measles-mumps-rubella vaccine has not been substantiated (AAP Committee on Children with Disabilities, 2001; Fombonne, 2001, 2003).

Autism has no known cure, but improvement, sometimes substantial, can occur, especially with early diagnosis and intervention. Some autistic children can be taught to speak, read, and write. Behavior therapy can help them learn such basic social skills as paying attention, sustaining eye contact, and feeding and dressing themselves and can help control problem behaviors. Physical and occupational therapy, highly structured social play situations, and extensive parent training may be part of the prescribed treatment. Newer, safer medications have shown effectiveness in managing specific symptoms (AAP Committee on Children with Disabilities, 2001). However, only about 2 percent of autistic children grow up to live independently; most need some degree of care throughout life. Children with Asperger's syndrome generally fare better ("Autism—Part II," 2001).

Checkpoint

Can you . . .

- ✔ Assess the evidence for genetic and environmental influences on obesity, intelligence, and temperament?
- ✔ Name and describe two mental disorders that show a strong genetic influence?

Prenatal Development

Guidepost

6. What are the three stages of prenatal development, and what happens during each stage?

If you had been born in China, you would probably celebrate your birthday on your estimated date of conception rather than your date of birth. This Chinese custom recognizes the importance of *gestation,* the approximately 9-month (or 266-day) period of development between conception and birth. Scientists, too, date *gestational age* from conception.

What turns a fertilized ovum, or *zygote,* into a creature with a specific shape and pattern? Research suggests that an identifiable group of genes is responsible for this transformation in vertebrates, presumably including human beings. These genes produce molecules called *morphogens,* which are switched on after fertilization and begin sculpting arms, hands, fingers, vertebrae, ribs, a brain, and other body parts (Echeland et al., 1993; Krauss, Concordet, & Ingham, 1993; Riddle, Johnson, Laufer, & Tabin, 1993). Scientists are also learning about the environment inside the womb and how it affects the developing person.

In this section we trace the course of gestation, or prenatal development. We discuss environmental factors that can affect the developing person-to-be, assess techniques for determining whether development is proceeding normally, and explain the importance of prenatal care.

Stages of Prenatal Development

Prenatal development takes place in three stages: *germinal, embryonic,* and *fetal.* (Table 3-4 on pages 88–89 gives a month-by-month description.) During these three stages of gestation, the original single-celled zygote grows into an *embryo* and then a *fetus.*

Both before and after birth, development proceeds according to two fundamental principles. Growth and motor development occur from top to bottom and from the center of the body outward.

The **cephalocaudal principle** (from Latin, meaning "head to tail") dictates that development proceeds from the head to the lower part of the trunk. An embryo's head, brain, and eyes develop earliest and are disproportionately large until the other parts catch up. At 2 months of gestation, the embryo's head is half the length of the body. By the time of birth, the head is only one-fourth the length of the body but is still disproportionately large. According to the **proximodistal principle** (from Latin, "near to far"), development proceeds from parts near the center of the body to outer ones. The embryo's head and trunk develop before the limbs, and the arms and legs before the fingers and toes.

cephalocaudal principle Prin-ciple that development proceeds in a head-to-tail direction; that is, that upper parts of the body develop before lower parts.

proximodistal principle Prin-ciple that development proceeds from within to without; that is, that parts of the body near the center develop before the extremities.

Germinal Stage (Fertilization to 2 Weeks) During the **germinal stage,** from fertilization to about 2 weeks of gestational age, the zygote divides, becomes more complex, and is implanted in the wall of the uterus (see Figure 3-8).

germinal stage First 2 weeks of prenatal development, characterized by rapid cell division, increasing complexity and differentiation, and implantation in the wall of the uterus.

Within 36 hours after fertilization, the zygote enters a period of rapid cell division and duplication, or *mitosis.* Seventy-two hours after fertilization, it has divided into 16 to 32 cells; a day later it has 64 cells. This division continues until the original single cell has developed into the 800 billion or more specialized cells that make up the human body.

While the fertilized ovum is dividing, it is also making its way down the fallopian tube to the uterus, a journey of 3 or 4 days. Its form changes into a fluid-filled sphere, a *blastocyst,* which floats freely in the uterus for a day or two and then begins to implant itself in the uterine wall. The blastocyst actively participates in this process through a complex system of hormonally regulated signaling (Norwitz, Schust, & Fisher, 2001). As cell differentiation begins, some cells around the edge of the blastocyst cluster on

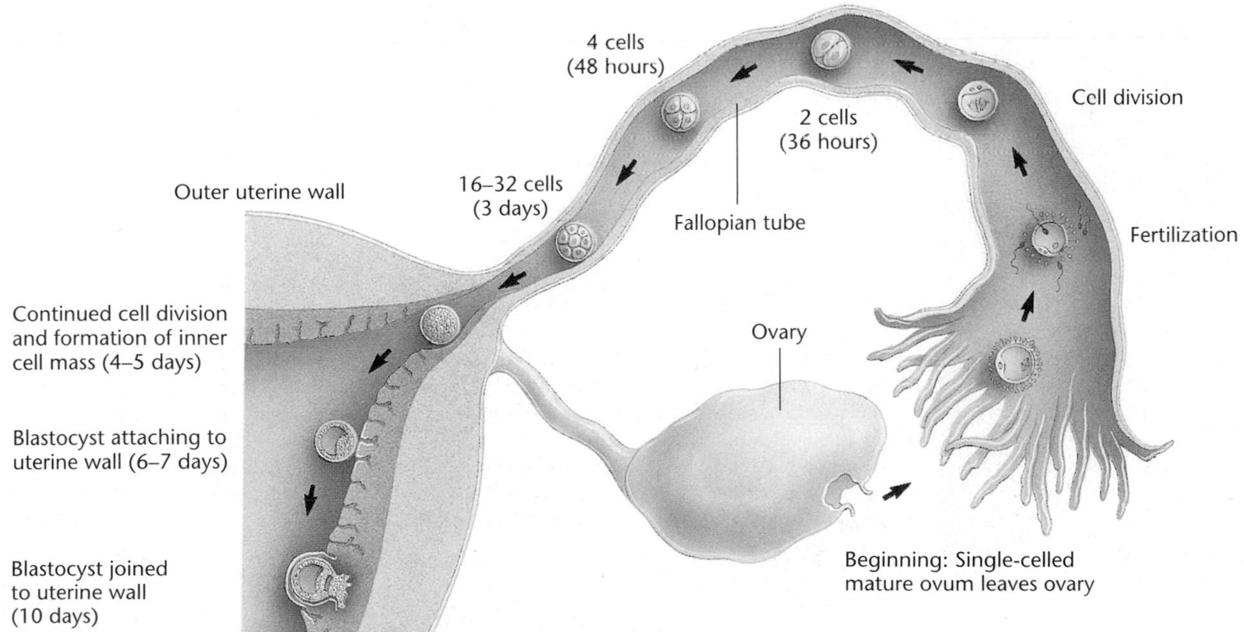

Figure 3-8
Early development of a human embryo. This simplified diagram shows the progress of the ovum as it leaves the ovary, is fertilized in the fallopian tube, and then divides while traveling to the lining of the uterus. Now a blastocyst, it is implanted in the uterus, where it will grow larger and more complex until it is ready to be born.

Table 3-4 Prenatal Development

Month	Description
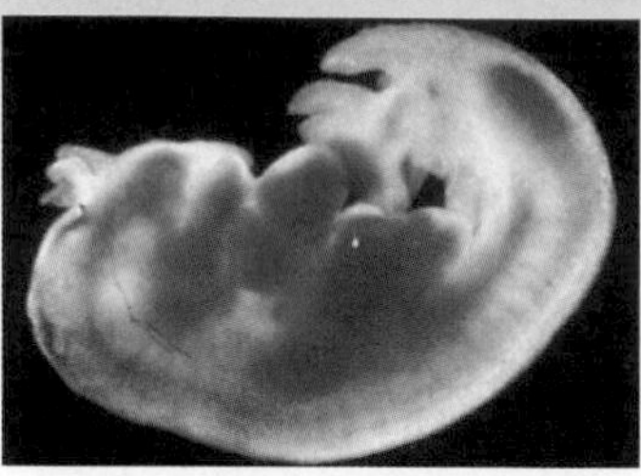 *1 month*	During the first month, growth is more rapid than at any other time during prenatal or postnatal life; the embryo reaches a size 10,000 times greater than the zygote. By the end of the first month, it measures about ½ inch in length. Blood flows through its veins and arteries, which are very small. It has a minuscule heart, beating 65 times a minute. It already has the beginning of a brain, kidneys, liver, and digestive tract. The umbilical cord, its lifeline to the mother, is working. By looking very closely through a microscope, it is possible to see the swellings on the head that will eventually become eyes, ears, mouth, and nose. Its sex cannot yet be determined.
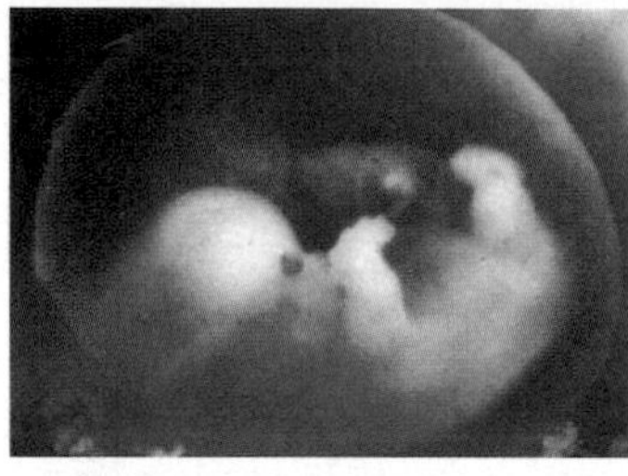 *7 weeks*	By the end of the second month, the organism is less than 1 inch long and weighs only ⅓ ounce. Its head is half its total body length. Facial parts are clearly developed, with tongue and teeth buds. The arms have hands, fingers, and thumbs, and the legs have knees, ankles, and toes. It has a thin covering of skin and can make handprints and footprints. Bone cells appear at about 8 weeks. Brain impulses coordinate the function of the organ system. Sex organs are developing the heartbeat is steady. The stomach produces digestive juices; the liver, blood cells. The kidneys remove uric acid from the blood. The skin is now sensitive enough to react to tactile stimulation. If an aborted 8-week-old fetus is stroked, it reacts by flexing its trunk, extending its head, and moving back its arms.
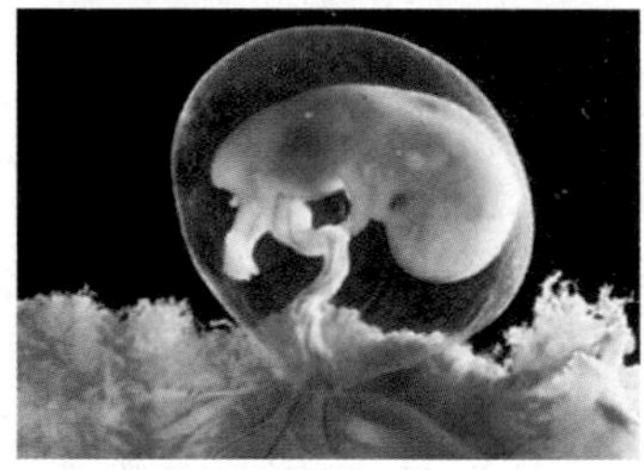 *3 months*	By the end of the third month, the fetus weighs about 1 ounce and measures about 3 inches in length. It has fingernails, toenails, eyelids (still closed), vocal cords, lips, and a prominent nose. Its head is still large—about ⅓ its total length—and its forehead is high. Sex can easily be determined. The organ systems are functioning, and so the fetus may now breathe, swallow amniotic fluid into the lungs and expel it, and occasionally urinate. Its ribs and vertebrae have turned into cartilage. The fetus can now make a variety of specialized responses; it can move its legs, feet, thumbs, and head; its mouth can open and close and swallow. If its eyelids are touched, it squints; if its palm is touched, it makes a partial fist; if its lip is touched, it will suck; and if the sole of the foot is stroked, the toes will fan out. These reflexes will be present at birth but will disappear during the first months of life.
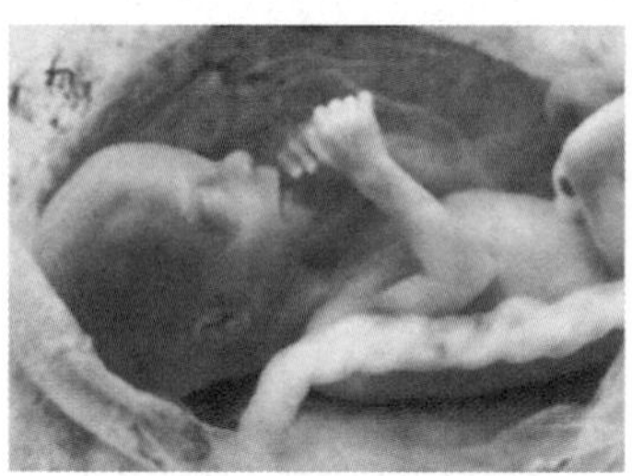 *4 months*	The body is catching up to the head, which is now only ¼ the total body length, the same proportion it will be at birth. The fetus now measures 8 to 10 inches and weighs about 6 ounces. The umbilical cord is as long as the fetus and will continue to grow with it. The placenta is now fully developed. The mother may be able to feel the fetus kicking, a movement known as *quickening,* which some societies and religious groups consider the beginning of human life. The reflex activities that appeared in the third month are now brisker because of increased muscular development.
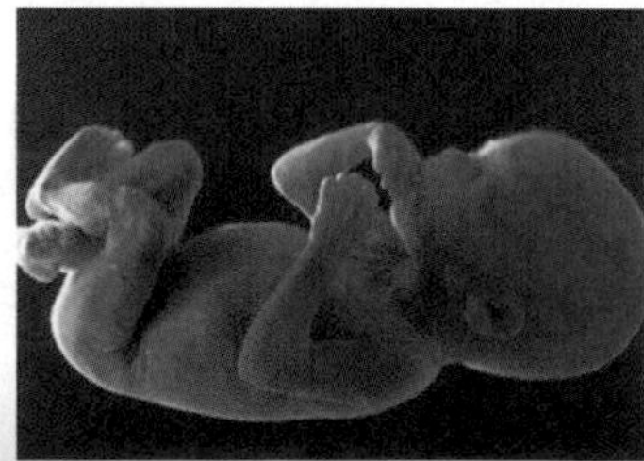 *5 months*	The fetus, now weighing about 12 ounces to 1 pound and measuring about 1 foot, begins to show signs of an individual personality. It has definite sleep-wake patterns, has a favorite position in the uterus (called its *lie*), and becomes more active—kicking, stretching, squirming, and even hiccuping. By putting an ear to the mother's abdomen, it is possible to hear the fetal heartbeat. The sweat and sebaceous glands are functioning. The respiratory system is not yet adequate to sustain life outside the womb; a baby born at this time does not usually survive. Coarse hair has begun to grow for eyebrows and eyelashes, fine hair is on the head, and a woolly hair called *lanugo* covers the body.

Month	Description
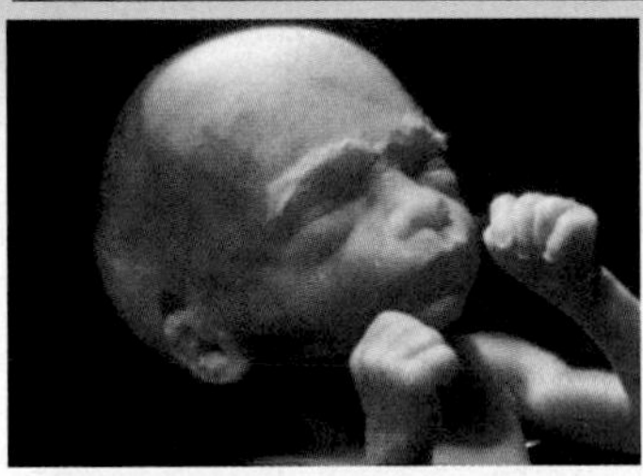 6 months	The rate of fetal growth has slowed down a little—by the end of the sixth month, the fetus is about 14 inches long and weighs $1\frac{1}{4}$ pounds. It has fat pads under the skin; the eyes are complete, opening, closing, and looking in all directions. It can hear, and it can make a fist with a strong grip. A fetus born during the sixth month still has only a slight chance of survival, because the breathing apparatus has not matured. However, some fetuses of this age do survive outside the womb.
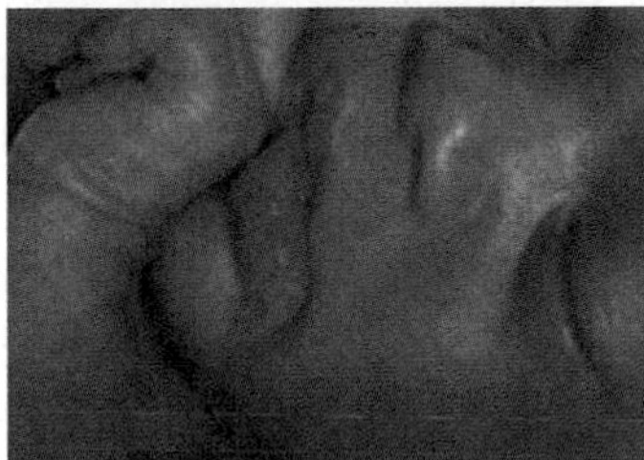 7 months	By the end of the seventh month, the fetus, about 16 inches long and weighing 3 to 5 pounds, now has fully developed reflex patterns. It cries, breathes, swallows, and may suck its thumb. The lanugo may disappear at about this time, or it may remain until shortly after birth. Head hair may continue to grow. The chances that a fetus weighing at least $3\frac{1}{2}$ pounds will survive are fairly good, provided it receives intensive medical attention. It will probably need to be kept in an isolette until a weight of 5 pounds is attained.
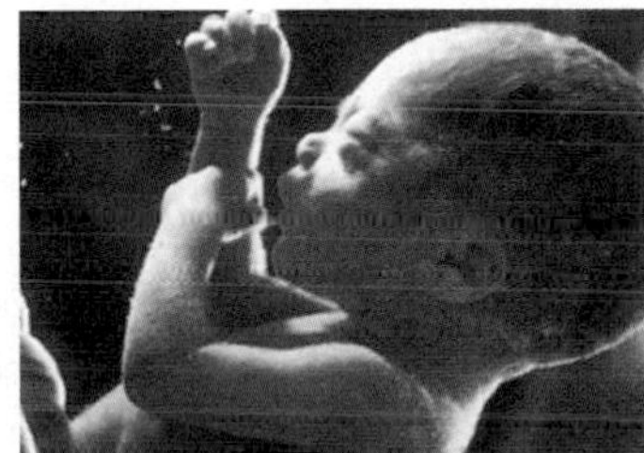 8 months	The 8-month old fetus is 18 to 20 inches long and weighs between 5 and 7 pounds. Its living quarters are becoming cramped, and so its movements are curtailed. During this month and the next, a layer of fat is developing over the fetus's entire body, which will enable it to adjust to varying temperatures outside the womb.
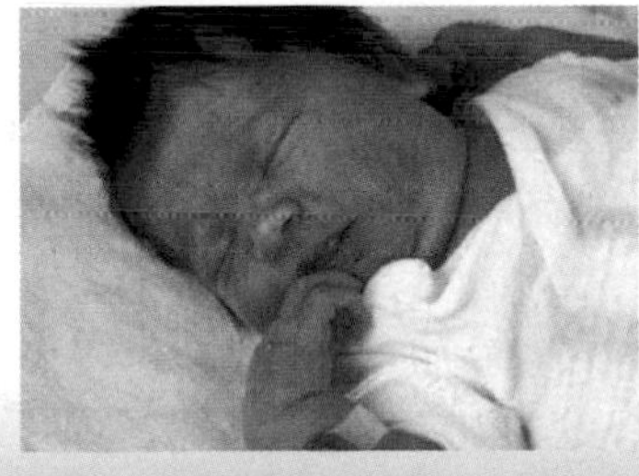 9 months—newborn	About a week before birth, the fetus stops growing, having reached an average weight of about $7\frac{1}{2}$ pounds and a length of about 20 inches, with boys tending to be a little longer and heavier than girls. Fat pads continue to form, the organ systems are operating more efficiently, the heart rate increases, and more wastes are expelled through the umbilical cord. The reddish color of the skin is fading. At birth, the fetus will have been in the womb for about 266 days, although gestational age is usually estimated at 280 days because most doctors date the pregnancy from the mother's last menstrual period.

Note: Even in these early stages, individuals differ. The figures and descriptions given here represent averages.

one side to form the *embryonic disk,* a thickened cell mass from which the embryo begins to develop. This mass is already differentiating into two layers. The upper layer, the *ectoderm,* will become the outer layer of skin, the nails, hair, teeth, sensory organs, and the nervous system, including the brain and spinal cord. The lower layer, the *endoderm,* will become the digestive system, liver, pancreas, salivary glands, and respiratory system. Later a middle layer, the *mesoderm,* will develop and differentiate into the inner layer of skin, muscles, skeleton, and excretory and circulatory systems.

Other parts of the blastocyst begin to develop into organs that will nurture and protect the unborn child: the *placenta,* the *umbilical cord,* and the *amniotic sac* with its outermost membrane, the *chorion.* The *placenta,* which has several important functions, will be connected to the embryo by the *umbilical cord.* Through this cord the placenta delivers oxygen and nourishment to the developing baby and removes its body wastes. The placenta also helps to combat internal infection and gives the unborn child immunity to various diseases. It produces the hormones that support pregnancy, prepare the mother's breasts for lactation, and eventually stimulate the uterine contractions that will expel the baby from the mother's body. The *amniotic sac* is a fluid-filled membrane that encases the developing baby, protecting it and giving it room to move. The *trophoblast,* the outer cell layer of the blastocyst (which becomes part of the placenta), produces tiny threadlike structures that penetrate the lining of the uterine wall and enable the developing organism to cling there until it is fully implanted in the uterine lining.

Only about 10 percent to 20 percent of fertilized eggs complete the crucial task of implantation and continue to develop. Researchers have now identified a gene called *Hoxa10,* which appears to control whether an embryo will be successfully implanted in the uterine wall (Taylor, Arici, Olive, & Igarashi, 1998).

embryonic stage Second stage of gestation (2 to 8 weeks), characterized by rapid growth and development of major body systems and organs.

Embryonic Stage (2 to 8 Weeks) During the **embryonic stage,** the second stage of gestation, from about 2 to 8 weeks, the organs and major body systems—respiratory, digestive, and nervous—develop rapidly. This is a critical period (refer back to Chapter 1), when the embryo is most vulnerable to destructive influences in the prenatal environment (see Figure 3-9). An organ system or structure that is still developing at the time of exposure is most likely to be affected. Defects that occur later in pregnancy are likely to be less serious.

spontaneous abortion Natural expulsion from the uterus of a conceptus that cannot survive outside the womb; also called *miscarriage.*

The most severely defective embryos usually do not survive beyond the first *trimester,* or 3-month period, of pregnancy. A **spontaneous abortion,** commonly called a *miscarriage,* is the expulsion from the uterus of an embryo or fetus that is unable to survive outside the womb. Most miscarriages result from abnormal pregnancies; about 50 to 70 percent involve chromosomal abnormalities.

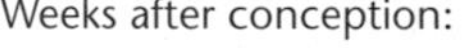
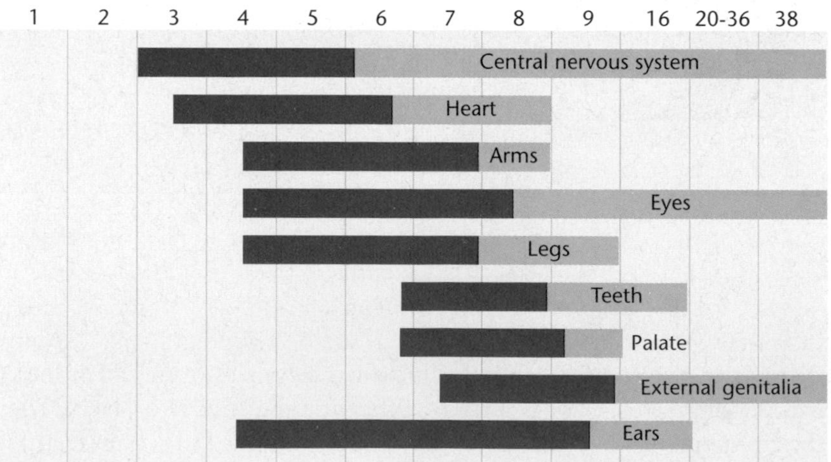

Figure 3-9

When birth defects occur. Body parts and systems are most vulnerable to damage during critical periods when they are developing most rapidly *(darkly shaded areas)*, generally within the first trimester of pregnancy. *Note:* Intervals of time are not all equal. (*Source:* J. E. Brody, 1995; data from March of Dimes.)

Males are more likely than females to be spontaneously aborted or *stillborn* (dead at birth). Thus, although about 125 males are conceived for every 100 females—a fact that has been attributed to the greater mobility of sperm carrying the smaller Y chromosome—only 105 boys are born for every 100 girls. Males' greater vulnerability continues after birth: more of them die early in life, and at every age they are more susceptible to many disorders. As a result, there are only 96 males for every 100 females in the United States (Martin, Hamilton, et al., 2002; U.S. Department of Health and Human Services, USDHHS, 1996a). Furthermore, the proportion of male births appears to be falling slightly in the United States, Canada, and several European countries, while the incidence of birth defects among males is rising, perhaps reflecting effects of environmental pollutants (Davis, Gottlieb, and Stampnitzky, 1998).

Checkpoint

Can you . . .

- ✔ Identify two principles that govern physical development and give examples of how they apply prenatally?
- ✔ Describe how a zygote becomes an embryo, and explain why defects and miscarriages most often occur during the embryonic stage?

Fetal Stage (8 Weeks to Birth) The appearance of the first bone cells at about 8 weeks signals the beginning of the **fetal stage,** the final stage of gestation. During this period, the fetus grows rapidly to about twenty times its previous length, and organs and body systems become more complex. Right up to birth, "finishing touches" such as fingernails, toenails, and eyelids develop.

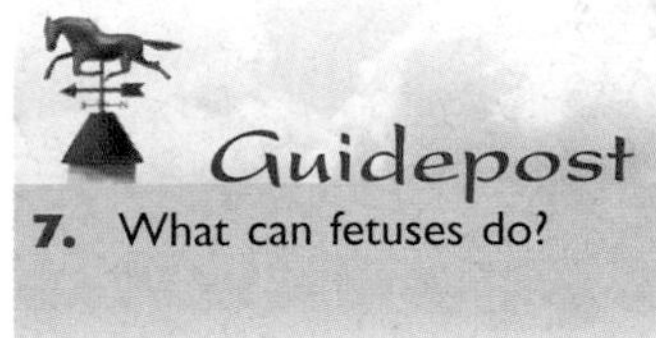

Guidepost

7. What can fetuses do?

Fetuses are not passive passengers in their mothers' wombs. Fetuses breathe, kick, turn, flex their bodies, do somersaults, squint, swallow, make fists, hiccup, and suck their thumbs. The flexible membranes of the uterine walls and amniotic sac, which surround the protective buffer of amniotic fluid, permit and even stimulate limited movement.

fetal stage Final stage of gestation (from 8 weeks to birth), characterized by increased detail of body parts and greatly enlarged body size.

ultrasound Prenatal medical procedure using high-frequency sound waves to detect the outline of a fetus and its movements, so as to determine whether a pregnancy is progressing normally.

Scientists can observe fetal movement through **ultrasound,** using high-frequency sound waves to detect the outline of the fetus. Other instruments can monitor heart rate, changes in activity level, states of sleep and wakefulness, and cardiac reactivity. The movements and activity level of fetuses show marked individual differences, and their heart rates vary in regularity and speed. There also are differences between males and females. Male fetuses, regardless of size, are more active and tend to move more vigorously than female fetuses throughout gestation. Thus infant boys' tendency to be more active than girls may be at least partly inborn (DiPietro, Hodgson, Costigan, Hilton, & Johnson, 1996).

Beginning at about the twelfth week of gestation, the fetus swallows and inhales some of the amniotic fluid in which it floats. The amniotic fluid contains substances that cross the placenta from the mother's bloodstream and enter the fetus's own bloodstream. Partaking of these substances may stimulate the budding senses of taste and smell and may contribute to the development of organs needed for breathing and digestion (Mennella & Beauchamp, 1996a; Ronca & Alberts, 1995; Smotherman & Robinson, 1995, 1996). Mature taste cells appear at about 14 weeks of gestation. The olfactory system, which controls the sense of smell, is also well developed before birth (Bartoshuk & Beauchamp, 1994; Mennella & Beauchamp, 1996a).

Fetuses also respond to the mother's voice and heartbeat and the vibrations of her body, showing that they can hear and feel. Familiarity with the mother's voice may have a basic survival function: to help newborns locate the source of food (Rovee-Collier, 1996). Responses to sound and vibration seem to begin at 26 weeks of gestation, rise, and then reach a plateau at about 32 weeks (Kisilevsky, Muir, & Low, 1992).

Fetuses seem to learn and remember. In one experiment, 3-day-old infants sucked more on a nipple that activated a recording of a story their mother had frequently read aloud during the last 6 weeks of pregnancy than on nipples that activated recordings of two other stories. Apparently, the infants recognized the story they had heard in the womb. A control group, whose mothers had not recited a story before birth, responded equally to all three recordings (DeCasper & Spence, 1986). Similar experiments have found that newborns 2 to 4 days old prefer musical and speech sequences heard before birth. They also prefer their mother's voice to those of other women,

Checkpoint

Can you . . .

- ✔ List several changes that occur during the fetal stage?
- ✔ Describe findings about fetal activity, sensory development, and memory?

female voices to male voices, and their mother's native language to another language (DeCasper & Fifer, 1980; DeCasper & Spence, 1986; Fifer & Moon, 1995; Lecanuet, Granier-Deferre, & Busnel, 1995; Moon, Cooper, & Fifer, 1993).

How do we know that these preferences develop before rather than after birth? Newborns were given the choice of sucking to turn on a recording of the mother's voice or a "filtered" version of her voice as it might sound in the womb. The newborns sucked more often to turn on the filtered version, suggesting that fetuses develop a preference for the kinds of sounds they hear before birth (Fifer & Moon, 1995; Moon & Fifer, 1990).

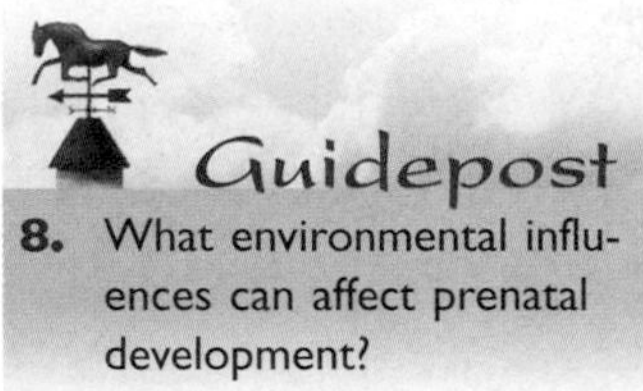

Guidepost

8. What environmental influences can affect prenatal development?

teratogenic Capable of causing birth defects.

Environmental Influences: Maternal Factors

Since the prenatal environment is the mother's body, virtually everything that impinges on her well-being, from her diet to her moods, may alter her unborn child's environment and affect its growth.

Not all environmental hazards are equally risky for all fetuses. Some factors that are **teratogenic** (birth defect-producing) in some cases have little or no effect in others. The timing of exposure to a teratogen, its intensity, and its interaction with other factors may be important (refer back to Figure 3-9).

Sometimes vulnerability may depend on a gene either in the fetus or in the mother. For example, fetuses with a particular variant of a growth gene, called *transforming growth factor alpha,* have six times more risk than other fetuses of developing a cleft palate if the mother smokes while pregnant (Hwang et al., 1995).

Nutrition Pregnant women typically need 300 to 500 additional calories a day, including extra protein. Those who gain 26 or more pounds are less likely to bear babies whose weight at birth is dangerously low. However, desirable weight gain depends on individual factors, such as weight and height before pregnancy (Martin et al., 2002).

Malnutrition during fetal growth may have long-range effects. In rural Gambia, in western Africa, people born during the "hungry" season, when foods from the previous harvest are badly depleted, are ten times more likely to die in early adulthood than people born during other parts of the year (Moore et al., 1997). Psychiatric examinations of Dutch military recruits whose mothers had been exposed to wartime famine during pregnancy suggest that severe prenatal nutritional deficiencies in the first or second trimesters affect the developing brain, increasing the risk of antisocial personality disorders at age 18 (Neugebauer, Hoek, & Susser, 1999). And, as we have already reported, a Finnish study found a link between fetal undernutrition and schizophrenia (Wahlbeck et al., 2001).

Malnourished women who take dietary supplements while pregnant tend to have bigger, healthier, more active, and more visually alert infants (J. L. Brown, 1987; Vuori et al., 1979); and women with low zinc levels who take daily zinc supplements are less likely to have babies with low birthweight and small head circumference (Goldenberg et al., 1995). However, certain vitamins (including A, B_6, C, D, and K) can be harmful in excessive amounts. Iodine deficiency, unless corrected before the third trimester of pregnancy, can cause cretinism, which may involve severe neurological abnormalities or thyroid problems (Cao et al., 1994; Hetzel, 1994).

Only recently have we learned of the critical importance of folic acid, or folate (a B vitamin) in a pregnant woman's diet. For some time, scientists have known that China has the highest incidence in the world of babies born with the neural tube defects anencephaly and spina bifida (refer back to Table 3-1), but it was not until the 1980s that researchers linked that fact with the timing of the babies' conception. Traditionally, Chinese couples marry in January or February and try to conceive as soon as possible. That means pregnancies often begin in the winter, when rural women have little access to fresh fruits and vegetables, important sources of folic acid.

After medical detective work established the lack of folic acid as a cause of neural tube defects, China embarked on a massive program to give folic acid supplements to prospective mothers. The result was a large reduction in the prevalence of these defects (Berry et al., 1999). Addition of folic acid to enriched grain products has been mandatory in the United States since 1998, and the incidence of neural tube defects has fallen by 19 percent (Honein, Paulozzi, Mathews, Erickson, & Wong, 2001). Women of childbearing age are urged to take folate supplements and to include this vitamin in their diets by eating plenty of fresh fruits and vegetables even before becoming pregnant, since damage from folic acid deficiency can occur during the early weeks of gestation (AAP Committee on Genetics, 1999; Mills & England, 2001).

Physical Activity Moderate exercise does not seem to endanger the fetuses of healthy women (Committee on Obstetric Practice, 2002; Riemann & Kanstrap Hansen, 2000). Regular exercise prevents constipation and improves respiration, circulation, muscle tone, and skin elasticity, all of which contribute to a more comfortable pregnancy and an easier, safer delivery. However, pregnant women should avoid activities that could cause a high degree of abdominal trauma (Committee on Obstetric Practice, 2002).

Employment during pregnancy generally entails no special hazards. However, strenuous working conditions, occupational fatigue, and long working hours may be associated that could cause a greater risk of premature birth (Luke et al., 1995).

The American College of Obstetrics and Gynecology (1994) recommends that women in low-risk pregnancies be guided by their own abilities and stamina. The safest course seems to be for pregnant women to exercise moderately, not pushing themselves and not raising their heart rate above 150, and, as with any exercise, to taper off at the end of each session rather than stop abruptly.

Drug Intake Practically everything an expectant mother takes in makes its way to the uterus. Drugs may cross the placenta, just as oxygen, carbon dioxide, and water do. Vulnerability is greatest in the first few months of gestation, when development is most rapid. What are the effects of the use of specific drugs during pregnancy? Let's look first at medical drugs; then at alcohol, nicotine, and caffeine; and finally at some illegal drugs: marijuana, opiates, and cocaine. Some of these risks, such as the danger of rubella during pregnancy and the risk of transmitting HIV, have been lessened by vaccines and other treatments and thus can be viewed as history-graded influences (refer back to Chapter 1).

Medical Drugs It once was thought that the placenta protected the fetus against drugs the mother took during pregnancy. Today, nearly thirty drugs have been found to be teratogenic in clinically recommended doses (Koren, Pastuszak, & Ito, 1998). Among them are the antibiotic tetracycline; certain barbiturates, opiates, and other central nervous system depressants; several hormones, including diethylstilbestrol (DES) and androgens; certain anticancer drugs, such as methotrexate; Accutane, a drug often prescribed for severe acne; and aspirin and other nonsteroidal anti-inflammatory drugs, which should be avoided during the third trimester.

The effects of taking a drug during pregnancy do not always show up immediately. In the late 1940s and early 1950s, the synthetic hormone diethylstilbestrol (DES) was widely prescribed (ineffectually, as it turned out) to prevent miscarriage. Not until years later, after the daughters of women who had taken DES during pregnancy reached puberty, did as many as 1 in 1,000 develop a rare form of vaginal or cervical cancer (Giusti, Iwamoto, & Hatch, 1995; Swan, 2000; Treffers, Hanselaar, Helmerhorst, Koster, & van Leeuwen, 2001). DES daughters may have abnormalities of the genital tract and may have trouble bearing children, with higher risks of miscarriage or

What's Your View?

- Thousands of adults now alive suffered gross abnormalities because, during the 1950s, their mothers took the tranquilizer thalidomide during pregnancy. As a result, the use of thalidomide was banned in the United States and some other countries. Now thalidomide has been found to be effective in many illnesses, from mouth ulcers to brain cancer. Should its use for these purposes be permitted even though there is a risk that pregnant women might take it? If so, what safeguards should be required?

premature delivery (Mittendorf, 1995; Swan, 2000; Treffers et al., 2001). DES sons also have had malformations in the genital tract, which did not seem to affect fertility (Treffers et al., 2001; Wilcox, Baird, Weinberg, Hornsby, & Herbst, 1995). Findings of an association between DES exposure and testicular cancer are controversial (Giusti et al., 1995). However, in male mice early exposure to DES led to long-term adverse effects on testicular development and sperm function (Fielden et al., 2002), as well as genital tumors (Treffers et al., 2001). DES mothers may have a heightened risk of breast cancer (Mittendorf, 1995; Treffers et al., 2001).

The American Academy of Pediatrics (AAP) Committee on Drugs (1994) recommends that *no* medication be prescribed for a pregnant or breast-feeding woman unless it is essential for her health or her child's. Pregnant women should not take over-the-counter drugs without consulting a doctor (Koren et al., 1998). Certain antipsychotic drugs used to manage severe psychiatric disorders may have serious potential effects on the fetus, and withdrawal symptoms may occur at birth. It is advisable to taper off and then discontinue the use of such drugs as the delivery date approaches, or, if necessary, to prescribe the lowest dose possible (AAP Committee on Drugs, 2000).

fetal alcohol syndrome (FAS) Combination of mental, motor, and developmental abnormalities affecting the offspring of some women who drink heavily during pregnancy.

Alcohol Like Abel Dorris, about 1 infant in 750 suffers from **fetal alcohol syndrome (FAS),** a combination of slow prenatal and postnatal growth, facial and bodily malformations, and disorders of the central nervous system. Problems related to the central nervous system can include, in infancy, poor sucking response, brain-wave abnormalities, and sleep disturbances; and, throughout childhood, slow information processing, short attention span, restlessness, irritability, hyperactivity, learning disabilities, retarded growth, and motor impairments. Prebirth exposure to alcohol seems to affect a portion of the *corpus callosum,* which coordinates signals between the two hemispheres of the brain (Miller, Astley, & Clarren, 1999).

A mother who drinks during pregnancy risks having a child born with fetal alcohol syndrome, as this 4-year-old boy was.

For every child with FAS, as many as ten others may be born with *fetal alcohol effects.* This less severe condition can include mental retardation, retardation of intrauterine growth, and minor congenital abnormalities.

Even moderate drinking may harm a fetus, and the more the mother drinks, the greater the effect. Moderate or heavy drinking during pregnancy seems to disturb an infant's neurological and behavioral functioning, and this may affect early social interaction with the mother, which is vital to emotional development (Nugent, Lester, Greene, Wieczorek-Deering, & O'Mahony, 1996). In a longitudinal study of 501 women at an urban university's maternity clinic, women who consumed even small amounts of alcohol tended to have children who were unusually aggressive at ages 6 to 7, and mothers who drank moderately to heavily during pregnancy tended to have problem or delinquent children (Sood et al., 2001).

Some FAS problems recede after birth, but others, such as retardation, behavioral and learning problems, and hyperactivity, tend to persist, as with Abel Dorris. Unfortunately, enriching these children's education or general environment does not seem to enhance their cognitive development (Kerns, Don, Mateer, & Streissguth, 1997; Spohr, Willms, & Steinhausen, 1993; Streissguth et al., 1991; Strömland & Hellström, 1996). Children whose mothers had at least one drink a day during the first trimester tend to show stunted growth at age 14 (Day et al., 2002). Since there is no known safe level of drinking during pregnancy, it is best to avoid alcohol from the time a woman begins *thinking* about becoming pregnant until she stops breast-feeding (AAP Committee on Substance Abuse and Committee on Children with Disabilities, 1993; Day et al., 2002).

Nicotine Tobacco use during pregnancy is estimated to cause 115,000 miscarriages every year in the United States and the deaths of some 5,600 babies. It may contribute to the births of 53,000 low-birthweight babies (weighing less than $5\frac{1}{2}$ pounds at birth) annually and 22,000 babies who need intensive care (DiFranza & Lew, 1995). It also brings increased risks of prenatal growth retardation, miscarriage, infant death, and long-term cognitive and behavioral problems (AAP Committee on Substance Abuse, 2001; Martin et al., 2002).

Since women who smoke during pregnancy also tend to smoke after giving birth, it is hard to separate the effects of prenatal and postnatal exposure. One study did this by examining 500 newborns about 48 hours after birth, while they were still in the hospital's nonsmoking maternity ward and thus had not been exposed to smoking outside the womb. Newborns whose mothers had smoked during pregnancy were shorter and lighter and had poorer respiratory functioning than babies of nonsmoking mothers (Stick, Burton, Gurrin, Sly, & LeSouëf, 1996). A Danish study found that mothers who smoke during pregnancy tend to have colicky babies (Sondergaard, Henriksen, Obel, & Wisborg, 2001). A mother's smoking during pregnancy also may increase her child's risk of cancer (Lackmann et al., 1999).

Smoking during pregnancy seems to have some of the same effects on children when they reach school age as drinking during pregnancy: poor attention span, hyperactivity, anxiety, learning and behavior problems, perceptual-motor and linguistic problems, poor IQ scores, low grade placement, and neurological problems (Landesman-Dwyer & Emanuel, 1979; Milberger, Biederman, Faraone, Chen, & Jones, 1996; Naeye & Peters, 1984; D. Olds, Henderson, & Tatelbaum, 1994a, 1994b; Streissguth et al., 1984; Wakschlag et al., 1997; Weitzman, Gortmaker, & Sobol, 1992; Wright et al., 1983). A ten-year longitudinal study of 6- to 23-year-old offspring of women who reported having smoked heavily during pregnancy found a fourfold increase in risk of conduct disorder in boys, beginning before puberty, and a fivefold increased risk of drug dependence in girls, beginning in adolescence, in comparison with young people whose mothers had not smoked during pregnancy (Weissman, Warner, Wickramaratne, & Kandel, 1999).

Caffeine Can the caffeine a pregnant woman swallows in coffee, tea, cola, or chocolate cause trouble for her fetus? For the most part, the answer is no (Leviton & Cowan, 2002). It does seem clear that caffeine is not a teratogen for human babies (Christian & Brent, 2001; Hinds, West, Knight, & Harland, 1996). A controlled study of 1,205 new mothers and their babies showed no effect of reported caffeine use on low birthweight, premature birth, or retarded fetal growth (Santos, Victora, Huttly, & Carvalhal, 1998). On the other hand, four or more cups of coffee a day during pregnancy may dramatically increase the risk of sudden death in infancy (Ford et al., 1998). Studies of a possible link between caffeine consumption and spontaneous abortion have had mixed results (Cnattingius et al., 2000; Dlugosz et al., 1996; Infante-Rivard, Fernández, Gauthier, David, & Rivard, 1993; Klebanov, Levine, DerSimonian, Clemens, & Wilkins, 1999; Mills et al., 1993; Signorello et al., 2001).

Marijuana, Opiates, and Cocaine Although findings about marijuana use by pregnant women are mixed (Dreher, Nugent, & Hudgins, 1994; Lester & Dreher, 1989), some evidence suggests that heavy use can lead to birth defects. A Canadian study found temporary neurological disturbances, such as tremors and startles, as well as higher rates of low birthweight in the infants of marijuana smokers (Fried, Watkinson, & Willan, 1984). An analysis of blood samples from the umbilical cords of thirty-four newborns found a greater prevalence of cancer-causing mutations in the infants of mothers who smoked marijuana. These women did not use tobacco, cocaine, or opiates, suggesting that marijuana use alone can increase cancer risk (Ammenheuser, Berenson, Babiak, Singleton, & Whorton, 1998).

BOX 3-2

Digging Deeper
Fetal Welfare versus Mothers' Rights

A Wisconsin woman persists in using cocaine while pregnant. A juvenile court orders her unborn child placed in protective custody by forcing the expectant mother into inpatient treatment. The Wisconsin Supreme Court later holds that she was wrongfully detained (Lewin, 1997).

A South Carolina hospital routinely tests the urine of pregnant women suspected to be using illegal drugs and reports the evidence to police. Ten women sue the hospital after being arrested. They argue that the urine tests constitute an unconstitutional search of their persons (Greenhouse, 2000b).

In Chicago, Cook County officials try to force a mother to have a cesarean delivery that doctors say is needed to protect her fetus. Before the dispute can be resolved in court, the woman gives birth normally—to a healthy boy ("Woman Delivers," 1993).

In all these cases, the issue is the conflict between protection of a fetus and a woman's right to privacy or to make her own decisions about her body. It is tempting to require a pregnant woman to adopt practices that will ensure her baby's health, or to stop or punish her if she doesn't. But what about her personal freedom? Can civil rights be abrogated for the protection of the unborn?

The argument about the right to choose abortion, which rests on similar grounds, is far from settled. But the examples just given deal with a different aspect of the problem. What can or should society do about a woman who does *not* choose abortion, but instead goes on carrying her baby while engaging in behavior destructive to it, or refuses tests or treatment that medical providers consider essential to its welfare?

Ingesting Harmful Substances Does a woman have the right to knowingly ingest a substance, such as alcohol or another drug, which can permanently damage her unborn child, as Abel Dorris's birth mother did? Some advocates for fetal rights think it should be against the law for pregnant women to smoke or use alcohol, even though these activities are legal for other adults. Other experts argue that incarceration for substance abuse is unworkable and self-defeating. They say that expectant mothers who have a drinking or drug problem need education and treatment, not prosecution (Marwick, 1997, 1998).

Since 1985 at least 240 women in thirty-five states have been prosecuted for using illegal drugs or alcohol during pregnancy, even though no state legislature has criminalized such activity (Nelson & Marshall, 1998). Most of the cases were dismissed or the convictions overturned ("States Look," 1998; Terry, 1996), but one South Carolina woman received an eight-year prison sentence for criminal child neglect for using crack cocaine during her pregnancy. The U.S. Supreme Court declined to hear an appeal ("Condon Pleased," 1997; "Supreme Court Ruling," 1998). In 1998, South Dakota and Wisconsin adopted laws permitting pregnant women who abuse alcohol or drugs to be involuntarily confined or committed to treatment programs, and similar legislation was pending in several other states ("States Look," 1998).

The wind may be starting to shift, however. In March 2001, the U.S. Supreme Court invalidated the South Carolina hospital's urine testing policy. Criticism of the

Women addicted to heroin or to opiates such as morphine and codeine are likely to bear premature babies who will be addicted to the same drugs. Prenatally exposed newborns are restless and irritable and often have tremors, convulsions, fever, vomiting, and breathing difficulties (Cobrinick, Hood, & Chused, 1959; Henly & Fitch, 1966; Ostrea & Chavez, 1979). They cry often, are less alert and less responsive than other babies (Strauss, Lessen-Firestone, Starr, & Ostrea, 1975), and tend to show acute withdrawal symptoms and sleep disturbances during the neonatal period, requiring prompt treatment (O'Brien & Jeffery, 2002; Wagner, Katikaneni, Cox, & Ryan, 1998).

At 1 year, these infants are likely to show somewhat slowed psychomotor development (Bunikowski et al., 1998). In early childhood they weigh less than average, are shorter, are less well adjusted, and score lower on tests of perceptual and learning abilities (G. Wilson, McCreary, Kean, & Baxter, 1979). These children tend not to do well in school, to be unusually anxious in social situations, and to have trouble making friends (Householder, Hatcher, Burns, & Chasnoff, 1982).

Digging Deeper

BOX 3-2

—continued

policy, along with a decline in cocaine use, has led to a statewide policy stressing treatment, rather than punishment (Greenhouse, 2000c).

Intrusive Medical Procedures Should a woman be forced to submit to intrusive procedures that pose a risk to her, such as a surgical delivery or intrauterine transfusions, when doctors say such procedures are essential to the delivery of a healthy baby? Should a woman from a fundamentalist sect that rejects modern medical care be taken into custody until she gives birth? Such measures have been invoked to "protect the rights of the unborn." But women's rights advocates claim that they reflect a view of women as mere vehicles for carrying offspring, and not as persons in their own right (Greenhouse, 2000c).

Medical professionals warn that such measures may have important practical drawbacks. Legal coercion could jeopardize the doctor-patient relationship. Coercion also could open the door to go further into pregnant women's lives—demanding prenatal screening and fetal surgery or restricting their diet, work, and athletic and sexual activity (Kolder, Gallagher, & Parsons, 1987). If failure to follow medical advice can bring forced surgery, confinement, or criminal charges, some women may avoid doctors altogether and thus deprive their fetuses of needed prenatal care (Nelson & Marshall, 1998). Indeed, in South Carolina, where fetal rights laws are among the nation's toughest, fewer women are seeking prenatal care (Jonsson, 2001).

The overwhelming view of medical, legal, and social critics is that the state should intervene only when there is a high risk of serious disease or a high degree of accuracy in the test for a defect, strong evidence that the proposed treatment will be effective, danger that deferring treatment until after birth will cause serious damage, minimal risk to the mother and modest interference with her privacy, and persistent but unsuccessful efforts to educate her and obtain her informed consent.

What's Your View?

Does society's interest in protecting an unborn child justify coercive measures against pregnant women who ingest harmful substances or refuse medically indicated treatment? Should pregnant women who refuse to stop drinking or get treatment be incarcerated until they give birth? Should mothers who repeatedly give birth to children with FAS be sterilized? Should liquor companies be held liable if adequate warnings are not on their products? Would your answers be the same regarding smoking or use of cocaine or other potentially harmful substances?

Check It Out:

For more information on this topic, go to www.mhhc.com/papaliah9, where you will find a link to information on fetal alcohol syndrome and fetal alcohol effects.

Cocaine use during pregnancy has been associated with a variety of risks, including spontaneous abortion, delayed growth, and impaired neurological development (Chiriboga, Brust, Bateman, & Hauser, 1999; Macmillan et al., 2001; Scher, Richardson, & Day, 2000). So great has been the concern about "crack babies" that some states have taken action against expectant mothers suspected of using cocaine. However, the U.S. Supreme Court in 2001 overturned one such policy as contrary to mothers' personal rights (see Box 3-2). Since then a review of the literature has found no specific effects of prenatal cocaine exposure on physical growth, cognition, language skills, motor skills, neurophysiology, behavior, attention, and emotional expressiveness in early childhood that could not also be attributed to other risk factors, such as exposure to tobacco, alcohol, marijuana, or a poor home environment (Frank, Augustyn, Knight, Pell, & Zuckerman, 2001).

acquired immune deficiency syndrome (AIDS) Viral disease that undermines effective functioning of the immune system.

Sexually Transmitted Diseases **Acquired immune deficiency syndrome (AIDS)** is a disease caused by the human immunodeficiency virus (HIV), which

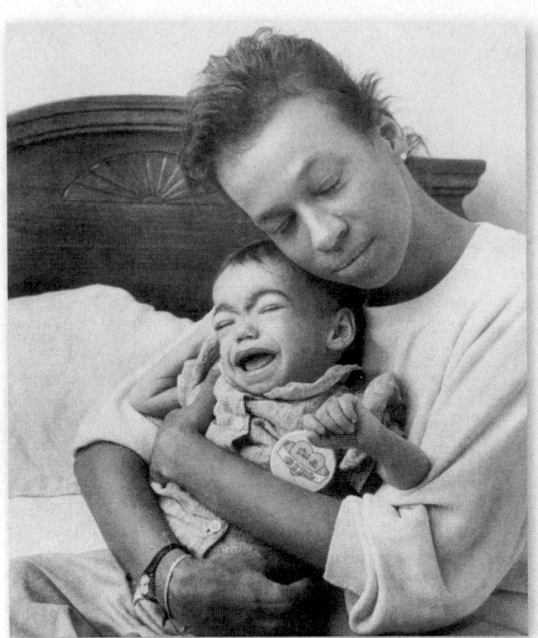

This 26-year-old mother contracted AIDS from her husband, who had gotten it from a former girlfriend, an intravenous drug user. The father died first of this modern plague, then the 21-month-old baby, and lastly the mother.

undermines functioning of the immune system. If an expectant mother has the virus in her blood, it may cross over to the fetus's bloodstream through the placenta. After birth, the virus can be transmitted through breast milk. Infants born to HIV-infected mothers tend to have small heads and slowed neurological development (Macmillan et al., 2001).

The drug zidovudine, commonly called AZT, has successfully curtailed transmission. Between 1992 and 1997, when zidovudine therapy became widespread, the number of babies who got AIDS from their mothers dropped by about two-thirds, raising the hope that mother-to-child transmission of the virus can be virtually eliminated (Lindegren et al., 1999). The risk of transmission also can be reduced by choosing cesarean delivery (International Perinatal HIV Group, 1999).

Syphilis can cause problems in fetal development, and gonorrhea and genital herpes can have harmful effects on the baby at the time of delivery. The incidence of genital herpes simplex virus (HSV) has increased among newborns, who may acquire the disease from the mother or father either at or soon after birth (Sullivan-Bolyai, Hull, Wilson, & Corey, 1983), causing blindness, other abnormalities, or death. Again, cesarean delivery may help avoid infection.

Other Maternal Illnesses Both prospective parents should try to prevent all infections—common colds, flu, urinary tract and vaginal infections, as well as sexually transmitted diseases. If the mother does contract an infection, she should have it treated promptly. Pregnant women also should be screened for thyroid deficiency, which can affect their children's future cognitive performance (Haddow et al., 1999).

Rubella (German measles), if contracted by a woman before her eleventh week of pregnancy, is almost certain to cause deafness and heart defects in her baby. Chances of catching rubella during pregnancy have been greatly reduced in Europe and the United States since the late 1960s, when a vaccine was developed that is now routinely administered to infants and children. However, rubella is still a serious problem in developing countries where inoculations are not routine (Plotkin, Katz, & Cordero, 1999).

An infection called *toxoplasmosis,* caused by a parasite harbored in the bodies of cattle, sheep, and pigs and in the intestinal tracts of cats, typically produces either no symptoms or symptoms like those of the common cold. In a pregnant woman, however, especially in the second and third trimesters of pregnancy, it can cause brain damage, severely impaired eyesight or blindness, seizures, or miscarriage, stillbirth, or death of the baby. Although as many as 9 out of 10 of these babies may appear normal at birth, more than half of them have later problems, including eye infections, hearing loss, and learning disabilities. To avoid infection, expectant mothers should not eat raw or very rare meat, should wash hands and all work surfaces after touching raw meat, should peel or thoroughly wash raw fruits and vegetables, and should not dig in a garden where cat feces are buried. Women who have a cat should have it checked for the disease, should not feed it raw meat, and, if possible, should have someone else empty the litter box (March of Dimes Foundation, 2002) or should do it often, wearing gloves (Kravetz & Federman, 2002).

Especially during the second and third trimesters of pregnancy, a diabetic mother's metabolic regulation, unless carefully managed, may affect her child's long-range neurobehavioral development and cognitive performance (Rizzo, Metzger, Dooley, & Cho, 1997). Risks in diabetic pregnancies can be greatly reduced by screening pregnant women for diabetes, followed by careful monitoring and a controlled diet (Kjos & Buchanan, 1999).

Maternal Age Women today typically start having children later in life than was true fifteen or twenty years ago, often because they spend their early adult years getting advanced education and establishing careers (Mathews & Ventura, 1997; Ventura et al., 1999). Births to women in their thirties and forties have steadily risen since the late 1970s (Ventura, Martin, Curtin, Menacker, & Hamilton, 2001)—another example of a history-graded influence.

How does delayed childbearing affect the risks to mother and baby? Pregnant women this age are more likely to suffer complications due to diabetes, high blood pressure, or severe bleeding. Most risks to the infant's health are not much greater than for babies born to younger mothers. Still, after age 35 there is more chance of miscarriage or stillbirth, and more likelihood of premature delivery, retarded fetal growth, other birth-related complications, or birth defects, such as Down syndrome. However, due to widespread screening for fetal defects among older expectant mothers, fewer malformed babies are born nowadays (Berkowitz, Skovron, Lapinski, & Berkowitz, 1990; P. Brown, 1993; Cunningham & Leveno, 1995).

Although multiple births generally tend to be riskier than single births, twins and triplets born to older mothers do as well or better than those born to younger mothers—unless the mothers have low socioeconomic status. Many multiple births to older women with higher SES are conceived through assisted reproductive technology (discussed in Chapter 13), and these pregnancies tend to be monitored closely (Zhang, Meikle, Grainger, & Trumble, 2002).

Adolescents tend to have premature or underweight babies—perhaps because a young girl's still-growing body consumes vital nutrients the fetus needs (Fraser, Brockert, & Ward, 1995). These newborns are at heightened risk of death in the first month, disabilities, or health problems (AAP Committee on Adolescence, 1999; Alan Guttmacher Institute, 1999a; Children's Defense Fund, 1998). Risks of teenage pregnancy are discussed further in Chapter 12.

Outside Environmental Hazards Chemicals, radiation, extremes of heat and humidity, and other hazards of modern life can affect prenatal development. Women who work with chemicals used in manufacturing semiconductor chips have about twice the rate of miscarriage as other female workers (Markoff, 1992), and women exposed to DDT tend to have more preterm births (Longnecker, Klebanoff, Zhou, & Brock, 2001). Infants exposed prenatally to high levels of lead score lower on tests of cognitive abilities than those exposed to low or moderate levels (Bellinger, Leviton, Watermaux, Needleman, & Rabinowitz, 1987; Needleman & Gatsonis, 1990). Children exposed prenatally to heavy metals have higher rates of childhood illness and lower measured intelligence than children not exposed to these metals (Lewis, Worobey, Ramsay, & McCormack, 1992).

Radiation can cause genetic mutations. In utero exposure to radiation has been linked to greater risk of mental retardation, small head size, chromosomal malformations, Down syndrome, seizure, and poor performance on IQ tests and in school. The critical period seems to be eight through fifteen weeks after fertilization (Yamazaki & Schull, 1990).

Environmental Influences: Paternal Factors

The father, too, can transmit environmentally caused defects. A man's exposure to marijuana or tobacco smoke, lead, large amounts of alcohol or radiation, DES, or certain pesticides may result in abnormal sperm. Men who smoke are at increased risk of impotence and of transmitting genetic abnormalities (AAP Committee on Substance Abuse, 2001); and a pregnant woman's exposure to the father's secondhand smoke has been linked with low birthweight and cancer in childhood and adulthood ((Ji et al.,

Checkpoint

Can you . . .

- Summarize recommendations concerning an expectant mother's diet and physical activity?
- Describe the short-term and long-term effects on the developing fetus of a mother's use of medical drugs, alcohol, tobacco, caffeine, marijuana, opiates, and cocaine during pregnancy?
- Summarize the risks of maternal illnesses, delayed childbearing, and exposure to chemicals and radiation?
- Identify at least three ways in which the father can influence environmentally caused defects?

1997; D. H. Rubin, Krasilnikoff, Leventhal, Weile, & Berget, 1986; Sandler, Everson, Wilcox, & Browder, 1985). Men with high lead exposure at work have an elevated risk of fathering a premature baby or one with low birthweight (Lin, Hwang, Marshall, & Marion, 1998). Offspring of male workers at a British nuclear processing plant had an elevated risk of stillbirth (Parker, Pearce, Dickinson, Aitkin, & Craft, 1999). Babies whose fathers had diagnostic X rays within the year prior to conception tend to have low birthweight and slowed fetal growth (Shea, Little, & the ALSPAC Study Team, 1997). And fathers whose diets are low in vitamin C are more likely to have children with birth defects and certain types of cancer (Fraga et al., 1991).

A man's use of cocaine can cause birth defects in his children. The cocaine seems to attach itself to his sperm, and this cocaine-bearing sperm then enters the ovum at conception. Other toxins, such as lead and mercury, may "hitchhike" onto sperm in the same way (Yazigi, Odem, & Polakoski, 1991).

A later paternal age (averaging in the late thirties) is associated with increases in the risk of several rare conditions, including Marfan's syndrome (deformities of the head and limbs) and dwarfism (G. Evans, 1976). Advanced age of the father also may be a factor in about 5 percent of cases of Down syndrome (Antonarakis & Down Syndrome Collaborative Group, 1991). More male cells than female ones undergo mutations, and mutations may increase with paternal age.

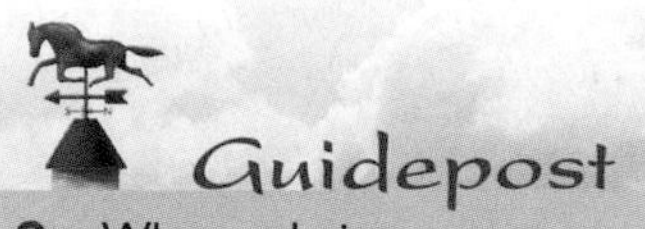

Guidepost

9. What techniques can assess a fetus's health and well-being, and what is the importance of prenatal care?

Monitoring Prenatal Development

Not long ago, almost the only decision parents had to make about their babies before birth was the decision to conceive; most of what happened in the intervening months was beyond their control. Now we have an array of tools to assess an unborn baby's progress and well-being and even to intervene to correct some abnormal conditions.

Ultrasound and Amniocentesis Some parents see their baby for the first time in a *sonogram,* a picture of the uterus, fetus, and placenta created by *ultrasound* directed into the mother's abdomen. Ultrasound is used to measure fetal growth, to judge gestational age, to detect multiple pregnancies, to evaluate uterine abnormalities, to detect major structural abnormalities in the fetus, and to determine

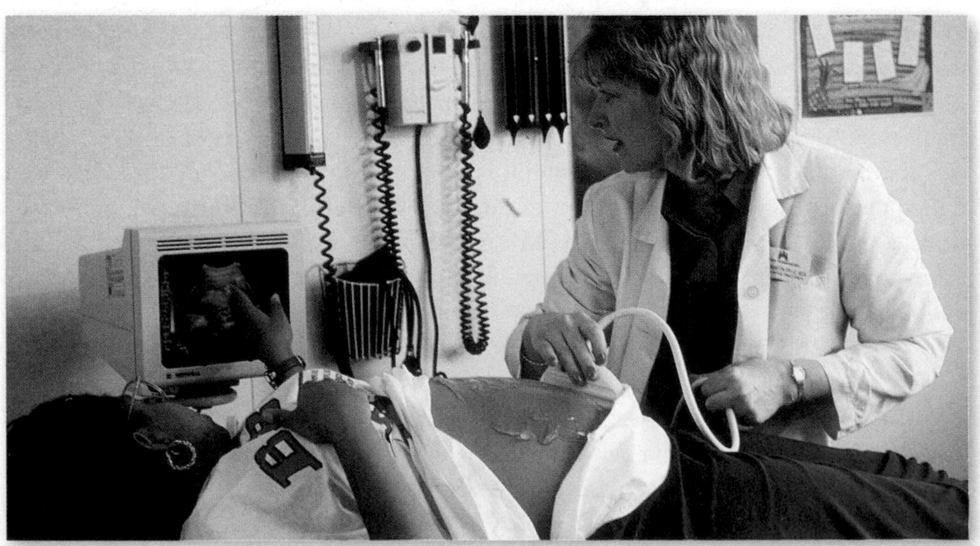

The most effective way to prevent birth complications is early prenatal care, which may include ultrasound checkups, such as this woman is having, to follow the fetus's development. Ultrasound is a diagnostic tool that presents an immediate image of the fetus in the womb.

whether a fetus has died, as well as to guide other procedures, such as amniocentesis. A newer technique called *sonoembriology,* which involves high-frequency transvaginal probes and digital image processing, has made possible earlier detection of unusual defects during the embryonic stage (Kurjak, Kupesic, Matijevic, Kos, & Marton, 1999).

In *amniocentesis,* a sample of the amniotic fluid, which contains fetal cells, is withdrawn and analyzed to detect the presence of certain genetic or multifactorial defects and all recognizable chromosomal disorders. Amniocentesis is usually recommended for pregnant women ages 35 and over. It is also recommended if the woman and her partner are both known carriers of such diseases as Tay-Sachs and sickle-cell anemia, or if they have a family history of such conditions as Down syndrome, spina bifida, Rh disease, and muscular dystrophy. However, a new ultrasound test that measures the nose bone of the fetus can improve early detection of Down syndrome and avoid the need for amniocentesis, which has a small risk of miscarriage (Cicero, Curcio, Papageorhiou, Sonek, & Nicolaides, 2001).

Both amniocentesis and ultrasound can reveal the sex of the fetus, which may help in diagnosing sex-linked disorders. In some Asian countries in which sons are preferred, both procedures have been used (in some places, illegally) for "sex screening" of unborn babies, with the result that in these populations males now predominate (Burns, 1994; Kristof, 1993; WuDunn, 1997).

Other Assessment Methods In *chorionic villus sampling (CVS),* tissue from the ends of *villi*—hairlike projections of the *chorion,* the membrane surrounding the fetus, which are made up of fetal cells—are tested for the presence of birth defects and disorders. This procedure can be performed between eight and thirteen weeks of pregnancy (earlier than amniocentesis), and it yields results within about a week. However, there is almost a 5 percent greater chance of miscarriage or neonatal death after CVS than after amniocentesis (D'Alton & DeCherney, 1993).

Embryoscopy, insertion of a tiny viewing scope into a pregnant woman's abdomen, can provide a clear look at embryos as young as 6 weeks. The procedure is promising for early diagnosis and treatment of embryonic and fetal abnormalities (Quintero, Abuhamad, Hobbins, & Mahoney, 1993).

Preimplantation genetic diagnosis can identify some genetic defects in embryos of four to eight cells, which were conceived by in vitro fertilization (IVF) (see Chapter 13) and have not yet been implanted in the mother's uterus. Defective embryos are not implanted. Ethical objections have been raised to preimplantation genetic diagnosis. If parents can choose to discard a defective embryo, will selection on the basis of sex or other genetically indicated physical characteristics follow? These objections must be weighed against the potential to avoid the birth of a child with a severe defect (Damewood, 2001).

By inserting a needle into tiny blood vessels of the umbilical cord under the guidance of ultrasound, doctors can take samples of a fetus's blood. This procedure, called *umbilical cord sampling* or *fetal blood sampling,* can test for infection, anemia, heart failure, and certain metabolic disorders and immunodeficiencies and seems to offer promise for identifying other conditions. However, the technique is associated with miscarriage, bleeding from the umbilical cord, early labor, and infection (Chervenak, Isaacson, & Mahoney, 1986; D'Alton & DeCherney, 1993; Kolata, 1988).

A blood sample taken from the mother between the sixteenth and eighteenth weeks of pregnancy can be tested for the amount of alpha fetoprotein (AFP) it contains. This *maternal blood test* is appropriate for women at risk of bearing children with defects in the formation of the brain or spinal cord, such as anencephaly or spina bifida, which may be detected by high AFP levels. To confirm or refute the presence of suspected conditions, ultrasound or amniocentesis, or both, may be performed. Blood tests of samples taken between the fifteenth and twentieth weeks of gestation can predict about 60 percent of cases of Down syndrome. This blood test is particularly important for women under 35, who bear 80 percent of all Down syndrome babies but usually are not targeted to receive amniocentesis because their individual risk is lower (Haddow et al., 1992).

The discovery that fetal cells that "leak" into the mother's blood early in pregnancy can be isolated and analyzed (Simpson & Elias, 1993) will make it possible to detect genetic as well as chromosomal disorders from a maternal blood test without using riskier procedures, such as amniocentesis, chorionic villus sampling, and fetal blood sampling. Already researchers have succeeded in screening fetal blood cells for single genes for sickle-cell anemia and thalassemia (Cheung, Goldberg, & Kan, 1996).

Prenatal Care

Screening for treatable defects and diseases is only one reason for the importance of prenatal care. Early, high-quality prenatal care, which includes educational, social, and nutritional services, can help prevent maternal and infant death and other complications of birth (Shiono & Behrman, 1995).

In the United States prenatal care is widespread, but not universal as in many European countries, and it lacks uniform national standards and guaranteed financial coverage. Use of early prenatal care (during the first three months of pregnancy) rose during the 1990s from 75.8 percent to 83.2 percent of pregnant women. Still, in 2000, nearly one in six expectant mothers got no care until after the first trimester, and one in twenty-five received no care until the last trimester or no care at all (Martin, Hamilton, et al., 2002).

Although prenatal care has increased, rates of low birthweight and premature birth have worsened (Kogan et al., 1998; Martin et al., 2001). Why?

One answer is the increasing number of multiple births, which require especially close prenatal attention. Twin pregnancies often end, for precautionary reasons, in early births, either induced or by cesarean delivery. Intensive prenatal care may allow early detection of problems requiring immediate delivery, as, for example, when one or both fetuses are not thriving. This may explain why a U.S. government study of twin births between 1981 and 1997 found parallel upward trends in use of prenatal care and rates of preterm birth—along with a decline in mortality of those twin infants whose mothers obtained intensive prenatal care (Kogan et al., 2000).

What's Your View?

- Can you suggest ways to persuade more pregnant women to seek early prenatal care?

Another possible explanation for these parallel trends is that the benefits of prenatal care are not evenly distributed. Although usage of prenatal care has grown, especially among ethnic groups that tend *not* to receive early care, the women most at risk of bearing low-birthweight babies—teenage and unmarried women, those with little education, and some minority women—still get the least prenatal care (Martin et al., 2001, Martin, Hamilton, et al., 2002; National Center for Health Statistics, 1994a, 1998a, 2001; U.S. Department of Health and Human Services, 1996a; see Figure 3-10).

Checkpoint

Can you . . .

- ✔ Describe seven techniques for identifying defects or disorders prenatally?
- ✔ Tell why early, high-quality prenatal care is important, and how it could be improved?

Merely increasing the quantity of prenatal care does not address the *content* of care (Misra & Guyer, 1998). Most prenatal care programs in the United States focus on screening for major complications and are not designed to attack the causes of low birthweight. A national panel has recommended that prenatal care be restructured to provide more visits early in the pregnancy and fewer in the last trimester. In fact, care should begin *before* pregnancy. Prepregnancy counseling could make more women aware, for example, of the importance of getting enough folic acid in their diet and making sure that they are immune to rubella. In addition, care needs to be made more accessible to poor and minority women (Shiono & Behrman, 1995).

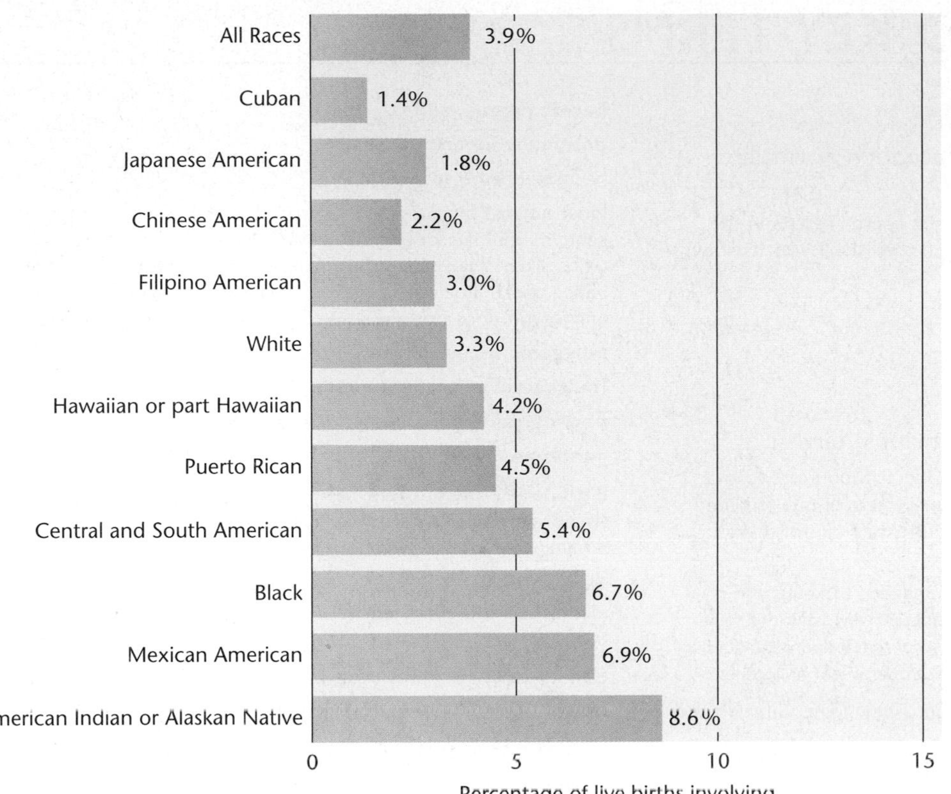

Figure 3-10
Proportion of U.S. mothers with late or no prenatal care, according to race or ethnicity, 2000. Late prenatal care begins in the last three months of pregnancy. (*Source:* Martin et al., 2002.)

Refocus

- What light does Abel Dorris's case shed on the role of the prenatal environment in a child's development?
- Why did Michael Dorris's belief that Abel would "catch up," given a positive adoptive home environment, prove unfounded?
- Does Abel's story illustrate the concept of reaction range? Of canalization? Of critical periods? If so, how?
- What sorts of information might be helpful in counseling prospective parents on adoption of a child whose prenatal history is unknown?

Good prenatal care can give every child the best possible chance for entering the world in good condition to meet the challenges of life outside the womb—challenges we discuss in the next three chapters.

SUMMARY AND KEY TERMS

Conceiving New Life

Guidepost 1. How does conception normally occur?

- Fertilization, the union of an ovum and a sperm, results in the formation of a one-celled zygote, which then duplicates itself by cell division.

  clone *(63)*

  fertilization *(63)*

  zygote *(63)*

Guidepost 2. What causes multiple births?

- Multiple births can occur either by the fertilization of two ova (or one ovum that has split) or by the splitting of one fertilized ovum. Larger multiple births result from either one of these processes or a combination of the two.
- Dizygotic (fraternal) twins have different genetic makeups and may be of different sexes; monozygotic (identical) twins have the same genetic makeup. Because of differences in prenatal and postnatal experience, "identical" twins may differ in temperament and other respects.

  dizygotic (two-egg) twins *(64)*

  monozygotic (one-egg) twins *(64)*

  temperament *(65)*

Mechanisms of Heredity

Guidepost 3. How does heredity operate in determining sex and transmitting normal and abnormal traits?

- The basic functional units of heredity are the genes, which are made of deoxyribonucleic acid (DNA). DNA carries the biochemical instructions, or genetic code, that governs bodily functions and determines inherited characteristics. Each gene seems to be located by function in a definite position on a particular chromosome. The complete sequence of genes in the human body is the human genome.

  deoxyribonucleic acid (DNA) *(65)*

  genetic code *(65)*

  chromosomes *(65)*

  genes *(65)*

  human genome *(65)*

- At conception, each normal human being receives 23 chromosomes from the mother and 23 from the father. These form 23 pairs of chromosomes—22 pairs of autosomes and 1 pair of sex chromosomes. A child who receives an X chromosome from each parent will be a female. If the child receives a Y chromosome from the father, a male will be conceived.
- The simplest patterns of genetic transmission are dominant and recessive inheritance. Sometimes codominance occurs. When a pair of alleles are the same, a person is homozygous for the trait; when they are different, the person is heterozygous.

  autosomes *(66)*

  sex chromosomes *(66)*

  alleles *(68)*

  homozygous *(68)*

  heterozygous *(68)*

  dominant inheritance *(68)*

  recessive inheritance *(68)*

- Most normal human characteristics are the result of polygenic or multifactorial transmission. Except for monozygotic twins, each child inherits a unique genotype. Dominant inheritance and multifactorial transmission explain why a person's phenotype does not always express the underlying genotype.

  polygenic inheritance *(68)*

  multifactorial transmission *(69)*

  phenotype *(69)*

  genotype *(69)*

- Birth defects and diseases may result from simple dominant, recessive, or sex-linked inheritance, from mutations, or from genome imprinting. Chromosomal abnormalities also can cause birth defects.
- Through genetic counseling, prospective parents can receive information about the mathematical odds of bearing children with certain defects.
- Genetic testing involves risks as well as benefits.

  mutations *(71)*

  incomplete dominance *(71)*

  sex-linked inheritance *(72)*

  Down syndrome *(73)*

  genetic counseling *(74)*

Nature and Nurture: Influences of Heredity and Environment

Guidepost 4. How do scientists study the relative influences of heredity and environment, and how do heredity and environment work together?

- Research in behavioral genetics is based on the assumption that the relative influences of heredity and environment can be measured statistically. If heredity is an important influence on a trait, genetically closer persons will be more similar in that trait. Family studies, adoption studies, and studies of twins enable researchers to measure the heritability of specific traits.
- The concepts of reaction range, canalization, genotype-environment interaction, genotype-environment correlation (or covariance), and niche-picking describe ways in which heredity and environment work together.
- Siblings tend to be more different than alike in intelligence and personality. According to some behavior geneticists, heredity accounts for most of the similarity, and nonshared environmental effects account for most of the difference. Critics claim that this research, for methodological reasons, minimizes the role of parenting and the complexity of developmental systems.

  behavioral genetics *(75)*

  heritability *(75)*

  concordant *(78)*

  reaction range *(79)*

  canalization *(79)*

  genotype-environment interaction *(80)*

  genotype-environment correlation *(81)*

  niche-picking *(81)*

  nonshared environmental effects *(82)*

Guidepost 5. What roles do heredity and environment play in physical health, intelligence, and personality?

- Obesity, longevity, intelligence, and temperament are influenced by both heredity and environment.
- Schizophrenia and autism are psychopathological disorders influenced by both heredity and environment.

schizophrenia *(84)*

autism *(84)*

Prenatal Development

Guidepost 6. What are the three stages of prenatal development, and what happens during each stage?

- Prenatal development occurs in three stages of gestation: the germinal, embryonic, and fetal stages.
- Growth and development both before and after birth follow the cephalocaudal principle (head to tail) and the proximodistal principle (center outward).
- Severely defective embryos usually are spontaneously aborted during the first trimester of pregnancy.

cephalocaudal principle *(87)*

proximodistal principle *(87)*

germinal stage *(87)*

embryonic stage *(90)*

spontaneous abortion *(90)*

fetal stage *(91)*

Guidepost 7. What can fetuses do?

- As fetuses grow, they move less, but more vigorously. Swallowing amniotic fluid, which contains substances from the mother's body, stimulates taste and smell. Fetuses seem able to hear, exercise sensory discrimination, learn, and remember.

ultrasound *(91)*

Guidepost 8. What environmental influences can affect prenatal development?

- The developing organism can be greatly affected by its prenatal environment. The likelihood of a birth defect may depend on the timing and intensity of an environmental event and its interaction with genetic factors.
- Important environmental influences involving the mother include nutrition, physical activity, smoking, intake of alcohol or other drugs, transmission of maternal illnesses or infections, maternal age, and external environmental hazards, such as chemicals and radiation. External influences also may affect the father's sperm.

teratogenic *(92)*

fetal alcohol syndrome (FAS) *(94)*

acquired immune deficiency syndrome (AIDS) *(97)*

Guidepost 9. What techniques can assess a fetus's health and well-being, and what is the importance of prenatal care?

- Ultrasound, amniocentesis, chorionic villus sampling, embryoscopy, preimplantation genetic diagnosis, umbilical cord sampling, and maternal blood tests can be used to determine whether an unborn baby is developing normally.
- Early, high-quality prenatal care is essential for healthy development. It can lead to detection of defects and disorders and, especially if begun early and targeted to the needs of at-risk women, may help reduce maternal and infant death, low birthweight, and other birth complications.

Chapter 4

Physical Development During the First Three Years

The experiences of the first three years of life are almost entirely lost to us, and when we attempt to enter into a small child's world, we come as foreigners who have forgotten the landscape and no longer speak the native tongue.

—Selma Fraiberg, *The Magic Years*, 1959

OUTLINE

Focus: The Birth of Elvis Presley*

Elvis Presley

Elvis Presley (1935–1977) was born in a 30- by 15-foot cottage in East Tupelo, Mississippi. Today, the modest birthplace of the now-legendary "king" of rock music is painted sparkling white, the walls are papered with primroses, and dainty curtains hang at the windows—among the many homey touches added for the benefit of tourists. But, like many of the popular myths about Elvis's early life, this "cute little doll house" (Goldman, 1981, p. 60) bears only slight resemblance to the reality: a bare board shack with no indoor plumbing or electricity, set in a dirt-poor hamlet that wasn't much more than "a wide spot in the road" (Clayton & Heard, 1994, p. 8).

During the Great Depression, Elvis's near-illiterate father, Vernon Presley, sometimes did odd jobs for a farmer named Orville Bean, who owned much of the town. Elvis's mother, Gladys, was vivacious and high-spirited, as talkative as Vernon was taciturn. She, like Vernon, came from a family of sharecroppers and migrant workers. She had moved to East Tupelo to be close to the garment factory where she worked.

Gladys first noticed handsome Vernon on the street and then, soon after, met him in church. They eloped on June 17, 1933. Vernon was 17 and Gladys, 21. They borrowed the three dollars for the license.

At first the young couple lived with friends and family. When Gladys became pregnant, Vernon borrowed $180 from his employer, Bean, to buy lumber and nails and, with the help of his father and older brother, built a two-room cabin next to his parents' house on Old Saltillo Road. Bean, who owned the land, was to hold title to the house until the loan was paid off.

*Sources of information about Elvis Presley's birth were Clayton & Heard (1994); Dundy (1985); Goldman (1981); Guralnick (1994); and Marling (1996).

Vernon and Gladys moved into their new home in December 1934, about a month before she gave birth. Her pregnancy was a difficult one; her legs swelled, and she finally quit her job at the garment factory, where she had to stand on her feet all day pushing a heavy steam iron.

When Vernon got up for work in the wee hours of January 8, a bitterly cold morning, Gladys was hemorrhaging. The midwife told Vernon to get the doctor, Will Hunt. (His $15 fee was paid by welfare.) At about 4 o'clock in the morning, Dr. Hunt delivered a stillborn baby boy, Jesse Garon. The second twin, Elvis Aron, was born about 35 minutes later. Gladys—extremely weak and losing blood—was taken to the hospital charity ward with baby Elvis. They stayed there for more than three weeks.

Baby Jesse remained an important part of the family's life. Gladys frequently talked to Elvis about his brother. "When one twin died, the one that lived got the strength of both," she would say (Guralnick, 1994, p. 13). Elvis took his mother's words to heart. Throughout his life, his twin's imagined voice and presence were constantly with him.

As for Elvis's birthplace, he lived there only until the age of 3. Vernon, who sold a pig to Bean for $4, was accused of altering the check to $40. He was sent to prison, and when the payment on the house loan came due, Bean evicted Gladys and her son, who had to move in with family members. In later years, Elvis would drive back to East Tupelo (now Tupelo's suburban Presley Heights). He would sit in his car in the dark, looking at the cottage on what is now called Elvis Presley Drive and "thinking about the course his life had taken" (Marling, 1996, p. 20).

Elvis Presley is just one of many well-known people—including almost all the presidents of the United States—who were born at home. At one time, medical care during pregnancy was rare, and most births were attended by midwives. Birth complications and stillbirth were common, and many women died in childbirth. A rising standard of living, together with medical advances, have eased childbirth and reduced its risks. Today, the overwhelming majority of births in the United States (but a smaller proportion in some European countries) occur in hospitals and are attended by physicians. However, there is a small but growing movement back to home births delivered by midwives (as is still the custom in many less developed countries) or to freestanding, homelike, professionally staffed birthing centers where the father can be present during the birth. In addition, doulas, experienced mothers who can furnish emotional support and can stay at the bedside throughout labor—common in traditional cultures—are gaining acceptance in the United States.

In this chapter, we describe how babies come into the world, how newborn babies look, and how their body systems work. We discuss ways to safeguard their life and health. We see how infants, who spend most of their time sleeping and eating, become busy, active toddlers and how parents and other caregivers can foster healthy growth and development. We see how sensory perception goes hand in hand with motor skills and helps shape the astoundingly rapid development of the brain.

After you have studied this chapter, you should be able to answer each of the following Guidepost questions. Look for them again in the margins, where they point to important concepts throughout the chapter. To check your understanding of these Guideposts, review the end-of-chapter summary. Checkpoints located at periodic spots throughout the chapter will help you verify your understanding of what you have read.

Guideposts for Study

1. What happens during each of the four stages of childbirth?
2. What alternative settings and methods of delivery are available today?
3. How do newborn infants adjust to life outside the womb?
4. How can we tell whether a new baby is healthy and is developing normally?
5. What complications of childbirth can endanger newborn babies' adjustment or even their lives?
6. How can we enhance babies' chances of survival and health?
7. What influences the growth of body and brain?
8. When do the senses develop?
9. What are some early milestones in motor development, and what are some influences on it?

The Birth Process

Birth is both a beginning and an end: the climax of all that has happened from the moment of fertilization. *Labor* is an apt term. Birth is hard work for both mother and baby—but work that yields a rich reward.

The uterine contractions that expel the fetus begin—typically, 266 days after conception—as mild tightenings of the uterus. A woman may have felt similar ("false") contractions at times during the final months of pregnancy, but she may recognize birth contractions as the "real thing" because of their greater regularity and intensity.

Guidepost

1. What happens during each of the four stages of childbirth?

parturition Process of uterine, cervical, and other changes, usually lasting about two weeks, preceding childbirth.

Parturition—the process of uterine, cervical, and other changes that brings on labor—typically begins about two weeks before delivery, when the balance between progesterone and estrogen shifts. During most of gestation, progesterone keeps the uterine muscles relaxed and the cervix firm. During parturition, sharply rising estrogen levels stimulate the uterus to contract and the cervix to become more flexible. The timing of parturition seems to be determined by the rate at which the placenta produces a protein called *corticotropin-releasing hormone (CRH)*, which also promotes maturation of the fetal lungs to ready them for life outside the womb. The rate of CRH production as early as the fifth month of pregnancy may predict whether a baby will be born early, "on time," or late (Smith, 1999).

Stages of Childbirth

Vaginal childbirth, or labor, takes place in four overlapping stages (see Figure 4-1 on page 110). The *first stage,* the longest, typically lasts 12 hours or more for a woman having her first child. In later births the first stage tends to be shorter. During this stage, regular and increasingly frequent uterine contractions cause the cervix to dilate, or widen.

The *second stage* typically lasts about $1\frac{1}{2}$ hours or less. It begins when the baby's head begins to move through the cervix into the vaginal canal, and it ends when the baby emerges completely from the mother's body. If this stage lasts longer than 2 hours,

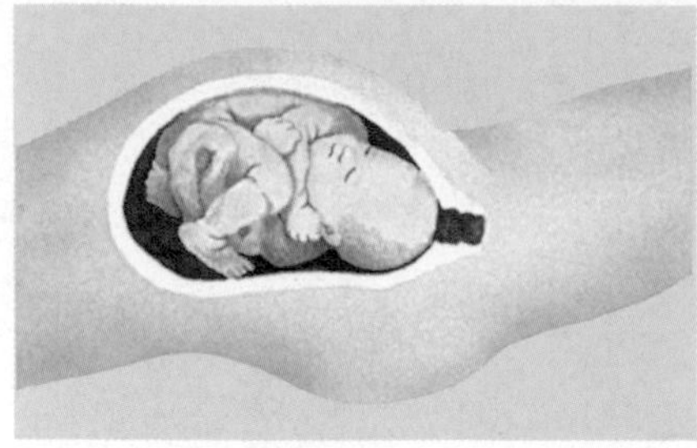

(*a*) First stage

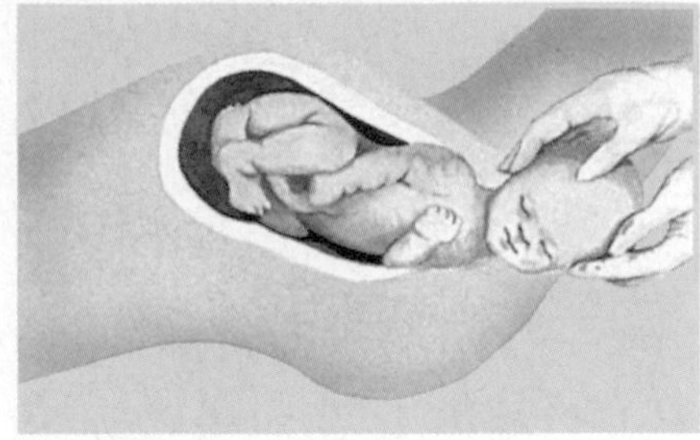

(*b*) Second stage

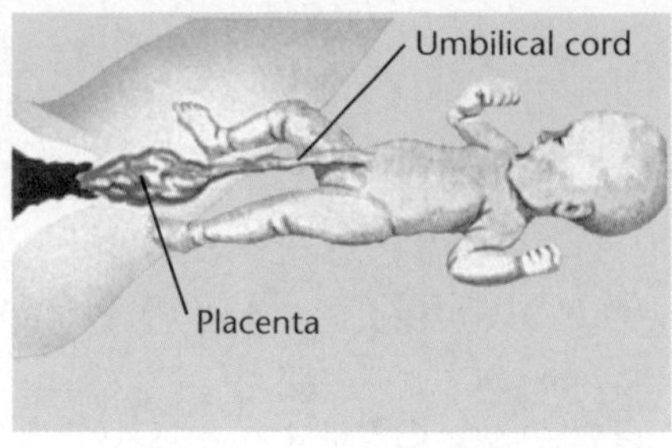

(*c*) Third stage

Figure 4-1

The first three stages of childbirth. (*a*) During the first stage of labor, a series of stronger and stronger contractions dilates the cervix, the opening to the mother's womb. (*b*) During the second stage, the baby's head moves down the birth canal and emerges from the vagina. (*c*) During the brief third stage, the placenta and umbilical cord are expelled from the womb. Then the cord is cut. During the fourth stage, recovery from delivery (not shown), the mother's uterus contracts. (*Source:* Adapted from Lagercrantz & Slotkin, 1986.)

signaling that the baby needs more help, a doctor may grasp the baby's head with forceps or, more often, use vacuum extraction with a suction cup to pull it out of the mother's body (Curtin & Park, 1999). At the end of this stage, the baby is born; but it is still attached to the placenta in the mother's body by the umbilical cord, which must be cut and clamped.

During the *third stage,* which lasts about 5 to 30 minutes, the placenta and the remainder of the umbilical cord are expelled from the mother. The couple of hours after delivery constitute the *fourth stage,* when the mother rests in bed while her recovery is monitored.

electronic fetal monitoring Mechanical monitoring of fetal heartbeat during labor and delivery.

Electronic fetal monitoring was used in 84 percent of live births in the United States in 2000 to track the fetus's heartbeat during labor and delivery (Martin, Hamilton, Ventura, Menacker, & Park, 2002). The procedure is intended to detect a lack of oxygen, which may lead to brain damage. It can provide valuable information in high-risk deliveries, including those in which the fetus is very small or seems to be in distress. Yet monitoring has drawbacks when used routinely in low-risk pregnancies. It is costly; it restricts the mother's movements during labor; and, most important, it has an extremely high "false positive" rate, suggesting that fetuses are in trouble when they are not. Such warnings may prompt doctors to deliver by the riskier cesarean method (described in the next section) rather than vaginally (Nelson, Dambrosia, Ting, & Grether, 1996).

Settings, Attendants, and Methods of Delivery

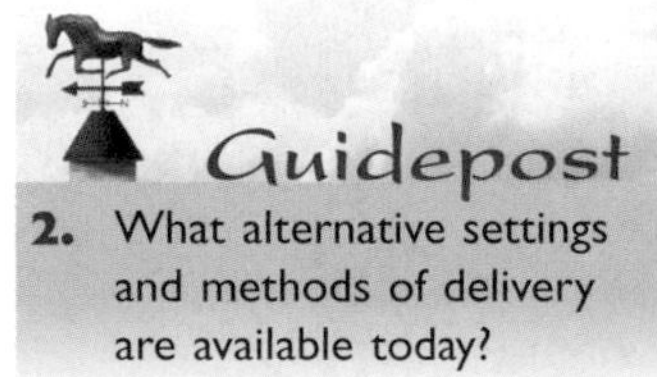

Guidepost

2. What alternative settings and methods of delivery are available today?

Settings and attendants for childbirth tend to reflect the overall cultural system. A Mayan woman in Yucatan gives birth in the hammock in which she sleeps every night; the father-to-be is expected to be present, along with the midwife. To evade evil spirits, mother and child remain at home for a week (Jordan, 1993). By contrast, among the Ngoni in East Africa, men are excluded from the event. In rural Thailand, a new mother generally resumes normal activity within a few hours after giving birth (Broude, 1995; Gardiner, Mutter, & Kosmitzki, 1998). In the United States, about 99 percent of babies are born in hospitals, and nearly 92 percent are attended by physicians. A growing percentage are attended by midwives (Martin, Hamilton, et al., 2002).

As safety has become more assured in most normal births in developed countries, health workers have focused on making the experience more pleasant and on meeting emotional needs by bringing the father and other family members into the process. Many hospitals have established homelike birth centers, where labor and delivery take

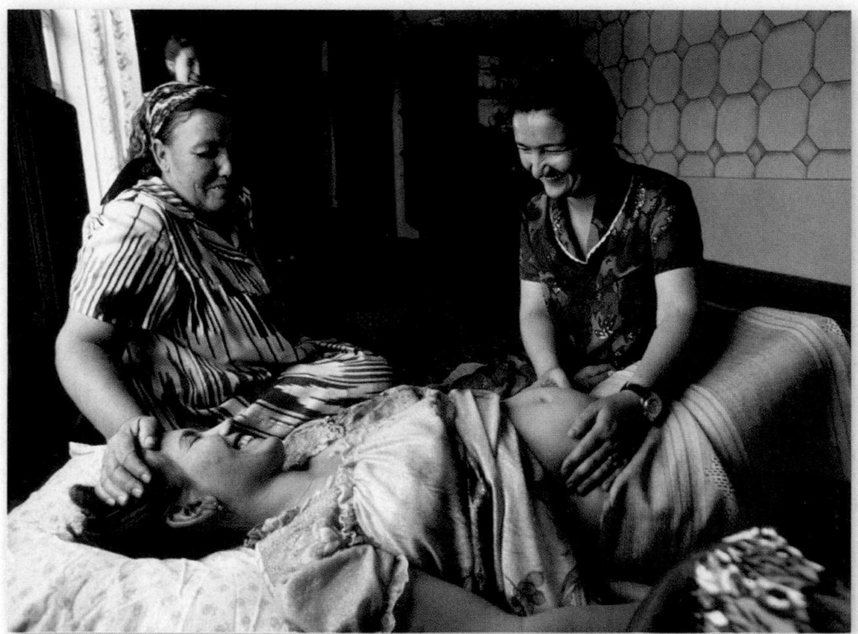

At a birth center in Princeton, New Jersey, a woman gives birth in a small house in a semiresidential area. Her husband and her mother give moral support as the midwife checks the fetal heartbeat. Informal, homelike settings for birth are growing in popularity for women with good medical histories and normal, uncomplicated pregnancies. However, it is essential to have arrangements with an ambulance service and a local hospital in case of emergency.

place under soft lights in the presence of the father or other companion. Rooming-in policies allow babies to stay in the mother's room much or all of the time.

A small but growing percentage of women opt for the intimate, personal experience of home birth, which can involve the whole family. A home birth usually is attended by a trained nurse-midwife, with the resources of medical science close at hand. Freestanding birth centers are another option. Studies suggest that both of these settings can be as safe and much less expensive than hospital births in low-risk deliveries attended by skilled practitioners (Anderson & Anderson, 1999; Durand, 1992; Guyer, Strobino, Ventura, & Singh, 1995; Korte & Scaer, 1984).

Vaginal versus Cesarean Delivery The usual method of childbirth, described in the preceding sections, is vaginal delivery. **Cesarean delivery** is a surgical procedure to remove the baby from the uterus by cutting through the abdomen.

cesarean delivery Delivery of a baby by surgical removal from the uterus.

The operation is commonly performed when labor progresses too slowly, when the fetus seems to be in trouble, or when the mother is bleeding vaginally. Often a cesarean is needed when the fetus is in the breech position (feet first) or in the transverse position (lying crosswise in the uterus), or when its head is too big to pass through the mother's pelvis. Surgical deliveries are more likely when the birth involves a first baby, a large baby, or an older mother. Thus the increase in cesarean rates since 1970 is in part a reflection of a proportional increase in first births, a rise in average birth weight, and a trend toward later childbirth (Guyer et al., 1999; Parrish, Holt, Easterling, Connell, & LeGerfo, 1994).

Cesarean birthrates in the United States are among the highest in the world, but rising rates in European countries during the past decade have narrowed the gap (Notzon, 1990; Sachs, Kobelin, Castro, & Frigoletto, 1999). The U.S. rate of cesarean births decreased by 9 percent during the early to mid-1990s, and the rate of vaginal births after a previous cesarean increased by half (from 18.9 percent in 1989 to 27.4 in 1997). These trends reflected a belief that cesarean delivery is unnecessary or harmful in many cases (Curtin & Park, 1999; Ventura, Martin, Curtin, Menacker, &

Hamilton, 2001). About 4 percent of cesareans result in serious complications, such as bleeding and infections (Nelson et al., 1996).

Still, some physicians argued that efforts to push for a further reduction in cesarean deliveries might be misguided, since it would entail greater reliance on operative vaginal deliveries (which use forceps or suction) and encouragement of vaginal delivery for women who have had previous cesarean deliveries. Although these procedures are fairly safe, they do carry risks, which must be weighed against the risks of cesarean delivery (Sachs et al., 1999). At greatest risk are women with previous cesarean births whose labor must be medically induced—who may suffer uterine rupture (Lydon-Rochelle, Holt, Easterling, & Martin, 2001)—and those whose labor is unsuccessful and who therefore must undergo a cesarean after all (McMahon, Luther, Bowes, & Olshan, 1996). A study of 313,238 births in Scotland found that for women with previous cesareans, the risk of the infant's dying during delivery was about eleven times higher in vaginal births than in planned repeat cesareans (Smith, Pell, Cameron, & Dobbie, 2002).

Perhaps because of these considerations, there has been a virtually complete reversal of the earlier trend. By 2000, the rate of vaginal births after previous cesareans dropped to 20.6 percent, a 27 percent decline since 1996, and in 2001, according to preliminary figures, this rate fell by another 20 percent. Meanwhile, the total cesarean rate rose to 24.4 percent of all births, a 17 percent increase since 1996 and the highest level since 1989 (Martin, Park, & Sutton, 2002).

Medicated versus Unmedicated Delivery In the mid–nineteenth century, England's Queen Victoria became the first woman in history to be sedated during delivery, that of her eighth child. Anesthesia became standard practice as more births took place in hospitals.

natural childbirth Method of childbirth that seeks to prevent pain by eliminating the mother's fear through education about the physiology of reproduction and training in breathing and relaxation during delivery.

prepared childbirth Method of childbirth that uses instruction, breathing exercises, and social support to induce controlled physical responses to uterine contractions and reduce fear and pain.

General anesthesia, which renders the woman completely unconscious, is rarely used today, even in cesarean births. The woman is given local anesthesia if she wants and needs it, but she can see and participate in the birth process and can hold her newborn immediately afterward. Regional (local) anesthesia blocks the nerve pathways that would carry the sensation of pain to the brain; or the mother can receive a relaxing analgesic. All these drugs pass through the placenta to enter the fetal blood supply and tissues, and thus may potentially pose dangers to the baby.

Alternative methods of childbirth were developed to minimize the use of drugs while maximizing both parents' active involvement. In 1914 a British physician, Dr. Grantly Dick-Read, suggested that pain in childbirth was caused mostly by fear. To eliminate fear, he advocated **natural childbirth:** educating women about the physiology of reproduction and training them in physical fitness and in breathing and relaxation during labor and delivery. By midcentury, Dr. Fernand Lamaze was using the **prepared childbirth** method. This technique substitutes voluntary, or learned, physical responses to the sensations of uterine contractions for the old responses of fear and pain.

Advocates of natural methods argue that use of drugs poses risks for babies and deprives mothers of what can be an empowering and transforming experience. In some early studies, infants appeared to show immediate ill effects of obstetric medication in poorer motor and physiologic responses (A. D. Murray, Dolby, Nation, & Thomas, 1981) and, through the first year, in slower motor development (Brackbill & Broman, 1979). However, later research suggested that medicated delivery may *not* do measurable harm (Kraemer, Korner, Anders, Jacklin, & Dimiceli, 1985).

What's Your View?

- If you or your partner were expecting a baby, and the pregnancy seemed to be going smoothly, would you prefer (a) medicated or nonmedicated delivery, (b) hospital, birth center, or home birth, and (c) attendance by a physician or midwife? Why? If you are a man, would you choose to be present at the birth? If you are a woman, would you want your partner present?

Improvements in medicated delivery during the past two decades have led more and more mothers to choose pain relief. Spinal or epidural injections have become increasingly common as physicians have found effective ways to relieve pain with smaller doses of medication (Hawkins, 1999). "Walking epidurals" enable a woman to feel sensations, move her legs, and fully participate in the birth. In an analysis of ten studies involving 2,369 births in Europe, the United States, and Canada, women who had

In a Lamaze class, expectant mothers learn breathing and muscular exercises to make labor easier. The prospective fathers learn how to assist their partners through labor and delivery.

Checkpoint

Can you . . .

- ✔ Describe the four stages of vaginal childbirth?
- ✔ Discuss the uses and disadvantages of cesarean births and electronic fetal monitoring?
- ✔ Discuss alternative settings for childbirth?
- ✔ Compare medicated delivery, natural childbirth, and prepared childbirth?

epidurals enjoyed more effective pain relief than women who had narcotic injections, and their babies tended to arrive in healthier condition. There was no significant difference in the rate of cesarean deliveries (Halpern, Leighton, Ohlsson, Barrett, & Rice, 1998).

The Newborn Baby

The first four weeks of life, the **neonatal period,** is a time of transition from the uterus, where a fetus is supported entirely by the mother, to an independent existence. What are the physical characteristics of newborn babies, and how are they equipped for this crucial transition?

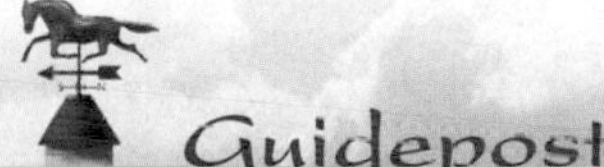

Guidepost

3. How do newborn infants adjust to life outside the womb?

Size and Appearance

An average newborn, or **neonate,** in the United States is about 20 inches long and weighs about $7\frac{1}{2}$ pounds. At birth, 95 percent of full-term babies weigh between $5\frac{1}{2}$ and 10 pounds and are between 18 and 22 inches long. Boys tend to be slightly longer and heavier than girls, and a firstborn child is likely to weigh less at birth than laterborns.

neonatal period First four weeks of life, a time of transition from intrauterine dependency to independent existence.

neonate Newborn baby, up to 4 weeks old.

In their first few days, neonates lose as much as 10 percent of their body weight, primarily because of a loss of fluids. They begin to gain weight again at about the fifth day and are generally back to birthweight by the tenth to the fourteenth day.

New babies have distinctive features, including a large head (one-fourth the body length) and a receding chin (which makes it easier to nurse). At first, a neonate's head may be long and misshapen because of the "molding" that eased its passage through the mother's pelvis. This temporary molding was possible because an infant's skull bones are not yet fused; they will not be completely joined for 18 months. The places on the head where the bones have not yet grown together—the soft spots, or *fontanels*—are covered by a tough membrane.

Many newborns have a pinkish cast; their skin is so thin that it barely covers the capillaries through which blood flows. During the first few days, some neonates are very hairy because some of the *lanugo,* a fuzzy prenatal hair, has not yet fallen off. All

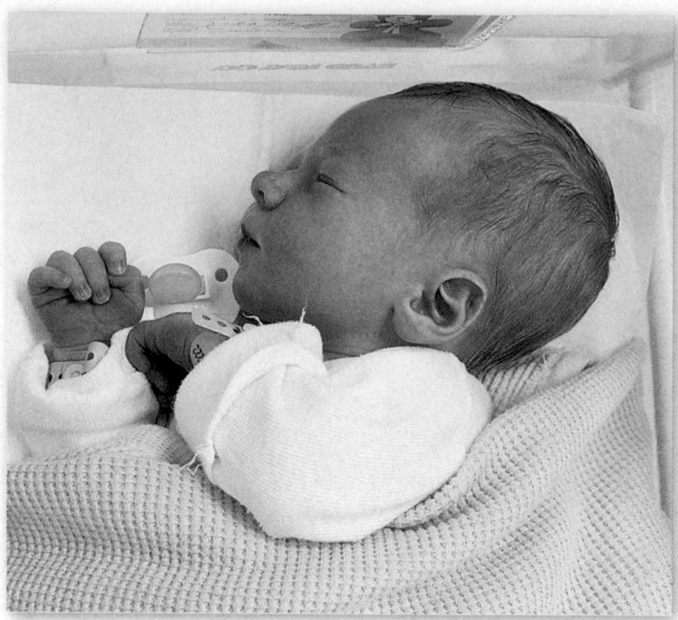

This 1-day-old boy's head is temporarily elongated from its passage through the birth canal. This "molding" of the head during birth occurs because the bones of the skull have not yet fused.

new babies are covered with *vernix caseosa* ("cheesy varnish"), an oily protection against infection that dries within the first few days.

Body Systems

Before birth, blood circulation, respiration, nourishment, elimination of waste, and temperature regulation were accomplished through the mother's body. The fetus and mother have separate circulatory systems and separate heartbeats; the fetus's blood is cleansed through the umbilical cord, which carries "used" blood to the placenta and returns a fresh supply. After birth, the baby's circulatory system must operate on its own. A neonate's heartbeat is fast and irregular, and blood pressure does not stabilize until about the tenth day of life.

The fetus gets oxygen through the umbilical cord, which also carries away carbon dioxide. A newborn needs much more oxygen than before and must now get it alone. Most babies start to breathe as soon as they are exposed to air. If breathing has not begun within about 5 minutes, the baby may suffer permanent brain injury caused by **anoxia,** lack of oxygen. Because infants' lungs have only one-tenth as many air sacs as adults' do, infants (especially those born prematurely) are susceptible to respiratory problems.

anoxia Lack of oxygen, which may cause brain damage.

In the uterus, the fetus relies on the umbilical cord to bring food from the mother and to carry fetal body wastes away. At birth, babies instinctively suck to take in milk, and their own gastrointestinal secretions digest it. During the first few days, infants secrete **meconium,** a stringy, greenish-black waste matter formed in the fetal intestinal tract. When the bowels and bladder are full, the sphincter muscles open automatically; a baby will not be able to control these muscles for many months.

meconium Fetal waste matter, excreted during the first few days after birth.

Three or four days after birth, about half of all babies (and a larger proportion of babies born prematurely) develop **neonatal jaundice:** their skin and eyeballs look yellow. This kind of jaundice is caused by the immaturity of the liver. Usually it is not serious, does not need treatment, and has no long-term effects. However, because most healthy U.S. newborns usually go home from the hospital within 48 hours or less, jaundice may go unnoticed and lead to complications (AAP Committee on Quality Improvement, 2002). Severe jaundice that is not monitored and treated promptly may result in brain damage.

neonatal jaundice Condition, in many newborn babies, caused by immaturity of liver and evidenced by yellowish appearance; can cause brain damage if not treated promptly.

The layers of fat that develop during the last two months of fetal life enable healthy full-term infants to keep their body temperature constant after birth despite changes in air temperature. Newborn babies also maintain body temperature by increasing their activity when air temperature drops.

States of Arousal

Babies have an internal "clock," which regulates their daily cycles of eating, sleeping, and elimination, and perhaps even their moods. These periodic cycles of wakefulness, sleep, and activity, which govern an infant's **state of arousal,** or degree of alertness (see Table 4-1), seem to be inborn and highly individual. Newborn babies average about 16 hours of sleep a day, but one may sleep only 11 hours while another sleeps 21 hours (Parmelee, Wenner, & Schulz, 1964). Changes in state are coordinated by multiple areas of the brain and are accompanied by changes in the functioning of virtually all body systems: heart rate and blood flow, breathing, temperature regulation, cerebral metabolism, and the workings of the kidneys, glands, and digestive system (Ingersoll & Thoman, 1999).

state of arousal An infant's physiological and behavioral status at a given moment in the periodic daily cycle of wakefulness, sleep, and activity.

Not many adults would want to "sleep like a baby." Most new babies wake up every two to three hours, day and night. Short stretches of sleep alternate with shorter

Table 4-1 States of Arousal in Infancy

State	Eyes	Breathing	Movements	Responsiveness
Regular sleep	Closed; no eye movement	Regular and slow	None, except for sudden, generalized startles	Cannot be aroused by mild stimuli
Irregular sleep	Closed; occasional rapid eye movements	Irregular	Muscles twitch, but no major movements	Sounds or light bring smiles or grimaces in sleep
Drowsiness	Open or closed	Irregular	Somewhat active	May smile, startle, suck, or have erections in response to stimuli
Alert inactivity	Open	Even	Quiet; may move head, limbs, and trunk while looking around	An interesting environment (with people or things to watch) may initiate or maintain this state.
Waking activity and crying	Open	Irregular	Much activity	External stimuli (such as hunger, cold, pain, being restrained, or being put down) bring about more activity, perhaps starting with soft whimpering and gentle movements and turning into a rhythmic crescendo of crying or kicking, or perhaps beginning and enduring as uncoordinated thrashing and spasmodic screeching.

Source: Adapted from information in Prechtl & Beintema, 1964; P. H. Wolff, 1966.

periods of consciousness, which are devoted mainly to feeding. Newborns have about six to eight sleep periods, which vary between quiet and active sleep. Active sleep is probably the equivalent of rapid eye movement (REM) sleep, which in adults is associated with dreaming. Active sleep appears rhythmically in cycles of about one hour and accounts for 50 to 80 percent of a newborn's total sleep time.

Parents and caregivers spend a great deal of time and energy trying to change babies' states—mostly by soothing a fussy infant to sleep. Although crying is usually more distressing than serious, it is particularly important to quiet low-birthweight babies, because quiet babies maintain their weight better. Steady stimulation is the time-proven way to soothe crying babies: by rocking or walking them, wrapping them snugly, or letting them hear rhythmic sounds.

As infants grow, their sleep needs diminish. At about 3 months, babies grow more wakeful in the late afternoon and early evening and start to sleep through the night. By 6 months, more than half their sleep occurs at night. The amount of REM (rapid-eye-movement) sleep decreases steadily throughout life.

Babies' sleep rhythms are not purely biological; they vary across cultures. In some cultures, such as those of the Micronesian Truk and the Canadian Hare peoples, babies and children have no regular sleep schedule; they fall asleep whenever they feel tired. Nor do infants necessarily have special places to sleep. Gusii infants in Kenya fall asleep in someone's arms or on a caregiver's back. In many cultures an infant sleeps in the parents' or mother's bed, and this practice may continue into early childhood (see Box 4-1 on page 116). Cultural variations in feeding practices may affect sleep patterns. Many U.S. parents time the evening feeding so as to encourage nighttime sleep. Mothers in rural Kenya allow their babies to nurse as they please, and their 4-month-olds continue to sleep only four hours at a stretch (Broude, 1995).

Checkpoint

Can you . . .

- ✔ Describe the normal size and appearance of a newborn, and name several changes that occur within the first few days?
- ✔ Compare four fetal and neonatal body systems?
- ✔ Identify two dangerous conditions that can appear soon after birth?
- ✔ Discuss variations in newborns' states of arousal?
- ✔ Tell how sleep patterns change after the first three months, and how cultural practices can affect these patterns?

Survival and Health

Although the great majority of births result in normal, healthy babies, some do not. How can we tell whether a newborn is at risk? What complications of birth can cause damage? How many babies die during infancy, and why? What can be done

Guidepost

4. How can we tell whether a new baby is healthy and is developing normally?

BOX 4-1

Window on the World

Sleep Customs

Newborns' sleeping arrangements vary considerably across cultures. In many societies, infants sleep in the same room with their mothers for the first few years of life, and frequently in the same bed, making it easier to nurse at night (Broude, 1995). In the United States, it is customary to have a separate bed and a separate room for the infant, but bed sharing is common in low-income, inner-city families (Brenner et al., 2003).

In interviews, middle-class U.S. parents and Mayan mothers in rural Guatemala revealed their societies' child-rearing values and goals in their explanations about sleeping arrangements (Morelli, Rogoff, Oppenheim, & Goldsmith, 1992). The U.S. parents, many of whom kept their infants in the same room but not in the same bed for the first three to six months, said they moved the babies to separate rooms because they wanted to make them self-reliant and independent. The Mayan mothers kept infants and toddlers in their beds until the birth of a new baby, when the older child would sleep with another family member or in a bed in the mother's room. The Mayan mothers valued close parent-child relationships and expressed shock at the idea that anyone would put a baby to sleep in a room all alone.

Some investigators find health benefits in the shared sleeping pattern. One research team monitoring sleep patterns of mothers and their 3-month-old infants found that those who sleep together tend to wake each other up during the night. The researchers suggested that this may prevent the baby from sleeping too long and too deeply and having long breathing pauses that might be fatal (McKenna & Mosko, 1993).

Bed sharing also promotes breast-feeding. Infants who sleep with their mothers breast-feed about three times longer during the night than infants who sleep in separate beds (McKenna, Mosko, & Richard, 1997). By snuggling up together, mother and baby stay oriented toward each other's subtle bodily signals. Mothers can respond more quickly and easily to an infant's first whimpers of hunger, rather than having to wait until the baby's cries are loud enough to be heard from the next room.

However, the American Academy of Pediatrics Task Force on Infant Positioning and SIDS (1997) found that, under some conditions, such as the use of soft bedding, or maternal smoking or drug use, bed sharing can increase the risk of sudden infant death syndrome (SIDS). There is also the possibility that the mother may roll over onto the baby while asleep. In a review of medical examiners' investigations of SIDS deaths in the St. Louis area between 1994 and 1997, a shared sleep surface was the site of death in nearly half (47.1 percent) of the cases investigated (Kemp et al., 2000). And, in an investigation of 84 SIDS cases in Cleveland, Ohio, bed sharing was associated with a younger age at death, especially when the mother was large (Carroll-Pankhurst & Mortimer, 2001). U.S. health experts also point out that adult beds are not designed to meet safety standards for infants, as cribs are (NICHD, 1997, updated 2000). Japan, where mothers and infants commonly sleep in the same bed, has one of the lowest SIDS rates in the world (Hoffman & Hillman, 1992), but this may be because Japanese families—as in many developing countries where bed sharing is practiced—generally sleep on thin mats on the floor.

Societal values influence parents' attitudes and behaviors. Throughout this book we will see many ways in which such culturally determined attitudes and behaviors affect children.

What's Your View?

In view of preliminary medical evidence that bed sharing between mother and infant may contribute to SIDS, should mothers from cultures in which sharing a bed is customary be discouraged from doing so?

Check It Out:

For more information on this topic, go to www.mhhe.com/papaliah9, where you will find a link to an article that explores infant sleep.

to prevent debilitating childhood diseases? How can we ensure that babies will live, grow, and develop as they should?

Medical and Behavioral Assessment

The first few minutes, days, and weeks after birth are crucial for development. It is important to know as soon as possible whether a baby has any problem that needs special care.

Apgar scale Standard measurement of a newborn's condition; it assesses appearance, pulse, grimace, activity, and respiration.

The Apgar Scale One minute after delivery, and then again five minutes after birth, most babies are assessed using the **Apgar scale** (see Table 4-2). Its name, after

Table 4-2 Apgar Scale

Sign*	0	1	2
Appearance (color)	Blue, pale	Body pink, extremities blue	Entirely pink
Pulse (heart rate)	Absent	Slow (below 100)	Rapid (over 100)
Grimace (reflex irritability)	No response	Grimace	Coughing, sneezing, crying
Activity (muscle tone)	Limp	Weak, inactive	Strong, active
Respiration (breathing)	Absent	Irregular, slow	Good, crying

*Each sign is rated in terms of absence or presence from 0 to 2; highest overall score is 10.
Source: Adapted from V. Apgar, 1953.

its developer, Dr. Virginia Apgar (1953), helps us remember its five subtests: *a*ppearance (color), *p*ulse (heart rate), *g*rimace (reflex irritability), *a*ctivity (muscle tone), and *r*espiration (breathing). In nonwhite children, color is assessed by examining the inside of the mouth, the whites of the eyes, the lips, palms, hands, and soles of the feet (Eisenberg, Murkoff, & Hathaway, 1989).

The newborn is rated 0, 1, or 2 on each measure, for a maximum score of 10. A 5-minute score of 7 to 10—achieved by approximately 98.6 percent of babies born in the United States in 2000—indicates that the baby is in good to excellent condition (Martin, Hamilton, et al., 2002). A score below 7 means the baby needs help to establish breathing; a score below 4 means the baby needs immediate lifesaving treatment. If resuscitation is successful, bringing the baby's score to 4 or more at 10 minutes, no long-term damage is likely to result (AAP Committee on Fetus and Newborn and American College of Obstetricians and Gynecologists [ACOG] Committee on Obstetric Practice, 1996).

In general, Apgar scores reliably predict survival during the first month of life (Casey, McIntire, & Leveno, 2001). However, care must be taken in interpreting the results. A low Apgar score alone does not necessarily indicate anoxia. Prematurity, medication given to the mother, and other conditions may affect the results (AAP Committee on Fetus and Newborn and ACOG Committee on Obstetric Practice, 1996).

Assessing Neurological Status: The Brazelton Scale The **Brazelton Neonatal Behavioral Assessment Scale (NBAS)** is used to assess neonates' responsiveness to their physical and social environment, to identify problems in neurological functioning, and to predict future development. The test is named for its designer, Dr. T. Berry Brazelton (1973, 1984; Brazelton & Nugent, 1995). It assesses *motor organization* as shown by such behaviors as activity level and the ability to bring a hand to the mouth; *reflexes; state changes,* such as irritability, excitability, and ability to quiet down after being upset; *attention and interactive capacities,* as shown by general alertness and response to visual and auditory stimuli; and indications of *central nervous system instability,* such as tremors and changes in skin color. The NBAS takes about 30 minutes, and scores are based on a baby's best performance.

Brazelton Neonatal Behavioral Assessment Scale (NBAS) Neurological and behavioral test to measure neonate's responses to the environment.

Neonatal Screening for Medical Conditions Children who inherit the enzyme disorder phenylketonuria, or PKU (refer back to Table 3-1), will become mentally retarded unless they are fed a special diet beginning in the first three to six weeks of life (National Institutes of Health [NIH] Consensus Development Panel, 2001). Screening tests administered soon after birth can often discover such correctable defects.

Checkpoint

Can you . . .

- ✔ Discuss the uses of the Apgar test and routine screening for rare disorders?
- ✔ Explain how infants' neurological status is assessed?

Routine screening of all newborn babies for such rare conditions as PKU (1 case in 15,000 births), congential hypothyroidism (1 in 3,600 to 5,000), galactosemia (1 in 60,000 to 80,000), and other, even rarer disorders is expensive. Yet the cost of testing thousands of newborns to detect one case of a rare disease may be less than the cost of caring for one mentally retarded person for a lifetime. All states require routine screening for PKU and congenital hypothyroidism; states vary on requirements for other screening tests (AAP Newborn Screening Task Force, 2000; NIH Consensus Development Panel, 2001). There is some risk in doing these tests. They can generate false-positive results, suggesting that a problem exists when it does not, and triggering anxiety and costly, unnecessary treatment.

Guidepost

5. What complications of childbirth can endanger newborn babies' adjustment or even their lives?

Complications of Childbirth

For a small minority of babies, the passage through the birth canal is a particularly harrowing journey. About 2 newborns in 1,000 are injured in the process (Wegman, 1994). **Birth trauma** (injury sustained at the time of birth) may be caused by anoxia (oxygen deprivation), diseases or infections, or mechanical injury. Sometimes the trauma leaves permanent brain damage, causing mental retardation, behavior problems, or even death. A larger proportion of infants remain in the womb too long or too briefly, or are born very small—complications that can impair their chances of survival and well-being.

birth trauma Injury sustained at the time of birth.

postmature Referring to a fetus not yet born as of two weeks after the due date or forty-two weeks after the mother's last menstrual period.

Postmaturity Close to 9 percent of pregnant women have not gone into labor two weeks after the due date, or forty-two weeks after the last menstrual period (Ventura, Martin, Curtin, & Mathews, 1998). At that point, a baby is considered **postmature.** Postmature babies tend to be long and thin, because they have kept growing in the womb but have had an insufficient blood supply toward the end of gestation. Possibly because the placenta has aged and become less efficient, it may provide less oxygen. The baby's greater size also complicates labor: the mother has to deliver a baby the size of a normal 1-month-old.

Since postmature fetuses are at risk of brain damage or even death, doctors sometimes induce labor with drugs or perform cesarean deliveries. However, if the due date has been miscalculated, a baby who is actually premature may be delivered. To help make the decision, doctors monitor the baby's status with ultrasound to see whether the heart rate speeds up when the fetus moves; if not, the baby may be short of oxygen. Another test examines the volume of amniotic fluid; a low level may mean the baby is not getting enough food.

low birthweight Weight of less than $5\frac{1}{2}$ pounds (2,500 grams) at birth because of prematurity or being small for date.

Prematurity and Low Birthweight In 2000 (and also in 2001, according to preliminary data), 7.6 percent of babies born in the United States had **low birthweight,** weighing less than 2,500 grams ($5\frac{1}{2}$ pounds) at birth. Very-low-birthweight babies, who weigh less than 1,500 grams ($3\frac{1}{2}$ pounds), accounted for 1.4 percent of births (Martin, Hamilton, et al., 2002; Martin, Park, & Sutton, 2002). Since low birthweight is the second leading cause of death in infancy, after birth defects (Anderson, 2002), preventing and treating low birthweight can greatly increase the number of babies who survive the first year of life.

Low-birthweight babies may be *preterm* or *small-for-date.* Babies born before completing the thirty-seventh week of gestation are called **preterm (premature) infants;** they may or may not be the appropriate size for their gestational age. **Small-for-date (small-for-gestational age) infants**, who may or may not be preterm, weigh less than 90 percent of all babies of the same gestational age. Their small size is generally the result of inadequate prenatal nutrition, which slows fetal growth.

preterm (premature) infants Infants born before completing the thirty-seventh week of gestation.

small-for-date (small-for-gestational age) infants Infants whose birthweight is less than that of 90 percent of babies of the same gestational age, as a result of slow fetal growth.

Although the United States is more successful than any other country in *saving* low-birthweight babies, the rate of such births to U.S. women is higher than in twenty-one other nations (UNICEF, 2002). Much of the increased prevalence of low birthweight in the United States since the mid-1980s is attributed to the increase in multiple births (Martin, Hamilton, et al., 2002). The increase in preterm births since 1990 may in part reflect the rise in cesarean deliveries and induced labor and in births to women ages 35 and up (Kramer et al., 1998).

Such measures as enhanced prenatal care, nutritional interventions, and administration of drugs, bed rest, and hydration for women who go into early labor have been tried, without success, to stem the tide of premature births. As many as 80 percent of these births are associated with uterine infection, which does not seem to respond to antibiotics once labor has begun. However, early antibiotic treatment of women with urinary or vaginal infections may be a promising approach (Goldenberg & Rouse, 1998).

Who Is More Likely to Have a Low-Birthweight Baby? Factors increasing the likelihood that a woman will have an underweight baby include: (1) *demographic and socioeconomic factors,* such as being under age 17 or over 40, poor, unmarried, or undereducated; (2) *medical factors predating the pregnancy,* such as having no children or more than four, being short or thin, having had previous low-birthweight infants or multiple miscarriages, having had low birthweight herself, or having genital or urinary abnormalities or chronic hypertension; (3) *prenatal behavioral and environmental factors,* such as poor nutrition, inadequate prenatal care, smoking, use of alcohol or other drugs, or exposure to stress, high altitude, or toxic substances; and (4) *medical conditions associated with the pregnancy,* such as vaginal bleeding, infections, high or low blood pressure, anemia, too little weight gain, and having last given birth less than six months or ten or more years before (S. S. Brown, 1985; Chomitz, Cheung, & Lieberman, 1995; Martin, Hamilton, et al., 2002; Nathanielsz, 1995; Shiono & Behrman, 1995; Wegman, 1992; Zhu, Rolfs, Nangle, & Horan, 1999). Many of these factors are interrelated, and low socioeconomic status cuts across many of them. The safest interval between pregnancies is eighteen to twenty-three months (Zhu et al., 1999).

A high proportion of low-birthweight babies in the African American population—more than twice as high as among white and Hispanic babies—is the major factor in the high mortality rates of black babies (Martin, Hamilton, et al., 2002; see Table 4-3). The higher risks of low birthweight and of preterm births among African American

Table 4-3 Birthweight, Mortality, and Race, 2000

	Low Birthweight (less than 5.5 pounds, or 2,500 grams), % of births	Very Low Birthweight (less than 3.3 pounds, or 1,500 grams), % of births	Infant Mortality Rate* per 1,000	Neonatal Mortality Rate** per 1,000	Postneonatal Mortality Rate*** per 1,000
Black infants	13.0	3.06	14.1	9.4	4.7
White (non-Hispanic) infants	6.6	1.13	5.7	3.8	1.9
Hispanic infants	6.4	1.14	5.6	3.7	1.9

Note: Black infants are more likely than white or Hispanic infants to die in the first year from birth defects or disorders, sudden infant death syndrome, respiratory distress syndrome, disorders related to short gestation and low birthweight, and as a result of maternal complications of pregnancy.

*Deaths during first year of life

**Deaths during first 4 weeks

***Deaths between 4 weeks and 12 months

Source: Anderson, 2002; Martin, Park, & Sutton., 2002.

babies largely reflect socioeconomic factors—greater poverty, less education, poorer health, less prenatal care, and greater incidence of teenage and unwed pregnancy. The cause does not seem to be genetic, since babies of *African-born* black women are not at such high risk (David & Collins, 1997).

Immediate Treatment and Outcomes The most pressing fear for very small babies is that they will die in infancy. Because their immune systems are not fully developed, they are especially vulnerable to infection. Because their nervous systems are immature, they may not be able to suck—a function basic to survival—and may instead need to be fed intravenously (through the veins). Because they do not have enough fat to insulate them and to generate heat, it is hard for them to stay warm. Respiratory distress syndrome, also called *hyaline membrane disease,* is common. Low Apgar scores in preterm newborns are a strong indication of heightened risk and of the need for intensive care (Weinberger et al., 2000). In a study of 122,754 live births at a Dallas hospital, full-term newborns who were at or below the third percentile of weight for their gestational age were at high risk of endangered health and neonatal death. Among preterm infants, the less they weighed, the higher their risk (McIntire, Bloom, Casey, & Leveno, 1999).

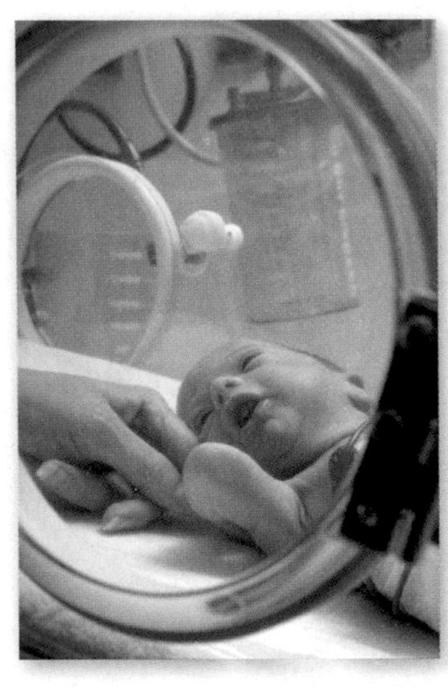

The antiseptic, temperature-controlled crib, or isolette, in which this premature baby lies has holes through which the infant can be examined, touched, and massaged. Frequent human contact helps low-birthweight infants thrive.

Many very small preterm babies lack surfactant, a lung-coating substance that keeps air sacs from collapsing; they may breathe irregularly or stop breathing altogether. Administering surfactant to high-risk preterm newborns, along with other medical interventions, has dramatically increased the survival rate of infants who weigh as little as 500 grams (about 1 pound 2 ounces), enabling four out of five in this lowest-weight group to survive (Corbet et al., 1995; Goldenberg & Rouse, 1998; Horbar et al., 1993). However, these infants are likely to be in poor health and to have neurological deficits—at 20 months, a 20 percent rate of mental retardation and 10 percent likelihood of cerebral palsy (Hack, Friedman, & Fanaroff, 1996).

A low-birthweight baby is placed in an *isolette* (an antiseptic, temperature-controlled crib) and fed through tubes. To counteract the sensory impoverishment of life in an isolette, hospital workers and parents are encouraged to give these small babies special handling. Gentle massage seems to foster growth, weight gain, motor activity, alertness, and behavioral organization, as assessed by the Brazelton NBAS (T. M. Field, 1986, 1998b; Schanberg & Field, 1987).

Long-Term Outcomes Even if low-birthweight babies survive the dangerous early days, as more and more do today, there is concern about their development. Small-for-gestational age infants are more likely to be neurologically and cognitively impaired than equally premature infants whose weight was appropriate for their gestational age (McCarton, Wallace, Divon, & Vaughan, 1996), and preterm infants who are neurologically impaired often remain so as they grow older (McGrath, Sullivan, Lester, & Oh, 2000).

A longitudinal study of 1,064 full-term British infants who were small-for-gestational-age found small but significant deficits in academic achievement at ages 5, 10, and 16 as compared with children of normal birthweight. At age 26, this group had lower incomes and professional attainments than the control group and were physically shorter. Still, they were just as likely to have completed their education and to be employed, married, and satisfied with life (Strauss, 2000).

Very-low-birthweight babies (less than 1,500 grams) may have a less promising prognosis. At school age, those who weighed the least at birth tend to have the worst cognitive, academic, behavioral, social, attentional, and linguistic problems (Klebanov, Brooks-Gunn, & McCormick, 1994; Taylor, Klein, Minich, & Hack, 2000). As teenagers, the less they weighed at birth, the lower their IQs and achievement test scores and the more likely they are to require special education or to have repeated a grade (Saigal, Hoult,

Streiner, Stoskopf, & Rosenbaum, 2000). As adults, they tend to have more neurosensory deficits and illnesses, lower IQs, and poorer educational achievement than adults who had normal birthweight. Still, in one longitudinal study of 242 adult survivors of very low birthweight, 51 percent had IQs in normal range, 74 percent had finished high school, and 41 percent had gone on to higher learning (Greene, 2002; Hack et al., 2002).

Among 179 Canadian infants of *extremely* low birthweight (501 to 1000 grams, or about 1 to 2 pounds) those who survived to adolescence tended to be smaller than a control group of full-term children and were far more likely to have neurological impairments and other problems (Saigal, Stoskopf, Streiner, & Burrows, 2001). But another longitudinal study of 296 very-low-birthweight infants found cognitive improvement in early childhood and intelligence in the normal range by age 8 (Ment et al., 2003).

Birthweight alone does not necessarily determine the outcome. Environmental factors make a difference, as we discuss in the next section.

Checkpoint

Can you . . .

- ✔ Explain the risks of postmaturity?
- ✔ Discuss risk factors, treatment, and outcomes for low-birthweight babies?

Can a Supportive Environment Overcome Effects of Birth Complications?

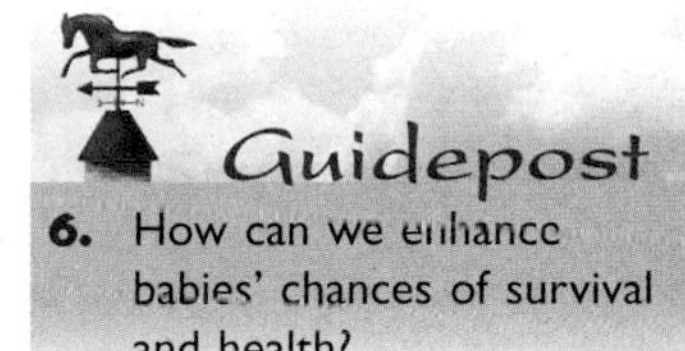
Guidepost

6. How can we enhance babies' chances of survival and health?

Prospects for overcoming the early disadvantage of birth complications depend on two interrelated factors: the family's socioeconomic circumstances and the quality of the early environment (Aylward, Pfeiffer, Wright, & Verhulst, 1989; McGauhey, Starfield, Alexander, & Ensminget, 1991; Ross, Lipper, & Auld, 1991).

The Infant Health and Development Studies The Infant Health & Development Program (IHDP) (1990) followed 985 preterm, low-birthweight babies of various ethnic origins—most of them from disadvantaged families—from birth to age 3. One-third of the heavier low-birthweight babies and one-third of the lighter ones were randomly assigned to "intervention" groups. Their parents received home visits, counseling, information about children's health and development, and instruction in children's games and activities; at 1 year, these babies entered an educational day care program.

When the program stopped, the 3-year-olds in both the lower- and higher-birthweight intervention groups were doing better on cognitive and social measures, were much less likely to show mental retardation, and had fewer behavioral problems than control groups of similar birthweight who had received only pediatric follow-up (Brooks-Gunn, Klebanov, Liaw, & Spiker, 1993). However, by age 5, the lower-birthweight intervention group lost their cognitive edge (Brooks-Gunn et al., 1994), and by age 8, the higher-birthweight intervention group averaged only four IQ points more than the controls. All groups had substantially below-average IQs and vocabulary scores (McCarton et al., 1997; McCormick, McCarton, Brooks-Gunn, Belt, & Gross, 1998). It seems, then, that for such an intervention to have lasting effects, it needs to continue beyond age 3.

Additional studies of the IHDP sample underline the importance of the home environment. Children whose mothers reported having experienced stressful events—illnesses, deaths of friends or family members, moves, or changes in schooling or work—during the last six months of the child's first year showed less cognitive benefit from the intervention at age 3 (Klebanov, Brooks-Gunn, & McCormick, 2001). Children who got little parental attention and care did more poorly on cognitive tests than children from more favorable home environments (Kelleher et al., 1993; McCormick et al., 1998). Those whose cognitive performance stayed high had mothers who scored high themselves on cognitive tests and who were responsive and stimulating. Babies who had more than one risk factor (such as poor neonatal health combined with having a mother who did not receive counseling or was less well educated or less responsive) fared the worst (Liaw & Brooks-Gunn, 1993).

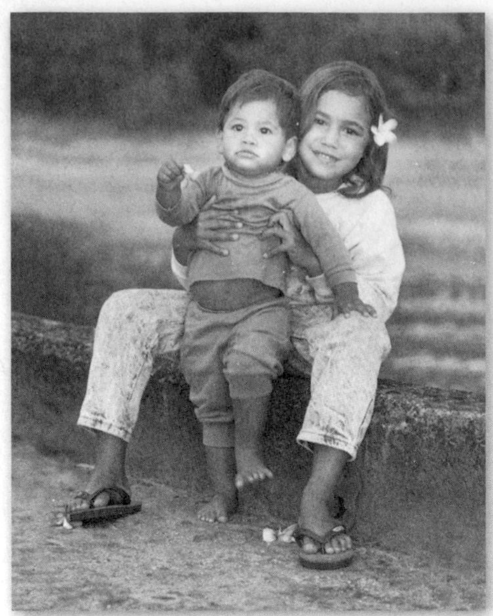

Thanks to their own resilience, fully a third of the at-risk children studied by Emmy Werner and her colleagues developed into self-confident, successful adults. These children had a positive and active approach to problem solving, the abilities to see some useful aspects of even painful experiences and to attract positive responses from other people, and faith in an optimistic vision of a fulfilling life.

The Kauai Study As the IHDP research suggests, given a supportive environment, many infants can overcome a poor start in life. That is also the conclusion of a long-term longitudinal study of 698 children born in 1955 on the Hawaiian island of Kauai.

For nearly five decades, Emmy E. Werner (1987, 1995; Werner & Smith, 2001) and a team of pediatricians, psychologists, public health workers, and social workers have followed these children from gestation to middle adulthood. The researchers interviewed the mothers-to-be, monitored their pregnancies, and interviewed them again when the children were 1, 2, and 10 years old. They observed the children at home, gave them aptitude, achievement, and personality tests in elementary and high school, and obtained progress reports from their teachers. The young people themselves were interviewed periodically as adults.

Physical and psychological development of children who had suffered low birthweight or other complications at or before birth was seriously impaired *only* when they grew up in persistently poor environmental circumstances. Unless the early damage was so serious as to require institutionalization, those children who had a stable and enriching environment did well (E. E. Werner, 1985, 1987). In fact, they had fewer language, perceptual, emotional, and school problems than children who had *not* experienced unusual stress at birth but who had received little intellectual stimulation or emotional support at home (E. E. Werner, 1989; E. E. Werner et al., 1968). The children who had been exposed to *both* birth-related problems and later stressful experiences had the worst health and the most retarded development (E. E. Werner, 1987).

Most remarkable is the resilience of children who escaped damage despite *multiple* sources of stress. Even when birth complications were combined with chronic poverty, family discord, divorce, or parents who were mentally ill, many children came through relatively unscathed. Of the 276 children who at age 2 had been identified as having four or more risk factors, two-thirds developed serious learning or behavior problems by the age of 10 or, by age 18, had become pregnant, gotten in trouble with the law, or become emotionally troubled. Yet, by age 30, one-third of these highly at-risk children had managed to become "competent, confident, and caring adults (E. E. Werner, 1995, p. 82). Of the full sample, about half of those on whom the researchers were able to obtain follow-up data successfully weathered the age-30 and age-40 transitions. Women tended to be better adapted than men (E. Werner & Smith, 2001).

protective factors Influences that reduce the impact of early stress and tend to predict positive outcomes.

Protective factors, which tended to reduce the impact of early stress, fell into three categories: (1) individual attributes that may be largely genetic, such as energy, sociability, and intelligence; (2) affectionate ties with at least one supportive family member; and (3) rewards at school, work, or place of worship that provide a sense of meaning and control over one's life (E. E. Werner, 1987). The home environment seemed to have the most marked effect in childhood, but in adulthood the individuals' own qualities made a greater difference (E. E. Werner, 1995).

Checkpoint

Can you . . .

- ✔ Discuss the effectiveness of the home environment and of intervention programs in overcoming effects of low birthweight and other birth complications?
- ✔ Name three protective factors identified by the Kauai study?

These studies underline the need to look at child development in context. They show how biological and environmental influences interact, making resiliency possible even in babies born with serious complications.

Death during Infancy

One of the most tragic losses is the death of an infant. Great strides have been made in protecting the lives of new babies, but these improvements are not evenly distributed throughout the population. Too many babies still die—some of them for no apparent reason, without warning or explanation.

Improving Infant Survival In recent decades, prospects for surviving the early years of life have improved. The improvement is especially dramatic in the developing regions of Africa, the Middle East, and Southeast Asia, yet the threat of early death remains the greatest in those regions (Wegman, 1999). Worldwide, in 2000, more than 1 in 20 infants died before their first birthday (UNICEF, 2002). Infant deaths represent an estimated 25 percent of all deaths in developing countries but only 1 percent of deaths in the developed world (U.S. Bureau of the Census, 1999).

In the United States, the **infant mortality rate**—the proportion of babies who die within the first year—is the lowest ever. In 2000, according to preliminary data, there were 6.9 deaths in the first year for every 1,000 live births, a 45 percent drop since 1980. About two-thirds of infant deaths take place during the neonatal period. Birth defects (congenital abnormalities), low birthweight, sudden infant death syndrome (SIDS), and maternal complications of pregnancy, in that order, are the leading causes, accounting for about half of all deaths in infancy (Miniño, Arias, Kochanek, Murphy, & Smith, 2002).

infant mortality rate Proportion of babies born alive who die within the first year.

The continuing improvement in infant survival rates during the 1990s, even at a time when more babies are born perilously small, has been due in part to effective treatment for respiratory distress and to prevention of SIDS (discussed in the next section), as well as to medical advances in keeping very small babies alive and treating sick newborns. Still, U.S. babies have a poorer chance of reaching their first birthday than babies in many other industrialized countries (Guyer et al., 1999; Mathews et al., 2000; see Figure 4-2). The higher survival rates of infants in western Europe and in

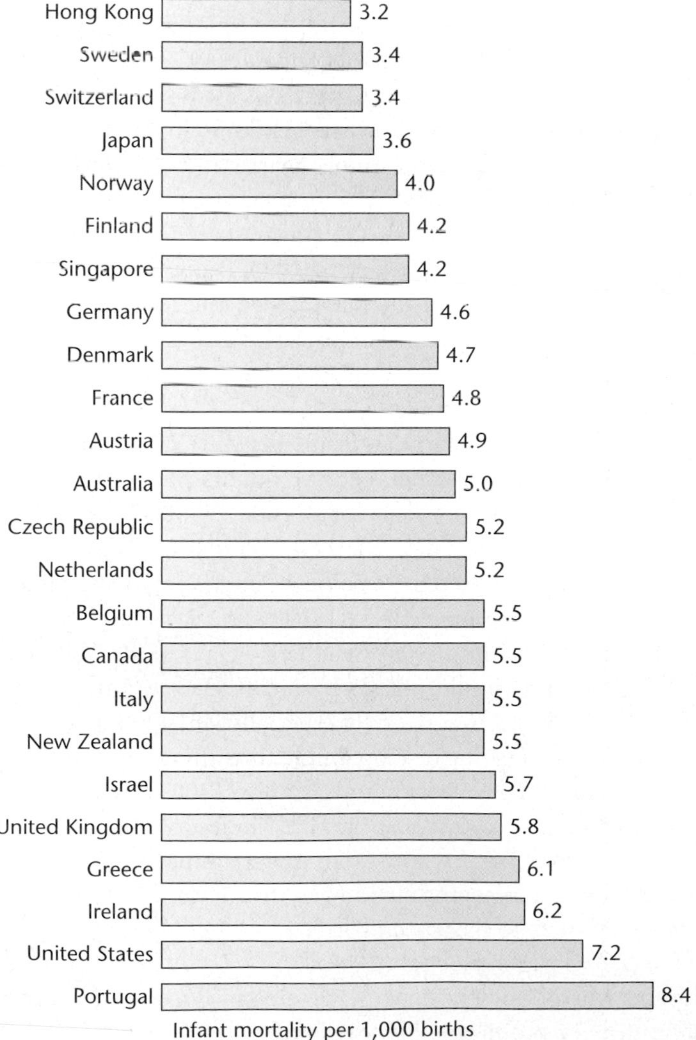

Figure 4-2
Infant mortality rates in industrialized countries. In 1998, the United States had a higher infant mortality rate than twenty-two other industrialized nations with populations of more than 250,000, largely because of its very high mortality rate for African American babies. In recent years most nations, including the United States, have shown dramatic improvement. *Note:* Rates for Sweden, Switzerland, and United Kingdom are for 1999. Rates for Canada and Italy are for 1997. Rates for Hong Kong, Sweden, Singapore, Germany, Denmark, France, Austria, Australia, Czech Republic, New Zealand, United Kingdom, Greece, Ireland, and Portugal are based on provisional data. (*Source:* Hoyert et al., 2001, Table 9, p. 1250.)

collectivist Pacific Rim societies, such as China, may be attributable to free pre- and postnatal health care and, in the Pacific Rim countries, to assistance from extended family members before and at birth (Gardiner et al., 1998).

Although infant mortality rates have declined for all races in the United States since 1980, racial disparities have increased—perhaps because black infants have not benefited as much as others from improvements in care of low-birthweight newborns (Alexander, Tompkins, Allen, & Hulsey, 2000). Black babies are two and a half times as likely to die in their first year as white and Hispanic babies (refer back to Table 4-3) and are about *four times* as likely as white babies to die of disorders related to low birthweight (Anderson, 2002; Miniño et al., 2002).

sudden infant death syndrome (SIDS) Sudden and unexplained death of an apparently healthy infant.

Sudden Infant Death Syndrome (SIDS)

Sudden infant death syndrome (SIDS), sometimes called "crib death," is the sudden death of an infant under 1 year of age in which the cause of death remains unexplained after a thorough investigation that includes an autopsy. In 2000, a total of 2,523 U.S. babies were victims of SIDS. It is the leading cause of death in infants after the neonatal period; it occurs most often between 1 and 4 months of age (Anderson, 2002; NICHD, 1997, updated 2000).

It seems likely that SIDS most often results from a combination of factors. An underlying biological defect may make some infants vulnerable, during a critical period in their development, to certain contributing or triggering experiences, such as exposure to smoke, prenatal exposure to caffeine, or sleeping on the stomach (AAP Task Force, 2000; Cutz, Perrin, Hackman, & Czegledy-Nagy, 1996; R. P. Ford et al., 1998). A gene that helps regulate heart rhythm and a defect in liver enzymes have been linked with small percentages of SIDS cases (Ackerman et al., 2001).

An important clue to what often happens in SIDS has emerged from the discovery of defects in chemical receptors, or nerve endings, in the brain stem, which receive and send messages that regulate breathing, heartbeat, body temperature, and arousal. These defects, which may originate early in fetal life, may prevent SIDS babies from awakening when they are breathing too much stale air containing carbon dioxide trapped under their blankets (Kinney et al., 1995; Panigrahy et al., 2000). This may be especially likely to happen when the baby is sleeping face down. Many SIDS babies may be deficient in a protective mechanism that allows an infant to become aroused enough to turn the head when breathing is restricted (AAP Task Force, 2000; Waters, Gonzalez, Jean, Morielli, & Brouillette, 1996).

Research strongly supports a relationship between SIDS and sleeping on the stomach. Side-sleeping is not safe either, because infants put to bed on their sides often turn onto their stomachs (AAP Task Force, 2000; Hauck et al., 2002; NICHD, 1997, updated 2000; Skadberg, Morild, & Markestad, 1998; J. A. Taylor et al., 1996). SIDS rates fell by as much as 70 percent in some countries following recommendations to put healthy babies to sleep on their backs (Dwyer, Ponsonby, Blizzard, Newman, & Cochrane, 1995; C. E. Hunt, 1996; Skadberg et al., 1998; Willinger, Hoffman, & Hartford, 1994). Infants should not sleep on soft surfaces, such as pillows, quilts, or sheepskin, or under loose covers, which, especially when the infant is face down, may increase the risk of overheating or rebreathing (breathing the infant's own waste products) (AAP Task Force, 2000; Guntheroth & Spiers, 2001). More effective educational outreach to urban African American families is needed. In a study of 260 Chicago SIDS babies, three-fourths of whom were African American, about one-third of the deaths were attributed to sleeping face down. African American mothers were less likely than the other mothers to have been correctly advised about sleeping position in the hospital after delivery (Hauck et al., 2002).

In cultures where bed-sharing with the mother is a common practice, its possible role in preventing or promoting SIDS is controversial (refer back to Box 4-1).

Immunization for Better Health

Such once-familiar and sometimes fatal childhood illnesses as measles, pertussis (whooping cough), and infantile paralysis (polio) are now largely preventable, thanks to the development of vaccines that mobilize the body's natural defenses. Unfortunately, many children still are not adequately protected, leaving themselves and those around them vulnerable to infection. In the developing world, 18 percent of deaths of children under age 5 are from vaccine-preventable diseases (Wegman, 1999).

Thanks to a nationwide immunization initiative, vaccine-preventable infectious diseases in the United States have dropped more than 95 percent since 1993 (AAP Committee on Infectious Diseases, 2000). In 1999, immunization rates for 19- to 35-month-olds reached record levels, ranging from nearly 80 percent to 96 percent. Still, about one child in six lacks one or more of the required shots, and there is substantial geographic variation in coverage (Centers for Disease Control and Prevention [CDC], 2000b; National Center for Health Statistics [NCHS], 2001). Native American children are at unusual risk of hepatitis A and B and certain types of influenza and pneumonia. Illnesses and deaths from these causes have declined as a result of special immunization recommendations for Native American communities (AAP Committee on Native American Child Health and Committee on Infectious Diseases, 1999).

One reason some parents hesitate to immunize their children is fear that vaccines (especially pertussis vaccine) may cause brain damage. However, the association between pertussis vaccine and neurologic illness appears very small (Gale et al., 1994). The potential damage from the diseases that this vaccine prevents is far greater than the risks of the vaccine.

Checkpoint

Can you . . .

- ✔ Summarize trends and risk factors for infant mortality?
- ✔ Discuss risk factors, causes, and prevention of sudden infant death syndrome?
- ✔ Explain why full immunization of infants and preschoolers is important?

Early Physical Development

Fortunately, most infants do survive, develop normally, and grow up healthy. What principles govern their development? What are the typical growth patterns of body and brain? How do babies' needs for nourishment and sleep change? How do their sensory and motor abilities develop?

Guidepost

7. What influences the growth of body and brain?

Principles of Development

As before birth, physical growth and development follow the *cephalocaudal principle* and *proximodistal principle.*

According to the cephalocaudal principle, growth occurs from the top down. Because the brain grows so rapidly before birth, a newborn baby's head is disproportionately large. The head becomes proportionately smaller as the child grows in height and the lower parts of the body develop (see Figure 4-3 on page 126). Sensory and motor development proceed according to the same principle: infants learn to use the upper parts of the body before the lower parts. They see objects before they can control their trunk, and they learn to do many things with their hands long before they can crawl or walk.

According to the proximodistal principle (inner to outer), growth and motor development proceed from the center of the body outward. In the womb, the head and trunk develop before the arms and legs, then the hands and feet, and then the fingers and toes. During infancy and early childhood, the limbs continue to grow faster than the hands and feet. Similarly, children first develop the ability to use their upper arms and upper legs (which are closest to the center of the body), then the forearms and forelegs, then hands and feet, and finally, fingers and toes.

Physical Growth

Children grow faster during the first three years, especially during the first few months, than ever again. At 5 months, the average baby boy's birthweight has doubled to 16

Figure 4-3
Changes in proportions of the human body during growth. The most striking change is that the head becomes smaller relative to the rest of the body. The fractions indicate head size as a proportion of total body length at several ages. More subtle is the stability of the trunk proportion (from neck to crotch). The increasing leg proportion is almost exactly the reverse of the decreasing head proportion.

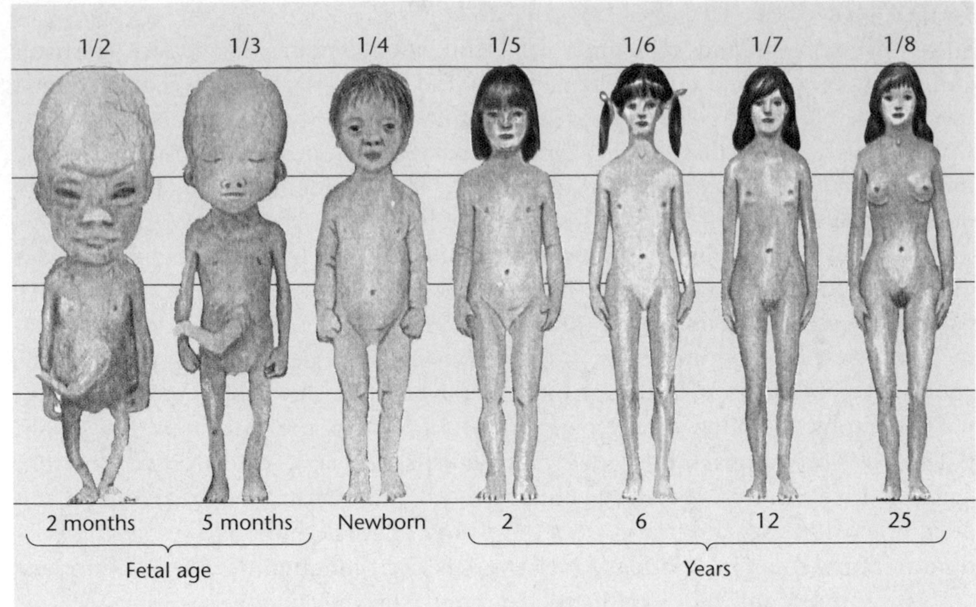

pounds, and, by 1 year, has nearly tripled to 23 pounds. This rapid growth rate tapers off during the second and third years (see Figure 4-4); a boy typically gains about 5 pounds by his second birthday and $3\frac{1}{2}$ pounds by his third.

A boy's height typically increases by 10 inches during the first year, by almost 5 inches during the second year, and by a little more than 3 inches during the third year, to top 37 inches. Girls follow a parallel pattern but are slightly smaller; at 3, the average girl weighs a pound less and is half an inch shorter than the average boy (Kuczmarski et al., 2000). As a baby grows, body shape and proportions change too; a 3-year-old typically is slender compared with a chubby, potbellied 1-year-old.

Teething usually begins around 3 or 4 months, when infants begin grabbing almost everything in sight to put into their mouths; but the first tooth may not actually arrive until sometime between 5 and 9 months of age, or even later. By the first birthday, babies generally have six to eight teeth. By age 3, all twenty primary, or deciduous, teeth are in place, and children can chew anything they want to.

Influences on Growth The genes an infant inherits have a strong influence on whether the child will be tall or short, thin or stocky, or somewhere in between. This genetic influence interacts with such environmental influences as nutrition and living

Figure 4-4
Growth in height and weight during infancy and toddlerhood. Babies grow most rapidly in both height and weight during the first few months of life, then taper off somewhat by age 3. Baby boys are slightly larger, on average, than baby girls. *Note:* Curves shown are for the 50th percentiles for each sex. (*Source:* Kuczmarski et al., 2000)

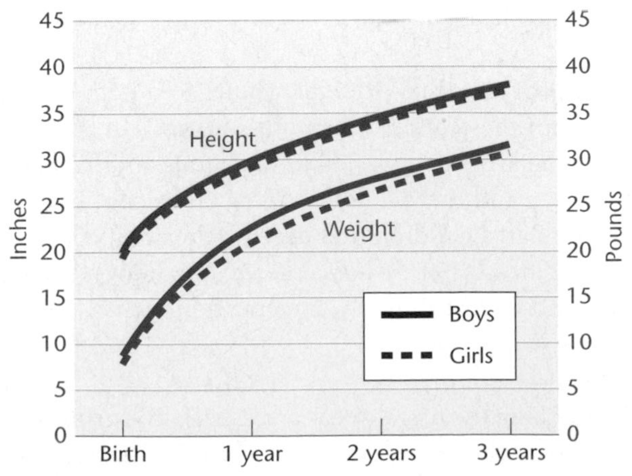

conditions, which also affect general health and well-being. For example, Japanese American children are taller and weigh more than children the same age in Japan, probably because of dietary differences (Broude, 1995).

Well-fed, well-cared-for children grow taller and heavier than less well nourished and nurtured children. They also mature sexually and attain maximum height earlier, and their teeth erupt sooner. Today, children in many developed countries are growing taller and maturing sexually at an earlier age than a century ago, probably because of better nutrition, improved sanitation and medical care, and the decrease in child labor.

Checkpoint

Can you . . .

- ✔ Summarize typical patterns of physical growth and change during the first three years?
- ✔ Identify several factors that affect growth?

Nutrition

Proper nutrition and adequate sleep are essential to healthy growth. Feeding and sleep needs change rapidly, especially during the first year of life.

Early Feeding: Past and Present From the beginnings of human history, babies were breast-fed. A woman who was either unable or unwilling to nurse her baby usually found another woman, a "wet nurse," to do it. Early in the twentieth century, with the advent of dependable refrigeration, pasteurization, and sterilization, manufacturers began to develop formulas to modify and enrich cow's milk for infant consumption.

During the next half-century, formula feeding became the norm in the United States and some other industrialized countries. By 1971, only 25 percent of American mothers even tried to nurse. Since then, recognition of the benefits of breast milk has brought about a reversal of this trend, so that today 70 percent of new mothers in the United States breast-feed. However, less than one-third are still breast-feeding at 6 months, and many of these supplement breast milk with formula (AAP Work Group on Breastfeeding, 1997; Ross Products Division, 2002; USDHHS, 2000a). Worldwide, only about one-half of all infants are breast-fed at any time from birth to 23 months (UNICEF, 2002).

Breast or Bottle? Breast milk is almost always the best food for infants. The only acceptable alternative is an iron-fortified formula based on either cow's milk or soy protein and containing supplemental vitamins and minerals. Because infants fed plain cow's milk in the early months of life may suffer from iron deficiency, the American Academy of Pediatrics (AAP, 1989b, 1996; AAP Committee on Nutrition, 1992b) recommends that babies receive breast milk or, alternatively, iron-fortified formula for at least the first year. At 1 year, babies can switch to cow's milk if they are getting a balanced diet of supplementary solid foods that provide one-third of their caloric intake (AAP, 1989b). To promote proper growth, the milk should be homogenized whole milk fortified with vitamin D (AAP, 1996).

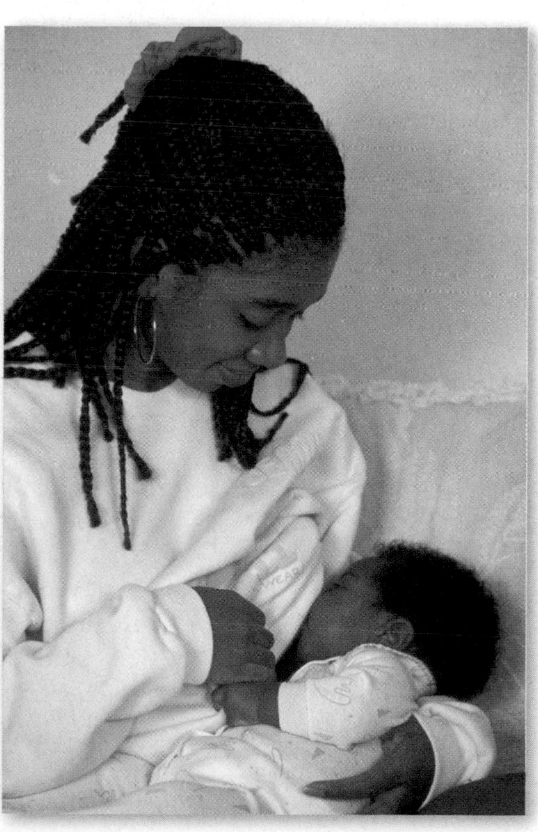

Breast milk has been called the "ultimate health food" because it offers so many benefits to babies—physical, cognitive, and emotional.

Why is breast-feeding best? Breast milk is more digestible and more nutritious than formula and is less likely to produce allergic reactions (AAP, 1989a, 1996; AAP Work Group on Breastfeeding, 1997; Eiger & Olds, 1999). Human milk is a complete source of nutrients for at least the first six months; during this time breast-fed babies normally do not need any other food. Neither they nor formula-fed infants need additional water (AAP Work Group on Breastfeeding, 1997).

The health advantages of breast-feeding are striking during the first two years and beyond (A. S. Cunningham, Jelliffe, & Jelliffe, 1991; J. Newman, 1995; A. L. Wright, Holberg, Taussig, & Martinez, 1995). Among the illnesses prevented or minimized by breast-feeding are diarrhea, respiratory infections (such as pneumonia and bronchitis), otitis media (an infection of the middle ear), and staphylococcal, bacterial, and urinary tract infections (AAP Work Group on Breastfeeding, 1997; A.S. Cunningham et al., 1991; Dewey, Heinig, & Nommsen-Rivers, 1995; J. Newman, 1995; Scariati, Grummer-Strawn, & Fein, 1997). Breast-feeding seems to have benefits for visual acuity (Makrides, Neumann, Simmer, Pater, & Gibson, 1995) and neurological development (Lanting, Fidler, Huisman, Touwen, & Boersma, 1994) and also may help prevent obesity, though findings on this point are inconclusive (Dietz, 2001; Gillman et al., 2001; Hediger, Overpeck, Kuczmarski, & Ruan, 2001; von Kries et al., 1999). Most studies also show benefits for cognitive development (AAP Work Group on Breastfeeding, 1997; Angelsen, Vik, Jacobsen, & Bakketeig, 2001; Horwood & Fergusson, 1998; Jacobson, Chiodo, & Jacobson, 1999), even into young adulthood (Mortensen, Michaelson, Sanders, & Reinisch, 2002). However, a literature review found that many had methodological flaws (Jain, Concato, & Leventhal, 2002).

Breast-feeding may reduce the risk of SIDS (National Institute of Child Health and Human Development [NICHD], 1997, updated 2000). According to data from a national survey of women of childbearing age, infants who are breast-fed are 80 percent more likely to survive the first year than infants who are never breast-fed.

Since 1991, 16,000 hospitals and birthing centers worldwide have been designated as "Baby-Friendly" under a United Nations initiative for encouraging institutional support of breast-feeding. The Baby-Friendly program includes staff information and training, offering new mothers rooming-in, telling them the benefits of breast-feeding, helping them start nursing within one hour of birth, showing them how to maintain lactation, encouraging on-demand feeding, giving infants nothing but breast milk (even pacifiers) unless medically necessary, and establishing ongoing breast-feeding support groups. At Boston Medical Center, breast-feeding increased substantially after the program went into effect (Philipp et al., 2001).

What's Your View?

- "Every mother who is physically able should breast-feed." Do you agree or disagree? Give reasons.

The more often and the longer babies are breast-fed, the better protected they are and the better their later cognitive performance (Angelsen et al., 2001). In a randomized controlled study of 17,046 new mothers in Belarus, mothers trained to promote successful breast-feeding through a program modeled after the Baby-Friendly initiative were more likely than a control group to breast-feed exclusively for the first three to six months and, to some degree, throughout the first year; and their infants were less likely to contract gastrointestinal infections and eczema (Kramer et al., 2001). However, programs to increase practical knowledge about breast-feeding may not be enough. Among 64 inner-city mothers who started breast-feeding, those who lacked confidence or who believed that their babies preferred formula stopped nursing within two weeks (Ertem, Votto, & Leventhal, 2001).

Nursing mothers need to be as careful as pregnant women about what they take into their bodies. Breast-feeding is inadvisable for a mother infected with the AIDS virus or any other infectious illness, if she has untreated active tuberculosis, or if she is taking any drug that would not be safe for the baby (AAP Committee on Drugs, 1994; AAP Committee on Infectious Diseases, 1994; AAP Work Group on Breastfeeding, 1997; Eiger & Olds, 1999; Miotti et al., 1999; Nduati et al., 2000; WHO/UNICEF Constitution on HIV Transmission and Breastfeeding, 1992).

Feeding a baby is an emotional as well as a physical act. Warm contact with the mother's body fosters emotional linkage between mother and baby. Such bonding can take place through either breast- or bottle-feeding and through many other caregiving activities, most of which can be performed by fathers as well as mothers. The quality of the relationship between parent and child and the provision of abundant affection and cuddling may be more important than the feeding method.

Obesity and Cholesterol Is obesity a problem in infancy? Not necessarily. In a study in Washington State, obese children under age 3 who did not have an obese parent were unlikely to grow up to be obese (Whitaker, Wright, Pepe, Seidel, & Dietz,

1997). However, a 1- or 2-year-old who has an obese parent—or especially two obese parents—may be a candidate for prevention efforts. At ages 3 and up, obesity is more likely to carry over to adulthood, regardless of whether the parents are obese.

Another concern is a potential buildup of *cholesterol,* a waxy substance found in human and animal tissue. High levels of LDL, or "bad" cholesterol, can dangerously narrow blood vessels, leading to heart disease. Since this condition, called *atherosclerosis,* can begin in childhood, so should heart disease prevention. In a controlled longitudinal study in Finland, a low-saturated fat, low-cholesterol diet beginning in the eighth month of infancy resulted in significant reductions in fat and cholesterol intake by age 5, with no adverse effect on growth or neurological development (Rask-Nissilä et al., 2000).

Checkpoint

Can you . . .

- ✔ Summarize pediatric recommendations regarding early feeding?
- ✔ Cite factors that contribute to obesity and cardiac problems in later life?

The Brain and Reflex Behavior

What makes newborns respond to a nipple? What tells them to start the sucking movements that allow them to control their intake of fluids? These are functions of the **central nervous system**—the brain and *spinal cord* (a bundle of nerves running through the backbone)—and of a growing peripheral network of nerves extending to every part of the body. Through this network, sensory messages travel to the brain, and motor commands travel back.

central nervous system Brain and spinal cord.

Building the Brain The growth of the brain is fundamental to future physical, cognitive, and emotional development. Through brain-imaging tools, researchers are gaining a clearer picture of how that growth occurs (Behrman, 1992; Casaer, 1993; Gabbard, 1996).* For example, from positron emission tomography (PET) scans we have learned that the brain's maturation takes much longer than was previously thought (Chugani, 1998).

The brain at birth weighs only about 25 percent of its eventual adult weight of $3\frac{1}{2}$ pounds. It reaches 70 percent of that weight at 1 year and nearly 90 percent by age 3. By age 6, it is almost adult size; but growth and functional development of specific parts of the brain continue into adulthood. The brain's growth occurs in fits and starts, and different parts of it grow rapidly at different times.

Major Parts of the Brain Beginning about two weeks after conception, the brain gradually develops from a long hollow tube into a spherical mass of cells (see Figure 4-5 on page 130). By birth, the growth spurt of the spinal cord and *brain stem* (the part of the brain responsible for such basic bodily functions as breathing, heart rate, body temperature, and the sleep-wake cycle) has almost run its course. The *cerebellum* (the part of the brain that maintains balance and motor coordination) grows fastest during the first year of life (Casaer, 1993).

The *cerebrum,* the largest part of the brain, is divided into right and left halves, or hemispheres, each with specialized functions. This specialization of the hemispheres is called **lateralization.** The left hemisphere is mainly concerned with language and logical thinking, the right hemisphere with visual and spatial functions such as map reading and drawing. The two hemispheres are joined by a tough band of tissue called the *corpus callosum,* which allows them to share information and coordinate commands. The corpus callosum grows dramatically during childhood, reaching adult size by about age 10.

lateralization Tendency of each of the brain's hemispheres to have specialized functions.

Each cerebral hemisphere has four lobes, or sections: the *occipital, parietal, temporal,* and *frontal* lobes, which control different functions (see Figure 4-6 on page 131)

*Unless otherwise referenced, the discussion in this section is largely based on Gabbard (1996).

Figure 4-5
Fetal brain development from 25 days of gestation through birth. The *brain stem,* which controls basic biological functions such as breathing, develops first. As the brain grows, the front part expands greatly to form the *cerebrum* (the large, convoluted upper mass). Specific areas of the gray outer covering of the brain have specific functions, such as sensory and motor activity; but large areas are "uncommitted" and thus are free for higher cognitive activity, such as thinking, remembering, and problem solving. The brain stem and other structures below the cortical layer handle reflex behavior and other lower-level functions. The *cerebellum,* which maintains balance and motor coordination, grows most rapidly during the first year of life. (*Source:* Casaer, 1993; Restak, 1984.)

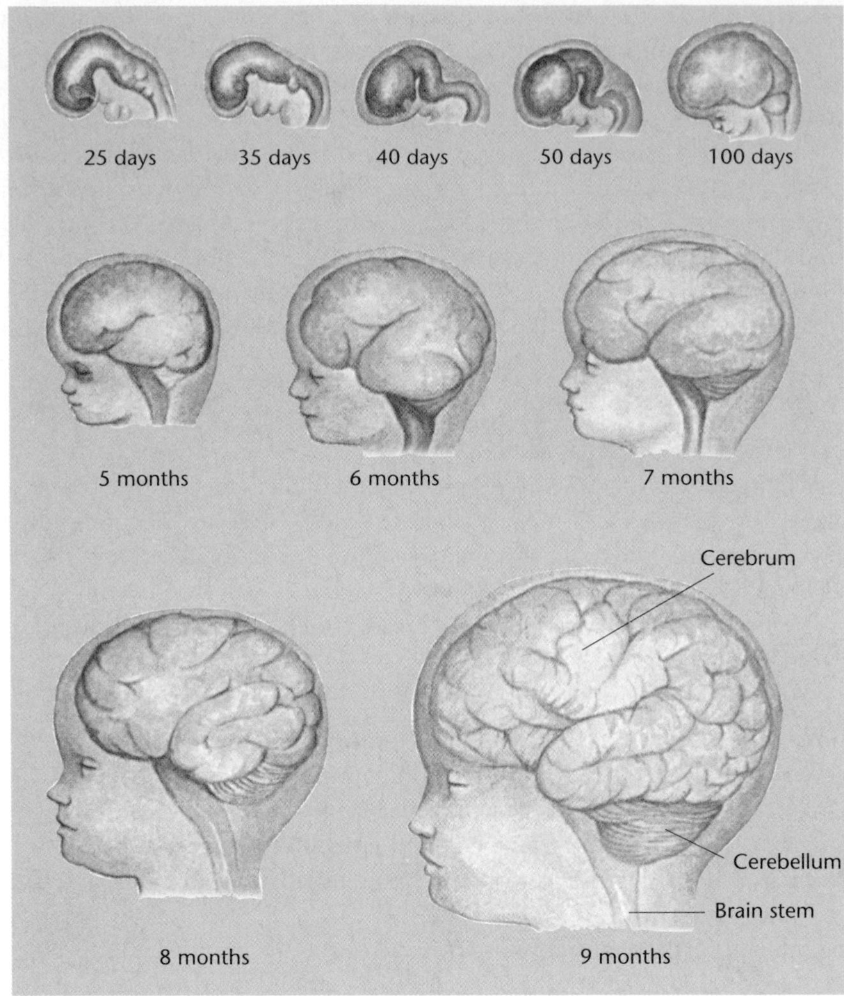

and develop at different rates. The regions of the *cerebral cortex* (the outer surface of the cerebrum) that govern vision and hearing are mature by 6 months of age, but the areas of the frontal lobe responsible for making mental associations, remembering, and producing deliberate motor responses remain immature for several years.

neurons Nerve cells.

Brain Cells The brain is composed of *neurons* and *glial cells.* **Neurons,** or nerve cells, send and receive information. *Glial cells* support and protect the neurons.

Beginning in the second month of gestation, an estimated 250,000 immature neurons are produced every minute through cell division (mitosis). At birth, most of the more than 100 billion neurons in a mature brain are already formed but are not yet fully developed. The number of neurons increases most rapidly between the twenty-fifth week of gestation and the first few months after birth. This cell proliferation is accompanied by a dramatic growth in cell size.

Originally the neurons are simply cell bodies with a nucleus, or center, composed of deoxyribonucleic acid (DNA), which contains the cell's genetic programming. As the brain grows, these rudimentary cells migrate to various parts of it. There they sprout *axons* and *dendrites*—narrow, branching extensions. Axons send signals to other neurons, and dendrites receive incoming messages from them, through *synapses,* the nervous system's communication links. The synapses are tiny gaps, which are bridged with the help of chemicals called *neurotransmitters.* Eventually a particular neuron may have anywhere from 5,000 to 100,000 synaptic connections to and from

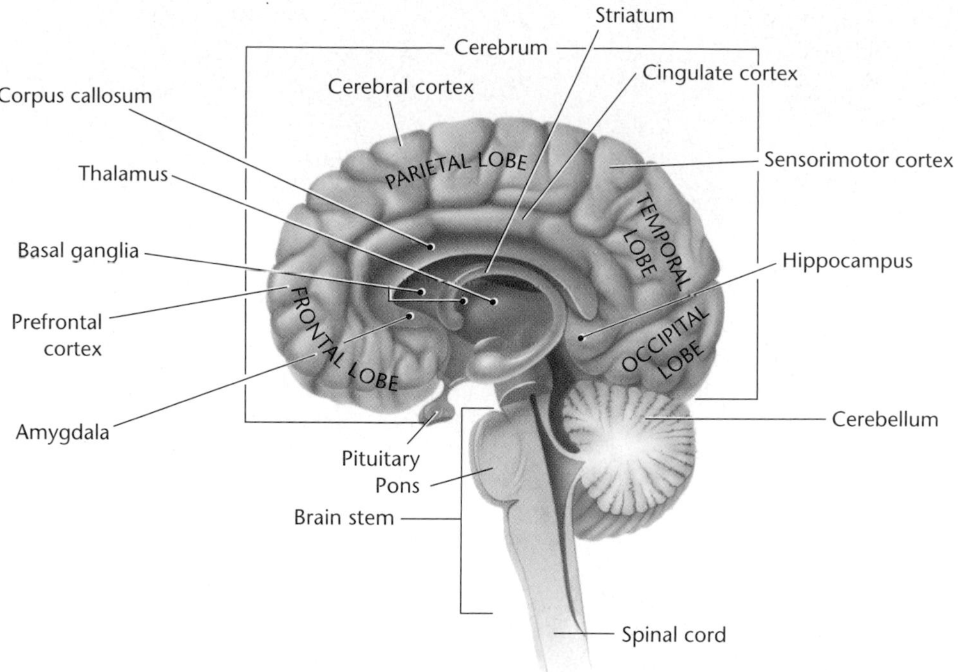

Figure 4-6
Parts of the brain, side view. The brain consists of three main parts: the brain stem, the cerebellum, and, above those, the large cerebrum. The brain stem, an extension of the spinal cord, is one of the regions of the brain most completely developed at birth. It controls such basic bodily functions as breathing, circulation, and reflexes. The cerebellum, at birth, begins to control balance and muscle tone; later it coordinates sensory and motor activity. The cerebrum constitutes almost 70 percent of the weight of the nervous system and handles thought, memory, language, and emotion. It is divided into two halves, or hemispheres, each of which has four sections, or lobes (right to left): (a) The occipital lobe processes visual information. (b) The temporal lobe helps with hearing and language. (c) The parietal lobe allows an infant to receive touch sensations and spatial information, which facilitates eye-hand coordination. (d) The frontal lobe develops gradually during the first year, permitting such higher-level functions as speech and reasoning. The cerebral cortex, the outer surface of the cerebrum, consists of gray matter; it is the seat of thought processes and mental activity. Parts of the cerebral cortex—the sensorimotor cortex and cingulate cortex—as well as several structures deep within the cerebrum, the thalamus, hippocampus, and basal ganglia, all of which control basic movements and functions, are largely developed at birth.

the body's sensory receptors, its muscles, and other neurons within the central nervous system.

The multiplication of dendrites and synaptic connections, especially during the last two and a half months of gestation and the first six months to two years of life (see Figure 4-7 on page 132), accounts for much of the brain's growth in weight and permits the emergence of new perceptual, cognitive, and motor abilities. Most of the neurons in the cortex, which is responsible for complex, high-level functioning, are in place by twenty weeks of gestation, and its structure becomes fairly well defined during the next twelve weeks. Only after birth, however, do the cells begin to form connections that allow communication to take place.

As the neurons multiply, migrate to their assigned locations, and develop connections, they undergo the complementary processes of *integration* and *differentiation.* Through **integration,** the neurons that control various groups of muscles coordinate their activities. Through **differentiation,** each neuron takes on a specific, specialized structure and function.

integration Process by which neurons coordinate the activities of muscle groups.

differentiation Process by which neurons acquire specialized structure and function.

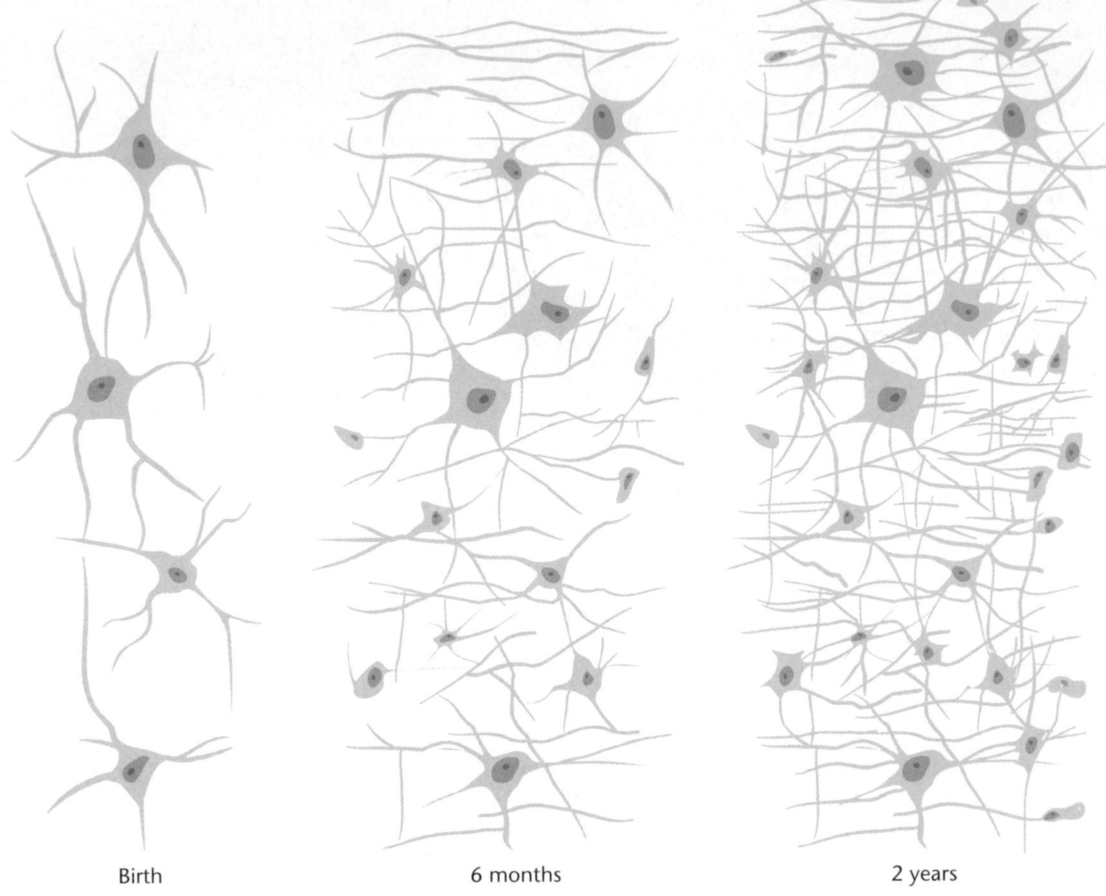

Figure 4-7
Growth of neural connections during first two years of life. The rapid increase in the brain's density and weight is due largely to the formation of dendrites, extensions of nerve cell bodies, and the synapses that link them. This mushrooming communications network sprouts in response to environmental stimulation and makes possible impressive growth in every domain of development. (*Source:* Conel, 1959.)

cell death Elimination of excess brain cells to achieve more efficient functioning.

At first the brain produces more neurons and synapses than it needs. Those that are not used or do not function well die out. This process of **cell death,** or pruning of excess cells, begins during the prenatal period and continues after birth (see Figure 4-8), helping to create an efficient nervous system. The number of synapses seems to peak at about age 2, and their elimination continues well into adolescence. Even as some neurons die out, others may continue to form during adult life (Eriksson et al., 1998; Gould, Reeves, Graziano, & Gross, 1999). Connections among cortical cells continue to improve into adulthood, allowing more flexible and more advanced motor and cognitive functioning.

myelination Process of coating neurons with a fatty substance (myelin) that enables faster communication between cells.

Myelination Much of the credit for improvement in efficiency of communication goes to the glial cells, which coat the neural pathways with a fatty substance called *myelin.* This process of **myelination** enables signals to travel faster and more smoothly, permitting the achievement of mature functioning.

Myelination begins about halfway through gestation in some parts of the brain and continues into adulthood in others. The pathways related to the sense of touch—the first sense to develop—are myelinated by birth. Myelination of visual pathways, which are slower to mature, begins at birth and continues during the first five months of life. Pathways related to hearing may begin to be myelinated as early as the fifth month of gestation, but the process is not complete until about age 4. The parts of the cortex that control attention and memory are not fully myelinated until young adult-

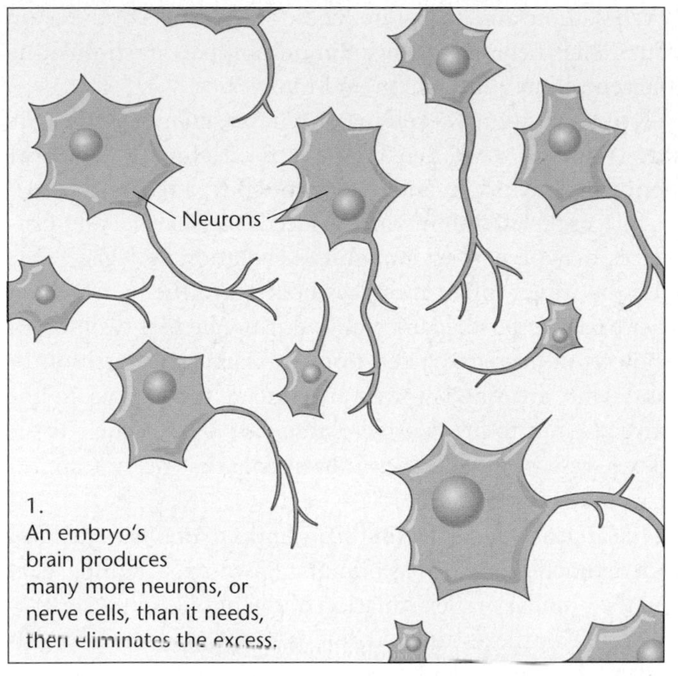

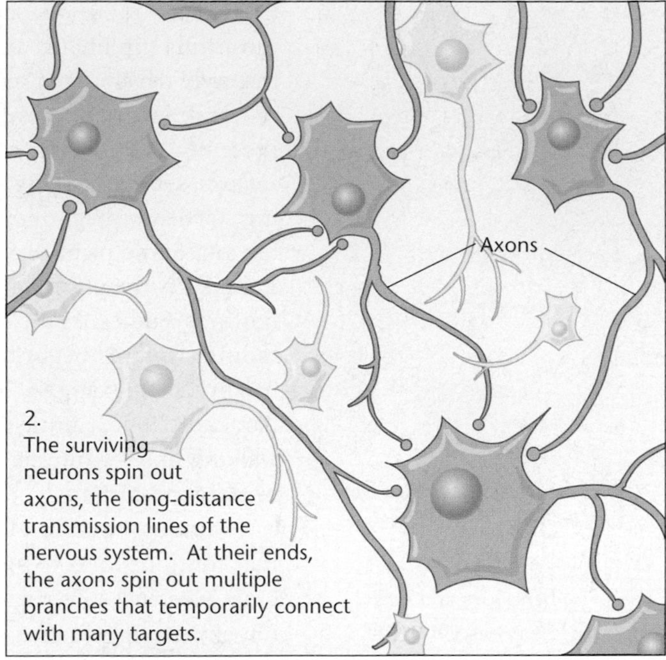

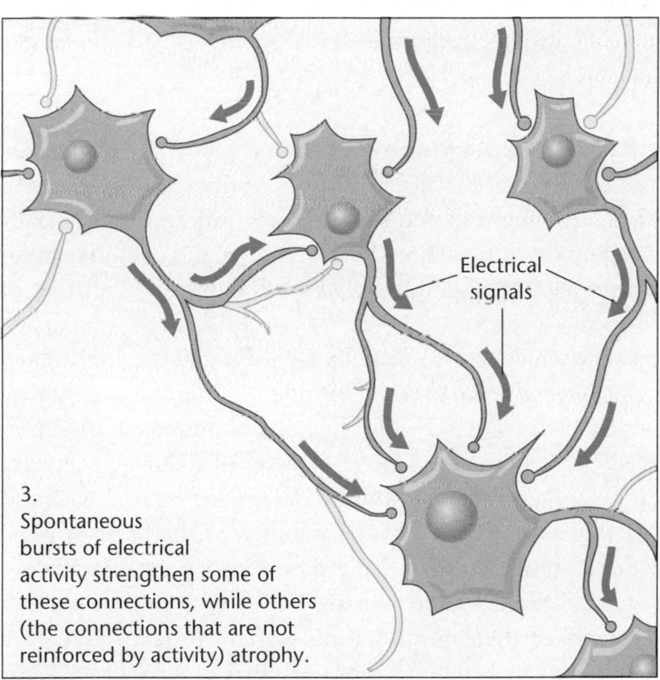

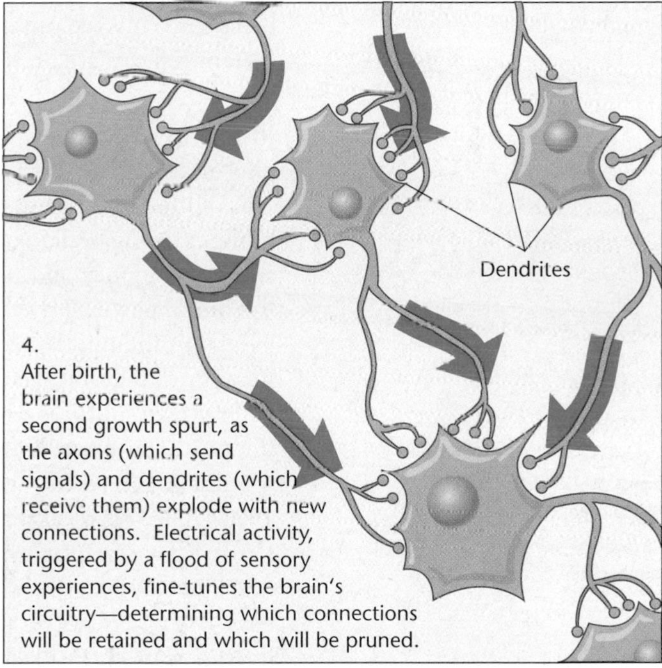

Figure 4-8
Wiring the brain: development of neural connections before and after birth. (*Source:* Nash, 1997, p. 51.)

hood. Myelination of the *hippocampus,* a structure deep in the temporal lobe that plays a key role in memory, continues to increase until at least age 70 (Benes, Turtle, Khan, & Farol, 1994).

Myelination of sensory and motor pathways, first in the fetus's spinal cord and later, after birth, in the cerebral cortex, may account for the appearance and disappearance of early reflexes.

Early Reflexes When you blink at a bright light, your eyelids are acting involuntarily. Such an automatic, innate response to stimulation is called a **reflex behavior.** Reflex behaviors are controlled by the lower brain centers that govern other

reflex behaviors Automatic, involuntary, innate responses to stimulation.

involuntary processes, such as breathing and heart rate. These are the parts of the brain most fully myelinated at birth. Reflex behaviors play an important part in stimulating the early development of the central nervous system and muscles.

Human infants have an estimated twenty-seven major reflexes, many of which are present at birth or soon after (Gabbard, 1996; see Table 4-4 for examples). *Primitive reflexes,* such as sucking, rooting for the nipple, and the Moro reflex (a response to being startled or beginning to fall), are related to instinctive needs for survival and protection. Some primitive reflexes may be part of humanity's evolutionary legacy. One example is the grasping reflex, by which infant monkeys hold on to the hair of their mothers' bodies. As the higher brain centers become active during the first two to four months, infants begin to show *postural reflexes:* reactions to changes in position or balance. For example, infants who are tilted downward extend their arms in the parachute reflex, an instinctive attempt to break a fall. *Locomotor reflexes,* such as the walking and swimming reflexes, resemble voluntary movements that do not appear until months after the reflexes have disappeared.

Most of the early reflexes disappear during the first six months to one year. Reflexes that continue to serve protective functions—such as blinking, yawning, coughing, gagging, sneezing, shivering, and the pupillary reflex (dilation of the pupils in the dark)—remain. Disappearance of unneeded reflexes on schedule is a sign that motor pathways in the cortex have been partially myelinated, enabling a shift to voluntary behavior. Thus we can evaluate a baby's neurological development by seeing whether certain reflexes are present or absent.

Checkpoint

Can you . . .

- ✔ Describe important features of early brain development?
- ✔ Explain the functions of reflex behaviors and why some drop out during the early months?

Molding the Brain: The Role of Experience The brain growth spurt that begins at about the third trimester of gestation and continues until at least the fourth year of life is important to the development of neurological functioning. Smiling, babbling, crawling, walking, and talking—all the major sensory, motor, and cognitive milestones of infancy and toddlerhood—are made possible by the rapid development of the brain, particularly the cerebral cortex.

Until the middle of the twentieth century, scientists believed that the brain grew in an unchangeable, genetically determined pattern. This does seem to be largely true before birth. But it is now widely believed, largely on the basis of animal studies, that the postnatal brain is "molded" by experience. This is so especially during the early months of life, when the cortex is still growing rapidly and organizing itself (J. E. Black, 1998). The technical term for this malleability, or modifiability, of the brain is **plasticity.** Early synaptic connections, some of which depend on sensory stimulation, refine and stabilize the brain's genetically designed "wiring." Thus early experience can have lasting effects on the capacity of the central nervous system to learn and store information (J. E. Black, 1998; Chugani, 1998; Greenough, Black, & Wallace, 1987; Pally, 1997; Wittrock, 1980).

plasticity Modifiability, or "molding," of the brain through experience.

We know that malnutrition can interfere with normal cognitive growth (Rose, 1994). By the same token, early abuse or sensory impoverishment may leave an imprint on the brain (J. E. Black, 1998). In one classic experiment, kittens fitted with goggles that allowed them to see only vertical lines grew up unable to see horizontal lines and bumped into horizontal boards in front of them. Other kittens, whose goggles allowed them to see only horizontal lines, grew up blind to vertical columns (Hirsch & Spinelli, 1970). This did not happen when the same procedure was carried out with adult cats. Apparently, neurons in the visual cortex became programmed to respond only to lines running in the direction the kittens were permitted to see. Thus, if certain cortical connections are not made early in life, and if no further intervention occurs (Bruer, 2001), these circuits may "shut down" forever.

Early emotional development, too, may depend on experience. Infants whose mothers are severely depressed show less activity in the left frontal lobe, the part of

Table 4-4 Early Human Reflexes

Reflex	Stimulation	Baby's Behavior	Typical Age of Appearance	Typical Age of Disappearance
Moro	Baby is dropped or hears loud noise.	Extends legs, arms, and fingers, arches back, draws back head.	7th month of gestation	3 months
Darwinian (grasping)	Palm of baby's hand is stroked.	Makes strong fist; can be raised to standing position if both fists are closed around a stick.	7th month of gestation	4 months
Tonic neck	Baby is laid down on back.	Turns head to one side, assumes "fencer" position, extends arms and legs on preferred side, flexes opposite limbs.	7th month of gestation	5 months
Babkin	Both of baby's palms are stroked at once.	Mouth opens, eyes close, neck flexes, head tilts forward.	Birth	3 months
Babinski	Sole of baby's foot is stroked.	Toes fan out; foot twists in.	Birth	4 months
Rooting	Baby's cheek or lower lip is stroked with finger or nipple.	Head turns; mouth opens; sucking movements begin.	Birth	9 months
Walking	Baby is held under arms, with bare feet touching flat surface.	Makes steplike motions that look like well-coordinated walking.	1 month	4 months
Swimming	Baby is put into water face down.	Makes well-coordinated swimming movements.	1 month	4 months

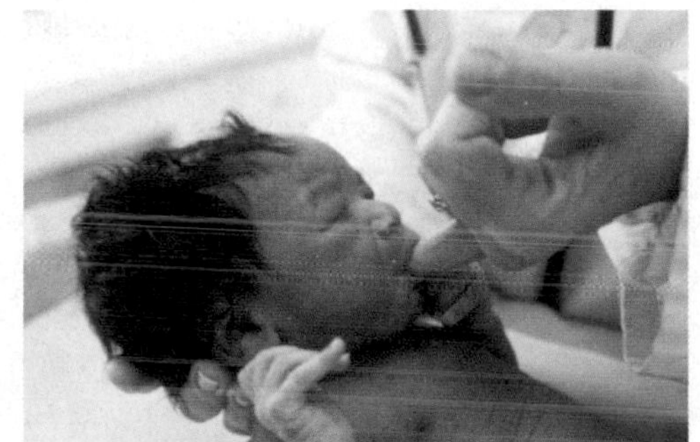

Rooting reflex

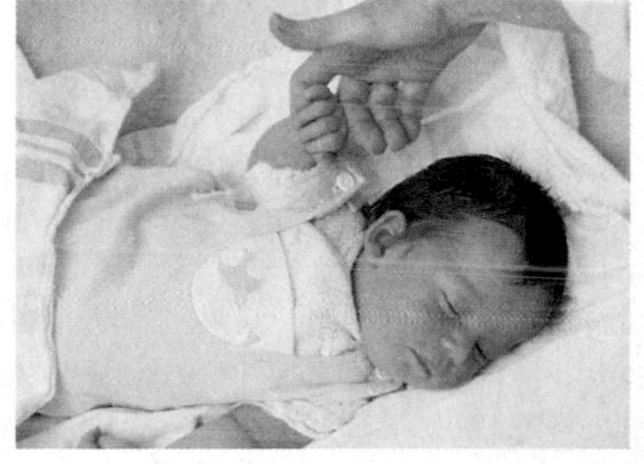

Darwinian reflex

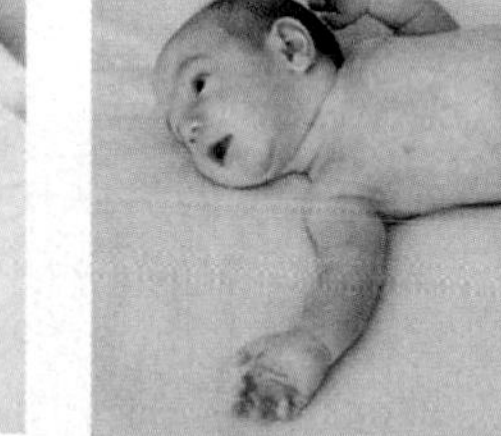

Tonic neck reflex

Moro reflex

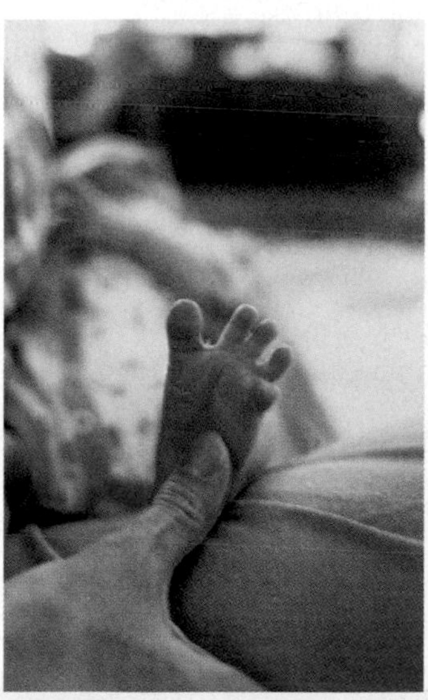

Babinski reflex

Walking reflex

Source: Adapted in part from Gabbard, 1996.

the brain that is involved in positive emotions such as happiness and joy, and more activity in the right frontal lobe, which is associated with negative emotions (Dawson, Frey, Panagiotides, Osterling, & Hessl, 1997; Dawson, Klinger, Panagiotides, Hill, & Spieker, 1992).

Plasticity continues throughout life as neurons change in size and shape in response to environmental experience (M. C. Diamond, 1988; Pally, 1997; Rutter, 2002). Sometimes corrective experience can make up for past deprivation (J. E. Black, 1998). Brain-damaged rats, when raised in an enriched setting, grow more dendritic connections (M. C. Diamond, 1988). Such findings have sparked successful efforts to stimulate the physical and mental development of children with Down syndrome and to help victims of brain damage recover function.

Ethical constraints prevent controlled experiments on the effects of environmental deprivation or enrichment on human infants. However, the discovery of thousands of infants and young children who had spent virtually their entire lives in overcrowded Romanian orphanages offered an opportunity for a natural experiment (Ames, 1997). Discovered after the fall of the dictator Nicolae Ceausescu in December 1989, these abandoned children appeared to be starving, passive, and emotionless. They had spent much of their time lying quietly in their cribs or beds, with nothing to look at. They had had little contact with one another or with their caregivers and had heard little conversation or even noise. Most of the 2- and 3-year-olds did not walk or talk, and the older children played aimlessly. PET scans of their brains showed extreme inactivity in the temporal lobes, which regulate emotion and receive sensory input.

Many of these children were adopted by Canadian families. At the time of adoption, all the children adopted into Canada showed delayed motor, language, or psychosocial development, and nearly eight out of ten were behind in all these areas. Three years later, when compared with children left behind in the Romanian institutions, many of the adopted children showed significant progress. About one-third had no serious problems and were doing well. Another one-third—generally those who had been in institutions the longest—still had serious developmental problems. The rest were moving toward average performance and behavior (Ames, 1997; Morison, Ames, & Chisholm, 1995).

At $4\frac{1}{2}$, those who had spent eight months or more in the orphanages and had been adopted into Canada by age 2 had average IQs and verbal comprehension. But the orphanage group as a whole had not caught up with Canadian-born nonadopted children nor with a control group of Romanian children adopted by 4 months of age, who had not been in orphanages. The previously institutionalized children were rated as having less stimulating home environments than the Canadian-born children (Morison & Ellwood, 2000). This is not surprising, since many of these children had severe behavioral problems, which tended to make parenting stressful (Mainemer, Gilman, & Ames, 1998). In preschool, these children showed poorer social skills and had more problems with social interaction than Canadian-born children or early Romanian adoptees (Thompson, 2001); and at age $8\frac{1}{2}$, PET scans found persistent underactivity in portions of their brains (Chugani et al., 2001).

What's Your View?

- In view of what is now known about the plasticity of the infant brain, how can we make sure that every baby has access to an appropriately stimulating environment?

Checkpoint

Can you . . .

- ✔ Discuss how early experience can affect brain growth and development both positively and negatively, and give examples?

Early Sensory Capacities

The developing brain enables newborn infants to make fairly good sense of what they touch, see, smell, taste, and hear; and their senses develop rapidly in the early months of life.

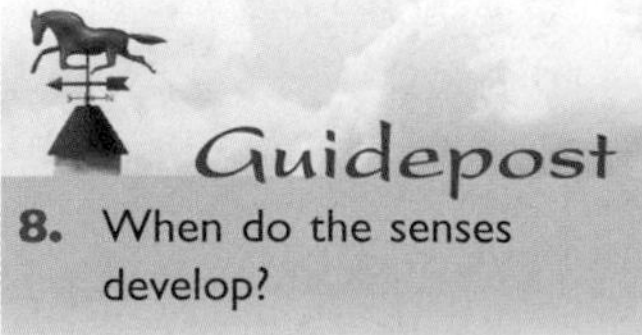

Guidepost

8. When do the senses develop?

Touch and Pain Touch is the first sense to develop, and for the first several months it is the most mature sensory system. When a newborn's cheek is stroked near the mouth, the baby responds by trying to find a nipple. Early signs of this rooting reflex (refer back to Table 4-4) occur two months after conception. By thirty-two weeks of gestation, all body parts are sensitive to touch, and this sensitivity increases during the first five days of life (Haith, 1986).

In the past, physicians performing surgery on newborn babies often used no anesthesia because of a mistaken belief that neonates cannot feel pain, or feel it only briefly. Actually, even on the first day of life, babies can and do feel pain; and they become more sensitive to it during the next few days. The American Academy of Pediatrics and Canadian Pediatric Society (2000) maintain that prolonged or severe pain can do long-term harm to newborns, and that pain relief is essential.

Smell and Taste The senses of smell and taste also begin to develop in the womb. The flavors and odors of foods an expectant mother consumes may be transmitted to the fetus through the amniotic fluid. After birth, a similar transmission occurs through breast milk (Mennella & Beauchamp, 1996b).

A preference for pleasant odors seems to be learned in utero and during the first few days after birth, and the odors transmitted through the mother's breast milk may further contribute to this learning (Bartoshuk & Beauchamp, 1994). Six-day-old breast-fed infants prefer the odor of their mother's breast pad over that of another nursing mother, but 2-day-olds do not, suggesting that babies need a few days' experience to learn how their mothers smell (Macfarlane, 1975).

Certain taste preferences seem to be largely innate (Bartoshuk & Beauchamp, 1994). Newborns prefer sweet tastes to sour or bitter ones (Haith, 1986). Sweetened water calms crying newborns, whether full-term or two to three weeks premature—evidence that not only the taste buds themselves (which seem to be fairly well developed by twenty weeks of gestation), but the mechanisms that produce this calming effect are functional before normal term (B. A. Smith & Blass, 1996).

Hearing Hearing, too, is functional before birth. Early recognition of voices and language heard in the womb (refer back to Chapter 3) may lay the foundation for the relationship between parents and child.

Auditory discrimination develops rapidly after birth. Three-day-old infants can tell new speech sounds from those they have heard before (L. R. Brody, Zelazo, & Chaika, 1984). At 1 month, babies can distinguish sounds as close as "ba" and "pa" (Eimas, Siqueland, Jusczyk, & Vigorito, 1971).

Because hearing is a key to language development, hearing impairments should be identified and treated as early as possible. The National Institutes of Health (1993) recommends that all infants be screened for hearing problems within the first three months.

Checkpoint

Can you . . .

- ✔ Give evidence for early development of the senses of touch, smell, and taste, and tell how breast-feeding plays a part in the latter two senses?
- ✔ Tell how auditory discrimination in newborns is related to fetal hearing?
- ✔ List three ways newborns' vision is underdeveloped?

Sight Vision is the least developed sense at birth. The eyes of newborns are smaller than those of adults, the retinal structures are incomplete, and the optic nerve is underdeveloped. Newborns blink at bright lights. Their peripheral vision is very narrow; it more than doubles between 2 and 10 weeks of age (E. Tronick, 1972). The ability to follow a moving target also develops rapidly in the first months, as does color perception.

Vision becomes more acute during the first year, reaching the 20/20 level by about the sixth month (Aslin, 1987). *Binocular vision*—the use of both eyes to focus, allowing perception of depth and distance—usually does not develop until 4 or 5 months (Bushnell & Boudreau, 1993).

Motor Development

Guidepost

9. What are some early milestones in motor development, and what are some influences on it?

Babies do not have to be taught such basic motor skills as grasping, crawling, and walking. They just need room to move and freedom to see what they can do. When the central nervous system, muscles, and bones are ready and the environment offers the right opportunities for exploration and practice, babies keep surprising the adults around them with new abilities.

systems of action Increasingly complex combinations of skills, which permit a wider or more precise range of movement and more control of the environment.

Denver Developmental Screening Test Screening test given to children 1 month to 6 years old to determine whether they are developing normally.

gross motor skills Physical skills that involve the large muscles.

fine motor skills Physical skills that involve the small muscles and eye-hand coordination.

Milestones of Motor Development Motor development is marked by a series of milestones: achievements that develop systematically, each newly mastered ability preparing a baby to tackle the next. Babies first learn simple skills and then combine them into increasingly complex **systems of action,** which permit a wider or more precise range of movement and more effective control of the environment. In developing the precision grip, for example, an infant first tries to pick things up with the whole hand, fingers closing against the palm. Later the baby masters the *pincer grasp,* in which thumb and index finger meet at the tips to form a circle, making it possible to pick up tiny objects. In learning to walk, an infant first gains control of separate movements of the arms, legs, and feet before putting these movements together to take that momentous first step.

The **Denver Developmental Screening Test** (Frankenburg, Dodds, Fandal, Kazuk, & Cohrs, 1975) is used to chart normal progress between the ages of 1 month and 6 years and to identify children who are not developing normally. The test measures **gross motor skills** (those using large muscles), such as rolling over and catching a ball, and **fine motor skills** (using small muscles), such as grasping a rattle and copying a

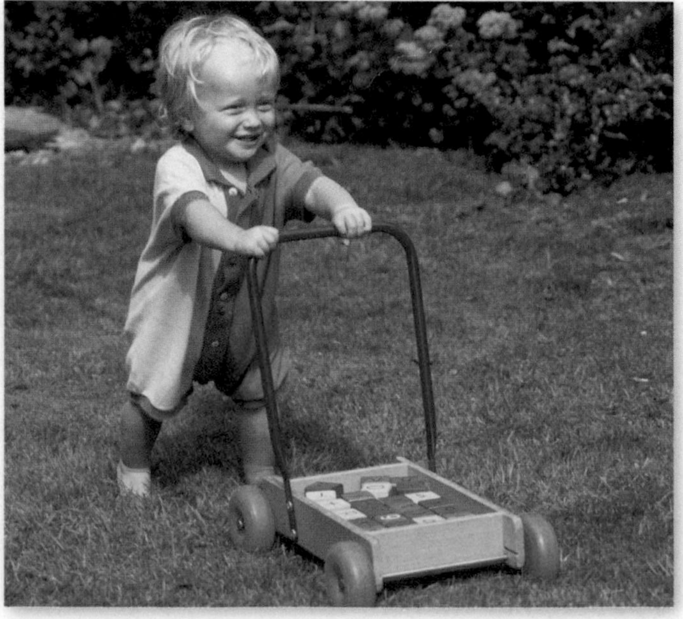

Lifting and holding up the head from a prone position, crawling along the floor to reach something enticing, such as a furry cat's tail, and walking well enough to push a doll's carriage are important early milestones of motor development.

circle. It also assesses language development (for example, knowing the definitions of words) and personality and social development (such as smiling spontaneously and dressing without help). The newest edition, the Denver II Scale (Frankenburg et al., 1992), includes revised norms (see Table 4-5 for examples).

When we talk about what the "average" baby can do, we refer to the 50 percent Denver norms. Actually, normality covers a wide range; about half of all babies master these skills before the ages given, and about half afterward. Also, the Denver norms were developed with reference to a western population and are not necessarily valid in assessing children from other cultures.

As we trace typical progress in head control, hand control, and locomotion, notice how these developments follow the *cephalocaudal* (head to tail) and *proximodistal* (inner to outer) principles outlined earlier.

Head Control At birth, most infants can turn their heads from side to side while lying on their backs. While lying chest down, many can lift their heads enough to turn them. Within the first two to three months, they lift their heads higher and higher—sometimes to the point where they lose their balance and roll over on their backs. By 4 months of age, almost all infants can keep their heads erect while being held or supported in a sitting position.

Hand Control Babies are born with a grasping reflex. If the palm of an infant's hand is stroked, the hand closes tightly. At about $3\frac{1}{2}$ months, most infants can grasp an object of moderate size, such as a rattle, but have trouble holding a small object. Next they begin to grasp objects with one hand and transfer them to the other, and then to hold (but not pick up) small objects. Some time between 7 and 11 months, their hands become coordinated enough to pick up a tiny object, such as a pea, using the pincer grasp. After that, hand control becomes increasingly precise. By 15 months, the average baby can build a tower of two cubes. A few months after the third birthday, the average toddler can copy a circle fairly well.

Locomotion After three months, the average infant begins to roll over deliberately (rather than accidentally, as before)—first from front to back and then from back to front. The average baby can sit without support by 6 months of age and can assume a sitting position without help about two and a half months later.

Table 4-5 Milestones of Motor Development

Skill	50 Percent	90 Percent
Rolling over	3.2 months	5.4 months
Grasping rattle	3.3 months	3.9 months
Sitting without support	5.9 months	6.8 months
Standing while holding on	7.2 months	8.5 months
Grasping with thumb and finger	8.2 months	10.2 months
Standing alone well	11.5 months	13.7 months
Walking well	12.3 months	14.9 months
Building tower of two cubes	14.8 months	20.6 months
Walking up steps	16.6 months	21.6 months
Jumping in place	23.8 months	2.4 years
Copying circle	3.4 years	4.0 years

Note: This table shows the approximate ages when 50 percent and 90 percent of children can perform each skill, according to the Denver Training Manual II.

Source: Adapted from Frankenburg et al., 1992.

BOX 4-2

Digging Deeper
The Far-Reaching Implications of Crawling

Between 7 and 9 months, babies change greatly in many ways. They show an understanding of such concepts as "near" and "far." They imitate more complex behaviors, and they show new fears; but they also show a new sense of security around their parents and other caregivers. Since these changes involve so many different psychological functions and processes and occur during such a short time span, some observers tie them all in with a reorganization of brain function. This neurological development may be set in motion by a skill that emerges at this time: crawling, which makes it possible for a baby to get around independently. Crawling has been called a "setting event" because it sets the stage for other changes in the infant and his or her relationships with the environment and the people in it (Bertenthal & Campos, 1987; Bertenthal, Campos, & Barrett, 1984; Bertenthal, Campos, & Kermoian, 1994).

Crawling exerts a powerful influence on babies' cognitive development by giving them a new view of the world. Infants become more sensitive to where objects are, how big they are, whether they can be moved, and how they look. Crawling helps babies learn to judge distances and perceive depth. As they move about, they see that people and objects look different close up than far away. Crawling babies can differentiate similar forms that are unlike in color, size, or location (J. Campos, Bertenthal, & Benson, 1980). Babies are more successful in finding a toy hidden in a box when they crawl around the box than when they are carried around it (Benson & Uzgiris, 1985).

The ability to crawl gets babies into new situations. As they become more mobile, they begin to hear such warnings as "Come back!" and "Don't touch!" They receive loving help as adult hands pick them up and turn them in a safer direction. They learn to look to caregivers for clues as to whether a situation is secure or frightening—a skill known as social referencing (see Chapter 6). Crawling babies do more social referencing than babies who have not yet begun to crawl (J. B. Garland, 1982). Crawling babies also may develop fear of heights; they learn to be afraid of places from which they might fall.

The ability to move from one place to another has other emotional and social implications. Crawling babies are no longer "prisoners" of place. If Ashley wants to be close to her mother and far away from a strange dog, she can move toward the one and away from the other. This is an important step in developing a sense of mastery, enhancing self-confidence and self-esteem.

Thus the physical milestone of crawling has far-reaching effects in helping babies see and respond to their world in new ways.

What's Your View?

Which do you think has more important overall effects on development: crawling or walking? Why? Would you consider walking to be a setting event? Can you think of any other milestones that might be considered setting events?

Check It Out:

For more information on this topic, go to www.mhhe.com/papaliah9, where you will find links to articles that discuss the movement of babies and young children.

Between 6 and 10 months, most babies begin to get around under their own power by means of creeping or crawling. This new achievement of *self-locomotion* has striking cognitive and psychosocial ramifications (see Box 4-2).

By holding onto a helping hand or a piece of furniture, the average baby can stand at a little past 7 months of age. A little more than four months later, most babies let go and stand alone. The average baby can stand well about two weeks or so before the first birthday.

All these developments lead up to the major motor achievement of infancy: walking. Humans begin to walk later than other species, possibly because babies' heavy heads and short legs make balance difficult. For some months before they can stand without support, babies practice "cruising" while holding onto furniture. Soon after they can stand alone well, at about $11\frac{1}{2}$ months, most infants take their first unaided steps. Within a few weeks, soon after the first birthday, the average child is walking well and thus achieves the status of toddler.

Many U.S. parents put their babies in mobile walkers in the belief that the babies will learn to walk earlier. Actually, by restricting babies' motor exploration, and sometimes their view of their own movements, walkers may *delay* motor skill development

(Siegel & Burton, 1999). Furthermore, walkers can be dangerous. In 1999, an estimated 8,800 children less than 15 months old were treated in emergency rooms for injuries connected with walkers. The American Academy of Pediatrics has therefore called for a ban on their manufacture and sale (AAP Committee on Injury and Poison Prevention, 2001b).

During the second year, children begin to climb stairs one at a time, putting one foot after another on the same step; later they will alternate feet. Walking down stairs comes later. In their second year, toddlers run and jump. By age $3\frac{1}{2}$, most children can balance briefly on one foot and begin to hop.

How Motor Development Occurs: Maturation in Context The sequence just described was traditionally thought to be genetically programmed—a largely automatic, preordained series of steps directed by the maturing brain. Today, many developmental scientists consider this view too simplistic. Instead, according to Esther Thelen (1995), motor development is a continuous process of interaction between baby and environment.

Thelen points to the *walking reflex:* stepping movements a neonate makes when held upright with the feet touching a surface. This behavior usually disappears by the fourth month. Not until the latter part of the first year, when a baby is getting ready to walk, do such movements appear again. The usual explanation is a shift to cortical control: an older baby's deliberate walking is seen as a new skill that reflects the brain's development. But, Thelen observes, a newborn's stepping involves the same kinds of movements the neonate makes while lying down and kicking. Why would stepping stop, only to reappear months later, whereas kicking continues? The answer, she suggests, may be that babies' legs become thicker and heavier during the early months, but not yet strong enough to carry the increased weight (Thelen & Fisher, 1982, 1983). In fact, when young infants are held in warm water, which helps support their legs, stepping reappears. Their ability to produce the movement has not changed—only the physical and environmental conditions that inhibit or promote it.

Maturation alone cannot explain such an observation, says Thelen. Infant and environment form an interconnected system, and development has interacting causes. One is the infant's motivation to do something (say, pick up a toy or get to the other side of the room). The infant's physical characteristics and his or her position in a particular setting (for example, lying in a crib or being held upright in a pool) offer opportunities and constraints that affect whether and how the baby can achieve the goal. Ultimately, a solution emerges as the baby tries out behaviors and retains those that most efficiently do the job. Rather than being solely in charge of this process, the maturing brain is only one part of it.

According to Thelen, normal babies develop the same skills in the same order because they are built approximately the same way and have similar physical challenges and needs. Thus they eventually discover that walking is more efficient than crawling in most situations. Thelen's hypothesis—that this discovery arises from each particular baby's experience in a particular context—may help explain why some babies learn to walk earlier than others.

Motor Development and Perception Sensory perceptions allow infants to learn about their environment so they can navigate in it. Motor experience sharpens and modifies their perceptions of what will happen if they move in a certain way. They "perceive in order to act, and . . . act in order to perceive" (Pick, 1992). This bidirectional connection between perception and action gives infants much useful information about themselves and their world.

Infants begin reaching for and grasping objects at about 4 to 5 months; by $5\frac{1}{2}$ months, they can adapt their reach to moving or spinning objects (Wentworth,

visual guidance The use of the eyes to guide the movement of the hands (or other parts of the body).

Benson, & Haith, 2000). Piaget and other researchers long believed that reaching depended on **visual guidance:** the use of the eyes to guide the movement of the hands (or other parts of the body). Now, research has found that infants in that age group can use other sensory cues to reach for an object. They can locate an unseen rattle by its sound, and they can reach for a glowing object in the dark, even though they cannot see their hands (Clifton, Muir, Ashmead, & Clarkson, 1993). They also can reach for an object based only on their memory of its location (McCarty, Clifton, Ashmead, Lee, & Goubet, 2001). Slightly older infants, 5 to $7\frac{1}{2}$ months old, can grasp a moving, fluorescent object in the dark—a feat that requires awareness, not only of how their own hands move, but also of the object's path and speed, so as to anticipate the likely point of contact (Robin, Berthier, & Clifton, 1996).

No matter how enticing a mother's arm are, this baby is staying away from them. As young as she is, she can perceive depth and wants to avoid falling off what looks like a cliff.

In a classic experiment by Richard Walk and Eleanor Gibson (1961), 6-month-old babies were placed on a plexiglass tabletop, over a checkerboard pattern that created the illusion of a vertical drop in the center of the table—a **visual cliff.** Would the infants perceive the illusion of depth? The babies did see a difference between the "ledge" and the "drop." They crawled freely on the "ledge" but avoided the "drop," even when they saw their mothers beckoning on the far side of the table.

visual cliff Apparatus designed to give an illusion of depth and used to assess depth perception in infants.

depth perception Ability to perceive objects and surfaces three-dimensionally.

haptic perception Ability to acquire information about properties of objects, such as size, weight, and texture, by handling them.

Depth perception, the ability to perceive objects and surfaces three-dimensionally, depends on several kinds of cues that affect the image of an object on the retina of the eye. These cues involve not only binocular coordination (both eyes working together), present by about 5 months, but also motor control (Bushnell & Boudreau, 1993). Kinetic cues are changes in an image with movement either of the object or of the observer. To find out which is moving, a baby might hold his or her head still for a moment, an ability that is well established by about 3 months.

Sometime between 5 and 7 months, babies respond to such cues as relative size and differences in texture and shading. To judge depth from these cues, babies depend on **haptic perception,** the ability to acquire information by handling objects rather than just looking at them. Haptic perception comes only after babies develop enough eye-hand coordination to reach for objects and grasp them (Bushnell & Boudreau, 1993).

affordance In the Gibsons' ecological theory of perception, the fit between a person's physical attributes and capabilities and characteristics of the environment.

ecological theory of perception Theory developed by Eleanor and James Gibson, which describes developing motor and perceptual abilities as interdependent parts of a functional system that guides behavior in varying contexts.

Eleanor and James Gibson's Ecological Theory How do crawling babies decide whether to try to cross a muddy patch or climb a hill? Crawling and, later, walking require infants to continually perceive, or size up, the "fit," or **affordance** between their own physical attributes and capabilities (such as arm and leg length, endurance, and strength) and the characteristics of the environment. (Is a moving ball close or far away? Is it low enough to catch? Is the ground too rough to walk on?)

Scientific awareness of the link between perception and action, and of the concept of affordances, is indebted to research beginning during the 1950s by Eleanor Gibson and James J. Gibson, which underlies their **ecological theory of perception** (E. J. Gibson, 1969; J. J. Gibson, 1979; Gibson & Pick, 2000). According to the Gibsons, sensory and motor activity are more or less coordinated from birth (Berthenthal & Clifton, 1998). Perceptual learning occurs through a growing ability to detect and distinguish, or differentiate, the many features of a rich sensory environment. It is this ability that permits infants and toddlers to recognize affordances, and this awareness is necessary to successfully negotiate a terrain.

With experience, babies become better able to gauge the environment in which they move and to adapt their locomotion accordingly. When crawling and walking babies (average ages $8\frac{1}{2}$ and 14 months) were placed on a walkway with an adjustable slope, neither the crawlers nor the walkers hesitated to climb uphill, a task that posed little danger. Going downhill was a different story. The inexperienced crawlers plunged down even the steepest slopes. The older and more experienced walkers walked down a shallow slope but slid down a steep one or avoided it altogether (Eppler, Adolph, & Weiner, 1996). Thus, as the Gibsonian perspective suggests, locomotor development seems to depend on increased sensitivity to affordances and is an outcome of both perception and action.

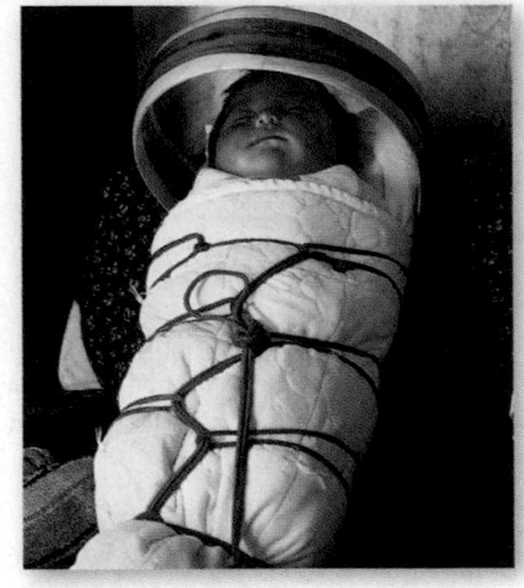

Some observers have suggested that babies from the Yucatan develop motor skills later than American babies because they are swaddled. However, Navajo babies like this one also are swaddled for most of the day, and they begin to walk at about the same time as other American babies, suggesting a hereditary explanation.

Cultural Influences on Motor Development Although motor development follows a virtually universal sequence, its *pace* does seem to respond to certain contextual factors. A normal rate of development in one culture may not be in another.

African babies tend to be more advanced than U. S. and European infants in sitting, walking, and running. In Uganda, for example, babies typically walk at 10 months, as compared with 12 months in the United States and 15 months in France (Gardiner et al., 1998). Asian babies tend to develop these skills more slowly. Such differences may in part be related to ethnic differences in temperament (H. Kaplan & Dove, 1987; see Chapter 6) or may reflect a culture's childrearing practices (Gardiner et al., 1998).

Some cultures actively encourage early development of motor skills. In many African and West Indian cultures with advanced infant motor development, adults use special "handling routines," such as bouncing and stepping exercises, to strengthen babies' muscles (Hopkins & Westra, 1988). In one study, Jamaican infants, whose mothers used such handling routines daily, sat, crawled, and walked earlier than English infants, whose mothers gave them no such special handling (Hopkins & Westra, 1990).

On the other hand, some cultures discourage early motor development. Children of the Ache in eastern Paraguay do not begin to walk until 18 to 20 months of age—about 9 months later than U.S. babies (H. Kaplan & Dove, 1987). Ache mothers pull their babies back to their laps when the infants begin to crawl away. The Ache mothers closely supervise their babies to protect them from the hazards of nomadic life. Yet, as 8- to 10-year-olds, Ache children climb tall trees, chop branches, and play in ways that enhance their motor skills (H. Kaplan & Dove, 1987). Normal development, then, need not follow the same timetable to reach the same destination.

Checkpoint

Can you . . .

- Trace a typical infant's progress in head control, hand control, and locomotion, according to the Denver norms?
- Explain and give examples of the bidirectional relationship between perception and action?
- Tell how Gibson's theory of ecological perception explains infants' or toddlers' behavior when confronted with challenging terrain?
- Discuss how cultural influences affect early motor development?

Refocus

- What changes in the customs and risks surrounding childbirth have occurred since Elvis Presley's birth?
- What resources available today might have changed the course of Gladys Presley's pregnancy and delivery?

By the time small children can run, jump, and play with toys requiring fairly sophisticated coordination, they are very different from the neonates described at the beginning of this chapter. The cognitive changes that have taken place are equally dramatic, as we discuss in Chapter 5.

SUMMARY AND KEY TERMS

The Birth Process

Guidepost 1. What happens during each of the four stages of childbirth?

- Birth normally occurs after a preparatory period of parturition and consists of four stages: (1) dilation of the cervix; (2) descent and emergence of the baby; (3) expulsion of the umbilical cord and the placenta; (4) contraction of the uterus and recovery of the mother.
- Electronic fetal monitoring is widely used (and may be overused) during labor and delivery. It is intended to detect signs of fetal distress, especially in high-risk births.

parturition *(109)*

electronic fetal monitoring *(110)*

Guidepost 2. What alternative settings and methods of delivery are available today?

- About 23 percent of births in the United States are by cesarean delivery—an unnecessarily high rate, according to critics.
- Natural or prepared childbirth can minimize the need for pain-killing drugs and maximize parents' active involvement. Modern epidurals can give effective pain relief with smaller doses of medication than in the past.
- Delivery at home or in birth centers, and attendance by midwives, are alternatives to physician-attended hospital delivery for women with normal, low-risk pregnancies who want to involve family members and make the experience more intimate and personal. The presence of a doula can provide physical benefits as well as emotional support.

cesarean delivery *(111)*

natural childbirth *(112)*

prepared childbirth *(112)*

The Newborn Baby

Guidepost 3. How do newborn infants adjust to life outside the womb?

- The neonatal period is a time of transition from intrauterine to extrauterine life. During the first few days, the neonate loses weight and then regains it; the lanugo (prenatal hair) falls off and the protective coating of vernix caseosa dries up. The fontanels (soft spots) in the skull close within the first eighteen months.
- At birth, the circulatory, respiratory, gastrointestinal, and temperature regulation systems become independent of the mother's. If a newborn cannot start breathing within about 5 minutes, brain injury may occur.
- Newborns have a strong sucking reflex and secrete meconium from the intestinal tract. They are commonly subject to neonatal jaundice, due to immaturity of the liver.
- A newborn's state of arousal is governed by periodic cycles of wakefulness, sleep, and activity, which seem to be inborn. Sleep takes up the major, but a diminishing, amount of a neonate's time. Newborns' activity levels show stability and may be early indicators of temperament. Parents' responsiveness to babies' states and activity levels is an important influence on development.

neonatal period *(113)*

neonate *(113)*

anoxia *(114)*

meconium *(114)*

neonatal jaundice *(114)*

state of arousal *(114)*

Survival and Health

Guidepost 4. How can we tell whether a new baby is healthy and is developing normally?

- At 1 minute and 5 minutes after birth, a neonate's Apgar score can indicate how well he or she is adjusting to extrauterine life. The Brazelton Neonatal Behavioral Assessment Scale can assess responses to the environment and predict future development.
- Neonatal screening is done for certain rare conditions, such as PKU and congenital hypothyroidism.

Apgar scale *(116)*

Brazelton Neonatal Behavioral Assessment Scale (NBAS) *(117)*

Guidepost 5. What complications of childbirth can endanger newborn babies' adjustment or even their lives?

- A small minority of infants suffer lasting effects of birth trauma. Other complications include low birthweight and postmature birth.
- Low-birthweight babies may be either preterm (premature) or small-for-date (small-for-gestational age). Low birthweight is a major factor in infant mortality and can cause long-term physical and cognitive problems. Very-low-birthweight babies have a less promising prognosis than those who weigh more.

birth trauma *(118)*

postmature *(118)*

low birthweight *(118)*

preterm (premature) infants *(118)*

small-for-date (small-for-gestational age) infants *(118)*

Guidepost 6. How can we enhance babies' chances of survival and health?

- A supportive postnatal environment and other protective factors often can improve the outcome for babies suffering from birth complications.
- Although infant mortality has diminished, it is still disturbingly high for African American babies, who are more likely to have low birthweight.
- Sudden infant death syndrome (SIDS) is the leading cause of death of U.S. infants after the first month. Major risk factors include exposure to smoke and, prenatally, to caffeine, and sleeping in the prone position.
- Vaccine-preventable diseases have declined as rates of immunization have improved, but many preschoolers are not fully protected.

protective factors *(122)*

infant mortality rate *(123)*

sudden infant death syndrome (SIDS) *(124)*

Early Physical Development

Guidepost 7. What influences the growth of body and brain?

- Normal physical growth and sensory and motor development proceed according to the cephalocaudal and proximodistal principles.
- A child's body grows most dramatically during the first year of life; growth proceeds at a rapid but diminishing rate throughout the first three years.
- Breast-feeding offers many health advantages and sensory and cognitive benefits, but only about two-thirds of mothers begin breast-feeding.
- Obese babies are *not* at special risk of becoming obese adults, unless they have obese parents. However, too much fat and cholesterol intake may lead to eventual cardiac problems.
- Sleep patterns change dramatically; by the second half of the first year, babies do most of their sleeping at night. Cultural customs affect sleep patterns.
- The central nervous system controls sensorimotor activity. Lateralization enables each hemisphere of the brain to specialize in different functions.
- The brain grows most rapidly during the months before and immediately after birth as neurons migrate to their assigned locations, form synaptic connections, and undergo integration and differentiation. Cell death and myelination improve the efficiency of the nervous system.
- Reflex behaviors—primitive, locomotor, and postural—are indications of neurological status. Most early reflexes drop out during the first year as voluntary, cortical control develops.
- Especially during the early period of rapid growth, environmental experience can influence brain development positively or negatively.

central nervous system *(129)*
lateralization *(129)*
neurons *(130)*
integration *(131)*
differentiation *(131)*
cell death *(132)*
myelination *(132)*
reflex behaviors *(133)*
plasticity *(134)*

Guidepost 8. When do the senses develop?

- Sensory capacities, present from birth and even in the womb, develop rapidly in the first months of life. Very young infants show pronounced abilities to discriminate between stimuli.
- Touch seems to be the first sense to develop and mature. Newborns are sensitive to pain. Smell, taste, and hearing also begin to develop in the womb.
- Vision is the least well developed sense at birth. Peripheral vision, color perception, acuteness of focus, binocular vision, and the ability to follow a moving object with the eyes all develop within the first few months.

Guidepost 9. What are some early milestones in motor development, and what are some influences on it?

- Motor skills develop in a certain sequence, which may depend largely on maturation but also on context, experience, and motivation. Simple skills combine into increasingly complex systems.
- Self-locomotion seems to be a "setting event," bringing about changes in all domains of development.
- Perception is intimately related to motor development. Depth perception and haptic perception develop in the first half of the first year.
- According to Eleanor and James Gibson's theory of ecological perception, awareness of affordances affects infants' and toddlers' ability to get around.
- Environmental factors, including cultural practices, may influence the pace of early motor development.

systems of action *(138)*
Denver Developmental Screening Test *(138)*
gross motor skills *(138)*
fine motor skills *(138)*
visual guidance *(142)*
visual cliff *(142)*
depth perception *(142)*
haptic perception *(142)*
affordance *(142)*
ecological theory of perception *(142)*

Chapter 5

Cognitive Development During the First Three Years

So runs my dream; but what am I?
An infant crying in the night;
An infant crying for the light,
And with no language but a cry.

—Alfred, Lord Tennyson, *In Memoriam*, Canto 54

Focus: "Doddy" Darwin, Naturalist's Son

Charles and "Doddy" Darwin

On December 27, 1839, when the naturalist Charles Darwin was 30 years old, his first baby, William Erasmus Darwin, affectionately known as Doddy, was born. That day—twenty years before the publication of Charles Darwin's *Origin of Species,* which outlined his theory of evolution based on natural selection—the proud father began keeping a diary of observations of his newborn son. It was these notes, published in 1877,* that first called scientific attention to the developmental nature of infant behavior.

What abilities are babies born with? How do they learn about their world? How do they communicate, first nonverbally and then through language? These were among the questions Darwin sought to answer—questions still central to the study of cognitive development.

Darwin's keen eye illuminates how coordination of physical and mental activity helps an infant adapt to the world—as in this entry written when Doddy was 4 months old:

> Took my finger to his mouth & as usual could not get it in, on account of his own hand being in the way; then he slipped his own back & so got my finger in.—This was not chance & therefore a kind of reasoning. (Diary, p. 12; quoted in Keegan & Gruber, 1985, p. 135)

In Darwin's notes, we can see Doddy developing new cognitive skills through interaction not only with his father's finger, but with other objects as well. The diary depicts a series of encounters with reflected images. In these episodes Doddy gains knowledge, not in sudden bursts or jumps, but through gradual integration of new experience with existing patterns of behavior. In Darwin's view—as, later, in Piaget's—this was not merely a matter of piling new knowledge upon old; it involved an actual transformation of the way the mind is organized.

*The source for analysis of Darwin's diary was Keegan and Gruber (1985).

OUTLINE

When Doddy, at $4\frac{1}{2}$ months, saw his likeness and his father's in a mirror, Darwin noted that the baby "seemed surprised at my voice coming from behind him, my image being in front" (Diary, p. 18; quoted in Keegan & Gruber, 1985, p. 135). Two months later, Doddy apparently had solved the mystery: now, when his father, standing behind him, made a funny face in the mirror, the infant "was aware that the image . . . was not real & therefore . . . turned round to look" (Diary, pp. 21–22; quoted in Keegan & Gruber, 1985, pp. 135–136).

At first, this newfound understanding did not generalize to other reflective materials. Two weeks later, Doddy seemed puzzled to see his father's reflection in a window. By 9 months, however, the boy realized that "the shadow of a hand, made by a candle, was to be looked for behind, in [the] same manner as in [a] looking glass" (Diary, p. 23; quoted in Keegan & Gruber, 1985, p. 136). His recognition that reflections could emanate from objects behind him now extended to shadows, another kind of two-dimensional image.

Darwin was particularly interested in documenting his son's progress in communication. He believed that language acquisition is a natural process, akin to earlier physical expressions of feelings. Through smiling, crying, laughing, facial expressions, and sounds of pleasure or pain, Doddy managed to communicate quite well with his parents even before uttering his first word. One of his first meaningful verbal expressions was "Ah!"—uttered when he recognized an image in a glass.

Darwin made these observations more than 160 years ago, at a time when infants' cognitive abilities were widely underestimated. We now know—as Darwin inferred from his observations of Doddy—that normal, healthy infants are born with the ability to learn and remember and with a capacity for acquiring and using speech. They use their growing sensory and cognitive capacities to exert control over their behavior and their world.

In this chapter we look at infants' and toddlers' cognitive abilities from three classic perspectives—behaviorist, psychometric, and Piagetian—and then from three newer perspectives: information processing, cognitive neuroscientific, and social-contextual. We trace the early development of language and discuss how it comes about. Finally, we see how adults help infants and toddlers become more competent with language.

After you have studied this chapter, you should be able to answer each of the following Guidepost questions. Look for them again in the margins, where they point to important concepts throughout the chapter. To check your understanding of these Guideposts, review the end-of-chapter summary. Checkpoints located at periodic spots throughout the chapter will help you verify your understanding of what you have read.

Guideposts for Study

1. How do infants learn, and how long can they remember?
2. Can infants' and toddlers' intelligence be measured, and how can it be improved?
3. How did Piaget describe infants' and toddlers' cognitive development, and how have his claims stood up?
4. How can we measure infants' ability to process information, and how does this ability relate to future intelligence?
5. When do babies begin to think about characteristics of the physical world?
6. What can brain research reveal about the development of cognitive skills?
7. How does social interaction with adults advance cognitive competence?
8. How do babies develop language?
9. What influences contribute to linguistic progress?

Studying Cognitive Development: Classic Approaches

How and when do babies begin to learn, to think, and to solve problems? How and when does memory develop? Are some babies smarter than others? Many investigators have taken one of three classic approaches to the study of such questions, which fall in the domain of *cognitive development:*

- The **behaviorist approach** studies the basic *mechanics* of learning. It is concerned with how behavior changes in response to experience.
- The **psychometric approach** seeks to *measure quantitative differences* in cognitive abilities by using tests that indicate or predict these abilities.
- The **Piagetian approach** looks at changes, or stages, in the *quality* of cognitive functioning. It is concerned with how the mind structures its activities and adapts to the environment.

behaviorist approach Approach to the study of cognitive development that is concerned with basic mechanics of learning.

psychometric approach Approach to the study of cognitive development that seeks to measure the quantity of intelligence a person possesses.

Piagetian approach Approach to the study of cognitive development that describes qualitative stages in cognitive functioning.

All three approaches, as well as the three newer ones we discuss in the following section—the information-processing, cognitive neuroscience, and social-contextual approaches—help us understand cognitive development.

Behaviorist Approach: Basic Mechanics of Learning

Babies are born with the ability to learn from what they see, hear, smell, taste, and touch, and they have some ability to remember what they learn. Of course, maturation is essential to this process. But while learning theorists recognize maturation as a limiting factor, their main interest is in mechanisms of learning.

Let's look first at two learning processes that behaviorists study: *classical conditioning* and *operant conditioning.* Later we will consider *habituation,* another form of learning that information-processing researchers study.

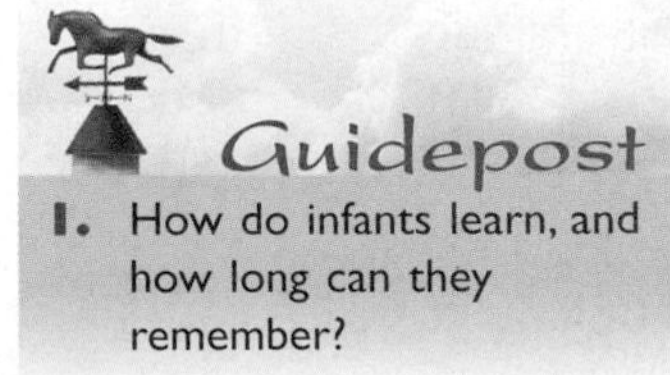

Guidepost

1. How do infants learn, and how long can they remember?

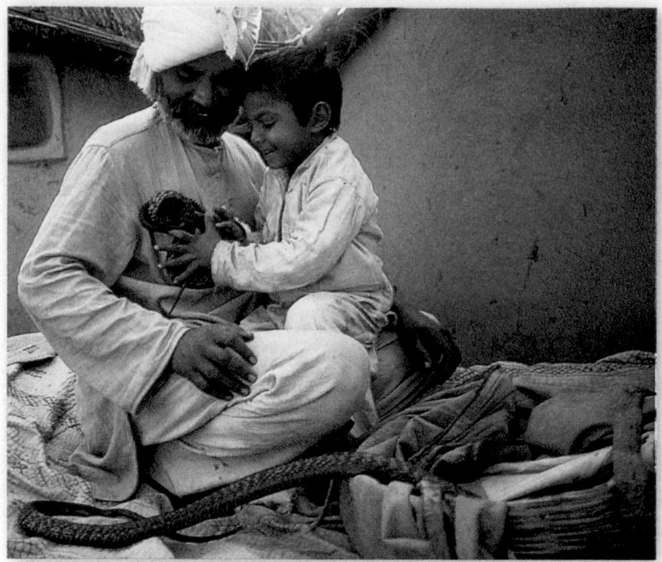

An Indian snake charmer's son eagerly plays with a snake the father has trained, showing that fear of snakes is a learned response. Children can be conditioned to fear animals that are associated with unpleasant or frightening experiences, as "Little Albert" was in a classic study by John B. Watson and Rosalie Rayner.

Classical and Operant Conditioning Eager to capture Anna's memorable moments on film, her father took pictures of the infant smiling, crawling, and showing off her other achievements. Whenever the flash went off, Anna blinked. One evening when Anna was 11 months old, she saw her father hold the camera up to his eye—and she blinked *before* the flash. She had learned to associate the camera with the bright light, so that the sight of the camera alone activated her blinking reflex.

Anna's blinking at the sight of the camera is an example of **classical conditioning,** in which a person learns to make a reflex, or involuntary, response to a stimulus (the camera) that originally did not provoke the response (see Figure 5-1). In classical conditioning, a person (or animal) learns to anticipate an event before it happens by forming associations between stimuli (such as the camera and the flash) that regularly occur together. Classically conditioned learning will fade, or become *extinct,* if it is not reinforced. Thus, if Anna frequently saw the camera without the flash, she eventually would stop blinking.

A baby's smiling to get loving attention from his parents (refer back to Chapter 2) is an example of **operant conditioning,** learning based on reinforcement (or punishment), in which the learner acts, or operates on, and influences the environment. The infant learns to make a certain response (smiling) in order to produce a particular effect (parental attention), which reinforces the learned response. Operant conditioning enables infants to learn voluntary behaviors, such as smiling, as opposed to involuntary behaviors, such as blinking.

classical conditioning Learning based on associating a stimulus that does not ordinarily elicit a response with another stimulus that does elicit the response.

operant conditioning Learning based on reinforcement or punishment.

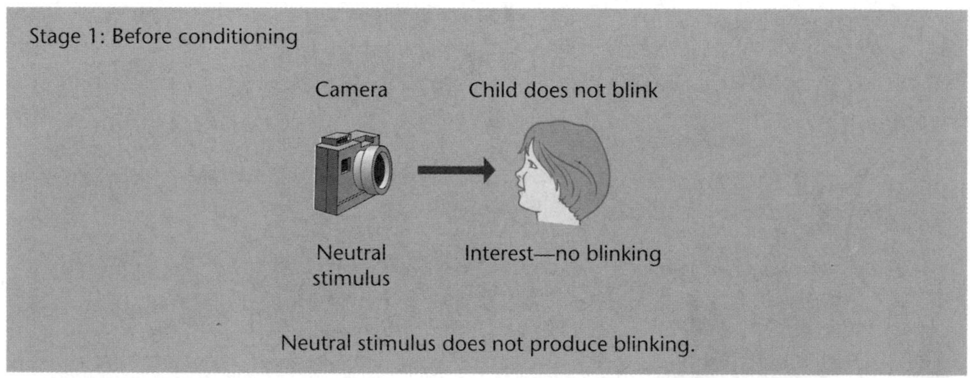

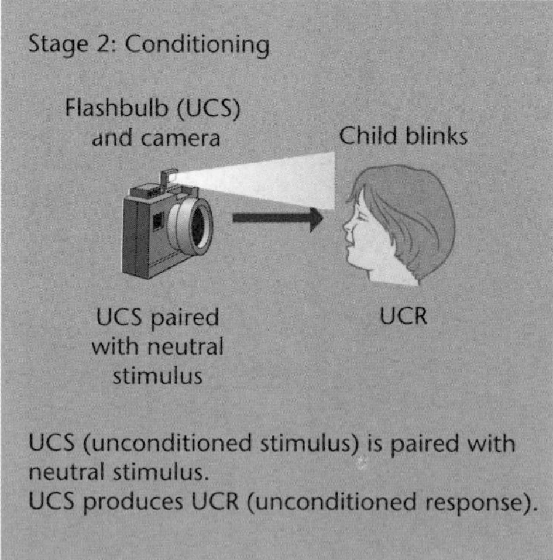

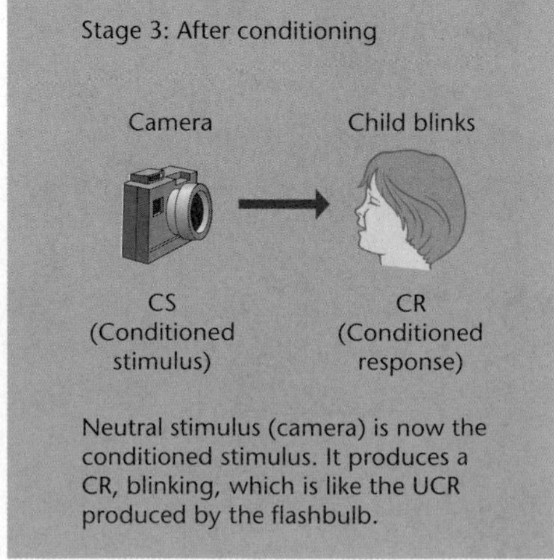

Figure 5-1
Three steps in classical conditioning.

Researchers often use operant conditioning to study other phenomena, such as fetal hearing and memory. In Chapter 4, we reported several studies in which infants' sucking of a nipple would start or stop a song or spoken passage. Newborns sucked more to turn on recordings of sounds they had heard in the womb than to turn on recordings of unfamiliar sounds. Studies such as these are based on infants' ability to learn that a behavior they already know how to do (suck) can bring on a desired effect (familiar sounds).

Babies 2 to 6 months old can remember, after a hiatus of two days to two weeks, that they were able to activate a mobile by kicking; they show this by kicking as soon as they see the mobile.

Infant Memory Can you remember anything that happened to you before you were 3 years old? The chances are you can't. This inability to remember early events is called *infantile amnesia.* One explanation, held by Piaget (1969) and others, is that early events are not stored in memory because the brain is not yet developed enough. Freud believed that early memories are stored but are repressed because they are emotionally troubling. Other researchers suggest that children cannot store events in memory until they can talk about them (Nelson, 1992).

Now, research using operant conditioning with nonverbal, age-appropriate tasks suggests that infants' memory processes may be much like those of older children and adults, except that their retention time is shorter. These studies have found that babies will repeat an action days or weeks later—*if* they are periodically reminded of the situation in which they learned it (Rovee-Collier, 1999).

In these experiments infants are operantly conditioned to kick to activate a mobile attached to one ankle by a ribbon. Babies 2 to 6 months old, when again shown the mobiles days or weeks later, repeat the kicking, even though their legs are no longer attached to the mobiles. When the infants see the mobiles, they kick more than before the conditioning, showing that recognition of the mobiles triggers a memory of their initial experience with them (Rovee-Collier, 1996, 1999).

In a similar task designed for older infants and toddlers, the child is conditioned to press a lever to make a miniature train go around a track. The length of time a conditioned response can be retained increases with age (see Figure 5-2), from two

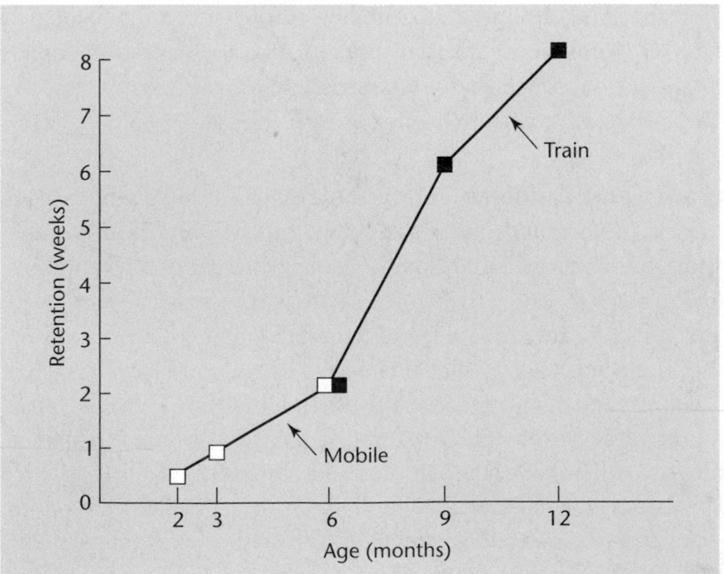

Figure 5-2
Maximum number of weeks that infants of varying ages show retention of how to operate either a mobile or a miniature train. Regardless of the task, retention improves with age. (*Source:* Rovee-Collier, 1999, Fig. 4, p. 83.)

Checkpoint

Can you . . .

- Distinguish the goals of the behaviorist, psychometric, and Piagetian approaches to the study of cognitive development?
- Identify conditions under which newborns can be classically or operantly conditioned?
- Summarize what studies of operant conditioning have shown about infant memory?

days for 2-month-olds to thirteen weeks for 18-month-olds (Hartshorn et al., 1998; Rovee-Collier, 1996, 1999). Furthermore, the memory span of very young infants can be increased by dividing their training time into more sessions (Hartshorn et al., 1998; Rovee-Collier, 1996).

Young infants' memory of a behavior seems to be specifically linked to the original cue. Two- to 6-month-olds will repeat a learned behavior only when they see the original mobile or train. However, older infants, between 9 and 12 months, will "try out" the behavior on a different train, if no more than two weeks have gone by since the training (Rovee-Collier, 1999).

Context can affect recollection when a memory has weakened. Three-, 9-, and 12-month-olds initially can recognize the mobile or train in a different setting from the one in which they were trained, but not after long delays. However, periodic brief exposure to the original stimulus can sustain a memory from early infancy through $1\frac{1}{2}$ to 2 years of age (Rovee-Collier, 1999).

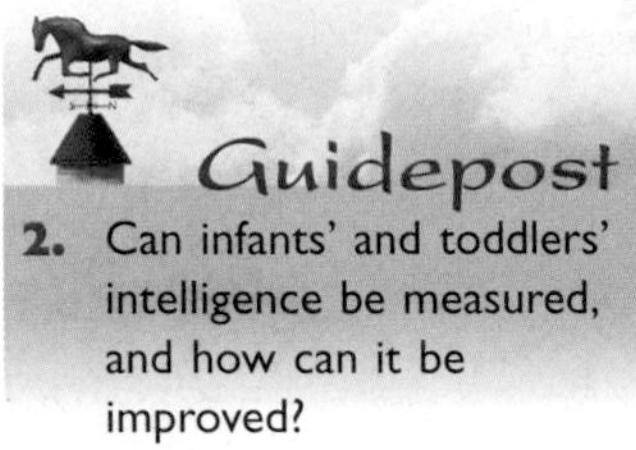

2. Can infants' and toddlers' intelligence be measured, and how can it be improved?

Psychometric Approach: Developmental and Intelligence Testing

When Doddy Darwin, at 4 months, figured out how to get his father's finger into his mouth by moving his own hand out of the way, he showed **intelligent behavior.** Intelligent behavior is *goal-oriented* and *adaptive:* directed at adjusting to the circumstances and conditions of life. Intelligence enables people to acquire, remember, and use knowledge; to understand concepts and relationships; and to solve everyday problems.

intelligent behavior Behavior that is goal-oriented and adaptive to circumstances and conditions of life.

The precise nature of intelligence has been debated for many years, as has the best way to measure it. Beginning in the nineteenth century, there were attempts to measure intelligence by such characteristics as head size and reaction time, and then by tests that scored strength of hand squeeze, pain sensitivity, weight discrimination, judgment of time, and rote recall. However, these tests had little predictive value.

Then, at the beginning of the twentieth century, school administrators in Paris asked the psychologist Alfred Binet to devise a way to identify children who could not handle academic work and who should be given special training. The test that Binet and his colleague Theodore Simon developed was the forerunner of psychometric tests, used for children of all levels of ability, which score intelligence by numbers. One is the Stanford-Binet Intelligence Scale, an American version of the traditional Binet-Simon tests (see Chapter 7).

The goals of psychometric testing are to measure quantitatively the factors that are thought to make up intelligence (such as comprehension and reasoning) and, from the results of that measurement, to predict future performance (such as school achievement). **IQ (intelligence quotient) tests** consist of questions or tasks that are supposed to show how much of the measured abilities a person has, by comparing that person's performance with that of other test-takers.

IQ (intelligence quotient) tests Psychometric tests that seek to measure intelligence by comparing a test-taker's performance with standardized norms.

Testing Infants and Toddlers For school-age children, intelligence test scores can predict academic performance fairly accurately and reliably. Testing infants and toddlers is another matter. Since babies cannot tell us what they know and how they think, the most obvious way to gauge their intelligence is by assessing what they can do. But if they do not grasp a rattle, it is hard to tell whether they do not know how, do not feel like doing it, do not realize what is expected of them, or have simply lost interest.

Although it is virtually impossible to measure infants' intelligence, it *is* possible to test their cognitive development. If parents are worried because a baby is not doing the same things as other babies the same age, developmental testing may reassure them that development is normal—or may alert them to a problem. Developmental tests compare a baby's performance on a series of tasks with norms established on the basis of observation of what large numbers of infants and toddlers can do at particular ages.

Table 5-1 Sample Tasks in the Bayley Scales of Infant Development

Age (in months)	Mental Scale*	Motor Scale*
1	Eyes follow moving person	Lifts head when held at shoulder
3	Reaches for suspended ring	Turns from back to side
6	Manipulates bell, showing interest in detail	Turns from back to stomach
9	Jabbers expressively	Raises self to standing position
12	Pats toy in imitation	Walks alone
14–16	Uses two different words appropriately	Walks up stairs with help
20–22	Names three objects	Jumps off floor with both feet
26–28	Matches four colors	Imitates hand movements
32–34	Uses past tense	Walks up stairs, alternating feet
38–42	Counts	Walks down stairs, alternating feet

*Task most children this age can do
Source: Bayley, 1993.

Bayley Scales of Infant Development Standardized test of infants' mental, motor, and behavioral development.

The **Bayley Scales of Infant Development** (Bayley, 1969, 1993; see Table 5-1) are designed to assess the developmental status of children from 1 month to $3\frac{1}{2}$ years. The Bayley-II has three sections: a *mental scale,* which measures such abilities as perception, memory, learning, and vocalization; a *motor scale,* which measures gross (large-muscle) and fine (manipulative) motor skills, including sensorimotor coordination; and a *behavior rating scale* to be completed by the examiner, in part on the basis of information from the child's caregiver. Separate scores, called *developmental quotients* (DQs), are calculated for each scale; they are based on deviation from the mean established by comparison with a normal sample. DQs are most useful for early detection of emotional disturbances and sensory, neurological, and environmental deficits.

Although these scores give a reasonably accurate picture of *current* developmental status, they are poor predictors of future functioning (Anastasi & Urbina, 1997). One likely reason is that environmental influences, such as family and neighborhood characteristics, seem to affect cognitive development more strongly as children approach age 3 (Klebanov, Brooks-Gunn, McCarton, & McCormick, 1998). Another reason is that developmental tests for babies measure mostly sensory and motor abilities, whereas intelligence tests for older children place more emphasis on verbal abilities (Bornstein & Sigman, 1986; Colombo, 1993; McCall & Carriger, 1993). Not until at least the third year of life, when children may be tested with the Stanford-Binet, do a child's IQ scores, along with other factors, such as the parents' IQ and educational level, usually help to predict later test scores (Kopp & Kaler, 1989; Kopp & McCall, 1982; McCall & Carriger, 1993). As children approach their fifth birthday, the relationship between current scores and those in later childhood becomes stronger (Bornstein & Sigman, 1986). IQ tests given near the end of kindergarten are among the best predictors of future school success (Tramontana, Hooper, & Selzer, 1988).

Assessing the Impact of the Home Environment Intelligence was once thought to be fixed at birth; we now know, as discussed in Chapter 3, that it is influenced by both inheritance and experience. What characteristics of the early home environment may influence intelligence? Using the **Home Observation for Measurement of the Environment (HOME)** (R. H. Bradley, 1989; Caldwell & Bradley, 1984), trained observers rate on a checklist the resources and atmosphere in a child's home.

Home Observation for Measurement of the Environment (HOME) Checklist to measure the influence of the home environment on children's cognitive growth.

One important factor that HOME assesses is parental responsiveness. HOME gives credit to the parent of an infant or toddler for caressing or kissing the child during an examiner's visit, to the parent of a preschooler for spontaneously praising the child, and to the parent of an older child for answering the child's questions. A longitudinal

The Home Observation for Measurement of the Environment (HOME) gives positive ratings to a parent who praises a child or answers his or her questions.

study found positive correlations between parents' responsiveness to their 6-month-olds and the children's IQ, achievement test scores, and teacher-rated classroom behavior through age 13 (Bradley, Corwyn, Burchinal, McAdoo, & Coll, 2001).

HOME also assesses the number of books in the home, the presence of playthings that encourage the development of concepts, and parents' involvement in children's play. High scores on all these factors are fairly reliable in predicting cognitive performance (Bradley, Corwyn, Burchinal, McAdoo, & Coll, 2001; Klebanov et al., 1998). In an analysis of HOME assessments of 29,264 European American, African American, and Hispanic American children in the National Longitudinal Study of Youth (NLSY), learning stimulation was consistently associated with kindergarten achievement tests, as well as with language competence and motor and social development (Bradley, Corwyn, Burchinal, McAdoo, & Coll, 2001).

Of course, some HOME items may be less culturally relevant in nonwestern than in western families (Bradley, Corwyn, McAdoo, & Coll, 2001). Also, we cannot be sure on the basis of HOME and correlational findings that parental responsiveness or an enriched home environment actually increases a child's intelligence. All we can say is that these factors are associated with high intelligence. Intelligent, well-educated parents may be more likely to provide a positive, stimulating home environment; and since they also pass their genes on to their children, there may be a genetic influence as well. (This is an example of a *passive genotype-environment correlation,* described in Chapter 3.) Adoption studies support a genetic influence (Braungart, Fulker, & Plomin, 1992; Coon, Fulker, DeFries, & Plomin, 1990).

Socioeconomic Status, Parenting Practices, and IQ The correlation between socioeconomic status and IQ is well documented (Neisser et al., 1996). Poverty can curb children's cognitive growth by limiting parents' ability to provide educational resources and by exerting a negative psychological effect on the parents and their parenting practices (McLoyd, 1990, 1998; see Chapter 10). In the NLSY sample mentioned in the previous section, poor children were less likely than nonpoor children to be exposed to developmentally enriching materials and experiences (Bradley, Corwyn, McAdoo, & Coll, 2001). Another longitudinal study suggests how specific aspects of parenting associated with SES can influence cognitive development (B. Hart & Risley, 1992, 1996).

Once a month for more than two years, until the participating children turned 3, researchers visited the homes of 40 families and observed parent-child interactions. Parents in higher-income families spent more time with their children, talked more with them, and showed more interest in what they had to say. Children whose parents did these things tended to do well on IQ tests six years later. They also did better than the other children in school and on language and achievement tests. Much more of the talk of the lower-income parents included such negative words as "stop," "quit," and "don't"; and the children of parents who talked that way had lower IQs and achievement (B. Hart & Risley, 1989, 1992, 1996; D. Walker, Greenwood, Hart, & Carta, 1994). This study pinpoints early parenting practices that *may* help account for differences in future IQ and school performance of children from higher- and lower-income families. We say "may" because, as we discuss in the next section, parenting practices may reflect parental intelligence, which itself predicts children's IQs.

Checkpoint

Can you . . .

- ✔ Tell why developmental tests are sometimes given to infants and toddlers and describe one such widely used test?
- ✔ Explain why tests of infants and toddlers are unreliable in predicting later IQ?
- ✔ Identify specific aspects of the home environment that may influence measured intelligence and other cognitive indicators, and explain why such influence is hard to show?
- ✔ Discuss the relationship between socioeconomic status, parenting practices, and cognitive development?

Early Intervention If an impoverished home environment can lower intelligence scores, can early intervention raise them? Research suggests that it can to some extent.

early intervention Systematic process of providing services to help families meet young children's developmental needs.

Early intervention, as defined under the Individuals with Disabilities Education Act, is a systematic process of planning and providing therapeutic and educational services to families that need help in meeting infants', toddlers', and preschool children's developmental needs.

Researchers have identified six **developmental priming mechanisms:**—aspects of the home environment that pave the way for normal cognitive and psychosocial development and help prepare children for school. The six mechanisms are: (1) encouragement to explore the environment; (2) mentoring in basic cognitive and social skills, such as labeling, sequencing, sorting, and comparing; (3) celebration of accomplishments; (4) guidance in practicing and expanding skills; (5) protection from inappropriate punishment, teasing, or disapproval for mistakes or unintended consequences of exploring and trying out skills; and (6) stimulation of language and other symbolic communication. The consistent presence of all six of these conditions early in life may be essential to normal brain development (C. T. Ramey & S. L. Ramey, 1998a, 1998b; S. L. Ramey & C. T. Ramey, 1992). Table 5-2 lists specific suggestions for helping babies develop cognitive competence.

developmental priming mechanisms Aspects of the home environment that seem necessary for normal cognitive and psychosocial development.

The goal of early intervention is to help children who may not be getting such developmental support. How effective is early intervention? Results from two randomly assigned, controlled studies have been positive (C. T. Ramey & S. L. Ramey, 1998b).

Project CARE (Wasik, Ramey, Bryant, & Sparling, 1990) and the Abecedarian Project (C. T. Ramey & Campbell, 1991) involved a total of 174 North Carolina babies from at-risk homes. In each project, from 6 weeks of age until kindergarten, an experimental group was enrolled in Partners for Learning, a full-day, year-round early childhood education program at a university child development center. The program had a low child-teacher ratio and used learning games to foster specific cognitive, linguistic, perceptual-motor, and social skills. Control groups received pediatric and

What's Your View?

- On the basis of the six developmental priming mechanisms listed in the text, can you suggest specific ways to help infants and toddlers get ready for schooling?

Table 5-2 Fostering Competence

Findings from the Harvard Preschool Project, from studies using the HOME scales, and from neurological studies and other research suggest the following guidelines for fostering infants' and toddlers' cognitive development:

1. In the early months, *provide sensory stimulation,* but avoid overstimulation and distracting noises.
2. As babies grow older, *create an environment that fosters learning*—one that includes books, interesting objects (which do not have to be expensive toys), and a place to play.
3. *Respond to babies' signals.* This establishes a sense of trust that the world is a friendly place and gives babies a sense of control over their lives.
4. *Give babies the power to effect changes,* through toys that can be shaken, molded, or moved. Help a baby discover that turning a doorknob opens a door, flicking a light switch turns on a light, and opening a faucet produces running water for a bath.
5. *Give babies freedom to explore.* Do not confine them regularly during the day in a crib, jump seat, or small room, and only for short periods in a playpen. Baby-proof the environment and let them go!
6. *Talk to babies.* They will not pick up language from listening to the radio or television; they need interaction with adults.
7. In talking to or playing with babies, *enter into whatever they are interested in* at the moment instead of trying to redirect their attention to something else.
8. *Arrange opportunities to learn basic skills,* such as labeling, comparing, and sorting objects (say, by size or color), putting items in sequence, and observing the consequences of actions.
9. *Applaud new skills, and help babies practice and expand them.* Stay nearby but do not hover.
10. *Read to babies in a warm, caring atmosphere from an early age.* Reading aloud and talking about the stories develop preliteracy skills.
11. *Use punishment sparingly.* Do not punish or ridicule results of normal trial-and-error exploration.

Sources: R. R. Bradley, & Caldwell, 1982; R. R. Bradley, Caldwell, & Rock, 1988; R. H. Bradley et al., 1989; C. T. Ramey & Ramey, 1998a, 1998b; S. L. Ramey & Ramey, 1992; Staso, quoted in Blakeslee, 1997; J. H. Stevens & Bakeman, 1985; B. L. White, 1971; B. L. White, Kaban, & Attanucci, 1979.

social work services, formula, and home visits, as the experimental groups did, but were not enrolled in Partners for Learning.

In both projects, the children who received the early intervention showed a widening advantage over the control groups in developmental test scores during the first eighteen months. By age 3, the average IQ of the Abecedarian children was 101, and of CARE children, 105—equal to or better than average for the general population—as compared with only 84 and 93 for the control groups (C. T. Ramey & S. L. Ramey, 1998b).

As often happens with early intervention programs, these early gains were not fully maintained. IQs dropped between ages 3 and 8, especially among children from the most disadvantaged homes. Still, scores tended to be higher and more stable among children who had been in Partners for Learning than in the control groups (Burchinal, Campbell, Bryant, Wasik, & Ramey, 1997). From then on into adulthood, both the experimental and control groups' IQs and math scores increasingly fell below national norms while reading scores held steady but below average. However, the children in the Abecedarian Project who had been enrolled in Partners for Learning continued to outdo the control group by all measures and were less likely to have repeated a grade in school (Campbell, Pungello, Miller-Johnson, Burchinal, & Ramey, 2001; C. T. Ramey et al., 2000).

Checkpoint

Can you . . .

- ✔ Identify six developmental priming mechanisms?
- ✔ Describe several early intervention programs, and summarize findings about the value of early intervention?

These findings suggest that early educational intervention can help moderate the effects of low socioeconomic status. The most effective early interventions are those that (1) start early and continue throughout the preschool years; (2) are highly time-intensive (i.e., occupy more hours in a day, or more days in a week, month, or year); (3) provide direct educational experiences, not just parental training; (4) take a comprehensive approach, including health, family counseling, and social services; and (5) are tailored to individual differences and needs. As in the two North Carolina projects, initial gains tend to diminish unless there is enough ongoing environmental support for further progress (C. T. Ramey & S. L. Ramey, 1996, 1998a).

Piagetian Approach: The Sensorimotor Stage

Guidepost

3. How did Piaget describe infants' and toddlers' cognitive development, and how have his claims stood up?

As a young man studying in Paris, Jean Piaget helped to standardize the tests Alfred Binet had developed to assess the intelligence of French schoolchildren. This work convinced him that psychometric tests miss much that is special and important about children's thinking. Piaget became intrigued by the children's wrong answers, finding in them clues to their thought processes, which were quite different from adult thought. Such observations led to Piaget's comprehensive theory of cognitive development.

Piaget's theory has inspired much research on cognition in infancy and childhood. Much of this research has supported Piaget's findings, but, as we will see, some of it has shown that he underestimated the cognitive abilities of infants and young children.

sensorimotor stage In Piaget's theory, the first stage in cognitive development, during which infants learn through senses and motor activity.

The first of Piaget's four stages of cognitive development (refer back to Table 2-2 in Chapter 2) is the **sensorimotor stage.** During this stage (birth to approximately age 2), infants learn about themselves and their world through their developing sensory and motor activity. Babies change from creatures who respond primarily through reflexes and random behavior into goal-oriented toddlers. In Darwin's diary, for example, we saw Doddy progress from simple exploration of the sucking potential of his father's finger to purposeful attempts to solve the mystery of mirrors and shadows.

schemes Piaget's term for organized patterns of behavior used in particular situations.

Substages of the Sensorimotor Stage The sensorimotor stage consists of six substages (see Table 5-3), which flow from one to another as a baby's **schemes,** organized patterns of behavior, become more elaborate. During the first five substages, babies learn to coordinate input from their senses and organize their activities in relation to their environment. They do this by the processes of *organization, adaptation,* and *equilibration,* which were described in Chapter 2. During the sixth and last substage, they progress from trial-and-error learning to the use of symbols and concepts to solve simple problems.

Table 5-3 Six Substages of Piaget's Sensorimotor Stage of Cognitive Development*

Substage	Ages	Description	Behavior
Use of reflexes	Birth to 1 month	Infants exercise their inborn reflexes and gain some control over them. They do not coordinate information from their senses. They do not grasp an object they are looking at.	Dorri begins sucking when her mother's breast is in her mouth.
Primary circular reactions	1 to 4 months	Infants repeat pleasurable behaviors that first occur by chance (such as thumb sucking). Activities focus on infant's body rather than the effects of the behavior on the environment. Infants make first acquired adaptations; that is, they suck different objects differently. They begin to coordinate sensory information and grasp objects.	When given a bottle, Jesse, who is usually breast-fed, is able to adjust his sucking to the rubber nipple.
Secondary circular reactions	4 to 8 months	Infants become more interested in the environment; they repeat actions that bring interesting results (such as shaking a rattle) and prolong interesting experiences. Actions are intentional but not initially goal-directed.	Benjamin pushes pieces of dry cereal over the edge of his high chair tray one at a time and watches each piece as it falls to the floor.
Coordination of secondary schemes	8 to 12 months	Behavior is more deliberate and purposeful (intentional) as infants coordinate previously learned schemes (such as looking at and grasping a rattle) and use previously learned behaviors to attain their goals (such as crawling across the room to get a desired toy). They can anticipate events.	Nancy pushes the button on her musical nursery rhyme book and "Twinkle, Twinkle, Little Star" plays. She pushes this button over and over again, choosing it instead of the buttons for the other songs.
Tertiary circular reactions	12 to 18 months	Toddlers show curiosity and experimentation; they purposefully vary their actions to see results (for example, by shaking different rattles to hear their sounds). They actively explore their world to determine what is novel about an object, event, or situation. They try out new activities and use trial and error in solving problems.	When Tony's big sister holds his favorite board book up to his crib bars, he reaches for it. His first efforts to bring the book into his crib fail because the book is too wide. Soon, Tony turns the book sideways and hugs it, delighted with his success.
Mental combinations	18 to 24 months	Since toddlers can mentally represent events, they are no longer confined to trial and error to solve problems. Symbolic thought allows toddlers to begin to think about events and anticipate their consequences without always resorting to action. Toddlers begin to demonstrate insight. They can use symbols, such as gestures and words, and can pretend.	Jenny plays with her shape box, searching carefully for the right hole for each shape before trying—and succeeding.

*Note: Infants show enormous cognitive growth during Piaget's sensorimotor stage, as they learn about the world through their senses and their motor activities. Note their progress in problem solving and the coordination of sensory information. All ages are approximate.

circular reactions Piaget's term for processes by which an infant learns to reproduce desired occurrences originally discovered by chance.

Much of this early cognitive growth comes about through **circular reactions,** in which an infant learns to reproduce pleasurable or interesting events originally discovered by chance. Initially, an activity produces a sensation so enjoyable that the baby wants to repeat it. The repetition then feeds on itself in a continuous cycle in which cause and effect keep reversing (see Figure 5-3 on page 158). The originally chance behavior has been consolidated into a new scheme.

In the *first substage* (birth to about 1 month), neonates begin to exercise some control over their inborn reflexes, engaging in a behavior even when its normal stimulus is not present. For example, newborns suck reflexively when their lips are touched. They soon learn to find the nipple even when they are not touched, and they suck at times when they are not hungry. Thus infants modify and extend the scheme for sucking.

In the *second substage* (about 1 to 4 months), babies learn to repeat a pleasant bodily sensation first achieved by chance (say, sucking their thumbs, as in the first part of Figure 5-3). Piaget called this a *primary circular reaction.* Also, they begin to turn toward sounds, showing the ability to coordinate different kinds of sensory information (vision and hearing).

Figure 5-3
Primary, secondary, and tertiary circular reactions.

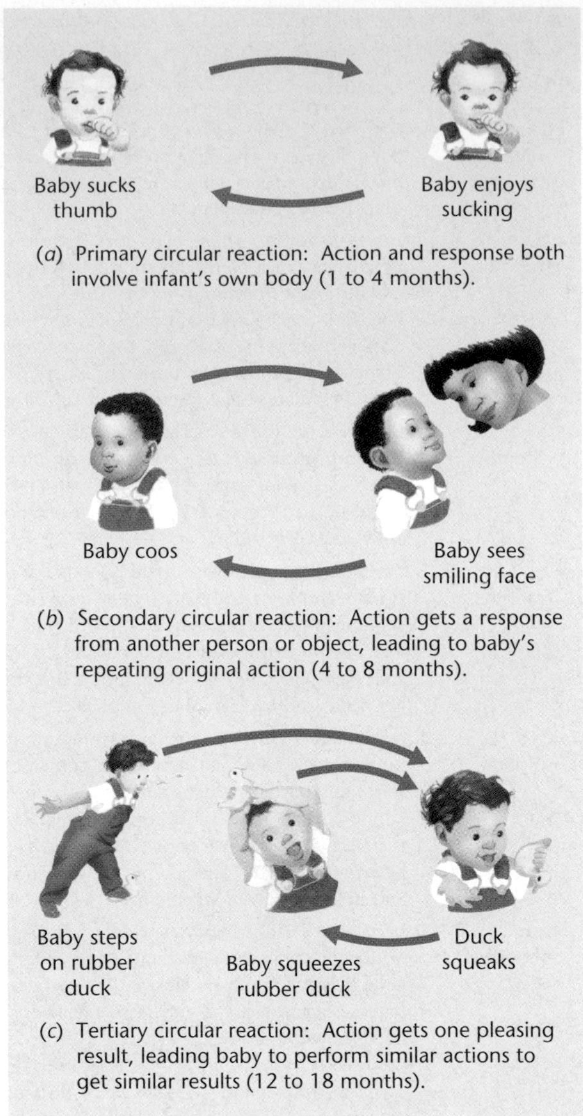

The *third substage* (about 4 to 8 months) coincides with a new interest in manipulating objects and learning about their properties. Babies engage in *secondary circular reactions:* intentional actions repeated not merely for their own sake, as in the second substage, but to get results *beyond the infant's own body.* For example, a baby this age will repeatedly shake a rattle to hear its noise, or (as in the second part of Figure 5-3) coo when a friendly face appears, so as to make the face stay longer.

By the time infants reach the *fourth substage, coordination of secondary schemes* (about 8 to 12 months), they have built on the few schemes they were born with. They have learned to generalize from past experience to solve new problems, and they can distinguish means from ends. They will crawl to get something they want, grab it, or push away a barrier to it (such as someone else's hand). They try out, modify, and coordinate previous schemes, to find one that works. This substage marks the development of complex, goal-directed behavior.

In the *fifth substage* (about 12 to 18 months), babies begin to experiment with new behavior to see what will happen. Once they begin to walk, they can more easily explore their environment. They now engage in *tertiary circular reactions,* varying an action to get a similar result, rather than merely repeating pleasing behavior they have accidentally discovered. For example, a toddler may squeeze a rubber duck that squeaked when stepped on, to see whether it will squeak again (as in the third part of Figure 5-3). For the first time, children show originality in problem solving. By trial and error, they try out behaviors until they find the best way to attain a goal.

The *sixth substage, mental combinations* (about 18 months to 2 years) is a transition into the preoperational stage of early childhood. **Representational ability**—the ability to mentally represent objects and events in memory, largely through symbols such as words, numbers, and mental pictures—blossoms. The ability to manipulate symbols frees children from immediate experience. They can now engage in **deferred imitation,** imitating actions they no longer see in front of them. They can pretend. They can think about actions before taking them. They no longer have to go through laborious trial and error to solve problems. Piaget's daughter Lucienne seemed to show representational ability when, in figuring out how to pry open a partially closed matchbox to remove a watch chain, she opened her mouth wider to represent her idea of widening the opening in the box (Piaget, 1936/1952).

representational ability Piaget's term for capacity to store mental images or symbols of objects and experiences.

deferred imitation Piaget's term for reproduction of an observed behavior after the passage of time.

Checkpoint

Can you . . .

- ✔ Summarize major developments in the six substages of the sensorimotor stage?
- ✔ Explain how primary, secondary, and tertiary circular reactions work?
- ✔ Tell why representational ability is important?

Development of Knowledge about Objects and Space The *object concept*—the idea that objects have their own independent existence, characteristics, and location in space—is fundamental to an orderly view of physical reality. The object concept is the basis for children's awareness that they themselves exist apart from objects and other people. It is essential to understanding a world full of objects and events. Doddy Darwin's struggle to understand the existence and location of reflective images was part of his development of an object concept.

Piaget believed that infants develop knowledge about objects and space by watching the results of their own actions: in other words, by coordinating visual and motor information. In both the United States and Africa's Ivory Coast, infants were observed using their hands to explore pictures as objects—feeling, rubbing, patting, or grasping them. Not until about 19 months—according to Piaget, the dawn of representational thought—did they show understanding that a picture is a representation of something else (DeLoache, Pierroutsakos, Uttal, Rosengren, & Gottlieb, 1998).

Object Permanence One aspect of the object concept is **object permanence,** the realization that an object or person continues to exist when out of sight. The development of this concept in many cultures can be seen in the game of peekaboo (see Box 5-1 on page 160).

object permanence Piaget's term for the understanding that a person or object still exists when out of sight.

According to Piaget, object permanence develops gradually during the sensorimotor stage. At first, infants have no such concept. By the third substage, from about 4 to 8 months, they will look for something they have dropped, but if they cannot see it, they act as if it no longer exists. In the fourth substage, about 8 to 12 months, they will look for an object in a place where they first found it after seeing it hidden, even if they later saw it being moved to another place. Piaget called this the **A, not-B error.** In the fifth substage, 12 to 18 months, they no longer make this error; they will search for an object in the *last* place they saw it hidden. However, they will *not* search for it in a place where they did *not* see it hidden. By the sixth substage, 18 to 24 months, object permanence is fully achieved; toddlers will look for an object even if they did not see it hidden.

A, not-B error Tendency for 8- to 12-month-old infants to search for a hidden object in a place where they previously found it, rather than in the place where they most recently saw it being hidden.

Piaget (1954) observed the A, not-B error when his son, Laurent, was $9\frac{1}{2}$ months old. Piaget placed Laurent on a sofa, with a small blanket (A) on his right and a wool garment (B) on his left. As the baby watched, Piaget hid his watch under the blanket. Laurent lifted the blanket and retrieved the watch. After repeating this game several times, Piaget placed the watch under the garment instead of under the blanket. Laurent watched intently, then again lifted the blanket and searched for the watch there. Two analyses of research on the A, not-B error have verified its prevalence (Marcovitch & Zelazo, 1999; Wellman, Cross, & Bartsch, 1986).

BOX 5-1

Window on the World

Playing Peekaboo

In rural South Africa, a Bantu mother smiles at her 9-month-old son, covers her eyes with her hands, and asks, "Uphi?" (Where?) After 3 seconds, the mother says, "Here!" and uncovers her eyes to the baby's delight. In Tokyo, a Japanese mother plays the same game with her 12-month-old daughter, who shows the same joyous response. In suburban Connecticut, a 15-month-old boy who sees his grandfather for the first time in two months raises his shirt to cover his eyes—as Grandpa did on his previous visit.

"Peekaboo!" This game, played the world over, helps babies to overcome anxiety about a parent's disappearance and to develop cognitive concepts, such as anticipation of future events. From N. Bayley in Scales in Infant Development, *Second Edition. Copyright © 1993 by The Psychological Corporation, a Harcourt Assessment Company. Reproduced by permission. All rights reserved.*

Peekaboo is played across diverse cultures, using similar routines (Fernald & O'Neill, 1993). In all cultures in which the game is played,* the moment when the mother or other caregiver reappears is exhilarating. It is marked by exaggerated gestures and voice tones. Infants' pleasure from the immediate sensory stimulation of the game is heightened by their fascination with faces and voices, especially the high-pitched tones the adult usually uses.

The game serves several important purposes. Psychoanalysts say that it helps babies master anxiety when their mother disappears. Cognitive psychologists see it as a way babies play with developing ideas about object permanence. It may also be a social routine that helps babies learn rules that govern conversation, such as taking turns. It may provide practice in paying attention, a prerequisite for learning.

As babies develop the cognitive competency to predict future events, the game takes on new dimensions. Between 3 and 5 months, the baby's smiles and laughter as the adult's face moves in and out of view signal the infant's developing expectation of what will happen next. At 5 to 8 months, the baby shows anticipation by looking and smiling as the adult's voice alerts the infant to the adult's imminent reappearance. By 1 year, babies are no longer merely observers but usually initiate the game, actively engaging adults in play. Now it is the adult who generally responds to the baby's physical or vocal cues, which can become quite insistent if the adult doesn't feel like playing.

To help infants who are in the process of learning peekaboo or other games, parents often use *scaffolding* (see Chapter 2). In an 18-month longitudinal study at the University of Montreal, 25 mothers were videotaped playing peekaboo with their babies, using a doll as a prop (Rome-Flanders, Cronk, & Gourde, 1995). The amount and type of scaffolding varied with the infant's age and skill. Mothers frequently tried to attract a 6-month-old's attention to begin the game; this became less and less necessary as time went on. Modeling (performing the peekaboo sequence to encourage a baby to imitate it) also was most frequent at 6 months and decreased significantly by 12 months, when there was an increase in direct verbal instruction ("Cover the doll") as babies became more able to understand spoken language. Indirect verbal instruction ("Where is the doll?"), used to focus attention on the next step in the game, remained constant throughout the entire age range. Reinforcement (showing satisfaction with the infant's performance, for example, by saying "Peekaboo!" when the infant uncovered the doll) was fairly constant from 9 months on. The overall amount of scaffolding dropped substantially at 24 months, by which time most babies have fully mastered the game.

*The cultures included in this report are found in Malaysia, Greece, India, Iran, Russia, Brazil, Indonesia, Korea, and South Africa.

What's Your View?

Have you ever played peekaboo periodically with the same infant? If so, did you notice changes with age in the child's participation, as described in this box?

Check It Out:

For more information on this topic, go to www.mhhe.com/papaliah9, where you'll find a link to an article about play therapy.

Piaget saw the A, not-B error as a sign of incomplete understanding of the object concept, together with an **egocentric** (self-centered) view of spatial relations. He reasoned that the infant must believe that the object's existence is linked to a particular location (the one where it was first found) and to the infant's own action in retrieving it from that location.

egocentric In Piaget's terminology, unable to consider any point of view other than one's own; a characteristic of young children's thought.

A more recent explanation is that infants—and even toddlers and preschoolers—may simply find it hard to restrain the impulse to repeat an earlier behavior that was previously reinforced by success (Diamond, Cruttenden, & Neiderman, 1994; Zelazo, Reznick, & Spinazzola, 1998). This interpretation may explain why even 2-year-olds and older preschoolers sometimes make the A, not-B error. If, on an earlier trial, they merely *observed* the object being found rather than finding it themselves, they are much less likely to make this error (Zelazo et al., 1998). In one study, 2-year-olds' tendency to make the A, not-B error lessened, the more times the hidden object was subsequently found in the B location (Spencer, Smith, & Thelen, 2001).

Objects in Space Before they can get around on their own, infants' knowledge about objects in space does not extend much farther than their own grasp. Because they are egocentric, they can see things only from their own point of view, which, given their immobility, is very limited.

With the coming of self-locomotion, babies can get close to an object, size it up, and compare its location with that of other objects (refer back to Box 4-2 in Chapter 4). This, said Piaget, is the beginning of a gradual decline in egocentrism. By the end of the sensorimotor stage, babies have begun to develop an **allocentric** (objective) view of the world. They can consider relationships among all objects in a given space, including themselves.

allocentric In Piaget's terminology, able to objectively consider relationships among objects or people.

Research generally supports Piaget's timetable of spatial development (Haith & Benson, 1998). Very young infants can follow their mother's gaze or her pointing finger to a nearby object. But not until 12 to 15 months, when most infants begin to walk, can they identify a distant object that is pointed out to them (Butterworth & Jarrett, 1991; Morissette, Ricard, & Decaric, 1995). At about that time, infants also become better able to judge the location of an object in relation to themselves (Newcombe, Huttenlocher, Drummey, & Wiley, 1998).

Which Abilities May Develop Earlier Than Piaget Thought? According to Piaget, the journey from reflex behavior to the beginnings of thought is a long, slow one. For a year and a half or so, babies learn only from their senses and movements; not until the last half of the second year do they make the breakthrough to conceptual thought. Today there is growing evidence that some of the limitations Piaget saw in infants' early cognitive abilities may instead have reflected immature linguistic and motor skills. Researchers using simplified tasks and modern research tools have built an impressive case for babies' cognitive strengths.

Object Permanence Piaget may have underestimated young infants' grasp of object permanence because of his testing methods. Babies may fail to search for hidden objects because they cannot yet carry out a two-step sequence of actions, such as moving a cushion or lifting the cover of a box before grasping the object. When object permanence is tested with a more age-appropriate procedure, in which the object is hidden only by darkness and thus can be retrieved in one motion, infants in the third substage (4 to 8 months) perform surprisingly well. In one study, $6\frac{1}{2}$-month-olds saw a ball drop down a chute and land in one of two spots, each identifiable by a distinctive sound. When the light was turned off, and the procedure was repeated, the babies reached for the ball in the appropriate location, guided only by the sound (Goubet & Clifton, 1998). This showed that they knew the ball continued to exist and could tell where it had gone.

Methods based only on what infants look at, and for how long, eliminate the need for *any* motor activity and thus can be used at even earlier ages. As we report later in this chapter, studies since the late 1970s, using information-processing methodology, suggest that very young infants may form mental representations—images or memories of objects not physically present—an ability Piaget said does not emerge before 18 months. According to this controversial research, infants as young as 3 or 4 months old not only seem to have a sense of object permanence, but also know certain principles about the physical world, understand categorization and causality, and have a rudimentary concept of number. Other research deals with infants' and toddlers' ability to remember and imitate what they see. (Table 5-4 compares these findings with Piaget's views; refer back to this table as you read on.)

Categorization According to Piaget, the ability to classify, or group things into categories, does not appear until the sixth substage, around 18 months. Yet even 3-month-olds seem to know that a dog is not a cat (Quinn, Eimas, & Rosenkrantz, 1993). Between 3 and 10 months, infants become better able to recognize a new example of a certain type, even when a pattern is complex (Younger, 1990).

Table 5-4 Key Developments of the Sensorimotor Stage

Concept or Skill	Piaget's View	More Recent Findings
Object permanence	Develops gradually between third and sixth substage. Infants in fourth substage (8–12 months) make A, not-B error.	Infants as young as $3\frac{1}{2}$ months (second substage) seem to show object knowledge, though interpretation of findings is in dispute. A, not-B error may persist into second year or longer.
Spatial knowledge	Development of object concept and spatial knowledge is linked to self-locomotion and coordination of visual and motor information.	Research supports Piaget's timetable and relationship of spatial judgments to decline of egocentrism. Link to motor development is less clear.
Causality	Develops slowly between 4–6 months and 1 year, based on infant's discovery, first of effects of own actions and then of effects of outside forces.	Some evidence suggests early awareness of specific causal events in the physical world, but general understanding of causality may be slower to develop.
Number	Depends on use of symbols, which begins in sixth substage (18–24 months).	Infants as young as 5 months may recognize and mentally manipulate small numbers, but interpretation of findings is in dispute.
Categorization	Depends on representational thinking, which develops during sixth substage (18–24 months).	Infants as young as 3 months seem to recognize perceptual categories and 7-month-olds categorize by function.
Imitation	Invisible imitation develops around 9 months, deferred imitation after development of mental representations in sixth substage (18–24 months).	Controversial studies have found invisible imitation of facial expressions in newborns and deferred imitation as early as 6 weeks. Deferred imitation of complex activities seems to exist at 6 months.

Much of the research in this area is based on infants' tendency to look longer at new sights that do not fit the same category they have been looking at. But is there a difference between this early *perceptual* categorizing, based on how things *look,* and *conceptual* categorizing, based on what things *are?*

To find out, Jean Mandler and Laraine McDonough (Mandler, 1998; Mandler & McDonough, 1993, 1996, 1998) encouraged infants to touch, examine, and manipulate objects. These experiments suggest that infants categorize objects by function, on the basis of their observation of, and experience with, those objects. For example, 7- to 11-month-olds seem to realize that a bird with wide wings is not in the same category as an airplane, even though they may look somewhat similar and both can fly (Mandler & McDonough, 1993). Mandler and McDonough propose that infants translate these functional perceptions into mental representations that lay the foundation for more sophisticated concepts (Mandler & McDonough, 1998).

In another, supporting series of experiments, 10- and 11-month-olds saw several examples in a single category, such as animals. Then they were shown a new animal and a piece of furniture. Another group were shown toy replicas of animals and furniture, as well as stylized, squared-off toy animals that looked somewhat like furniture and furniture with animal-like features, such as zebra-striped upholstery. In all situations, the infants looked longer at a new item from a different category than at a new item from the category they had been looking at, showing that they were responding to conceptual rather than perceptual similarities and differences (Pauen, 2002).

What's Your View?

- On the basis of observations by Piaget and the research they inspired, what factors would you consider in designing or purchasing a toy for an infant or toddler?

Invisible and Deferred Imitation Piaget maintained that **invisible imitation**—imitation using parts of the body that a baby cannot see, such as the mouth—develops at about 9 months, after **visible imitation**—the use of hands or feet, for example, which babies can see. Yet in a series of studies by Andrew Meltzoff and M. Keith Moore (1983, 1989), babies less than 72 hours old appeared to imitate adults by opening their mouths and sticking out their tongues, as well as by duplicating adults' head movements.

invisible imitation Imitation with parts of one's body that one cannot see.

visible imitation Imitation with parts of one's body that one can see.

However, a review of Meltzoff and Moore's work, and of attempts to replicate it, found clear, consistent evidence of only one apparently imitative movement—sticking out the tongue (Anisfeld, 1996)—and that response disappears by about 2 months of age. Because it seems unlikely that an early and short-lived imitative capacity would be limited to one gesture, some researchers have instead suggested that the tongue thrust may serve other purposes—perhaps as an early attempt to interact with the mother, or simply as exploratory behavior aroused by the intriguing sight of an adult tongue (Bjorklund, 1997; S. S. Jones, 1996). Pending further research, then, the age when invisible imitation begins will remain in doubt.

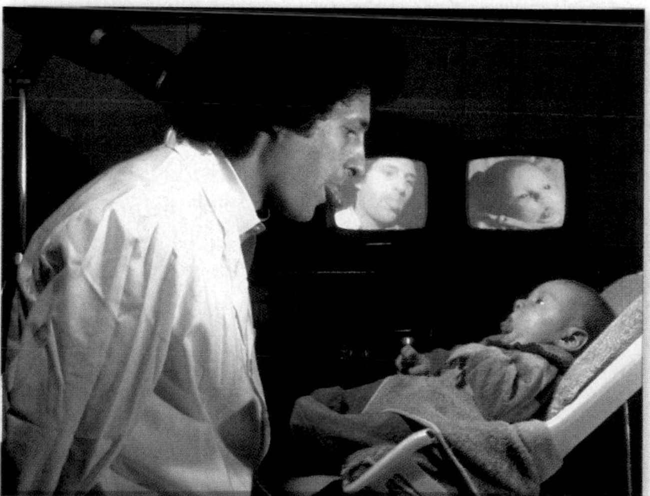

Is this infant imitating the researcher's stuck-out tongue? Studies by Andrew N. Meltzoff suggest that infants as young as 2 weeks are capable of invisible imitation. But other researchers found that only the youngest babies make this response, suggesting that the tongue movement may merely be exploratory behavior.

Piaget also held that children under 18 months cannot engage in *deferred imitation* of an act they saw some time before. Yet some research suggests that very young babies can retain a mental representation of an event. Babies as young as 6 weeks imitated facial movements they had seen an adult make the day before, when they again saw the same adult, this time expressionless (Meltzoff & Moore, 1994, 1998).

Early deferred imitation may be infants' way of exploring identities. When infants see an adult they previously saw making a distinct facial movement, they may imitate the

Checkpoint

Can you . . .

- ✔ Summarize Piaget's views on object permanence and spatial knowledge?
- ✔ Explain why Piaget may have underestimated some of infants' cognitive abilities, and summarize more recent research on object permanence, categorization, and imitation?
- ✔ Tell which of Piaget's ideas about major developments during the sensorimotor stage are supported by current research and which are not?

earlier movement as a way of probing whether or not this person is the person they saw before. Deferred imitation of novel or complex *actions* seems to begin by 6 to 9 months, again much earlier than Piaget thought (Meltzoff & Moore, 1998). In one study, 16- to 20-month-olds reproduced activities they had been shown two to four months earlier (Meltzoff, 1995). Thus the findings on deferred imitation agree with those on operant conditioning (Rovee-Collier, 1999): Infants and toddlers do seem capable of remembering over fairly long periods of time.

Overall, infants and toddlers seem to be far more cognitively competent than Piaget imagined and show earlier signs of conceptual thought. This does not mean that infants come into the world with minds fully formed. As Piaget observed, immature forms of cognition seem to give way to more mature forms. We can see this, for example, in the errors young infants make in searching for hidden objects. But Piaget may have been wrong in his emphasis on motor experience as the primary "engine" of cognitive growth. Infants' perceptions are far ahead of their motor abilities, and today's methods allow researchers to make observations and inferences about those perceptions. How perception relates to cognition is a major area of investigation, as we will see in the next section.

Studying Cognitive Development: Newer Approaches

During the past few decades, researchers have turned to three new approaches to add to our knowledge about infants' and toddlers' cognitive development:

- The **information-processing approach** focuses on the processes involved in perception, learning, memory, and problem solving. It seeks to discover what people do with information from the time they encounter it until they use it.
- The **cognitive neuroscience approach** examines the "hardware" of the central nervous system. It attempts to identify what brain structures are involved in specific aspects of cognition.
- The **social-contextual approach** examines environmental aspects of the learning process, particularly the role of parents and other caregivers.

information-processing approach Approach to the study of cognitive development by analyzing processes involved in perceiving and handling information.

cognitive neuroscience approach Approach to the study of cognitive development that links brain processes with cognitive ones.

social-contextual approach Approach to the study of cognitive development by focusing on environmental influences, particularly parents and other caregivers.

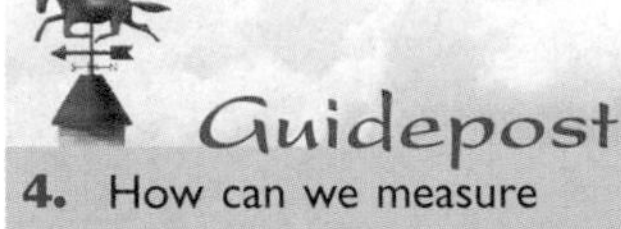

Guidepost

4. How can we measure infants' ability to process information, and how does this ability relate to future intelligence?

Information-Processing Approach: Perceptions and Representations

Like the psychometric approach, information-processing theory is concerned with individual differences in cognition. Unlike the psychometric approach, it aims to describe the mental processes involved when people acquire and remember information or solve problems, rather than merely inferring differences in mental functioning from answers given or problems solved. Information-processing research uses new methods to test ideas about cognitive development that sprang from the psychometric and Piagetian approaches. For example, information-processing researchers analyze the separate parts of a complex task, such as Piaget's object search tasks, to figure out what abilities are necessary for each part of the task and at what age these abilities develop. Information-processing researchers also measure, and draw inferences from, what infants pay attention to, and for how long.

Habituation At about 6 weeks, Stefan lies peacefully in his crib near a window, sucking a pacifier. It is a cloudy day, but suddenly the sun breaks through, and an angular shaft of light appears on the end of the crib. Stefan stops sucking for a few

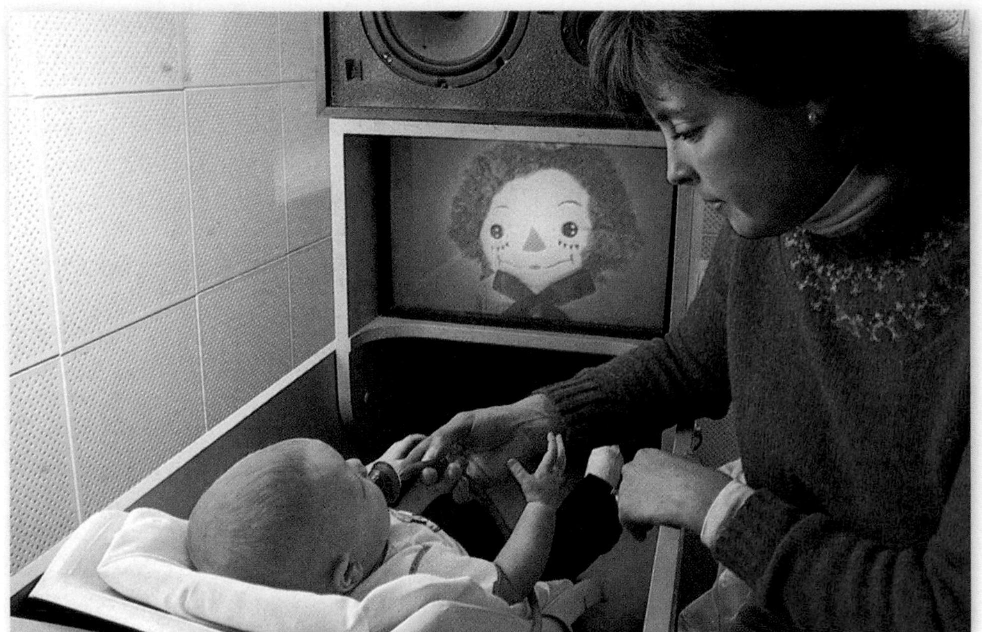

Can this baby tell the difference between Raggedy Ann and Raggedy Andy? This researcher may find out by seeing whether the baby has habituated—gotten used to one face—and then stops sucking on the nipple when a new face appears, showing recognition of the difference.

moments, staring at the pattern of light and shade. Then he looks away and starts sucking again.

We don't know what was going on in Stefan's mind when he saw the shaft of light, but we can tell by his sucking and looking behavior at what point he began paying attention and when he stopped. These simple behaviors can be indicators of sensory perception and discrimination and even of future intelligence.

Much information-processing research with infants is based on **habituation,** a type of learning in which repeated or continuous exposure to a stimulus (such as the shaft of light) reduces attention to that stimulus. In other words, familiarity breeds loss of interest. As infants habituate, they transform the novel into the familiar, the unknown into the known (Rheingold, 1985).

habituation Simple type of learning in which familiarity with a stimulus reduces, slows, or stops a response.

Researchers study habituation in newborns by repeatedly presenting a stimulus (usually a sound or visual pattern) and then monitoring such responses as heart rate, sucking, eye movements, and brain activity. A baby who has been sucking typically stops when the stimulus is first presented and does not start again until after it has ended. After the same sound or sight has been presented again and again, it loses its novelty and no longer causes the baby to stop sucking. Resumption of uninterrupted sucking shows that the infant has habituated to the stimulus. A new sight or sound, however, will capture the baby's attention and the baby will again stop sucking. This increased response to a new stimulus is called **dishabituation.** Habituation has been used to study topics ranging from infants' ability to detect differences between visual patterns to their ability to categorize people, objects, and events.

dishabituation Increase in responsiveness after presentation of a new stimulus.

Researchers gauge the efficiency of infants' information processing by measuring how quickly babies habituate to familiar stimuli, how fast their attention recovers when they are exposed to new stimuli, and how much time they spend looking at the new and the old. Efficiency of habituation correlates with later signs of cognitive development, such as a preference for complexity, rapid exploration of the environment, sophisticated play, quick problem solving, and the ability to match pictures. Indeed, as we will see, speed of habituation and other information-processing abilities show promise as predictors of intelligence (Bornstein & Sigman, 1986; Colombo, 1993; McCall & Carriger, 1993).

visual preference Tendency of infants to spend more time looking at one sight than another.

visual recognition memory Ability to distinguish a familiar visual stimulus from an unfamiliar one when shown both at the same time.

cross-modal transfer Ability to use information gained by one sense to guide another.

Early Perceptual and Processing Abilities The amount of time a baby spends looking at different sights is a measure of **visual preference,** which is based on the ability to make visual distinctions. Classic research by Robert Fantz and his colleagues revealed that babies less than 2 days old prefer curved lines to straight lines, complex patterns to simple patterns, three-dimensional objects to two-dimensional objects, pictures of faces to pictures of other things, and new sights to familiar ones (Fantz, 1963, 1964, 1965; Fantz, Fagen, & Miranda, 1975; Fantz & Nevis, 1967).

If infants pay more attention to new stimuli than to familiar ones—a phenomenon called *novelty preference*—they are showing that they can tell the new from the old. Therefore, say information-processing theorists, they must be able to remember the old. **Visual recognition memory** is the ability to distinguish familiar sights from unfamiliar ones when shown both at the same time, as measured by the tendency to look longer at the new. Visual recognition memory depends on comparing new information with information the infant already has—in other words, on the ability to form mental representations (P. R. Zelazo, Kearsley, & Stack, 1995). The efficiency of information processing depends on the speed with which infants form and refer to such images.

Contrary to Piaget's view, habituation and novelty preference studies suggest that this ability exists at birth or very soon after, and it quickly becomes more efficient. Newborns can tell sounds they have already heard from those they have not. In one study, infants who heard a certain speech sound 1 day after birth appeared to remember that sound 24 hours later, as shown by a reduced tendency to turn their heads toward the sound and even a tendency to turn away (Swain, Zelazo, & Clifton, 1993). Indeed, as we reported in Chapter 4, newborns seem to remember sounds they heard in the womb.

The way infants distribute their attention is an indicator of efficiency of processing. When shown two sights at the same time, infants who look a short time at one and then shift attention quickly to another tend to have better recognition memory and stronger novelty preference than infants who take longer looks at a single sight (Jankowski, Rose, & Feldman, 2001; Rose, Feldman, & Jankowski, 2001; Stoecker, Colombo, Frick, & Allen, 1998). Experiments with 5-month-olds found that infants can be trained to distribute attention more efficiently and thus to improve processing (Jankowski et al., 2001).

Piaget believed that the senses are unconnected at birth and are only gradually integrated through experience. If so, this integration begins almost immediately. The fact that neonates will look at a source of sound shows that they associate hearing and sight. A more sophisticated ability is **cross-modal transfer,** the ability to use information gained from one sense to guide another—as when a person negotiates a dark room by feeling for the location of familiar objects, or identifies objects by sight after feeling them with eyes closed. In one study, 1-month-old infants showed that they could transfer information gained from sucking (touch) to vision. When the infants saw a rigid object (a hard plastic cylinder) and a flexible one (a wet sponge) being manipulated by a pair of hands, the infants looked longer at the object they had just sucked (Gibson & Walker, 1984). The use of cross-modal transfer to judge some other properties of objects, such as shape, seems to develop a few months later (Maurer, Stager, & Mondloch, 1999). And, by 5 to 7 months, infants can link the feeling of their legs kicking to a visual image of that motion (Schmuckler & Fairhall, 2001).

Speed of processing increases rapidly during the first year of life. It continues to increase during the second and third years, as toddlers become better able to separate new information from information they have already processed (P. R. Zelazo et al., 1995).

Information Processing as a Predictor of Intelligence Because of the weak correlation between infants' scores on developmental tests and their later IQ, many psychologists believed that the cognitive functioning of infants had little in common with that of older children and adults—in other words, that there was a discontinuity in cognitive development (Kopp & McCall, 1982). Piaget believed this, too. However, when researchers assess how infants and toddlers process information, some aspects of mental development seem to be fairly continuous from birth (McCall & Carriger, 1993). Children who, from the start, were efficient at taking in and interpreting sensory information score well on intelligence tests.

In many longitudinal studies, habituation and attention-recovery abilities during the first 6 months to 1 year of life were moderately useful in predicting childhood IQ. So was visual recognition memory (Bornstein & Sigman, 1986; Colombo, 1993; McCall & Carriger, 1993). In one study, a combination of visual recognition memory at 7 months and cross-modal transfer at 1 year predicted IQ at age 11 and also showed a modest (but nonetheless remarkable after ten years!) relationship to processing speed and memory at that age (Rose & Feldman, 1995, 1997).

Visual reaction time and *visual anticipation* can be measured by the *visual expectation paradigm.* A series of computer-generated pictures briefly appears, some on the right and some on the left sides of an infant's peripheral visual field. The same sequence of pictures is repeated several times. Infants' eye movements are measured to see how quickly their gaze shifts to a picture that has just appeared (reaction time) or to the place where they expect the next picture to appear (anticipation). These measurements are taken to indicate attentiveness and processing speed, as well as the tendency to form expectations on the basis of experience. In a longitudinal study, visual reaction time and visual anticipation at $3\frac{1}{2}$ months correlated with IQ at age 4 (Dougherty & Haith, 1997). Reaction time and anticipation seem to improve up to 8 or 9 months of age. With complex patterns, younger infants may shift their gaze before the next pattern appears, but not to the precise place where it will appear. Also, if young infants show a perceptual expectation of a new sight, that does not mean they know what they expect to see (Reznick, Chawarska, & Betts, 2000).

All in all, there is much evidence that the abilities infants use to process sensory information are related to the cognitive abilities that intelligence tests measure. Still, we need to be cautious in interpreting these findings. Most of the studies used small samples. Also, the predictability of childhood IQ from measures of habituation and recognition memory is only modest. It is no higher than the predictability from parental education and socioeconomic status, and not as high as the predictability from some other infant behaviors, such as early vocalization. Predictions based on information-processing measures alone do not take into account the influence of environmental factors (Colombo & Janowsky, 1998; Laucht, Esser, & Schmidt, 1994; McCall & Carriger, 1993). For example, maternal responsiveness in early infancy seems to play a part in the link between early attentional abilities and cognitive abilities later in childhood (Bornstein & Tamis-LeMonda, 1994) and even at age 18 (Sigman, Cohen, & Beckwith, 1997).

Checkpoint

Can you . . .

- ✔ Distinguish three newer approaches to the study of cognitive development?
- ✔ Explain how habituation measures efficiency of infants' information processing?
- ✔ Identify several early perceptual and processing abilities that serve as predictors of intelligence?

Violation of Expectations and the Development of Thought According to some research, infants begin to think and reason about the physical world much earlier than Piaget believed. In the violation-of-expectations method, infants are first habituated to seeing an event happen as it normally would. Then the event is changed in a way that conflicts with (violates) normal expectations. An infant's tendency to look longer at the changed event (dishabituation) is interpreted as evidence that the infant recognizes it as surprising.

Guidepost

5. When do babies begin to think about characteristics of the physical world?

Researchers using the **violation-of-expectations** method claim that some of the concepts Piaget described as developing toward the end of the sensorimotor stage, such as object permanence, number, and causality—all of which depend on formation of mental representations—actually arise much earlier (refer back to Table 5-4). It has been proposed that infants may be born with reasoning abilities—*innate learning mechanisms* that help them make sense of the information they encounter—or may acquire these abilities very early (Baillargeon, 1994a). Some investigators go further, suggesting

violation-of-expectations Research method in which dishabituation to a stimulus that conflicts with experience is taken as evidence that an infant finds the new stimulus surprising.

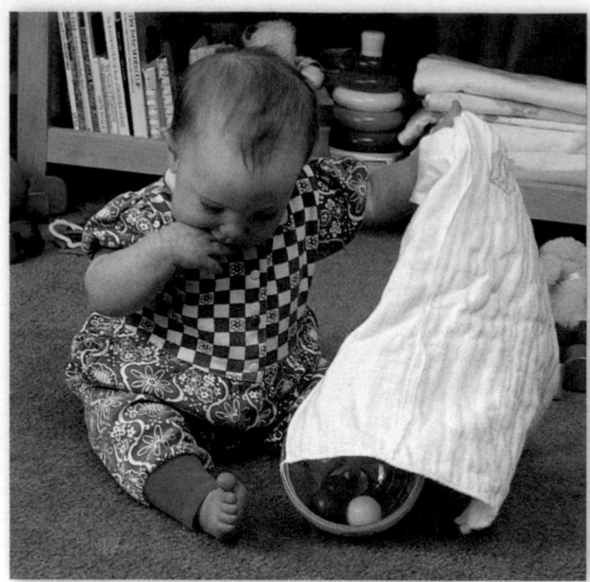

This baby seems to be showing some concept of object permanence by searching for an object that is partially hidden. The age when object permanence begins to develop is in dispute.

that infants at birth may already have intuitive *knowledge* about basic physical principles—knowledge that then develops further with experience (Spelke, 1994, 1998). As we will see, these interpretations and conclusions are highly controversial.

Object Permanence Using the violation-of-expectations method, Renée Baillargeon and her colleagues claim to have found evidence of object permanence in infants as young as $3\frac{1}{2}$ months. The babies appeared surprised by the failure of a tall carrot that slid behind a screen of the same height to show up in a large notch in the upper part of the screen before appearing again on the other side (Baillargeon & DeVos, 1991; see Figure 5-4). Of course, since this task is so different from Piaget's object permanence task, it may not assess precisely the same ability. Recognition that an object that disappeared on one side of a screen is the same as the object that reappears on the other side need not imply knowledge that the object should have continued to exist behind the screen (Meltzoff & Moore, 1998). Still, this experiment raises the possibility that at least a rudimentary form of object permanence may be present in the early months of life.

Number Violation-of-expectations research suggests that an understanding of number may begin long before Piaget's sixth substage, when he claimed children first begin to use symbols. Karen Wynn (1992) tested whether 5-month-old babies can add and subtract small numbers of objects. The infants watched as Mickey Mouse dolls were placed behind a screen, and a doll was either added or taken away. The screen then was lifted to reveal either the expected number or a different number of dolls. In a series of experiments, the babies looked longer at surprising "wrong" answers than at expected "right" ones, suggesting (says Wynn) that they had mentally "computed" the right answers. Other researchers who replicated these experiments got similar results (Baillargeon, 1994b; Koechlin, Dehaene, & Mehler, 1997; Simon, Hespos, & Rochat, 1995; Uller, Carey, Huntley-Fenner, & Klatt, 1999). Wynn (1996) also found that 6-month-olds seemed to know the difference between a puppet jumping twice in a row and three times in a row—numerical comparisons that could not be taken in at a glance.

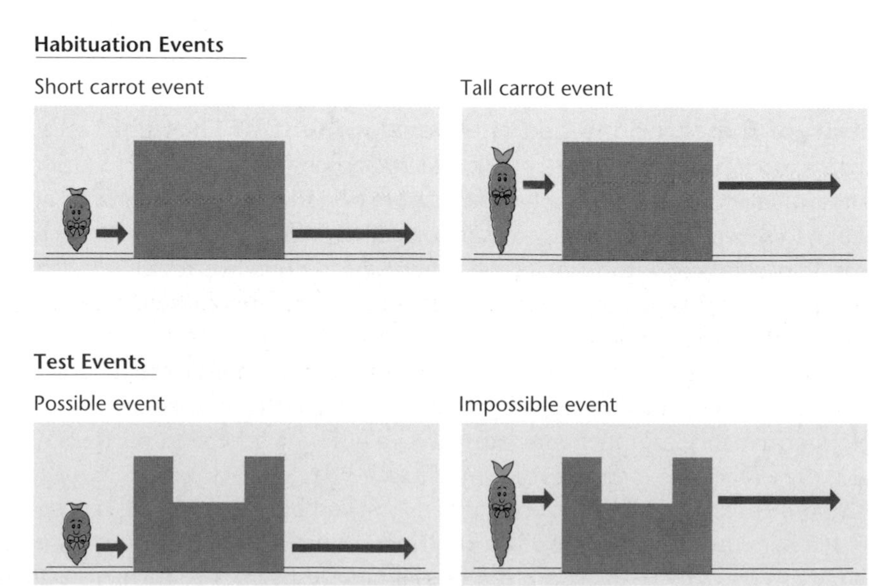

Figure 5-4
How early do infants show object permanence? In this experiment, $3\frac{1}{2}$-month-olds watched a short carrot and then a tall carrot slide along a track, disappear behind a screen, and then reappear. After they became accustomed to seeing these events, the opaque screen was replaced by a screen with a large notch at the top. The short carrot did not appear in the notch when passing behind the screen; the tall carrot, which should have appeared in the notch, also did not. The babies looked longer at the tall than at the short carrot event, suggesting that they were surprised that the tall carrot did not reappear. (*Source:* Baillargeon & DeVos, 1991.)

According to Wynn, this research raises the possibility that numerical concepts are inborn—that when parents teach their babies numbers, they may only be teaching them the names ("one, two, three") for concepts the babies already know. However, this is mere speculation, since the infants in these studies were already 5 and 6 months old. Furthermore, infants may simply be responding to the puzzling presence of a doll they saw removed from behind the screen, or the absence of a doll they saw placed there (Haith, 1998; Haith & Benson, 1998). Other studies suggest that although infants do seem to discriminate visually between sets of, say, two and three objects, they merely notice differences in the overall contours, area, or collective mass of the sets of objects rather than comparing the *number* of objects in the two sets (Clearfield & Mix, 1999; Mix, Huttenlocher, & Levine, 2002). Finally, a recent study—which Wynn (2000) disputes on procedural grounds—failed to replicate Wynn's findings consistently (Wakely, Rivera, & Langer, 2000a, 2000b).

Causality An understanding of *causality,* the principle that one event causes another, is important because it "allows people to predict and control their world" (L. B. Cohen, Rundell, Spellman, & Cashon, 1999). Piaget believed that this understanding develops slowly during the first year of life. At about 4 to 6 months, as infants become able to grasp objects, they begin to recognize that they can act on their environment. Thus the concept of causality is rooted in a dawning awareness of the power of their own intentions. However, according to Piaget, infants do not yet know that causes must come before effects; and not until close to 1 year do they realize that forces outside of themselves can make things happen.

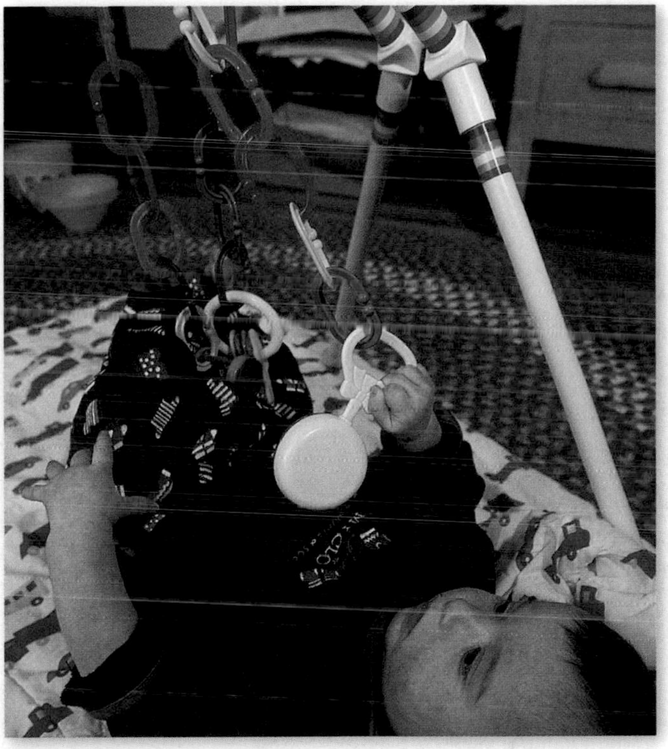

Some research suggests that a mechanism for recognizing causality exists much earlier, possibly in a special part of the brain (Mandler, 1998). In habituation-dishabituation experiments, infants $6\frac{1}{2}$ months old appear to see a difference between immediate causes of events (such as a brick striking a second brick, which is then pushed out of position) and events that occur with no apparent cause (such as a brick moving away from another brick without having been struck by it). Thus, at an early age, infants seem aware of continuity of relationships in time and space—perhaps a first step toward understanding causality. However, the infants in these studies may be responding simply to differences in the positions of objects in space and time, not to what caused those changes (L. B. Cohen & Amsel, 1998; Leslie, 1982, 1994).

This 5-month-old baby is discovering that he can make a dangling chain rattle and swing by pulling it. As infants this age become able to grasp objects, said Piaget, they become aware of the power of their own intentions—a first step toward understanding causality.

Investigators who support Piaget's slower timetable attribute the development of causal understanding to growth in information-processing skills. By 7 months, infants may make causal interpretations about a particular set of objects and simple events, but not until 10 to 15 months do they perceive causality in more complex circumstances involving a chain of several events. As infants accumulate more information about how objects behave, they are better able to see causality as a general principle operating in a variety of situations (L. B. Cohen & Amsel, 1998; L. B. Cohen & Oakes, 1993; L. B. Cohen et al., 1999; Oakes, 1994).

Evaluating Violation-of-Expectations Research There is some skepticism about what violation-of-expectations studies show. Does the infant's reaction reveal an understanding of the way things work, or merely awareness that something unusual has happened? The fact that an infant looks longer at one scene than at another may show only that the infant can see a difference between the two. It does not show what the infant knows about the difference, or that the infant is actually surprised. It's also possible that an infant, in becoming accustomed to the habituation event, develops the expectations that are then violated by the "surprising" event, and did not have such knowledge or expectations before (Goubet & Clifton, 1998; Haith, 1998; Haith & Benson, 1998; Mandler, 1998; Munakata, 2001; Munakata, McClelland, Johnson, & Siegler, 1997).

Defenders of the new research insist that a conceptual interpretation best accounts for the evidence (Baillargeon, 1999), but a recent variation on one of Baillargeon's experiments suggests otherwise. In her original research, Baillargeon (1994a) showed infants of various ages a "drawbridge" rotating 180 degrees. When the infants became habituated to the rotation, a barrier was introduced in the form of a box. At $4\frac{1}{2}$ months, infants seemed to show (by longer looking) that they realized the drawbridge could not move through the entire box (see Figure 5-5). When investigators replicated the experiment but eliminated the box, 5-month-olds still looked longer at the 180-degree rotation, even though no barrier was present—suggesting that the explanation might simply be a preference for greater movement (Rivera, Wakeley, & Langer, 1999).

Until further research clarifies these methodological issues, we must be cautious about inferring the existence of adultlike cognitive abilities from data that may have simpler explanations or may represent only partial achievement of those abilities (Haith, 1998).

Checkpoint

Can you . . .

- ✔ Describe the violation-of-expectations method, tell how and why it is used, and list some criticisms of it?
- ✔ Discuss three areas in which violation-of-expectations research seems to contradict Piaget's account of development?

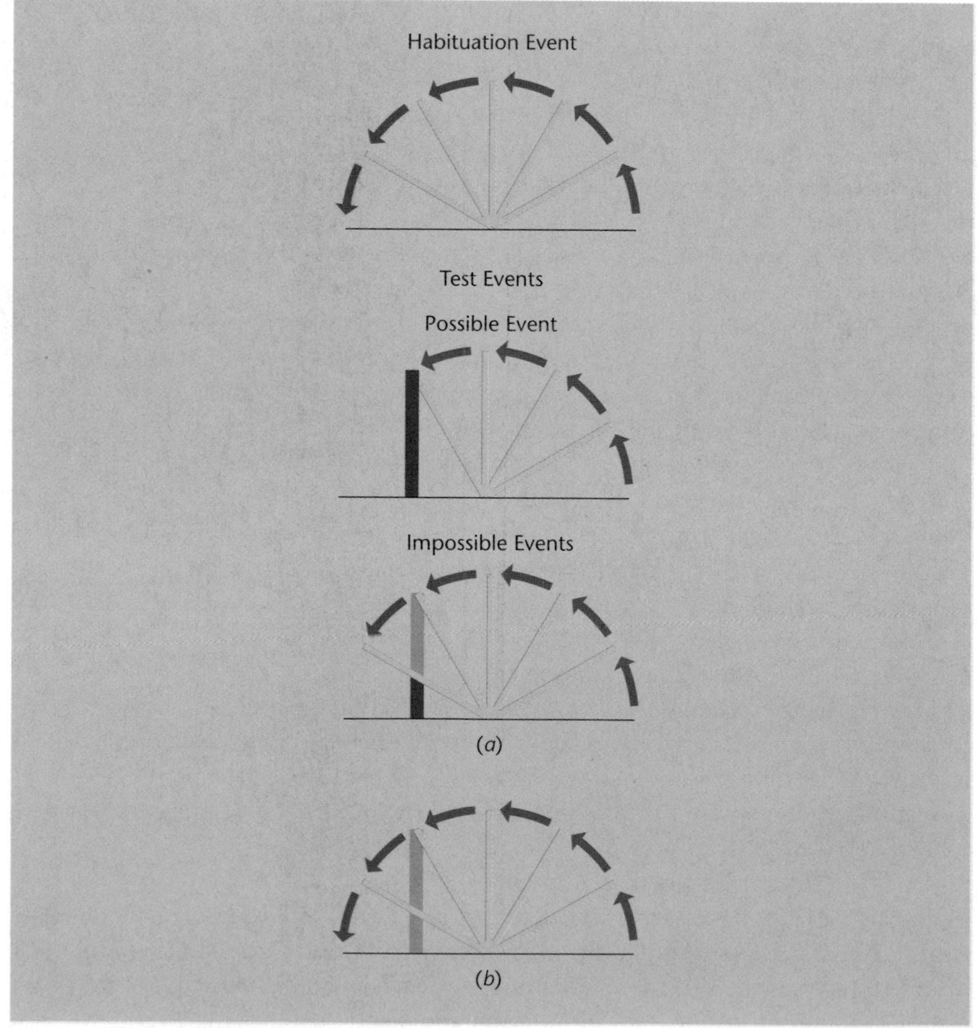

Figure 5-5
Test for infants' understanding of how a barrier works. Infants first become accustomed to seeing a "drawbridge" rotate 180 degrees on one edge. Then a box is placed beside the drawbridge. In the possible event, the drawbridge stops when it reaches the edge of the box. In the impossible events, the drawbridge rotates through part or all of the space occupied by the box. On the basis of how long they stare at each event, $4\frac{1}{2}$-month-old infants seem to know that the drawbridge cannot pass through the entire box (b); but not until $6\frac{1}{2}$ months do infants recognize that the drawbridge cannot pass through 80 percent of the box (a). (*Source:* Adapted from Baillargeon, 1994a.)

Cognitive Neuroscience Approach: The Brain's Cognitive Structures

Piaget's belief that neurological maturation is a major factor in cognitive development is borne out by current brain research. Studies of infant brain functioning have made use of behaviorist principles and Piagetian tasks. Other studies have recorded brain wave changes associated with information processing and have determined which brain structures affect which aspects of memory. Brain growth spurts, periods of rapid growth and development, coincide with changes in cognitive behavior similar to those Piaget described (Fischer & Rose, 1994, 1995).

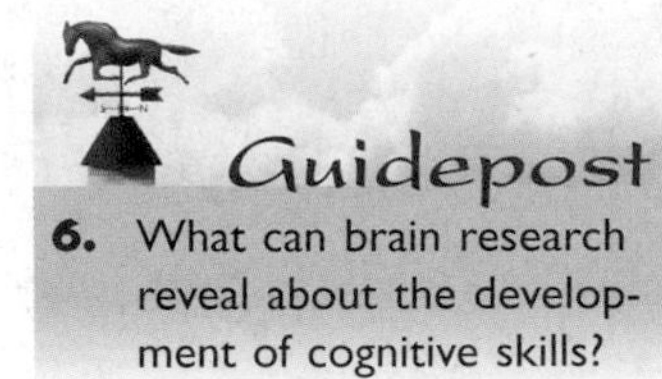

6. What can brain research reveal about the development of cognitive skills?

Studies of normal and brain-damaged adults point to two separate long-term memory systems—*explicit* and *implicit*—which acquire and store different kinds of information. Brain scans provide direct physical evidence of the location of these systems (Squire, 1992; Vargha-Khadem et al., 1997). **Explicit memory** is conscious or intentional recollection, usually of facts, names, events, or other things that people can state, or declare. **Implicit memory** refers to remembering that occurs without effort or even conscious awareness; it generally pertains to habits and skills, such as knowing how to throw a ball or ride a bicycle.

explicit memory Intentional and conscious memory, generally of facts, names, and events.

implicit memory Unconscious recall, generally of habits and skills; sometimes called *procedural memory*.

Implicit memory seems to develop earlier and mature faster. Two kinds of implicit memory are present during the first few months of life. One, an early form of procedural memory, is memory for sequences such as a series of lights, which seems to be centered in the *striatum*. The other type of early implicit memory is conditioning, which appears to depend on the *cerebellum* and cell nucleii deep in the *brain stem*. A reflexlike precursor of explicit memory is chiefly dependent on the *hippocampus*, a seahorse-shaped structure deep in the central portion of the brain, the *medial temporal lobe*. This preexplicit memory system permits infants to remember specific sights or sounds for a few seconds—long enough to show simple novelty preferences (Nelson, 1995; refer back to Figure 4-6 in Chapter 4 for locations of brain structures).

Sometime between 6 and 12 months, or perhaps earlier (Rovee-Collier, 1999), a more sophisticated form of explicit memory modifies or replaces the preexplicit form. It draws upon cortical structures, which are the primary site of general knowledge (*semantic memory*), as well as structures associated with the hippocampus, which govern memory of specific experiences (*episodic memory*) (Nelson, 1995; Vargha-Khadem et al., 1997). This advance is responsible for the emergence of complex forms of cross-modal transfer.

The *prefrontal cortex* (the large portion of the frontal lobe directly behind the forehead) is believed to control many aspects of cognition. During the second half of the first year, the prefrontal cortex and associated circuitry develop the capacity for **working memory**—short-term storage of information the brain is actively processing, or working on. It is in working memory that mental representations are prepared for, or recalled from, storage.

working memory Short-term storage of information being actively processed.

The relatively late appearance of working memory may be largely responsible for the slow development of object permanence, which seems to be seated in a rearward area of the prefrontal cortex (Nelson, 1995). This part of the brain develops more slowly than any other (M. H. Johnson, 1998). By 12 months, this region may be developed enough to permit an infant to avoid the A, not-B error by controlling the impulse to search in a place where the object previously was found (Bell & Fox, 1992; Diamond, 1991).

Although explicit memory and working memory continue to develop beyond infancy, the early emergence of the brain's memory structures underlines the importance of environmental stimulation during the first months of life. Social-contextual theorists and researchers pay particular attention to the impact of environmental influences.

Checkpoint

Can you . . .

- ✔ Identify the brain structures apparently involved in implicit, preexplicit, explicit, and working memory and mention a task made possible by each?
- ✔ Tell how brain research helps explain Piagetian developments and information-processing skills?

Social-Contextual Approach: Learning from Interactions with Caregivers

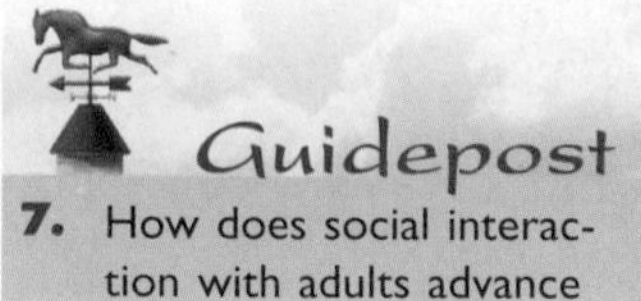

Guidepost

7. How does social interaction with adults advance cognitive competence?

guided participation Participation of an adult in a child's activity in a manner that helps to structure the activity and to bring the child's understanding of it closer to that of the adult.

Researchers influenced by Vygotsky's sociocultural theory study how the cultural context affects early social interactions that may promote cognitive competence.

The concept of **guided participation** (Rogoff, 1990, 1998; Rogoff, Mistry, Göncü, & Mosier, 1993) was inspired by Vygotsky's zone of proximal development (refer back to Chapter 2) and his view of learning as a collaborative process. Guided participation refers to mutual interactions with adults that help structure children's activities and bridge the gap between the child's understanding and the adult's. Guided participation often occurs in shared play and in ordinary, everyday activities in which children learn informally the skills, knowledge, and values important in their culture.

In one cross-cultural study (Rogoff et al., 1993), researchers visited the homes of 14 one- to two-year-olds in each of four places: a Mayan town in Guatemala, a tribal village in India, and middle-class urban neighborhoods in Salt Lake City and Turkey. The investigators interviewed caregivers about their childrearing practices and watched them help the toddlers learn to dress themselves and to play with unfamiliar toys.

Cultural differences affected the types of guided participation the researchers observed. In the Guatemalan town, where toddlers normally saw their mothers sewing and weaving at home to help support the family, and in the Indian village, where they accompanied their mothers at work in the fields, the children customarily played alone or with older siblings while the mother worked nearby. After initial demonstration and instruction, mostly nonverbal, the children took the lead in their own learning, while a parent or other caregiver remained available to help.

The U.S. toddlers, who had full-time homemaker mothers or were in day care, interacted with their parents in the context of child's play rather than in the parents' work or social worlds. Caregivers spoke with the children as peers and managed and motivated their learning with praise and mock excitement. Turkish families, who were in transition from a rural to an urban way of life, showed a pattern somewhere between the other two.

Checkpoint

Can you . . .

- ✔ Explain how the concept of guided participation relates to Vygotsky's theory?
- ✔ Compare two cultural patterns of guided participation in toddlers' learning?

The cultural context, then, influences the way caregivers contribute to cognitive development. These researchers suggest that direct adult involvement in children's play and learning may be better adapted to the environment in a middle-class urban community, in which homemaker mothers have more time, greater verbal skills, and possibly more interest in children's play and learning, than in a rural community in a developing country, in which children frequently observe and participate in adults' work activities. The ways adults involve themselves in children's learning in one culture may be no better or worse than in another—just different.

Language Development

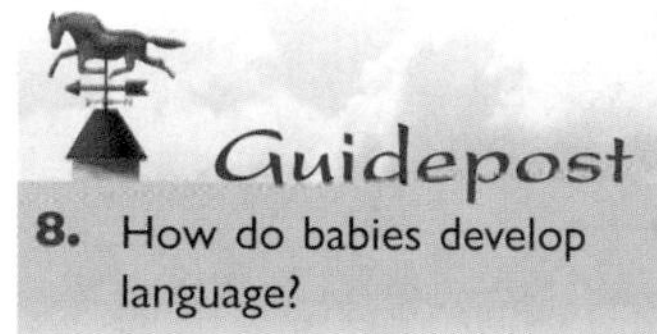

Guidepost

8. How do babies develop language?

language Communication system based on words and grammar.

literacy Ability to read and write.

Doddy Darwin's exclamation "Ah!" to express recognition of an image in a glass is a striking example of the connection between **language,** a communication system based on words and grammar, and cognitive development. Once children know words, they can use them to represent objects and actions. They can reflect on people, places, and things; and they can communicate their needs, feelings, and ideas in order to exert control over their lives.

The growth of language illustrates how all aspects of development interact. As the physical structures needed to produce sounds mature, and the neuronal connections necessary to associate sound and meaning become activated, social interaction with adults introduces babies to the communicative nature of speech. Let's look at the typical sequence of milestones in language development (see Table 5-5), at some characteristics of early speech, at how babies acquire language and make progress in using it, and at how parents and other caregivers help toddlers prepare for **literacy,** the ability to read and write.

Table 5-5 Language Milestones from Birth to 3 Years

Age in Months	Development
Birth	Can perceive speech, cry, make some response to sound.
$1\frac{1}{2}$ to 3	Coos and laughs.
3	Plays with speech sounds.
5 to 6	Makes consonant sounds, trying to match what she or he hears.
6 to 10	Babbles in strings of consonants and vowels.
9	Uses gestures to communicate and plays gesture games.
9 to 10	Begins to understand words (usually "no" and baby's own name); imitates sounds.
10 to 12	No longer can discriminate sounds not in own language.
9 to 12	Uses a few social gestures.
10 to 14	Says first word (usually a label for something).
10 to 18	Says single words.
13	Understands symbolic function of naming.
13	Uses more elaborate gestures.
14	Uses symbolic gesturing.
16 to 24	Learns many new words, expanding vocabulary rapidly, going from about 50 words to up to 400; uses verbs and adjectives.
18 to 24	Says first sentence (2 words).
20	Uses fewer gestures; names more things.
20 to 22	Has comprehension spurt.
24	Uses many two-word phrases; no longer babbles; wants to talk.
30	Learns new words almost every day; speaks in combinations of three or more words; understands very well; makes grammatical mistakes.
36	Says up to 1,000 words, 80 percent intelligible; makes some mistakes in syntax.

Source: Bates, O'Connell, & Shore, 1987; Capute, Shapiro, & Palmer, 1987; Lalonde & Werker, 1995; Lenneberg, 1969.

Sequence of Early Language Development

Before babies can use words, they make their needs and feelings known—as Doddy Darwin did—through sounds that progress from crying to cooing and babbling, then to accidental imitation, and then deliberate imitation. These sounds are known as **prelinguistic speech.** Infants also grow in the ability to recognize and understand speech sounds and to use meaningful gestures. Babies typically say their first word around the end of the first year, and toddlers begin speaking in sentences about eight months to a year later.

prelinguistic speech Forerunner of linguistic speech; utterance of sounds that are not words. Includes crying, cooing, babbling, and accidental and deliberate imitation of sounds without understanding their meaning.

Early Vocalization *Crying* is a newborn's only means of communication. Different pitches, patterns, and intensities signal hunger, sleepiness, or anger (Lester & Boukydis, 1985).

Between 6 weeks and 3 months, babies start *cooing* when they are happy—squealing, gurgling, and making vowel sounds like "ahhh." At about 3 to 6 months, babies begin to play with speech sounds, matching the sounds they hear from people around them.

Babbling—repeating consonant-vowel strings, such as "ma-ma-ma-ma"—occurs between 6 and 10 months of age and is often mistaken for a baby's first word. Babbling is not real language, since it does not hold meaning for the baby, but it becomes more wordlike.

Language development continues with accidental *imitation of language sounds* babies hear and then imitation of themselves making these sounds. At about 9 to 10 months, infants deliberately imitate sounds without understanding them. Once they have a repertoire of sounds, they string them together in patterns that sound like language but seem to have no meaning.

Recognizing Language Sounds The ability to perceive differences between sounds is essential to language development. As we have seen, this ability is present from or even before birth, and it becomes more refined during the first year of life. In getting ready to understand and use speech, infants first become familiar with the sounds of words and phrases and later attach meanings to them (Jusczyk & Hohne, 1997).

The process apparently begins in the womb. In one experiment, two groups of Parisian women in their thirty-fifth week of pregnancy each recited a different nursery rhyme, saying it three times a day for four weeks. At the end of that time, researchers played recordings of both rhymes close to the women's abdomens. The fetuses' heart rates slowed when the rhyme the mother had spoken was played, but not for the other rhyme. Since the voice on the tape was not that of the mother, the fetuses apparently were responding to the linguistic sounds they had heard the mother use. This suggests that hearing the "mother tongue" before birth may "pretune" an infant's ears to pick up its sounds (DeCasper, Lecanuet, Busnel, Granier-Deferre, & Maugeais, 1994).

By 6 months of age, babies have learned to recognize the basic sounds, or *phonemes,* of their native language, and to adjust to slight differences in the way different speakers form those sounds. In one study, 6-month-old Swedish and U.S. babies routinely ignored variations in sounds common in their own language but noticed variations in an unfamiliar language (Kuhl, Williams, Lacerda, Stevens, & Lindblom, 1992).

Before infants can connect sounds to meanings, they seem to recognize sound patterns they hear frequently, such as their own names. Four-and-a-half-month-olds listen longer to their own names than to other names, even names with stress patterns similar to theirs (Mandel, Jusczyk, & Pisoni, 1995). Six-month-olds look longer at a video of their mothers when they hear the word *mommy* and of their fathers when they hear *daddy,* suggesting that they are beginning to associate sound with meaning—at least with regard to special people (Tincoff & Jusczyk, 1999).

By about 10 months, babies lose their earlier sensitivity to sounds that are not part of the language they hear spoken. For example, Japanese infants no longer make a distinction between "ra" and "la," a distinction that does not exist in the Japanese language. Although the ability to perceive nonnative sounds is not entirely lost—it can be revived, with effort, in adulthood—the brain no longer routinely discriminates them (Bates et al., 1987; Lalonde & Werker, 1995; Werker, 1989).

Meanwhile, during the second half of the first year, as babies become increasingly familiar with the sounds of their language, they begin to become aware of its phonological rules—how sounds are arranged in speech. In one series of experiments (Marcus, Vijayan, Rao, & Vishton, 1999), 7-month-olds listened longer to "sentences" containing a different order of nonsense sounds (such as "wo fe wo," or ABA) from the order to which the infants had been habituated (such as "ga ti ti," or ABB). The sounds used in the test were different from those used in the habituation phase, so the infants' discrimination must have been based on the patterns of repetition alone. This finding suggests that infants may have a mechanism for discerning abstract rules of sentence structure.

Gestures At 9 months Maika *pointed* to an object, sometimes making a noise to show that she wanted it. Between 9 and 12 months, she learned some *conventional social gestures:* waving bye-bye, nodding her head to mean *yes,* and shaking her head to signify *no.* By about 13 months, she used more elaborate *representational gestures;* for example, she would hold an empty cup to her mouth to show that she wanted a drink or hold up her arms to show that she wanted to be picked up.

Symbolic gestures, such as blowing to mean *hot,* or sniffing to mean *flower,* often emerge around the same time as babies say their first words, and they function much like words. By using them, children show an understanding that symbols can refer to specific objects, events, desires, and conditions. Gestures usually appear before children have a vocabulary of 25 words and drop out when children learn the word for the idea they were gesturing and can say it instead (Lock, Young, Service, & Chandler, 1990).

Gesturing seems to come naturally. In an observational study, blind children and adolescents used gestures while speaking, as much as sighted children did, and even while speaking to a blind listener. Thus the use of gestures does not depend on having either a model or an observer, but seems to be an inherent part of the speaking process (Iverson & Goldin-Meadow, 1998).

Learning gestures seems to help babies learn to talk. In one experiment (Goodwyn & Acredolo, 1998), 11-month-olds learned gestures by watching their parents perform them and say the corresponding words. Between 15 and 36 months, when tested on vocal language development, these children outperformed two other groups—one whose parents had only said words and another who had received neither vocal nor gestural training. Gestures, then, can be a valuable alternative or supplement to words, especially during the period of early vocabulary formation.

This toddler is communicating with his father by pointing at something that catches his eye. Gesturing seems to come naturally to young children and may be an important part of language learning.

First Words Doddy Darwin, at 11 months, said his first word—"ouchy"—which he attached to a number of objects. Doddy's development was typical in this respect. The average baby says a first word sometime between 10 and 14 months, initiating **linguistic speech**—verbal expression that conveys meaning. Before long, the baby will use many words and will show some understanding of grammar, pronunciation, intonation, and rhythm. For now, an infant's total verbal repertoire is likely to be "mama" or "dada." Or it may be a simple syllable that has more than one meaning depending on the context in which the child utters it. "Da" may mean "I want that," "I want to go out," or "Where's Daddy?" A word like this, which expresses a complete thought, is called a **holophrase.**

linguistic speech Verbal expression designed to convey meaning.

holophrase Single word that conveys a complete thought.

Babies understand many words before they can use them. The first words most babies understand are the ones they are likely to hear most often: their own names and the word *no,* as well as words with special meaning for them.

By 13 months, most children understand that a word stands for a specific thing or event, and they can quickly learn the meaning of a new word (Woodward, Markman, & Fitzsimmons, 1994). Addition of new words to their *expressive* (spoken) vocabulary is slower at first. As children come to rely more on words than on gestures to express themselves, the sounds and rhythms of speech grow more elaborate.

Vocabulary continues to grow throughout the single-word stage, which generally lasts until about 18 months of age. At this age toddlers—especially those with larger vocabularies and faster reaction times—can recognize spoken words from just the first part of the word. For example, upon hearing "daw" or "ki," they will point to a picture of a dog or kitten (Fernald, Swingley, & Pinto, 2001). Sometime between 16 and 24 months a "naming explosion" occurs. Within a few weeks, a toddler may go from saying about 50 words to saying about 400 (Bates, Bretherton, & Snyder, 1988). These rapid gains in spoken vocabulary reflect the increase in speed and accuracy of word recognition during the second year of life (Fernald, Pinto, Swingley, Weinberg, & McRoberts, 1998). Toddlers actively seek to learn new words. In one study, $2\frac{1}{2}$-year-olds were just as good at learning new words from overheard speech as from speech directly addressed to them (Akhtar, Jipson, & Callanan, 2001).

First Sentences The next important linguistic breakthrough comes when a toddler puts two words together to express one idea ("Dolly fall"). Generally, children do this between 18 and 24 months, about 8 to 12 months after they say their first word. However, this age range varies greatly. Although prelinguistic speech is fairly closely tied to chronological age, linguistic speech is not. Most children who begin talking fairly late catch up eventually—and many make up for lost time by talking nonstop to anyone who will listen! (True delayed language development is discussed in Chapter 7.)

A child's first sentences typically deal with everyday events, things, people, or activities (Braine, 1976; Rice, 1989; Slobin, 1973). Darwin noted instances in which Doddy expressed his developing moral sense in words. At 27 months the boy gave his sister the last bit of his gingerbread, exclaiming, "Oh, kind Doddy, kind Doddy!"

telegraphic speech Early form of sentence consisting of only a few essential words.

At first children typically use **telegraphic speech,** consisting of only a few essential words. When Rita says, "Damma deep," she seems to mean "Grandma is sweeping the floor." Children's use of telegraphic speech, and the form it takes, vary, depending on the language being learned (Braine, 1976; Slobin, 1983). Word order generally conforms to what a child hears; Rita does not say "Deep Damma" when she sees her grandmother pushing a broom.

Does the omission of functional words such as *is* and *the* mean that a child does not know these words? Not necessarily; the child may merely find them hard to reproduce. Even during the first year, infants are sensitive to the presence of functional words; at $10\frac{1}{2}$ months, they can tell a normal passage from one in which the functional words have been replaced by similar-sounding nonsense words (Jusczyk, in press).

syntax Rules for forming sentences in a particular language.

Sometime between 20 and 30 months, children show increasing competence in ***syntax,*** the rules for putting sentences together in their language. They become somewhat more comfortable with articles *(a, the),* prepositions *(in, on),* conjunctions *(and, but),* plurals, verb endings, past tense, and forms of the verb *to be (am, are, is).* They also become increasingly aware of the communicative purpose of speech and of whether their words are being understood (Shwe & Markman, 1997)—a sign of growing sensitivity to the mental lives of others (see Box 5-2). By age 3, speech is fluent, longer, and more complex; although children often omit parts of speech, they get their meaning across well.

Characteristics of Early Speech

Early speech has a character all its own—no matter what language a child is speaking (Slobin, 1971).

As we have seen, children *simplify.* They use telegraphic speech to say just enough to get their meaning across ("No drink milk!").

Children *understand grammatical relationships they cannot yet express.* At first, Nina may understand that a dog is chasing a cat, but she cannot string together enough words to express the complete action. Her sentence comes out as "Puppy chase" rather than "Puppy chase kitty."

Children *underextend word meanings.* Lisa's uncle gave her a toy car, which the 13-month-old called her "koo-ka." Then her father came home with a gift, saying, "Look, Lisa, here's a little car for you." Lisa shook her head. "Koo-ka," she said, and ran and got the one from her uncle. To her, *that* car—and *only* that car—was a little car, and it took some time before she called any other toy cars by the same name. Lisa was underextending the word *car* by restricting it to a single object.

Children also *overextend word meanings.* At 14 months, Eddie jumped in excitement at the sight of a gray-haired man on the television screen and shouted, "Gampa!" Eddie was overgeneralizing, or *overextending,* a word; he thought that because his grandfather had gray hair, all gray-haired men could be called "Grandpa." As children develop a larger vocabulary and get feedback from adults on the appropriateness of what they say, they overextend less. ("No, honey, that man looks a little like Grandpa, but he's somebody else's grandpa, not yours.")

Checkpoint

Can you . . .

- ✔ Trace the typical sequence of milestones in early language development, pointing out the influence of the language babies hear around them?
- ✔ Describe five ways in which early speech differs from adult speech?

Digging Deeper

Can Toddlers "Read" Others' Wishes?

BOX 5-2

At what age can babies begin to "read" what is on other people's minds? Twelve-month-olds will give an object to a person who points to it and asks for it. But does the baby realize that the request reflects an inner desire, or is the child merely responding to observable behavior (pointing)? Eighteen-month-olds will offer a toy to a crying child. But do they realize that their comforting may change the other child's mental state, or are they merely trying to change an overt behavior (crying)? And, since they usually offer a toy they themselves would find comforting, are they capable of distinguishing another person's state of mind from their own?

Since most toddlers can't talk well enough to tell us what they are thinking, one research team (Repacholi & Gopnik, 1997) designed a nonverbal experiment to test their ability to discern another person's food preferences.

Each of 159 children—about half of them 14 months and the other half 18 months old—took part in an individual free play session. During the session, the child and an experimenter were offered two bowls of snacks: one that young children typically like (goldfish crackers) and one that they typically do not like (raw broccoli flowerets). First the child tasted the snacks, and then the experimenter did. As expected, more than 9 out of 10 children preferred the crackers.

Equal numbers of boys and girls of each age were randomly assigned to two testing conditions: one in which the experimenter's apparent food preference matched the child's expected preference and one in which it did not. In the "matched" condition, the experimenter showed pleasure after tasting the cracker ("Mmm!") and disgust after tasting the broccoli ("Eww"). In the "mismatched" condition, the experimenter acted as if she preferred the broccoli.

Next, the experimenter asked the child to give her some food. The child also had another opportunity to taste the snacks. This was done to see whether the children's food preferences had been influenced by the experimenter's preferences. Only 6 children (4 percent) changed their apparent preference.

What did the children do when the experimenter asked for food? Nearly 7 out of 10 of the 14-month-olds did not respond. About 1 in 3 "teased" the experimenter by offering the crackers and then pulling back. Most of the 14-month-olds who did respond offered crackers, regardless of which food the experimenter seemed to prefer. By contrast, only 3 out of 10 of the 18-month-olds failed to respond to the request; and, of those who did, 3 out of 4 gave the experimenter the food she had shown a liking for, whether or not it was the one they themselves liked.

Thus 18-month-olds, but not 14-month-olds, seem able to use another person's emotional cues to figure out what that person likes and wants, even when that person's desire is different from their own, and then to apply the information in a different situation in which there are no visible cues to the other person's preference. This suggests a rather sophisticated understanding of mental states: an awareness that two people can have opposite feelings about the same thing.

Young children who can interpret another person's desire are on their way to developing a *theory of mind,* a topic we discuss in Chapter 7.

What's Your View?

Have you ever been in a conversation with a toddler who seemed aware of your mental state? How could you tell?

Check It Out:

For more information on this topic, go to www.mhhe.com/papaliah9. You will find a link to the webpage of Alison Gopnik, whose work is the basis for this box.

Children *overregularize rules:* they apply them rigidly, not knowing that some rules have exceptions. When John says "mouses" instead of "mice" or Megan says "I thinked" rather than "I thought," this represents progress. Both children initially used the correct forms of these irregular words, but merely in imitation of what they heard. Once children learn the rules for plurals and past tense (a crucial step in learning language), they apply them universally. The next step is to learn the exceptions to the rules, which they generally do by early school age.

Classic Theories of Language Acquisition: The Nature-Nurture Debate

How do children gain access to the secrets of verbal communication? Is linguistic ability learned or inborn? In the 1950s, a debate raged between two schools of thought: one

the infant brain seems to allow functions to be transferred from damaged areas to other regions. Thus, whereas an adult whose left hemisphere is removed or injured will be severely language-impaired, a young child who undergoes this procedure may eventually have nearly normal speech and comprehension (Nobre & Plunkett, 1997; Owens, 1996).

Brains of normal infants also show plasticity. In one study, researchers measured brain activity at various places on the scalp as babies listened to a series of words, some of which they did not understand. Between ages 13 and 20 months, a period of marked vocabulary growth, the infants' comprehension appeared to be increasingly lateralized (Mills, Cofley-Corina, & Neville, 1997). Other evidence of neural plasticity comes from findings that the upper regions of the temporal lobe, which are involved in hearing and understanding speech, can be activated by a born-deaf person's use of sign language (Nishimura et al., 1999). Such findings suggest that the assignment of language functions to brain structures may be a gradual process linked to verbal experience and cognitive development (Nobre & Plunkett, 1997).

Checkpoint

Can you . . .

- ✔ Name two areas of the brain involved in early language development, and tell the function of each?
- ✔ Give evidence for plasticity in the brain's linguistic areas?

Social Interaction: The Role of Parents and Caregivers Language is a social act. Parents or other caregivers play an important role at each stage of language development.

Prelinguistic Period At the babbling stage, adults help an infant advance toward true speech by repeating the sounds the baby makes. The baby soon joins in the game and repeats the sounds back. Parents' imitation of babies' sounds affects the pace of language learning (Hardy-Brown & Plomin, 1985; Hardy-Brown, Plomin, & DeFries, 1981). It also helps babies experience the social aspect of speech, the sense that a conversation consists of taking turns, an idea most babies seem to grasp at about $7\frac{1}{2}$ to 8 months of age. Even as early as 4 months, babies in a game of peekaboo show sensitivity to the structure of social exchange with an adult (Rochat, Querido, & Striano, 1999; refer back to Box 5-1).

Caregivers may help babies understand spoken words by, for example, pointing to a doll and saying, "Please give me Kermit." If the baby doesn't respond, the adult may pick up the doll and say, "Kermit." In one longitudinal study, mothers' responsiveness to 9-month-olds' and, even more so, to 13-month-olds' vocalization and play predicted the timing of language milestones, such as first spoken words and sentences. By 13 months, when children become better able to communicate, responses to their verbal initiatives become especially important (Tamis-LeMonda, Bornstein, & Baumwell, 2001).

Vocabulary Development When babies begin to talk, parents or caregivers often help them by repeating their first words and pronouncing them correctly. Vocabulary gets a boost when an adult seizes an appropriate opportunity to teach a child a new word. If Jordan's mother says, "This is a ball" when Jordan is looking at the ball, he is more likely to remember the word than if he were playing with something else and she tried to divert his attention to the ball (Dunham, Dunham & Curwin, 1993). Adults help a toddler who has begun to put words together by expanding on what the child says. If Christina says "Mommy sock," her mother may reply, "Yes, that is Mommy's sock."

Babies learn by listening to what adults say. A strong relationship has appeared between the frequency of various words in mothers' speech and the order in which children learn these words (Huttenlocher, Haight, Bryk, Seltzer, & Lyons, 1991), as well as between mothers' talkativeness and the size of toddlers' vocabularies (Huttenlocher, 1998).

However, sensitivity and responsiveness to a child's level of development count more than the number of words a mother uses. In one longitudinal study, in which toddlers were observed interacting with their mothers at 13 and 20 months, the mothers used an increasing number of words to match their children's growing language abilities; and the children with the biggest vocabularies had mothers who were most responsive (Bornstein, Tamis-LeMonda, & Haynes, 1999).

In households where two languages are spoken, babies often use elements of both languages at first, sometimes in the same utterance—a phenomenon called **code mixing.** Still, as we have seen, even young infants do learn to discriminate between languages. A naturalistic observation in Montreal (Genesee, Nicoladis, & Paradis, 1995) suggests that children as young as 2 in dual-language households differentiate between the two languages, using French, for example, with a predominantly French-speaking father and English with a predominantly English-speaking mother. This ability to shift from one language to another is called **code switching.** (Chapter 13 discusses second-language learning.)

code mixing Use of elements of two languages, sometimes in the same utterance, by young children in households where both languages are spoken.

code switching Changing one's speech to match the situation, as in people who are bilingual.

Child-Directed Speech You do not have to be a parent to speak "parentese." If, when you talk to an infant or toddler, you speak slowly in a high-pitched voice with exaggerated ups and downs, simplify your speech, exaggerate vowel sounds, and use short words and sentences and much repetition, you are using **child-directed speech (CDS).** Most adults, and even children, do it naturally. Such "baby talk" may well be universal; it has been documented in many languages and cultures (Kuhl et al., 1997).

Many researchers believe that CDS helps children to learn their native language, or at least to pick it up faster. In one cross-cultural observational study, mothers in the United States, Russia, and Sweden were audiotaped speaking to their 2- to 5-month-old infants. Whether the mothers were speaking English, Russian, or Swedish, they produced more exaggerated vowel sounds when talking to the infants than when talking to other adults. Apparently this kind of linguistic input helps infants hear the distinguishing features of speech sounds. At 20 weeks, the babies' babbling contained distinct vowels that reflected the phonetic differences to which their mothers' speech had alerted them (Kuhl et al., 1997).

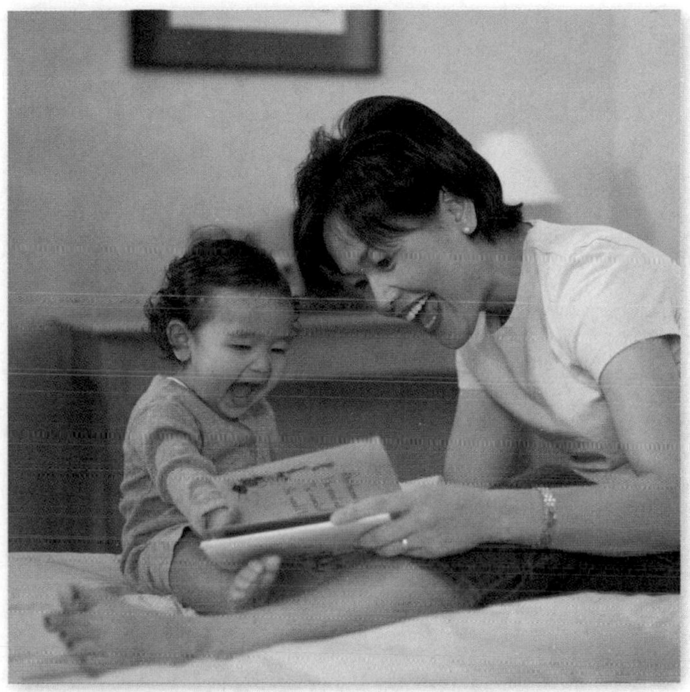

Despite controversy over the value of child-directed speech, or "parentese," this simplified way of speaking does *appeal to babies.*

child-directed speech (CDS) Form of speech often used in talking to babies or toddlers; includes slow, simplified speech, a high-pitched tone, exaggerated vowel sounds, short words and sentences, and much repetition. Also called *parentese.*

Some investigators challenge the value of CDS. They contend that babies speak sooner and better if they hear and can respond to more complex adult speech. In fact, some researchers say, children discover the rules of language faster when they hear complex sentences that use these rules more often and in more ways (Gleitman, Newport, & Gleitman, 1984; Oshima-Takane, Goodz, & Derevensky, 1996).

Nonetheless, infants themselves prefer simplified speech. This preference is clear before 1 month of age, and it does not seem to depend on any specific experience (Cooper & Aslin, 1990; Kuhl et al., 1997; Werker, Pegg, & McLeod, 1994).

The preference for CDS is not limited to spoken language. In an observational study in Japan, deaf mothers were videotaped reciting everyday sentences in sign language, first to their deaf 6-month-old infants and then to deaf adult friends. The mothers signed more slowly and with more repetition and exaggerated movements when directing the sentences to the infants, and other infants the same age paid more attention and appeared more responsive when shown these tapes (Masataka, 1996). What's more, 6-month-old *hearing* infants who had never been exposed to sign language also showed a preference for infant-directed sign (Masataka, 1998). This is powerful evidence that infants, whether hearing or deaf, are universally attracted to child-directed communication.

Checkpoint

Can you . . .

- ✔ Explain the importance of social interaction and give at least three examples of how parents or caregivers help babies learn to talk?
- ✔ Assess the value of child-directed speech (CDS)?

Preparing for Literacy: The Benefits of Reading Aloud

Most babies love to be read to, and the frequency with which parents or caregivers read to them, as well as the way they do it, can influence how well children speak and eventually how well they read. Children who learn to read early are generally those whose parents read to them very frequently when they were very young.

Reading to an infant or toddler offers opportunities for emotional intimacy and communication and fosters parent-child conversation. Read-aloud sessions offer a perfect opportunity for this kind of interaction.

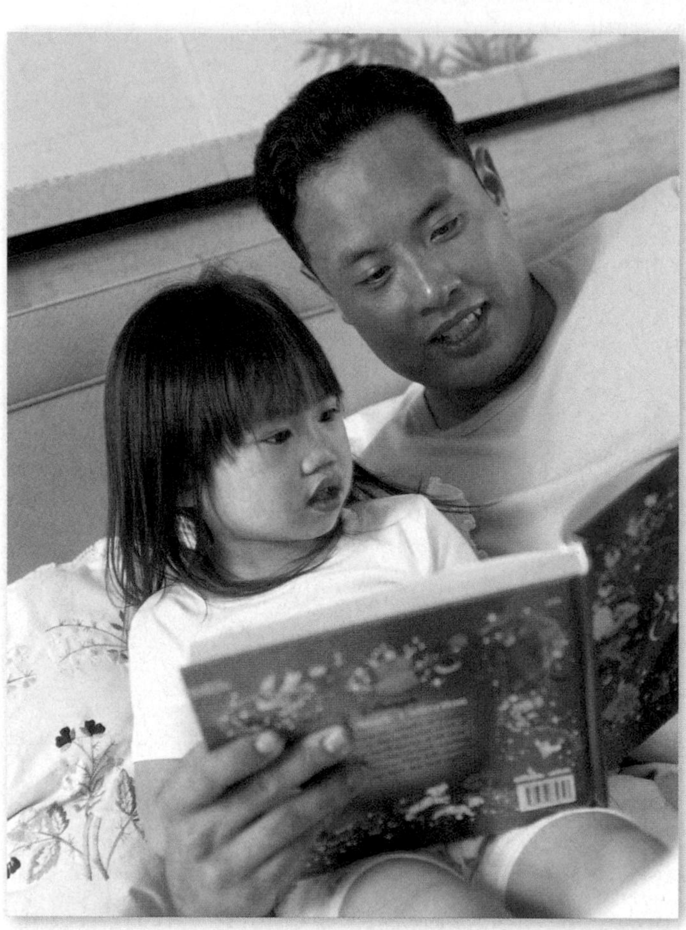

By reading aloud to his young daughter and asking questions about the pictures in the book, this father is helping her build language skills and learn how letters look and sound.

Adults tend to have one of three styles of reading to children: the *describer style, comprehender style,* and *performance-oriented style.* A *describer* focuses on describing what is going on in the pictures, and inviting the child to do so ("What are the Mom and Dad having for breakfast?"). A *comprehender* encourages the child to look more deeply at the meaning of a story and to make inferences and predictions ("What do you think the lion will do now?"). A *performance-oriented* reader reads the story straight through, introducing the main themes beforehand and asking questions afterward.

An adult's read-aloud style is best tailored to the needs and skills of the child. In an experimental study of fifty 4-year-olds in Dunedin, New Zealand, the describer style resulted in the greatest overall benefits for vocabulary and print skills, but the performance-oriented style was more beneficial for children who started out with large vocabularies (Reese & Cox, 1999).

A promising technique, both for normal children and for those who show language delays or are at risk of developing reading problems, is called *dialogic reading,* or shared reading. In this method (mentioned in Chapter 2), which is similar to the describer style, "the child learns to become the storyteller" while the adult acts as an active listener (Whitehurst & Lonigan, 1998, p. 859). Parents are taught to ask challenging, open-ended questions rather than those calling for a simple yes or no ("What is the cat doing?" instead of "Is the cat asleep?"). They follow up the child's answers with more questions, repeat and expand on what the child says, correct wrong answers and give alternative possibilities, help the child as needed, and give praise and encouragement. They encourage the child to relate a story to the child's own experience ("Have you ever seen a duck swimming? What did it look like?").

Children who are read to often, especially in this way, when they are 1 to 3 years old show better language skills at ages $2\frac{1}{2}$, $4\frac{1}{2}$, and 5 and better reading comprehension at age 7 (Crain-Thoreson & Dale, 1992; Wells, 1985). In one study, 21- to 35-month-olds whose parents used this method scored six months higher in vocabulary and expressive language skills than a control group. The experimental group also got a boost in *prereading skills,* the competencies helpful in learning to read, such as learning how letters look and sound (Arnold & Whitehurst, 1994; Whitehurst et al., 1988).

Why is shared reading more effective than just talking with a child? Shared reading affords a natural opportunity for giving information and increasing vocabulary. It provides a focus for both the adult's and child's attention and for asking and responding to questions. In addition, it is enjoyable for both children and adults; it offers a way to foster emotional bonding while enhancing cognitive development.

Checkpoint

Can you . . .

- ✔ Tell why reading aloud to children at an early age is beneficial?
- ✔ Describe an effective way of reading aloud to infants and toddlers?

Refocus

- Which approach to cognitive development seems closest to the one Darwin took in observing and describing his son's development? Why?
- How might a behaviorist, a Piagetian, a psychometrician, an information-processing researcher, a cognitive neuroscientist, and a social-contextual theorist attempt to study and explain the developments Darwin described?
- Did Doddy's early linguistic development seem more consistent with Skinner's or Chomsky's theory of language development? How does it illustrate the role of social interaction?

Social interaction in reading aloud, play, and other daily activities is a key to much of childhood development. Children call forth responses from the people around them and, in turn, react to those responses. In Chapter 6, we look more closely at these bidirectional influences as we explore early psychosocial development.

SUMMARY AND KEY TERMS

Studying Cognitive Development: Classic Approaches

Guidepost 1. How do infants learn, and how long can they remember?

- Two types of learning that behaviorists study are classical conditioning and operant conditioning.
- Rovee-Collier's research suggests that infants' memory processes are much like those of adults, but their memories fade quickly without periodic reminders.

behaviorist approach *(149)*
classical conditioning *(150)*
operant conditioning *(150)*

Guidepost 2. Can infants' and toddlers' intelligence be measured, and how can it be improved?

- Psychometric tests measure factors presumed to make up intelligence.

psychometric approach *(149)*
intelligent behavior *(152)*
IQ (intelligence quotient) tests *(152)*

- Developmental tests, such as the Bayley Scales of Infant Development, can indicate current functioning but are generally poor predictors of later intelligence.
- Socioeconomic status, parenting practices, and the home environment may affect measured intelligence.
- If developmental priming mechanisms are not present, early intervention may be needed.

Bayley Scales of Infant Development *(153)*
Home Observation for Measurement of the Environment (HOME) *(153)*
early intervention *(154)*
developmental priming mechanisms *(155)*

Guidepost 3. How did Piaget describe infants' and toddlers' cognitive development, and how have his claims stood up?

- During Piaget's sensorimotor stage, infants' schemes become more elaborate. They progress from primary to secondary to tertiary circular reactions and finally to the development of representational ability, which makes possible deferred imitation, pretending, and problem solving.

Piagetian approach *(149)*
sensorimotor stage *(156)*
schemes *(156)*
circular reactions *(157)*
representational ability *(159)*
deferred imitation *(159*

- Object permanence develops gradually. Piaget saw the A, not-B error as a sign of incomplete object knowledge and the persistence of egocentric thought.
- Research suggests that a number of abilities develop earlier than Piaget described. He may have underestimated young infants' grasp of object permanence and their imitative abilities.

object permanence *(159)*
A, not-B error *(159)*
egocentric *(161)*
allocentric *(161)*
invisible imitation *(163)*
visible imitation *(163)*

Studying Cognitive Development: Newer Approaches

Guidepost 4. How can we measure infants' ability to process information, and how does this ability relate to future intelligence?

- Information-processing researchers measure mental processes through habituation and other signs of perceptual abilities. Contrary to Piaget, such research suggests that representational ability is present virtually from birth.
- Indicators of the efficiency of infants' information processing, such as speed of habituation, tend to predict later intelligence.

information-processing approach *(164)*
habituation *(165)*
dishabituation *(165)*
visual preference *(166)*
visual recognition memory *(166)*
cross-modal transfer *(166)*

Guidepost 5. When do babies begin to think about characteristics of the physical world?

- Violation-of-expectations research suggests that infants as young as $3\frac{1}{2}$ to 5 months may have a rudimentary grasp of object permanence, a sense of number, the beginning of an understanding of causality, and an ability to reason about other characteristics of the physical world. Some researchers suggest that infants may have innate learning mechanisms for acquiring such knowledge. However, the meaning of these findings is in dispute.

violation-of-expectations *(167)*

Guidepost 6. What can brain research reveal about the development of cognitive skills?

- Brain studies have found that some forms of implicit memory and a primitive form of preexplicit memory develop during the first few months of life. Explicit memory and working memory emerge between 6 and 12 months of age. Neurological developments help explain the emergence of Piagetian skills and information-processing abilities.

cognitive neuroscience approach *(164)*
explicit memory *(171)*
implicit memory *(171)*
working memory *(171)*

Guidepost 7. How does social interaction with adults advance cognitive competence?

- Social interactions with adults contribute to cognitive competence through shared activities that help children learn skills, knowledge, and values important in their culture.

social-contextual approach *(164)*
guided participation *(172)*

Language Development

Guidepost 8. How do babies develop language?

- The acquisition of language is an important aspect of cognitive development.
- Prelinguistic speech includes crying, cooing, babbling, and imitating language sounds. By 6 months, babies have learned the basic sounds of their language and begin to become aware of its phonological rules and to link sound with meaning.
- Use of gestures is an important part of language development.
- Babies begin to recognize and understand words before they can say them. The first word typically comes sometime between 10 and 14 months, initiating linguistic speech. A "naming explosion" typically occurs sometime between 16 and 24 months of age.
- The first brief sentences generally come between 18 and 24 months. By age 3, syntax and communicative abilities are fairly well developed.
- Early speech is characterized by simplification, underextending and overextending word meanings, and overregularizing rules.
- Two classic theoretical views about how children acquire language are learning theory and nativism. Today, most developmentalists hold that an inborn capacity to learn language may be activated or constrained by experience.

language *(172)*
literacy *(172)*
prelinguistic speech *(173)*
linguistic speech *(175)*
holophrase *(175)*
telegraphic speech *(176)*
syntax *(176)*
nativism *(178)*
language acquisition device (LAD) *(178)*

Guidepost 9. What influences contribute to linguistic progress?

- Influences on language development include brain maturation and social interaction.
- Family characteristics, such as socioeconomic status and household size, may affect language learning.
- Child-directed speech (CDS) seems to have cognitive, emotional, and social benefits, and infants show a preference for it. However, some researchers dispute its value.
- Reading aloud to a child from an early age helps pave the way for literacy.

code mixing *(181)*
code switching *(181)*
child-directed speech (CDS) *(181)*

Psychosocial Development During the First Three Years

Chapter 6

*I'm like a child
trying to do everything
say everything
and be everything
all at once*

—John Hartford, "Life Prayer," 1971

Focus: Mary Catherine Bateson, Anthropologist

Mary Catherine Bateson

Mary Catherine Bateson (b. 1939) is an anthropologist, the daughter of two famous anthropologists: Margaret Mead (refer back to Chapter 2 Focus vignette) and Gregory Bateson, Mead's third husband and research partner. Hers was probably one of the most documented infancies on record—her mother taking notes, her father behind the camera. Margaret Mead's memoir, *Blackberry Winter* (1972), and Mary Catherine Bateson's *With a Daughter's Eye* (1984) together provide a rare and fascinating dual perspective on a child's emotional development.

Cathy—Mead's only child—was born when her mother was 38 years old. Her parents divorced when she was 11. Their work during World War II often necessitated long absences and separations. But during her infancy and toddlerhood, when they were still together, Cathy was the focus of their love and wholehearted attention. Her fondest early recollections are of sitting with her parents on a blanket outdoors, being read to on her mother's lap; and watching the two of them hold up their breakfast spoons to reflect the morning light, making a pair of "birds" flash across the walls for her amusement.

To avoid subjecting her to frustration, her parents tried to respond quickly to her needs. Mead arranged her professional commitments around breastfeeding and nursed "on demand," like the mothers in the island cultures she had studied. Like their friend Erik Erikson, Mead and Bateson placed great importance on the development of trust. They never left Cathy in a strange place with a strange person; she always met a new caregiver in a familiar place. As an adult, Catherine observed that, during difficult periods in her life, she often found "resources of faith and strength, a foundation that must have been built

OUTLINE

in those [first] two years" (Bateson, 1984, p. 35). Yet, as Mead wrote, reflecting on the contributions of nature and nurture, "How much was temperament? How much was felicitous accident? How much could be attributed to upbringing? We may never know" (1972, p. 268).

Mead tried to avoid overprotectiveness and to let Cathy be herself. Catherine remembers her father pushing her swing so high that he could run under it. Later he taught her to climb tall pine trees, testing every branch for firmness and making sure that she could find her way back down, while her mother, watching, tried not to show her fear.

When she was 2 and her parents' need to be away for wartime work increased, they merged households and moved in with a friend and colleague in New York City. The decision fit in with Mead's belief, gleaned from her studies, that children benefit from having multiple caregivers and learning to adapt to different situations.

The ménage in Frank's brownstone in Greenwich Village included his infant son, Colin, and five older children. "Thus," Catherine writes, "I did not grow up in a nuclear family or as an only child, but as a member of a flexible and welcoming extended family . . . , in which five or six pairs of hands could be mobilized to shell peas or dry dishes." Her summertime memories are of a lakeside retreat in New Hampshire, where "each child was cared for by enough adults so that there need be no jealousy, where the garden bloomed and the evenings ended in song. . . . I was rich beyond other children . . . and yet there were all those partings. There were all those beloved people, yet often the people I wanted most were absent" (Bateson, 1984, pp. 38–39).

In the story of Mary Catherine Bateson's early upbringing, we can see the importance of emotional and social development during the first two years. The joyful hours Cathy spent with her parents during those years provided a strong foundation for the rest of her life.

Margaret Mead's and Mary Catherine Bateson's complementary memoirs show how Mead put into practice the beliefs she had developed about child rearing, in part from memories of her own childhood and in part from observations of distant cultures. We see her seeking solutions to a problem that has become increasingly common: child care for children of working parents. And we see a bidirectionality of influence: how early experiences with parents help shape a child's development, and how a child's needs can shape parents' lives.

This chapter is about the shift from the dependence of infancy to the independence of childhood. We first examine foundations of *psychosocial development:* emotions, temperament, and early experiences with parents. We consider Erikson's views about the development of trust and autonomy. We look at relationships with caregivers, at the emerging sense of self, and at the foundations of conscience. We explore relationships with siblings and other children and with grandparents. Finally, we consider the increasingly widespread impact of parental employment and early child care.

After you have studied this chapter, you should be able to answer each of the following Guidepost questions. Look for them again in the margins, where they point to important concepts throughout the chapter. To check your understanding of these Guideposts, review the end-of-chapter summary. Checkpoints located at periodic spots throughout the chapter will help you verify your understanding of what you have read.

Guideposts for Study

1. What are emotions, when do they develop, and how do babies show them?
2. How do infants show temperamental differences, and how enduring are those differences?
3. What roles do mothers and fathers play in early personality development?
4. How do infants gain trust in their world and form attachments?
5. How do infants and caregivers "read" each other's nonverbal signals, and what happens when communication breaks down?
6. When and how do the self and self-concept arise?
7. How do toddlers develop autonomy and standards for socially acceptable behavior?
8. How do infants and toddlers interact with siblings and other children?
9. How do parental employment and early child care affect infants' and toddlers' development?

Foundations of Psychosocial Development

While babies share common patterns of development, they also—from the start—show distinct personalities, which reflect both inborn and environmental influences. From infancy on, personality development is intertwined with social relationships (see Table 6-1 on page 190).

Guidepost

1. What are emotions, when do they develop, and how do babies show them?

Emotions

Emotions, such as sadness, joy, and fear, are subjective reactions to experience, which are associated with physiological and behavioral changes (Sroufe, 1997).* Fear, for example, is accompanied by a faster heartbeat and, often, by self-protective action.

emotions Subjective reactions to experience that are associated with physiological and behavioral changes.

All normal human beings have the capacity to feel emotions, but people differ in how often they experience a particular emotion, in the kinds of events that may produce it, in the physical manifestations they show (such as heart rate changes), and in how they act as a result. One child may be easily angered; another is not. Culture influences the way people feel about a situation and the way they show their emotions. For example, some Asian cultures, which stress social harmony, discourage expression of anger but place much importance on shame. The opposite is often true in American culture, which stresses self-expression, self-assertion, and self-esteem (Cole, Bruschi, & Tamang, 2002).

Because emotions are subjective, they are difficult to study. Researchers disagree about how many emotions there are, when they arise, how they should be defined and measured, and even about what is or is not an emotion. Individuals themselves often do not know why they feel the way they do, and if they think they understand their emotions, the reason they give may not be the actual, underlying cause. How much more difficult it is, then, to study emotions in infants and young children!

*The discussion in this section is largely indebted to Sroufe (1997).

Table 6-1 Highlights of Infants' and Toddlers' Psychosocial Development, Birth to 36 Months

Approximate Age, Months	Characteristics
0–3	Infants are open to stimulation. They begin to show interest and curiosity, and they smile readily at people.
3–6	Infants can anticipate what is about to happen and experience disappointment when it does not. They show this by becoming angry or acting warily. They smile, coo, and laugh often. This is a time of social awakening and early reciprocal exchanges between the baby and the caregiver.
6–9	Infants play "social games" and try to get responses from people. They "talk" to, touch, and cajole other babies to get them to respond. They express more differentiated emotions, showing joy, fear, anger, and surprise.
9–12	Infants are intensely preoccupied with their principal caregiver, may become afraid of strangers, and act subdued in new situations. By 1 year, they communicate emotions more clearly, showing moods, ambivalence, and gradations of feeling.
12–18	Toddlers explore their environment, using the people they are most attached to as a secure base. As they master the environment, they become more confident and more eager to assert themselves.
18–36	Toddlers sometimes become anxious because they now realize how much they are separating from their caregiver. They work out their awareness of their limitations in fantasy and in play and by identifying with adults.

Source: Adapted from Sroufe, 1979.

Early investigators attempted to identify when various emotions are first shown. Learning theorists explained these developments as the result of conditioning. Later, ethologists became interested in the purposes emotions serve in people's survival and well-being as social animals.

In guiding and regulating behavior, emotions perform several protective functions. One such function is to communicate needs, intentions, or desires and to call forth a response. This communicative function is central to the development of social relationships and is especially important for infants, who must depend on adults to meet their basic needs. A second protective function, served by such emotions as fear and surprise, is to mobilize action in emergencies. A third function, that of such emotions as interest and excitement, is to promote exploration of the environment, which leads to learning that can protect or sustain life.

Today many developmental scientists view emotional development as an orderly process in which complex emotions unfold from simpler ones. A person's characteristic pattern of emotional reactions begins to develop during infancy and is a basic element of personality. Indeed, as we will see, an infant's earliest awareness of self is intimately tied in with emotional development. However, as children grow older, some emotional responses may change. A baby who, at 3 months of age, smiled at a stranger's face may, at 8 months, show wariness, or *stranger anxiety.* Also, different events may call forth the same emotion at different ages. An infant may smile or laugh when he sits on a plastic duck and hears a squeak; a toddler is likely to smile when she finds she can push a switch to turn on a light.

Emotion is closely tied to other aspects of development. For example, a newborn baby who is emotionally neglected—not hugged, caressed, or talked to—may show *nonorganic failure to thrive,* that is, failure to grow and gain weight despite adequate nutrition. The baby often will improve when moved to a hospital and given emotional support. Among both children and adults, anxiety has been linked to asthma, irritable bowel syndrome, ulcers, inflammatory bowel disease, coronary heart disease, and shortened life (Twenge, 2000). Such emotions as anger and fear, and especially shame, guilt, and sympathy, may motivate moral behavior (Ben-Ze'ev, 1997; Eisenberg, 2000; Eisenberg, Guthrie, et al., 1999; Kochanska, 1997a).

First Signs of Emotion Newborns plainly show when they are unhappy. They let out piercing cries, flail their arms and legs, and stiffen their bodies. It is harder to tell when they are happy. During the first month, they become quiet at the sound of a human voice or when they are picked up, and they may smile when their hands are moved together to play pat-a-cake. Later, infants respond more to people—smiling, cooing, reaching out, and eventually going to them.

These early signals or clues to babies' feelings are important steps in development. When babies want or need something, they cry; when they feel sociable, they smile or laugh. When their messages bring a response, their sense of connection with other people grows. Their sense of control over their world grows, too, as they see that their cries bring help and comfort and that their smiles and laughter elicit smiles and laughter in return. They become more able to actively participate in regulating their states of arousal and their emotional life.

The meaning of babies' emotional signals changes. At first, crying signifies physical discomfort; later, it more often expresses psychological distress. An early smile comes spontaneously as an expression of well-being; around 3 to 6 weeks, a smile may show pleasure in social contact. As babies get older, smiles and laughter at novel or incongruous situations reflect increasing cognitive awareness and growing ability to handle excitement (Sroufe, 1997).

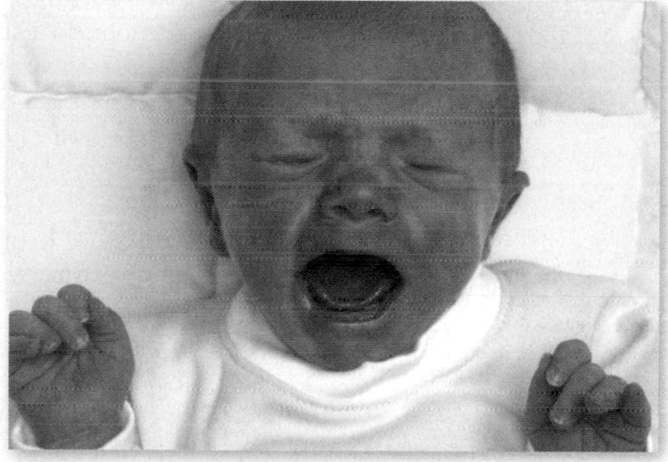

Crying is the most powerful way, and sometimes the only way, that babies can communicate their needs. Parents may soon learn to recognize whether their baby is crying because of hunger, anger, frustration, or pain.

Crying Crying is the most powerful way—and sometimes the only way—infants can communicate their needs. Some research has distinguished four patterns of crying (Wolff, 1969): the basic *hunger cry* (a rhythmic cry, which is not always associated with hunger); the *angry cry* (a variation of the rhythmic cry, in which excess air is forced through the vocal cords); the *pain cry* (a sudden onset of loud crying without preliminary moaning, sometimes followed by holding the breath); and the *frustration cry* (two or three drawn-out cries, with no prolonged breath-holding).

The more distressed a baby sounds, the more immediate the response is likely to be. However, the response may depend on the situation. Caregivers may wait longer to respond if, for example, they believe the baby's cry is a prelude to falling asleep (Wood & Gustafson, 2001).

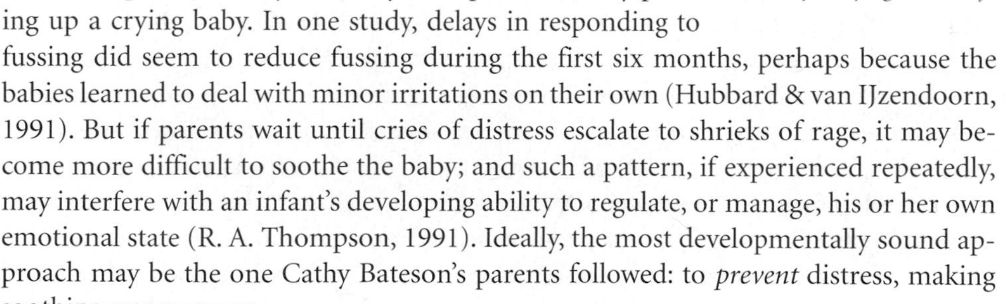

Some parents worry that they will spoil a child by picking up a crying baby. In one study, delays in responding to fussing did seem to reduce fussing during the first six months, perhaps because the babies learned to deal with minor irritations on their own (Hubbard & van IJzendoorn, 1991). But if parents wait until cries of distress escalate to shrieks of rage, it may become more difficult to soothe the baby; and such a pattern, if experienced repeatedly, may interfere with an infant's developing ability to regulate, or manage, his or her own emotional state (R. A. Thompson, 1991). Ideally, the most developmentally sound approach may be the one Cathy Bateson's parents followed: to *prevent* distress, making soothing unnecessary.

Smiling and Laughing The earliest faint smiles occur spontaneously soon after birth, apparently as a result of subcortical nervous system activity. These involuntary smiles frequently appear during periods of REM sleep (refer back to Chapter 4). They become less frequent during the first three months as the cortex matures (Sroufe, 1997).

At 6 months, butting heads with his grandfather makes Jackson laugh. Laughter at unusual or unexpected occurrences reflects growing cognitive understanding.

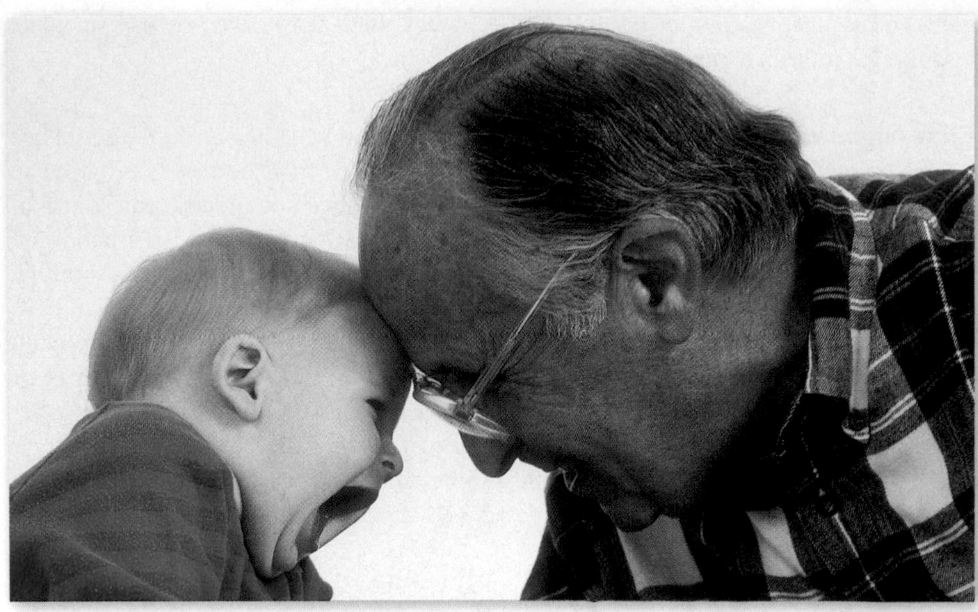

Checkpoint

Can you . . .

- ✔ Explain why emotions are difficult to study?
- ✔ Name three functions of emotions that aid in survival and well-being?
- ✔ Give examples of the role of emotions in other domains of development?
- ✔ Explain the significance of patterns of crying, smiling, and laughing?

The earliest *waking* smiles may be elicited by mild sensations, such as gentle jiggling or blowing on the infant's skin. In the second week, a baby may smile drowsily after a feeding. By the third week, most infants begin to smile when they are alert and paying attention to a caregiver's nodding head and voice. At about 1 month, smiles generally become more frequent and more social. During the second month, as visual recognition develops, babies smile more at visual stimuli, such as faces they know (Sroufe, 1997; Wolff, 1963).

At about the fourth month, infants start to laugh out loud when kissed on the stomach or tickled. As babies grow older, they become more actively engaged in mirthful exchanges. A 6-month-old may giggle in response to the mother making unusual sounds or appearing with a towel over her face; a 10-month-old may laughingly try to put the towel back on her face. This change reflects cognitive development: by laughing at the unexpected, babies show that they know what to expect. By turning the tables, they show awareness that they can make things happen. Laughter also helps babies discharge tension, such as fear of a threatening object (Sroufe, 1997).

When Do Emotions Appear? At what age do sadness, joy, fear, and other emotions develop? To answer that question, we need first to determine that an infant of a certain age is *showing* a particular emotion. Identifying infants' emotions is a challenge because babies cannot tell us what they feel. Still, parents, caregivers, and researchers learn to recognize clues. For example, Carroll Izard and his colleagues videotaped infants' facial expressions and interpreted them as showing joy, sadness, interest, and fear, and to a lesser degree anger, surprise, and disgust (Izard, Huebner, Resser, McGinness, & Dougherty, 1980). Of course, we do not know that these babies actually had the feelings they were credited with, but their facial expressions were remarkably similar to adults' expressions when experiencing these emotions.

Facial expressions are not the only, or necessarily the best, index of infants' emotions; motor activity, body language, and physiological changes also are important indicators. An infant can be fearful without showing a "fear face"; the baby may show fear by turning away or averting the gaze, or by a faster heartbeat, and these signs do not necessarily accompany each other. Different criteria may point to different conclusions about the timing of emergence of specific emotions. In addition, this timetable shows a good deal of individual variation (Sroufe, 1997).

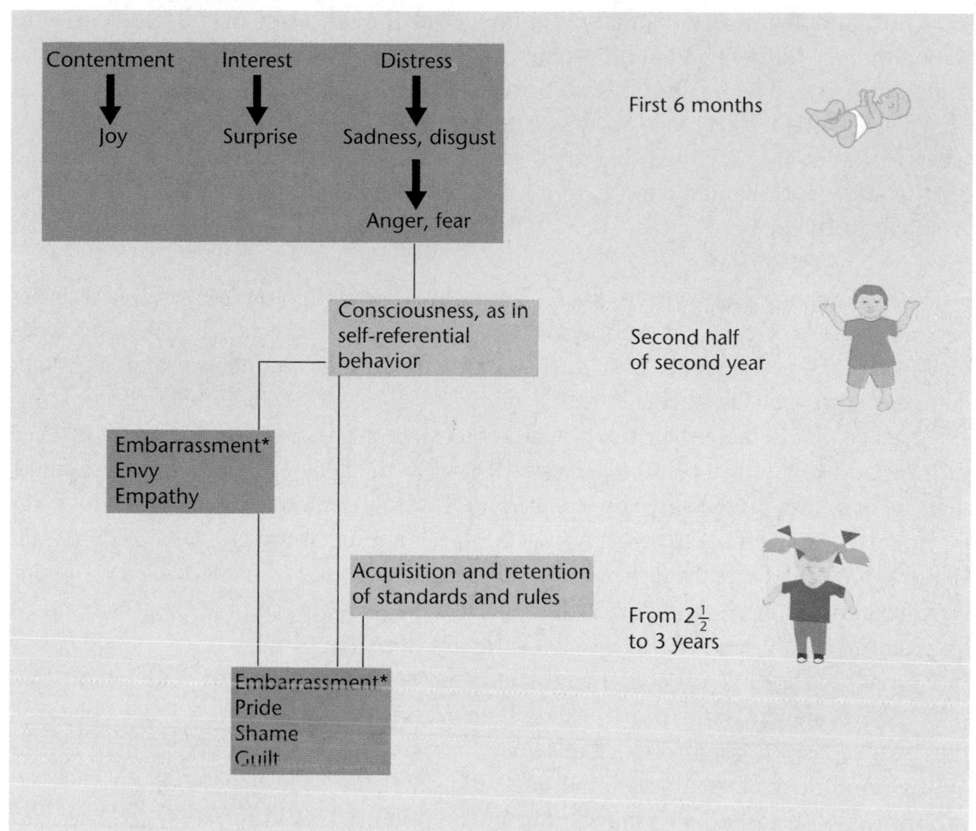

Figure 6-1
Differentiation of emotions during the first three years. The primary, or basic, emotions emerge during the first six months or so; the self-conscious emotions develop beginning in the second half of the second year, as a result of the emergence of self-awareness (consciousness of self) together with accumulation of knowledge about societal standards and rules. **Note:* There are two kinds of embarrassment. The earlier form does not involve evaluation of behavior and may simply be a response to being singled out as the object of attention. The second kind, evaluative embarrassment, which emerges during the third year, is a mild form of shame. (*Source:* Adapted from Lewis, 1997, Figure 1, p. 120.)

Basic Emotions According to one model (Lewis, 1997; see Figure 6-1), soon after birth babies show signs of contentment, interest, and distress. These are diffuse, reflexive, mostly physiological responses to sensory stimulation or internal processes. During the next six months or so, these early emotional states differentiate into true emotions: joy, surprise, sadness, disgust, and last, anger and fear—reactions to events that have meaning for the infant. As we'll discuss in the next section, the emergence of these basic, or primary, emotions is related to the biological "clock" of neurological maturation.

Although the repertoire of basic emotions seems to be universal, there are cultural variations in their expression. In laboratory observations, videotaped faces of 11-month-old Chinese infants whose arms were briefly restrained were less expressive of emotion than those of American and Japanese infants who underwent the same treatment (Camras et al., 1998). Whether these findings reflect cultural attitudes or innate differences in emotional reactivity is unclear.

Emotions Involving the Self **Self-conscious emotions,** such as embarrassment, empathy, and envy, arise only after children have developed **self-awareness:** the cognitive understanding that they have a recognizable identity, separate and different from the rest of their world. Consciousness of self seems to emerge between 15 and 24 months, when (according to Piaget) infants become able to make mental representations—of themselves as well as other people and things. Self-awareness is necessary before children can be aware of being the focus of attention, identify with what other "selves" are feeling, or wish they had what someone else has. By about age 3, having acquired self-awareness plus a good deal of knowledge about their society's accepted standards, rules, and goals, children show **self-evaluative emotions:** pride, shame, and guilt. They now can evaluate their own thoughts, plans, desires, and behavior against what is considered socially appropriate (Lewis, 1995, 1997, 1998).

self-conscious emotions Emotions, such as embarrassment, empathy, and envy, that depend on self-awareness.

self-awareness Realization that one's existence and functioning are separate from those of other people and things.

self-evaluative emotions Emotions, such as pride, shame, and guilt, which depend on both self-awareness and knowledge of socially accepted standards of behavior.

Guilt and shame are distinct emotions, even though both may be responses to wrongdoing. Children who fail to live up to behavioral standards may feel guilty (that is, regret their behavior), but they do not necessarily feel a lack of self-worth, as when they feel ashamed. Their focus is on a bad *act,* not a bad *self.* A guilty child will often try to make amends, say, by trying to put together a broken dish that the child knocked off the table; an ashamed child is more likely to try to hide the results of a misdeed (Eisenberg, 2000).

empathy Ability to put oneself in another person's place and feel what the other person feels.

Empathy: Feeling What Others Feel **Empathy**—the ability to put oneself in another person's place and feel what that person feels, or would be expected to feel, in a particular situation—is thought to arise during approximately the second year and, like guilt, increases with age (Eisenberg, 2000; Eisenberg & Fabes, 1998). As toddlers become increasingly able to differentiate their own mental state from that of another person, they can respond to another child's distress as if it were their own. A child who recognizes that she or he has caused such distress, perhaps by grabbing a toy that another child was playing with, may decide to give it back; and this empathic impulse may be akin to guilt (Hoffman, 1998). Empathy differs from *sympathy,* which merely involves sorrow or concern for another person's plight. Both empathy and sympathy tend to be accompanied by *prosocial behavior,* such as giving back the toy (see Chapter 8).

social cognition Ability to understand that other people have mental states and to gauge their feelings and intentions.

Empathy depends on **social cognition,** the cognitive ability to understand that others have mental states and to gauge their feelings and intentions. Piaget believed that egocentrism (a focus on a child's own viewpoint) delays the development of this ability until the concrete operational stage. But other research suggests that social cognition begins so early that it may be "an innate potential, like the ability to learn language" (Lillard & Curenton, 1999, p. 52). One-year-olds pick up emotional cues from television performers (Mumme & Fernald, 2003), and 18 month-olds seem to impute mental states to others (Meltzoff, 1995; refer back to Chapter 5).

Brain Growth and Emotional Development The growth of the brain after birth is closely connected with changes in emotional life. A newborn has only a diffuse sense of consciousness and is easily overstimulated and upset by sounds, lights, and other sources of sensory arousal. As the structures of the central nervous system develop and sensory pathways become myelinated, the baby's reactions become more focused and tempered, or modulated. Sensory processing becomes less reflexive as the cortex begins to function. This is a bidirectional process: emotional experiences not only are affected by brain development but can have long-lasting effects on the structure of the brain (Mlot, 1998; Sroufe, 1997).

There appear to be four major shifts in brain organization, which roughly correspond to changes in emotional processing (Schore, 1994; Sroufe, 1997, refer back to Figure 4-6). During the first three months, differentiation of basic emotions begins as the *cerebral cortex* becomes functional. The second shift occurs around 9 or 10 months, when the *frontal lobes* begin to interact with the limbic system, a seat of emotional reactions. At the same time, limbic structures such as the *hippocampus* become larger and more adultlike. Connections between the frontal cortex and the *hypothalamus* and limbic system, which process sensory information, may facilitate the relationship between the cognitive and emotional spheres. As these connections become denser and more elaborate, an infant can experience and interpret emotions at the same time.

Checkpoint

Can you . . .

✔ Trace a typical sequence of emergence of the basic, self-conscious, and evaluative emotions, and explain its connection with cognitive and neurological development?

The third shift takes place during the second year, when infants develop self-awareness, self-conscious emotions, and a greater capacity for regulating their own emotions and activities. These changes, which coincide with greater physical mobility and exploratory behavior, may be related to myelination of the frontal lobes. The fourth shift occurs around age 3, when hormonal changes in the autonomic nervous system coincide with the emergence of evaluative emotions.

Neurological factors also may play a part in temperamental differences (Mlot, 1998), the topic we turn to next.

Temperament

Temperament—sometimes defined as a person's characteristic, biologically based way of approaching and reacting to people and situations—has been described as the *how* of behavior: not *what* people do, but how they go about doing it (Thomas & Chess, 1977). Two toddlers, for example, may be equally able to dress themselves and may be equally motivated, but one may do it more quickly than the other, be more willing to put on a new outfit, and be less distracted if the cat jumps on the bed. Some researchers look at temperament more broadly. A child may not act the same way in all situations. And temperament may affect not only the way children approach and react to the outside world, but the way they regulate their own mental, emotional, and behavioral functioning (Rothbart, Ahadi, & Evans, 2000).

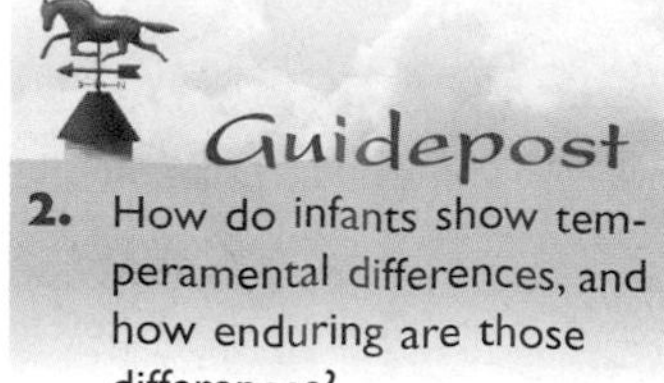

2. How do infants show temperamental differences, and how enduring are those differences?

temperament Characteristic disposition, or style of approaching and reacting to situations.

Temperament has an emotional basis; but while emotions such as fear, excitement, and boredom come and go, temperament is relatively consistent and enduring. Individual differences in temperament, which are thought to derive from a person's basic biological makeup, form the core of a developing personality—the relatively consistent patterns of feeling, thought, and behavior that make a person unique (Eisenberg, Fabes, Guthrie, & Reiser, 2000).

Studying Temperamental Patterns In the New York Longitudinal Study (NYLS), a pioneering study on temperament, researchers followed 133 infants into adulthood, interviewing, testing, and observing them and interviewing their parents and teachers. The researchers looked at how active the children were; how regular they were in hunger, sleep, and bowel habits; how readily they accepted new people and situations; how they adapted to changes in routine; how sensitive they were to noise, bright lights, and other sensory stimuli; how intensely they responded; whether their mood tended to be pleasant, joyful, and friendly or unpleasant, unhappy, and unfriendly; and whether they persisted at tasks or were easily distracted (A. Thomas, Chess, & Birch, 1968). The children differed in all these characteristics, almost from birth, and the differences tended to continue.

Almost two-thirds of the children fell into one of three categories (see Table 6-2 on page 196). Forty percent were **"easy" children:** generally happy, rhythmic in biological

"easy" children Children with a generally happy temperament, regular biological rhythms, and readiness to accept new experiences.

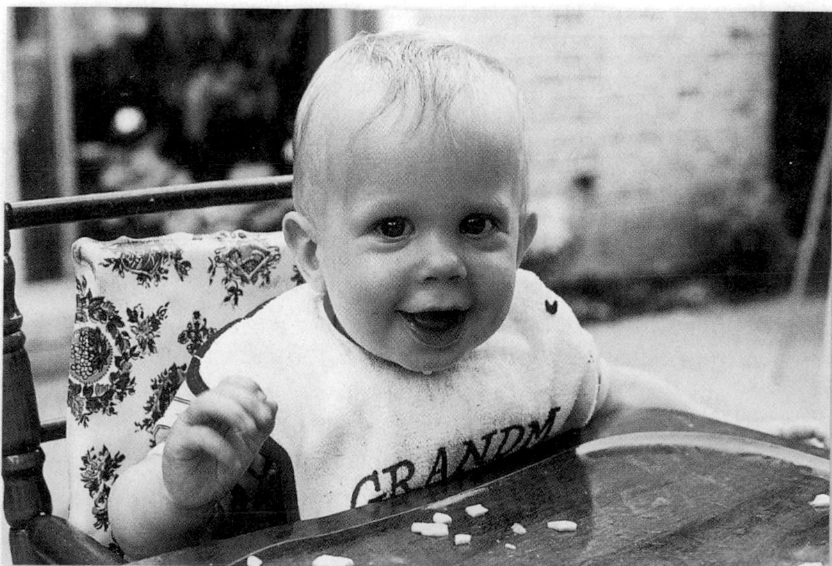

Seven-month-old Daniel's ready smile and willingness to try a new food are signs of an easy temperament.

Table 6-2 Three Temperamental Patterns (according to the New York Longitudinal Study)

"Easy" Child	"Difficult" Child	"Slow-to-Warm-Up" Child
Has moods of mild to moderate intensity, usually positive	Displays intense and frequently negative moods; cries often and loudly; also laughs loudly	Has mildly intense reactions, both positive and negative
Responds well to novelty and change	Responds poorly to novelty and change	Responds slowly to novelty and change
Quickly develops regular sleep and feeding schedules	Sleeps and eats irregularly	Sleeps and eats more regularly than difficult child, less regularly than easy child
Takes to new foods easily	Accepts new foods slowly	Shows mildly negative initial response to new stimuli (a first encounter with a new person, place, or situation)
Smiles at strangers	Is suspicious of strangers	
Adapts easily to new situations	Adapts slowly to new situations	
Accepts most frustrations with little fuss	Reacts to frustration with tantrums	
Adapts quickly to new routines and rules of new games	Adjusts slowly to new routines	Gradually develops liking for new stimuli after repeated, unpressured exposures

Source: Adapted from A. Thomas & Chess, 1984.

"difficult" children Children with irritable temperament, irregular biological rhythms, and intense emotional responses.

"slow-to-warm-up" children Children whose temperament is generally mild but who are hesitant about accepting new experiences.

goodness of fit Appropriateness of environmental demands and constraints to a child's temperament.

functioning, and accepting of new experiences. This is how Margaret Mead described the infant Cathy. Ten percent were what the researchers called **"difficult" children:** more irritable and harder to please, irregular in biological rhythms, and more intense in expressing emotion. Fifteen percent were **"slow-to-warm-up" children:** mild but slow to adapt to new people and situations (A. Thomas & Chess, 1977, 1984).

Many children (including 35 percent of the NYLS sample) do not fit neatly into any of these three groups. A baby may eat and sleep regularly but be afraid of strangers. A child may be easy most of the time, but not always. Another child may warm up slowly to new foods but adapt quickly to new baby-sitters (A. Thomas & Chess, 1984). A child may laugh intensely but not show intense frustration, and a child with rhythmic toilet habits may show irregular sleeping patterns (Rothbart et al., 2000). All these variations are well within the normal range.

"Difficult" children are not necessarily maladjusted. According to the NYLS, the key to healthy adjustment is **goodness of fit:** the match between a child's temperament and the environmental demands and constraints the child must deal with, including caregivers' temperaments. If a very active child is expected to sit still for long periods, if a slow-to-warm-up child is constantly pushed into new situations, or if a persistent child is constantly taken away from absorbing projects, trouble may occur. When parents recognize that a child acts in a certain way, not out of willfulness, laziness, or stupidity, but largely because of inborn temperament, they are less likely to feel guilty, anxious, or hostile or to be rigid or impatient. They can anticipate the child's reactions and help the child adapt—for example, by giving early warnings of the need to stop an activity, or, as Mead and Bateson did, gradually introducing a child to new situations.

Because the complex interviewing and scoring procedures used in the NYLS are cumbersome, many researchers now use questionnaires. A parental self-report instrument—the Rothbart Infant Behavior Questionnaire, or IBQ (Rothbart et al., 2000)—focuses on several dimensions of infant temperament similar to those in the NYLS: fear, frustration, positive emotion, soothability, and duration of orienting (a combination of distractibility and attention span). A companion Children's Behavior Questionnaire, or CBQ (Rothbart, Ahadi, Hershey, & Fisher, 2001), covers three clusters of personality characteristics: (1) *extraversion* (impulsiveness, intense pleasure, high activity level, boldness, risk taking, comfort in new social situations), (2) *negative affect* (sadness, discomfort, anger, frustration, fear, high reactivity), and (3) *effortful control* (inhibitory control, low-intensity pleasure, ability to focus attention, perceptual sensitivity).

How Stable Is Temperament? Temperament appears to be largely inborn, probably hereditary (Braungart, Plomin, DeFries, & Fulker, 1992; Emde et al., 1992; Schmitz et al., 1996; A. Thomas & Chess, 1977, 1984), and fairly stable. Newborn babies show different patterns of sleeping, fussing, and activity, and these differences tend to persist to some degree (Korner, 1996; Korner et al., 1985).

That does not mean temperament is fully formed at birth. Temperament develops as various emotions and self-regulatory capacities appear (Rothbart et al., 2000) and can change in response to parental attitudes and treatment (Belsky, Fish, & Isabella, 1991; J. V. Lerner & Galambos, 1985). In the NYLS, many children switched temperamental styles, especially during the early months, apparently reacting to special experiences or parental handling (Lerner & Galambos, 1985; A. Thomas & Chess, 1984).

Still, studies using the IBQ during infancy and the CBQ at age 7 found strong links between infant temperament and childhood personality (Rothbart et al., 2000, 2001). Other researchers, using temperamental types similar to those of the NYLS, have found that temperament at age 3 closely predicts personality at ages 18 and 21 (Caspi, 2000; Caspi & Silva, 1995; Newman, Caspi, Moffitt, & Silva, 1997).

Biological Bases of Temperament Temperament, like emotion, seems to have a biological basis. In longitudinal research with about 400 children starting in infancy, Jerome Kagan and his colleagues have studied an aspect of temperament called *inhibition to the unfamiliar,* or shyness, which has to do with how sociable a child is with strange children and how boldly or cautiously the child approaches unfamiliar objects and situations. This characteristic is associated with differences in physical features, such as eye color, and in brain functioning, as reflected in physiological signs such as heart rate, blood pressure, and pupil dilation. When asked to solve problems or learn new information, the shyest children (about 15 percent of the sample) showed higher and less variable heart rates than bolder children, and the pupils of their eyes dilated more. The boldest children (about 10 to 15 percent) tended to be energetic and spontaneous and to have very low heart rates (Arcus & Kagan, 1995).

Four month olds who were highly reactive—that is, who showed much motor activity and distress, or who fretted or cried readily in response to new stimuli—were likely to show the inhibited pattern at 14 and 21 months. Babies who were highly inhibited or uninhibited seemed to maintain these patterns to some degree during childhood and adolescence (Kagan, 1997; Kagan & Snidman, 1991a, 1991b). However, behavioral distinctions between these two types of children tend to "smoothe out" by preadolescence, even though the physiological distinctions remain (Woodward et al., 2001).

Again, experience can moderate or accentuate early tendencies. Male toddlers who were inclined to be fearful and shy were more likely to remain so at age 3 if their parents were highly accepting of the child's reactions. But if parents encouraged their sons to venture into new situations, the boys tended to become less inhibited (Park, Belsky, Putnam, & Crnic, 1997).

In a separate four-year longitudinal study of 153 infants, those whose behavior patterns changed from inhibited to uninhibited showed different patterns of brain activity from those who remained inhibited. The infants who changed in temperament also were more likely to have had nonparental caregiving during the first two years (Fox, Henderson, Rubin, Calkins, & Schmidt, 2001).

What's Your View?

- In the United States, many people consider shyness undesirable. How should a parent handle a shy child? Do you think it is best to accept the child's temperament or try to change it?

Cross-Cultural Differences As Margaret Mead observed, temperament may be affected by culturally influenced childraising practices. Infants in Malaysia, an island group in Southeast Asia, tend to be less adaptable, more wary of new experiences, and more readily responsive to stimuli than U.S. babies. This may be because Malay parents do not often expose young children to situations that require adaptability, and

Checkpoint

Can you . . .

- List and describe nine aspects and three patterns of temperament indentified by the New York Longitudinal Study?
- Explain the importance of "goodness of fit"?
- Assess evidence for the stability of temperament?
- Discuss evidence of biological and cultural differences in temperament?

they encourage infants to be acutely aware of sensations, such as the need for a diaper change (Banks, 1989).

A cross-cultural study of Chinese and Canadian 2-year-olds casts further light on the concept of goodness of fit. Canadian mothers of inhibited children tended to be punitive or overprotective, whereas Chinese mothers of shy children were warm and accepting and encouraged them to achieve. The Chinese toddlers were significantly more inhibited than the Canadian ones. In western countries such as Canada, shy, inhibited children tend to be seen as incompetent, immature, and unlikely to accomplish much; their mothers may emotionally reject them or give them special guidance and protection. In China, shyness and inhibition are socially approved. Thus a naturally inhibited Chinese child may be less motivated to come out of his or her shell. However, because this was a correlational study, we don't know whether the children's temperament was a consequence or a cause of their mothers' treatment, or perhaps a bidirectional effect (Chen et al., 1998).

Earliest Social Experiences: The Infant in the Family

Guidepost

3. What roles do mothers and fathers play in early personality development?

Infant care practices and patterns of interaction vary greatly around the world, depending on the culture's view of infants' nature and needs. In Bali, infants are believed to be ancestors or gods brought to life in human form and thus must be treated with utmost dignity and respect. The Beng of West Africa think that young babies can understand all languages, whereas people in the Micronesian atoll of Ifaluk believe that babies cannot understand language at all, and therefore adults do not speak to them (DeLoache & Gottlieb, 2000).

Among the Efe people of central Africa, infants typically receive care from five or more people in a given hour and are routinely breast-fed by other women besides the mother (Tronick, Morelli, & Ivey, 1992). Among the Gusii in western Kenya, where infant mortality is high, parents are more likely than those in industrial societies to keep their infants close to them, respond quickly when they cry, and feed them on demand (LeVine, 1974, 1989, 1994). The same is true of Aka foragers (hunter-gatherers) in central Africa, who move around frequently in small, tightly knit groups marked by extensive sharing, cooperation, and concern about danger. However, Ngandu farmers in the same region, who tend to live farther apart and to stay in one place for long periods of time, are more likely to leave their infants alone and to let them fuss or cry, smile, vocalize, or play (Hewlett, Lamb, Shannon, Leyendecker, & Schölmerich, 1998).

A highly physical style of play, characteristic of the way many U.S. fathers play with their infants, is not typical of fathers in all cultures. Swedish and German fathers usually do not play with their babies this way (Lamb, Frodi, Frodi, & Hwang, 1982; Parke, Grossman, & Tinsley, 1981). Nor do African Aka fathers (Hewlett, 1987) and those in New Delhi, India (Roopnarine, Hooper, Ahmeduzzaman, & Pollack, 1993; Roopnarine, Talokder, Jain, Josh, & Srivastav, 1992). Such cross-cultural variations suggest that rough play is *not* a function of male biology, but instead is culturally influenced.

We need to remember, then, that patterns of adult-infant interaction we take for granted may be culture-based. With that caution in mind, let's look first at the roles of the mother and father—how they care for and play with their babies, and how their influence begins to shape personality differences between boys and girls. Later in this chapter, we look more deeply at relationships with parents and, finally, at interactions with siblings.

The Mother's Role In a series of pioneering experiments by Harry Harlow and his colleagues, rhesus monkeys were separated from their mothers six to twelve hours after birth and raised in a laboratory. The infant monkeys were put into cages with one of two kinds of surrogate "mothers": a plain cylindrical wire-mesh form or a form covered with terry cloth. Some monkeys were fed from bottles connected to the wire "mothers"; others were "nursed" by the warm, cuddly cloth ones. When the monkeys were allowed to spend time with either kind of "mother," they all spent more time clinging to the cloth surrogates, even if they were being fed only by the wire ones. In an unfamiliar room, the babies "raised" by cloth surrogates showed more natural interest in exploring than those "raised" by wire surrogates, even when the appropriate "mothers" were there.

Apparently, the monkeys also remembered the cloth surrogates better. After a year's separation, the "cloth-raised" monkeys eagerly ran to embrace the terry-cloth forms, whereas the "wire-raised" monkeys showed no interest in the wire forms (Harlow & Zimmerman, 1959). None of the monkeys in either group grew up normally, however (Harlow & Harlow, 1962), and none were able to nurture their own offspring (Suomi & Harlow, 1972).

It is hardly surprising that a dummy mother would not provide the same kinds of stimulation and opportunities for development as a live mother. These experiments show that feeding is not the only, or even the most important thing babies get from their mothers. Mothering includes the comfort of close bodily contact and, in monkeys, the satisfaction of an innate need to cling. Human infants also have social needs that must be satisfied if they are to grow up normally. In the next major section of this chapter we discuss the importance of trust, attachment, and emotional communication.

In a series of classic experiments, Harry Harlow and Margret Harlow showed that food is not the most important way to a baby's heart. When infant rhesus monkeys could choose whether to go to a wire surrogate "mother" or a warm, soft terry-cloth "mother," they spent more time clinging to the cloth mother, even if they were being fed by bottles connected to the wire mother.

The Father's Role In the past, research on infant psychosocial development focused almost exclusively on mothers and babies, but now researchers are studying relationships between infants and their fathers, as well as siblings and other caregivers. By looking at the family as a functioning unit, we get a fuller picture of the network of relationships among all its members.

All cultures recognize the fathering role; but, beyond the initial act of insemination, it may be seen as a social construction (Doherty, Kouneski, & Erickson, 1998; refer back to Chapter 1). The role may be taken or shared by someone other than the biological father: the mother's brother, as in Botswana (where young mothers remain with their own childhood family until their partners are in their forties), or a grandfather, as in Vietnam (Engle & Breaux, 1998; Richardson, 1995; Townsend, 1997).

The father's role, like the mother's, entails emotional commitments, and often direct involvement in the care and upbringing of children (Engle & Breaux, 1998). Still, while fathers' involvement varies greatly (see Box 6-1 on page 200), women are children's primary caregivers in most cultures. In the United States, fathers' involvement in caregiving and play has greatly increased since 1970 as more mothers work outside the home and concepts of fathering change (Cabrera et al., 2000; Casper, 1997; Pleck, 1997). A father's frequent and positive involvement with his child, from infancy on, is directly related to the child's well-being and cognitive and social development (Cabrera et al., 2000).

What's Your View?

- "Despite the increasingly active role many of today's fathers play in child raising, a mother will always be more important to babies and young children than a father." Do you agree or disagree?

BOX 6-1

Window on the World

Fatherhood in Three Cultures

Fatherhood has different meanings in different cultures. In some societies, fathers are more involved in their young children's lives—economically, emotionally, and in time spent—than in other cultures. In many parts of the world, what it means to be a father has changed—and is changing (Engle & Breaux, 1998).*

Urbanization in West Africa and Inner Mongolia In Cameroon and other rural areas of West Africa (Nsamenang, 1987, 1992a, 1992b), men have more than one wife, and children grow up in large extended families linked to kinship-based clans. Although children guarantee the perpetuation of a man's family line, they belong to the kinship group, not just to the parents. After weaning, children may have multiple caregivers or may even be given to other members of the group to raise.

The father has the dominant position in the family and gives his children their connection with the clan. The mother is literally the breadwinner, responsible for providing her children's food, but the father controls his wives and their earnings; and wives compete for their husbands' favor. Fathers are primarily disciplinarians and advisers. They have little contact with infants but serve as guides, companions, and models for older children.

With the coming of urbanization and western values, these traditional gender roles are breaking up. Many men are pursuing financial goals and are spending almost no time with their children. With the vanishing of traditional folkways, these men no longer know how to be fathers. They can no longer tell folktales to young children around the fire or teach their sons how to do a man's work.

Among the Huhot of Inner Mongolia, a province of China, fathers traditionally are responsible for discipline and mothers for nurturing; but fathers also provide economic support (Jankowiak, 1992). Children have strong bonds with mothers, who live in the homes of their mothers-in-law and have no economic power. Fathers are stern and aloof, and their children respect and fear them. Men almost never hold infants; they are believed to be incapable of it. Fathers interact more with toddlers but perform child care duties reluctantly, and only if the mother is absent.

Here, as in Cameroon, urbanization is changing these traditionally gender-typed attitudes—but in the opposite direction. Families now live in very small quarters, and women work outside the home. Fathers—especially college-educated ones—now seek more intimate relationships with children, especially sons. China's official one-child policy has accentuated this change, leading both parents to be more deeply involved with their only child.

Aka Pygmies The Aka are hunter-gatherers in the tropical forests of central Africa who move frequently from camp to camp in small, tightly knit groups and are highly protective of young children. In contrast with fathers in the other two cultures just described, Aka fathers are as nurturant and emotionally supportive as Aka mothers. In fact, "Aka fathers provide more direct infant care than fathers in any other known society" (Hewlett, 1992, p. 169). They hold their babies frequently and hug, kiss, clean, and play gently with them (Hewlett, 1987).

This behavior is in line with *family systems theory,* which predicts that fathers will be more involved in the care of young children in cultures in which husbands and wives frequently cooperate in subsistence tasks and other activities (Hewlett, 1992). Among the Aka and other societies with high paternal involvement in infant care, the key is not just that both parents participate in such activities, but that they do it together. The father's role in child care is part and parcel of his role in the family.

What's Your View?

How do you think your relationship with your father might have been different if you had grown up in Cameroon? Among the Huhot of Inner Mongolia? Among Aka Pygmies?

Check It Out:

For more information on this topic, go to www.mhhe.com/papaliah9, where you'll find a link to an article that discusses the influence of fathers on their children's development.

*Unless otherwise referenced, this box is based on Engle & Breaux, 1998.

At the same time, many fathers are not even present in the household (Cabrera et al., 2000; Coley, 2001); 32 percent of families in the United States are headed by women (mostly single mothers), and even higher rates are reported in Norway and in some African and Caribbean countries (Engle & Breaux, 1998). A father's absence may affect a child in many ways, from economic loss to psychological distress (Cabrera et al., 2000).

What conditions promote "responsible fathering"—a father's active involvement in meeting his child's financial, physical, and emotional needs? Factors may include his motivation and commitment, his beliefs about fathering, his confidence in his parenting skills, his success as a breadwinner, his relationship with the mother, and the extent to which she encourages his involvement (Coley, 2001; Doherty et al., 1998; Lamb, Pleck, Charnov, & Levine, 1985; Pleck, 1997).

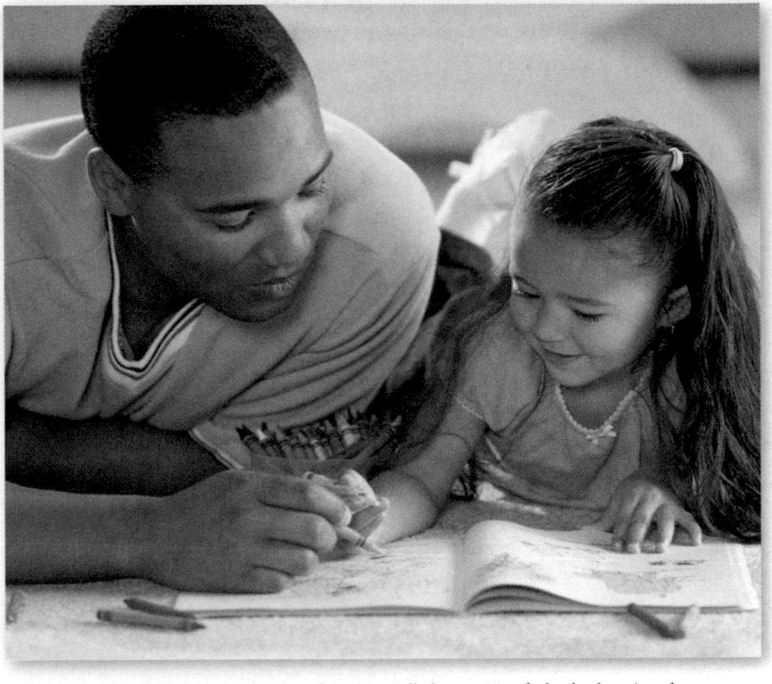

Coloring with Daddy is an activity after this girl's heart. Her father's close involvement contributes to her cognitive, as well as emotional, development.

How Parents Shape Gender Differences

Being male or female affects how people look, how they move their bodies, and how they work, play, and dress. It influences what they think about themselves and what others think of them. All those characteristics—and more—are included in the word **gender:** what it means to be male or female.

Measurable differences between baby boys and girls are few. Males are physically more vulnerable than females from conception on. On the other hand, baby boys are a bit longer and heavier than baby girls and may be slightly stronger. Newborn boys and girls react differently to stress, possibly suggesting genetic, hormonal, or temperamental differences (Davis & Emory, 1995). An analysis of a large number of studies found baby boys more active than baby girls, though this difference is not consistently documented (Eaton & Enns, 1986). The two sexes are equally sensitive to touch and tend to teethe, sit up, and walk at about the same ages (Maccoby, 1980).

gender Significance of being male or female.

gender-typing Socialization process by which children, at an early age, learn appropriate gender roles.

Parental shaping of boys' and girls' personalities appears to begin very early. Fathers, especially, promote **gender-typing,** the process by which children learn behavior that their culture considers appropriate for each sex (Bronstein, 1988). Fathers treat boys and girls more differently than mothers do, even during the first year (M. E. Snow, Jacklin, & Maccoby, 1983). During the second year, fathers talk more and spend more time with sons than with daughters (Lamb, 1981). Mothers talk more, and more supportively, to daughters than to sons. Overall, fathers are less talkative and supportive—but also less negative—in their speech than mothers are. These differences are especially pronounced with toddlers, whose mothers typically spend much more time with them than fathers do (Leaper, Anderson, & Sanders, 1998). Fathers of toddlers play more roughly with sons and show more sensitivity to daughters (Kelley, Smith, Green, Berndt, & Rogers, 1998).

We discuss gender-typing and gender differences in more depth in Chapter 8.

Checkpoint

Can you . . .

- ✔ Give examples of cultural differences in care and treatment of infants?
- ✔ Compare the roles of fathers and mothers in meeting infants' needs?
- ✔ Describe how mothers and fathers influence gender-typing?

Developmental Issues in Infancy

How does a dependent newborn, with a limited emotional repertoire and pressing physical needs, become a child with complex feelings and the abilities to understand and control them? Much of this development revolves around issues regarding relationships with caregivers.

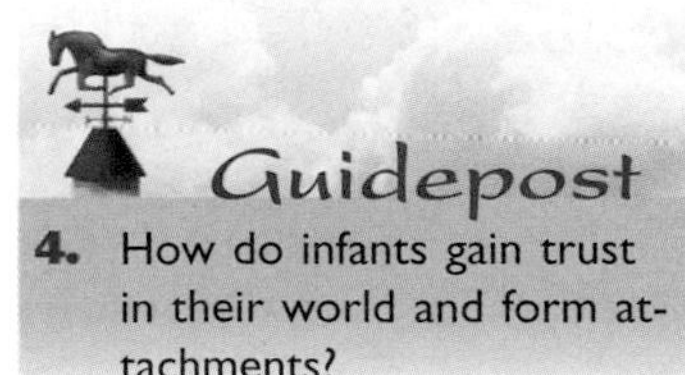

Guidepost

4. How do infants gain trust in their world and form attachments?

Developing Trust

For a far longer period than the young of other mammals, human babies are dependent on other people for food, for protection, and for their very lives. How do they come to trust that their needs will be met? According to Erikson (1950), early experiences are the key.

According to Erikson, this newborn infant will develop trust in the world through reliance on the mother's sensitive, responsive, consistent caregiving.

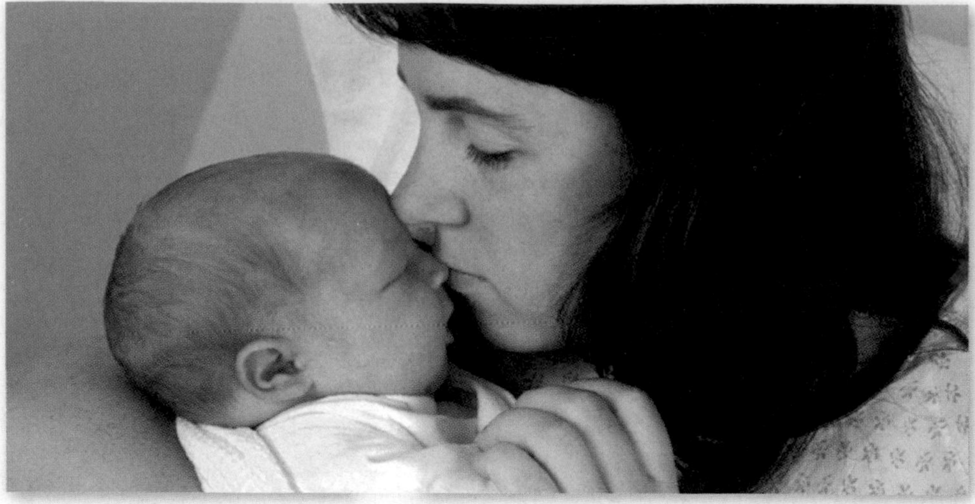

basic trust versus basic mistrust Erikson's first stage in psychosocial development, in which infants develop a sense of the reliability of people and objects.

The first stage in psychosocial development that Erikson identified is **basic trust versus basic mistrust** (refer back to Table 2-2 in Chapter 2). This stage begins at birth and continues until about 12 to 18 months. In these early months, babies develop a sense of the reliability of the people and objects in their world. They need to develop a balance between trust (which lets them form intimate relationships) and mistrust (which enables them to protect themselves). If trust predominates, as it should, children develop the "virtue" of *hope:* the belief that they can fulfill their needs and obtain their desires (Erikson, 1982). If mistrust predominates, children will view the world as unfriendly and unpredictable and will have trouble forming relationships.

Checkpoint

Can you . . .

✔ Explain the importance of Erikson's stage of basic trust versus basic mistrust and identify what he saw as the critical element in its resolution?

The critical element in developing trust is sensitive, responsive, consistent caregiving. In an echo of Freud's oral stage (described in Chapter 2), Erikson saw the feeding situation as the setting for establishing the right mix of trust and mistrust. Can the baby count on being fed when hungry, and can the baby therefore trust the mother as a representative of the world? Trust enables an infant to let the mother out of sight "because she has become an inner certainty as well as an outer predictability" (Erikson, 1950, p. 247). It is this inner trust that, for Cathy Bateson, may have formed a solid foundation for the more difficult periods ahead.

Developing Attachments

attachment Reciprocal, enduring tie between infant and caregiver, each of whom contributes to the quality of the relationship.

Attachment is a reciprocal, enduring emotional tie between an infant and a caregiver, each of whom contributes to the quality of the relationship. Attachments have adaptive value for babies, ensuring that their psychosocial as well as physical needs will be met. According to ethological theory, infants and parents are biologically predisposed to become attached to each other, and attachment promotes a baby's survival.

Studying Patterns of Attachment Mary Ainsworth first studied attachment in the early 1950s with John Bowlby. On the basis of ethological studies of bonding in animals and observation of disturbed children in a London psychoanalytic clinic, Bowlby (1951), was convinced of the importance of the mother-baby bond; he warned against separating mother and baby without providing good substitute caregiving. Ainsworth, after studying attachment in African babies in Uganda through naturalistic observation in their homes (Ainsworth, 1967), devised the **Strange Situation,** a now-standard laboratory-based technique designed to assess attachment patterns between an infant and an adult. Typically, the adult is the mother (though other adults have taken part as well), and the infant is 10 to 24 months old.

Strange Situation Laboratory technique used to study attachment.

The Strange Situation consists of a sequence of eight episodes, which takes less than half an hour. During that time, the mother twice leaves the baby in an unfamiliar room, the first time with a stranger. The second time she leaves the baby alone, and the stranger comes back before the mother does. The mother then encourages the baby to explore and play again and gives comfort if the baby seems to need it (Ainsworth, Blehar, Waters, & Wall, 1978). Of particular concern is the baby's response each time the mother returns.

When Ainsworth and her colleagues observed 1-year-olds in the Strange Situation and at home, they found three main patterns of attachment: *secure* (the most common category, into which 66 percent of U.S. babies fell) and two forms of anxious, or insecure, attachment: *avoidant* (20 percent of U.S. babies) and *ambivalent,* or *resistant* (12 percent).

Babies with **secure attachment** cry or protest when the mother leaves and greet her happily when she returns. They use her as a **secure base,** leaving her to go off and explore but returning occasionally for reassurance. They are usually cooperative and relatively free of anger. Babies with **avoidant attachment** rarely cry when the mother leaves, and they avoid her on her return. They tend to be angry and do not reach out in time of need. Babies with **ambivalent (resistant) attachment** become anxious even before the mother leaves and are very upset when she goes out. When she returns, they show their ambivalence by seeking contact with her while at the same time resisting it by kicking or squirming. These three attachment patterns are universal in all cultures in which they have been studied—cultures as different as those in Africa, China, and Israel—though the percentage of infants in each category varies (van IJzendoorn & Kroonenberg, 1988; van IJzendoorn & Sagi, 1999).

Other research (Main & Solomon, 1986) has identified a fourth pattern, **disorganized-disoriented attachment.** Babies with the disorganized pattern often show inconsistent, contradictory behaviors. They greet the mother brightly when she returns but then turn away or approach without looking at her. They seem confused and afraid. This may be the least secure pattern and is most likely to occur in babies whose mothers are insensitive, intrusive, or abusive (Carlson, 1998). (Table 6-3 describes how babies with each of the four patterns of attachment typically react to the Strange Situation.)

Although much research on attachment has been based on the Strange Situation, some investigators have questioned its validity. The Strange Situation *is* strange; it is also artificial. It asks mothers not to initiate interaction, exposes babies to repeated comings and goings of adults, and expects the infants to pay attention to them. Since attachment influences a wider range of behaviors than are seen in the Strange Situation, some researchers have called for a more comprehensive, sensitive method to measure it, one that would show how mother and infant interact during natural, nonstressful situations (T. M. Field, 1987).

secure attachment Pattern in which an infant cries or protests when the primary caregiver leaves and actively seeks out the caregiver upon his or her return.

secure base Infant's use of a parent or other familiar caregiver as a departure point for exploration and a safe place to return periodically for emotional support.

avoidant attachment Pattern in which an infant rarely cries when separated from the primary caregiver and avoids contact upon his or her return.

ambivalent (resistant) attachment Pattern in which an infant becomes anxious before the primary caregiver leaves, is extremely upset during his or her absence, and both seeks and resists contact on his or her return.

disorganized-disoriented attachment Pattern in which an infant, after separation from the primary caregiver, shows contradictory behaviors upon his or her return.

Table 6-3 Attachment Behaviors in Strange Situation

Attachment Classification	Behavior
Secure	Gloria plays and explores freely when her mother is nearby. She responds enthusiastically when her mother returns.
Insecure-Avoidant	When Sam's mother returns; Sam does not make eye contact or greet her. It is almost as if he has not noticed her return.
Insecure-Resistant	James hovers close to his mother during much of the Strange Situation, but he does not greet her positively or enthusiastically during the reunion episode. Instead, he is angry and upset.
Disorganized-Disoriented	Erica responds to the Strange Situation with inconsistent, contradictory behavior. She seems to fall apart, overwhelmed by the stress.

Source: Based on Thompson, 1998, pp. 37–39.

It has been suggested that the Strange Situation may be especially inappropriate for studying attachment in children of employed mothers, since these children are used to routine separations and the presence of other caregivers. However, a comparison of 1,153 randomly sampled 15-month-olds born in ten U.S. cities, who had received varying amounts, types, and quality of day care starting at various ages, found "no evidence . . . that the Strange Situation was less valid for children with extensive child care experience than for those without" (NICHD Early Child Care Research Network, 1997a, p. 867).

The Strange Situation may be less valid in some nonwestern cultures, which have different expectations for babies' interaction with their mothers and in which mothers may encourage different kinds of attachment-related behavior. Research on Japanese infants, who are less commonly separated from their mothers than U.S. babies, showed high rates of resistant attachment, which may reflect the extreme stressfulness of the Strange Situation for these babies (Miyake, Chen, & Campos, 1985).

Some researchers have begun to supplement the Strange Situation with methods that can be used in natural settings. In the Q-sort technique, observers sort a set of descriptive words or phrases ("cries a lot"; "tends to cling") into categories ranging from most to least characteristic of a child. The Waters and Deane (1985) Attachment Q-set (AQS) has mothers or other observers compare descriptions of children's everyday behavior with expert descriptions of the "hypothetical most secure child." The Preschool Assessment of Attachment (PAA) (Crittenden, 1993) measures attachment after 20 months of age, taking into account preschoolers' more complex relationships and language abilities.

In a cross-cultural study using the AQS, mothers in China, Colombia, Germany, Israel, Japan, Norway, and the United States decribed their children as behaving more like than unlike the "most secure child." Furthermore, the mothers' descriptions of "secure-base" behavior were about as similar across cultures as within a culture. Thus the tendency to use the mother as a secure base may be universal (Posada et al., 1995).

How Attachment Is Established Both mothers and babies contribute to security of attachment by the way they respond to each other. Virtually any activity on a baby's part that leads to a response from an adult can be an attachment-seeking behavior: sucking, crying, smiling, clinging, or looking into the caregiver's eyes. As early as the eighth week of life, Ainsworth (1969) observed, babies direct these behaviors particularly to their mothers. The overtures are successful when the mother responds warmly, expresses delight, and gives the baby frequent physical contact and freedom to explore.

Although similar attachment *patterns* have been found in such remote cultures as the Dogon population of Mali in West Africa (True, Pisani, & Oumar, 2001), attachment *behaviors* vary across cultures. Among the Gusii of east Africa, on the western edge of Kenya, infants are greeted with handshakes, and Gusii infants reach out for a parent's hand much as western infants cuddle up for a hug (van IJzendoorn & Sagi, 1999).

On the basis of a baby's interactions with the mother, said Ainsworth and Bowlby, the baby builds a "working model" of what can be expected from her. The various patterns of emotional attachment represent different cognitive representations that result in different expectations. As long as the mother continues to act the same way, the model holds up. If her behavior changes—not just once or twice but consistently—the baby may revise the model, and security of attachment may change.

A baby's working model of attachment is related to Erikson's concept of basic trust. (Margaret Mead's and Gregory Bateson's success as new parents reflected their grasp of this concept.) Secure attachment reflects trust; insecure attachment, mistrust. Securely attached babies have learned to trust not only their caregivers but their own ability to get what they need. Babies who cry a lot, and whose mothers respond by

Both Anna and Diane contribute to the attachment between them by the way they act toward each other. The way the baby molds herself to her mother's body shows her trust and reinforces Diane's feelings for her child, which she displays through sensitivity to Anna's needs.

soothing them, tend to be securely attached (Del Carmen, Pedersen, Huffman, & Bryan, 1993).

Contrary to Ainsworth's original findings, babies seem to develop attachments to both parents at about the same time, and security of attachment to father and mother is usually quite similar, as it seems to have been with Cathy (Fox, Kimmerly, & Schafer, 1991). If not, a secure attachment to one parent can sometimes offset an insecure attachment to the other parent (Engle & Breaux, 1998; Verschueren & Marcoen, 1999).

Influences on Attachment Why does one baby show secure attachment while another seems insecure? The reason is probably not genetic; dizygotic twins are as likely to be similarly attached as monozygotic twins, suggesting that parental treatment may be a more important factor (O'Connor & Kroft, 2001). The key to attachment may lie in an interplay between the quality of the relationship with the caregiver and the infant's emotional makeup (Braungart-Rieker, Garwood, Powers, & Wang, 2001; Kochanska, 1998; Seifer, Schiller, Sameroff, Resnick, & Riordan, 1996).

Like Ainsworth and her colleagues (1978), many studies have found that mothers of securely attached infants and toddlers tend to be sensitive and responsive (Braungart-Rieker et al., 2001; De Wolff & van IJzendoorn, 1997; Isabella, 1993; NICHD Early Child Care Research Network, 1997a), though sensitivity may be expressed in different ways across cultures (Posada et al., 2002). Equally important are mutual interaction, stimulation, a positive attitude, warmth and acceptance, and emotional support (De Wolff & van IJzendoorn, 1997).

Contextual factors, such as a mother's employment and her attitude toward her work and the separation it causes, may play a part (De Wolff & van IJzendoorn, 1997). In one study, infants of employed mothers who were highly anxious about being away from home tended to develop avoidant attachments, as measured at 18 months by the Strange Situation (Stifter, Coulehan, & Fish, 1993).

The Role of Temperament How much influence does a child's temperament exert on attachment, and in what ways? Findings vary (Susman-Stillman, Kalkoske, Egeland, & Waldman, 1996; Vaughn et al., 1992). Some studies have identified frustration levels, amounts of crying, irritability, and fearfulness as predictors of attachment

(Calkins & Fox, 1992; Izard, Porges, Simons, Haynes, & Cohen, 1991; Kochanska, 1998). Indicators such as variability in heart rate, which is associated with irritability, may reflect underlying neurological or physiological conditions (Izard, Porges, et al., 1991).

A baby's temperament may indirectly affect attachment through its impact on the parents. In a series of studies in the Netherlands (van den Boom, 1989, 1994), 15-day-old infants classified as irritable were much more likely than nonirritable infants to be insecurely attached at 1 year. However, irritable infants whose mothers received home visits, with instruction on how to soothe their babies, were as likely to be securely attached as the nonirritable infants. Thus an infant's irritability may prevent the development of secure attachment, but not if the mother has the skills to cope with the baby's temperament (Rothbart et al., 2000). "Goodness of fit" may well be a key to security of attachment.

Intergenerational Transmission of Attachment Patterns The way a mother remembers her attachment to her parents seems to predict the way her children will be attached to *her.* The *Adult Attachment Interview (AAI)* (George, Kaplan, & Main, 1985; Main, 1995; Main, Kaplan, & Cassidy, 1985) is a semistructured interview that asks adults to recall and interpret feelings and experiences related to their childhood attachments. An analysis of eighteen studies using the AAI found that the clarity, coherence, and consistency with which these early attachments are remembered and interpreted reliably predicts the security with which the respondent's own child will be attached to him or her (van IJzendoorn, 1995).

Apparently, the way adults recall early experiences with parents or caregivers affects the way they respond to the children they care for (Dozier, Stovall, Albus, & Bates, 2001; Slade, Belsky, Aber, & Phelps, 1999). A mother who was securely attached to *her* mother, or who understands why she was insecurely attached, can accurately recognize the baby's attachment behaviors, respond encouragingly, and help the baby form a secure attachment to her (Bretherton, 1990).

The important thing is not the way a mother *actually* was attached as a child, but the way she *remembers* her attachment. Adults' perceptions of their own early attachments may be influenced by later experiences, such as physical or sexual abuse, serious illness, or the death of a parent. Adults who have experienced such events tend to be preoccupied with their early attachment relationships (Beckwith, Cohen, & Hamilton, 1999).

Long-Term Effects of Attachment As attachment theory predicts, security of attachment seems to affect emotional, social, and cognitive competence (van IJzendoorn & Sagi, 1997). The more secure a child's attachment to a nurturing adult, the easier it is for the child eventually to become independent of that adult, as Cathy Bateson did in midadolescence, and to develop good relationships with others. The link between attachment in infancy and characteristics observed years later underscores the continuity of development and the interrelationships of its various aspects.

If, on the basis of early experience, children have positive expectations about their ability to get along with others and to engage in social give-and-take, and if they think well of themselves, they may set up social situations that tend to reinforce these beliefs and the gratifying interactions that result from them (Elicker, Englund, & Sroufe, 1992; Sroufe, Carlson, & Shulman, 1993). And if children, as infants, had a secure base and could count on parents' or caregivers' responsiveness, they are likely to feel confident enough to be actively engaged in their world (Jacobsen & Hofmann, 1997).

Children who were securely attached as infants tend to get along well with other children and form close friendships.

Securely attached toddlers have larger, more varied vocabularies than those who are insecurely attached (Meins, 1998). They also are more sociable (Elicker et al., 1992; Main, 1983). They have more positive interactions with peers, and their friendly overtures are more likely to be accepted (Fagot, 1997). Insecurely attached toddlers show more negative emotions (fear and distress, and anger), while securely attached children show more joyfulness, even in the same situations (Kochanska, 2001).

From ages 3 to 5, securely attached children are more curious, competent, empathic, resilient, and self-confident than those who are insecurely attached; get along better with other children; and are more likely to form close friendships (Elicker et al., 1992; J. L. Jacobson & Wille, 1986; Youngblade & Belsky, 1992). They interact more positively with parents, preschool teachers, and peers and are better able to resolve conflicts (Elicker et al., 1992). They tend to have a more positive self-image (Elicker et al., 1992; Verschueren, Marcoen, & Schoefs, 1996).

The advantages of secure attachment continue into middle childhood and beyond. In a French-Canadian laboratory observation, attachment patterns and the emotional quality of 6-year-olds' interactions with their mothers predicted the strength of the children's communicative skills, cognitive engagement, and mastery motivation at age 8 (Moss & St-Laurent, 2001).

The intimacy of secure attachment seems to prepare children for the intimacy of friendship. Securely attached children (at least in western cultures, where most studies have been done) tend to have the closest, most stable friendships (Schneider, Atkinson, & Tardif, 2001). When 10- and 11-year-olds were observed in summer day camp, those with histories of secure attachment were better at making and keeping friends and functioning in a group than children who had been classified as avoidant or resistant. They also were more self-reliant, self-assured, and adaptable and better physically coordinated. In a reunion of 15-year-olds who had gone to camp together, the adolescents who had been securely attached in infancy were rated higher on emotional health, self-esteem, ego resiliency, and peer competence by their counselors and peers and by researchers who observed them (Sroufe et al., 1993).

Insecurely attached infants, by contrast, often have later problems: inhibitions and negative emotions in toddlerhood, hostility toward other children at age 5, and dependency during the school years (Calkins & Fox, 1992; Kochanska, 2001; Lyons-Ruth, Alpern, & Repacholi, 1993; Sroufe et al., 1993). Those with disorganized attachment tend to have behavior problems at all levels of schooling and psychiatric disorders at age 17 (Carlson, 1998). However, it is possible that correlations between attachment in infancy and later development stem, not from attachment itself, but from underlying personality characteristics that may affect both attachment and parent-child interactions *after* infancy (Lamb, 1987).

Checkpoint

Can you . . .

- ✔ Describe four patterns of attachment?
- ✔ Discuss how attachment is established and the influences of parent-child relationships and of the baby's temperament?
- ✔ Describe long-term behavioral differences influenced by attachment patterns?

Emotional Communication with Caregivers: Mutual Regulation

5. How do infants and caregivers "read" each other's nonverbal signals, and what happens when communication breaks down?

mutual regulation Process by which infant and caregiver communicate emotional states to each other and respond appropriately.

Interactions that influence the quality of attachment depend on **mutual regulation**—the ability of both infant and caregiver to respond appropriately to signals about each other's emotional states. Infants take an active part in this process by influencing the way caregivers behave toward them.

Healthy interaction occurs when a caregiver "reads" a baby's signals accurately and responds appropriately. When a baby's goals are met, the baby is joyful, or at least interested, as Cathy was when her parents made bird images with their shiny spoons (E. Z. Tronick, 1989). If a caregiver ignores an invitation to play or insists on playing when the baby has signaled "I don't feel like it," the baby may feel frustrated or sad. When babies do not achieve desired results, they keep on sending signals to repair the interaction. Normally, interaction moves back and forth between well-regulated and poorly regulated states, and babies learn from these shifts how to send signals and what to do when their initial signals do not result in a comfortable emotional balance.

Mutual regulation with parents and other caregivers helps babies learn to "read" others' behavior and to develop expectations about it. Infants as young as 2 to 4 months can perceive emotions expressed by others and can adjust their own behavior accordingly (Legerstee & Varghese, 2001; Montague & Walker-Andrews, 2001; Termine & Izard, 1988); and they respond differently to emotional expressions of familiar people, such as their mothers, than to expressions of unfamiliar people (Kahana-Kalman & Walker-Andrews, 2001).

"still-face" paradigm Research method used to measure mutual regulation in infants 2 to 9 months old.

The **"still-face" paradigm** (Tronick, Als, Adamson, Wise, & Brazelton, 1978) is a research method used to measure mutual regulation in infants from 2 to 9 months old. In the *still-face* episode, which follows a normal face-to-face interaction, the mother suddenly becomes stony-faced, silent, and unresponsive. Then, a few minutes later, she resumes normal interaction (the *reunion* episode). During the still-face episode, infants tend to stop smiling and looking at the mother. They may make faces, sounds, or gestures or may touch themselves, their clothing, or a chair, apparently to comfort themselves or to relieve the emotional stress created by the mother's unexpected behavior (Cohn & Tronick, 1983; E. Z. Tronick, 1980, 1989; Weinberg & Tronick, 1996).

How do infants react during the reunion episode? One study combined a microanalysis of 6-month-olds' facial expressions during this episode with measures of heart rate and nervous system reactivity. The infants' reactions were mixed. On the one hand, they showed even more positive behavior—joyous expressions and utterances, and gazes and gestures directed toward the mother—than before the still-face episode. On the other hand, the persistence of sad or angry facial expressions, "pick-me-up" gestures, distancing, and indications of stress, as well as an increased tendency to fuss and cry, suggested that while infants welcome the resumption of interaction with the mother, the negative feelings stirred by a breakdown in mutual regulation are not readily eased (Weinberg & Tronick, 1996).

The way a mother sees and responds to her infant affects the infants' reactions to the still-face procedure (Rosenblum, McDonough, Muzik, Miller, & Sameroff, 2002). Infants whose parents are normally sensitive and responsive to their emotional needs seem better able to comfort themselves during the still-face episode and to recover during the reunion episode. This is important because infants' ability to regulate emotions during the still-face procedure at 4 months has been shown to predict security of attachment at 12 months (Braungart-Rieker et al., 2001; Rosenblum et al., 2002). In home observations, infants who failed to smile during a still-face episode at 6 months tended, at 18 months, to be reported by their mothers to show such problem behaviors as misbehaving, hitting, and yelling. Depressed mothers were especially likely to perceive their toddlers as having such problem behaviors (Moore, Cohn, & Campbell, 2001). (Box 6-2 discusses how a mother's depression may contribute to developmental problems in her baby.)

Digging Deeper

BOX 6–2

How a Mother's Depression Affects Mutual Regulation

Reading emotional signals lets mothers assess and meet babies' needs; and it lets babies influence or respond to the mother's behavior toward them. What happens, then, if that communication system seriously breaks down, and what can be done about it?

Temporary postpartum depression, which affects 10 to 40 percent of new mothers (Kendall-Tackett, 1997), may have little or no impact on the way a mother interacts with her baby, but severe or chronic depression lasting six months or more (which is far less common) can have serious effects (Campbell, Cohn, & Meyers, 1995; Teti, Gelfand, Messinger, & Isabella, 1995).

Chronically depressed mothers tend to be either withdrawn or intrusive (T. Field, 1998a, 1998c). They are less sensitive and less engaged with their infants than nondepressed mothers, and their interactions with their babies are less positive (NICHD Early Child Care Research Network, 1999b). Depressed mothers are less able to interpret and respond to an infant's cries (Donovan, Leavitt, & Walsh, 1998). Babies of depressed mothers may give up on sending emotional signals and try to comfort themselves by sucking or rocking. If this defensive reaction becomes habitual, babies learn that they have no power to draw responses from other people, that their mothers are unreliable, and that the world is untrustworthy. They also tend to become depressed themselves (Gelfand & Teti, 1995; Teti et al., 1995).

We cannot be sure, however, that such infants become depressed through a failure of mutual regulation. They may inherit a predisposition to depression, or acquire it prenatally through exposure to hormonal or other biochemical influences. Newborns of mothers with depressive symptoms are less expressive, less active and robust, more excitable, and less oriented to sensory stimuli than other newborns, suggesting an inborn tendency (Lundy, Field, & Pickens, 1996).

Infants of depressed mothers tend to show unusual patterns of brain activity, similar to the mothers' own patterns. Within twenty-four hours after birth, they show relatively less activity in the left frontal region of the brain, which seems to be specialized for "approach" emotions such as joy and anger, and more activity in the right frontal region, which controls "withdrawal" emotions, such as distress and disgust (G. Dawson et al., 1992, 1999; T. Field, 1998a, 1998c; T. Field, Fox, Pickens, Nawrocki, & Soutollo, 1995; N. A. Jones, Field, Fox, Lundy, & Davalos, 1997). Newborns of depressed mothers also have lower scores on the Brazelton Neonatal Behavior Assessment Scale (T. Field, 1998a, 1998c; N. A. Jones et al., 1998). In a study of sixty-three pregnant women, depressed expectant mothers had higher levels of stress hormones (cortisol and norepinephrine) and lower levels of the neurotransmitter dopamine—and so did their newborns, who also had low Brazelton scores (Lundy et al., 1999). These findings suggest that a mother's depression during pregnancy may affect her newborn's neurological and behavioral functioning.

A combination of genetic, prenatal, and environmental factors may put infants of depressed mothers at risk of becoming depressed. It is likely that a bidirectional influence is at work; an infant who does not respond normally may further depress the mother, and her unresponsivness may in turn increase the infant's depression (T. Field, 1995, 1998a, 1998c; Lundy et al., 1999). Interactions with a nondepressed adult—the father or a child care worker or nursery school teacher—can help infants compensate for the effects of depressed mothering (T. Field, 1995, 1998a, 1998c).

Both as infants and as preschoolers, children with severely or chronically depressed mothers tend to be insecurely attached to them (Gelfand & Teti, 1995; Teti et al., 1995). They are less motivated to explore and more apt to prefer relatively unchallenging tasks (Hart, Field, del Valle, & Pelaez-Nogueras, 1998; Redding, Harmon, & Morgan, 1990).

As toddlers these children tend to have trouble suppressing frustration and tension (Cole, Barrett, & Zahn-Waxler, 1992; Seiner & Gelfand, 1995). They are likely to grow poorly, to perform poorly on cognitive and linguistic measures, and to have behavior problems (T. Field, 1998a, 1998c; T. M. Field et al., 1985; Gelfand & Teti, 1995; NICHD Early Child Care Research Network, 1999b; B. S. Zuckerman & Beardslee, 1987).

Besides antidepressant medications and psychotherapy ("Depression During Pregnancy and After," 2002), techniques that may help improve a depressed mother's mood include listening to music, visual imagery, aerobics, yoga, relaxation, and massage therapy (T. Field, 1995, 1998a, 1998c). Massage also can help depressed babies (T. Field, 1998a, 1998b; T. Field et al., 1996), possibly through effects on neurological activity (N. A. Jones et al., 1997). In one study, mood-brightening measures plus social, educational, and vocational rehabilitation for the mother and day care for the infant improved their interaction behavior. The infants showed faster growth and had fewer pediatric problems, more normal biochemical values, and better developmental test scores than a control group (T. Field, 1998a, 1998b).

What's Your View?

Can you suggest ways to help depressed mothers and babies, other than those mentioned here?

Check It Out:

For further information on this topic, go to www.mhhe.com/papaliah9, where you'll find links to articles about depression in women.

What's Your View?

- Do you see any ethical problems with the still-face paradigm or the Strange Situation? Are the benefits of these kinds of research worth the risks?

The still-face reaction seems to be similar in eastern and western cultures and in interactions with both fathers and mothers (Braungart-Rieker, Garwood, Powers, & Notaro, 1998; Kisilevsky et al., 1998). However, gender differences have been found. In one laboratory observation, 6-month-old sons seemed to have a harder time than daughters in regulating their emotions during the still-face episode. In *normal* face-to-face interaction, sons maintained better coordination of emotional signals with their mothers than daughters did, but also took longer to repair mismatches (Weinberg, Tronick, Cohn, & Olson, 1999).

Stranger Anxiety and Separation Anxiety

stranger anxiety Wariness of strange people and places, shown by some infants during the second half of the first year.

separation anxiety Distress shown by an infant when a familiar caregiver leaves.

Sophie used to be a friendly baby, smiling at strangers and going to them, continuing to coo happily as long as someone—anyone—was around. Now, at 8 months, she turns away when a new person approaches, and she howls when her parents try to leave her with a baby-sitter. Sophie is experiencing both **stranger anxiety,** wariness of a person she does not know, and **separation anxiety,** distress when a familiar caregiver leaves her.

Separation anxiety and stranger anxiety used to be considered emotional and cognitive milestones of the second half of infancy, reflecting attachment to the mother. However, newer research suggests that although stranger anxiety and separation anxiety are fairly typical, they are not universal. Whether a baby cries when a parent leaves or when someone new approaches may say more about the baby's temperament or life circumstances than about security of attachment (R. J. Davidson & Fox, 1989).

Babies rarely react negatively to strangers before 6 months of age, commonly do so by 8 or 9 months, and do so more and more throughout the rest of the first year (Sroufe, 1997). This change may reflect cognitive development. Sophie's stranger anxiety involves memory for faces, the ability to compare the stranger's appearance with her mother's, and perhaps the recollection of situations in which she has been left with a stranger. If Sophie is allowed to get used to the stranger gradually in a familiar setting, she may react more positively (Lewis, 1997; Sroufe, 1997). (As we've mentioned, Margaret Mead and Gregory Bateson made sure that Cathy always met a new caregiver in a familiar place.)

This baby is showing separation anxiety about being left with a baby-sitter. Separation anxiety is common in the last half of the first year.

Separation anxiety may be due not so much to the separation itself as to the quality of substitute care. When substitute caregivers are warm and responsive and play with 9-month-olds *before* they cry, the babies cry less than when they are with less responsive caregivers (Gunnar, Larson, Hertsgaard, Harris, & Brodersen, 1992).

Stability of care is important. Pioneering work by René Spitz (1945, 1946) on institutionalized children emphasizes the need for substitute care to be as close as possible to good mothering. Research has underlined the value of continuity and consistency in caregiving, so children can form early emotional bonds with their caregivers. As Mead observed in southeast island cultures, bonds can be formed with multiple caregivers, as long as the caregiving situation is stable.

Today, neither intense fear of strangers nor intense protest when the mother leaves is considered to be a sign of secure attachment. Researchers measure attachment more by what happens when the mother returns than by how many tears the baby sheds at her departure.

Social Referencing

Have you ever, at a formal dinner party, cast a sidelong glance to see which fork the person next to you was using? If so, you engaged in **social referencing:** forming an understanding of how to act in an ambiguous, confusing, or unfamiliar situation by seeking out another person's reaction to it. Babies seem to use social referencing when they look at their caregivers upon encountering a new person or toy. This pattern of behavior may emerge during the latter part of the first year, when infants begin to judge the possible consequences of events, imitate complex behaviors, and distinguish among and react to various emotional expressions (Baldwin & Moses, 1996).

social referencing Understanding an ambiguous situation by seeking out another person's perception of it.

In a study using the visual cliff (a test of depth perception described in Chapter 4), when the drop looked very shallow or very deep, 1 year olds did not look to their mothers; they were able to judge for themselves whether to cross over or not. When they were uncertain about the depth of the "cliff," however, they paused at the "edge," looked down, and then looked up at their mothers. Most of the babies whose mothers showed joy or interest crossed the "drop," but very few whose mothers looked angry or afraid crossed it (Sorce, Emde, Campos, & Klinnert, 1985).

The idea that infants engage in social referencing has been challenged. When infants spontaneously look at caregivers in ambiguous situations, it is not clear that they are looking for information; they may be seeking comfort, attention, sharing of feelings, or simply reassurance of the caregiver's presence—typical attachment behaviors (Baldwin & Moses, 1996). However, newer research provides experimental evidence of social referencing at 1 year (Moses, Baldwin, Rosicky, & Tidball, 2001). When exposed to jiggling or vibrating toys fastened to the floor or ceiling, both 12- and 18-month-olds moved closer to, or farther from, the toys depending on the experimenters' expressed emotional reactions ("Yecch!" or "Nice!").

Checkpoint

Can you . . .

- ✔ Describe how mutual regulation works?
- ✔ Discuss how a mother's depression can affect her baby?
- ✔ Discuss reasons for stranger anxiety and separation anxiety?
- ✔ Tell what social referencing is, and give examples of how infants seem to use it?

Developmental Issues in Toddlerhood

About halfway between their first and second birthdays, babies become toddlers. This transformation can be seen not only in such physical and cognitive skills as walking and talking, but in the ways children express their personalities and interact with others. Let's look at three psychological issues that toddlers—and their caregivers—have to deal with: the emerging *sense of self;* the growth of *autonomy,* or self-determination; and the *internalization of behavioral standards.*

Guidepost

6. When and how do the self and self-concept arise?

The Emerging Sense of Self

I-self James's term for the subjective entity that seeks to know about itself.

Me-self James's term for what a person objectively knows about himself or herself. Also called *self-concept.*

self-concept Sense of self; descriptive and evaluative mental picture of one's abilities and traits.

William James, in the late nineteenth century, described two selves: the *I-self* and the *Me-self,* the knower and the known (James, 1950). The **I-self** is a subjective entity that constructs and seeks to know the Me-self. The **Me-self,** is what can objectively be known about the self. It is called the *self-concept.*

The **self-concept** is our image of ourselves. It is what the I-self believes about the Me-self—our total picture of our abilities and traits. The self-concept involves both cognition and emotion. It describes what we (our I-selves) know and feel about ourselves (our Me-selves) and guides our actions (Harter, 1996, p. 207). Children incorporate into their self-image the picture that others reflect back to them.

When and how do the two main aspects of the self develop?

Emergence of the I-Self (Birth to 15 months) The I-self is believed to be the first aspect of the self to emerge. It does so in the context of the infant-caregiver relationship, which profoundly shapes it.* From a jumble of seemingly isolated experiences (say, from one breast-feeding session to another), infants begin to extract consistent patterns that form rudimentary concepts of self and other. Depending on what kind of care the infant receives and how she or he responds, pleasant or unpleasant emotions become connected with sensorimotor experiences (such as sucking) that play an important part in the growing organization of the self.

self-efficacy Sense of capability to master challenges and achieve goals.

Between 4 and 10 months, when infants learn to reach, grasp, and make things happen, they may begin to experience a sense of personal *agency* ("I can make the mobile move"), a feature of the I-self. The sense of agency—the realization that one can control external events—is a forerunner of what Bandura (1994) calls **self-efficacy,** a sense of being able to master challenges and achieve goals. At about this time infants develop *self-coherence,* the sense of being a physical whole with boundaries, within which agency resides.

These developments occur in interaction with caregivers in games such as peekaboo, in which the infant becomes increasingly aware of the difference between self and other ("I see you!"). It is this awareness that allows attachment to occur—a manifestation of both individuation and connectedness.

Between 10 and 15 months, "infants come to realize that their subjective experiences, their attention, intentions, and affective states can be shared with another" who is also an independent agent (Harter, 1998, p. 561). When a crawling infant looks at the mother's face to see whether or not it's all right to touch a pretty vase, an emotional communication has occurred between two selves.

What's Your View?

- Given the integral importance of relationships with caregivers to infants' self-development, what kinds of caregiving practices do you think would lead to a healthy sense of self?

Emergence of the Me-Self (15 to 30 months) The emergence of *self-awareness*—conscious knowledge of the self as a distinct, identifiable being—may be a gradual process that builds on an earlier dawning of perceptual discrimination between self and others. In an experiment with ninety-six 4- and 9-month-olds, the infants showed more interest in images of others than of themselves. The 4-month-olds looked and smiled more at images of an experimenter imitating their facial expressions and movements than at a mirror image of themselves. The 9-month-olds appeared to attempt social initiatives such as reaching toward the other image (Rochat & Striano, 2002).

This early *perceptual* discrimination may be the foundation of the Me-self, the *conceptual* self-awareness that develops between 15 and 18 months. In a classic line of research, investigators dabbed rouge on the noses of 6- to 24-month-olds and sat them in front of a mirror. Three-fourths of 18-month-olds and all 24-month-olds touched their red noses more often than before, whereas babies younger than 15 months never

*The discussion in this section is indebted to Harter, 1998.

This toddler shows self-awareness by touching the spot on her face where she sees in the mirror that experimenters have placed a dot of rouge. According to this research, toddlers come to recognize their own image between 18 and 24 months of age.

did. This behavior suggests that the older babies knew they didn't normally have red noses and that they recognized the image in the mirror as their own (Lewis, 1997; Lewis & Brooks, 1974).

By 20 to 24 months, toddlers begin to use first-person pronouns, another sign of self-awareness (Lewis, 1997). The use of "I," "me," and "you" enables toddlers to represent and refer to both the self and the other. Once they have a concept of themselves as distinct beings, children begin to apply descriptive terms ("big" or "little"; "straight hair" or "curly hair") and evaluative ones ("good," "pretty," or "strong") to themselves. This normally occurs sometime between 19 and 30 months, as representational ability and vocabulary expand. The rapid development of language during this period makes it possible for children to think and talk about the self and to incorporate parents' verbal descriptions ("You're so smart!" "What a big boy!") into their own emerging self-image (Stipek, Gralinski, & Kopp, 1990). Self-evaluation and evaluation by others are steps toward the development of conscience.

Checkpoint

Can you . . .

- ✔ Explain the difference between the I-self and the Me-self, and discuss how they emerge and develop in infancy and toddlerhood?

Development of Autonomy

Erikson (1950) identified the period from about 18 months to 3 years as the second stage in personality development, **autonomy versus shame and doubt,** which is marked by a shift from external control to self-control. Having come through infancy with a sense of basic trust in the world and an awakening self-awareness, toddlers begin to substitute their own judgment for their caregivers'. The "virtue" that emerges during this stage is *will.* Toilet training is an important step toward autonomy and self-control. So is language; as children are better able to make their wishes understood, they become more powerful and independent.

Guidepost

7. How do toddlers develop autonomy and standards for socially acceptable behavior?

autonomy versus shame and doubt Erikson's second stage in psychosocial development, in which children achieve a balance between self-determination and control by others.

Since unlimited freedom is neither safe nor healthy, said Erikson, shame and doubt have a necessary place. As in all of Erikson's stages, an appropriate balance is crucial. Toddlers need adults to set appropriate limits, and shame and doubt help them recognize the need for those limits.

In the United States, the "terrible twos" are considered a normal manifestation of the early drive for autonomy. Toddlers feel impelled to test the new notion that they are

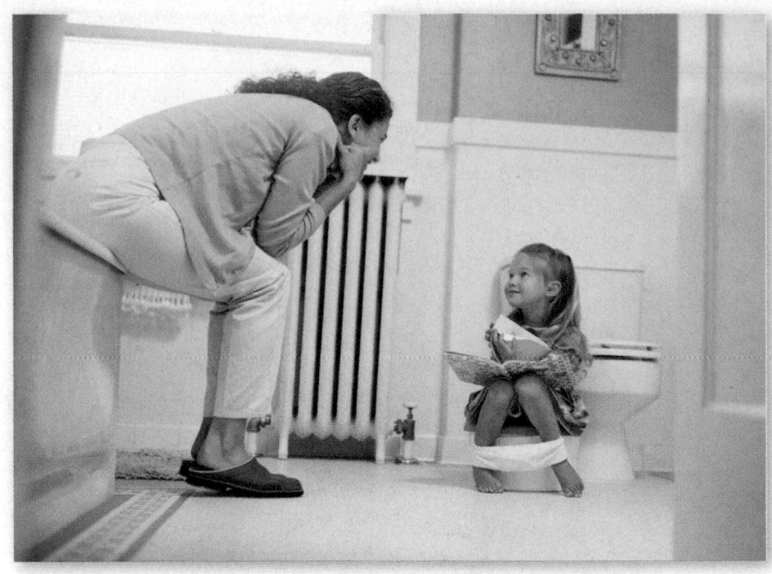

According to Erikson, toilet training is an important step toward autonomy and self-control.

individuals, that they have some control over their world, and that they have new, exciting powers. They are driven to try out their own ideas, exercise their own preferences, and make their own decisions. This drive typically shows itself in the form of *negativism,* the tendency to shout "No!" just for the sake of resisting authority. Almost all children show negativism to some degree; it usually begins before 2 years of age, tends to peak at about $3\frac{1}{2}$ to 4, and declines by age 6.

Parents and other caregivers who view children's expressions of self-will as a normal, healthy striving for independence, not as stubbornness, can help them learn self-control, contribute to their sense of competence, and avoid excessive conflict. In one observational study of 65 two-and-a-half-year-olds and their mothers, conflict occurred an average of nineteen times an hour. Children whose mothers clarified or gave reasons for their requests, or who compromised or bargained with the child, tended at age 3 to show higher levels of emotional understanding, social competence, and early conscience development than children whose mothers had threatened, teased, insisted, or given in (Laible & Thompson, 2002). (Table 6-4 gives specific, research-based suggestions for dealing with the "terrible twos.")

Socialization and Internalization: Developing a Conscience

socialization Development of habits, skills, values, and motives shared by responsible, productive members of a society.

internalization Process by which children accept societal standards of conduct as their own; fundamental to socialization.

Socialization is the process by which children develop habits, skills, values, and motives that make them responsible, productive members of society. Socialization rests on the **internalization** of societal standards—taking those standards as one's own. Once internalized, such standards as taking turns and learning to use words instead of blows become almost automatic.

Compliance with parental expectations can be seen as a first step toward compliance with societal standards. Some rules of socialization have to do with safety: how to cross streets, for example. A child begins to learn these rules within the family at an early age. Children who are successfully socialized no longer merely obey rules or commands to get rewards or avoid punishment; they have made parental and social standards their own (Grusec & Goodnow, 1994; Kochanska & Aksan, 1995; Kochanska, Tjebkes, & Forman, 1998).

Some children are socialized more readily than others. The way parents go about their job, together with a child's temperament and the quality of the parent-child relationship, may help predict how hard or easy it will be to socialize a particular child (Kochanska, 1993, 1995, 1997a, 1997b). Factors in the success of socialization may include security of attachment, observational learning of parents' behavior, and the mutual responsiveness of parent and child (Maccoby, 1992).

conscience Internal standards of behavior, which usually control one's conduct and produce emotional discomfort when violated.

self-regulation Child's independent control of behavior to conform to understood social expectations.

Conscience includes both emotional discomfort about doing something wrong and the ability to refrain from doing it. According to Freud, the *superego,* or conscience, emerges at age 5 or 6, marking the beginning of moral development. Today developmental scientists are seeking the origins of conscience at a much earlier age. How readily does a preschooler or even a toddler comply with parental commands? Does the child comply even when the parent is not present? **Self-regulation**—the ability to inhibit impulses and control one's own behavior in the absence of imme-

Table 6-4 Dealing with the "Terrible Twos"

The following research-based guidelines can help parents of toddlers discourage negativism and encourage socially acceptable behavior:

- *Be flexible.* Learn the child's natural rhythms and special likes and dislikes.
- *Think of yourself as a safe harbor,* with safe limits, from which a child can set out and discover the world—and keep coming back for support.
- *Make your home "child-friendly."* Fill it with unbreakable objects that are safe to explore.
- *Avoid physical punishment.* It is often ineffective and may even lead a toddler to do more damage.
- *Offer a choice*—even a limited one—to give the child some control. ("Would you like to have your bath now, or after we read a book?")
- *Be consistent* in enforcing necessary requests.
- *Don't interrupt an activity unless absolutely necessary.* Try to wait until the child's attention has shifted.
- *If you must interrupt, give warning.* ("We have to leave the playground soon.")
- *Suggest alternative activities* when behavior becomes objectionable. (When Ashley is throwing sand in Keiko's face, say, "Oh, look! Nobody's on the swings now. Let's go over and I'll give you a good push!")
- *Suggest; don't command.* Accompany requests with smiles or hugs, not criticism, threats, or physical restraint.
- *Link requests with pleasurable activities.* ("It's time to stop playing, so that you can go to the store with me.")
- *Remind the child of what you expect:* "When we go to this playground, we *never* go outside the gate."
- *Wait a few moments before repeating a request* when a child doesn't comply immediately.
- *Use "time out"* to end conflicts. In a nonpunitive way, remove either yourself or the child from a situation.
- *Expect less self-control during times of stress* (illness, divorce, the birth of a sibling, or a move to a new home).
- *Expect it to be harder for toddlers to comply with "do's" than with "don'ts."* "Clean up your room" takes more effort than "Don't write on the furniture."
- *Keep the atmosphere as positive as possible.* Make your child *want* to cooperate.

Sources: Haswell, Hock, & Wenar, 1981; Kochanska & Aksan, 1995; Kopp, 1982; Kuczynski & Kochanska, 1995; Power & Chapieski, 1986.

diate external control—has repeatedly been correlated with measures of conscience development, such as resisting temptation and making amends for wrongdoing (Eisenberg, 2000).

Developing Self-Regulation Katy, age 2, is about to poke her finger into an electric outlet. In her "child-proofed" apartment, the sockets are covered, but not here in her grandmother's home. When Katy hears her father shout "No!" the toddler pulls her arm back. The next time she goes near an outlet, she starts to point her finger, hesitates, and then says "No." She has stopped herself from doing something she remembers she is not supposed to do. She is beginning to show *self-regulation.*

Self-regulation is the foundation of socialization, and it links all domains of development—physical, cognitive, social, and emotional. Until Katy was physically able to get around on her own, electric outlets posed no hazard. To stop herself from poking her finger into an outlet requires that she consciously understand and remember what her father told her. Cognitive awareness, however, is not enough; restraining herself also requires emotional control.

By "reading" their parents' emotional responses to their behavior, children continually absorb information about what conduct their parents approve of. As children process, store, and act upon this information, their strong desire to please their parents leads them to do as they know their parents want them to, whether or not the parents are there to see. Mutual regulation of emotional states during infancy contributes to the development of self-control, especially in temperamentally "difficult" children, who may need extra help in achieving it (R. Feldman, Greenbaum, & Yirmiya, 1999).

Self-regulation requires flexibility and the ability to wait for gratification. When young children want very badly to do something, however, they easily forget the rules; they may run into the street after a ball or take a forbidden cookie. In most children, the full development of self-regulation extends well into early childhood, taking at least three years (Kopp, 1982).

Before they can control their own behavior, children may need to be able to regulate, or control, their *attentional processes* and to modulate negative emotions. Children who frequently become angry or frustrated and are unable to control these emotions, and who also are restless or have short attention spans, are more likely than other children to become aggressive and antisocial or to have other conduct problems (Eisenberg, 2000). Attentional regulation is a skill that varies among children and remains with them, at least into early childhood, enabling them to develop willpower and cope with frustration (Sethi, Mischel, Aber, Shoda, & Rodriguez, 2000).

Committed Compliance Before children can develop a conscience, they need to have internalized moral standards. Conscience depends on willingness to do the right thing because a child believes it is right, not (as in self-regulation) just because someone else said so. **Inhibitory control**—conscious, or effortful, holding back of impulses, a mechanism of self-regulation that emerges during toddlerhood—may contribute to the development of conscience by first enabling the child to comply voluntarily with parental do's and don'ts (Kochanska, Murray, & Coy, 1997).

inhibitory control Conscious, effortful holding back of impulses.

Grazyna Kochanska (1993, 1995, 1997a, 1997b) and her colleagues have sought the origins of conscience in a longitudinal study of a group of toddlers and mothers in Iowa. Researchers videotaped 103 children ages 26 to 41 months and their mothers playing together with toys for two to three hours, both at home and in a homelike laboratory setting (Kochanska & Aksan, 1995). After a free-play period, the mother gave the child 15 minutes to put the toys away. The laboratory had a special shelf with other, unusually attractive toys, such as a bubble gum machine, a walkie-talkie, and a music box. The child had been told not to touch anything on the shelf. After about an hour, the experimenter asked the mother to go into an adjoining room, leaving the child alone with the toys. A few minutes later, a woman entered, played with several of the forbidden toys, and then left the child alone again for 8 minutes.

committed compliance Kochanska's term for wholehearted obedience of a parent's orders without reminders or lapses.

situational compliance Kochanska's term for obedience of a parent's orders only in the presence of signs of ongoing parental control.

Children were judged to show **committed compliance** if they willingly followed the orders to clean up and not to touch the toys, without reminders or lapses—thus showing inhibitory control. Children showed **situational compliance** if they needed prompting to obey; their compliance depended on ongoing parental control.

Committed compliance is strongly related to internalization of parental values and rules. Children whose mothers rated them as having internalized household rules refrained from touching the forbidden toys even when left alone with them, whereas children whose compliance was only situational tended to yield to temptation when their mothers were out of sight.

Committed compliance and situational compliance can be distinguished in children as young as 13 months, but their roots go back to infancy. Committed compliers, who are more likely to be girls than boys, tend to be those who, at 8 to 10 months, could refrain from touching when told "No!" Committed compliance tends to increase with age, while situational compliance decreases (Kochanska, Tjebkes, & Forman, 1998).

Secure attachment and a warm, mutually responsive parent-child relationship seem to foster conscience development (Eisenberg, 2000; Kochanska & Aksan, 1995). Mothers

Checkpoint

Can you . . .

- ✔ Describe Erikson's stage of autonomy versus shame and doubt?
- ✔ Explain why the "terrible twos" are considered a normal phenomenon?
- ✔ Tell when and how self-regulation develops and how it contributes to socialization?
- ✔ Explain the importance of attentional regulation and inhibitory control?
- ✔ Distinguish between committed and situational compliance?

of 2- and 3-year-old committed compliers, as contrasted with mothers of situational compliers, tend to rely on gentle guidance rather than force, threats, or other forms of negative control (Kochanska & Aksan, 1995). Children may more readily comply with parental demands when the parent has repeatedly affirmed the child's autonomy—for example, by following the child's lead during play. Mothers who can readily see a child's point of view seem to be most successful in doing this (Kochanska, 1997b).

Contact with Other Children

Although parents exert a major influence on children's lives, relationships with other children—both in the home and out of it—are important, too, from infancy on.

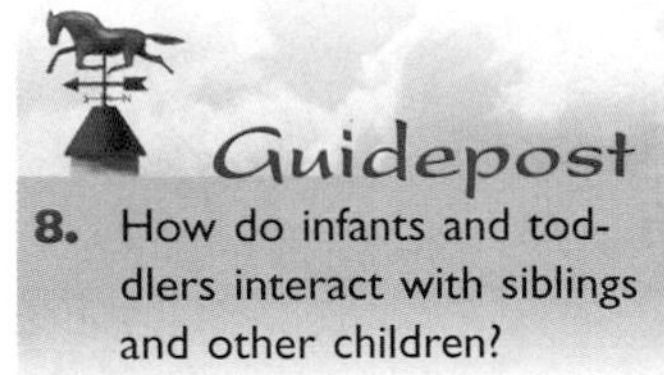

Guidepost

8. How do infants and toddlers interact with siblings and other children?

Siblings

Sibling relationships play a distinct role in socialization, different from those with parents or peers (Vandell, 2000). Sibling conflicts can become a vehicle for understanding social relationships (Dunn & Munn, 1985; Ram & Ross, 2001). Lessons and skills learned from interactions with siblings carry over to relationships outside the home (Brody, 1998).

Babies usually become attached to their older brothers and sisters. The more securely attached each sibling is to the parents, the better they get along with each other (Teti & Ablard, 1989). Nevertheless, as babies begin to move around and become more assertive, they inevitably come into conflict with siblings. Sibling conflict increases dramatically after the younger child reaches 18 months of age (Vandell & Bailey, 1992).

As cognitive and social understanding grows, sibling conflict tends to become more constructive, and the younger sibling participates in attempts to reconcile. Constructive conflict helps children recognize each other's needs, wishes, and point of view, and it helps them learn how to fight, disagree, and compromise within the context of a safe, stable relationship (Vandell & Bailey, 1992).

In many nonwestern cultures, it is common to see older siblings caring for younger siblings, as with these Chinese children.

Sociability with Nonsiblings

Infants and—even more so—toddlers show interest in people outside the home, particularly people their own size. During the first few months, they look, smile, and coo at other babies (T. M. Field, 1978). During the last half of the first year, they increasingly smile at, touch, and babble to another infant (Hay, Pedersen, & Nash, 1982).

At about 1 year, when babies are learning to walk and to manipulate objects, they pay more attention to toys and less to other people (T. M. Field & Roopnarine, 1982). This stage does not last long, though; from about $1\frac{1}{2}$ years of age to almost 3, they show more interest in what other children do and increasing understanding of how to deal with them. This insight seems to accompany awareness of themselves as separate individuals (Eckerman, Davis, & Didow, 1989; Eckerman & Stein, 1982).

Toddlers learn by imitating one another. Games such as follow-the-leader help toddlers connect with other children and pave the way for more complex games during the preschool years (Eckerman et al., 1989). As with siblings, conflict, too, can have a purpose: helping children learn how to negotiate and resolve disputes (Caplan, Vespo, Pedersen, & Hay, 1991).

Some children, of course, are more sociable than others, reflecting underlying temperamental traits. Sociability is also influenced by experience; babies who spend time with other babies tend to become sociable earlier than those who spend all their time at home alone.

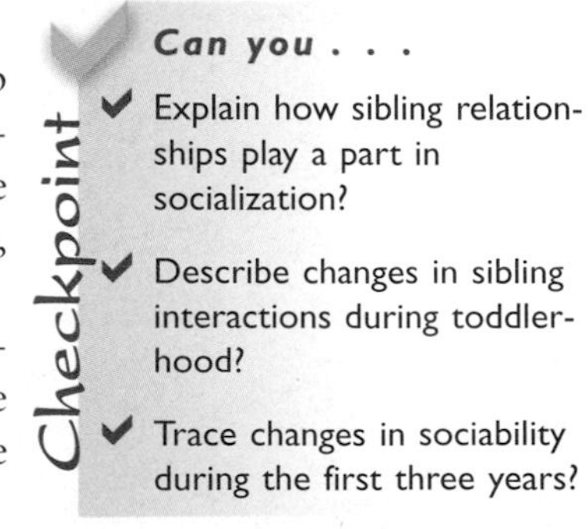

Checkpoint

Can you . . .

- ✔ Explain how sibling relationships play a part in socialization?
- ✔ Describe changes in sibling interactions during toddlerhood?
- ✔ Trace changes in sociability during the first three years?

Children of Working Parents

Guidepost

9. How do parental employment and early child care affect infants' and toddlers' development?

A significant influence on the atmosphere in the home is the work one or both parents do for pay. Parents' work determines more than the family's financial resources. Much of adults' time, effort, and emotional involvement go into their occupations. How do their work and their child care arrangements affect young children? Most research on this subject pertains to mothers' work. (We'll discuss the impact of parents' work on older children in Chapter 10 and on adolescents in Chapter 12.)

Effects of Parental Employment

More than half (50.6 percent) of mothers of infants in their first year of life and 56 percent of women with children under 3 were in the labor force in 2001 (Bureau of Labor Statistics, 2002). How does early maternal employment impact an infant or a young child?

The National Longitudinal Survey of Youth (NLSY) is an annual survey of some 12,600 women, accompanied by assessments of their children. An analysis of 1994 NLSY data (Harvey, 1999) found little or no effect of early maternal employment on children's compliance, behavior problems, self-esteem, cognitive development, or academic achievement. As in a number of other studies, early maternal employment did seem to benefit children in low-income families by increasing the family's resources. The study found no significant effects of fathers' working hours.

On the other hand, longitudinal data on 900 European American children from the National Institute of Child Health and Human Development Study of Early Child Care, discussed in the next section, showed negative effects on cognitive development at 15 months to 3 years when mothers go to work 30 or more hours a week by a child's ninth month. Maternal sensitivity, the quality of the home environment, and quality of child care made a difference, but did not fully account for the findings (Brooks-Gunn, Han, & Waldfogel, 2002). These findings suggest a need for generous family-leave policies to help mothers—and fathers—combine parenting and work.

The Impact of Early Child Care

Parental leave policies, which encourage working parents to stay home for an extended period to care for a new baby, can help them avoid or postpone the use of outside care. In the United States, however, legally required parental leave is unpaid and limited to three months, as compared with an average *paid* leave of nine months in member nations of the European Union. Thus many U.S. infants are in child care by the time they are 3 months old (Kamerman, 2000). More than two out of five children under age 5 receive regular nonparental child care. Those whose mothers are employed spend an average of 30 hours a week in child care. About 30 percent of these children stay with grandparents, who have become the nation's leading (and usually unpaid) care providers (Smith, 2002).

Effects of early child care may depend on the type, amount, overall quality, and stability of care, as well as the age at which children start receiving it. In home settings, where infants are likely to stay, quality of paid care is related to family income; the higher the income, the better the care. This is less true in child care centers, more commonly used for older preschoolers; there poor children who benefit from federal subsidies may receive better care than those from middle-class families (NICHD Early Child Care Research Network, 1997b). With an average cost for child care of $4,000 to $6,000 a year, affordability of care is a pressing issue for many families (Gardner, 2002). In 1999 only 12 percent of children eligible for federal child care subsidies got them, and, in seventeen states surveyed, only 15 to 20 percent of children eligible for

These children in a high-quality group day care program are likely to do at least as well cognitively and socially as children cared for full time at home. The most important element of infant day care is the caregiver or teacher, who exerts a strong influence on the children in her care.

state aid received it (USDHHS, 2000b). Most child care centers do not meet all recommended guidelines for child-staff ratios, group sizes, teacher training, and teacher education (Bergen, Reid, & Torelli, 2000; NICHD Early Child Care Research Network, 1998c). Table 6-5 lists guidelines for judging quality of care.

The most important element in quality of care is the caregiver; stimulating interactions with responsive adults are crucial to early cognitive, linguistic, and psychosocial development. Low staff turnover is critical; infants need consistent caregiving in order to develop trust and secure attachments (Burchinal, Roberts, Nabors, & Bryant, 1996; Howes, Matheson, & Hamilton, 1994).

Table 6-5 Checklist for Choosing a Good Child Care Facility

- Is the facility licensed? Does it meet minimum state standards for health, fire, and safety? (Many centers and home care facilities are not licensed or regulated.)
- Is the facility clean and safe? Does it have adequate indoor and outdoor space?
- Does the facility have small groups, a high adult-to-child ratio, and a stable, competent, highly involved staff?
- Are caregivers trained in child development?
- Are caregivers warm, affectionate, accepting, responsive, and sensitive? Are they authoritative but not too restrictive, and neither too controlling nor merely custodial?
- Does the program promote good health habits?
- Does it provide a balance between structured activities and free play? Are activities age-appropriate?
- Do the children have access to educational toys and materials, which stimulate mastery of cognitive and communicative skills at a child's own pace?
- Does the program nurture self-confidence, curiosity, creativity, and self-discipline?
- Does it encourage children to ask questions, solve problems, express feelings and opinions, and make decisions?
- Does it foster self-esteem, respect for others, and social skills?
- Does it help parents improve their childrearing skills?
- Does it promote cooperation with public and private schools and the community?

Sources: American Academy of Pediatrics [AAP]; 1986; Belsky, 1984; K. A. Clarke-Stewart, 1987; NICHD Early Child Care Research Network, 1996; S. W. Olds, 1989; Scarr, 1998.

The most comprehensive research on early child care to date is sponsored by the National Institute of Child Health and Human Development (NICHD). This ongoing longitudinal study of 1,364 children and their families began in 1991 in ten university centers across the United States, shortly after the children's birth. The sample was diverse socioeconomically, educationally, and ethnically; nearly 35 percent of the families were poor or near-poor. Most infants entered nonmaternal care before 4 months of age and received, on average, 33 hours of care each week. Child care arrangements varied widely in type and quality (Peth-Pierce, 1998).

The study was designed to measure the contribution child care makes to developmental outcomes, apart from the influences of family characteristics, the child's characteristics, and the care the child receives at home. Through observation, interviews, questionnaires, and tests, researchers measured the children's social, emotional, cognitive, and physical development at frequent intervals from 1 month of age through the first seven years of life. What do the findings show?

What's Your View?

- What advice would you give a new mother about the timing of her return to work and the selection of child care?

The quantity and quality of care children receive, as well as the type and stability of care, influence specific aspects of development (Peth-Pierce, 1998; see Table 6-6). However, factors related to child care seem to be less influential than family characteristics, such as income. These characteristics strongly predict developmental outcomes, regardless of how much time children spend in child care (NICHD Early Child Care Research Network, 1998b). While caregivers' sensitivity and responsiveness influence toddlers' self-control and compliance and the likelihood of problem behavior, the mother's sensitivity has a greater influence (NICHD Early Child Care Research Network, 1998a).

Maternal sensitivity also is the strongest predictor of attachment. Child care has no direct effect on attachment (as measured at 15 and 36 months by the Strange Situation), no matter how early infants enter care or how many hours they spend in it. Nor do the stability or quality of care matter, in and of themselves. However, when unstable, poor quality, or more-than-minimal amounts of child care (ten or more hours a week) are added to the impact of insensitive, unresponsive mothering, insecure attachment is more likely. On the other hand, high-quality care may help to offset insensitive mothering (NICHD Early Child Care Research Network, 1997a, 2001b).

Quality of care does contribute to cognitive and psychosocial development (NICHD Early Child Care Research Network, 2002; Peisner-Feinberg et al., 2001). Children in child care centers with low child-staff ratios, small group sizes, and trained, sensitive, responsive caregivers who provide positive interactions and language stimulation score higher on tests of language comprehension, cognition, and readiness for school; and their mothers report fewer behavior problems (NICHD Early Child Care Research Network, 1999a, 2000, 2002). Once again, though, family income, the

Table 6-6 Aspects of Development Affected by Characteristics of Early Child Care*

	Attachment	Parent-Child Relationships	Cooperation	Problem Behaviors	Cognitive Development and School Readiness	Language Development
Quality	•	•		+	+	+
Amount	•	•		•		
Type			•	•	+	+
Stability	•		•			

*Results after taking into account all family and child variables.

Source: Peth-Pierce, 1998, summary table of findings, p. 15.

+ Consistent effects

• Effects under some conditions

mother's vocabulary, the home environment, and the amount of mental stimulation the mother provides are even more influential (NICHD Early Child Care Research Network, 2000).

It should not be surprising that what look on the surface like effects of child care often may be effects of family characteristics. After all, stable families with high incomes and educational backgrounds and favorable home environments are more able, and therefore more likely, to place their children in high-quality care.

One area in which child care seems to have direct effects, independent of characteristics of the family and child, is in interactions with peers. Between ages 2 and 3, children whose caregivers are sensitive and responsive tend to become more positive and competent in the way they play with other children than before (NICHD Early Child Care Research Network, 2001a).

Checkpoint

Can you . . .

- ✔ Evaluate the impact of a mother's employment on her baby's well-being?
- ✔ List at least five criteria for good child care?
- ✔ Compare the impact of child care and of family characteristics on emotional, social, and cognitive development?

Refocus

- Which of the four types of temperament did Cathy Bateson show? Was there goodness of fit in her relationship with her parents?
- Did Cathy appear to be securely or insecurely attached?
- How did the childraising practices Cathy's parents followed seem to contribute to her psychosocial development?
- Did Cathy's tree-climbing technique suggest that she had internalized her parents' safety rules?
- How did her mother's professional life affect Cathy as an infant? As a toddler? On balance, as an only child, did she seem to benefit from her family's unusual child care arrangement?

However infants and toddlers are cared for, the experiences of the first three years lay the foundation for future development. In Part 4, we'll see how young children build on that foundation.

SUMMARY AND KEY TERMS

Foundations of Psychosocial Development

Guidepost 1. What are emotions, when do they develop, and how do babies show them?

- Emotions, by guiding and regulating behavior, serve protective needs.
- Emotional development can be seen as an orderly process, in which complex emotions unfold from simpler ones.
- Crying, smiling, and laughing are early signs of emotion.
- The repertoire of basic emotions seems to be universal, but there are individual and cultural variations in their expression.
- Self-conscious and evaluative emotions arise after the development of self-awareness.
- The emergence and expression of emotions seem to be tied to brain maturation and cognitive development.

emotions *(189)*
self-conscious emotions *(193)*
self-awareness *(193)*
self-evaluative emotions *(193)*
empathy *(194)*
social cognition *(194)*

Guidepost 2. How do infants show temperamental differences, and how enduring are those differences?

- Many children seem to fall into three categories of temperament: "easy," "difficult," and "slow-to-warm-up." Temperamental patterns appear to be largely inborn and to have a biological basis. They are generally stable but can be modified by experience.
- Cross-cultural differences in temperament may reflect childraising practices.

temperament *(195)*
"easy" children *(195)*
"difficult" children *(196)*
"slow-to-warm-up" children *(196)*
goodness of fit *(196)*

Guidepost 3. What roles do mothers and fathers play in early personality development?

- Childraising practices and caregiving roles vary around the world. Fathers in some cultures have different styles of play with babies.
- Infants have strong needs for maternal closeness and warmth as well as physical care.
- In most cultures, mothers do more infant care than fathers, but fathers' involvement is important.
- Although significant gender differences typically do not appear until after infancy, parents begin gender-typing boys and girls almost from birth.

gender *(201)*
gender-typing *(201)*

Developmental Issues in Infancy

Guidepost 4. How do infants gain trust in their world and form attachments?

- According to Erikson, infants in the first eighteen months experience the first stage in personality development, basic trust versus basic mistrust. Sensitive, responsive, consistent caregiving is the key to successful resolution of this conflict.
- Research based on the Strange Situation has found four patterns of attachment: secure, avoidant, ambivalent (resistant), and disorganized-disoriented.
- Newer instruments measure attachment in natural settings and in cross-cultural research.
- Attachment patterns may depend on a baby's temperament, as well as on the quality of parenting, and may have long-term implications for development. A parent's memories of childhood attachment can influence his or her own child's attachment.

basic trust versus basic mistrust *(202)*
attachment *(202)*
Strange Situation *(202)*
secure attachment *(203)*
secure base *(203)*
avoidant attachment *(203)*
ambivalent (resistant) attachment *(203)*
disorganized-disoriented attachment *(203)*

Guidepost 5. How do infants and caregivers "read" each other's nonverbal signals, and what happens when communication breaks down?

- Mutual regulation enables babies to play an active part in regulating their emotional states.
- A mother's depression, especially if severe or chronic, may have serious consequences for her infant's development.
- Separation anxiety and stranger anxiety may arise during the second half of the first year and appear to be related to temperament and circumstances.
- There is evidence that 1-year-olds show social referencing.

mutual regulation *(207)*
"still-face" paradigm *(208)*
stranger anxiety *(209)*
separation anxiety *(209)*
social referencing *(210)*

Developmental Issues in Toddlerhood

Guidepost 6. When and how do the self and self-concept arise?

- William James identified two "selves": the I-self and the Me-self, or self-concept.
- The I-self is believed to develop early in infancy, in the context of emotional experiences involving the relationship with a caregiver.
- The Me-self is believed to emerge between 15 and 30 months in conjunction with the development of self-awareness.

I-self *(212)*
Me-self *(212)*
self-concept *(212)*
self-efficacy *(212)*

Guidepost **7.** How do toddlers develop autonomy and standards for socially acceptable behavior?

- Erikson's second stage concerns autonomy versus shame and doubt. Negativism is a normal manifestation of the shift from external control to self-control.
- Socialization, which rests on internalization of societally approved standards, begins with the development of self-regulation.
- Parenting practices, a child's temperament, and the quality of the parent-child relationship may be factors in the ease and success of socialization.
- Toddlers who show committed compliance tend to internalize adult rules more readily than those who show situational compliance.

autonomy versus shame and doubt *(213)*

socialization *(214)*

internalization *(214)*

conscience *(214)*

self-regulation *(214)*

inhibitory control *(216)*

committed compliance *(216)*

situational compliance *(216)*

Contact with Other Children

Guidepost **8.** How do infants and toddlers interact with siblings and other children?

- Siblings influence each other's socialization, partly through practice in conflict resolution.
- Even during the first few months, infants show interest in other babies. This interest increases during the second half of the first year.
- Sociability may depend on temperament and exposure to other babies.

Children of Working Parents

Guidepost **9.** How do parental employment and early child care affect infants' and toddlers' development?

- Mothers' workforce participation during a child's first three years seems to have little independent impact on development.
- Substitute child care varies widely in type and quality. The most important element in quality of care is the caregiver.
- Although quality, quantity, stability, and type of care have some influence on psychosocial and cognitive development, the influence of family characteristics seems greater.
- Low-income children, especially, benefit from good child care.

PART 3

During the years from 3 to 6, often called the preschool years, children make the transition from toddlerhood to childhood. Their bodies become slimmer, their motor and mental abilities sharper, and their personalities and relationships more complex.

The 3-year-old is no longer a baby, but a sturdy adventurer, at home in the world and eager to explore its possibilities as well as the developing capabilities of his or her own body and mind. A child of this age has come through a relatively dangerous time of life—the years of infancy and toddlerhood—to enter a healthier, less threatening phase.

Growth and change are less rapid in early childhood than in infancy and toddlerhood, but, as we see in Chapters 7 and 8, all aspects of development—physical, cognitive, emotional, and social—continue to intertwine. ▸

Linkups to look for

- As muscles come under more conscious control, children can tend to more of their own personal needs, such as dressing and toileting, and thus gain a greater sense of competence and independence.
- Eating and sleep patterns are influenced by cultural attitudes.
- Even the common cold can have emotional and cognitive implications. Occasional minor illnesses not only build immunity; they help children learn to cope with physical distress and understand its causes.
- Social interaction plays a major role in the development of preliteracy skills, memory, and measured intelligence.
- Cognitive awareness of gender has far-reaching psychosocial implications, affecting children's sense of self and their attitudes toward the roles the two sexes play in their society.
- Environmental influences, including the parents' life circumstances, affect health and safety. The link between developmental realms is especially evident in the tragic results of child abuse and neglect; although the most obvious effects may be physical, these conditions can stunt cognitive growth and can leave lasting emotional scars.

Early Childhood

PREVIEW

CHAPTER 7

Physical and Cognitive Development in Early Childhood

Growth is steady; appearance becomes more slender and proportions more adultlike.

Appetite diminishes, and sleep problems are common.

Handedness appears; fine and gross motor skills and strength improve.

Thinking is somewhat egocentric, but understanding of other people's perspectives grows.

Cognitive immaturity leads to some illogical ideas about the world.

Memory and language improve.

Intelligence becomes more predictable.

Preschool experience is common, and kindergarten more so.

CHAPTER 8

Psychosocial Development in Early Childhood

Self-concept and understanding of emotions become more complex; self-esteem is global.

Independence, initiative, and self-control increase.

Gender identity develops.

Play becomes more imaginative, more elaborate, and usually more social.

Altruism, aggression, and fearfulness are common.

Family is still the focus of social life, but other children become more important.

Chapter 7

Physical and Cognitive Development in Early Childhood

Children live in a world of imagination and feeling. . . . They invest the most insignificant object with any form they please, and see in it whatever they wish to see.

—**Adam G. Oehlenschlager**

OUTLINE

Focus: Wang Yani, Self-Taught Artist*

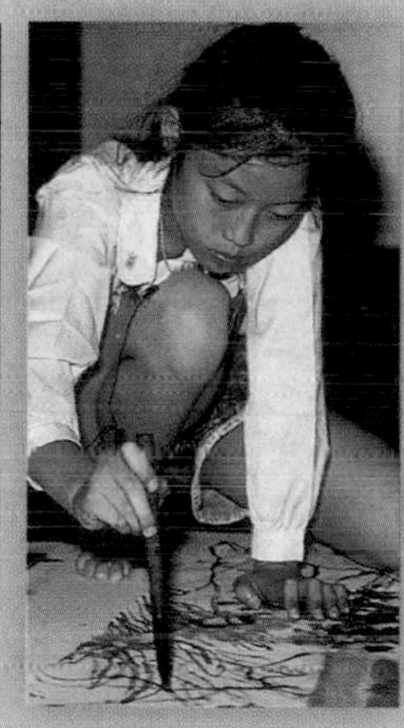

Wang Yani

Wang Yani (b. 1975) is a gifted young Chinese artist. Now in her twenties, she had her first exhibit in Shanghai at the age of 4 and produced four thousand paintings by the time she turned 6. Her work has been shown throughout Asia and in Europe and the United States since she was 10.

Yani (her given name)** began painting at $2\frac{1}{2}$ by imitating her father, Wang Shiqiang. A professional artist and educator, Wang gave her big brushes and large sheets of paper to permit bold strokes. Rather than teach her, he let her learn by doing, in her own way, and always praised her work. In contrast with traditional Chinese art edu cation, which emphasizes conformity and imitation, he al lowed his daughter's imagination free rein.

Yani went through the usual stages in preschoolers' drawing, but far more quickly than usual. Her early paintings after the scribble stage were made up of dots, circles, and apparently meaningless lines, which stood for people, birds, or fruit. By the age of 3, she painted recognizable but highly original forms.

Yani's father encouraged her to paint what she saw outdoors near their home in the scenic riverside town of Gongcheng. Like traditional Chinese artists, she did not paint from life but constructed her brightly colored compositions from mental images of what she had seen. Her visual memory has been called astounding. When she was only 4, her father taught her Chinese characters (letters) of as many as twenty-five strokes by "writing" them in the air with his finger. Yani immediately put them down on paper.

*Sources of biographical information about Wang Yani were Bond (1989), Costello (1990), Ho (1989), Stuart (1991), and Zhensun & Low (1991).
**In Chinese custom, the given name follows the family name.

Her father helped develop her powers of observation and imagery by carrying her on his shoulders as he hiked in the fields and mountains or lying with her in the grass and telling stories about the passing clouds. The pebbles along the riverbank reminded her of the monkeys at the zoo, which she painted over and over between the ages of 3 and 6. Yani made up stories about the monkeys she portrayed. They often represented Yani herself—eating a snack, refereeing an argument among friends, or trying to conquer her fear of her first shot at the doctor's office. Painting, to Yani, was not an objective representation of reality; it was a mirror of her mind, a way to transform her sensory impressions into simple but powerful semiabstract images onto which she projected her thoughts, feelings, and dreams.

Because of her short arms, Yani's brush strokes at first were short. Her father trained her to hold her brush tightly, by trying to grab it from behind when she was not looking. She learned to paint with her whole arm, twisting her wrist to produce the effect she wanted. As her physical dexterity and experience grew, her strokes became more forceful, varied, and precise: broad, wet strokes to define an animal's shape; fuzzy, nearly dry ones to suggest feathers, fur, or tree bark. The materials she used—bamboo brushes, ink sticks, and rice paper—were traditional, but her style—popularly called *xieyi,* "idea writing"—was not. It was, and remains, playful, free, and spontaneous.

With quick reflexes, a fertile imagination, remarkable visual abilities, strong motivation, and her father's sensitive guidance, Yani's artistic progress has been swift. As a young adult, she is considered an artist of great promise. Yet she herself finds painting very simple: "You just paint what you think about. You don't have to follow any instruction. Everybody can paint" (Zhensun & Low, 1991, p. 9).

Although Wang Yani's artistic growth has been unusual, it rested on typical developments of early childhood: rapid improvement in muscular control and eye-hand coordination, accompanied by a growing understanding of the world around her—an understanding guided by her powers of observation and memory and her verbal interactions with her father. Together these physical, cognitive, and social influences helped her express her thoughts and emotions through art.

In this chapter, we look at physical and cognitive development during the years from 3 to 6. Youngsters in this age group grow more slowly than before, but still at a fast pace; and they make so much progress in muscle development and coordination that they can do much more. Children also make enormous advances in the abilities to think, speak, and remember. In this chapter, we trace all these developing capabilities and consider several health concerns. We also discuss an experience increasingly common in many places: early childhood education.

After you have read and studied this chapter, you should be able to answer each of the following Guidepost questions. Look for them again in the margins, where they point to important concepts throughout the chapter. To check your understanding of these Guideposts, review the end-of-chapter summary. Checkpoints located at periodic spots throughout the chapter will help you verify your understanding of what you have read.

Guideposts for Study

1. How do children's bodies change between ages 3 and 6, and what are their nutritional and dental needs?
2. What sleep patterns and problems tend to develop during early childhood?
3. What are the main motor achievements of early childhood?
4. What are the major health and safety risks for young children?
5. What are typical cognitive advances and immature aspects of preschool children's thinking?
6. How does language improve, and what happens when its development is delayed?
7. What memory abilities expand in early childhood?
8. How is preschoolers' intelligence measured, and what are some influences on it?
9. What purposes does early childhood education serve, and how do children make the transition to kindergarten?

PHYSICAL DEVELOPMENT

Aspects of Physical Development

In early childhood, children slim down and shoot up. They need less sleep than before and are more likely to develop sleep problems. They improve in running, hopping, skipping, jumping, and throwing balls. They also become better at tying shoelaces, drawing with crayons, and pouring cereal; and they begin to show a preference for either the right or left hand.

Guidepost

1. How do children's bodies change between ages 3 and 6, and what are their nutritional and dental needs?

Bodily Growth and Change

Children grow rapidly between ages 3 and 6, but less quickly than before. At about 3, children begin to lose their babyish roundness and take on the slender, athletic appearance of childhood. As abdominal muscles develop, the toddler potbelly tightens. The trunk, arms, and legs grow longer. The head is still relatively large, but the other parts of the body continue to catch up as body proportions steadily become more adultlike.

The pencil mark on the wall that shows Eve's height is $37\frac{1}{2}$ inches from the floor, and this "average" 3-year-old now weighs about 30 pounds. Her twin brother Isaac, like most boys this age, is a little taller and heavier and has more muscle per pound of body weight, whereas Eve, like most girls, has more fatty tissue. Both boys and girls typically grow 2 to 3 inches a year during early childhood and gain 4 to 6 pounds annually (see Table 7-1 on page 230). Boys' slight edge in height and weight continues until the growth spurt of puberty.

Muscular and skeletal growth progresses, making children stronger. Cartilage turns to bone at a faster rate than before, and bones become harder and stronger, giving the child a firmer shape and protecting the internal organs. These changes, coordinated

Table 7-1 Physical Growth, Ages 3 to 6 (50th percentile)*

Age	Height, Inches		Weight, Pounds	
	Boys	Girls	Boys	Girls
3	37½	37	32	30
3½	39	38½	34	32½
4	40½	39½	36	35
4½	41½	41	38	37
5	43	42½	40	40
5½	44½	44	43	42
6	45½	45½	46	45

*Fifty percent of children in each category are above this height or weight level, and 50 percent are below it.
Source: Kuczmarski et al., 2000.

Checkpoint

Can you . . .

✔ Describe typical physical changes around the age of 3, and compare boys' and girls' growth patterns?

by the maturing brain and nervous system, promote the development of a wide range of motor skills. The increased capacities of the respiratory and circulatory systems build physical stamina and, along with the developing immune system, keep children healthier.

Nutrition and Oral Health

Preschoolers eat less in proportion to their size than infants do; as growth slows, they need fewer calories per pound of body weight. Preschoolers who are allowed to eat when they are hungry and are not pressured to eat everything given to them are more likely to regulate their own caloric intake than are children fed on schedule (Johnson & Birch, 1994). However, children vary in their ability to recognize their internal cues of hunger and fullness, and parents' eating habits have an influence. In a study of forty families in two child care facilities, a six-week intervention program designed to teach children to recognize their own cues improved their ability to self-regulate, independent of what they saw their mothers do (Johnson, 2000).

As children move through the preschool period, their eating patterns become more environmentally influenced, like those of adults. Whereas most 3-year-olds will eat only until they are full, 5-year-olds tend to eat more when a larger portion is put in front of them. Thus a key to preventing overweight may be to make sure older preschoolers are served appropriate portions—and not to admonish them to clean their plates (Rolls, Engell, & Birch, 2000).

What's Your View?

- Much television advertising aimed at young children fosters poor nutrition by promoting fats and sugars rather than proteins and vitamins. How might parents counteract these pressures?

To avoid overweight and prevent cardiac problems, young children should get only about 30 percent of their total calories from fat, and less than 10 percent of the total from saturated fat. Lean meat and dairy foods should remain in the diet to provide protein, iron, and calcium. Milk and other dairy products can now be skim or low-fat (AAP Committee on Nutrition, 1992a). Studies have found no negative effects on height, weight, body mass, or neurological development from a moderately low-fat diet (Rask-Nissilä et al., 2000; Shea et al., 1993).

obesity Extreme overweight in relation to age, sex, height, and body type; defined in childhood as having a body mass index (weight-for-height) at or above the 95th percentile of growth curves for children of the same age and sex.

Obesity, or extreme overweight, is defined in childhood as having a *body mass index (BMI)*—comparison of weight to height—at or above the 95th percentile for age and sex. A child whose BMI is higher than that of 95 percent of children of the same age and sex in a standardized sample is considered obese. Obesity today is more common among preschoolers (especially girls, who tend to be less active than boys) than twenty-five years ago (Ogden et al., 1997). More than 10 percent of 2- to 5-year-olds are obese, compared with 7 percent in 1994 (Ogden, Flegal, Carroll, & Johnson, 2002). Worldwide, an International Obesity Task Force estimates that 22 million children under age 5 are obese (Belizzi, 2002). As "junk food" spreads through the developing world, in some countries, such as Egypt, Morocco, and Zambia, as many as 20 to 25 percent of 4-year-olds are overweight or obese—a larger proportion than are malnourished. (Malnutrition, a serious problem especially in the developing world, is discussed in Chapter 9.)

Overweight children, especially those who have overweight parents, tend to become overweight adults (Whitaker et al., 1997), and excess body mass can be a threat to health. A tendency to obesity is partly hereditary, but it also depends on fat intake and exercise (Jackson et al., 1997; Klesges, Klesges, Eck, & Shelton, 1995; Leibel, 1997; Ogden et al., 1997). Early to middle childhood is a good time to treat obesity, when a child's diet is still subject to parental influence or control (Whitaker et al., 1997).

By age 3, all the primary, or deciduous, teeth are in place. The permanent teeth, which will begin to appear at about age 6, are developing. Use of fluoride and improved dental care have dramatically reduced the incidence of tooth decay since the 1970s, but disadvantaged children still have more untreated cavities than other children (Brown, Wall, & Lazar, 2000).

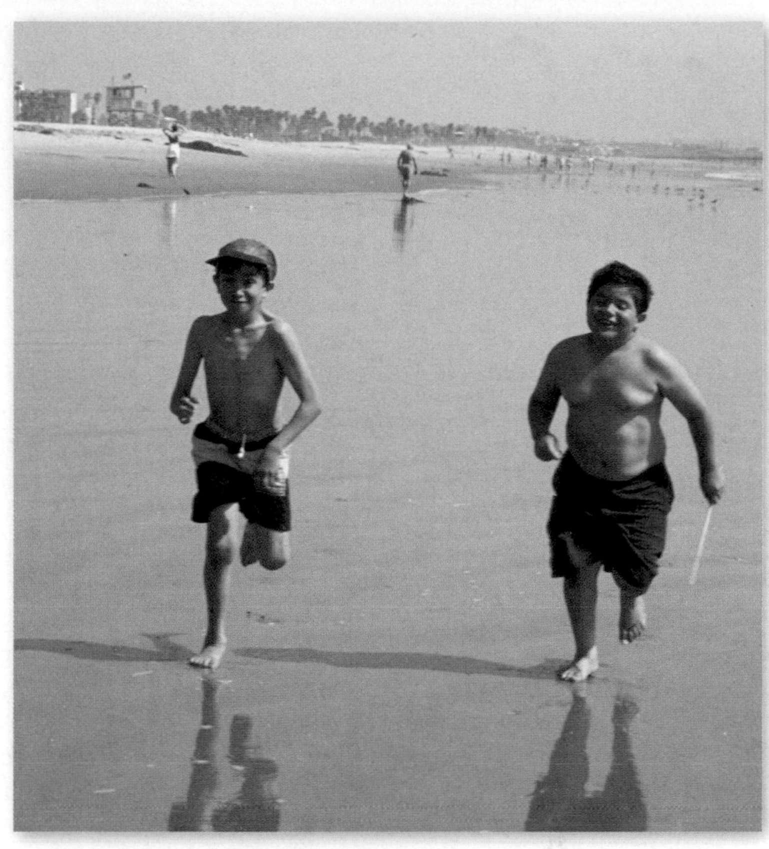

An obese child is likely to find it hard to keep up with slimmer peers, both physically and socially. Obesity among preschool and school-age children is more common than in the past.

Sleep Patterns and Problems

Sleep patterns change throughout the growing-up years. Young children usually sleep more deeply at night than they will later in life.

Guidepost

2. What sleep patterns and problems tend to develop during early childhood?

Children in different cultures may get the same amount of sleep each day, but its timing may vary. In many traditional cultures, such as the Gusii of Kenya, the Javanese in Indonesia, and the Zuni in New Mexico, young children have no regular bedtime. Among the Canadian Hare, 3-year-olds do not take naps but are put to sleep right after dinner and are allowed to sleep as long as they wish in the morning (Broude, 1995). Most U.S. children still take a daytime nap or quiet rest until about age 5.

Young children may develop elaborate routines to put off going to bed, and it may take them longer than before to fall asleep. Bedtime may bring on a form of separation anxiety, and the child may do all she or he can to avoid it. Regular, consistent sleep routines can help minimize this common problem. Children past infancy should not be put to sleep by feeding or rocking, as this may make it hard for them to fall asleep on their own (American Academy of Child and Adolescent Psychiatry [AACAP], 1997).

Sleep Disturbances and Disorders About 20 to 30 percent of children in their first four years engage in *bedtime struggles* lasting more than an hour and wake their parents frequently at night. Five experiences tend to distinguish children with these problems. One is sleeping in the same bed with parents; it is simply more tempting and easier to wake someone in the same bed than in the next room. The other four conditions signal family stress. The family is likely to have experienced a stressful accident or illness; or the mother is likely to be depressed, to have mixed feelings about the child, or to have recently changed her schedule so as to be away for most of the day (Lozoff, Wolf, & Davis, 1985).

Walking and talking during sleep are fairly common in early childhood. Although sleepwalking itself is harmless, sleepwalkers may be in danger of hurting themselves (AACAP, 1997; Vgontzas & Kales, 1999). This and such other sleep disturbances as nightmares and sleep terrors are caused by accidental activation of the brain's motor control system (Hobson & Silvestri, 1999). They are mostly occasional and usually outgrown. However, persistent sleep problems may indicate an emotional, physiological, or neurological condition that needs to be examined.

A *nightmare* is a frightening dream, often brought on by staying up too late, eating a heavy meal close to bedtime, or overexcitement—for example, from watching an overstimulating television program, seeing a terrifying movie, or hearing a frightening bedtime story (Vgontzas & Kales, 1999). Nightmares usually come toward morning and are often vividly recalled. They are quite common, especially among girls (AACAP, 1997; Hobson & Silvestri, 1999). An occasional bad dream is no cause for alarm, but frequent or persistent nightmares, especially those that make a child fearful or anxious during waking hours, may signal excessive stress.

A child who experiences a *sleep terror* awakens abruptly from a deep sleep in a state of panic. The child may scream and sit up in bed, breathing rapidly and staring. Yet he is not really awake, quiets down quickly, and the next morning remembers nothing about the episode. Unlike nightmares, sleep terrors tend to occur within an hour after falling asleep. They typically begin between ages 4 and 12. Like sleepwalking, sleep terrors are most common among boys and run in families (AACAP, 1997; Hobson & Silvestri, 1999). They may be triggered by disordered breathing or restless leg movements (Guilleminault, Palombini, Pelayo, & Chervin, 2003). Sleep terrors rarely signify a serious emotional problem. While the first concern is to protect the child from injury, it is best not to interrupt sleepwalking or sleep terrors; interruptions may confuse and further frighten the child (Vgontzas & Kales, 1999).

Bed-Wetting Most children stay dry, day and night, by 3 to 5 years of age; but **enuresis,** repeated urination in clothing or in bed, is common, especially at night. About 7 percent of 5-year-old boys and 3 percent of girls that age wet the bed regularly (American Psychiatric Association [APA], 1994; Schmitt, 1997).

enuresis Repeated urination in clothing or in bed.

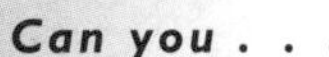

Checkpoint

Can you . . .

- ✔ Summarize preschoolers' dietary needs and explain why obesity and tooth decay can become concerns at this age?
- ✔ Discuss cultural variations in sleep patterns?
- ✔ Identify five common sleep problems and give recommendations for handling them?

Children this age normally recognize the sensation of a full bladder while asleep and awaken to empty it in the toilet. Children who wet the bed do not have this awareness. Fewer than 1 percent of bed-wetters have a physical disorder, though they may have a small bladder capacity. Nor is persistent enuresis primarily an emotional, mental, or behavioral problem—though such problems can develop because of the way bed-wetters are treated by playmates and family (National Enuresis Society, 1995; Schmitt, 1997). The discovery of the approximate site of a gene linked to enuresis (Eiberg, 1995; Eiberg, Berendt, & Mohr, 1995) points to heredity as a major factor in the condition, possibly in combination with such other factors as slow motor maturation, allergies, and poor behavioral control (Goleman, 1995b).

Children and their parents need to be reassured that enuresis is common and not serious. The child is not to blame and should not be punished. Generally parents need not do anything unless children themselves see bed-wetting as a problem.

Motor Skills

Guidepost

3. What are the main motor achievements of early childhood?

Preschool children make great advances in **gross motor skills,** such as running and jumping, which involve the large muscles (see Table 7-2). Development of the sensory and motor areas of the cortex permits better coordination between what children want to do and what they can do. Their bones and muscles are stronger, and their lung capacity is greater, making it possible to run, jump, and climb farther, faster, and better.

gross motor skills Physical skills that involve the large muscles.

Children vary in adeptness, depending on their genetic endowment and their opportunities to learn and practice motor skills. Those under age 6 are rarely ready to take part in any organized sport. Only 20 percent of 4-year-olds can throw a ball well, and only 30 percent can catch well (AAP Committee on Sports Medicine and Fitness, 1992). Physical development blossoms best in active, unstructured free play.

(a)

(b)

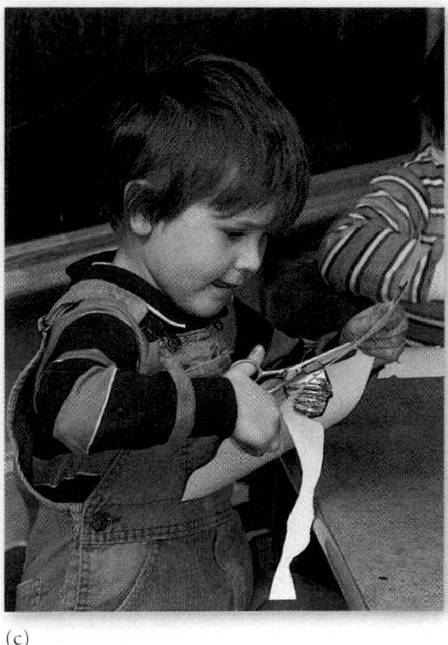
(c)

Children make significant advances in motor skills during the preschool years. As they develop physically, they are better able to make their bodies do what they want. Large-muscle development lets them run or ride a tricycle; increasing eye-hand coordination helps them to use scissors or chopsticks. Children with disabilities can do many normal activities with the aid of special devices.

Fine motor skills, such as buttoning shirts and drawing pictures, involve eye-hand and small-muscle coordination, skills in which Wang Yani clearly excelled. Gains in these skills allow young children to take more responsibility for their personal care.

fine motor skills Physical skills that involve the small muscles and eye-hand coordination.

As they develop both types of motor skills, preschoolers continually merge abilities they already have with those they are acquiring, to produce more complex capabilities. Such combinations of skills are known as **systems of action.**

systems of action Increasingly complex combinations of skills, which permit a wider or more precise range of movement and more control of the environment.

Artistic Development Changes in young children's drawings seem to reflect maturation of the brain as well as of the muscles (Kellogg, 1970; see Figure 7-1 on page 234). Two-year-olds *scribble*—not randomly but in patterns, such as vertical and zigzag lines. By age 3, children draw *shapes*—circles, squares, rectangles, triangles, crosses, and Xs—and then begin combining the shapes into more complex *designs.* The *pictorial* stage typically begins between ages 4 and 5; Wang Yani reached this stage at age 3.

The switch from abstract form and design to depicting real objects marks a fundamental change in the purpose of children's drawing, reflecting cognitive development

Table 7-2 Gross Motor Skills in Early Childhood

3-Year-Olds	4-Year-Olds	5-Year-Olds
Cannot turn or stop suddenly or quickly	Have more effective control of stopping, starting, and turning	Can start, turn, and stop effectively in games
Can jump a distance of 15 to 24 inches	Can jump a distance of 24 to 33 inches	Can make a running jump of 28 to 36 inches
Can ascend a stairway unaided, alternating feet	Can descend a long stairway alternating feet, if supported	Can descend a long stairway unaided, alternating feet
Can hop, using largely an irregular series of jumps with some variations added	Can hop four to six steps on one foot	Can easily hop a distance of 16 feet

Source: Corbin, 1973.

Figure 7-1
Artistic development in early childhood. There is a great difference between the very simple shapes shown in (a) and the detailed pictorial drawings in (e). The challenge for adults is to encourage children's creativity while acknowledging their growing facility in drawing.
(*Source:* Kellogg, 1970.)

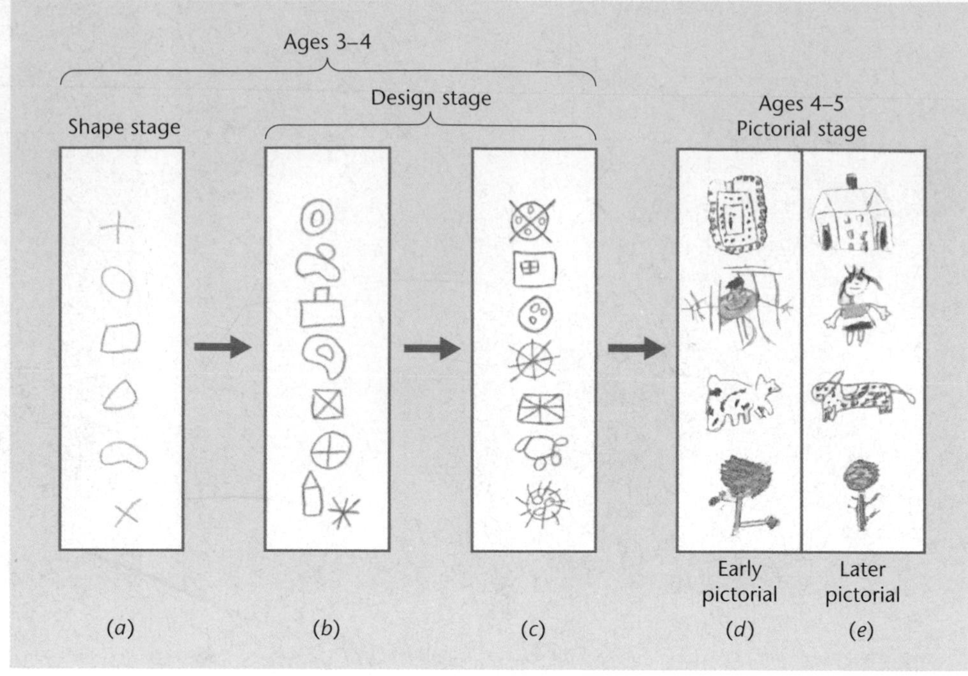

What's Your View?

- Drawings from children's early pictorial stage show energy and freedom; those from the later pictorial stage show care and accuracy. Why do you think these changes occur? How would you evaluate them?

of representational ability. However, greater pictorial accuracy—often encouraged by adults—may come at the cost of the energy and freedom shown in children's early efforts. This was not so in Yani's case, of course. While her father refrained from influencing her artistic style, he gave her big sheets of paper and trained her to paint with her whole arm, using large muscles as well as small ones. Her pictorial forms retained a free-flowing, semiabstract quality that gave them the stamp of originality.

handedness Preference for using a particular hand.

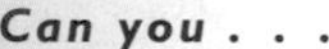

Handedness **Handedness,** the preference for using one hand over the other, is usually evident by age 3. Since the left hemisphere of the brain, which controls the right side of the body, is usually dominant, most people favor their right side. In people whose brains are more symmetrical, the right hemisphere tends to dominate, making them left-handed. Handedness is not always clear-cut; not everybody prefers one hand for every task. Boys are more likely to be left-handed than girls.

Is handedness genetic or learned? That question has been controversial. A new theory proposes the existence of a single gene for right-handedness. According to this theory, people who inherit this gene from either or both parents—about 82 percent of the population—are right-handed. Those who do not inherit the gene still have a 50-50 chance of being right-handed; otherwise they will be left-handed or ambidextrous. Random determination of handedness among those who do not receive the gene could explain why some monozygotic twins have differing hand preferences, as well as why 8 percent of the offspring of two right-handed parents are left-handed. The theory closely predicted the proportion of left-handed offspring in a three-generational sample of families recruited through advertisements (Klar, 1996).

Checkpoint

Can you . . .

- ✔ List at least three gross motor skills, and tell when they typically develop?
- ✔ Identify four stages in young children's drawing?
- ✔ Tell how brain functioning is related to physical skills and handedness?

Health and Safety

Guidepost

4. What are the major health and safety risks for young children?

What used to be a very vulnerable time of life is much safer now. Because of widespread immunization, many of the major diseases of childhood are now fairly rare in western industrialized countries. In the developing world, however, such vaccine-preventable diseases as measles, pertussis (whooping cough), and tuberculosis still take a large toll. Diarrheal infections account for nearly one-fifth of the 11.2 million deaths of children under age 5 in these regions each year (Wegman, 1999).

In the United States, children's death rates from virtually all kinds of illness have come down in recent years. Deaths in childhood are relatively few compared with deaths in adulthood, and most are caused by injury rather than illness (National Center for Health Statistics [NCHS], 2001). Still, environmental influences make this a less healthy time for some children than for others.

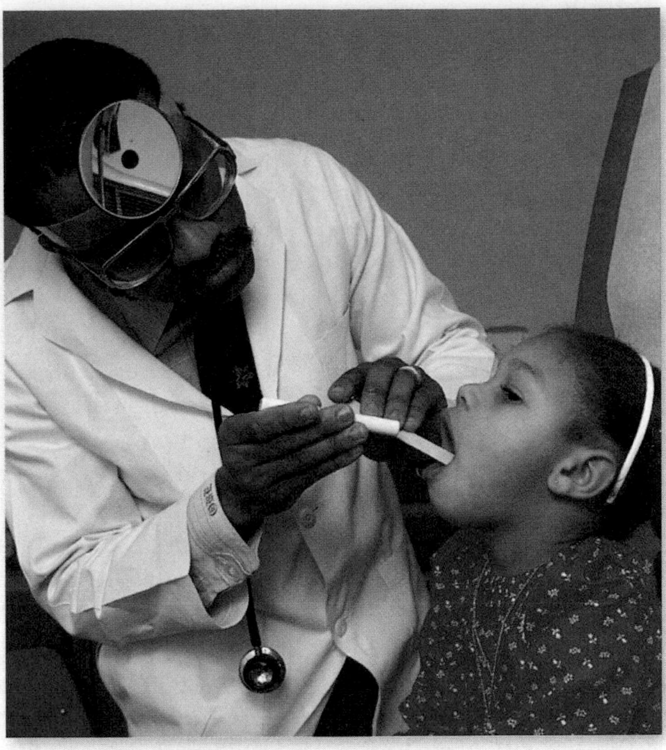

Although sore throats and other minor illnesses are common among 3- to 6-year-olds, they are usually not serious enough to require visits to the doctor. This 5-year-old will probably have fewer colds and sore throats in the next few years, as her respiratory and immune systems mature.

Minor Illnesses

Coughs, sniffles, stomachaches, and runny noses are a part of early childhood. These minor illnesses typically last a few days and are seldom serious enough to need a doctor's attention. Because the lungs are not fully developed, respiratory problems are common, though less so than in infancy. Three- to 5-year-olds catch an average of seven to eight colds and other respiratory illnesses a year. It's a good thing they do, since these illnesses help build natural immunity (resistance to disease). During middle childhood, when the respiratory system is more fully developed, children average fewer than six such illnesses a year (Denny & Clyde, 1983).

Accidental Injuries and Deaths

Accidents are the leading cause of death throughout childhood and adolescence in the United States. Most of these deaths are from motor vehicle injuries (Rivara, 1999; NCHS, 2001). Deaths from pedestrian injuries have fallen by 65 percent since the late 1970s, but the risk of serious brain damage and lifelong disability from head injuries remains high (Rivara, 1999).

Many deaths from car accidents are preventable. In 1996, 1 in 5 children's deaths in automobile crashes—whether as passengers, pedestrians, or bicyclists—were alcohol-related. In 2 out of 3 of these deaths, the child's own driver had been drinking (Margolis, Foss, & Tolbert, 2000), and in most of these cases the child was riding unrestrained (Quinlan, Brewer, Sleet, & Dellinger, 2000).

More than one million cases of ingestion of toxic substances by children under 6 were reported to poison control centers in 1998, and the true figure may be more than 4 million. Medications are responsible for more than half (52 percent) of deaths from poisoning. Safe storage could prevent many of these deaths (Litovitz et al., 1999; Shannon, 2000).

U.S. laws requiring automobile seat belts and child restraints, "childproof" caps on medicine bottles and other dangerous household products, regulation of product safety, mandatory helmets for bicycle riders, and safe storage of firearms have improved child safety. Making playgrounds safer would be another valuable measure. An estimated 3 percent of children in day care are hurt badly enough each year to need medical attention, and about half of accidents at child care centers occur on playgrounds. Nearly 1 in 5 are from falls, often resulting in skull injury and brain damage (Briss, Sacks, Addiss, Kresnow, & O'Neil, 1994). Children are less likely to be injured in day care, however, than in and around the home (Thacker, Addiss, Goodman, Holloway, & Spencer, 1992), where most fatal nonvehicular accidents occur.

Temperament may make some children injury-prone. In a longitudinal study of 59 children, those who were more extraverted and had less inhibitory control as toddlers and preschoolers tended to overestimate their physical abilities at age 6, and they also had had considerably more injuries requiring medical treatment (Schwebel & Plumert, 1999).

Checkpoint

Can you . . .

- Identify a benefit of minor illnesses?
- Tell where and how young children are most likely to be injured, and list ways in which injuries can be avoided?

Also at special risk are children whose primary caregivers are young, uneducated, and overburdened. In a study of all children born in Tennessee between 1985 and 1994, children born to mothers under 20 years old, with less than a high school education and three or more other children, were fifteen times as likely to die of injuries before the age of 5 as children whose mothers were college educated, more than 30 years old, and had fewer than three other children. If the mortality rate for all children could be reduced to that of this lowest-risk group, injury-related deaths might be reduced by more than 75 percent (Scholer, Mitchel, & Ray, 1997).

Health in Context: Environmental Influences

Why do some children have more illnesses or injuries than others? The genetic heritage contributes: some children seem predisposed toward some medical conditions. In addition, as Bronfenbrenner's bioecological theory would predict, the home, the child care facility, the neighborhood, and the larger society play major roles.

Exposure to Smoking Parental smoking is an important preventable cause of childhood illness and death. In the United States, 43 percent of children 2 months to 11 years old live with smokers and are exposed daily to secondhand smoke (AAP Committee on Substance Abuse, 2001; Pirkle et al., 1996). This passive exposure increases the risk of contracting a number of medical conditions, including pneumonia, bronchitis, serious infectious illnesses, otitis media (middle ear infection), burns, and asthma. It also may lead to cancer in adulthood (Aligne & Stoddard, 1997; AAP Committee on Environmental Health, 1997; U.S. Environmental Protection Agency, 1994). The American Academy of Pediatrics Committee on Environmental Health (1997) recommends that children be raised in a smoke-free environment.

SES and Poverty There is a striking relationship between socioeconomic status and health: the lower a family's SES, the greater a child's risks of illness, injury, and death (Chen, Matthews, & Boyce, 2002). Low income is the *chief* factor associated with poor health of children and adolescents, over and above race and family structure (Montgomery, Kiely, & Pappas, 1996; refer back to Table 1-2 in Chapter 1).

More than 1 in 6 U.S. children were poor in the year 2000, and the youngest children tend to be the poorest. Although poverty strikes all parts of the population, it besets young families—including working families—and minorities disproportionately. About 31 percent of black children and 28 percent of Hispanic children are poor, as compared with 13 percent of white children and 14.5 percent of Asian and Pacific Islander children. Furthermore, the safety net for needy families in a sluggish economy has weakened with the end of national welfare assistance (Children's Defense Fund, 2001, 2002b).

The health problems of poor children often begin before birth. Many poor mothers do not eat well and do not receive adequate prenatal care; their babies are more likely than babies of nonpoor mothers to be of low birthweight or to die in infancy. Poor children who do not eat properly do not grow properly, and thus are weak and susceptible to disease. Many poor families live in crowded, unsanitary housing, and the children may lack adequate supervision, especially when the parents are at work. They are more likely than other children to suffer lead poisoning, hearing and vision loss, and iron-deficiency anemia, as well as such stress-related conditions as asthma, headaches, insomnia, and irritable bowel. They also tend to have more behavior problems, psychological disturbances, and learning disabilities (J. L. Brown, 1987; Chen et al., 2002; Egbuono & Starfield, 1982; Santer & Stocking, 1991; Starfield, 1991).

Many poor children do not get the medical care they need (Chen et al., 2002). One in 10 U.S. children is uninsured; this proportion has improved from 1 in 7 in

1997, due to the Children's Health Insurance Program (CHIP), a federally underwritten state program that covers poor families who earn too much to qualify for Medicaid (Associated Press, 2002b). Latino children, now the nation's largest racial/ethnic minority, are more likely to lack regular, quality care and insurance than white or black children. They are especially at risk for asthma, obesity, diabetes, and tuberculosis and behavioral and developmental problems. Language and cultural barriers and the need for more Latino care providers may help explain these disparities (Flores et al., 2002).

Exposure to Lead An estimated 890,000 children in the United States have high levels of lead in their blood (AAP Committee on Environmental Health, 1998; Children's Defense Fund, 2000). Children can get lead in the bloodstream from lead-contaminated food or water, from putting contaminated fingers in their mouths, or from inhaling dust in homes or schools where there is lead-based paint. Lead poisoning can seriously interfere with cognitive development and can bring on a variety of neurological and behavioral problems (AAP Committee on Environmental Health, 1998; Needleman, Riess, Tobin, Biesecker, & Greenhouse, 1996; Tesman & Hills, 1994). Yet it can be completely prevented by removing sources of lead from children's environment (Tesman & Hills, 1994).

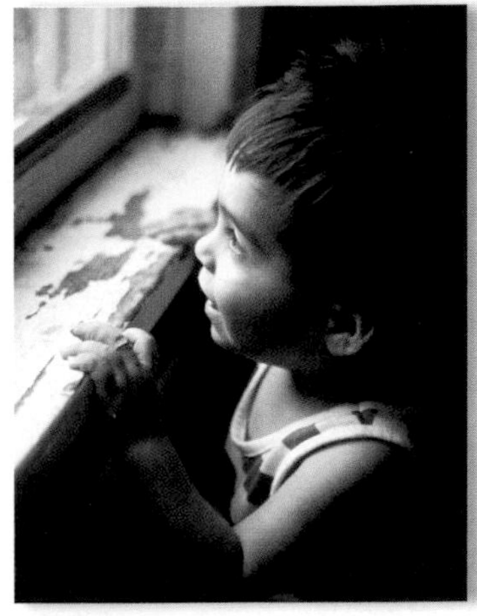

Young children who live in old, dilapidated buildings with peeling lead paint are at risk for lead poisoning, which can adversely affect the developing brain.

There is no safe level of exposure to lead. However, the degree of toxicity depends on the dose, how long a child is exposed, and the child's developmental and nutritional vulnerability (AAP Committee on Environmental Health, 1998). Even low levels of exposure may have detrimental behavioral effects in very young preschoolers, particularly those who have other risk factors, such as poverty and maternal depression (Mendelsohn et al., 1998). Moderate lead poisoning can be treated (Ruff, Bijur, Markowitz, Ma, & Rosen, 1993), but reduced exposure may only partially reverse the cognitive effects (Tong, Baghurst, Sawyer, Burns, & McMichael, 1998).

Laws mandating removal of lead from gasoline, paints, and soldered food cans have helped prevention efforts, but dust and soil in many places are still contaminated (Pirkle et al., 1994; Tesman & Hills, 1994). The Centers for Disease Control and Prevention (1997) calls for universal screening of residential areas with at least 27 percent of housing built before 1950 and in populations in which the percentage of 1- and 2-year-olds with elevated blood lead levels is 12 percent or more. Parents can reduce lead exposure (AAP Committee on Environmental Health, 1998) by washing children's hands before meals and before bed, keeping fingernails clipped, and providing a well-balanced diet. They should also carefully remove chipping or peeling paint and put up barriers to keep children away from areas that contain lead (Kimbrough, LeVois, & Webb, 1994).

Homelessness It is difficult to find and count homeless people (Smith & Smith, 2001). According to one estimate, 850,000 children, about one-fourth of them preschoolers, are homeless in the United States (Children's Defense Fund, 2000). Typically, homeless families are headed by single mothers in their twenties (Buckner, Bassuk, Weinreb, & Brooks, 1999).

Many homeless children spend their crucial early years in unstable, insecure, and often unsanitary environments. They and their parents may be cut off from a supportive community, family ties, and institutional resources and from ready access to medical care and schooling. They are at high risk of being separated from their families and placed in foster care (Children's Defense Fund, 2000).

From birth, these children suffer more health problems than poor children who have homes, and they are more likely to die in infancy. They are three times more

What's Your View?

- What can communities do to provide for children's well-being when parents cannot furnish adequate food, clothing, shelter, and health care?

likely than other children to lack immunizations, and two to three times more likely to have iron deficiency anemia. They experience high rates of diarrhea; hunger and malnourishment; obesity (from eating excessive carbohydrates and fats); tooth decay; asthma and other chronic diseases; respiratory, skin, and eye and ear infections; scabies and lice; trauma-related injuries; and elevated levels of lead. Homeless children also tend to suffer severe depression and anxiety and to have neurological and visual deficits, developmental delays, behavior problems, and learning difficulties. Uprooted from their neighborhoods, many do not go to school; if they do, they tend to have problems, partly because they miss a lot of it and have no place to do homework. They tend to do poorly on standardized reading and math tests, even when their cognitive functioning is normal, and they are more likely to repeat a grade or be placed in special classes than are children with homes (AAP Committee on Community Health Services, 1996; Bassuk, 1991; Bassuk, Weinreb, Dawson, Perloff, & Buckner, 1997; Burt et al., 1999; Rafferty & Shinn, 1991; Rubin et al., 1996).

To combat homelessness, a number of communities and community development groups are building low-income housing units and reclaiming neighborhoods with the help of federal, state, local, foundation, and private financing (Children's Defense Fund, 1998).

Checkpoint

Can you . . .

✔ Discuss several environmental influences that endanger children's health and development?

COGNITIVE DEVELOPMENT

Guidepost

5. What are typical cognitive advances and immature aspects of preschool children's thinking?

Piagetian Approach: The Preoperational Child

Jean Piaget named early childhood, from approximately ages 2 to 7, the **preoperational stage** because children are not yet ready to engage in mental *operations,* or manipulations, that require logical thinking. The characteristic development in this second major stage of cognitive development is a great expansion in the use of symbolic thought, or representational ability, which first emerges at the end of the sensorimotor stage (refer back to Chapter 5).

preoperational stage In Piaget's theory, the second major stage of cognitive development, in which children become more sophisticated in their use of symbolic thought but are not yet able to use logic.

Let's look at some advances and immature aspects of preoperational thought (see Tables 7-3 and 7-4) and at recent research findings, some of which challenge Piaget's conclusions.

Advances of Preoperational Thought

Advances in symbolic thought are accompanied by a growing understanding of space, causality, identities, categorization, and number. Some of these understandings have roots in infancy and toddlerhood; others begin to develop in early childhood but are not fully achieved until middle childhood.

The Symbolic Function "I want ice cream!" announces Kerstin, age 4, trudging indoors from the hot, dusty backyard. She has not seen anything that triggered this desire—no open freezer door, no television commercial. She no longer needs this kind of sensory cue to think about something. She remembers ice cream, its coldness and taste, and she purposefully seeks it out.

symbolic function Piaget's term for ability to use mental representations (words, numbers, or images) to which a child has attached meaning.

This absence of sensory or motor cues characterizes the **symbolic function:** the ability to use symbols, or mental representations—words, numbers, or images to which a person has attached meaning. The use of symbols is a universal mark of

Table 7-3 Cognitive Advances During Early Childhood

Advance	Significance	Example
Use of symbols	Children do not need to be in sensorimotor contact with an object, person, or event in order to think about it.	Simon asks his mother about the elephants they saw on their trip to the circus several months earlier.
	Children can imagine that objects or people have properties other than those they actually have.	Rolf pretends that a slice of apple is a vacuum cleaner "vrooming" across the kitchen table.
Understanding of identities	Children are aware that superficial alterations do not change the nature of things.	Boris knows that his teacher is dressed up as a pirate but is still his teacher underneath the costume.
Understanding of cause and effect	Children realize that events have causes.	Seeing a ball roll from behind a wall, Anasa looks behind the wall for the person who kicked the ball.
Ability to classify	Children organize objects, people, and events into meaningful categories.	Sigrid sorts the pine cones she collected on a nature walk into two piles according to their size: "big" and "little."
Understanding of number	Children can count and deal with quantities.	Minjee shares some candy with her friends, counting to make sure that each girl gets the same amount.
Empathy	Children become more able to imagine how others might feel.	Carlos tries to comfort his friend when he sees that his friend is upset.
Theory of mind	Children become more aware of mental activity and the functioning of the mind.	Oxana wants to save some cookies for herself, so she hides them from her younger brother in a pasta box. She knows her cookies will be safe there because her brother will not look in a place where he doesn't expect to find cookies.

Table 7-4 Limitations of Preoperational Thought (according to Piaget)

Limitation	Description	Example
Centration: inability to decenter	Children focus on one aspect of a situation and neglect others.	Timothy teases his younger sister that he has more juice than she does because his juice box has been poured into a tall, skinny glass, but hers has been poured into a short, wide glass.
Irreversibility	Children fail to understand that some operations or actions can be reversed, restoring the original situation.	Timothy does not realize that the juice in each glass can be poured back into the juice box from which it came, contradicting his claim that he has more than his sister.
Focus on states rather than transformations	Children fail to understand the significance of the transformation between states.	In the conservation task, Timothy does not understand that transforming the shape of a liquid (pouring it from one container into another) does not change the amount.
Transductive reasoning	Children do not use deductive or inductive reasoning; instead they jump from one particular to another and see cause where none exists.	Sarah was mean to her brother. Then her brother got sick. Sarah concludes that she made her brother sick.
Egocentrism	Children assume everyone else thinks, perceives, and feels as they do.	Kara doesn't realize that she needs to turn a book around so that her father can see the picture she is asking him to explain to her. Instead, she holds the book directly in front of her, where only she can see it.
Animism	Children attribute life to objects not alive.	Amanda says that spring is trying to come but winter is saying, "I won't go! I won't go!"
Inability to distinguish appearance from reality	Children confuse what is real with outward appearance.	Courtney is confused by a sponge made to look like a rock. She states that it looks like a rock and it really is a rock.

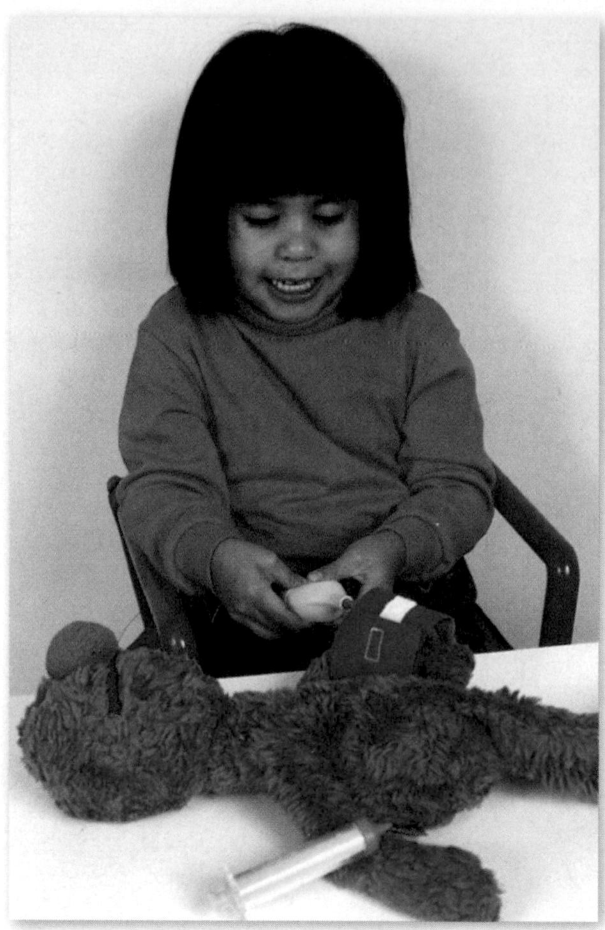

As Anna pretends to take Grover's blood pressure, she is showing a major cognitive achievement: deferred imitation, the ability to act out an action she observed some time before.

human culture. Without symbols, people could not communicate verbally, make change, read maps, or treasure photos of distant loved ones.

Having symbols for things helps children to remember and think about them without having them physically present, as Wang Yani did when she drew or painted from memory. Preschool children show the symbolic function through the growth of deferred imitation, pretend play, and language. *Deferred imitation* (which begins in the last substage of the sensorimotor stage) is based on having kept a mental representation of an observed action (like Yani's early imitation of her father's artwork). In *pretend play* (discussed in Chapter 8), children make an object, such as a doll, represent, or symbolize, something else, such as a person. *Language,* discussed later in this chapter, uses a system of symbols (words) to communicate.

An understanding of symbolism comes only gradually. Very young children often spend a good deal of time watching television, but how clearly do they realize that they are seeing a representation of reality? In one experiment, $2\frac{1}{2}$-year-olds who watched on a video monitor as an object was being hidden found it easily. Two-year-olds did not, even though they had found it when watching through a window (Troseth & DeLoache, 1998). Even 3-year-olds sometimes show confusion about screen images. When asked whether a televised bowl of popcorn would spill if the television set were turned upside down, a significant number of 3-year-olds said yes (Flavell, Flavell, Green, & Korfmacher, 1990).

Symbolic Development and Spatial Thinking The growth of representational thinking enables children to make more accurate judgments about spatial relationships. By 19 months children understand that a picture is a representation of something else (DeLoache, Pierroutsakos, et al., 1998), but until age 3 or later, most children do not reliably grasp the relationships between pictures, maps, or scale models and the objects or spaces they represent (DeLoache, Miller, & Pierroutsakos, 1998). This was the age by which Wang Yani began painting recognizable forms.

In one experiment, a group of $2\frac{1}{2}$-year-olds were told that a "shrinking machine" had shrunk a room to the size of a miniature model. The children in this group were more successful in finding a toy hidden in the room on the basis of its position in the model than were those in another group who were told that the "little room" was just like the "big room." According to the **dual representation hypothesis,** what makes the second task harder is that it requires a child to mentally represent both the symbol (the "little room") and its relationship to the thing it stands for (the "big room") at the same time. With the "shrinking machine," children do not have to perform this dual operation, because they are told that the room and the model are one and the same. Three-year-olds do not seem to have this problem with models (DeLoache, Miller, & Rosengren, 1997).

dual representation hypothesis Proposal that children under the age of 3 have difficulty grasping spatial relationships because of the need to keep more than one mental representation in mind at the same time.

Older preschoolers can use simple maps, and they can transfer the spatial understanding gained from working with models to maps and vice versa (DeLoache, Miller, & Pierroutsakos, 1998). In one experiment, 4-year-olds and most 3-year-olds were able to use a rectangle with a dot inside to find the corresponding location of a small black disk in a similarly shaped (but much larger) sandbox (Huttenlocher, Newcombe, & Vasilyeva, 1999).

Causality Although Piaget recognized that toddlers have some understanding of a connection between actions and reactions, he believed that even preoperational children cannot yet reason logically about cause and effect. Instead, he said, they reason by **transduction.** They view one situation as the basis for another situation—often one occurring at about the same time—whether or not there is logically a causal relationship. For example, they may think that their "bad" thoughts or behavior caused their own or another child's illness or their parents' divorce.

transduction Piaget's term for a preoperational child's tendency to mentally link particular phenomena, whether or not there is logically a causal relationship.

Yet when tested on situations they can understand, young children do accurately link cause and effect. One research team set up a series of microgenetic experiments using a device called a "blicket detector," which was rigged to light up and play music when certain objects (but not others) were placed on it. By observing the device in operation, even 2-year-olds showed logical reasoning in deciding which objects were "blickets" and which to remove in order to turn the blicket detector off (Gopnick, Sobel, Schulz, & Glymour, 2001).

Apparently, then, young children's understanding of familiar events in the physical world enables them to think logically about causation (Wellman & Gelman, 1998). Studies have found that children under 5 also seem to understand "how biological entities cause growth, inheritance, and illness; and how desires, emotions, and beliefs cause human actions" (Gopnick et al., 2001, p. 620). In naturalistic observations of $2\frac{1}{2}$- to 5-year-olds' everyday conversations with their parents, children showed flexible causal reasoning appropriate to the subject. For example, "I talking very quiet because I don't want somebody to wake up" shows psychological reasoning. "I won't chew gum because Daddy says I shouldn't" shows social-conventional reasoning. "I got medicine because it makes my fever go away" shows biological reasoning (Hickling & Wellman, 2001). However, preschoolers often have unrealistic views about causes of illness, which may reflect a belief that all causal relationships are equally and absolutely predictable. In one series of experiments, 3- to 5-year-olds, unlike adults, were just as sure that a person who does not wash his or her hands before eating will get sick as they were that a person who jumps up will come down (Kalish, 1998).

Some research suggests that preschoolers can see analogies involving familiar items—an ability that, according to Piaget, does not develop until the stage of formal operations in adolescence. This may have been because the verbal analogies he tested them on were too abstract for young children. When shown a picture of a chocolate bar paired with a picture of melted chocolate, even some 3-year-olds realize that the analogous pair for a picture of a snowman is a melted snowman, and not a melted crayon, a dirty snowman, a scarecrow, or a sled (Goswami & Brown, 1989).

Understanding of Identities and Categorization The world becomes more orderly and predictable as preschool children develop a better understanding of *identities:* the concept that people and many things are basically the same even if they change in form, size, or appearance. This understanding underlies the developing self-concept.

Categorization, or classification, requires a child to identify similarities and differences—as Yani did in comparing the "faces" of pebbles on the riverbank with monkeys in the zoo. By age 4, many children can classify by two criteria, such as color and shape. Children use this ability to order many aspects of their lives, categorizing people as "good," "bad," "friend," "nonfriend," and so forth. Thus categorization is a cognitive ability that has emotional and social implications.

How do children distinguish living from nonliving things? When Piaget asked young children whether the wind and clouds were alive, their answers led him to think they were confused about what is alive and what is not. (The tendency to attribute life to objects that are not alive is called **animism.**) But when later researchers questioned 3- and 4-year-olds about something more familiar to them—differences between a rock, a person, and a doll—the children showed they understood that people are alive

animism Tendency to attribute life to objects that are not alive.

and rocks and dolls are not (Gelman, Spelke, & Meck, 1983). They did not attribute thoughts or emotions to rocks, and they cited the fact that dolls cannot move on their own as evidence that dolls are not alive.

Of course, plants do not move on their own either, nor do they utter sounds, as most animals do. Yet preschoolers know that both plants and animals can grow and decay and, when injured, can heal themselves (Rosengren, Gelman, Kalish, & McCormick, 1991; Wellman & Gelman, 1998).

Culture can affect such beliefs. In a cross-cultural study, 5- to 9-year-old Israeli children, whose tradition views plants primarily in terms of their usefulness as food, were less likely than U.S. and Japanese children to attribute to plants the qualities of living things, such as respiration, growth, and death. On the other hand, Japanese children were more likely to attribute such qualities to inanimate objects, such as a stone and a chair, which, in their culture, are sometimes viewed as if they were alive and had feelings (Hatano et al., 1993).

Number In early childhood, children come to recognize five principles of counting (Gelman & Gallistel, 1978; Sophian, 1988):

1. The *1-to-1 principle:* Say only one number-name for each item being counted ("One . . . two . . . three . . .").
2. The *stable-order principle:* Say number-names in a set order ("One, two, three . . ." rather than "Three, one, two . . .").
3. The *order-irrelevance principle:* Start counting with any item, and the total count will be the same.
4. The *cardinality principle:* The last number-name used is the total number of items being counted. (If there are five items, the last number-name will be "5.")
5. The *abstraction principle:* The principles above apply to any kind of object.

It was previously believed that an understanding of these principles enables children to count (Gelman & Gallistel, 1978). However, more recent findings suggest the reverse: that children extract the principles from their experience with counting (Ho & Fuson, 1998; Siegler, 1998).

When asked to count six items, children younger than $3\frac{1}{2}$ tend to recite the number-names (one through six) but not to say how many items there are altogether (six). In other words, children that age do not yet seem to understand the cardinality principle (Wynn, 1990), or they may have trouble applying or interpreting it.

By age 5, most children can count to 20 or more and know the relative sizes of the numbers 1 through 10, and some can do single-digit addition and subtraction (Siegler, 1998). Children intuitively devise strategies for adding, by counting on their fingers or by using other objects.

How quickly children learn to count depends in part on the number system of their culture and in part on schooling (Naito & Miura, 2001). Through age 3, when most number learning is focused on counting from 1 through 10, U.S. and Chinese children perform about equally well. Then, at ages 4 and 5, when U.S. youngsters are learning separate names for the numbers between 11 and 20, Chinese youngsters learn their language's more efficient system based on tens and ones (10 + 1, 10 + 2, and so forth). It's not surprising, then, that U.S. children's math performance begins to lag (Miller, Smith, Zhu, & Zhang, 1995). This lag continues when they begin to do arithmetic (Fuson & Kwon, 1992; Geary, Bow-Thomas, Liu, & Siegler, 1996; Ho & Fuson, 1998).

Ordinality—the concept of *more* or *less, bigger* or *smaller*—seems to begin around 12 to 18 months and, like cardinality, at first is limited to comparisons involving very few objects (Siegler, 1998). By 5 months, infants may be able to tell the difference between one object and two, and between two and three. Three- and 4-year olds know that if they have one cookie and then get another cookie, they have more cookies than before, and if they give one cookie to another child, they have fewer cookies. By age 4 or 5, when the ability to compare numerical quantities is localized in the parietal lobes (Byrnes & Fox, 1998), children can solve ordinality problems ("Megan picked six apples, and Joshua picked four apples; which child picked more?") with sets of up to nine objects.

Ordinal knowledge appears to be universal. However, it develops at different rates, depending on how important counting is in a particular family or culture and how much instruction parents, teachers, or educational television programs provide (Resnick, 1989; Saxe, Guberman, & Gearhart, 1987; Siegler, 1998).

Checkpoint

Can you . . .

✔ Summarize findings about preschool children's understanding of symbols, space, causality, identities, categorization, and number?

Immature Aspects of Preoperational Thought

According to Piaget, one of the main characteristics of preoperational thought is **centration:** the tendency to focus on one aspect of a situation and neglect others. He said preschoolers come to illogical conclusions because they cannot **decenter**—think about several aspects of a situation at one time. Centration can limit young children's thinking about both physical and social relationships.

centration In Piaget's theory, tendency of preoperational children to focus on one aspect of a situation and neglect others.

decenter In Piaget's terminology, to think simultaneously about several aspects of a situation.

conservation Piaget's term for awareness that two objects that are equal according to a certain measure remain equal in the face of perceptual alteration so long as nothing has been added to or taken away from either object.

Conservation A classic example is the failure to understand **conservation,** the fact that two things that are equal remain so if their appearance is altered, so long as nothing is added or taken away. Piaget found that children do not fully grasp this principle until the stage of concrete operations and that they develop different kinds of conservation at different ages. Table 7-5 shows how various dimensions of conservation have been tested.

Table 7-5 Tests of Various Kinds of Conservation

Conservation Task	Show Child (and Have Child Acknowledge) That Both Items Are Equal	Perform Transformation	Ask Child	Preoperational Child Usually Answers
Number	Two equal, parallel rows of candies	Space the candles in one row farther apart.	"Are there the same number of candles in each row or does one row have more?"	"The longer one has more."
Length	Two parallel sticks of the same length	Move one stick to the right.	"Are both sticks the same size or is one longer?"	"The one on the right (or left) is longer."
Liquid	Two identical glasses holding equal amounts of liquid	Pour liquid from one glass into a taller, narrower glass.	"Do both glasses have the same amount of liquid or does one have more?"	"The taller one has more."
Matter (mass)	Two balls of clay of the same size	Roll one ball into a sausage shape.	"Do both pieces have the same amount of clay or does one have more?"	"The sausage has more."
Weight	Two balls of clay of the same weight	Roll one ball into a sausage shape.	"Do both weigh the same or does one weigh more?"	"The sausage weighs more."
Area	Two toy rabbits, two pieces of cardboard (representing grassy fields), with blocks or toys (representing barns on the fields), same number of "barns" on each board	Rearrange the blocks on one piece of board.	"Does each rabbit have the same amount of grass to eat or does one have more?"	"The one with the blocks close together has more to eat."
Volume	Two glasses of water with two equal-sized balls of clay in them	Roll one ball into a sausage shape.	"If we put the sausage back in the glass, will the water be the same height in each glass, or will one be higher?"	"The water in the glass with the sausage will be higher."

In one type of conservation task, conservation of liquid, a 5-year-old we'll call Timothy is shown two identical clear glasses, each one short and wide and each holding the same amount of water. Timothy is asked, "Is the amount of water in the two glasses equal?" When he agrees, the researcher pours the water in one glass into a third glass, a tall, thin one. Timothy is now asked, "Do both glasses contain the same amount of water? Or does one contain more? Why?" In early childhood—after watching the water being poured out of one of the short, fat glasses into a tall, thin glass or even after pouring it himself—Timothy will say that either the taller glass or the wider one contains more water. When asked why, he says, "This one is bigger this way," stretching his arms to show the height or width. Preoperational children cannot consider height *and* width at the same time. Since they center on one aspect, they cannot think logically, said Piaget.

irreversibility Piaget's term for a preoperational child's failure to understand that an operation can go in two or more directions.

The ability to conserve is also limited by **irreversibility:** failure to understand that an operation or action can go two or more ways. Once Timothy can imagine restoring the original state of the water by pouring it back into the other glass, he will realize that the amount of water in both glasses is the same.

Preoperational children commonly think as if they were watching a slide show with a series of static frames: they *focus on successive states,* said Piaget, and do not recognize the transformation from one state to another. In the conservation experiment, they focus on the water as it stands in each glass rather than on the water being poured from one glass to another, and so they fail to realize that the amount of water is the same.

egocentrism Piaget's term for inability to consider another person's point of view.

Egocentrism **Egocentrism** is a form of centration. According to Piaget, young children center so much on their own point of view that they cannot take in another's. Three-year-olds are not as egocentric as newborn babies; but, said Piaget, they still think the universe centers on them. Egocentrism may help explain why young children (as we will see) sometimes have trouble separating reality from what goes on inside their own heads and why they may show confusion about what causes what. When Jeffrey believes that his "bad thoughts" have made his sister sick, or that he caused his parents' marital troubles, he is thinking egocentrically.

To study egocentrism, Piaget designed the *three-mountain task* (see Figure 7-2). A child sits facing a table that holds three large mounds. A doll is placed on a chair at the opposite side of the table. The investigator asks the child how the "mountains" would look to the doll. Piaget found that young children usually could not answer the question correctly; instead, they described the "mountains" from their own perspec-

Figure 7-2
Piaget's three-mountain task. A preoperational child is unable to describe the "mountains" from the doll's point of view—an indication of egocentrism, according to Piaget.

tive. Piaget saw this as evidence that preoperational children cannot imagine a different point of view (Piaget & Inhelder, 1967).

However, another experimenter who posed a similar problem in a different way got different results (Hughes, 1975). A child sat in front of a square board divided by "walls" into four sections. A toy police officer stood at the edge of the board; a doll was moved from one section to another. After each move the child was asked, "Can the police officer see the doll?" Then another toy police officer was brought into the action, and the child was told to hide the doll from both officers. Thirty children between ages $3\frac{1}{2}$ and 5 were correct nine out of ten times.

Why were these children able to take another person's point of view (the police officer's) when those doing the mountain task were not? It may be because the "police officer" task calls for thinking in more familiar, less abstract ways. Most children do not look at mountains and do not think about what other people might see when looking at one, but most 3-year-olds know about dolls and police officers and hiding. Thus young children may show egocentrism primarily in situations beyond their immediate experience.

Checkpoint

Can you . . .

- ✔ Tell how centration limits preoperational thought?
- ✔ Give several reasons why preoperational children have difficulty with conservation?
- ✔ Discuss research that challenges Piaget's views on egocentrism in early childhood?

Do Young Children Have Theories of Mind?

Piaget (1929) was the first scholar to investigate children's **theory of mind,** their emerging awareness of their own mental processes and those of other people. He asked children such questions as "Where do dreams come from?" and "What do you think with?" On the basis of the answers, he concluded that children younger than 6 cannot distinguish between thoughts or dreams and real physical entities and have no theory of mind. However, more recent research indicates that between ages 2 and 5, children's knowledge about mental processes—their own and others'—grows dramatically (Astington, 1993; Bower, 1993; Flavell et al., 1995; Wellman, Cross, & Watson, 2001).

theory of mind Awareness and understanding of mental processes.

Again, methodology seems to have made the difference. Piaget's questions were abstract, and he expected children to be able to put their understanding into words. Contemporary researchers use vocabulary and objects children are familiar with. Instead of talking in generalities, they observe children in everyday activities or give them concrete examples. In this way, we have learned, for example, that 3-year-olds can tell the difference between a boy who has a cookie and a boy who is thinking about a cookie; they know which boy can touch, share, and eat it (Astington, 1993). Let's look at several aspects of theory of mind.

Knowledge about Thinking and Mental States Between ages 3 and 5, children come to understand that thinking goes on inside the mind; that it can deal with either real or imaginary things; that someone can be thinking of one thing while doing or looking at something else; that a person whose eyes and ears are covered can think about objects; that someone who looks pensive is probably thinking; and that thinking is different from seeing, talking, touching, and knowing (Flavell et al., 1995).

However, preschoolers generally believe that mental activity starts and stops. Not until middle childhood do children know that the mind is continuously active (Flavell, 1993; Flavell et al., 1995). Preschoolers also have little or no awareness that they or other people think in words, or "talk to themselves in their heads," or that they think while they are looking, listening, reading, or talking (Flavell, Green, Flavell, & Grossman, 1997). Not until age 7 or 8 do most children realize that people who are asleep do *not* engage in conscious mental activity—that they do not know they are asleep (Flavell, Green, Flavell, & Lin, 1999). Preschoolers tend to equate dreams with imagining; they believe they can dream about anything they wish. Five-year-olds show a more adult-like understanding, recognizing that physical experiences, emotions, knowledge, and thoughts can affect the content of dreams. Not until age 11, however, do children fully realize that they cannot control their dreams (Woolley & Boerger, 2002).

Social cognition, the recognition that others have mental states (refer back to Chapter 6) is a distinctly human capacity (Povinelli & Giambrone, 2001) that accompanies the decline of egocentrism and the development of empathy. At 14 to 18 months, children may be able to infer the intentions of another person from vocal expressions, by whether that person expresses, say, satisfaction ("There!") or surprise ("Woops!") (Carpenter, Akhtar, & Tomasello, 1998). By age 3, children realize that a person who does not immediately find what she wants will keep looking. They know that if someone gets what he wants he will be happy, and if not, he will be sad (Wellman & Woolley, 1990). Four-year-olds begin to understand that people have differing beliefs about the world—true or mistaken—and that these beliefs affect their actions.

False Beliefs and Deception A researcher shows 3-year-old Mariella a candy box and asks what is in it. "Candy," she says. But when Mariella opens the box, she finds crayons, not candy. "What will a child who hasn't opened the box think is in it?" the researcher asks. "Crayons," says Mariella, not understanding that another child would be fooled by the box, as she was. And then she says that she herself originally thought crayons would be in the box (Flavell, 1993; Flavell et al., 1995).

The understanding that people can hold false beliefs flows from the realization that people hold mental representations of reality, which can sometimes be wrong. Three-year-olds like Mariella appear to lack such an understanding (Flavell et al., 1995). An analysis of 178 studies in various countries, using a number of variations on, and simplifications of, false belief tasks, found this consistent developmental pattern (Wellman & Cross, 2001; Wellman, Cross, & Watson, 2001). However, some researchers claim that 3-year-olds do have a rudimentary understanding of false beliefs but may not show it when presented with complicated situations (Hala & Chandler, 1996). According to modular theory, the ability to develop understanding of false beliefs, as well as other aspects of theory of mind, may be seated in specific *modules,* or functional structures, in the brain (Leslie, 1994; Leslie & Polizzi, 1998; Scholl & Leslie, 2001).

Three-year-olds' failure to recognize false beliefs may stem from egocentric thinking. At that age, children tend to believe that everyone else knows what they know and believes what they do, and, like Mariella, they have trouble understanding that their own beliefs can be false (Lillard & Curenton, 1999). Four-year-olds understand that people who see or hear different versions of the same event may come away with different beliefs. Not until about age 6, however, do children realize that two people who see or hear the *same* thing may interpret it differently (Pillow & Henrichon, 1996).

Deception is an effort to plant a false belief in someone else's mind, and it requires a child to suppress the impulse to be truthful. In other words, lying represents cognitive development! Some studies have found that children become capable of deception as early as age 2 or 3, others, at 4 or 5. The difference may have to do with the means of deception children are expected to use. In a series of experiments, 3-year-olds were asked whether they would like to play a trick on an experimenter by giving a false clue about which of two boxes a ball was hidden in. The children were better able to carry out the deception when asked to put a picture of the ball on the wrong box, or to point to that box with an arrow, than when they pointed with their fingers, which children this age are accustomed to doing truthfully (Carlson, Moses, & Hix, 1998).

Piaget maintained that young children regard all falsehoods—intentional or not—as lies. However, when 3- to 6-year-olds were told a story about the danger of eating contaminated food and were given a choice between interpreting a character's action as a lie or a mistake, about three-fourths of the children in all age groups characterized it accurately (Siegal & Peterson, 1998). Apparently, then, even 3-year-olds have some understanding of the role of intent in deception.

Distinguishing between Appearance and Reality Related to awareness of false beliefs is the ability to distinguish between appearance and reality: both require a child to refer to two conflicting mental representations at the same time. According to Piaget, not until about age 5 or 6 do children understand the distinction between what *seems* to be and what *is.* Much research bears him out, though some studies have found this ability beginning to emerge before age 4 (Friend & Davis, 1993; C. Rice, Koinis, Sullivan, Tager-Flusberg, & Winner, 1997).

In one series of experiments (Flavell, Green, & Flavell, 1986), 3-year-olds apparently confused appearance and reality in a variety of tests. For example, when the children put on special sunglasses that made milk look green, they said the milk *was* green, even though they had just seen white milk. However, when shown a sponge that looked like a rock and asked to help trick someone else into believing it was a rock, the children were able to distinguish between the way the sponge looked (like a rock) and what it actually was (a sponge). Apparently, putting the task in the context of a deception helped the children realize that an object can be perceived as other than what it is (Rice et al., 1997).

As with other theory-of-mind tasks, the methods researchers use to determine whether 3-year-olds can distinguish appearance from reality can affect the results. Language can be a limitation at this age. When children were asked questions about how to use a candle wrapped like a crayon, only 3 out of 10 answered correctly. But when asked to respond with actions rather than words ("I want a candle to put on a birthday cake"), 9 out of 10 handed the experimenter the crayon-like candle (Sapp, Lee, & Muir, 2000).

Distinguishing between Fantasy and Reality Sometime between 18 months and 3 years, children learn to distinguish between real and imagined events. Three-year-olds know the difference between a real dog and a dog in a dream, and between something invisible (such as air) and something imaginary. They can pretend and can tell when someone else is pretending (Flavell et al., 1995).

Still, the line between fantasy and reality may seem to blur at times, as it did for Yani when she made up stories about her monkey friends. In one study (Harris, Brown, Marriott, Whittall, & Harmer, 1991), 4- to 6-year-olds, left alone in a room, preferred to touch a box holding an imaginary bunny rather than a box holding an imaginary monster, even though most of the children claimed they were just pretending. However, in a partial replication of the study, in which the experimenter stayed in the room and clearly ended the pretense, only about 10 percent of the children touched or looked in either of the boxes, and almost all showed a clear understanding that the creatures were imaginary (Golomb & Galasso, 1995). Thus it is difficult to know, when questioning children about "pretend" objects, whether children are giving "serious" answers or are keeping up the pretense (M. Taylor, 1997).

The belief that "wishing will make it so" may be linked more to a belief in magic than to preschoolers' otherwise realistic understanding of how causality works in the real world. Both of these beliefs tend to decrease near the end of the preschool period (Woolley, Phelps, Davis, & Mandell, 1999). A review of the literature suggests that magical or wishful thinking in children age 3 and older does *not* stem from confusion

Is it really the Cookie Monster and Elmo? These young boys don't seem quite sure. The ability to distinguish appearance from reality develops between ages 3 and 6.

BOX 7-1

Digging Deeper
Imaginary Companions

At $3\frac{1}{2}$, Anna had twenty-three "sisters" with such names as Och, Elmo, Zeni, Aggie, and Ankie. She often talked to them on the telephone, since they lived about 100 miles away, in the town where her family used to live. During the next year, most of the sisters disappeared, but Och continued to visit, especially for birthday parties. Och had a cat and a dog (which Anna had begged for in vain), and whenever Anna was denied something she saw advertised on television, she announced that she already had one at her sister's house. But when a live friend came over and Anna's mother happened to mention one of her imaginary companions, Anna quickly changed the subject.

All twenty-three sisters—and some "boys" and "girls" who have followed them—lived only in Anna's imagination, as she well knew. Like an estimated 25 to 65 percent of children between ages 3 and 10 (Woolley, 1997), she created imaginary companions, with whom she talked and played. This normal phenomenon of childhood is seen most often in firstborn and only children, who lack the close company of siblings. Like Anna, most children who create imaginary companions have many of them (Gleason, Sebanc, & Hartup, 2000). Girls are more likely than boys to have imaginary "friends" (or at least to acknowledge them). Girls' imaginary playmates are usually other children, whereas boys' are more often animals (D. G. Singer & Singer, 1990).

Children who have imaginary companions can distinguish fantasy from reality, but in free-play sessions they are more likely to engage in pretend play than are children without imaginary companions (M. Taylor, Cartwright, & Carlson, 1993). They play more happily and more imaginatively than other children and are more cooperative with other children and adults (D. G. Singer & Singer, 1990; J. L. Singer & Singer, 1981); and they do not lack for friends at preschool (Gleason et al., 2000). They are more fluent with language, watch less television, and show more curiosity, excitement, and persistence during play. In one study, 4-year-olds—regardless of verbal intelligence—who reported having imaginary companions did better on theory-of-mind tasks (such as differentiating appearance and reality and recognizing false beliefs) than children who did not create such companions (M. Taylor & Carlson, 1997).

Children's relationships with imaginary companions are like peer relationships; they are usually sociable and friendly, in contrast with the way children "take care of" personified objects, such as stuffed animals and dolls (Gleason et al., 2000). Imaginary playmates are good company for an only child like Anna. They provide wish-fulfillment mechanisms ("There was a monster in my room, but Elmo scared it off with magic dust"), scapegoats ("I didn't eat those cookies—Och must have done it!"), displacement agents for the child's own fears ("Aggie is afraid she's going to be washed down the drain"), and support in difficult situations. (One 6-year-old "took" her imaginary companion with her to see a scary movie.)

What's Your View?

How should parents respond to children's talk about imaginary companions?

Check It Out:

OLC

For more information on this topic, go to www.mhhe.com/papaliah9, where you'll find a link to a web page about children's imaginary companions.

between fantasy and reality. Often magical thinking is a way to explain events that do not seem to have obvious realistic explanations (usually because children lack knowledge about them), or simply to indulge in the pleasures of pretending—as with the belief in imaginary companions (see Box 7-1). Children, like adults, generally are aware of the magical nature of such fantasy figures as witches and dragons but are more willing to entertain the possibility that they may be real (Woolley, 1997).

Influences on Theory-of-Mind Development Some children develop theory-of-mind abilities earlier than others. This development reflects brain maturation and improvements in cognition. Hereditary and environmental influences play a large part.

Difficulties in social interaction associated with Turner's syndrome, and typical delays in autistic children's understanding of false beliefs, support a strong genetic influence on social cognition, since both of these disorders have genetic origins. Brain imaging shows increased activity in the left frontal lobe (a brain region in which autistic persons have abnormalities) during theory-of-mind tasks (Sabbagh & Taylor, 2000). A study of 119 same-sex 3-year-old twins found a heritability of 67 percent in understanding of false beliefs and deception (Hughes & Cutting, 1999).

The way mothers talk with preschoolers can affect theory-of-mind development. In one study, mothers talked with their 3-year-olds about photographs of people in situations involving emotions, preferences, or false beliefs (much like Mariella's candy-box task). What the mothers said about mental states while talking about the pictures turned out to be directly correlated with the children's theory-of-mind understanding—not only at the time, but at two later times over the course of a year (Ruffman, Slade, & Crowe, 2002).

Children whose teachers rate them high on social skills are better able to recognize false beliefs (Watson, Nixon, Wilson, & Capage, 1999). So are children with several siblings (Hughes & Cutting, 1999) and children with advanced language development, who are better able to take part in family discussions about such matters (Astington & Jenkins, 1999; Cutting & Dunn, 1999).

Different cultures have different ways of looking at the mind, and these cultural attitudes influence children (Lillard, 1998). For example, middle-class Northern Europeans and Americans pay a lot of attention to how mental states affect behavior ("Sorry I snapped at you—I'm in a bad mood today"), whereas Asians focus on situations that call for certain behaviors. Japanese parents and teachers frequently talk to children about how their behavior affects other people's feelings (Azuma, 1994). A Japanese child who refuses to finish a meal may be told that the farmer who worked hard to grow the food will be hurt if the child doesn't eat it.

Talking with children about mental states, and about how the characters in a story feel (as Yani and her father did), helps them develop social understanding (Lillard & Curenton, 1999). Younger siblings, who have older siblings to talk to, understand false beliefs earlier than older siblings do. Families that encourage pretend play stimulate the development of theory-of-mind skills. As children play roles, they assume others' perspectives. When children pretend together, they must deal with other children's views of their imaginary world (Lillard & Curenton, 1999).

Checkpoint

Can you . . .

- ✔ Give examples of research that challenges Piaget's views on young children's cognitive limitations?
- ✔ Describe changes between the ages of 3 and 6 in children's knowledge about the way their minds work, and identify influences on that development?

Language and Other Cognitive Abilities

Preschoolers are full of questions: "How many sleeps until tomorrow?" "Who filled the river with water?" "Do babies have muscles?" "Do smells come from inside my nose?" Young children's growing facility with language helps them express their own unique view of the world.

Guidepost

6. How does language improve, and what happens when its development is delayed?

Language Development

Preschoolers make rapid advances in vocabulary, grammar, and syntax. The child who, at 3, describes how Daddy "hatches" wood (chops with a hatchet), or asks Mommy to "piece" her food (cut it into little pieces) may, by the age of 5, tell her mother, "Don't be ridiculous!" or proudly point to her toys and say, "See how I organized everything?" And, as we'll see, language may play a part in the development of memory and the predictability of intelligence.

Vocabulary At 3 the average child can use 900 to 1,000 different words and uses about 12,000 each day. By the age of 6, a child typically has a spoken vocabulary of 2,600 words and understands more than 20,000 (Owens, 1996), having learned an average of 9 new words a day since about $1\frac{1}{2}$ years of age (M. L. Rice, 1982). With the help of formal schooling, a youngster's passive, or receptive, vocabulary (words she can understand) will grow four times as large—to 80,000 words—by the time of entry into high school (Owens, 1996).

fast mapping Process by which a child absorbs the meaning of a new word after hearing it once or twice in conversation.

How do children expand their vocabularies so quickly? Apparently they do it by **fast mapping,** which allows them to absorb the meaning of a new word after hearing it only once or twice in conversation. From the context, children seem to form a quick hypothesis about the meaning of the word and store it in memory. Linguists are not sure how fast mapping works, but it seems likely that children draw on what they know about the rules for forming words, about similar words, about the immediate context, and about the subject under discussion.

Theory-of-mind development—the increasing ability to infer another's mental state—seems to play a role in vocabulary learning. In one study, preschoolers learned "nonsense" words better from a speaker who seemed certain what the word meant than from one who seemed unsure (Sabbagh & Baldwin, 2001).

Names of objects (nouns) seem to be easier to fast map than names of actions (verbs), which are less concrete. Yet one experiment showed that children just under 3 years old can fast map a new verb and apply it to another situation in which the same action is being performed (Golinkoff, Jacquet, Hirsh-Pasek, & Nandakumar, 1996).

Many 3- and 4-year-olds seem able to tell when two words, such as "doggy" and "puppy," refer to the same object or action (Savage & Au, 1996). They know that a single object cannot have two proper names (a dog cannot be both Spot and Fido). They also know that more than one adjective can apply to the same noun ("Fido is spotted and furry") and that an adjective can be combined with a proper name ("smart Fido!") (Hall & Graham, 1999).

Grammar and Syntax The ways in which children combine syllables into words and words into sentences grow increasingly sophisticated during early childhood (Owens, 1996). At 3, children typically begin to use plurals, possessives, and past tense and know the difference between *I*, *you,* and *we.* However, their sentences are generally short and simple, often leaving out small words such as *a* and *the,* but including some pronouns, adjectives, and prepositions. Most of their sentences are declarative ("Kitty wants milk"), but they can ask—and answer—*what* and *where* questions. (*Why* and *how* are harder to grasp.)

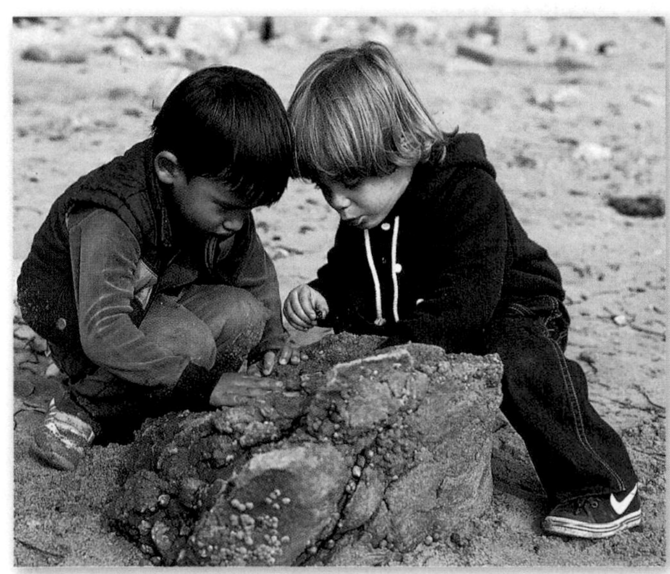

Although Piaget believed that most of young children's speech is egocentric, research shows that children like these boys playing on the beach communicate, both verbally and through gestures, from an early age.

Children this age still tend to make errors of irregularization because they have not yet learned exceptions to rules. Saying "holded" instead of "held," or "eated" instead of "ate," is a normal sign of linguistic progress. Eventually, they notice that *-ed* is not always used to form the past tense of a verb. Children are more likely to overgeneralize the use of transitive or intransitive verbs in constructions that call for the other type of verb ("He disappeared it" or "He's hitting") if the verb they are using is not very familiar to them (Brooks, Tomasello, Dodson, & Lewis, 1999).

Between ages 4 and 5, sentences average four to five words and may be declarative, negative ("I'm not hungry"), interrogative ("Why can't I go outside?"), or imperative ("Catch the ball!"). Four-year-olds use complex, multiclause sentences ("I'm eating because I'm hungry") more frequently if their parents often use such sentences (Huttenlocher, Vasilyeva, Cymerman, & Levine, in preparation). Children this age tend to string sentences together in long run-on stories (". . . And then . . . And then . . ."). In some respects, comprehension may be immature. For example, 4-year-old Noah can carry out a command that includes more than one step ("Pick up your toys and put them in the cupboard"). However, if his mother tells him "You may watch TV after you pick up your toys," he may process the words in the order in which he hears them and think he can first watch television and then pick up his toys.

By ages 5 to 7, children's speech has become quite adultlike. They speak in longer and more complicated sentences. They use more conjunctions, prepositions, and articles. They use compound and complex sentences and can handle all parts of speech. Still, while they speak fluently, comprehensibly, and fairly grammatically, they have yet to master many fine points of language. They rarely use the passive voice (as in "The sidewalk is being shoveled"), verb tenses that include the auxiliary *have* ("I have already shoveled the sidewalk"), and conditional sentences ("If Barbara were home, she would help shovel the sidewalk") (C. S. Chomsky, 1969).

Pragmatics and Social Speech As children learn vocabulary, grammar, and syntax, they become more competent in **pragmatics**—the practical knowledge of how to use language to communicate. This includes knowing how to ask for things, how to tell a story or joke, how to begin and continue a conversation, and how to adjust comments to the listener's perspective (M. L. Rice, 1982). These are all aspects of **social speech:** speech intended to be understood by a listener.

pragmatics The practical knowledge needed to use language for communicative purposes.

social speech Speech intended to be understood by a listener.

With improved pronunciation and grammar, it becomes easier for others to understand what children say. Most 3-year-olds are quite talkative, and they pay attention to the effect of their speech on others. If people cannot understand them, they try to explain themselves more clearly. Four-year-olds, especially girls, simplify their language and use a higher register when speaking to 2-year-olds (Owens, 1996; Shatz & Gelman, 1973).

Most 5-year-olds can adapt what they say to what the listener knows. They can now use words to resolve disputes, and they use more polite language and fewer direct commands in talking to adults than to other children. Almost half of all 5-year-olds can stick to a conversational topic for about a dozen turns—if they are comfortable with their partner and if the topic is one they know and care about (Owens, 1996).

Private Speech Anna, age 4, was alone in her room painting. When she finished, she was overheard saying aloud, "Now I have to put the pictures somewhere to dry. I'll put them by the window. They need to get dry now. I'll paint some more dinosaurs."

Private speech—talking aloud to oneself with no intent to communicate with others—is normal and common in childhood, accounting for 20 to 50 percent of what 4- to 10-year-old children say (Berk, 1986a). Two- to 3-year-olds engage in "crib talk," playing with sounds and words. Four- and 5-year-olds use private speech as a way to express fantasies and emotions (Berk, 1992; Small, 1990). Older children "think out loud" or mutter in barely audible tones.

private speech Talking aloud to oneself with no intent to communicate.

Piaget (1962/1923) saw private speech as a sign of cognitive immaturity. According to Piaget, young children are *egocentric*—unable to to recognize others' viewpoints and therefore unable to communicate meaningfully. Instead, they simply vocalize whatever is on their own minds. Another reason young children talk while they do things, said Piaget, is that they do not yet distinguish between words and the actions the words stand for, or symbolize. By the end of the preoperational stage, he said, with cognitive maturation and social experience, children become less egocentric and more capable of symbolic thought, and so discard private speech.

Like Piaget, Vygotsky (1962/1934) believed that private speech helps young children to integrate language with thought. However, Vygotsky did not look upon private speech as egocentric. He saw it as a special form of communication: conversation with the self. As such, he said, it serves a very important function in the transition between early social speech (often experienced in the form of adult commands) and inner speech (thinking in words)—a transition toward internal rather than external control of behavior ("Now I have to put the pictures somewhere to dry"). Vygotsky suggested that private speech follows a bell-shaped curve: it increases during the preschool years and fades away during the early elementary school years as children become more able to guide and master their actions.

Research generally supports Vygotsky as to the functions of private speech. In an observational study of 93 low- to middle-income 3- to 5-year-olds, 86 percent of the children's remarks were *not* egocentric (Berk, 1986a). The most sociable children, and those who engage in the most social speech, tend to use the most private speech as well, apparently supporting Vygotsky's view that private speech is stimulated by social experience (Berk, 1986a, 1986b, 1992; Berk & Garvin, 1984; Kohlberg, Yaeger, & Hjertholm, 1968).

There also is evidence for the role of private speech in self-regulation, a child's efforts to control his or her own behavior (Berk & Garvin, 1984; Furrow, 1984). Private speech tends to increase when children are trying to do difficult tasks, especially without adult supervision (Berk, 1992; Berk & Garvin, 1984).

How much do children engage in private speech? Some studies have reported no age changes in its overall use; others have found variations in the timing of its decline. Whereas Vygotsky considered the need for private speech a universal stage of cognitive development, studies have found a wide range of individual differences, with some children using it very little or not at all (Berk, 1992).

Understanding the significance of private speech has practical implications, especially in school (Berk, 1986a). Talking to oneself or muttering should not be considered misbehavior; a child may be struggling with a problem and may need to think out loud.

Checkpoint

Can you . . .

- ✔ Trace normal progress in 3- to 6-year-olds' vocabulary, grammar, syntax, and conversational abilities?
- ✔ Give reasons why children of various ages use private speech?

Delayed Language Development About 3 percent of preschool-age children show language delays, though their intelligence is usually average or better (M. L. Rice, 1989). Boys are more likely than girls to be late talkers (Plomin et al., 1998).

It is unclear why some children speak late. They do not necessarily lack linguistic input at home. These children may have a cognitive limitation that makes it hard for them to learn the rules of language (Scarborough, 1990). Some late speakers have a history of otitis media (an inflammation of the middle ear) between 12 and 18 months of age and improve in language ability when the infection, with its related hearing loss, clears up (Lonigan, Fischel, Whitehurst, Arnold, & Valdez-Menchaca, 1992).

Some current investigations focus on problems in fast mapping. Children with delayed language skills may need to hear a new word more often than other children do before they can incorporate it into their vocabularies (M. L. Rice, 1989; M. Rice, Oetting, Marquis, Bode, & Pae, 1994). Heredity seems to play a role in the most severe cases of language delay. Among 3,039 pairs of 2-year-old twins, if one monozygotic twin fell in the bottom 5 percent in vocabulary knowledge, the other twin had an 80 percent chance of being equally delayed. With dizygotic twins, the chances of equivalent delays were only 42 percent (Plomin et al., 1998).

Many children who speak late—especially those whose comprehension is normal—eventually catch up (Girolametto, Wiigs, Smyth, Weitzman, & Pearce, 2001; Thal, Tobias, & Morrison, 1991). Still, delayed language development can have far-reaching cognitive, social, and emotional consequences. Children who show an unusual tendency to mispronounce words at age 2, who have poor vocabulary at age 3, or who have trouble naming objects at age 5 are apt to have reading disabilities later on (M. Rice et al., 1994; Scarborough, 1990). Children who do not speak or understand as well as their peers tend to be judged negatively by adults and other children (M. L. Rice, Hadley, & Alexander, 1993) and to have trouble finding playmates or friends (Gertner, Rice, & Hadley, 1994). Children viewed as unintelligent or immature may "live down" to these expectations, and their self-image may suffer.

Speech and language therapy for children with delayed language development should begin with professional assessment of both child and family. In a promising technique called *dialogic reading* (described in Chapter 5), reading picture books becomes a vehicle for parent-child dialogue about the story. Three- to 6-year-olds with mild-to-moderate language delays whose mothers were trained in dialogic reading improved more than a comparison group whose mothers had been trained to use similar principles in talking with their children, but not about books (Dale, Crain-Thoreson, Notari-Syverson, & Cole, 1996).

Why is shared reading more effective than just talking with a child? Shared reading affords a natural opportunity for giving information and increasing vocabulary. It provides a focus for attention and for asking and responding to questions. In addition, it is enjoyable for both children and adults; it fosters emotional bonding while enhancing cognitive development.

What's Your View?

- Suppose you wanted to set up a program for children with delayed language development. What elements would you include in your program? How would you judge its success?

Social Interaction and Preparation for Literacy To understand what is on the printed page, children first need to master certain prereading skills (Lonigan, Burgess, & Anthony, 2000). **Emergent literacy** refers to the development of these skills, along with the knowledge and attitudes that underlie reading (and writing).

emergent literacy Preschoolers' development of skills, knowledge, and attitudes that underlie reading and writing.

Prereading skills include (1) general linguistic skills, such as vocabulary, syntax, narrative structure, and the understanding that language is used to communicate; and (2) specific skills, such as *phonemic awareness*—the realization that words are composed of distinct sounds, or *phonemes*—and *phoneme-grapheme correspondence,* the ability to link sounds with the corresponding letters or combinations of letters (Whitehurst & Lonigan, 1998; Lonigan et al., 2000). One phonemic awareness curriculum for 280 low-income preschoolers was combined with dialogic reading techniques. The program produced gains in emergent literacy that the children maintained through the end of kindergarten (Whitehurst et al., 1999).

As children learn the skills they will need to translate the written word into speech, they also learn that writing can express ideas, thoughts, and feelings. Preschool children pretend to write by scribbling, lining up their marks from left to right (Brenneman, Massey, Machado, & Gelman, 1996). Later they begin using letters, numbers, and letterlike shapes to represent words, syllables, or phonemes. Often their spelling is so inventive that they may not be able to read it themselves (Whitehust & Lonigan, 1998)!

Social interaction can promote emergent literacy. Children are more likely to become good readers and writers if, during the preschool years, parents provide conversational challenges the children are ready for—if they use a rich vocabulary and center dinner-table talk on the day's activities or on questions about why people do things and how things work (Snow, 1990, 1993). It is likely that Yani's frequent hiking expeditions with her father, when he told her stories about the clouds and they talked about the things they saw around them, contributed to her emergent literacy.

In a longitudinal study of 24 white, middle-class two-parent families, the quality of mother-child conversation at ages 3 and 4—particularly about past events—was a strong predictor of literacy skills prior to entering first grade. Most influential was mothers' use of questions and comments that helped children elaborate on events or link them with other incidents (Reese, 1995).

Checkpoint

Can you . . .

- Discuss possible causes, consequences, and treatment of delayed language development?
- Explain how social interaction promotes preparation for literacy?

Reading to children is one of the most effective paths to literacy. Children who are read to from an early age learn that reading and writing in English move from left to right and from top to bottom and that words are separated by spaces (Siegler, 1998; Whitehurst & Lonigan, 1998). Children who have been taught the alphabet and other prereading skills before entering school tend to become better readers (Siegler, 1998; Lonigan et al., 2000; Whitehurst & Lonigan, 1998).

Moderate exposure to educational television can help prepare children for literacy, especially if parents talk with children about what they see. In one study, the more time 3- to 5-year-olds spent watching *Sesame Street,* the more their vocabulary improved (M. L. Rice, Huston, Truglio, & Wright, 1990). What young children watch on television can have long-range effects. In a longitudinal study, the content of television programs viewed at ages 2 and 4 predicted academic skills three years later (Wright et al., 2001).

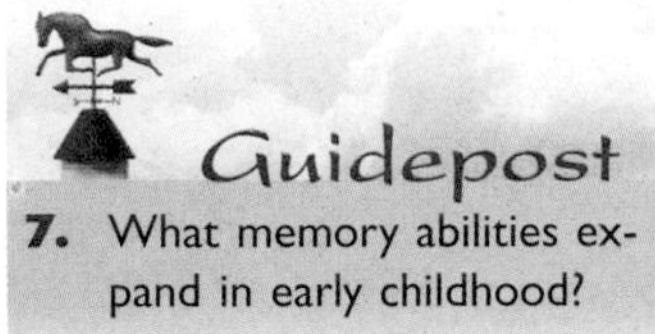

Guidepost

7. What memory abilities expand in early childhood?

Information-Processing Approach: Memory Development

encoding Process by which information is prepared for long-term storage and later retrieval.

storage Retention of memories for future use.

retrieval Process by which information is accessed or recalled from memory storage.

Memory is often compared to a filing system that has three steps, or processes: *encoding, storage,* and *retrieval.* To file something in memory, we first must decide which "folder" to put it in—for example, "people I know" or "places I've been." **Encoding** attaches a "code" or "label" to the information to prepare it for storage, so that it will be easier to find when needed. **Storage** is putting the folder away in the filing cabinet. The last step, **retrieval,** occurs when the information is needed; we then search for the file and take it out. Difficulties in any of these processes can interfere with efficiency.

During early childhood, children show significant improvement in attention and in the speed and efficiency with which they process information; and they begin to form long-lasting memories. Still, young children do not remember as well as older ones. For one thing, in encoding, young children tend to focus on exact details of an event, which are easily forgotten, whereas older children and adults generally concentrate on the gist of what happened. (Here Yani's memory was remarkable; she not only remembered details of the letters her father "wrote" in the air, but also retained rich mental images of the essence of what she saw, which enabled her to paint imaginatively from memory.) Also, young children, because of their lesser knowledge of the world, may fail to notice and encode important aspects of a situation, such as when and where it occurred, which could help jog retrieval.

recognition Ability to identify a previously encountered stimulus.

recall Ability to reproduce material from memory.

Recognition and Recall

When trying to retrieve information from memory, preschool children, like people of all ages, do better on **recognition,** identifying something encountered before, than on **recall,** reproducing information from memory. For example, they can more readily recognize a missing mitten in a lost-and-found box than recall how the lost mitten looks. Both recognition and recall are forms of explicit memory, and both abilities improve with age. The more familiar children are with information, the better they can recall it. Recall also depends on motivation and on the strategies a child uses to enhance it (Lange, MacKinnon, & Nida, 1989).

Young children often fail to use strategies for remembering—even strategies they already know—unless reminded (Flavell, 1970). This tendency not to generate efficient strategies may reflect lack of awareness of how a strategy would be useful (Sophian, Wood, & Vong, 1995). Older children tend to become more efficient in the spontaneous use of memory strategies (see Chapter 9).

prospective memory Remembering to perform future actions.

By contrast with the ability to call up past memories, young children's **prospective memory**—the ability to remember to do something at a later time, such as bringing a book to preschool the next day—is relatively developed by ages 4 and 5 and improves only modestly by age 7 (Kvavilashvili, Messer, & Ebdon, 2001).

Forming Childhood Memories Memory of experiences in early childhood is rarely deliberate: young children simply remember events that made a strong impression, and most of these early conscious memories seem to be short-lived. How do children begin to form permanent memories? To answer that question, one investigator has distinguished between three types of childhood memory that serve different functions: *generic, episodic,* and *autobiographical* (Nelson, 1993b).

Generic memory, which begins at about age 2, produces a **script,** or general outline of a familiar, repeated event without details of time or place. The script contains routines for situations that come up again and again; it helps a child know what to expect and how to act. For example, a child may have scripts for riding the bus to preschool or having lunch at Grandma's house.

generic memory Memory that produces scripts of familiar routines to guide behavior.

script General remembered outline of a familiar, repeated event, used to guide behavior.

Episodic memory refers to awareness of having experienced a particular incident that occurred at a specific time and place. Young children remember more clearly events that are unique or new to them. Three-year-olds may recall details about a trip to the circus for a year or longer (Fivush, Hudson, & Nelson, 1983), whereas generic memories of frequent events (such as going to the park) tend to blur together. However, given a young child's limited memory capacity, episodic memories are temporary. Unless they recur several times (in which case they are transferred to generic memory), they last for a few weeks or months and then fade. The reliability of children's episodic memory has become an important issue in lawsuits involving charges of child abuse (see Box 7-2 on pages 256–257).

episodic memory Long-term memory of specific experiences or events, linked to time and place.

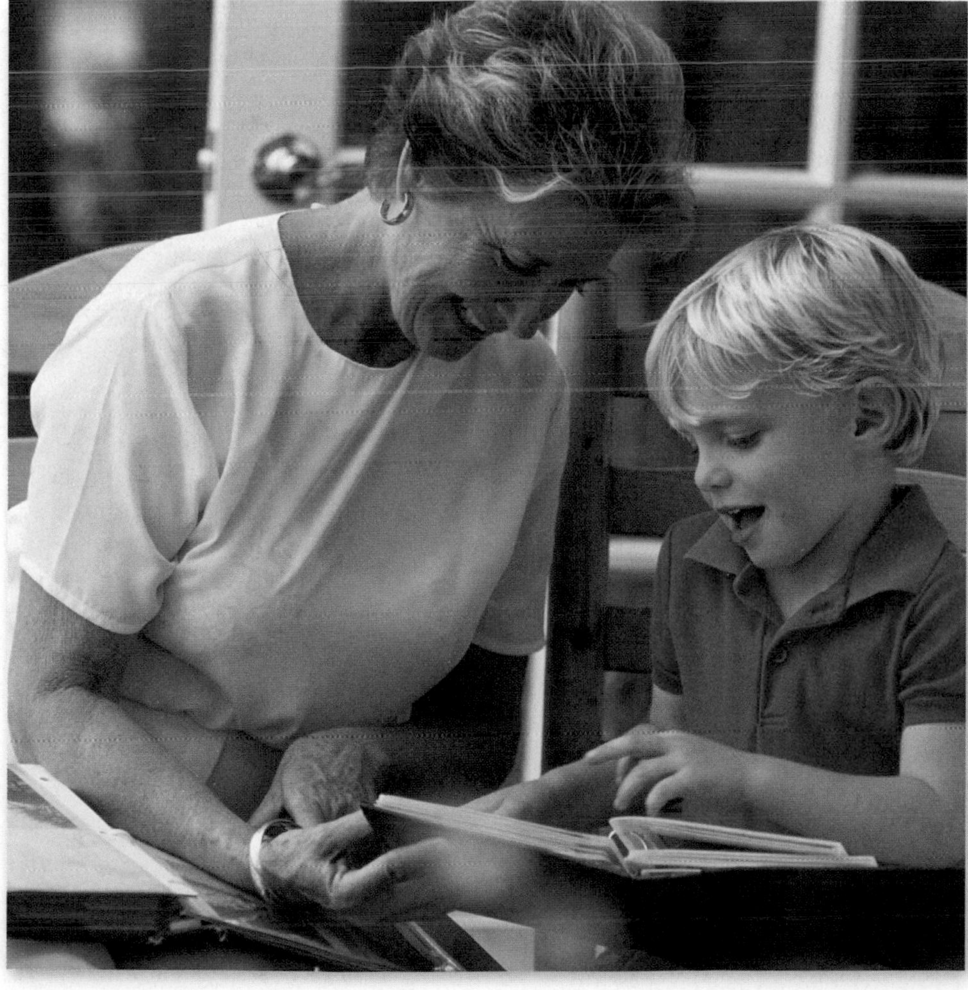

"Remember when we went to the zoo?" Young children remember better events that are unique and new, and they may recall details from a special trip for a year or longer.

BOX 7-2

Practically Speaking

How Reliable Is Children's Eyewitness Testimony?

Child abuse is a crime that often can be proved only by the testimony of a preschool child. If a child's testimony is inaccurate, an innocent adult may be unfairly punished. On the other hand, if a child's testimony is not believed, a dangerous adult may be set free.

Children responding to adults' suggestions have been known to "remember" events that never occurred. In one study, for eleven consecutive weeks, an interviewer told a 4-year-old, "You went to the hospital because your finger got caught in a mousetrap. Did this ever happen to you?" At first the boy said, "No, I've never been to the hospital." In the second interview he said, "Yes, I cried." By the eleventh interview, he gave a detailed recital of the event and the trip to the hospital, which he now said had happened the day before (Ceci, in Goleman, 1993).

On the other hand, among 96 children ages 2 to 12 in Newfoundland who had been hospitalized with serious injuries, children as young as 3 volunteered memories of the injuries and the hospital stays as much as two years later. This study suggests that young children can accurately describe events that are important to them after long periods of time—*if* they are questioned neutrally (Peterson, 1999).

Preschoolers tend to be more suggestible than older children. This difference may be due to younger children's weaker memory for specific events and their greater vulnerability to bribes, threats, and adult expectations (Bruck, Ceci, & Hembrooke, 1998; Ceci & Bruck, 1993; Leichtman & Ceci, 1995). Suggestibility seems to diminish after age $4\frac{1}{2}$ (Portwood & Repucci, 1996). However, some children, regardless of age, are more suggestible than others (Bruck & Ceci, 1997).

Young children may not know whether they "remember" something from experience or from imagining or being told or asked about it (Woolley & Bruell, 1996). In one experiment, researchers had a man called "Sam Stone" drop in at a child care center for a few minutes (Leichtman & Ceci, 1995). The visitor commented on a story that was being read, strolled around the room, and then waved goodbye and left. Some of the children who witnessed the event had repeatedly been told stories about "Sam Stone" before his visit, depicting him as a well-meaning bumbler, and/or were given false suggestions afterward that he had ripped a book and dirtied a teddy bear.

After four weekly interviews, nearly half of the 3- and 4-year-olds and 30 percent of 5- and 6-year-olds who had received *both* the stereotyped advance preparation and the misleading questioning spontaneously reported the book-ripping and teddy-bear-dirtying to a new interviewer; and when asked probing questions, nearly three out of four of the younger children said the visitor had done one or both. Lesser proportions of children who had received *only* advance preparation or suggestive questioning gave false reports. By contrast, *none* of the children in a control group, which had received neither advance preparation nor suggestive questioning, made false reports, showing that young children's testimony *can* be accurate when elicited neutrally. In other research, kindergartners modified their recall of a character in a story according to what they were told about that character, either before or after hearing the story (Greenhoot, 2000).

Reports are likely to be more reliable if children are interviewed only once, soon after the event, by people who do not have an opinion about what took place; if the

autobiographical memory Memory of specific events in one's own life.

Autobiographical memory refers to memories that form a person's life history. These memories are specific and long-lasting. Although autobiographical memory is a type of episodic memory, not everything in episodic memory becomes part of it—only those memories that have a special, personal meaning to the child.

Autobiographical memory begins for most people around age 4, and rarely before age 3. It increases slowly between ages 5 and 8; memories from then on may be recalled for twenty, forty, or more years. Individuals differ in the onset of autobiographical memory; some people have vivid memories from the age of 3, while others do not remember much before age 8 (Nelson, 1992).

This timetable suggests that autobiographical memory is linked with the development of language. The ability to talk about an event, as Yani and her father often did, may not be necessary for a young child to remember it, but verbal skills may affect whether and how memories can be carried forward into later life (Fivush & Schwarzmueller, 1998). Not until children can put memories into words can they hold them in their minds, reflect on them, and compare them with the memories of others.

Practically Speaking

BOX 7-2

—continued

interviewers do not ask leading questions, ask open-ended rather than yes/no questions, and do not repeatedly ask the same questions; if they are patient and nonjudgmental; and if they do not selectively reward or reinforce responses or convey veiled threats or accusations (Bruck & Ceci, 1997; Bruck et al., 1998; Leichtman & Ceci, 1995; Steward & Steward, 1996).

Often young children are given anatomically correct dolls to point out where they were touched. According to some research, many children will insert fingers or sticks into a doll's vagina or anus, reporting that someone did that to them, even when it did not happen (Bruck & Ceci, 1997; Ceci & Bruck, 1993). In interviews with 72 children, ages $2\frac{1}{2}$ to 4, the children gave more accurate information about where they had been touched by an experimenter when asked directly or told to point to the place on their own bodies than when asked to show it by using a doll (DeLoache, 1995). In other studies, however, use of dolls to jog memory did *not* increase false reports but rather produced more complete reports (Steward & Steward, 1996).

Young children are apt to err in recalling precise details of an event that varies with repetition (Powell & Thomson, 1996). They tend to confuse what happened during a particular episode with what happened during other, similar episodes; all may blur together in memory into a generic "script." Thus a child may have trouble answering questions about a *specific instance* of abuse, even though the child accurately remembers a *pattern* of abuse.

Often young children's testimony is excluded because they cannot demonstrate a clear understanding of the difference between truth and falsehood and of the morality and consequences of telling a lie. Often they do not understand such questions the way they are asked or cannot explain the concepts involved. Furthermore, abused children often have seriously delayed language skills. The Lyon-Saywitz Oath-Taking Competency Picture Task avoids these problems by simply asking a prospective young witness whether a child in a story is telling the truth about a pictured event and what would happen if the child told a lie. Among 192 maltreated 4- to 7-year-olds awaiting court appearances, a majority of 5-year-olds successfully performed this task, and even 4-year-olds did better than chance would predict (Lyon & Saywitz, 1999).

Issues concerning the reliability of young children's testimony are still being sorted out, but it appears that children *can* give reliable testimony if care is taken to avoid biased interviewing techniques. Researchers are trying to develop and validate "model" interview techniques that will expose adults who harm children while protecting those who may be falsely accused (Bruck et al., 1998).

What's Your View?

What information would you seek and what factors would you consider in deciding whether to believe a preschooler's testimony in a child abuse case?

Check It Out:

For more information on this topic, go to www.mhhe.com/papaliah9, where you'll find links to information about child victims and witnesses in court.

It's important to keep in mind that most research on memory has focused on middle-class American or western European children, who have been talking since about age 2. We know little about the relationship between memory and language among children who begin to speak later because of different social and cultural practices, or among deaf children of hearing parents who cannot as easily converse with them (Nelson, 1993b).

Influences on Autobiographical Memory Why do some early memories last longer than others? One factor, as we've already noted, is the uniqueness of the event. Let's look at two other factors: children's active participation, either in the event itself or in its retelling or reenactment, and parents' way of talking with children about past events.

Preschoolers tend to remember things they *did* better than things they merely *saw* (D. C. Jones, Swift, & Johnson, 1988; Murachver, Pipe, Gordon, Owens, & Fivush, 1996). In one study, $2\frac{1}{2}$- to 3-year-olds engaged in pretend play with their mothers about a camping trip, a birdwatching adventure, and the opening of an ice cream shop.

Children who jointly handled *and* jointly discussed with their mothers various items connected with these events recalled them better one to three days later than children who had only handled or only discussed the items (Haden, Ornstein, Eckerman, & Didow, 2001).

The way adults talk with a child about a shared experience can influence how well the child will remember it (Haden & Fivush, 1996; Reese & Fivush, 1993). When a child gets stuck, adults with a *repetitive* conversational style tend to repeat their own previous statements or questions. Adults with an *elaborative* style are more likely to move on to a new aspect of the event or add more information. A repetitive-style parent might ask, "Do you remember how we traveled to Florida?" and then, receiving no answer, ask, "How did we get there? We went in the _____." An elaborative-style parent might instead follow up the first question by saying, "Did we go by car or by plane?" Elaborative parents seem more focused on having a mutually rewarding conversation and affirming the child's responses, whereas repetitive parents are more focused on checking the child's memory performance. Three-year-olds of elaborative-style parents take part in longer conversations about events and remember more details, and they tend to remember the events better at ages 5 and 6 (Reese, Haden, & Fivush, 1993). Even as early as 19 to 32 months, a mother's elaborative reminiscing predicts children's ability to repeat and elaborate on shared memories (Harley & Reese, 1999).

Checkpoint

Can you . . .

- ✔ Compare preschoolers' recognition and recall ability?
- ✔ Explain how language development may contribute to the onset of autobiographical memory?
- ✔ Identify factors that affect how well a preschool child will remember an event?

Intelligence: Psychometric and Vygotskian Approaches

One factor that may affect how early children develop both language and memory is intelligence. Let's look at two ways intelligence is measured in early childhood—through traditional psychometric tests and through newer tests of cognitive potential. Then we'll consider some influences on children's performance.

Guidepost

8. How is preschoolers' intelligence measured, and what are some influences on it?

Traditional Psychometric Measures Because 3-, 4-, and 5-year-olds are more proficient with language than younger children, intelligence tests can now include more verbal items; and these tests, if well standardized (refer back to Chapter 2), produce more reliable results than the largely nonverbal tests used in infancy. As children approach age 5, there is a higher correlation between their scores on intelligence tests and the scores they will achieve later (Bornstein & Sigman, 1986).

Although preschool children are easier to test than infants and toddlers, they still need to be tested individually. The two most commonly used individual tests for preschoolers are the Stanford-Binet Intelligence Scale and the Wechsler Preschool and Primary Scale of Intelligence.

Stanford-Binet Intelligence Scale Individual intelligence test used to measure memory, spatial orientation, and practical judgment.

The **Stanford-Binet Intelligence Scale** takes thirty to forty minutes. The child is asked to define words, string beads, build with blocks, identify the missing parts of a picture, trace mazes, and show an understanding of numbers. The child's score is supposed to measure memory, spatial orientation, and practical judgment in real-life situations. The fourth edition, revised in 1985, includes an equal balance of verbal and nonverbal, quantitative, and memory items. Instead of providing the IQ as a single overall measure of intelligence, the revised version assesses patterns and levels of cognitive development.

Wechsler Preschool and Primary Scale of Intelligence, Revised (WPPSI-R) Individual intelligence test for children ages 3 to 7, which yields verbal and performance scores as well as a combined score.

The **Wechsler Preschool and Primary Scale of Intelligence, Revised (WPPSI-R),** an hour-long individual test used with children ages 3 to 7, yields separate verbal and performance scores as well as a combined score. Its separate scales are similar to those in the Wechsler Intelligence Scale for Children (WISC-III), discussed in Chapter 9. The 1989 revision includes new subtests and new picture items.

Both the Stanford-Binet and the WPPSI-R have been restandardized on a sample of children representing the population of preschool-age children in the United States.

Influences on Measured Intelligence At one time it was believed that the family environment played a major role in cognitive development. Now the extent of that influence is in question. We don't know how much of parents' influence on intelligence comes from their genetic contribution, and how much from the fact that they provide a child's earliest environment for learning.

Twin and adoption studies suggest that family life has its strongest influence in early childhood, and this influence diminishes greatly by adolescence (McGue, 1997; Neisser et al., 1996). However, these studies have been done largely with white, middle-class samples; their results may not apply to low-income and nonwhite families (Neisser et al., 1996).

In two longitudinal studies of low-income African American children, the influence of the home environment did diminish between infancy and middle childhood but remained substantial—at least as strong as the influence of the mother's IQ (Burchinal et al., 1997). Among 175 African American 3-year-olds, a father's satisfaction with his parenting role was associated with his child's IQ, and paternal involvement and nurturance were associated with language skills and other aspects of well-being (Black et al., 1999).

Giving suggestions and strategies for solving a puzzle or problem—without showing strong approval or disapproval—can foster cognitive growth.

Family economic circumstances can exert a powerful influence, not so much in themselves as in the way they affect parenting practices and the atmosphere in the home. But socioeconomic status is only one of several social and family risk factors. Assessments of 152 children at ages 4 and 13 revealed no single pattern of risk. Instead, a child's IQ was related to *the total number* of such risk factors as the mother's behavior, mental health, anxiety level, education, and beliefs about children's development; family size and social support; stressful life events; parental occupations; and disadvantaged status. The more risk factors there were, the lower the child's IQ score (Sameroff, Seifer, Baldwin, & Baldwin, 1993).

Children's temperament—or at least, the way parents perceive it—may contribute to the way parents treat them, and both of these factors may affect children's cognitive potential. In a three-and-a-half-year longitudinal study of 93 toddlers, mothers who rated their 18-month-olds as "difficult" tended, a year later, to give them more assistance and instruction in a laboratory problem-solving task or to be more critical and coercive; and their children were likely to give up, make errors, and develop learning problems. Children whose mothers, when the children were $2\frac{1}{2}$, gave them suggestions for solving problems or showed them effective strategies did better on the arithmetic and vocabulary subtests of the WPPSI at age 5. Children whose mothers had given *either* more approval *or* disapproval or had told them what to do did worse (Fagot & Gauvain, 1997).

Testing and Teaching Based on Vygotsky's Theory According to Vygotsky, intelligence grows with the interaction between child and environment, and assessments should seek to capture—and guide—this ongoing process. *Dynamic testing,* based on the concept of the zone of proximal development (ZPD), introduced in Chapter 2, offers an alternative to traditional "static" tests that measure a child's abilities at a given moment. Unlike static tests, dynamic tests measure potential abilities by giving the child leading questions, examples, and demonstrations that may help the child master a task.

The ZPD, in combination with the related concept of *scaffolding* (refer back to Chapter 2), can help parents and teachers guide children's cognitive progress. The less

What's Your View?

- If you were a preschool or kindergarten teacher, how helpful do you think it would be to know a child's IQ? The child's ZPD?

Checkpoint

Can you . . .

- ✔ Describe two commonly used individual intelligence tests for preschoolers?
- ✔ Discuss several influences on measured intelligence?
- ✔ Explain why dynamic testing may be useful?

able a child is to do a task, the more direction an adult must give. As the child can do more and more, the adult helps less and less. When the child can do the job alone, the adult takes away the "scaffold" that is no longer needed.

In one study, 3- and 4-year-olds were asked to give their parents directions for finding a hidden mouse in a dollhouse. The parents gave the children feedback when their directions needed clarifying. The parents proved to be highly sensitive to the children's scaffolding needs; they gave more directive prompts to 3-year-olds, whose directions tended to be less clear than those of 4-year-olds. The parents used fewer directive prompts as the children gained experience in giving clear directions (Plumert & Nichols-Whitehead, 1996).

Early Childhood Education

Guidepost

9. What purposes does early childhood education serve, and how do children make the transition to kindergarten?

Going to preschool is an important step, widening a child's physical, cognitive, and social environment. Today more 4-year-olds than ever, and even many 3-year-olds, are enrolled in early childhood education. The transition to kindergarten, the beginning of "real school," is another momentous step.

Goals and Types of Preschools: A Cross-Cultural View

In some countries, such as China, preschools are expected to provide academic preparation for schooling. In contrast, most preschools in the United States and many other western countries traditionally have followed a "child-centered" philosophy stressing social and emotional growth in line with young children's developmental needs—though some, such as those based on the theories of Piaget or the Italian educator Maria Montessori, have a stronger cognitive emphasis. As part of a debate over how to improve education, pressures have grown to offer instruction in basic academic skills in U.S. preschools. Defenders of the traditional developmental approach maintain that academically oriented programs neglect young children's need for exploration and free play and that too much teacher-initiated instruction may stifle their interest and interfere with self-initiated learning (Elkind, 1986; Zigler, 1987).

These preschoolers playing Candyland are improving in physical coordination, counting skills, and the ability to take turns and cooperate in play. A good preschool stimulates all aspects of development through interaction with trained teachers, playmates, and carefully chosen materials.

Preschools in Japan are different from preschools in the United States, but similar issues have surfaced there (Holloway, 1999). The typical Japanese preschool, in line with accepted cultural values, is *society-centered;* it emphasizes skills and attitudes that promote group harmony, such as greeting the teacher properly. Two other types of preschools have emerged in Japan in recent years: *child-centered* and *role-centered.*

Child-centered preschools arose in response to criticism that society-centered preschools discourage self-expression and creativity—qualities needed in the modern industrial society Japan has become. Child-centered programs are more individualized, like western ones. Children freely choose activities and interact individually with their teachers.

Role-centered programs—about 30 percent of private Japanese preschools—reject western individualism and stress traditional Japanese principles. They concentrate on preparing children for roles in society. Whereas society-centered preschools downplay academic learning, children in role-centered preschools study not only "the basics"—reading, writing, and mathematics—but also English, art, gymnastics, swordsmanship, tea ceremonies, and Japanese dance.

What type of preschool is best for children? Studies in the United States support the child-centered, developmental approach. One field study (Marcon, 1999) compared 721 randomly selected, predominantly low-income and African American 4- and 5-year-olds from three types of preschool classrooms in Washington, D.C.: *child-initiated, academically directed,* and *middle-of-the-road* (a blend of the other two approaches). Children from child-initiated programs, in which they actively directed their own learning experiences, excelled in basic academic skills. They also had more advanced motor skills than the other two groups and scored higher than the middle-of-the-road group in behavioral and communicative skills. These findings suggest that a single, coherent philosophy of education may work better than an attempt to blend diverse approaches and that a child-centered approach seems more effective than an academically oriented one.

What's Your View?

- Should the primary purpose of preschool be to provide a strong academic foundation or to foster social and emotional development?

Compensatory Preschool Programs

Estimates are that more than two-thirds of children in poor urban areas enter school poorly prepared to learn (Zigler, 1998). Since the 1960s large-scale programs have been developed to help such children compensate for what they have missed and to prepare them for school.

The best-known compensatory preschool program for children of low-income families in the United States is Project Head Start, a federally funded program launched in 1965. Its goals are to improve physical health, enhance cognitive skills, and foster self-confidence, relationships with others, social responsibility, and a sense of dignity and self-worth for the child and the family.

Has Head Start lived up to its name? By and large, yes. Data strongly support its effectiveness in improving school readiness (Ripple, Gilliam, Chanana, & Zigler, 1999). The most successful Head Start programs have been those with the most parental participation, the best-trained teachers, the lowest staff-to-child ratios, the longest school days and weeks, and the most extensive services. Outcomes are best when the programs last at least two years (S. Ramey, 1999).

However, when compensatory programs do not continue after children start school, cognitive benefits tend to fade (Ripple et al., 1999). Although Head Start children do better on intelligence tests than other children from comparable backgrounds, this advantage disappears after the children start school. Nor have Head Start children equaled the average middle-class child in school achievement or on standardized tests (Collins & Deloria, 1983; Zigler & Styfco, 1993, 1994). Still, children from Head Start and other such programs are less likely to be placed in special education or to repeat a grade and are more likely to finish high school than low-income children who did not attend compensatory preschool programs (Neisser et al., 1996). "Graduates" of high-quality compensatory programs, such as the Perry Preschool Project, were much less likely than a comparison group who lacked preschool experience to become juvenile delinquents; and the girls were less likely to become pregnant in their teens (Berrueta-Clement, Schweinhart, Barnett, Epstein, & Weikart, 1985; Schweinhart, Barnes, & Weikart 1993; see Chapter 12).

Results seem to be best with earlier and longer-lasting intervention (Reynolds & Temple, 1998; Zigler & Styfco, 1993, 1994, 2001). The Chicago Child Parent Centers, a large-scale intensive federally funded compensatory program, extends from preschool through third grade. The added years of academic enrichment significantly increased participants' reading achievement and decreased grade retention and special education placement through seventh grade, as compared with children who participated for only two or three years (Reynolds, 1994; Reynolds & Temple, 1998). At age 20, among 989 poverty-level children who had begun the program by age 4, nearly half (49.7 percent) had graduated from high school, as compared with 38.5 percent of a control group who had attended less intensive preschools or no preschool; and 16.9 percent had been arrested for juvenile crimes as compared with 25.1 percent of the control group (Reynolds, Temple, Robertson, & Mann, 2001).

In 1995, an Early Head Start program began offering child and family development services to pregnant women and to infants and toddlers from birth to age 3. In a preliminary evaluation of the 635 Early Head Start programs serving 45,000 low-income children and families, 2-year-old participants scored higher on standardized developmental and vocabulary tests, spoke in more complex sentences, and were at less risk of slowed developmental learning than children *not* in the program. The Early Head Start parents read more to their children, played with them in more structured ways, set more regular bedtimes, and used less physical punishment (Commissioner's Office of Research and Evaluation and Head Start Bureau, 2001).

The Transition to Kindergarten

Originally a year of transition between the relative freedom of home or preschool and the structure of "real school," kindergarten is now more like first grade. Children spend less time on self-chosen activities and more time on worksheets and preparing to read. Many kindergartners now spend a full day in school rather than the traditional half day. And, as academic and emotional pressures mount, many parents hold children back a year so that they now start kindergarten at age 6.

Children with extensive preschool experience tend to adjust to kindergarten more easily than those who spent little or no time in preschool. Children who start kindergarten with peers they know and like generally do better (Ladd, 1996).

One group of studies, which followed 399 full-day kindergarten students throughout the year, found a number of interlocking factors that influence cognitive achievement and social adjustment. Preexisting risk and protective factors having to do with the child and the home environment interact with features of the classroom environment, such as the child's developing relationships with teacher and peers; and the effects become stronger as time goes on. Children who show prosocial behavior during the early weeks become more well liked, whereas children who initially show antisocial behavior become more disliked. They tend to get into conflicts with teachers, to participate less, and to be lower achievers. Children who are more cognitively mature tend to participate more, and those who participate more achieve better. A supportive family background also influences achievement (Ladd, Birch, & Buhs, 1999). Children who are rejected by peers tend to participate less in

Checkpoint

Can you . . .

- ✔ Compare goals of varying types of preschool programs in the United States and Japan?
- ✔ Summarize findings on the short-term and long-term effects of academic and child-centered preschool programs?
- ✔ Assess the benefits of compensatory preschool education?
- ✔ Discuss factors that affect adjustment to kindergarten?

class and achieve less. They tend to feel lonely and to want to stay home from school (Buhs & Ladd, 2001).

There are proposals to lengthen the school year, for kindergarten as well as for higher grades. When an elementary school in a midsize, southeastern city added 30 days to its school year, kindergartners who went through the resulting 210-day program outperformed students in a traditional 180-day program on tests of math, reading, general knowledge, and cognitive competence at the beginning of first grade (Frazier & Morrison, 1998).

Refocus

- What aspects of Wang Yani's physical and cognitive development in early childhood seem to have been fairly typical, and in what ways was her development advanced?
- Can you give examples of how Yani's physical, cognitive, and psychosocial development interacted?
- What more would you like to know about Yani's early development if you had the chance to interview her or her parents?

The burgeoning physical and cognitive skills of early childhood have psychosocial implications, as we'll see in Chapter 8.

SUMMARY AND KEY TERMS

PHYSICAL DEVELOPMENT

Aspects of Physical Development

Guidepost 1. How do children's bodies change between ages 3 and 6, and what are their nutritional and dental needs?

- Physical growth increases during the years from 3 to 6, but more slowly than during infancy and toddlerhood. Boys are on average slightly taller, heavier, and more muscular than girls. Internal body systems are maturing, and all primary teeth are present.
- Preschool children generally eat less for their weight than before—and need less—but the prevalence of obesity has increased.
- Tooth decay has decreased since the 1970s but remains a problem among disadvantaged children.

Guidepost 2. What sleep patterns and problems tend to develop during early childhood?

- Sleep patterns change during early childhood and are affected by cultural expectations.
- It is normal for preschool children to develop bedtime rituals that delay going to sleep. Prolonged bedtime struggles or persistent sleep terrors or nightmares may indicate emotional disturbances that need attention.
- Bed-wetting is common and is usually outgrown without special help.

obesity *(230)*
enuresis *(232)*

Guidepost 3. What are the main motor achievements of early childhood?

- Children progress rapidly in gross and fine motor skills and eye-hand coordination, developing more complex systems of action.
- Stages of art production, which appear to reflect brain development and fine motor coordination, are the scribbling stage, shape stage, design stage, and pictorial stage.
- Handedness is usually evident by age 3, reflecting dominance by one hemisphere of the brain.

gross motor skills *(232)*
fine motor skills *(233)*
systems of action *(233)*
handedness *(234)*

Health and Safety

Guidepost 4. What are the major health and safety risks for young children?

- Although major contagious illnesses are rare today in industrialized countries due to widespread immunization, preventable disease continues to be a major problem in the developing world.
- Minor illnesses, such as colds and other respiratory illnesses, are common during early childhood and help build immunity to disease.
- Accidents, most commonly motor vehicle injuries, are the leading cause of death in childhood in the United States. Most fatal nonvehicular accidents occur at home.

- Environmental factors such as exposure to smoking, poverty, and homelessness increase the risks of illness or injury. Lead poisoning can have serious physical, cognitive, and behavioral effects.

COGNITIVE DEVELOPMENT

Piagetian Approach: The Preoperational Child

Guidepost 5. What are typical cognitive advances and immature aspects of preschool children's thinking?

- Children in the preoperational stage show several important advances, as well as some immature aspects of thought.
- The symbolic function enables children to reflect upon people, objects, and events that are not physically present. It is shown in deferred imitation, pretend play, and language.
- Early symbolic development helps preoperational children make more accurate judgments of spatial relationships. They can understand the concept of identity, link cause and effect, categorize living and nonliving things, and understand principles of counting.
- Centration keeps preoperational children from understanding principles of conservation. Their logic also is limited by irreversibility and a focus on states rather than transformations.
- Preoperational children appear to be less egocentric than Piaget thought.
- The theory of mind, which develops markedly between the ages of 3 and 5, includes awareness of a child's own thought processes, social cognition, understanding that people can hold false beliefs, ability to deceive, ability to distinguish appearance from reality, and ability to distinguish fantasy from reality. Hereditary and environmental influences affect individual differences in theory-of-mind development.

preoperational stage *(238)*
symbolic function *(238)*
dual representation hypothesis *(240)*
transduction *(241)*
animism *(241)*
centration *(243)*
decenter *(243)*
conservation *(243)*
irreversibility *(244)*
egocentrism *(244)*
theory of mind *(245)*

Language Development and Other Cognitive Abilities

Guidepost 6. How does language improve, and what happens when its development is delayed?

- During early childhood, vocabulary increases greatly, and grammar and syntax become fairly sophisticated. Children become more competent in pragmatics.
- Private speech is normal and common; it may aid in the shift to self-regulation and usually disappears by age 10.
- Causes of delayed language development are unclear. Although many children who speak late catch up, treatment may be needed to avoid serious cognitive, social, and emotional consequences.
- Interaction with adults can promote emergent literacy.

fast mapping *(250)*
pragmatics *(251)*
social speech *(251)*
private speech *(251)*
emergent literacy *(253)*

Guidepost 7. What memory abilities expand in early childhood?

- Information-processing models describe three steps in memory: encoding, storage, and retrieval.
- At all ages, recognition is better than recall, but both increase during early childhood.
- Early episodic memory is only temporary; it fades or is transferred to generic memory. Autobiographical memory begins at about age 3 or 4 and may be related to early self-recognition ability and language development.
- Children are more likely to remember unusual activities that they actively participate in. The way adults talk with children about events influences memory formation.

encoding *(254)*
storage *(254)*
retrieval *(254)*
recognition *(254)*
recall *(254)*
prospective memory *(254)*
generic memory *(255)*
script *(255)*
episodic memory *(255)*
autobiographical memory *(256)*

Guidepost 8. How is preschoolers' intelligence measured, and what are some influences on it?

- The two most commonly used psychometric intelligence tests for young children are the Stanford-Binet Intelligence Scale and the Wechsler Preschool and Primary Scale of Intelligence, Revised (WPPSI-R).
- Intelligence test scores may be influenced by social and emotional functioning, as well as by parent-child interaction and socioeconomic factors.
- Newer tests based on Vygotsky's concept of the zone of proximal development (ZPD) indicate immediate potential for achievement. Such tests, when combined with scaffolding, can help parents and teachers guide children's progress.

Stanford-Binet Intelligence Scale *(258)*
Wechsler Preschool and Primary Scale of Intelligence, Revised (WPPSI-R) *(258)*

Early Childhood Education

Guidepost 9. What purposes does early childhood education serve, and how do children make the transition to kindergarten?

- Goals of preschool education vary in different cultures. Since the 1970s the academic content of early childhood education programs in the United States has increased.
- For low-income U.S. children, academically oriented programs seem less effective than child-centered ones.
- Compensatory preschool programs have had positive outcomes, but participants generally have not equaled the performance of middle-class children. Compensatory programs that begin early and extend into the primary grades have better long-term results.
- Adjustment to kindergarten may depend on interaction among the child's characteristics and those of the home, school, and neighborhood environments.

Psychosocial Development in Early Childhood

Chapter 8

Children's playings are not sports and should be deemed as their most serious actions.

—**Montaigne, *Essays***

Focus: Isabel Allende, Militant Writer

Isabel Allende

Isabel Allende* has been called Latin America's foremost woman writer. Her best-selling novels and short stories, which evoke her imaginative inner world, have been translated into thirty languages and have sold an estimated 11 million copies worldwide. Perhaps her most moving work is *Paula* (1995), the memoir she began scribbling on yellow pads as she sat at the bedside of her 27-year-old daughter, Paula Frías, in a Madrid hospital, waiting for her to awaken from a coma that never lifted. The words Allende poured out were as much a reminiscence of her own tempestuous life as a tribute to her dying daughter.

Born August 2, 1942, in Lima, Peru, Isabel Allende was the daughter of a Chilean diplomat, a cousin of the Chilean revolutionary hero Salvador Allende, who was assassinated in a military coup in 1973. Her emotional connection with the cause of her oppressed people became the backdrop for much of her later writing. Her major theme is the role of women in a highly patriarchal society.

When she was almost 3, Isabel's father abandoned her mother, Doña Panchita, in childbirth. Left with no means of support and humiliated by the failure of her marriage, Doña Panchita returned in disgrace with her three young children to her parents' household in Santiago. She got a low-paying job in a bank and supplemented her salary by making hats. Although there was no divorce in Chile, the marriage was annulled. "Those were difficult years for my mother," Allende (1995, p. 32) writes; "she had to contend with poverty, gossip, and the snubs of people who had been her friends."

*Sources of information on Isabel Allende were Agosin (1999), Allende (1995), Perera (1995), Piña (1999), Rodden (1999), and various biographical materials from Allende's website, http://www.isabelallende.com.

OUTLINE

A second blow to young Isabel was the death of her beloved grandmother. Suddenly the house became dim and cheerless. A small, fearful, isolated child often left in the care of a harsh, threatening maid, Isabel found refuge in silent games and in the fanciful stories her mother told at night in the dark. She felt "different," "like an outcast" (Allende, 1995, p. 50), and she had a rebellious streak. Although she loved her mother deeply and wanted to protect her, she did not want to be like her. She wanted to be strong and independent like her grandfather. "I think Tata was always sorry I wasn't a boy," she writes in *Paula* (p. 37); "had I been, he could have taught me to play jai alai, and use his tools, and hunt." He tacitly condoned the "character-building" tactics of the two bachelor uncles who lived in the household and played rough "games" with the children that today would be considered physically or emotionally abusive.

When Isabel was about 5, Ramón Huidobro, the Chilean consul who had helped the family return to Chile, moved in with Doña Panchita and eventually married her, displacing Isabel and her brothers from their mother's bedroom. It was during these pivotal early years that Allende's fervent feminism was born. "When I was a little girl," she says, "I felt anger towards my grandfather, my stepfather, and all the men in the family, who had all the advantages while my mother was the victim. . . . She had to please everyone and everyone told her what to do" (Piña, 1999, pp. 174–175).

It took Isabel years to accept her stepfather. "He raised us with a firm hand and unfailing good humor; he set limits and sent clear messages, without sentimental demonstrations, and without compromise. . . . he put up with my contrariness without trying to buy my esteem or ceding an inch of his authority, until he won me over totally," she writes (Allende, 1995, pp. 48–49).

Through her books, Allende has come to a greater understanding and acceptance of herself and her gender. Many of her characters are extraordinary women who break with tradition despite their place in society. Being a woman, she says, "was like being handicapped in many ways. In that macho culture where I was brought up. . . . I would have liked to be a man." Not until she was 40 did she "finally accept that I was always going to . . . be the person I am" (Foster, 1999, p. 107).

The years from ages 3 to 6 are pivotal ones in children's psychosocial development, as they were for Isabel Allende. Even without such tumultuous changes as she went through, a child's emotional development and sense of self are rooted in the experiences of those years. Yet the story of the self is not completed in early childhood; like Allende, we continue to write it even as adults.

Allende's story also highlights the importance of the cultural context. As a girl growing up in a male-dominated culture, she faced attitudes very different from what she might have experienced in a less tightly gender-based society.

In this chapter we discuss preschool children's understanding of themselves and their feelings. We see how their identification of themselves as male or female arises and how it affects their behavior. We describe the activity on which children typically spend most of their time: play. We consider the influence, for good or ill, of what parents do. Finally, we discuss relationships with siblings and other children.

After you have read and studied this chapter, you should be able to answer each of the following Guidepost questions. Look for them again in the margins, where they point to important concepts throughout the chapter. To check your understanding of these Guideposts, review the end-of-chapter summary. Checkpoints located at periodic spots throughout the chapter will help you verify your understanding of what you have read.

Guideposts for Study

1. How does the self-concept develop during early childhood?
2. How do young children advance in understanding their emotions and develop initiative and self-esteem?
3. How do boys and girls become aware of the meaning of gender, and what explains differences in behavior between the sexes?
4. How do preschoolers play, and how does play contribute to and reflect development?
5. What forms of discipline do parents use, and how do parenting styles and practices influence development?
6. Why do young children help or hurt others, and why do they develop fears?
7. What causes child abuse and neglect, and what are the effects of maltreatment?
8. How do young children get along with—or without—siblings?
9. How do young children choose playmates and friends, and why are some children more popular than others?

The Developing Self

"Who in the world am I? Ah, *that's* the great puzzle," said Alice in Wonderland, after her size had abruptly changed—again. Solving Alice's "puzzle" is a lifelong process of getting to know one's self.

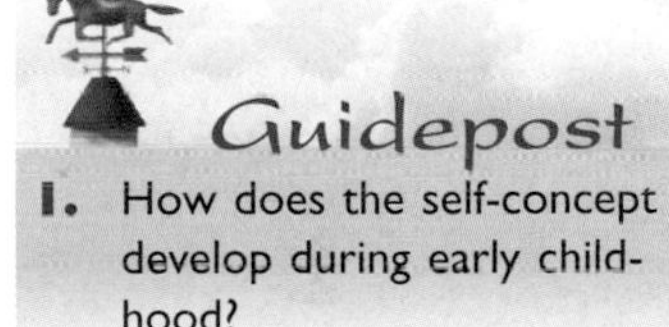

Guidepost

1. How does the self-concept develop during early childhood?

The Self-Concept and Cognitive Development

The **self-concept** is our total image of ourselves. It is what we believe about who we are—our total picture of our abilities and traits. It is "a *cognitive construction,* . . . a system of descriptive and evaluative representations about the self," which determines how we feel about ourselves and guides our actions (Harter, 1996, p. 207). The sense of self also has a social aspect: children incorporate into their self-image their growing understanding of how others see them.

self-concept Sense of self; descriptive and evaluative mental picture of one's abilities and traits.

The picture of the self comes into focus in toddlerhood, as children develop self-awareness. The self-concept becomes clearer and more compelling as a person gains in cognitive abilities and deals with the developmental tasks of childhood, of adolescence, and then of adulthood.

How does the self-concept change in early childhood? By age 4, Jason's attempts at **self-definition** are becoming more comprehensive as he begins to identify a cluster of characteristics to describe himself:

self-definition Cluster of characteristics used to describe oneself.

> My name is Jason and I live in a big house with my mother and father and sister, Lisa. I have a kitty that's orange and a television set in my own room. . . . I like pizza and I have a nice teacher. I can count up to 100, want to hear me? I love my dog, Skipper. I can climb to the top of the jungle gym, I'm not scared! Just happy. You can't be happy *and* scared, no way! I have brown hair, and I go to preschool. I'm really strong. I can lift this chair, watch me! (Harter, 1996, p. 208)

A young child's self-concept is based mainly on external characteristics, such as physical features.

The way Jason describes himself is typical of children his age. He talks mostly about concrete, observable behaviors; external characteristics, such as physical features; preferences; possessions; and members of his household. He mentions particular skills (running and climbing) rather than general abilities (being athletic). His self-descriptions are unrealistically positive, and they frequently spill over into demonstrations; what he *thinks* about himself is almost inseparable from what he *does.* Not until around age 7 will he describe himself in terms of generalized traits, such as *popular, smart,* or *dumb;* recognize that he can have conflicting emotions; and be self-critical while holding a positive overall self-concept.

During the past twenty-five years, researchers have become interested in pinpointing the intermediate changes that make up this "age 5 to 7 shift." An analysis based on neo-Piagetian theory (Case, 1985, 1992; Fischer, 1980) describes the 5 to 7 shift as occurring in three steps, which actually form a continuous progression.* At 4, Jason is at the first step: his statements about himself are **single representations**—isolated, one-dimensional items. His thinking jumps from particular to particular, without logical connections. At this stage he cannot imagine having two emotions at once ("You can't be happy *and* scared"). He cannot decenter, in part because of his limited working memory capacity, and so he cannot consider different aspects of himself at the same time. His thinking is all-or-nothing. He cannot acknowledge that his **real self,** the person he actually is, is not the same as his **ideal self,** the person he would like to be. So he describes himself as a paragon of virtue and ability.

single representations In neo-Piagetian terminology, first stage in development of self-definition, in which children describe themselves in terms of individual, unconnected characteristics and in all-or-nothing terms.

real self The self one actually is.

ideal self The self one would like to be.

At about age 5 or 6, Jason moves up to the second step, as he begins to link one aspect of himself to another: "I can run fast, and I can climb high. I'm also strong. I can throw a ball real far, I'm going to be on a team some day!" (Harter, 1996, p. 215). However, these **representational mappings**—logical connections between parts of his image of himself—are still expressed in completely positive, all-or-nothing terms. Since good and bad are opposites, he cannot see how he might be good at some things and not at others.

representational mappings In neo-Piagetian terminology, second stage in development of self-definition, in which a child makes logical connections between aspects of the self but still sees these characteristics in all-or-nothing terms.

The third step, *representational systems,* takes place in middle childhood (see Chapter 10), when children begin to integrate specific features of the self into a general, multidimensional concept and to articulate a sense of self-worth. As all-or-nothing thinking declines, Jason's self-descriptions will become more balanced ("I'm good at hockey but bad at arithmetic"). He will have come a long way from the 4-year-old who declared, "You can't be happy *and* scared, no way!"

Understanding Emotions

Guidepost

2. How do young children advance in understanding their emotions and develop initiative and self-esteem?

Understanding their own emotions helps children to guide their behavior in social situations and to talk about feelings (Laible & Thompson, 1998). It enables them to control the way they show their feelings and to be sensitive to how others feel (Garner & Power, 1996). Understanding one's emotions, then, is a cognitive process that can lead to action.

Because early emotional experience occurs within the family, it should not be surprising that family relationships affect the development of emotional understanding, as they did with Isabel Allende. A study of 41 preschoolers found a relationship between security of attachment to the mother and a child's understanding of others' neg-

*This discussion of children's developing understanding of themselves from age 4 on, including their understanding of their emotions, is indebted to Susan Harter (1990, 1993, 1996, 1998).

ative emotions, such as fear, anger, and sadness—both as observed among their peers, and as inferred from stories enacted by puppets (Laible & Thompson, 1998).

Preschoolers can talk about their feelings and often can discern the feelings of others, and they understand that emotions are connected with experiences and desires (Saarni, Mumme, & Campos, 1998). By age 3, children know that if someone gets what he wants he will be happy, and if not, he will be sad (Wellman & Woolley, 1990). However, they still lack a full understanding of such self-directed emotions as shame and pride, and they have trouble reconciling conflicting emotions, such as being happy about getting a new bicycle but disappointed because it's the wrong color (Kestenbaum & Gelman, 1995).

Emotions Directed Toward the Self As we have mentioned, emotions directed toward the self, such as guilt, shame, and pride, typically develop by the end of the third year, after children gain self-awareness and accept the standards of behavior their parents have set. Violating accepted standards can bring shame or guilt, or both; living up to, or surpassing, standards can bring pride. But even children a few years older often lack the cognitive sophistication to *recognize* these emotions and what brings them on—a necessary step toward emotional control.

In one study (Harter, 1993), 4- to 8-year-olds were told two stories. In the first story, a child takes a few coins from a jar after being told not to do so; in the second story, a child performs a difficult gymnastic feat—a flip on the bars. Each story was presented in two versions: one in which a parent sees the child doing the act, and another in which no one sees the child. The children were asked how they and the parent would feel in each circumstance.

The answers revealed a gradual progression in understanding of feelings about the self (Harter, 1996). At ages 4 to 5, children did not say that either they or their parents would feel pride or shame. Five- to 6-year-olds said their parents would be ashamed or proud of them but did not acknowledge feeling these emotions themselves. At 6 to 7, children said they would feel proud or ashamed, but only if they were observed. Not until ages 7 to 8 did children say that they would feel ashamed or proud of themselves even if no one saw them. By this age, the standards that produce pride and shame appear to be fully internalized and to affect children's opinion of themselves (Harter, 1993, 1996). It is also in middle childhood that children seem to develop a clearer idea of the difference between guilt and shame (Harris, Olthof, Meerum Terwogt, & Hardman, 1987; Olthof, Schouten, Kuiper, Stegge, & Jennekens-Schinkel, 2000).

Simultaneous Emotions Part of the confusion in younger children's understanding of their feelings is difficulty in recognizing that they can experience different emotional reactions at the same time, as Isabel Allende did toward her grandfather, both resenting and admiring him.

Individual differences in understanding conflicting emotions are evident by age 3. Three-year-olds who could identify whether a face looked happy or sad and could tell how a puppet felt when enacting a situation involving happiness, sadness, anger, or fear were better able at the end of kindergarten to explain a story character's conflicting emotions. These children tended to come from families that often discussed why people behave as they do (J. R. Brown & Dunn, 1996). Children acquire a more sophisticated understanding of simultaneous emotions during middle childhood (see Chapter 10).

Checkpoint

Can you . . .

- ✔ Trace self-concept development between ages 3 and 6?
- ✔ Explain the difficulties young children have in understanding emotions directed toward the self and simultaneous emotions?

Erikson: Initiative versus Guilt

The need to deal with conflicting feelings about the self is at the heart of the third stage of personality development identified by Erik Erikson (1950): **initiative versus guilt.** The conflict arises from the growing sense of purpose, which lets a child plan and carry out activities, and the growing pangs of conscience the child may have about such plans.

initiative versus guilt
Erikson's third stage in psychosocial development, in which children balance the urge to pursue goals with moral reservations that may prevent carrying them out.

Preschool children can do—and want to do—more and more. At the same time, they are learning that some of the things they want to do meet social approval, while others do not, as when Isabel Allende, at 6, was expelled from a parochial school for organizing her classmates to show their underpants. How do children reconcile their desire to *do* with their desire for approval?

This conflict marks a split between two parts of the personality: the part that remains a child, full of exuberance and a desire to try new things and test new powers, and the part that is becoming an adult, constantly examining the propriety of motives and actions. Children who learn how to regulate these opposing drives develop the "virtue" of *purpose,* the courage to envision and pursue goals without being unduly inhibited by guilt or fear of punishment (Erikson, 1982).

Self-Esteem

self-esteem The judgment a person makes about his or her self-worth.

Self-esteem is the self-evaluative part of the self-concept, the judgment children make about their overall worth. From a neo-Piagetian perspective, self-esteem is based on children's growing cognitive ability to describe and define themselves.

Developmental Changes in Self-Esteem Children do not generally articulate a concept of self-worth until about age 8, but younger children show by their behavior that they have one. Recent attempts to measure young children's self-esteem often incorporate teacher and parent reports (Davis-Kean & Sandler, 2001) or puppets and doll play (Measelle, Ablow, Cowan, & Cowan, 1998) in addition to self-reports.

In a study in Belgium (Verschueren, Buyck, & Marcoen, 2001), researchers measured 5-year-olds' self-representations, using two measures: (1) the Harter (1985b) Self-Perception Profile for Children (SPPC), which covers overall (global) self-worth, as well as specific perceptions about physical appearance, scholastic and athletic competence, social acceptance, and behavioral conduct; and (2) the Puppet Interview (Cassidy, 1988; Verschueren et al., 1996), in which puppets are used to reveal a child's perception of what another person thinks of him or her. Children's positive or negative self-perceptions at age 5 tended to predict their self-perceptions and socioemotional functioning (as reported by teachers) at age 8.

Still, before the 5 to 7 shift, young children's self-esteem is not necessarily based on a realistic appraisal. Although they can make judgments about their competence at various activities, they are not yet able to rank them in importance. They tend to

This mother's approval of her 3-year-old son's artwork is an important contributor to his self-esteem. Not until middle childhood do children develop strong internal standards of self-worth.

accept the judgments of adults, who often give positive, uncritical feedback, and thus may overrate their abilities (Harter, 1990, 1993, 1996, 1998).

Self-esteem in early childhood tends to be all-or-none: "I am good" or "I am bad" (Harter, 1996, 1998). Not until middle childhood do personal evaluations of competence and adequacy (based on internalization of parental and societal standards) normally become critical in shaping and maintaining a sense of self-worth (Harter, 1990, 1996, 1998).

Contingent Self-Esteem: The "Helpless" Pattern When self-esteem is high, a child is motivated to achieve. However, if self-esteem is *contingent* on success, children may view failure or criticism as an indictment of their worth and may feel helpless to do better. About one-third to one-half of preschoolers, kindergartners, and first-graders show elements of this "helpless" pattern: self-denigration or self-blame, negative emotion, lack of persistence, and lowered expectations for themselves (Burhans & Dweck, 1995; Ruble & Dweck, 1995). Instead of trying a different way to complete a puzzle, as a child with unconditional self-esteem might do, "helpless" children feel ashamed and give up, or go back to an easier puzzle they have already done. They do not expect to succeed, and so they do not try. Whereas older children who fail may conclude that they are dumb, preschoolers interpret poor performance as a sign of being "bad." Furthermore, they believe that "badness" is permanent. This sense of being a bad person may persist into middle childhood and on into adulthood.

Individual differences in self-esteem may hinge on whether children think their traits and attributes are fixed or can be changed (Harter, 1998). Children who believe their attributes are permanent tend to become demoralized when, say, they fail a test, believing there is nothing they can do to improve. Often these children attribute poor performance or social rejection to their own personality deficiencies, which they believe they are helpless to change. Rather than trying new ways to gain approval, they repeat unsuccessful strategies or just give up. Children with high self-esteem, by contrast, tend to attribute failure or disappointment to factors outside themselves or to the need to try harder. If initially unsuccessful or rejected they persevere, trying new strategies until they find one that works (Erdley, Cain, Loomis, Dumas-Hines, & Dweck, 1997; Pomerantz & Saxon, 2001). Children with high self-esteem tend to have parents and teachers who give specific, focused feedback rather than criticizing the child as a person ("Look, the tag on your shirt is showing in front," not "Can't you see your shirt is on backwards? When are you going to learn to dress yourself?").

What's Your View?

- Can you think of ways in which your parents or other adults helped you develop self-esteem?

Checkpoint

Can you . . .

- ✔ Explain the significance of Erikson's third stage of personality development?
- ✔ Tell how young children's self-esteem differs from that of older children?
- ✔ Describe how the "helpless pattern" arises and how it can affect children's reactions to social rejection?

Gender

Gender identity, awareness of one's femaleness or maleness and all it implies in a particular society, is an important aspect of the developing self-concept. As we have seen, Isabel Allende's awareness of what it meant to be female in a "man's world" went back to her early years.

How different are young boys and girls? What causes those differences? How do children develop gender identity, and how does it affect their attitudes and behavior?

Guidepost

3. How do boys and girls become aware of the meaning of gender, and what explains differences in behavior between the sexes?

gender identity Awareness, developed in early childhood, that one is male or female.

Gender Differences

Gender differences are psychological or behavioral differences between males and females. How pronounced are these differences?

Measurable differences between baby boys and girls are few. The two sexes are equally sensitive to touch and tend to teethe, sit up, and walk at about the same ages (Maccoby, 1980). Girls do seem to have a *biological* advantage; they are less vulnerable than boys from conception on, develop faster, are less reactive to stress, and are more likely to survive infancy (Keenan & Shaw, 1997). On the other hand, baby boys are a bit longer and heavier than baby girls and may be slightly stronger. An analysis of a large number of

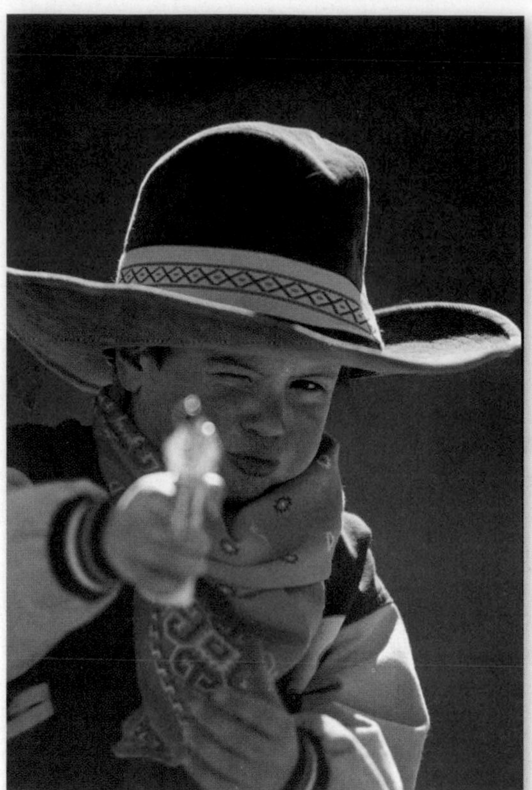

This preschool boy dressed as a gunslinger has developed a strong sense of gender roles. The clearest behavioral difference between young boys and young girls is boys' greater aggressiveness.

studies found baby boys more active than baby girls, though this difference is not consistently documented (Eaton & Enns, 1986).

One of the earliest *behavioral* differences, appearing as early as age 2, is in the choice of toys and play activities and of playmates of the same sex (Turner & Gervai, 1995). While some gender differences become more pronounced after age 3, boys and girls on average remain more alike than different. The clearest difference is that boys, from preschool age on, show more overt aggression than girls, both physically and verbally (Coie & Dodge, 1998; Turner & Gervai, 1995). Most studies find that girls are more empathic and prosocial (Keenan & Shaw, 1997), and some find that girls are more compliant and cooperative with parents and seek adult approval more than boys do (N. Eisenberg, Fabes, Schaller, & Miller, 1989; M. L. Hoffman, 1977; Maccoby, 1980; Turner & Gervai, 1995).

Intelligence test scores show no overall gender differences (Keenan & Shaw, 1997). This is not surprising, since the most widely used tests are designed to eliminate gender bias (Neisser et al., 1996). However, there are differences in scores on specific abilities. Females tend to do better at verbal tasks (but not analogies), at mathematical computation, and at tasks requiring fine motor and perceptual skills, while males excel in most spatial abilities and in abstract mathematical and scientific reasoning (Halpern, 1997).

Some of these cognitive differences begin quite early in life. Girls' superiority in perceptual speed and verbal fluency appears during infancy and toddlerhood, and boys' greater ability to mentally manipulate figures and shapes and solve mazes becomes evident early in the preschool years. Other differences do not become apparent until preadolescence or beyond (Halpern, 1997; Levine et al., 1999).

As toddlers, boys and girls are equally likely to hit, bite, and throw temper tantrums, and they are just as likely to show "difficult" temperaments. Around age 4, however, problem behavior diminishes in girls, whereas boys tend to get in trouble or "act up." This absence of problem behavior among girls persists until adolescence, when they become more prone to anxiety and depression (Keenan & Shaw, 1997).

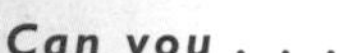

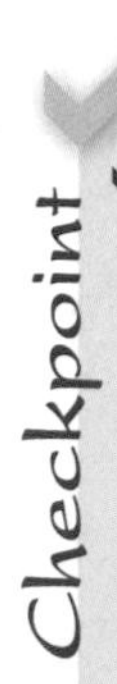

Checkpoint

Can you . . .

✔ Summarize the main behavioral and cognitive differences between boys and girls?

Possible reasons for this divergence may lie in the biological and cognitive differences just discussed. Lower reactivity to stress may enable girls to deal with frustration or anger in a more controlled way, and girls' greater facility with language may enable them to communicate their feelings in healthier ways. Another reason may be a difference in the way boys and girls are socialized. Girls, more than boys, are taught to control themselves, to share toys, and to think about how their actions affect others; and their greater empathic ability may help them internalize social standards (Keenan & Shaw, 1997). Girls talk about their experiences in more detail than boys do, and they tend to talk more about feelings, people, and relationships (Buckner & Fivush, 1998).

We need to remember, of course, that gender differences are valid for large groups of boys and girls but not necessarily for individuals. By knowing a child's sex, we cannot predict whether that *particular* boy or girl will be faster, stronger, smarter, more obedient, or more assertive than another child.

Perspectives on Gender Development: Nature and Nurture

What accounts for gender differences, and why do some of them emerge with age? The most influential explanations, until recently, centered on the differing experiences and social expectations that boys and girls meet almost from birth (Halpern, 1997; Neisser et al., 1996). These experiences and expectations concern three related aspects of gender identity: *gender roles, gender-typing,* and *gender stereotypes.*

Gender roles are the behaviors, interests, attitudes, skills, and personality traits that a culture considers appropriate for males or females. All societies have gender roles. Historically, in most cultures, as in Isabel Allende's Chile, women have been expected to devote most of their time to caring for the household and children, while men were providers and protectors. Women were expected to be compliant and nurturant; men, to be active, aggressive, and competitive. It is these culturally defined roles that Allende rebelled against. Today, gender roles in western cultures have become more diverse and more flexible than before.

gender roles Behaviors, interests, attitudes, skills, and traits that a culture considers appropriate for males or for females.

Gender-typing, the process by which children learn and acquire a gender role, takes place early in childhood, but children vary in the degree to which they become gender-typed. **Gender stereotypes** are preconceived generalizations about male or female behavior, such as, "All females are passive and dependent; all males are aggressive and independent." Gender stereotypes pervade many cultures. They are seen to some degree in children as young as $2\frac{1}{2}$ or 3, increase during the preschool years, and reach a peak at age 5 (Haugh, Hoffman, & Cowan, 1980; Ruble & Martin, 1998; J. E. Williams & Best, 1982). Preschoolers—and even much older children—often attribute positive qualities to their own sex and negative qualities to the other sex (Egan & Perry, 2001; Ruble & Martin, 1998; Underwood, Schockner, & Hurley, 2001). Still, among preschoolers, *both* boys and girls call boys strong, fast, and cruel, and girls fearful and helpless (Ruble & Martin, 1998).

gender-typing Socialization process whereby children, at an early age, learn appropriate gender roles.

gender stereotypes Preconceived generalizations about male or female role behavior.

How do children acquire gender roles, and why do they adopt gender stereotypes? Are these purely social constructs, or do they reflect underlying biological differences between males and females? Do social and cultural influences create gender differences, or merely accentuate them?

Today investigators are uncovering evidence of biological explanations for gender differences: genetic, hormonal, and neurological. These explanations are not either or. Both nature and nurture probably play important parts in what it means to be male or female. Biological influences are not necessarily universal, inevitable, or unchangeable; nor are social and cultural influences easily overcome.

Let's look, then, at four perspectives on gender development (summarized in Table 8-1 on page 276): *biological, psychoanalytic, cognitive,* and *socialization-based* approaches. Each of these perspectives can contribute to our understanding, but none fully explains why boys and girls turn out differently in some respects and not in others.

Biological Approach The existence of similar gender roles in many cultures suggests that some gender differences may be biologically based. How do biological differences affect behavior?

By age 5, when the brain reaches approximate adult size, boys' brains are about 10 percent larger than girls' brains, mostly because boys have more gray matter in the cerebral cortex, whereas girls have greater neuronal density. What these findings may tell us about brain organization and functioning is unknown (Reiss, Abrams, Singer, Ross, & Denckla, 1996).

We do have evidence that size differences in the *corpus callosum,* the band of tissue joining the right and left cortical hemispheres, are correlated with verbal fluency (Hines, Chiu, McAdams, Bentler, & Lipcamon 1992). Since girls have a larger corpus callosum, better coordination between the two hemispheres may help explain girls' superior verbal abilities (Halpern, 1997).

Hormones in the bloodstream before or about the time of birth may affect the developing brain and influence gender differences. The male hormone testosterone, along with low levels of the neurotransmitter serotonin, seems related to aggressiveness, competitiveness, and dominance, perhaps through action on certain brain structures, such as the hypothalamus and amygdala (Bernhardt, 1997). Attempts also have been made to link prenatal hormonal activity with other aspects of brain

Table 8-1 Four Perspectives on Gender Development

Theories	Major Theorists	Key Processes	Basic Beliefs
Biological Approach		Genetic, neurological, and hormonal activity	Many or most behavioral differences between the sexes can be traced to biological differences.
Psychoanalytic Approach			
Psychosexual theory	Sigmund Freud	Resolution of unconscious emotional conflict	Gender identity occurs when child identifies with same-sex parent.
Cognitive Approach			
Cognitive-developmental theory	Lawrence Kohlberg	Self-categorization	Once child learns she is a girl or he is a boy, child sorts information about behavior by gender and acts accordingly.
Gender-schema theory	Sandra Bem, Carol Lynn Martin, & Charles F. Halverson	Self-categorization based on processing of cultural information	Child organizes information about what is considered appropriate for a boy or a girl on the basis of what a particular culture dictates, and behaves accordingly. Child sorts by gender because the culture dictates that gender is an important schema.
Socialization Approach			
Social cognitive theory	Albert Bandura	Modeling, reinforcement, and teaching	Gender-typing is a result of interpretation, evaluation, and internalization of socially transmitted standards.

functioning, such as those involved in spatial and verbal skills (Neisser et al., 1996), but this research is controversial (Ruble & Martin, 1998).

Other research focuses on children with unusual hormonal histories. Girls with a disorder called congenital adrenal hyperplasia (CAH) have unusually high prenatal levels of *androgens* (male sex hormones). Although raised as girls, they tend to prefer "boys' toys," rough play, and male playmates, and to show strong spatial skills. *Estrogens* (female hormones), on the other hand, seem to have less influence on boys' gender-typed behavior. Since these studies are natural experiments, they cannot establish cause and effect; other factors besides hormonal differences, such as early interactions with parents, may play a role. Also, hormonal differences may themselves be affected by environmental or other factors. In any case, such atypical patterns of behavior have not been found in children with normal hormonal variations (Ruble & Martin, 1998).

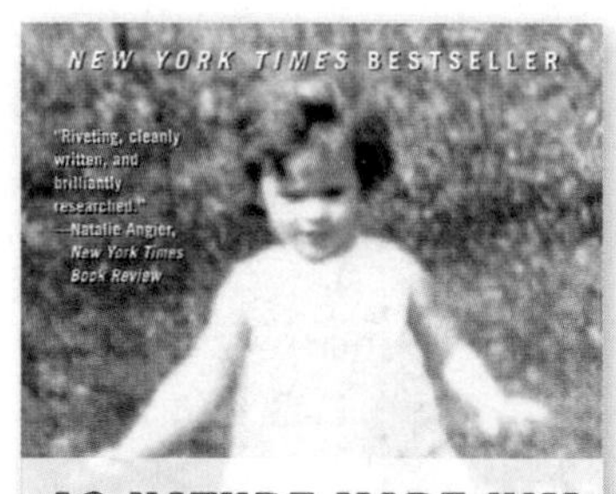

Is gender identity rooted in biology? In the famous case described in this book, an infant boy whose penis was cut off during circumcision was raised as a girl but later rejected female identity and lived as a male.

Perhaps the most dramatic examples of biologically based research have to do with infants born with ambiguous sexual organs (part male and part female). John Money and his colleagues (Money, Hampson, & Hampson, 1955) developed guidelines for such cases, recommending that the child be assigned as early as possible to the gender that holds the potential for the most nearly normal functioning. These guidelines also have been applied when sexual organs were accidentally damaged.

In the case of a 7-month-old boy whose penis was accidentally cut off during circumcision, the decision was made at 17 months to rear the child as a girl, and four months later doctors performed surgical reconstruction (Money & Ehrhardt, 1972). Although initially described as developing into a normal female, the child later rejected female identity and, at puberty, switched to living as a male. After a second surgical reconstruction, he married a woman and adopted her children. The implicit lesson was that gender identity may be rooted in chromosomal structure or prenatal development and cannot easily be changed (Diamond & Sigmundson, 1997).

A recent study of 27 male children born without penises supports this conclusion. Although 25 of these infants were raised as girls, in childhood they considered themselves boys and engaged in rough-and-tumble play, suggesting that hormones do play a powerful role in gender identity (Reiner, 2000).

Psychoanalytic Approach "Daddy, where will you live when I grow up and marry Mommy?" asks Timmy, age 4. From the psychoanalytic perspective, Timmy's question is part of his acquisition of gender identity. That process, according to Freud, is one of **identification,** the adoption of characteristics, beliefs, attitudes, values, and behaviors of the parent of the same sex. Freud and other classical psychoanalytic theorists considered identification an important personality development of early childhood. Some social learning theorists also have used the term.

identification In Freudian theory, the process by which a young child adopts characteristics, beliefs, attitudes, values, and behaviors of the parent of the same sex.

According to classical Freudian theory, identification will occur for Timmy when he represses or gives up the wish to possess the parent of the other sex (his mother) and identifies with the parent of the same sex (his father). Although this explanation for gender development has been influential, it has been difficult to test. Despite some evidence that preschoolers tend to act more affectionately toward the opposite-sex parent and more aggressively toward the same-sex parent (Westen, 1998), the theory has little research support. (Certainly it does not seem to apply to Allende, who felt protective toward her mother and resentful of the men in her family.) Most developmental psychologists today favor other explanations.

Cognitive Approach Sarah figures out she is a girl because people call her a girl. She figures out that she will always be a girl. She comes to understand gender the same way she comes to understand everything else: by actively thinking about and constructing her own gender-typing. This is the heart of Lawrence Kohlberg's (1966) cognitive-developmental theory.

According to Kohlberg, children classify themselves as male or female and then organize their behavior around that classification. They do this by adopting behaviors they perceive as consistent with their gender. Thus, Sarah prefers dolls to trucks because she views playing with dolls as consistent with her idea of herself as a girl. According to Kohlberg, **gender constancy,** more recently called *sex-category constancy*—a child's realization that his or her sex will always be the same—leads to the acquisition of gender roles. Once children realize they are permanently male or female, they adopt what they see as gender-appropriate behaviors.

gender constancy Awareness that one will always be male or female. Also called *sex-category constancy.*

Gender constancy seems to develop in three stages (Ruble & Martin, 1998; Szkrybalo & Ruble, 1999). First, children become aware of their own gender and that of others. Next, a girl realizes that she will grow up to be a woman, and a boy that he will grow up to be a man—in other words, that gender remains the same across time. Children at this stage may base judgments about gender on superficial external appearances and stereotyped behaviors. Finally—sometime between ages 3 and 7, or

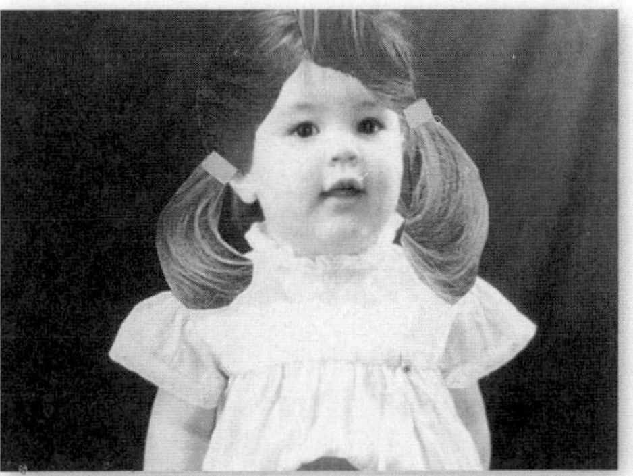

In one study, children saw three photos of this little boy: nude, dressed in boys' clothes, and dressed in girls' clothes. Preschoolers who identified the child's sex by genitals rather than by dress were more likely to show gender constancy—to know that they themselves would remain the sex they were.

even later—comes the realization that a girl remains a girl even if she has a short haircut and wears pants, and a boy remains a boy even if he has long hair and earrings.

There is little evidence for Kohlberg's view that gender constancy is the key to gender-typing. Long before children attain the final stage of gender constancy, they show gender-typed preferences (Bussey & Bandura, 1992; Ruble & Martin, 1998). They categorize activities and objects by gender, know a lot about what males and females do, and often acquire gender-appropriate behaviors (G. D. Levy & Carter, 1989; Luecke-Aleksa, Anderson, Collins, & Schmitt, 1995). Even at $2\frac{1}{2}$, girls show more interest in dolls and boys in cars, and both begin to prefer being with children of their own sex (Ruble & Martin, 1998).

It is possible that gender constancy, once achieved, may further sensitize children to gender-related information (Ruble & Martin, 1998). Five-year-old boys who have reached or are on the brink of gender constancy pay more attention to male characters on television and watch more sports and action programs than other boys their age (Luecke-Aleksa et al., 1995). Later, children develop more complex beliefs about gender and become more flexible in their views about gender roles (Ruble & Martin, 1998; M. G. Taylor, 1996).

A second cognitive approach, which combines elements of cognitive-developmental and social learning theory, is **gender-schema theory.** Among its leading proponents is Sandra Bem (1983, 1985, 1993); others are Carol Lynn Martin and Charles F. Halverson (1981).

gender-schema theory Theory, proposed by Bem, that children socialize themselves in their gender roles by developing a mentally organized network of information about what it means to be male or female in a particular culture.

A *schema* is a mentally organized network of information that influences a particular category of behavior. According to gender-schema theory, children begin (very likely in infancy) to categorize events and people, organizing their observations around the schema, or category, of gender. They organize information on this basis because they see that their society classifies people that way: males and females wear different clothes, play with different toys, and use separate bathrooms. Once children know what sex they are, they take on gender roles by developing a concept of what it means to be male or female in their culture. Children then match their own behavior to their culture's gender schema—what boys and girls are "supposed" to be and do.

According to this theory, gender schemas promote gender stereotypes by influencing judgments about behavior. When a new boy his age moves in next door, 4-year-old Brandon knocks on his door, carrying a toy truck. He assumes that the new boy will like the same toys he likes: "boys' toys." Children are quick to accept gender labels; when told that an unfamiliar toy is for the other sex, they will drop it like a hot potato, and they expect others to do the same (C. L. Martin, Eisenbud, & Rose, 1995; Ruble & Martin, 1998). However, it is not clear that gender schemas are at the root of this behavior. Nor does gender-schema theory explain why some children show less stereotyped behavior than others (Bussey & Bandura, 1992, 1999; Ruble & Martin, 1998).

Another problem with both gender-schema theory and Kohlberg's theory is that gender-typing does not necessarily become stronger with increased gender knowledge; in fact, the opposite is often true (Bussey & Bandura, 1999). One explanation, which has some research support, is that while children are constructing and then consolidating their gender schemas (around ages 4 to 6), they notice and remember only information consistent with them. Later, around age 8, schemas become more complex as children begin to take in and integrate contradictory information, such as the fact that some girls like trucks (Ruble & Martin, 1998; Welch-Ross & Schmidt, 1996).

Cognitive approaches to gender development have made an important contribution by exploring how children think about gender and what they know about it at various ages. However, these approaches do not fully explain the link between knowledge and conduct. What prompts children to act out gender roles, and why do some children become more strongly gender-typed than others? Some investigators point to the role of selective socialization (Bussey & Bandura, 1992).

Socialization-Based Approach According to Albert Bandura's (1986; Bussey & Bandura, 1999) **social cognitive theory** (an expanded version of social learning theory), children learn gender roles through *socialization,* the process by which they acquire socially accepted standards of behavior in their culture. Bandura sees gender identity as the outcome of a complex array of interacting influences, personal and social. The way a child interprets experiences with parents, teachers, peers, and cultural institutions plays a central part.

social cognitive theory Albert Bandura's expansion of social learning theory; holds that children learn gender roles through socialization.

As in traditional social learning theory, children initially acquire gender roles by observing models. Children generally pick models they see as powerful or nurturing. Typically, one model is a parent, often of the same sex, but children also pattern their behavior after other adults or after peers. (Isabel Allende, uncomfortable with the subordinate roles of the women she saw, sought to model herself after her grandfather.) Behavioral feedback, together with direct teaching by parents and other adults, reinforces gender-typing. A boy who models his behavior after his father or male peers is commended for acting "like a boy." A girl gets compliments on a pretty dress or hairstyle.

The socialization process begins in infancy, long before a conscious understanding of gender begins to form. Gradually, as children begin to regulate their own activities, standards of gender-related behavior become internalized. A child no longer needs praise, rebukes, or a model's presence to act in socially appropriate ways. Children feel good about themselves when they live up to their internal standards and feel bad if they don't. A substantial part of this shift from socially guided control to self-regulation of gender preferences may take place between ages 3 and 4 (Bussey & Bandura, 1992).

Early childhood is a prime period for socialization. Let's look more closely at how parents, peers, and the media influence gender development.

Family Influences As we discussed in Chapter 6, parental shaping of boys' and girls' personalities appears to begin very early. However, it is not clear how much effect parental influences actually have (Ruble & Martin, 1998). Some studies have found that parental treatment affects children's gender *knowledge* more than their *behavior* (Fagot & Leinbach, 1995; Turner & Gervai, 1995). A girl may know that baseball bats are "supposed" to be for boys but may use one anyway.

One reason for discrepancies in findings may be that researchers study different kinds of gender-related behavior and use different measuring instruments (Turner & Gervai, 1995). Gender-typing has many facets, and the particular combination of "masculine" and "feminine" traits and behaviors that a child acquires is an individual matter. Also, today many parents' own gender roles are less sterotyped than they once were.

In general, boys are more strongly gender-socialized with regard to play preferences than girls. Parents, especially fathers, tend to show more discomfort if a boy plays with a doll than if a girl plays with a truck (Lytton & Romney, 1991; Sandnabba & Ahlberg, 1999). Girls have more freedom than boys in their clothes, games, and choice of playmates (Miedzian, 1991; Sandnabba & Ahlberg, 1999).

A father who encourages his son to engage in traditionally masculine activities, such as adjusting a bicycle seat, delivers a powerful message about what kinds of interests are appropriate for a boy.

What's Your View?

- Should parents encourage girls to play with trucks and boys with dolls?
- Which is closer to your own views? Explain.
  1. Family A thinks girls should wear only ruffly dresses and boys should never wash dishes or cry.
  2. Family Z treats sons and daughters exactly alike, without making any references to the children's sex.

In egalitarian households, the father's role in gender socialization seems especially important (Fagot & Leinbach, 1995). In an observational study of 4-year-olds in Cambridge, England, and Budapest, Hungary, children whose fathers did more housework and child care were less aware of gender stereotypes and engaged in less gender-typed play (Turner & Gervai, 1995). Gender-role socialization also tends to be untraditional in families headed by single mothers or fathers who must play both the customary masculine and feminine roles (Leve & Fagot, 1997).

Do siblings influence each other's gender development? Yes, according to a three-year longitudinal study of 198 first- and secondborn siblings (median ages of 10 and 8) and their parents. Secondborns tended to become more like their older siblings in attitudes, personality, and leisure activities. Firstborns were more influenced by their parents and less by their younger siblings (McHale, Updegraff, Helms-Erikson, & Crouter, 2001).

Peer Influences Anna, at age 5, insisted on dressing in a new way. She wanted to wear leggings with a skirt over them, and boots—indoors and out. When her mother asked her why, Anna replied, "Because Katie dresses like this—and Katie's the king of the girls!"

Even in early childhood, the peer group is a major influence on gender-typing (Turner & Gervai, 1995). Peers begin to reinforce gender-typed behavior by age 3, and their influence increases with age. Children show more disapproval of boys who act "like girls" than of girls who act "like boys" (Ruble & Martin, 1998). Although both 3- and 4-year-olds know what behaviors peers consider gender-appropriate, 4-year-olds more consistently apply these judgments to themselves (Bussey & Bandura, 1992).

In the study of British and Hungarian 4-year-olds (Turner & Gervai, 1995), play preferences seemed less affected by parents' gender-typing than were other aspects of the children's behavior; at this age, such choices may be more strongly influenced by peers and the media than by the models children see at home. Generally, however, peer and parental attitudes reinforce each other. Social cognitive theory sees peers not as an independent influence for socialization but as part of a complex cultural system that encompasses parents and other socializing agents as well (Bussey & Bandura, 1999).

Cultural Influences The Russian psychologist Lev Vygotsky analyzed how cultural practices affect development. When, for example, a Hindu girl in a village in Nepal touched the plow that her brother was using, she was severely rebuked. In this way she learned that as a female she was restricted from acts her brother was expected to perform (Skinner, 1989). Isabel Allende, at 5, received similar instruction when told that she must sit and knit with her legs together while her brothers were out climbing trees.

Television is a major channel for transmission of cultural attitudes toward gender (Durkin & Bradley, 1998). Although women in programs and commercials are now more likely to be working outside the home and men sometimes care for children or do the marketing, for the most part life as portrayed on screen continues to be more stereotyped than life in the real world (Coltrane & Adams, 1997; Ruble & Martin, 1998).

Social cognitive theory predicts that children who watch a lot of television will become more gender-typed by imitating the models they see on the screen. Dramatic supporting evidence emerged from a natural experiment in several Canadian towns that obtained access to television transmission for the first time. Children who had had relatively unstereotyped attitudes showed marked increases in traditional views two years later (Kimball, 1986). In another study, children who watched a series of nontraditional episodes, such as a father and son cooking together, had less stereotyped views than children who had not seen the series (J. Johnston & Ettema, 1982).

Children's books have long been a source of gender stereotypes. Today friendship between boys and girls is portrayed more often, and girls are braver and more resourceful. Still, male characters predominate, females are more likely to need help, and males are more likely to give it (Beal, 1994; Evans, 1998).

Major strengths of the socialization approach include the breadth and multiplicity of processes it examines and the scope for individual differences it reveals. But this very complexity makes it difficult to establish clear causal connections between the way children are raised and the way they think and act. Just what aspects of the home environment and the peer culture promote gender-typing? Underlying this question is a chicken-and-egg problem: Do parents and peers treat boys and girls differently because they *are* different, or because the culture says they *should be* different? Does differential treatment *produce* or *reflect* gender differences? Perhaps, as social cognitive theory suggests, there is a bidirectional relationship. Further research may help to show how socializing agents mesh with children's own tendencies with regard to gender-related attitudes and behavior.

Checkpoint

Can you . . .

- ✔ Distinguish among four approaches to the study of gender development?
- ✔ Assess evidence for biological explanations of gender differences?
- ✔ Compare how various theories explain the acquisition of gender roles, and assess the support for each theory?

Play: The Business of Early Childhood

Play is the work of the young, and it contributes to all domains of development. Through play, children stimulate the senses, learn how to use their muscles, coordinate sight with movement, gain mastery over their bodies, and acquire new skills. As they sort blocks of different shapes, count how many they can pile on each other, or announce that "my tower is bigger than yours," they lay the foundation for mathematical concepts (Jarrell, 1998). As they play with computers, they learn new ways of thinking (Silvern, 1998).

Guidepost

4. How do preschoolers play, and how does play contribute to and reflect development?

Preschoolers engage in different types of play at different ages. Particular children have different styles of play, and they play at different things. Researchers categorize children's play by its *content* (what children do when they play) and its *social dimension* (whether they play alone or with others).

Types of Play

Carol, at 3, "talked for" a doll, using a deeper voice than her own. Miguel, at 4, wore a kitchen towel as a cape and "flew" around as Batman. These children were engaged in pretend play involving make-believe people or situations.

functional play Play involving repetitive muscular movements.

constructive play Play involving use of objects or materials to make something.

pretend play Play involving imaginary people or situations; also called *fantasy play, dramatic play,* or *imaginative play.*

Pretend play is one of four categories of play identified by Piaget and others as showing increasing levels of cognitive complexity (Piaget, 1951; Smilansky, 1968). The simplest form, which begins during infancy, is active **functional play** involving repetitive muscular movements (such as rolling or bouncing a ball). As gross motor skills improve, preschoolers run, jump, skip, hop, throw, and aim.

The second level of cognitive complexity is seen in toddlers' and preschoolers' **constructive play** (using objects or materials to make something, such as a house of blocks or a crayon drawing). Four-year-olds in preschools or day care centers may spend more than half their time in this kind of play, which becomes more elaborate by ages 5 and 6 (J. E. Johnson, 1998).

The third level, **pretend play,** also called *fantasy play, dramatic play,* or *imaginative play,* rests on the symbolic function, which emerges during the last part of the second year, near the end of the sensorimotor stage (Piaget, 1962). Pretend play typically increases during the preschool years and then declines as school-age children become more involved in the fourth cognitive level of play, *formal games with rules*—organized games with known procedures and penalties, such as hopscotch and marbles.

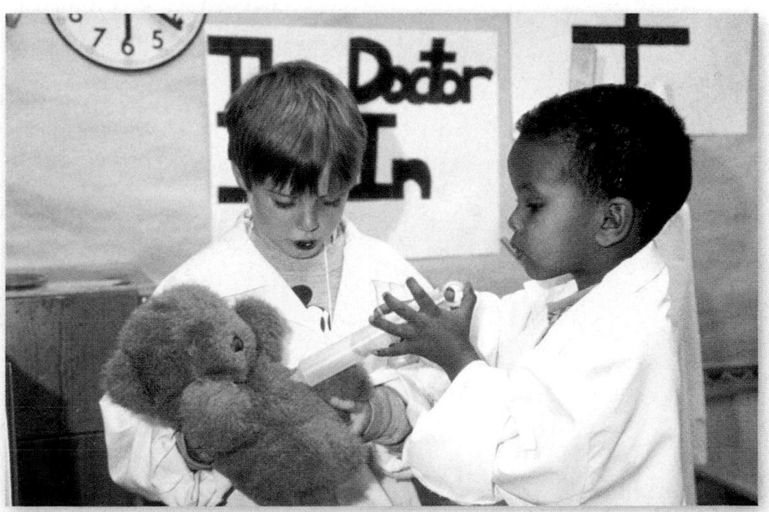

This young "veterinarian" examining his toy dog is showing an important cognitive development of early childhood, which underlies imaginative play: the ability to use symbols to stand for people or things in the real world.

In pretend play, children try out roles (as Miguel did in playing Batman), cope with uncomfortable emotions, gain understanding of other people's viewpoints, and construct an image of the social world. They develop problem-solving and language skills and experience the joy of creativity (Bodrova & Leong, 1998; J. I. F. Davidson, 1998; Furth & Kane, 1992; J. E. Johnson, 1998; Nourot, 1998; Singer & Singer, 1990). By making "tickets" for an imaginary train trip or "reading" eye charts in a "doctor's office," they build emergent literacy (Christie, 1991, 1998).

An estimated 10 to 17 percent of preschoolers' play and 33 percent of kindergartners' is pretend play, often using dolls and real or imaginary props (Bretherton, 1984; Garner, 1998; J. E. Johnson, 1998; K. H. Rubin, Fein, & Vandenberg, 1983). Children who often play imaginatively tend to cooperate more with other children and to be more popular and more joyful than those who don't (Singer & Singer, 1990). Children who watch a great deal of television tend to play less imaginatively, perhaps because they are accustomed to passively absorbing images rather than generating their own (Howes & Matheson, 1992).

The Social Dimension of Play

In a classic study done in the 1920s, Mildred B. Parten (1932) identified six types of early play, ranging from the least to the most social (see Table 8-2). She found that as children get older, their play tends to become more social—that is, more interactive and cooperative. At first children play alone, then alongside other children, and finally, together.

Today most researchers view Parten's characterization of children's play development as too simplistic. Children of all ages engage in all of Parten's categories of play (K. H. Rubin, Bukowski, & Parker, 1998).

Is solitary play less mature than social play? Parten and others suggested that children who play alone may be at risk of developing social, psychological, and edu-

Table 8-2 Parten's Categories of Social and Nonsocial Play

Category	Description
Unoccupied behavior	The child does not seem to be playing, but watches anything of momentary interest.
Onlooker behavior	The child spends most of the time watching other children play. The onlooker talks to them, asking questions or making suggestions, but does not enter into the play. The onlooker is definitely observing particular groups of children rather than anything that happens to be exciting.
Solitary independent play	The child plays alone with toys that are different from those used by nearby children and makes no effort to get close to them.
Parallel play	The child plays independently, but among the other children, playing with toys like those used by the other children, but not necessarily playing with them in the same way. Playing *beside* rather than *with* the others, the parallel player does not try to influence the other children's play.
Associative play	The child plays with other children. They talk about their play, borrow and lend toys, follow one another, and try to control who may play in the group. All the children play similarly if not identically; there is no division of labor and no organization around any goal. Each child acts as she or he wishes and is interested more in being with the other children than in the activity itself.
Cooperative or organized supplementary play	The child plays in a group organized for some goal—to make something, play a formal game, or dramatize a situation. One or two children control who belongs to the group and direct activities. By a division of labor, children take on different roles and supplement each other's efforts.

Source: Adapted from Parten, 1932, pp. 249–251.

cational problems. Actually, much nonsocial play consists of activities that *foster* cognitive, physical, and social development. In one study of 4-year-olds, some kinds of nonsocial play, such as *parallel constructive play* (for example, working on puzzles near another child who is also doing so) were most common among children who were good problem solvers, were popular with other children, and were seen by teachers as socially skilled (K. Rubin, 1982). Such play may reflect independence and maturity or simple preference, not poor social adjustment (Harrist, Zain, Bates, Dodge, & Pettit, 1997; K. H. Rubin et al., 1998). On the other hand, a Canadian study found that kindergarten boys (but not girls) who engage in solitary passive play—drawing pictures or building with blocks while peers are playing nearby—tend to be shy or maladjusted (Coplan, Gavinski-Molina, Lagacé-Séguin, & Wichman, 2001).

One kind of play that generally becomes more social during the preschool years is imaginative play, which shifts from solitary pretending to dramatic play involving other children (K. H. Rubin et al., 1998; Singer & Singer, 1990). Young children follow unspoken rules in organizing dramatic play, staking out territory ("I'm the daddy; you're the mommy"), negotiating ("Okay, I'll be the daddy tomorrow"), or setting the scene ("Watch out—there's a train coming!"). As imaginative play becomes increasingly collaborative, story lines become more complex and more innovative. Dramatic play offers rich opportunities to practice interpersonal and language skills and to explore social roles and conventions (Bodrova & Leong, 1998; Christie, 1991; J. E. Johnson, 1998; Nourot, 1998).

What's Your View?

- How do you think use of computers might affect preschool children's cognitive and social development?

How Gender Influences Play

A tendency toward sex segregation in play seems to be universal across cultures. It is common among preschoolers as young as 3 and becomes even more common in middle childhood (Maccoby, 1988, 1990, 1994; Ramsey & Lasquade, 1996; Snyder, West, Stockemer, Gibbons, & Almquist-Parks, 1996).

Boys and girls play differently (Serbin, Moller, Gulko, Powlishta, & Colburne, 1994). Most boys like physical play in fairly large groups; girls are inclined to quieter play with one playmate (Benenson, 1993). The difference is not just based on liking different kinds of activities. Even when boys and girls play with the same toys, they play more socially with others of the same sex (Neppl & Murray, 1997). Boys play more boisterously; girls play more cooperatively, taking turns to avoid clashes (Maccoby, 1980).

Children's developing gender concepts seem to influence dramatic play. Whereas boys' stories often involve danger and discord, such as mock battles, girls' plots generally focus on maintaining or restoring orderly social relationships, as in playing house (Fagot & Leve, 1998; Nourot, 1998).

From an evolutionary viewpoint, gender differences in children's play provide practice for adult behaviors important for reproduction and survival. Boys' rough-and-tumble play mirrors adult males' competition for dominance and status, and for fertile mates. Girls' play parenting prepares them to care for the young (Geary, 1999).

How Culture Influences Play

The frequency of specific forms of play differs across cultures and is influenced by the play environments adults set up for children, which in turn reflect cultural values (Bodrova & Leong, 1998).

One observational study compared 48 middle-class Korean American and 48 middle-class Anglo-American children in separate preschools (Farver, Kim, & Lee, 1995). The Anglo-American preschools, in keeping with typical American values, encouraged independent thinking, problem solving, and active involvement in learning by letting children select from a wide range of activities. The Korean American preschool, in keeping with traditional Korean values, emphasized development of academic skills and completion of tasks. The Anglo-American preschools encouraged social interchange among children and collaborative activities with teachers. In the Korean American preschool, children were allowed to talk and play only during outdoor recess.

Not surprisingly, the Anglo-American children engaged in more social play, whereas the Korean Americans engaged in more unoccupied or parallel play. Korean American children played more cooperatively, often offering toys to other children—very likely a reflection of their culture's emphasis on group harmony. Anglo-American children were more aggressive and often responded negatively to other children's suggestions, reflecting the competitiveness of their culture.

An ethnographic study compared pretend play among middle-class $2\frac{1}{2}$- to 4-year-olds in five Irish American families in the United States and nine Chinese families in Taiwan. Play was primarily social in both cultures, but Irish American children were more likely to pretend with other children and Chinese children with caregivers, who often used the play as a vehicle to teach proper conduct—a major emphasis in Chinese culture (Haight, Wang, Fung, Williams, & Mintz, 1999). Broadening the study of play to a wider variety of cultures can enhance our knowledge of the meanings and purposes of play.

Checkpoint

Can you . . .

- ✔ Describe four cognitive levels of play, according to Piaget and others, and six categories of social and nonsocial play, according to Parten?
- ✔ Explain how cognitive and social dimensions of play may be connected?
- ✔ Tell how gender and culture influence the way children play, and give examples?

Parenting

Guidepost

5. What forms of discipline do parents use, and how do parenting styles and practices influence development?

As children gradually become their own persons, their upbringing can be a complex challenge. Parents must deal with small people who have minds and wills of their own, but who still have a lot to learn about what kinds of behavior work well in society. How do parents handle discipline? Are some ways of parenting more effective than others?

Forms of Discipline

discipline Methods of molding children's character and of teaching them to exercise self-control and engage in acceptable behavior.

Discipline refers to methods of teaching children character, self-control, and moral values and behavior. It can be a powerful tool for socialization with the goal of developing *self*-discipline. What forms of discipline work best? Researchers have looked at a wide range of techniques.

Behaviorist Techniques: Reinforcement and Punishment "What are we going to do with that child?" Noel's mother says. "The more we punish him, the more he misbehaves!"

Parents sometimes punish children to stop undesirable behavior, but children usually learn more from being reinforced for good behavior (refer back to Chapter 2). *External* reinforcements may be tangible (candy, money, toys, or gold stars) or intangible (a smile, a word of praise, a hug, extra attention, or a special privilege). Whatever the reinforcement, the child must see it as rewarding and must receive it fairly consistently after showing the desired behavior. Eventually, the behavior should provide its own *internal* reward: a sense of pleasure or accomplishment. In Noel's case, his parents often ignore him when he behaves well but scold or spank him when he acts up. In other words, they unwittingly reinforce his *mis*behavior by giving him attention when he does what they do *not* want him to do.

Still, at times punishment—such as isolation, or denial of privileges—is necessary. Children may have to be prevented from running out into traffic or hitting another child. Sometimes a child is willfully defiant. In such situations, punishment, if consistent, immediate, and clearly tied to the offense, may be effective. It should be administered calmly, in private, and aimed at eliciting compliance, not guilt. It is most effective when accompanied by a short, simple explanation (AAP Committee on Psychosocial Aspects of Child and Family Health, 1998; Baumrind, 1996a, 1996b).

However, some punishment can be counterproductive. Children who are punished harshly and frequently may have trouble interpreting other people's actions and words; they may attribute hostile intentions where none exist (B. Weiss, Dodge, Bates, & Pettit, 1992). Young children who have been punished harshly may later act aggressively, even though the punishment is intended to stop what a parent sees as purposely aggressive behavior (Nix et al., 1999). Or such children may become passive because they feel helpless. Children may become frightened if parents lose control and may eventually try to avoid a punitive parent, undermining the parent's ability to influence behavior (Grusec & Goodnow, 1994).

Corporal punishment has been defined as "the use of physical force with the intention of causing a child to experience pain, but not injury, for the purpose of correction or control of the child's behavior" (Straus, 1994a, p. 4). It can include spanking, hitting, slapping, pinching, shaking (which can be fatal to infants), and other physical acts. Corporal punishment is a pervasive part of the socialization of many children. Many people believe that it is more effective than other remedies and harmless if done in moderation by loving parents. However, a growing body of evidence suggests that these beliefs are untrue, that corporal punishment can have serious negative consequences, and that it should not be used (Straus, 1999; Straus & Stewart, 1999; see Box 8-1 on page 286).

corporal punishment Use of physical force with the intention of causing pain, but not injury, to correct or control behavior.

Power Assertion, Induction, and Withdrawal of Love Looking at reinforcement and punishment alone may be an oversimplification of how parents influence behavior. Contemporary research has focused on three broader categories of discipline: *power assertion, induction,* and *temporary withdrawal of love.*

Power assertion is intended to stop or discourage undesirable behavior through physical or verbal enforcement of parental control; it includes demands, threats, withdrawal of privileges, spanking, and other punishments. These were the kinds of techniques used by the feared maid who took care of Isabel Allende and her brothers. **Inductive techniques** are designed to encourage desirable behavior (or discourage undesirable behavior) by reasoning with a child; they include setting limits, demonstrating logical consequences of an action, explaining, discussing, and getting ideas from the child about what is fair. **Withdrawal of love** may include ignoring, isolating, or showing dislike for a child. The choice and effectiveness of a disciplinary strategy may depend on the parent's personality, the child's personality and age, and the quality of their relationship, as well as on culturally based customs and expectations (Grusec & Goodnow, 1994).

power assertion Disciplinary strategy designed to discourage undesirable behavior through physical or verbal enforcement of parental control.

inductive techniques Disciplinary techniques designed to induce desirable behavior by appealing to a child's sense of reason and fairness.

withdrawal of love Disciplinary strategy that may involve ignoring, isolating, or showing dislike for a child.

Induction is usually the most effective method, and power assertion the least effective, of getting children to accept parental standards (M. L. Hoffman, 1970a, 1970b; Jagers, Bingham, & Hans, 1996; McCord, 1996). Inductive reasoning tends to arouse empathy for the victim of wrongdoing, as well as guilt on the part of the wrongdoer (Krevans & Gibbs, 1996). Kindergartners whose mothers reported using reasoning were more likely to see the moral wrongness of behavior that hurts other people (as opposed to merely breaking rules) than children whose mothers took away privileges (Jagers et al., 1996). This may be because removal of privileges encourages children to focus on themselves and their own feelings rather than on the way their behavior affects others (McCord, 1996).

Most parents call upon more than one disciplinary strategy, depending on the situation and their knowledge of their particular child (Grusec, Goodnow, & Kuczynski, 2000). Parents tend to use reasoning to get a child to show concern for others. They use power assertion to stop play that gets too rough, and they use both power assertion and reasoning to deal with lying and stealing (Grusec & Goodnow, 1994).

The strategy parents choose may depend not only on their belief in its effectiveness but on their confidence that they can carry it out. In one observational study of

BOX 8-1

Practically Speaking

The Case Against Corporal Punishment

"Spare the rod and spoil the child" may sound old-fashioned, but corporal punishment has become a live issue today (Gershoff, 2002). While some professionals view corporal punishment as verging on child abuse (Straus, 1994b), others defend it as necessary or desirable in moderation, when prudently administered by loving parents (Baumrind, 1996a, 1996b).

Corporal punishment has diminished in many European countries since the passage of laws against it in Sweden in 1979, followed by Austria, Croatia, Cyprus, Denmark, Finland, Germany, Israel, Italy, Latvia, and Norway. Yet in the United States some professionals—and politicians—advocate corporal punishment more strongly than ever. In 1999 the Arizona and Arkansas legislatures adopted resolutions urging parents and teachers to exercise their right to use it. All states allow parents to do it, though some insist that it be reasonable, appropriate, moderate, or necessary, and some recognize that excessive corporal punishment can be abusive (Gershoff, 2002).

Some form of corporal, or bodily, punishment is widely used on U.S. infants, and it is virtually universal among parents of toddlers. In interviews with a nationally representative sample of 991 parents in 1995, 35 percent reported using corporal punishment—usually hand slapping—on infants during the previous year, and fully 94 percent on 3- and 4-year-olds. About half of the parents continued to use corporal punishment by the time their children were 12, one-third at age 14, and 13 percent at age 17 (Straus & Stewart, 1999).

Why do so many parents use corporal punishment? Probably because it does get children to comply (Gershoff, 2002). However, a large body of research, including analyses of 88 studies conducted over the past six decades, consistently finds negative short-term and long-term outcomes from its use. Apart from the risk of escalation into injury or abuse, these outcomes may include, in childhood, increased physical aggressiveness, antisocial behavior, and delinquency, lack of moral internalization, poor parent-child relationships, and diminished mental health. Outcomes in adulthood can include aggression, criminal or antisocial be-

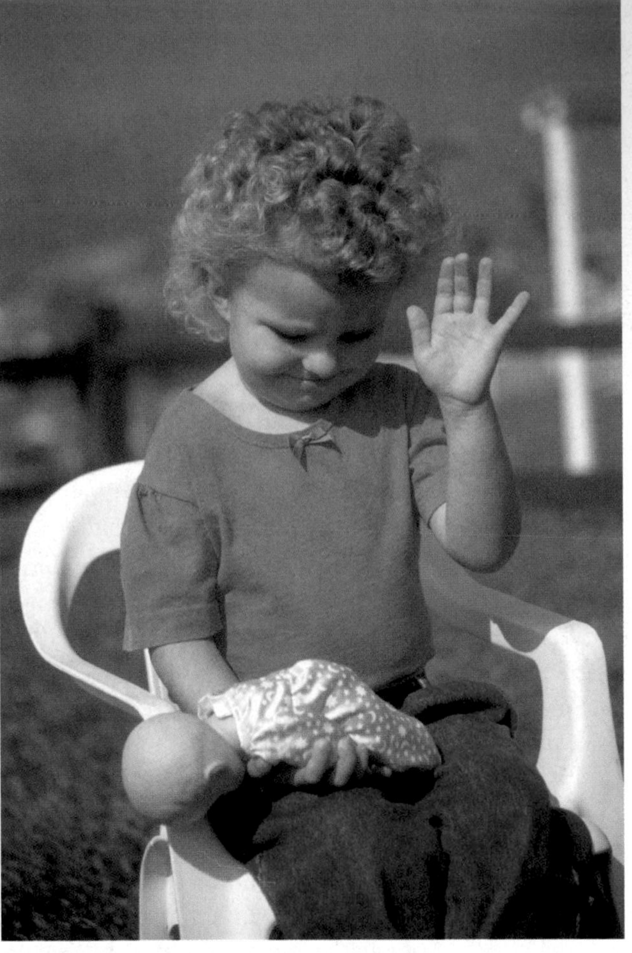

A child who is spanked is likely to imitate that behavior. Studies show that children who are spanked tend to become aggressive.

parental handling of sibling conflicts, mothers were more likely to use inductive techniques, while fathers were more likely to use power-assertive strategies. Still, what both mothers and fathers did most often was not to intervene at all (Perozynski & Kramer, 1999).

The child's cognitive level, temperament, and emotionality may affect the child's response (Grusec et al., 2000). Gentle guidance seems particularly suited to temperamentally fearful or anxious children, who tend to become upset when they misbehave. Such a child will readily internalize parental messages with a minimum of prodding; displays of power would merely make the child more anxious (Kochanska, 1995, 1997a). Shame tends to arise when parents are angry or rejecting and do not use appropriate discipline of any kind (Eisenberg, 2000). Children in such situations may feel unworthy of their parents' attention.

Practically Speaking

BOX 8-1

—continued

havior, anxiety disorders, depression, alcohol problems, and partner or child abuse (Gershoff, 2002; MacMillan et al., 1999; Strassberg, Dodge, Pettit, & Bates, 1994).

Most of this research was cross-sectional or retrospective, or did not consider that the spanked children may have been aggressive in the first place, and that their aggressive behavior (or some other factor) might have led their parents to spank them. Also, corporal punishment rarely occurs in isolation, so we cannot be sure that the observed outcomes are attributable to it, and not to some other form of discipline, such as threats, time-outs, or withdrawal of privileges (Gershoff, 2002).

Since 1997 several large, nationally representative landmark studies (Brezina, 1999; Gunnoe & Mariner, 1997; Simons, Lin, & Gordon, 1998; Strauss & Paschall, 1999; Straus, Sugarman, & Giles-Sims, 1997) have sought to overcome the former defect by taking account of the child's own behavior at the time of first measurement. These studies, which included youngsters ranging from age 3 through adolescence, found that corporal punishment is counterproductive: the more a child receives, the more aggressive or antisocial the child's behavior becomes, and the more likely that child is to show antisocial or other maladaptive behavior as a child and as an adult (Straus & Stewart, 1999).

Why is this so? One answer is that physical punishment stimulates aggressive behavior by leading children to imitate the punisher and to consider infliction of pain an acceptable response to problems. Corporal punishment also may arouse anger and resentment, causing children to focus on their own hurts rather than on the wrong they have done to others, and making them less receptive to parental teachings. Furthermore, as with any punishment, the effectiveness of spanking diminishes with repeated use; children may feel free to misbehave if they are willing to take the consequences. Reliance on physical punishment may weaken parents' authority when children become teenagers, too big and strong to spank, even if spanking were appropriate (AAP Committee on Psychosocial Aspects of Child and Family Health, 1998; Gershoff, 2002; McCord, 1996).

Spanking may even inhibit cognitive development, according to data on 2- to 4-year-olds and 5- to 9-year-olds from the National Longitudinal Study of Youth. Children whose mothers used little or no corporal punishment (such as spanking or hand-slapping) during a two-week period showed greater cognitive gains than children who were hit (Straus & Paschall, 1999).

Opponents of corporal punishment are not against disciplining children, but they maintain there are more effective, less risky or harmful ways to do it. The American Academy of Pediatrics Committee on Psychosocial Aspects of Child and Family Health (1998) urges parents to avoid spanking. Instead, the committee suggests such inductive methods as teaching children to use words to express feelings, giving them choices and helping them evaluate the consequences, and modeling orderly behavior and cooperative conflict resolution. The committee recommends positive reinforcement to encourage desired behaviors; and verbal reprimands, "time-outs" (isolating the child for a short time, to give the child a chance to cool down), or removal of privileges to discourage undesired behaviors—all within the context of a positive, supportive, loving parent-child relationship.

What's Your View?

Did your parents ever spank you? If so, how often and in what kinds of situations? Would you spank, or have you ever spanked, your own child? Why or why not?

Check It Out:

OLC

For more information on this topic, go to www.mhhe.com/papaliah9, where you'll find links to information about discipline and corporal punishment.

The effectiveness of parental discipline may hinge on how well the child understands and accepts the parents' message, both cognitively and emotionally (Grusec & Goodnow, 1994). The child has to recognize the message as appropriate; so parents need to be fair and accurate, and clear and consistent about their expectations. They need to fit their actions to the misdeed and to the child's temperament and cognitive and emotional level. The child may be more motivated to accept the message if the parents normally are warm and responsive, if they arouse the child's empathy for someone harmed by the misdeed, and if they make the child feel less secure in their affections as a result of the misbehavior. It may help if parents deliver the message in humorous or indirect terms ("Who was your servant last year?" to a child who leaves things strewn around the house, and "What's the magic word?" to a child who doesn't say "Please.")

What's Your View?

- As a parent, what forms of discipline would you favor in what situations? Give specific examples, and tell why.

Because a child interprets and responds to discipline in the context of an ongoing relationship with a parent, some researchers have looked beyond specific parental practices to overall styles, or patterns, of parenting.

Parenting Styles

Why does Stacy hit and bite the nearest person when she cannot finish a jigsaw puzzle? What makes David sit and sulk when he cannot finish the puzzle, even though his teacher offers to help him? Why does Consuelo work on the puzzle for twenty minutes and then shrug and try another? Why are children so different in their responses to the same situation? Temperament is a major factor, of course; but some research suggests that styles of parenting may affect children's competence in dealing with their world.

Baumrind's Model Are some ways of socializing children more effective than others? In pioneering research, Diana Baumrind (1971, 1996b; Baumrind & Black, 1967) studied 103 preschool children from 95 families. Through interviews, testing, and home studies, she measured how the children were functioning, identified three parenting styles, and described typical behavior patterns of children raised according to each. Baumrind's findings were correlational and did not consider innate factors, such as temperament. However, Baumrind's work and the large body of research it inspired have established strong associations between each parenting style and a particular set of child behaviors (Baumrind, 1989; Darling & Steinberg, 1993; Pettit, Bates, & Dodge, 1997).

authoritarian In Baumrind's terminology, parenting style emphasizing control and obedience.

Authoritarian parents, according to Baumrind, value control and unquestioning obedience. They try to make children conform to a set standard of conduct and punish them arbitrarily and forcefully for violating it. They are more detached and less warm than other parents. Their children tend to be more discontented, withdrawn, and distrustful.

permissive In Baumrind's terminology, parenting style emphasizing self-expression and self-regulation.

Permissive parents value self-expression and self-regulation. They make few demands and allow children to monitor their own activities as much as possible. When they do have to make rules, they explain the reasons for them. They consult with children about policy decisions and rarely punish. They are warm, noncontrolling, and undemanding. Their preschool children tend to be immature—the least self-controlled and the least exploratory.

authoritative In Baumrind's terminology, parenting style blending respect for a child's individuality with an effort to instill social values.

Authoritative parents value a child's individuality but also stress social constraints. They have confidence in their ability to guide children, but they also respect children's independent decisions, interests, opinions, and personalities. They are loving and accepting, but also demand good behavior, are firm in maintaining standards, and are willing to impose limited, judicious punishment when necessary, within the context of a warm, supportive relationship. They explain the reasoning behind their stands and encourage verbal give-and-take. Their children apparently feel secure in knowing that they are both loved and firmly guided. Preschoolers with authoritative parents tend to be the most self-reliant, self-controlled, self-assertive, exploratory, and content. (Isabel Allende's description of how her stepfather, Tió Ramón, took charge and raised her and her brothers fits this description perfectly; his parenting style was more effective than those of their authoritarian grandfather and permissive mother.)

Eleanor Maccoby and John Martin (1983) added a fourth parenting style—*neglectful,* or *uninvolved*—to describe parents who, sometimes because of stress or depression, focus on their own needs rather than on those of the child. Neglectful parenting has been linked with a variety of behavioral disorders in childhood and adolescence (Baumrind, 1991; Parke & Buriel, 1998; R. A. Thompson, 1998).

Why does authoritative parenting seem to enhance children's social competence? It may be because authoritative parents like Ramón set sensible expectations and realistic standards. By making clear, consistent rules, they let children know what is expected of them. In authoritarian homes, children are so strictly controlled that often they cannot make independent choices about their own behavior. In permissive homes, children receive so little guidance that they may become uncertain and anxious about whether they are doing the right thing. In authoritative homes, children know when they are meeting expectations and can decide whether it is worth risking parental displeasure to pursue a goal. These children are expected to perform well, fulfill commitments, and participate actively in family duties as well as family fun. They know the satisfaction of accepting responsibilities and achieving success. Parents who make reasonable demands show that they believe their children can meet them—and that the parents care enough to insist that they do.

When conflict arises, an authoritative parent can teach the child positive ways to communicate his or her own point of view and negotiate acceptable alternatives. ("If you don't want to throw away those rocks you found, where do you think we should keep them?") Internalization of this broader set of skills, not just of specific behavioral demands, may well be a key to the success of authoritative parenting (Grusec & Goodnow, 1994).

Cultural Factors Baumrind's categories reflect the dominant North American view of child development and may be misleading when applied to some cultures or socioeconomic groups. Among Asian Americans, obedience and strictness—rather than being associated with harshness and domination—seem to have more to do with caring, concern, and involvement and with maintaining family harmony. Traditional Chinese culture, with its emphasis on respect for elders, stresses adults' responsibility to maintain the social order by teaching children socially proper behavior. This obligation is carried out through firm control of the child—and even by physical punishment if necessary (Zhao, 2002).

Although Asian American parenting is frequently described as authoritarian, the warmth and supportiveness that characterize Chinese American family relationships more closely resemble Baumrind's authoritative parenting—but without the emphasis on the American values of individuality, choice, and freedom (Chao, 1994). In a comparative study of five hundred Chinese American and European American adolescents, it was close parent-child relationships that tended to explain the positive effect of authoritative parenting on school performance. Authoritative parenting had less effect on second generation Chinese Americans than on European Americans, and no effect on first generation Chinese Americans, who may have had the benefit of warm, supportive parenting but with stricter parental control (Chao, 2001).

Researchers have identified a parenting style in some African American families that falls between Baumrind's authoritarian and authoritative styles. This style, called "no nonsense parenting," combines warmth and affection with firm parental control. "No nonsense" parents regard stringent control and insistence on obedience to rules as necessary safeguards for children growing up in dangerous neighborhoods, and such children see this kind of parenting as evidence of concern about their well-being (Brody & Flor, 1998). It can be misleading, then, to consider parenting styles without looking at the goals parents are trying to achieve and the constraints their life circumstances present.

Checkpoint

Can you . . .

- ✔ Compare various forms of discipline, and identify factors that influence their effectiveness?
- ✔ Describe and evaluate Baumrind's model of parenting styles, and give reasons for cultural variations on it?

Promoting Altruism and Dealing with Aggression and Fearfulness

Three specific issues of especial concern to parents, caregivers, and teachers of preschool children are how to promote altruism, curb aggression, and deal with fears that often arise at this age.

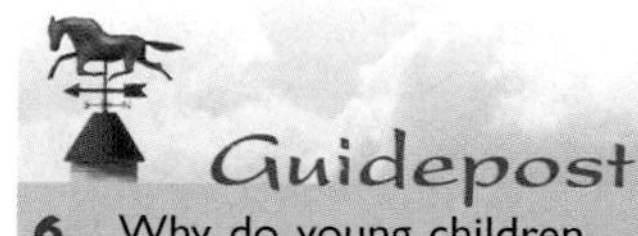

Guidepost

6. Why do young children help or hurt others, and why do they develop fears?

Prosocial Behavior Alex, at $3\frac{1}{2}$, responded to two fellow preschoolers' complaints that they did not have enough modeling clay, his favorite plaything, by giving them half of his. By acting out of concern for another person with no expectation of

altruism Behavior intended to help others out of inner concern and without expectation of external reward; may involve self-denial or self-sacrifice.

prosocial behavior Any voluntary behavior intended to help others.

reward, Alex was showing **altruism.** Altruistic acts like Alex's often entail cost, self-sacrifice, or risk. Altruism is the heart of **prosocial behavior,** voluntary activity intended to benefit another.

Even before the second birthday, children often help others, share belongings and food, and offer comfort. Such behaviors may reflect a growing ability to imagine how another person might feel (Zahn-Waxler, Radke-Yarrow, Wagner, & Chapman, 1992). An analysis of 179 studies found increasing evidence of concern for others from infancy throughout childhood and adolescence (Fabes & Eisenberg, 1996). Although girls tend to be more prosocial than boys, the differences are small (Eisenberg & Fabes, 1998).

Is there a prosocial personality, or disposition? A longitudinal study that followed 32 four- and five-year-olds into early adulthood suggests that there is, and that it emerges early and remains somewhat consistent throughout life (Eisenberg, Guthrie, et al., 1999). Preschoolers who were sympathetic and spontaneously shared with classmates tended to show prosocial understanding and empathic behavior as much as seventeen years later. This prosocial disposition may be partly temperamental or genetic. It involves inhibitory control—self-control or self-denial—and reflects individual differences in moral reasoning, which may be reinforced within the family.

Children given responsibilities at home tend to develop prosocial qualities, such as cooperation and helpfulness. This 3-year-old girl, who is learning to care for plants, is likely to have caring relationships with people as well.

The family is important as a model and as a source of explicit standards of behavior (Eisenberg & Fabes, 1998). Parents of prosocial children typically are prosocial themselves. They point out models of prosocial behavior and steer children toward stories, films, and television programs that depict cooperation, sharing, and empathy and encourage sympathy, generosity, and helpfulness (Singer & Singer, 1998). Relationships with siblings (discussed later in this chapter) provide an important "laboratory" for trying out caring behavior and learning to see another person's point of view. Peers and teachers also can model and reinforce prosocial behavior (Eisenberg, 1992; Eisenberg & Fabes, 1998).

Parents encourage prosocial behavior when they use inductive disciplinary methods instead of power-assertive techniques (Eisenberg & Fabes, 1998). When Sara took candy from a store, her father did not lecture her on honesty, spank her, or tell her what a bad girl she had been. Instead, he explained how the owner of the store would be harmed by her failure to pay for the candy, and he took her back to the store to return it. When such incidents occur, Sara's parents ask "How do you think Mr. Jones feels?" or "How would you feel if you were Mr. Jones?"

What's Your View?

- In a society in which "good Samaritans" are sometimes reviled for "butting into other people's business" and sometimes attacked by the very persons they try to help, is it wise to encourage children to offer help to strangers?

Motives for prosocial behavior may change as children grow older and develop more mature moral reasoning (see Chapters 9 and 11). Preschoolers tend to show egocentric motives; they want to earn praise and avoid disapproval. They weigh costs and benefits and consider how they would like others to act toward them. As children grow older, their motives become less self-centered. They adopt societal standards of "being good," which eventually become internalized as principles and values (Eisenberg & Fabes, 1998).

Cultures vary in the degree to which they foster prosocial behavior. Cultures in which people live in extended family groups and share work seem to foster prosocial values more than cultures that stress individual achievement (Eisenberg & Fabes, 1998).

instrumental aggression Aggressive behavior used as a means of achieving a goal.

Aggression When Peter roughly snatches a ball away from Tommy, he is interested only in getting the ball, not in hurting or dominating Tommy. This is **instrumental aggression,** or aggression used as an instrument to reach a goal—the most common type of aggression in early childhood. Between ages $2\frac{1}{2}$ and 5, children commonly struggle over toys and control of space. Aggression surfaces mostly during social play; children who fight the most also tend to be the most sociable and competent. In fact, the ability to show some instrumental aggression may be a necessary step in social development.

Between ages 2 and 4, as children develop more self-control and become better able to express themselves verbally and to wait for what they want, they typically shift from showing aggression with blows to doing it with words (Coie & Dodge, 1998). However, individual differences remain; children who more frequently hit or grab toys from other children at age 2 are likely to be more physically aggressive at age 5 (Cummings, Iannotti, & Zahn-Waxler, 1989).

The kind of aggression involved in fighting over a toy, without intention to hurt or dominate the other child, is known as instrumental aggression. *It surfaces mostly during social play and normally declines as children learn to ask for what they want.*

After age 6 or 7, most children become less aggressive as they become more cooperative, less egocentric, more empathic, and better able to communicate. They can now put themselves in someone else's place, can understand why the other person may be acting in a certain way, and can develop more positive ways of asserting themselves in social relationships. However, children who, as preschoolers, often engaged in pretend play involving violent fantasy may, at age 6, lack self-control and empathy and be prone to displays of anger and conflict with peers (Dunn & Hughes, 2001).

Are boys more aggressive than girls? Many studies say yes. Indeed, it has been suggested that the male hormone testosterone, which boys have in greater amounts than girls, may underlie aggressive behavior. From infancy, boys are more likely to grab things from others. As children learn to talk, girls are more likely to rely on words to protest and to work out conflicts (Coie & Dodge, 1998).

However, girls may be more aggressive than they seem; they just show aggressiveness differently (McNeilly-Choque, Hart, Robinson, Nelson, & Olsen, 1996). Boys engage in more **overt aggression,** physical force or verbal threats openly directed against a target. Girls commonly practice **relational aggression** (also called *covert, indirect,* or *psychological aggression*), or find it directed against them. This more subtle kind of aggression consists of manipulation and damaging or threatening to damage relationships, reputation, or psychological well-being. It may involve "putting down," spreading rumors, name-calling, teasing, withholding friendship, or excluding someone from a group. Among preschoolers, it tends to be direct and face-to-face ("You can't come to my party if you don't give me that toy"). In middle childhood and adolescence, relational aggression becomes more sophisticated and indirect (Crick, Casas, & Nelson, 2002).

overt aggression Aggression that is openly directed at its target.

relational aggression Aggression aimed at damaging or interfering with another person's relationships, reputation, or psychological well-being; also called *covert, indirect,* or *psychological aggression.*

Sources of Aggression

What produces an aggressive child? Why are some children more aggressive than others?

Biology may play a part. So may temperament: children who are intensely emotional and low in self-control tend to express anger aggressively (Eisenberg, Fabes, Nyman, Bernzweig, & Pinuelas, 1994).

Aggressive behavior tends to be bred from early childhood by a combination of a stressful and unstimulating home atmosphere; harsh discipline; lack of maternal warmth and social support; exposure to aggressive adults and neighborhood violence; and transient peer groups, which prevent stable friendships. Through such negative socializing experiences, children growing up in poor, high-risk surroundings may absorb antisocial attitudes despite their parents' best efforts (Dodge, Pettit, & Bates, 1994; Grusec & Goodnow, 1994).

A negative early relationship with a rejecting mother—often a poor single mother—is an important factor. In longitudinal studies, insecure attachment and lack of maternal warmth and affection in infancy have predicted aggressiveness in early childhood (Coie & Dodge, 1998; MacKinnon-Lewis, Starnes, Volling, & Johnson, 1997). Negative parent-child relationships may set the stage for prolonged, destructive sibling conflicts, in which children imitate their parents' hostile behavior. These coercive family processes may foster aggressive tendencies that are carried over to peer relations (MacKinnon-Lewis et al., 1997). Among 180 low-income 5-year-olds with close-in-age siblings, a combination of rejecting parents (by age 2) and high levels of destructive sibling conflict predicted aggressive or antisocial conduct at home and at school at age 6 (Garcia, Shaw, Winslow, & Yaggi, 2000).

Parents of children who become antisocial often fail to reinforce good behavior and are harsh or inconsistent, or both, in stopping or punishing misbehavior (Coie & Dodge, 1998). Parents who back down when confronted with a preschooler's coercive demands (such as whining or yelling when scolded for not going to bed) may reinforce repetition of the undesirable behavior (G. R. Patterson, 1995). On the other hand, harsh punishment, especially spanking, often backfires; children who are spanked not only suffer frustration, pain, and humiliation (which can be spurs to aggression) but also see aggressive behavior in an adult model (refer back to Box 8-1). A study of 69 kindergartners who had been harshly disciplined and physically harmed found that such treatment in the first five years increases the likelihood of aggressive conduct in school (Dodge, Pettit, & Bates, 1997).

Aggressors tend to be unpopular and to have social and psychological problems, but it is not clear whether aggression causes these problems or is an expression of them (Crick & Grotpeter, 1995). Highly aggressive children tend to seek out friends like themselves and to egg each other on to antisocial acts (Hartup, 1989, 1992, 1996a; Hartup & Stevens, 1999; Masten & Coatsworth, 1998).

Triggers of Aggression Exposure to violence, real or televised, can trigger aggression. In a classic social learning experiment (Bandura, Ross, & Ross, 1961), 3- to 6-year-olds individually watched adult models play with toys. Children in one experimental group saw the adult play quietly. The model for a second experimental group began to assemble Tinker Toys, but then spent the rest of the ten-minute session punching, throwing, and kicking a life-size inflated doll. A control group did not see any model. After the sessions, the children, who were mildly frustrated by seeing toys they were not allowed to play with, went into another playroom. The children who had seen the aggressive model acted much more aggressively than those in the other groups, imitating many of the same things they had seen the model say and do. The children who had been with the quiet model were less aggressive than the control group. This finding suggests that parents may be able to moderate the effects of frustration by modeling nonaggressive behavior.

Influence of Culture How much influence does culture have on aggressive behavior? One research team asked closely matched samples of 30 Japanese and 30 U.S. middle- to upper-middle-class preschoolers to choose pictured solutions to hypothetical conflicts or stressful situations (such as having one's block tower knocked down, having to stop playing and go to bed, being hit, hearing parents argue, or fighting on a jungle gym). The children also were asked to act out and complete such situations using dolls and props. The U.S. children showed more anger, more aggressive behavior and language, and less control of emotions than the Japanese children (Zahn-Waxler, Friedman, Cole, Mizuta, & Hiruma, 1996).

These results are consistent with childrearing values in the two cultures. In Japan, anger and aggression are seen as clashing with the emphasis on harmonious relationships. Japanese mothers are more likely than U.S. mothers to use reasoning and induce guilt, pointing out how aggressive behavior hurts others. Japanese mothers also strongly show their disappointment when children fail to meet their behavioral standards. However, the cross-cultural difference in children's anger and aggressiveness was significant even apart from mothers' behavior, suggesting that temperamental differences may also be at work (Zahn-Waxler et al., 1996).

What's Your View?

- Are there situations in which a child should be encouraged to be aggressive?

Fearfulness "My childhood was a time of unvoiced fears," writes Isabel Allende (1995, p. 50): fear of her family's tyrannical maid; fear that her mother would die and her father would come back to claim her; fear of the devil; fear of her sadistic uncles; fear of gypsies; and fear of what "bad men can do to little girls."

Passing fears are common in early childhood. Many 2- to 4-year-olds are afraid of animals, especially dogs. By 6 years, children are more likely to be afraid of the dark. Other common fears are of thunderstorms, doctors, and imaginary creatures (DuPont, 1983; Stevenson-Hinde & Shouldice, 1996). Most of these disappear as children grow older and lose their sense of powerlessness.

Young children's fears stem largely from their intense fantasy life and their tendency to confuse appearance with reality. Sometimes their imaginations get carried away, making them worry about being attacked by a lion or being abandoned. Young children are more likely to be frightened by something that looks scary, such as a cartoon monster, than by something capable of doing great harm, such as a nuclear explosion (Cantor, 1994). For the most part, older children's fears are more realistic and self-evaluative (for example, fear of failing a test), since they know they are being evaluated by others (Stevenson-Hinde & Shouldice, 1996; see Table 8-3).

Fears may come from personal experience or from hearing about other people's experiences (Muris, Merckelbach, & Collaris, 1997). A preschooler whose mother is sick in bed may become upset by a story about a mother's death, even if it is an animal mother. Often fears come from appraisals of danger, such as the likelihood of being bitten by a dog, or are triggered by events, as when a child who was hit by a car becomes afraid to cross the street. Children who have lived through an earthquake, a kidnapping, or some other frightening event may fear that it will happen again (Kolbert, 1994).

Table 8-3 Childhood Fears

Age	Fears
0–6 months	Loss of support, loud noises
7–12 months	Strangers; heights; sudden, unexpected, and looming objects
1 year	Separation from parent, toilet, injury, strangers
2 years	Many stimuli, including loud noises (vacuum cleaners, sirens and alarms, trucks, and thunder), animals, dark rooms, separation from parent, large objects or machines, changes in personal environment, unfamiliar peers
3 years	Masks, dark, animals, separation from parent
4 years	Separation from parent, animals, dark, noises (including noises at night)
5 years	Animals, "bad" people, dark, separation from parent, bodily harm
6 years	Supernatural beings (e.g., ghost, witches), bodily injury, thunder and lightning, dark, sleeping or staying alone, separation from parent
7–8 years	Supernatural beings, dark, media events (e.g., news reports on the threat of nuclear war or child kidnapping), staying alone, bodily injury
9–12 years	Tests and examinations in school, school performances, bodily injury, physical appearance, thunder and lightning, death, dark

Source: Adapted from Morris & Kratochwill, 1983; Stevenson-Hinde & Shouldice, 1996.

Checkpoint

Can you . . .

- Discuss how parental and other influences contribute to altruism, aggression, and fearfulness?

Parents can help prevent children's fears by instilling a sense of trust and normal caution without being too protective, and also by overcoming their own unrealistic fears. They can help a fearful child by reassurance and by encouraging open expression of feelings. Ridicule ("Don't be such a baby!"), coercion ("Pat the nice doggie—it won't hurt you"), and logical persuasion ("The closest bear is twenty miles away, locked in a zoo!") are not helpful. Not until elementary school can children tell themselves that what they fear is not real (Cantor, 1994).

Children also can be helped to overcome fears by *systematic desensitization,* a therapeutic technique involving gradual exposure to a feared object or situation. This technique has been used successfully to help children overcome fears ranging from snakes to elevators (Murphy & Bootzin, 1973; Sturges & Sturges, 1998).

Families in Trouble: Child Abuse and Neglect

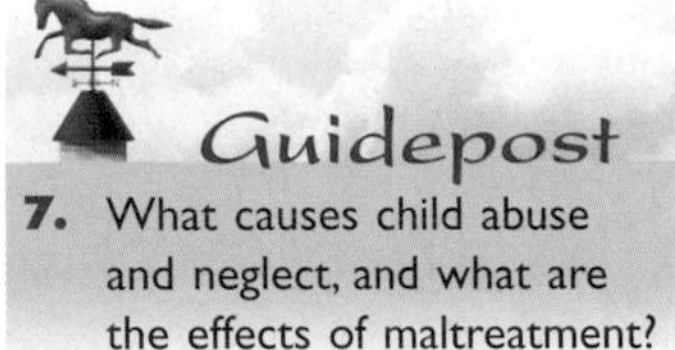

Guidepost

7. What causes child abuse and neglect, and what are the effects of maltreatment?

Although most parents are loving and nurturing, some cannot or will not take proper care of their children, and some deliberately hurt or kill them. *Maltreatment,* by parents or others, is deliberate or avoidable endangerment of a child. Maltreatment takes several forms (U.S. Department of Health and Human Services [USDHHS], 1999a); any one form is likely to be accompanied by one or more of the others (Belsky, 1993).

In general, *abuse* refers to action that inflicts harm; *neglect* refers to inaction: omission of care that can lead to harm. **Physical abuse** involves injury to the body through punching, beating, kicking, or burning. **Neglect** is failure to meet a child's basic physical, emotional, or educational needs. **Sexual abuse** is sexual activity involving a child and another person. **Emotional maltreatment** includes acts of abuse or neglect that may cause behavioral, cognitive, emotional, or mental disorders. It may include rejection, terrorization, isolation, exploitation, degradation, ridicule, or failure to provide emotional support, love, and affection. Emotional maltreatment is hard to identify; its effects may not surface immediately and may be difficult to distinguish from signs of emotional disturbance and other developmental problems (Dubowitz, 1999; USDHHS, 1999a).

physical abuse Infliction of bodily injury on a child.

neglect Failure to meet a child's basic needs.

sexual abuse Sexual activity involving a child and an older person.

emotional maltreatment Action or inaction that may cause behavioral, cognitive, emotional, or mental disorders.

Maltreatment: Facts and Figures

How common is maltreatment? It is hard to say. Many, if not most, cases—like the "rough games" Isabel Allende's uncles played with her and her brothers—are never reported to agencies, and many of those reported are not investigated (USDHHS, 1999a). On the other hand, some reported claims filed in the context of divorce proceedings, for example, are false. The steep rise in reported cases and serious injuries since 1976, when the first national statistics were compiled, may reflect an increase in maltreatment, an increase in reporting, or (more likely) both.

Since its peak in 1993 the reported number of abused and neglected children in the United States has declined. Still, state child protective services agencies investigated and confirmed some 826,000 cases in 1999, and the actual number may well have been considerably higher. In that year almost three-fifths (58.4 percent) of reported maltreatment cases involved neglect, and one-fifth (21.3 percent) involved physical abuse. About 11 percent of victims were sexually abused (National Child Abuse and Neglect Data System [NCANDS], 2001).

Abused and neglected children are of all ages, but the highest rates are for ages 3 and younger. Girls are four times as likely as boys to be sexually abused (NCANDS, 2001). Some studies suggest that as many as 25 percent of girls and 10 percent of boys become victims of sexual abuse by age 18 (AAP Committee on Child Abuse and Neglect, 1999). In almost nine out of ten cases, the perpetrators of abuse are the child's parents—usually the mother, except in cases of sexual abuse (NCANDS, 2001).

Maltreatment is a major cause of death among young children. An estimated 1,100 children died of abuse or neglect in 1999; 86 percent of these were under 6 years old. More than 38 percent of these cases were attributed to neglect (NCANDS, 2001).

Contributing Factors: An Ecological View

Maltreatment by parents is a symptom of extreme disturbance in child rearing, usually aggravated by other problems, such as poverty, alcoholism, or antisocial behavior. A disproportionate number of abused and neglected children are in large, poor, or single-parent families, which often are under stress. They may live in crowded conditions in high-risk neighborhoods and may move frequently (Dubowitz, 1999; Sedlak & Broadhurst, 1996). Yet, what pushes one parent over the edge, another may take in stride. Although most neglect cases occur in very poor families, most low-income parents do not neglect their children. Abuse and neglect reflect the interplay of many contributing factors involving the family and the neighborhood community (Dubowitz, 1999; USDHHS, 1999a).

Characteristics of Abusive Families Abuse may begin when a parent who is already anxious, depressed, or hostile tries to control a child physically but loses self-control and ends up shaking or beating the child (USDHHS, 1999a). When parents who are emotionally fragile have children who are particularly needy or unresponsive, the likelihood of maltreatment increases (National Research Council [NRC], 1993b; J. R. Reid, Patterson, & Loeber 1982; USDHHS, 1999a).

Abusive parents tend to fight physically. Their households tend to be disorganized, and they experience more stressful events than other families (J. R. Reid et al., 1982; Sedlak & Broadhurst, 1996). Many abusive parents cut themselves off from others, leaving the family isolated, with no one to turn to in times of stress and no one to see what is happening.

Characteristics of Neglectful Families Neglectful parents tend to be apathetic, incompetent, irresponsible, or emotionally withdrawn (Wolfe, 1985). The family atmosphere tends to be chaotic, with people moving in and out.

Neglectful parents tend to distance themselves from their children. They may be critical or uncommunicative. Often the mothers were neglected themselves as children and are depressed or feel hopeless. They may be mentally retarded or have limited knowledge about children's needs. Many are substance abusers. The fathers are not involved in their children's lives; many have deserted or do not give enough financial or emotional support. The child may be unresponsive or may have a "difficult" temperament, and thus may be hard to care for. Often the children are of low birthweight. This may be related to SES and to lack of adequate prenatal care (Dubowitz, 1999).

Abuse and neglect often happen in the same households. Like abusive families, neglectful families tend to be socially isolated. Lack of social support makes it harder for these families to cope with difficult circumstances (Dubowitz, 1999). Substance abuse is a factor in at least one-third of cases of abuse and neglect (USDHHS, 1999a).

Neighborhood and Social Support The outside world can create a climate for family violence. What makes one low-income neighborhood a place where children are highly likely to be maltreated, while another, matched for ethnic population and income levels, is safer?

In one inner-city Chicago neighborhood, the proportion of children who died from maltreatment (1 death for every 2,541 children) was about twice the proportion in another inner-city neighborhood. Researchers who interviewed community leaders found a depressed atmosphere in the high-abuse community. Criminal activity was rampant, and facilities for community programs were dark and dreary. This was an

Checkpoint

Can you . . .

- Name four types of child abuse and neglect?
- Discuss the incidence of maltreatment and explain why it is hard to measure?
- Identify contributing factors having to do with family and community?

environment with "an ecological conspiracy against children" (Garbarino & Kostelny, 1993, p. 213). In the low-abuse neighborhood, people described their community as a poor but decent place to live. They painted a picture of a neighborhood with robust social support networks, well-publicized community services, and strong political leadership. In a community like this, maltreatment is less likely to occur.

Effects of Maltreatment

Maltreatment can produce grave consequences—physical, cognitive, emotional, and social.

Neglected children tend to grow poorly and often have medical problems (Dubowitz, 1999). Maltreated children often show language delays (Coster, Gersten, Beeghly, & Cicchetti, 1989). They often do poorly on cognitive tests and in school and show problem behavior (Dubowitz, 1999; Eckenrode, Laird, & Doris, 1993; Shonk & Cicchetti, 2001).

Maltreated children often have disorganized-disoriented attachments and negative, distorted self-concepts. They do not develop social skills and, because they act aggressively, tend to be rejected by peers (Bolger & Patterson, 2001; Price, 1996). Chronic neglect in early childhood can have negative effects on school performance, social relationships, adaptability, and problem solving (NRC, 1993b).

Maltreated children may become either overly aggressive or withdrawn (Dubowitz, 1999; Shonk & Cicchetti, 2001; USDHHS, 1999a). Physically abused youngsters tend to be fearful, uncooperative, less able to respond appropriately to friendly overtures, and, consequently, unpopular (Coie & Dodge, 1998; Haskett & Kistner, 1991; Salzinger, Feldman, Hammer, & Rosario, 1993). Neglected children tend to lack enthusiasm, creativity, and self-esteem and to be angry and dependent (Egeland, Sroufe, & Erickson, 1993).

Although most abused children do not become delinquent, criminal, or mentally ill, abuse makes it likelier that they will (Dodge, Bates, & Pettit, 1990; NRC, 1993b; Widom, 1989). Neglected children, too, often become delinquents and adult criminals (Dubowitz, 1999). Teenagers who were abused when they were younger may run away, which may be self-protective, or may abuse drugs, which is not (NRC, 1993b).

Consequences of sexual abuse vary with age (see Table 8-4). Sexually abused children may become sexually active at an early age (Fiscella, Kitzman, Cole, Sidora, &

Table 8-4 Developmentally Related Reactions to Sexual Abuse

Age	Most Common Symptoms
Preschoolers	Anxiety
	Nightmares
	Inappropriate sexual behavior
School-age children	Fear
	Mental illness
	Aggression
	Nightmares
	School problems
	Hyperactivity
	Regressive behavior
Adolescents	Depression
	Withdrawn, suicidal, or self-injurious behaviors
	Physical complaints
	Illegal acts
	Running away
	Substance abuse

Source: Adapted from Kendall-Tackett, Williams, & Finkelhor, 1993.

Olds, 1998). Fearfulness and low self-esteem often continue into adulthood. Adults who were sexually abused as children tend to be anxious, depressed, angry, hostile, or mistrustful; to feel isolated and stigmatized; to be sexually maladjusted (Browne & Finkelhor, 1986); and to abuse alcohol or drugs (NRC, 1993b; USDHHS, 1999a).

Emotional maltreatment is more subtle than physical maltreatment. It has been linked to lying, stealing, low self-esteem, emotional maladjustment, dependency, underachievement, depression, aggression, learning disorders, homicide, and suicide, as well as to psychological distress later in life (S. N. Hart & Brassard, 1987).

Still, many maltreated children show remarkable resilience, especially if they have been able to form an attachment to a supportive person (Egeland & Sroufe, 1981). Above average intelligence, advanced cognitive abilities, and high self-esteem seem to help (Garmezy, Masten, & Tellegen, 1984; Zimrin, 1986). Most abused children do not grow up to abuse their own children (Kaufman & Zigler, 1987; USDHHS, 1999a). Abused children who grow up to be *non*abusing parents are likely to have had someone to whom they could turn for help, to have received therapy, and to have good marital or love relationships. They are likely to have been abused by only one parent and to have had a loving, supportive relationship with the other (Egeland, Jacobvitz, & Sroufe, 1988; Kaufman & Zigler, 1987; NRC, 1993b).

Helping Families in Trouble or at Risk Since maltreatment is a multifactorial problem, it needs many-pronged solutions. Effective prevention and intervention strategies should be comprehensive, neighborhood-based, centered on protecting children, and aimed at strengthening families if possible and removing children if necessary (USDHHS, 1999a). Some abuse-prevention programs teach basic parenting skills. Others offer subsidized day care, volunteer homemakers, home visitors, and temporary "respite homes" or "relief parents" to take over occasionally.

Services for abused children and adults include shelters, education in parenting skills, and therapy. Parents Anonymous and other organizations offer free, confidential support groups. Abused children may receive play or art therapy and day care in a therapeutic environment. In communities where abuse or neglect is widespread, school-based programs can be effective.

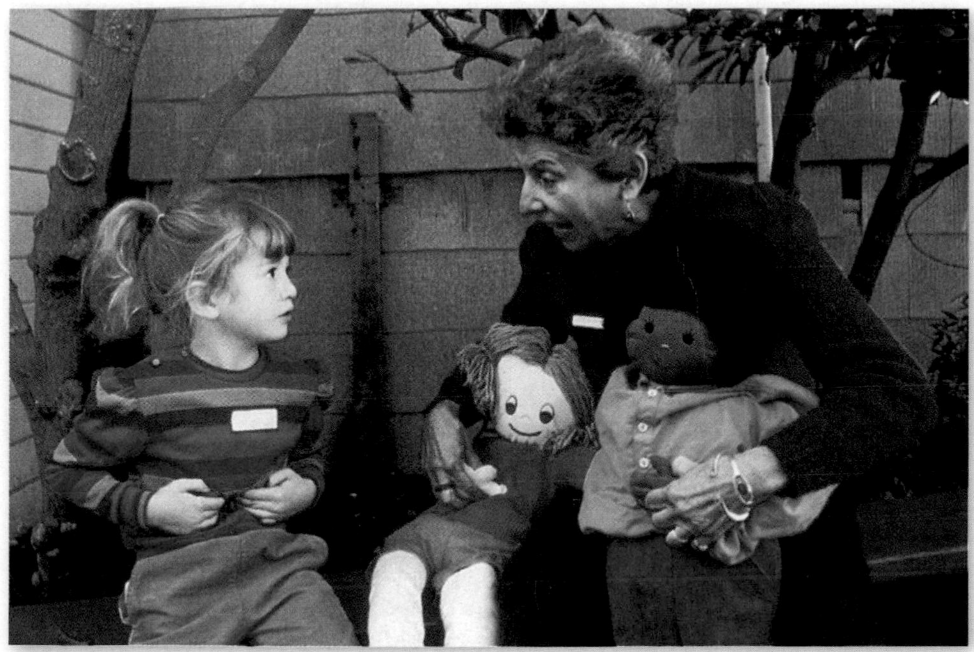

This adult volunteer uses dolls to help young children realize that they have control over their bodies and need not let anyone—even friends or family members—touch them. Such programs for preventing sexual abuse need to walk a fine line between alerting children to danger and frightening them or discouraging appropriate affection.

Checkpoint

Can you . . .

- ✔ Give examples of effects of child abuse and neglect?
- ✔ Describe ways to prevent or stop maltreatment and help its victims?

When authorities remove children from their homes, the usual alternative is foster care, which has increased markedly since the 1980s. Foster care removes a child from immediate danger, but it is often unstable, may also turn out to be an abusive situation, and further alienates the child from the family. It is intended as a temporary, emergency measure; but in some cities the average stay is five years, often with a series of placements in different homes (NRC, 1993b).

The plight of abused and neglected children is one for which our society needs to find more effective remedies. Without help, maltreated children often grow up with serious problems, at great cost to themselves and to society, and may continue the cycle of maltreatment when they have children of their own.

Relationships with Other Children

Although the most important people in young children's world are the adults who take care of them, relationships with siblings and playmates become more important in early childhood. Virtually every characteristic activity and personality issue of this age, from gender development to prosocial or aggressive behavior, involves other children. Sibling and peer relationships provide a measuring stick for *self-efficacy,* children's growing sense of capability to master challenges and achieve their goals. By competing with and comparing themselves with other children, they can gauge their physical, social, cognitive, and linguistic competencies and gain a more realistic sense of self (Bandura, 1994).

Siblings—or Their Absence

Ties between brothers and sisters often set the stage for later relationships. Let's look at sibling relationships, and then at children who grow up with no siblings.

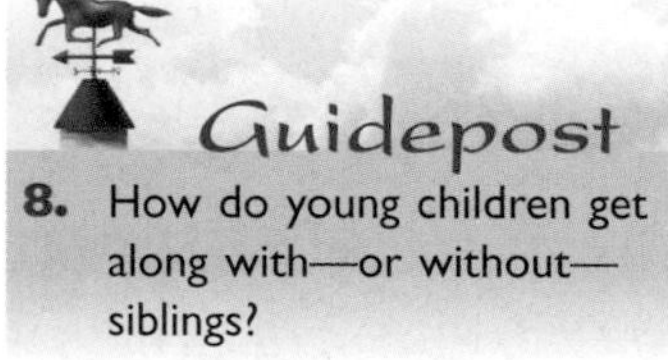

Guidepost

8. How do young children get along with—or without—siblings?

Brothers and Sisters

"It's mine!"
"No, it's mine!"
"Well, I was playing with it first!"

The earliest, most frequent, and most intense disputes among siblings are over property rights—who owns a toy or who is entitled to play with it. Although exasperated adults may not always see it that way, sibling disputes and their settlement can be viewed as socialization opportunities, in which children learn to stand up for moral principles.

In one study of 40 pairs of 2- and 4-year-old siblings, property disputes arose, on average, about every 15 minutes during a 9-hour observation period. Even children as young as $2\frac{1}{2}$ argued on the basis of clear principles: the owner's right to a toy should take precedence over who was currently using it, but when the toy belonged to both children (as was true in about half the disputes), the current user should have exclusive rights. Parents did not clearly favor claims based on either ownership or possession but were more inclined to stress sharing and avoiding damage, or to suggest alternate playthings (Ross, 1996).

However, sibling rivalry is *not* the main pattern between brothers and sisters early in life. While some rivalry exists, so do affection, interest, companionship, and influence, the main pattern for Isabel Allende and her younger brothers. Observations spanning three and a half years, which began when younger siblings were about $1\frac{1}{2}$ years old and the older ones ranged from 3 to $4\frac{1}{2}$, found prosocial and play-oriented behaviors to be more common than rivalry, hostility, and competition (Abramovitch, Corter, & Lando, 1979; Abramovitch, Corter, Pepler, & Stanhope, 1986; Abramovitch, Pepler, & Corter, 1982). Older siblings initiated more behavior, both friendly and unfriendly; younger siblings tended to imitate the older ones. Siblings got along better when their mother was not with them. (Squabbling can be a bid for parental attention.) As the younger children reached their fifth birthday, the siblings became less physical and more verbal, both in showing aggression (through commands, insults, threats, tattling, put-downs, bribes, and teasing) and in showing care and affection (by compliments and comforting rather than hugs and kisses).

At least one finding of this research has been replicated in many studies: same-sex siblings, particularly girls, are closer and play together more peaceably than boy-girl pairs (Kier & Lewis, 1998). The quality of relationships with brothers and sisters often carries over to relationships with other children; a child who is aggressive with siblings is likely to be aggressive with friends as well. However, a child who is dominated by an older sibling may be able to take a dominant role with a playmate (Abramovitch et al., 1986).

The Only Child Are only children spoiled, selfish, lonely, or maladjusted? Research does not bear out this stereotype. According to an analysis of 115 studies, "onlies" do comparatively well (Falbo & Polit, 1986; Polit & Falbo, 1987). In occupational and educational achievement and intelligence, they surpass children with siblings. Only children also tend to be more mature and motivated to achieve and to have higher self-esteem. Perhaps these children do better in these areas because their parents spend more time and focus more attention on them, talk to them more, do more with them, and expect more of them. Onlies do not differ from other children, however, in overall adjustment or sociability.

Research in China, which mandates one-child families, also has produced encouraging findings about only children (see Box 8-2 on page 300).

Checkpoint

Can you . . .

- ✔ Explain how the resolution of sibling disputes contributes to socialization?
- ✔ Tell how birth order and gender affect typical patterns of sibling interaction?
- ✔ Compare development of only children with that of children with siblings?

Playmates and Friends

Friendships develop as people develop. Toddlers play alongside or near each other, but not until about age 3 do children begin to have friends. Through friendships and interactions with casual playmates, young children learn how to get along with others. They learn that being a friend is the way to have a friend. They learn how to solve problems in relationships and how to put themselves in another person's place, and they see models of various kinds of behavior. They learn moral values and gender-role norms, and they practice adult roles.

Guidepost

9. How do young children choose playmates and friends, and why are some children more popular than others?

Choosing Playmates and Friends Preschoolers usually like to play with children of their own age and sex. In preschool, they tend to spend most of their time with a few other children with whom they have had positive experiences and whose behavior is like their own. Children who have frequent positive experiences with each other are most likely to become friends (Rubin et al., 1998; Snyder et al., 1996). About three out of four preschoolers have such mutual friendships (Hartup & Stevens, 1999).

The traits that young children look for in a playmate are similar to the traits they look for in a friend (C. H. Hart, DeWolf, Wozniak, & Burts, 1992). In one study, 4- to 7-year-olds rated the most important features of friendships as: doing things together, liking and caring for each other, sharing and helping one another, and to a lesser degree, living nearby or going to the same school. Younger children rated physical traits, such as appearance and size, higher than did older ones and rated

Young children learn the importance of being *a friend in order to* have *a friend. One way of being a friend is for a sighted child to help a blind playmate enjoy the feel of the sand and the sound of the surf.*

BOX 8-2

Window on the World

A Nation of Only Children

In 1979, to control an exploding population, the People's Republic of China established an official policy of limiting families to one child each. In addition to propaganda campaigns and incentives (housing, money, child care, health care, and preference in school placement) to induce voluntary compliance, millions of involuntary abortions and sterilizations have taken place. People who have had children without first getting a permit faced fines and loss of jobs. By 1985, at least eight out of ten young urban couples and half of those in rural areas had only one child (Yang, Ollendick, Dong, Xia, & Lin, 1995), and by 1997, the country's estimated population growth was holding steady at a little more than 1 percent.

Today the one-child policy is unevenly enforced (Faison, 1997). The State Family Planning Commission has now prohibited forced sterilizations and abortions and has begun to switch to a system stressing education, contraceptive choice, and heavy taxation for families with more than one child. In a small but growing number of counties, fixed quotas and permit requirements have been eliminated (Rosenthal, 1998).

Still, in many Chinese cities, kindergartens and primary classrooms are almost completely filled with children who have no brothers or sisters. This situation marks a great change in Chinese society, in which newlyweds were traditionally congratulated with the wish, "May you have a hundred sons and a thousand grandsons."

What kind of future population are the Chinese raising? Among 4,000 third- and sixth-graders, personality differences between only children and those with siblings—as rated by parents, teachers, peers, and the children themselves—were few. In academic achievement and physical growth, only children did about the same as, or better than, those with siblings (Falbo & Poston, 1993). A review of the literature found no significant differences in behavior problems; the small number of severe problems that did appear in only children were attributed to parental overindulgence and overprotection (Tao, 1998).

Indeed, only children seem to be at a distinct psychological advantage in China. When questionnaires were administered to 731 urban children and adolescents, children with siblings reported higher levels of fear, anxiety, and depression than only children, regardless of sex or age. Apparently children with siblings are less well adjusted in a society that favors and rewards the only child (Yang et al., 1995).

Only children seem to do better cognitively, too. A randomized study in Beijing schools (Jiao, Ji, & Jing, 1996) found that only children outperformed first-grade classmates with siblings in memory, language, and mathematics skills. This finding may reflect the greater attention, stimulation, hopes, and expectations that parents shower on a baby they know will be their first and last. Fifth-grade only children, who were born before the one-child policy was strongly enforced—and whose parents originally may have planned on a larger family—did not show a pronounced cognitive edge.

Both of these studies used urban samples. Further research may reveal whether the findings hold up in rural areas and small towns, where children with siblings are more numerous, and whether only children maintain their cognitive superiority as they move through school.

China's population policy has wider implications. If it succeeds, most Chinese will eventually lack aunts, uncles, nephews, nieces, and cousins, as well as siblings. How this will affect individuals, families, and the social fabric is incalculable.

A more sinister question is this: what happened to the girls? A 1990 census suggests that 5 percent of all infant girls born in China (some half a million infants born alive each year) are unaccounted for. Suspicions are that many parents, being permitted only one child, had their baby girls killed or let them die of neglect to allow the parents the chance to bear and raise more highly valued sons. A more benign explanation is that these girls were hidden and raised secretly to evade the one-child policy (Kristof, 1991, 1993). In either case, China's one-child policy appears to be having ramifications its developers may not have considered, and concern about these unforeseen effects may be one factor in the current relaxation of enforcement.

What's Your View?

Governmental control of reproduction may seem like the ultimate in totalitarianism, but what course of action would you propose for a country that cannot support an exploding population?

Check It Out:

OLC

For more information on this topic, go to www.mhhe.com/papaliah9, where you'll find links to information about China and reproductive issues.

affection and support lower (Furman & Bierman, 1983). Preschool children prefer prosocial playmates (C. H. Hart et al., 1992). They reject disruptive, demanding, intrusive, or aggressive children and ignore those who are shy or withdrawn (Ramsey & Lasquade, 1996; Roopnarine & Honig, 1985).

Well-liked preschoolers and kindergartners, and those who are rated by parents and teachers as socially competent, generally cope well with anger. They avoid insults and threats. Instead, they respond directly in ways that minimize further conflict and keep relationships going. Unpopular children tend to hit back or tattle (Fabes & Eisenberg, 1992).

Not all children without playmates have poor social adjustment, however. Among 567 kindergartners, almost 2 out of 3 socially withdrawn children were rated (through direct observation, teacher questionnaires, and interviews with classmates) as socially and cognitively competent; they simply preferred to play alone (Harrist et al., 1997).

Characteristics and Benefits of Friendships Preschoolers act differently with their friends than with other children. They have more positive interactions, but also more quarrels (Rubin et al., 1998). Children may get just as angry with a friend as with someone they dislike, but they are more likely to control their anger and express it constructively (Fabes, Eisenberg, Smith, & Murphy, 1996). Friendships are more satisfying—and more likely to last—when children see them as relatively harmonious and as validating their self-worth (Ladd, Kochenderfer, & Coleman, 1996).

Children with friends enjoy school more (Ladd & Hart, 1992). Among 125 kindergartners, those who had friends in their class when they entered in August liked school better two months later, and those who kept up these friendships continued to like school better the following May. Children whose friendships are a source of help and self-validation are happier, feel better about school, and can look to classmates for support (Ladd et al., 1996).

Parenting and Popularity Parenting styles and practices can influence peer relationships. Popular children generally have warm, positive relationships with both parents. The parents are likely to be authoritative, and the children to be both assertive and cooperative (Isley, O'Neil, & Parke, 1996; Kochanska, 1992; Roopnarine & Honig, 1985). Children who are insecurely attached or whose parents are harsh, neglectful, or depressed or have troubled marriages are at risk of developing unattractive social and emotional patterns and of being rejected by peers (Rubin et al., 1998).

Children whose parents rely on power-assertive discipline tend to use coercive tactics in peer relations; children whose parents engage in give-and-take reasoning are more likely to resolve conflicts with peers that way (Crockenberg & Lourie, 1996). Children whose parents clearly communicate disapproval rather than anger, as well as strong positive feelings, are more prosocial, less aggressive, and better liked (Boyum & Parke, 1995).

Checkpoint

Can you . . .

- ✔ Explain how preschoolers choose playmates and friends, how they behave with friends, and how they benefit from friendships?
- ✔ Discuss how relationships at home can influence relationships with peers?

Refocus

- From what you have read, would you guess that Isabel Allende had high or low self-esteem as a young child? Why?
- Which of the theories of gender formation seems to best describe Allende's development? Which do you think she would agree with most?
- Isabel Allende describes herself as a solitary child, who lived and played largely in the world of her own imagination. Would Parten have considered her immature? Would you?
- Allende and her mother shared an unconditional love, yet she seemed to have greater respect for her stepfather. Why?
- Allende says little about relationships with other children besides her younger brothers. Thinking about her personality, would you expect her to have been popular or unpopular with peers?

Peer relationships become even more important during middle childhood, which we examine in Chapters 12, 13, and 14.

SUMMARY AND KEY TERMS

The Developing Self

Guidepost 1. How does the self-concept develop during early childhood?

- The self-concept undergoes major change in early childhood. According to neo-Piagetians, self-definition shifts from single representations to representational mappings. Young children do not see the difference between the real self and the ideal self.

self-concept *(269)*
self-definition *(269)*
single representations *(270)*
real self *(270)*
ideal self *(270)*
representational mappings *(270)*

Guidepost 2. How do young children advance in understanding their emotions and develop initiative and self-esteem?

- Understanding of emotions directed toward the self and of simultaneous emotions develops gradually.
- According to Erikson, the chief developmental conflict of early childhood is initiative versus guilt. Successful resolution of this conflict results in the "virtue" of *purpose*.
- Self-esteem in early childhood tends to be global and unrealistic, reflecting adult approval.

initiative versus guilt *(271)*
self-esteem *(272)*

Gender

Guidepost 3. How do boys and girls become aware of the meaning of gender, and what explains differences in behavior between the sexes?

- Gender identity is an aspect of the developing self-concept.
- The main gender difference in early childhood is boys' greater aggressiveness. Girls tend to be more empathic and prosocial and less prone to problem behavior. Some cognitive differences appear early, others not until preadolescence or later.
- Children learn gender roles at an early age through gender-typing. Gender stereotypes peak during the preschool years.
- Four major perspectives on gender development are biological, psychoanalytic, cognitive, and socialization-based.
- Evidence suggests that some gender differences may be biologically based.
- In Freudian theory, a child identifies with the same-sex parent after giving up the wish to possess the other parent.
- Cognitive-developmental theory maintains that gender identity develops from thinking about one's gender. According to Kohlberg, gender constancy leads to acquisition of gender roles. Gender-schema theory holds that children categorize gender-related information by observing what males and females do in their culture.
- According to social cognitive theory, children learn gender roles through socialization. Parents, peers, and the media influence gender-typing.

gender identity *(273)*
gender roles *(275)*
gender-typing *(275)*
gender stereotypes *(275)*
identification *(277)*
gender constancy *(277)*
gender-schema theory *(278)*
social cognitive theory *(279)*

Play: The Business of Early Childhood

Guidepost 4. How do preschoolers play, and how does play contribute to and reflect development?

- Play has physical, cognitive, and psychosocial benefits. Changes in the types of play children engage in reflect cognitive and social development.
- According to Piaget and Smilansky, children progress cognitively from functional play to constructive play, pretend play, and then formal games with rules. Pretend play becomes increasingly common during early childhood and helps children develop social and cognitive skills. Rough-and-tumble play also begins during early childhood.
- According to Parten, play becomes more social during early childhood. However, later research has found that nonsocial play is not necessarily immature.
- Children prefer to play with (and play more socially with) others of their sex.
- Cognitive and social aspects of play are influenced by the culturally approved environments adults create for children.

functional play *(281)*
constructive play *(281)*
pretend play *(281)*

Parenting

Guidepost 5. What forms of discipline do parents use, and how do parenting styles and practices influence development?

- Discipline can be a powerful tool for socialization.
- Both positive reinforcement and prudently administered punishment can be appropriate tools of discipline within the context of a positive parent-child relationship.
- Power assertion, inductive techniques, and withdrawal of love each can be effective in certain situations. Reasoning is generally the most effective and power assertion the least effective in promoting internalization of parental standards. Spanking and other forms of corporal punishment can have negative consequences.
- Baumrind identified three childrearing styles: authoritarian, permissive, and authoritative. A fourth style, neglectful or uninvolved, was identified later. Authoritative parents tend to raise more competent children. However, Baumrind's findings may be misleading when applied to some cultures or socioeconomic groups.

discipline *(284)*
corporal punishment *(285)*
power assertion *(285)*
inductive techniques *(285)*
withdrawal of love *(285)*
authoritarian *(288)*
permissive *(288)*
authoritative *(288)*

Guidepost 6. Why do young children help or hurt others, and why do they develop fears?

- The roots of altruism and prosocial behavior appear early. This may be an inborn disposition, which can be cultivated by parental modeling and encouragement.
- Instrumental aggression—first physical, then verbal—is most common in early childhood.
- Most children become less aggressive after age 6 or 7.
- Boys tend to practice overt aggression, whereas girls often engage in relational aggression.
- Preschool children show temporary fears of real and imaginary objects and events; older children's fears tend to be more realistic.

altruism *(290)*

prosocial behavior *(290)*

instrumental aggression *(290)*

overt aggression *(291)*

relational aggression *(291)*

Families in Trouble: Child Abuse and Neglect

Guidepost 7. What causes child abuse and neglect, and what are the effects of maltreatment?

- The incidence of reported maltreatment of children has increased greatly.
- Forms of maltreatment are physical abuse, neglect, sexual abuse, and emotional maltreatment.
- Characteristics of the family and the community contribute to child abuse and neglect.
- Maltreatment can interfere with physical, cognitive, emotional, and social development, and its effects can continue into adulthood. Still, many maltreated children show remarkable resilience.

physical abuse *(294)*

neglect *(294)*

sexual abuse *(294)*

emotional maltreatment *(294)*

Relationships with Other Children

Guidepost 8. How do young children get along with—or without—siblings?

- Sibling and peer relationships contribute to self-efficacy.
- Most sibling interactions are positive. Older siblings tend to initiate activities, and younger ones to imitate. Same-sex siblings, especially girls, get along best.
- Siblings tend to resolve disputes on the basis of moral principles.
- The kind of relationship children have with siblings often carries over into other peer relationships.
- Only children seem to develop at least as well as children with siblings.

Guidepost 9. How do young children choose playmates and friends, and why are some children more popular than others?

- Preschoolers choose playmates and friends who are like them. Aggressive children are less popular than prosocial children.
- Friends have more positive and negative interactions than other playmates.
- Parenting can affect children's social competence with peers.

PART 4

Linkups to look for

- Malnutrition can hamper cognitive and psychosocial development.
- Moral development may be linked to cognitive growth.
- IQ can be affected by nutrition, socioeconomic status, culture, rapport with the examiner, and familiarity with the surroundings.
- Parenting styles can affect school achievement.
- Physical appearance plays a large part in self-esteem.
- A decline in egocentric thinking permits deeper, more intimate friendships.
- Children who are good learners and problem solvers tend to be resilient in coping with stress.

The middle years of childhood, from about age 6 to about age 11, are often called the school years. School is the central experience during this time—a focal point for physical, cognitive, and psychosocial development. As we see in Chapter 9, children grow taller, heavier, and stronger and acquire the motor skills needed to participate in organized games and sports. They also make major advances in thinking, in moral judgment, in memory, and in literacy. Individual differences become more evident and special needs more important, as competencies affect success in school.

Competencies also affect self-esteem and popularity, as we see in Chapter 10. Although parents continue to be important, the peer group is more influential than before. Children develop physically, cognitively, and emotionally, as well as socially, through contacts with other youngsters. ▸

Middle Childhood

PREVIEW

CHAPTER 9

Physical and Cognitive Development in Middle Childhood

Growth slows.

Strength and athletic skills improve.

Respiratory illnesses are common, but health is generally better than at any other time in the life span.

Egocentrism diminishes. Children begin to think logically but concretely.

Memory and language skills increase.

Cognitive gains permit children to benefit from formal schooling.

Some children show special educational needs and strengths.

CHAPTER 10

Psychosocial Development in Middle Childhood

Self-concept becomes more complex, affecting self-esteem.

Coregulation reflects gradual shift in control from parents to child.

Peers assume central importance.

Chapter 9

Physical and Cognitive Development in Middle Childhood

What we must remember above all in the education of our children is that their love of life should never weaken.

—Natalia Ginzburg, *The Little Virtues*, 1985

Focus: Ann Bancroft, Polar Explorer

Ann Bancroft

Ann Bancroft* is the first woman in history to reach both the North and South Poles by nonmotorized means. In 1986, she dogsledded 1,000 miles from the Northwest Territories in Canada to the North Pole as the only female member of an international expedition. After surviving eight months of grueling training and enduring temperatures as low as −70 degrees for 56 days, Bancroft stood on top of the world. Seven years later she led three other women in a 67-day, 660-mile ski trek to the South Pole, reaching it on January 14, 1993. For these exploits, she was inducted into the National Women's Hall of Fame. In 2000, she and Liv Arneson of Norway became the first team of women to ski across the landmass of Antarctica; and in 2002 the two women reunited for a kayaking voyage from the north shore of Lake Superior to the St. Lawrence Seaway.

How did this five-foot-three-inch, 125-pound woman achieve these remarkable feats? The answers go back to her childhood in Mendota Heights, Minnesota.

Born September 29, 1955, into what she calls a family of risk takers, Ann showed her climbing instincts as soon as she could walk. As a toddler, she would climb her grandmother's bookcase to reach things on top. Instead of trying to stop her from climbing, her parents said, "Go ahead and try; you might just get what you want."

Ann was an outdoor girl. She and her two brothers and two sisters spent hours roaming the fields surrounding their farmhouse. Ann would "pretend she was a pirate building rafts to float down the creek, or an adventurer canoeing in the far north. During the winter she would build snow forts, sleeping shacks, and tunnels" (Wenzel, 1990, p. 15).

Her father often took the family on camping and canoe trips in the wilds of northern Minnesota. When she was 8, Ann started camping out in her backyard in winter with her cousins and the family dog. When she was 10, her parents went to Africa as missionaries. Ann's two years in Kenya kindled her thirst to see other parts of the world.

In school Ann was a poor student and had to be tutored to keep up. A natural athlete, her favorite class was gym. Not until seventh grade did she learn that she had dyslexia, a reading disability. Around that time Ann came across a book about Sir Ernest Shackleton's unsuccessful effort to reach the South Pole

*Biographical information about Ann Bancroft came primarily from Noone (2000), Wenzel (1990), and Bancroft's website, http://www.yourexpedition.com. Other sources were "Ann Bancroft, 1955- " (1998), "Ann Bancroft, 1955- " (1999), "Ann Bancroft, Explorer" (undated), "First Woman to Both Poles" (1997), and "Minnesota Explorer Ann Bancroft" (2002).

OUTLINE

in 1914. She was drawn to the photographs. "I was so fascinated by the images that I no longer was intimidated by the words and thickness of the book," Ann recalls. "I wanted to know about this adventure at the bottom of the world. This began my curiosity with Antarctica and the dream of one day crossing it."

Ann became a physical education teacher and athletic director in St. Paul. In 1983, she and a friend climbed Alaska's Mount McKinley, the highest peak in North America—an expedition that could have ended in disaster for her partner, who developed hypothermia, had it not been for Ann's training in first aid and emergency medicine. Two years later, Ann was invited to join the Steger International Polar Expedition to the North Pole as a medic and trip photographer.

"The goal was not so much reaching the pole itself," Bancroft recalls. "It was . . . more universal. Why do we all take on struggles? Why run a marathon? I think we're all striving to push ourselves. And in the process of overcoming struggle and challenges, we get to know ourselves better."

Bancroft's childhood struggle with dyslexia helps explain the determination that helped her succeed as a polar explorer. "I get stubborn and dig in when people tell me I can't do something and I think I can," she explains. "I never wanted to be perceived as handicapped or limited in any way."

Today Bancroft is an instructor for Wildnerness Inquiry, a program for both able-bodied people and those with disabilities. During her first South Pole expedition, she lugged a 30-pound radio set across the ice so she could send progress reports to students around the world. On her last expedition to Antarctica with Arneson, children in more than forty countries followed the journey with the help of an interactive website. She has coauthored a book about her adventures (Loewen & Bancroft, 2001)—for her, perhaps the greatest challenge of all.

Her goal is to "inspire children around the globe to pursue their dreams" as she has (Noone, 2000, p. 1). "It is totally energizing," she says, "to step out each day living a dream."

As a schoolgirl, Ann Bancroft may not have seemed extraordinary except that her dyslexia marked her as a child with special needs. Yet her achievements, based on her indomitable energy and will, are impressive indeed. Her story illustrates how a dream formed in childhood can inspire later accomplishments. She is a living example of the power of attitudes and desires to shape physical and cognitive development.

Although motor abilities improve less dramatically in middle childhood than before, these years are an important time for the development of the strength, stamina, endurance, and motor proficiency needed for sports and outdoor activities. In this chapter we look at these and other physical developments. Cognitively, we see how entrance into Piaget's stage of concrete operations enables children to think logically and to make more mature judgments. We see how children improve in memory and problem solving, how their intelligence is tested, and how the abilities to read and write open the door to participation in a wider world. We look at factors affecting school achievement, and we examine the controversies over IQ testing, methods of teaching reading, and second-language education. Finally, we see how schools educate children with exceptional needs, like Ann Bancroft.

After you have read and studied this chapter, you should be able to answer each of the the following Guidepost questions. Look for them again in the margins, where they point to important concepts throughout the chapter. To check your understanding of these Guideposts, review the end-of-chapter summary. Checkpoints located at periodic spots throughout the chapter will help you verify your understanding of what you have read.

Guideposts for Study

1. What gains in growth and motor development occur during middle childhood, and what nutritional hazards do children face?
2. What are the principal health and safety concerns about school-age children?
3. How do school-age children's thinking and moral reasoning differ from those of younger children?
4. What advances in memory and other information-processing skills occur during middle childhood?
5. How accurately can schoolchildren's intelligence be measured?
6. How do communicative abilities and literacy expand during middle childhood?
7. What influences school achievement?
8. How do schools meet the needs of non-English-speaking children and those with learning problems?
9. How is giftedness assessed and nurtured?

PHYSICAL DEVELOPMENT

Aspects of Physical Development

If we were to walk by a typical elementary school just after the three o'clock bell, we would see a virtual explosion of children of all shapes and sizes. Tall ones, short ones, husky ones, and slender ones would be bursting out of the school doors into the open air. We would see that school-age children look very different from children a few years younger. They are taller, and most are fairly wiry; but more are likely to be overweight than in past decades, and some may be malnourished. Some of these children, who have spent much of the day sitting in school, will go home, get a snack, and dash outside to jump rope, play ball, skate, cycle, or throw snowballs. Some, especially those with working parents, may stay at school for organized after-school programs. Many children, however, go inside after school, not to emerge for the rest of the day. Instead of practicing skills that stretch their bodies, they do homework or sit in front of the television set. When we talk about physical development in middle childhood, then, we need to look closely at individual children.

Guidepost

1. What gains in growth and motor development occur during middle childhood, and what nutritional hazards do children face?

Growth

Growth during middle childhood slows considerably. Still, although day-by-day changes may not be obvious, they add up to a startling difference between 6-year-olds, who are still small children, and 11-year-olds, many of whom are now beginning to resemble adults.

School-age children grow about 1 to 3 inches each year and gain about 5 to 8 pounds or more, doubling their average body weight. Girls retain somewhat more fatty tissue than boys, a characteristic that will persist through adulthood. Of course, these figures are just averages. Individual children vary widely—so widely that a child of average height at age 7 who did not grow at all for two years would still be within the normal limits of height at age 9.

African American boys and girls tend to grow faster than white children. By about age 6, African American girls have more muscle and bone mass than European American (white) or Mexican American (Hispanic) girls, while the Hispanic girls have a higher percentage of body fat than white girls the same size (Ellis, Abrams, & Wong, 1997).

Although most children grow normally, some do not. One type of growth disorder arises from the body's failure to produce enough growth hormone—or sometimes any growth hormone at all. Administration of synthetic growth hormone in such cases can result in rapid growth in height, especially during the first two years (Albanese & Stanhope, 1993; Vance & Mauras, 1999). However, synthetic growth hormone also is being used for children who are much shorter than other children their age, but whose bodies *are* producing normal quantities of the hormone. Its use for this purpose is highly controversial (Macklin, 2000; Vance & Mauras, 1999). The American Academy of Pediatrics Committee on Drugs and Committee on Bioethics (1997) and other medical experts recommend extreme caution in prescribing growth hormone except as a replacement for an insufficiency of natural hormone.

Checkpoint

Can you . . .

- ✔ Summarize typical growth patterns of boys and girls in middle childhood and give reasons for variations?
- ✔ Discuss the advisability of administering synthetic growth hormone?

Nutrition

Most schoolchildren have good appetites and eat far more than younger children. To support their steady growth and constant exertion, children need, on average, 2,400 calories every day—more for older children and less for younger ones.

What's Your View?

- Much television advertising aimed at young children fosters poor nutrition. How might parents counteract these pressures?

Nutritionists recommend a varied diet including plenty of grains, fruits, and vegetables, which are high in natural nutrients, and high levels of complex carbohydrates, found in potatoes, pasta, bread, and cereals. Simple carbohydrates, found in sweets, should be kept to a minimum. U.S. children of all ages eat too much fat and sugar and artificially fortified or low-nutrient food (Muñoz, Krebs-Smith, Ballard-Barbash, & Cleveland, 1997; Subar, Krebs-Smith, Cook, & Kahle, 1998). To avoid overweight and prevent cardiac problems, young children should get only about 30 percent of their total calories from fat, and less than 10 percent of the total from saturated fat. Lean meat and dairy foods should remain in the diet to provide protein, iron, and calcium. Milk and other dairy products can now be skim or low-fat (AAP Committee on Nutrition, 1992a). Studies have found no negative effects on height, weight, body mass, or neurological development from a moderately low-fat diet (Rask-Nissilä et al., 2000; Shea et al., 1993).

Malnutrition Nearly half (46 percent) of young children in south Asia, 30 percent in sub-Saharan Africa, 8 percent in Latin America and the Caribbean, and 27 percent worldwide are believed to suffer from malnutrition (UNICEF, 2002). In the United States in 1998, one child in 5 did not get enough to eat (U.S. Department of Agriculture, 1999).

Because undernourished children usually live in poverty and suffer other kinds of environmental deprivation, the specific effects of malnutrition may be hard to isolate. However, taken together, these deprivations can affect not only growth and physical well-being but cognitive and psychosocial development as well. In an analysis of data on a nationally representative sample of 3,286 six- to eleven-year-olds living in households, those whose families lacked sufficient food were more likely to have low arithmetic test scores, to have repeated a grade, to have seen a psychologist, and to have had difficulty getting along with other children (Alaimo, Olson, & Frongillo, 2001).

Since malnutrition may affect all aspects of development, its treatment may need to go beyond physical care. One longitudinal study (Grantham-McGregor, Powell, Walker, Chang, & Fletcher, 1994) followed two groups of poor Jamaican children with low developmental levels who were hospitalized for severe malnourishment in infancy or toddlerhood. Health care paraprofessionals played with an experimental group in the hospital and, after discharge, visited them at home every week for three years, showing the mothers how to use homemade toys and encouraging them to interact with their children. A control group received only standard medical care. The mothers in the experimental group also enrolled their children in preschools at earlier ages than in the control group.

Three years after the program stopped, the experimental group's IQs were well above those of the control group (though not as high as those of a third, well-nourished group); and their IQs remained significantly higher seven, eight, nine, and fourteen years after leaving the hospital.

Malnutrition of children is a major problem worldwide. Its effects can be counteracted by improved diet.

Can schooling help counteract cognitive losses? One longitudinal study followed about 1,400 Guatemalan children in impoverished rural villages, many of whom had stunted growth due to malnutrition and who lived in unsanitary, infection-causing conditions. Those who completed at least four years of school did better on tests of cognition during adolescence than those who dropped out earlier (Gorman & Pollitt, 1996). However, it is quite possible that the children who stayed in school had better cognitive abilities to begin with than those who dropped out, so the schooling may not have been the cause of their greater cognitive development.

What's Your View?

- In view of childhood malnutrition's apparent long-term effects on physical, social, and cognitive development, what can be done to combat it?

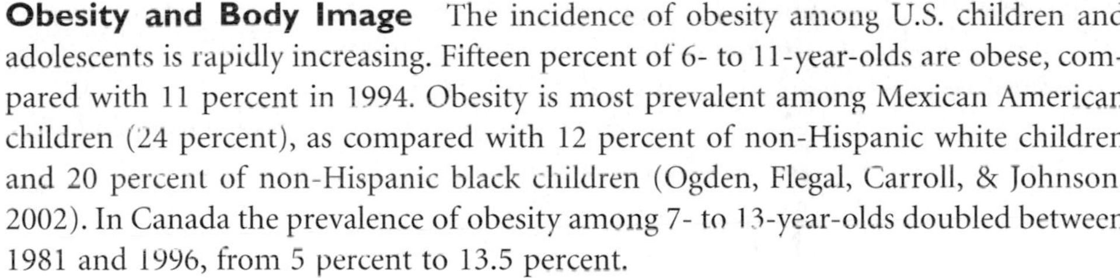

Obesity and Body Image The incidence of obesity among U.S. children and adolescents is rapidly increasing. Fifteen percent of 6- to 11-year-olds are obese, compared with 11 percent in 1994. Obesity is most prevalent among Mexican American children (24 percent), as compared with 12 percent of non-Hispanic white children and 20 percent of non-Hispanic black children (Ogden, Flegal, Carroll, & Johnson, 2002). In Canada the prevalence of obesity among 7- to 13-year-olds doubled between 1981 and 1996, from 5 percent to 13.5 percent.

As we reported in Chapter 3, obesity often results from an *inherited tendency,* aggravated by too little exercise and too much, or the wrong kinds of, food. Among the genes that seem to be involved in obesity is one that governs production of a brain protein called *leptin,* which seems to help regulate body fat (Campfield, Smith, Guisez, Devos, & Burn, 1995; Friedman & Halaas, 1998; Halaas et al., 1995; Kristensen et al., 1998; Montague et al., 1997; Pelleymounter et al., 1995; Zhang et al., 1994).

Environment is also influential, since children tend to eat the same kinds of foods and develop the same kinds of habits as the people around them. High body mass index (BMI) and high blood pressure, both risk factors for heart disease, tend to be more common in African American and Mexican American children than in white children (Winkleby, Robinson, Sundquist, & Kraemer, 1999).

Inactivity may be a major factor in the sharp rise in obesity (Freedman et al., 1997; Harrell, Gansky, Bradley, & McMurray, 1997). For example, children who watch four or more hours of television each day have more body fat and a higher BMI than those who watch less than two hours a day (Andersen, Crespo, Bartlett, Cheskin, & Pratt, 1998).

Obese children often suffer because of taunts from peers, and they may compensate by indulging themselves with treats, making their physical and social problems even worse. Especially if they have overweight parents, they also tend to become overweight adults (Whitaker et al., 1997), at risk of high blood pressure, heart disease, orthopedic problems, and diabetes (Must, Jacques, Dallal, Bajema, & Dietz, 1992).

body image Descriptive and evaluative beliefs about one's appearance.

Checkpoint

Can you . . .

- ✔ Discuss nutritional needs of preschool and school-age children?
- ✔ Describe effects of malnutrition and identify factors that may influence its long-term outcome?
- ✔ Discuss why obesity has increased and how it can be treated?

For these reasons, a panel of pediatric obesity experts recommends that any child with a BMI in the ninety-fifth percentile or higher be screened for possible treatment (Barlow & Dietz, 1998). Parents need to find constructive, blame-free ways to help children lose weight, by encouraging physical activity and providing a wide variety of healthful, low-fat foods (Davison & Birch, 2001). In a 12-week experiment with ten obese 8- to 12-year-olds, those whose television-viewing was limited to the amount of time they spent pedaling an exercise bicycle watched much less television and showed significantly greater reductions in body fat than a control group (Faith et al., 2001).

Unfortunately, children who try to lose weight are not always the ones who need to do so. Concern with **body image**—how one believes one looks—becomes increasingly important toward the end of middle childhood, especially for girls, and may develop into eating disorders that become more common in adolescence (see Chapter 12).

Motor Development

Motor skills continue to improve in middle childhood (see Table 9-1). By this age, however, children in most nonliterate and transitional societies go to work, and this plus more household labor, especially for girls, leaves them little time and freedom for physical play (Larson & Verma, 1999). In the United States, children's lives today are more tightly organized than they were when Ann Bancroft was camping out in her backyard. They spend less time in free, unstructured activities, such as rough-and-tumble play and informal games, and more time in organized sports (Hofferth & Sandberg, 1998).

rough-and-tumble play Vigorous play involving wrestling, hitting, and chasing, often accompanied by laughing and screaming.

Rough-and-Tumble Play About 10 percent of schoolchildren's free play at recess in the early grades consists of **rough-and-tumble play,** vigorous play that involves wrestling, kicking, tumbling, grappling, and sometimes chasing, often accompanied by laughing and screaming. This kind of play peaks in middle childhood; the proportion typically drops to about 5 percent at age 11, about the same as in early childhood (Pellegrini, 1998; Pellegrini & Smith, 1998).

This kind of play reminds us of our evolutionary heritage. Unlike symbolic play, which is distinctly human, rough-and-tumble play was first described in monkeys. It also seems to be universal, since it takes place from early childhood through adolescence

Table 9-1 Motor Development in Middle Childhood

Age	Selected Behaviors
6	Girls are superior in movement accuracy; boys are superior in forceful, less complex acts.
	Skipping is possible.
	Children can throw with proper weight shift and step.
7	One-footed balancing without looking becomes possible.
	Children can walk 2-inch-wide balance beams.
	Children can hop and jump accurately into small squares.
	Children can execute accurate jumping-jack exercise.
8	Children have 12-pound pressure on grip strength.
	Number of games participated in by both sexes is greatest at this age.
	Children can engage in alternate rhythmic hopping in a 2-2, 2-3, or 3-3 pattern.
	Girls can throw a small ball 40 feet.
9	Boys can run 16½ feet per second.
	Boys can throw a small ball 70 feet.
10	Children can judge and intercept pathways of small balls thrown from a distance.
	Girls can run 17 feet per second.
11	Standing broad jump of 5 feet is possible for boys; 6 inches less for girls.

Source: Adapted from Cratty, 1986.

in such diverse places as India, Mexico, Okinawa, Africa, the Philippines, Great Britain, and the United States (Humphreys & Smith, 1984).

Anthropologists suggest that rough-and-tumble play evolved to provide practice in skills used in fighting and hunting (Symons, 1978). Today it serves other purposes, aside from physical exercise. Rough-and-tumble play helps children jockey for dominance in the peer group by assessing their own and each other's strength. Boys around the world engage in rough-and-tumble play more than girls do, a fact generally attributed to a combination of hormonal differences and socialization (Pellegrini, 1998; Pellegrini & Smith, 1998).

Not enough children engage in active after-school play, as this girl is doing.

Physical Fitness Although most U.S. schoolchildren get enough exercise to meet national goals, many children are not as active as they should be—and could be. Among a nationally representative sample of 8- through 16-year-olds examined between 1988 and 1994, 80 percent said they play or exercise vigorously—enough to work up a sweat or breathe hard—at least three times a week outside of physical education classes. However, 15 percent of boys and 26 percent of girls did not meet that standard (Andersen et al., 1998).

Exercise—or lack of it—affects both physical and mental health. It improves strength and endurance, helps build healthy bones and muscles, helps control weight, reduces anxiety and stress, and increases self confidence. Even moderate physical activity has health benefits if done regularly for at least thirty minutes on most, and preferably all, days of the week. A sedentary lifestyle that carries over into adulthood may result in obesity, with increased risk of diabetes, heart disease, and cancer (Centers for Disease Control [CDC], 2000a; National Institutes of Health [NIH] Consensus Development Panel on Physical Activity and Cardiovascular Health, 1996).

Unfortunately, most physical activities, in and out of school, are team and competitive sports and games aimed at the fittest and most athletic children, like Ann Bancroft. Too often, parents and coaches pressure children to practice long hours, focus on winning rather than playing the game, criticize children's skills, or offer bribes to make them do well (Wolff, 1993). All these tactics discourage rather than encourage participation. Furthermore, most children will drop these activities after leaving school.

To help children improve their motor skills, organized athletic programs should offer the chance to try a variety of sports, should gear coaching to building skills rather than winning games, and should include as many children as possible rather than concentrating on a few star athletes. Programs should include a variety of sports that can be part of a lifetime fitness regimen, such as tennis, bowling, running, swimming, golf, and skating (AAP Committee on Sports Medicine & Fitness, 1997).

Checkpoint

Can you . . .

- ✔ Explain the significance of rough-and-tumble play?
- ✔ Describe changes in the types of physical play children engage in as they grow older?
- ✔ Explain why some children are not as physically fit as they should be?

Health and Safety

The development of vaccines for major childhood illnesses has made middle childhood a relatively safe time of life, especially in developed countries. Since immunizations are required for school admission in the United States, children this age are likely to be protected. The death rate in these years is the lowest in the life span. Still, some children suffer from acute or chronic medical conditions; and some are injured in accidents. As children's experience with illness increases, so does their cognitive understanding of the causes of health and illness and of how people can promote their own health (see Box 9-1 on page 314).

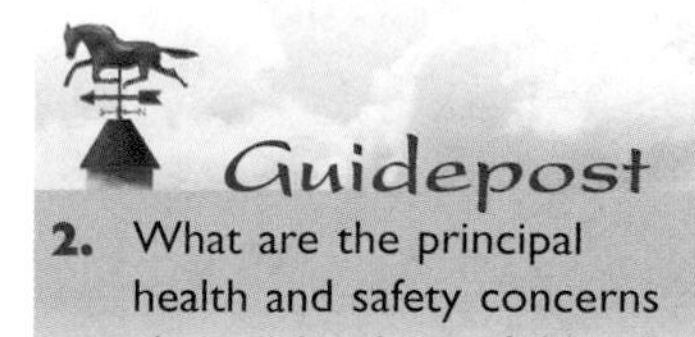

Guidepost

2. What are the principal health and safety concerns about school-age children?

BOX 9-1

Digging Deeper
Children's Understanding of Illness

From a Piagetian perspective, children's understanding of health and illness is tied to cognitive development. As they mature, their explanations for disease change. Before middle childhood, children are egocentric; they tend to believe that illness is magically produced by human actions, often their own ("I was a bad boy, so now I feel bad"). Later they explain all diseases—only a little less magically—as the doing of all-powerful germs; the only "protection" is a variety of superstitious behaviors to ward them off. "Watch out for germs," a child may say. As children approach adolescence, they see that there can be multiple causes of disease, that contact with germs does not automatically lead to illness, and that people can do much to keep healthy.

Children's understanding of AIDS increases with age, like their understanding of colds and of cancer, but they understand the cause of colds earlier than they do the causes of the other two illnesses, probably because they are more familiar with colds (Kistner et al., 1997; Schonfeld, Johnson, Perrin, O'Hare, & Cicchetti, 1993). Although most 6- and 7-year-olds have heard of HIV/AIDS, misconceptions about its causes and symptoms persist. Among 231 African American children, ages 6 through 11, those whose mothers were infected showed fewer misconceptions than their peers (Armistead et al., 1999). Misconceptions about the disease can be harmful, because children who harbor them are likely to avoid contact with classmates with AIDS (Kistner et al., 1997).

Interviews with 361 children in kindergarten through sixth grade (Schonfeld et al., 1993) found that children often give superficially correct explanations but lack real understanding of the processes involved in AIDS. For example, although 96 children mentioned drug use as a cause, most did not seem to realize that the disease is spread through blood adhering to a needle shared by drug users. One second-grader gave this version of how someone gets AIDS: "Well, by doing drugs and something like that . . . by going by a drug dealer who has AIDS. . . . Well, you go by a person who's a drug dealer and you might catch the AIDS from 'em by standing near 'em" (Schonfeld et al., 1993, p. 393).

From a young child's point of view, such a statement may be a logical extension of the belief that germs cause disease. The child may wrongly assume that AIDS can be caught, as colds are, from sharing cups and utensils, from being near someone who is coughing or sneezing, or from hugging and kissing. One AIDS education program (Sigelman et al., 1996) sought to replace such intuitive "theories" with scientifically grounded ones and to test Piaget's idea that if children have not mastered a concept, they are probably not yet ready to do so. The developers of the program hypothesized that what young children lack is knowledge about the disease, not the ability to think about it.

A carefully scripted program was tried on 306 third-, fifth-, and seventh-graders in Catholic schools in Tucson. Trained health instructors conducted two 50-minute sessions consisting of lectures, video clips, drawings, and discussion, and using vocabulary appropriate for third-graders. The curriculum emphasized that there are only a few ways to get AIDS and that normal contact with infected people is not one of them.

Experimental and control groups were tested before the program began and again about two weeks afterward. Students who had received instruction knew more about AIDS and its causes than those who had not, were no more (and no less) worried about it than before, and were more willing to be with people with AIDS. Almost a year later, the gains generally were retained. The success of this program shows that, contrary to Piaget, even relatively young children can grasp complex scientific concepts about disease if teaching is geared to their level of understanding.

What's Your View?

How old do you think children should be before being taught about AIDS?

Check It Out:

OLC

For more information on this topic, go to www.mhhe.com/papaliah9, where you'll find links to information about children's understanding of illness.

Medical Problems

acute medical conditions Illnesses that last a short time.

Illness in middle childhood tends to be brief. **Acute medical conditions**—occasional, short-term conditions, such as infections, allergies, and warts—are common. Six or seven bouts a year with colds, flu, or viruses are typical at this age, as germs pass among children at school or at play (Behrman, 1992). Upper-respiratory illnesses, sore throats, strep throats, and ear infections decrease with age; but acne, headaches, and transitory emotional disturbances increase as children approach puberty (Starfield et al., 1984).

chronic medical conditions Illnesses or impairments that persist for at least three months.

According to a nationwide survey of 30,032 families, an estimated 18 percent of children under age 18 in 1994 had **chronic medical conditions:** physical, developmental, behavioral, and/or emotional conditions requiring special health services.

Children with special health needs spend three times as many days sick in bed and miss school three times as often as other children (Newacheck et al., 1998). Poor children (who are disproportionately minority children) and those living with a single parent are more likely than other children to have chronic conditions and to face barriers to health care (Flores et al., 2002; Newacheck et al., 1998).

Children with chronic conditions tend to be remarkably resilient. Most do not show problems in mental health, behavior, or schooling (AAP Committee on Children with Disabilities and Committee on Psychosocial Aspects of Child and Family Health, 1993). Still, certain conditions—such as vision and hearing problems, asthma, and AIDS—can greatly affect everday living.

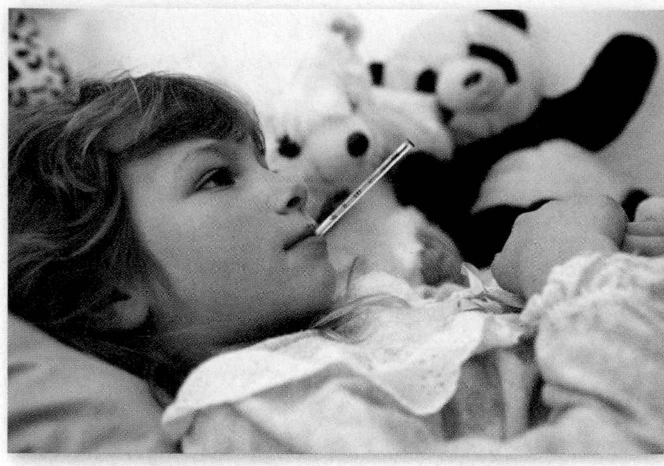

Colds, flu, and viruses are common in middle childhood. Illnesses at this age tend to be brief and transient.

Vision and Hearing Problems Most school-age children have keener vision than when they were younger. Children under 6 years old tend to be farsighted. By age 6, vision typically is more acute; and because the two eyes are better coordinated, they can focus better.

Almost 13 percent of children under 18 are estimated to be blind or to have impaired vision. Vision problems are reported more often for white and Latino children than for African Americans (Newacheck, Stoddard, & McManus, 1993). About 15 percent of 6- to 19-year olds, mostly boys, have some hearing loss. Current screening guidelines may miss many children with very high-frequency impairments. This is of concern, since even slight hearing loss can affect communication, behavior, and social relationships (Niskar et al., 1998).

Asthma **Asthma,** a chronic respiratory disease, is the number one cause of childhood disability, affecting an estimated 1.4 percent of U.S. children. Its prevalence has increased 232 percent since 1969 (Newacheck & Halfon, 2000). Apparently allergy-based, it is characterized by sudden attacks of coughing, wheezing, and difficulty in breathing; and it can be fatal. Children's asthma death rates have tripled since 1984, but the number of deaths fell nearly 20 percent in 1997 compared with the year before, probably due to improved diagnosis and treatment. The cause of the asthma explosion is unknown, but some experts point to more tightly insulated houses that permit less air circulation and early exposure to environmental toxins and allergens (Nugent, 1999; Sly, 2000; Stapleton, 1998). Tobacco smoke in the home, use of a gas stove for heat, and allergies to household pets are important risk factors (Lanphear, Aligne, Auinger, Weitzman, & Byrd, 2001). Psychosocial factors also may play a part. Infants with family histories of asthma whose mothers were rated by clinicians as likely to have parenting difficulties tended to develop asthma by ages 6 to 8 (Klinnert et al., 2001).

asthma A chronic respiratory disease characterized by sudden attacks of coughing, wheezing, and difficulty in breathing.

Poor, minority children, especially boys, are most likely to be affected, perhaps because of inadequate access to health care, as are children in single-parent families (Newacheck & Halfon, 2000; Stapleton, 1998). Children with asthma miss an average of ten days of school each year and experience twenty days of limited activity—almost twice as often as children with other chronic ailments (Newacheck & Halfon, 2000). Some of this sickness may be avoidable; most children with moderate to severe asthma do not get adequate treatment (Halterman, Aligne, Auinger, McBride, & Szilagyi, 2000).

HIV and AIDS Children infected with the human immunodeficiency virus (HIV) are at high risk to develop AIDS. Ninety percent of these children acquired the AIDS virus from their mothers, almost all of them in the womb (AAP Committee on Pediatric AIDS and Committee on Infectious Diseases, 1999; refer back to Chapter 3).

What's Your View?

- Medical evidence shows virtually no evidence that children with HIV infection who are symptom-free can transmit the virus to others except through bodily fluids. Yet many parents are afraid to have their children go to school with a child who is HIV-positive. Can you suggest ways to deal with parents who have this concern?

Most children infected with HIV who reach school age function normally. Those with symptoms of AIDS may develop central nervous system dysfunction that can interfere with their ability to learn, but antiretroviral therapy can improve their functioning (AAP Committee on Pediatric AIDS, 2000). A combination therapy including protease inhibitors has markedly reduced mortality among HIV-infected children and adolescents (Gortmaker et al., 2001).

Since there is virtually no risk of infecting classmates (refer back to Box 9-1), children who carry the AIDS virus do not need to be isolated, either for their own health or for that of other children. They should be encouraged to participate in all school activities, including athletics, to the extent they are able (AAP Committee on Sports Medicine and Fitness, 1999; AAP Committee on Pediatric AIDS, 2000).

Accidental Injuries

Injuries increase between ages 5 and 14, as children take part in more physical activities and are supervised less. As in early childhood, accidental injuries are the leading cause of death (Anderson, 2002).

In 1998, approximately 275 children died and about 430,000 went to emergency rooms for treatment of nonfatal injuries as a result of bicycle accidents. An estimated 23,000 of these were serious brain injuries. As many as 88 percent of these injuries could be prevented by using helmets (AAP Committee of Injury and Poison Prevention, 2001a). Protective headgear also is vital for baseball and softball, football, roller skating, roller blading, skateboarding, scooter riding, horseback riding, hockey, speed sledding, and tobogganing. For soccer, protective goggles and mouth guards may help reduce head and facial injuries. "Heading" the ball should be minimized because of the danger of brain injury (AAP Committee on Sports Medicine and Fitness, 2000, 2001).

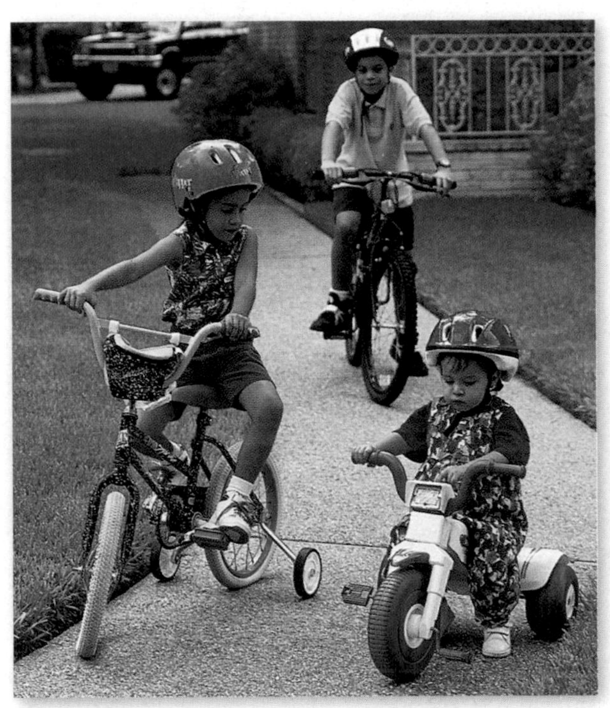

Safety-approved helmets protect children of all ages from disabling or fatal head injuries.

Children under 14 suffered more than 1,260 snowmobile-related injuries, many of them severe and some fatal, in 1997 (Rice, Alvanos, & Kenney, 2000). The AAP Committee on Accident and Poison Prevention (1988) recommends that children under 16 *not* use snowmobiles, and that older riders be required by law to be licensed and to wear helmets at all times.

For a growing number of children, an important source of danger is the trampoline in the backyard (Furnival, Street, & Schunk, 1999; Smith & Shields, 1998). In 1996, an estimated 83,400 trampoline-related injuries were treated in U.S. hospital emergency rooms—a 140 percent increase since 1990—and more than two-thirds of the victims were 5 to 14 years old. Many of these children required surgery or hospitalization (AAP Committee on Injury and Poison Prevention and Committee on Sports Medicine and Fitness, 1999). Because of the need for stringent safety precautions and constant supervision, the American Academy of Pediatrics Committee on Injury and Poison Prevention and Committee on Sports Medicine and Fitness (1999) recommend that parents never buy trampolines, nor should children use them on playgrounds or at school.

Unfortunately, the media do not encourage safety consciousness. In the twenty-five most popular G- and PG-rated nonanimated movies between 1995 and 1997, most characters did not wear automobile safety belts, look both ways when crossing streets, use crosswalks, wear helmets when bicycling, or wear flotation devices while boating (Pelletier et al., 2000).

Checkpoint

Can you . . .

- ✔ Distinguish between acute and chronic medical conditions, and discuss how vision and hearing problems, asthma, and HIV can affect everyday life?
- ✔ Identify factors that increase the risks of accidental injury?

COGNITIVE DEVELOPMENT

Piagetian Approach: The Concrete Operational Child

At about age 7, according to Piaget, children enter the stage of **concrete operations,** so named because children can now use mental operations to solve concrete (actual) problems. Children can think more logically than before because they can take multiple aspects of a situation into account. However, they are still limited to thinking about real situations in the here and now.

Guidepost

3. How do school-age children's thinking and moral reasoning differ from those of younger children?

concrete operations Third stage of Piagetian cognitive development (approximately from ages 7 to 12), during which children develop logical but not abstract thinking.

Cognitive Advances

Children in the stage of concrete operations can perform many tasks at a much higher level than they could in the preoperational stage (see Table 9-2). They have a better understanding of spatial concepts, of causality, of categorization, of inductive and deductive reasoning, and of conservation.

Space and Causality Children in the stage of concrete operations can better understand spatial relationships. They have a clearer idea of how far it is from one place to another and how long it will take to get there, and they can more easily remember the route and the landmarks along the way. Experience plays a role in this development: a child who walks to school becomes more familiar with the neighborhood outside the home.

The abilities to use maps and models and to communicate spatial information improve with age (Gauvain, 1993). Although 6-year-olds can search for and find hidden objects, they usually do not give clear directions for finding the same objects—

Table 9-2 Advances in Selected Cognitive Abilities During Middle Childhood

Ability	Example
Spatial thinking	Danielle can use a map or model to help her search for a hidden object and can give someone else directions for finding the object. She can find her way to and from school, can estimate distances, and can judge how long it will take her to go from one place to another.
Cause and effect	Douglas knows which physical attributes of objects on each side of a balance scale will affect the result (i.e., number of objects matters but color does not). He does not yet know which spatial factors, such as position and placement of the objects, make a difference.
Classification	Elena can sort objects into categories, such as shape, color or both. She knows that a subclass (roses) has fewer members than the class of which it is a part (flowers).
Seriation and transitive inference	Catherine can arrange a group of sticks in order, from the shortest to the longest, and can insert an intermediate-size stick into the proper place. She knows that if one stick is longer than a second stick, and the second stick is longer than a third, then the first stick is longer than the third.
Inductive and deductive reasoning	Dara can solve both inductive and deductive problems and knows that inductive conclusions (based on particular premises) are less certain than deductive ones (based on general premises).
Conservation	Felipe, at age 7, knows that if a clay ball is rolled into a sausage, it still contains the same amount of clay (conservation of substance). At age 9, he knows that the ball and the sausage weigh the same. Not until early adolescence will he understand that they displace the same amount of liquid if dropped in a glass of water.

perhaps because they lack the appropriate vocabulary or do not realize what information the other person needs (Plumert, Pick, Marks, Kintsch, & Wegesin, 1994).

Judgments about cause and effect also improve during middle childhood. When 5- to 12-year-olds were asked to predict how levers and balance scales would perform with varying numbers and weights of objects placed at varying distances from the center, the older children gave more correct answers than the younger children (Amsel, Goodman, Savoie, & Clark, 1996).

Categorization The ability to categorize helps children think logically. Categorization now includes such sophisticated abilities as *seriation, transitive inference,* and *class inclusion.* Children show that they understand **seriation** when they can arrange objects in a series according to one or more dimensions, such as weight (lightest to heaviest) or color (lightest to darkest). By 7 or 8, children can grasp the relationships among a group of sticks on sight and arrange them in order of size (Piaget, 1952).

seriation Ability to order items along a dimension.

transitive inference Understanding of the relationship between two objects by knowing the relationship of each to a third object.

class inclusion Understanding of the relationship between a whole and its parts.

Transitive inference is the ability to recognize a relationship between two objects by knowing the relationship between each of them and a third object. Catherine is shown three sticks: a yellow one, a green one, and a blue one. She is shown that the yellow stick is longer than the green one, and the green one is longer than the blue. Without physically comparing the yellow and blue sticks, she knows that the yellow one is longer than the blue one (Chapman & Lindenberger, 1988; Piaget & Inhelder, 1967).

Class inclusion is the ability to see the relationship between a whole and its parts. If preoperational children are shown a bunch of ten flowers—seven roses and three carnations—and are asked whether there are more roses or more flowers, they are likely to say there are more roses, because they are comparing the roses with the carnations rather than with the whole bunch. Not until the stage of concrete operations do children come to realize that roses are a subclass of flowers and that, therefore, there cannot be more roses than flowers (Flavell, 1963).

Inductive and Deductive Reasoning According to Piaget, children in the stage of concrete operations use **inductive reasoning.** Starting with observations about particular members of a class of people, animals, objects, or events, they then draw general conclusions about the class as a whole. ("My dog barks. So does Terry's dog and Melissa's dog. So it looks as if all dogs bark.") Inductive conclusions must be tentative because it is always possible to come across new information (a dog that does not bark) that does not support the conclusion.

inductive reasoning Type of logical reasoning that moves from particular observations about members of a class to a general conclusion about that class.

deductive reasoning Type of logical reasoning that moves from a general premise about a class to a conclusion about a particular member or members of the class.

Deductive reasoning, which Piaget believed does not develop until adolescence, starts with a general statement (premise) about a class and applies it to particular members of the class. If the premise is true of the whole class, and the reasoning is sound, then the conclusion must be true: "All dogs bark. Spot is a dog. Spot barks."

Researchers gave 16 inductive and deductive problems to 16 kindergartners, 17 second-graders, 16 fourth-graders, and 17 sixth-graders. The problems were designed so as *not* to call upon knowledge of the real world. For example, one deductive problem was: "All poggops wear blue boots. Tombor is a poggop. Does Tombor wear blue boots?" The corresponding inductive problem was: "Tombor is a poggop. Tombor wears blue boots. Do all poggops wear blue boots?" Contrary to Piagetian theory, second-graders (but not kindergartners) were able to correctly answer both kinds of problems, to see the difference between them, and to explain their responses, and they (appropriately) expressed more confidence in their deductive answers than in their inductive ones (Galotti, Komatsu, & Voelz, 1997).

What's Your View?

- How can parents and teachers help children improve their reasoning ability?

Conservation In solving various types of conservation problems, children in the stage of concrete operations can work out the answers in their heads; they do not have to measure or weigh the objects.

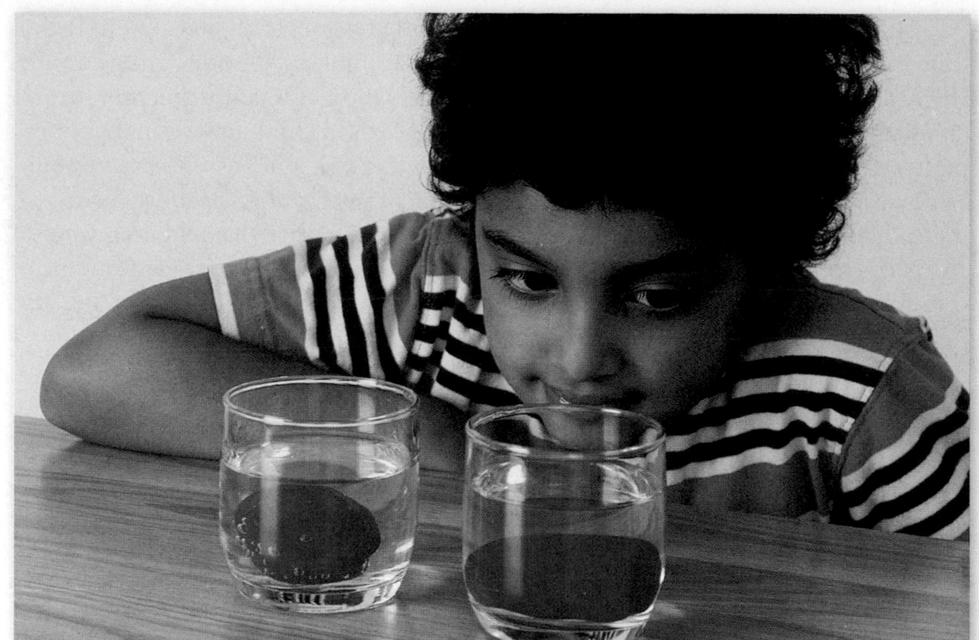

Does one ball of clay displace more water than the other? A child who has acheived conservation of volume knows that the answer does not depend on the ball's shape.

If one of two identical clay balls is rolled or kneaded into a different shape, say, a long, thin "sausage," Felipe, who is in the stage of concrete operations, will say that the ball and the "sausage" still contain the same amount of clay. Stacy, who is in the preoperational stage, is deceived by appearances. She says the long, thin roll contains more clay because it looks longer.

Felipe, unlike Stacy, understands the principle of *identity:* he knows the clay is still the same clay, even though it has a different shape. He also understands the principle of *reversibility:* he knows he can change the sausage back into a ball. And he can *decenter:* he can focus on both length and width. He recognizes that although the ball is shorter than the "sausage," it is also thicker. Stacy centers on one dimension (length) while excluding the other (thickness).

Typically, children can solve problems involving conservation of substance, like this one, by about age 7 or 8. However, in tasks involving conservation of weight—in which they are asked, for example, whether the ball and the "sausage" weigh the same—children typically do not give correct answers until about age 9 or 10. In tasks involving conservation of volume—in which children must judge whether the "sausage" and the ball displace an equal amount of liquid when placed in a glass of water—correct answers are rare before age 12.

Piaget's term for this inconsistency in the development of different types of conservation is **horizontal décalage.** Children's thinking at this stage is so concrete, so closely tied to a particular situation, that they cannot readily transfer what they have learned about one type of conservation to another type, even though the underlying principles are the same.

horizontal décalage Piaget's term for inability to transfer learning about one type of conservation to other types, which causes a child to master different types of conservation tasks at different ages.

Piaget maintained that mastery of skills such as conservation depends on neurological maturation and adaptation to the environment and is not tied to cultural experience. Support for a neurological basis of conservation of volume comes from scalp measurements of brain activity during a conservation task. Children who had achieved conservation of volume showed different brain wave patterns from those who had not yet achieved it, suggesting that they were using different brain regions for the task (Stauder, Molenaar, & Van der Molen, 1993).

Although cross-cultural studies support a progression from the rigid, illogical thinking of younger children to the flexible, logical thinking of older ones (Broude, 1995; Gardiner et al., 1998), abilities such as conservation also may depend in part on familiarity with the materials being manipulated. Mexican children who make pottery understand that a clay ball that has been rolled into a coil still has the same amount of clay sooner than they understand other types of conservation (Broude, 1995); and these children show signs of conservation of substance earlier than children who do not make pottery (Price-Williams, Gordon, & Ramirez, 1969). Thus, understanding of conservation may come not only from new patterns of mental organization, but also from culturally defined personal experience with the physical world.

Moral Reasoning

To draw out children's moral thinking, Piaget (1932) would tell them a story about two little boys: "One day Augustus noticed that his father's inkpot was empty and decided to help his father by filling it. While he was opening the bottle, he spilled a lot of ink on the tablecloth. The other boy, Julian, played with his father's inkpot, even though he knew he shouldn't, and spilled a little ink on the cloth." Then Piaget would ask, "Which boy was naughtier, and why?"

Children younger than 7 usually considered Augustus naughtier, since he made the bigger stain. Older children recognized that Augustus meant well and made the large stain by accident, whereas Julian made a small stain while doing something he should not have been doing. Immature moral judgments, Piaget concluded, center only on the degree of offense; more mature judgments consider intent.

Piaget (1932; Piaget & Inhelder, 1969) proposed that moral reasoning develops in three stages. Children move gradually from one stage to another, at varying ages.

The first stage (approximately ages 2–7, corresponding with the preoperational stage), is based on obedience to authority. Young children think rigidly about moral concepts. Because they are egocentric, they cannot imagine more than one way of looking at a moral issue. They believe that rules come from adult authorities and cannot be bent or changed, that behavior is either right or wrong, and that any offense (like Augustus's) deserves punishment, regardless of intent.

The second stage (ages 7 or 8 to 10 or 11, corresponding with the stage of concrete operations) is characterized by increasing flexibility and some degree of autonomy based on mutual respect and cooperation. As children interact with more people and come into contact with a wider range of viewpoints, they begin to discard the idea that there is a single, absolute standard of right and wrong and to develop their own sense of justice based on fairness, or equal treatment for all. Because they can consider more than one aspect of a situation, they can make more subtle moral judgments, such as taking into consideration the intent behind Augustus's and Julian's behavior.

Around age 11 or 12, when children may become capable of formal reasoning (see Chapter 11), the third stage of moral development arrives. Now "equality" takes on a different meaning for the child. The belief that everyone should be treated alike gradually gives way to the idea of *equity,* of taking specific circumstances into account. Thus, a child of this age might say that a 2-year-old who spilled ink on the tablecloth should be held to a less demanding moral standard than a 10-year-old who did the same thing.

Lawrence Kohlberg's theory of moral reasoning, which builds on Piaget's, is discussed in Chapter 11.

What's Your View?

- Do you think intent is an important factor in morality? In what ways does the criminal justice system reflect or contradict this view?

Checkpoint

Can you . . .

- ✔ Identify five kinds of cognitive abilities that emerge or strengthen during middle childhood?
- ✔ Name three principles that help school-aged children understand conservation, and explain why children master different kinds of conservation at different ages?
- ✔ Give evidence for influences of neurological development and cultural experience on Piagetian tasks?
- ✔ Describe Piaget's three stages of moral development and explain their links to cognitive maturation?

Information Processing and Intelligence

Unlike Piaget, who described broad changes in the way school-age children's minds operate, information-processing researchers focus on improvements in the *efficiency* of mental operations: how much information children can handle at a given time and how quickly and accurately they can process it. More efficient processing makes it easier for children to learn and remember. Differences in efficiency of processing may help account for the range of scores on psychometric intelligence tests, which now become more reliable predictors of school performance.

Memory and Other Processing Skills

As children move through the school years, they make steady progress in their abilities to process and retain information. They understand more about how memory works, and this knowledge enables them to use strategies, or deliberate plans, to help them remember. In addition, as their knowledge expands, they become more aware of what kinds of information are important to pay attention to and remember.

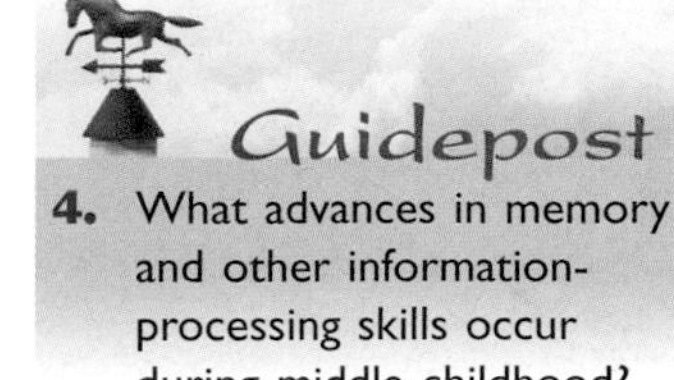

4. What advances in memory and other information-processing skills occur during middle childhood?

Basic Processes and Capacities The way the brain stores information is believed to be universal, though the efficiency of the system varies from person to person (Siegler, 1998). Information-processing models depict the brain as containing three "storehouses": *sensory memory, working memory,* and *long-term memory.*

sensory memory Initial, brief, temporary storage of sensory information.

Sensory memory is the storage system's initial entry point; a temporary "holding tank" for incoming sensory information. Sensory memory shows little change with age; as we have seen, even infants show it. And a 5-year-old's immediate recall is about as good as that of an adult (Siegler, 1998). However, without processing (encoding), sensory memories fade quickly.

working memory Short-term storage of information being actively processed.

Information that is being encoded or retrieved is kept in **working memory,** a short-term "storehouse" for information a person is actively working on; that is, information the person is trying to understand, remember, or think about. It is in working memory that mental representations are prepared for, or recalled from, storage. Brain imaging studies have found that working memory is located partly in the *prefrontal cortex,* the large portion of the frontal lobe directly behind the forehead (Nelson et al., 2000). This region of the brain develops more slowly than any other (M. H. Johnson, 1998); not until the second half of the first year do the prefrontal cortex and associated circuitry develop the capacity for working memory (Nelson, 1995).

The efficiency of working memory is limited by its capacity. Researchers may assess the capacity of working memory by asking children to recall a series of digits in reverse order (for example, "2-8-3-7-5-1" if they heard "1-5-7-3-8-2"). The capacity of working memory, that is, the number of digits a child can recall, increases rapidly in middle childhood (Cowan, Nugent, Elliott, Ponomarev, & Saults, 1999). At ages 5 to 6, children usually remember only two digits; the typical adolescent remembers six.

central executive In Baddeley's model, element of working memory that controls the processing of information.

long-term memory Storage of virtually unlimited capacity, which holds information for very long periods.

According to a widely used information-processing model, a **central executive** controls the processing operations that go on in working memory (Baddeley, 1981, 1986). The central executive orders information encoded for transfer to **long-term memory,** a "storehouse" of virtually unlimited capacity that holds information for long periods of time. The central executive also retrieves information from long-term memory for processing in working memory. The central executive can temporarily expand the capacity of working memory by moving information into two separate subsidiary systems, one of which holds verbal information and the other, visual/spatial images, while the central executive is occupied with other tasks. The central executive, which may be located in the frontal lobes, seems to mature sometime between ages 8 and 10.

During middle childhood, reaction time improves, and processing speed for such tasks as matching pictures, adding numbers in one's head, and recalling spatial information increases rapidly as unneeded synapses, or neural connections in the brain, are pruned away (Hale, Bronik, & Fry, 1997; Janowsky & Carper, 1996; Kail, 1991, 1997; Kail & Park, 1994). Faster, more efficient processing increases the amount of information a child can keep in working memory, making possible better recall and more complex, higher-level thinking (Flavell et al., 1993).

Contestants in a spelling bee can make good use of mnemonic strategies—devices to aid memory—such as rehearsal (repetition), organization, and elaboration.

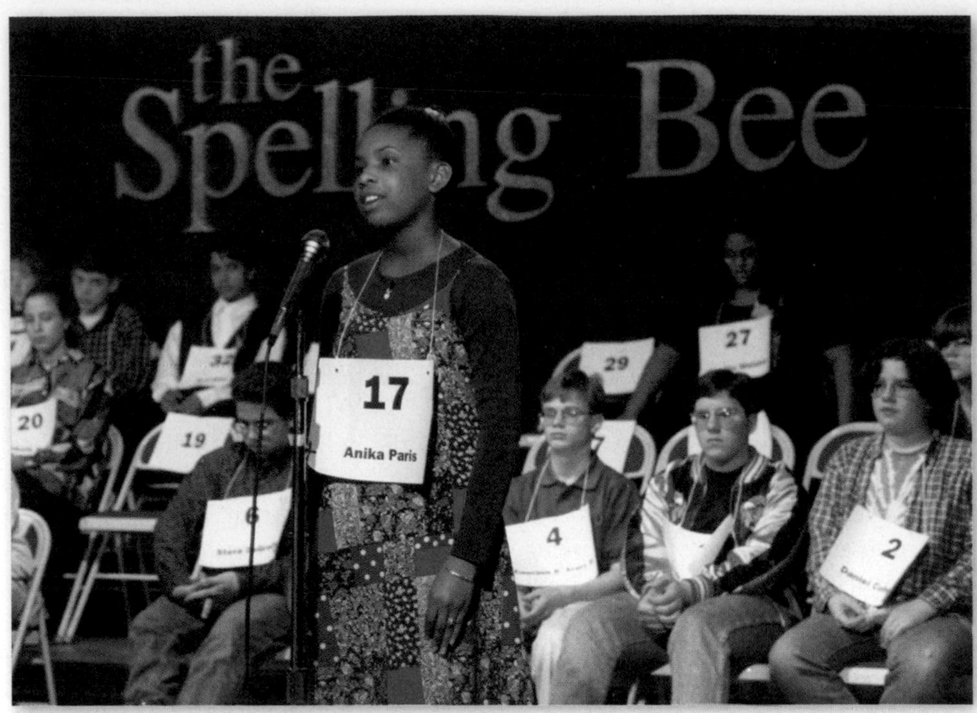

metamemory Understanding of processes of memory.

Metamemory: Understanding Memory Between ages 5 and 7, the brain's frontal lobes undergo significant development and reorganization, making possible improved recall and **metamemory,** knowledge about the processes of memory (Janowsky & Carper, 1996). From kindergarten through fifth grade, children advance steadily in understanding of memory (Flavell et al., 1993; Kreutzer, Leonard, & Flavell, 1975). Kindergartners and first-graders know that people remember better if they study longer, that people forget things with time, and that it is easier to relearn something than to learn it for the first time. By third grade, children know that some people remember better than others and that some things are easier to remember than others.

One pair of experiments looked at preschoolers', first-graders', and third-graders' beliefs about what influences remembering and forgetting. Most children in all three age groups believed that important events in a story about a birthday party (such as a guest falling into the cake) were more likely to be retained than minor details (such as a guest bringing a ball as a present). Most first- and third-graders, but not most preschoolers, believed that a later experience (playing with a friend who was not at the party) might color a child's recollection of who was at the party. Not until third grade did most children recognize that memory can be distorted by suggestions from others—say, that the friend *was* at the party (O'Sullivan, Howe, & Marche, 1996).

mnemonic strategies Techniques to aid memory.

external memory aids Mnemonic strategies using something outside the person.

rehearsal Mnemonic strategy to keep an item in working memory through conscious repetition.

organization Mnemonic strategy of categorizing material to be remembered.

elaboration Mnemonic strategy of making mental associations involving items to be remembered.

Mnemonics: Strategies for Remembering Devices to aid memory are called **mnemonic strategies.** The most common mnemonic strategy among both children and adults is use of *external memory aids.* Other common strategies include *rehearsal, organization,* and *elaboration* (see Table 9-3).

Writing down a telephone number, making a list, setting a timer, and putting a library book by the front door are examples of **external memory aids:** prompting by something outside the person. Saying a telephone number over and over after looking it up, so as not to forget it before dialing, is a form of **rehearsal,** or conscious repetition. **Organization** is mentally placing information into categories (such as animals, furniture, vehicles, and clothing) to make it easier to recall. In **elaboration,**

Table 9-3 Four Common Memory Strategies

Strategy	Definition	Development in Middle Childhood	Example
External memory aids	Prompting by something outside the person	5- and 6-year-olds can do this, but 8-year-olds are more likely to think of it.	Dana makes a list of the things she has to do today.
Rehearsal	Conscious repetition	6-year-olds can be taught to do this; 7-year-olds do it spontaneously.	Tim says the letters in his spelling words over and over until he knows them.
Organization	Grouping by categories	Most children do not do this until at least age 10, but younger children can be taught to do it.	Luis recalls the animals he saw in the zoo by thinking first of the mammals, then the reptiles, then the amphibians, then the fish, and then the birds.
Elaboration	Associating items to be remembered with something else, such as a phrase, scene, or story	Older children are more likely to do this spontaneously and remember better if they make up their own elaboration; younger children remember better if someone else makes it up.	Yolanda remembers the lines of the musical staff (E, G, B, D, F) by associating them with the phrase "*E*very *g*ood *b*oy *d*oes *f*ine."

children associate items with something else, such as an imagined scene or story. To remember to buy lemons, ketchup, and napkins, for example, a child might imagine a ketchup bottle balanced on a lemon, with a pile of napkins handy to wipe up spilled ketchup.

As children get older, they develop better strategies, use them more effectively, and tailor them to meet specific needs (Bjorklund, 1997). Even kindergartners recognize the value of *external aids,* and as children mature, they use them more (Kreutzer et al., 1975). Children usually do not use *rehearsal* spontaneously until after first grade; and if taught to do so in one situation, they usually do not apply it to another (Flavell, Beach, & Chinsky, 1966; Flavell et al., 1993; Keeney, Canizzo, & Flavell, 1967). The picture is similar for the other two types of mnemonic strategies, though there is some evidence that even preschoolers, when taught to use *organization,* can generalize this learning to other situations. Again, older children are more likely than younger ones to use *elaboration* spontaneously and to transfer it to other tasks (Flavell et al., 1993). Children often use more than one strategy for a task and choose different kinds of strategies for different problems (Coyle & Bjorklund, 1997).

Checkpoint

Can you . . .

- ✔ Identify at least three ways in which information processing improves during middle childhood?
- ✔ Describe three types of memory storage?
- ✔ Name four common mnemonic strategies and discuss developmental differences in their use?

Selective Attention School-age children can concentrate longer than younger children and can focus on the information they need and want while screening out irrelevant information. For example, they can summon up the appropriate meaning of a word they read and suppress other meanings that do not fit the context (Simpson & Foster, 1986; Simpson & Lorsbach, 1983). Fifth-graders are better able than first-graders to keep discarded information from reentering working memory and vying with other material for attention (Harnishfeger & Pope, 1996). This growing ability to control the intrusion of older thoughts and associations and redirect attention to current, relevant ones is believed to be due to neurological maturation. It is one of the reasons memory functioning improves during middle childhood (Bjorklund & Harnishfeger, 1990; Harnishfeger & Bjorklund, 1993).

The ability to consciously direct attention may help explain why older children make fewer mistakes in recall than younger ones. It may enable them to select what they want to remember and what they can forget (Lorsbach & Reimer, 1997).

Information Processing and Piagetian Tasks Improvements in information processing may help explain the advances Piaget described. For example, 9-year-olds may be better able than 5-year-olds to find their way to and from school because they can scan a scene, take in its important features, and remember objects in context, in the order in which the children encountered them (Allen & Ondracek, 1995).

Improvements in memory may contribute to the mastery of conservation tasks. Young children's working memory is so limited that, even if they are able to master the concept of conservation, they may not be able to remember all the relevant information (Siegler & Richards, 1982). They may forget that two differently shaped pieces of clay were originally identical. Gains in short-term memory may contribute to the ability to solve problems like this in middle childhood.

Robbie Case (1985, 1992), a neo-Piagetian theorist (refer back to Chapter 2), suggested that as a child's application of a concept or scheme becomes more automatic, it frees space in working memory to deal with new information. This may help explain horizontal décalage: children may need to become comfortable enough with one kind of conservation to use it without conscious thought before they can extend and adapt that scheme to other kinds of conservation.

Case (1999; Case & Okamoto, 1996; Case, Demetriou, Platsidou, & Kazl, 2001) tested a model that modifies Piaget's idea of cognitive structures and coordinates well with classic psychometric notions of general and special abilities. Unlike Piaget's *operational* structures, such as concrete and formal operations, which apply to any domain of thought, Case proposed *conceptual* structures, rooted in a culture, within specific domains such as number, story understanding, and spatial relations. As children acquire knowledge, they go through stages in which their conceptual structures become more complex, better coordinated, and multidimensional. For example, a child's understanding of spatial concepts begins by recognizing the shapes of objects, moves on to a sense of their relative size and location, and then to an understanding of perspective.

Checkpoint

Can you . . .

- ✔ Explain the importance of metamemory and selective attention?
- ✔ Give examples of how improved information processing may help explain cognitive advances Piaget described?

Psychometric Approach: Testing Intelligence

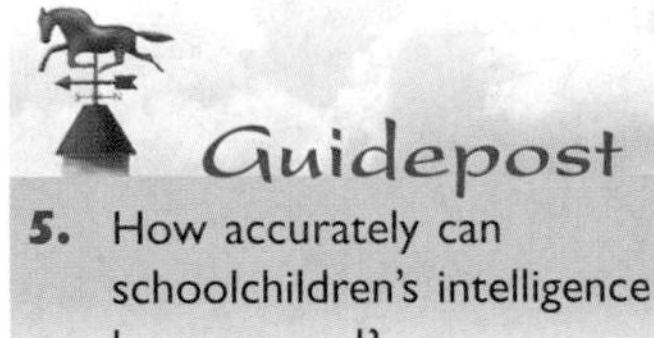

Guidepost

5. How accurately can schoolchildren's intelligence be measured?

Intelligence (IQ) tests claim to measure the capacity to learn, as contrasted with *achievement tests,* which assess how much children already have learned in various subject areas. However, as we'll see, it is virtually impossible to design a test that requires no prior knowledge. In addition, intelligence tests are validated against measures of achievement, such as school performance, and such measures are affected by factors beyond innate intelligence. For this and other reasons, there is strong disagreement over how accurately IQ tests assess differences among children.

Traditional Group and Individual Tests The original IQ tests, such as those of Alfred Binet and Theodore Simon (refer back to Chapter 5), were designed to be given to individuals, and their modern versions still are used that way. The first group tests, developed during World War I to screen army recruits for appropriate assignments, became models for the group tests now given in schools. As both individual and group tests have been refined, their developers have turned from the original emphasis on general intelligence to more sophisticated distinctions among various kinds of abilities and have sought to adapt the tests to special needs (Anastasi & Urbina, 1997; Daniel, 1997).

One popular group test, the **Otis-Lennon School Ability Test,** has levels for kindergarten through twelfth grade. Children are asked to classify items, to show an understanding of verbal and numerical concepts, to display general information, and to follow directions. Separate scores for verbal comprehension, verbal reasoning, pictorial reasoning, figural reasoning, and quantitative reasoning can identify strengths and weaknesses.

Otis-Lennon School Ability Test Group intelligence test for kindergarten through twelfth grade.

The most widely used individual test is the **Wechsler Intelligence Scale for Children (WISC-III).** This test for ages 6 through 16 measures verbal and performance abilities, yielding separate scores for each, as well as a total score. With separate subtest scores, it is easier to pinpoint a child's strengths and to diagnose specific problems. For example, if a child does well on verbal tests (such as general information and basic arithmetic operations) but poorly on performance tests (such as doing a puzzle or drawing the missing part of a picture), the child may be slow in perceptual or motor development. A child who does well on performance tests but poorly on verbal tests may have a language problem. Another commonly used individual test is the Stanford-Binet Intelligence Scale, described in Chapter 7.

Wechsler Intelligence Scale for Children (WISC-III) Individual intelligence test for schoolchildren, which yields verbal and performance scores as well as a combined score.

The IQ Controversy The use of psychometric intelligence tests is controversial. On the positive side, because IQ tests have been standardized and widely used, there is extensive information about their norms, validity, and reliability (refer back to Chapters 2, 5, and 7). IQ scores taken during middle childhood are fairly good predictors of school achievement, especially for highly verbal children, and scores are more reliable than during the preschool years. IQ at age 11 even has been found to predict length of life, functional independence late in life, and the presence or absence of dementia (Starr, Deary, Lemmon, & Whalley, 2000; Whalley & Deary, 2001; Whalley et al., 2000).

But are IQ tests fair? Critics claim that the tests underestimate the intelligence of children who, for one reason or another, do not do well on tests (Anastasi, 1988; Ceci, 1991). Because the tests are timed, they equate intelligence with speed and penalize a child who works slowly and deliberately. A more fundamental criticism is that IQ tests infer intelligence from what children already know; much of this knowledge is derived from schooling or culture and thus cannot measure native ability.

Influence of Schooling Schooling does seem to increase tested intelligence (Ceci & Williams, 1997; Neisser et al., 1996). In one study, differences in IQ between identical twins raised in different homes were directly related to the amount of education each twin had had (Bronfenbrenner, 1979). Children whose school entrance was significantly delayed (as happened, for example, in South Africa due to a teacher shortage and in the Netherlands during the Nazi occupation) lost as many as five IQ points per year, and some of these losses were never recovered (Ceci & Williams, 1997).

IQ scores also drop during summer vacation (Ceci & Williams, 1997). Among a national sample of 1,500 children, language, spatial, and conceptual scores improved much more between October and April, the bulk of the school year, than between April and October, which includes summer vacation and the beginning and end of the school year (Huttenlocher, Levine, & Vevea, 1998).

Influences of Ethnicity and Culture Average test scores vary among ethnic groups, inspiring claims that the tests are unfair to minorities. Although some African Americans score higher than most whites, black children, on average, score about fifteen points lower than white children and show a comparable lag on school achievement tests. Average IQ scores of Hispanic children fall between those of black and white children, and their scores, too, tend to predict school achievement. Yet Asian Americans, whose scholastic achievements consistently outstrip those of other ethnic groups, do not seem to have a significant edge in IQ—a reminder of the limited predictive power of intelligence testing (Neisser et al., 1996). Instead, as we'll show later in this chapter, Asian American children's strong scholastic achievement seems to be best explained by cultural factors.

What accounts for ethnic differences in IQ? Some writers have argued that part of the cause is genetic (Herrnstein & Murray, 1994; Jensen, 1969). However, while there is strong evidence of a genetic influence on *individual* differences in intelligence, there is *no* direct evidence that differences among ethnic, cultural, or racial groups are hereditary (Neisser et al., 1996).

Many scholars attribute such differences to inequalities in environment—in income, in nutrition, in living conditions, in intellectual stimulation, in schooling, in culture, or in other circumstances such as the effects of oppression and discrimination, which can affect self-esteem, motivation, and academic performance (Kamin, 1974, 1981; Kottak, 1994; Miller-Jones, 1989). The IQ and achievement test gaps between white and black Americans appear to be narrowing (Neisser et al., 1996) as the life circumstances and educational opportunities of many African American children improve.

cultural bias Tendency of intelligence tests to include items calling for knowledge or skills more familiar or meaningful to some cultural groups than to others.

culture-free Describing an intelligence test that, if it were possible to design, would have no culturally linked content.

culture-fair Describing an intelligence test that deals with experiences common to various cultures, in an attempt to avoid cultural bias.

In one study of 5-year-olds of low birthweight, when analysts adjusted for socioeconomic differences between black and white children (including differences in home environment), they virtually eliminated the difference in average IQ (Brooks-Gunn, Klebanov, & Duncan, 1996). Generally, however, while socioeconomic status and IQ are strongly correlated, SES does not seem to explain the entire intergroup variance in IQ (Neisser et al., 1996; Suzuki & Valencia, 1997).

Some critics attribute ethnic differences in IQ to **cultural bias:** a tendency to include questions that use vocabulary or call for information or skills more familiar or meaningful to some cultural groups than to others (Sternberg, 1985a, 1987). These critics argue that intelligence tests are built around the dominant thinking style and language of white people of European ancestry, putting minority children at a disadvantage (Heath, 1989; Helms, 1992). Cultural bias also may affect the testing situation. For example, a child from a culture that stresses sociability and cooperation may be handicapped taking a test alone (Kottak, 1994). Still, while cultural bias may play a part in some children's performance, controlled studies have failed to show that it contributes substantially to overall group differences in IQ (Neisser et al., 1996).

Checkpoint

Can you . . .

- Name and describe two traditional intelligence tests for schoolchildren?
- Give arguments for and against IQ tests?
- Assess explanations that have been advanced for ethnic differences in performance on intelligence tests?

Test developers have tried to design **culture-free** tests—tests with no culture-linked content—by posing tasks that do not require language, such as tracing mazes, putting the right shapes in the right holes, and completing pictures. But they have been unable to eliminate all cultural influences. Test designers also have found it virtually impossible to produce **culture-fair** tests consisting only of experiences common to people in various cultures.

Is There More Than One Intelligence? Another serious criticism of IQ tests is that they focus almost entirely on abilities that are useful in school. They do *not* assess other important aspects of intelligent behavior, such as common sense, social skills, creative insight, and self-knowledge. Yet these abilities, in which some children with modest academic skills excel, may become equally or more important in later life (Gardner, 1993; Sternberg, 1985a, 1987) and may even be considered separate forms of intelligence. Two of the chief advocates of this position are Howard Gardner and Robert Sternberg.

Gardner's Theory of Multiple Intelligences Is a child who is good at analyzing paragraphs and making analogies more intelligent than someone who can play a difficult violin solo, or someone who can organize a closet or design a group project, or someone who can pitch a curveball at the right time? The answer is no, according to Gardner's (1993) **theory of multiple intelligences.**

theory of multiple intelligences Gardner's theory that each person has several distinct forms of intelligence.

Gardner, a neuropsychologist and educational researcher at Harvard University, originally proposed that there are seven distinct kinds of intelligence. This hypothesis makes sense, he says, since different parts of the brain process different kinds of information (Kirschenbaum, 1990). According to Gardner, conventional intelligence tests tap only three "intelligences": linguistic, logical-mathematical, and, to some extent, spatial. The other four, which are not reflected in IQ scores, are musical, bodily-kinesthetic, interpersonal, and intrapersonal. Gardner (1998) recently added an eighth intelligence, naturalist, to his original list. (See Table 9-4 for definitions and examples of fields in which each intelligence is particularly useful.)

According to Howard Gardner, musical ability—which includes the ability to perceive and create patterns of pitch and rhythm—is one of several separate kinds of intelligence.

High intelligence in one area is not necessarily accompanied by high intelligence in any of the others. A person may be extremely gifted in art (a spatial ability), precision of movement (bodily-kinesthetic), social relations (interpersonal), or self-understanding (intrapersonal), but not have a high IQ. Thus Albert Einstein, the poet T. S. Eliot, and the cellist Pablo Casals may have been equally intelligent, each in a different area.

Gardner would assess each intelligence directly by observing its products—how well a child can tell a story, remember a melody, or get around in a strange area—and not by standardized tests. To monitor spatial ability, for example, the examiner might hide an object from a 1-year-old, ask a 6-year-old to do a jigsaw puzzle, and give a Rubik's cube to a preadolescent. Extended observation could reveal strengths and weaknesses so as to help children realize their potential, rather than to compare individuals (Gardner, 1995; Scherer, 1985). Of course, such assessments would be far more time-consuming and more open to observer bias than paper-and-pencil tests.

What's Your View?

- Which of Gardner's types of intelligence are you strongest in? Did your education include a focus on any of these?

Table 9-4 Eight Intelligences, According to Gardner

Intelligence	Definition	Fields or Occupations Where Used
Linguistic	Ability to use and understand words and nuances of meaning	Writing, editing, translating
Logical-mathematical	Ability to manipulate numbers and solve logical problems	Science, business, medicine
Musical	Ability to perceive and create patterns of pitch and rhythm	Musical composition, conducting
Spatial	Ability to find one's way around in an environment and judge relationships between objects in space	Architecture, carpentry, city planning
Bodily-kinesthetic	Ability to move with precision	Dancing, athletics, surgery
Interpersonal	Ability to understand and communicate with others	Teaching, acting, politics
Intrapersonal	Ability to understand the self	Counseling, psychiatry, spiritual leadership
Naturalist	Ability to distinguish species	Hunting, fishing, farming, gardening, cooking

Source: Based on Gardner, 1993, 1998.

Sternberg's Triarchic Theory of Intelligence Sternberg (1997) defines *intelligence* as a group of mental abilities necessary for children or adults to adapt to any environmental context, and also to select and shape the contexts in which they live and act. By limiting his definition of intelligence to universally necessary mental abilities, Sternberg would exclude some of Gardner's "intelligences," such as musical and bodily-kinesthetic abilities.

triarchic theory of intelligence Sternberg's theory describing three types of intelligence: componential, experiential, and contextual.

componential element Sternberg's term for the analytic aspect of intelligence.

experiential element Sternberg's term for the insightful or creative aspect of intelligence.

contextual element Sternberg's term for the practical aspect of intelligence.

Sternberg's (1985a) **triarchic theory of intelligence** embraces three elements, or aspects, of intelligence: *componential, experiential,* and *contextual.*

- The **componential element** is the *analytic* aspect of intelligence; it determines how efficiently people process information. It tells people how to solve problems, how to monitor solutions, and how to evaluate the results.
- The **experiential element** is *insightful* or *creative;* it determines how people approach novel or familiar tasks. It allows people to compare new information with what they already know and to come up with new ways of putting facts together—in other words, to think originally.
- The **contextual element** is *practical;* it determines how people deal with their environment. It is the ability to size up a situation and decide what to do: adapt to it, change it, or get out of it.

According to Sternberg, everyone has these three kinds of abilities to a greater or lesser extent. A person may be strong in one, two, or all three.

Conventional IQ tests measure mainly componential ability, and since this ability is the kind most school tasks require, it's not surprising that the tests are fairly good predictors of school performance. Their failure to measure experiential (insightful or creative) and contextual (practical) intelligence, says Sternberg, may explain why they are less useful in predicting success in the outside world.

Sternberg Triarchic Abilities Test (STAT) Test that seeks to measure componential, experiential, and contextual intelligence.

The **Sternberg Triarchic Abilities Test (STAT)** (Sternberg, 1993) seeks to measure each of the three components of intelligence—analytic, creative, and practical—through multiple-choice and essay questions in three domains: *verbal, quantitative,* and *figural* (or spatial). For example, a test of practical-quantitative intelligence might be to solve an everyday math problem having to do with buying tickets to a ball game or following a recipe for making cookies. A creative-verbal item might ask children to solve deductive reasoning problems that start with factually false premises (such as, "Money falls off trees"). An analytical-figural item might ask children to identify the missing piece of a figure.

Preliminary validation has found correlations with several other tests of critical thinking, creativity, and practical problem solving. As predicted, the three kinds of abilities are only weakly correlated with each other (Sternberg, 1997; Sternberg & Clinkenbeard, 1995).

Other New Directions in Intelligence Testing Ever since intelligence tests were born, one psychologist after another has tried to overcome their shortcomings. Wechsler's addition of performance tasks to lessen the verbal emphasis of earlier IQ tests was one such innovation. In recent years, several other approaches in addition to Gardner's and Sternberg's have emerged.

Kaufman Assessment Battery for Children (K-ABC) Nontraditional individual intelligence test designed to provide fair assessments of minority children and children with disabilities.

Some new diagnostic and predictive tools are based on neurological research and information-processing theory. The **Kaufman Assessment Battery for Children (K-ABC)** (Kaufman & Kaufman, 1983), an individual test for children $2\frac{1}{2}$ to $12\frac{1}{2}$ years old, has separate scales for aptitude (mental processing abilities) and achievement. There is also a completely nonverbal scale for children with hearing impairments or speech or language disorders and for those whose primary language is not English. The K-ABC incorporates the concept of scaffolding: if a child fails any of the first three items on a subtest, the examiner can clarify what kind of response is expected by using different words or gestures or a different language.

Other tests, as mentioned in Chapter 7, are based on Vygotsky's concept of *dynamic testing.* Used for decades in the Soviet Union, dynamic testing captured attention in the United States in the 1960s and 1970s, when psychometric tests came under criticism (Grigorinko & Sternberg, 1998).

Tests based on the zone of proximal development (ZPD) contain items up to two years above a child's current level of competence. Examiners help the child, when necessary, by asking leading questions, giving examples or demonstrations, and offering feedback; thus, the test itself is a learning situation. The difference between the items a child can answer alone and the items the child can answer with help is the child's ZPD.

Vygotsky (1956) gave an example of two children, each with a mental age of 7 years. With help, Natasha can easily solve problems geared to a mental age of 9, two years beyond her mental age; but Ivan, with the same kind of help, can do tasks at only a $7\frac{1}{2}$-year-old level. Measured by what they can do on their own, these two children's cognitive development is about the same. But measured by their immediate potential development—their ZPD—they are quite different.

By pointing to what a child is ready to learn and how much help is needed, dynamic testing may give teachers more useful information than a psychometric test does and can aid in designing interventions to help children reach their potential. It can be particularly effective with disadvantaged children, who often do not do well on conventional psychometric tests (Grigorinko & Sternberg, 1998; Rutland & Campbell, 1996). However, the ZPD has had little experimental validation (Grigorinko & Sternberg, 1998) and may be inherently difficult to measure precisely.

What's Your View?

- If you were a teacher in the primary grades, would you rather know a pupil's IQ or ZPD?

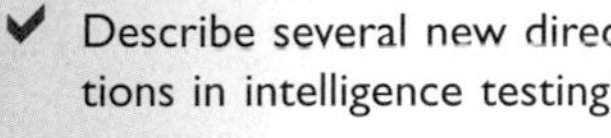

Checkpoint

Can you . . .

- ✔ Compare Gardner's and Sternberg's theories of intelligence, and the specific abilities proposed by each?
- ✔ Describe several new directions in intelligence testing?
- ✔ Explain the difference between dynamic testing and traditional psychometric testing?

Language and Literacy

Language abilities continue to grow during middle childhood. Children are now better able to understand and interpret oral and written communication and to make themselves understood.

Guidepost

6. How do communicative abilities and literacy expand during middle childhood?

Vocabulary, Grammar, and Syntax

As vocabulary grows during the school years, children use increasingly precise verbs to describe an action *(hitting, slapping, striking, pounding).* They learn that a word like *run* can have more than one meaning, and they can tell from the context which meaning is intended. They learn not only to use many more words but to select the right word for a particular use. *Simile* and *metaphor,* figures of speech in which a word or phrase that usually designates one thing is compared or applied to another, become increasingly common (Owens, 1996; Vosniadou, 1987). Although grammar is quite complex by age 6, children during the early school years rarely use the passive voice (as in "The sidewalk is being shoveled"), verb tenses that include the auxiliary *have* ("I have already shoveled the sidewalk"), and conditional sentences ("If Barbara were home, she would help shovel the sidewalk") (C. S. Chomsky, 1969).

Up to and possibly after age 9, children's understanding of rules of *syntax* (how words are organized into phrases and sentences) becomes more sophisticated. Sentence structure continues to become more elaborate. Older children use more subordinate clauses ("The boy *who delivers the newspapers* rang the doorbell"), and they now look at the semantic effect of a sentence as a whole, rather than focusing on word order as a signal of meaning. Still, some constructions, such as clauses beginning with *however* and *although,* do not become common until early adolescence (Owens, 1996).

Pragmatics: Knowledge about Communication

pragmatics Set of linguistic rules that govern the use of language for communication.

The major area of linguistic growth during the school years is in **pragmatics:** the practical use of language to communicate.* This includes both conversational and narrative skills.

Good conversationalists probe by asking questions before introducing a topic with which the other person may not be familiar. They quickly recognize a breakdown in communication and do something to repair it. There are wide individual differences in such conversational skills; some 7-year-olds are better conversationalists than some adults (Anderson, Clark, & Mullin, 1994).

Schoolchildren are highly conscious of adults' power and authority. First-graders respond to adults' questions with simpler, shorter answers than they give their peers. They tend to speak differently to parents than to other adults, issuing more demands and engaging in less extended conversation.

When children this age tell stories, they usually do not make them up; they are more likely to relate a personal experience. Most 6-year-olds can retell the plot of a short book, movie, or television show. They are beginning to describe motives and causal links.

By second grade, children's stories become longer and more complex. Fictional tales often have conventional beginnings and endings ("Once upon a time . . . " and "They lived happily ever after," or simply "The end"). Word use is more varied than before, but characters do not show growth or change, and plots are not fully developed.

Older children usually "set the stage" with introductory information about the setting and characters, and they clearly indicate changes of time and place during the story. They construct more complex episodes than younger children do, but with less unnecessary detail. They focus more on the characters' motives and thoughts, and they think through how to resolve problems in the plot.

Literacy

How do children begin to read and write, and how do these skills improve?

Identifying Words: Decoding versus Visually Based Retrieval Children can identify a printed word in two ways. One is called *decoding:* the child "sounds out" the word, translating it from print to speech before retrieving it from long-term memory. To do this, the child must master the phonetic code that matches the printed alphabet to spoken sounds. The second method is *visually based retrieval:* the child simply looks at the word and then retrieves it.

phonetic, or code emphasis approach Approach to teaching reading that emphasizes decoding of unfamiliar words.

whole-language approach Approach to teaching reading that emphasizes visual retrieval and use of contextual clues.

These two methods have inspired contrasting approaches to reading instruction. The traditional approach, which emphasizes decoding, is called the **phonetic, or code emphasis approach.** The more recent **whole-language approach** emphasizes visual retrieval and the use of contextual cues. Whole-language programs are built around real literature and open-ended, student-initiated activities, in contrast with the more rigorous, teacher-directed tasks involved in phonics instruction.

The whole-language approach is based on the belief that children can learn to read and write naturally, much as they learn to understand and use speech. To foster this natural process, children are encouraged to experience from the beginning the purpose of written language: to communicate meaning. Whole-language proponents assert that children learn to read with better comprehension and more enjoyment if they see written language as a way to gain information and express ideas and feelings, not as a system of isolated sounds and syllables that must be learned by memorization and drill.

*This section is largely indebted to Owens (1996).

Reviews of the literature, however, have found little support for these claims (Stahl, McKenna, & Pagnucco, 1994; Stahl & Miller, 1989). Critics say that whole-language teaching encourages children to skim through a text, guessing at words and their meaning, and not to try to correct reading or spelling errors. Reading, they say, is a skill that must be taught; the brain is not programmed to acquire it. A long line of research supports the view that phonemic awareness and early phonics training are keys to reading proficiency (Booth, Perfetti, & MacWhinney, 1999; Hatcher, Hulme, & Ellis, 1994; Jeynes & Littell, 2000; Liberman & Liberman, 1990; National Reading Panel, 2000).

Many experts now recommend a blend of the best of both the phonetic and whole-language approaches (National Reading Panel, 2000). Children learn phonetic skills along with strategies to help them understand what they read. Such a combined approach seems best suited to the way children's brains work. Because academic skills such as reading are the product of many functions in different parts of the brain working together, instruction focused solely on specific subskills (phonetics or comprehension) is less likely to succeed than a program that covers a broad constellation of skills (Byrnes & Fox, 1998). Children who can choose either visually based or phonetic strategies—using visual retrieval for familiar words and phonetic decoding as a backup for unfamiliar words—become better, more versatile readers (Siegler, 1998).

Comprehension The developmental processes that improve comprehension, or understanding of written passages, are the same as those that improve memory. As word identification becomes more automatic, and as the capacity of working memory increases, children can focus more on the meaning of what they read. New, more sophisticated strategies enable children to adjust their reading speed and attention to the importance and difficulty of the material. **Metacognition**—awareness of what is going on in one's own mind—helps children to monitor their understanding of what they read and to develop strategies, such as rereading difficult passages, reading more slowly, trying to visualize what is being described, and thinking of examples, to clear up any problems. As children's store of knowledge increases, they can more readily check new information against what they already know (Siegler, 1998).

metacognition Awareness of a person's own mental processes.

Some teaching methods help children develop interpretive strategies through literary discussion. Teachers can model effective strategies (such as making associations with prior knowledge, summarizing, visualizing relationships, and making predictions) and coach students on how to select and use them. After a year in one such program, low-achieving second-graders did significantly better than a control group on standardized measures of comprehension (Brown & Pressley, 1994; Brown, Pressley, Schuder, & Van Meter, 1994).

Writing The acquisition of writing skill goes hand in hand with the development of reading. As children learn to translate the written word into speech, they also learn that they can use written words to express ideas, thoughts, and feelings. Older preschoolers begin using letters, numbers, and letterlike shapes as symbols to represent words or parts of words—syllables or phonemes. Often their spelling is quite inventive—so much so that they may not be able to read it themselves (Whitehurst & Lonigan, 1998)!

Writing is difficult for young children, and early compositions usually are quite short. Often school writing assignments involve unfamiliar topics; children must draw together and organize diverse information from long-term memory and other sources. Unlike conversation, which offers constant feedback, writing requires the child to judge independently whether the goal has been met. The child also must keep in mind a variety of other constraints: spelling, punctuation, grammar, and capitalization, as well as the basic physical task of forming letters. Children who type or use word processors write better, since they do not have to deal with the mechanical demands of handwriting (Siegler, 1998).

Checkpoint

Can you . . .

- ✔ Summarize improvements in language skills during middle childhood?
- ✔ Compare and evaluate the whole-language and code emphasis (phonetic) methods of teaching reading?
- ✔ Tell how comprehension can be improved?
- ✔ Explain why writing is hard for young children?

The Child in School

Guidepost

7. What influences school achievement?

"What will the teacher be like?" 6-year-old Julia wonders as she walks up the steps to her new school, wearing her new backpack. "Will the work be too hard? Will the kids like me? What games will we play at recess?"

Even today, when many children go to preschool and most go to kindergarten, children often approach the start of first grade with a mixture of eagerness and anxiety. The first day of "regular" school is a milestone—a sign of the developmental advances that make this new status possible.

Entering First Grade

A child's first-grade performance can affect the entire school career. Just as the curriculum in each grade builds on what went before, so does the file that follows the child from year to year. This "paper trail" helps shape each new teacher's perceptions and expectations—expectations that can affect achievement in the middle grades and even in high school (Entwisle & Alexander, 1998).

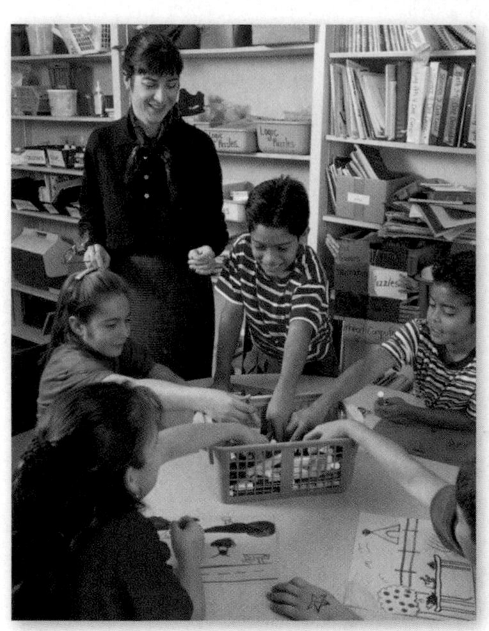

Children who participate actively tend to do well in school.

The Beginning School Study (BSS), which followed 790 randomly selected African American and white Baltimore children from first grade on, identified factors that can ease the first-grade transition (Entwisle & Alexander, 1998). One is the amount of kindergarten a child has had. Children who had attended full-day kindergarten did better on achievement tests and got higher marks in reading and math early in first grade than those who had attended kindergarten half days or not at all. Children in two-parent families tended to do better than children in single-parent families, apparently because of economic disparities.

To make the most academic progress, a child needs to be involved in what is going on in class. The better first-graders feel about their academic skills, the more engaged they tend to be; and conversely, the harder children work in school, the more self-confidence they develop about their academic ability (Valeski & Stipek, 2001). Interest, attention, and active participation are associated with achievement test scores and, even more so, with teachers' marks from first grade through at least fourth (K. L. Alexander, Entwisle, & Dauber, 1993). Since patterns of classroom behavior seem to be established in first grade, this crucial year offers a "window of opportunity" for parents and teachers to help a child form good learning habits.

Checkpoint

Can you . . .

- ✔ Explain the impact of the first-grade experience on a child's school career, and identify factors that affect success in first grade?

Influences on School Achievement

As Bronfenbrenner's bioecological theory (refer back to Chapter 2) would predict, in addition to children's own characteristics, each level of the context of their lives, from the immediate family to what goes on in the classroom to the messages children receive from peers and from the larger culture (such as "It's not cool to be smart"), influences how well they do in school. Let's look at this web of influences.

The Child: Self-Efficacy Beliefs and Academic Motivation According to Albert Bandura (Bandura, Barbaranelli, Caprara, & Pastorelli, 1996; Zimmerman, Bandura, & Martinez-Pons, 1992), whose social cognitive theory we discussed in Chapters 2 and 8, students who are high in *self-efficacy*—who believe that they can master schoolwork and regulate their own learning—are more likely to try to achieve and more likely to succeed than students who do not believe in their own abilities. It was Ann Bancroft's belief in her self-efficacy that helped her get through school despite her learning disability.

A parent's attitude about the importance of homework tends to "rub off" on a child. A parent whose child is motivated to achieve does not need to bribe or threaten to make sure that homework gets done.

Parenting Practices Parents of achieving children create an environment for learning. They provide a place to study and to keep books and supplies; they set times for meals, sleep, and homework; they monitor how much television their children watch and what their children do after school; and they show interest in their children's lives by talking with them about school and being involved in school activities. As children get older, the responsibility for seeing that schoolwork gets done shifts from parent to child (Cooper, Lindsay, Nye, & Greathouse, 1998).

How do parents motivate children to do well? Some use *extrinsic* (external) means—giving children money or treats for good grades or punishing them for bad ones. Others encourage children to develop *intrinsic* (internal) motivation by praising them for ability and hard work. Intrinsic motivation seems more effective. In a study of 77 third- and fourth-graders, those who were interested in the work itself did better in school than those who mainly sought grades or parents' approval (Miserandino, 1996).

Parenting styles may affect motivation. In one study, the highest-achieving fifth-graders had *authoritative* parents. These children were curious and interested in learning; they liked challenging tasks and enjoyed solving problems by themselves. *Authoritarian* parents, who kept after children to do their homework, supervised closely, and relied on extrinsic motivation, tended to have lower-achieving children. So did children of *permissive* parents, who were uninvolved and did not seem to care how the children did in school (G. S. Ginsburg & Bronstein, 1993).

Socioeconomic Status Socioeconomic status (SES) can be a powerful factor in educational achievement—not in and of itself, but through its influence on family atmosphere, on choice of neighborhood, on quality of available schooling, and on parents' way of rearing children (National Research Council [NRC], 1993a). When researchers followed 1,253 second- through fourth-graders for two to four years, those from low-income families tended to have lower reading and math achievement test scores, and the income gap in math achievement widened as time went on (Pungello, Kupersmidt, Burchinal, & Patterson, 1996).

SES can affect parents' ability to provide an environment that enhances learning. Among 229 two-parent and single-parent families with school-age children, parents who reported adequate financial resources were more likely to have confidence in their effectiveness as parents, to set positive goals for their children, and to use parenting practices that promote children's competence. They established consistent routines, had harmonious family relationships, and were actively involved at school (G. H. Brody, Stoneman, & Flor, 1995; G. H. Brody, Flor, & Gibson, 1999).

However, SES is not the only factor. In one longitudinal study, 8-year-olds whose home environment was cognitively stimulating had higher intrinsic motivation for academic learning at ages 9, 10, and 13 than children who lived in less stimulating homes. This was true over and above effects of SES (Gottfried, Fleming, & Gottfried, 1998).

The neighborhood a family can afford generally determines the quality of schooling available; and this, together with attitudes in the neighborhood peer group, affects motivation (Pong, 1997). Still, many young people from disadvantaged neighborhoods do well in school. What may make the difference is **social capital:** the family and community resources that families with children can draw upon. In a three-year experimental intervention called the New Hope Project, working parents were given wage supplements to raise their income above poverty level and were offered subsidies for child care and health insurance. These parents expressed less stress and more optimism than a control group, and their school-age sons' academic achievement and behavior improved (Huston et al., 2001).

social capital Family and community resources on which a child can draw.

self-fulfilling prophecy Expectation or prediction of behavior that tends to come true because it leads people to act as if it already were true.

Teacher Expectations According to the principle of the **self-fulfilling prophecy,** children live up—or down—to other people's expectations for them. In the "Oak School" experiment, teachers were falsely told at the beginning of the term that some students had shown unusual potential for cognitive growth, when these children actually had been chosen at random. Yet several months later, many of them showed unusual gains in IQ (R. Rosenthal & Jacobson, 1968).

Later analyses cast doubt on the power of the self-fulfilling prophecy: its effects, on average, have generally been found to be small. Still, under certain conditions—such as when teachers favor, or are perceived to favor, high over low achievers, or when teachers have lower expectations for poor children—teachers' expectations do seem to function as self-fulfilling prophecies, both predicting and influencing students' learning (Alvidrez & Weinstein, 1999; Jussim, Eccles, & Madon, 1996; Kuklinski & Weinstein, 2001).

If self-fulfilling prophecies are at work, early entries in a student's cumulative file can be vitally important. Performance can become self-perpetuating by fueling teacher expectations, which, in turn, influence student achievement as a child passes from class to class (Entwisle & Alexander, 1998).

Teacher expectations remain important as children approach and enter adolescence. In one study, sixth-graders at two suburban middle schools, one predominantly European American and the other predominantly African American, filled out questionnaires about their classroom experiences. In both schools, high teacher expectations significantly predicted students' motivation, goals, and interests. On the other hand, students' perceptions of negative feedback and lack of encouragement consistently predicted academic and social problems, as rated by peers and teachers (Wentzel, 2002).

The Educational System How can school best enhance children's development? Throughout the twentieth century, conflicting educational philosophies, along with historical events, brought great swings in educational theory and practice—from the "three R's" (reading, 'riting, and 'rithmetic), to "child-centered" methods that focused on children's interests, and then, when competition from Russia and then from Japan loomed and test scores plummeted, back to the "basics." In the 1980s, a series of governmental and educational commissions proposed plans for improvement, ranging from more homework (see Box 9-2 on page 336) to a longer school day and school year to a total reorganization of schools and curricula.

Today, many educators recommend teaching children in the early grades by integrating subject matter fields and building on children's natural interests and talents: teaching reading and writing, for example, in the context of a social studies project or teaching math concepts through the study of music. They favor cooperative projects, hands-on problem solving, and close parent-teacher cooperation (Rescorla, 1991).

Many contemporary educators also emphasize a "fourth R": reasoning. Children who are taught thinking skills in the context of academic subject matter perform better on intelligence tests and in school (R. D. Feldman, 1986; Sternberg, 1984, 1985a, 1985b). Everyday activities also can be routes to enhancing thinking skills (see Table 9-5). Research on Sternberg's triarchic theory suggests that students learn better when taught in a variety of ways, emphasizing creative and practical skills as well as memorization and critical thinking (Sternberg, Torff, & Grigorenko, 1998).

When the Chicago public schools in 1996 ended **social promotion,** the practice of promoting children who do not meet academic standards, many observers hailed the change. However, some educators maintain that the alternative—forcing failing students to go to summer school before they can graduate, or to repeat a grade—is shortsighted (Bronner, 1999). Although retention in some cases can be a "wake-up call," more often it is the first step on a remedial track that leads to lowered expectations, poor performance, and ultimately dropping out of school (J. M. Fields & Smith, 1998; McLeskey, Lancaster, & Grizzle, 1995). A number of countries with well-regarded educational systems, such as Denmark, Sweden, Norway, Japan, and South Korea, have automatic promotion policies.

Many educators say the only real solution to a high failure rate is to identify at-risk students early and intervene *before* they fail (Bronner, 1999). In a longitudinal study of kindergarten through eighth-graders in the Chicago schools, retained students did more poorly on math and reading achievement tests than peers who had been promoted, and also did more poorly in math than their new, younger classmates

What's Your View?

- Which approach to education do you favor for children in the primary grades: instruction in the "basics," or a more flexible, "child-centered" curriculum, or a combination of the two?

social promotion Policy of automatically promoting children even if they do not meet academic standards.

Table 9-5 Everyday Ways to Enhance Children's Thinking Skills

- When reading to children, ask open-ended questions (beginning with what, why, and how).
- Help children find the most important points in what they read, see, or hear.
- Ask children to compare new information with what they already know. Identifying commonalities and differences can help children organize information, which helps them think as well as remember.
- Teach children not to accept a statement that contradicts common knowledge without reliable proof.
- Encourage children to write. Putting thoughts on paper forces them to organize their thoughts. Projects may include keeping a journal, writing a letter to a famous person, and presenting an argument to parents (say, for an increase in allowance or a special purchase or privilege).
- Encourage children to think imaginatively about what they have learned. ("How do you think the soldiers in the American Revolution felt at Valley Forge? What do you suppose they wore?")
- When writing a poem or drawing a picture, encourage children to produce a first version and then to polish or revise it.
- Show children how to approach a problem by identifying what they do and don't know about it, designing a plan to solve it, carrying out the plan, and then deciding whether it has worked.
- Ask children to invent a new product, such as a gadget to ease a household chore.
- Teach children such skills as reading a map and using a microscope, and provide opportunities to practice them.

Sources: Marzano & Hutchins, 1987; Maxwell, 1987.

BOX 9–2

Practically Speaking

The Homework Debate

The homework debate is far from new. In the United States, historical swings in homework use have reflected shifts in educational philosophy (Cooper, 1989; Gill & Schlossman, 1996).

During the nineteenth century, the mind was considered a muscle, and homework a means of exercising it. But anti-homework crusaders argued that children had too much homework: assignments lasting far into the evening endangered children's physical and emotional health and interfered with family life (Gill & Schlossman, 1996). Some parents complained that children had no time for household chores (Buell, 2000).

By the 1940s, progressive, child-centered education held sway, and homework had lost favor. Homework time declined, and a number of states and school districts banned it (Cooper, 1989).

In the 1950s, when the Soviet Union's *Sputnik* launch brought calls for more rigorous science and math education, and again in the early 1980s, amid worries about the United States' competitive position toward Japan, "More homework!" became a battle cry in campaigns to upgrade U.S. educational standards (Cooper, 1989).

By 1997, according to one survey, first- through third-graders were spending about two hours a week on homework, three times as much as in 1981 (Hofferth & Sandberg, 1998). Still, U.S. children, especially adolescents, spend less time on homework than students in other developed countries (Larson & Verma, 1999).

Homework advocates claim that it disciplines the mind, develops good work habits, improves retention, and lets students cover more ground than they could in the classroom alone. Homework is a bridge between home and school, increasing parental involvement. Opponents claim that too much homework leads to boredom, anxiety, or frustration, overburdens children, discourages intrinsic motivation, and usurps time from family life and other worthwhile activities—including sleep (Buell, 2000; Cooper, 1989). Child psychologists report an increase in homework-related anxieties (Winerip, 1999). Once again, some critics (Kralovec & Buell, 2000) want to ban homework, at least for young children.

Research supports a balanced view, recognizing that homework can improve achievement and long-term success but also has costs (Larson & Verma, 1999). A comprehensive review of nearly 120 studies found that the value of homework depends on many factors, including the age, ability, and motivation of the child; the amount and purpose of homework; the home situation; and classroom follow-up. The older the child, the more effective homework can be: while it has strong benefits for high school students, it has only moderate benefits for junior high school students (and then only if limited to two hours a night), and virtually no benefits for elementary school students as compared with in-class study. Homework seems to work best when assignments are not overly complicated or completely unfamiliar, when material is spread out over several assignments, and when the need for parental involvement (which varies in effectiveness and can create tension at home) is kept to a minimum (Cooper, 1989).

Junior high and high school students who spend more time on homework tend to get better grades (Cooper et al., 1998; Cooper, Valentine, Nye, & Lindsay, 1999), but this is less true at the elementary level. The more homework younger children get, the more negatively they feel toward it. In a survey of 709 second- through twelfth-graders, about one-third of lower-grade students said they typically did not finish their homework. Even in the upper grades, students who received lengthy assignments tended not to complete them (Cooper et al., 1998).

Homework, then, has value—but only in moderation and when geared to students' developmental levels. Assignments in the elementary grades should be short and easy enough for children to succeed. Research-based recommendations range from one to three 15-minute assignments a week in the primary grades to four or five assignments a week, each lasting 75 to 120 minutes, in grades 10 to 12. Instead of grading homework, teachers should use it to diagnose learning problems (Cooper, 1989).

What's Your View?

How much homework do you think is appropriate for children of various ages?

Check It Out:

OLC

For more information on this topic, go to www.mhhe.com/papaliah9, where you'll find links to information about schoolchildren and homework.

(McCoy & Reynolds, 1999). In a second study of the same sample, those who had been in a high-quality early childhood education program were less likely to be held back in school or to drop out of high school (Temple, Reynolds, & Miedel, 2000).

Summer school may be helpful as an early intervention. Disadvantaged children, during the summer months, tend to fall behind their more advantaged peers, who have more opportunities for summer reading and other learning experiences. A three-year study is following about 450 low-income Baltimore elementary school students randomly assigned to summer instruction in reading and writing. In the first year of the study, kindergartners who attended at least 75 percent of the time outscored 81 percent of their peers who did not participate, and first-graders outscored 64 percent (Borman, Boulay, Kaplan, Rachuba, & Hewes, 1999).

Computer literacy and the ability to navigate the World Wide Web are opening new possibilities for individualized instruction, global communication, and early training in independent research skills. Under the Telecommunications Act of 1997, the U.S. Federal Communications Commission has allotted $2.25 billion to help schools acquire the equipment necessary to make universal classroom Internet service a reality.

However, this tool poses dangers. Beyond the risk of exposure to harmful or inappropriate material, students need to learn to critically evaluate information they find in cyberspace and to separate facts from opinion and advertising (J. Lee, 1998). A focus on "visual literacy" may divert financial resources from other areas of the curriculum. Nor does computer use necessarily improve basic skills. In a major international math and science examination, fourth-graders from 7 countries out of 26 significantly outperformed U.S. fourth-graders in math, and teachers in 5 of these countries reported that students never or almost never used computers in class (Mullis et al., 1997).

The Culture Why do so many children of East Asian origin do so well in U.S. schools? Cultural influences and educational practices in these children's countries of origin may hold the key (Song & Ginsburg, 1987; H. W. Stevenson, 1995; Stigler, Lee, & Stevenson, 1987). The school day and year are longer than in U.S. schools, and the curriculum is set centrally. Classes are larger (about forty to fifty students), and teachers spend more time teaching the whole class, whereas U.S. children spend more time working alone or in small groups and thus receive more individual attention but less total instruction.

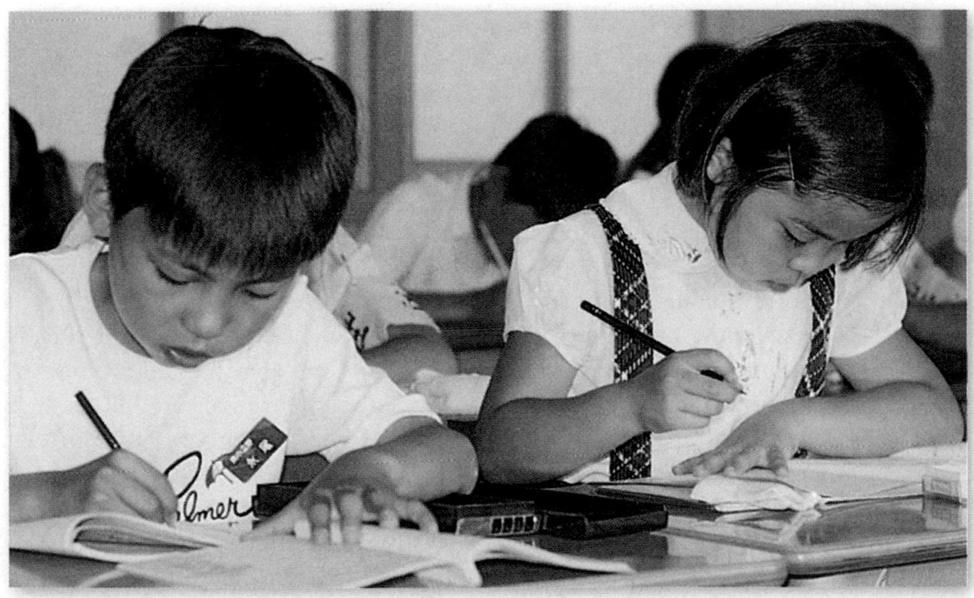

Children of East Asian extraction often do better in school than other U.S. youngsters. The reasons seem to be cultural, not genetic.

East Asian cultures share values that foster educational success (Chao, 1994). In Japan, a child's entrance into school is a major occasion for celebration. Japanese and Korean parents spend a great deal of time helping children with schoolwork. Japanese children who fall behind are tutored or go to *jukus,* private remedial and enrichment schools (McKinney, 1987; Song & Ginsburg, 1987).

Chinese and Japanese mothers view academic achievement as a child's most important pursuit (H. W. Stevenson, 1995; H. W. Stevenson, Chen, & Lee, 1993; H. W. Stevenson, Lee, Chen, & Lummis, 1990; H. W. Stevenson, Lee, Chen, Stigler, et al., 1990). Their children spend more time on homework, like it better, and get more parental help than U.S. children (C. Chen & Stevenson, 1989). Whereas U.S. students socialize after school and engage in sports and other activities, Asian students devote themselves almost entirely to study (Fuligni & Stevenson, 1995; H. W. Stevenson, 1995; H. W. Stevenson et al., 1993).

Checkpoint

Can you . . .

- ✔ Tell how students' self-efficacy beliefs and parental practices can influence school success?
- ✔ Discuss the impact of socioeconomic status on school achievement?
- ✔ Evaluate the effects of teachers' perceptions and expectations?
- ✔ Trace major changes in educational philosophy and practice during the twentieth century, including views about homework?
- ✔ Give reasons for the superior achievement of children of East Asian origin?

East Asians carry over these values and practices to their new land. Many Asian American families see education as the best route to upward mobility (Chao, 1996; Sue & Okazaki, 1990). The child's school success is a prime goal of parenting (Chao, 1994, 1996, 2000; Huntsinger & Jose, 1995). Nor is this academic success at the price of social skills. In a study of 36 first- and second-grade children of Chinese immigrants, the Chinese American children were equally well adjusted as a control group of European American children and had more advanced academic skills (Huntsinger, Jose, & Larson, 1998).

Of course, as Asian American children grow up in U.S. culture and absorb its values, their attitudes toward learning may change (C. Chen & Stevenson, 1995; Huntsinger et al., 1998). Research on second-, third-, and fourth-generation Asian Americans may help sort out cultural influences on educational achievement.

Guidepost

8. How do schools meet the needs of non-English-speaking children and those with learning problems?

Second-Language Education

Between 1979 and 1999, with rising immigration, the number of U.S. schoolchildren who have difficulty speaking English more than doubled, from 1.25 million to 2.6 million. Approximately 8.8 million U.S. children speak a language other than English at home (U.S. Bureau of the Census, 2002). Similar trends exist in Western European countries, and schools there also are under pressure to meet these special needs. Whereas a main goal of European programs is to preserve students' cultural identity, most U.S. programs, as mandated by the federal Equal Education Opportunity Act, aim chiefly at helping non-English-speaking students learn English well enough to compete academically with native English speakers (NCES, 1996).

English-immersion Approach to teaching English as a second language in which instruction is presented only in English.

bilingual education System of teaching non-English-speaking children in their native language while they learn English, and later switching to all-English instruction.

bilingual Fluent in two languages.

Some schools use an **English-immersion** approach, in which minority children are immersed in English from the beginning, in special classes. Other schools have adopted programs of **bilingual education,** in which children are taught in two languages, first learning in their native language with others who also speak it, and then switching to regular classes in English when they become more proficient in it. These programs can encourage children to become **bilingual** (fluent in two languages) and to feel pride in their cultural identity.

Advocates of early English immersion claim that the sooner children are exposed to English and the more time they spend speaking it, the better they learn it (Rossel & Ross, 1986). Support for this view comes from findings that the effectiveness of second-language learning declines from early childhood through late adolescence (Newport, 1991). On the other hand, proponents of bilingual programs claim that children progress faster academically in their native language and later make a smoother transition to all-English classrooms (Padilla et al., 1991, Thomas & Collier, 1999). Some educators maintain that the English-immersion approach stunts children's cognitive growth; because foreign-speaking children can understand only

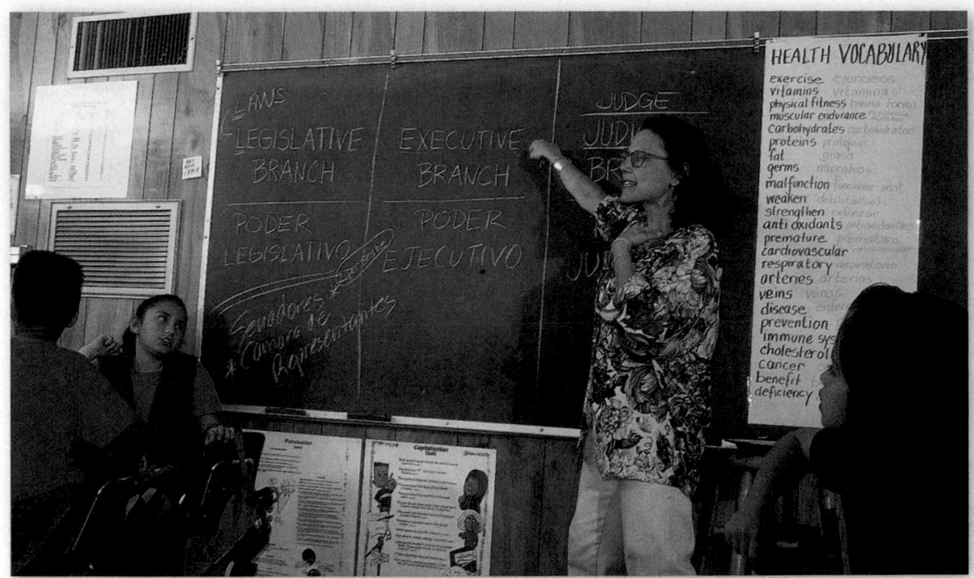

Advocates of bilingual instruction claim that children who learn in their native language as well as in English, like these fourth-graders, make faster academic progress than in English alone.

simple English at first, the curriculum must be watered down, and children are less prepared to handle complex material later (Collier, 1995).

A study of 70,000 non-English-speaking students in high-quality second-language programs in five districts across the United States offers strong support for a bilingual approach (Collier, 1995; W. P. Thomas & Collier, 1997). The study compared not only English proficiency but also long-term academic achievement. In the primary grades, whether the children were in bilingual or English-immersion programs made little difference; but from seventh grade on, children who had remained in bilingual programs at least through sixth grade caught up with or even surpassed their native English-speaking peers. At the same time, the relative performance of children who had been in traditional immersion programs began to decline. By the end of high school, those in part-time immersion programs trailed 80 percent of native English speakers their age.

Most successful was a third, less common approach: **two-way,** or **dual-language learning,** in which English-speaking and foreign-speaking children learn together in their own and each other's languages. This approach avoids any need to place non-English-speaking children in separate classes. By valuing both languages equally, it helps build self-esteem and thus improve school performance. An added advantage is that English speakers learn a foreign language at an early age, when they can acquire it most easily (Collier, 1995; W. P. Thomas & Collier, 1997, 1998, 1999). These findings echo earlier ones: the more bilingually proficient children are, the higher their cognitive and linguistic achievement—as long as school personnel value bilingualism and the second language is added at no sacrifice to the first (Diaz, 1983; Padilla et al., 1991).

two-way (dual-language) learning Approach to second-language education in which English speakers and non-English speakers learn together in their own and each other's languages.

In a study of 46 Spanish-speaking Mexican American children, participation in a bilingual preschool program promoted competency in both Spanish and English in comparison with a control group who remained at home (Winsler, Díaz, Espinosa, & Rodríguez, 1999). When bilingualism rises to the level of *biliteracy* (proficiency in reading and writing two languages), which makes possible full participation in both cultures, we see the most positive effects (Huang, 1995).

Despite such findings, critics claim that bilingual education has produced children who do not know enough English to hold a job. In 1998, a California referendum outlawed bilingual education there and required English immersion. Other states are considering similar moves (Holloway, 2000).

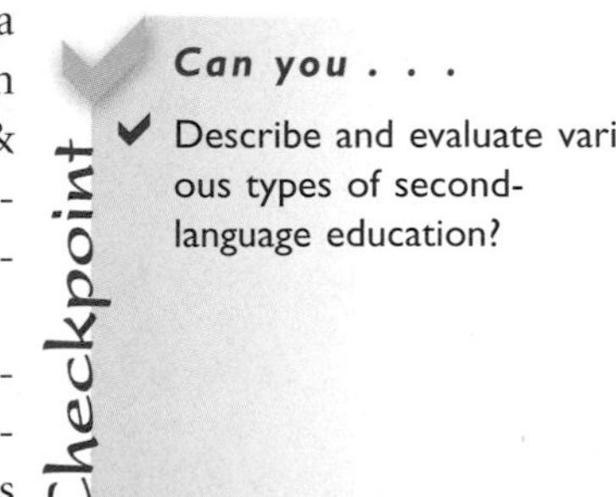

Can you . . .

✔ Describe and evaluate various types of second-language education?

Children with Learning Problems

Just as educators have become more sensitive to teaching children from varied cultural backgrounds, they also have sought to meet the needs of children with special educational needs.

mental retardation Significantly subnormal cognitive functioning.

Mental Retardation **Mental retardation** is significantly subnormal cognitive functioning. It is indicated by an IQ of about 70 or less, coupled with a deficiency in age-appropriate adaptive behavior (such as communication, social skills, and self-care), appearing before age 18. Both IQ and behavior are considered in making a diagnosis. About 1 percent of the U.S. population are mentally retarded, about three males for every two females (American Psychiatric Association [APA], 1994).

In about 30 to 40 percent of cases the cause of mental retardation is unknown. Known causes (in declining order) include problems in embryonic development, such as in fetal alcohol syndrome; mental disorders, such as autism; environmental influences, such as lack of nurturance; problems in pregnancy and childbirth, such as fetal malnutrition or birth trauma; hereditary conditions, such as Tay-Sachs disease; and medical problems in childhood, such as trauma or lead poisoning (APA, 1994). Many cases of retardation may be preventable through genetic counseling, prenatal care, amniocentesis, routine screening and health care for newborns, and nutritional services for pregnant women and infants.

Most retarded children can benefit from schooling. Intervention programs have helped many mildly or moderately retarded adults and those considered "borderline" (with IQs ranging from 70 up to about 85) to hold jobs, live in the community, and function fairly well in society. The profoundly retarded need constant care and supervision, usually in institutions. For some, day care centers, hostels for retarded adults, and homemaking services for caregivers can be less costly and more humane alternatives.

dyslexia Developmental disorder in which reading achievement is substantially lower than predicted by IQ or age.

Learning Disabilities Ann Bancroft is far from the only eminent person who has struggled with learning problems. Nelson Rockefeller, former vice president of the United States, had so much trouble reading that he ad-libbed speeches instead of using a script. Others who reportedly have suffered from **dyslexia,** a developmental reading disorder in which reading achievement is substantially below the level pre-

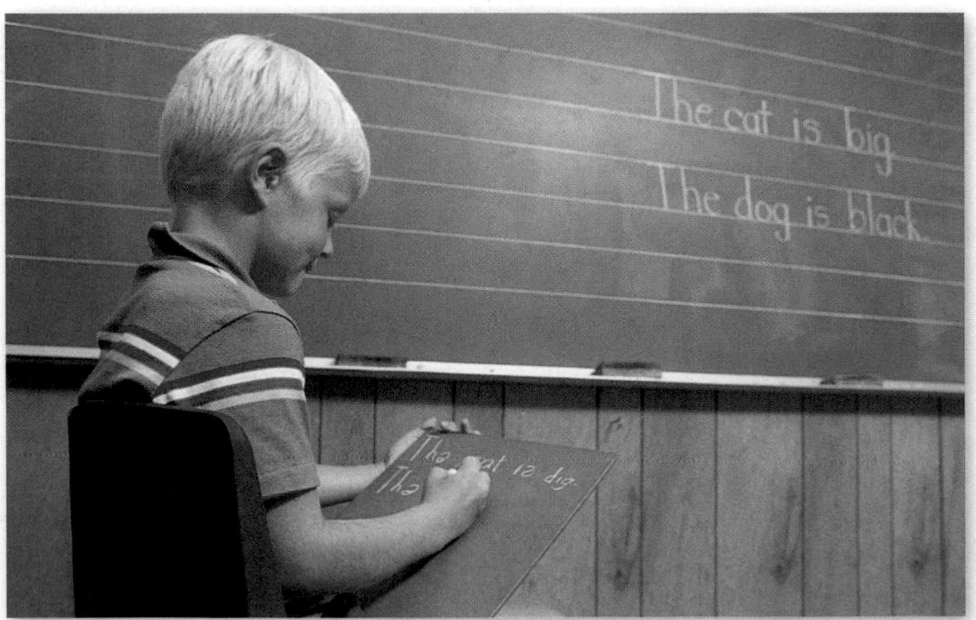

Children with dyslexia have trouble reading and writing, and often doing arithmetic, because they may confuse up and down and left and right. Dyslexia may be part of a more general language impairment.

dicted by IQ or age, include the World War II hero General George Patton, the inventor Thomas Edison, and the actress Whoopi Goldberg.

Dyslexia is the most commonly diagnosed of a large number of **learning disabilities (LDs),** disorders that interfere with specific aspects of school achievement, resulting in performance substantially lower than would be expected given a child's age, intelligence, and amount of schooling (APA, 1994). A growing number of children are classified as learning disabled (LD)—2.8 million in 2001 (National Center for Learning Disabilities, 2001).

learning disabilities (LDs) Disorders that interfere with specific aspects of learning and school achievement.

Children with LDs often have near-average to higher-than-average intelligence and normal vision and hearing, but they have trouble processing sensory information. They tend to be less task oriented and more easily distracted than other children; they are less well organized as learners and less likely to use memory strategies (Feagans, 1983). Learning disabilities can have devastating effects on self-esteem as well as on the report card.

Four out of five children with LDs have dyslexia. Estimates of its prevalence range from 5 to 17.5 percent of the school population; it seems to affect boys and girls equally (S. E. Shaywitz, 1998).

The term *dyslexia* refers to any type of reading problem. Most cases are believed to result from a neurological defect in processing speech sounds: an inability to recognize that words consist of smaller units of sound, which are represented by printed letters. This defect in phonological processing makes it hard to decode words. This and other language and communication disorders show substantial genetic influence (Plomin, 2001). Dyslexic children also may be weak in short-term verbal memory and other linguistic and cognitive skills (Morris et al., 1998; S. E. Shaywitz, 1998).

Brain imaging has revealed differences in the regions of the brain activated during phonological tasks in dyslexic as compared with normal readers (Horwitz, Rumsey, & Donohue, 1998; Shaywitz, Shaywitz, Pugh, Fulbright, Constable, et al., 1998; T. L. Richards et al., 1999). Although dyslexic children can be taught to read through systematic phonological training, the process never becomes automatic, as it does with most readers (S. E. Shaywitz, 1998).

Mathematical disabilities include difficulty in counting, comparing numbers, calculating, and remembering basic arithmetic facts. Each of these may involve distinct disabilities. One cause may be a neurological deficit.

Of course, not all children who have trouble with reading or arithmetic are learning disabled. Some haven't been taught properly, are anxious or have trouble reading or hearing directions, lack motivation to learn math, or have a developmental delay, which eventually disappears (Geary, 1993; Ginsburg, 1997; Roush, 1995).

Hyperactivity and Attention Deficits **Attention-deficit/hyperactivity disorder (ADHD)** affects an estimated 2 to 11 percent or more of school-age children worldwide (Zametkin & Ernst, 1999) and 3 to 6 percent in the United States (Bloom & Tonthat, 2002; USDHHS, 1999c), though some research suggests that its prevalence there may be underestimated (Rowland et al., 2002). It is marked by persistent inattention, distractibility, impulsivity, low tolerance for frustration, and a great deal of activity at the wrong time and the wrong place, such as the classroom (APA, 1994). Boys are three to four times as likely to be diagnosed as girls (Barkley, 1998b; USDHHS, 1999c; Zametkin & Ernst, 1999).

attention-deficit/hyperactivity disorder (ADHD) Syndrome characterized by persistent inattention and distractibility, impulsivity, low tolerance for frustration, and inappropriate overactivity.

The disorder has two different sets of symptoms. Some children are inattentive but not hyperactive; others show the reverse pattern (USDHHS, 1999c). However, in 85 percent of cases, the two behaviors go together (Barkley, 1998a). These characteristics appear to some degree in most children; there is cause for concern when they are unusually frequent and so severe as to interfere with the child's functioning in school and in daily life (AAP Committee on Children with Disabilities and Committee on Drugs, 1996; Barkley, 1998b; USDHHS, 1999c).

ADHD has a substantial genetic basis, with heritability approaching 80 percent (APA, 1994; Barkley, 1998b; Elia, Ambrosini, & Rapoport, 1999; USDHHS, 1999c; Zametkin, 1995; Zametkin & Ernst, 1999). One gene linked strongly with ADHD also is related to novelty seeking, a behavior that may once have helped humans adapt to rapidly changing environments. This evolutionary advantage may explain why the disorder became relatively common (Ding et al., 2002).

Birth complications that may play a part include prematurity, a prospective mother's alcohol or tobacco use, exposure to high levels of lead, and oxygen deprivation, which may lead to inadequate availability of the neurotransmitter dopamine (Barkley, 1998b; USDHHS, 1999c). However, the belief that ADHD children are brain damaged has been discredited by brain imaging studies (USDHHS, 1999c). Imaging studies do suggest that children with ADHD have unusually small brain structures in the prefrontal cortex and basal ganglia, the regions that inhibit impulses and regulate attention and self-control. Research has failed to substantiate any link between ADHD and food additives, such as artificial colorings and flavorings and the sugar substitute aspartame—or, for that matter, sugar itself (Barkley, 1998b; B. A. Shaywitz et al., 1994; Zametkin, 1995).

Although symptoms tend to decline with age, ADHD often persists into adolescence and adulthood and, if untreated, can lead to excessive injuries, academic problems, antisocial behavior, risky driving, substance abuse, and anxiety or depression (Barkley, 1998b; Barkley, Murphy, & Kwasnik, 1996; Elia et al., 1999; McGee, Partridge, Williams, & Silva, 1991; USDHHS, 1999c; Wender, 1995; Zametkin, 1995).

ADHD is often treated with drugs, sometimes combined with behavioral therapy, counseling, training in social skills, and special classroom placement. Psychotropic stimulants such as methylphenidate ("Ritalin"), used in proper doses, appear to be safe and effective in the short run, but long-term effects are unknown (AAP Committee on Children with Disabilities and Committee on Drugs, 1996; Elia et al., 1999; NIH, 1998; Rodrigues, 1999; USDHHS, 1999c; Zametkin, 1995; Zametkin & Ernst, 1999). A fourteen-month randomized study of 579 seven- to nine-year-olds with ADHD found a carefully monitored program of Ritalin treatment, alone or in combination with behavior modification, more effective than the behavioral therapy alone or standard community care (MTA Cooperative Group, 1999). A newer drug called *atomoxetine* also seems to be safe and effective for ADHD (Michelson et al., 2001).

A disturbing trend is the increasing use of drugs such as Ritalin on preschoolers, even though their effectiveness on children that young has not been shown, and despite concerns about effects on the developing brain. One study suggests that up to 1.5 percent of 2- to 4-year-olds on Medicaid or in HMOs are on stimulants, antidepressants, or antipsychotic medications (Coyle, 2000; Zito et al., 2000).

What's Your View?

- Long-term effects of drug treatment for ADHD are unknown, and leaving the condition untreated also carries risks. If you had a child with ADHD, what would you do?

Educating Children with Disabilities The Individuals with Disabilities Education Act (IDEA) of 1975 (amended 1997) ensures a free, appropriate public education for all children with disabilities in the United States. An individualized program must be designed for each child, with parental involvement. Children must be educated in the "least restrictive environment" appropriate to their needs: that means, whenever possible, the regular classroom. Many of these students can be served by "inclusion" programs, in which they are integrated with nondisabled children for all or part of the day. Inclusion can help children with disabilities learn to get along in society and can let nondisabled children know and understand people with disabilities.

A potential problem with inclusion is that children with learning disabilities may be evaluated by unrealistic standards, resulting in their being held back and made to repeat grades. This has already happened on a large scale in some schools, despite evidence that retention is ineffective even with children of normal abilities (McLeskey et al., 1995).

Checkpoint

Can you . . .

- ✔ Describe the causes and prognoses for three common types of conditions that interfere with learning?
- ✔ Discuss the impact of federal requirements for the education of children with disabilities?

Gifted Children

Giftedness is hard to define and measure. Educators disagree on who qualifies as gifted and on what basis, and what kinds of educational programs these children need. Another source of confusion is that creativity and artistic talent are sometimes viewed as aspects or types of giftedness and sometimes as independent of it (Hunsaker & Callahan, 1995).

Guidepost

9. How is giftedness assessed and nurtured?

Identifying Gifted Children The traditional criterion of giftedness is high general intelligence, as shown by an IQ score of 130 or higher. This definition tends to exclude highly creative children (whose unusual answers often lower their test scores), disadvantaged children (whose abilities may not be well developed, though the potential is there), and children with specific aptitudes (who may be only average or even show learning problems in other areas). Most states and school districts therefore have adopted a broader definition, which includes children who have shown high *potential* or *achievement* in one or more of the following: general intellect, specific aptitude (such as in mathematics or science), creative or productive thinking, leadership, talent in the arts (such as painting, writing, music, or acting), and psychomotor ability (Cassidy & Hossler, 1992). Many school districts now use multiple criteria for admission to programs for the gifted, including achievement test scores, grades, classroom performance, creative production, parent and teacher nominations, and student interviews; but IQ remains an important, and sometimes the determining, factor (Reis, 1989).

What's Your View?

- Should IQ carry more or less weight than other factors in admitting students to gifted education programs?

The Lives of Gifted Children A classic longitudinal study of gifted children began in 1921, when Lewis M. Terman (who brought the Binet intelligence test to the United States) identified more than 1,500 California children with IQs of 135 or higher. The study demolished the widespread stereotype of the bright child as a puny, pasty-faced bookworm. These children were taller, healthier, better coordinated, better adjusted, and more popular than the average child (Wallach & Kogan, 1965), and their cognitive, scholastic, and vocational superiority has held up through their adult years (Shurkin, 1992; Terman & Oden, 1959).

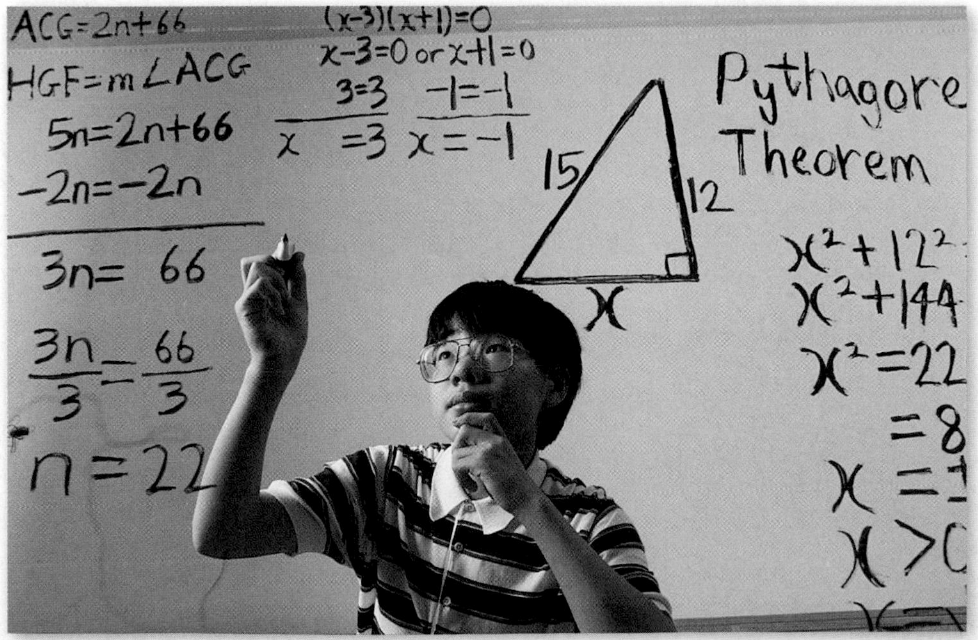

Mahito Takahashi of New Jersey made a perfect score in a worldwide mathematics Olympiad and has won close to 200 other awards. A well-rounded youngster, he sings in a chamber choir and acted in a school production of Shakespeare's Romeo and Juliet. *The key to helping such children achieve lies in recognizing and nurturing their natural gifts.*

On the other hand, none of Terman's sample grew up to be Einsteins, and those with the highest IQs became no more illustrious than those who were only moderately gifted. This lack of a close correlation between childhood giftedness and adult eminence has been supported by later research (Winner, 1997). Although most gifted children are highly motivated, they may lack the insatiable drive and "furious impulse to understand" (Michelmore, 1962, p. 24) that characterize an Einstein. When Benjamin Bloom (1985) of the University of Chicago asked distinguished pianists, sculptors, athletes, mathematicians, and neurologists to recall their childhoods, he found that many of them had shown less talent initially than a sibling. What made the difference in ultimate achievement were love of the field, a drive to excel, and hard work, as well as the encouragement and guidance of a special teacher, parent, or relative.

creativity Ability to see situations in a new way, to produce innovations, or to discern previously unidentified problems and find novel solutions.

Defining and Measuring Creativity One definition of **creativity** is the ability to see things in a new light—to produce something never seen before or to discern problems others fail to recognize and find new and unusual solutions. High creativity and high academic intelligence (IQ) do not necessarily go hand in hand (Anastasi & Schaefer, 1971; Getzels, 1964, 1984; Getzels & Jackson, 1962, 1963).

Creative thinking may require different abilities from those needed to do exceptionally well in school (Renzulli & McGreevy, 1984). Creativity seems to involve a greater role for emotions and attitudes, offbeat methods, and unconscious thought processes leading to sudden moments of illumination (Torrance, 1988), usually after long periods of slow, deliberate effort (Gruber, 1998). (Table 9-6 lists some research-based suggestions for fostering creativity.)

convergent thinking Thinking aimed at finding the one right answer to a problem.

divergent thinking Thinking that produces a variety of fresh, diverse possibilities.

Much as intelligence tests attempt to measure abilities that predict success in school, psychometric tests of creativity attempt to measure abilities that predict creative productivity. J. P. Guilford (1956, 1959, 1960, 1967, 1986) distinguished between two kinds of thinking: *convergent* and *divergent.* **Convergent thinking**—the kind IQ tests measure—seeks a single correct answer; **divergent thinking** comes up with a wide array of fresh possibilities. Tests of creativity call for divergent thinking. The Torrance Tests of Creative Thinking (Torrance, 1966, 1974; Torrance & Ball, 1984), among the most widely known tests of creativity, include such tasks as listing unusual uses for a paper clip, completing a figure, and writing down what a sound brings to mind.

One problem with many of these tests is that the score depends partly on speed, which is not a hallmark of creativity. Moreover, although the tests yield fairly reliable results, there is dispute over whether they are valid—whether they identify children who are creative in everyday life (Anastasi, 1988; Mansfield & Busse, 1981; Simonton, 1990). Torrance's (1988) claim to validity rests on longitudinal studies of elementary and high school students, begun when the tests were in preparation (Torrance, 1972a,

Table 9-6 Fostering Creativity

The following attributes and values in a child's home and school environments may encourage creative expression.

- *Intrinsic motivation:* Pursuing an activity for its own sake, not to please others or reap rewards, such as fame or money
- *Choice:* Having the opportunity to choose a task to perform and then to select a way of doing it
- *Stimulation:* Having experiences that are cognitively and perceptually stimulating
- *Inspirational models:* Coming into contact with creative people who serve as examples or mentors
- *Freedom from evaluation:* Performing a task without fear of being judged foolish or inadequate
- *Independence:* Performing a task without a sense of being observed by others in a critical way

Source: Amabile (1983).

1972b, 1981). Follow-up studies after intervals ranging from seven to twenty-two years found that the tests had successfully predicted which youngsters would become creative achievers. However, we know very little about their predictive value across the adult life span.

As Guilford recognized, divergent thinking may not be the only, or even the most important, factor in creative performance. More research needs to be done to find ways to identify youngsters who can become unusually creative adults.

enrichment Approach to educating the gifted, which broadens and deepens knowledge and skills through extra activities, projects, field trips, or mentoring.

acceleration Approach to educating the gifted, which moves them through the curriculum at an unusually rapid pace.

Educating Gifted Children A powerful argument for special education for the gifted is that the achievement of the most promising U.S. students lags behind that in other technologically advanced countries. About half of those in the top 5 percent, as measured by IQ, are underachievers (Feldhusen & Moon, 1992; Winner, 1997).

Most states have programs for the gifted, with about 6 percent of public school children participating (U.S. Department of Education, 1996). But competition for funding and opposition to what some critics consider elitism threatens the continuation of these programs (Purcell, 1995; Winner, 1997). Furthermore, supporters of gifted education disagree on what form it should take.

Programs for the gifted generally follow one of two approaches: *enrichment* or *acceleration.* **Enrichment** broadens and deepens knowledge and skills through extra classroom activities, research projects, field trips, or coaching by experts. **Acceleration,** often recommended for highly gifted children, speeds up their education by early school entrance, by grade skipping, by placement in fast-paced classes, or by advanced courses in specific subjects. Moderate acceleration does not seem to harm social adjustment, at least in the long run (Winner, 1997).

Children in gifted programs not only make academic gains but also tend to improve in self-concept and social adjustment (Ford & Harris, 1996). Some educators advocate moving away from an all-or-nothing definition of giftedness and including a wider range of students in more flexible programs (J. Cox, Daniel, & Boston, 1985; Feldhusen, 1992; R. D. Feldman, 1985). Some say that if the level of education were significantly improved for all children, only the most exceptional would need special classes (Winner, 1997).

Checkpoint

Can you . . .

- ✔ Tell how gifted children are identified?
- ✔ Discuss the relationship between giftedness and life achievements and between IQ and creativity?
- ✔ Describe how creativity is measured, and evaluate the effectiveness of such instruments?
- ✔ Describe two approaches to education of gifted children?

Refocus

- How much impact do you think psychosocial factors such as motivation, determination, and self-confidence had in Ann Bancroft's physical and cognitive development?
- How did Bancroft's childhood experiences influence her later achievements?
- What can we learn from Bancroft's experience about the diagnosis and treatment of a child who is not doing well in reading? About the kinds of activities that can lead to lifetime fitness?

There is no firm dividing line between being gifted and not being gifted, creative and not creative. All children benefit from being encouraged in their areas of interest and ability. What we learn about fostering intelligence and creativity in the most able youngsters may help all children make the most of their potential. The degree to which they do this will affect their self-concept and other aspects of personality, as we discuss in Chapter 10.

SUMMARY AND KEY TERMS

PHYSICAL DEVELOPMENT

Aspects of Physical Development

Guidepost **1.** What gains in growth and motor development occur during middle childhood, and what nutritional hazards do children face?

- Growth slows in middle childhood, and wide differences in height and weight exist.
- Children with retarded growth due to growth hormone deficiency may be given synthetic growth hormone.
- Proper nutrition is essential for normal growth and health.
- Malnutrition can affect all aspects of development.
- Obesity, which is increasingly common among U.S. children, entails health risks. It is influenced by genetic and environmental factors and can be treated.
- Concern with body image, especially among girls, may lead to eating disorders.
- Because of improved motor development, boys and girls in middle childhood can engage in a wide range of motor activities.
- About 10 percent of schoolchildren's play, especially among boys, is rough-and-tumble play.
- Many children, mostly boys, go into organized, competitive sports. A sound physical education program should aim at skill development and fitness for all children.
- Many children, especially girls, do not meet fitness standards.

body image *(312)*

rough-and-tumble play *(312)*

Health and Safety

Guidepost **2.** What are the principal health and safety concerns about school-age children?

- Middle childhood is a relatively healthy period; most children are immunized against major illnesses, and the death rate is the lowest in the life span.
- Respiratory infections and other acute medical conditions are common. Chronic conditions such as asthma are most prevalent among poor and minority children.
- Children's understanding of health and illness is related to their cognitive level.
- Vision becomes keener during middle childhood, but some children have defective vision or hearing.
- Most children who are HIV-positive function normally in school and should not be excluded from any activities of which they are capable.
- Accidents are the leading cause of death in middle childhood. Use of helmets and other protective devices and avoidance of trampolines, snowmobiling, and other dangerous sports can greatly reduce injuries.

acute medical conditions *(314)*

chronic medical conditions *(314)*

asthma *(315)*

COGNITIVE DEVELOPMENT

Piagetian Approach: The Concrete Operational Child

Guidepost **3.** How do school-age children's thinking and moral reasoning differ from those of younger children?

- A child at about age 7 enters the stage of concrete operations. Children are less egocentric than before and are more proficient at tasks requiring logical reasoning, such as spatial thinking, understanding of causality, categorization, inductive and deductive reasoning, and conservation. However, their reasoning is largely limited to the here and now.
- Cultural experience, as well as neurological development, seems to contribute to the rate of development of conservation and other Piagetian skills.
- According to Piaget, moral development is linked with cognitive maturation and occurs in three stages, as children move from rigid to more flexible thinking.

concrete operations *(317)*

seriation *(318)*

transitive inference *(318)*

class inclusion *(318)*

inductive reasoning *(318)*

deductive reasoning *(318)*

horizontal décalage *(319)*

Information Processing and Intelligence

Guidepost **4.** What advances in memory and other information-processing skills occur during middle childhood?

- Although sensory memory shows little change with age, the capacity of working memory increases greatly during middle childhood.
- The central executive, which controls the flow of information to and from long-term memory, seems to mature between ages 8 and 10.
- Metamemory, selective attention, and use of mnemonic strategies improve during these years. Gains in information-processing abilities may help explain the advances Piaget described.

sensory memory *(321)*

working memory *(321)*

central executive *(321)*

long-term memory *(321)*

metamemory *(322)*

mnemonic strategies *(322)*

external memory aids *(322)*

rehearsal *(322)*

organization *(322)*

elaboration *(322)*

Guidepost 5. How accurately can schoolchildren's intelligence be measured?

- The intelligence of school-age children is assessed by group or individual tests.
- IQ tests are fairly good predictors of school success but may be unfair to some children.
- Differences in IQ among ethnic groups appear to result to a considerable degree from socioeconomic and other environmental differences.
- Schooling seems to increase measured intelligence.
- Attempts to devise culture-free or culture-fair tests have been unsuccessful.
- IQ tests tap only three of the "intelligences" in Howard Gardner's theory of multiple intelligences.
- According to Robert Sternberg's triarchic theory, IQ tests measure mainly the componential element of intelligence, not the experiential and contextual elements.
- New directions in intelligence testing include the Sternberg Triarchic Abilities Tests (STAT), Kaufman Assessment Battery for Children (K-ABC), and tests based on Vygotsky's concept of dynamic testing.

Otis-Lennon School Ability Test *(325)*
Wechsler Intelligence Scale for Children (WISC-III) *(325)*
cultural bias *(326)*
culture-free *(326)*
culture-fair *(326)*
theory of multiple intelligences *(327)*
triarchic theory of intelligence *(328)*
componential element *(328)*
experiential element *(328)*
contextual element *(328)*
Sternberg Triarchic Abilities Test (STAT) *(328)*
Kaufman Assessment Battery for Children (K-ABC) *(328)*

Language and Literacy

Guidepost 6. How do communicative abilities and literacy expand during middle childhood?

- Use of vocabulary, grammar, and syntax become increasingly sophisticated, but the major area of linguistic growth is in pragmatics.
- Despite the popularity of whole-language programs, early phonics training is a key to reading proficiency.
- Metacognition contributes to reading comprehension.
- Acquisition of writing skills accompanies development of reading.

pragmatics *(330)*
phonetic, or code emphasis approach *(330)*
whole-language approach *(330)*
metacognition *(331)*

The Child in School

Guidepost 7. What influences school achievement?

- Because schooling is cumulative, the foundation laid in first grade is very important.
- Parents influence children's learning by becoming involved in their schooling, motivating them to achieve, and transmitting attitudes about learning. Socioeconomic status can influence parental beliefs and practices that, in turn, influence achievement.
- Although the power of the self-fulfilling prophecy may not be as great as was once thought, teachers' perceptions and expectations can have a strong influence.
- Historical philosophical shifts affect such issues as amount of homework assigned, social promotion, and computer literacy.
- The superior achievement of children of East Asian extraction seems to stem from cultural factors.

social capital *(334)*
self-fulfilling prophecy *(334)*
social promotion *(335)*

Guidepost 8. How do schools meet the needs of non-English-speaking children and those with learning problems?

- Methods of second-language education are controversial. Issues include speed and facility with English, long-term achievement in academic subjects, and pride in cultural identity.
- Three frequent sources of learning problems are mental retardation, learning disabilities (LDs), and attention-deficit/hyperactivity disorder (ADHD). Dyslexia is the most common learning disability.
- In the United States, all children with disabilities are entitled to a free, appropriate education. Children must be educated in the least restrictive environment possible, often in the regular classroom.

English-immersion *(338)*
bilingual education *(338)*
bilingual *(338)*
two-way (dual-language) learning *(339)*
mental retardation *(340)*
dyslexia *(340)*
learning disabilities (LDs) *(341)*
attention-deficit/hyperactivity disorder (ADHD) *(341)*

Guidepost 9. How is giftedness assessed and nurtured?

- An IQ of 130 or higher is a common standard for identifying gifted children. Broader definitions include creativity, artistic talent, and other attributes and rely on multiple criteria for identification.
- In Terman's classic longitudinal study of gifted children, most turned out to be well adjusted and successful, but not outstandingly so.
- Creativity and IQ are *not* closely linked. Tests of creativity seek to measure divergent thinking, but their validity has been questioned.
- Special educational programs for gifted children stress enrichment or acceleration.

creativity *(344)*
convergent thinking *(344)*
divergent thinking *(344)*
enrichment *(345)*
acceleration *(345)*

Psychosocial Development in Middle Childhood

Chapter 10

Have you ever felt like nobody?
Just a tiny speck of air.
When everyone's around you,
And you are just not there.

—Karen Crawford, age 9

OUTLINE

Focus: Marian Anderson, Operatic Trailblazer*

Marian Anderson

The African American contralto Marian Anderson (1902–1993) had—in the words of the great Italian conductor Arturo Toscanini—a voice heard "once in a hundred years." She was also a pioneer in breaking racial barriers. Turned away by a music school in her hometown of Philadelphia, she studied voice privately and in 1925 won a national competition to sing with the New York Philharmonic. When she was refused the use of a concert hall in Washington, D.C., First Lady Eleanor Roosevelt arranged for her to sing on the steps of the Lincoln Memorial. The unprecedented performance on Easter Sunday, 1939, drew 75,000 people and was broadcast to millions. Several weeks later, Marian Anderson was the first black singer to perform at the White House. But not until 1955 did Anderson, at age 57, become the first African American to sing with New York's Metropolitan Opera.

A remarkable story lies behind this woman's "journey from a single rented room in South Philadelphia" (McKay, 1992, p. xxx). It is a story of nurturing family ties—bonds of mutual support, care, and concern that extended from generation to generation.

Marian Anderson was the eldest of three children of John and Annie Anderson. Two years after her birth, the family left their one-room apartment to move in with her father's parents and then into a series of small rented houses nearby.

At the age of 6, Marian joined the junior choir at the Union Baptist Church. There she made a friend, Viola Johnson. Within a year or two, they performed a duet together—Marian's first public performance.

When Marian was 12, her beloved father died, and the family again moved in with his parents. The household included his sister and her two daughters, as well as, from time to time, various other relatives. Marian became attached to her kind, soft-spoken grandfather, but he too died a year later.

*The chief sources of biographical material about Marian Anderson and her family were Anderson (1992) and Keller (2000). Some details come from Kernan (1993) and from obituaries published in *Time* (April 19, 1993), *People Weekly, The New Yorker,* and *Jet* (April 26, 1993).

Her grandmother took care of all the children, giving them chores and teaching them lessons about sharing and respect for others. Marian's aunt ran the house, and her mother contributed by cooking dinners, working as a cleaning woman, and taking in laundry, which Marian and her sister Alyce delivered.

The most important influence in Marian Anderson's life was the counsel, example, and spiritual guidance of her hardworking, unfailingly supportive mother. Annie Anderson placed great importance on her children's schooling and saw to it that they didn't skimp on homework. Even when she was working full time, she cooked their dinner every night, and she taught Marian to sew her own clothes.

When Marian Anderson became a world-renowned concert artist, she often returned to her old neighborhood in Philadelphia. Her mother and sister Alyce shared a modest house, and the other sister, Ethel, lived next door with her son.

"It is the pleasantest thing in the world to go into that home and feel its happiness, . . ." the singer wrote. "They are all comfortable, and they cherish and protect one another. . . . I know that it warms [Mother] to have her grandson near her as he grows up, just as I think that when he gets to be a man, making his own life, he will have pleasant memories of his home and family" (Anderson, 1992, p. 93). In 1992, Marian Anderson—widowed, childless, and frail at age 95—went to live with that nephew, James DePriest, then music director of the Oregon Symphony. She died of a stroke at his home the following year.

Marian Anderson "lived through momentous changes in America and the world" and in African American life (McKay, 1992, p. xxiv), but one thing that never changed was the strong, supportive network of relationships that sustained her and her family.

The kind of household a child lives in, and the relationships within the household, can have profound effects on psychosocial development in middle childhood, when children are developing a stronger sense of what it means to be responsible, contributing members, first of a family, and then of society. The family is part of a web of contextual influences, including the peer group, the school, and the neighborhood in which the family lives. Marian Anderson's first friend, her church choir, and the neighbors for whom she did odd jobs all played parts in her development. Above and beyond these influences were the overarching cultural patterns of time and place, which presented special challenges to African American families and communities and called forth mutually supportive responses.

In this chapter, we see how children develop a more realistic self-concept and become more self-reliant and in control of their emotions. Through being with peers they make discoveries about their own attitudes, values, and skills. Still, the family remains a vital influence. Children's lives are affected not only by the way parents approach the task of child raising but also by whether and how they are employed, by the family's economic circumstances, and by the makeup of the household. Although most children are emotionally healthy, some have mental health problems; we look at several of these. We also describe resilient children, who emerge from the stresses of childhood healthier and stronger.

After you have read and studied this chapter, you should be able to answer each of the following Guidepost questions. Look for them again in the margins, where they point to important concepts throughout the chapter. To check your understanding of these Guideposts, review the end-of-chapter summary. Checkpoints located at periodic spots throughout the chapter will help you verify your understanding of what you have read.

Guideposts for Study

1. How do school-age children develop a realistic self-concept, and what contributes to self-esteem?
2. How do school-age children show emotional growth?
3. How do parent-child relationships change in middle childhood?
4. What are the effects of parents' work and of poverty on family atmosphere?
5. What impact does family structure have on children's development?
6. How do siblings influence and get along with one another?
7. How do relationships with peers change in middle childhood, and what influences popularity and choice of friends?
8. What are the most common forms of aggressive behavior in middle childhood, and what influences contribute to it?
9. What emotional disorders may develop in childhood, and how are they treated?
10. How do the stresses of modern life affect children, and why are some children more resilient than others?

The Developing Self

The cognitive growth that takes place during middle childhood enables children to develop more complex concepts of themselves and to grow in emotional understanding and control.

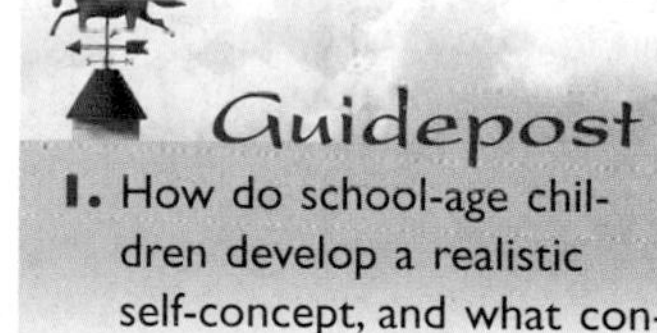

Guidepost

1. How do school-age children develop a realistic self-concept, and what contributes to self-esteem?

Representational Systems: A Neo-Piagetian View

Judgments about the self become more realistic, more balanced, more comprehensive, and more consciously expressed in middle childhood (Harter, 1996, 1998). Around age 7 or 8, children reach the third of the neo-Piagetian stages of self-concept development described in Chapter 8. Children now have the cognitive ability to form **representational systems:** broad, inclusive self-concepts that integrate different aspects of the self (Harter, 1993, 1996, 1998).

representational systems In neo-Piagetian terminology, the third stage in development of self-definition, characterized by breadth, balance, and the integration and assessment of various aspects of the self.

"At school I'm feeling pretty smart in certain subjects, Language Arts and Social Studies," says 8-year-old Lisa. "I got A's in these subjects on my last report card and was really proud of myself. But I'm feeling really dumb in Arithmetic and Science, particularly when I see how well the other kids are doing. . . . I still like myself as a person, because Arithmetic and Science just aren't that important to me. How I look and how popular I am are more important" (Harter, 1996, p. 208).

Lisa's self-description shows that she can focus on more than one dimension of herself. She has outgrown an all-or-nothing, black-or-white self-definition; she recognizes that she can be "smart" in certain subjects and "dumb" in others. Her self-descriptions are more balanced; she can verbalize her self-concept better, and she can weigh different aspects of it ("How I look and how popular I am are more important."). She can

Middle childhood, according to Erikson, is a time for learning the skills one's culture considers important. In driving geese to market, this Vietnamese girl is developing a sense of competence and gaining self-esteem. In addition, by taking on responsibilities to match her growing capabilities, she learns about how her society works, her role in it, and what it means to do a job well.

compare her *real self* with her *ideal self* and can judge how well she measures up to social standards in comparison with others. All of these changes contribute to the development of self-esteem, her assessment of her *global self-worth* ("I like myself as a person").

Self-Esteem

industry versus inferiority Erikson's fourth stage of psychosocial development, in which children must learn the productive skills their culture requires or else face feelings of inferiority.

According to Erikson (1982), a major determinant of self-esteem is children's view of their capacity for productive work. The issue to be resolved in middle childhood is **industry versus inferiority.** The "virtue" that develops with successful resolution of this crisis is *competence,* a view of the self as able to master skills and complete tasks.

Children have to learn skills valued in their society. Arapesh boys in New Guinea learn to make bows and arrows and to lay traps for rats; Arapesh girls learn to plant, weed, and harvest. Inuit children of Alaska learn to hunt and fish. Children in industrialized countries learn to read, write, count, and use computers. Like Marian Anderson, many children learn household skills and help out with odd jobs. Children compare their abilities with those of their peers; if they feel inadequate, they may retreat to the protective embrace of the family. If, on the other hand, they become too industrious, they may neglect social relationships and turn into workaholics.

A different view of the sources of self-worth comes from research by Susan Harter (1985a, 1990, 1993). Harter (1985a) asked 8- to 12-year-olds to rate their appearance, behavior, school performance, athletic ability, and acceptance by other children and to assess how much each of these areas affected their opinion of themselves. The children rated physical appearance most important. Social acceptance came next. Less critical were schoolwork, conduct, and athletics. In contrast, then, to the high value Erikson placed on mastery of skills, Harter suggests that today's school-age children, at least in North America, judge themselves more by good looks and popularity.

A major contributor to self-esteem is social support—first, from parents and classmates, then from friends and teachers. Do they like and care about the child? Do they treat the child as a person who matters and has valuable things to say? Even if Mike thinks it's important to be handsome and smart and considers himself both, his self-esteem will suffer if he does not feel valued by the important people in his life. Still, social support generally will not compensate for a low self-evaluation. If Juanita thinks sports are important but that she is not athletic, she will lose self-esteem no matter how much praise she gets from others.

Children who are socially withdrawn or isolated may be overly concerned about their performance in social situations. They may attribute rejection to their own personality deficiencies, which they believe they are helpless to change. Rather than trying new ways to gain approval, they repeat unsuccessful strategies or just give up. (This is similar to the "helpless pattern" in younger children, described in Chapter 8.) Children with high self-esteem, by contrast, tend to attribute failure to factors outside themselves or to the need to try harder. If initially unsuccessful, they persevere, trying new strategies until they find one that works (Erdley et al., 1997).

Checkpoint

Can you . . .

- ✔ Discuss how the self-concept develops in middle childhood?
- ✔ Compare Erikson's and Harter's findings about sources of self-esteem?
- ✔ Describe how the "helpless pattern" can affect children's reactions to social rejection?

Emotional Growth

Guidepost

2. How do school-age children show emotional growth?

As children grow older, they are more aware of their own and other people's feelings. They can better regulate their emotional expression in social situations, and they can respond to others' emotional distress (Saarni et al., 1998).

By age 7 or 8, shame and pride, which depend on awareness of the implications of their actions and on what kind of socialization children have received, affect their opinion of themselves (Harter, 1993, 1996). Increasingly, children can verbalize conflicting emotions (see Table 10-1). As Lisa says, "Most of the boys at school are pretty yukky. I don't feel that way about my little brother Jason, although he does get on my nerves. I love him but at the same time, he also does things that make me mad. But I control my temper, I'd be ashamed of myself if I didn't" (Harter, 1996, p. 208).

Children become more empathic and more inclined to prosocial behavior in middle childhood. Prosocial behavior is a sign of positive adjustment. Prosocial children tend to act appropriately in social situations, to be relatively free from negative emotion, and to cope with problems constructively (Eisenberg, Fabes, & Murphy, 1996).

Control of negative emotions is an aspect of emotional growth. Children learn what makes them angry, fearful, or sad and how other people react to a display of these

Table 10-1 Levels of Understanding of Conflicting Emotions

Level	Approximate Age	What Children Understand	What a Child Might Say
Level 0	3–6 years	Children do not understand that *any* two feelings can coexist. They cannot even acknowledge feeling two *similar* emotions at once (such as mad and sad).	Carlos says, "You can't have two feelings at the same time because you only have one mind!"
Level 1	6–7 years	Children are developing separate categories for positive and negative emotions. They can be aware of two emotions at the same time, but only if both are either positive or negative and are directed toward the same target.	Kayla says, "If my brother hit me, I would be mad and sad."
Level 2	7–8 years	Children can recognize having two feelings of the same kind directed toward different targets. However, they cannot acknowledge holding contradictory feelings.	Dominic says, "I was excited about going to Mexico and glad to see my grandparents. I wasn't scared; I couldn't feel glad and scared at the same time; I would have to be two people at once!"
Level 3	8–10 years	Children can integrate sets of positive and negative emotions. They can understand having contrary feelings at the same time, but only if they are directed toward different targets.	Ashley can express a negative feeling toward her baby brother ("I was mad at Tony, so I pinched him") and a positive feeling toward her father ("I was happy my father didn't spank me"), but she cannot recognize that she has positive and negative feelings (anger and love) toward both.
Level 4	11 years	Children can describe conflicting feelings toward the same target.	Lisa says, "I'm excited about going to my new school, but I'm a little scared too."

Source: Harter, 1996.

emotions, and they learn to adapt their behavior accordingly. They also learn the difference between having an emotion and expressing it. Kindergartners believe that a parent can make a child less sad by telling the child to stop crying, or can make a child less afraid of a dog by telling the child there is nothing to be afraid of. Sixth-graders know that an emotion may be suppressed, but it still exists (Rotenberg & Eisenberg, 1997).

By middle childhood, children are well aware of their culture's "rules" for emotional displays. In interviews with 223 second-, fourth-, and fifth-graders in the United States and Nepal, three distinct cultural patterns emerged. Lower-caste Tamang children in Nepal, who are taught to be submissive, were more likely to report feeling shame in difficult situations than either uppercaste Brahman children in Nepal or U.S. children, both of whom tend to have high self-esteem. Brahman children, who are taught to be highly self-aware and self-controlled, were less likely to express anger than U.S. children, who are taught to be self-assertive (Cole, Bruschi, & Tamang, 2002).

Such cultural rules are communicated through parents' reactions to children's displays of feelings. U.S. children whose mothers encourage them to express feelings constructively and help them focus on solving the root problem tend to cope more effectively and have better social skills than children whose mothers devalue their feelings by minimizing the seriousness of the situation (Eisenberg et al., 1996). Parents who acknowledge and legitimize children's own feelings of distress encourage empathy and prosocial development (Bryant, 1987). When parents show disapproval of, or punish, negative emotions, the emotions may become more intensely expressed and may impair children's social adjustment (Fabes, Leonard, Kupenoff, & Martin, 2001). Or such children may learn to hide negative emotions but may become anxious in situations that evoke them. As children approach early adolescence, parental intolerance of negative emotion may heighten parent-child conflict (Eisenberg, Fabes, et al., 1999). As we'll see in the next section, this is one of many ways in which the family environment affects children's development.

Checkpoint

Can you . . .

✔ Identify some aspects of emotional growth in middle childhood and tell how parental treatment may affect children's handling of negative emotions?

The Child in the Family

Guidepost

3. How do parent-child relationships change in middle childhood?

School-age children spend more time away from home than when they were younger and become less close to their parents (Hofferth, 1998). With the upsurge in dual-earner and single-parent families, greater emphasis on education, and the tighter pace of family life, children spend more time at school or in child care and in organized activities than a generation ago. They have less free time for unstructured play, outdoor activities, and leisurely family dinners. Much of the time parents and children spend together is task-centered: shopping, preparing meals, cleaning house, and doing homework (Hofferth & Sandberg, 1998). Still, home and the people who live there remain an important part of a child's life.

To understand the child in the family we need to look at the family environment—its *atmosphere* and its *structure,* or composition. These in turn are affected by what goes on beyond the walls of the home. As Bronfenbrenner's bioecological theory describes, additional layers of influence—including parents' work and socioeconomic status and societal trends such as urbanization, changes in family size, divorce, and remarriage—help shape the family environment and, thus, children's development.

Beyond these influences are cultural experiences and values that influence family life and the roles of family members. For example, African American families like Marian Anderson's have carried on African extended-family traditions, which have helped them adapt to life in the United States. These traditions include living near or with kin, frequent contacts with relatives, a strong sense of family obligation, willingness to take additional relatives into the household, and a system of mutual aid.

Important goals of parenting include teaching children how to deal with racial discrimination (such as Anderson's rejection by the music school) and instilling ethnic pride (Parke & Buriel, 1998).

As we look at the child in the family, then, we need to be aware of outside influences that impinge upon it.

Family Atmosphere

The most important influences of the family environment on children's development come from the atmosphere within the home (Bronfenbrenner & Morris, 1998; Demo, 1991). Is it supportive and loving, or conflict-ridden? Does the family have enough money to provide for basic needs? Often these two facets of family atmosphere are interrelated.

Parenting Issues: Coregulation and Discipline As children's lives change, so do the issues between them and their parents, and the ways in which issues are resolved. During the course of childhood, control of behavior gradually shifts from parents to child.

Middle childhood is the transitional stage of **coregulation,** in which parent and child share power: parents oversee, but children exercise moment-to-moment self-regulation (Maccoby, 1984). With regard to problems with peers, for example, parents now rely less on direct management or supervision and more on consultation and discussion with their own child (Parke & Buriel, 1998). Children are more apt to follow their parents' wishes or advice when they recognize that the parents are fair and are concerned about the child's welfare and that they may "know better" because of experience. It also helps if parents try to defer to children's maturing judgment and take strong stands only on important issues (Maccoby, 1984).

coregulation Transitional stage in the control of behavior in which parents exercise general supervision and children exercise moment-to-moment self-regulation.

The way parents and children resolve conflicts may be more important than the specific outcomes. If family conflict is constructive, it can help children see the need for rules and standards of behavior. They also learn what kinds of issues are worth arguing about and what strategies can be effective (A. R. Eisenberg, 1996).

As children become preadolescents, and their striving for autonomy becomes more insistent, the quality of family problem solving and negotiation often deteriorates. In

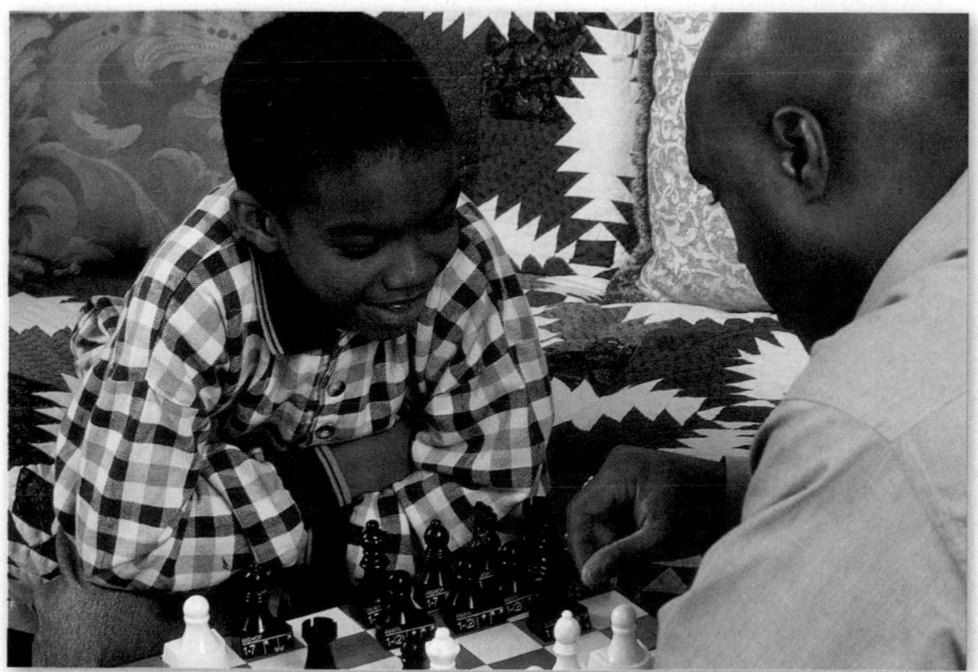

Although school-age children spend less time at home than before, parents continue to be very important in children's lives. Parents who enjoy being with their children tend to raise children who feel good about themselves—and about their parents.

one study, 63 two-parent families with fourth-grade children videotaped home discussions of two problems (for example, over allowance, bedtime, or chores) that had come up within the past month—one topic of the child's choosing and one of the parents' choosing. The families repeated the procedure two years later. Between the ages of 9 and 11, the children's participation became more negative, especially when discussing topics the parents had chosen. It made no difference what the topic was; the basic issue, apparently, was "who is in charge" (Vuchinich, Angelelli, & Gatherum, 1996).

The shift to coregulation affects how parents handle discipline (Maccoby, 1984; Roberts, Block, & Block, 1984). Parents of school-age children are more likely to use inductive techniques that include reasoning. For example, 8-year-old Jared's father points out how his actions affect others: "Hitting Jermaine hurts him and makes him feel bad." In other situations, Jared's parents may appeal to his self-esteem ("What happened to the helpful boy who was here yesterday?"), sense of humor ("If you go one more day without a bath, we'll know when you're coming without looking!"), moral values ("A big, strong boy like you shouldn't sit on the train and let an old person stand"), or appreciation ("Aren't you glad that your father cares enough to remind you to wear boots so that you won't catch a cold?"). Above all, Jared's parents let him know he must bear the consequences of his behavior ("No wonder you missed the school bus today—you stayed up too late last night! Now you'll have to walk to school").

Checkpoint

Can you . . .

✔ Describe how coregulation works and how discipline and the handling of family conflict change during middle childhood?

Guidepost

4. What are the effects of parents' work and of poverty on family atmosphere?

Effects of Parents' Work Today, about three out of four U.S. mothers of school-age children and about the same proportion of Canadian women ages 25 to 34 are in the workforce (Bureau of Labor Statistics, 2000; Sorrentino, 1990). With more than half of all new mothers in the United States going to work within a year after giving birth (Bureau of Labor Statistics, 2000), many children have never known a time when their mothers were *not* working for pay.

As we mentioned earlier, most studies of the impact of parents' work on children's well-being have focused on employed mothers. The impact of a mother's work depends on many factors, including the child's age, sex, temperament, and personality; whether the mother works full or part time; why she is working, and how she feels about her work; whether she has a supportive or unsupportive mate, or none; the family's socioeconomic status; and the kind of care the child receives before and/or after school (Parke & Buriel, 1998).

Another factor is whether there are two parents or only one in the household. Often a single mother like Marian Anderson's must work to stave off economic disaster. How her working affects her children may hinge on how much time and energy she has left over to spend with them and what sort of role model she provides (B. L. Barber & Eccles, 1992)—clearly, a positive one in Annie Anderson's case.

The more satisfied a mother is with her employment status, the more effective she is likely to be as a parent (Parke & Buriel, 1998). School-age children of employed mothers tend to live in more structured homes than children of full-time homemakers, with clear-cut rules giving them more household responsibilities. They are also encouraged to be more independent (Bronfenbrenner & Crouter, 1982), and they have more egalitarian attitudes about gender roles (Parke & Buriel, 1998).

How does a mother's employment affect school achievement? Both boys and girls in low-income families seem to benefit academically from the more favorable environment a working mother's income can provide (Goldberg, Greenberger, & Nagel, 1996; Vandell & Ramanan, 1992). In middle-class families, however, sons of working mothers tend to do less well in school than sons of homemakers, whereas daughters usually do as well or better when mothers work (Goldberg et al., 1996; Heyns & Catsambis, 1986). These gender differences in middle-class families may have to do with boys' greater need for supervision and guidance (Goldberg et al., 1996).

Some children of employed mothers are supervised after school by their fathers, grandparents, other relatives, or baby-sitters. Some go to structured programs, either at school or in child care settings. Like good child care for preschoolers, good after-school programs have relatively low enrollment, low child-staff ratios, and well-educated staff (Posner & Vandell, 1999; Rosenthal & Vandell, 1996). Children, especially boys, in organized after-school programs marked by flexible programming and a positive emotional climate tended to adjust better in first grade (Pierce, Hamm, & Vandell, 1999).

Eight percent of 8- to 10-year-olds and 23 percent of 11- and 12-year-olds in a nationally representative sample of 1,500 children regularly care for themselves at home without adult supervision. However, each child spends an average of only one hour alone each day (Hofferth & Jankuniene, 2000). This arrangement is advisable only for older children who are mature, responsible, and resourceful and know how to get help in an emergency, and if a parent stays in touch by telephone.

What's Your View?

- If finances permit, should either the mother or the father stay home to take care of the children?

Poverty and Parenting About one U.S. child in five is born poor, and one in three spends part of childhood in poverty (Children's Defense Fund, 2001). Poverty can inspire people like Marian Anderson's mother to work hard and make a better life for their children—or it can crush their spirits.

Poverty can harm children's development through its impact on parents' emotional state and parenting practices and on the home environment they create (Brooks-Gunn & Duncan, 1997; Brooks-Gunn et al., 1998). Vonnie McLoyd's (1990, 1998; Mistry, Vandewater, Huston, & McLoyd, 2002) ecological analysis of the effects of poverty traces a route that leads to adult psychological distress, to effects on child rearing, and finally to emotional, behavioral, and academic problems in children. Parents who live in poor housing (or have none), who have lost their jobs, who are worried about their next meal, and who feel a lack of control over their lives are likely to become anxious, depressed, or irritable. They may become less affectionate with, and less responsive to, their children. They may discipline inconsistently, harshly, and arbitrarily. They may ignore good behavior and pay attention only to misbehavior. The children, in turn, tend to become depressed themselves, to have trouble getting along with peers, to lack self-confidence, to have behavioral problems, and to engage in antisocial acts (Brooks-Gunn et al., 1998; McLoyd, 1990, 1998; Mistry et al., 2002). This linkage of poverty, family stress, and children's social and emotional problems exists among rural, low-income white children as well as among inner city ethnic minorities (Evans & English, 2002).

Families under economic stress are less likely to monitor their children's activities, and lack of monitoring is associated with poorer school performance and social adjustment (Bolger, Patterson, Thompson, & Kupersmidt, 1995). In a nationally representative study of 11,760 children ages 6 to 17, one-third of those with family incomes below poverty level were behind the normal grade level for their age (J. M. Fields & Smith, 1998).

A father's involvement with his children tends to be related to his economic success; when a father feels like a failure as a breadwinner, his demoralization is likely to carry over to his fathering role and to negatively affect his relationships with his children. Thus, fathering is especially vulnerable to economic and social forces that affect occupational opportunities (Doherty et al., 1998).

Poverty can sap parents' confidence in their ability to affect their children's development. Lack of financial resources also can make it harder for mothers and fathers to support each other in parenting. One study looked at 9- to 12-year-olds and their married parents with incomes ranging from $2,500 to $57,500. In many of the poor families, parents worked several fatiguing jobs to make ends meet. These parents were less optimistic and more depressed than parents in better-off families. They found it harder to communicate and cooperate with each other and often fought over child raising. Contradictory parental messages led to behavioral and scholastic problems in the children (Brody et al., 1994).

Persistent poverty can be particularly damaging. Among 534 schoolchildren in Charlottesville, Virginia, those from persistently deprived families had lower self-esteem, got along less well with peers, and were more likely to have behavior problems than children whose families experienced intermittent hardship or none at all (Bolger et al., 1995).

Checkpoint

Can you . . .

- ✔ Identify ways in which parents' work can affect children?
- ✔ Discuss effects of poverty on child raising?

However, this bleak picture is not etched in stone. Parents who can turn to relatives (as Annie Anderson did) or to community representatives for emotional support, help with child care, and childrearing information often can parent their children more effectively. Also, as we will see, some children are more adaptable than others; their temperament enables them to cope more successfully with a stressful environment (Ackerman, Kogos, Youngstrom, Schoff, & Izard, 1999).

Family Structure

Guidepost

5. What impact does family structure have on children's development?

The structure, or makeup, of families in the United States has changed dramatically. In earlier generations, the vast majority of children grew up in traditional families, with two married, heterosexual biological or adoptive parents. Today, although most children under 18 live with two parents, the proportion has declined drastically (see Figure 10-1). In addition, many two-parent families are cohabiting families or stepfamilies, resulting from divorce and remarriage. There also are a growing number of other family types, including single-parent families, gay and lesbian families, and grandparent-headed families (see Chapter 16). The proportion of all households in which a married couple live with their biological, adopted, or stepchildren fell from about 40 percent in 1970 to only 24 percent in 2000 (Fields & Casper, 2001).

Other things being equal, children tend to do better in a traditional two-parent family than in a divorced, single-parent, or stepfamily (Bramlett & Mosher, 2001; Bray & Hetherington, 1993; Bronstein, Clauson, Stoll, & Abrams, 1993; D. A. Dawson, 1991; Hetherington, Bridges, & Insabella, 1998). However, structure in itself is not the key; the parents' relationship with each other and their ability to create a favorable

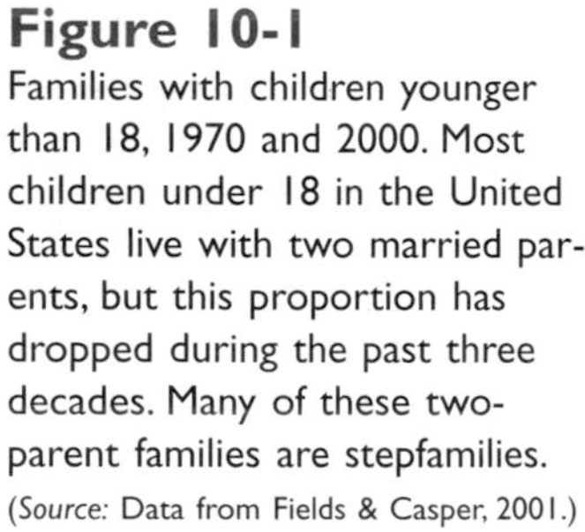

Figure 10-1
Families with children younger than 18, 1970 and 2000. Most children under 18 in the United States live with two married parents, but this proportion has dropped during the past three decades. Many of these two-parent families are stepfamilies.
(*Source:* Data from Fields & Casper, 2001.)

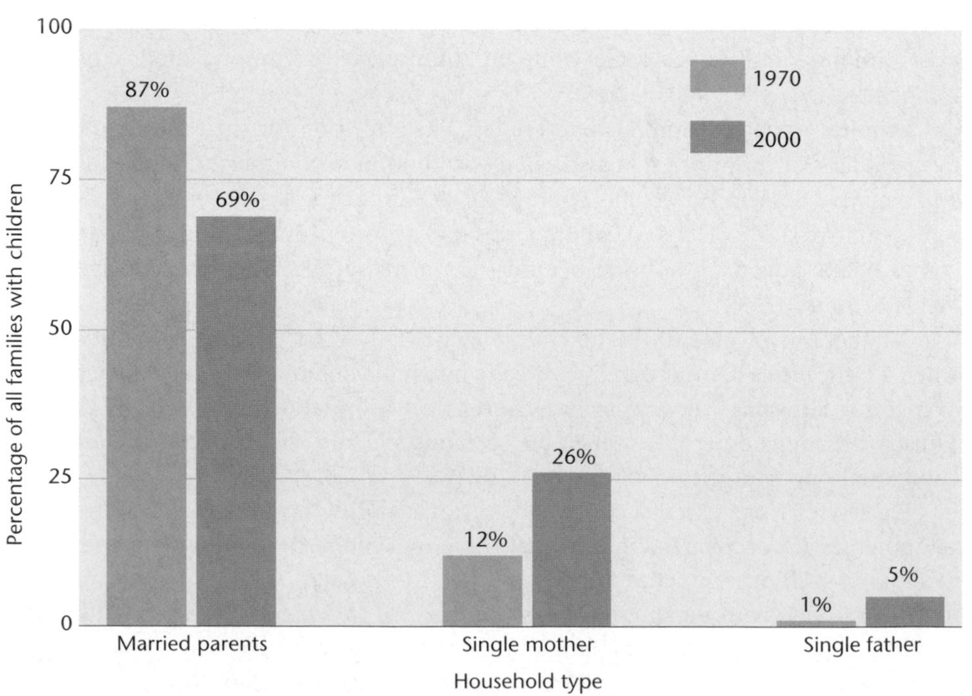

Because of a decrease in the number of adoptable American babies, many children adopted today are of foreign birth. Adoptive parents face special challenges, such as the need to explain the adoption to the child. But most adoptive children view their adoption positively and see it as playing only a minor role in their identity.

atmosphere affect children's adjustment more than does marital status (Bray & Hetherington, 1993; Bronstein et al., 1993; D. A. Dawson, 1991; Emery, 1988; Hetherington, 1989).

Adoptive Families Adoption is found in all cultures throughout history. It is not only for infertile people; single people, older people, gay and lesbian couples, and people who already have biological children have become adoptive parents. Adoptions take place through public or private agencies or through independent agreements between birth parents and adoptive parents. Independent adoptions have become increasingly common (Brodzinsky, 1997; Goodman, Emery, & Haugaard, 1998).

About 60 percent of legal adoptions in the United States are by relatives, usually stepparents or grandparents (Goodman et al., 1998; Haugaard, 1998). An increasing percentage of children available for adoption by *non*relatives are beyond infancy, are of foreign birth, or have special needs. This is because advances in contraception and legalization of abortion have reduced the number of adoptable healthy white U.S. babies. The percentage of babies, born to never-married white women, who were placed for adoption dropped from 19.3 percent in the early 1970s to only 1.7 percent in the early 1990s (Chandra, Abma, Maza, & Bachrach, 1999), and black women have consistently been far less likely to put up their babies for adoption (Brodzinsky, 1997).

About 8 percent of adoptions are transracial, often involving an Asian or Latin American child being adopted into a household with a white mother. The resulting families are among the far greater, and increasing, number of multiracial U.S. families—about 1.4 million of them in 1995—formed by interracial marriage (Rosenblatt, 1999). Rules governing interracial adoption vary from state to state; some give priority to same-race adoption, whereas others require that race not be a factor in approval of an adoption.

Adopting a child carries special challenges. Besides the usual issues of parenthood, adoptive parents need to deal with integrating the adopted child into the family, explaining the adoption to the child, helping the child develop a healthy sense of self, and perhaps eventually helping the child to contact the biological parents.

There are few significant differences in adjustment between adopted and nonadopted children, according to a review of the literature (Haugaard, 1998). Children

What's Your View?

- If you were infertile, do you think you would try to adopt? If so, would you consider transracial or foreign adoption? Open adoption?

adopted in infancy are least likely to have adjustment problems (Sharma, McGue, & Benson, 1996b). Any problems that do occur seem to surface around the time of sexual maturation (Goodman et al., 1998; Sharma, McGue, & Benson, 1996a).

Does adopting a foreign-born child lead to special difficulties? A number of studies have found no such effects (Sharma et al., 1996a). One study looked at 100 Israeli families, half of whom had adopted South American children and half Israeli children. The two groups of 7- to 13-year-olds, all of whom had been adopted soon after birth, showed no significant differences in psychological adjustment, in school adjustment and performance, in observed behavior at home, or in the way they coped with being adopted (Levy-Shiff, Zoran, & Shulman, 1997).

open adoption Adoption in which the birth parents and the adoptive parents know each other's identities and share information or have direct contact.

Traditionally, adoptions were confidential, with no contact between the birth mother and the adoptive parents, and the identity of the birth mother was kept secret. In recent years, **open adoption,** in which the parties share information or have direct contact, has become more common. Contrary to what are sometimes considered the risks of open adoption, one study found that with direct contact the adoptive parents tend to feel more confident that the arrangement is permanent and that the birth mother will not try to reclaim the child. At the same time, they are more likely to recognize the child's interest in knowing about her or his origins (Grotevant, McRoy, Elde, & Fravel, 1994). In one survey of 1,059 California families who had adopted children three years earlier, whether or not an adoption was open seemed to bear no relation to the children's adjustment or to the parents' satisfaction with the adoption, both of which were very high (Berry, Dylla, Barth, & Needell, 1998).

When Parents Divorce The annual number of divorces has tripled since 1960 (Harvey & Pauwels, 1999). One-third of first marriages dissolve within ten years (Bramlett & Mosher, 2001), and more than 1 million children are involved in divorces each year. How do these children adjust?

Influences on a child's adjustment to divorce include the child's age or maturity, gender, temperament, and psychological and social adjustment before the divorce. The ways parents handle such issues as custody and visitation arrangements, finances, reorganization of household duties, contact with the noncustodial parent, remarriage, and the child's relationship with a stepparent also make a difference.

Younger children are more anxious about divorce, have less realistic perceptions of what caused it, and are more likely to blame themselves; but they may adapt more quickly than older children, who better understand what is going on. School-age children are sensitive to parental pressures and loyalty conflicts; like younger children, they may fear abandonment and rejection. Boys generally find it harder to adjust than girls do. However, this difference may be less significant than was once thought and may depend largely on how involved the father remains (Bray, 1991; Hetherington, Stanley-Hagan, & Anderson, 1989; Hetherington et al., 1998; Hines, 1997; Masten, Best, & Garmezy, 1990; Parke & Buriel, 1998).

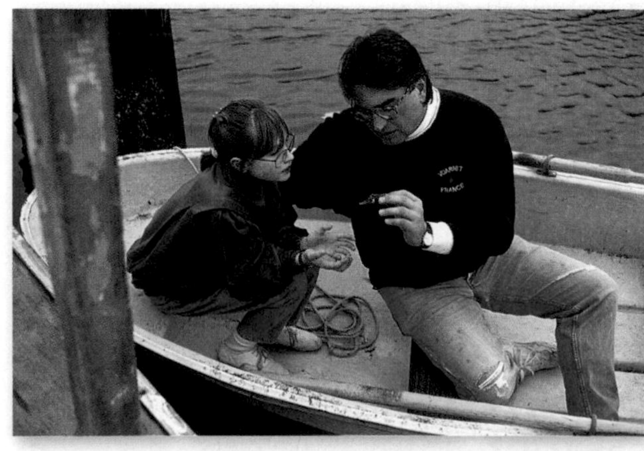

Children of divorce tend to be better adjusted if they have reliable, frequent contact with the noncustodial parent, usually the father.

In most divorce cases the mother gets custody, but paternal custody is a growing trend (Meyer & Garasky, 1993). The more recent the separation, the closer the father lives to his children, and the higher his socioeconomic status, the more involved he is likely to be (Amato & Keith, 1991; Parke & Buriel, 1998).

Children adjust better when the custodial parent creates a stable, structured, nurturing environment and does not expect the children to take on more responsibility than they are ready for (Hetherington et al., 1989). According to an analysis of sixty-three studies, children living with divorced mothers do better when the father pays child support, which may be a barometer of the tie between father and child and also of relative lack of rancor between the ex-spouses. Frequency of contact with the father is not as important as the quality of the father-child relationship. Children who are close to their nonresident fathers, and whose fathers use authoritative parenting, tend to do better in school; children who do not enjoy such relationships with their fathers are likely to have behavior problems (Amato & Gilbreth, 1999). Children also perform better academically if their nonresident fathers are involved in their schools (National Center for Education Statistics [NCES], 1998b) and if their custodial mothers use effective parenting practices and provide skill-building activities at home (DeGarmo, Forgatch, & Martinez, 1999).

Emotional or behavioral problems may stem from parental conflict, both before and after divorce, as well as from the separation itself (Amato, Kurdek, Demo, & Allen, 1993; E. M. Cummings, 1994; Furstenberg & Kiernan, 2001; Parke & Buriel, 1998; Shaw, Winslow, & Flanagan, 1999; see Box 10-1 on page 362). If parents can control their anger, cooperate in parenting, and avoid exposing the children to quarreling, the children are less likely to have problems (Bray & Hetherington, 1993; Hetherington et al., 1989). Unfortunately, the strains of divorce make it harder for a couple to be effective parents (Hines, 1997). Parent education programs that teach separated or divorced couples how to prevent or deal with conflict, keep lines of communication open, develop an effective coparenting relationship, and help children adjust to divorce have been introduced in many courts, with measurable success (Amato & Gilbreth, 1999; Shifflet & Cummings, 1999). One program—a series of structured group sessions either for mothers alone or for mothers and their 9- to 12-year-old children—dramatically reduced the children's likelihood six years later of showing mental health problems such as aggression, substance use, and sexual promiscuity, as compared with a control group who merely received books on adjusting to divorce (Wolchik et al., 2002).

Joint custody, custody shared by both parents, can be advantageous in some cases, since both parents can continue to be closely involved with the child. When parents have joint *legal* custody, they share the right and responsibility to make decisions regarding the child's welfare. When parents have joint *physical* custody (which is less common), the child is supposed to live part time with each of them. Joint legal custody tends to encourage nonresident fathers to visit their children more often (Seltzer, 1998), by encouraging them to maintain their parental role (Amato & Gilbreth, 1999).

The main determinant of the success of joint custody is the amount of conflict between the parents (Parke & Buriel, 1998). An analysis of 33 studies of 814 children in joint custody and 1,846 children in sole custody found that children in either legal or physical joint custody were better adjusted and had higher self-esteem and better family relationships than children in sole custody, and their families experienced less conflict. In fact, the joint custody children were as well-adjusted as children in nondivorced families (Bauserman, 2002). Of course, it is likely that couples who choose joint custody are those that have less conflict.

Most children of divorce eventually adjust reasonably well (Chase-Lansdale, Cherlin, & Kiernan, 1995). Still, they are more than twice as likely as children in nondivorced families to drop out of high school (McLanahan & Sandefur, 1994). They also are more likely to marry young and to form unstable, unsatisfying relationships (Ross & Mirowsky, 1999), which themselves end in divorce (Amato, 1999, 2000)—though this pattern is less prevalent than it was thirty years ago (Wolfinger, 1999). Having experienced their parents' divorce as children, some young adults are afraid of making commitments that might end in disappointment (Wallerstein & Corbin, 1999). Yet many overcome their fears and form solid, loving relationships (Wallerstein & Lewis, 1998). Much depends on how they resolve and interpret the experience of parental divorce. Some, who saw a high degree of conflict between their parents, are

BOX 10-1

Digging Deeper
Should Parents Stay Together for the Sake of the Children?

A generation ago, when divorce was far less common than it is today, it was widely believed that parents in troubled marriages should stay together for the sake of the children. More recent research has found that marital strife harms children more than divorce does—that children are better adjusted if they grow up in a harmonious single-parent household than in a two-parent home marked by discord and discontent (Hetherington et al., 1998; Hetherington & Stanley-Hagan, 1999). However, that finding may need some qualifying.

Clearly, watching parents' spats can be hard on children. Aside from the distress, worry, or fear children may feel, marital dissension may diminish parents' responsiveness to children's needs. Both before and after divorce, children tend to show behavior problems (Shaw, Winslow, & Flanagan, 1999). Boys growing up in an atmosphere of parental anger and discord tend to become aggressive; girls to become withdrawn and anxious. Children do not get used to marital conflict; the more they are exposed to it, the more sensitive they become (E. M. Cummings, 1994). Children see destructive parental quarrels as threatening their own security and that of the family (Davies & Cummings, 1998). Violent clashes, conflicts about a child to which the child is directly exposed, and those in which a child feels caught in the middle are the most damaging (Hetherington & Stanley-Hagan, 1999).

The *amount* of conflict in a marriage may make a difference. A fifteen-year longitudinal study, which followed a nationwide sample originally consisting of 2,033 married people (Amato & Booth, 1997), suggests that in only about 30 percent of divorces involving children is there so much discord that the children are better off if the marriage ends. About 70 percent of cases, according to this research, involve low-conflict marriages, in which children would benefit "if parents remained together until children are grown" (p. 238).

In as many as one in five divorced families, parental conflict continues or escalates. Two years after a divorce, children suffer more from dissension in a divorced family than do children in a nondivorced family. Thus, if conflict is going to *continue,* children may be better off in an acrimonious two-parent household than if the parents divorce. On the other hand, if conflict *lessens* after a divorce, the children may be better off than they were before. Unfortunately, the amount of bickering after a divorce is not always easy to anticipate (Hetherington & Stanley-Hagan, 1999).

To test the theory that children are better off if their parents wait to divorce, one team of researchers (Furstenberg & Kiernan, 2001) examined data from a longitudinal cohort of 11,407 men and women born in England in March, 1958. Sixteen percent of them reported at age 33 that their parents had been divorced at some point. Two-thirds of these divorces had occurred by the time the children were 16. Thus it was possible to compare young adults who had experienced parental divorce as children with those whose parents had divorced after the children were grown and those whose parents had not divorced at all. The researchers also were able to control for early characteristics of the children.

Despite some differences, men and women who had experienced parental divorce at *any* age showed similar outcomes in several respects. They tended to exhibit more malaise than those whose parents had remained married. By and large, they tended to have lower educational and occupational qualifications and were more likely to be unemployed. They seemed to form cohabiting partnerships earlier and to dissolve them more quickly. However, early and unwed parenthood were more common among products of early divorce (Furstenberg & Kiernan, 2001).

In evaluating the effects of divorce, we need to look at particular circumstances. Sometimes divorce may improve a child's situation by reducing the amount of conflict within the family, and sometimes not. Children's personal characteristics make a difference; intelligent, socially competent children without serious behavior problems, who have a sense of control over their own lives, can cope better with both parental conflict and divorce (Hetherington & Stanley-Hagan, 1999). As we point out in this chapter, ongoing contact with both parents is an important factor. And, while the immediate effects of a marital breakup may be traumatic, in the long run some children may benefit from having learned new coping skills that make them more competent and independent (B. L. Barber & Eccles, 1992).

What's Your View?

Would you advise parents who want a divorce to stay married until their children have grown up? Why or why not? What factors might you consider in giving your advice?

Check It Out:

OLC

For more information on this topic, go to www.mhhe.com/papaliah9, where you'll find links to information on children and divorce.

able to learn from that negative example and to form highly intimate relationships themselves (Shulman, Scharf, Lumer, & Maurer, 2001).

Of course, since all research on effects of divorce is correlational, we cannot be sure that a parental divorce *caused* children's later behavior. Children may still be reacting to conflict preceding or surrounding the dissolution of the marriage, or to some other factor.

Living in a One-Parent Family One-parent families result from divorce or separation, unwed parenthood, or death. The number of single-parent families in the United States has more than doubled since 1970 (Fields & Casper, 2001) with rising rates of divorce and of parenthood outside of marriage. Today one child in four lives with only one parent (Children's Defense Fund, 2001), and a child has at least a 50 percent chance of living with only one parent at some point (Bianchi, 1995; Hines, 1997; NCES, 1998).

Although the growth of one-parent families is slowing, in 2000 they comprised almost one-third (about 31 percent) of U.S. families with children under 18, as compared with 13 percent of all families in 1970 (Fields & Casper, 2001). In Canada, the proportion of such families in 1996 (the most recent date for which such data are available) was 15 percent, less than half the current U.S. rate (Statistics Canada, 1996).

About one in six single-parent U.S. families is headed by the father (Fields & Casper, 2001). The number of father-only families has more than quadrupled since 1974, apparently due largely to an increase in the number of fathers having custody after divorce (Garasky & Meyer, 1996; U.S. Bureau of the Census, 1998).

In 2000 about one in three births—up from fewer than one in twenty-five in 1940—was to an unwed mother (Martin, Hamilton, Ventura, Menacker, & Park, 2002; National Center for Health Statistics [NCHS], 1993, 1994b). Births to single mothers have increased dramatically in many other industrialized countries as well (Bruce, Lloyd, & Leonard, 1995; WuDunn, 1996). However, these data can be misleading because many of these women are in cohabiting unions, some of them with the child's biological father (Seltzer, 2000). In the early 1990s, 39 percent of U.S. nonmarital births were to cohabiting couples (Bumpass & Lu, 2000).

Children in one-parent families tend to do less well socially and educationally than children in two-parent families, partly because one-parent families are more likely to be poor (Seltzer, 2000). Children in one-parent families are more on their own than children living with two parents. They tend to have more household responsibility, more conflict with siblings, less family cohesion, and less support, control, or discipline from fathers, if it is the father who is absent from the household (Amato, 1987; Coley, 1998; Walker & Hennig, 1997). Divorced mothers particularly tend to have trouble with school-age sons (Forgatch & DeGarmo, 1999). However, poor outcomes are far from inevitable. Not only the father's involvement, but also the child's age and level of development, the parents' financial circumstances, whether or not there are frequent moves, and other aspects of the family situation affect how children turn out (Seltzer, 2000).

Checkpoint

Can you . . .

- ✔ Discuss trends in adoption and the adjustment of adopted children?
- ✔ List the psychological "tasks" children face in adjusting to divorce, and identify factors that affect adjustment?
- ✔ Assess the impact of parental divorce on children?
- ✔ Tell three ways in which a one-parent family can be formed, and how living in such a household can affect children's well-being?

Living in a Stepfamily Since about 75 percent of divorced mothers and 80 percent of divorced fathers remarry, families made up of "yours, mine, and ours" are common (Bray & Hetherington, 1993). Stepfamilies often start out as cohabiting families, when a single parent brings a new partner into the house (Seltzer, 2000).

The stepfamily is different from the "natural" family. It has a larger cast, which may include the relatives of up to four adults (the remarried pair, plus one or two former spouses); and it has many stressors. A child's loyalties to an absent or dead parent may interfere with forming ties to a stepparent. Adjustment is harder when there are many children, including those from both the man's and the woman's previous marriages, or when a new child is born (Hetherington et al., 1989).

Findings on the impact of remarriage on children are mixed (Parke & Buriel, 1998). Some studies have found that boys—who often have more trouble than girls in adjusting to divorce and single-parent living, usually with the mother—benefit from a stepfather. A girl, on the other hand, may find the new man in the house a threat to her independence and to her close relationship with her mother and may be less likely to accept him (Bray & Hetherington, 1993; Hetherington, 1987; Hetherington et al., 1989; Hetherington et al., 1998; Hines, 1997). In a longitudinal study of a nationally represented sample of U.S. adults, mothers who remarried or formed new cohabiting relationships used less harsh discipline than mothers who remained single, and their children reported better relationships with them. On the other hand, supervision was greatest in stable single-mother families (Thomson, Mosley, Hanson, & McLanahan, 2001). (Stepfamilies are further discussed in Chapter 14.)

Living with Gay or Lesbian Parents It is estimated that between 1 and 9 million U.S. children have at least one gay or lesbian parent. Some gays and lesbians are raising children born of previous heterosexual relationships. Others conceive by artificial means, employ surrogate mothers, or adopt children (Perrin and AAP Committee on Psychosocial Aspects of Child and Family Health, 2002).

This baby has two fathers—and both obviously dote on the child. Contrary to popular stereotypes, children living with homosexual parents are no more likely than other children to have social or psychological problems or to turn out to be homosexual themselves.

Several studies have focused on the personal development of children of gays and lesbians, including physical and emotional health, intelligence, adjustment, sense of self, moral judgment, and social and sexual functioning. A considerable body of research has indicated no concerns (AAP Committee on Psychosocial Aspects of Child and Family Health, 2002; Mooney-Somers & Golombok, 2000; C. J. Patterson, 1992, 1995a, 1995b, 1997; Perrin and AAP Committee on Psychosocial Aspects of Child and Family Health, 2002). There is no consistent difference between homosexual and heterosexual parents in terms of emotional health or parenting skills and attitudes (Perrin and AAP Committee on Psychosocial Aspects of Child and Family Health, 2002). Openly gay or lesbian parents usually have positive relationships with their children, and the children are no more likely than children raised by heterosexual parents to have social or psychological problems (Chan, Raboy, & Patterson, 1998; C. J. Patterson, 1992, 1995a, 1997).

Children of gays and lesbians are no more likely to be homosexual themselves, or to be confused about their gender, than are children of heterosexuals (Anderssen, Amlie, & Ytteroy, 2002; B. M. King, 1996; C. J. Patterson, 1997). In one study, the vast majority of adult sons of gay fathers were heterosexual (Bailey, Bobrow, Wolfe, & Mikach, 1995). Likewise, in a longitudinal study of adult children of lesbians, a large majority identified themselves as heterosexual (Golombok & Tasker, 1996).

Such findings have social policy implications for legal decisions on custody and visitation disputes, foster care, and adoptions. The American Academy of Pediatrics supports legislative and legal efforts to permit a partner in a same-sex couple to adopt the other partner's child, so that the child may enjoy the benefits of two parents (AAP Committee on Psychosocial Aspects of Child and Family Health, 2002).

Checkpoint

Can you . . .

- ✔ Discuss how parents and stepparents handle the issues and challenges of a stepfamily?
- ✔ Discuss the outcomes of child raising by gay and lesbian parents?

Sibling Relationships

In remote rural areas or villages of Asia, Africa, Oceania, and Central and South America, it is common to see older girls caring for three or four younger siblings: feeding, comforting, and toilet training them; disciplining them; assigning chores; and generally keeping an eye on them. In a poor agricultural or pastoral community, older siblings have an important, culturally defined role. Parents train children early to teach younger sisters and brothers how to gather firewood, carry water, tend animals, and grow food. Younger siblings absorb intangible values, such as respecting elders and placing the welfare of the group above that of the individual. Siblings may fight and compete, but they do so within societal rules and roles (Cicirelli, 1994a).

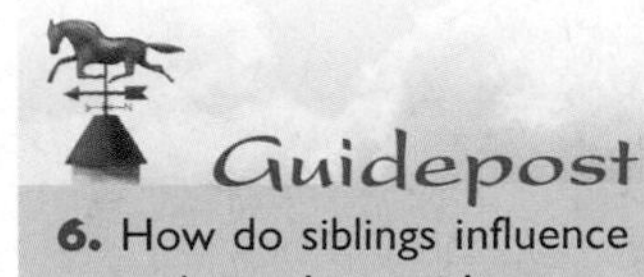

6. How do siblings influence and get along with one another?

Often teaching arises spontaneously as older siblings care for the younger. In an ethnographic study of 72 Mayan children and their 2-year-old younger siblings in a highland village in Mexico, the older ones taught the younger ones how to do such everyday tasks as washing, cooking, taking care of baby dolls, and making tortillas—all in the context of play. The older children's teaching skills increased so that by age 8, they were able to use a combination of techniques—showing, telling, explaining, manual guidance, scaffolding, and giving verbal feedback. Thus older siblings participate in socializing the younger ones in culturally important tasks (Maynard, 2002).

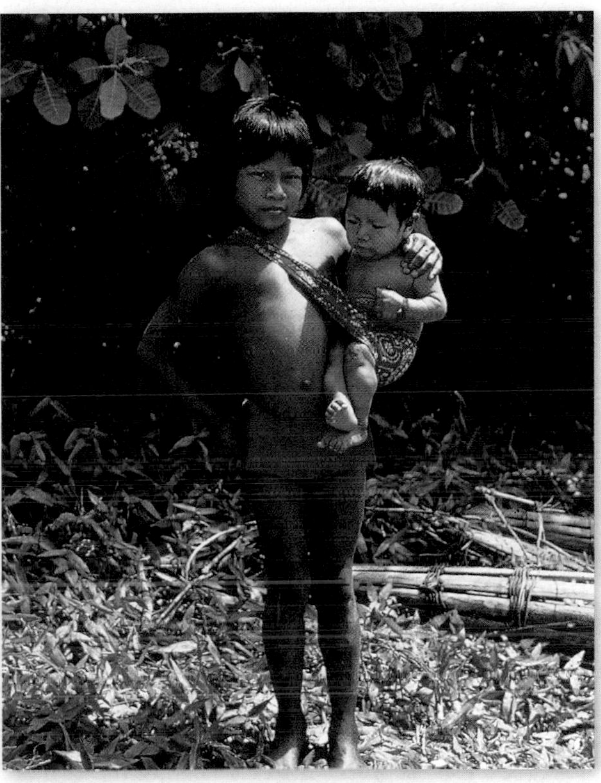

This boy in Surinam has an important responsibility: taking care of his younger brother. Siblings in nonindustrialized societies have clear, culturally defined roles throughout life.

In industrialized societies such as the United States, parents generally try not to "burden" older children with the care of younger ones (Weisner, 1993). Although some caretaking takes place, it is generally sporadic. Older siblings do teach younger ones, but this usually happens by chance, and not as an established part of the social system (Cicirelli, 1994a).

The number of siblings in a family and their spacing, birth order, and gender often determine roles and relationships. The larger number of siblings in nonindustrialized societies helps the family carry on its work and provide for aging members. In industrialized societies, siblings tend to be fewer and farther apart in age, making it easier for parents to pursue careers or other interests and to focus more resources and attention on each child (Cicirelli, 1994a).

Two longitudinal studies, one in England and one in Pennsylvania, based on naturalistic observation of siblings and mothers and interviews with the mothers, found that changes in sibling relationships were most likely to occur when one sibling was between ages 7 and 9. Both mothers and children often attributed these changes to outside friendships, which led to jealousy and competitiveness or loss of interest in, and intimacy with, the sibling. Sometimes the younger sibling's growing assertiveness played a part (Dunn, 1996).

Sibling relations are a laboratory for conflict resolution. Siblings are impelled to make up after quarrels, since they know they will see each other every day. They learn that expressing anger does not end a relationship. Children are more apt to squabble with same-sex siblings; two brothers quarrel more than any other combination (Cicirelli, 1976, 1995).

Siblings influence each other, not only *directly*, through their own interactions, but *indirectly* through their impact on each other's relationship with the parents. Conversely, behavior patterns established with parents tend to "spill over" into behavior with siblings. An older child's positive relationship with the mother or father can mitigate the effects of that child's "difficult" temperament on sibling interactions (Brody, Stoneman, & Gauger, 1996).

Checkpoint

Can you . . .

- ✔ Compare the roles and responsibilities of siblings in industrialized and nonindustrialized countries?
- ✔ Discuss how siblings affect each other's development?

The Child in the Peer Group

Guidepost

7. How do relationships with peers change in middle childhood, and what influences popularity and choice of friends?

In the preschool years, children play together, but in the school years the peer group comes into its own. Groups form naturally among children who live near one another or go to school together. Children who play together are usually close in socioeconomic status and age, though a neighborhood play group may include mixed ages. Too wide an age range brings differences, not only in size, but in interests and ability levels. Groups are usually all girls or all boys (Hartup, 1992). Children of the same sex have common interests; girls are generally more mature than boys, and girls and boys play and talk to one another differently. Same-sex groups help children to learn gender-appropriate behaviors and to incorporate gender roles into their self-concept (Hibbard & Buhrmester, 1998).

Positive and Negative Influences of Peer Relations

What's Your View?

- How can parents and schools reduce racial, religious, and ethnic prejudice?

As children begin to move away from parental influence, the peer group opens new perspectives and frees them to make independent judgments. Testing values they previously accepted unquestioningly against those of their peers helps them decide which to keep and which to discard. In comparing themselves with others their age, children can gauge their abilities more realistically and gain a clearer sense of self-efficacy (Bandura, 1994). The peer group helps children learn how to get along in society—how to adjust their needs and desires to those of others, when to yield, and when to stand firm.

The peer group also can have negative effects. It is usually in the company of peers that children shoplift, begin to use drugs, and act in other antisocial ways. Preadolescent children are especially susceptible to pressure to conform, and this pressure may change a troublesome child into a delinquent one (Hartup, 1992). Of course, some degree of conformity to group standards is healthy. It is unhealthy when it becomes destructive or prompts people to act against their own better judgment.

prejudice Unfavorable attitude toward members of certain groups outside one's own, especially racial or ethnic groups.

Another negative influence of the peer group may be a tendency to reinforce **prejudice:** unfavorable attitudes toward "outsiders," especially members of certain racial or ethnic groups. Broadening children's experience may lessen or eliminate prejudice. The most effective programs get children from different groups to work together toward a common goal, as on athletic teams (Gaertner, Mann, Murrell, & Dovidio, 1989).

Among their peers, children get a sense of how smart, how athletic, and how likable they are. Both competition and shared confidences build the self-concept, helping children develop social skills and a sense of belonging. Peer groups tend to be of the same sex, enabling boys and girls to learn gender-appropriate behaviors.

Popularity

Popularity becomes more important in middle childhood. Children spend more time with other children, and peers' opinions greatly affect their self-esteem. Peer relationships in middle childhood are strong predictors of later adjustment (Masten & Coatsworth, 1998). Schoolchildren whose peers like them are likely to be well adjusted as adolescents. Those who have trouble getting along with peers are more likely to develop psychological problems, drop out of school, or become delinquent (Hartup, 1992; Kupersmidt & Coie, 1990; Morison & Masten, 1991; Newcomb, Bukowski, & Pattee, 1993; Parker & Asher, 1987).

Popular children typically have good cognitive abilities, are high achievers, are good at solving social problems, help other children, and are assertive without being disruptive or aggressive. They are trustworthy, loyal, and self-disclosing and provide emotional support. Their superior social skills make others enjoy being with them (Masten & Coatsworth, 1998; Newcomb et al., 1993). However, this picture is not universally true. Some aggressive or antisocial boys are among the most popular in the classroom, suggesting that criteria for popularity vary (Rodkin, Farmer, Pearl, & Van Acker, 2000). In a study of "rejected" fourth-graders, aggressive boys tended to gain in status by the end of fifth grade, suggesting that behavior shunned by younger children may be seen as "cool" or glamorous by preadolescents (Sandstrom & Coie, 1999).

Children can be unpopular for many reasons, some of which may not be fully within their control. While some unpopular children are aggressive, some are hyperactive and inattentive, and some are withdrawn (Dodge, Coie, Pettit, & Price, 1990; Masten & Coatsworth, 1998; Newcomb et al., 1993; A. W. Pope, Bierman, & Mumma, 1991). Others act silly and immature or anxious and uncertain. They are often insensitive to other children's feelings and do not adapt well to new situations (Bierman, Smoot, & Aumiller, 1993). Some show undue interest in being with groups of the other sex (Sroufe, Bennett, Englund, Urban, & Shulman, 1993). Some unpopular children *expect* not to be liked, and this becomes a self-fulfilling prophecy (Rabiner & Coie, 1989).

It is often in the family that children acquire behaviors that affect popularity (Masten & Coatsworth, 1998). Authoritative parents tend to have more popular children than authoritarian parents (Dekovic & Janssens, 1992). Children of authoritarian parents who punish and threaten are likely to threaten or act mean with other children; they are less popular than children whose authoritative parents reason with them and try to help them understand how another person might feel (C. H. Hart, Ladd, & Burleson, 1990).

In both western and Chinese cultures, there is a bidirectional link between academic achievement and social competence. High achievers tend to be popular and socially skilled; and well-adjusted, well-liked children tend to do well in school (X. Chen, Rubin, & Li, 1997). One difference is that shyness and sensitivity are valued in China, but not in western cultures. Thus, children who show these traits are more likely to be popular in China—at least in middle childhood (see Box 10-2 on page 368).

Checkpoint

Can you . . .

- ✔ Tell some ways in which members of a peer group tend to be alike?
- ✔ Identify positive and negative effects of the peer group?
- ✔ Describe characteristics of popular and unpopular children, and tell how they may vary?
- ✔ Identify family and cultural influences on popularity?

Friendship

Children may spend much of their free time in groups, but only as individuals do they form friendships. Popularity is the peer group's opinion of a child, but friendship is a two-way street.

Children look for friends who are like them: of the same age, sex, and ethnic group and with common interests. A friend is someone a child feels affection for, is comfortable with, likes to do things with, and can share feelings and secrets with. Friends know each other well, trust each other, feel a sense of commitment to one another, and treat each other as equals. The strongest friendships involve equal commitment and mutual give-and-take. Even unpopular children can make friends; but

BOX 10-2

Window on the World

Popularity: A Cross-Cultural View

How does culture affect popularity? Would a child who is popular in one culture be equally popular in another? Researchers compared 480 second- and fourth-graders in Shanghai, China, with 296 children the same ages in Ontario, Canada (X. Chen, Rubin, & Sun, 1992). Although the two samples were quite different—for example, none of the Canadian children came from peasant families, but many of the Chinese children did—both samples were representative of school-age children in the two countries.

The researchers assessed the children's popularity by two kinds of peer perceptions. The children filled out a sociometric rating telling which three classmates they most and least liked to be with and which three classmates were their best friends. The results showed that certain traits are valued similarly in both cultures. A sociable, cooperative child is likely to be popular in both China and Canada, and an aggressive child is likely to be rejected in both countries. However, one important difference emerged: shy, sensitive children are well liked in China, but not in Canada. This is not surprising. Chinese children are encouraged to be cautious, to restrain themselves, and to inhibit their urges; thus a quiet, shy youngster is considered well behaved. In a western culture, by contrast, such a child is likely to be seen as socially immature, fearful, and lacking in self-confidence.

A follow-up study at ages 8 and 10 (X. Chen, Rubin, & Li, 1995) again found that shy, sensitive Chinese children were popular with peers. They also were rated by teachers as socially competent, as leaders, and as academic achievers. However, by age 12, an interesting twist had occurred: shy, sensitive Chinese children were no longer popular. They tended to be rejected by their peers, just as in western cultures.

It may be, then, that shyness and sensitivity take on different social meanings in China as children enter adolescence, when peer relationships become more important and adult approval becomes less so. As in the west, a shy early adolescent may lack the assertiveness and communication skills needed to establish and maintain strong peer relationships.

This research suggests that the influence of culture may be tempered by developmental processes that are more or less universal. Even in China, with its strong tradition of obedience to authority, the influence of adult social standards may wane as children's urge to make their own independent judgments of their peers asserts itself.

What's Your View?

How would you advise parents of a shy, sensitive child who complains of being rejected by other children?

Check It Out:

For more information on this topic, go to www.mhhe.com/papaliah9, where you'll find links to information on children's cliques in China.

they have fewer friends than popular children and tend to find friends among younger children, other unpopular children, or children in a different class or a different school (George & Hartmann, 1996; Hartup, 1992, 1996a, 1996b; Newcomb & Bagwell, 1995).

Why is friendship important? With their friends, children learn to communicate and cooperate. They learn about themselves and others. They can help each other get through stressful transitions, such as starting a new school or adjusting to parents' divorce. The inevitable quarrels help children learn to resolve conflicts (Furman, 1982; Hartup, 1992, 1996a, 1996b; Hartup & Stevens, 1999; Newcomb & Bagwell, 1995).

Friendship seems to help children to feel good about themselves, though it's also likely that children who feel good about themselves have an easier time making friends. Peer rejection and friendlessness in middle childhood may have long-term effects. In one longitudinal study, fifth-graders who had no friends were more likely than their classmates to show symptoms of depression in young adulthood. Young adults who had had friends in childhood had higher self-esteem (Bagwell, Newcomb, & Bukowski, 1998).

Children's concepts of friendship, and the ways they act with their friends, change with age, reflecting cognitive and emotional growth. Preschool friends play together,

During middle childhood, shy, sensitive children are better liked in China than in western cultures, because they are considered well behaved. Children this age tend to accept adult standards of behavior.

but friendship among school-age children is deeper and more stable. Children cannot be or have true friends until they achieve the cognitive maturity to consider other people's views and needs as well as their own (Hartup, 1992; Hartup & Stevens, 1999; Newcomb & Bagwell, 1995).

On the basis of interviews with more than 250 people between ages 3 and 45, Robert Selman (1980; Selman & Selman, 1979) traced changing conceptions of friendship through five overlapping stages (see Table 10-2). He found that most

Table 10-2 Selman's Stages of Friendship

Stage	Description	Example
Stage 0: Momentary playmateship (ages 3 to 7)	On this *undifferentiated* level of friendship, children are egocentric and have trouble considering another person's point of view; they tend to think only about what they want from a relationship. Most very young children define their friends in terms of physical closeness and value them for material or physical attributes.	"She lives on my street" or "He has the Power Rangers."
Stage 1: One-way assistance (ages 4 to 9)	On this *unilateral* level, a "good friend" does what the child wants the friend to do.	"She's not my friend anymore, because she wouldn't go with me when I wanted her to" or "He's my friend because he always says yes when I want to borrow his eraser."
Stage 2: Two-way fair-weather cooperation (ages 6 to 12)	This *reciprocal* level overlaps stage 1. It involves give-and-take but still serves many separate self-interests, rather than the common interests of the two friends.	"We are friends; we do things for each other" or "A friend is someone who plays with you when you don't have anybody else to play with."
Stage 3: Intimate, mutually shared relationships (ages 9 to 15)	On this *mutual* level, children view a friendship as having a life of its own. It is an ongoing, systematic, committed relationship that incorporates more than doing things for each other. Friends become possessive and demand exclusivity.	"It takes a long time to make a close friend, so you really feel bad if you find out that your friend is trying to make other friends too."
Stage 4: Autonomous interdependence (beginning at age 12)	In this *interdependent* stage, children respect friends' needs for both dependency and autonomy.	"A good friendship is a real commitment, a risk you have to take; you have to support and trust and give, but you have to be able to let go too."

Source: Selman, 1980; Selman & Selman, 1979.

School-age friends often share secrets—and laughs—as Anna and her friend Christina are doing. Friendship becomes deeper and more stable in middle childhood, reflecting cognitive and emotional growth. Girls tend to have fewer friends, but more intimate ones, than boys do.

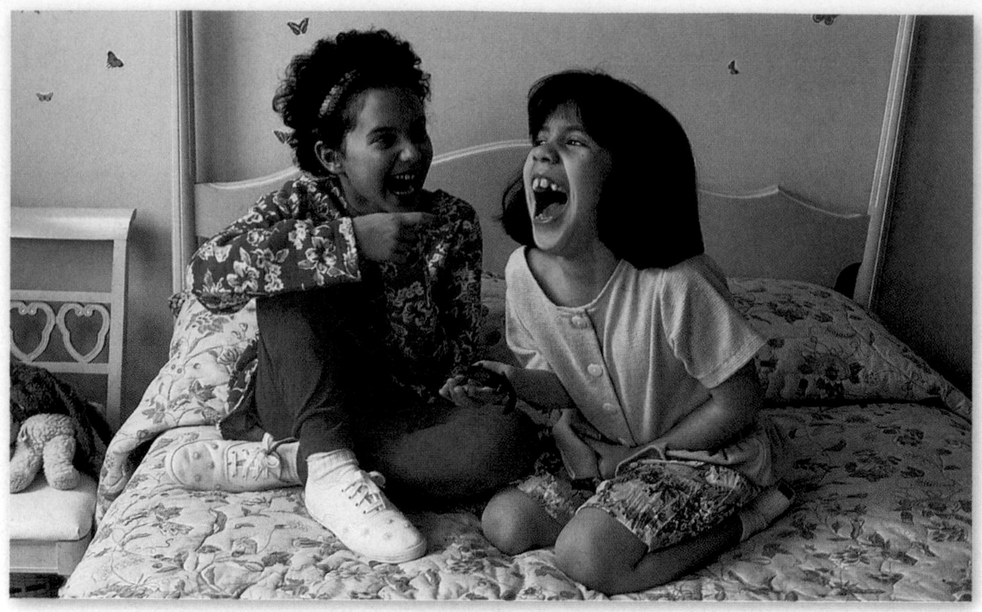

school-age children are in stage 2 (reciprocal friendship based on self-interest). Older children, from about age 9 up, may be in stage 3 (intimate, mutually shared relationships).

School-age children distinguish "best friends," "good friends," and "casual friends" on the basis of how intimate they are and how much time they spend together (Hartup & Stevens, 1999). Children this age typically have three to five "best" friends with whom they spend most of their free time, but they usually play with only one or two at a time (Hartup, 1992; Hartup & Stevens, 1999). Twelve percent of children this age have only one friend or none (Hofferth, 1998).

Checkpoint

Can you . . .

✔ Distinguish between popularity and friendship?

✔ List characteristics children look for in friends?

✔ Tell how age and gender affect friendships?

School-age girls care less about having many friends than about having a few close friends they can rely on. Boys have more friendships, but they tend to be less intimate and affectionate (Furman, 1982; Furman & Buhrmester, 1985; Hartup & Stevens, 1999). In one study, 56 same-sex threesomes of third-, fourth-, and fifth-graders were observed discussing personal issues, doing a puzzle together, playing a competitive game, and engaging in free play. Although intimate sharing was more common among girls and aggressive behavior among boys, there were no differences in responsiveness, dominance, exuberance, or ability to cooperate (Lansford & Parker, 1999).

Aggression and Bullying

Guidepost

8. What are the most common forms of aggressive behavior in middle childhood, and what influences contribute to it?

hostile aggression Aggressive behavior intended to hurt another person.

During the school years, aggression declines and changes in form (Coie & Dodge, 1998). ***Hostile aggression*** (aggression aimed at hurting its target) largely replaces *instrumental aggression* (aggression aimed at achieving an objective), the hallmark of the preschool period (Coie & Dodge, 1998). *Overt* aggression (physical force or verbal threats) becomes less common than *relational,* or social, aggression (refer back to Chapter 8). This may take such subtle, indirect forms as "putting down" or spreading rumors about another person, as well as direct retaliation, such as not choosing that person for a team (Crick et al., 2002). Nine-year-olds and older children recognize such behavior as "mean"; they realize that it stems from anger and is aimed at hurting others (Crick, Bigbee, & Howes, 1996; Crick et al., 2002; Galen & Underwood, 1997). It is not clear whether relational aggression is more frequent among girls than among boys, but its consequences may be more serious for girls, who tend to be more concerned with relationships than boys are (Crick et al., 2002).

Some children do not learn to control aggression (Coie & Dodge, 1998). Aggressors tend to be unpopular and to have social and psychological problems, but it is not clear whether aggression causes these problems or is a reaction to them (Crick & Grotpeter, 1995). Highly aggressive children tend to seek out friends like themselves and to egg each other on to antisocial acts (Hartup, 1989, 1992, 1996a; Hartup & Stevens, 1999; Masten & Coatsworth, 1998).

Aggression and Social Information Processing What makes children act aggressively? One answer may lie in the way they process social information: what features of the social environment they pay attention to, and how they interpret what they perceive (Crick & Dodge, 1994, 1996).

A child who is accidentally bumped in line may push back hard, assuming that the other child bumped her on purpose. This child may be a hostile (also called *reactive*) aggressor. These children often have a *hostile attribution bias,* or *hostile attribution of intent;* they see other children as trying to hurt them, and they strike out angrily in retaliation or self-defense (Crick & Dodge, 1996; de Castro, Veerman, Koops, Bosch, & Monshouwer, 2002; Waldman, 1996). Children who seek dominance and control may be especially sensitive to slights, provocations, or other threats to their status, especially if their cognitive abilities to process these experiences are limited. They may attribute such behavior to hostility and react aggressively (de Castro et al., 2002; Erdley et al., 1997). Rejected children and those exposed to harsh parenting also tend to have a hostile attribution bias (Coie & Dodge, 1998; Masten & Coatsworth, 1998; Weiss et al., 1992). Since people often *do* become hostile toward someone who acts aggressively toward them, a hostile attribution bias may become a self-fulfilling prophecy, setting in motion a cycle of aggression that eventually becomes a behavior problem. An analysis of 41 studies with 6,017 participants found a significant association between hostile attribution of intent and aggressive behavior (de Castro et al., 2002).

Instrumental (or *proactive*) aggressors view force and coercion as effective ways to get what they want. They act deliberately, not out of anger. In social learning terms, they are aggressive because they expect to be rewarded for it; and when they *are* rewarded, their belief in the effectiveness of aggression is reinforced (Crick & Dodge, 1996).

Both types of aggressors need help in altering the way they process social information, so that they do not interpret aggression as either justified or useful. Adults can help children curb hostile aggression by teaching them how to recognize when they are getting angry and how to control their anger. Instrumental aggression tends to stop if it is not rewarded (Crick & Dodge, 1996).

Research shows that children who see televised violence tend to act aggressively. The long-term influence is particularly great in middle childhood.

Does Televised Violence Lead to Aggression? Children see an enormous amount of violence on television. More than half (57 percent) of U.S. 8- to 16-year-olds have television sets in their bedrooms (Woodward & Gridina, 2000), and many watch before bedtime as a form of relaxation (Larson & Verma, 1999). U.S. and Canadian children watch television somewhere between twelve and twenty-five hours a week (Hofferth, 1998; Sege & Dietz, 1994; Statistics Canada, 1997). In the United States, about six out of ten programs contain violence, and few show alternatives to violence. The worst culprits are movies, including those on premium cable channels, which show violence 85 percent of the time (National Television Violence Study, 1995). Thirty-nine percent of children's programs on British television contain violence, mostly shootings or other physical assaults (Gunter & Harrison, 1997).

Experimental and longitudinal studies support a causal relationship between watching televised violence and acting aggressively (Coie & Dodge, 1998; Geen, 1994; Huston et al., 1992; Strasburger & Donnerstein, 1999). Children, especially those whose parents use harsh discipline, are more vulnerable than adults to the influence of televised violence (Coie & Dodge, 1998). Classic social learning research suggests that children imitate filmed models even more than live ones (Bandura, Ross, & Ross, 1963). The influence is stronger if the child believes the violence on the screen is real, identifies with the violent character, and watches without parental supervision (Coie & Dodge, 1998; Huesmann & Eron, 1986).

When children see televised violence, they may absorb the values depicted and come to view aggression as acceptable behavior. Most programs glorify and glamorize violence. In 73 percent of violent scenes, perpetrators go unpunished; in 47 percent, victims go unharmed, suggesting that violence has no unpleasant consequences (National Television Violence Study, 1995). Children who see both heroes and villains on television getting what they want through violence are likely to conclude that violence is an effective way to resolve conflicts. They may become less sensitive to the pain it causes. They may learn to take violence for granted and may be less likely to intervene when they see it (Gunter & Harrison, 1997; National Television Violence Study, 1995, 1996; National Institute of Mental Health [NIMH], 1982; Sege & Dietz, 1994; Singer, Slovak, Frierson, & York, 1998; M. E. Smith, 1993; Strasburger & Donnerstein, 1999). Of course, some children are more impressionable, more impulsive, and more easily influenced than others (M. O. Johnson, 1996).

The larger the dose of television, the more harmful its apparent effects. In a survey of 2,245 third- through eighth-graders in 11 Ohio public schools, the more television children said they watched each day, especially among those who preferred action programs, the more trauma symptoms (such as anxiety, depression, stress, and anger) and violent behavior they reported. Children with psychological and behavior problems may watch more television than children without such problems, and a heavy diet of television may well worsen such problems. Thus heavy television viewing may indicate problems that may need treatment (Singer et al., 1998).

What's Your View?

- What can and should be done about children's exposure to violent television programs?

The long-term influence of televised violence is greater in middle childhood than at earlier ages; 8- to 12-year-olds seem particularly susceptible (Eron & Huesmann, 1986). Among 427 young adults whose viewing habits had been studied at age 8, the best predictor of aggressiveness in 19-year-old men and women was the degree of violence in the shows they had watched as children (Eron, 1980, 1982). In a follow-up study, the amount of television viewed at age 8, and the preference among boys for violent shows, predicted the severity of criminal offenses at age 30 (Huesmann, 1986; Huesmann & Eron, 1984).

Checkpoint

Can you . . .

✔ Tell how aggression changes in form during middle childhood and how social information processing and televised violence can contribute to it?

Aggressiveness can be reduced by cutting down on television use. In one intervention, third- and fourth-graders who received a six-month curriculum geared at motivating them to monitor and reduce the time they spent on television, videotapes, and video games showed significant decreases in peer-rated aggression, as compared with a control group who did not participate in the program (Robinson, Wilde, Navacruz, Haydel, & Varady, 2001).

bullying Aggression deliberately and persistently directed against a particular target, or victim, typically one who is weak, vulnerable, and defenseless.

Bullies and Victims Aggression becomes **bullying** when it is deliberately, persistently directed against a particular target: a victim who typically is weak, vulnerable, and defenseless.

More than 2 million U.S. schoolchildren—about 30 percent of those in grades 6 through 10—are either bullies or victims, according to a survey of nearly 16,000 students (Nansel et al., 2001). Male bullies tend to use physical force (overt aggression) and to select either boys or girls as victims. Female bullies may use verbal or psychological means (relational aggression) and are more likely to victimize other girls (Boulton, 1995; Nansel et al., 2001). Victims of relational aggression tend to have poor relationships with peers, depressive symptoms, or antisocial behavior. Children who, perhaps because of unsupportive family backgrounds, are highly sensitive to relational aggression tend to be victimized again and again (Crick et al., 2002).

Patterns of bullying and victimization may become established as early as kindergarten. As tentative peer groups form, children initially direct aggression at various targets. Aggressors soon get to know which children make the easiest "marks" and focus their aggression on them.

Middle childhood is a prime time for bullying (Boulton & Smith, 1994). Bullies tend to have poor grades and to smoke or drink (Nansel et al., 2001). Victims tend to be anxious and submissive and to cry easily, or to be argumentative and provocative (Hodges, Boivin, Vitaro, & Bukowski, 1999; Olweus, 1995). They tend to be lonely and to have trouble making friends (Nansel et al., 2001). They are apt to have low self-esteem—though it is not clear whether low self-esteem leads to or follows from victimization. Male victims tend to be physically weak (Boulton & Smith, 1994; Olweus, 1995). Risk factors for victimization seem to be similar across cultures. Among 296 Chinese fifth- and sixth-graders, victims tended to be either submissive and withdrawn or aggressive, rather than assertive and prosocial, and they tended to do poorly in school—all factors associated with victimization in western cultures (Schwartz, Chang, & Farver, 2001).

Bullying tends to peak in the middle grades. Boys are more likely to use overt aggression; girls, relational aggression.

Children who are bullied often have few friends and come from harsh, punitive family environments that leave them vulnerable to further punishment or rejection (Schwartz, Dodge, Pettit, & Bates, 2000). Having friends seems to provide some protection against this pattern (Hodges et al., 1999; Schwartz et al., 2000). Victims of bullying may develop such behavior problems as hyperactivity and overdependence, and they may become more aggressive themselves (Schwartz, McFadyen-Ketchum, Dodge, Pettit, & Bates, 1998). In the wave of school shootings since 1994, the perpetrators often had been victims of bullying (Anderson et al., 2001).

What's Your View?

- What can and should adults do to help unpopular children, bullies, and victims?

The likelihood of being bullied seems to decrease steadily throughout middle childhood and adolescence. As children get older, most of them may learn how to discourage bullying, leaving a smaller "pool" of available victims (P. K. Smith & Levan, 1995).

Bullying can be stopped or prevented. One intervention program in grades 4 through 7 in Norwegian schools cut bullying in half and also reduced other antisocial behavior. This was accomplished by creating an authoritative atmosphere marked by warmth, interest, and involvement combined with firm limits and consistent, nonphysical punishment. Better supervision and monitoring at recess and lunch time, class rules against bullying, and serious talks with bullies, victims, and parents were part of the program (Olweus, 1995). A growing number of U.S. schools are adopting such programs (Guerrero, 2001).

Checkpoint

Can you . . .

- ✔ Tell how patterns of bullying and victimization become established and change?
- ✔ Describe characteristics associated with bullies and victims?

Mental Health

Guidepost

9. What emotional disorders may develop in childhood, and how are they treated?

The term *mental health* is somewhat of a misnomer, since it usually refers to emotional health. Just as some children have physical or mental abnormalities, some children do not develop normally in the emotional sphere. Let's look at several common emotional disturbances and then at types of treatment.

Common Emotional Disorders

Although most children are fairly well adjusted emotionally, beginning in elementary school increasing numbers are referred for mental health treatment. An estimated one in five children and adolescents ages 9 to 17 in the United States has a diagnosable mental or emotional disorder that causes some interference with everyday functioning; and more than one in ten—about 4 million in all—suffer significant functional impairment (USDHHS, 1999c). Most common are *anxiety* or *mood disorders* (feeling sad, depressed, unloved, nervous, fearful, or lonely); and *disruptive conduct disorders* (aggression, defiance, or antisocial behavior). Some problems seem to be associated with a particular phase of a child's life and will go away on their own, but others need to be treated to prevent future trouble (Achenbach & Howell, 1993; USDHHS, 1999c). A study of parent-reported mental health problems of more than 13,000 children in Australia, Belgium, China, Germany, Greece, Israel, Jamaica, the Netherlands, Puerto Rico, Sweden, Thailand, and the United States found remarkably similar complaints across cultures (Crijnen, Achenbach, & Verhulst, 1999).

oppositional defiant disorder (ODD) Pattern of behavior, persisting into middle childhood, marked by negativity, hostility, and defiance.

conduct disorder (CD) Repetitive, persistent pattern of aggressive, antisocial behavior violating societal norms or the rights of others.

school phobia Unrealistic fear of going to school; may be a form of *separation anxiety disorder* or *social phobia*.

separation anxiety disorder Condition involving excessive, prolonged anxiety concerning separation from home or from people to whom a child is attached.

Disruptive Behavior Disorders Temper tantrums and defiant, argumentative, hostile, deliberately annoying behavior—common among 4- and 5-year-olds—typically are outgrown by middle childhood. When such a pattern of behavior persists until age 8, children (usually boys) may be diagnosed with **oppositional defiant disorder (ODD),** a pattern of defiance, disobedience, and hostility toward adult authority figures. Children with ODD constantly fight, argue, lose their temper, snatch things, blame others, are angry and resentful, and generally test the limits of adults' patience (APA, 1994; USDHHS, 1999c).

Some children with ODD move on to a repetitive, persistent pattern of aggressive, antisocial acts, such as truancy, setting fires, habitual lying, fighting, vandalism, rape or prostitution, and use of guns. This is called **conduct disorder (CD)** (APA, 1994). About 1 to 4 percent of noninstitutionalized 9- to 17-year-olds in the United States has CD (USDHHS, 1999c). Many children with CD also have attention-deficit hyperactivity disorder (ADHD), discussed in Chapter 9. Some 11- to 13-year-olds progress from CD to criminal violence—mugging, rape, and break-ins—and by age 17 may be frequent, serious offenders (Coie & Dodge, 1998). Many of these highly antisocial children become antisocial adults (USDHHS, 1999c), but most do not (Maughan & Rutter, 2001).

School Phobia and Other Anxiety Disorders Children with **school phobia** have an unrealistic fear of going to school. Some children have realistic reasons to avoid going to school: a sarcastic teacher, overly demanding work, or a bully in the schoolyard (Kochenderfer & Ladd, 1996). In such instances, the environment may need changing, not the child.

True school phobia may be a type of **separation anxiety disorder,** a condition involving excessive anxiety for at least four weeks concerning separation from home or from people to whom the child is attached. Separation anxiety disorder (not to be confused with separation anxiety in infancy) affects some 4 percent of children and young adolescents and may persist through the college years. These children often come from close-knit, caring families. They may develop the disorder after the death of a pet, an illness, or a move to a new school (APA, 1994). Many children with separation anxiety disorder also show symptoms of depression: sadness, withdrawal, apathy, or difficulty in concentrating (USDHHS, 1999c).

School-phobic children tend to be average or good students. They tend to be timid and inhibited away from home, but willful, stubborn, and demanding with their parents (G. A. Bernstein & Garfinkel, 1988). The most important element in treatment is an early, gradual return to school. Usually children go back without too much trouble once treatment is begun.

School phobia also may be a form of **social phobia:** extreme fear and/or avoidance of social situations. Social-phobic children may be so afraid of embarrassment that they break into blushes, sweats, or palpitations when asked to speak in class or when meeting an acquaintance on the street (USDHHS, 1999c). Social phobia is much more common than was once believed, affecting about 5 percent of children and 8 percent of adults. Social phobias run in families, so there may be a genetic component. Often these phobias are triggered by traumatic experiences, such as a child's mind going blank when the child is called on in class. Children also can develop social phobias by observing how their parents respond to social situations (Beidel & Turner, 1998).

social phobia Extreme fear and/or avoidance of social situations.

Some children have a **generalized anxiety disorder,** which is not focused on one specific part of their lives, such as school or social relationships. These children worry about just about everything: school grades, being on time, wars, or earthquakes. Their worry seems independent of their performance or of how they are regarded by others. They tend to be perfectionists, conformists, and self-doubters. They seek approval and need constant reassurance (APA, 1994; USDHHS, 1999c). Far less common is **obsessive-compulsive disorder;** sufferers are obsessed by repetitive, intrusive thoughts, images, or impulses and often show compulsive behaviors, such as constant hand-washing, in an attempt to get rid of these obsessions (APA, 1994; USDHHS, 1999c).

generalized anxiety disorder Anxiety not focused on any single target.

obsessive-compulsive disorder Anxiety aroused by repetitive, intrusive thoughts, images, or impulses, often leading to compulsive ritual behaviors.

Anxiety disorders of all these types are among the most prevalent mental health problems in the United States for children and adolescents (USDHHS, 1999c) and have increased greatly. The *average* U.S. child in the 1980s reported more anxiety than did children under psychiatric care in the 1950s. The reasons are related to such social conditions as rising divorce and crime and a general decline in connectedness. Children and adolescents seem to feel these problems even more keenly than adults. These findings underline the importance of cohort and of the wider social environment in emotional development (Twenge, 2000).

Anxiety disorders are twice as common among girls as among boys. The heightened female vulnerability to anxiety begins as early as age 6. Females also are more susceptible to depression, which is similar to anxiety in some ways and often goes hand in hand with it (Lewinsohn, Gotlib, Lewinsohn, Seeley, & Allen, 1998). A tendency to anxiety and depression may stem from early experiences that make children feel a lack of control over what happens around them (Chorpita & Barlow, 1998).

Childhood Depression "Nobody likes me" is a not an unusual complaint among school-age children, who tend to be popularity-conscious; but a prolonged sense of friendlessness may be one sign of **childhood depression,** a disorder of mood that goes beyond normal, temporary sadness. At any given time, between 10 and 15 percent of children and adolescents have symptoms of depression (USDHHS, 1999c), such as inability to have fun or concentrate, fatigue, extreme activity or apathy, crying, sleep problems, feelings of worthlessness, weight change, physical complaints, or frequent thoughts about death or suicide. Any five of these symptoms, lasting at least two weeks, may point to depression (APA, 1994). If symptoms persist, the child should be given psychological help. Depression may lead to an attempted suicide and often signals the beginning of a recurrent problem that, if present during adolescence, is likely to persist into adulthood (Birmaher, 1998; Birmaher et al., 1996; Cicchetti & Toth, 1998; Kye & Ryan, 1995; USDHHS, 1999c; Weissman et al., 1999).

childhood depression Mood disorder characterized by such symptoms as a prolonged sense of friendlessness, inability to have fun or concentrate, fatigue, extreme activity or apathy, feelings of worthlessness, weight change, physical complaints, and thoughts of death or suicide.

The exact causes of childhood depression are not known. Twin studies have found the heritability of childhood depression to be only modest, though 20 to 50 percent of depressed children and adolescents have a family history of it. Depressed children tend to come from families with high levels of parental depression, anxiety, substance abuse, or antisocial behavior; and the atmosphere in such families may increase children's risk of depression. Early interactions with caregivers may lay the groundwork for childhood depression (Cicchetti & Toth, 1998; USDHHS, 1999c). Children as young as 5 or 6 can accurately report depressed moods and feelings that forecast later trouble, from academic problems to major depression and ideas of suicide (Ialongo, Edelsohn, & Kellam, 2001).

Depression often emerges when children move from elementary school to middle school; it may be related to stiffer academic pressures (Cicchetti & Toth, 1998). The transition to middle school seems especially stressful and depression-producing in young people who do not have strong self-efficacy beliefs and who have little personal investment in academic success (Rudolph, Lambert, Clark, & Kurlakowsky, 2001).

individual psychotherapy Psychological treatment in which a therapist sees a troubled person one-on-one.

family therapy Psychological treatment in which a therapist sees the whole family together to analyze patterns of family functioning.

behavior therapy Therapeutic approach using principles of learning theory to encourage desired behaviors or eliminate undesired ones; also called *behavior modification.*

Treatment Techniques

Psychological treatment for emotional disturbances can take several forms. In **individual psychotherapy,** a therapist sees a child one-on-one, to help the child gain insights into his or her personality and relationships and to interpret feelings and behavior. Such treatment may be helpful at a time of stress, such as the death of a parent or parental divorce, even when a child has not shown signs of disturbance. Child psychotherapy is usually more effective when combined with counseling for the parents.

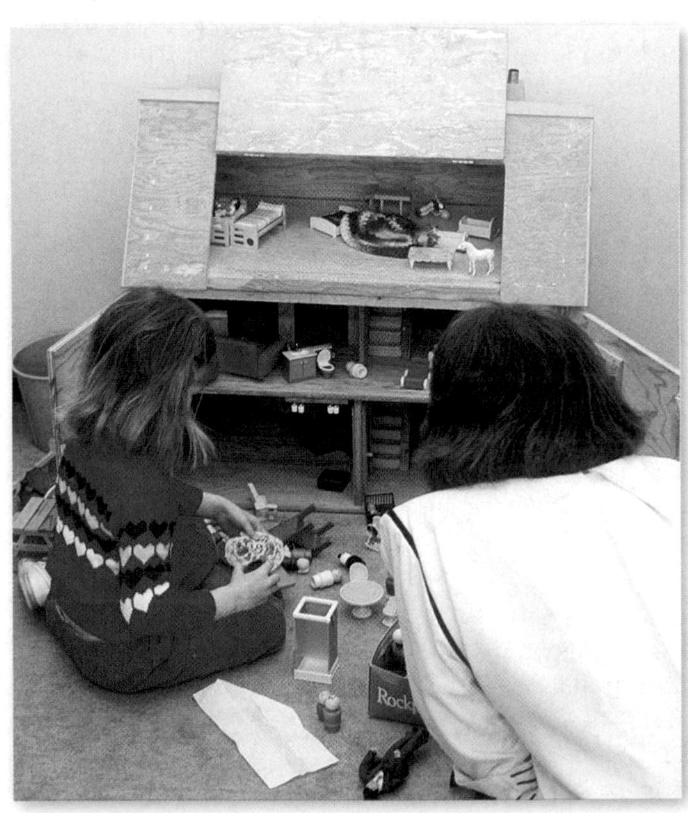

In play therapy, the therapist observes as a child acts out troubled feelings, using developmentally appropriate materials.

In **family therapy,** the therapist sees the family together, observes how members interact, and points out both growth-producing and growth-inhibiting or destructive patterns of family functioning. Sometimes the child whose problem brings the family into therapy is, ironically, the healthiest member, responding openly to a troubled family situation. Therapy can help parents confront their own conflicts and begin to resolve them. This is often the first step toward resolving the child's problems as well.

Behavior therapy, or *behavior modification,* is a form of psychotherapy that uses principles of learning theory to eliminate undesirable behaviors (such as temper tantrums) or to develop desirable ones (such as putting away toys after play). In the latter example, every time the child puts toys away, she or he gets a reward, such as praise, a treat, or a token to be exchanged for a new toy.

A statistical analysis of many studies found that, in general, psychotherapy is effective with children and adolescents, especially with adolescent girls. Behavior therapy was more effective than nonbehavioral methods. Results were best when treatment was targeted to specific problems and desired outcomes (Weisz, Weiss, Han, Granger, & Morton, 1995).

play therapy Therapeutic approach in which a child plays freely while a therapist observes and occasionally comments, asks questions, or makes suggestions.

To assess developmental problems, therapists may observe a young child in unstructured play with materials appropriate to the child's developmental level. A team member may be assigned to play with the child, so that the child may be observed in social and communicative interactions (Meisels & Atkins-Burnett, 2000). **Play therapy,** in which a child plays freely while a therapist occasionally comments, asks questions, or makes suggestions, has proven effective with a variety of emotional, cognitive, and social problems, especially when consultation with parents or other close family members is part of the process (Athansiou, 2001; Bratton & Ray, 2002; Leblanc & Ritchie, 2001; Ryan & Needham, 2001; Wilson & Ryan, 2001).

When children have limited verbal and conceptual skills, or have suffered emotional trauma, **art therapy** can help them express or describe what is troubling them without having to put their feelings into words (Kozlowska & Hanney, 1999). The child may express deep emotions through choice of colors and subjects to depict (Garbarino, Dubrow, Kostelny, & Pardo, 1992). In family therapy, observing how a family plans, carries out, and then discusses an art project can reveal patterns of family interactions. Family members often "speak" more freely through such a shared activity (Kozlowska & Hanney, 1999).

art therapy Therapeutic approach that allows a child to express troubled feelings without words, using a variety of art materials and media.

The use of **drug therapy** to treat childhood emotional disorders greatly increased during the 1990s, often in combination with one or more forms of psychotherapy. However, there is insufficient research on its long-term effect and safety for children and adolescents (USDHHS, 1999c; Zito et al., 2003), and developmental scientists generally decry its use. Antidepressants are commonly prescribed for depression, and antipsychotics for severe psychological problems. Yet many studies have found most antidepressants no more effective than *placebos* (substances with no active ingredients) in treating depression in children and adolescents (Fisher & Fisher, 1996; Sommers-Flanagan & Sommers-Flanagan, 1996).

drug therapy Administration of drugs to treat emotional disorders.

Two exceptions are the use of stimulants such as methylphenidate (Ritalin) to treat ADHD and the use of *serotonin selective reuptake inhibitors (SSRIs)* to treat obsessive-compulsive, depressive, and anxiety disorders. These drugs have been shown to be effective (Research Unit on Pediatric Psychopharmacology Anxiety Study Group, 2001; Rodrigues, 1999; USDHHS, 1999c). A randomly controlled trial found fluoxetine (Prozac), the most popular of the SSRIs, superior to placebos. It is safer and has more tolerable side effects than other classes of drugs (Birmaher, 1998). However, Prozac can produce sleep disturbances and behavioral changes, and its long-term effects are unknown. There also is concern that SSRIs may be used instead of psychological therapies, rather than along with them (Rushton, Clark, & Freed, 1999).

Checkpoint

Can you . . .

- ✔ Discuss the prevalence of mental health problems in childhood and adolescence?
- ✔ Identify causes and symptoms of aggressive conduct disorders, social phobias, other anxiety disorders, and childhood depression?
- ✔ Describe and evaluate six common types of therapy for emotional disorders?

Stress and Resilience: Protective Factors

Guidepost

10. How do the stresses of modern life affect children, and why are some children more resilient than others?

Stress is a response to physical or psychological demands on a person. Stressful events, or **stressors,** are part of childhood, and most young people learn to cope. Stress that becomes overwhelming, however, can lead to psychological problems. Severe stressors, such as kidnapping or child abuse, or dramatically destructive acts such as school shootings or the attack on the World Trade Centers, may have long-term effects on physical and psychological well-being. Yet some indivuals show remarkable resilience in surviving such ordeals.

stress Response to physical or psychological demands.

stressors Stress-producing experiences.

Stresses of Modern Life

The child psychologist David Elkind (1981, 1984, 1986, 1997) has called today's child the "hurried child." He warns that the pressures of modern life are forcing children to grow up too soon and are making their childhood too stressful. Today's children are expected to succeed in school, to compete in sports, and to meet parents' emotional needs. Children are exposed to many adult problems on television and in real life before they have mastered the problems of childhood. They know about sex and violence, and they often must shoulder adult responsibilities. Many children move frequently and have to change schools and leave old friends (Fowler, Simpson, & Schoendorf, 1993; G. A. Simpson & Fowler, 1994). The tightly scheduled pace of life also can be stressful (Hofferth & Sandberg, 1998). Yet children are not small adults. They feel and think like children, and they need the years of childhood for healthy development.

Given how much stress children are exposed to, it should not be surprising that they worry a lot. Anxiety in childhood has increased greatly (Twenge, 2000). Fears of danger and death are the most consistent fears of children at all ages (Gullone, 2000). These findings have been corroborated in a wide range of developed societies, including Australia, the United Kingdom, Israel, Italy, and Northern Ireland, as well as the United States. Poor children—who may see their environment as threatening—tend to be more fearful than children of higher socioeconomic status.

In a survey and interviews of 272 ethnically diverse second- through sixth-graders in a large U.S. metropolitan area (Silverman, La Greca, & Wasserstein, 1995), school emerged as one of the children's chief concerns. So did health—their own or someone else's. However, the worry reported by the largest number of children (56 percent of the sample) was personal harm from others: being robbed, stabbed, or shot.

These children were not in a high-crime area, nor had they personally experienced many attacks. Their intense anxiety about their safety seemed to reflect the high rates of crime and violence in the larger society—even including killings in schools (Garbarino et al., 1992, 1998). Between 1994 and 1999, 253 people died in school shootings in the United States, 68 percent of them students (Anderson et al., 2001).

How did children in New York City react to the terrorist attack on the World Trade Center on September 11, 2001? According to a survey of 8,266 fourth- through twelfth-graders in 94 public schools, an estimated 10.5 percent, or 75,000 children, showed symptoms of post-traumatic stress disorder. Symptoms included trouble sleeping, chronic nightmares, shortened attention spans, and obsessively thinking about the attack or trying *not* to think, hear, or talk about it. Fifteen percent experienced agoraphobia, fear of public places (Board of Education of City of New York, 2002).

Children who grow up *surrounded* by violence often have trouble concentrating and sleeping. They may be afraid that their mothers will abandon them. Some become aggressive, and some come to take brutality for granted. Many do not allow themselves to become attached to other people, for fear of more hurt and loss (Garbarino et al., 1992, 1998). Children with multiple risks—those who live in violent communities, who are poor, and who receive inadequate parenting, education, and health care—are the most likely to suffer permanent developmental damage (Rutter, 1987).

Safety may be an even greater concern in some less developed countries. In a large cross-cultural study (Ollendick, Yang, King, Dong, & Akande, 1996), Nigerian and Chinese children and adolescents had more safety-related fears, as well as fears of failure and criticism, than their U.S. and Australian counterparts, perhaps reflecting their cultures' emphasis on self-control and conformity with societal norms. Also, Nigerian and Chinese children did not become less fearful with age, as children in western countries, with their emphasis on individual self-reliance, generally do.

School-based programs designed to prevent violent behavior by promoting social competence have been modestly successful in the United States. One such program, Providing Alternative Thinking Strategies (PATH), presumes that thoughts and behavior are based on emotional awareness and control. Emotional and cognitive development are guided through carefully sequenced lessons that include instruction, worksheets, discussion, role playing, and modeling and reinforcement by teachers and peers. Experience with such programs suggests the desirability of school reforms aimed at integrating social-emotional and academic development, since children who are socially competent and have little conflict with classmates may be able to better concentrate on schoolwork (Henrich, Brown, & Aber, 1999).

Checkpoint

Can you . . .

- ✔ Explain Elkind's concept of the "hurried child"?
- ✔ Name the most common sources of fear in western children, and tell how fears change with age?

Coping with Stress: The Resilient Child **Resilient children** are those who weather circumstances that might blight others, who maintain their composure and competence under challenge or threat, or who bounce back from traumatic events. These children do not possess extraordinary qualities. They simply manage, despite

resilient children Children who weather adverse circumstances, function well despite challenges or threats, or bounce back from traumatic events.

Table 10-3 Characteristics of Resilient Children and Adolescents

Source	Characteristic
Individual	Good intellectual functioning
	Appealing, sociable, easygoing disposition
	Self-efficacy, self-confidence, high self-esteem
	Talents
	Faith
Family	Close relationship to caring parent figure
	Authoritative parenting: warmth, structure, high expectations
	Socioeconomic advantages
	Connections to extended supportive family networks
Extrafamilial context	Bonds to prosocial adults outside the family
	Connections to prosocial organizations
	Attending effective schools

Source: Masten & Coatsworth, 1998, p. 212.

adverse circumstances, to hold onto the basic systems and resources that promote positive development in normal children (Masten, 2001; see Table 10-3). The two most important **protective factors,** which seem to help children and adolescents overcome stress and contribute to resilience, are good *family relationships* and *cognitive functioning* (Masten & Coatsworth, 1998).

protective factors Influences that reduce the impact of early stress and tend to predict positive outcomes.

Resilient children are likely to have good relationships and strong bonds with at least one supportive parent (Pettit et al., 1997) or caregiver. If not, the child may be close to at least one other caring, competent adult (Masten, 2001; Masten & Coatsworth, 1998).

Resilient children tend to have high IQs and to be good problem solvers. Their superior information-processing skills may help them cope with adversity, protect themselves, regulate their behavior, and learn from experience. They may attract the interest of teachers, who can act as guides, confidants, or mentors (Masten & Coatsworth, 1998).

Other frequently cited protective factors (Eisenberg et al., 1997; Masten, 2001; Masten et al., 1990; Masten & Coatsworth, 1998; E. E. Werner, 1993) include:

- *The child's personality:* Resilient children are adaptable, friendly, well liked, independent, and sensitive to others. They are competent and have high self-esteem. They are creative, resourceful, independent, self-regulated, and self-motivated.
- *Reduced risk:* Children who have been exposed to only one of a number of factors strongly related to psychiatric disorder (such as parental discord, low social status, a disturbed mother, a criminal father, and experience in foster care or an institution) are often better able to overcome stress than children who have been exposed to more than one risk factor.
- *Compensating experiences:* A supportive school environment or successful experiences in studies, in sports, in music, or with other children or adults can help make up for a destructive home life. In adulthood, a good marriage can compensate for poor relationships earlier in life.

What's Your View?

- Do you recall an experience with a caring adult that helped you deal with adversity?

All this does not mean that bad things which happen in a child's life do not matter. In general, children with unfavorable backgrounds have more problems in adjustment than children with more favorable backgrounds. Some outwardly resilient children may suffer internal distress that may have long-term consequences (Masten & Coatsworth, 1998). Still, what is heartening about these findings is that

Checkpoint

Can you . . .

- ✔ Identify factors that tend to protect children and adolescents from emotional health risks?

negative childhood experiences do not necessarily determine the outcome of a person's life and that many children have the strength to navigate through the most difficult passages.

Refocus

- What do you think were major sources of self-esteem for Marian Anderson as a child? Would you estimate her self-esteem as high or low?
- How would you describe the family atmosphere in Anderson's home? Was her upbringing authoritarian, authoritative, or permissive?
- How did poverty, and the need for her mother to work outside the home, affect Anderson?
- How did Anderson's experience living in an extended-family household affect her?
- Was Anderson's choice of her first friend consistent with what you have learned in this chapter about children's choice of friends?
- Can you point to examples of resilience in Marian Anderson's childhood and adult life? What do you think accounted for her resilience?

Adolescence, too, is a stressful, risk-filled time—more so than middle childhood. Yet most adolescents develop the skills and competence to deal with the challenges they face, as we'll see in Chapters 11 and 12.

SUMMARY AND KEY TERMS

The Developing Self

Guidepost 1. How do school-age children develop a realistic self-concept, and what contributes to self-esteem?

- The self-concept becomes more realistic during middle childhood, when, according to neo-Piagetian theory, children form representational systems.
- According to Erikson, the chief source of self-esteem is children's view of their productive competence. This "virtue" develops through resolution of the conflict of industry versus inferiority. According to Susan Harter's research, however, self-esteem arises primarily from self-evaluation and social support.

representational systems *(351)*

industry versus inferiority *(352)*

Guidepost 2. How do school-age children show emotional growth?

- School-age children have internalized shame and pride and can better understand and control negative emotions.
- Empathy and prosocial behavior increase.
- Emotional growth is affected by parents' reactions to displays of negative emotions.

The Child in the Family

Guidepost 3. How do parent-child relationships change in middle childhood?

- School-age children spend less time with, and are less close to, parents than before; but relationships with parents continue to be important. Culture influences family relationships and roles.
- Development of coregulation may affect the way a family handles conflicts and discipline.

coregulation *(355)*

Guidepost 4. What are the effects of parents' work and of poverty on family atmosphere?

- The most important influence of the family environment on children's development comes from the atmosphere in the home.
- The impact of mothers' employment depends on many factors concerning the child, the mother's work and her feelings about it; whether she has a supportive mate; the family's socioeconomic status; and the kind of care the child receives.
- Homes with employed mothers tend to be more structured and more egalitarian than homes with at-home mothers. Maternal employment has a positive influence on school achievement in low-income families, but boys in middle-class families tend to do less well.

- Parents living in persistent poverty may have trouble providing effective discipline and monitoring and emotional support.

Guidepost 5. What impact does family structure have on children's development?

- Many children today grow up in nontraditional family structures. Children tend to do better in traditional two-parent families. The structure of the family, however, is less important than its effects on family atmosphere.
- Adopted children are generally well adjusted, though they face special challenges.
- Children's adjustment to divorce depends on factors concerning the child; the parents' handling of the situation; custody and visitation arrangements; financial circumstances; contact with the noncustodial parent (usually the father); and a parent's remarriage.
- The amount of conflict in a marriage and the likelihood of its continuing after divorce may influence whether or not children are better off if the parents stay together.
- Children living with only one parent are at heightened risk of behavioral and academic problems, in part related to socioeconomic status.
- Boys tend to have more trouble than girls in adjusting to divorce and single-parent living but tend to adjust better to the mother's remarriage.
- Studies have found no ill effects on children living with homosexual parents.

open adoption *(360)*

Guidepost 6. How do siblings influence and get along with one another?

- The roles and responsibilities of siblings in nonindustrialized societies are more structured than in industrialized societies.
- Siblings learn about conflict resolution from their relationships with each other. Relationships with parents affect sibling relationships.

The Child in the Peer Group

Guidepost 7. How do relationships with peers change in middle childhood, and what influences popularity and choice of friends?

- The peer group becomes more important in middle childhood. Peer groups generally consist of children who are similar in age, sex, and socioeconomic status, and who live near one another or go to school together.
- The peer group helps children develop social skills, allows them to test and adopt values independent of parents, gives them a sense of belonging, and helps develop the self-concept. It also may encourage conformity and prejudice.
- Popularity influences self-esteem and future adjustment. Popular children tend to have good cognitive abilities and social skills. Behaviors that affect popularity may derive from family relationships and cultural values.
- Intimacy and stability of friendships increase during middle childhood. Boys tend to have more friends, whereas girls have closer friends.

prejudice *(366)*

Guidepost 8. What are the most common forms of aggressive behavior in middle childhood, and what influences contribute to it?

- During middle childhood, aggression typically declines. Instrumental aggression gives way to hostile aggression. Relational aggression becomes more common than overt aggression, especially among girls. Highly aggressive children tend to be unpopular and maladjusted.
- Aggressiveness promoted by exposure to televised violence can extend into adult life.
- Middle childhood is a prime time for bullying; patterns may be established in kindergarten. Victims tend to be weak and submissive, or argumentative and provocative, and to have low self-esteem.

hostile aggression *(370)*

bullying *(372)*

Mental Health

Guidepost 9. What emotional disorders may develop in childhood, and how are they treated?

- Common emotional and behavioral disorders among school-age children include anxiety or mood disorders and disruptive behavioral disorders.
- Childhood depression often emerges during the transition to middle school; its prevalence increases during adolescence.
- Treatment techniques include individual psychotherapy, family therapy, behavior therapy, play therapy, art therapy, and drug therapy. Often therapies are used in combination.

oppositional defiant disorder (ODD) *(374)*

conduct disorder (CD) *(374)*

school phobia *(374)*

separation anxiety disorder *(374)*

social phobia *(375)*

generalized anxiety disorder *(375)*

obsessive-compulsive disorder *(375)*

childhood depression *(375)*

individual psychotherapy *(376)*

family therapy *(376)*

behavior therapy *(376)*

play therapy *(376)*

art therapy *(377)*

drug therapy *(377)*

Guidepost 10. How do the stresses of modern life affect children, and why are some children more resilient than others?

- As a result of the pressures of modern life, many children experience stress. Children tend to worry about school, health, and, especially, personal safety.
- Resilient children are better able than others to withstand stress. Protective factors include cognitive ability, family relationships, personality, degree of risk, and compensating experiences.

stress *(377)*

stressors *(377)*

resilient children *(378)*

protective factors *(379)*

PART 5

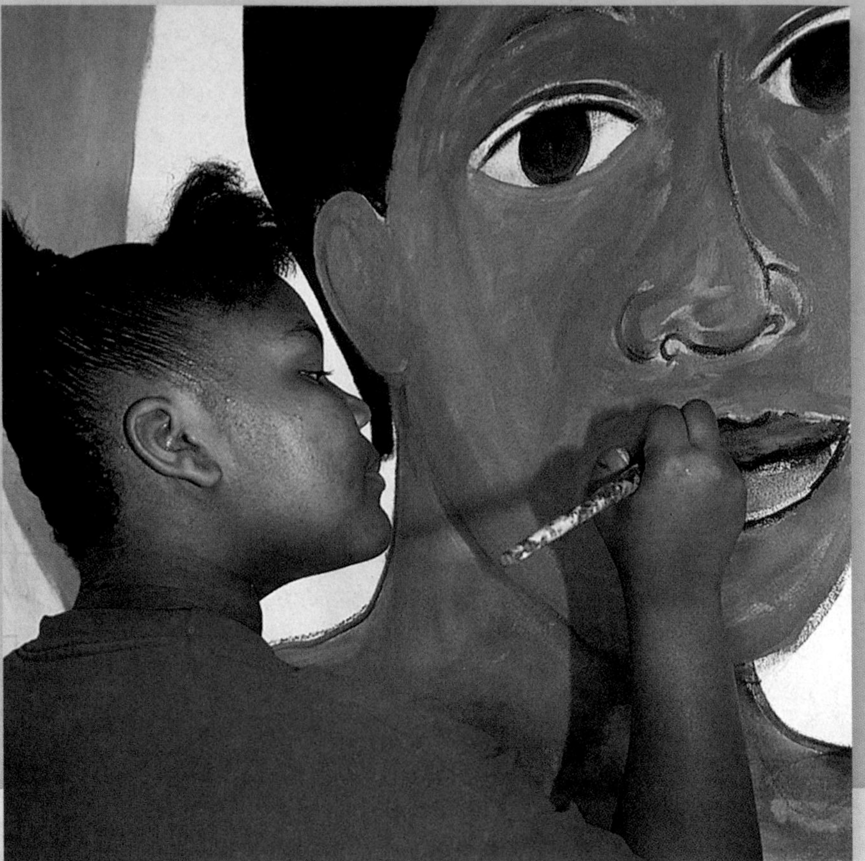

Linkups to look for

- Both hormonal and social influences may contribute to heightened emotion and moodiness in adolescence.
- Early or late physical maturation can affect emotional and social adjustment.
- Conflict between adolescents and their parents may sometimes stem from immature aspects of adolescent thinking.
- Parental involvement and parenting styles influence academic achievement.
- The ability of low-income children to do well in school may depend on the availability of family and community resources.
- Physical characteristics play an important part in molding adolescents' self-concept.
- Girls who are knowledgeable about sex are most likely to postpone sexual activity.
- The intensity and intimacy of adolescent friendships is in part due to cognitive development.

In adolescence, young people's appearance changes; as a result of the hormonal events of puberty, they take on the bodies of adults. Their thinking changes, too; they are better able to think abstractly and hypothetically. Their feelings change about almost everything. All areas of development converge as adolescents confront their major task: establishing an identity—including a sexual identity—that will carry over to adulthood.

In Chapters 11 and 12, we see how adolescents incorporate their drastically changed appearance, their puzzling physical yearnings, and their new cognitive abilities into their sense of self. We see how the peer group serves as the testing ground for teenagers' ideas about life and about themselves. We look at risks and problems that arise during the teenage years, as well as at characteristic strengths of adolescents. ▸

Adolescence

PREVIEW

CHAPTER 11

Physical and Cognitive Development in Adolescence

- Physical growth and other changes are rapid and profound.
- Reproductive maturity occurs.
- Major health risks arise from behavioral issues, such as eating disorders and drug abuse.
- Ability to think abstractly and use scientific reasoning develops.
- Immature thinking persists in some attitudes and behaviors.
- Education focuses on preparation for college or vocations.

CHAPTER 12

Psychosocial Development in Adolescence

- Search for identity, including sexual identity, becomes central.
- Peer groups help develop and test self-concept but also may exert an antisocial influence.
- Relationships with parents are generally good.

Chapter 11

Physical and Cognitive Development in Adolescence

What I like in my adolescents is that they have not yet hardened. We all confuse hardening and strength. Strength we must achieve, but not callousness.

—**Anaïs Nin, *The Diaries of Anaïs Nin,* Vol. IV**

OUTLINE

Focus: Anne Frank, Diarist of the Holocaust*

Anne Frank

For her thirteenth birthday on June 12, 1942, Anne Frank's parents gave her a diary. This small, cloth-covered volume was the first of several notebooks in which Anne recorded her experiences and reflections during the next two years. Little did she dream that her jottings would become one of the most famous published accounts by victims of the Holocaust during World War II.

Anne Frank (1929–1945), her parents, Otto and Edith Frank, and her older sister, Margot, were German Jews who fled to Amsterdam after Hitler came to power in 1933, only to see the Netherlands fall to Nazi conquest seven years later. In the summer of 1942, when the Nazis began rounding up Dutch Jews for deportation to concentration camps, the family went into hiding on the upper floors of the building occupied by Otto Frank's pharmaceutical firm. Behind a door concealed by a movable cupboard, a steep stairway led to the four rooms Anne called the "Secret Annexe." For two years, they stayed in those confined quarters with a couple named "Van Daan,"** their 15-year-old son, "Peter,"** and a middle-aged dentist, "Albert Dussel,"** who shared Anne's room. Then, on August 4, 1944, German and Dutch security police raided the Secret Annexe and sent its occupants to concentration camps, where all but Anne's father died.

Anne's writings, published by Otto Frank after the war, describe the life the fugitives led. During the day they had to be completely quiet so as not to alert people in the offices below. They saw no one except a few trusted Christian helpers who risked their lives to bring food, books, newspapers, and

*Sources of biographical information about Anne Frank were Bloom (1999); Frank (1958, 1995), Lindwer (1991), Müller (1998), and Netherlands State Institute for War Documentation (1989). Page references are to the 1958 paperback version of the diary.

**Fictional names Anne invented for use in her diary.

essential supplies. To venture outside—which would have been necessary to replace Anne's quickly outgrown clothes or to correct her worsening nearsightedness—was unthinkable.

The diary reveals the thoughts, feelings, daydreams, and mood swings of a high-spirited, introspective adolescent coming to maturity under traumatic conditions. Anne wrote of her concern about her "ugly" appearance, of her wish for "a real mother who understands me," and of her adoration for her father (Frank, 1958, pp. 36, 110). She expressed despair at the adults' constant criticism of her failings and at her parents' apparent favoritism toward her sister. She wrote about her fears, her urge for independence, her hopes for a return to her old life, and her aspirations for a writing career.

As tensions rose in the "Secret Annexe," Anne lost her appetite and began taking antidepressant medication. But as time went on, she became less self-pitying and more serious-minded. When she thought back to her previous carefree existence, she felt like a different person from the Anne who had "grown wise within these walls" (p. 149).

She was deeply conscious of her sexual awakening: "I think what is happening to me is so wonderful, and not only what can be seen on my body, but all that is taking place inside. . . . Each time I have a period . . . I have the feeling that . . . I have a sweet secret, and . . . I always long for the time that I shall feel that secret within me again" (pp. 115–116).

Anne originally had regarded Peter as shy and gawky—a not-very-promising companion; but eventually she began visiting his attic room for long, intimate talks and, finally, her first kiss. Her diary records the conflict between her stirring sexual passion and her strict moral upbringing.

One of the last diary entries is dated July 15, 1944, less than three weeks before the raid and eight months before Anne's death in the concentration camp at Bergen-Belsen: " . . . in spite of everything, I still believe that people are really good at heart. . . . I hear the ever approaching thunder, which will destroy us too, I can feel the suffering of millions and yet, if I look up into the heavens, I think that it will all come right, that this cruelty too will end, and that peace and tranquillity will return again" (p. 233).

The moving story of Anne Frank's tragically abbreviated adolescence points up the insistent role of biology and its interrelationships with inner and outer experience. Anne's "coming of age" occurred under highly unusual conditions. Yet her normal physical maturation went on, along with a host of cognitive and psychosocial changes heightened by her stressful circumstances.

In this chapter, we describe the physical transformations of adolescence and how they affect young people's feelings. We consider the impact of early and late maturation, and we discuss health issues associated with this time of life. Turning to cognitive development, we examine the Piagetian stage of formal operations, which makes it possible for a young person like Anne Frank to visualize an ideal world. We also look at some immature aspects of adolescents' thought and at their linguistic and moral development. Finally, we explore practical aspects of cognitive growth—issues of education and vocational choice, which continued to concern Anne Frank no matter how narrowly circumscribed her life became.

After you have read and studied this chapter, you should be able to answer each of the following Guidepost questions. Look for them again in the margins, where they point to important concepts throughout the chapter. To check your understanding of these Guideposts, review the end-of-chapter summary. Checkpoints located at periodic spots throughout the chapter will help you verify your understanding of what you have read.

1. What is adolescence, when does it begin and end, and what opportunities and risks does it entail?
2. What physical changes do adolescents experience, and how do these changes affect them psychologically?
3. What are some common health problems in adolescence, and how can they be prevented?
4. How do adolescents' thinking and use of language differ from younger children's?
5. On what basis do adolescents make moral judgments?
6. What influences affect school success, and why do some students drop out?
7. What factors affect educational and vocational planning and preparation?

Guideposts for Study

Adolescence: A Developmental Transition

In modern industrial societies, the passage from childhood to adulthood is marked by a long transitional period known as **adolescence.** Adolescence is generally considered to begin with **puberty,** the process that leads to sexual maturity, or fertility—the ability to reproduce.* Adolescence lasts from about age 11 or 12 until the late teens or early twenties, and it entails major, interrelated changes in all realms of development.

Guidepost

1. What is adolescence, when does it begin and end, and what opportunities and risks does it entail?

adolescence Developmental transition between childhood and adulthood entailing major physical, cognitive, and psychosocial changes.

puberty Process by which a person attains sexual maturity and the ability to reproduce.

Adolescence is a social construction (refer back to Chapter 1). Before the twentieth century, there was no concept of adolescence; children in western cultures entered the adult world when they matured physically or when they began a vocational apprenticeship. Today entry into adulthood takes longer and is less clear-cut. Puberty begins earlier than it used to; and entrance into a vocation tends to occur later, since complex societies require longer periods of education or vocational training before a young person can take on adult responsibilities.

Contemporary U.S. society has a variety of markers of entrance into adulthood. There are *legal* definitions: at 17, young people may enlist in the armed forces; at age 18, in most states, they may marry without their parents' permission; at 18 to 21 (depending on the state), they may enter into binding contracts. Using *sociological* definitions, people may call themselves adults when they are self-supporting or have chosen a career, have married or formed a significant relationship, or have started a family. There also are *psychological* definitions. Cognitive maturity is often considered to coincide with the capacity for abstract thought. Emotional maturity may depend on such achievements as discovering one's identity, becoming independent of parents, developing a system of values, and forming relationships. Some people never leave adolescence, no matter what their chronological age.

*Some people use the term *puberty* to mean the end point of sexual maturation and refer to the process as *pubescence,* but our usage conforms to that of most psychologists today.

In many cultures, special celebrations herald entrance to puberty. These 9-year-old schoolgirls in Tehran celebrate the ceremony of Taqlif, which marks their readiness to begin the religious duties of Islam.

Early adolescence (approximately ages 11 or 12 to 14), the transition out of childhood, offers opportunities for growth—not only in physical dimensions, but also in cognitive and social competence, autonomy, self-esteem, and intimacy. This period also carries great risks. Some young people have trouble handling so many changes at once and may need help in overcoming dangers along the way. Adolescence is a time of increasing divergence between the majority of young people, who are headed for a fulfilling and productive adulthood, and a sizable minority (about one out of five) who will be dealing with major problems (Offer, 1987; Offer & Schonert-Reichl, 1992).

U.S. adolescents today face greater hazards to their physical and mental well-being than did their counterparts in earlier years (Petersen, 1993; Takanishi, 1993). Among these hazards are early pregnancy and childbearing (see Chapter 12) and high death rates from accidents, homicide, and suicide (Anderson, 2002; National Center for Health Statistics [NCHS], 2001). Behavior patterns that contribute to these risks, such as heavy drinking, drug abuse, sexual and gang activity, motorcycling without helmets, and use of firearms, are established early in adolescence (Petersen, 1993; Rivara & Grossman, 1996). However, a government survey shows encouraging trends: recent declines in ninth- to twelfth-graders' tobacco and marijuana use, risky sexual behavior, carrying of weapons, and riding in cars without seat belts or with drivers who have been drinking (Grunberg et al., 2002). Diminishing such risky behaviors increases the chances that young people will come through the teenage years in good physical and mental health.

Checkpoint

Can you . . .

- ✔ Compare three ways of defining entrance into adulthood?
- ✔ Identify risky behavior patterns common during adolescence?

PHYSICAL DEVELOPMENT

Puberty: The End of Childhood

The biological changes of puberty, which signal the end of childhood, result in rapid growth in height and weight, changes in body proportions and form, and attainment of sexual maturity. These dramatic physical changes are part of a long, complex process of maturation that begins even before birth, and their psychological ramifications continue into adulthood.

How Puberty Begins

Puberty begins with a sharp increase in production of sex hormones. First, sometime between ages 5 and 9, the adrenal glands begin secreting larger amounts of androgens, which will play a part in the growth of pubic, axillary (armpit), and facial hair. A few years later, in girls, the ovaries step up their output of estrogen, which stimulates growth of female genitals and development of breasts. In boys, the testes increase the manufacture of androgens, particularly testosterone, which stimulate growth of male genitals, muscle mass, and body hair. Boys and girls have both types of hormones, but girls have higher levels of estrogen and boys have higher levels of androgens; in girls, testosterone influences growth of the clitoris, as well as of the bones and of pubic and axillary hair.

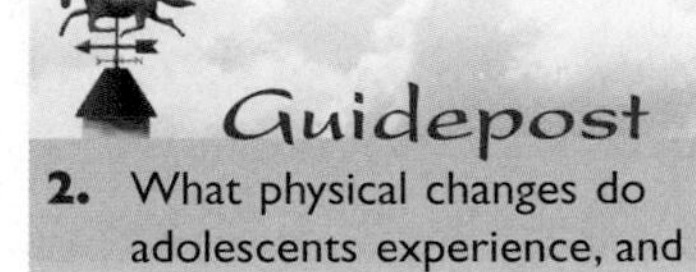

2. What physical changes do adolescents experience, and how do these changes affect them psychologically?

The precise time when this burst of hormonal activity begins seems to depend on reaching a critical weight level. Studies of mice and humans show that leptin, a protein hormone secreted by fatty tissue and identified as having a role in obesity (refer back to Chapter 12), is needed to trigger the onset of puberty (Chehab, Mounzih, Lu, & Lim, 1997; Clément et al., 1998; O'Rahilly, 1998; Strobel, Camoin, Ozata, & Strosberg, 1998). An accumulation of leptin in the bloodstream may stimulate the hypothalamus, a structure at the base of the brain, to send pulsating signals to the nearby pituitary gland, which in turn, may signal the sex glands to increase their secretion of hormones. This may explain why overweight girls tend to enter puberty earlier than thin girls.

Some research attributes the heightened emotionality and moodiness of early adolescence—so apparent in Anne Frank's diary—to hormonal changes. However, other influences, such as gender, age, temperament, and the timing of puberty, may moderate or even override hormonal ones. Hormones seem more strongly related to moods in boys than in girls, and especially in early adolescents, who are still adjusting to pubertal changes (Buchanan et al., 1992).

Timing, Sequence, and Signs of Maturation

There is about a seven-year range for the onset of puberty in both boys and girls. The process typically takes about four years for both sexes and begins about two or three years earlier in girls than in boys.

Physical changes in both boys and girls during puberty include the adolescent growth spurt, the development of pubic hair, a deeper voice, and muscular growth. The maturation of reproductive organs brings the beginning of ovulation and menstruation in girls and the production of sperm in boys. These changes unfold in a sequence that is much more consistent than their timing (see Table 11-1 on page 390), though it does vary somewhat. One girl, for example, may be developing breasts and body hair at about the same rate; in another, body hair may grow so fast that it shows an adult pattern a year or so before her breasts develop. Similar variations occur among boys.

On the basis of historical sources, developmental scientists have found a **secular trend** (a trend that spans several generations) in the onset of puberty: a lowering of the age when puberty begins and when young people reach adult height and sexual maturity. The trend, which also involves increases in adult height and weight, began about 100 years ago and has occurred in the United States, western Europe, and Japan. The most likely explanation seems to be a higher standard of living. Children who are healthier, better nourished, and better cared for mature earlier and grow bigger. Thus, the average age of sexual maturity is earlier in industrialized countries than in less developed ones.

secular trend Trend that can be seen only by observing several generations, such as the trend toward earlier attainment of adult height and sexual maturity, which began a century ago.

In the United States, the average age for boys' entry into puberty is 12, but boys may begin to show changes any time between 9 and 16. Girls, on average, begin to show pubertal changes at 8 to 10 years of age.

Table 11-1 Usual Sequence of Physiological Changes in Adolescence

Female Characteristics	Age of First Appearance
Growth of breasts	6–13
Growth of pubic hair	6–14
Body growth	9.5–14.5
Menarche	10–16.5
Underarm hair	About 2 years after appearance of pubic hair
Increased output of oil- and sweat-producing glands (which may lead to acne)	About the same time as appearance of underarm hair
Male Characteristics	**Age of First Appearance**
Growth of testes, scrotal sac	10–13.5
Growth of pubic hair	12–16
Body growth	10.5–16
Growth of penis, prostate gland, seminal vesicles	11–14.5
Change in voice	About the same time as growth of penis
First ejaculation of semen	About one year after beginning of growth of penis
Facial and underarm hair	About two years after appearance of pubic hair
Increased output of oil- and sweat-producing glands (which may lead to acne)	About the same time as appearance of underarm hair

Some girls begin to show breast budding and pubic hair as early as age 6 (for African American girls) or 7 (for white girls) and as late as 14. African American girls, who tend to be heavier than white girls, enter puberty about a year earlier (Ellis et al., 1997; Herman-Giddens et al., 1997; Kaplowitz et al., 1999). Overweight is associated with early puberty, especially in white 6- to 9-year-old girls (Kaplowitz, Slora, Wasserman, Pedlow, & Herman-Giddens, 2001). One research team found a link between early female puberty and a gene that controls the breakdown of the male hormone testosterone. A reduction in a girl's testosterone level may trigger breast development (Kadlubar et al., 2001).

adolescent growth spurt Sharp increase in height and weight that precedes sexual maturity.

The Adolescent Growth Spurt In Anne Frank's diary, she made rueful references to her physical growth—to shoes she could no longer get into and vests "so small that they don't even reach my tummy" (p. 71). Anne apparently was in the **adolescent growth spurt**—a rapid increase in height and weight, which generally begins in girls between ages $9\frac{1}{2}$ and $14\frac{1}{2}$ (usually at about 10) and in boys, between $10\frac{1}{2}$ and 16 (usually at 12 or 13). The growth spurt typically lasts about two years; soon after it ends, the young person reaches sexual maturity. Since girls' growth spurt usually occurs earlier than that of boys, girls between ages 11 and 13 are taller, heavier, and stronger than boys the same age. Muscular growth peaks at age $12\frac{1}{2}$ for girls and $14\frac{1}{2}$ for boys. After their growth spurt, boys are again larger than girls, as before. Both boys and girls reach virtually their full height by age 18.

Boys and girls grow differently, of course. A boy becomes larger overall: his shoulders wider, his legs longer relative to his trunk, and his forearms longer relative to his upper arms and his height. A girl's pelvis widens to make childbearing easier, and layers of fat are deposited under the skin, giving her a more rounded appearance.

The adolescent growth spurt affects practically all skeletal and muscular dimensions. Even the eye grows faster, causing (as in Anne Frank's case) an increase in nearsightedness, a problem that affects about one-fourth of 12- to 17-year-olds (Gans,

1990). The lower jaw becomes longer and thicker, the jaw and nose project more, and the incisor teeth become more upright. Because each of these changes follows its own timetable, parts of the body may be out of proportion for a while. The result is the familiar teenage gawkiness Anne noticed in Peter Van Daan, which accompanies unbalanced, accelerated growth.

Many girls of junior high school age tower above their male classmates. At ages 11 to 13, girls are, on average, taller, heavier, and stronger than boys, who reach their adolescent growth spurt later than girls do.

These dramatic physical changes have psychological ramifications. Most young teenagers are more concerned about their looks than about any other aspect of themselves, and many do not like what they see in the mirror. Girls tend to be unhappier about their looks than boys, reflecting the greater cultural emphasis on women's physical attributes (Rosenblum & Lewis, 1999). Girls, especially those who are advanced in pubertal development, tend to think they are too fat (Richards, Boxer, Petersen, & Albrecht, 1990; Swarr & Richards, 1996), and this negative body image can lead to eating problems. Concern with body image may be related to the stirring of sexual attraction, which, as we shall see, has been found to begin as early as age 9 or 10.

Primary and Secondary Sex Characteristics The **primary sex characteristics** are the organs necessary for reproduction. In the female, the sex organs are the ovaries, fallopian tubes, uterus, and vagina; in the male, the testes, penis, scrotum, seminal vesicles, and prostate gland. During puberty, these organs enlarge and mature. In boys, the first sign of puberty is the growth of the testes and scrotum. In girls, the growth of the primary sex characteristics is not readily apparent because these organs are internal.

primary sex characteristics Organs directly related to reproduction, which enlarge and mature during adolescence.

The **secondary sex characteristics** are physiological signs of sexual maturation that do not directly involve the sex organs: for example, the breasts of females and the broad shoulders of males. Other secondary sex characteristics are changes in the voice and skin texture, muscular development, and the growth of pubic, facial, axillary, and body hair.

secondary sex characteristics Physiological signs of sexual maturation (such as breast development and growth of body hair) that do not involve the sex organs.

The first reliable sign of puberty in girls is the growth of the breasts. The nipples enlarge and protrude, the *areolae* (the pigmented areas surrounding the nipples) enlarge, and the breasts assume first a conical and then a rounded shape. Some adolescent boys, much to their distress, experience temporary breast enlargement; this is normal and may last up to eighteen months.

The voice deepens, partly in response to the growth of the larynx and partly, especially in boys, in response to the production of male hormones. The skin becomes coarser and oilier. Increased activity of the sebaceous glands (which secrete a fatty substance) may give rise to pimples and blackheads. Acne is more common in boys and seems related to increased amounts of testosterone.

Pubic hair, which at first is straight and silky and eventually becomes coarse, dark, and curly, appears in different patterns in males and females. Adolescent boys are usually happy to see hair on the face and chest; but girls are generally dismayed at the appearance of even a slight amount of hair on the face or around the nipples, though this is normal.

Signs of Sexual Maturity: Sperm Production and Menstruation In males, the principal sign of sexual maturity is the production of sperm. A boy may wake up to find a wet spot or a hardened, dried spot on the sheets—the result of a spermarche Boy's first ejaculation.

menarche Girl's first menstruation.

nocturnal emission, an involuntary ejaculation of semen (commonly referred to as a *wet dream*). Most adolescent boys have these emissions, sometimes in connection with an erotic dream. There is little research on boys' feelings about the first ejaculation (**spermarche**), which occurs at an average age of 13; most boys in one study reported positive reactions, though about two-thirds were somewhat frightened (Gaddis & Brooks-Gunn, 1985).

The principal sign of sexual maturity in girls is *menstruation,* a monthly shedding of tissue from the lining of the womb—what Anne Frank called her "sweet secret." The first menstruation, called **menarche,** occurs fairly late in the sequence of female development (refer back to Table 11-1) and indicates that ovulation is occurring. On average, a white girl in the United States first menstruates at about $12\frac{1}{2}$, and a Hispanic or black girl three to six months earlier (Chumlea et al., 2003). However, the normal timing of menarche can vary from ages 10 to $16\frac{1}{2}$.

A combination of genetic, physical, emotional, and environmental influences may affect the timing of menarche. Age of first menstruation tends to be similar to that of the mother. Bigger girls and those whose breasts are more developed tend to menstruate earlier. Strenuous exercise, as in competitive athletics, can delay menarche. Nutrition also is a factor. Even when these factors are controlled, girls with early menarche tend to be aggressive or depressed or to have poor family relationships (Ellis & Garber, 2000; Graber, Brooks-Gunn, & Warren, 1995; Moffitt, Caspi, Belsky, & Silva, 1992; Steinberg, 1988).

A longitudinal study suggests that the relationship with the father may be a key to pubertal timing. Girls who, as preschoolers, had close, supportive relationships with their parents—especially with an affectionate, involved father—showed later pubertal development than girls whose parental relationships had been cold or distant, or those raised by single mothers (Ellis, McFadyen-Ketchum, Dodge, Pettit, & Bates, 1999).

The mechanism by which family relationships might affect pubertal development is not clear. One suggestion is that human males, like some animals, may give off *pheromones,* odorous chemicals that attract mates. As a natural incest-prevention mechanism, sexual development may be inhibited in girls who are heavily exposed to their fathers' pheromones, as would happen in a close father-daughter relationship. On the other hand, frequent exposure to the pheromones of unrelated adult males, such as stepfathers or a single mother's boyfriends, may speed up pubertal development (Ellis & Garber, 2000). Since both the father's absence and early pubertal tim-

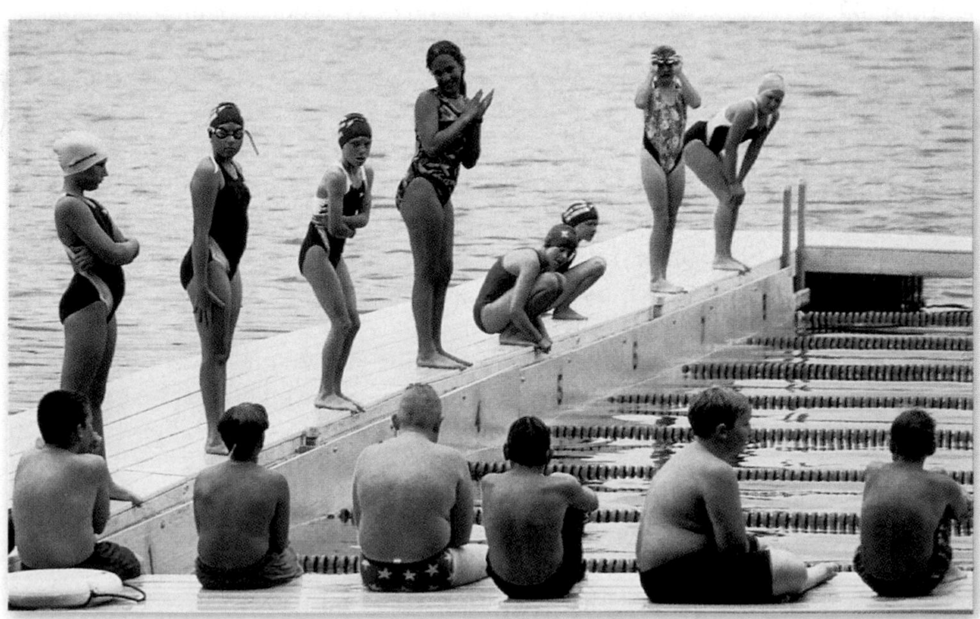

The wide range of sizes and body shapes that can be seen among a group of early adolescents results from the six- to seven-year variation in the onset of puberty. Boys tend to like maturing early, but girls do not.

ing have been identified as risk factors for sexual promiscuity and teenage pregnancy, the father's early presence and active involvement may be important to girls' healthy sexual development (Ellis et al., 1999).

A contrasting, genetic explanation is that both a father's tendency toward marital conflict and family abandonment and his daughter's tendency toward early puberty and precocious sexual activity may stem from the same shared genes. A genetic analysis of 121 men and 164 unrelated women focused on a sex-linked variant of the androgen receptor (AR) gene, which is carried on the X chromosome of affected fathers and can be transmitted to daughters, but not to sons. Men with this allele tended to be aggressive, impulsive, and sexually promiscuous, whereas women with the same allele tended to have had early menarche and to have experienced parental divorce and the absence of their biological fathers before age 7 (Comings, Muhleman, Johnson, & MacMurray, 2002). This hypothesis needs to be tested by genetic analysis of absent fathers and their biological daughters.

Psychological effects of pubertal timing depend on how the adolescent and other people in his or her world interpret the accompanying changes. However, early menarche has been associated with depression and substance abuse (Stice, Presnell, & Bearman, 2001). Effects of early or late maturation are most likely to be negative when adolescents are much more or less developed than their peers, when they do not see the changes as advantageous, and when several stressful events occur at about the same time (Petersen, 1993; Simmons, Blyth, & McKinney, 1983). Adults need to be sensitive to the potential impact of pubertal changes so as to help young people experience these changes as positively as possible.

What's Your View?

- Did you mature early, late, or "on time"? How did the timing of your maturation affect you psychologically?

Checkpoint

Can you . . .

- ✔ Tell how puberty begins and how its timing and length vary?
- ✔ Describe typical pubertal changes in boys and girls, and identify factors that affect psychological reactions to these changes?

Physical and Mental Health

These years are generally healthy, as most adolescents recognize. Nine out of ten early and midadolescents consider themselves healthy, according to an international school-based survey of more than 120,000 eleven-, thirteen-, and fifteen-year-olds in the United States and twenty-seven other western industrialized countries* under the auspices of the World Health Organization (WHO) (Scheidt, Overpeck, Wyatt, & Aszmann, 2000). Still, despite their general good health, many younger adolescents—especially girls—reported frequent health problems and symptoms, such as headache, stomachache, backache, nervousness, and feeling tired, lonely, or "low." Such reports were most common in the United States and Israel, perhaps because life in those cultures tends to be fast-paced and stressful (Scheidt et al., 2000).

Guidepost

3. What are some common health problems in adolescence, and how can they be prevented?

Most adolescents have low rates of disability and chronic disease, and dental health has improved among both children and adolescents. Still, about one-fifth of 10- to 18-year-olds in the United States have at least one serious physical or mental health problem, and many more need counseling or other health services (Dougherty, 1993).

Many health problems are preventable, stemming from lifestyle or poverty. In industrialized countries, according to the WHO survey, adolescents from less affluent families tend to report poorer health and more frequent symptoms. More well-off adolescents tend to have healthier diets and to be more physically active. On the other hand, socioeconomic status seems to have no effect on smoking and drinking among 15-year-olds (Mullan & Currie, 2000).

Within the United States, across ethnic and social-class lines, many early adolescents use drugs, drive while intoxicated, and become sexually active, and these behaviors increase throughout the teenage years (see Figure 11-1 on page 394). Adolescents whose families have been disrupted by parental separation or death are more likely to

*Belgium, Canada, Czech Republic, Denmark, England, Estonia, Finland, France, Germany, Greece, Greenland, Hungary, Republic of Ireland, Israel, Latvia, Lithuania, Northern Ireland, Norway, Poland, Portugal, Russian Federation, Scotland, Slovak Republic, Spain, Sweden, Switzerland, and Wales.

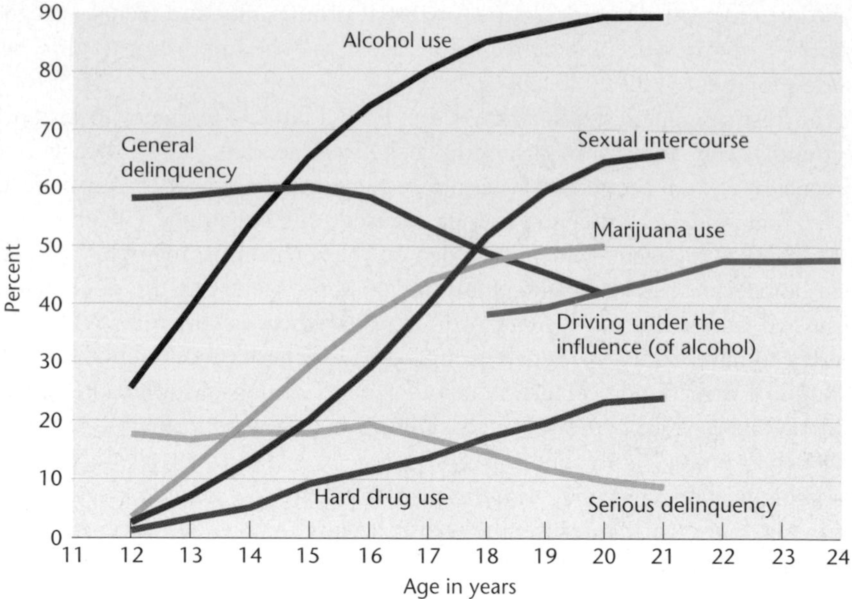

Figure 11-1
Age-specific rates for prevalence of some high-risk behaviors, averaged out over 3 years. (*Source:* Adapted from Elliott, 1993).

start these activities early and to engage in them more frequently during the next few years (Millstein et al., 1992). Boys and girls who enter puberty early or whose cognitive maturation comes late are especially prone to risky behavior (D. P. Orr & Ingersoll, 1995). So are gay, lesbian, and bisexual young people (Garofalo, Wolf, Kessel, Palfrey, & DuRant, 1998).

Adolescents are less likely than younger children to see a physician regularly; they more frequently go to school-based health centers. An estimated 18.7 percent of young people in grades 7 through 12 do not receive the medical care they need—most of the time because of procrastination or fear of what a doctor will say, but in about 14 percent of cases because of inability to pay (Ford, Bearman, & Moody, 1999). Young people who do not receive needed care are at increased risk of physical and mental health problems, including frequent smoking and drinking (Ford et al., 1999).

Let's look at several specific health concerns: physical fitness, sleep needs, eating disorders, drug abuse, depression, and causes of death in adolescence.

Physical Fitness

Exercise—or lack of it—affects both physical and mental health. It improves strength and endurance, helps build healthy bones and muscles, helps control weight, reduces anxiety and stress, and increases self-confidence. Even moderate physical activity has health benefits if done regularly for at least 30 minutes on most, and preferably all, days of the week. A sedentary lifestyle that carries over into adulthood may result in increased risk of obesity, diabetes, heart disease, and cancer (Centers for Disease Control and Prevention [CDC], 2000a; National Institutes of Health [NIH] Consensus Development Panel on Physical Activity and Cardiovascular Health, 1996).

Many boys and, especially, girls become less active during adolescence. Adolescents in the United States exercise less often than in past years and less frequently than adolescents in most other western industrialized countries. Still, most young Americans get some exercise at least two hours a week (CDC, 2000a; Hickman, Roberts, & de Matos, 2000).

Young people who exercise generally feel better than those who do not. They tend to be more confident and spend more time with friends, suggesting that they may use sports as a means of socializing (Hickman et al., 2000). On the other hand, many high school students are injured in sports. Some of these injuries could be avoided by grouping players by size, skill, and maturational level instead of by age; by improved equipment design; and by better supervision and enforcement of safety rules (AAP Committee on Sports Medicine and Committee on School Health, 1989; Cheng et al., 2000).

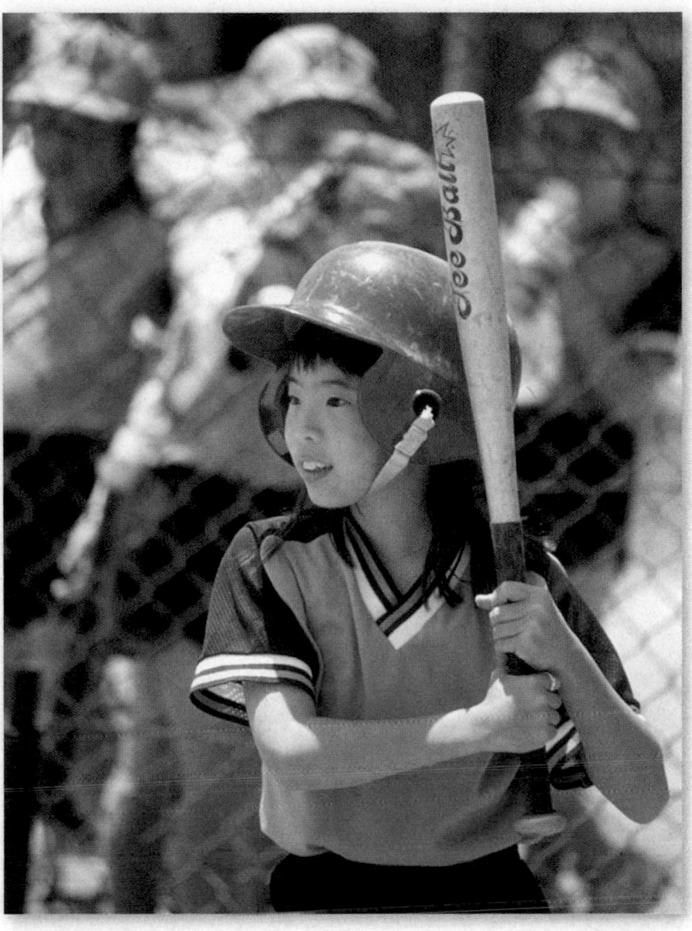

Adolescents who engage in sports tend to feel better than those who do not. Those who take safety precautions, such as wearing helmets while batting, are less likely to be injured in organized sports.

Sleep Needs

Many adolescents do not get enough sleep. They go to bed later than younger children and, on school days, get up as early or earlier. Yet early adolescents need almost as much sleep as before—about nine hours per night (Iglowstein, Jenni, Molinari, & Largo, 2003). Nor does "sleeping in" on weekends make up for the loss. Adolescents or preadolescents who have irregular sleep schedules tend to be chronically sleep-deprived and to be sleepy in the daytime (Sadeh, Raviv, & Gruber, 2000; Scheidt, Overpeck, Wyatt, & Aszmann, 2000; Wolfson & Carskadon, 1998).

Sleep-deprived adolescents tend to show symptoms of depression, have sleep problems, and do poorly in school. In a survey of 3,120 Rhode Island high school students, total sleep time diminished by forty to fifty minutes between ages 13 and 19, and students who got the least sleep got the worst grades (Wolfson & Carskadon, 1998).

Why do teenagers stay up late? In part it may be because they need to do homework, like to talk on the phone with friends or surf the Web, or want to act "grown up." However, physiological changes also may be involved (Sadeh et al., 2000). Adolescents undergo a shift in the brain's natural sleep cycle, or *circadian timing system.* The timing of secretion of *melatonin,* a hormone detectable in saliva, is a gauge of when the brain is ready for sleep. After puberty, this secretion takes place later at night (Carskadon, Acebo, Richardson, Tate, & Seifer, 1997). Thus adolescents need to go to bed later and get up later than younger children. Yet most secondary schools start earlier than elementary schools. Their schedules are out of sync with students' biological rhythms.

These findings fit in with adolescents' daily mood cycles, which also may be hormonally related. Teenagers tend to be least alert and most stressed early in the morning. Starting school later, or at least offering difficult courses later in the day, would maximize students' ability to concentrate (Crouter & Larson, 1998).

Checkpoint

Can you . . .

- ✔ Discuss adolescents' health status and health risks?
- ✔ Explain why physical activity is important in adolescence, and why adolescents often get too little sleep?

Nutrition and Eating Disorders

U.S. adolescents have less healthy diets than those in most other western industrialized countries. They eat fewer fruits and vegetables and more sweets, chocolate, soft drinks, and other "junk" foods, which are high in cholesterol, fat, and calories, and low in nutrients (Vereecken & Maes, 2000). Deficiencies of calcium, zinc, and iron are common at this age (Lloyd et al., 1993; Bruner, Joffe, Duggan, Casella, & Brandt, 1996) and may have cognitive effects: iron deficiency has been linked to lower standardized math scores (Halterman, Kaczorowski, Aligne, Auinger, & Szilagyi, 2001).

Eating disorders—both extreme overeating and extreme undereating—are most prevalent in industrialized societies, where food is abundant and attractiveness is equated with slimness (APA, 1994; Becker, Grinspoon, Klibanski, & Herzog, 1999).

Obesity The average teenage girl needs about 2,200 calories per day; the average teenage boy needs about 2,800. Many adolescents eat more calories than they expend and thus accumulate excess body fat. The percentage of U.S. young people who are overweight has almost doubled in the past two decades (CDC, 2000a). Today more than 15 percent of 12- to 19-year-olds are obese. The rise in obesity has been especially marked among Mexican American and non-Hispanic black adolescents (Ogden, Flegal, Carroll, & Johnson, 2002).

Some causes of obesity—too little physical activity and poor eating habits—are, to some extent, within a young person's control. Weight-loss programs that use behavioral modification techniques to help adolescents make changes in diet and exercise have had some success. However, as we have pointed out, genetic and other factors having nothing to do with willpower or lifestyle choices seem to make some people susceptible to obesity. Among these factors are faulty regulation of metabolism, inability to recognize body cues about hunger and satiation, and development of an abnormally large number of fat cells.

Obese teenagers tend to become obese adults, subject to physical, social, and psychological risks (Gortmaker, Must, Perrin, Sobol, & Dietz, 1993). Overweight in adolescence can lead to life-threatening chronic conditions in adulthood, even if the excess weight is lost (Must et al., 1992).

body image Descriptive and evaluative beliefs about one's appearance.

Body Image and Eating Disorders Sometimes a determination *not* to become obese can result in graver problems than obesity itself. Concern with **body image**—one's perception of one's own appearance—often begins in middle childhood or earlier and intensifies in adolescence. It may lead to obsessive efforts at weight control (Davison & Birch, 2001; Schreiber et al., 1996; Vereecken & Maes, 2000). This pattern is more common among girls than among boys and is less likely to be related to actual weight problems. Because of girls' normal increase in body fat during puberty, many—especially those who are advanced in pubertal development—become unhappy about their looks, reflecting the cultural emphasis on women's physical attributes (Richards et al., 1990; Rosenblum & Lewis, 1999; Swarr & Richards, 1996), and this negative body image can lead to eating problems. Girls' dissatisfaction with their bodies increases over the course of early to midadolescence, while boys, who are becoming more muscular, become more satisfied with theirs (Feingold & Mazella, 1998; Rosenblum & Lewis, 1999; Swarr & Richards, 1996). By age 15, more than half the girls sampled in sixteen countries were dieting or thought they should be. The United States was at the top of the list, with 47 percent of 11-year-old girls and 62 percent of 15-year-olds concerned about overweight (Vereecken & Maes, 2000). According to a large prospective cohort study, parental attitudes and media images play a greater part in encouraging weight concerns than do peer influences. Girls who try to look like the unrealistically thin models they see in the media tend to develop excessive concern about weight. And both girls and boys who believe that thinness is important to their parents, especially to their fathers, tend to become constant dieters (Field et al., 2001). Girls with single or divorced parents, and those who frequently eat alone, are at risk of eating disorders (Martínez-González et al., 2003).

anorexia nervosa Eating disorder characterized by self-starvation.

Anorexia nervosa and *bulimia nervosa* are eating disorders that involve abnormal patterns of food intake. **Anorexia nervosa,** or self-starvation, is potentially life-threatening; it may be accompanied by irregularity or cessation of menstruation and growth of soft, fuzzy body hair. Anorexics have a distorted body image; though they are constantly dieting and eat next to nothing, they think they are too fat. They often are good students, described by their parents as "model" children. They may be withdrawn or depressed and engage in repetitive, perfectionist behavior. An estimated 0.5 percent of adolescent girls and young women and a smaller but growing percentage of boys and men in western countries are affected (Committee on Adolescence, 2003; Martínez-González et al., 2003).

bulimia nervosa Eating disorder in which a person regularly eats huge quantities of food and then purges the body by laxatives, induced vomiting, fasting, or excessive exercise.

In **bulimia nervosa,** a person regularly goes on huge eating binges within a short time, usually two hours or less, and then may try to undo the high caloric intake by self-induced vomiting, strict dieting or fasting, engaging in excessively vigorous exercise, or taking laxatives, enemas, or diuretics to purge the body. These episodes occur at least twice a week for at least three months. People with bulimia are obsessed with their weight and shape. They become overwhelmed with shame, self-contempt, and depression over their eating habits. They have low self-esteem and a history of wide weight fluctuation, dieting, or frequent exercise (Kendler et al., 1991).

Recently the American Psychiatric Association has tentatively identified a related *binge eating disorder,* which involves frequent bingeing but without subsequent fasting, exercise, or vomiting. About 3 percent of women and 0.3 percent of men have developed bulimia or binge eating disorder at some time in their lives, and much larger numbers have an occasional eating binge or bulimic episode (Harvard Medical School, 2002b).

What's Your View?

- Can you suggest ways to reduce the prevalence of eating disorders?

Anorexia and bulimia tend to run in families, suggesting a possible genetic basis. A variant of a gene that may lead to decreased feeding signals has been found in anorexic patients (Vink et al., 2001). Other possible causes are neurochemical, developmental, and social-cultural (Becker et al., 1999; "Eating Disorders—Part I, Part II," 1997; Kendler et al., 1991).

Researchers in London, Sweden, and Germany have found reduced blood flow to certain parts of the brain in anorexics, including an area thought to control visual self-perception and appetite (Gordon, Lask, Bryantwaugh, Christie, & Timini, 1997). Bulimia seems to be related to low levels of the brain chemical serotonin ("Eating Disorders—Part I," 1997; K. A. Smith, Fairburn, & Cowen, 1999). Some psychologists see anorexia as related to fear of growing up or fear of sexuality or to a malfunctioning family ("Eating Disorders—Part I," 1997; Garner, 1993). People with bulimia are thought to use food to satisfy their hunger for love and attention ("Eating Disorders—Part I," 1997; Humphrey, 1986). Excessive concern with body image, weight, and dieting can be an early warning sign (Harvard Medical School, 2002b).

Anorexia and bulimia may be treated with behavior therapy, followed by individual, group, or family psychotherapy or cognitive behavioral therapy (getting patients to rethink their attitudes, eating habits, and self-defeating beliefs). Since these patients are at risk for depression and suicide, antidepressant drugs such as Prozac can be helpful when combined with psychotherapy (Becker et al., 1999; Edwards, 1993; Fluoxetine-Bulimia Collaborative Study Group, 1992; Harvard Medical School, 2002b; Hudson & Pope, 1990; Kaye, Weltzin, Hsu, & Bulik, 1991).

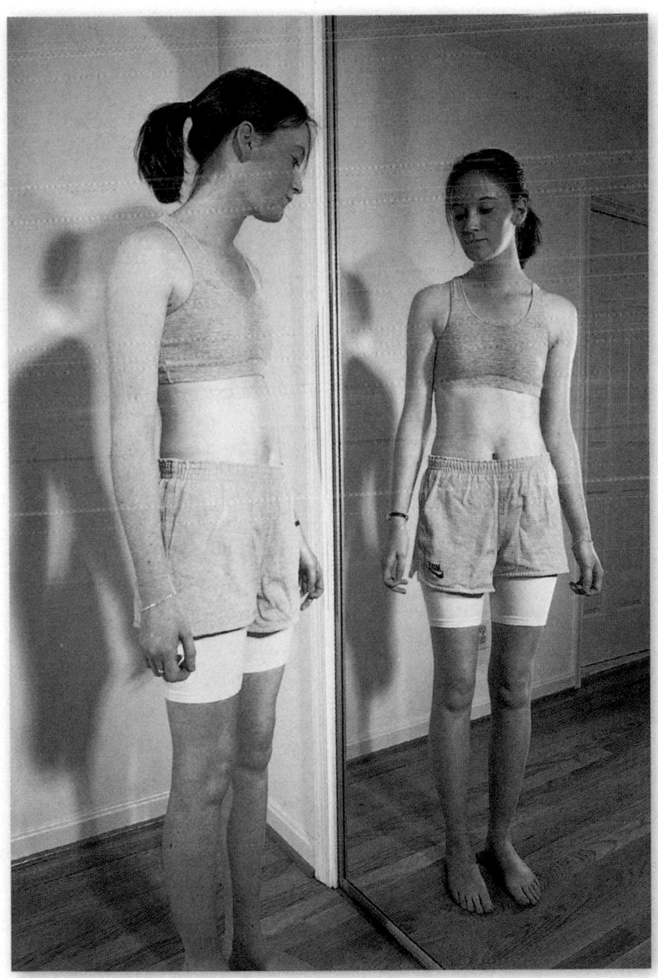

Anorexics, like this adolescent girl, have a distorted body image. They are so afraid of obesity that they see themselves as fat even when they are emaciated.

The outlook for people with bulimia is better than for those with anorexia, because the patients generally want treatment ("Eating Disorders—Part II," 1997; Herzog et al., 1999; Keel & Mitchell, 1997). Researchers have found an average recovery rate of 50 percent after periods ranging from 6 months to five years in patients treated for bulimia (Harvard Medical School, 2002b). People with anorexia often have long-term

Checkpoint

Can you . . .

- Summarize dietary deficiencies of U.S. adolescents, and tell why concerns about body image arise?
- Discuss risk factors, effects, treatment, and prognosis for obesity, anorexia, and bulimia?

psychological problems even after they have stopped starving themselves (Sullivan, Bulik, Fear, & Pickering, 1998). Up to 25 percent of patients with anorexia progress to chronic invalidism, and between 2 and 10 percent die prematurely (APA, 1994; Beumont, Russell, & Touyz, 1993; "Eating Disorders—Part I," 1997; Herzog, Keller, & Lavori, 1988).

Use and Abuse of Drugs

Use of illicit drugs among U.S. adolescents has declined slightly overall since its recent high levels in 1996 and 1997 and is well below the peak during the late 1970s and early 1980s (see Figure 11-2). The upsurge during the early 1990s accompanied a decline in perception of the dangers of drug use and a softening of peer disapproval, but that trend has now begun to reverse itself, including, for the first time in 1999, a drop in use of crack cocaine. Two exceptions to the general trend have been increased use of MDMA ("ecstasy"), a hallucinatory "club drug" popular at night-long "raves," and of anabolic steroids to enhance muscle strength among tenth-grade boys. However, ecstasy use declined in 2002 (Johnston, O'Malley, & Bachman, 2000, 2001, 2002a, 2002b; Mathias, 1999).

These findings come from the latest in a series of annual government surveys of a nationally representative sample of more than 43,000 eighth-, tenth-, and twelfth-graders in 394 schools across the United States (Johnston et al., 2002a). These surveys probably underestimate adolescent drug use since they do not reach high school dropouts, who are likely to have higher rates.

Risk Factors for Drug Abuse What makes it likely that a particular young person will abuse drugs? Research has pinpointed a number of risk factors: (1) poor impulse control and a tendency to seek out sensation (which may have a biochemical basis), (2) family influences (such as a genetic predisposition to alcoholism, parental use or acceptance of drugs, poor or inconsistent parenting practices, family conflict, and troubled or distant family relationships), (3) "difficult" temperament, (4) early and persistent behavior problems, particularly aggression, (5) academic failure and lack of commitment to education, (6) peer rejection, (7) associating with drug users, (8) alienation and rebelliousness, (9) favorable attitudes toward drug use, and (10) early initiation

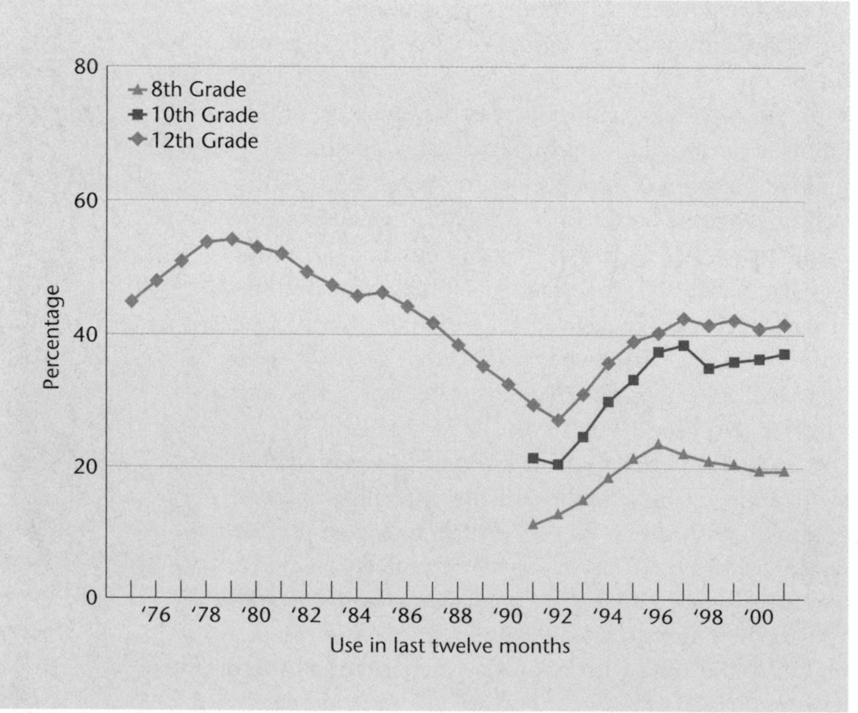

Figure 11-2
Trends in past-year use of drugs by eighth-, tenth-, and twelfth-graders. Only twelfth-graders were surveyed before 1991.
(*Source:* Johnson, O'Malley, & Bachman, 2002b.)

into drug use (Hawkins, Catalano, & Miller, 1992; Johnson, Hoffmann, & Gerstein, 1996; Masse & Tremblay, 1997; USDHHS, 1996b). The more risk factors that are present, the greater the chance that an adolescent or young adult will abuse drugs.

Drug use often begins as children move from elementary school to middle school, where they meet new friends and become more vulnerable to peer pressure. Fourth- to sixth-graders may start using cigarettes, beer, and inhalants and, as they get older, move on to marijuana or harder drugs (National Parents' Resource Institute for Drug Education, 1999). The earlier young people start using a drug, the more frequently they are likely to use it and the greater the tendency to abuse it.

Gateway Drugs Alcohol, marijuana, and tobacco, the three drugs most popular with adolescents, are sometimes called **gateway drugs,** because their use may lead to use of more addictive substances, such as cocaine and heroin. Young people who smoke, drink, or use marijuana often associate with peers who introduce them to harder drugs as they grow older. Marijuana not only tends to lead to hard drug use (Lynskey et al., 2003), but can be harmful in itself; long-term heavy use can impair memory and attention (Solowij et al., 2002).

gateway drugs Drugs such as alcohol, tobacco, and marijuana, the use of which may lead to use of more addictive drugs.

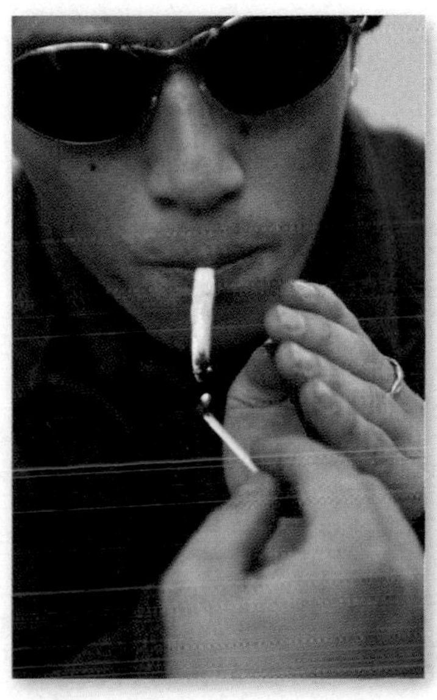

Marijuana is the most widely used illicit drug in the United States. Aside from its own ill effects, marijuana use may lead to addiction to hard drugs.

Frequency of alcohol and tobacco use is high in many industrial countries and is starting earlier than in the past (Gabhainn & François, 2000). However, cigarette smoking has declined among U.S. adolescents since 1996 (Johnston, O'Malley, & Bachman, 2002b).

An important early influence may be the omnipresence of substance use in the media. According to one study, alcohol, tobacco, or illicit drugs are shown in 70 percent of prime-time network television dramas, thirty-eight out of forty top-grossing movies, and half of all music videos (Gerbner & Ozyegin, 1997). Among fifty children's animated feature films available on videotape from five major Hollywood studios, more than two-thirds show characters smoking or drinking, with no indication or warning of negative health effects (Goldstein, Sobel, & Newman, 1999). Although the tobacco industry has claimed that it does not target adolescents, cigarette brands popular with 10- to 15-year-olds are widely advertised in magazines popular with young readers (King, Siegel, Celebucki, & Connolly, 1998). Receptivity to tobacco advertising is heightened in adolescents suffering from depression (Tercyak, Goldman, Smith, & Audrain, 2002).

Authoritative parenting can help young people internalize standards that may insulate them against negative peer influences (Collins et al., 2000). Among 500 ninth- through eleventh-graders, students whose close friends were drug users were less likely to report increased drug use if they saw their parents as highly authoritative (Mounts & Steinberg, 1995).

Contrary to popular impression, adolescents do seem to care what parents think. Adolescents who believe their parents disapprove of smoking are less likely to smoke (Sargent & Dalton, 2001). Rational discussions with parents can counteract harmful media influences and discourage or limit drinking (Austin, Pinkleton, & Fujioka, 2000; Turrisi, Wiersman, & Hughes, 2000).

Checkpoint

Can you . . .

- ✔ Summarize recent trends in drug use among adolescents?
- ✔ Discuss factors and risks connected with use of drugs, specifically alcohol, marijuana, and tobacco?

Depression

It is not surprising that Anne Frank took an antidepressant in view of the desperate situation in which she found herself. But even in normal surroundings, the prevalence of depression increases during adolescence. As many as 2.5 percent of children and 8.3 percent of adolescents have major depression at a given time (USDHHS, 1999c), and 15 to 20 percent may experience an episode sometime during adolescence (Petersen et al., 1993).

Adolescent girls, especially early-maturing girls—like adult women—are especially subject to depression (Birmaher et al., 1996; Cicchetti & Toth, 1998; Ge, Conger, & Elder, 2001; Stice & Bearman, 2001). This gender difference may be related to

This teenage boy may be worried about his grades on a test or about a rejection by a girlfriend. Such worries are not unusual in adolescence; but if sadness persists, accompanied by such symptoms as inability to concentrate, fatigue, apathy, and feelings of worthlessness, the young person may be depressed. As many as one in five adolescents experience at least one episode of depression.

biological changes connected with puberty or to the way girls are socialized (Birmaher et al., 1996) and their greater vulnerability to stress in social relationships (Ge et al., 2001; USDHHS, 1999c). Body-image and eating disturbances can aggravate depressive symptoms (Stice & Bearman, 2001).

Death in Adolescence

Not every death in adolescence is as poignant as Anne Frank's. Still, death this early in life is always tragic, and (unlike Anne's) usually accidental (Anderson, 2002)—but not entirely so. The frequency of car crashes, handgun deaths, and suicide in this age group reflects a violent culture, as well as adolescents' inexperience and immaturity, which often lead to risk taking and carelessness.

Deaths from Vehicle Accidents and Firearms Motor vehicle collisions are the leading cause of death among U.S. teenagers; they account for more than one-third of all deaths of 15- to 19-year-olds (CDC, 1999). Collisions are more likely to be fatal when a 16- or 17-year-old driver carries passengers, perhaps because adolescents tend to drive more recklessly in the presence of peers (Chen, Baker, Braver, & Li, 2000).

Death rates for this age group have dropped 26 percent in the past twenty years, largely because of decreases in alcohol-related motor vehicle accidents (USDHHS, 1999b). Some states have adopted graduated licensing systems, which allow beginning drivers to drive only with supervision at first and lift the restrictions gradually.

Firearm-related deaths of 15- to 19-year-olds (including homicide, suicide, and accidental deaths) are far more common in the United States than in other industrialized countries, comprising about one-third of all injury deaths and more than 85 percent of all homicides. Guns are the number one killer of African American youth. The chief reason for these grim statistics seems to be the ease of obtaining a gun in the United States (AAP Committee on Injury and Poison Prevention, 2000). This is evident from the fact that youth death rates from firearms have declined since 1993 (AAP Committee on Injury and Poison Prevention, 2000), a period during which police have been confiscating guns on the street (T. B. Cole, 1999) and fewer young people carry them (USDHHS, 1999b).

For many adolescents, the easiest place to get a gun is at home (Stennies, Ikeda, Leadbetter, Houston, & Sacks, 1999). Contrary to the claims of gun-rights defenders, guns in the home are forty-three times more likely to kill a family member or acquaintance than to be used in self-defense (AAP Committee on Injury and Poison Prevention, 2000).

Suicide Ready availability of guns in the home also is a major factor in teenage suicide, which increased by 11 percent among 15- to 19-year-olds and more than doubled among 10- to 14-year-olds between 1980 and 1997 (Centers for Disease Control & Prevention [CDC], 2002b). Although most young people who *attempt* suicide do it by taking pills or ingesting other substances, those who succeed are most likely to use or carry firearms (Borowsky, Ireland, & Resnick, 2001; Garland & Zigler, 1993). Firearms are used in 67 percent of completed suicides (AAP Committee on Adolescence, 2000). Thus, limiting access to firearms might well reduce the suicide rate, which is currently about 8 suicides per 100,000 15- to 19-year-olds, making suicide the third leading cause of death in this age group (Anderson, 2002).

Boys this age are six times as likely as girls to take their lives. Although suicide affects all ethnic groups, Native American boys have the highest rates and African American girls the lowest. Homosexual and bisexual youths, who have high rates of depression, also have high rates of suicide and attempted suicide (AAP Committee on Adolescence, 2000; Remafedi, French, Story, Resnick, & Blum, 1998).

Practically Speaking

BOX 11-1

Preventing Teenage Suicide

What can be done to stem the alarming rise in suicide among young people? Many people intent on killing themselves keep their plans secret, but others send out signals well in advance. An attempt at suicide is sometimes a call for help, and some people die because they are more successful than they intended to be.

Warning signs include withdrawal from relationships; talking about death, the hereafter, or suicide; giving away prized possessions; drug or alcohol abuse; personality changes, such as a rise in anger, boredom, or apathy; unusual neglect of appearance; difficulty concentrating at work or in school; staying away from work, school, or other usual activities; complaints of physical problems when nothing is organically wrong; and eating or sleeping much more or much less than usual. Friends or family may be able to help by talking to a young person about his or her suicidal thoughts to bring them out in the open; telling others who are in a position to do something—the person's parents or partner, other family members, a close friend, a therapist, or a counselor; and showing the person that she or he has other options besides death, even though none of them may be ideal.

Telephone hotlines are the most prevalent type of suicide intervention for adolescents, but their effectiveness appears to be minimal. In fact, some of these programs may do harm by exaggerating the extent of teenage suicide and painting it as a reaction to normal stresses of adolescence rather than a pathological act. Instead, programs should identify and treat young people at particular risk of suicide, including those who have already attempted it. Equally important is to attack the risk factors—for example, through programs to reduce substance abuse, violence, and access to guns and to strengthen families and improve parenting skills (Borowsky et al., 2001; Garland & Zigler, 1993). Programs to enhance self-esteem and build problem-solving and coping abilities can be directed toward young children and continued throughout the school years (Meehan, 1990).

What's Your View?

Have you ever experienced any of the warning signs described in this box? What would you do if a close friend or family member showed one or more of them?

Check It Out:

For more information on this topic, go to http://www.mhhe.com/papaliah9, where you'll find links to information about teenage suicide and prevention.

In a national survey of seventh- to twelfth-graders, almost one-fourth of the students reported that they had seriously considered suicide during the past year (AAP Committee on Adolescence, 2000). Other surveys show that as many as 12 percent of girls and 6 percent of boys actually attempt to kill themselves (Borowsky et al., 2001). Young people who attempt suicide tend to have histories of emotional illness: commonly depression, substance abuse, antisocial or aggressive behavior, or unstable personality. They tend to be either perpetrators or victims of violence. They also tend to have attempted suicide before, or to have friends or family members who did (Borowsky et al., 2001; Garland & Zigler, 1993; National Institute of Mental Health [NIMH], 1999a, 1999b; Slap, Vorters, Chaudhuri, & Centor, 1989; "Suicide—Part I," 1996). Alcohol plays a part in fully half of all teenage suicides (AAP Committee on Adolescence, 2000).

Suicidal teenagers tend to think poorly of themselves, to feel hopeless, and to have poor impulse control and low tolerance for frustration and stress. Feelings of depression may be masked as boredom, apathy, hyperactivity, or physical problems. These young people are often alienated from their parents and have no one outside the family to turn to. Many come from troubled families—often with a history of unemployment, imprisonment, or suicidal behavior—and a high proportion of these young people have been abused or neglected (Deykin, Alpert, & McNamara, 1985; Garland & Zigler, 1993; Slap et al., 1989; "Suicide—Part I," 1996; Swedo et al., 1991). School problems—academic or behavioral—are common among would-be suicides (Borowsky et al., 2001; National Committee for Citizens in Education [NCCE], 1986).

Protective factors that reduce the risk of suicide include a sense of connectedness to family and school, emotional well-being, and academic achievement (Borowsky et al., 2001). Box 11-1 discusses ways of preventing suicide.

Checkpoint

Can you . . .

- ✔ Discuss factors affecting gender differences in adolescent depression?
- ✔ Name the three leading causes of death among adolescents, and discuss the dangers of firearm injury?
- ✔ Assess risk and protective factors and prevention programs for teenage suicide?

COGNITIVE DEVELOPMENT

Aspects of Cognitive Maturation

Guidepost

4. How do adolescents' thinking and use of language differ from younger children's?

Despite the perils of adolescence, most young people emerge from the teenage years with mature, healthy bodies and a zest for life. Their cognitive development has continued, too. Adolescents not only look different from younger children; they also think differently. Although their thinking may remain immature in some ways, many are capable of abstract reasoning and sophisticated moral judgments and can plan more realistically for the future.

Piaget's Stage of Formal Operations

formal operations Piaget's final stage of cognitive development, characterized by the ability to think abstractly.

According to Piaget, adolescents enter the highest level of cognitive development—**formal operations**—when they develop the capacity for abstract thought. This development, usually around age 11, gives them a new, more flexible way to manipulate information. No longer limited to the here and now, they can understand historical time and extraterrestrial space. They can use symbols for symbols (for example, letting the letter X stand for an unknown numeral) and thus can learn algebra and calculus. They can better appreciate metaphor and allegory and thus can find richer meanings in literature. They can think in terms of what *might* be, not just what *is.* They can imagine possibilities and can form and test hypotheses.

People in the stage of formal operations can integrate what they have learned in the past with the challenges of the present and make plans for the future. Thought at this stage has a flexibility not possible in the stage of concrete operations. The ability to think abstractly has emotional implications, too. Earlier, a child could love a parent or hate a classmate. Now "the adolescent can love freedom or hate exploitation. . . . The possible and the ideal captivate both mind and feeling" (H. Ginsburg & Opper, 1979, p. 201). Thus could Anne Frank, in her attic hideout, express her ideals and her hopes for the future.

Hypothetical-Deductive Reasoning To appreciate the difference formal reasoning makes, let's follow the progress of a typical child in dealing with a classic Piagetian problem, the pendulum problem.* The child, Adam, is shown the pendulum—an object hanging from a string. He is then shown how he can change any of four factors: the length of the string, the weight of the object, the height from which the object is released, and the amount of force he may use to push the object. He is asked to figure out which factor or combination of factors determines how fast the pendulum swings. (This and other Piagetian tasks for assessing the achievement of formal operations are pictured in Figure 11-3.)

When Adam first sees the pendulum, he is not yet 7 years old and is in the preoperational stage. Unable to formulate a plan for attacking the problem, he tries one thing after another in a hit-or-miss manner. First he puts a light weight on a long string and pushes it; then he tries swinging a heavy weight on a short string; then he removes the weight entirely. Not only is his method random; he also cannot understand or report what has happened.

Adam next encounters the pendulum at age 10, when he is in the stage of concrete operations. This time, he discovers that varying the length of the string and the weight of the object affects the speed of the swing. However, because he varies both factors at the same time, he cannot tell which is critical or whether both are.

Adam is confronted with the pendulum for a third time at age 15, and this time he goes at the problem systematically. He designs an experiment to test all the possi-

*This description of age-related differences in the approach to the pendulum problem is adapted from H. Ginsburg and Opper (1979).

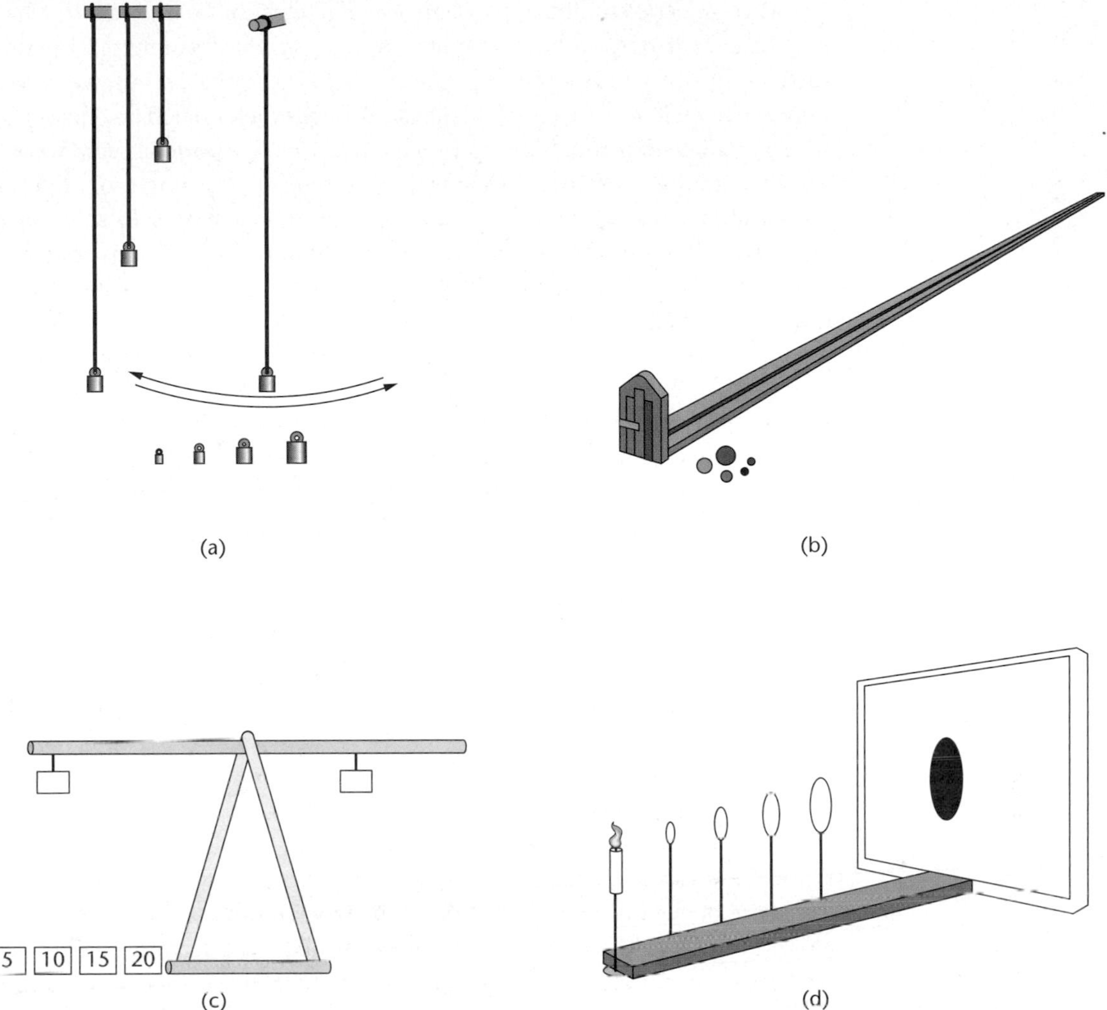

Figure 11-3
Piagetian tasks for measuring attainment of formal operations.
(a) Pendulum. The pendulum's string can be shortened or lengthened, and weights of varying sizes can be attached to it. The student must determine what variables affect the speed of the pendulum's swing.
(b) Motion in a horizontal plane. A spring device launches balls of varying sizes, which roll in a horizontal plane. The student must predict their stopping points.
(c) Balance beam. A balance scale comes with weights of varying sizes, which can be hung at different points along the crossbar. The student must determine what factors affect whether or not the scale will balance.
(d) Shadows. A board containing a row of peg holes is attached perpendicular to the base of a screen. A light source and rings of varying diameters can be placed in the holes, at varying distances from the screen. The student must produce two shadows of the same size, using different-sized rings. (*Source:* Adapted from Small, 1990, Figure 8-12.)

ble hypotheses, varying one factor at a time—first, the length of the string; next, the weight of the object; then the height from which it is released; and finally, the amount of force used—each time holding the other three factors constant. In this way, he is able to determine that only one factor—the length of the string—determines how fast the pendulum swings.

Adam's solution of the pendulum problem shows that he has arrived at the stage of formal operations. He is now capable of **hypothetical-deductive reasoning.** He can develop a hypothesis and can design an experiment to test it. He considers all the relationships he can imagine and goes through them systematically, one by one, to eliminate the false and arrive at the true. Hypothetical-deductive reasoning gives him a tool to solve problems, from fixing the family car to constructing a political theory.

hypothetical-deductive reasoning Ability, believed by Piaget to accompany the stage of formal operations, to develop, consider, and test hypotheses.

Microgenetic studies of problem-solving behavior (refer back to Chapter 2) support Piaget's analysis of how concrete operations differ from formal operations. In one such study, fifth- and sixth-graders and noncollege-educated adults were asked to design experiments to understand physical phenomena, such as factors affecting the speed of a vessel through a canal (Schauble, 1996). Preadolescents were less systematic than adults in exploring such problems, typically varying more than one factor at the same time, as Adam did with the pendulum at that age. To solve such problems, people need to think like scientists. They should not rule out a hypothesis before testing it, just because it seems unlikely to be true—a common mistake among children (DeLoache, Miller, & Pierroutsakos, 1998). They need to know what theories and strategies they are following—something many preadolescents do not do (Kuhn, Garcia-Mila, Zohar, & Andersen, 1995).

What's Your View?

- How can parents and teachers help adolescents improve their reasoning ability?

What brings about the shift to formal reasoning? Piaget attributed it to a combination of brain maturation and expanding environmental opportunities. Both are essential: even if young people's neurological development has advanced enough to permit formal reasoning, they can attain it only with appropriate stimulation. One way this can happen is through cooperative effort (Johnson, Johnson, & Tjosvold, 2000). When college students (average age, $18\frac{1}{2}$) were told to set up their own experiments to solve a chemistry problem, students randomly assigned to work in pairs solved more problems than those who worked alone. The more the partners challenged each other's reasoning, the greater were their advances in thinking (Dimant & Bearison, 1991).

Culture and schooling seem to play a role—as Piaget (1972) ultimately recognized. French 10- to 15-year-olds in the 1990s did better on Piagetian tests of formal operations than their counterparts two to three decades earlier, when fewer had secondary school educations (Flieller, 1999). When adolescents in New Guinea and Rwanda were tested on the pendulum problem, none were able to solve it. On the other hand, Chinese children in Hong Kong, who had been to British schools, did at least as well as U.S. or European children. Schoolchildren in Central Java and New South Wales also showed some formal operational abilities (Gardiner et al., 1998). Apparently, this kind of thinking is a learned ability that is not equally necessary or equally valued in all cultures.

Evaluating Piaget's Theory Piaget's influence on the field of developmental psychology has been compared with Shakespeare's influence on English literature and Aristotle's influence on philosophy (Beilin, 1994). His theory has pointed the way to countless avenues of investigation and continues to do so. Piaget's theory also has had an enormous influence on education. It has given parents and teachers benchmarks for what to expect, roughly, at various ages and has helped educators design curricula appropriate to children's levels of development.

Although research has not seriously challenged the overall *sequence* of development Piaget described (Lourenco & Machado, 1996), it has questioned his assertion of definite stages of development. His own writings provide many examples of children displaying aspects of scientific thinking well before adolescence. At the same time, Piaget seems to have *over*estimated some older children's abilities. In most of his writings, he paid little attention to individual differences, to variations in a child's performance of different kinds of tasks, or to social and cultural influences. He failed to adequately take into account the gradual accumulation of knowledge and expertise in specific fields and the role of *metacognition,* awareness and monitoring of one's own mental processes and strategies (Flavell et al., 2002).

In his later years, Piaget himself "came to view his earlier model of the development of children's thinking, particularly formal operations, as flawed because it failed to capture the essential *role of the situation* in influencing and constraining . . . children's thinking" (Brown, Metz, & Campione, 1996, pp. 152–153). Neo-Piagetian research suggests that children's cognitive processes are closely tied to specific content (what a child is thinking *about*), as well as to the context of a problem and the kinds of information and thought a culture considers important (Case & Okamoto, 1996).

Although Piaget described the stage of formal operations as the pinnacle of cognitive achievement, other research (reported in Chapters 13 and 15) suggests that developmental changes in cognition extend well into adulthood. According to Piaget's critics, formal reasoning is not the only, and perhaps not even the most important, aspect of mature thinking (Moshman, 1998). Piaget's theory may not give enough weight to such aspects of mature intelligence as the role of experience and intuition and the wisdom that helps people cope with an often chaotic world.

Language Development

Although school-age children are quite proficient in use of language, adolescence brings further refinements. Vocabulary continues to grow as reading matter becomes more adult. Although individual differences are great, by ages 16 to 18 the average young person knows about 80,000 words (Owens, 1996).

With the advent of formal thought, adolescents can define and discuss such abstractions as *love, justice,* and *freedom.* They more frequently use such terms as *however, otherwise, anyway, therefore, really,* and *probably* to express logical relations between clauses or sentences. They become more conscious of words as symbols that can have multiple meanings; they enjoy using irony, puns, and metaphors (Owens, 1996).

Adolescents also become more skilled in *social perspective-taking,* the ability to understand another person's point of view and level of knowledge and to speak accordingly. This ability is essential in order to persuade or just to engage in conversation. Conscious of their audience, adolescents speak a different language with peers than with adults (Owens, 1996; see Box 11-2 on page 406). Teenage slang is part of the process of developing an independent identity separate from parents and the adult world. In creating such expressions as "awesome" and "geek," young people use their newfound ability to play with words "to define their generation's unique take on values, tastes, and preferences" (Elkind, 1998, p. 29).

Checkpoint

Can you . . .

- ✔ Explain the difference between formal operational and concrete operational thinking, as exemplified by the pendulum problem?
- ✔ Cite factors influencing adolescents' development of formal reasoning?
- ✔ Evaluate strengths and weaknesses of Piaget's theory of formal operations?
- ✔ Identify characteristics of adolescents' language development that reflect cognitive advances?

Elkind: Immature Characteristics of Adolescent Thought

We have seen how children develop from egocentric beings whose interest extends not much beyond the nipple to persons able to solve abstract problems and imagine ideal societies. Yet in some ways adolescents' thinking seems strangely immature. They may be rude to adults, they have trouble making up their minds what to wear each day, and they often act as if the whole world revolved around them.

According to the psychologist David Elkind (1984, 1998), such behavior stems from adolescents' inexperienced ventures into formal operational thought. This new way of thinking, which fundamentally transforms the way they look at themselves and their world, is as unfamiliar to them as their reshaped bodies, and they sometimes feel just as awkward in its use. As they try out their new powers, they may sometimes stumble, like an infant learning to walk.

This immaturity of thinking manifests itself in at least six characteristic ways, according to Elkind:

1. *Idealism and criticalness:* As adolescents envision an ideal world, they realize how far the real world, for which they hold adults responsible, falls short by comparison. They become super-conscious of hypocrisy, and, with their sharpened verbal reasoning, they relish magazines and entertainers that attack public figures with satire and parody. They are convinced that they know better than adults how to run the world, and they frequently find fault with their parents.

BOX 11-2

Window on the World

Pubilect: The Dialect of Adolescence

"That guy's hot!"
"She's fine!"
"Chill!"
"Let's bounce!"

Adolescents' conversation is mainly about the people and events in their everyday world (Labov, 1992). They use slang (nonstandard speech) to label people ("dork" or "loser"), to pronounce positive or negative judgments ("That's cool!" or "What a beast!"), and to describe alcohol or drug-related activity ("She's wasted" or "He's blazed").

The Canadian linguist Marcel Danesi (1994)* argues that adolescent speech is more than just slang (which, of course, adults can use, too). Instead, it constitutes a dialect of its own: *pubilect,* "the social dialect of puberty" (p. 97).

Pubilect is more than an occasional colorful expression. It is the primary mode of verbal communication among teenagers, by which they differentiate themselves from adults. As they approach puberty, youngsters absorb this dialect from slightly older peers. Like any other linguistic code, pubilect serves to strengthen group identity and to shut outsiders (adults) out. Teenage vocabulary is characterized by rapid change. Although some of its terms have entered common discourse, adolescents keep inventing new ones all the time.

Analysis of recorded samples of adolescent conversation reveals several key features of pubilect. First, it is an *emotive* code. Through exaggerated tone, slow and deliberate delivery, prolonged stress, accompanying gestures, and vulgar interjections, it draws attention to feelings and attitudes ("Yeah, riiight!" "Well, duuuh!"). Such emotive utterances seem to constitute about 65 percent of adolescent speech. The use of fillers, such as the word *like,* as well as the typical pattern of narrative intonation, in which each phrase or sentence seems to end with a question mark, reflects unconscious uncertainty and serves to draw the listener into the speaker's state of mind.

A second feature of pubilect is its *connotative* function. Teenagers coin descriptive words (or extend the meaning of existing words) to convey their view of their world and the people in it—often, in highly metaphorical ways. A person does not need a dictionary to figure out the meanings of such expressions as "space cadet" and "ditz." Such terms provide a ready lexicon for quick, automatic value judgments about others.

In the United States, there is not just a single youth culture, but many subcultures. Vocabulary may differ by gender, ethnicity, age, geographical region, neighborhood (city, suburban, or rural) and type of school (public or private) (Labov, 1992). Also, pubilect is *clique-coded:* it varies from one clique to another. "Druggies" and "jocks" engage in different kinds of activities, which form the main subjects of their conversation. This talk, in turn, cements bonds within the clique. Males use verbal dueling to assert power. Contenders for leadership trade insults and clever retorts in an effort to symbolically gain the upper hand in front of the group.

A study of teenage speech patterns in Naples, Italy, suggests that similar features may emerge "in any culture where teenagerhood constitutes a distinct social category" (Danesi, 1994, p. 123). Neapolitan teenagers use "mmmm" much as U.S. teenagers use "like": "Devo, mmmm, dire che, mmmm, non capisco, mmmm, . . ." ("I have, mmmm, to say that, mmmm, I don't understand, mmmm, . . ."). Exaggerated tone and rising intonation at the ends of phrases are also common. The Italian young people have terms roughly equivalent to the English "cool" (*togo*), "loser" (*grasta*), and "dork" or "nerd" (*secchione*). Other investigators report that adolescents in Milan, Bologna, and other northern Italian cities speak "the language of rock and roll." This cultural borrowing—the result of wide dissemination of English-language television channels, such as MTV—may well be creating a "symbolic universe" for teenagers around the world (Danesi, 1994, p. 123).

*Unless otherwise referenced, the source of this discussion is Danesi, 1994.

What's Your View?

Can you remember "pubilect" expressions from your own adolescence? When and why did you use such expressions? What was their effect on others your age? On adults?

Check It Out:

For more information on this topic, go to http://www.mhhe.com/papaliah9, where you will find a link to a website called "American Slanguages."

2. *Argumentativeness:* Adolescents are constantly looking for opportunities to try out—and show off—their newfound formal reasoning abilities. They often become argumentative as they marshal facts and logic to build a case for, say, staying out late.
3. *Indecisiveness:* Adolescents can keep many alternatives in mind at the same time, but because of their inexperience, they lack effective strategies for choosing among

them. Thus they may have trouble making up their minds even about such a simple thing as what to wear.

4. *Apparent hypocrisy:* Young adolescents often do not recognize the difference between expressing an ideal and making the sacrifices necessary to live up to it. In one example Elkind (1998) gives, teenagers concerned about animal welfare demonstrated in front of a furrier's shop but waited until a warm spring day to do it—thus avoiding having to stand outside in cloth coats in wintry weather. To an adult observer, this behavior might seem hypocritical; but actually, these earnest young people did not realize the connection between their behavior and the ideal they were advocating.

Argumentativeness—usually with parents—is a typical characteristic of adolescent thought, according to David Elkind.

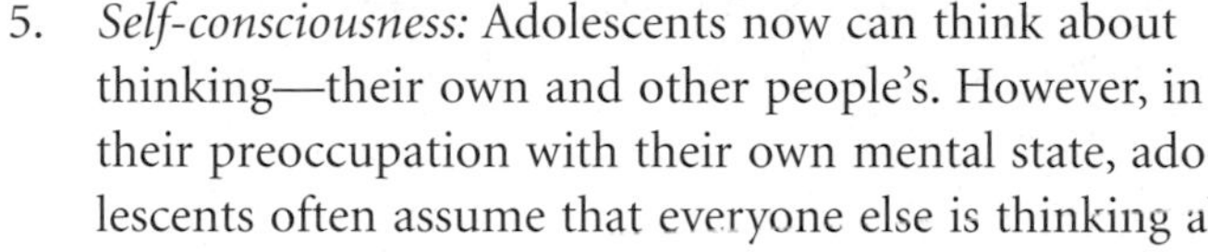

5. *Self-consciousness:* Adolescents now can think about thinking—their own and other people's. However, in their preoccupation with their own mental state, adolescents often assume that everyone else is thinking about the same thing they are thinking about: themselves. A teenage girl may be mortified if she wears "the wrong thing" to a party, thinking that everyone else must be looking askance at her. Elkind refers to this self-consciousness as the **imaginary audience,** a conceptualized "observer" who is as concerned with a young person's thoughts and behavior as he or she is. The imaginary audience, says Elkind, is especially strong in the early teens but persists to a lesser degree into adult life. It may surface when, for example, a person drops a fork on the tile floor of a noisy restaurant and imagines that everyone in the room is watching.

imaginary audience Elkind's term for an observer who exists only in an adolescent's mind and is as concerned with the adolescent's thoughts and actions as the adolescent is.

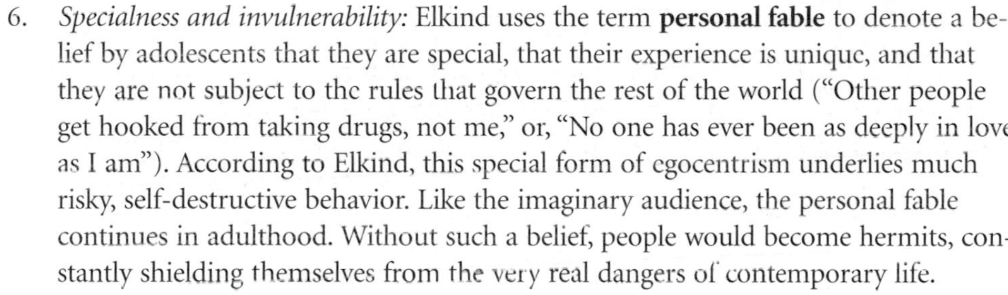

6. *Specialness and invulnerability:* Elkind uses the term **personal fable** to denote a belief by adolescents that they are special, that their experience is unique, and that they are not subject to the rules that govern the rest of the world ("Other people get hooked from taking drugs, not me," or, "No one has ever been as deeply in love as I am"). According to Elkind, this special form of egocentrism underlies much risky, self-destructive behavior. Like the imaginary audience, the personal fable continues in adulthood. Without such a belief, people would become hermits, constantly shielding themselves from the very real dangers of contemporary life.

personal fable Elkind's term for the conviction that one is special, unique, and not subject to the rules that govern the rest of the world.

The concepts of the imaginary audience and the personal fable have been widely accepted, but their validity as distinct earmarks of adolescence has little independent research support. In some studies of the personal fable, adolescents were *more* likely than college students or adults to see themselves as vulnerable to certain risks, such as alcohol and other drug problems, rather than *less* likely, as the personal fable would predict (Quadrel, Fischoff, & Davis, 1993). Rather than universal features of adolescents' cognitive development, it has been suggested that the imaginary audience and personal fable may be related to specific social experiences. And, since these concepts grew out of Elkind's clinical observations, they may be more characteristic of youngsters who are experiencing difficulties in adjustment (Vartanian & Powlishta, 1996).

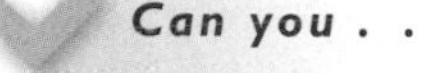

Checkpoint

Can you . . .

✔ Describe Elkind's six proposed aspects of immature adolescent thought, and explain how they may grow out of the transition to formal operations?

Moral Reasoning: Kohlberg's Theory

A woman is near death from cancer. A druggist has discovered a drug that doctors believe might save her. The druggist is charging $2,000 for a small dose—ten times what the drug costs him to make. The sick woman's husband, Heinz, borrows from everyone he knows but can scrape together only $1,000. He begs the druggist to sell him the drug for $1,000 or let him pay the rest later. The druggist refuses, saying "I discovered the drug and I'm going to make money from it." Heinz, desperate, breaks into the man's store and steals the drug. Should Heinz have done that? Why or why not? (Kohlberg, 1969).

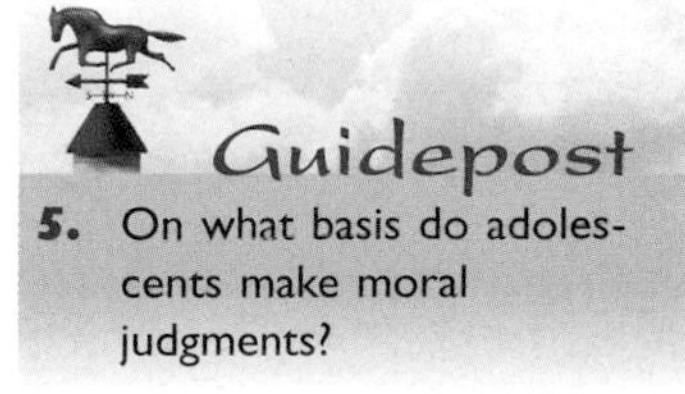

Guidepost

5. On what basis do adolescents make moral judgments?

Heinz's problem is the most famous example of Lawrence Kohlberg's approach to studying moral development. Starting in the 1950s, Kohlberg and his colleagues posed hypothetical dilemmas like this one to 75 boys ages 10, 13, and 16 and continued to question them periodically for more than thirty years. At the heart of each dilemma was the concept of justice. By asking respondents how they arrived at their answers, Kohlberg concluded that the way people look at moral issues reflects cognitive development.

Kohlberg's Levels and Stages Moral development in Kohlberg's theory bears some similarity to Piaget's (refer back to Chapter 9), but his model is more complex. On the basis of thought processes shown by responses to his dilemmas, Kohlberg (1969) described three levels of moral reasoning, each divided into two stages (see Table 11-2):

preconventional morality First level of Kohlberg's theory of moral reasoning, in which control is external.

conventional morality Second level of Kohlberg's theory of moral reasoning, in which standards of authority figures are internalized.

postconventional morality Third level of Kohlberg's theory of moral reasoning, in which people follow internally held moral principles and can decide among conflicting moral standards.

- *Level I:* ***Preconventional morality.*** People act under external controls. They obey rules to avoid punishment or reap rewards, or act out of self-interest. This level is typical of children ages 4 to 10.
- *Level II:* ***Conventional morality (or morality of conventional role conformity).*** People have internalized the standards of authority figures. They are concerned about being "good," pleasing others, and maintaining the social order. This level is typically reached after age 10; many people never move beyond it, even in adulthood.
- *Level III:* ***Postconventional morality (or morality of autonomous moral principles).*** People now recognize conflicts between moral standards and make their own judgments on the basis of principles of right, fairness, and justice. People generally do not reach this level of moral reasoning until at least early adolescence, or more commonly in young adulthood, if ever.

Kohlberg later added a transitional level between levels II and III, when people no longer feel bound by society's moral standards but have not yet reasoned out their own principles of justice. Instead, they base their moral decisions on personal feelings.

In Kohlberg's theory, it is the reasoning underlying a person's response to a moral dilemma, not the answer itself, that indicates the stage of moral development. As illustrated in Table 11-2, two people who give opposite answers may be at the same stage if their reasoning is based on similar factors.

Kohlberg's early stages correspond roughly to Piaget's stages of moral development in childhood, but his advanced stages go into adulthood. Some adolescents, and even some adults, remain at Kohlberg's level I. Like young children, they seek to avoid punishment or satisfy their own needs. Most adolescents, and most adults, seem to be at level II. They conform to social conventions, support the status quo, and do the "right" thing to please others or to obey the law. (Toward the end of Anne Frank's diary, we can see her begin to emerge from this stage as she argues with her father and herself about the morality of a more physically intimate relationship with Peter.)

Very few people reach level III, when they can choose between two socially accepted standards. In fact, at one point Kohlberg questioned the validity of stage 6, since so few people seem to attain it. Later, however, he proposed a seventh, "cosmic" stage (see Chapter 13), in which people consider the effect of their actions not only on other people but on the universe as a whole (Kohlberg, 1981; Kohlberg & Ryncarz, 1990).

Evaluating Kohlberg's Theory Kohlberg and Piaget brought about a profound shift in the way we look at moral development. Instead of viewing morality solely as

Table 11-2 Kohlberg's Six Stages of Moral Reasoning

Levels	Stages of Reasoning	Typical Answers to Heinz's Dilemma
Level I: Preconventional morality (ages 4 to 10)	*Stage 1: Orientation toward punishment and obedience.* "What will happen to me?" Children obey rules to avoid punishment. They ignore the motives of an act and focus on its physical form (such as the size of a lie) or its consequences (for example, the amount of physical damage).	*Pro:* "He should steal the drug. It isn't really bad to take it. It isn't as it he hadn't asked to pay for it first. The drug he'd take is worth only $200; he's not really taking a $2,000 drug." *Con:* "He shouldn't steal the drug. It's a big crime. He didn't get permission; he used force and broke and entered. He did a lot of damage and stole a very expensive drug."
	Stage 2: Instrumental purpose and exchange. "You scratch my back, I'll scratch yours." Children conform to rules out of self-interest and consideration for what others can do for them. They look at an act in terms of the human needs it meets and differentiate this value from the act's physical form and consequences.	*Pro:* "It's all right to steal the drug, because his wife needs it and he wants her to live. It isn't that he wants to steal, but that's what he has to do to save her." *Con:* "He shouldn't steal it. The druggist isn't wrong or bad; he just wants to make a profit. That's what you're in business for—to make money."
Level II: Conventional morality (ages 10 to 13 or beyond)	*Stage 3: Maintaining mutual relations, approval of others, the golden rule.* "Am I a good boy or girl?" Children want to please and help others, can judge the intentions of others, and develop their own ideas of what a good person is. They evaluate an act according to the motive behind it or the person performing it, and they take circumstances into account.	*Pro:* "He should steal the drug. He is only doing something that is natural for a good husband to do. You can't blame him for doing something out of love for his wife. You'd blame him if he didn't love his wife enough to save her." *Con:* "He shouldn't steal. If his wife dies, he can't be blamed. It isn't because he's heartless or that he doesn't love her enough to do everything that he legally can. The druggist is the selfish or heartless one."
	Stage 4: Social concern and conscience. "What if everybody did it?" People are concerned with doing their duty, showing respect for higher authority, and maintaining the social order. They consider an act always wrong, regardless of motive or circumstances, if it violates a rule and harms others.	*Pro:* "You should steal it. If you did nothing, you'd be letting your wife die. It's your responsibility if she dies. You have to take it with the idea of paying the druggist." *Con:* "It is a natural thing for Heinz to want to save his wife, but it's still always wrong to steal. He knows he's taking a valuable drug from the man who made it."
Level III: Postconventional morality (early adolescence, or not until young adulthood, or never)	*Stage 5: Morality of contract, of individual rights, and of democratically accepted law.* People think in rational terms, valuing the will of the majority and the welfare of society. They generally see these values as best supported by adherence to the law. While they recognize that there are times when human need and the law conflict, they believe it is better for society in the long run if they obey the law.	*Pro:* "The law wasn't set up for these circumstances. Taking the drug in this situation isn't really right, but it's justified." *Con:* "You can't completely blame someone for stealing, but extreme circumstances don't really justify taking the law into your own hands. You can't have people stealing whenever they are desperate. The end may be good, but the ends don't justify the means."
	Stage 6: Morality of universal ethical principles. People do what they as individuals think is right, regardless of legal restrictions or the opinions of others. They act in accordance with internalized standards, knowing that they would condemn themselves if they did not.	*Pro:* "This is a situation that forces him to choose between stealing and letting his wife die. In a situation where the choice must be made, it is morally right to steal. He has to act in terms of the principle of preserving and respecting life." *Con:* "Heinz is faced with the decision of whether to consider the other people who need the drug just as badly as his wife. Heinz ought to act not according to his feelings for his wife, but considering the value of all the lives involved."

Source: Adapted from Kohlberg, 1969; Lickona, 1976.

the attainment of control over self-gratifying impulses, investigators now look at how children make moral judgments based on their growing understanding of the social world.

Research has supported some aspects of Kohlberg's theory but has left others in question. The American boys whom Kohlberg and his colleagues followed through adulthood progressed through Kohlberg's stages in sequence, and none skipped a stage. Their levels of moral judgments correlated positively with increasing age, education, IQ, and socioeconomic status (Colby, Kohlberg, Gibbs, & Lieberman, 1983). However, a Canadian study of children's judgments about laws and lawbreaking suggests that children can reason flexibly about such issues at an earlier age than either Piaget or Kohlberg proposed. Even children as young as 6 weighed the perceived justice of a law, its social purpose, and its potential for infringement on individual freedoms and rights in evaluating whether the law was "good or bad" and whether or not it should be obeyed (Helwig & Jasiobedzka, 2001).

Furthermore, research has generally noted the lack of a clear relationship between moral reasoning and moral behavior. People at postconventional levels of reasoning do not necessarily act more morally than those at lower levels (Colby & Damon, 1992; Kupfersmid & Wonderly, 1980). Perhaps one problem is the remoteness from young people's experience of such dilemmas as the "Heinz" situation. On the other hand, juvenile delinquents (particularly boys) consistently show developmental delays in Kohlbergian tests of moral reasoning (Gregg, Gibbs, & Basinger, 1994).

Critics claim that a cognitive approach to moral development gives insufficient attention to the importance of emotion. Moral activity, they say, is motivated not only by abstract considerations of justice, but by such emotions as empathy, guilt, and distress and the internalization of prosocial norms (Gibbs, 1991, 1995; Gibbs & Schnell, 1985).

Some theorists today seek to synthesize Kohlberg's cognitive-developmental approach with the role of emotion and the insights of socialization theory (Gibbs, 1991, 1995; Gibbs & Schnell, 1985). Kohlberg himself did recognize that noncognitive factors such as emotional development and life experience affect moral judgments. One reason the ages attached to Kohlberg's levels are so variable is that people who have achieved a high level of cognitive development do not always reach a comparably high level of moral development. A certain level of cognitive development is *necessary* but not *sufficient* for a comparable level of moral development. Thus other processes besides cognition must be at work.

What's Your View?

- Kohlberg's method of assessing moral development by evaluating participants' reactions to moral dilemmas is widely used. Does this seem to you the most appropriate method? Why or why not? Can you suggest an alternative measure?
- Can you think of a time when you acted contrary to your own moral judgment? Why do you think this happened?

Family Influences Neither Piaget nor Kohlberg considered parents important to children's moral development. More recent research, however, emphasizes parents' contribution in both the cognitive and the emotional realms.

In one study, parents of 63 students in grades 1, 4, 7, and 10 were asked to talk with their children about hypothetical and real dilemmas (L. J. Walker & Taylor, 1991). The children and adolescents who, during the next two years, showed the greatest progress through Kohlberg's stages were those whose parents had used humor and praise, listened to them, and asked their opinions. These parents had asked clarifying questions, reworded answers, and checked to be sure the children understood the issues. They reasoned with their children at a slightly higher level than the children were currently at, much as in the method of scaffolding. The children who advanced the least were those whose parents had lectured them or challenged or contradicted their opinions.

Validity for Women and Girls Carol Gilligan (1982) has argued that Kohlberg's theory is oriented toward values more important to men than to women. According to

Gilligan, women see morality not so much in terms of justice and fairness as of responsibility to show care and avoid harm.

Research has not supported Gilligan's claim of a male bias in Kohlberg's stages; and she has since modified her position, suggesting that both men and women value an "ethic of care" (see Chapter 13). However, some research has found gender differences in moral judgments in early adolescence, with girls scoring *higher* than boys (Garmon, Basinger, Gregg, & Gibbs, 1996; Skoe & Gooden, 1993). This may be because girls generally mature earlier and have more intimate social relationships (Garmon et al., 1996; Skoe & Diessner, 1994). Early adolescent girls do tend to emphasize care-related concerns more than boys do, especially when tested with open-ended questions ("How important is it to keep promises to a friend?") or self-chosen moral dilemmas related to their own experience (Garmon et al., 1996).

Cross-cultural Validity Cross-cultural studies support Kohlberg's sequence of stages—up to a point. Older people from countries other than the United States do tend to score at higher stages than younger people. However, people in nonwestern cultures rarely score above stage 4 (Edwards, 1981; Nisan & Kohlberg, 1982; Snarey, 1985). Does this mean that these cultures do not foster higher moral development? It seems more likely that some aspects of Kohlberg's definition of morality may not fit the cultural values of some societies.

When Kohlberg's dilemmas were tested in India, Buddhist monks from Ladakh, a Tibetan enclave, scored lower than laypeople. Apparently Kohlberg's model, while capturing the preconventional and conventional elements of Buddhist thinking, was inadequate for understanding postconventional Buddhist principles of cooperation and nonviolence (Gielen & Kelly, 1983). It also has been argued that stages 5 and 6 cannot fairly be called the most mature stages of moral development, since they restrict "maturity" to a select group of people who are given to philosophical reflection (Gibbs, 1995).

Kohlberg's own view was that before people can develop a fully principled morality, they must recognize the relativity of moral standards. Many young people question their earlier views about morality when they enter high school or college or the world of work and encounter people whose values, culture, and ethnic background are different from their own. They begin to understand that every society evolves its own definitions of right and wrong; in some cases, the values of one culture may even seem shocking to members of another. For example, the practice of circumcising girls before puberty, or *female genital mutilation*—widely practiced in some parts of the world as a way of preserving virginity before marriage, reducing sexual appetite, enhancing beauty, and affirming femininity—has been condemned as harmful and abusive by the American Medical Association and World Health Organization but continues to be practiced in many cultures (AAP, 1998; Council on Scientific Affairs, 1995; Samad, 1996).

Checkpoint

Can you . . .

- ✔ List Kohlberg's levels and stages, and discuss factors that influence how rapidly children progress through them?
- ✔ Evaluate Kohlberg's theory in the light of more recent research, especially with regard to family influences, gender, and cultural validity?

Educational and Vocational Issues

School is a central organizing experience in most adolescents' lives. It offers opportunities to learn information, master new skills, and sharpen old ones; to participate in sports, the arts, and other activities; to explore vocational choices; and to be with friends. It widens intellectual and social horizons. Some adolescents, however, experience school not as an opportunity but as one more hindrance on the road to adulthood.

Guidepost

6. What influences affect school success, and why do some students drop out?

Let's examine influences on school achievement and at how adolescents divide their time among school, work, and other activities. Then we'll look at why some young people drop out of school, and what penalties they and society pay. Finally, we'll consider planning for higher education and vocations.

Influences on School Achievement

In the year 2000, 88 percent of Americans ages 25 to 29 had completed high school, as compared with only 71 percent in 1971 (National Center for Education Statistics [NCES], 2001). As in the elementary grades, such factors as socioeconomic status, the quality of the home environment, and parental involvement continue to influence the course of school achievement. In a longitudinal study of 174 disadvantaged children, these factors, as measured in first grade, closely predicted improvement or deterioration in academic performance by age 16 (Jimerson, Egeland, & Teo, 1999). Other factors include peer influence, quality of schooling, and—perhaps most important—students' (and parents') belief in their ability to succeed.

Self-Efficacy Beliefs and Academic Motivation According to Albert Bandura (Bandura et al., 1996; Zimmerman et al., 1992), students who are high in *self-efficacy*—who believe that they can master academic material and regulate their own learning—are more likely to try to achieve and more likely to succeed than students who do not believe in their own abilities.

Self-regulated learners set challenging goals and use appropriate strategies to achieve them. They try hard, persist in the face of difficulties, and seek help when necessary. Students who do not believe in their ability to succeed tend to become frustrated and depressed—feelings that make success harder to attain.

In one study that found a link between self-efficacy beliefs and academic achievement, 116 ninth- and tenth-graders of various ethnic backgrounds in two eastern high schools answered a questionnaire about their ability to learn and to regulate their own learning (Zimmerman et al., 1992). They were asked such questions as: How well can you finish homework assignments by deadlines? Concentrate on school subjects? Use the library to get information? Plan and organize your schoolwork? Motivate yourself to do schoolwork? Participate in class discussions?

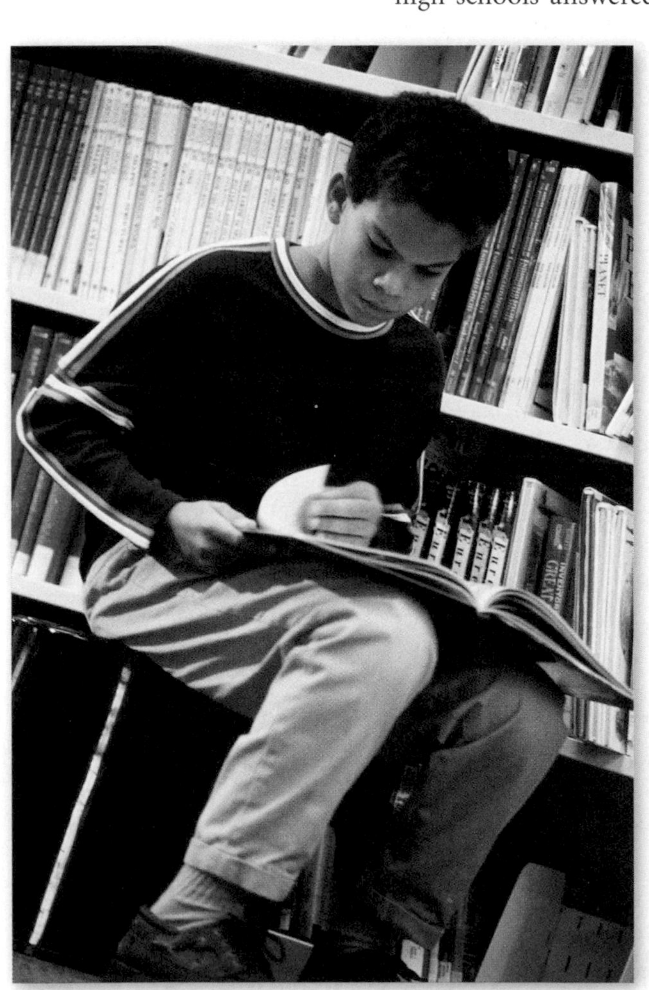

Adolescents who take responsibility for their own learning, like this boy doing library research, are most likely to get good grades.

The students' perceived self-efficacy predicted the social studies grades they hoped for, expected, and actually achieved. Students' goals were influenced by their parents' goals for them, but students' beliefs about their own abilities seemed more important. The message is clear: if parents want their children to do well in school, they must see that children have learning experiences that build a belief in their ability to succeed.

Several factors, including parental beliefs and practices, socioeconomic status, and peer influence, affect parents' power to strengthen children's achievement. Parents' own perceived self-efficacy—their belief in their ability to promote their children's academic growth—affects their success in doing so. Parents who are economically secure and who have high aspirations for their children and a strong sense of parental efficacy tend to have children with high academic goals and achievement (Bandura et al., 1996).

Peer influence may explain the downward trend in academic motivation and achievement that begins for many students in early adolescence. In a longitudinal study of students entering an urban middle school after sixth grade, motivation and grades declined, on average, during the seventh-grade year. However, students whose peer group were high achievers showed less decline in achievement and enjoyment of school, while those who associated with low achievers showed greater declines. This was true for both boys and girls across ethnic groups (Ryan, 2001).

Use of Time Academic motivation and efficacy beliefs may affect the way adolescents use their time. Some seem so busy with extracurricular activities, household chores, and outside work that it seems a wonder that they can also get good grades. Yet many can and do, while others who seem to have plenty of time on their hands do not do so well.

In a four-year longitudinal study of 1,010 randomly selected ninth-graders in the St. Paul, Minnesota, public schools (Shanahan & Flaherty, 2001), students annually filled out questionnaires about how much time they spent on school, home, and social activities, and how much (if any) on paid work. The students also were asked about their plans for the future and their attitudes toward various aspects of their present and future lives.

Although patterns of time use shifted somewhat from year to year, more than half of the students were consistently active in a number of areas: homework, other school activities, time with friends, household chores, and in some cases, paid work, such as baby-sitting and yard work. These young people tended to do well in school and to have more ambitious plans for future schooling, marriage, occupation, and citizenship than those who showed fewer commitments. Students with more limited involvements and less engagement in school tended to have less ambitious educational and occupational plans, less optimism about their prospects for marriage, and less interest in responsible citizenship, whether or not they had outside employment.

Socioeconomic Status and the Family Environment Socioeconomic status can be a powerful factor in educational achievement through its influence on family atmosphere, on choice of neighborhood, and on parents' way of rearing children (National Research Council [NRC], 1993a). Children of poor, uneducated parents are more likely to experience negative family and school atmospheres and stressful events (Felner et al., 1995). The neighborhood a family can afford generally determines the quality of schooling and opportunities for higher education; and the availability of such opportunities, together with attitudes in the neighborhood peer group, affects motivation.

Still, many young people from disadvantaged neighborhoods do well in school and improve their condition in life. What may make the difference is *social capital:* the family and community resources children and adolescents can draw upon. Parents who invest time and effort in their children and who have a strong network of community support build the family's social capital (J. S. Coleman, 1988).

In a twenty-year study of 252 children born to mostly poor and African American teenage mothers in Baltimore, those who—regardless of parents' income, education, and employment—had more social capital were more likely by the end of adolescence to have completed high school and in some cases to have gone to college, or to have entered the labor force and to be enjoying stable incomes (Furstenberg & Hughes, 1995).

Parental Involvement and Parenting Styles Parents can affect their children's educational achievement by becoming involved in their children's schooling: acting as advocates for their children and impressing teachers with the seriousness of the family's educational goals (Bandura et al., 1996). Students whose parents are closely involved in their school lives and monitor their progress fare best in high school (National Center for Education Statistics [NCES], 1985).

Even though adolescents are more independent than younger children, the home atmosphere continues to influence school achievement. Parents help not only by monitoring homework but by taking an active interest in other aspects of teenagers' lives. Children of authoritative parents, who discuss issues openly and offer praise and encouragement, tend to do best in school.

Parenting style can make a difference. Research has consistently found that the benefits of authoritative parenting continue during adolescence. *Authoritative parents* urge adolescents to look at both sides of issues, admit that children sometimes know more than parents, and welcome their participation in family decisions. These parents strike a balance between making demands and being responsive. Their children receive praise and privileges for good grades; poor grades bring encouragement to try harder and offers of help.

Authoritarian parents, by contrast, tell adolescents not to argue with or question adults and tell them they will "know better when they are grown up." Good grades bring admonitions to do even better; poor grades upset the parents, who may punish by reducing allowances or "grounding." *Permissive parents* seem not to care about grades, make no rules about watching television, do not attend school functions, and neither help with nor check their children's homework. These parents may not be neglectful or uncaring, but simply convinced that teenagers should be responsible for their own lives.

Among about 6,400 California high school students, children of authoritative parents tended to do better in school than children of authoritarian and permissive parents (Dornbusch, Ritter, Leiderman, Roberts, & Fraleigh, 1987; Steinberg & Darling, 1994; Steinberg, Lamborn, Dornbusch, & Darling, 1992). Adolescents raised authoritatively not only achieve better academically but are more socially competent, are more emotionally healthy, and show fewer behavior problems than children raised in an authoritarian or permissive manner (Glasgow, Dornbusch, Troyer, Steinberg, & Ritter, 1997).

What accounts for the academic success of authoritatively raised adolescents? Authoritative parents' greater involvement in schooling may be a factor, as well as their encouragement of positive attitudes toward work. A more subtle mechanism, consistent with Bandura's findings on self-efficacy, may be parents' influence on how children explain success or failure. In a study of 2,353 students at six high schools in California and three high schools in Wisconsin, youngsters who saw their parents as nonauthoritative were more likely than their peers to attribute poor grades to external causes or to low ability—forces beyond their control—rather than to their own efforts. A year later, such students tended to pay less attention in class and to spend less time on homework (Glasgow et al., 1997). Thus a sense of helplessness associated with nonauthoritative parenting may become a self-fulfilling prophecy, discouraging students from trying to succeed.

The findings about the value of authoritative parenting do *not* seem to hold true among some ethnic and cultural groups. In one study, Latino and African American students—even those with authoritative parents—did not do as well as white students, apparently because of lack of peer support for academic achievement (Steinberg, Dornbusch, & Brown, 1992). On the other hand, Asian American students, whose parents are sometimes described as authoritarian, get high grades and score higher than white students on math achievement tests, apparently because they like math and because both parents *and* peers prize achievement. In addition, Asian Americans tend to go to good schools and take challenging courses. They spend more time studying than white students and less time socializing with friends, and they are less likely to hold outside jobs (C. Chen & Stevenson, 1995).

Among some ethnic groups, then, parenting styles may be less important than other factors that affect motivation. Young people who are interested in what they are learning and whose parents and peers value education are more motivated to succeed. The strong school achievement of many first- and second-generation young people from immigrant backgrounds—not only Asian, but also Filipino, Mexican, and European—reflects their families' and friends' strong emphasis on and support of educational success (Fuligni, 1997).

Checkpoint

Can you . . .

- ✔ Explain how self-efficacy beliefs can contribute to adolescents' motivation to learn?
- ✔ Assess the influences of parents, teachers, and peers on academic achievement?
- ✔ Discuss ethnic differences in attitudes toward school?

School Factors The quality of a school strongly influences student achievement. A good high school has an orderly, unoppressive atmosphere; an active, energetic principal; and teachers who take part in making decisions. Principal and teachers have high expectations for students, emphasize academics more than extracurricular activities, and closely monitor student performance (Linney & Seidman, 1989).

Students who like their school do better academically and also are healthier. Adolescents, particularly boys, in most western industrialized countries like school less than younger children. Adolescents are more satisfied with school if they are allowed to participate in making rules and feel support from teachers and other students (Samdal & Dür, 2000).

Schools that tailor teaching to students' abilities get better results than schools that try to teach all students in the same way. Research on Sternberg's triarchic theory of intelligence (refer back to Chapter 9) found that students high in practical or creative intelligence do better when taught in a way that allows them to capitalize on those strengths and compensate for their weaknesses (Sternberg, 1997). Indeed, a combination of teaching styles may be most effective for all students. In an experiment in teaching psychology to gifted eighth-graders, groups whose teachers used methods that tap creative and practical abilities as well as analysis and memory did better, even on multiple-choice tests, than groups taught by traditional memory-based or critical thinking approaches alone (Sternberg, Torff, & Grigorenko, 1998).

Asian American students tend to do well in school because both they and their parents and friends seriously value learning and achievement.

Some big-city school systems, such as New York's, Philadelphia's, and Chicago's, are experimenting with small schools (either freestanding or within larger schools)—small enough for students, teachers, and parents to form a learning community. The curriculum may have a special focus, such as ethnic studies. Teaching is flexible, innovative, and personalized; teachers work together closely and get to know students well (Meier, 1995; Rossi, 1996). In Central Park East, a complex of four small, ethnically diverse elementary and secondary schools in New York's East Harlem, 90 percent of the students finish high school and nine out of ten of those go on to college, as compared with an average citywide graduation rate of 50 percent (Meier, 1995).

Dropping out of High School

Historically in the United States, education has been the ticket to economic and social advancement. However, for some students, school does not serve this vital purpose. Society suffers when young people do not finish school. Dropouts are more likely to be unemployed or to have low incomes, to end up on welfare, and to become involved with drugs, crime, and delinquency. In addition, the loss of taxable income burdens the public treasury (NCES, 1987, 1999, 2001). What can be done to prevent dropouts?

In 1999, 11 percent of 16- to 24-year-olds had dropped out of high school. Hispanic students are more likely to drop out than African Americans, who are more likely to drop out than non-Hispanic whites (NCES, 2001). Hispanic immigrants have the highest rates, but even Hispanics born in the United States have higher rates than the other two groups.

Dropout and high school completion rates vary among states. In 1999–2000, among thirty-three states reporting sufficient data, completion rates ranged from 89.3 percent in Wisconsin to 62.6 in Louisiana. Most states reported annual dropout rates ranging from 4 to 6 percent (Young, 2002).

Low-income students are much more likely to drop out than middle- or high-income students (NCES, 1999). The higher dropout rates among minority groups living in poverty may stem in part from the poor quality of their schools as compared with those attended by more advantaged children. Among other possible reasons for the high Latino dropout rates are language difficulties, financial pressures, and a culture that puts family first, since these students often leave school to help support their families (U.S. Department of Education, 1992).

What's Your View?

- How can parents, educators, and societal institutions encourage young people to finish high school?

Students in single-parent and remarried households—even relatively affluent ones—are more likely to drop out than students living with both parents (Finn & Rock, 1997; Zimiles & Lee, 1991). Frequent moves may contribute to the effects of family instability, and changing schools may reduce a family's social capital. Families that move a lot generally have weaker social connections, know less about the children's school, and are less able to make wise decisions about schooling (Teachman, Paasch, & Carver, 1996).

Preschool experience—or the lack of it—may set the stage for high school success or failure. In the Chicago longitudinal study mentioned earlier, young people who had been in a high-quality early childhood education program were less likely to be held back or to drop out of high school (Temple, Reynolds, & Miedel, 2000).

Time use can be an index of risk for dropping out of school. In the St. Paul time use study reported in a previous section, 65 percent of young people who dropped out of school before eleventh grade had no extracurricular activities and spent little time on homework, even though they did not have outside jobs. On the other hand, *full-time* work (25 to 40 hours a week) was a risk factor. One-third of all eleventh-grade dropouts and half of all twelfth-grade dropouts had begun working full time by eleventh grade (Shanahan & Flaherty, 2001).

Time use is one way of looking at the key factor of **active engagement,** or involvement in schooling. On the most basic level, active engagement means coming to class on time, being prepared, listening and responding to the teacher, and obeying school rules. A second level of engagement consists of getting involved with the coursework—asking questions, taking the initiative to seek help when needed, or doing extra projects. Both levels of active engagement tend to pay off in positive school performance by at-risk students (Finn & Rock, 1997). Students who participate in extracurricular activities also are less likely to drop out (Mahoney, 2000).

active engagement
Involvement in schooling.

What factors promote active engagement? Family encouragement is undoubtedly one. Others may be small class size and a warm, supportive school environment. Since engaged or alienated behavior patterns tend to be set early in a child's school career, dropout prevention should start early, too (Finn & Rock, 1997).

Checkpoint

Can you . . .

- ✔ Give examples of educational practices that help high school students do better?
- ✔ Discuss factors that promote or discourage dropping out of school?

Educational and Vocational Preparation

How do young people develop career goals? How do they decide whether or not to go to college and, if not, how to enter the world of work? Many factors enter in, including individual ability and personality, education, socioeconomic and ethnic background, the advice of school counselors, life experiences, and societal values. Let's look at some influences on educational and vocational aspirations. Then we'll look at what provisions exist for young people who do not plan to go to college.

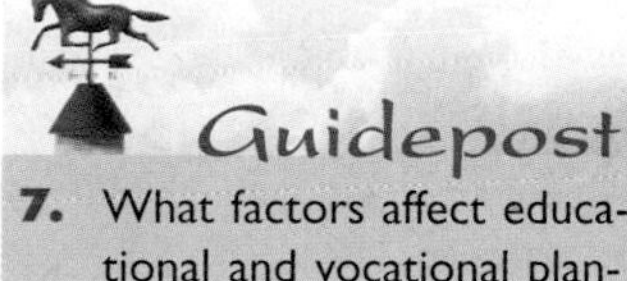

7. What factors affect educational and vocational planning and preparation?

Influences on Students' Aspirations Students' self-efficacy beliefs—their confidence in their educational and vocational prospects—shape the occupational options they consider and the way they prepare for careers. These beliefs and aspirations are often influenced by parents' own self-efficacy beliefs and aspirations (Bandura, Barbaranelli, Caprara, & Pastorelli, 2001; Bandura et al., 1996). Parents' values regarding academic achievement influence adolescents' values and occupational goals (Jodl, Michael, Malanchuk, Eccles, & Sameroff, 2001).

Gender also may have an influence. A 1992 report by the American Association of University Women [AAUW] Educational Foundation claimed that schools shortchange girls by steering them away from science and math and into gender-typed pursuits. Six years later, a follow-up study (AAUW Educational Foundation, 1998a, 1998b) reported that girls were taking more science and math than before and doing better in those subjects. According to the National Center for Education Statistics (1997), male and female high school seniors are now equally likely to plan careers in math or science, although boys are much more likely to expect to go into engineering. Boys take fewer English classes and lag in communications skills (AAUW Educational Foundation, 1998b; Weinman, 1998).

The educational system itself may act as a subtle brake on vocational aspirations. The relatively narrow range of abilities valued in many schools gives certain students the inside track. Students who can memorize and analyze tend to do well on intelligence tests and in classrooms where teaching is geared to those abilities. Thus, as predicted by the tests, these students are achievers in a system that stresses the abilities in which they excel.

Meanwhile, students whose strength is in creative or practical thinking—areas critical to success in certain fields—never get a chance to show what they can do. They may be frozen out of career paths or forced into less challenging and rewarding ones because of test scores and grades too low to put them on track to success (Sternberg, 1997). Recognition of a broader range of "intelligences" (see Chapter 9), combined with more flexible teaching and career counseling, could allow more students to get the education and enter the occupations they desire and to make the contributions of which they are capable.

Guiding Students Not Bound for College About 37 percent of high school graduates in the United States do not immediately go on to college (NCES, 2001). Yet most vocational counseling in high schools is oriented toward college-bound youth.

Most industrialized countries offer some kind of structured guidance to non-college-bound students. Germany, for example, has an apprenticeship system, in which high school students go to school part time and spend the rest of the week in paid on-the-job training supervised by an employer-mentor (Hopfensperger, 1996).

In the United States, whatever vocational training programs do exist tend to be less comprehensive and less closely tied to the needs of businesses and industries. Most young people get training on the job or in community college courses. Many, ignorant about the job market, do not obtain needed skills. Others take jobs beneath their abilities. Some do not find work at all (NRC, 1993a).

In some communities, demonstration programs help in the school-to-work transition. The most successful ones offer instruction in basic skills, counseling, peer support, mentoring, apprenticeship, and job placement (NRC, 1993a). In 1994, Congress passed the School to Work Opportunities Act, which allocated $1.1 billion to help states and local governments develop vocational training programs.

What's Your View?

- Would you favor an apprenticeship program like Germany's in the United States? How successful do you think it would be in helping young people make realistic career plans? What negative effects, if any, might it have?
- Did you work full or part time in high school? If so, do you feel the effects on your schoolwork and occupational prospects were primarily positive or negative, and why?

Should High School Students Work Part Time? Many high school students hold part-time jobs. This may be financially necessary in many families, and it fits in with a basic American belief in the benefits of work. Paid work may teach young people to handle money, develop good work habits, manage time, and assume responsibility. It can help a student learn workplace skills, such as how to find a job. It may build confidence, independence, and status with peers. By helping them learn more about a particular field of work, it may guide them in choosing careers (Elder & Caspi, 1990; Mortimer, 2003; Mortimer & Shanahan, 1991; National Commission on Youth, 1980; Phillips & Sandstrom, 1990; Steel, 1991). Also, by showing adolescents how demanding and difficult the world of work is and how unprepared they are for it, part-time jobs sometimes motivate young people to stay in school longer.

On the other hand, most high school students who work part time have low-level, repetitive jobs in which they do not learn skills useful later in life. According to some research, teenagers who work are no more independent in making financial decisions and are unlikely to earn any more money as adults than those who do not hold jobs during high school. By assuming adult burdens they are not yet ready to deal with, young people may miss out on the opportunity to explore their interests and to develop close relationships. Outside work may require a stressful juggling of other commitments and cut down on involvement in school (Greenberger & Steinberg, 1986). More than fifteen to twenty hours of work a week may undermine school performance and increase the likelihood of dropping out (Larson & Verma, 1999; NCES, 1987).

Paid work can have other hidden costs. Young people who work long hours are less likely to eat breakfast, exercise, get enough sleep, or have enough leisure time (Bachman & Schulenberg, 1993). They spend less time with their families and may feel less close to them. Some teenagers take jobs because they are uninterested in school or feel alienated from their families. Some spend their earnings on alcohol or drugs (Greenberger & Steinberg, 1986; Steinberg, Fegley, & Dornbusch, 1993).

However, some of the alleged harmful effects of work may be overstated (Mortimer, 2003). In the St. Paul time use study, most of the students who worked were also heavily engaged in school and other activities (Shanahan & Flaherty, 2001). According to students' self-reports, the number of hours a student worked did not seem to reduce self-esteem, mental health, or mastery motivation. Working had no effect on homework time or grades until senior year, when students who worked more than twenty hours a week tended to do less homework than other students. Even so, their grades and achievement motivation did not suffer. And students who worked *fewer* hours had *higher* grades than those who did not work at all. Working was not related to smoking or behavioral problems at school. However, working more than twenty hours a week *was* associated with increased alcohol use (Mortimer, Finch, Ryu, Shanahan, & Call, 1996). Another study of more than 12,000 randomly selected seventh- through twelfth-graders nationwide (also based largely on self-reports) found that teenagers who work twenty or more hours a week are more likely to feel stress, to smoke, drink, or use marijuana, and to begin sexual activity early (Resnick et al., 1997).

This research does not give a definitive answer as to whether outside work is good or bad for adolescents. For one thing, the data come entirely from self-reports, which are always subjective. Furthermore, these studies address only how *much* young people work, and not the quality of their work experience. Other studies suggest that such factors as advancement opportunity, the chance to learn useful skills, and the kinds of responsibilities adolescents have at work may determine whether the experience is positive or negative (Call, Mortimer, & Shanahan, 1995; Finch, Shanahan, Mortimer, & Ryu, 1991; Shanahan, Finch, Mortimer, & Ryu, 1991).

Checkpoint

Can you . . .

- ✔ Discuss influences on educational and vocational planning?
- ✔ Describe programs for non-college-bound students?
- ✔ Give evidence for and against the value of part-time work for adolescents?

Refocus

- What typical pubertal changes did Anne Frank's diary describe? How did these changes affect Anne psychologically?
- What evidence did Anne show of cognitive maturation and moral development?
- In what ways might Anne's development have been similar, and in what ways different, under normal circumstances?

Vocational planning is one aspect of an adolescent's search for identity. The question "What shall I do?" is very close to "Who shall I be?" People who feel they are doing something worthwhile, and doing it well, feel good about themselves. Those who feel that their work does not matter—or that they are not good at it—may wonder about the meaning of their lives. A prime personality issue in adolescence, which we discuss in Chapter 12, is the effort to define the self.

SUMMARY AND KEY TERMS

Adolescence: A Developmental Transition

Guidepost 1. What is adolescence, when does it begin and end, and what opportunities and risks does it entail?

- Adolescence, in modern industrial societies, is the transition from childhood to adulthood. It lasts from age 11 or 12 until the late teens or early twenties.
- Legal, sociological, and psychological definitions of entrance into adulthood vary.
- Adolescence is full of opportunities for physical, cognitive, and psychosocial growth, but also of risks to healthy development. Risky behavior patterns, such as drinking alcohol, drug abuse, sexual and gang activity, and use of firearms, tend to be established early in adolescence. About four out of five young people experience no major problems.

adolescence *(387)*

puberty *(387)*

PHYSICAL DEVELOPMENT

Puberty: The End of Childhood

Guidepost 2. What physical changes do adolescents experience, and how do these changes affect them psychologically?

- Puberty is triggered by hormonal changes, which may affect moods and behavior. Puberty takes about four years, typically begins earlier in girls than in boys, and ends when a person can reproduce. A secular trend toward earlier attainment of adult height and sexual maturity began about 100 years ago, probably because of improvements in living standards.
- During puberty, both boys and girls undergo an adolescent growth spurt. Primary sex characteristics (the reproductive organs) enlarge and mature, and secondary sex characteristics appear.
- The principal signs of sexual maturity are production of sperm (for males) and menstruation (for females). Spermarche typically occurs at age 13. Menarche occurs, on average, between the ages of 12 and 13 in the United States.
- Psychological effects of early or late maturation depend on how adolescents and others interpret the accompanying changes.

secular trend *(389)*

adolescent growth spurt *(390)*

primary sex characteristics *(391)*

secondary sex characteristics *(391)*

spermarche *(392)*

menarche *(392)*

Physical and Mental Health

Guidepost 3. What are some common health problems in adolescence, and how can they be prevented?

- For the most part, the adolescent years are relatively healthy. Health problems often are associated with poverty or a risk-taking lifestyle. Adolescents are less likely than younger children to get regular medical care.
- Many adolescents, especially girls, do not engage in regular, vigorous physical activity.
- Many adolescents do not get enough sleep, in part because the high school schedule is out of sync with their natural body rhythms.
- Concern with body image often leads to obsessive dieting.
- Three common eating disorders in adolescence are obesity, anorexia nervosa, and bulimia nervosa. All can have serious long-term effects. Anorexia and bulimia affect mostly girls. Outcomes for bulimia tend to be better than for anorexia.
- Adolescent substance abuse and dependence have lessened in recent years; still, drug use often begins as children move into middle school.
- Marijuana, alcohol, and tobacco are the most popular drugs with adolescents and can be gateways to the use of hard drugs.
- The prevalence of depression increases in adolescence, especially among girls.
- Leading causes of death among adolescents include motor vehicle accidents, firearm use, and suicide.

body image *(396)*

anorexia nervosa *(396)*

bulimia nervosa *(397)*

gateway drugs *(399)*

COGNITIVE DEVELOPMENT

Aspects of Cognitive Maturation

Guidepost 4. How do adolescents' thinking and use of language differ from younger children's?

- People in Piaget's stage of formal operations can engage in hypothetical-deductive reasoning. They can think in terms of possibilities, deal flexibly with problems, and test hypotheses.
- Brain maturation and environmental stimulation play important parts in attaining this stage. Schooling and culture also play a role.
- Not all people become capable of formal operations; and those who are capable do not always use it.
- Piaget's theory does not take into account accumulation of knowledge and expertise and the growth of metacognition. Piaget also paid little attention to individual differences, between-task variations, and the role of the situation.
- Vocabulary and other aspects of language development, especially those related to abstract thought, improve in adolescence. Adolescents enjoy wordplay and create their own "dialect."
- According to Elkind, immature thought patterns can result from adolescents' inexperience with formal thinking. These thought patterns include idealism and criticalness, argumentativeness, indecisiveness, apparent hypocrisy, self-consciousness, and an assumption of specialness and invulnerability. Research has cast doubt on the special prevalence of the latter two patterns during adolescence.

formal operations *(402)*

hypothetical-deductive reasoning *(403)*

imaginary audience *(407)*

personal fable *(407)*

Guidepost 5. On what basis do adolescents make moral judgments?

- According to Kohlberg, moral reasoning is based on a developing sense of justice and growing cognitive abilities. Kohlberg proposed that moral development progresses from external control to internalized societal standards to personal, principled moral codes.
- Kohlberg's theory has been criticized on several grounds, including failure to credit the roles of emotion, socialization, and parental guidance. The applicability of Kohlberg's system to women and girls and to people in nonwestern cultures has been questioned.

preconventional morality *(408)*

conventional morality *(408)*

postconventional morality *(408)*

Educational and Vocational Issues

Guidepost 6. What influences affect school success, and why do some students drop out?

- Self-efficacy beliefs, academic motivation, socioeconomic status, parental involvement, parenting styles, ethnicity, peer influences, and quality of schooling affect adolescents' educational achievement. Poor families whose children do well in school tend to have more social capital than poor families whose children do not do well.
- Although most Americans graduate from high school, the dropout rate is higher among poor minority students and among those not living with both parents. Active engagement in studies is an important factor in keeping adolescents in school.

active engagement *(417)*

Guidepost 7. What factors affect educational and vocational planning and preparation?

- Educational and vocational aspirations are influenced by several factors, including students' and parents' self-efficacy beliefs and parents' values and aspirations. Gender stereotypes still have an influence, but less so than in the past.
- High school graduates who do not immediately go on to college can benefit from vocational training.
- Part-time work seems to have both positive and negative effects on educational, social, and occupational development.

Chapter 12

Psychosocial Development in Adolescence

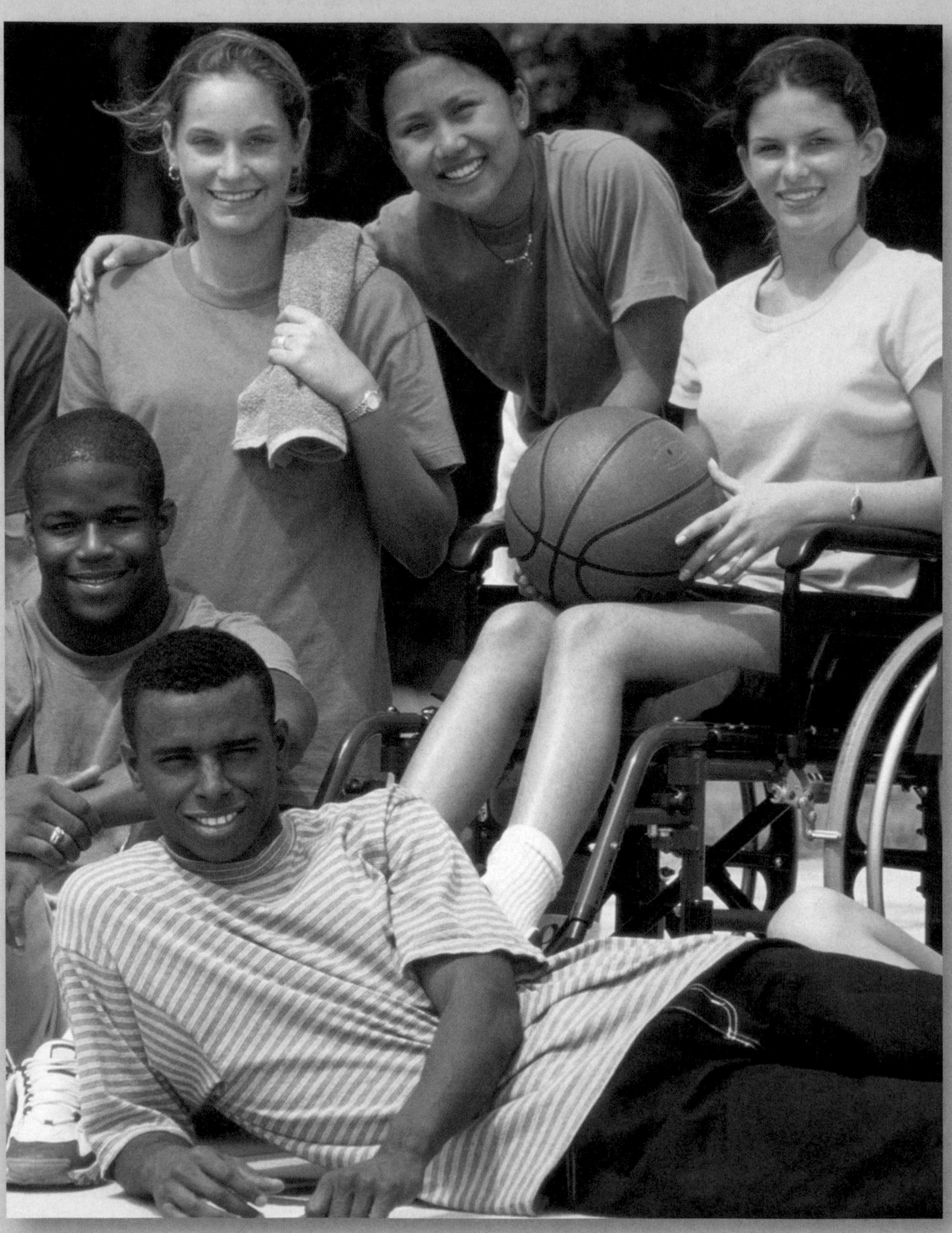

This face in the mirror
stares at me
demanding *Who are you? What will you become?*
And taunting, *You don't even know.*
Chastened, I cringe and agree
and then
because I'm still young,
I stick out my tongue.

—Eve Merriam, "Conversation with Myself," 1964

Focus: Jackie Robinson, Baseball Legend*

Jackie Robinson

On April 15, 1947, when 28-year-old Jack Roosevelt ("Jackie") Robinson (1919–1972) put on a Brooklyn Dodgers uniform and strode onto Ebbets Field, he became the first African American in the twentieth century to play major league baseball. By the end of a spectacular first season in which he was named Rookie of the Year, Robinson's name had become a household word. Two years later, he was voted baseball's Most Valuable Player. During his ten years with the Dodgers, the team won six pennants, and Robinson played in six consecutive All-Star games. After his retirement, he won first-ballot election to the Hall of Fame.

His triumph did not come easily. When the Dodgers' manager, Branch Rickey, decided to bring Robinson up from the Negro Leagues, several players petitioned to keep him off the team. But Robinson's athletic prowess and dignified demeanor in the face of racist jibes, threats, hate mail, and attempts at bodily harm won the respect of the baseball world. Within the next decade, most major league teams signed African American players. Baseball had become "one of the first institutions in modern society to accept blacks on a relatively equal basis" (Tygiel, 1983).

Behind the Jackie Robinson legend is the story of a prodigiously talented boy growing up in a nation in which opportunities for black youth were extremely limited. His grandfather had been a slave. Jackie's father, a Georgia sharecropper, abandoned his wife and five children when the boy was 6 months old. His mother, Mallie Robinson, was a determined, deeply religious

*Sources of biographical information about Jackie Robinson were Falkner (1995), Rampersad (1997), J. Robinson (1995), S. Robinson (1996), and Tygiel (1983, 1997).

OUTLINE

woman, who imbued her children with moral strength and pride. Intent on providing them with a good education, she moved her family to Pasadena, California. But Pasadena turned out to be almost as rigidly segregated as the Deep South.

Jackie Robinson lived for sports. He idolized his older brother Mack, who won a silver medal in the 1936 Olympics. By the time Jackie was in junior high school, he was a star in his own right. He also did odd jobs after school.

Still, he had time on his hands. He joined a street gang of poor black, Mexican, and Japanese boys who seethed with "a growing resentment at being deprived of some of the advantages the white kids had" (J. Robinson, 1995, p. 6). The gang's activities were serious enough to get them in trouble—throwing rocks at cars and street lamps, smashing windows, and swiping apples from fruitstands. But once they were taken to jail at gunpoint merely for swimming in the reservoir when they were not allowed entrance to the whites-only municipal pool.

Robinson later reflected that he "might have become a full-fledged juvenile delinquent" had it not been for the influence of two men. One was an auto mechanic, Carl Anderson, who pointed out that "it didn't take guts to follow the crowd, that courage and intelligence lay in being willing to be different" (J. Robinson, 1995, pp. 6–7). The other was a young African American minister, Karl Downs, who lured Robinson and his friends into church-sponsored athletics, listened to their worries, helped them find jobs, and got them to help build a youth center—"an alternative to hanging out on street corners" (J. Robinson, 1995, p. 8). Later, while in college, Robinson served as a volunteer Sunday school teacher at the church.

Adolescence is a time of both opportunities and risks. Teenagers are on the threshold of love, of life's work, and of participation in adult society. Yet adolescence is also a time when some young people engage in behavior that closes off their options and limits their possibilities. Today, research is increasingly focusing on how to help young people whose environments are not optimal to avoid hazards that can keep them from fulfilling their potential. What saved Jackie Robinson—in addition to the influence of his indomitable, hardworking mother, his older brothers, and his adult mentors—were his talent and his passion for athletics, which ultimately enabled him to channel his drive, energy, audacity, and rebellion against racism in a positive direction.

In Chapter 11 we looked at some physical and cognitive factors that contribute to an adolescent's sense of self, such as appearance and school achievement. In this chapter, we turn to psychosocial aspects of the quest for identity. We discuss how adolescents come to terms with their sexuality. We consider how teenagers' burgeoning individuality expresses itself in relationships with parents, siblings, and peers. We examine sources of antisocial behavior and ways of reducing the risks of adolescence so as to make it a time of positive growth and expanding possibilities.

After you have read and studied this chapter, you should be able to answer each of the following Guidepost questions. Look for them again in the margins, where they point to important concepts throughout the chapter. To check your understanding of these Guideposts, review the end-of-chapter summary. Checkpoints located at periodic spots throughout the chapter will help you verify your understanding of what you have read.

1. How do adolescents form an identity?
2. What determines sexual orientation?
3. What sexual practices are common among adolescents, and what leads some teenagers to engage in risky sexual behavior?
4. How common are sexually transmitted diseases and teenage pregnancy, and what are their usual outcomes?
5. How typical is "adolescent rebellion"?
6. How do adolescents relate to parents, siblings, and peers?
7. What are the root causes of antisocial behavior and juvenile delinquency, and what can be done to reduce these and other risks of adolescence?

Guideposts for Study

The Search for Identity

The search for **identity**—which Erikson defined as a coherent conception of the self, made up of goals, values, and beliefs to which the person is solidly committed—comes into focus during the teenage years. Adolescents' cognitive development now enables them to construct a "theory of the self" (Elkind, 1998). As Erikson (1950) emphasized, a teenager's effort to make sense of the self is not "a kind of maturational malaise." It is part of a healthy, vital process that builds on the achievements of earlier stages—on trust, autonomy, initiative, and industry—and lays the groundwork for coping with the psychosocial issues of adult life.

Guidepost

1. How do adolescents form an identity?

identity According to Erikson, a coherent conception of the self, made up of goals, values, and beliefs to which a person is solidly committed.

identity versus identity confusion Erikson's fifth stage of psychosocial development, in which an adolescent seeks to develop a coherent sense of self, including the role she or he is to play in society. Also called *identity versus role confusion.*

Erikson: Identity versus Identity Confusion

The chief task of adolescence, said Erikson (1968), is to resolve the "crisis" of **identity versus identity confusion** (or *identity versus role confusion*), so as to become a unique adult with a coherent sense of self and a valued role in society. This "identity crisis" is seldom fully resolved in adolescence; issues concerning identity crop up again and again throughout adult life.

According to Erikson, adolescents form their identity not by modeling themselves after other people, as younger children do, but by modifying and synthesizing earlier identifications into "a new psychological structure, greater than the sum of its parts" (Kroger, 1993, p. 3). To form an identity, adolescents must ascertain and organize their abilities, needs, interests, and desires so they can be expressed in a social context.

Erikson saw the prime danger of this stage as identity (or role) confusion, which can greatly delay reaching psychological adulthood. (He himself did not resolve his own identity crisis until his midtwenties.) Some degree of identity confusion is normal. It accounts for both the seemingly chaotic nature of much adolescent behavior and teenagers' painful self-consciousness. Cliquishness and intolerance of differences—both hallmarks of the adolescent social scene—are defenses against identity confusion. Adolescents also may show confusion by regressing into childishness to avoid resolving conflicts or by committing themselves impulsively to poorly thought-out courses of action.

Identity forms as young people resolve three major issues: the choice of an occupation, the adoption of values to believe in and live by, and the development of a satisfying sexual identity. During the crisis of middle childhood, that of *industry versus inferiority,* children acquire skills needed for success in their culture. Now, as adolescents, they need to find ways to use these skills. When young people have trouble settling on an occupational identity—or when their opportunities are artificially limited, as they were for Jackie Robinson and his friends—they are at risk of behavior with serious negative consequences, such as criminal activity or early pregnancy.

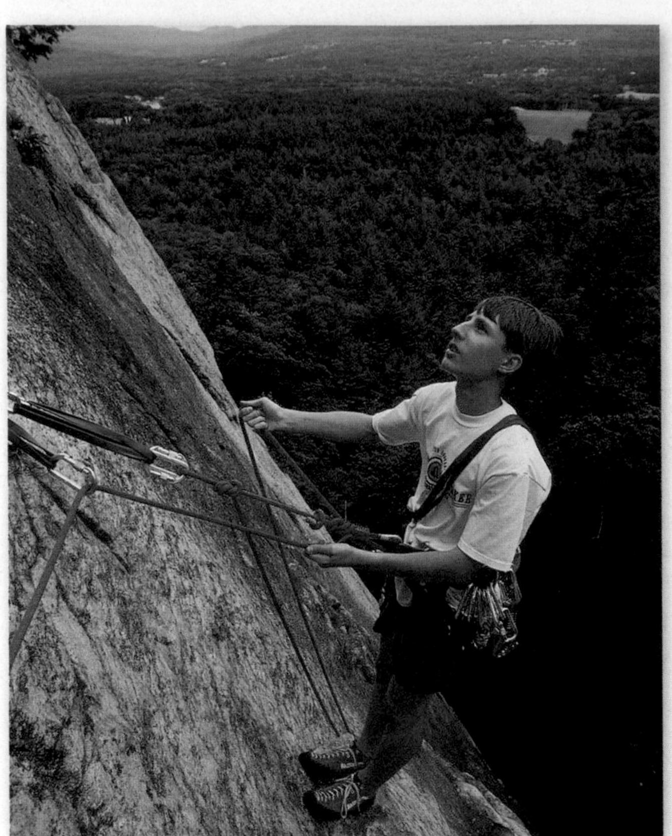

Mastering the challenge of rock climbing may help this adolescent boy assess his abilities, interests, and desires. According to Erikson, this process of self-assessment helps adolescents resolve the crisis of identity versus identity confusion.

During the *psychosocial moratorium*—the "time out" period that adolescence provides—many young people search for commitments to which they can be faithful. These youthful commitments may shape a person's life for years to come. Jackie Robinson's commitments were to develop his athletic potential and to help improve the position of African Americans in society. The extent to which young people remain faithful to commitments, as Robinson did, influences their ability to resolve the identity crisis. Adolescents who satisfactorily resolve that crisis develop the "virtue" of *fidelity:* sustained loyalty, faith, or a sense of belonging to a loved one or to friends and companions. Fidelity also can mean identification with a set of values, an ideology, a religion, a political movement, a creative pursuit, or an ethnic group (Erikson, 1982). Self-identification emerges when young people choose values and people to be loyal to, rather than simply accepting their parents' choices.

Fidelity is an extension of trust. In infancy, it is important for trust of parents to outweigh mistrust; in adolescence, it becomes important to be trustworthy oneself. In addition, adolescents now extend their trust to mentors or loved ones. In sharing thoughts and feelings, an adolescent clarifies a tentative identity by seeing it reflected in the eyes of the beloved. However, these adolescent "intimacies" differ from mature intimacy, which involves greater commitment, sacrifice, and compromise.

Erikson's theory describes male identity development as the norm. According to Erikson, a man is not capable of real intimacy until after he has achieved a stable identity, whereas women define themselves through marriage and motherhood (something that may have been truer when Erikson developed his theory than it is today). Thus, said Erikson, women (unlike men) develop identity *through* intimacy, not before it. As we'll see, this male orientation of Erikson's theory has prompted criticism. Still, Erikson's concept of the identity crisis has inspired much valuable research.

Marcia: Identity Status—Crisis and Commitment

Kate, Andrea, Nick, and Mark are all about to graduate from high school. Kate has considered her interests and her talents and plans to become an engineer. She has narrowed her college choices to three schools that offer good programs in this field.

Andrea knows exactly what she is going to do with her life. Her mother, a union leader at a plastics factory, has arranged for Andrea to enter an apprenticeship program there. Andrea has never considered doing anything else.

Nick, on the other hand, is agonizing over his future. Should he attend a community college or join the army? He cannot decide what to do now or what he wants to do eventually.

Mark still has no idea of what he wants to do, but he is not worried. He figures he can get some sort of a job and make up his mind about the future when he is ready.

These four young people are involved in identity formation. What accounts for the differences in the way they go about it, and how will these differences affect the outcome? According to research by the psychologist James E. Marcia (1966, 1980), these students are in four different states of ego (self) development, or **identity statuses,** which seem to be related to certain aspects of personality.

identity statuses Marcia's term for states of ego development that depend on the presence or absence of crisis and commitment.

Through thirty-minute, semistructured *identity-status interviews* (see Table 12-1), Marcia found four types of identity status: *identity achievement, foreclosure, moratorium,* and *identity diffusion.* The four categories differ according to the presence or absence of **crisis** and **commitment,** the two elements Erikson saw as crucial to forming identity. Marcia defines *crisis* as a period of conscious decision making, and *commitment* as a personal investment in an occupation or system of beliefs (ideology). He found relationships between identity status and such characteristics as anxiety, self-esteem, moral reasoning, and patterns of behavior. Building on Marcia's theory, other researchers have identified other personality and family variables related to identity status (see Table 12-2 on page 428). Here is a thumbnail sketch of people in each of the four identity statuses:

crisis Marcia's term for a period of conscious decision making related to identity formation.

commitment Marcia's term for personal investment in an occupation or system of beliefs.

1. **Identity achievement** *(crisis leading to commitment).* Kate has resolved her identity crisis. During the crisis period, she devoted much thought and some emotional struggle to major issues in her life. She has made choices and expresses strong commitment to them. Her parents have encouraged her to make her own decisions; they have listened to her ideas and given their opinions without pressuring her to adopt them. Kate is thoughtful but not so introspective as to be unable to act. She has a sense of humor, functions well under stress, is capable of intimate relationships, and holds to her standards while being open to new ideas. Research in a number of cultures has found people in this category to be more mature and more competent in relationships than people in the other three (Marcia, 1993).

identity achievement Identity status, described by Marcia, that is characterized by commitment to choices made following a crisis, a period spent in exploring alternatives.

Table 12-1 Identity-Status Interview

Sample Questions	Typical Answers for the Four Statuses
About occupational commitment. "How willing do you think you'd be to give up going into ______ if something better came along?"	*Identity achievement.* "Well, I might, but I doubt it. I can't see what 'something better' would be for me." *Foreclosure.* "Not very willing. It's what I've always wanted to do. The folks are happy with it and so am I." *Moratorium.* "I guess if I knew for sure, I could answer that better. It would have to be something in the general area—something related . . ." *Identity diffusion.* "Oh, sure. If something better came along, I'd change just like that."
About ideological commitment. "Have you ever had any doubts about your religious beliefs?"	*Identity achievement.* "Yes, I started wondering whether there is a God. I've pretty much resolved that now. The way it seems to me is . . ." *Foreclosure.* "No, not really; our family is pretty much in agreement on these things." *Moratorium.* "Yes, I guess I'm going through that now. I just don't see how there can be a God and still so much evil in the world . . ." *Identity diffusion.* "Oh, I don't know. I guess so. Everyone goes through some sort of stage like that. But it really doesn't bother me much. I figure that one religion is about as good as another!"

Source: Adapted from Marcia, 1966.

Table 12-2 Family and Personality Factors Associated with Adolescents in Four Identity Statuses*

Factor	Identity Achievement	Foreclosure	Moratorium	Identity Diffusion
Family	Parents encourage autonomy and connection with teachers; differences are explored within a context of mutuality.	Parents are overly involved with their children; families avoid expressing differences.	Adolescents are often involved in an ambivalent struggle with parental authority.	Parents are laissez-faire in childrearing attitudes; are rejecting or not available to children.
Personality	High levels of ego development, moral reasoning, self-certainty, self-esteem, performance under stress, and intimacy.	Highest levels of authoritarianism and stereotypical thinking, obedience to authority, dependent relationships, low level of anxiety.	Most anxious and fearful of success; high levels of ego development, moral reasoning, and self-esteem.	Mixed results, with low levels of ego development, moral reasoning, cognitive complexity, and self-certainty; poor cooperative abilities.

*These associations have emerged from a number of separate studies. Since all the studies have been correlational, it is impossible to say that any factor caused placement in any identity status.
Source: Kroger, 1993.

foreclosure Identity status, described by Marcia, in which a person who has not spent time considering alternatives (that is, has not been in crisis) is committed to other people's plans for his or her life.

moratorium Identity status, described by Marcia, in which a person is currently considering alternatives (in crisis) and seems headed for commitment.

identity diffusion Identity status, described by Marcia, that is characterized by absence of commitment and lack of serious consideration of alternatives.

2. **Foreclosure** *(commitment without crisis).* Andrea has made commitments, not as a result of a crisis, which would involve questioning and exploring possible choices, but by accepting someone else's plans for her life. She is happy and self-assured, perhaps even smug and self-satisfied, and she becomes dogmatic when her opinions are questioned. She has close family ties, is obedient, and tends to follow a powerful leader (like her mother), who accepts no disagreement.
3. **Moratorium** *(crisis with no commitment yet).* Nick is in crisis, struggling with decisions. He is lively, talkative, self-confident, and scrupulous, but also anxious and fearful. He is close to his mother but also resists her authority. He wants to have a girlfriend but has not yet developed a close relationship. He will probably come out of his crisis eventually with the ability to make commitments and achieve identity.
4. **Identity diffusion** *(no commitment, no crisis).* Mark has not seriously considered options and has avoided commitments. He is unsure of himself and tends to be uncooperative. His parents do not discuss his future with him; they say it's up to him. People in this category tend to be unhappy. They are often lonely because they have only superficial relationships.

These categories are not permanent, of course; they may change as people continue to develop (Marcia, 1979, 2002). From late adolescence on, more and more people are in moratorium or achievement: seeking or finding their own identity. Still, many people, even as young adults, remain in foreclosure or diffusion (Kroger, 1993). Although people in foreclosure seem to have made final decisions, that is often not so; when adults in midlife look back on their lives, they most commonly trace a path from foreclosure to moratorium to identity achievement (Kroger & Haslett, 1991).

What's Your View?

- Which of Marcia's identity statuses do you think you fit into as an adolescent? Has your identity status changed since then? If so, how?

Gender Differences in Identity Formation

Much research supports Erikson's view that, for women, identity and intimacy develop together. Indeed, intimacy matters more to girls than to boys even in grade school friendships (Blyth & Foster-Clark, 1987). Rather than view this pattern as a departure from a male norm, however, some researchers see it as pointing to a weakness in Erikson's theory, which, they claim, is based on male-centered western concepts of individuality, autonomy, and competitiveness. According to Carol Gilligan (1982, 1987a, 1987b; L. M. Brown & Gilligan, 1990), the female sense of self develops not so much through achieving a separate identity as through establishing relationships. Girls and women, says Gilligan, judge themselves on their handling of their responsibilities and on their ability to care for others as well as for themselves.

Some developmental scientists, however, have begun to question how different the male and female paths to identity really are—especially today—and to suggest that individual differences may be more important than gender differences (Archer, 1993; Marcia, 1993). Indeed, Marcia (1993) argues that relationships and an ongoing tension between independence and connectedness are at the heart of all of Erikson's psychosocial stages for *both* men and women.

Self-esteem, during adolescence, develops largely in the context of relationships with peers, particularly those of the same sex. In line with Gilligan's view, male self-esteem seems to be linked with striving for individual achievement, whereas female self-esteem depends more on connections with others. In one longitudinal study, 84 mostly white, socioeconomically diverse young adults, whose self-esteem had been measured at ages 14 and 18, described memories about important experiences with others. Men who had had high self-esteem during adolescence tended to recall wanting to assert themselves with male friends, whereas women who had had high self-esteem recalled efforts to help female friends—efforts that involved asserting themselves in a collaborative rather than a competitive way (Thorne & Michaelieu, 1996).

Some research suggests that adolescent girls have lower self-esteem than adolescent boys (Chubb, Fertman, & Ross, 1997). Highly publicized studies during the early 1990s found that girls' self-confidence and self-esteem stay fairly high until age 11 or 12 and then tend to falter (American Association of University Women [AAUW] Educational Foundation, 1992; L. M. Brown & Gilligan, 1990). A recent analysis of hundreds of studies involving nearly 150,000 respondents concluded that boys and men do have higher self-esteem than girls and women, especially in late adolescence, but the difference is small. Contrary to the earlier finding, both males and females seem to gain self-esteem with age (Kling, Hyde, Showers, & Buswell, 1999).

Ethnic Factors in Identity Formation

What happens to young people's identity when the values of their ethnic community conflict with those of the larger society—for example, when American Indians are expected to participate in a tribal ceremony on a day when they are also supposed to be in school? Or when young people face and perhaps internalize (take into their own value system) prejudice against their own ethnic group? Or when discrimination limits their occupational choices, as it did for Jackie Robinson's brother Mack, who, after his Olympic glory, came home to a succession of menial jobs? All these situations can lead to identity confusion.

Identity formation is especially complicated for young people in minority groups. In fact, for some adolescents ethnicity may be central to identity formation. Skin color and other physical features, language differences, and stereotyped social standing can be extremely influential in molding minority adolescents' self-concept (Spencer & Dornbusch, 1998).

Teenagers have wider social networks and more mobility than younger children, and greater cognitive awareness of cultural attitudes and distinctions. Caught between two cultures, many minority youth are keenly conscious of conflicts between the values stressed at home and those dominant in the wider society. Despite positive appraisals by parents, teachers, community, and peers, minority adolescents' self-perceptions may, as Erikson (1968) noted, reflect negative views of their group by the majority culture (Spencer & Dornbusch, 1998).

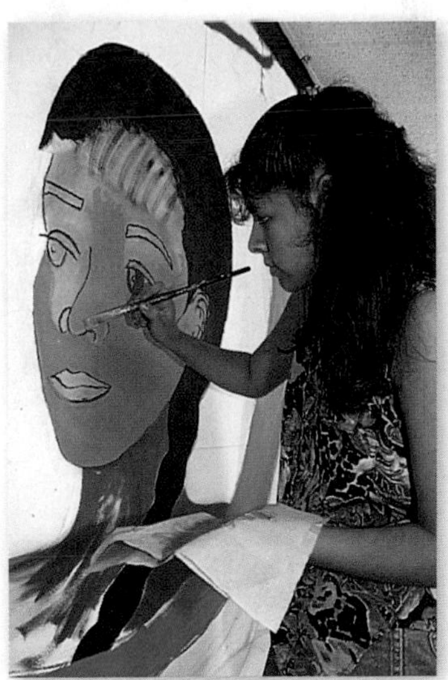

Identity development can be especially complicated for young people from minority groups. Ethnicity—and the conflicts with the dominant culture it entails—may play a central part in their self-concept.

Research dating back to the late 1970s and early 1980s has identified four stages of ethnic identity based on Marcia's identity statuses (Phinney, 1998):

1. *Diffuse:* Juanita has done little or no exploration of her ethnicity and does not clearly understand the issues involved.

2. *Foreclosed:* Kwame has done little or no exploration of his ethnicity but has clear feelings about it. These feelings may be positive or negative, depending on the attitudes he absorbed at home.
3. *Moratorium:* Cho-san has begun to explore her ethnicity but is confused about what it means to her.
4. *Achieved:* Diego has explored his ethnicity and understands and accepts it.

In a study of 64 African American, Asian American, and Hispanic American tenth-graders from two Los Angeles high schools (Phinney, 1998), researchers who coded the adolescents' responses to interviews and questionnaires were able to reliably assign all but four young people to three categories. About half of the sample (33) were *diffuse/foreclosed.* (The researchers combined these two categories—both involving lack of exploration of ethnicity—because they could not clearly distinguish between them on the basis of the young people's responses.) The other half were either in *moratorium* (14) or had apparently *achieved* identity (13).

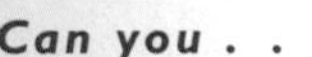

Checkpoint

Can you . . .

- ✔ List the three major issues involved in identity formation, according to Erikson?
- ✔ Describe four types of identity status found by Marcia?
- ✔ Discuss how gender and ethnicity can affect identity formation?

Members of different ethnic groups found different issues critical. Hispanics were highly conscious of prejudice against their group. Asian Americans struggled with pressures for academic achievement. African American girls were keenly aware that they did not meet white standards of beauty. African American boys were more concerned about job discrimination and the negative societal image of black males.

About one-fifth of the participants (some at each stage) had negative attitudes toward their own ethnic group. However, those in the achieved stage showed better overall adjustment than those in the other groups. They thought more highly of themselves, had a greater sense of mastery, and reported more positive family relationships and social and peer interactions.

Sexuality

Seeing oneself as a sexual being, recognizing one's sexual orientation, coming to terms with sexual stirrings, and forming romantic or sexual attachments all are parts of achieving sexual identity. The urgent awareness of sexuality is an important aspect of identity formation, profoundly affecting self-image and relationships. Although this process is biologically driven, its expression is in part culturally defined.

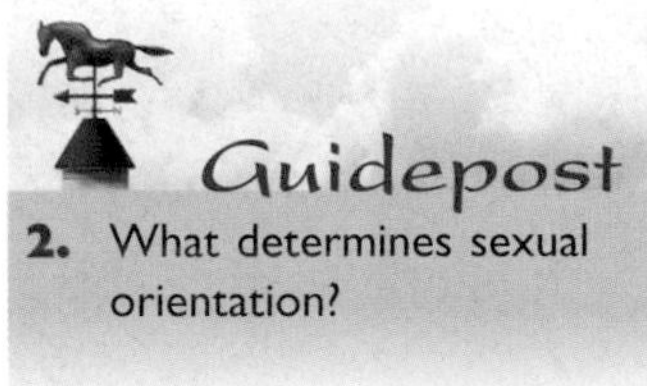

Guidepost

2. What determines sexual orientation?

sexual orientation Focus of consistent sexual, romantic, and affectionate interest, either heterosexual, homosexual, or bisexual.

Sexual Orientation

Although present in younger children, it is in adolescence that a person's **sexual orientation** generally becomes a pressing issue: whether that person will consistently be sexually, romantically, and affectionately attracted to persons of the other sex *(heterosexual)* or of the same sex *(homosexual)* or of both sexes *(bisexual).*

Homosexuality is common in some cultures, such as the Melanesian islands in the South Pacific (King, 1996), but not in the United States and other western countries. In one study of 38,000 American students in grades 7 through 12, about 88 percent described themselves as predominantly heterosexual and only 1 percent as predominantly homosexual or bisexual. About 11 percent, mostly younger students, were unsure of their sexual orientation (Remafedi, Resnick, Blum, & Harris, 1992). However, social stigma may bias such self-reports, underestimating the prevalence of homosexuality and bisexuality.

Research into sexual orientation has been focused primarily on efforts to explain the less common condition, homosexuality. Homosexuality once was considered a mental illness, but several decades of research have found no association between sexual orientation and emotional or social problems (American Psychological Association, undated; C. J. Patterson, 1992, 1995a, 1995b). These findings eventually led the psychiatric profession to stop classifying homosexuality as a mental disorder.

Other common explanations for homosexuality—all scientifically discredited—point to disturbed relationships with parents; parental encouragement of unconventional, cross-gender behavior; imitation of homosexual parents; or chance learning through seduction by a homosexual. Many young people have one or more homosexual experiences as they are growing up, usually before age 15. However, isolated experiences, or even homosexual attractions or fantasies, do not determine sexual orientation.

According to one theory, sexual orientation may be influenced by a complex prenatal process involving both hormonal and neurological factors (Ellis & Ames, 1987). If the levels of sex hormones in a fetus of either sex between the second and fifth months of gestation are in the typical female range, the person is likely to be attracted to males after puberty. If the hormone levels are in the male range, the person is likely to be attracted to females. Whether and how hormonal activity may affect brain development, and whether and how differences in brain structure may affect sexual orientation have not been established (Golombok & Tasker, 1996), but an anatomical difference between homosexual and heterosexual men in an area of the brain that governs sexual behavior has been reported (LeVay, 1991).

Sexual orientation seems to be at least partly genetic. An identical twin of a homosexual has about a 50 percent probability of also being homosexual, while a fraternal twin has only about a 20 percent likelihood and an adopted sibling 10 percent or less (Gladue, 1994). In a large-scale nationally representative survey that included 794 twin pairs, the concordance rate for nonheterosexual orientation among monozygotic ("identical") twins was 31.6 percent, compared with 8.3 percent for dizygotic ("fraternal") twins (Kendler et al., 2000). One series of studies linked male homosexuality to a small region of the X chromosome inherited from the mother (Hamer, Hu, Magnuson, Hu, & Pattatucci, 1993; Hu et al., 1995). However, later research failed to replicate this finding (G. Rice, Anderson, Risch, & Ebers, 1999).

Controversy remains as to whether or not sexual orientation is decisively shaped either before birth or at an early age. There also is dispute as to the relative contributions of biological, psychological, and social influences (Baumrind, 1995; C. J. Patterson, 1995b). These influences may well be "impossible to untangle," and their relative strength may differ among individuals (Baumrind, 1995, p. 132).

Checkpoint

Can you . . .

✔ Discuss theories and research regarding origins of sexual orientation?

Sexual Behavior

It is difficult to do research on sexual behavior. People willing to answer questions about sex tend to be sexually active and liberal in their attitudes toward sex and thus are not representative of the population. Also, a discrepancy often exists between what people say about sex and what they do, and there is no way to corroborate what people say. Some may conceal sexual activity; others may exaggerate. Problems multiply in surveying young people. For one thing, parental consent is often required, and parents who grant permission may not be typical. Methodology can make a difference: adolescent boys are more open in reporting certain types of sexual activity when surveys are self-administered by computer (C. F. Turner et al., 1998). Still, within the groups that take part in surveys we can see trends that reveal cultural differences and changes in sexual mores.

Guidepost

3. What sexual practices are common among adolescents, and what leads some teenagers to engage in risky sexual behavior?

Heterosexual Activity Internationally, there are wide variations in timing of sexual initiation. The percentage of women who report having first intercourse by 17 is ten times as great in Mali (72 percent) as in Thailand (7 percent) or the Philippines (6 percent). Similar differences exist for men. Although earlier male initiation is the norm in most cultures, in Mali and Ghana more women than men become sexually active at an early age (Singh, Wulf, Samara, & Cuca, 2000).

Since the 1920s the United States has witnessed an evolution in sexual behavior. Premarital sexual activity has become more common, especially among girls. In the

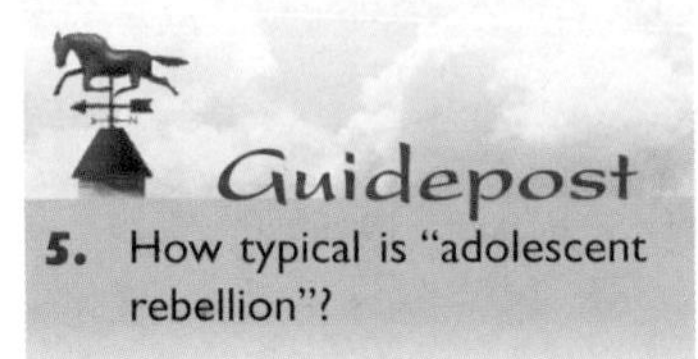

5. How typical is "adolescent rebellion"?

adolescent rebellion Pattern of emotional turmoil, characteristic of a minority of adolescents, which may involve conflict with family, alienation from adult society, reckless behavior, and rejection of adult values.

Is Adolescent Rebellion a Myth?

The teenage years have been called a time of **adolescent rebellion,** involving emotional turmoil, conflict within the family, alienation from adult society, reckless behavior, and rejection of adults' values. Yet research in schools the world over suggests that only about one in five adolescents fits this pattern (Offer & Schonert-Reichl, 1992).

The idea of adolescent rebellion may have been born in the first formal theory of adolescence, that of the psychologist G. Stanley Hall. Hall (1904/1916) believed that young people's efforts to adjust to their changing bodies and to the imminent demands of adulthood usher in a period of emotional "storm and stress," which produces conflict between the generations. Sigmund Freud (1935/1953) and his daughter, Anna Freud (1946), described "storm and stress" as universal and inevitable, growing out of a resurgence of early sexual drives toward the parents.

However, Margaret Mead, who studied adolescence in Samoa and other South Pacific islands, concluded that when a culture provides a gradual, serene transition from childhood to adulthood, "storm and stress" is not typical. Although her research in Samoa was later challenged (Freeman, 1983), this conclusion was eventually supported by research in 186 preindustrial societies (Schlegel & Barry, 1991).

Full-fledged rebellion now appears to be uncommon even in western societies, at least among middle-class youngsters who are in school. Only 15 to 25 percent of families with adolescents report significant conflict, and many of those families had problems before the children reached their teens (W. A. Collins, 1990; J. P. Hill, 1987; Offer, Ostrov, & Howard, 1989; Offer & Schonert-Reichl, 1992). Although adolescents may defy parental authority with some regularity, the emotions attending this transition do not normally lead to family conflict of major proportions or to a sharp break with parental or societal standards (Arnett, 1999; Offer & Church, 1991; Offer, Ostrov, Howard, & Atkinson, 1988; Offer et al., 1989; Offer & Schonert-Reichl, 1992). In a study of 5,938 adolescents in ten countries,* the young people overwhelmingly reported that they were usually happy and relaxed, enjoyed life, and felt able to exercise self-control. They enjoyed relationships, school, and work; felt comfortable with their sexuality; and looked forward to the future, confident of their ability to cope with the problems life might bring (Offer et al., 1988).

What's Your View?

- Looking back over your adolescence, did it seem to be a time of high emotionality, or was it on a fairly even keel? Were emotional ups and downs connected with any specific events?

Still, adolescence in western cultures can be a difficult time. Family conflict, depression, and risky behavior are more common than during other parts of the life span (Arnett, 1999; Petersen et al., 1993). Many adolescents feel self-conscious, embarrassed, awkward, lonely, nervous, or ignored (Larson & Richards, 1994), and most take occasional risks (Arnett, 1999). Negative emotionality and mood swings are most intense during early adolescence, perhaps due to the stressful events connected with puberty. By late adolescence, emotionality tends to become more stable (Larson, Moneta, Richards, & Wilson, 2002).

Recognizing that adolescence may be a difficult time can help parents and teachers put troubling behavior in perspective. Adults who assume that adolescent turmoil is normal and necessary may fail to heed the signals of the occasional young person who needs special help.

Changing Time Use and Changing Relationships

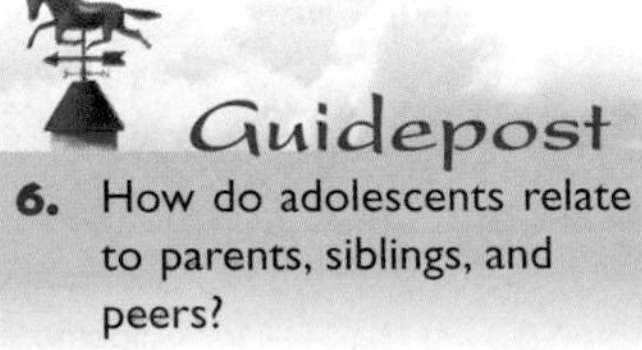

6. How do adolescents relate to parents, siblings, and peers?

One way to assess changes in adolescents' relationships with the important people in their lives is to see how they spend their discretionary time. Young people who grow up in tribal or peasant societies, who must focus on production of the bare necessities of life, have much less time for socializing than adolescents in technologically advanced societies (Larson & Verma, 1999). By comparison even with some

*Australia, Bangladesh, Hungary, Israel, Italy, Japan, Taiwan, Turkey, the United States, and West Germany.

postindustrial societies, as in Asia, where schoolwork and family obligations are strongly stressed, European and U.S. adolescents have a great deal of discretionary time. Much of this time is spent talking and "hanging out" with peers, and increasingly with peers of the other sex (Larson & Verma, 1999).

According to sequential research with 220 white middle- and working-class suburban U.S. youngsters, who carried beepers and reported what they were doing each time the beepers sounded, the amount of time spent with families declines dramatically between ages 10 and 18, from 35 percent to 14 percent of waking hours (Larson, Richards, Moneta, Holmbeck, & Duckett, 1996). This disengagement is not a rejection of the family, but a response to developmental needs. Early adolescents often retreat to their rooms; they seem to need time alone to step back from the demands of social relationships, regain emotional stability, and reflect on identity issues (Larson, 1997). High schoolers spend more of their free time with peers, with whom they identify and feel comfortable (Larson & Richards, 1991, 1998).

In contrast with young people in developing countries, U.S. adolescents have a great deal of free, discretionary time, and they spend much of it "hanging out" with peers.

Ethnic and cultural variations in time use tell us much about how culture affects psychosocial development. African American teenagers, who may look upon their families as havens in a hostile world, tend to maintain more intimate family relationships and less intense peer relations than white teenagers. Black teenagers also tend to be more flexible in their choice of friends and less dependent on peer approval (Giordano, Cernkovich, & DeMaris, 1993). Mexican American boys—but not girls—tend to become closer to their parents during puberty. This may reflect the unusually close-knit nature of Mexican American families, as well as the importance these families place on the traditional male role (Molina & Chassin, 1996). For Chinese American youth from immigrant families, the need to adapt to U.S. society often conflicts with the pull of traditional family obligations. Time use diaries of 140 first and second-generation Chinese American high school students in New York City showed that these young people spent a little less time with family than in studying and socializing with peers (Fuligni, Yip, & Tseng, 2002).

With such variations in mind, let's look more closely at relationships with parents, and then with siblings and peers.

Checkpoint

Can you . . .

- ✔ Explain why adolescence is no longer considered a time of "storm and stress"?
- ✔ Identify age and cultural differences in how young people spend their time, and discuss their significance?

Adolescents and Parents

Just as adolescents feel tension between dependency on their parents and the need to break away, parents often have mixed feelings, too. They want their children to be independent, yet they find it hard to let go. Parents have to walk a fine line between giving adolescents enough independence and protecting them from immature lapses in judgment. These tensions often lead to family conflict, and parenting styles can influence its shape and outcome. Also, as with younger children, parents' life situation—their work and marital and socioeconomic status—affects their relationships with teenage children.

Conversation, Autonomy, and Conflict The character of family interactions changes during the teenage years. Adolescents and their parents may spend less time than before watching television together, but just as much—and among girls, more—

(Berndt & Perry, 1990; Buhrmester, 1990, 1996; Hartup & Stevens, 1999; Laursen, 1996). Intimacy with same-sex friends increases during early to midadolescence, after which it typically declines as intimacy with the other sex grows (Laursen, 1996).

The increased intimacy of adolescent friendship reflects cognitive, as well as emotional, development. Adolescents are now better able to express their private thoughts and feelings. They also can more readily consider another person's point of view, and so it is easier for them to understand a friend's thoughts and feelings. Increased intimacy also reflects early adolescents' concern with getting to know themselves. Confiding in a friend helps young people explore their own feelings, define their identity, and validate their self-worth. Friendship provides a safe place to venture opinions, admit weaknesses, and get help with problems (Buhrmester, 1996).

The capacity for intimacy is related to psychological adjustment and social competence. Adolescents who have close, stable, supportive friendships generally have a high opinion of themselves, do well in school, are sociable, and are unlikely to be hostile, anxious, or depressed (Berndt & Perry, 1990; Buhrmester, 1990; Hartup & Stevens, 1999). A bidirectional process seems to be at work: good friendships foster adjustment, which in turn fosters good friendships.

Shared confidences and emotional support seem to be more vital to female friendships than to male friendships. Boys' friendships focus less on conversation than on shared activity, usually sports and competitive games (Blyth & Foster-Clark, 1987; Buhrmester, 1996; Bukowski & Kramer, 1986). Girls feel better after telling a friend about an upsetting experience than boys do; boys may express support by just spending time doing things together (Denton & Zarbatany, 1996). Boys tend to gain self-esteem from competing with friends, girls from helping them.

Checkpoint

Can you . . .

- ✔ Describe typical changes in sibling relationships during adolescence?
- ✔ List several functions of the peer group in adolescence?
- ✔ Describe characteristics that affect adolescents' popularity?
- ✔ Discuss important features of adolescent friendships?

Adolescents in Trouble: Antisocial Behavior and Juvenile Delinquency

Guidepost

7. What are the root causes of antisocial behavior and juvenile delinquency, and what can be done to reduce these and other risks of adolescence?

What influences young people to engage in—or refrain from—violence (see Box 12-2 on page 450) or other antisocial acts? How do "problem behaviors" escalate into chronic delinquency—an outcome Jackie Robinson managed to avoid? Research suggests that early and continuing patterns of parent-child interaction often pave the way for negative peer influence, which reinforces and promotes antisocial behavior.

Becoming a Delinquent: How Influences Interact Parents often worry about a teenager's "falling in with the wrong crowd"; but actually, parental upbringing influences the choice of peer groups and friends. Young people generally gravitate to others brought up like themselves, who are similar in school achievement, adjustment, and prosocial or antisocial tendencies (Collins et al., 2000; B. B. Brown, Mounts, Lamborn, & Steinberg, 1993).

In the early years, parents begin to shape prosocial or antisocial behavior by whether they meet children's basic emotional needs (Krevans & Gibbs, 1996; Staub, 1996). Parents of chronic delinquents often failed to reinforce good behavior in early childhood and were harsh or inconsistent, or both, in punishing misbehavior. Through the years these parents typically have not been closely and positively involved in their children's lives (G. R. Patterson, DeBaryshe, & Ramsey, 1989). The children may get payoffs for antisocial behavior: when they act up, they may gain attention or get their own way.

Children with behavior problems tend to do poorly in school and do not get along with well-behaved classmates. Unpopular and low-achieving children gravitate toward each other and egg each other on to further misconduct (G. R. Patterson, Reid, & Dishion, 1992; Vitaro, Tremblay, Kerr, Pagani, & Bukowski, 1997).

These "problem" children continue to elicit ineffective parenting, which often leads in adolescence to delinquent behavior and association with deviant peers (Simons, Chao, Conger, & Elder, 2001). Antisocial teens tend to have conflictual relationships with parents, for reasons that may be largely genetic (Neiderhiser, Reiss, Hetherington, & Plomin, 1999).

As in childhood, antisocial adolescents tend to have antisocial friends, and their antisocial behavior increases when they associate with each other (Dishion, McCord, & Poulin, 1999; Hartup & Stevens, 1999; Vitaro et al., 1997). The way antisocial teenagers talk, laugh, or smirk about rule-breaking and nod knowingly among themselves constitutes what has been called "deviancy training" (Dishion et al., 1999).

Authoritative parenting can help young people internalize standards that may insulate them against negative peer influences and open them to positive ones (Collins et al., 2000; Mounts & Steinberg, 1995). Improvements in parenting during adolescence can reduce delinquency by discouraging association with deviant peers (Simons et al., 2001). In disadvantaged neighborhoods, a combination of nurturant, involved parenting and collective socialization practices, such as adults monitoring or supervising each other's children, can minimize deviant relationships (Brody et al., 2001).

Most juvenile delinquents do not become adult criminals; many simply outgrow their "wild oats" (Kosterman, Graham, Hawkins, Catalano, & Herrenkohl, 2001; Moffitt, 1993). Delinquency peaks at about age 15 and then declines (Petersen, 1993) as most adolescents and their families come to terms with young people's need to assert independence. However, teenagers who do not see positive alternatives are more likely to adopt a permanently antisocial lifestyle (Elliott, 1993).

Preventing and Treating Delinquency Since juvenile delinquency has roots early in childhood, so must preventive efforts. Adolescents who took part in certain early childhood intervention programs were less likely to get in trouble (Reynolds, Temple, Robertson, & Mann, 2001; Yoshikawa, 1994; Zigler, Taussig, & Black, 1992). Programs that have achieved impressive long-term results in preventing antisocial behavior and delinquency include the Perry Preschool Project (refer back to Chapter 7), the Syracuse Family Development Research Project, the Yale Child Welfare Project, and the Houston Parent Child Development Center. Each of these model programs targeted high-risk urban children and lasted at least two years during the child's first five years of life. All influenced children directly, through high-quality day care or education, and indirectly, by offering families assistance and support geared to their needs (Berrueta-Clement et al., 1985; Berrueta-Clement, Schweinhart, Barnett, & Weikart, 1987; Schweinhart et al., 1993; Seitz, 1990; Yoshikawa, 1994; Zigler et al., 1992).

What's Your View?

- How should society deal with youthful offenders?

These programs operated on Bronfenbrenner's mesosystem (refer back to Chapter 2) by affecting interactions between the home and the school or child care center. The programs also went one step further to the exosystem, by creating supportive parent networks and linking parents with community services, including prenatal and postnatal health care and educational and vocational counseling (Yoshikawa, 1994; Zigler et al., 1992). Through their multipronged approach, these interventions had an impact on several early risk factors for delinquency.

The Chicago Child-Parent Centers, a preschool program for disadvantaged children in the Chicago Public Schools that is followed by special services through age 9, shows that early intervention can work on a large scale. At age 20, participants had better educational and social outcomes and fewer juvenile arrests than a comparison group who had received less extensive early interventions (Reynolds et al., 2001).

A preventive program for first- through sixth-graders in multiethnic high-crime areas of Seattle, mentioned earlier in this chapter, reduced adolescent criminal behavior, as well as heavy drinking and risky sexual activity. Rather than targeting those issues directly, the program was designed to make youngsters more competent academically and socially and more committed to school. At age 18, youths who had been in the program were 19 percent less likely than a control group to have committed violent acts (Hawkins, Catalano, Kosterman, Abbott, & Hill, 1999).

BOX 12-2

Digging Deeper
The Youth Violence Epidemic

On April 20, 1999, 18-year-old Eric Harris and 17-year-old Dylan Klebold entered Columbine High School in Littleton, Colorado, wearing black trench coats and carrying a rifle, a semiautomatic pistol, two sawed-off shotguns, and more than thirty homemade bombs. Laughing and taunting, they began spraying bullets at fellow students, killing twelve classmates and one teacher before fatally shooting themselves.

The massacre in Littleton was one of a string of school shootings. A ten-year epidemic of youth violence peaked in 1993 and has since declined (Cook & Laub, 1998), but the number of arrests of young people for aggravated assault has not. Nor have young people's confidential reports of their own violent behavior. The occasional youth killing may make the headlines, but other crimes such as forcible rape, robbery, and assault are much more prevalent (Snyder, 2000).

Why do some young people engage in such destructive behavior? One answer lies in the immaturity of the adolescent brain, particularly the prefrontal cortex, which is critical to judgment and impulse suppression. Another answer is ready access to guns in a culture that "romanticizes gunplay" (Weinberger, 2001, p. 2). Violence often accompanies drug use, gang membership, early sexual activity, and other risky behaviors ("Youth Violence," 2001).

Psychologists point to potential warning signs that might avert future tragedies. Adolescents who are likely to commit violence often refuse to listen to authority figures, such as parents and teachers; ignore the feelings and rights of others; mistreat people; rely on violence or threatened violence to solve problems; and believe that life has treated them unfairly. They often look older than their peers. They tend to do poorly in school; cut classes or play truant; be held back or suspended or drop out; use alcohol, inhalants, and/or drugs; join gangs; and fight, steal, or destroy property (American Psychological Association and American Academy of Pediatrics [AAP], 1996; Resnick et al., 1997). Harris and Klebold showed some of these characteristics.

In three out of four assaults or murders by young people, the perpetrators are members of gangs (American Psychological Association, undated). For many adolescents, gangs satisfy unfulfilled needs for identity, connection, and a sense of power and control. For youngsters who lack positive family relationships, a gang can become a substitute family. Gangs promote a sense of "us-versus-them"; violence against outsiders strengthens bonds of loyalty and support within the gang (Staub, 1996).

Teenage violence and antisocial behavior have roots in childhood. Eight-year-olds who are unusually aggressive in school are likely to be antisocial in adolescence and adult-

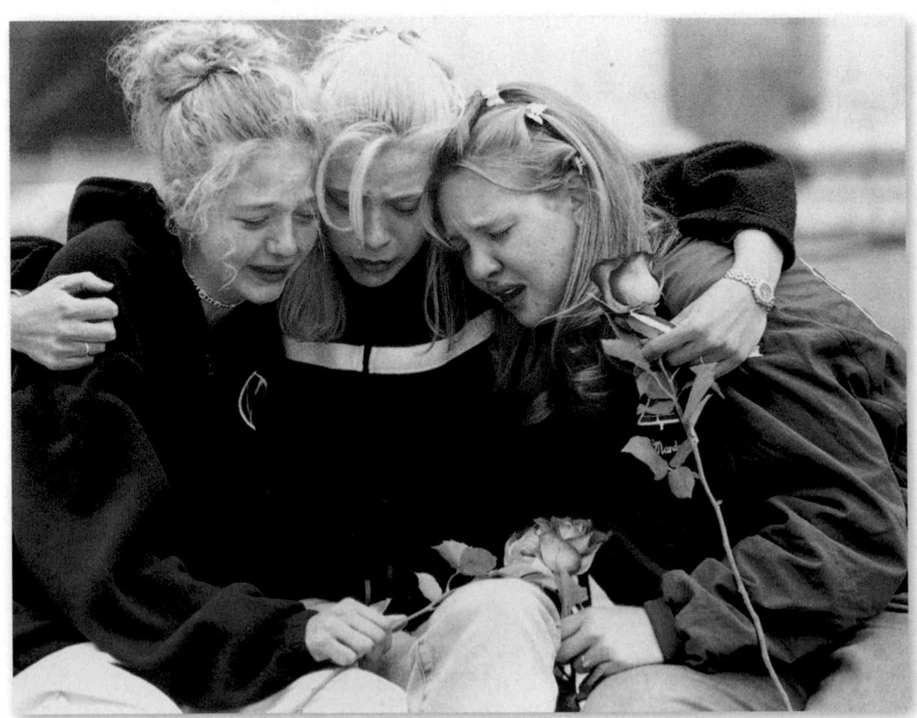

These sixteen-year-old girls console each other at a vigil service for victims of a shooting spree by teenage gunmen at Columbine High School in Littleton, Colorado, on April 20, 1999. This and other school shootings are part of what has been called an epidemic of youth violence.

—continued

hood (American Psychological Association Commission on Violence and Youth, 1994). Children raised in a rejecting or coercive atmosphere, or in an overly permissive or chaotic one, tend to show aggressive behavior; and the hostility they evoke in others increases their own aggression. Their negative self-image prevents them from succeeding at school or developing other constructive interests, and they generally associate with peers who reinforce their antisocial attitudes and behavior (Staub, 1996). Young people who are impulsive or fearless, or who have low IQs or learning difficulties, also may be violence-prone. Boys in poor, unstable neighborhoods are most likely to become involved in violence—one reason that the incident at Columbine, a middle-class suburban school, was so shocking (American Psychological Association, undated).

Adolescents are more likely to turn violent if they have witnessed or have been victims of violence, such as physical abuse or neighborhood fights. Exposure to media violence has a significant impact by desensitizing viewers to violence and depicting situations in which aggression is rewarded or justified (American Psychological Association, undated; Strasburger & Donnerstein, 1999; refer back to Chapter 10). One in five rock music videos portrays overt violence, and one in four depicts weapon carrying (DuRant et al., 1997). In a community sample of 707 adolescents and young adults, the amount of time spent watching television predicted the likelihood of aggression, even when previous aggressive behavior and other risk factors were controlled (Johnson, Cohen, Smailes, Kasen, & Brook, 2002).

Despite occasional widely publicized tragedies, the epidemic of youth violence seems to be abating. Between 1991 and 1997, the percentage of high school students nationwide who reported carrying a weapon dropped by about one-third, from 26 percent to 18 percent—still a dangerously high number (Brener, Simon, Krug, & Lowry, 1999).

A report by the Surgeon General of the United States challenges several myths, or stereotypes, about youth violence ("Youth Violence," 2001; see table). One of the worst is the myth that nothing can be done to prevent or treat violent behavior. Unfortunately, about half of the hundreds of programs being used in schools and communities fall short when rigorously evaluated, and some may actually be counterproductive, according to the report. Effective programs address both individual risks and environmental conditions. They focus on the individual youth by building skills and competencies. They provide parent effectiveness training. And they try to improve the school's social climate through interventions addressed to peer groups. A program in Galveston, Texas, that addressed specific risk factors led to a drop in arrests for juvenile crime (Thomas, Holzer, & Wall, 2002).

What's Your View?

What methods for controlling youth violence seem to you most likely to work?

Check It Out:

For more information on this topic, go to http://www.mhhe.com/papaliah9, where you'll find links to a site on preventing youth violence by raising responsible children and teenagers.

Five Myths About Youth Violence

Myth	Fact
Most future offenders can be identified in early childhood.	Children with conduct disorders or uncontrolled behavior do not necessarily turn out to be violent adolescents.
African American and Hispanic youth are more likely than other ethnic youth to become involved in violence.	Although arrest rates differ, self-reports suggest that race and ethnicity have little effect on the overall proportion of nonfatal violent behavior.
A new breed of "super-predators," who grew to adolescence in the 1990s, threatens to make the United States an even more violent place than it is.	There is no evidence that young people involved in violence during the peak 1990s were more violent or more vicious than youths in earlier years.
Trying young offenders in tough adult criminal courts makes them less likely to commit more violent crimes.	Juveniles handled in adult courts have significantly higher rates of repeat offenses and of later felonies than young offenders handled in juvenile courts.
Most violent youths will end up being arrested for violent crimes.	Most youths involved in violent behavior will never be arrested for a violent crime.

Source: Based on data from "Youth Violence," 2001.

Interventions need to target older students as well. In addition to spotting characteristics of troubled adolescents, it is important to find ways to reduce young people's exposure to high-risk settings that encourage antisocial behavior. Again, adult monitoring is important, especially after school, on weekend evenings, and in summer, when adolescents are most likely to be idle and get into trouble. As Jackie Robinson's experience shows, getting teenagers involved in constructive activities during their free time can pay long-range dividends (Larson, 1998). Participation in extracurricular school activities tends to cut down on dropout and criminal arrest rates among high-risk boys and girls (Mahoney, 2000).

Delinquent and predelinquent teenagers tend to be "stuck" in Kohlberg's stage 2: like preschoolers, they are deterred from misconduct only by the threat of punishment and fear of getting caught. By moving to stage 3, where they are more concerned with meeting social norms and expectations, they may develop a "cognitive buffer" against temptation (Gibbs, Arnold, Ahlborn, & Cheesman, 1984). This may happen through interaction with a partner who is of higher peer status and at a higher level of moral reasoning—as was found when 40 institutionalized young male offenders were paired off with peers for face-to-face discussion of moral issues (Taylor & Walker, 1997). Thus peer interaction can stimulate moral growth—if the peer climate is positive (Dishion et al., 1999).

Fortunately, the great majority of adolescents do not get into serious trouble. Those who do show disturbed behavior can—and should—be helped. With love, guidance, and support, adolescents can avoid risks, build on their strengths, and explore their possibilities as they approach adult life.

Checkpoint

Can you . . .

- ✔ Explain how parental, peer, and neighborhood influences may interact to promote antisocial behavior and delinquency?
- ✔ Give examples of programs that have been successful in preventing or stopping delinquency and other risky behavior?

Refocus

- What evidence suggests that Jackie Robinson may have gone through Erikson's stage of identity versus identity confusion?
- Which of Marcia's identity statuses did Robinson seem to fall into, both with regard to his identity in general and his ethnicity in particular?
- Did Robinson's relationships with his mother and his peers seem consistent with the findings reported in this chapter?
- Would you say that Robinson showed adolescent rebellion?
- Based on the material in this chapter, why do you think Robinson did not become a full-fledged juvenile delinquent?

The normal developmental changes in the early years of life are obvious and dramatic signs of growth. The infant lying in the crib becomes an active, exploring toddler. The young child enters and embraces the worlds of school and society. The adolescent, with a new body and new awareness, prepares to step into adulthood.

Growth and development do not screech to a stop after adolescence. People change in many ways throughout early, middle, and late adulthood, as we will see in the remaining chapters of this book.

SUMMARY AND KEY TERMS

The Search for Identity

Guidepost 1. How do adolescents form an identity?

- A central concern during adolescence is the search for identity, which has occupational, sexual, and values components. Erik Erikson described the psychosocial conflict of adolescence as *identity versus identity confusion.* The "virtue" that should arise from this crisis is *fidelity.*
- James Marcia, in research based on Erikson's theory, described four identity statuses with differing combinations of crisis and commitment: identity achievement, foreclosure, moratorium, and identity diffusion.
- Researchers differ on whether girls and boys take different paths to identity formation. Although some research suggests that girls' self-esteem tends to fall in adolescence, later research does not support that finding.
- Ethnicity is an important part of identity. Minority adolescents seem to go through stages of ethnic identity development much like Marcia's identity statuses.

identity *(425)*
identity versus identity confusion *(425)*
identity statuses *(427)*
crisis *(427)*
commitment *(427)*
identity achievement *(427)*
foreclosure *(428)*
moratorium *(428)*
identity diffusion *(428)*

Sexuality

Guidepost 2. What determines sexual orientation?

- Sexual orientation appears to be influenced by an interaction of biological and environmental factors and may be at least partly genetic.

sexual orientation *(430)*

Guidepost 3. What sexual practices are common among adolescents, and what leads some teenagers to engage in risky sexual behavior?

- Sexual behaviors are more liberal than in the past. Teenage sexual activity involves risks of pregnancy and sexually transmitted disease. Adolescents at greatest risk are those who begin sexual activity early, have multiple partners, do not use contraceptives, and are ill-informed about sex.
- Regular condom use is the best safeguard for sexually active teens.
- Comprehensive sex education programs delay sexual initiation and encourage contraceptive use. Abstinence-only programs have not been effective.
- Many teenagers get misleading information about sexuality from the media.

sexually transmitted diseases (STDs) *(433)*

Guidepost 4. How common are sexually transmitted diseases and teenage pregnancy, and what are their usual outcomes?

- Rates of sexually transmitted diseases (STDs) in the United States are among the highest in the industrialized world; one in three cases occurs in adolescents. STDs can be transmitted by oral sex as well as intercourse. They are more likely to develop undetected in girls than in boys.
- Teenage pregnancy and birthrates in the United States have declined but are still highest in the industrialized world. Most of the pregnancies are unintended, and most of the births are to unmarried mothers.
- Teenage childbearing often has negative outcomes. Teenage mothers and their families tend to suffer ill health and financial hardship, and the children often suffer from ineffective parenting.

Relationships with Family, Peers, and Adult Society

Guidepost 5. How typical is "adolescent rebellion"?

- Although relationships between adolescents and their parents are not always smooth, full-scale adolescent rebellion is unusual.

adolescent rebellion *(440)*

Guidepost 6. How do adolescents relate to parents, siblings, and peers?

- Adolescents in the United States, who have a large amount of discretionary time, spend an increasing amount of it with peers, but relationships with parents continue to be close and influential, especially among some ethnic minorities.
- Family interactions change during the teenage years. There is more intimacy, but also more conflict over issues of autonomy. Conflict with parents tends to be most frequent during early adolescence and most intense during mid-adolescence. Authoritative parenting is associated with the most positive outcomes.
- Effects of divorce and single parenting on adolescents' development depend on the way they affect family atmosphere. Genetic factors may affect the way young adolescents adapt to divorce.
- Effects of maternal employment depend on such factors as the presence or absence of the other parent, how closely parents monitor adolescents' activity, and the mother's workload. A mother's working may help shape attitudes toward gender roles.
- Economic stress affects relationships in both single-parent and two-parent families.
- Relationships with siblings tend to become more equal and more distant during adolescence.
- The peer group can have both positive and negative influences. Adolescents who are rejected by peers tend to have the greatest adjustment problems.
- Friendships, especially among girls, become more intimate and supportive in adolescence.

Guidepost 7. What are the root causes of antisocial behavior and juvenile delinquency, and what can be done to reduce these and other risks of adolescence?

- Chronic delinquency is associated with multiple interacting risk factors, including ineffective parenting, school failure, peer influence, neighborhood influences, and low socioeconomic status. Programs that attack such risk factors from an early age have had success.

PART 6

At one time, developmental scientists considered the years from the end of adolescence to the onset of old age a relatively uneventful plateau, but research tells us that this is not so. Growth and decline go on throughout life, in a balance that differs for each individual. Choices and events during young adulthood (which we define approximately as the span between ages 20 and 40) have much to do with how that balance is struck.

During these two decades, as we see in Chapters 13 and 14, human beings build a foundation for much of their later development. This is when people typically leave their parents' homes, start jobs or careers, get married or establish other intimate relationships, have and raise children, and begin to contribute significantly to their communities. They make decisions that will affect the rest of their lives—their health, their happiness, and their success. ▸

Linkups to look for

- Income, education, and marital status affect health.
- Emotions may play a part in intelligence.
- Cognitive and moral development reflects life experience.
- Gender-typing may affect women's choice of careers and use of their talents.
- The gender revolution has diminished differences in men's and women's life course and health patterns.
- Infertility can lead to marital problems.
- Pressures at work can affect family relationships.
- People without friends or family are more likely to become ill and die.

Young Adulthood

PREVIEW

CHAPTER 13

Physical and Cognitive Development in Young Adulthood

Physical condition peaks, then declines slightly.

Lifestyle choices influence health.

Cognitive abilities and moral judgments assume more complexity.

Educational and career choices are made.

CHAPTER 14

Psychosocial Development in Young Adulthood

Personality traits and styles become relatively stable, but changes in personality may be influenced by life stages and events.

Decisions are made about intimate relationships and personal lifestyles.

Most people marry, and most become parents.

Chapter 13

Physical and Cognitive Development in Young Adulthood

If . . . happiness is the absence of fever, then I will never know happiness. For I am possessed by a fever for knowledge, experience, and creation.

—*Diary of Anaïs Nin* (1931–1934), written when she was between 28 and 31

OUTLINE

FOCUS:
Arthur Ashe, Tennis Champion

PHYSICAL DEVELOPMENT

Health and Physical Condition
- Health Status
- Genetic Influences on Health
- Behavioral Influences on Health and Fitness
- Indirect Influences on Health and Fitness

Sexual and Reproductive Issues
- Premenstrual Syndrome
- Sexually Transmitted Diseases (STDs)

COGNITIVE DEVELOPMENT

Perspectives on Adult Cognition
- Beyond Piaget: The Shift to Postformal Thought
- Schaie: A Life-Span Model of Cognitive Development
- Sternberg: Insight and Know-How
- Emotional Intelligence

Moral Development
- The Seventh Stage
- Gender and Moral Development

Education and Work
- The Transition to College
- Entering the World of Work
- Cognitive Complexity of Work
- Adult Education and Literacy

BOXES

13-1
Practically Speaking: Sleep Deprivation

13-2
Digging Deeper: Development of Faith Across the Life Span

Focus: Arthur Ashe, Tennis Champion*

Arthur Ashe

The tennis champion Arthur Ashe (1943–1993) was one of the most respected athletes of all time. "Slim, bookish and bespectacled" (Finn, 1993, p. B1), he was known for his quiet, dignified manner on and off the court. He did not dispute calls, indulge in temper tantrums, or disparage opponents.

The only African American to win the Wimbledon tournament and the United States and Australian Opens, Ashe grew up in Richmond, Virginia, where he began playing on segregated public courts and was barred from a city tennis tournament because of his race. As a young adult, the only black star in a white-dominated game, Ashe was a target for bigotry; but he maintained his composure and channeled his aggressive impulses into the game.

Ashe used his natural physical gifts and stellar reputation to combat racism and increase opportunity for disadvantaged youth. He conducted tennis clinics and helped establish tennis programs for inner-city youngsters. Twice refused a visa to play in the South African Open, he was finally allowed to compete in 1973 and again in 1974 and 1975. Despite South Africa's rigid apartheid system of racial separation, he insisted on nonsegregated seating at his matches.

Ashe continued to work against apartheid, for the most part quietly, behind the scenes. Accused of being an "Uncle Tom" by angry militants who shouted him down while he was giving a speech, he politely rebuked them: "What do you expect to achieve when you give in to passion and invective and surrender the high moral ground that alone can bring you to victory?" (Ashe & Rampersad, 1993, pp. 117, 118). Several years later, he was arrested in a protest outside the South African embassy in Washington, D.C. He felt tremendous

*Sources of biographical information about Arthur Ashe were Ashe and Rampersad (1993), Finn (1993), and Witteman (1993).

pride when he saw Nelson Mandela, the symbol of opposition to apartheid, released from prison in 1990, riding in a ticker-tape parade in New York City. But Ashe would not live to see Mandela become president of South Africa.

In 1979, at age 36, at the height of a brilliant career, Ashe suffered the first of several heart attacks and underwent quadruple bypass surgery. Forced to retire from competitive play, he served for five years as captain of the U.S. Davis Cup team. In 1985, barely past young adulthood, he was inducted into the Tennis Hall of Fame.

One summer morning in 1988, Ashe woke up and could not move his right arm. He was given two options: immediate brain surgery, or wait and see. He opted for action. Preparatory blood tests showed that he was HIV-positive, probably from a blood transfusion during his heart surgery five years earlier. The brain surgery revealed a parasitic infection linked to AIDS, which had progressed to AIDS itself. Like an athlete who is outscored but still in the game, Ashe refused to panic or to give up. Relying on the best medical knowledge, he chose to do all he could to fight his illness. He also chose to keep quiet about it—in part to protect his family's privacy and in part because, as he insisted, "I am not sick." He played golf, appeared on the lecture circuit, wrote columns for the *Washington Post,* was a television commentator for HBO and ABC Sports, and composed a three-volume history of African American athletes.

In 1992, warned that *USA Today* planned to reveal his secret, Ashe called a press conference and announced that he had AIDS. He became a tireless leader in the movement for AIDS research, establishing a foundation and launching a $5 million fund-raising campaign.

Ashe died of AIDS-related pneumonia in 1993, at age 49. Shortly before, he had summed up his situation in his usual style: "I am a fortunate, blessed man. Aside from AIDS and heart disease, I have no problems" (Ashe & Rampersad, 1993, p. 328).

Arthur Ashe's characteristic way of coping with trouble or bigotry was to meet it as he did an opponent on the tennis court: with grace, determination, moral conviction, and coolness under fire. Again and again, he turned adversity into opportunity. Arthur Ashe was a "can-do" person.

Even for people who lack Ashe's outstanding athletic skills, young adulthood typically is a "can-do" period. Most people at this age are on their own for the first time, setting up and running households and proving themselves in their chosen pursuits. Every day, they test and expand their physical and cognitive abilities. They encounter the "real world" and find their way through or around problems of everyday living. They make decisions that help determine their health, their careers, and the kinds of people they wish to be.

In this chapter, we look at young adults' physical functioning, which is usually at its height; and we note factors that can affect health in young adulthood and in later life. We discuss aspects of cognition that come to the fore in adulthood, and how education can stimulate cognitive growth. We examine how culture and gender affect moral development. Finally, we discuss one of the most important tasks during this period: entering the world of work.

After you have read and studied this chapter, you should be able to answer each of the following Guidepost questions. Look for them again in the margins, where they point to important concepts throughout the chapter. To check your understanding of these Guideposts, review the end-of-chapter summary. Checkpoints located at periodic spots throughout the chapter will help you verify your understanding of what you have read.

1. In what physical condition is the typical young adult, and what factors affect health and well-being?
2. What are some sexual and reproductive issues at this time of life?
3. What is distinctive about adult thought and intelligence?
4. How does moral reasoning develop?
5. How do higher education and work affect cognitive development?
6. How can continuing education help adults meet workplace demands?

Guideposts for Study

PHYSICAL DEVELOPMENT

Health and Physical Condition

Your favorite spectator sport may be tennis, basketball, figure skating, or football. Whatever it is, most of the athletes you root for (like Arthur Ashe in his time) are young adults, people in prime physical condition.

Guidepost

1. In what physical condition is the typical young adult, and what factors affect health and well-being?

Young adults typically are at the peak of health, strength, energy, and endurance. They also are at a peak of sensory and motor functioning. By the middle twenties, most body functions are fully developed. Visual acuity is keenest from about age 20 to age 40; and taste, smell, and sensitivity to pain and temperature generally remain undiminished until at least 45. However, a gradual hearing loss, which typically begins during adolescence, becomes more apparent after 25, especially for higher-pitched sounds.

Health Status

Most young adults in the United States are in good to excellent health; less than 6 percent of 25- to 44-year-olds call their health fair or poor (NCHS, 2002b). Many are never seriously ill or incapacitated, and the vast majority have no chronic conditions or impairments. The most common is chronic back pain (Rizzo, Abbott, & Berger, 1998), which may be work-related (Bernard, 1997).

Accidents are the leading cause of death for Americans ages 20 to 34, followed by homicide and suicide; these three causes account for 72 percent of deaths in the early twenties and 51 percent among 25- to 34-year-olds (Anderson, 2002). Death rates for young adults have been nearly cut in half during the past half-century, and mortality rates for other age groups have dropped as well (Pastor, Makuc, Reuben, & Xia, 2002). Heart disease, strokes, and most other life-threatening diseases are down (Minino & Smith, 2001; NCHS, 2002b). On the other hand, too many adults—even young ones—are overweight and not active enough and engage in health-threatening behaviors.

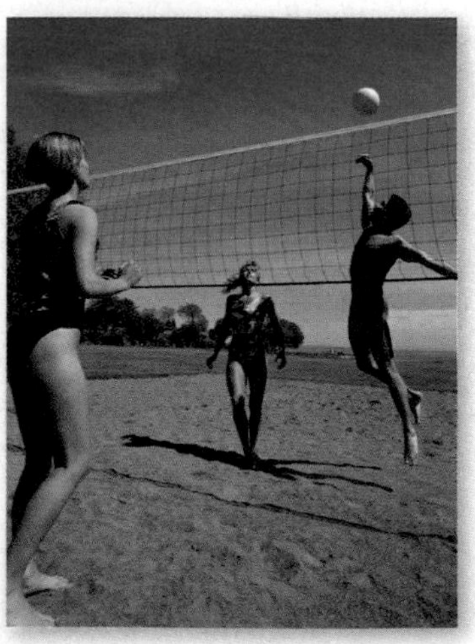

Playing volleyball takes strength, energy, endurance, and muscular coordination. Young adults like these typically are in prime physical condition.

In young adulthood, the foundation for physical functioning throughout the rest of the life span is laid. Although health may in part be influenced by the genes, behavioral factors—what young adults eat, whether they get enough sleep, how physically active they are, and whether they smoke, drink, or use drugs—contribute greatly to present and future health and well-being.

Genetic Influences on Health

The mapping of the human genome is enabling scientists to discover genetic bases for many disorders, from obesity to certain cancers (notably lung, prostate, and breast cancer) to mental health conditions, such as alcoholism (discussed later in this chapter).

Most diseases are multifactorial, involving both genetic and environmental causes. An example is non-insulin-dependent diabetes mellitus, which affects about 4 percent of the world's population. Researchers have found a gene on chromosome 2 that contributes to susceptibility to this disease in Mexican Americans (Horikawa et al., 2000). However, the single most important predictor of this type of diabetes is obesity. Other behavioral factors such as lack of exercise, poor nutrition, and smoking also contribute (Hu et al., 2001).

Risk factors for atherosclerosis, or narrowing of the arteries—which may begin in childhood and can become a threat by the forties or fifties—include high blood pressure, smoking, and elevated cholesterol levels in the blood. Cholesterol, in combination with proteins and triglycerides (fatty acids), circulates through the bloodstream, carried by low-density lipoprotein (LDL), commonly called "bad" cholesterol. High-density lipoprotein (HDL), or "good" cholesterol, flushes cholesterol out of the system. An estimated 80 percent of the variation in HDL levels within the population is due to genetic factors ("How to Raise HDL," 2001). However, as we discuss in the next section, cholesterol levels also are influenced by behavioral factors.

Behavioral Influences on Health and Fitness

Good health is not just a matter of luck. People can seek health by pursuing some activities and refraining from others.

In a longitudinal study of 7,000 adults ages 20 to 70, health was directly related to several common habits: eating regular meals, including breakfast, and not snacking; eating and exercising moderately; sleeping regularly seven to eight hours each night; not smoking; and drinking in moderation. After ten or more years, people who did not follow these health habits were twice as likely to be disabled as people who followed most or all of them (Breslow & Breslow, 1993).

Preventive measures can pay dividends. Regular screening tests, such as Pap smears to detect cervical cancer and testicular self-examinations to detect testicular cancer, can prevent diseases or catch them in early, treatable stages.

Many musculoskeletal disorders are work related and preventable. Back injuries often result from overexertion in lifting, pushing, pulling, or carrying objects. Repetitive motion injuries, such as carpal tunnel syndrome, can be controlled by such measures as proper placement of computer keyboards and good posture (Bernard, 1997; National Research Council, 1998, 2001).

The link between behavior and health illustrates the interrelationship among physical, cognitive, and emotional aspects of development. What people know about health affects what they do, and what they do affects how they feel. Knowing about good health habits is not enough, however. Personality, emotions, and social surroundings often outweigh what people know they should do and lead them into unhealthful behavior.

Let's look at several lifestyle factors that are strongly and directly linked with health and fitness: nutrition and obesity, sleep (see Box 13-1), physical activity, and alcohol and drug use. (In Chapter 15 we'll discuss the influence of stress.) In the next section of this chapter we consider indirect influences: socioeconomic status, race or ethnicity, gender, and relationships.

Practically Speaking

BOX 13-1

Sleep Deprivation

If you have ever experienced jet lag—fatigue due to rapid time change during a cross-country or overseas flight—you know how it feels to have your *circadian rhythms* disrupted. Circadian rhythms are daily cycles of physiological and behavioral changes (such as falling asleep and waking up) that are linked to the cycles of light and dark in nature. These rhythmic cycles are governed by a biological clock in the brain, which may be genetically based. They go on even in the absence of natural external cues—for example, in a windowless room that is kept constantly light or constantly dark (Vitaterna, Takahashi, & Turek, 2001).

Human beings can override their circadian rhythms by choosing when and how long they will sleep (for example, by setting an alarm clock). Normally, when the light-dark cycle changes (as in daylight savings time or travel across time zones), the internal clock will adjust. But when the sleep-wake cycle is seriously and chronically out of phase with circadian rhythms, health, safety, and productivity may suffer (Vitaterna et al., 2001).

Adverse health effects may include gastrointestinal and cardiovascular problems, altered hormonal functioning, and depression (Monk, 2000; Vitaterna et al., 2001). In a large-scale poll by the National Sleep Foundation (2001), respondents said they were more likely to make mistakes, to become impatient or aggravated when waiting, or to get upset with their children or others when they had not had enough sleep the night before. Sleep deprivation can be lethal on the road; drowsy drivers cause an estimated 3.6 percent of all fatal crashes (Peters et al., 1994). Sleep deprivation may even lead to premature aging. In one study, 36 hours of sleep deprivation in young adults produced effects on the prefrontal cortex—a part of the brain heavily involved in working memory and verbal fluency—similar to those found in non-sleep-deprived 60-year-olds (Harrison, Horne, & Rothwell, 2000).

Many young adults, especially those who work abnormal hours, go without adequate sleep. Night shift workers may find it difficult to fall asleep in the daytime, when it is light out and family activities are going on (Monk, 2000). Furthermore, not everyone has the same pattern of circadian rhythms. Some people call themselves "morning people" or "evening people" because they are more alert at one time or the other. Chronobiologists—scientists who study circadian rhythms—call such people "larks" and "owls." If work or school schedules force an "owl" to get up early every morning or a "lark" to regularly burn the midnight oil, trouble can ensue (McEnany & Lee, 2000).

Adequate sleep improves learning of complex motor skills (Walker, Brakefield, Morgan, Hobson, & Stickgold, 2002) and consolidates previous learning. Even a short nap can prevent burnout—oversaturation of the brain's perceptual processing systems (Mednick et al., 2002). Sleep deprivation tends to impair verbal learning (Horne, 2000), some aspects of memory (Harrison & Horne, 2000b), and speech articulation (Harrison & Horne, 1997), and to increase distractibility (Blagrove, Alexander, & Horne, 1995). Impairment seems to be selective, mainly affecting dull, monotonous tasks. Complex tasks that involve decisions tend to call forth greater motivation and effort to make up for lost sleep (Horne, 2000). However, high-level decision making can be impaired, especially in emergency situations that require innovation, flexibility, avoidance of distraction, realistic risk assessment, metamemory, and communication skills (Harrison & Horne, 2000a).

Brain imaging studies show how compensatory changes in the brain can help maintain initial cognitive performance after short-term loss of sleep. In an experiment on 13 healthy young adults, the prefrontal cortex was more responsive during verbal memory tasks after 35 sleepless hours than after normal sleep. In addition, while sleep-deprived participants showed reduced verbal recall, activation of the parietal lobes, not normally involved in verbal tasks, tended to lessen the impairment (Drummond et al., 2000). However, chronic sleep deprivation (less than six hours a night for three or more nights) can seriously worsen cognitive performance even when a person is not aware of it (Van Dongen, Maislin, Mullington, & Dinges, 2003).

What's Your View?

Do the findings about sleep deprivation and circadian rhythms suggest desirable changes in the workplace?

Check It Out:

For more information on this topic, go to http://www.mhhe.com/papaliah9, where you'll find links to information on sleep and sleep deprivation.

Nutrition and Cholesterol The saying "You are what you eat" sums up the importance of nutrition for physical and mental health. What people eat affects how they look, how they feel, and how likely they are to get sick.

Eating habits play an important part in heart disease—which, as Arthur Ashe's story shows, is not necessarily limited to later life. People who eat a variety of fruits and vegetables, especially those rich in carotenoids (such as carrots, sweet potatoes, broccoli, spinach, and cantaloupe) may lessen their chances of heart disease (Liu, Manson, Lee, et al., 2000; Rimm et al., 1996), and stroke (Gillman et al., 1995).

This juicy hamburger is dripping with calories and also is high in animal fat, which has been linked with heart disease and some cancers.

A review of many epidemiological studies found that following a mostly plant-based diet—together with staying active, maintaining a healthy weight, and refraining from tobacco use—could cut the risk of most cancers by as much as 70 percent (World Cancer Research Fund and American Institute for Cancer Research, 1997). Since then some studies have disputed the protective power of fruit and vegetable consumption against specific cancers (Michels et al., 2000; Smith-Warner et al., 2001), while others have supported it (Feskanich et al., 2000; Michaud et al., 2000; Terry et al., 2001). It may be that methodological differences account for the varying findings (Slattery, 2001).

A diet high in animal fat has been linked with colon cancer (Willett, Stampfer, Colditz, Rosner, & Speizer, 1990) and prostate cancer (Giovannucci et al., 1993; Hebert et al., 1998; Willett, 1994; Willett et al., 1992), but not breast cancer (Holmes et al., 1999). Fat consumption increases cardiovascular risks, particularly cholesterol levels (Brunner et al. 1997; Matthews et al., 1997)). In a twenty-five-year study of more than 12,000 men in five European countries, the United States, and Japan, cholesterol levels were directly related to the risk of death from coronary heart disease (Verschuren et al., 1995). Controlling cholesterol through diet and medication can significantly lower this risk (Lipid Research Clinics Program, 1984a, 1984b; Scandinavian Simvastatin Survival Study Group, 1994; Shepherd et al., 1995).

obesity Extreme overweight, often measured in adults by a body mass index of 30 or more, or by more than 25 percent body fat in men and more than 30 percent in women.

Obesity **Obesity** in adults is generally measured by *body mass index,* the number of kilograms of weight per square meter of height. An adult with a BMI of 25 or more is overweight, and one with a BMI of 30 or more is obese. Another criterion for obesity is percentage of body fat; men with more than 25 percent body fat and women with more than 30 percent may be considered obese (National Center for Biotechnology Information, [NCBI], 2002).

The World Health Organization (WHO) has called obesity a worldwide epidemic (WHO, 1998). Obesity more than doubled in the United Kingdom between 1980 and 1994, and similar increases have been reported in Brazil, Canada, and several countries in Europe, the Western Pacific, Southeast Asia, and Africa (Taubes, 1998). In the United States, 30.5 percent of the adult population were obese in 1999–2000, up from 22.9 percent in 1988–1994. Obesity is especially prevalent among black and Mexican American women (Flegal, Carroll, Ogden, & Johnson, 2002). Young adults are less likely to be obese than older ones, but about 20 percent of 20- to 39-year-olds were obese in 2001 (NCHS, 2002a).

What explains the obesity epidemic? Experts point to an increase in snacking (Zizza, Siega-Riz, & Popkin, 2001), availability of inexpensive "fast foods," "supersized" portions, high-fat diets, labor-saving technologies, and sedentary recreational pursuits, such as television and computers (Brownell, 1998; Hill & Peters, 1998; Taubes, 1998; Young & Nestle, 2002).

A tendency toward obesity can be inherited, and this genetic tendency may interact with environmental and behavioral factors (Comuzzie & Allison, 1998; NCBI, 2002). Researchers have identified a genetic mutation in mice that may disrupt the appetite control center in the brain by inhibiting production of the protein *leptin,* which tells the brain when the body has consumed enough (Campfield, Smith, Guisez, Devos, & Burns, 1995; Halaas et al., 1995, Pelleymounter et al., 1995; Zhang et al., 1994). In humans, overeating may result from the brain's failure to respond to this protein's signals (Campfield, Smith, & Burn, 1998; Travis, 1996). Eventually this research may lead to identification and treatment of people predisposed to obesity (NCBI, 2002).

In a society that values slenderness, being overweight can lead to emotional problems. It also carries risks of high blood pressure, heart disease, stroke, diabetes, gallstones, and some cancers and diminishes quality of life (Hu et al., 2001; Mokdad, Bowman et al., 2001; Mokdad, Ford et al., 2003; National Task Force on the Prevention and Treatment of Obesity, 1993; Sturm, 2002; Wickelgren, 1998). Obese people have 30 to 50 percent more chronic medical problems than smokers or problem drinkers (Sturm, 2002). Each year an estimated 300,000 U.S. adults die from obesity-related causes (Allison, Fontaine, Manson, Stevens, & Vanltallie, 1999). Obesity at 40—alone or combined with smoking—can take six to fourteen years off life (Peeters et al., 2003). In a fourteen-year longitudinal study of more than 1 million U.S. men and women, the risk of death from all causes, especially cardiovascular disease, increased with the degree of overweight (Calle, Thun, Petrelli, Rodriguez, & Heath, 1999). People at healthy weight levels need to maintain them, since both modest and large weight gains are associated with increased risks of disease (USDHHS, 2002b).

It is not clear whether these increased risks come from overweight itself or from inactivity and lack of cardiovascular fitness, which often accompany overweight. Since overweight becomes more prevalent with age, prevention of weight gain during young adulthood through healthy diet and regular physical activity is the most prudent approach (Wickelgren, 1998).

Physical Activity Adults who are physically active reap many benefits. Aside from helping to maintain desirable body weight, physical activity builds muscles; strengthens heart and lungs; lowers blood pressure; protects against heart disease, stroke, diabetes, cancer, and osteoporosis (a thinning of the bones that is most prevalent in middle-aged and older women, causing fractures); relieves anxiety and depression; and lengthens life (American Heart Association [AHA], 1995; Boulé, Haddad, Kenny, Wells, & Sigal, 2001; I. M. Lee & Paffenbarger, 1992; Pratt, 1999; USDHHS, 2002b; WHO, 2002a). Inactivity is a global public health problem. A sedentary lifestyle is one of the world's ten leading causes of death and disability (WHO, 2002a).

Young adults like these, who engage in regular physical activity, are likely to be healthier, happier, and live longer than if they rarely exercised.

Even moderate exercise has health benefits (I. M. Lee, Hsieh, & Paffenbarger, 1995; NIH Consensus Development Panel on Physical Activity and Cardiovascular Health, 1996; USDHHS, 2002b; WHO, 2002a). Incorporating more physical activity into daily life—for example, by walking instead of driving short distances, and climbing stairs instead of taking elevators—can be as effective as structured exercise (Andersen et al., 1999; Dunn et al., 1999; Pratt, 1999). In a longitudinal study of 15,902 healthy Finnish men and women ages 25 to 64, those who got even occasional exercise were less likely to die within the next nineteen years, regardless of genetic or familial factors (Kujala, Kaprio, Sarna, & Koskenvuo, 1998).

Despite all these advantages of exercise, only 44.3 percent of U.S. 18- to 24-year-olds—52.6 percent of men and 36 percent of women—engage in regular leisure-time physical activity, and the percentages drop with age (NCHS, 2002a). If adults—and children as well—engaged in thirty minutes of moderate physical activity daily, an estimated 250,000 deaths a year could be avoided, most of them from cardiovascular disease (NIH Consensus Development Panel, 1996; Pate, Pratt, Blair, Haskell, & Macera, 1995).

Smoking Smoking is the leading preventable cause of death in the United States (AHA, 1995). It kills about 400,000 people yearly and disables millions. When victims of passive smoking—inhaling other people's smoke—are added, the death toll may reach more than 450,000 (Bartecchi, MacKenzie, & Schrier, 1995). Despite these risks, 25 percent of the U.S. population uses tobacco regularly (AAP Committee on Substance Abuse, 2001).

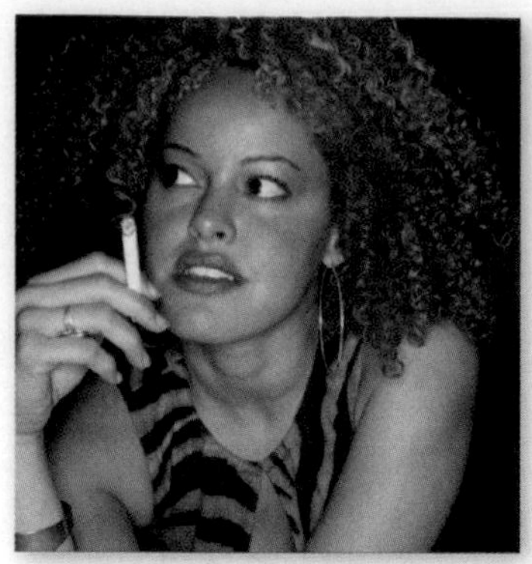

Because smoking is addictive, it is hard for some smokers to quit despite knowledge of the health risks. Smoking is especially harmful to African Americans, who metabolize more nicotine in their blood and are more subject to lung cancer than white Americans.

Worldwide, one-third of adults smoke cigarettes, and half of all persistent smokers—more than 4 million people each year—die from smoking-related diseases. By 2020, if current trends continue, tobacco will account for one-third of all adult deaths in the world (International Agency for Cancer Research, 2002; WHO, 2002b).

The link between smoking and lung cancer is well established. Smoking and exposure to environmental smoke are estimated to be responsible for about 90 percent of lung cancer in the United States (Wingo et al., 1999). Smoking is also linked to cancer of the stomach, liver, larynx, mouth, esophagus, bladder, kidney, pancreas, and cervix; to gastrointestinal problems, such as ulcers; to respiratory illnesses, such as bronchitis and emphysema; to osteoporosis; and to heart disease (He, Vupputuri, Prerost, Hughes, & Whelton, 1999; Hopper & Seeman, 1994; International Agency for Cancer Research, 2002; National Institute on Aging [NIA], 1993; Slemenda, 1994). Secondhand smoke exposes nonsmokers to the same carcinogens as active smokers inhale. Not only cigarettes, but also cigars, pipes, and other forms of smoking can be harmful (International Agency for Cancer Research, 2002).

Smokers are five times as likely as nonsmokers to have heart attacks in their thirties or forties (Parish et al., 1995). Passive smoke—even for as short a time as thirty minutes—has been shown to cause circulatory dysfunction and to increase the risk of cardiovascular disease in young Japanese men (Otsuka et al., 2001).

As the risks became known, smoking in the United States declined more than 37 percent after 1965 (AHA, 1995). Currently about 22 percent of American adults ages 18 and over—24.5 percent of men and 20 percent of women—are smokers (NCHS, 2002a). However, smoking is more prevalent among 18- to 25-year-olds; about 38 percent smoke cigarettes and about 10 percent smoke cigars (SAMHSA, 2001).

In view of the known risks of smoking, why do so many people do it? One reason is that smoking is addictive. A tendency to addiction may be genetic, and certain genes may affect the ability to quit (Lerman et al., 1999; Pianezza, Sellers, & Tyndale 1998; Sabol et al., 1999).

Giving up smoking reduces the risks of heart disease and stroke (Kawachi et al., 1993; NIA, 1993; Wannamethee, Shaper, Whincup, & Walker, 1995). Men and women who stop smoking have virtually no greater risk of heart attack, or of dying from heart disease within three to twenty years, than those who never have smoked (Rosenberg, Palmer, & Shapiro, 1990; Stamler, Dyer, Shekelle, Neaton, & Stamler, 1993).

Nicotine chewing gum, nicotine patches, and nicotine nasal sprays and inhalers, especially when combined with counseling, can help addicted persons taper off gradually and safely (Cromwell, Bartosch, Fiore, Hasselblad, & Baker, 1997; Hughes, Goldstein, Hurt, & Shiffman, 1999; NIA, 1993).

Alcohol The United States is a drinking society. Advertising equates liquor, beer, and wine with the good life and with being "grown up." About 60 percent of 21- to 35-year-olds report using alcohol at least once a month; 21-year-olds are the heaviest drinkers (Substance Abuse and Mental Health Services Administration [SAMHSA], 2001).

College is a prime time and place for drinking. Although frequent drinking is common at this age, college students tend to drink more, and more heavily, than their noncollegiate peers. About four out of five college students use alcohol, and about two out of five binge drink (down five or more drinks at a time) at least once in two weeks (National Institute on Alcohol Abuse and Alcoholism [NIAAA], 2002; SAMHSA, 2001). Individual drinking patterns are influenced by genetic and other biological characteristics, family and cultural backgrounds, previous drinking in high school, and the college environment.

Alcohol use is associated with other risks characteristic of young adulthood, such as traffic accidents, crime, and HIV infection (Leigh, 1999). Some 1,400 college students die each year from alcohol-related injuries, and drinking contributes to 500,000 injuries and 70,000 cases of date rape or sexual assault each year. Students who drink heavily tend to miss classes, fall behind in school, get lower grades, develop health problems, cause property damage, drive after drinking, get arrested, and engage in unplanned, unsafe sexual activity (SAMHSA, 2001; NIAAA, 2002).

Light-to-moderate alcohol consumption seems to reduce the risk of fatal heart disease and stroke, and also of dementia later in life (Ruitenberg et al., 2002). However, heavy drinking over the years may lead to cirrhosis of the liver, other gastrointestinal disorders (including ulcers), pancreatic disease, certain cancers, heart failure, stroke, damage to the nervous system, psychoses, and other medical problems (AHA, 1995; Fuchs et al., 1995). The risks of cancer of the mouth, throat, and esophagus are greater for excessive drinkers who smoke (NIAAA, 1998). Regular, long-term drinking increases the risk of breast cancer (Singletary & Gapstur, 2001; Smith-Warner et al., 1998).

Alcoholism is a chronic disease involving pathological dependence on alcohol, causing interference with normal functioning and fulfillment of obligations. Alcoholism runs in families; close relatives of people who are addicted to alcohol are three to four times as likely to become dependent on it as people whose relatives are not addicted (APA, 1994; McGue, 1993).

alcoholism Chronic disease involving dependence on use of alcohol, causing interference with normal functioning and fulfillment of obligations.

Alcoholism, like other addictions, seems to result from long-lasting changes in patterns of neural signal transmission in the brain. Exposure to a substance that creates a euphoric mental state brings about neurological adaptations that produce feelings of discomfort and craving when it is no longer present. Six to forty-eight hours after the last drink, alcoholics experience strong physical withdrawal symptoms (anxiety, agitation, tremors, elevated blood pressure, and sometimes seizures). Alcoholics, like drug addicts, develop a tolerance for the substance and need more and more to get the desired high (NIAAA, 1996b).

Depending on the severity of the condition, current treatment for alcoholism may include detoxification (removing all alcohol from the body), hospitalization, medication, individual and group psychotherapy, involvement of the family, and referral to a support organization, such as Alcoholics Anonymous. While not a cure, treatment can give alcoholics new tools for coping with their addiction and leading a productive life (Friedmann, Saitz, & Samet, 1998).

Drug Use Use of illicit drugs peaks at ages 18 to 20, with nearly 20 percent of this age group indulging at least monthly. Rates currently decline with age until the early forties, the cohort who were teenagers during the 1970s, when drug use was very high. Although college students' rate of current drug use (about 18 percent) is virtually the same as for others the same age, college graduates are less likely than other adults to use drugs (SAMHSA, 2001).

As in adolescence, marijuana is by far the most popular illicit drug among young adults. In 2000, 13.6 percent of 18- to 25-year-olds had used marijuana within the previous month, as compared with 3.6 percent who used psychotherapeutic drugs for nonmedical purposes, 1.8 percent who used hallucinogens, 1.4 percent who used cocaine, and less than 1 percent who used inhalants (SAMHSA, 2001). Collegiate marijuana users, like binge drinkers, tend to get lower grades, to spend less time studying and more time socializing, and to participate in other high-risk behaviors (Bell, Wechsler, & Johnston, 1997; Wechsler, Dowdall, Davenport, & Castillo, 1995).

As young adults mature, settle down, and take more responsibility for their future, they tend to cut down on drug use. Although 38.5 percent of all adults age 26 and older have tried illicit drugs, most commonly marijuana, only 4.2 percent are current users (SAMHSA, 2001).

Long-term marijuana use is associated with significant losses in memory and attention (Solowij et al., 2002). Chronic, heavy cocaine use also can impair cognitive

Checkpoint

Can you . . .

- ✔ Summarize the typical health status of young adults in the United States?
- ✔ List the leading causes of death in young adulthood?
- ✔ Tell how diet can affect the likelihood of cancer and heart disease?
- ✔ Give reasons for the "obesity epidemic"?
- ✔ Cite benefits of exercise?
- ✔ Discuss risks involved in smoking and substance use?

What's Your View?

- What specific things could you do to have a healthier lifestyle?

functioning (Bolla, Cadet, & London, 1998; Bolla, Rothman, & Cadet, 1999). Many baby boomers who began using drugs in their teens or early twenties, and continued to do so, now have severe drug-related medical problems (SAMHSA, 1998).

Indirect Influences on Health and Fitness

Apart from the things people do, or refrain from doing, which affect their health directly, there are indirect influences on health. Among the most important are income, education, race/ethnicity, and gender. Relationships also seem to make a difference.

Socioeconomic Status and Race/Ethnicity The connection between socioeconomic status and health has been widely documented. Higher-income people rate their health as better and live longer than lower-income people. Education is important, too. The less schooling people have had, the greater the chance that they will develop and die from communicable diseases, injuries, or chronic ailments (such as heart disease), or that they will become victims of homicide or suicide (Pamuk, Makuc, Heck, Reuben, & Lochner, 1998).

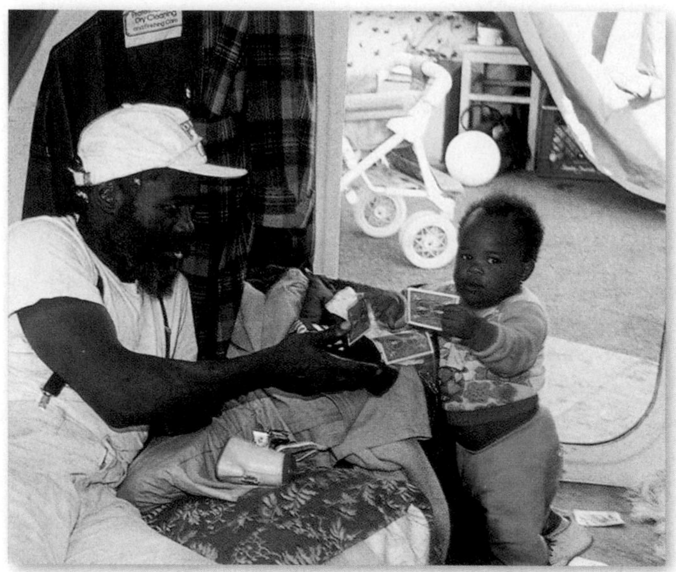

Income and living conditions are major influences on health. This homeless family may not be getting the nutrition and medical care needed for good health.

This does not mean that income and education *cause* good health; instead, they are related to environmental and lifestyle factors that are likely to be causative. Poverty is associated with poor nutrition, substandard housing, exposure to pollutants and violent behavior, and limited access to health care (Adler & Newman, 2002; Otten, Teutsch, Williamson, & Marks, 1990; Pamuk et al., 1998). Indeed, the gap in health care access between rich and poor in the United States has widened (Kiefe et al., 2000). Better-educated and more affluent people have healthier diets and better preventive health care and medical treatment. They exercise more, are less likely to be overweight, and smoke less. They are more likely to use alcohol, but to use it in moderation (Pamuk et al., 1998; SAMHSA, 1998, 2001).

The associations between income, education, living conditions, and health help shed light on the relatively poor state of health in some minority populations (Kiefe et al., 2000). Young black adults are twenty times more likely to have high blood pressure than young white adults (Agoda, 1995). And African Americans are more than twice as likely as white people to die in young adulthood, in part because young black men are about seven times as likely to be victims of homicide (Hoyert et al., 1999).

Ethnic differences in health are not wholly attributable to socioeconomic factors. For example, although African Americans smoke less than white Americans, they metabolize more nicotine in the blood, are more subject to lung cancer, and have more trouble breaking the habit. Possible reasons may be genetic, biological, or behavioral (Caraballo et al., 1998; Pérez-Stable, Herrera, Jacob III, & Benowitz, 1998; Sellers, 1998). In a study of coronary risk factors among women ages 30 and under (Palaniappan et al., 2002), Caucasian American women were found to have lower cardiac risk factors than African American or Asian Indian American women and to engage in more physical activity. The African American women consumed more fat and cholesterol than the other two groups and had higher percentages of body fat and higher body mass indexes (BMIs).

Disparities in most indicators of health lessened during the 1990s for most racial and ethnic groups, though not for American Indians and Alaska Natives. However,

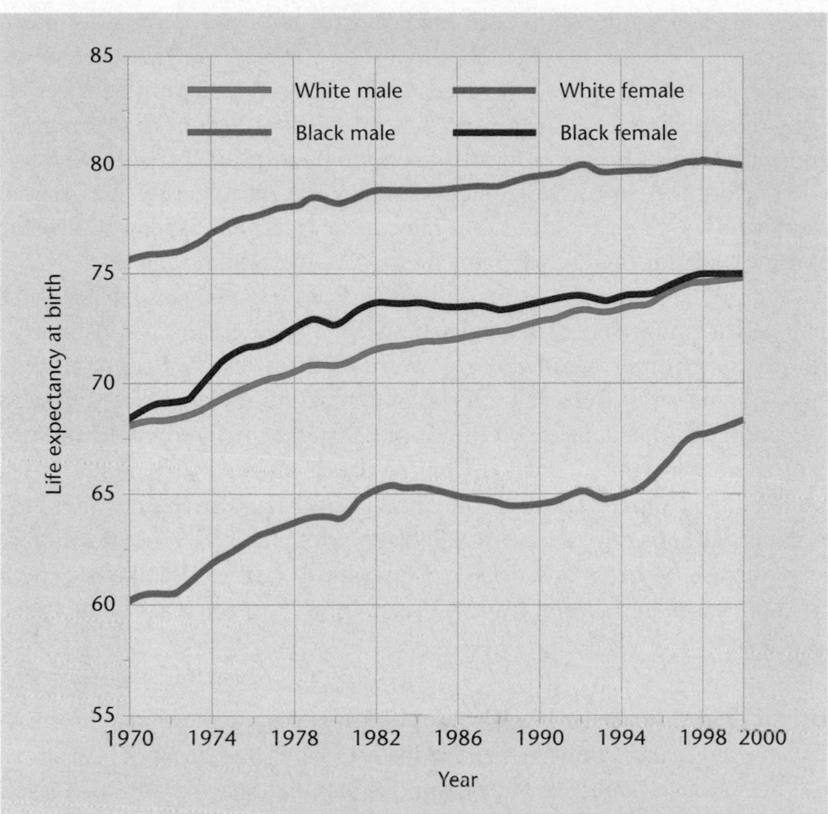

Figure 13-1
Life expectancy by sex and race, 1970–2000. (*Source:* Anderson, 2001b; data for 2000 from Miniño et al., 2002.)

racial and ethnic disparities in deaths from work-related injuries, motor vehicle crashes, and suicide widened (Keppel, Pearcy, & Wagener, 2002). A congressionally mandated research review of more than 100 studies found that racial and ethnic minorities tend to receive lower-quality health care than whites do, even when insurance status, income, age, and severity of conditions are similar (Smedley, Stith, & Nelson, 2002).

We further discuss the relationship between ethnicity and health in Chapter 15.

Gender Which sex is healthier: women or men? One reason this question is hard to answer is that until recently women have been excluded from many important studies of health problems that affect both sexes (Healy, 1991; Rodin & Ickovics, 1990). As a result, much of what we know applies only to men.

We do know that women have a higher life expectancy than men and lower death rates throughout life (Anderson, 2001b; Hoyert et al., 1999; see Figure 13-1 and Chapter 17). Women's greater longevity has been attributed to genetic protection given by the second X chromosome (which men do not have) and, before menopause, to beneficial effects of the female hormone estrogen, particularly on cardiovascular health (Rodin & Ickovics, 1990; USDHHS, 1992). However, psychosocial and cultural factors, such as men's greater propensity for risk taking and their preference for meat and potatoes rather than fruits and vegetables, also may play a part (Liebman, 1995a; Schardt, 1995).

Despite their longer life, women report being ill more often than men, are more likely to seek treatment for minor illnesses, and report more unexplained symptoms. Men, by contrast, have longer hospital stays, and their health problems are more likely to be chronic and life-threatening (Kroenke & Spitzer, 1998; NCHS, 1998; Rodin & Ickovics, 1990).

Women's greater tendency to seek medical care does not necessarily mean that women are in worse health than men, nor that they are imagining ailments or are preoccupied with illness (Kroenke & Spitzer, 1998). They may simply be more health-conscious. Women generally know more than men about health, think and do more about preventing illness, are more aware of symptoms and susceptibility, and are more likely to talk about their medical worries. Men may feel that illness is not "masculine" and thus may be less likely to admit that they do not feel well. It may be that the better care women take of themselves helps them live longer than men.

However, public awareness of men's health issues has increased. The availability of impotence treatment and of screening tests for prostate cancer is bringing more men into doctor's offices. Meanwhile, as women's lifestyles have become more like men's, so—in some ways—have their health patterns. Women now account for 39 percent of all smoking-related deaths in the United States. More women die of lung cancer than of any other type of cancer, including breast cancer (Satcher, 2001). The gap between men's and women's use of alcohol and illicit drugs also has narrowed (Center on Addiction and Substance Abuse [CASA], 1996), as has the gender gap in deaths from heart disease. Such trends help explain why the difference between women's and men's life expectancy shrank from 7.8 years in 1979 to 5.4 years in 2000 (Miniño et al., 2002).

Relationships and Health Personal relationships seem to be vital to health. People isolated from friends and family are twice as likely to fall ill and die as people who maintain social ties (House, Landis, & Umberson, 1988). Of course, because this research is correlational, we cannot be sure that relationships contribute to good health. It may be that healthy people are more likely to maintain relationships.

This happy couple are the picture of good health. Although there is a clear association between relationships and health, it isn't clear which is the cause and which the effect.

What is it about relationships that might promote good health? Social ties may foster a sense of meaning or coherence in life. Emotional support may help minimize stress. People who are in touch with others may be more likely to eat and sleep sensibly, get enough exercise, avoid substance abuse, and get necessary medical care (House et al., 1988).

Married people, especially men, tend to be healthier physically and, in some research, psychologically than those who are never-married, widowed, separated, or, especially, divorced (de Vaus, 2002; Horwitz, White, & Howell-White, 1996; Ross, Mirowsky, & Goldsteen, 1990). Contrary to previous belief, marriage seems to be as good for wives' mental health as for husbands'. This conclusion comes from a study of a random sample of 10,641 Australian adults. The study found that men are more likely to have substance use disorders, while women are more likely to have anxiety or depression, and marriage equally reduces the risk of both. One in four of the divorced participants had emotional problems (de Vaus, 2002).

Married people also tend to be better off financially, a factor associated with physical and mental health (Ross et al., 1990). In a study of more than 36,000 men and women ages 25 to 64, married people were less likely to die than unmarrieds. However, people with high incomes, married or single, were more likely to survive than were married people with low incomes; the highest mortality was among low-income singles (Rogers, 1995).

Marriage is related differently to mental and physical health in husbands than in wives. In a seven-year longitudinal survey of 1,201 young white, middle-class adults, men who got married and stayed married were less likely to become depressed, and the women who did so were less likely to develop alcohol problems, than those who remained single (Horwitz et al., 1996).

Checkpoint

Can you . . .

- ✔ Point out some differences in health and mortality that reflect income, education, race or ethnicity, and gender?
- ✔ Discuss how relationships, particularly marriage, may affect physical and mental health?

Sexual and Reproductive Issues

Sexual and reproductive activity can bring pleasure and sometimes parenthood. These natural and important functions also may involve physical concerns. Three such concerns are premenstrual syndrome (PMS), sexually transmitted diseases (STDs), and infertility.

Guidepost

2. What are some sexual and reproductive issues at this time of life?

Premenstrual Syndrome

Premenstrual syndrome (PMS) is a disorder that produces physical discomfort and emotional tension during the one to two weeks before a menstrual period. Symptoms may include fatigue, food cravings, headaches, swelling and tenderness of the breasts, swollen hands or feet, abdominal bloating, nausea, constipation, weight gain, anxiety, depression, irritability, mood swings, tearfulness, and difficulty concentrating or remembering ("PMS: It's Real," 1994; Reid & Yen, 1981). PMS typically affects women in their thirties or older. Up to 70 percent of menstruating women may have some symptoms, but in fewer than 10 percent do they create significant health problems (Freeman, Rickels, Sondheimer, & Polansky, 1995; "PMS: It's Real," 1994). Although some people believe PMS has emotional origins, a double-blind study established that it is an abnormal response to normal monthly surges of the female hormones estrogen and progesterone (Schmidt, Nieman, Danaceau, Adams, & Rubinow, 1998).

premenstrual syndrome (PMS) Disorder producing symptoms of physical discomfort and emotional tension during the one to two weeks before a menstrual period.

How to treat PMS is controversial. One widely used treatment—administration of progesterone in the form of a pill or suppository—proved in a large, randomized, controlled study to be no more beneficial than a placebo (Freeman, Rickels, Sondheimer, & Polansky, 1990). In a follow-up study, anti-anxiety pills proved more effective (Freeman et al., 1995). For milder symptoms, some doctors recommend exercise and dietary changes, such as avoiding fat, sodium, caffeine, and alcohol ("PMS: It's Real," 1994).

Sexually Transmitted Diseases (STDs)

An estimated 15 million people in the United States become infected with one or more STDs each year, and about half contract lifelong infections. Not surprisingly, the highest rates for most STDs are among adolescents and young adults, the age groups most likely to engage in risky sexual activity (CDC, 2000c; refer back to Chapter 12).

While some STDs—notably syphilis—have become less prevalent, others, such as gonorrhea and genital herpes, are on the rise. Although STDs are found in all racial and ethnic groups, they tend to be higher among African Americans than among white Americans, in part due to such factors as poverty, drug use, and sexual networks in which STDs are widespread (CDC, 2000c).

At the end of 2001, 40 million people worldwide were estimated to have HIV, the virus that causes AIDS; about 95 percent were in the developing world. The majority of new infections occur in young adults, especially young women. Worldwide, AIDS is the fourth leading cause of death; in sub-Saharan Africa, it is first (WHO, 2001).

Globally, most HIV-infected adults are heterosexual (Altman, 1992). In the United States, HIV has been most prevalent among homosexual and bisexual men, drug abusers who share contaminated hypodermic needles, and people who have heterosexual contact with infected partners. Only about 1 percent of cases are in people who (like Arthur Ashe) have received transfusions of infected blood or blood products (CDC, 2001b).

In the United States, the AIDS epidemic has begun to come under control. In 1995 AIDS became the leading cause of death for 25- to 44-year-olds. In 2000 it was fifth (Hoyert et al., 1999; Miniño et al., 2002). Of the total 793,026 AIDS cases reported since 1981, 484,067 have been in young adults (CDC, 2001b).

As many as 300,000 persons may be unaware that they are infected with HIV (CDC, 2001c): nearly half of 25- to 34-year-olds and two-thirds of 18- to 24-year-olds never have been tested (NCHS, 2002a).

Getting men to use condoms, the most effective means of preventing STDs, is often not easy. In a study of 822 young inner-city women, only 7 percent reported that their main partners consistently used condoms. Percentages were higher among women with a strong sense of self-efficacy, perhaps because they were more assertive with their partners (Stark et al., 1998). A three-session intervention among U.S. Marine security guards resulted in increased perception of social support for condom use and stronger intentions to practice safe sex (Booth-Kewley, Minagawa, Shaffer, & Brodine, 2002).

infertility Inability to conceive after twelve months of trying.

Infertility An estimated 7 percent of U.S. couples experience **infertility:** inability to conceive a baby after twelve months of trying (CDC, 2001a). Women's fertility begins to decline in the late twenties, with substantial decreases during the thirties. Men's fertility is less affected by age but declines significantly by the late thirties (Dunson, Colombo, & Baird, 2002).

The most common cause of infertility in men is production of too few sperm. Although only one sperm is needed to fertilize an ovum, a sperm count lower than 60 to 200 million per ejaculation makes conception unlikely. Sometimes an ejaculatory duct is blocked, preventing the exit of sperm; or sperm may be unable to "swim" well enough to reach the cervix. Some cases of male infertility seem to have a genetic basis (King, 1996; Phillips, 1998; Reijo, Alagappan, Patrizio, & Page, 1996).

If the problem is with the woman, she may not be producing ova; the ova may be abnormal; mucus in the cervix may prevent sperm from penetrating it; or a disease of the uterine lining may prevent implantation of the fertilized ovum. A major cause of declining fertility in women after age 30 is deterioration in the quality of their ova (van Noord-Zaadstra et al., 1991). However, the most common female cause is blockage of the fallopian tubes, preventing ova from reaching the uterus. In about half of these cases, the tubes are blocked by scar tissue from STDs (King, 1996).

Infertility burdens a marriage emotionally. Partners may become frustrated and angry with themselves and each other and may feel empty, worthless, and depressed (Abbey, Andrews, & Halman, 1992; H. W. Jones & Toner, 1993). Such couples may benefit from professional counseling or support from other infertile couples.

Hormone treatment may raise a man's sperm count or increase a woman's ovulation. Sometimes drug therapy or surgery can correct the problem. However, fertility drugs increase the likelihood of multiple, and often premature, births (King, 1996). Also, men undergoing fertility treatment are at increased risk of producing sperm with chromosomal abnormalities (Levron et al., 1998).

New research suggests that couples who have been unable to bear children after one year should not necessarily rush into fertility treatments. Unless there is a known cause for failure to conceive, the chances of success after eighteen months to two years are high. Among 782 women in six European countries, 9 out of 10 even of those in their late thirties were able to conceive by the end of the second year of trying, unless the male partner was over 40 (Dunson, 2002).

For couples who give up on the natural way, science today offers several alternative ways to parenthood.

Assisted Reproduction Assisted reproduction began in 1978 with the birth of Louise Brown of England, the first child born by means of *in vitro fertilization (IVF),* fertilization outside the mother's body. Today the field of assisted reproduction has mushroomed. In 1998, more than 20,000 U.S. women delivered with technological help, giving birth to more than 29,000 babies (Society for Assisted Reproductive Technology and the American Society for Reproductive Medicine, 2002).

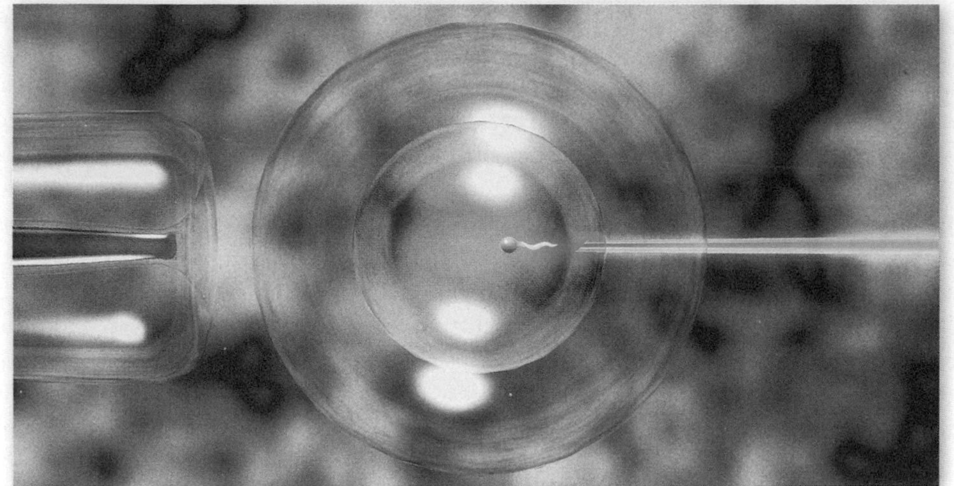

In in vitro fertilization, *a microscopically tiny needle (right) injects a single male sperm cell into a ripe egg (center), which has been surgically removed from the woman's body. A flat-nosed pipette (left) is used to hold the egg steady during the insertion. The fertilized egg is then implanted in the womb. This technique is one of several forms of assisted reproduction that are helping some infertile couples to reproduce.*

In IVF, the most common procedure, fertility drugs are given to increase production of ova. Then one or more mature ova are surgically removed, fertilized in a laboratory dish, and implanted in the woman's uterus. Usually 50,000 to 100,000 sperm are used to increase the chances of fertilization, and several embryos are transferred to the uterus to increase the chances of pregnancy. (This also increases the likelihood of multiple births.)

Many of the women, like Louise Brown's mother, who have successfully conceived in this way have fallopian tubes blocked or scarred beyond surgical repair. This method also can address severe male infertility, since a single sperm can be injected into the ovum—a technique called *intracytoplasmic sperm injection (ICSI)*. However, there is a significant risk of transmission of a genetic defect, which increases the likelihood that the resulting offspring will be infertile. Preimplantation genetic diagnosis (refer back to Chapter 3) can help ensure that only normal embryos are implanted (Parikh et al., 2001).

Artificial insemination—injection of sperm into a woman's vagina, cervix, or uterus—can be done when a man has a low sperm count. Sperm from several ejaculations can be combined for one injection, enabling the couple to produce their own biological offspring. If the man is infertile, a couple may choose *donor insemination (DI)*. If the woman has no explainable cause of infertility, the chances of success can be greatly increased by stimulating her ovaries to produce excess ova and injecting semen directly in the uterus (Colón, 1997; Guzick et al., 1999).

A woman who is producing poor-quality ova or who has had her ovaries removed may try *ovum transfer*. In this procedure, *donor egg*—an ovum provided, usually anonymously, by a fertile young woman—is fertilized in the laboratory and implanted in the prospective mother's uterus. Alternatively, the ovum can be fertilized in the donor's body by artificial insemination. The donor's uterus is flushed out a few days later, and the embryo is retrieved and inserted into the recipient's uterus.

In the United States in 1998, 390 clinics offered IVF and related fertility procedures, and 81,899 were carried out—an increase of nearly 27 percent in just two years. However, the success rate was low—about one live birth for every four procedures done; and more than half of the procedures produced multiple births, with high risks for complications such as major birth defects and low birthweight. Two newer techniques with higher success rates are *gamete intrafallopian transfer (GIFT)* and *zygote intrafallopian transfer (ZIFT)*, in which either the egg and sperm or the fertilized egg are inserted in the fallopian tube (CDC, 2002c; Schieve et al., 2002; Society for Assisted Reproductive Technology, 1993, 2002).

In *surrogate motherhood,* a fertile woman is impregnated by the prospective father, usually by artificial insemination. She carries the baby to term and gives the child to the father and his mate. Surrogate motherhood is in legal limbo; courts in most states view surrogacy contracts as unenforceable, and some states have either banned the practice or placed strict conditions on it. The American Academy of Pediatrics (AAP) Committee on Bioethics (1992) recommends that surrogacy be considered a tentative preconception adoption agreement in which the surrogate is the sole decision maker before the birth. The AAP committee also recommends a prebirth agreement on the period of time in which the surrogate may assert her parental rights.

What's Your View?

- If you or your partner were infertile, would you seriously consider or undertake one of the methods of assisted reproduction described here? Why or why not?

Perhaps the most objectionable aspect of surrogacy, aside from the possibility of forcing the surrogate to relinquish the baby, is the payment of money. The creation of a "breeder class" of poor and disadvantaged women who carry the babies of the well-to-do strikes many people as wrong. Similar concerns have been raised about payment for donor eggs. Exploitation of the would-be parents is an issue, too (Gabriel, 1996).

Checkpoint

Can you . . .

- ✔ Discuss ways to control the spread of STDs?
- ✔ Identify several causes of male and female infertility?
- ✔ Describe several means of assisted reproduction, and discuss issues they raise?

How do children conceived by artificial means turn out? Among babies born in Western Australia between 1993 and 1997, those conceived by IVF or ICSI were twice as likely to show major birth defects during the first year as infants conceived naturally (Hansen, Kurinczuk, Bower, & Webb, 2002). It is not known whether these increased risks are due to the fertility procedures themselves or to characteristics connected with infertility. There is no evidence of adverse cognitive effects from IVF, other than those associated with the increased risk of premature or multiple births (Saunders, Spensley, Munro, & Halasz, 1996). Socially and emotionally, artificially conceived children tend to be well adjusted. Two longitudinal studies—one of 34 children conceived by IVF (but genetically related to both parents) and the other of 37 children conceived by DI—found little or no difference in socioemotional development at age 12 between these children and naturally conceived or adopted children (Golombok, MacCallum, & Goodman, 2001; Golombok, MacCallum, Goodman, & Rutter, 2002).

One thing seems certain: as long as there are people who want children but are unable to conceive or bear them, human ingenuity and technology will come up with ways to satisfy their need.

COGNITIVE DEVELOPMENT

Perspectives on Adult Cognition

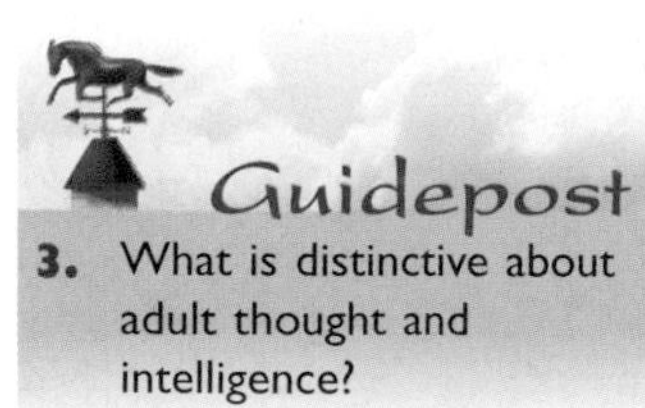

Guidepost

3. What is distinctive about adult thought and intelligence?

Common sense tells us that adults think differently from children or adolescents. They hold different kinds of conversations, understand more complicated material, and use their broader experience to solve practical problems. Is common sense correct? Developmental theorists and researchers have studied adult cognition from a variety of perspectives. Some investigators, such as K. Warner Schaie, take a stage approach, seeking to identify what is distinctive about the way adults think, as Piaget did for children's thinking. Other investigators, such as Robert Sternberg, focus on types or aspects of intelligence, overlooked by psychometric tests, that tend to come to the fore in adulthood. One current theory highlights the role of emotion in intelligent behavior.

Beyond Piaget: The Shift to Postformal Thought

Although Piaget described the stage of formal operations as the pinnacle of cognitive achievement, some developmental scientists maintain that changes in cognition extend beyond that stage. According to Piaget's critics, formal reasoning is not the only, and perhaps not even the most important, capability of mature thought (Moshman, 1998). Research and theoretical work since the 1970s suggest that mature thinking may be far richer and more complex than the abstract intellectual manipulations Piaget described (Arlin, 1984; Labouvie-Vief, 1985, 1990a; Labouvie-Vief & Hakim-Larson, 1989; Sinnott, 1984, 1989a, 1989b, 1991, 1998). For example, when asked whether there was the same amount of space in differently shaped houses made with the same number of blocks, one woman said no: "When you start getting fancy, you always lose some space because [you] have to have a hallway upstairs as well as downstairs, which takes away space" (Roberts, Papalia-Finlay, Davis, Blackburn, & Dellman, 1982, p. 191). This apparently preformal response actually was the result of experience and nuanced thinking.

Thought in adulthood often appears to be flexible, open, adaptive, and individualistic. It draws on intuition and emotion as well as on logic to help people cope with a seemingly chaotic world. It applies the fruits of experience to ambiguous situations. It is characterized by the ability to deal with uncertainty, inconsistency, contradiction, imperfection, and compromise (as Arthur Ashe did when faced with physical limitations on his ability to continue his tennis career). This higher stage of adult cognition is sometimes called **postformal thought.**

postformal thought Mature type of thinking, which relies on subjective experience and intuition as well as logic and is useful in dealing with ambiguity, uncertainty, inconsistency, contradiction, imperfection, and compromise.

Postformal thought is relativistic. Immature thinking sees black and white (right versus wrong, intellect versus feelings, mind versus body); postformal thinking sees shades of gray. It often develops in response to events and interactions that open up unaccustomed ways of looking at things and challenge a simple, polarized view of the world. It enables adults to transcend a single logical system (such as a particular theory of human development, or an established political system) and reconcile or choose among conflicting ideas or demands (such as those of the Israelis and Palestinians), each of which, from its own perspective, may have a valid claim to truth (Labouvie-Vief, 1990a, 1990b; Sinnott, 1996, 1998).

One prominent researcher, Jan Sinnott (1984, 1998), has proposed several criteria of postformal thought. Among them are the following:

- *Shifting gears.* Ability to shift back and forth between abstract reasoning and practical, real-world considerations. ("This might work on paper but not in real life.")
- *Multiple causality, multiple solutions.* Awareness that most problems have more than one cause and more than one solution, and that some solutions are more likely to work than others. ("Let's try it your way; if that doesn't work, we can try my way.")
- *Pragmatism.* Ability to choose the best of several possible solutions and to recognize criteria for choosing. ("If you want the most practical solution, do this; if you want the quickest solution, do that.")
- *Awareness of paradox.* Recognition that a problem or solution involves inherent conflict. ("Doing this will give him what he wants, but it will only make him unhappy in the end.")

Postformal thinking deals with information in a social context. Unlike the problems Piaget studied, which involve physical phenomena and require dispassionate, objective observation and analysis, social dilemmas are less clearly structured and often fraught with emotion. It is in these kinds of situations that mature adults tend to call on postformal thought (Berg & Klaczynski, 1996; Sinnott, 1996, 1998).

One study (Labouvie-Vief, Adams, Hakim-Larson, Hayden, & DeVoe, 1987) asked people from preadolescence through middle age to consider the following problem:

> John is a heavy drinker, especially at parties. His wife, Mary, warns him that if he gets drunk once more, she will take the children and leave him. John does come home drunk after an office party. Does Mary leave John?

Preadolescents and most early adolescents answered "yes": Mary would leave John because she had said she would. More mature adolescents and adults took into account the problem's human dimensions; they realized that Mary might not go through with her threat. The *most* mature thinkers recognized that there are a number of ways to interpret the same problem, and that the way people look at such questions often depends on their life experience. The ability to envision multiple outcomes was only partly age related; although it did not appear until late adolescence or early adulthood, adults in their forties did not necessarily think more maturely than adults in their twenties.

Other research, however, has found a general, age-related progression toward postformal thought throughout young and middle adulthood, especially when emotions are involved (Blanchard-Fields, 1986). In one study, participants were asked to judge what caused the outcomes of a series of hypothetical situations, such as a marital conflict. Adolescents and young adults tended to blame individuals, whereas middle-aged people were more likely to attribute behavior to the interplay among persons and environment. The more ambiguous the situation, the greater were the age differences in interpretation (Blanchard-Fields & Norris, 1994).

Although a number of studies support the existence of postformal thought (Berg & Klaczynski, 1996; Sinnott, 1996, 1998), critics say the concept has a thin research base. Much of the supporting research has taken the form of extensive, time-consuming interviews that probe participants' views of hypothetical situations and then compare their responses to subjective criteria. Such studies are not easy to replicate, so the validity of their conclusions cannot easily be tested.

Empirical evidence of the value of postformal thought did emerge from a longitudinal study of 130 freshman medical students. Their degree of tolerance for ambiguity, together with their empathy as juniors and seniors (a combination of emotion and cognition), predicted their clinical performance as rated by patients (Morton et al., 2000). (We further discuss postformal thought in Chapter 15.)

Checkpoint

Can you . . .

- ✔ Explain the difference between formal and postformal thinking, and tell why postformal thought may be especially suited to solving social problems?

Schaie: A Life-Span Model of Cognitive Development

One of the few investigators to propose a full life-span model of cognitive development is K. Warner Schaie (1977–1978; Schaie & Willis, 2000). Schaie's model looks at the developing *uses* of intellect within a social context. His seven stages revolve around objectives that come to the fore at various stages of life. These objectives shift from acquisition of information and skills *(what I need to know)* to practical integration of knowledge and skills *(how to use what I know)* to a search for meaning and purpose *(why I should know)*. The seven stages are as follows:

1. **Acquisitive stage** (childhood and adolescence). Children and adolescents acquire information and skills mainly for their own sake or as preparation for participation in society.
2. **Achieving stage** (late teens or early twenties to early thirties). Young adults no longer acquire knowledge merely for its own sake; they use what they know to pursue goals, such as career and family.
3. **Responsible stage** (late thirties to early sixties). Middle-aged people use their minds to solve practical problems associated with responsibilities to others, such as family members or employees.
4. **Executive stage** (thirties or forties through middle age). People in the executive stage, which may overlap with the achieving and responsible stages, are responsible for societal systems (such as governmental or business organizations) or social movements. They deal with complex relationships on multiple levels.

acquisitive stage First of Schaie's seven cognitive stages, in which children and adolescents learn information and skills largely for their own sake or as preparation for participation in society.

achieving stage Second of Schaie's seven cognitive stages, in which young adults use knowledge to gain competence and independence.

responsible stage Third of Schaie's seven cognitive stages, in which middle-aged people are concerned with long-range goals and practical problems related to their responsibility for others.

executive stage Fourth of Schaie's seven cognitive stages, in which middle-aged people responsible for societal systems deal with complex relationships on several levels.

5. **Reorganizational stage** (end of middle age, beginning of late adulthood). People who enter retirement reorganize their lives and intellectual energies around meaningful pursuits that take the place of paid work.
6. **Reintegrative stage** (late adulthood). Older adults, who may have let go of some social involvement and whose cognitive functioning may be limited by biological changes, are often more selective about what tasks they expend effort on. They focus on the purpose of what they do and concentrate on tasks that have the most meaning for them.
7. **Legacy-creating stage** (advanced old age). Near the end of life, once reintegration has been completed (or along with it), older people may create instructions for the disposition of prized possessions, make funeral arrangements, provide oral histories, or write their life stories as a legacy for their loved ones. All of these tasks involve the exercise of cognitive competencies within a social and emotional context.

reorganizational stage Fifth of Schaie's seven cognitive stages, in which adults entering retirement reorganize their lives around nonwork-related activities.

reintegrative stage Sixth of Schaie's seven cognitive stages, in which older adults choose to focus limited energy on tasks that have meaning to them.

legacy-creating stage Seventh of Schaie's seven cognitive stages, in which very old people prepare for death by recording their life stories, distributing possessions, and the like.

Not everyone goes through these stages within the suggested time frames. Indeed, Arthur Ashe, by the time of his premature death, had moved through all of them. As a boy in the *acquisitive stage,* Ashe gained the knowledge and skills needed to become a top tennis player. While still in high school and college, he was already entering the *achieving stage,* refining his knowledge and skills as he used them to win amateur tournaments and lay the groundwork for a professional tennis career. In his thirties he moved into the *responsible stage,* helping to found a tennis players' union, serving as its president, and then becoming captain of the U.S. Davis Cup team. He also became more keenly aware of his responsibility to use his position to promote racial justice and equal opportunity. Shifting into the *executive stage,* he served as chairman of the National Heart Association and on the boards of directors of corporations and established tennis programs for inner-city youths in several cities. Meanwhile, his early retirement from tennis and then his struggle with AIDS led him into the *reorganizational stage,* lecturing, writing, playing golf, and acting as a television sports commentator. His ultimate decision to "go public" with the news of his illness pushed him into the *reintegrative* and *legacy creating stages:* spearheading a nationwide movement for AIDS research and education and writing books on African American history—projects that would have a lasting impact.

If adults do go through stages such as these, then traditional psychometric tests, which use the same kinds of tasks to measure intelligence at all periods of life, may be inappropriate for them. Tests developed to measure knowledge and skills in children may not be suitable for measuring cognitive competence in adults, who use knowledge and skills to solve practical problems and achieve self-chosen goals. Thus we may need measures that show competence in dealing with real-life challenges, such as balancing a checkbook, reading a railroad timetable, and making informed decisions about medical problems. Robert Sternberg has taken a step in this direction.

Checkpoint

Can you . . .

✔ Describe Schaie's seven stages of cognitive development and give reasons why intelligence tests devised for children may not be valid for adults?

Sternberg: Insight and Know-How

> Each of us knows individuals who succeed in school but fail in their careers, or conversely, who fail in school but succeed in their careers. We have watched as graduate students, at the top of their class in the initial years of structured coursework, fall by the wayside when they must work independently on research and a dissertation. Most of us know of colleagues whose brilliance in their academic fields is matched only by their incompetence in social interactions. (Sternberg, Wagner, Williams, & Horvath, 1995, p. 912)

Alix, Barbara, and Courtney applied to graduate programs at Yale University. Alix had earned almost straight A's in college, scored high on the Graduate Record Examination (GRE), and had excellent recommendations. Barbara's grades were only fair, and her GRE scores were low by Yale's standards, but her letters of recommendation enthusiastically praised her exceptional research and creative ideas. Courtney's grades, GRE scores, and recommendations were good but not among the best.

Alix and Courtney were admitted to the graduate program. Barbara was not admitted but was hired as a research associate and took graduate classes on the side. Alix did very well for the first year or so, but less well after that. Barbara confounded the admissions committee by doing outstanding work. Courtney's performance in graduate school was only fair, but she had the easiest time getting a good job afterward (Trotter, 1986).

experiential element Sternberg's term for the insightful or creative aspect of intelligence.

contextual element Sternberg's term for the practical aspect of intelligence.

componential element Sternberg's term for the analytic aspect of intelligence.

According to Sternberg's (1985a, 1987) triarchic theory of intelligence (introduced in Chapter 9), Barbara and Courtney were strong in two aspects of intelligence that psychometric tests miss: creative insight (what Sternberg calls the **experiential element**) and practical intelligence (the **contextual element**). Since insight and practical intelligence are very important in adult life, psychometric tests are much less useful in gauging adults' intelligence and predicting their life success than in measuring children's intelligence and predicting their school success. As an undergraduate, Alix's **componential** (analytical) ability helped her sail through examinations. However, in graduate school, where original thinking is expected, Barbara's superior experiential intelligence—her fresh insights and innovative ideas—began to shine. So did Courtney's practical, contextual intelligence—her "street smarts." She knew her way around. She chose "hot" research topics, submitted papers to the "right" journals, and knew where and how to apply for jobs.

Studies suggest that creative production and the ability to solve practical problems grow at least until midlife (see Chapter 15), while the ability to solve academic problems generally declines (Sternberg et al., 1995). Practical problems emerge from personal experience, as does the information needed to solve them. Being more relevant to the solver, they evoke more careful thinking and provide a better gauge of cognitive ability than academic problems, which are made up by someone else, provide all necessary information, and are disconnected from everyday life. Academic problems generally have a definite answer and one right way to find it; practical problems are often ill-defined and have a variety of possible solutions and ways of reaching them, each with its advantages and disadvantages (Neisser, 1976; Sternberg & Wagner, 1989; Wagner & Sternberg, 1985). Life experience helps adults solve such problems.

tacit knowledge Sternberg's term for information that is not formally taught or openly expressed but is necessary to get ahead.

An important aspect of practical intelligence is **tacit knowledge:** "inside information," "know-how," or "savvy" that is not formally taught or openly expressed (Sternberg, Grigorenko, & Oh, 2001; Sternberg & Wagner, 1993; Sternberg et al., 1995; Wagner & Sternberg, 1986). Tacit knowledge, acquired largely on one's own, is "commonsense" knowledge of how to get ahead—how to win a promotion or cut through red tape. It is not well correlated with measures of general cognitive ability, but it may be a better predictor of managerial success (Sternberg, Grigorenko, & Oh, 2001).

Tacit knowledge may include *self-management* (knowing how to motivate oneself and organize time and energy), *management of tasks* (knowing, for example, how to write a term paper or grant proposal), and *management of others* (knowing when and how to reward or criticize subordinates). Employers can increase effective use of tacit knowledge by rewarding team effort and information sharing, linking employees with electronic networks, and maintaining a database of "tips" and "war stories" to which employees contribute (Smith, 2001).

Sternberg's method of testing tacit knowledge is to compare a test-taker's chosen course of action in hypothetical, work-related situations (such as how best to angle for a promotion) with the choices of experts in the field and with accepted "rules of thumb." Tacit knowledge, measured in this way, seems to be unrelated to IQ and predicts job performance better than do psychometric tests (Sternberg et al., 1995).

One study posed simulated critical situations to 16 registered nurses who averaged almost fifteen years' experience. One task called for dressing a slightly infected wound on the forearm of a patient who had fallen from a motor bike, and who showed signs of hypoglycemia (weakness, perspiring, trembling, and hunger) and possible head trauma. The nurses who dealt most successfully with the situation showed no greater explicit (consciously learned) knowledge than those who did poorly; the difference was in their application of tacit knowledge: their willingness to use their feelings and intuitions in deciding how to act and their organization of knowledge in a holistic, interactive way (Herbig, Büssing, & Ewert, 2001).

These colleagues conferring informally about their work will be helped to achieve professional success by their tacit knowledge—practical, "inside" information about how things are done, which is not formally taught but must be gained from experience.

Of course, tacit knowledge is not all that is needed to succeed; other aspects of intelligence count, too. In studies of business managers, tests of tacit knowledge together with IQ and personality tests predicted virtually *all* of the variance in performance, as measured by such criteria as salary, years of management experience, and the company's success (Sternberg et al., 1995). In one study, tacit knowledge was related to the salaries managers earned at a given age and to how high their positions were, independent of family background and education. The most knowledgeable managers were not those who had spent many years with a company or many years as managers, but those who had worked for the most companies, perhaps gaining a greater breadth of experience (Sternberg et al., 2000).

Further research is needed to determine how and when tacit knowledge is acquired, why some people acquire it more efficiently than others, and how it can best be measured. In the meantime, tests of practical intelligence such as these can be a valuable supplement to the aptitude tests now widely used in hiring and promotion.

Emotional Intelligence

In the 1960s, the U.S. State Department asked the psychologist David McClelland to find a better way of selecting foreign service officers. The test of general knowledge then in use was a poor predictor of performance and tended to screen out women and minorities. McClelland found that the characteristics that set top performers apart had nothing to do with cognitive abilities. Most important were sensitivity to others, positive expectations of others, and speed in learning social networks. On the basis of these findings McClelland devised a new selection process that proved a far better predictor of success than the old cognitive test—and eliminated the discrimination against women and minorities (Spencer & Spencer, 1993).

The finding that emotions influence success is not new, nor does it apply only to adults. However, it is in adult life, with its "make-or-break" challenges, that we can perhaps see most clearly the role of the emotions in influencing how effectively people use their minds—as Arthur Ashe demonstrated again and again.

In 1990, two psychologists, Peter Salovey and John Mayer, coined the term **emotional intelligence** (sometimes called *EI*). It refers to the ability to recognize and deal with one's own feelings and the feelings of others. Daniel Goleman (1995, 1998, 2001), the psychologist and science writer who popularized the concept, expanded it to include such qualities as optimism, conscientiousness, motivation, empathy, and social competence.

emotional intelligence Salovey and Mayer's term for ability to understand and regulate emotions; an important component of effective, intelligent behavior.

According to Goleman, these abilities may be more important to success, on the job and elsewhere, than is IQ. Goleman cites studies of nearly 500 corporations in which people who scored highest on EI rose to the top. EI seems to underlie competencies that contribute to effective performance at work. These competencies, according to Goleman (1998, 2001), fall under the heads of *self-awareness* (emotional self-awareness, accurate self-assessment, and self-confidence), *self-management* (self-control, trustworthiness, conscientiousness, adaptability, achievement drive, and initiative), *social awareness* (empathy, service orientation, and organizational awareness), and *relationship management* (developing others, exerting influence, communication, conflict management, leadership, being a catalyst for change, building bonds, and teamwork and collaboration. Excelling in at least one competency in each of these four areas seems to be a key to success in almost any job (Cherniss, 2002; Cherniss & Adler, 2000; Goleman, 1998).

Emotional intelligence may play a part in the ability to acquire and use tacit knowledge, as in the nurses' study discussed in the previous section. In nursing, as in other fields, EI may be vital to the abilities to work effectively in teams, to recognize and respond appropriately to one's own and another's feelings, and to motivate oneself and others (Cadman & Brewer, 2001). It also may affect how well people navigate intimate relationships and how healthy they remain under stress (Cherniss, 2002).

Emotional intelligence is not the opposite of cognitive intelligence, says Goleman; some people are high in both, while others have little of either. He speculates that EI may be largely set by midadolescence, when the parts of the brain that control how people act on their emotions mature. Men and women tend to have differing emotional strengths. On an EI test given to 4,500 men and 3,200 women, the women scored higher on empathy and social responsibility, the men on stress tolerance and self-confidence (Murray, 1998).

Emotional intelligence echoes some other developmental theories and concepts. It is reminiscent of Gardner's proposed intrapersonal and interpersonal intelligences (refer back to Chapter 9). It also resembles postformal thought in its connection between emotion and cognition.

Although research supports the role of emotions in intelligent behavior, the concept of EI is controversial. Hard as it is to assess cognitive intelligence, EI may be even harder to measure. For one thing, lumping the emotions together can be misleading. How do we assess someone who can handle fear but not guilt, or who can face stress better than boredom? Then too, the usefulness of a certain emotion may depend on the circumstances. Anger, for example, can lead to either destructive or constructive behavior. Anxiety may alert a person to danger but also may block effective action (Goleman, 1995). Furthermore, most of the alleged components of EI are usually considered personality traits. One investigation found that objective measures of EI, as currently defined, are unreliable, and those that depend on self-ratings are almost indistinguishable from personality tests (Davies, Stankov, & Roberts, 1998).

Ultimately, acting on emotions often comes down to a value judgment. Is it smarter to obey or disobey authority? To inspire others or exploit them? "Emotional skills, like intellectual ones, are morally neutral. . . . Without a moral compass to guide people in how to employ their gifts, emotional intelligence can be used for good or evil" (Gibbs, 1995, p. 68). Let's look next at the development of that "moral compass" in adulthood.

What's Your View?

- In what kinds of situations would postformal thought be most useful? Give specific examples. Do the same for tacit knowledge and emotional intelligence.
- Who is the most intelligent person you know? Why do you consider this person exceptionally intelligent? Would you ask this person for advice about a personal problem? Why or why not?

Checkpoint

Can you . . .

- ✔ Compare several theoretical views on adult cognition?
- ✔ Cite support for, and criticisms of, the concept of emotional intelligence?

Moral Development

In Kohlberg's theory, moral development of children and adolescents accompanies cognitive maturation. Youngsters advance in moral judgment as they shed egocentrism and become capable of abstract thought. In adulthood, however, moral judgments often become more complex.

According to Kohlberg, advancement to the third level of moral reasoning—fully principled, postconventional morality—is chiefly a function of experience (refer back to Chapter 11). Most people do not reach this level until their twenties, if ever. Although cognitive awareness of higher moral principles often develops in adolescence, people

Guidepost

4. How does moral reasoning develop?

typically do not commit themselves to such principles until adulthood (Kohlberg, 1973). Two experiences that spur moral development in young adults are encountering conflicting values away from home (as happens in college or the armed services or sometimes in foreign travel) and being responsible for the welfare of others (as in parenthood).

Experience may lead adults to reevaluate their criteria for what is right and fair. Some adults spontaneously offer personal experiences as reasons for their answers to moral dilemmas. For example, people who have had cancer, or whose relatives or friends have had cancer, are more likely to condone a man's stealing an expensive drug to save his dying wife, and to explain this view in terms of their own experience (Bielby & Papalia, 1975). Arthur Ashe's experiences in a highly competitive environment, captaining the U.S. Davis Cup team, led him to be more activist and outspoken in his advocacy of an end to apartheid in South Africa. Such experiences, strongly colored by emotion, trigger rethinking in a way that hypothetical, impersonal discussions cannot and are more likely to help people see other points of view.

With regard to moral judgments, then, cognitive stages do not tell the whole story. Of course, someone whose thinking is still egocentric is unlikely to make moral decisions at a postconventional level; but even someone who can think abstractly may not reach the highest level of moral development unless experience catches up with cognition. Many adults who are capable of thinking for themselves do not break out of a conventional mold unless their experiences have prepared them for the shift. Furthermore, experience is interpreted within a cultural context.

Culture and Moral Development Israelis raised on a kibbutz, a collective farming or industrial settlement, are imbued with a socialist perspective. How do such people score on a problem such as Heinz's dilemma, which weighs the value of human life against a druggist's right to charge what the traffic will bear? Interviewers using Kohlberg's standardized scoring manual ran into trouble in trying to classify the following response:

> The medicine should be made available to all in need; the druggist should not have the right to decide on his own. . . . The whole community or society should have control of the drug.

Responses such as this one were coupled with statements about the importance of obeying the law and thus were confusing to the interviewers, who estimated them as fitting in with conventional stage 4 reasoning or as being in transition between stages 4 and 5. However, from the perspective of an Israeli kibbutz dweller, such a response may represent a postconventional moral principle missing from Kohlberg's description of stage 5. If membership in a kibbutz is viewed as a commitment to certain social values, including cooperation and equality for all, then concern about upholding the system may be not merely for its own sake, but aimed at protecting those principles (Snarey, 1985).

When Kohlberg's dilemmas were tested in India, Buddhist monks scored lower than laypeople. Apparently Kohlberg's model, while capturing the preconventional and conventional elements of Buddhist thinking, was inadequate for understanding postconventional Buddhist principles of cooperation and nonviolence (Gielen & Kelly, 1983).

Heinz's dilemma was revised for use in Taiwan. In the revision, a shopkeeper will not give a man *food* for his sick wife. This version would seem unbelievable to Chinese villagers, who are more accustomed to hearing a shopkeeper in such a situation say, "You have to let people have things whether they have money or not" (Wolf, 1968, p. 21).

Whereas Kohlberg's system is based on justice, the Chinese ethos leans toward conciliation and harmony. In Kohlberg's format, respondents make an either-or decision based on their own value systems. In Chinese society, people faced with moral dilemmas are expected to discuss it openly, be guided by community standards, and try to find a way of resolving the problem to please as many parties as possible. In the west, even good people may be harshly punished if, under the force of circumstances, they break a law. The Chinese are unaccustomed to universally applied laws; they are taught to abide by the decisions of a wise judge (Dien, 1982).

However, we need to be careful to avoid making broad-brush generalizations about cultural attitudes. Concepts of rights, welfare, and justice exist in all cultures, though they may be differently applied. To say that western cultures are individualistic and eastern cultures are collectivist ignores individual differences and even diametrically opposed attitudes within each culture, and the specific contextual situations in which moral judgments are applied (Turiel, 1998). For example, it became apparent in the days and weeks following the terrorist attacks of September 11, 2001, that cooperation may be as strong a part of the American ethos as competition.

What's Your View?

- Have you ever had an experience with a person from another culture involving differences in moral principles?

The Seventh Stage

Kohlberg, shortly before his death in 1987, proposed a seventh stage of moral reasoning, which moves beyond considerations of justice and has much in common with the concept of self-transcendence in eastern traditions. In the seventh stage, adults reflect on the question, "*Why* be moral?" (Kohlberg & Ryncarz, 1990, p. 192; emphasis added). The answer, said Kohlberg, lies in achieving a cosmic perspective: "a sense of unity with the cosmos, nature, or God," which enables a person to see moral issues "from the standpoint of the universe as a whole" (Kohlberg & Ryncarz, 1990, pp. 191, 207). In experiencing oneness with the universe, people come to see that everything is connected; each person's actions affect everything and everyone else, and the consequences rebound on the doer.

This idea was eloquently expressed in a letter written in the mid-nineteenth century by the American Indian Chief Seattle, leader of the Suquamish and Duwamish tribes, when the U.S. government sought to buy tribal land:

> We are part of the earth and it is part of us. . . . Man did not weave the web of life, he is merely a strand in it. Whatever he does to the web, he does to himself. . . . So, if we sell you our land, love it as we have loved it. Care for it as we have cared for it. . . . As we are part of the land, you too are part of the land. We are brothers after all. (Chief Seattle, quoted in Campbell & Moyers, 1988, pp. 34–35)

The achievement of such a perspective is so rare that Kohlberg himself had questions about calling it a stage of development, and it has had little research exploration. Kohlberg did note that it parallels the most mature stage of faith that the theologian James Fowler (1981) identified (see Box 13-2, on page 482), in which "one experiences a oneness with the ultimate conditions of one's life and being" (Kohlberg & Ryncarz, 1990, p. 202).

Carol Gilligan (center) studied moral development in women and, later, in men and concluded that concern for others is at the highest level of moral thought.

Gender and Moral Development

Because Kohlberg's original studies were done on boys and men, Carol Gilligan (1982, 1987a, 1987b) argued that his system gives a higher place to "masculine" values of justice and fairness than to "feminine" values of compassion, responsibility, and caring. Gilligan suggested that a woman's central moral dilemma is the conflict between her own needs and those of others. While most societies typically expect assertiveness and independent judgment from men, they expect from women self-sacrifice and concern for others.

To find out how women make moral choices, Gilligan (1982) interviewed 29 pregnant women about their decisions to continue or end their pregnancies. These women saw morality in terms of selfishness versus responsibility,

Table 13-1 Gilligan's Levels of Moral Development in Women

Stage	Description
Level 1: Orientation of individual survival	The woman concentrates on herself—on what is practical and what is best for her.
Transition 1: From selfishness to responsibility	The woman realizes her connection to others and thinks about what the responsible choice would be in terms of other people (including her unborn baby), as well as herself.
Level 2: Goodness as self-sacrifice	This conventional feminine wisdom dictates sacrificing the woman's own wishes to what other people want—and will think of her. She considers herself responsible for the actions of others, while holding others responsible for her own choices. She is in a dependent position, one in which her indirect efforts to exert control often turn into manipulation, sometimes through the use of guilt.
Transition 2: From goodness to truth	The woman assesses her decisions not on the basis of how others will react to them but on her intentions and the consequences of her actions. She develops a new judgment that takes into account her own needs, along with those of others. She wants to be "good" by being responsible to others, but also wants to be "honest" by being responsible to herself. Survival returns as a major concern.
Level 3: Morality of nonviolence	By elevating the injunction against hurting anyone (including herself) to a principle that governs all moral judgment and action, the woman establishes a "moral equality" between herself and others and is then able to assume the responsibility for choice in moral dilemmas.

Source: Based on Gilligan, 1982.

defined as an obligation to exercise care and to avoid hurting others. Gilligan concluded that women think less about abstract justice and fairness than men do and more about their responsibilities to specific people. (Table 13-1 lists Gilligan's proposed levels of moral development in women.)

However, other research has not, on the whole, found significant differences in moral reasoning. One large-scale analysis comparing results from 66 studies found no significant differences in men's and women's responses to Kohlberg's dilemmas across the life span (L. J. Walker, 1984). In the few studies in which men scored slightly higher, the findings were not clearly gender-related, since the men generally were better educated and had better jobs than the women. A more recent analysis of 113 studies reached a slightly more nuanced conclusion. Although women were more likely to think in terms of care, and men were more oriented to justice, these differences were small, especially among university students. Ages of respondents and the types of dilemmas or questions presented were more significant factors than gender (Jaffee & Hyde, 2000). Thus the weight of evidence does not appear to back up either of Gilligan's original contentions: a male bias in Kohlberg's theory or a distinct female perspective on morality (L. Walker, 1995). As Jaffee and Hyde state, "researchers may benefit from turning their attention away from the study of gender differences in moral orientation and toward a more sophisticated characterization of moral orientation or to questions of how moral orientations develop over time" (2000, p. 720).

In her own later research, Gilligan has described moral development in *both* men and women as evolving beyond abstract reasoning. In studies using real-life moral dilemmas (such as whether a woman's lover should confess their affair to her husband), rather than hypothetical dilemmas like the ones Kohlberg used, Gilligan and her colleagues found that many people in their twenties become dissatisfied with a narrow moral logic and become more able to live with moral contradictions (Gilligan, Murphy, & Tappan, 1990). It seems, then, that if the "different voice" in Gilligan's earlier research reflected an alternative value system, it was not gender-based. At the same time, with the inclusion of his seventh stage, Kohlberg's thinking evolved to a point of greater agreement with Gilligan's. Both theories now place responsibility to others at the highest level of moral thought. Both recognize the importance for both sexes of connections with other people and of compassion and care.

What's Your View?

- Which (if either) do you consider to be higher moral priorities: justice and rights, or compassion and care?

Checkpoint

Can you . . .

- ✔ Give examples of the role of experience and culture in adult moral development?
- ✔ Compare Kohlberg's proposed seventh stage with Gilligan's highest stage of moral development?
- ✔ State Gilligan's original position on gender differences in moral development, and summarize research findings on the subject?

BOX 13-2

Digging Deeper
Development of Faith Across the Life Span

Can faith be studied from a developmental perspective? Yes, according to James Fowler (1981, 1989). Fowler defined faith as a way of seeing or knowing the world. To find out how people arrive at this knowledge, Fowler and his students at Harvard Divinity School interviewed more than 400 people of all ages with various ethnic, educational, and socioeconomic backgrounds and various religious or secular identifications and affiliations.

Fowler's theory focuses on the *form* of faith, not its content or object; it is not limited to any particular belief system. Faith can be religious or nonreligious: people may have faith in a god, in science, in humanity, or in a cause to which they attach ultimate worth and which gives meaning to their lives.

According to Fowler, faith develops—as do other aspects of cognition—through interaction between the maturing person and the environment. As in other stage theories, Fowler's stages of faith progress in an unvarying sequence, each building on those that went before. New experiences—crises, problems, or revelations—that challenge or upset a person's equilibrium may prompt a leap from one stage to the next. The ages at which these transitions occur are variable, and some people never leave a particular stage.

Fowler's stages correspond roughly to those described by Piaget, Kohlberg, and Erikson. The beginnings of faith, says Fowler, come at about 18 to 24 months of age, after children become self-aware, begin to use language and symbolic thought, and have developed what Erikson called *basic trust:* the sense that their needs will be met by powerful others.

- *Stage 1: Intuitive-projective faith* (ages 18–24 months to 7 years). As young children struggle to understand the forces that control their world, they form powerful, imaginative, often terrifying, and sometimes lasting images of God, heaven, and hell, drawn from the stories adults read to them. These images are often irrational, since preoperational children tend to be confused about cause and effect and may have trouble distinguishing between reality and fantasy. Still egocentric, they have difficulty distinguishing God's point of view from their own or their parents'. They think of God mainly in terms of obedience and punishment.
- *Stage 2: Mythic-literal faith* (ages 7 to 12 years). Children are now more logical and begin to develop a more coherent view of the universe. Not yet capable of abstract thought, they tend to take religious stories and symbols literally, as they adopt their family's and community's beliefs and observances. They can now see God as having a perspective beyond their own, which takes into account people's effort and intent. They believe that God is fair and that people get what they deserve.
- *Stage 3: Synthetic-conventional faith* (adolescence or beyond). Adolescents, now capable of abstract thought, begin to form ideologies (belief systems) and commitments to ideals. As they search for identity, they seek a more personal relationship with God. However, their identity is not on firm ground; they look to others (usually peers) for moral authority. Their faith is unquestioning and conforms to community standards. This stage is typical of followers of organized religion; about 50 percent of adults may never move beyond it.
- *Stage 4: Individuative-reflective faith* (early to middle twenties or beyond). Adults who reach this postconventional stage examine their faith critically and think out their own beliefs, independent of external authority and group norms. Since young adults are deeply concerned with intimacy, movement into this

Education and Work

Guidepost

5. How do higher education and work affect cognitive development?

Educational and vocational choices after high school flow from the cognitive developments of earlier years and often present opportunities for further cognitive growth.

The Transition to College

College enrollment is at a record high and is still growing, in part because of older women going back to school (Snyder & Hoffman, 2002). Today nearly all graduating high school students plan to continue their education at some point, and nearly two out of three go directly to college, as compared with only about one in two in 1972 (NCES Digest of Education Statistics, 2001).

In the 1970s, women were less likely than men to go to college and less likely to finish. Today, women earn more than half of all bachelor's degrees. However, women

Digging Deeper

BOX 13-2

—*continued*

stage is often triggered by divorce, the death of a friend, or some other stressful event.

- *Stage 5: Conjunctive faith* (midlife or beyond). Middle-aged people become more aware of the limits of reason. They recognize life's paradoxes and contradictions, and they often struggle with conflicts between fulfilling their own needs and sacrificing for others. As they begin to anticipate death, they may achieve a deeper understanding and acceptance by integrating into their faith aspects of their earlier beliefs.
- *Stage 6: Universalizing faith* (late life). In this rare, ultimate category Fowler placed such moral and spiritual leaders as Mahatma Gandhi, Martin Luther King, and Mother Teresa, whose breadth of vision and commitment to the well-being of all humanity profoundly inspire others. Consumed with a sense of "participation in a power that unifies and transforms the world," they seem "more lucid, more simple, and yet somehow more fully human than the rest of us" (Fowler, 1981, p. 201). Because they threaten the established order, they often become martyrs; and though they love life, they do not cling to it. This stage parallels Kohlberg's proposed seventh stage of moral development.

As one of the first researchers to systematically study how faith develops, Fowler has had great impact; his work has become required reading in many divinity schools. It also has been criticized on several counts (Koenig, 1994). Critics say Fowler's concept of faith is at odds with conventional definitions, which involve acceptance, not introspection. They challenge his emphasis on cognitive knowledge and claim that he underestimates the maturity of a simple, solid, unquestioning faith (Koenig, 1994). Critics also question whether faith develops in universal stages—at least in those Fowler identified. Fowler himself has cautioned that his advanced stages should not be seen as better or truer than others, though he does portray people at his highest stage as moral and spiritual exemplars.

Fowler's sample was not randomly selected; it consisted of paid volunteers who lived in or near North American cities with major colleges or universities. Thus, the findings may be more representative of people with above average intelligence and education (Koenig, 1994). Nor are the findings representative of nonwestern cultures. Also, the initial sample included few people over age 60. To remedy this weakness, Richard N. Shulik (1988) interviewed 40 older adults and found a strong relationship between their stages of faith and their Kohlbergian levels of moral development. However, he also found that older people at intermediate levels of faith development were less likely to be depressed than older people at higher or lower stages. Thus, Fowler's theory may overlook the adaptive value of conventional religious belief for many older adults (Koenig, 1994; see Chapter 18).

Some of these criticisms resemble those made against other models of life-span development. Piaget's, Kohlberg's, and Erikson's initial samples were not randomly selected either. More research is needed to confirm, modify, or extend Fowler's theory, especially in nonwestern cultures.

What's Your View?

- Is faith in God necessary to be a religious person?
- Do you fit into one of the stages of faith that Fowler described?

Check It Out:

For more information on this topic, go to http://www.mhhe.com/papaliah9.

still tend to major in traditionally "feminine" fields, such as education, nursing, and psychology. The great majority of engineering and computer science degrees still go to men, but the gender gap has reversed in the life sciences and is closing in mathematics and physical sciences (NCES Digest, 2001).

Socioeconomic status plays a major part in access to postsecondary education. In 1999, 76 percent of high school graduates from high-income families, as compared with only 49 percent from low-income families, enrolled immediately in college (NCES Digest, 2001).

A majority of undergraduate students attend four-year, degree-granting institutions, and most of those who complete their first year go on to earn degrees (NCES, 1999, 2001). However, enrollment patterns have shifted since 1970: increasing numbers of students attend college part time or go to two-year community colleges (Seftor

& Turner, 2002). In 1996, nearly half of all post-high-school students who were *not* working toward bachelor's degrees were enrolled in vocational education, mostly in community colleges and chiefly in business, health, and engineering and science technology (U.S. Department of Education, 2000).

Most young adults who do not enroll in postsecondary education, or do not finish, enter the job market, but many return later to finish their schooling. In 1999, about 39 percent of postsecondary students were ages 25 and over (Snyder & Hoffman, 2002). A college graduate can expect to earn nearly twice as much over a lifetime as someone with only a high school diploma (Day & Newburger, 2002).

Increasingly, college courses and even complete degree or certificate programs are available by *distance learning,* in which instructor and student are separated by space and, sometimes, by time. Courses may be delivered via mail, e-mail, the Internet, telephone, video (either live and interactive or prerecorded), or other technological means (Mariani, 2001). Older students, especially women, who are financially independent, work full time, are married, or have dependent children are most likely to participate in distance learning (Sikora & Carroll, 2002).

For young people in transition from adolescence to adulthood, exposure to a new educational or work environment, sometimes far away from the childhood home, offers a chance to hone abilities, question long-held assumptions, and try out new ways of looking at the world. For the increasing number of students of nontraditional age, college or workplace education can rekindle intellectual curiosity, improve employment opportunities, and enhance work skills.

Cognitive Growth in College College can be a time of intellectual discovery and personal growth. Students change in response to the curriculum, which offers new insights and new ways of thinking; to other students who challenge long-held views and values; to the student culture, which is different from the culture of society at large; and to faculty members, who provide new role models.

The choice of a college major can represent the pursuit of a passionate interest or a prelude to a future career. It also tends to affect thinking patterns. In a longitudinal study of 165 undergraduates, freshmen majoring in the natural sciences, humanities, and social sciences showed improvement in everyday reasoning by their senior year, but different courses of study promoted different *kinds* of reasoning. Training in the social sciences led to gains in *statistical and methodological* reasoning—the ability to general-

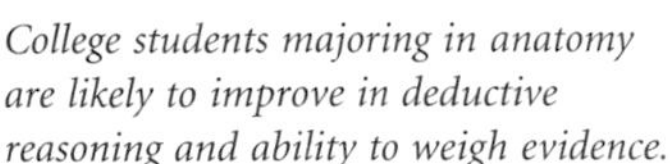

College students majoring in anatomy are likely to improve in deductive reasoning and ability to weigh evidence.

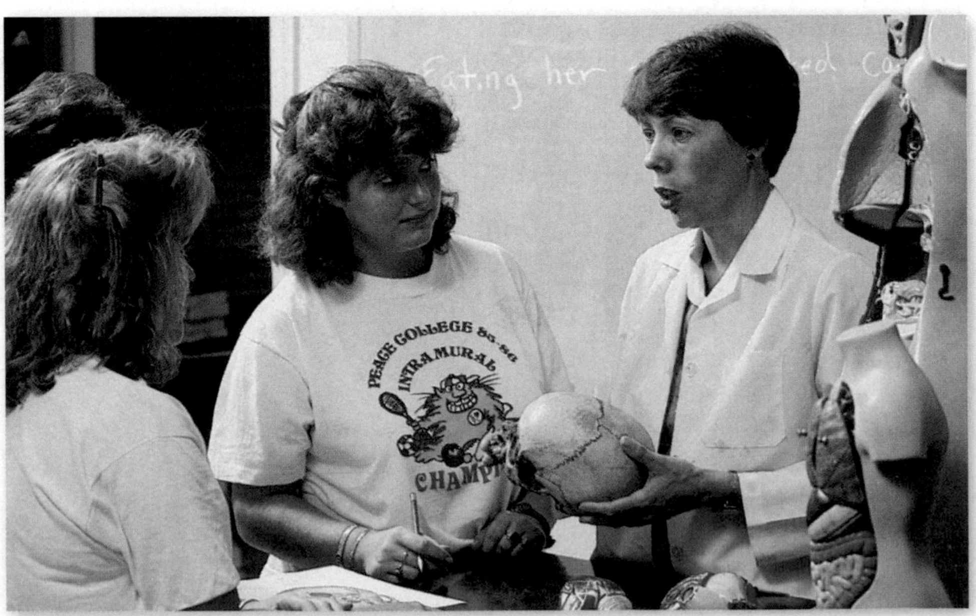

ize patterns. Students majoring in the humanities and natural sciences had better *conditional* reasoning—formal deductive logic, like that used in computer programming and mathematics. These two groups also improved in *verbal* reasoning—the ability to recognize arguments, evaluate evidence, and detect analogies (Lehman & Nisbett, 1990).

Beyond improvement in reasoning abilities, the college experience may lead to a fundamental change in the way students think. In a classic study that foreshadowed current research on the shift to postformal thought, William Perry (1970) interviewed 67 Harvard and Radcliffe students throughout their undergraduate years and found that their thinking progressed from *rigidity* to *flexibility* and ultimately to *freely chosen commitments*. Many students come to college with rigid ideas about truth; they cannot conceive of any answer but the "right" one. As students begin to encounter a wide range of ideas and viewpoints, said Perry, they are assailed by uncertainty. They consider this stage temporary, however, and expect to learn the "one right answer" eventually. Next, they come to see all knowledge and values as relative. They recognize that different societies and different individuals have their own value systems. They now realize that their opinions on many issues are as valid as anyone else's, even those of a parent or teacher; but they cannot find meaning or value in this maze of systems and beliefs. Chaos has replaced order. Finally, they achieve *commitment within relativism:* they make their own judgments and choose their own beliefs and values despite uncertainty and the recognition of other valid possibilities—a key aspect of postformal thought.

Can college students be taught to use postformal thought? Sinnott (1998) has developed specific methods for doing so. Jointly creating a grading system, brainstorming ways to design a research project, debating fundamental questions about the meaning of life, presenting arguments in a mock courtroom trial, and trying to find several explanations for an event are a few of many ways instructors can help students to recognize that there is more than one way of examining and solving a problem, to appreciate the logic of competing systems, and to see the ultimate need to commit to one.

What's Your View?

- From your observation, does college students' thinking typically seem to follow the stages Perry outlined?

Checkpoint

Can you . . .

- ✔ Discuss factors affecting who goes to college?
- ✔ Tell how college, and working while in college, can affect cognitive development?

Entering the World of Work

Along with promoting cognitive development, education expands employment opportunities and earning power. The fastest-growing and best-paying occupations usually require at least a bachelor's degree (Bureau of Labor Standards, 2000, 2001). In 2000, median earnings of holders of bachelor's degrees ($46,300) were more than twice the earnings of high school dropouts ($21,400), and people with professional degrees earned more than three and a half times as much (Bureau of Labor Standards, 2002). Even in a booming economy, in mid-1999, the unemployment rate for adults age 25 and over with no more than a high school diploma was twice as high—and for high school dropouts more than three times as high—as for college graduates (Bureau of Labor Statistics, 1999c).

On average, for every dollar U.S. men earn, women who work full time earn only 76 cents. However, the picture is brighter for college-educated women; their earnings (adjusted for inflation) have risen 30.4 percent since 1979, while college-educated men's real earnings increased only 16.7 percent. The gender gap in earnings exists mainly in older age groups; young women ages 20 to 24 earn nearly as much as their male counterparts (91.9 percent), suggesting that the gap may close as this cohort moves up in the working world (Bureau of Labor Statistics, 2001a).

An estimated one-third of full-time and two-thirds of part-time college students work to help pay their bills. How does juggling work and study affect cognitive development and career preparation? One longitudinal study followed a random sample of incoming freshmen at 23 two- and four-year colleges and universities in 16 states through their first three years of college. Each year the students took tests in reading comprehension skills, mathematical reasoning, and critical thinking. During the first two years, on- or off-campus work had little or no effect on the test results. By the third year, part-time work had a positive effect, perhaps because employment forces students to organize their time efficiently and learn better work habits. However, working on campus more than fifteen hours a week or off campus more than twenty hours a week tended to have a negative impact (Pascarella, Edison, Nora, Hagedorn, & Terenzini, 1998).

A much higher proportion—80 percent—of graduate and professional students are employed, 63 percent full time and year-round. About 70 percent of these employed students say their jobs help them prepare for careers. However, they also report drawbacks, such as limitations on scheduling and number and choice of classes (Snyder & Hoffman, 2002).

Cognitive Complexity of Work

The nature of work is changing. By 2000, there were almost four times as many Americans in service and retail jobs (61 million workers) as in manufacturing (18.4 million) (Bureau of Labor Statistics, 2001b). Work arrangements are becoming more varied and less stable. More and more adults are self-employed, working at home, telecommuting, on flexible work schedules, or acting as independent contractors (Clay, 1998; McGuire, 1998; Bureau of Labor Statistics, 1998).

substantive complexity Degree to which a person's work requires thought and independent judgment.

spillover hypothesis Hypothesis that there is a positive correlation between intellectuality of work and of leisure activities because of a carryover of cognitive gains from work to leisure.

Do people change as a result of the kind of work they do? Some research says yes: people seem to grow in challenging jobs, the kind that are becoming increasingly prevalent today. A combination of cross-sectional and longitudinal studies (Kohn, 1980) revealed a reciprocal relationship between the **substantive complexity** of work—the degree of thought and independent judgment it requires—and a person's flexibility in coping with cognitive demands (Kohn, 1980).

Brain research casts light on how people deal with complex work. Full development of the frontal lobes during young adulthood may equip people to handle several tasks at the same time. Magnetic resonance imaging reveals that the most frontward part of the frontal lobes, the *fronto-polar prefrontal cortex (FPPC),* has a special function in problem solving and planning. The FPPC springs into action when a person needs to put an unfinished task "on hold" and shift attention to another task—a process called *branching.* The FPPC permits a worker to keep the first task in working memory while attending to the second—for example, to resume reading a report after being interrupted by the telephone (Koechlin, Basso, Pietrini, Panzer, & Grafman, 1999).

Checkpoint

Can you . . .

- ✔ Summarize current changes in the workplace?
- ✔ Explain the relationship between substantive complexity of work and cognitive development?

Cognitive growth need not stop at the end of the workday. According to the **spillover hypothesis,** cognitive gains from work carry over to nonworking hours. Studies support this hypothesis: substantive complexity of work strongly influences the intellectual level of leisure activities (Kohn, 1980; K. Miller & Kohn, 1983).

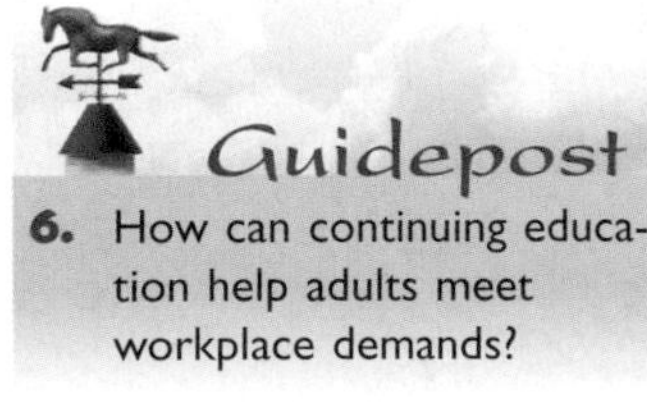

Guidepost

6. How can continuing education help adults meet workplace demands?

Adult Education and Literacy

About 48 percent of adults in the United States participate in educational activities. Three out of four participants take courses from postsecondary institutions and the rest from business or other organizations (NCES Digest, 2001).

Many of these adults seek to improve their work skills. Much of this work-related education and training is employer-supported (Kopka, Schantz, & Korb, 1998)—and for good reason. Most occupations, especially high-paying ones, that do not require a college degree do require on-the-job training (Bureau of Labor Standards, 2000–2001). Employers see benefits of workplace education in improved morale, increased quality of work, better teamwork and problem solving, and greater ability to cope with new technology and other changes in the workplace. Employees also gain in such basic skills as reading, math, and critical thinking (Conference Board, 1999).

literacy In an adult, ability to use printed and written information to function in society, achieve goals, and develop knowledge and potential.

Literacy is a fundamental requisite for participation not only in the workplace but in all facets of a modern, information-driven society. Literate adults are those who can use printed and written information to function in society, achieve their goals, and develop their knowledge and potential. At the turn of the century, a person with a fourth-grade education was considered literate; today, a high school diploma is barely adequate.

Nearly half of U.S. adults cannot understand written material, manipulate numbers, and use documents well enough to succeed in today's economy. This finding comes from an analysis of national and international literacy surveys conducted by the Educational Testing Service (ETS) during the 1990s (Sum, Kirsch, & Taggart, 2002).

In literacy comparisons of adults in 17 higher-income, industrialized countries, the U.S. performance was only mediocre, ranking slightly above the mean for all participating countries.* This is true even though the United States spends more on education per capita than nearly all these other countries (Sum et al., 2002) and has higher rates of secondary school completion than many of them (NCES Digest, 2001).

The literacy surveys revealed wide internal disparities. The United States ranked near the top of the list of countries both in percentages of adults at the lowest level of literacy and in those at the highest levels (Sum et al., 2002).

The international survey found, not surprisingly, that literacy was directly related to occupational status and earnings; the least literate workers tended to be in blue-collar jobs or to be unemployed or out of the labor force, while those at the highest literacy level held professional or managerial positions (Binkley, Matheson, & Williams, 1997). For U.S. test-takers, the single most important factor in literacy was the level of educational attainment, and the disparity based on education was greater than in any other country. U.S. college graduates did better on the literacy test than college graduates in every other country except Belgium; but U.S. high school dropouts did more poorly than in any other high-income country (NCES, 1999).

Globally, almost 1 billion adults are illiterate (UNESCO, 1998). Illiteracy is especially common among women in developing countries, where education typically is considered unimportant for females. In 1990, the United Nations launched literacy programs in such developing countries as Bangladesh, Nepal, and Somalia (Linder, 1990). In the United States, the National Literacy Act requires the states to establish literacy training centers with federal funding assistance.

Technological literacy is increasingly necessary for success in the modern world. The increase in Internet use is a global phenomenon. More than half of all Americans use the Internet, and more than 2 million people go online for the first time each month. In a single year, between August 2000 and September 2001, Internet use at work among employed adults ages 25 and over increased from 26.1 percent to 41.7 percent. Young and middle-aged adults are more likely to use the Internet and e-mail at work than employed older adults (Department of Commerce, 2002).

Checkpoint

Can you . . .

- ✔ Explain the need for workplace education?
- ✔ Discuss current trends in print and technological literacy?

Refocus

- What direct and indirect influences on health and fitness does Arthur Ashe's story illustrate?
- Do you see evidence of postformal thought, tacit knowledge, emotional intelligence, or moral reasoning in the way Ashe handled the opportunities and challenges of his career and personal life?

Work affects day-to-day life, not only on the job but at home, and it brings both satisfaction and stress. In Chapter 14, we explore the effects of work on relationships as we look at psychosocial development in young adulthood.

*Australia, Belgium (Flanders), Canada, Denmark, Finland, France, Germany, Great Britain, Ireland, Italy, Netherlands, New Zealand, Northern Ireland, Norway, Sweden, Switzerland, and the United States.

SUMMARY AND KEY TERMS

PHYSICAL DEVELOPMENT

Health and Physical Condition

Guidepost 1. In what physical condition is the typical young adult, and what factors affect health and well-being?

- The typical young adult is in good condition; physical and sensory abilities are usually excellent.
- Accidents are the leading cause of death in young adults. Others are homicide and suicide.
- The mapping of the human genome is enabling the discovery of genetic bases for certain disorders.
- Lifestyle factors such as diet, obesity, exercise, smoking, and substance use or abuse can affect health and survival.
- Good health is related to higher income and education. African Americans and some other minorities tend to be less healthy than other Americans, in part due to lower SES.
- Women tend to live longer than men, in part for biological reasons, but perhaps also because they are more health-conscious.
- Social relationships, especially marriage, tend to be associated with physical and mental health.

obesity *(462)*

alcoholism *(465)*

Sexual and Reproductive Issues

Guidepost 2. What are some sexual and reproductive issues at this time of life?

- Premenstrual syndrome, sexually transmitted diseases, and infertility can be concerns during young adulthood.
- While some STDs have become less prevalent, others are on the rise.
- The AIDS epidemic is coming under control in the United States, but heterosexual transmission has increased, particularly among young women.
- The most common cause of infertility in men is a low sperm count; the most common cause in women is blockage of the fallopian tubes.
- Infertile couples now have several options for assisted reproduction, but these techniques may involve thorny ethical and practical issues. Fertility clinics are expensive and have low success rates, and there is heightened risk of birth defects and low birthweight.

premenstrual syndrome (PMS) *(469)*

infertility *(470)*

COGNITIVE DEVELOPMENT

Perspectives on Adult Cognition

Guidepost 3. What is distinctive about adult thought and intelligence?

- Some investigators propose a distinctively adult stage of cognition beyond formal operations, called postformal thought. It is generally applied in social situations and involves intuition and emotion as well as logic. Criteria include ability to shift between reasoning and practical considerations, awareness that problems can have multiple causes and solutions, pragmatism in choosing solutions, and awareness of inherent conflict.
- Schaie proposed seven stages of age-related cognitive development: acquisitive (childhood and adolescence), achieving (young adulthood), responsible and executive (middle adulthood), and reorganizational, reintegrative, and legacy-creating (late adulthood). This model suggests a need to develop intelligence tests that have validity for adults.
- According to Sternberg's triarchic theory of intelligence, the experiential and contextual elements become particularly important during adulthood. Tests that measure tacit knowledge are useful complements to traditional intelligence tests.
- Emotional intelligence may play an important part in life success. However, emotional intelligence as a distinct construct is controversial and hard to measure.

postformal thought *(473)*

acquisitive stage *(474)*

achieving stage *(474)*

responsible stage *(474)*

executive stage *(474)*

reorganizational stage *(475)*

reintegrative stage *(475)*

legacy-creating stage *(475)*

experiential element *(476)*

contextual element *(476)*

componential element *(476)*

tacit knowledge *(476)*

emotional intelligence *(477)*

Moral Development

Guidepost 4. How does moral reasoning develop?

- According to Lawrence Kohlberg, moral development in adulthood depends primarily on experience, though it cannot exceed the limits set by cognitive development. Experience may be interpreted differently in various cultural contexts.
- Kohlberg, shortly before his death, proposed a seventh stage of moral development, which involves seeing moral issues from a cosmic perspective. This is similar to the highest stage of faith proposed by James Fowler.
- Carol Gilligan initially proposed that women have an ethic of care, whereas Kohlberg's theory emphasizes justice. However, later research, including her own, has not supported a distinction between men's and women's moral outlook.

Education and Work

Guidepost 5. How do higher education and work affect cognitive development?

- Depending on their major field, college students often show specific kinds of improvement in reasoning abilities.
- According to Perry, college students' thinking tends to progress from rigidity to flexibility to freely chosen commitments.
- Research has found a relationship between substantive complexity of work and cognitive growth. Also, people who do more complex work tend to engage in more intellectually demanding leisure activities.
- The workplace poses special challenges for adults who lack college education.

- Although more women than men now are going to college, they tend to choose different major fields. Still, an increasing number of women are pursuing careers in traditionally male-dominated fields and are moving into managerial and professional positions.

  substantive complexity *(486)*

  spillover hypothesis *(486)*

Guidepost 6. How can continuing education help adults meet workplace demands?

- Workplace education can help adults develop basic job skills, which many lack.
- Adults with low literacy skills are at a severe disadvantage in a modern economy. The average American's literacy level is mediocre compared with other industrialized countries, and there are great disparities between Americans with high and low literacy levels. In developing countries, illiteracy is more common among women than among men.

  literacy *(486)*

Psychosocial Development in Young Adulthood

Chapter 14

Every adult is in need of help, of warmth, of protection . . . in many ways differing [from] and yet in many ways similar to the needs of the child.

—**Erich Fromm, *The Sane Society,* 1955**

Focus: Ingrid Bergman, "Notorious" Actress*

Ingrid Bergman

Ingrid Bergman (1915–1982) was one of the world's most distinguished stage and screen actresses. Perhaps best remembered for her starring role in *Casablanca,* she won Academy Awards for *Gaslight, Anastasia,* and *Murder on the Orient Express;* the New York Film Critics' Award for *Autumn Sonata;* and an Emmy for *The Turn of the Screw.* In 1981, a year before her death, she came out of retirement to play the Israeli prime minister Golda Meir in the Emmy-winning *A Woman Called Golda.*

Bergman's personal life was as dramatic as any movie plot. One of her film titles, *Notorious,* sums up the abrupt change in her public image in 1949, when Bergman—known as a paragon of wholesomeness and purity—shocked the world by leaving her husband and 10-year-old daughter for the Italian film director Roberto Rossellini. Compounding the scandal was the news that Bergman was pregnant by Rossellini, a married man.

Bergman had been obsessed with acting since she had seen her first play at the age of 11 in her native Sweden. Tall, awkward, and shy, she came alive onstage. Plucked out of Stockholm's Royal Dramatic School at 18 to make her first film, she braved the wrath of the school's director, who warned that movies would destroy her talent.

At 22, she married Dr. Petter Lindstrom, a handsome, successful dentist eight years her senior, who later became a prominent brain surgeon. It was he who urged her to accept the producer David Selznick's invitation to go to Hollywood to make *Intermezzo.* At 23, she arrived, to be joined later by her husband and infant daughter, Pia.

Her filmmaking was punctuated by periodic spells of domesticity. "I have plenty to do as usual, and having a home, husband and child ought to be enough for any woman's life," she wrote during one such interlude. "But still I think every day is a lost day. As if only half of me is alive" (Bergman & Burgess, 1980, p. 110).

*Sources of biographical information about Ingrid Bergman are Bergman and Burgess (1980) and Spoto (1997).

OUTLINE

Bergman began to see her husband—whom she had always leaned on for help and decision making—as overprotective, controlling, jealous, and critical. The couple spent long hours, days, and weeks apart—she at the studio or on tour, he at the hospital.

Meanwhile, Bergman was becoming dissatisfied with filming on studio lots. When she saw Rossellini's award-winning *Open City,* she was stunned by its power and realism and by Rossellini's artistic freedom and courage. She wrote to him, offering to come to Italy and work with him. The result was *Stromboli*—and the end of what she now saw as a constrictive, unfulfilling marriage. "It was not my intention to fall in love and go to Italy forever," she wrote to Lindstrom apologetically. "But how can I help it or change it?"

At 33, Bergman, who had been number one at the box office, became a Hollywood outcast. Her affair made headlines worldwide. So did the illegitimate birth of Robertino in 1950, Bergman's hurried Mexican divorce and proxy marriage there to Rossellini (who had had his own marriage annulled), the birth of twin daughters in 1952, and the struggle over visitation rights with Pia, who took her father's side and did not see her guilt-ridden mother for six years.

The tempestuous Bergman-Rossellini love match did not last. Every picture they made together failed, and finally, so did the marriage. But their mutual bond with their children, to whom Bergman gave Rossellini custody to avoid another bitter battle, made these ex-spouses a continuing part of each other's lives. In 1958, at the age of 43, Ingrid Bergman—her career, by this time, rehabilitated and peace made with her eldest daughter—began her third marriage, to Lars Schmidt, a Swedish-born theatrical producer. It lasted sixteen years, despite constant work-related separations, and ended in an amicable divorce. Schmidt and Bergman remained close friends for the rest of her life.

Ingrid Bergman's story is a dramatic reminder of the impact of cultural change on personal attitudes and behavior. The furor over her affair with Rossellini may seem strange today, when cohabitation, extramarital sex, divorce, and out-of-wedlock birth, all of which were shocking fifty years ago, have become more common. Still, now as then, personal choices made in young adulthood establish a framework for the rest of life. Bergman's marriages and divorces, the children she bore and loved, her passionate pursuit of her vocation, and her agonizing over her unwillingness to put family before work were much like the life events and issues that confront many young women today.

Did Bergman change with maturity and experience? On the surface, she seemed to keep repeating the same cycle again and again. Yet, in her handling of her second and third divorces, she seemed calmer, more pragmatic, and more in command. Still, her basic approach to life remained the same: she did what she felt she must, come what may.

Does personality stop growing when the body does? Or does it keep developing throughout life? In this chapter, we look at theories and research on adult personality and at effects of cultural attitudes and social change. We examine the choices that frame personal and social life: adopting a sexual lifestyle; marrying, cohabiting, or remaining single; having children or not; and establishing and maintaining friendships.

After you have read and studied this chapter, you should be able to answer each of the following Guidepost questions. Look for them again in the margins, where they point to important concepts throughout the chapter. To check your understanding of these Guideposts, review the end-of-chapter summary. Checkpoints located at periodic spots throughout the chapter will help you verify your understanding of what you have read.

Guideposts for Study

1. Does personality change during adulthood, and if so, how?
2. What is intimacy, and how is it expressed in friendship, love, and sexuality?
3. Why do some people remain single?
4. How do homosexuals deal with "coming out," and what is the nature of gay and lesbian relationships?
5. What are the pros and cons of cohabitation?
6. What do adults gain from marriage, what cultural patterns surround entrance into marriage, and why do some marriages succeed while others fail?
7. When do most adults become parents, and how does parenthood affect a marriage?
8. How do dual-earner couples divide responsibilities and deal with role conflicts?
9. Why have divorce rates risen, and how do adults adjust to divorce, remarriage, and stepparenthood?

Personality Development: Four Views

Whether personality primarily shows stability or change depends in part on how we study and measure personality (Caspi, 1998). Four approaches to adult psychosocial development are represented by *normative-stage models,* the *timing-of-events model, trait models,* and *typological models.*

Guidepost

1. Does personality change during adulthood, and if so, how?

Normative-stage models portray a typical sequence of age-related development that continues throughout the adult life span, much as in childhood and adolescence. Normative-crisis research has found major, predictable changes in adult personality. The **timing-of-events model** holds that change is related not so much to age as to the expected or unexpected occurrence and timing of important life events. This model emphasizes individual and contextual differences.

Trait models focus on mental, emotional, temperamental, and behavioral traits, or attributes, such as cheerfulness and irritability. Trait-based studies find that adult personality changes very little. **Typological models** identify broader personality types, or styles, that represent how personality traits are organized within the individual. These models, too, tend to find considerable stability in personality.

normative-stage models Theoretical models that describe psychosocial development in terms of a definite sequence of age-related changes.

timing-of-events model Theoretical model that describes adult psychosocial development as a response to the expected or unexpected occurrence and timing of important life events.

trait models Theoretical models that focus on mental, emotional, temperamental, and behavioral traits, or attributes.

typological models Theoretical models that identify broad personality types, or styles.

Normative-Stage Models

Erik Erikson believed that personality changes throughout life. Variations on Erikson's theory grew out of pioneering studies by George Vaillant and Daniel Levinson. These *normative-stage models,* all of which originally were based on research with men, hold that everyone follows the same basic sequence of age-related social and emotional changes. The changes are *normative* in that they seem to be common to most members of a population; and they emerge in successive periods, or *stages,* sometimes marked by emotional crises that pave the way for further development.

as marriage, parenthood, grandparenthood, and retirement. Events that occur when expected are *on time;* events that occur earlier or later than usual are *off time.* Events that are normative when they are "on time" become nonnormative when they are "off time." According to this model, people usually are keenly aware of their own timing and of the **social clock,** their society's norms or expectations for the appropriate timing of life events.

social clock Set of cultural norms or expectations for the times of life when certain important events, such as marriage, parenthood, entry into work, and retirement, should occur.

Crises may result, not from reaching a certain age (as in normative-stage models), but from the unexpected occurrence and timing of life events. If events occur on time, development proceeds smoothly. If not, stress can result. Stress may come from an unexpected event (such as losing a job), an event that happens off time (being widowed at age 35, having a first child at 45, being forced to retire at 55), or the failure of an expected event to occur at all (never being married, or being unable to have a child). Personality differences influence the way people respond to life events and may even influence their timing. For example, a resilient person is likely to experience an easier transition to adulthood and the tasks and events that lie ahead than an overly anxious person, who may put off relationship or career decisions.

Architect Harold Fisher, who at age 100 was named America's oldest worker, is living proof that there is no longer a single "right time" for retirement in U.S. society.

The typical timing of events varies from culture to culture and from generation to generation. One illustration is the rise in the average age when adults first marry in the United States (Fields & Casper, 2001); another is the trend toward delayed first childbirth (Martin et al., 2002). A timetable that seems right to people in one cohort may not seem so to the next.

Since the mid-twentieth century western societies have become less age-conscious; the feeling that there is a "right time" to do certain things is less rigid, and the acceptable range of age norms is wider (C. C. Peterson, 1996). Today people are more accepting of 40-year-old first-time parents and 40-year-old grandparents, 50-year-old retirees and 75-year-old workers, 60-year-olds in jeans and 30-year-old college presidents. Such rapid social change undermines the predictability on which the timing-of-events model is based.

The timing-of-events model has made an important contribution to our understanding of adult personality by emphasizing the individual life course and challenging the idea of universal, age-related change. However, its usefulness may well be limited to cultures and historical periods in which norms of behavior are stable and widespread.

Trait Models: Costa and McCrae's Five Factors

Rather than looking at the course of typical lives, trait models look for stability or change in personality traits. Paul T. Costa and Robert R. McCrae, researchers with the National Institute on Aging, have developed and tested a **five-factor model** consisting of factors that seem to underlie five groups of associated traits (known as the "Big Five"). They are (1) *neuroticism,* (2) *extraversion,* (3) *openness to experience,* (4) *conscientiousness,* and (5) *agreeableness* (see Figure 14-1).

five-factor model Theoretical model, developed and tested by Costa and McCrae, based on the "Big Five" factors underlying clusters of related personality traits: neuroticism, extraversion, openness to experience, conscientiousness, and agreeableness.

Neuroticism is a cluster of six negative traits indicating emotional instability: anxiety, hostility, depression, self-consciousness, impulsiveness, and vulnerability. Highly neurotic people are nervous, fearful, irritable, easily angered, and sensitive to criticism. They may feel sad, hopeless, lonely, guilty, and worthless. *Extraversion* also has six facets: warmth, gregariousness, assertiveness, activity, excitement-seeking, and positive emotions. Extraverts are sociable and like attention. They keep busy and active; they are constantly looking for excitement, and they enjoy life. We can speculate that Ingrid Bergman would have had fairly high scores on some facets of neuroticism and extraversion and low scores on others.

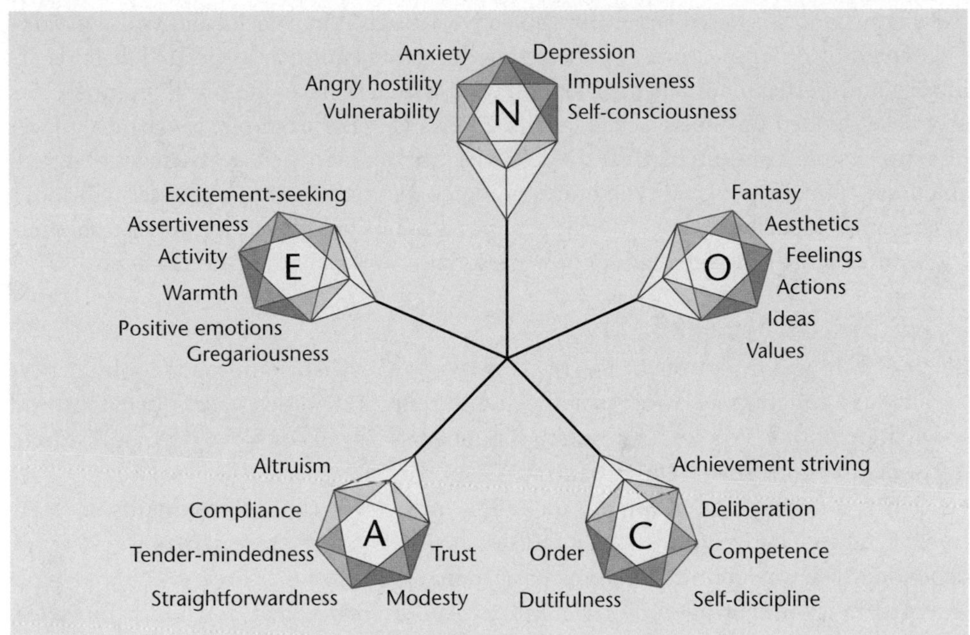

Figure 14-1
Costa and McCrae's five-factor model. Each factor, or domain of personality, represents a cluster of related traits or facets. N = neuroticism, E = extraversion, O = openness to experience, A = agreeableness, C = conscientiousness. (*Source:* Adapted from Costa & McCrae, 1980.)

People who are *open to experience* are willing to try new things and embrace new ideas. They have vivid imagination and strong feelings. They appreciate beauty and the arts and question traditional values. Ingrid Bergman probably would have scored high in these areas.

Conscientious people are achievers: they are competent, orderly, dutiful, deliberate, and disciplined. *Agreeable* people are trusting, straightforward, altruistic, compliant, modest, and easily swayed. Some of these characteristics could be identified with Ingrid Bergman in her youth but less and less as she got older.

By analyzing cross-sectional, longitudinal, and sequential data from several large samples of men and women of all ages, Costa and McCrae (1980, 1988, 1994a, 1994b; Costa et al., 1986; McCrae & Costa, 1984; McCrae, Costa, & Busch, 1986) found remarkable stability in all five domains. However, they did find age-related differences between college students and young and middle-aged adults (Costa & McCrae, 1994b). "Somewhere between age 21 and age 30 personality appears to take its final, fully developed form," these researchers conclude (Costa & McCrae, 1994a, p. 34). Adaptations may occur in response to new responsibilities and demands, traumatic events, or major cultural transformations (such as the feminist movement), but basic tendencies remain unchanged and influence the way a person adapts (Caspi, 1998; Clausen, 1993; Costa & McCrae, 1994a).

This body of work has made a powerful case for continuity of personality. Other researchers using somewhat different systems of trait classification have had similar results (Costa & McCrae, 1995). Comparable systems have emerged when personality was rated in languages other than English (Saucier & Ostendorf, 1999). In a study of representative samples of adults ages 25 to 65 in the United States and Germany, the "Big Five" (especially neuroticism) and other personality dimensions largely accounted for variations in subjective feelings of health and well-being (Staudinger, Fleeson, & Baltes, 1999). Furthermore, at least one of the "Big Five" seems to be identifiable in childhood. In a longitudinal study of 194 boys and girls in central Finland, teacher and peer reports of aggression, compliance, and self-control at age 8 predicted the degree of agreeability at age 36 (Laursen, Pulkkinen, & Adams, 2002).

Still, the five-factor model has critics. Jack Block (1995a, 1995b) argues that analysis of personality factors presents statistical and methodological problems. Because the five-factor model is based largely on subjective ratings, it may lack validity unless supplemented by other measures. The selection of factors and their associated facets is arbitrary and perhaps not all-inclusive; other researchers have chosen different factors and have divided up the associated traits differently. (For example, is warmth a facet of extraversion, as in the Big Five model, or is it better classified as an aspect of agreeableness?) Finally, personality is more than a collection of traits. A model that looks only at individual differences in trait groupings is limited in that it offers no theoretical framework for understanding how personality works within the person.

Typological Models

Block (1971) was a pioneer in the *typological approach.* This approach looks at personality as a functioning whole that affects and reflects attitudes, values, behavior, and social interactions. Typological research is not necessarily in conflict with trait research, but seeks to complement and expand it (Caspi, 1998).

Using a variety of techniques, including interviews, clinical judgments, Q-sorts (refer back to Chapter 6), behavior ratings, and self-reports, researchers working independently have identified several basic personality types. Three types that have emerged in a number of studies are *ego-resilient, overcontrolled,* and *undercontrolled.* People of these three types differ in **ego-resiliency,** or adaptability under stress, and **ego-control,** or self-control. *Ego-resilient* people are well adjusted: self-confident, independent, articulate, attentive, helpful, cooperative, and task-focused. *Overcontrolled* people are shy, quiet, anxious, and dependable; they tend to keep their thoughts to themselves and to withdraw from conflict, and they are the most subject to depression. *Undercontrolled* people are active, energetic, impulsive, stubborn, and easily distracted. These or similar personality types seem to exist in both sexes, across cultures and ethnic groups, and in children, adolescents, and adults (Caspi, 1998; Hart, Hofmann, Edelstein, & Keller, 1997; Pulkkinen, 1996; Robins, John, Caspi, Moffitt, & Stouthamer-Loeber, 1996; van Lieshout, Haselager, Riksen-Walraven, & van Aken, 1995).

ego-resiliency Adaptability under potential sources of stress.

ego-control Self-control.

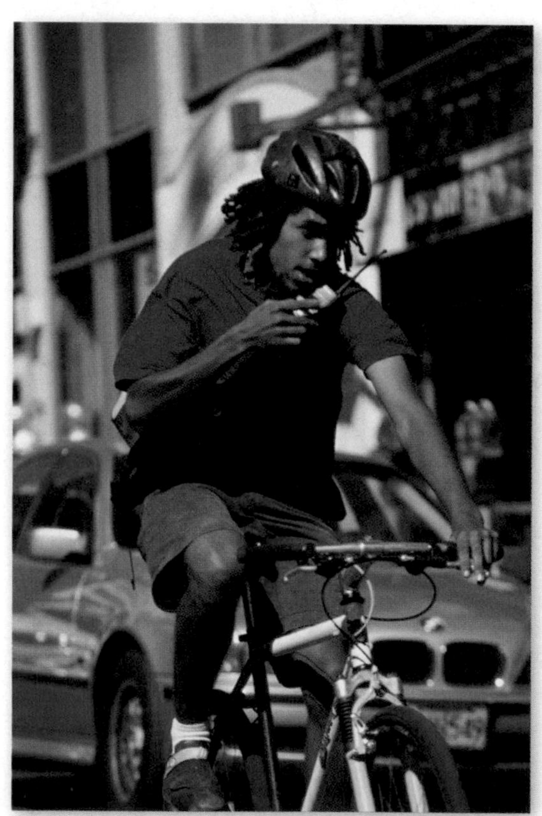

A bicycle messenger's job requires energy, spontaneity, and risk taking—qualities that adults who were undercontrolled in childhood are likely to show.

In a longitudinal study of 1,024 three-year-olds in New Zealand, observer-rated personality types, similar to the three categories just described, showed predictable relationships to self-reported personality characteristics at age 19 (Caspi & Silva, 1995). Of course, the finding of a tendency toward continuity of attitudes and behavior does not mean that personalities never change, or that certain people are condemned to a life of maladjustment. Undercontrolled children may get along better in early adulthood if they find niches in which their energy and spontaneity are considered a plus rather than a minus. Overcontrolled youngsters, like Ingrid Bergman in her youth, may come out of their shell if they find that their quiet dependability is valued.

Although personality traits or types established in childhood may predict *trajectories,* or long-term patterns of behavior, certain events may change the life course (Caspi, 1998). For some young adults, military service offers a "time-out" period and an opportunity to redirect their lives. For young people with adjustment problems, marriage to a supportive spouse can be a turning point, leading to more positive outcomes.

Integrating Approaches to Personality Development

The four approaches to personality development described in the preceding sections (see Table 14-1) ask different questions about adult development, look at different aspects of development, and use different methods. For example, normative-stage

Table 14-1 Four Views of Personality Development

Models	Questions Asked	Methods Used	Change or Stability
Normative-stage models	Does personality change in typical ways at certain periods throughout the life course?	In-depth interviews, biographical materials	Normative personality changes, having to do with personal goals, work, and relationships, occur in stages.
Timing-of-events model	When do important life events typically occur? What if they occur earlier or later than usual?	Statistical studies, interviews, questionnaires	Nonnormative timing of life events can cause stress and affect personality development.
Trait models	Do personality traits fall into groups, or clusters? Do these clusters of traits change with age?	Personality inventories, questionnaires, factor analysis	Personality changes very little after age 30.
Typological models	Can basic personality types be identified, and how well do they predict the life course?	Interviews, clinical judgments, Q-sorts, behavior ratings, self-reports	Personality types tend to show continuity from childhood through adulthood; but certain events can change the life course.

models were built on in-depth interviews and biographical materials, whereas trait researchers rely heavily on personality inventories and questionnaires. It is not surprising, then, that researchers within each of these traditions often come out with results that are difficult to reconcile or even to compare.

Advocates of personality stability and advocates of change often defend their positions zealously, but personality development clearly entails some of both. In the 1970s, theories of normative change took center stage, only to yield to the timing-of-events model. Since then, trait and typological researchers have redirected attention to the essential stability of personality.

Recently, efforts have been made to pull these diverse approaches together. One leading team of trait researchers (Costa & McCrae, 1994a) has mapped six interrelated elements that "make up the raw material of most personality theories" (p. 23). These elements are *basic tendencies, external influences, characteristic adaptations, self-concept, objective biography,* and *dynamic processes.*

Basic tendencies include not only personality traits, but physical health, appearance, gender, sexual orientation, intelligence, and artistic abilities. These tendencies, which may be either inherited or acquired, interact with *external* (environmental) *influences* to produce certain *characteristic adaptations:* social roles, attitudes, interests, skills, activities, habits, and beliefs. For example, it takes a combination of musical inclination (a basic tendency) and exposure to an instrument (an external influence) to produce musical skill (a characteristic adaptation). Basic tendencies and characteristic adaptations, in turn, help shape the *self-concept,* which bears only a partial resemblance to the *objective biography,* the actual events of a person's life. Thus a woman may think of herself as having more musical ability than she has objectively demonstrated, and her behavior may be influenced by that self-image. *Dynamic processes* link the other five elements; one such process is learning, which enables people to adapt to external influences (for example, to become accomplished in playing a musical instrument).

Various theorists emphasize one or another of these elements. Trait models focus on basic tendencies, which are the least likely to change, though they may manifest themselves differently at different times. For example, an extraverted 25-year-old shoe salesman may, at 70, be lobbying against cuts in social security. Typological models seek to identify certain characteristic adaptations, such as resiliency. Normative-crisis models and the timing-of-events model highlight dynamic processes that reflect universal or particular aspects of the objective biography.

Another attempt to integrate various approaches to personality development is that of Ravenna Helson, whose work we discuss further in Chapter 16. For more than

What's Your View?

- Which of the models presented here seems to you to most accurately describe psychosocial development in adulthood?

Can you . . .

- ✔ Summarize and compare four major theoretical approaches to adult psychosocial development?

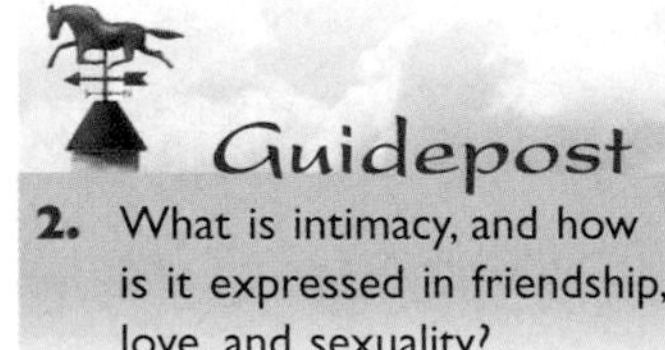

Guidepost

2. What is intimacy, and how is it expressed in friendship, love, and sexuality?

three decades Helson and her associates have followed 140 women from the classes of 1958 and 1960 at Mills College in Oakland, California. Using a combination of techniques, such as personality ratings, Q-sorts, and self-reports in response to open-ended questions, these researchers found evidence of systematic personality change.

One normative change in young adulthood was an increase and then a decline in traits associated with femininity (sympathy and compassion combined with a sense of vulnerability, self-criticism, and lack of confidence and initiative). Between ages 27 and 43, the women developed more self-discipline and commitment, independence, confidence, and coping skills (Helson & Moane, 1987). The Mills researchers also found certain changes related to specific personality patterns. For example, women identified as willful, or excessively self-absorbed, at age 21 became more effective, happier, more sociable, and more confident by age 27 but by midlife tended to have problems with drugs, relationships, and careers (Wink, 1991, 1992).

The Mills studies found that "personality does change from youth to middle age in consistent and often predictable ways" (Helson & Moane, 1987, p. 185), but there were important areas of stability as well. For example, certain persistent traits, such as optimism, affected quality of life at various ages (Mitchell & Helson, 1990).

Of course, the experience of these Mills graduates has to be considered in terms of their socioeconomic status, cohort, and culture. They are a group of educated, predominantly white, upper-middle-class women who lived through a time of great change in women's roles. Thus the normative changes found in the Mills research are not necessarily the same as maturational changes. Today's young women, in turn, may be developing differently from the women in the Mills sample.

Foundations of Intimate Relationships

Young adulthood typically is a time of dramatic change in personal relationships as people establish, renegotiate, or cement bonds based on friendship, love, and sexuality. How do young adults enter into relationships? What skills are necessary for healthy relationships in young adulthood?

As young adults enter college or the workplace—as they take responsibility for themselves and make their own decisions—they must complete the negotiation of autonomy begun in adolescence and redefine their relationships with their parents (Lambeth & Hallett, 2002; Mitchell, Wister, & Burch, 1989). Unless young adults can resolve conflicts with parents in a wholesome way, they may find themselves reenacting similar conflicts in the new relationships they develop with friends, colleagues, and partners. They may also—perhaps for the first time—encounter peers of diverse ethnic groups; and they need to become aware of how intercultural differences shape perceptions and attitudes (Lambeth & Hallett, 2002).

As they become their own persons, young adults seek emotional and physical intimacy in relationships with peers and romantic partners. These relationships require such skills as self-awareness, empathy, the ability to communicate emotions, sexual decision making, conflict resolution, and the ability to sustain commitments. Such skills are pivotal as young adults decide to marry, form unwed or homosexual partnerships, or live alone, and to have or not to have children (Lambeth & Hallett, 2002).

Erikson saw the development of intimate relationships as the crucial task of young adulthood. *Intimacy* may or may not include sexual contact. An important element of intimacy is *self-disclosure:* "revealing important information about oneself to another" (Collins & Miller, 1994, p. 457). People become intimate—and remain intimate—through shared disclosures, responsiveness to one another's needs, and mutual acceptance and respect (Harvey & Omarzu, 1997; Reis & Patrick, 1996).

Intimacy includes a sense of belonging. The need to form strong, stable, close, caring relationships is a powerful motivator of human behavior. The strongest emotions—

both positive and negative—are evoked by intimate attachments. And, as we mentioned in Chapter 13, people tend to be healthier, physically and mentally, and to live longer, if they have satisfying close relationships (Baumeister & Leary, 1995; Myers & Diener, 1995).

The Internet has brought a new dimension to relationships. Online relationships tend to be weaker than face-to-face ones. In a longitudinal study of 93 Pittsburgh families from diverse neighborhoods, Internet users tended to become less socially involved, to communicate less within the family, and to have fewer friends. Internet use also was associated with increases in loneliness and depression (Kraut et al., 1998). However, a follow-up study suggests that these negative effects may have been related to initial use of a new technology and may diminish with accustomed use (Kraut et al., 2002).

Friendship

Friendships during young and middle adulthood tend to center on work and parenting activities and the sharing of confidences and advice (Hartup & Stevens, 1999). Of course, friendships vary in character and quality. Some are extremely intimate and supportive; others are marked by frequent conflict. Some friends have many interests in common; others are based on a single shared activity, such as bowling or bridge. Some friendships are lifelong; others are fleeting (Hartup & Stevens, 1999). Some "best friendships" are more stable than ties to a lover or spouse.

Young singles rely more on friendships to fulfill their social needs than young marrieds or young parents do (Carbery & Buhrmester, 1998); but newlyweds have the greatest *number* of friends. The number of friends and the amount of time spent with them generally decreases by middle age. Young adults who are building careers and perhaps caring for babies have limited time to spend with friends. Still, friendships are important to them. People with friends tend to have a sense of well-being; either having friends makes people feel good about themselves, or people who feel good about themselves have an easier time making friends (Hartup & Stevens, 1999; Myers, 2000).

triangular theory of love Sternberg's theory that patterns of love hinge on the balance among three elements: intimacy, passion, and commitment.

Young women—whether single or married, and whether or not they have children—tend to have more of their social needs met by friends than young men do (Carbery & Buhrmester, 1998). Women typically have more intimate friendships than men and find friendships with other women more satisfying than those with men. Men are more likely to share information and activities, not confidences, with friends (Rosenbluth & Steil, 1995).

Couples in love tend to have similar interests and temperament. These rollerbladers may have been drawn together by their sense of adventure and enjoyment of risk taking.

Love

Most people like love stories, including their own. In a sense, says Robert J. Sternberg (1995), love *is* a story. The lovers are its authors, and the kind of story they make up reflects their personalities and their feelings about the relationship. Love "stories" also differ historically and across cultures (see Box 14-1 on page 502).

Thinking of love as a story may help us see how people select and mix the elements of the "plot." According to Sternberg's **triangular theory of love** (1986; Sternberg & Barnes, 1985; Sternberg & Grajek, 1984), the three elements of love are intimacy, passion, and commitment. *Intimacy,* the emotional element, involves self-disclosure, which leads to connection, warmth, and trust. *Passion,* the motivational element, is based on inner drives that translate physiological arousal into sexual desire. *Commitment,* the cognitive

BOX 14-1

Window on the World

Cultural Conceptions of Love

In William Shakespeare's *A Midsummer Night's Dream,* a fairy king who wants to play a trick on his queen squeezes the juice of a magic flower into her sleeping eyes so that she will fall in love with the first person she sees upon awakening—who turns out to be an actor wearing a donkey's head. That tale is one source of the old saying, "Love is blind."

Actually, students of love find that chance plays a much smaller role than the cultural context. Although love seems to be virtually universal (Goleman, 1992), its meaning and expression vary across time and space.

According to Anne E. Beall and Robert Sternberg (1995),* people in different cultures define love differently, and the way they think about love affects what they feel. Love, say these investigators, is a *social construction*—a concept people create out of their culturally influenced perceptions of reality. This concept influences what is considered normal, acceptable, or ideal. Culture influences not only the definition of love, but the features considered desirable in choosing a beloved, the feelings and thoughts expected to accompany love, and how lovers act toward each other. Social approval and support from family and friends reinforce satisfaction with and commitment to a relationship.

In many cultures, love has been considered a dangerous distraction, disruptive of a social order based on arranged marriages. During the past two centuries, in western societies and in some nonwestern ones as well (Goleman, 1992), marriage has come to be built on love—a trend accelerated by women's increasing economic self-sufficiency. Romantic love is more commonly accepted in individualistic societies than in collectivist ones. In Communist China, for example, such love is frowned upon. Chinese see themselves in terms of social roles and relationships and view self-indulgent emotional displays as weakening the social fabric.

Within western civilization, ideas about love have changed radically. In ancient Greece, homosexual love was prized above heterosexual relationships. In some cultures, love has been separated from sexuality. In King Arthur's court, love involved a nonsexual chivalry rather than intimacy; knights undertook feats of bravery to impress fair ladies but didn't seek to marry them. In the Roman Catholic Church, love of God is considered superior to love of a human being. In Victorian England, love was viewed as a noble emotion, but sex was considered a necessary evil, required only for producing children. The Victorian poets placed the beloved on a pedestal. A more modern view is that of loving a person for who he or she is, warts and all.

Ideas about love are influenced by how a culture looks at human nature. For example, during the eighteenth-century European Enlightenment, love—like other aspects of human experience—was thought to be subject to scientific understanding and rational control, and people were expected to hold their passions in check. By the nineteenth century, disillusionment with the power of science and reason had set in. People were seen as creatures of sensation, prejudice, and irrational emotion, and love was described as an uncontrollable passion. Today, the popularity of marriage counseling suggests a reassertion of the possibility of consciously affecting the course of love.

*Unless otherwise noted, this discussion is indebted to Beall and Sternberg (1995).

What's Your View?

How do you imagine ideas about love may change in the future?

Check It Out:

For more information on this topic, go to http://www. mhhe.com/papaliah9.

What's Your View?

- Other than sexual attraction, what difference, if any, do you see between a friend and a lover?
- If you have ever been in love, do any of the theories and hypotheses presented in this section ring true, in your experience?

element, is the decision to love and to stay with the beloved. The degree to which each of the three elements is present determines what kind of love people have (see Table 14-2). Mismatches can lead to problems.

Do opposites attract? Not as a rule. Just as people choose friends with whom they have something in common, they tend to choose life partners much like themselves (E. Epstein & Gutmann, 1984). According to the *matching hypothesis,* dating partners who are about equally attractive are most likely to develop close relationships (Harvey & Pauwels, 1999). Lovers often resemble each other in physical appearance, mental and physical health, intelligence, popularity, and warmth. They are likely to be similar in the degree to which their parents are happy as individuals and as couples, and in such factors as socioeconomic status, race, religion, education, and income (Murstein, 1980). Couples often have similar temperaments, too; risk takers tend to marry other risk takers—though they may be risking early divorce (Zuckerman, 1994)!

Table 14-2 Patterns of Loving

Type	Description
Nonlove	All three components of love—intimacy, passion, and commitment—are absent. This describes most interpersonal relationships, which are simply casual interactions.
Liking	Intimacy is the only component present. There is closeness, understanding, emotional support, affection, bondedness, and warmth. Neither passion nor commitment is present.
Infatuation	Passion is the only component present. This is "love at first sight," a strong physical attraction and sexual arousal, without intimacy or commitment. Infatuation can flare up suddenly and die just as fast—or, given certain circumstances, can sometimes last for a long time.
Empty love	Commitment is the only component present. Empty love is often found in long-term relationships that have lost both intimacy and passion, or in arranged marriages.
Romantic love	Intimacy and passion are both present. Romantic lovers are drawn to each other physically and bonded emotionally. They are not, however, committed to each other.
Companionate love	Intimacy and commitment are both present. This is a long-term, committed friendship, often occurring in marriages in which physical attraction has died down but in which the partners feel close to each other and have made the decision to stay together.
Fatuous love	Passion and commitment are present without intimacy. This is the kind of love that leads to a whirlwind courtship, in which a couple make a commitment on the basis of passion without allowing themselves the time to develop intimacy. This kind of love usually does not last, despite the initial intent to commit.
Consummate love	All three components are present in this "complete" love, which many people strive for, especially in romantic relationships. It is easier to achieve it than to hold onto it. Either partner may change what he or she wants from the relationship. If the other partner changes, too, the relationship may endure in a different form. If the other partner does not change, the relationship may dissolve.

Source: Based on Sternberg, 1986.

Sexuality: Issues and Attitudes

Views about sexual activity fall into three main categories, according to a major national survey of sexual attitudes and behavior. About 30 percent of Americans have traditional, or *reproductive* attitudes about sex—that sex is permissible only for reproductive purposes within marriage. Another 25 percent (more men than women) have a *recreational* view of sex: that whatever feels good and doesn't hurt anyone is fine. Roughly 45 percent take a *relational* view: that sex should be accompanied by love or affection, but not necessarily marriage (Laumann & Michael, 2000). These three views structure the national debate about what is right and wrong when it comes to sexual behavior.

The change in attitudes toward premarital sex among young adults in the United States since the 1960s is striking. Between 1965 and 1994, disapproval of sex before marriage fell from 63 percent to 30 percent among men and from 80 percent to 44 percent among women (Scott, 1998).

In some other respects, however, the change in sexual attitudes and behavior is not so dramatic. Neither men nor women appear to be as promiscuous as is sometimes thought. The median number of sex partners after age 18 is two for women and six for men. Most people meet their partners through mutual acquaintances and thus tend to be similar in age, educational level, and racial, ethnic, and religious background. About 30 percent of adults, because of the threat of AIDS, say they have modified their sexual behavior by having fewer partners, choosing them more carefully, using condoms, or abstaining from sex (Feinleib & Michael, 2000; Laumann, Gagnon, Michael, & Michaels, 1994; Michael, Gagnon, Laumann, & Kolata, 1994).

Acquaintance rape is a problem on many college campuses (Lambeth & Hallett, 2002). College women are approximately three times more likely to become rape victims than women in the population as a whole (Gidycz, Hanson, & Layman, 1995). Rape-prevention programs have had some success. In one study, college men who participated in an hour-long session designed to provide accurate information about rape and debunk myths about it became more empathic toward rape victims than a control group and also became more aware of what constitutes rape (Pinzone-Glover, Gidycz, & Jacobs, 1998).

Between adolescence and young adulthood, gender differences in frequency of intercourse and incidence of masturbation increase. American men are much more likely than American women to masturbate and to approve of casual premarital sex. However, an overview of 177 studies done from 1966 through 1990, which included nearly 59,000 males and 70,000 females (largely young adults), found *no* gender differences in sexual satisfaction or participation in oral sex. Also, the sexes were quite similar in *attitudes* about masturbation, homosexuality, and civil liberties for gays and lesbians (Oliver & Hyde, 1993).

Negative attitudes toward homosexuality are slowly diminishing in the United States, but nearly three out of four men and more than two out of three women still disapprove (Gardiner et al., 1998). According to a *Newsweek* poll (2000), nearly half of the population surveyed consider homosexuality a sin, and one-third of the respondents in another survey (*Americans on Values,* 1999) believe that it is an illness—contrary to the stated position of the American Psychiatric Association (APA, 2000).

The social stigma against homosexuality, and the discrimination that reflects it, may have significant effects on gays' and lesbians' mental health. Studies have found a higher risk of anxiety, depression, and other psychiatric disorders among gays and lesbians than among heterosexuals (Cochran, 2001).

Disapproval of extramarital sex today is even greater in U.S. society than disapproval of homosexuality—94 percent—though perhaps not as intense or as publicly expressed as in Ingrid Bergman's time. The pattern of strong disapproval of homosexuality, even stronger disapproval of extramarital sex, and far weaker disapproval of premarital sex also holds true in European countries such as Britain, Ireland, Germany, Sweden, and Poland, though degrees of disapproval differ from one country to another. The United States has more restrictive attitudes than any of these countries except Ireland, where the influence of the Catholic Church is strong. For example, in Germany and Sweden only 3 to 7 percent of adults disapprove of premarital sex (Scott, 1998). In China, sexual attitudes and premarital and extramarital sexual activity have liberalized dramatically despite official prohibition of sex outside marriage (Gardiner et al., 1998). Surveys taken at five-year intervals in the Netherlands found that, much as in the United States, attitudes toward extramarital sex liberalized between 1965 and 1975 and then became more restrictive. Younger, more educated, and less religious people tend to have more liberal attitudes about sex, and men are still more liberal than women (Kraaykamp, 2002).

Checkpoint

Can you . . .

- ✔ Mention several challenges young adults face with regard to relationships?
- ✔ Identify factors that promote and maintain intimacy?
- ✔ Describe characteristic features of friendship in young adulthood?
- ✔ Discuss theories and research about the nature of love and how men and women choose mates?
- ✔ Summarize recent trends in sexual attitudes and behavior?

Nonmarital and Marital Lifestyles

Today's rules for acceptable behavior are more elastic than they were during the first half of the twentieth century. Current norms no longer dictate that people must get married, stay married, or have children, and at what ages. People may stay single, live with a partner of either sex, divorce, remarry, be single parents, or remain childless; and a person's choices may change during the course of adulthood.

The proportion of U.S. households consisting of married couples with their own children dropped from 40 percent in 1970 to 24 percent in 2000. Meanwhile, the proportion of households in which one person lives alone increased from 17 percent to 26 percent (Fields & Casper, 2001). People marry later nowadays, if at all; more have children outside of marriage, if at all; and more break up their marriages (Fields & Casper, 2001; T. Smith, 1999). Still, an overwhelming 95 percent of men and women have been married at some time before age 65, "indicating that marriage is still very much a part of American life" (Fields & Casper, 2001, p. 10).

In this section, we look at marriage and its alternatives. In the next section we examine parenthood.

Single Life

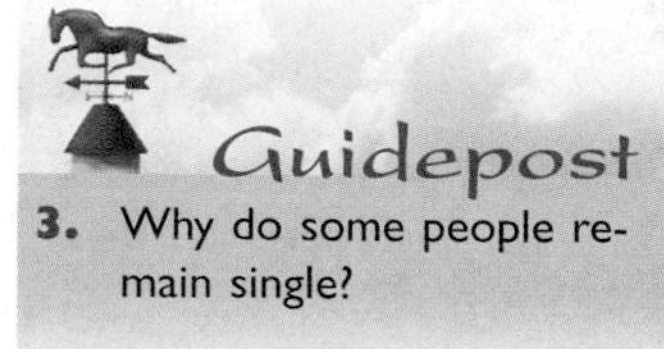

3. Why do some people remain single?

The number of young adults who have not yet married has increased dramatically. In 2000, about 45 percent of 25- to 29-year-olds had never married, a threefold increase since 1970. Even among 35- to 44-year-olds, 15.5 percent still had never married (Fields & Casper, 2001). The trend is particularly pronounced among African American women, 35 percent of whom remain unmarried in their late thirties (Teachman, Tedrow, & Crowder, 2000).

In a study of 300 black, white, and Latina single women in the Los Angeles area (Tucker & Mitchell-Kernan, 1998), members of all three groups had difficulty finding eligible men with similar educational and social backgrounds; but unlike the other two groups, African American women, whose average age was 40, seemed relatively untroubled by the situation. Perhaps, as the timing-of-events model might predict, this is because they saw singlehood as normative in their ethnic group.

These African American women seem to enjoy their single status, which is not unusual in their ethnic group.

While some young adults stay single because they have not found the right mates, others are single by choice. More women today are self-supporting, and there is less social pressure to marry. Some people want to be free to take risks, experiment, and make changes—move across the country or across the world, pursue careers, further their education, or do creative work without worrying about how their quest for self-fulfillment affects another person. Some enjoy sexual freedom. Some find the lifestyle exciting. Some just like being alone. And some postpone or avoid marriage because of fear that it will end in divorce. Postponement makes sense, since, as we'll see, the younger people are when they first marry, the likelier they are to split up. By and large, singles like their status (Austrom & Hanel, 1985). Most are not lonely (Cargan, 1981; Spurlock, 1990); they are busy and active and feel secure about themselves.

Gay and Lesbian Relationships

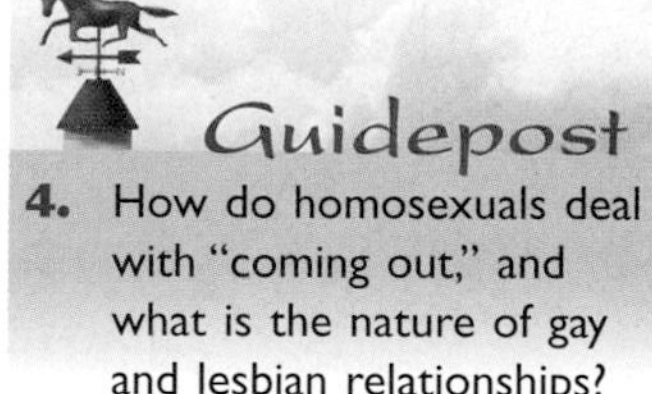

4. How do homosexuals deal with "coming out," and what is the nature of gay and lesbian relationships?

Adults are more likely than adolescents to identify themselves as homosexual (refer back to Chapter 12). Still, fewer than 3 percent of U.S. men and $1\frac{1}{2}$ percent of women call themselves homosexual or bisexual. Slightly more—5 percent of men and 4 percent of women—report at least one homosexual encounter in adulthood. Gay or lesbian identification is more common in big cities—9 percent for men and 3 percent for women (Laumann et al., 1994; Laumann & Michael, 2000; Michael et al., 1994).

Because of strong societal disapproval of homosexuality, **coming out**—the process of openly disclosing a homosexual orientation—is often slow and painful. Coming out generally occurs in four stages, which may never be fully achieved (King, 1996):

coming out Process of openly disclosing one's homosexual orientation.

1. *Recognition of being homosexual.* This may take place early in childhood or not until adolescence or later. It can be a lonely, painful, confusing experience.
2. *Getting to know other homosexuals* and establishing sexual and romantic relationships. This may not happen until adulthood. Contact with other homosexuals can diminish feelings of isolation and improve self-image.
3. *Telling family and friends.* Many homosexuals cannot bring themselves to do this for a long time—if ever. The revelation can bring disapproval, conflict, and rejection; or it may deepen family solidarity and support (Mays, Chatters, Cochran, & Mackness, 1998).

Most gays and lesbians, like most heterosexuals, seek love, companionship, and sexual fulfillment in a committed relationship.

4. *Complete openness.* This includes telling colleagues, employers, and others. Homosexuals who reach this stage have achieved healthy acceptance of their sexuality as part of who they are.

Gay and lesbian relationships take many forms, but most homosexuals (like most heterosexuals) seek love, companionship, and sexual fulfillment through a relationship with one person. Such relationships are more common in societies that tolerate, accept, or support them (Gardiner et al., 1998). The ingredients of long-term satisfaction are very similar in homosexual and heterosexual relationships (Patterson, 1995b).

Lesbians are more likely to have stable, monogamous relationships than gay men. Since the AIDS epidemic, however, gay men have become more interested in long-term relationships. Gay and lesbian partners who live together tend to be as committed as married couples (Kurdek, 1995).

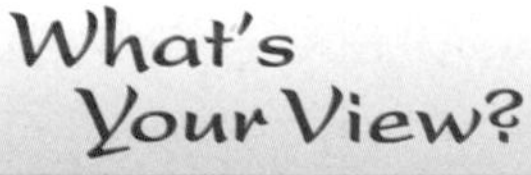

What's Your View?

- Should gays and lesbians be allowed to marry? Adopt children? Be covered by a partner's health care plan?

Today, gays and lesbians in the United States and Europe are struggling to obtain legal recognition of their unions, as in the Netherlands and the state of Vermont, and the right to adopt children or raise their own. Many homosexuals who have been married and had children before coming out have been unable to gain or keep custody. Others are adopting children or conceiving via assisted reproduction techniques. To give these children the benefit of two parents, the American Academy of Pediatrics Committee on Psychosocial Aspects of Child and Family Health (2002) supports laws permitting adoption by the parent's same-sex partner.

Gays and lesbians also are pressing for an end to discrimination in employment and housing. A current issue is whether unmarried domestic partners—homosexual or heterosexual—should be entitled to coverage under each other's health insurance and pension plans, should be able to file joint tax returns, and should receive bereavement leave and other customary benefits of marriage. Such provisions already are in effect in France, Sweden, Norway, Denmark, and the Netherlands (Trueheart, 1999).

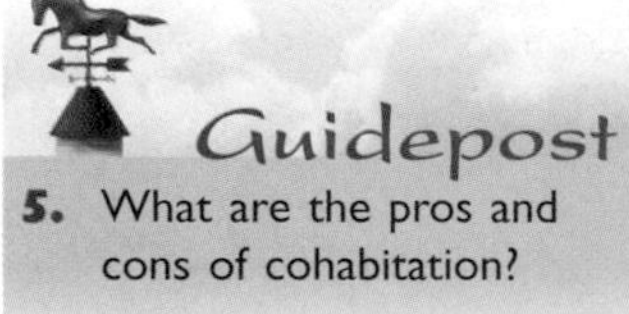

Guidepost

5. What are the pros and cons of cohabitation?

cohabitation Status of an unmarried couple who live together and maintain a sexual relationship.

Cohabitation

Cohabitation is a lifestyle in which an unmarried couple involved in a sexual relationship live together in what is sometimes called a *consensual* or *informal union.* Such unions have become the norm in many European countries, such as Sweden and Denmark, where cohabiting couples have practically the same legal rights as married ones, and are becoming increasingly common in the United States and Canada

(Popenoe & Whitehead, 1999; Seltzer, 2000). In Britain, 70 percent of first partnerships are cohabitations, and 60 percent of cohabiting couples eventually marry (Ford, 2002). In Canada, 12 percent of couples were cohabiting in 1996, twice as many as in 1981 (Wu, 1999).

The widespread acceptance of cohabitation in the United States is remarkable, considering that until about 1970 it was against the law, and still is in some states (Popenoe & Whitehead, 1999). A total of 7.6 million men and women classified themselves as cohabiting in 2000, representing 3.7 percent of all households—and the actual numbers may well be higher. Forty-one percent of these unmarried-partner households included children under 18 (Fields & Casper, 2001). Much larger numbers have *ever* cohabitated—about 41 percent of 15- to 44-year-olds as of 1995 (Bramlett & Mosher, 2002).

Cohabitation can be either a substitute for marriage or a "trial marriage." Consensual unions have long been accepted as an alternative to marriage in many Latin American countries; this may explain why, for example, Puerto Ricans have higher rates of cohabitation and are less likely than non-Hispanic white Americans to marry their live-in partners. Although family law in the United States gives cohabitors few of the rights and benefits of marriage, this is changing, particularly with regard to protections for children of cohabiting couples. And, as cohabitation becomes increasingly common, cohabiting couples are under less social pressure to marry (Seltzer, 2000). It is easy to keep extending the "trial period" before making a long-term commitment (Wu, 1999). There also is an increasing trend toward cohabitation after divorce as an alternative to remarriage (Coleman, Ganong, & Fine, 2000). However, cohabiting relationships tend to be less satisfying than marriages. Cohabitants miss out on some of the economic, psychological, and health benefits of marriage, which come from the security of a long-term commitment, greater sharing of economic and social resources, and a stronger community connection (Popenoe & Whitehead, 1999).

Premarital cohabitation has accompanied the trend toward delayed marriage, discussed in the next section (Seltzer, 2000). More than half of all U.S. couples who marry have lived together first, as did Ingrid Bergman and Roberto Rossellini (Popenoe & Whitehead, 1999; Seltzer, 2000). Looking at the data another way, more than half (58 percent) of first cohabitations that last three years, and 70 percent of those that last five years, end in marriage (Bramlett & Mosher, 2002). However, cohabiting unions tend to be less stable than marriages (Bramlett & Mosher, 2002; Popenoe & Whitehead, 1999; Seltzer, 2000). Thirty-nine percent break up within three years and 49 percent within five years (Bramlett & Mosher, 2002). Many adults have two or more live-in partners before marriage (Michael et al., 1994; Popenoe & Whitehead, 1999). Couples who have a child together are less likely to break up, whether or not they marry (Seltzer, 2000).

According to national surveys, most young adults think cohabitation before marriage is a good idea. Yet, according to some research, couples who live together before marriage tend to have unhappier marriages and greater likelihood of divorce (Bramlett & Mosher, 2002; Popenoe & Whitehead, 1999; Seltzer, 2000). In part, the higher divorce rates of couples who cohabit before marriage may reflect the kinds of people who choose cohabitation, and not the effects of cohabitation itself. Cohabitants tend to have unconventional attitudes about family life, and they are less likely than most other people to select partners like themselves in age, race or ethnicity, and previous marital status. They are more likely to have divorced parents and stepchildren and to have liberal attitudes toward divorce. All these factors tend to predict unstable marriages (Cohan & Kleinbaum, 2002; Fields & Casper, 2001; D. R. Hall & Zhao, 1995; Popenoe & Whitehead, 1999; Seltzer, 2000).

What's Your View?

- From your experience or observation, is it a good idea to cohabit before marriage? Why or why not? Does it make a difference whether children are involved?

Checkpoint

Can you . . .

- ✔ State reasons why people remain single?
- ✔ List four stages of "coming out" for homosexuals and describe typical characteristics of gay and lesbian relationships?
- ✔ Give reasons for the rise in cohabitation and differentiate between two types of cohabitation?

Marriage

Guidepost

6. What do adults gain from marriage, what cultural patterns surround entrance into marriage, and why do some marriages succeed while others fail?

Marriage customs vary widely, but the universality of some form of marriage throughout history and around the world suggests that it meets fundamental needs. *Monogamy*—marriage to one mate—is the norm in most developed societies. *Polygyny*—a man's marriage to more than one woman at a time—is common in Islamic countries, African societies, and parts of Asia. In *polyandrous* societies, where women generally wield more economic power, a woman may take several husbands—in some Himalayan regions, a set of brothers (Gardiner et al., 1998; Kottak, 1994).

In most societies, marriage is considered the best way to ensure orderly raising of children. It allows for a division of labor within a consuming and working unit. Ideally, it offers intimacy, commitment, friendship, affection, sexual fulfillment, companionship, and an opportunity for emotional growth, as well as new sources of identity and self-esteem (Gardiner et al., 1998; Myers, 2000). In certain Eastern philosophical traditions, the harmonious union of male and female is considered essential to spiritual fulfillment and the survival of the species (Gardiner et al., 1998).

Today some benefits of marriage, such as sex, intimacy, and economic security, are not confined to matrimony. Still, many surveys in Europe and North America show that married people tend to be happier than unmarried people—though those in unhappy marriages are less happy than those who are unmarried or divorced. Contrary to common belief, women are as happy in marriage as men (Myers, 2000). People who marry and stay married, especially women, also tend to accumulate more wealth than those who do not marry or who divorce (Wilmoth & Koso, 2002). In a national sample of more than 2,000 U.S. adults ages 18 to 90, both genders reported equal benefit from a marital attachment: women from economic support and men from emotional support (Ross, 1995).

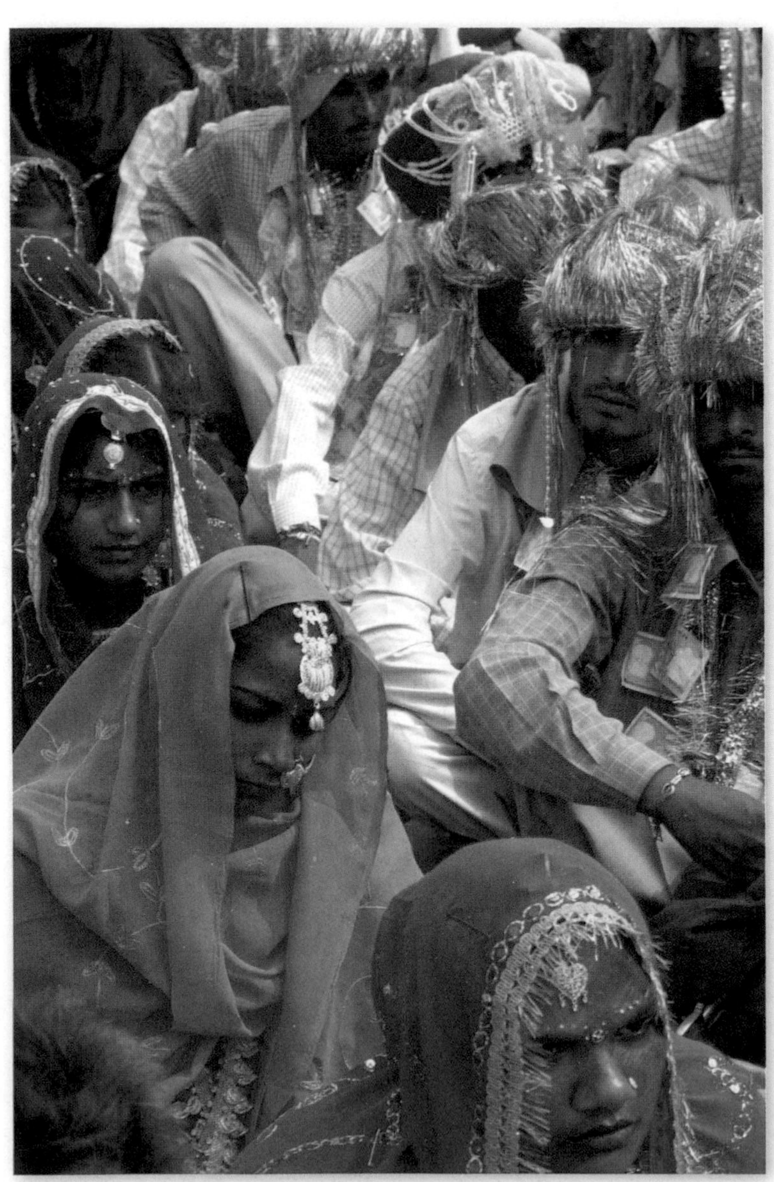

The mass wedding in India is an example of the variety of marriage customs around the world.

Entering Matrimony Historically and across cultures, the most common way of selecting a mate has been through arrangement, either by the parents or by professional matchmakers. Sometimes betrothal takes place in childhood. The bride and groom may not even meet until their wedding day. Free choice of mates on the basis of love has become the norm in the western world (Broude, 1994; Ingoldsby, 1995; refer back to Box 14-1); but in Japan, 25 to 30 percent of marriages still are arranged (Applbaum, 1995).

The typical "marrying age" varies across cultures. In eastern Europe, people tend to marry in or before their early twenties, as Ingrid Bergman did. But industrialized nations such as her native Sweden are seeing a trend toward later marriage as young adults take time to pursue educational and career goals or to explore relationships (Bianchi & Spain, 1986). In France, the average bridegroom is 30 and his bride, 28, five years older than their counterparts a quarter-century ago (Ford, 2002). In Canada, the average age of first marriage for women has risen from about 23 to 27, and for men from about 26 to 29, since 1961 (Wu, 1999). In the United States, the median age of first-time bridegrooms is about 27, and of first-time brides, 25—a rise of about three and a half years since the early 1940s (Fields & Casper, 2001; Kreider & Fields, 2002).

The transition to married life brings major changes in sexual functioning, living arrangements, rights and responsibilities, attachments, and loyalties. Among other things, marriage partners need to redefine the connection with their original families, balance intimacy with autonomy, and establish a fulfilling sexual relationship (Wallerstein & Blakeslee, 1995).

To help newlyweds adjust, some traditional societies give them extra privacy; in other societies, their sexual and other activities are subject to prescribed rules and supervision. In some cultures, newlyweds set up their own household; in other cultures, they live with parents, temporarily or permanently. In some societies, such as the Rajputs of Khalapur, India, husband and wife live, eat, and sleep apart (Broude, 1994). In contrast to Anglo-American cultures, where the chief purpose of marriage is seen as love and companionship (T. Smith, 1999), the sole purpose of marriage in Rajput society is reproduction; emotional and social support come from same-sex relatives and friends (Broude, 1994).

Sexual Activity After Marriage Americans apparently have sex less often than media images suggest, and married people do so more often than singles, though not as often as cohabitors. Face-to-face interviews with a random sample of 3,432 men and women ages 18 to 59 found that only about one-third, including 40 percent of married couples, have intercourse two or more times a week (Laumann et al., 1994; Laumann & Michael, 2000; Michael et al., 1994). However, married couples report more emotional satisfaction from sex than single or cohabiting couples (Waite & Joyner, 2000). Frequency of sexual relations in marriage drops sharply after the early months and then declines gradually as time goes on. Satisfaction with the marriage is the second most important factor after age—though it is unclear whether satisfaction influences frequency of sex or the other way around (Call, Sprecher, & Schwartz, 1995).

Some married people seek sexual intimacy outside of marriage, especially after the first few years, when the excitement of sex with the spouse wears off or problems in the relationship surface. It is hard to know just how common extramarital sex is, because there is no way to tell how truthful people are about their sexual practices, but surveys suggest that it is much less common than is generally assumed. In one survey, only about 21 percent of men and 11.5 percent of women who were ever married reported having had extramarital relations during their married lives. Extramarital activity was more prevalent among younger cohorts than among those born before 1940 (T. W. Smith, 1994). However, fear of AIDS and other sexually transmitted diseases may have curtailed extramarital sex since its reported peak in the late 1960s and early 1970s. In a nationwide survey, only about 2 percent of married respondents admitted having been unfaithful during the previous year (Choi, Catania, & Dolcini, 1994).

Factors in Marital Success or Failure One of the most important factors in marital success is a sense of commitment. Among a national sample of 2,331 married people, the partners' dependence on each other played a part in commitment to marriage, but the strongest factor was a feeling of obligation to the spouse (Nock, 1995).

Success in marriage is closely associated with how partners communicate, make decisions, and deal with conflict (Brubaker, 1983, 1993). Arguing and openly expressing anger seem to be good for a marriage; whining, defensiveness, stubbornness, and withdrawal are signs of trouble (Gottman & Krokoff, 1989). Among 150 couples who

BOX 14-2

Practically Speaking

Dealing with Domestic Violence

Domestic violence, or *partner abuse,* is the physical, sexual, or psychological maltreatment of a spouse, a former spouse, or an intimate partner so as to gain or maintain power or control. Its full extent is unknown (Walker, 1999) because it generally takes place in private, and victims often do not report it because they are ashamed or afraid (Bachman, 1994). Wife beating is most prevalent in societies marked by aggressive behavior, restrictive sexual practices, inferior status of women, and use of physical force to resolve disputes. It is fairly rare in societies based on extended-family households (Broude, 1994).

More than nine out of ten victims in the United States are women, and they are more likely than men to be seriously harmed. Once a woman has been abused, she is likely to be abused again (Holtzworth-Munroe & Stuart, 1994; U.S. Bureau of Justice Statistics, 1994).

Partner abuse occurs at every level of society, in all income groups; but the women at greatest risk are young, poor, uneducated, and divorced or separated (U.S. Bureau of Justice Statistics, 1994; Walker, 1999). Men who intentionally injure women tend to have less than a high school education, to be unemployed or intermittently employed, to have low incomes and alcohol or other drug problems, and to be the former or estranged husbands or former boyfriends of their victims (Heyman, O'Leary, & Jouriles, 1995; Kyriacou et al., 1999; McKenry, Julian, & Gavazzi, 1995). There is no appreciable difference in domestic violence against black and white women (Bachman, 1994).

Pushing, shoving, and slapping often begin even before marriage. Among 625 newlywed couples, 36 percent reported premarital violence (McLaughlin, Leonard, & Senchak, 1992). If nothing is done about it, the violence tends to continue or increase (Heyman et al., 1995; Holtzworth-Munroe & Stuart, 1994; O'Leary et al., 1989). In a population-based North Carolina study, about 7 percent of women were abused during the year before becoming pregnant, and most of them continued to be abused during pregnancy, some even after giving birth (Martin, Mackie, Kupper, Buescher, & Moracco, 2001).

Most victims of domestic violence are women, and they are more likely to be seriously hurt. Men who abuse their partners often seek to control or dominate. Many were brought up in violent homes themselves.

Spousal abuse is more frequent in marriages in which the man seeks to control or dominate (Yllo, 1984, 1993). Such relationships may be products of a socialization process in which boys are taught by example to prevail through aggression and physical force. Eight out of ten men who physically assault their wives saw their fathers beat their mothers (Reiss & Roth, 1994).

were followed through the first ten years of marriage, those who learned to "fight fair" were 50 percent less likely to divorce (Markman, Renick, Floyd, Stanley, & Clements, 1993).

Age at marriage is a major predictor of whether a union will last. Teenagers have high divorce rates; people who wait until their twenties to marry have a better chance of success. College graduates and couples with high family income are less likely to end their marriages than those with less education and income (Bramlett & Mosher, 2001, 2002). Cohabitation before marriage and having divorced parents are predictive of divorce; so are becoming pregnant or bearing a child before marriage, having no children, and having stepchildren in the home (Bramlett & Mosher, 2002; Schoen, 1992; White, 1990). People who attach high importance to religion are less likely to experience marital dissolution (Bramlett & Mosher, 2002).

Economic hardship can put severe emotional stress on a marriage. In a four-year longitudinal study of more than 400 married couples, those who were most resilient when faced with economic pressures were those who showed mutual supportiveness—who listened to each other's concerns, tried to help, were sensitive to

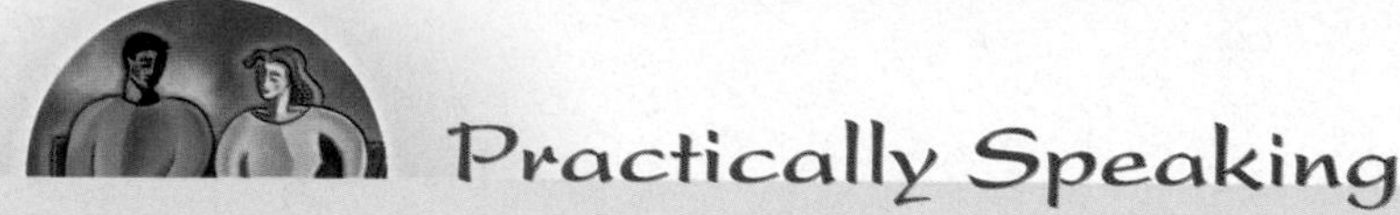

Practically Speaking

BOX 14-2

—continued

The effects of domestic violence often extend beyond the couple. The children, especially sons, are likely to be abused by both parents (Jouriles & Norwood, 1995), and boys exposed to abuse are likely to grow up to be abusers themselves (Walker, 1999).

Why do women stay with men who abuse them? Some cannot bring themselves to face and admit what is happening. Some have low self-esteem and feel they deserve to be beaten. Constant ridicule, criticism, threats, punishment, and psychological manipulation may destroy their self-confidence and overwhelm them with self-doubt (Fawcett, Heise, Isita-Espejel, & Pick, 1999; NOW Legal Defense and Education Fund & Chernow-O'Leary, 1987). Some minimize the extent of the abuse or hold themselves responsible for not living up to their marital obligations. Many see abuse as a private issue to be resolved within the family (Fawcett et al., 1999). Some women feel they have nowhere to turn. Their abusive partners isolate them from family and friends. They are often financially dependent and lack outside social support (Kalmuss & Straus, 1982; McKenry et al., 1995; Strube & Barbour, 1984).

Often the risks of acting seem to outweigh the benefits (Fawcett et al., 1999). If the woman tries to end the relationship or call the police, she gets more abuse (Geller, 1992). Some women are afraid to leave—a realistic fear, since some abusive husbands later track down, harass, and beat or even kill their estranged wives (Reiss & Roth, 1994; Walker, 1999).

In some cases, marital or family therapy may stop mild to moderate abuse before it escalates (Gelles & Maynard, 1987; Holtzworth-Munroe & Stuart, 1994; Walker, 1999). Men who are arrested for family violence are less likely to repeat the abuse, and communities are increasingly adopting this approach (Bouza, 1990; L. W. Sherman & Berk, 1984; L. W. Sherman & Cohn, 1989; Walker, 1999). Sometimes, however, especially when the perpetrator has antisocial tendencies, arrest only worsens the abuse afterward (Walker, 1999).

In the United States, the Violence Against Women Act, adopted in 1994, provides for tougher law enforcement, funding for shelters, a national domestic violence hotline, and educating judges and court personnel, as well as young people, about domestic violence. Canada has similar programs to help battered women. Efforts to protect women and eliminate gender-based violence also are under way in various European and Latin American countries. In England and Brazil, police are being trained to understand gender-based violence and to help women feel comfortable in reporting it (Walker, 1999).

In the long run, the best hope for eliminating partner abuse is to "change men's socialization patterns so that power over women will no longer be a necessary part of the definition of what it means to be a man" and to "renegotiat[e] the balance of power between women and men at all levels of society" (Walker, 1999, pp. 25, 26).

What's Your View?

What do you think can or should be done about domestic abuse?

Check It Out:

OLC

For more information on this topic, go to http://www. mhhe.com/papaliah9.

each other's point of view, and expressed approval of each other's qualities (Conger, Rueter, & Elder, 1999).

Looking back on their marriages, 130 divorced women who had been married an average of eight years showed remarkable agreement on the reasons for the failure of their marriages. The most frequently cited reasons were incompatibility and lack of emotional support; for more recently divorced, presumably younger women, this included lack of career support. Spousal abuse was third, suggesting that domestic violence may be more frequent than is generally realized (Dolan & Hoffman, 1998; see Box 14-2).

A subtle factor underlying marital conflict and marital failure may be a difference in what the man and woman expect from marriage. To many women, marital intimacy entails sharing of feelings and confidences. Men tend to express intimacy through sex, practical help, companionship, and shared activities (Thompson & Walker, 1989). The mismatch between what women expect of their husbands and the way men look at themselves may be promoted by the media. The headlines, text, and pictures in men's magazines continue to reinforce the traditional masculine role as breadwinner, while women's magazines show men in nurturing roles (Vigorito & Curry, 1998).

Checkpoint

Can you . . .

- ✔ Identify several benefits of marriage?
- ✔ Note cultural differences in methods of mate selection, marrying age, and household arrangements?
- ✔ Discuss how sexual relations change after marriage?
- ✔ Identify factors in marital success or failure?

Parenthood

Guidepost

7. When do most adults become parents, and how does parenthood affect a marriage?

Although the institution of the family is universal (Kottak, 1994), the "traditional" family—a husband, a wife, and their biological children—is not. In many African, Asian, and Latin American cultures the extended-family household is the traditional form. In western industrialized countries, family size, composition, structure, and division of labor have changed dramatically. Most mothers now work for pay, in or outside the home, and a small but growing number of fathers are primary caregivers. More single women and cohabiting couples are having or adopting children and raising them (Teachman et al., 2000). Millions of children live with gay or lesbian parents or with stepparents (refer back to Chapter 10).

On the other hand, an increasing number of couples remain childless by choice (Seccombe, 1991). Some of these couples want to concentrate on careers or social causes. Some feel more comfortable with adults or think they would not make good parents. Some want to retain the intimacy of the honeymoon. Some enjoy an adult lifestyle, with freedom to travel or to make spur-of-the-moment decisions. Some women worry that pregnancy will make them less attractive and that parenthood will change their relationship with their spouse (Callan, 1986).

Some people may be discouraged by the financial burdens of parenthood and the difficulty of combining parenthood with employment. In 2000 the estimated expenditures to raise a child to age 18 in a middle-income two-parent, two-child family were $165,630 (Lino, 2001). Better child care and other support services might help couples make truly voluntary decisions.

Becoming Parents

At one time, a blessing offered to newlyweds in the Asian country of Nepal was, "May you have enough sons to cover the hillsides!" Today, Nepali couples are wished, "May you have a very bright son" (B. P. Arjyal, personal communication, February 12, 1993). While sons still are preferred over daughters, even boys are not wished for in such numbers as in the past.

In preindustrial farming societies, large families were a necessity: children helped with the family's work and would eventually care for aging parents. The death rate in childhood was high, and having many children made it more likely that some would reach maturity. Today, infant and child mortality rates have improved greatly, and, in industrial societies, large families are no longer an economic asset. In developing countries, too, where overpopulation and hunger are major problems, there is recognition of the need to limit family size and to space children further apart.

Not only do people typically have fewer children today, but they also start having them later in life, often because they spend their early adult years getting an education and establishing a career. (Ingrid Bergman, like most women of her generation, did not wait to establish her career before becoming a mother; she had her first child at 23, just before coming to Hollywood.)

Today the median age of first-time mothers in the United States is 24.6, having risen consistently for three decades. Since the mid-1970s the percentage of women who give birth in their thirties and even after 40 has increased steadily, often thanks to fertility treatments. Meanwhile, birthrates for women in their late twenties, which had declined after 1990, are again on the rise. For the first time in almost thirty years, the total fertility rate in 2000 (a projected total of 2.1 births per woman) exceeded "replacement level," the number of births needed to offset deaths. The U.S. fertility rate is higher than in several other developed countries; the rate is 1.2 in Spain, 1.5 in Japan, and 1.7 in the United Kingdom (Martin, Hamilton, Ventura, Menacker, & Park, 2002; see Figure 14-2).

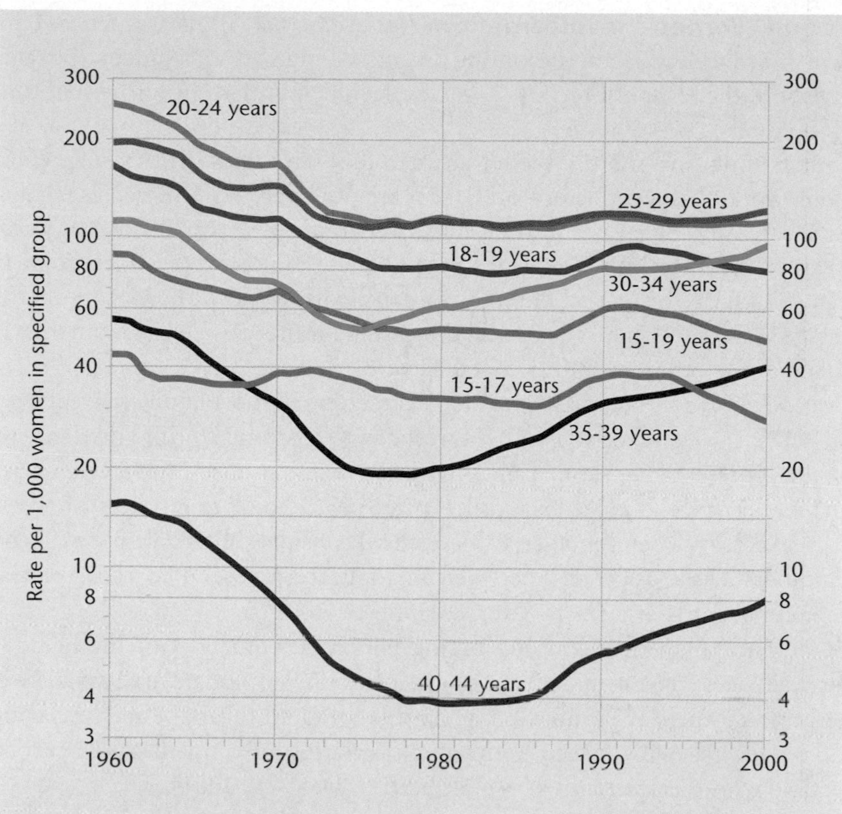

Figure 14-2
Birthrates by age of mother, 1960 to 2000. (*Source:* Martin et al., 2002, Figure 2.)

Economically, delaying childbirth may pay off for women who intend to work later on. Among women born between 1944 and 1954, the first cohort to combine child raising and employment on a large scale, those who gave birth between ages 20 and 27 tend to earn less than women who gave birth at later ages (Taniguchi, 1999). Further research may show whether this holds true in later cohorts.

Babies of older mothers may benefit from their mothers' greater ease with parenthood. When 105 new mothers ages 16 to 38 were interviewed and observed with their infants, the older mothers reported more satisfaction with parenting and spent more time at it. They were more affectionate and sensitive to their babies and more effective in encouraging desired behavior (Ragozin, Basham, Crnic, Greenberg, & Robinson, 1982). And, among a large, nationally representative sample, a subsample of 47 men who became fathers after their thirty-fifth birthdays spent more leisure time with their children, had higher expectations for the children's behavior, and were more nurturing than a comparison group who became fathers before age 35 (Heath, 1994). On the other hand, looking far down the road, older parents are more likely to become a burden when their children reach middle age (see Chapters 16 and 18).

Couples today tend to have fewer children than in past generations, and to have them later in life. Infants may benefit from mature parents' ease with parenthood and willingness to invest more time in it.

Parenthood as a Developmental Experience

A first baby marks a major transition in parents' lives. This totally dependent new person changes individuals and changes relationships. As children develop, parents do, too.

Men's and Women's Involvement in Parenthood Both women and men often have mixed feelings about becoming parents. Along with excitement, they may feel anxiety about the responsibility of caring for a child and the commitment of time and energy it entails.

Fathers today are more involved in their children's lives, and even in child care and housework, than ever before. Still, most are not nearly as involved as mothers are (Coley, 2001; W. T. Bailey, 1994). In a study of parents of 4-year-olds in 10 European, Asian, and African countries and the United States, fathers averaged less than 1 hour a day in sole charge of their children during the work week, while U.S. mothers spent an average of nearly 11 hours each weekday caring for preschoolers—more than mothers in any of the other 10 countries (Olmsted & Weikart, 1994).

Even working mothers are the primary caregivers in most families (Deutsch, 2001; Pleck, 1997). This is especially true on weekdays, according to time diaries kept by a nationally representative sample of 2,400 intact U.S. families in 1997. However, the time fathers spend with children becomes more nearly equal to mothers' on weekends, and increases as children get older. Fathers spend considerably *more* time with children than mothers in television or video viewing, outdoor play, and coaching or teaching sports (Yeung, Sandberg, Davis-Kean, & Hofferth, 2001).

Some fathers do much more, sharing parenting equally with mothers. Such a choice challenges still-prominent social expectations that fathers are primarily breadwinners and mothers are primarily responsible for child raising. Equally sharing parents do not reverse roles; instead, both parents make job adjustments and career choices compatible with their parenting responsibilities (Deutsch, 2001).

Petter Lindstrom's decision to care for his baby daughter when his wife, Ingrid Bergman, went to Hollywood was very unusual for that time. Today, fathers are the primary caregivers for 11.4 percent of preschoolers with employed mothers (Casper, 1998). Studies show that fathers who are primary caregivers can be nearly as nurturing as mothers (Geiger, 1996).

Checkpoint

Can you . . .

- ✔ Describe trends in family size and age of parenthood?
- ✔ Compare men's and women's attitudes toward and exercise of parental responsibilities?

Besides time spent in direct child care, fatherhood may change men in other ways. Among 5,226 men ages 19 to 65, fathers living with their dependent children were less involved in outside social activities than those who had no children, but *more* likely to be engaged in school-related activities, church groups, and community service organizations. They tended to work more hours and were less likely to be unemployed. The most involved fathers were more satisfied with their lives and more involved in work, family, community, and socializing (Eggebeen & Knoester, 2001).

How Parenthood Affects Marital Satisfaction Marital satisfaction typically declines during the childraising years (see Chapter 16). In a ten-year longitudinal study of predominantly white couples who married in their late twenties, both husbands and wives reported a sharp decline in satisfaction during the first four years, followed by a plateau and then another decline. Spouses who had children, especially those who became parents early in their marriage and those who had many children, showed a steeper decline. Although there was a high attrition rate—429 out of the original 522 couples divorced or separated during the course of the study or did not complete it—the presumably greater dissatisfaction of the couples who ultimately left the study did not seriously skew the findings while they were in it. The pattern of decline held true, though less strongly, even when this factor was controlled (Kurdek, 1999).

Of course, this statistical pattern is an average; it is not necessarily true of all couples. One research team followed 128 middle- and working-class couples in their late twenties from the first pregnancy until the child's third birthday. Some marriages got stronger, while others deteriorated, especially in the eyes of the wives. In these marriages, the partners tended to be younger and less well educated, to earn less money, to have been married a shorter time, and to have lower self-esteem. The mothers who had the hardest time were those whose babies had difficult temperaments. Surprisingly, women who had planned their pregnancies were unhappier, possibly because they had expected life with a baby to be better than it turned out to be (Belsky & Rovine, 1990).

Among young Israeli first-time parents, fathers who saw themselves as caring, nurturing, and protecting experienced less decline in marital satisfaction than other fathers and felt better about parenthood. Men who were less involved with their babies, and whose wives were more involved, tended to be more dissatisfied. The mothers who became most dissatisfied with their marriages were those who saw themselves as disorganized and unable to cope with the demands of motherhood (Levy-Shiff, 1994).

How Dual-Earner Families Cope

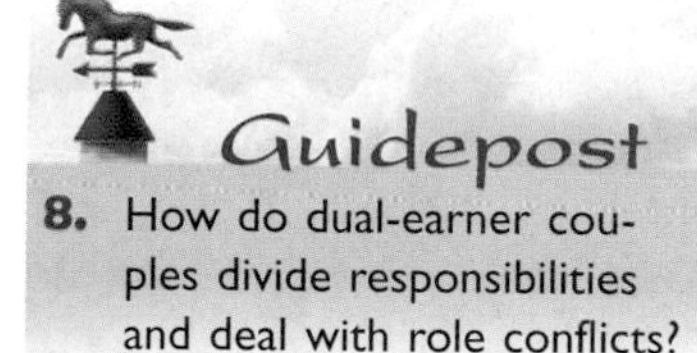

Guidepost

8. How do dual-earner couples divide responsibilities and deal with role conflicts?

Nearly two out of three U.S. families consisting of a married couple with children under 18 are dual-earner families (Bureau of Labor Statistics, 1999a). Fewer women than ever are taking time out for motherhood. Two out of three prospective first-time mothers work during pregnancy, and three-fourths of them return to work within a year after giving birth. In 1940 women made up one-quarter of the labor force; by 1997 they constituted nearly half of it (Smith & Bachu, 1999).

Why do so many women work? Many factors may play a part—the rising cost of living; changes in the divorce, social security, and tax laws; changing attitudes about gender roles; availability of labor-saving household appliances; and the reduced income gap between male and female workers. Some women simply want to be gainfully employed (Jones, McGrattan, & Manuelli, 2002).

It is important in studying dual-earner couples to recognize the diversity of these families (Barnett & Hyde, 2001). Besides the more traditional pattern of a main provider (usually the man) and a secondary provider (usually the woman), there are families in which both earners have high-powered careers and high earnings (like Petter Lindstrom and Ingrid Bergman). There also are many middle-class families in which one or both partners "scale back": cut back on working hours or refuse overtime or turn down jobs that require excessive travel, so as to increase family time and reduce stress (Becker & Moen, 1999; Crouter & Manke, 1994). Or a couple may make trade-offs: trading a career for a job, or trading off whose work takes precedence, depending on shifts in career opportunities and family responsibilities. Wives are more likely to do the scaling back, which usually occurs during the early years of child rearing (Becker & Moen, 1999). Race, ethnicity, sexual orientation, life stage, and social class may make a difference (Barnett & Hyde, 2001). For example, a study of newlyweds in Wayne County, Michigan, found that African American couples were more egalitarian than white couples (Orbuch & Eyster, 1997).

Benefits and Drawbacks of a Dual-Earner Lifestyle Dual-earner marriages present both opportunities and challenges. On the positive side, a second income raises some families from poverty to middle-income status and makes others affluent. It makes women more independent and gives them a greater share of economic power, and it reduces the pressure on men to be providers; 47 percent of working wives contribute half or more of family income (Louis Harris & Associates, 1995). Less tangible benefits may include a more equal relationship between husband and wife, better health for both, greater self-esteem for the woman, and a closer relationship between a father and his children (Gilbert, 1994).

On the downside, working couples face extra demands on time and energy, conflicts between work and family, possible rivalry between spouses, and anxiety and guilt about meeting children's needs. The family is most demanding, especially for women who are employed full time, when there are young children (Milkie & Peltola, 1999; Warren & Johnson, 1995). Careers are especially demanding when a worker is getting established or being promoted. Both kinds of demands frequently occur in young adulthood.

Working men and women seem equally affected by physical and psychological stress, whether due to work interfering with family life or the other way around (Frone, Russell, & Barnes, 1996). However, men and women may be stressed by different aspects of the work-family situation. Among 314 spouses with relatively high income and education, husbands were more likely to suffer from overload (perhaps because they had not been socialized to deal with domestic as well as occupational responsibilities). Women were more likely to feel the strain of conflicting role expectations—the need to be aggressive and competitive at work but compassionate and nurturing at home (Paden & Buehler, 1995).

Overall, two researchers in women's studies suggest, combining work and family roles is generally beneficial to both men and women in terms of mental and physical health and the strength of their relationship (Barnett & Hyde, 2001). That conclusion is based on a large body of empirical research, including findings that most psychological gender differences are not large or immutable enough to require highly differentiated roles (refer back to Chapter 7). Besides added income, factors that contribute to the beneficial effects of multiple roles include increased opportunities for social support; opportunities to experience success in more than one arena; balancing of failure or stress in one role by success and satisfaction in another role; broader perspective or frame of reference; increased complexity of the self-concept, which may buffer swings in mood and self-esteem; and similarity of experiences, which can enhance communication and marital quality. However, the benefits of multiple roles depend on how many roles each partner carries, the time demands of each role, and—most important—the success or satisfaction the partners derive from their roles. The benefits also can be moderated by the extent to which couples hold traditional or nontraditional attitudes about gender roles.

Division of Domestic Work and Effects on the Marriage In almost all known societies, women—even if they work full time—have primary responsibility for housework and child raising (Gardiner et al., 1998). However, the ways couples divide breadwinning and household work, and the psychological effects of those decisions, vary.

What's Your View?

- What advice would you give a dual-earner couple on how to handle family responsibilities?

The division of labor among dual-income couples in U.S. society tends to be different from that in one-paycheck families. The father is likely to do more housework and child care than the husband of a full-time homemaker (Almeida, Maggs, & Galambos, 1993; Demo, 1991; Parke & Buriel, 1998) and to do more monitoring of older children's activities, especially in summer, when school is not in session (Crouter, Helms-Erikson, Updegraff, & McHale, 1999; Crouter & McHale, 1993).

Nevertheless, the burdens of the dual-earner lifestyle generally fall most heavily on the woman. In 1997, employed married men spent nearly one hour more on household chores and one-half hour more with their children on workdays than in 1977; yet the husbands still did only about two-thirds as much domestic work and child care as employed married women (Bond & Galinsky, 1998).

The effects of a dual-earner lifestyle on a marriage may depend largely on how husband and wife view their roles. Unequal roles are not necessarily seen as inequitable, and it may be a *perception* of unfairness that contributes most to marital instability. A national longitudinal survey of 3,284 women in two-income families found greater likelihood of divorce the more hours the woman worked—*if* she had a nontraditional view of marital roles. Given that men generally do less household work than women, an employed woman who believes in an equal division of labor is likely to perceive as unfair the greater burden she carries in comparison with her husband; and this perception of unfairness will probably be magnified the more hours she puts in on the job (Greenstein, 1995).

What spouses perceive as fair may depend on the size of the wife's financial contribution, whether she thinks of herself as a coprovider or merely as supplementing her husband's income, and the meaning and importance she and her husband place on her work (Gilbert, 1994). In nearly one in four dual-earner households, the wife earns more than the husband. In such households, women may have a greater say in family financial and career decisions. When the woman is regarded as the primary breadwinner, there may be a reversal of traditional gender roles (Winkler, 1998). Whatever the actual division of labor, couples who agree on their assessment of it and who enjoy a harmonious, caring, involved family life are more satisfied than those who do not (Gilbert, 1994).

Checkpoint

Can you . . .

- ✔ Discuss how parenthood affects marital satisfaction?
- ✔ Identify benefits and drawbacks of a dual-earner household, and discuss how division of labor can affect the stability of the marriage?

When Marriage Ends

A popular play in the 1950s was *The Seven-Year Itch* by George Axelrod. The title still reflects reality: in the United States, the average marriage that ends in divorce does so after seven to eight years (Kreider & Fields, 2002). The high divorce rate shows how hard it is to attain the goals for which people marry, but the high remarriage rate shows that people keep trying, as Ingrid Bergman did. Divorce, more often than not, leads to remarriage with a new partner and the formation of a stepfamily, which includes children born to or adopted by one or both partners before the current marriage.

Guidepost

9. Why have divorce rates risen, and how do adults adjust to divorce, remarriage, and stepparenthood?

Divorce

The United States has one of the highest divorce rates in the world: in 2000 and 2001, according to provisional data, about 4 divorces a year per 1,000 population (Centers for Disease Control, 2001, 2002). Nearly half (43 percent) of first marriages end in separation or divorce within fifteen years, and 90 percent of separated couples go on to divorce within five years (Bramlett & Mosher, 2001, 2002). A woman born in 1945 to 1954 is almost three times as likely to have been divorced as a woman born in 1925 to 1934 (Kreider & Fields, 2002). Divorce also has skyrocketed in many other developed countries (Burns, 1992).

Why Has Divorce Increased? The increase in divorce has accompanied the passage of more liberal divorce laws, which eliminate the need to find one partner at fault. No-fault laws were a response to societal developments that prompted a greater demand for divorce (Nakonezny, Shull, & Rodgers, 1995). A woman who is financially independent is less likely to remain in a bad marriage; and women today are more likely than men to initiate a divorce (Braver & O'Connell, 1998; Crane, Soderquist, & Gardner, 1995). Instead of staying together "for the sake of the children," many embattled spouses conclude that exposing children to continued parental conflict does greater damage—though research suggests that that is not always true (refer back to Box 10-1 in Chapter 10). And, for the increasing number of childless couples, it's easier to return to a single state (Eisenberg, 1995). Perhaps most important, while most people today hope their marriages will endure, fewer *expect* them to last. Indeed, so expectable has divorce become that some sociologists refer to "starter marriages"—first marriages without children, from which a person moves on as from a first house (Amato & Booth, 1997).

On the other hand, in some ways young people today may expect *too much* from marriage. Young adults who live far from their families of origin may expect their spouses to take the place of parents and friends, as well as being confidantes and lovers—an impossibly tall order. Conflicts between men's and women's expectations may produce tension.

Finally, divorce breeds more divorce. Adults with divorced parents are more likely to become divorced themselves than those whose parents remained together (Shulman, Scharf, Lumer, & Maurer, 2001).

What's Your View?

- Has divorce become too easy to obtain in the United States?

Adjusting to Divorce Divorce is not a single event. It is a *process*—"a sequence of potentially stressful experiences that begin before physical separation and continue after it" (Morrison & Cherlin, 1995, p. 801). Ending even an unhappy marriage can be painful, especially when there are children. (Issues concerning children's adjustment to divorce are discussed in Chapter 10.)

Even though some people may seem to adjust rather quickly, divorce tends to reduce long-term well-being, especially for the partner who did not initiate the divorce or does not remarry. Reasons may include disruption of parent-child relationships, discord with a former spouse, economic hardship, loss of emotional support, and having to move out of the family home (Amato, 2000). Divorce can bring feelings of failure, blame, hostility, and self-recrimination, as well as high rates of depression, illness, and death (Kitson & Morgan, 1990; Thabes, 1997). On the other hand, when a marriage was highly conflicted, its ending can improve well-being (Amato, 2000).

Among 272 divorced women surveyed an average of fourteen years after divorce, about half had initiated the breakup, but about 80 percent of the whole sample said it had taken them three years or more to feel comfortable being unattached. Older women, those without young children, those who had not been abused during their marriage, those with higher incomes, and those who had had good legal representation during the divorce tended to adjust better (Thabes, 1997). Women are more likely than men to live in poverty after separation or divorce (Kreider & Fields, 2002). Many have to deal with continued struggles with an ex-spouse who may default on child support (Kitson & Morgan, 1990).

An important factor in adjustment is emotional detachment from the former spouse. People who argue with their ex-mates or have not found a new lover or spouse experience more distress. An active social life, both at the time of divorce and afterward, helps (Amato, 2000; Thabes, 1997; Tschann, Johnston, & Wallerstein, 1989).

Remarriage and Stepparenthood

Remarriage, said the essayist Samuel Johnson, "is the triumph of hope over experience." The high divorce rate is not a sign that people do not want to be married. Instead, it often reflects a desire to be *happily* married and a belief that divorce is like surgery—painful and traumatic, but necessary for a better life. In the survey of 272 divorced women reported in the preceding section, while more than 50 percent said they did not miss marriage, more than 90 percent said they would consider marrying again if they met the right person (Thabes, 1997).

Three-quarters of divorced women in the United States remarry within ten years. Young women (under age 25) are more likely to remarry than older ones, but also more likely to redivorce (Bramlett & Mosher, 2001, 2002). Men are even likelier to remarry than women (U.S. Bureau of the Census, 1998). Thus only 8 percent of men and 10 percent of women are currently divorced. Half of those who remarry after divorce from a first marriage do so within about three years (Kreider & Fields, 2002). Remarriage rates are somewhat lower in Canada and Europe (Coleman et al., 2000).

Remarriages are more likely than first marriages to end in divorce. The likelihood of redivorce is greatest during the first five years, especially when there are stepchildren (Parke & Buriel, 1998). Remarried partners may be less likely than partners in first marriages to have similar interests and values. And, having once divorced, they may be more likely to see divorce as a solution to marital problems (Booth & Edwards, 1992). Also, the adjustment to living in a stepfamily can be stressful for both adults and children (refer back to Chapter 10). Because the increase in stepfamilies is fairly recent, social expectations for such families have not caught up. In combining two family units, each with its own web of customs and relationships, remarried families must invent their own ways of doing things (Hines, 1997).

Becoming a stepparent may be especially challenging for women. Interviews with 138 stepparents who also had biological children in the home found that women have more trouble than men do in raising stepchildren, as compared with raising biological children. This may be because women generally spend more time with the children than men do. It does not seem to matter whether the biological children are from a previous marriage or the present one. The more recent the current marriage and the older the stepchildren, the harder stepparenting seems to be (MacDonald & DeMaris, 1996).

Stepparents seem less able to separate their feelings about the marriage from their feelings about their success as stepparents than they can with regard to their relationships with their biological children (Fine & Kurdek, 1995). The connection between satisfaction with stepparenting and with the marriage may have to do with the fact that both begin at the same time and are inextricably linked. When problems arise in raising stepchildren, the stepparent is likely to blame the biological parent (for example, for taking the child's side in an argument). The biological parent, whose relationship with the child is more secure, is less likely to blame the stepparent for trouble involving the child.

Still, for people who have been bruised by loss, the blended family has the potential to provide a warm, nurturing atmosphere, as does any family that cares about all its members. One researcher (Papernow, 1993) identified several stages of adjustment. At first adults expect a smooth, rapid adjustment, while children fantasize that the stepparent will go away and the original parent will return. As internal conflicts develop, each parent may side with his or her own biological children. Eventually the adults form a strong alliance to meet the needs of all the children. The stepparent gains the role of a significant adult figure, and the family becomes an integrated unit with its own identity.

Checkpoint

Can you . . .

- ✔ Explain why divorce has increased?
- ✔ Discuss factors in adjustment to divorce?
- ✔ Discuss factors in adjustment to remarriage and stepparenthood after divorce, and explain why remarriages tend to be less stable than first marriages?

Refocus

- How would a normative-stage theorist, a timing-of-events theorist, a trait theorist, and a typological theorist describe Ingrid Bergman's personality development?
- Which of Sternberg's patterns of love did Bergman's three marriages seem to illustrate?
- How have attitudes toward extramarital sex, cohabitation, and having a baby out of wedlock changed since Ingrid Bergman's day?
- What factors in marital success or failure do or do not seem to apply to Bergman's marriages?
- Why did Bergman have difficulty balancing her career with marriage and parenthood?
- Does Bergman's story argue for more liberal or less liberal divorce laws?

The bonds forged in young adulthood with friends, lovers, spouses, and children often endure throughout life and influence development in middle and late adulthood. The changes people experience in their more mature years also affect their relationships, as we'll see in Parts Seven and Eight.

SUMMARY AND KEY TERMS

Personality Development: Four Views

Guidepost 1. Does personality change during adulthood, and if so, how?

- Whether and how personality changes during adulthood is an important issue among developmental theorists. Four important perspectives on adult personality are offered by normative-stage models, the timing-of-events model, trait models, and typological models.
- Normative-stage models hold that age-related social and emotional change emerges in successive periods sometimes marked by crises. In Erikson's theory, the major issue of young adulthood is intimacy versus isolation. In Levinson's theory, transitions lead to reevaluation and modification of the life structure. In the Grant study, mature adaptive mechanisms were associated with greater well-being.
- The timing-of-events model, advocated by Neugarten, proposes that adult psychosocial development is influenced by the occurrence and timing of normative life events. As society becomes less age-conscious, however, the social clock has less meaning.
- The five-factor model of Costa and McCrae is organized around five groupings of related traits: neuroticism, extraversion, openness to experience, conscientiousness, and agreeableness. Studies find that people change very little in these respects after age 30.
- Typological research, pioneered by Jack Block, has identified personality types that differ in ego-resiliency and ego-control. These types seem to persist from childhood through adulthood.
- Recently there have been attempts to synthesize various approaches to adult personality development.

normative-stage models *(493)*
timing-of-events model *(493)*
trait models *(493)*
typological models *(493)*
intimacy versus isolation *(494)*
adaptive mechanisms *(494)*
life structure *(494)*
normative life events *(495)*
social clock *(496)*
five-factor model *(496)*
ego-resiliency *(498)*
ego-control *(498)*

Foundations of Intimate Relationships

Guidepost 2. What is intimacy, and how is it expressed in friendship, love, and sexuality?

- Young adulthood is a time of dramatic change in personal relationships. Young adults seek emotional and physical intimacy in relationships with peers and romantic partners.
- Self-disclosure and a sense of belonging are important aspects of intimacy. Intimate relationships are associated with physical and mental health.
- While the Internet offers expanded opportunities for communication, it may lead to a weakening of intimacy and a decline in psychological well-being.
- Most young adults have friends but have increasingly limited time to spend with them. Women's friendships tend to be more intimate than men's.
- According to Sternberg's triangular theory of love, love has three aspects: intimacy, passion, and commitment. These combine into eight types of love relationships.
- People tend to choose partners like themselves.
- Attitudes toward premarital sex have been greatly liberalized, but men and women are less promiscuous than is sometimes believed. Disapproval of homosexuality has declined but remains strong. Disapproval of extramarital sex is even greater.

triangular theory of love *(501)*

Nonmarital and Marital Lifestyles

Guidepost 3. Why do some people remain single?

- Today more adults than in the past postpone marriage or never marry. Reasons for staying single include career opportunities, travel, sexual and lifestyle freedom, a desire for self-fulfillment, women's greater self-sufficiency, reduced social pressure to marry, fear of divorce, and difficulty in finding a suitable mate.

Guidepost 4. How do homosexuals deal with "coming out," and what is the nature of gay and lesbian relationships?

- For homosexuals, the process of coming out may last well into adulthood, and complete openness about their sexual orientation may never be fully achieved. Both gay men and lesbians form enduring sexual and romantic relationships. Gays and lesbians in the United States are fighting for rights married people enjoy.

coming out *(505)*

Guidepost 5. What are the pros and cons of cohabitation?

- Cohabitation has become common and is the norm in many countries. Cohabitation can be a "trial marriage" or a substitute for marriage. Couples who cohabit before marriage tend to have weaker marriages.

cohabitation *(506)*

Guidepost 6. What do adults gain from marriage, what cultural patterns surround entrance into marriage, and why do some marriages succeed while others fail?

- Marriage (in a variety of forms) is universal and meets basic economic, emotional, sexual, social, and childraising needs.
- Mate selection and marrying age vary across cultures. People in industrialized nations have been marrying later than in past generations.
- Frequency of sexual relations in marriage declines with age and loss of novelty. Fewer people appear to be having extramarital sexual relationships than in the past.
- Success in marriage may depend on strength of commitment and patterns of interaction set in young adulthood. Age at marriage is a major predictor of whether a marriage will last. Resilience in facing economic hardship, compatibility, emotional support, and men's and women's differing expectations may be important factors.

Parenthood

Guidepost **7.** When do most adults become parents, and how does parenthood affect a marriage?

- Family patterns vary across cultures and have changed greatly in western societies. Today women are having fewer children and having them later in life, and an increasing number choose to remain childless.
- Fathers are usually less involved in child raising than mothers, but some share parenting equally and some are primary caregivers.
- Marital satisfaction typically declines during the childbearing years. Expectations and division of tasks can contribute to a marriage's deterioration or improvement.

Guidepost **8.** How do dual-earner couples divide responsibilities and deal with role conflicts?

- Nearly two out of three families with children are dual-earner families. Dual-earner families show several patterns and offer both benefits and drawbacks.
- Women and men are equally affected by the stress of a dual-earner lifestyle, but they may be affected in different ways. Family-friendly workplace policies may help alleviate stress.
- In most cases, the burdens of a dual-earner lifestyle fall most heavily on the woman. Whether an unequal division of labor contributes to marital distress may depend on how the spouses perceive their roles.
- A new theory of gender roles proposes that both men and women generally benefit from combining multiple roles, but this depends on the number of roles they carry, time demands, and satisfaction derived.

When Marriage Ends

Guidepost **9.** Why have divorce rates risen, and how do adults adjust to divorce, remarriage, and stepparenthood?

- The United States has one of the highest divorce rates in the world. Among the reasons for the rise in divorce are women's greater financial independence, reluctance to expose children to parental conflict, and the greater "expectability" of divorce.
- Divorce usually entails a painful period of adjustment. Adjustment may depend on the way the divorce is handled, people's feelings about themselves and their ex-partners, emotional detachment from the former spouse, social support, and personal resources.
- Adjusting to divorce is a long-term process that tends to reduce well-being.
- Most divorced people remarry within a few years, but remarriages tend to be less stable than first marriages.
- Stepfamilies may go through several stages of adjustment. Women tend to have more difficulty being stepparents than men do.

PART 7

When does middle age begin? Is it at the birthday party when you see your cake ablaze with forty candles? Is it the day your "baby" leaves home? Is it the day when you notice that police officers seem to be getting younger?

When does middle age end? Is it at your retirement party? Is it the day you get your Medicare card? Is it the first time someone younger gets up to give you a seat on the bus?

Middle adulthood has many markers, and they are not the same for everyone. At 40, some people become parents for the first time, while others become grandparents. At 50, some people are starting new careers, while others are taking early retirement.

As in earlier years, all aspects of development are interrelated. In Chapters 15 and 16, we note, for example, the psychological impact of menopause (and debunk some myths about it!), and we see how mature thinkers combine logic and emotion. ▸

Linkups to look for

- Some physical skills improve with age, due to practice, experience, and judgment.
- Physical symptoms associated with menopause seem to be affected by cultural attitudes toward aging.
- Stressful experiences often lead to illness.
- Postformal thinking is especially useful with regard to social problems.
- Personality characteristics play an important role in creative performance.
- Modifications in men's and women's personalities at midlife have been attributed both to hormonal changes and to cultural shifts in gender roles.
- Responsibility for aging parents can affect physical and mental health.

Middle Adulthood

PREVIEW

CHAPTER 15

Physical and Cognitive Development in Middle Adulthood

- **Some deterioration of sensory abilities, health, stamina, and prowess may take place.**
- **Women experience menopause.**
- **Most basic mental abilities peak; expertise and practical problem-solving skills are high.**
- **Creative output may decline but improve in quality.**
- **For some, career success and earning powers peak; for others, burnout or career change may occur.**

CHAPTER 16

Psychosocial Development in Middle Adulthood

- **Sense of identity continues to develop; midlife transition may occur.**
- **Double responsibilities of caring for children and elderly parents may cause stress.**
- **Launching of children leaves empty nest.**

Chapter 15

Physical and Cognitive Development in Middle Adulthood

The primitive, physical, functional pattern of the morning of life, the active years before forty or fifty, is outlived. But there is still the afternoon opening up, which one can spend not in the feverish pace of the morning but in having time at last for those intellectual, cultural, and spiritual activities that were pushed aside in the heat of the race.

—**Anne Morrow Lindbergh, *Gift from the Sea*, 1955**

OUTLINE

Focus:
Mahatma Gandhi, Father of a Nation

Mahatma Gandhi

Mohandas Karamchand Gandhi (1869–1948)* was called *Mahatma* (Great Soul) by the people of his native India, whom he led to freedom from British colonial rule through a decades-long campaign of nonviolent resistance. His revolutionary ideas and practices profoundly influenced other world leaders, notably Nelson Mandela and Martin Luther King, Jr. He is considered one of the greatest moral exemplars of all time.

The son of an uneducated merchant, Gandhi admitted to less than average intellectual ability, but his linguistic and interpersonal skills were strong. He had a keen moral sense and was a lifelong seeker of truth. He had the courage to challenge authority and take risks for what he saw as a worthy goal.

As a lawyer in South Africa, another British colony, he saw and experienced the discrimination the Indian minority suffered. It was in South Africa that Gandhi began to develop his philosophy of *satyagraha,* nonviolent social action. He organized civil disobedience campaigns and peaceful marches. Time and again, he invited arrest; in 1908, approaching his fortieth year, he was jailed for the first time. Eventually he would spend a total of seven years in prison.

Gandhi "felt he could not proceed as an ethical agent, seeking a better life for his people, unless he had himself attained and come to embody moral authority. He had to purify himself before he could make demands of others" (Gardner, 1997, p. 115). He moved with his wife and four sons from the South African capital, Johannesburg, to a farm outside Durban. He did daily

*Sources of biographical information about Gandhi included J. M. Brown (1989), Gandhi (1948), Gardner (1997), and Kumar and Puri (1983).

exercises, prepared his own food, and gave up western dress for simple Indian garb. In 1910, he founded a collective farm based on ascetic and cooperative principles.

Returning to India in 1915, Gandhi became the acknowledged leader of a nationalist movement. He taught his people to show forbearance. When a street mob in a small town rioted and killed police, he called off political actions throughout India. When mill owners were unbending and strikers became restive, he put his own physical well-being on the line by fasting until a satisfactory settlement was reached.

In 1930, to protest a tax on manufactured salt, Gandhi, then 60, led a 200-mile march to the sea, where hundreds of followers illegally extracted salt from seawater. The event, reminiscent of the Boston Tea Party, triggered protests all over India. When British police attacked and beat a line of peaceful marchers, their brutality made headlines around the world. It was the beginning of the end for British domination.

Gandhi's influence was the product of a seamless web of body, mind, and spirit. By living out his ideals, he was effective in solving real, almost intractable problems that affected millions of people. In his efforts to defuse conflict and inspire cooperation, he showed wisdom grounded in moral vision.

Few of us reach the heights of intelligence and creativity or achieve the moral and spiritual heights Gandhi did, and few of us have such influential careers. But caring and concern for others, including the generations to follow, are important in any adult, as is the work to which one chooses to devote one's life. As with Gandhi, these features tend to intensify or come to fruition in middle age.

In this chapter, we examine physical changes common in middle adulthood. We discuss how health problems may be worsened by poverty, racial discrimination, and other stresses. We consider how intelligence changes, how thought processes mature, what underlies creative performance and moral leadership such as Gandhi's, and how careers develop.

After you have read and studied this chapter, you should be able to answer each of the following Guidepost questions. Look for them again in the margins, where they point to important concepts throughout the chapter. To check your understanding of these Guideposts, review the end-of-chapter summary. Checkpoints located at periodic spots throughout the chapter will help you verify your understanding of what you have read.

Guideposts for Study

1. What are the distinguishing features of middle age?
2. What physical changes generally occur during the middle years, and what is their psychological impact?
3. What factors affect health at midlife?
4. What cognitive gains and losses occur during middle age?
5. Do mature adults think differently than younger people do?
6. What accounts for creative achievement, and how does it change with age?
7. How have work patterns changed, and how does work contribute to cognitive development?
8. What is the value of education for mature learners?

Middle Age: A Cultural Construct

Until recently, middle adulthood was the least studied part of the life span. The middle years were considered a relatively uneventful hiatus between the more dramatic changes of young adulthood and old age. Now that the baby-boom generation is in middle age, research on that period is booming (Lachman, 2001; Lachman & James, 1997; Moen & Wethington, 1999). In the United States, by 2015, the 45- to 64-year-old population is expected to reach 80 million, 72 percent more than in 1990. This is the best educated and most affluent cohort ever to reach middle age anywhere, and it is changing our perspective on the importance and meaning of that time of life (Willis & Reid, 1999).

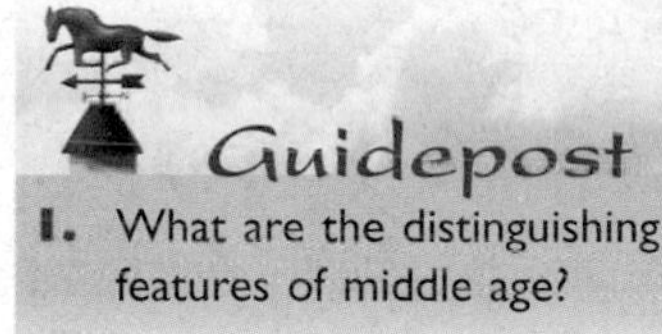

Guidepost

1. What are the distinguishing features of middle age?

The term "middle age" came into use in Europe and the United States around the turn of the twentieth century as life expectancy began to lengthen. Today, in industrial societies, middle adulthood is considered to be a distinct stage of life with its own societal norms, roles, opportunities, and challenges. Thus, some scholars describe middle age as a socially constructed concept, with culturally ascribed meaning (Gullette, 1998; Menon, 2001; Moen & Wethington, 1999). Some traditional societies, such as upper-caste Hindus in rural India (Menon, 2001) and the Gusii in Kenya (see Box 16-1 in Chapter 16), do not recognize a middle stage of adulthood between youth and old age at all. In other parts of India and in Japan, maturation and aging are thought of primarily as social processes involving relationships and roles, rather than in terms of chronological years and biological changes (Menon, 2001).

Ironically, as medical and nutritional advances have opened up an unprecedented second half of life in more developed societies, anxiety about physical and other losses has become a major theme in popular descriptions of middle age. In a youth-oriented culture, adults' expectations for these years may be influenced more by images in literature and the media than by what is going on in their own bodies and minds (Gullette, 1998). A life-span developmental perspective (refer back to Chapter 1) presents a more balanced, more complex picture. Middle age can be a time, not only or

What's Your View?

- When would you say middle age begins and ends?
- Think of people you know who call themselves middle-aged. How old are they? Do they seem to be in good health? How involved are they in work or other activities?

even primarily of decline and loss, but also of growth. The concept of plasticity suggests that what people do and how they live has much to do with how they age (Heckhausen, 2001; Lachman, 2001; Lock, 1998; Moen & Wethington, 1999; Staudinger & Bluck, 2001).

When Is Middle Age?

There is no consensus on specific biological or social events that mark the beginning and end of middle age (Staudinger & Bluck, 2001). With improvements in health and length of life, the subjective upper limits of middle age are rising (Lachman, 2001; Stewart & Ostrove, 1998). One-third of Americans in their seventies, and half of those between 65 and 69, think of themselves as middle-aged (National Council on Aging, 2000). Middle age in U.S. society is increasingly a state of mind (Menon, 2001).

In this book, we define *middle adulthood* in chronological terms, as the years between ages 40 and 65, but this definition is arbitrary. Middle age also can be defined contextually, and the two definitions may differ. One context is the family: a middle-aged person is sometimes described as one with grown children and/or elderly parents. Yet today some people in their forties and beyond are still raising young children; and some adults at any age have no children at all. Those with grown children may find the nest emptying—or filling up again. Age also has a biological aspect: a 50-year-old who has exercised regularly is likely to be biologically younger than a 35-year-old whose most strenuous exercise is clicking the remote control. Still, typically there are important differences between the issues and tasks of early and late middle age (Staudinger & Bluck, 2001).

Many middle-aged people, like the musician Carlos Santana, are at the height of their careers, enjoying a sense of freedom and control over their lives.

The Meaning of Middle Age

The meaning of middle age varies with health, gender, ethnicity, socioeconomic status, cohort, and culture (Helson, 1997; Moen & Wethington, 1999; Staudinger & Bluck, 2001). Most middle-aged people in the United States today are in good physical, cognitive, and emotional shape—more so than in any previous generation—and feel good about the quality of their lives (see Figure 15-1). The middle years are marked by growing individual differences based on prior choices and experiences, as well as on genetic makeup (Lachman & James, 1997). Some middle-aged people can run a marathon; others get winded climbing a steep stairway. Some have a sharper memory than ever; others feel their memory beginning to slip. Some, like Gandhi, are at the height of creativity or careers; others have gotten a slow start or have reached dead ends. Still others dust off mothballed dreams or pursue new goals.

Middle age is often filled with heavy responsibilities and multiple, demanding roles—responsibilities and roles that most adults feel competent to handle: running households, departments, or enterprises; launching children; and perhaps caring for aging parents or starting new careers (Gallagher, 1993; Lachman, 2001; Lachman, Lewkowicz, Marcus, & Peng, 1994; Merrill & Verbrugge, 1999). At the same time, many middle-aged adults, having

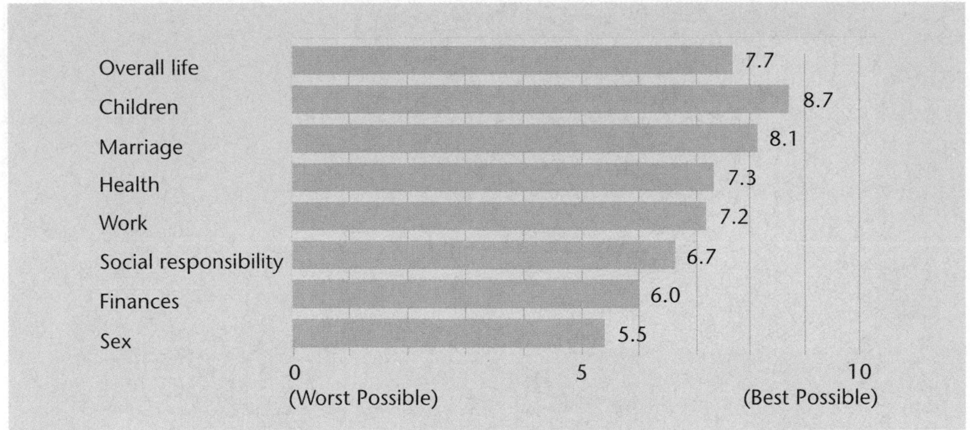

Figure 15-1
How middle-aged adults rate aspects of their quality of life.
(*Source:* Goode, 1999; data from MacArthur Foundation Research Network on Successful Midlife Development.)

made their mark and raised their children, have an increased feeling of freedom and independence (Lachman, 2001). Many experience a heightened sense of success and control in work and social relationships, along with a more realistic awareness of their limitations and of outside forces they *cannot* control (Clark-Plaskie & Lachman, 1999).

Middle adulthood can be a time of reevaluating goals and aspirations and how well they have been fulfilled, and deciding how best to use the remaining part of the life span (Lachman & James, 1997).

Checkpoint

Can you . . .

- ✔ Explain why middle age is considered a cultural construct?
- ✔ Differentiate between chronological, contextual, and biological meanings of middle age?

PHYSICAL DEVELOPMENT

Physical Changes

"Use it or lose it!" Research bears out the wisdom of that popular creed. Although some physiological changes are direct results of biological aging and genetic makeup, behavioral and lifestyle factors dating from youth can affect the likelihood, timing, and extent of physical change. By the same token, health and lifestyle habits in the middle years influence what happens in the years beyond (Merrill & Verbrugge, 1999; Whitbourne, 2001). People who limit their exposure to the sun can minimize wrinkling and avoid skin cancer; and people who are physically active can retain muscle strength—a powerful predictor of physical condition in old age (Rantanen et al., 1999).

Guidepost

2. What physical changes generally occur during the middle years, and what is their psychological impact?

The more people do, the more they *can* do. People who become active early in life reap the benefits of more stamina and more resilience after age 60 (Spirduso & MacRae, 1990). People who lead sedentary lives lose muscle tone and energy and become even less inclined to exert themselves physically. Still, as Gandhi realized, it is never too late to adopt a healthier lifestyle. Middle-aged people who had unhealthful habits in their youth can improve their physical well-being by changing their behavior (Merrill & Verbrugge, 1999).

The mind and the body have ways of compensating for changes that do occur. Most middle-aged people are realistic enough to take in stride alterations in appearance, in sensory, motor, and systemic functioning, and in reproductive and sexual capacities; and some experience a sexual renaissance.

Sensory and Psychomotor Functioning

From young adulthood through the middle years, sensory and motor changes are small, gradual, and almost imperceptible (Merrill & Verbrugge, 1999)—until one day a 45-year-old man realizes that he cannot read the telephone directory without eyeglasses, or a 60-year-old woman has to admit that she is not as quick on her feet as she was.

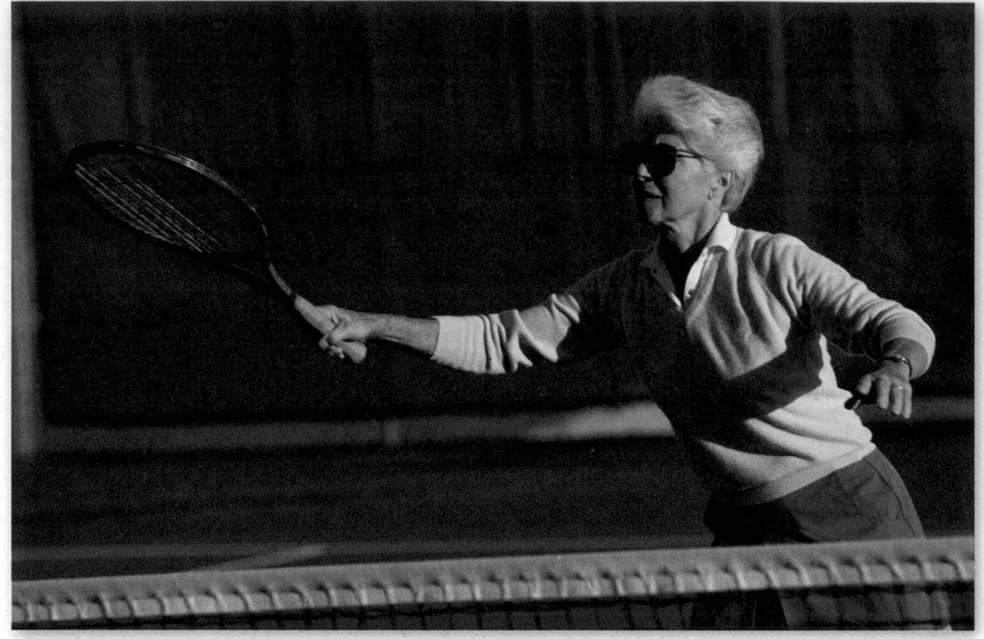

Many middle-aged people find that their improved ability to use strategies in a sport as a result of experience and better judgment outweighs changes in strength, coordination, and reaction time. A consistent exercise program beginning in young adulthood, such as playing tennis regularly, can help build muscles and maintain stamina and resilience in middle and old age.

Age-related visual problems occur mainly in five areas: *near vision, dynamic vision* (reading moving signs), *sensitivity to light, visual search* (for example, locating a sign), and *speed of processing* visual information (Kline et al., 1992; Kline & Scialfa, 1996; Kosnik, Winslow, Kline, Rasinski, & Sekuler, 1988). Also common is a slight loss in *visual acuity,* or sharpness of vision. Because of changes in the pupil of the eye, middle-aged people may need about one-third more brightness to compensate for the loss of light reaching the retina (Belbin, 1967; Troll, 1985).

Because the lens of the eye becomes progressively less flexible, its ability to shift focus diminishes. This change usually becomes noticeable in early middle age and is practically complete by age 60 (Kline & Scialfa, 1996). Many people age 40 and older need reading glasses for **presbyopia,** a lessened ability to focus on near objects—a condition associated with aging. (The prefix *presby-* means "with age.") The incidence of **myopia** (nearsightedness) also increases through middle age (Merrill & Verbrugge, 1999). Bifocals and trifocals—eyeglasses in which lenses for reading are combined with lenses for distant vision—aid the eye in adjusting between near and far objects.

presbyopia Farsightedness associated with aging, resulting when the lens of the eye becomes less elastic.

myopia Nearsightedness.

A gradual hearing loss, rarely noticed earlier in life, speeds up in the fifties (Merrill & Verbrugge, 1999). This condition, **presbycusis,** normally is limited to higher-pitched sounds than those used in speech (Kline & Scialfa, 1996). By the end of middle age, one in four people has significant hearing loss (Horvath & Davis, 1990). Hearing loss proceeds twice as quickly in men as in women (Pearson et al., 1995). Today, a preventable increase in hearing loss is occurring among 45- to 64-year-olds due to continuous or sudden exposure to noise at work, at loud concerts, through earphones, and elsewhere (Wallhagen, Strawbridge, Cohen, & Kaplan, 1997). Hearing losses due to environmental noise can be avoided by wearing hearing protectors, such as earplugs or special earmuffs.

presbycusis Gradual loss of hearing, which accelerates after age 55, especially with regard to sounds at the upper frequencies.

Sensitivity to taste and smell generally begins to decline in midlife (Cain, Reid, & Stevens, 1990; Stevens, Cain, Demarque, & Ruthruff, 1991). As the taste buds become less sensitive and the number of olfactory cells diminishes, foods may seem more bland (Merrill & Verbrugge, 1999; Troll, 1985). Women tend to retain these senses longer than men. There are individual differences, however. A woman might lose her sweet tooth; her husband might find his martinis not sour enough. One person could become less sensitive to salty foods, another to sweet, bitter, or sour foods. And the same person may remain more sensitive to some of these tastes than to others (Stevens, Cruz, Hoffman, & Patterson, 1995; Whitbourne, 1999).

Adults begin to lose sensitivity to touch after age 45, and to pain after age 50. However, pain's protective function remains: although people feel pain less, they become less able to tolerate it (Katchadourian, 1987).

Strength and coordination decline gradually from their peak during the twenties. Some loss of muscle strength is usually noticeable by age 45; 10 to 15 percent of maximum strength may be gone by 60. Most people notice a weakening first in the back and leg muscles and then in the arm and shoulder—the latter, not until well into the sixties. The reason for this loss of strength is a loss of muscle fiber, which is replaced by fat. By middle age, body fat, which comprised only 10 percent of body weight during adolescence, typically reaches at least 20 percent (Katchadourian, 1987; Merrill & Verbrugge, 1999; Spence, 1989). But individual differences are great, and become greater with each passing decade (Spirduso & MacRae, 1990; Vercruyssen, 1997). Strength training can prevent muscle loss and even regain strength (Whitbourne, 2001).

Endurance often holds up much better than strength (Spirduso & MacRae, 1990). Loss of endurance results from a gradual decrease in the rate of **basal metabolism** (use of energy to maintain vital functions) after age 40 (Merrill & Verbrugge, 1999). "Overpracticed" skills are more resistant to effects of age than those that are used less; thus, athletes show a smaller-than-average loss in endurance (Stones & Kozma, 1996).

basal metabolism Use of energy to maintain vital functions.

Manual dexterity generally becomes less efficient after the midthirties (Vercruyssen, 1997)—though some pianists, such as Vladimir Horowitz, have continued to perform brilliantly in their eighties. Simple reaction time, which involves a single response to a single stimulus (such as pressing a button when a light flashes) slows by about 20 percent, on average, between ages 20 and 60 (Birren, Woods, & Williams, 1980). When a vocal rather than a manual response is called for, age differences in simple reaction time are substantially less (S. J. Johnson & Rybash, 1993).

Tasks that involve a choice of responses (such as hitting one button when a light flashes and another button when a tone is heard) and complex motor skills involving many stimuli, responses, and decisions (as in driving a car) decline more, but the decline does not necessarily result in poorer performance. Typically, middle-aged adults are better drivers than younger ones (McFarland, Tune, & Welford, 1964), and 60-year-old typists are as efficient as 20-year-olds (Spirduso & MacRae, 1990; Salthouse, 1984).

In these and other activities, knowledge based on experience may more than make up for physical changes. Skilled industrial workers in their forties and fifties are often more productive than ever, partly because they tend to be more conscientious and careful. Middle-aged workers are less likely than younger workers to suffer disabling injuries on the job (Salthouse & Maurer, 1996)—a likely result of experience and good judgment, which compensate for any lessening of coordination and motor skills.

Structural and Systemic Changes

Changes in appearance, often reflecting changes in body structure and systems, may become noticeable during the middle years. By the fifth or sixth decade, the skin may become less taut and smooth as the layer of fat below the surface becomes thinner, collagen molecules become more rigid, and elastin fibers more brittle. Hair may become thinner, due to a slowed replacement rate, and grayer as production of melanin, the pigmenting agent, declines. People perspire less as the number of sweat glands decreases. They tend to gain weight, due to accumulation of body fat, and lose height due to shrinkage of the intervertebral disks (Merrill & Verbrugge, 1999; Whitbourne, 2001).

Bone density normally peaks in the twenties or thirties. From then on, people typically experience some net loss of bone as more calcium is absorbed than replaced, causing bones to become thinner and more brittle. Bone loss accelerates in the fifties and sixties; it occurs twice as rapidly in women as in men, sometimes leading to osteoporosis

vital capacity Amount of air that can be drawn in with a deep breath and expelled.

Checkpoint

Can you . . .

- Summarize changes in sensory and motor functioning and body structure and systems that may begin during middle age?
- Identify factors that contribute to individual differences in physical condition?

(discussed later in this chapter) (Merrill & Verbrugge, 1999; Whitbourne, 2001). Bone loss can be affected by lifestyle factors earlier in adulthood. Smoking, alcohol use, and a poor diet tend to speed bone loss; it can be slowed by aerobic exercise, resistance training with weights, increased calcium intake, and vitamin C. Joints may become stiffer as a result of accumulated stress. Exercises that expand range of motion and strengthen the muscles supporting a joint can improve functioning (Whitbourne, 2001).

Large proportions of middle-aged and even older adults show little or no decline in organ functioning (Gallagher, 1993). In some, however, the heart begins to pump more slowly and irregularly in the midfifties; by 65, it may lose up to 40 percent of its aerobic power. Arterial walls may become thicker and more rigid. Heart disease becomes more common beginning in the late forties or early fifties, especially among men. **Vital capacity**—the maximum volume of air the lungs can draw in and expel—may begin to diminish at about age 40 and may drop by as much as 40 percent by age 70. Temperature regulation and immune response may begin to weaken, and sleep may become less deep (Merrill & Verbrugge, 1999; Whitbourne, 2001).

Sexuality and Reproductive Functioning

Sexuality is not just a hallmark of youth. Although both sexes experience losses in reproductive capacity sometime during middle adulthood—women become unable to bear children and men's fertility begins to decline—sexual enjoyment can continue throughout adult life. (Changes in the male and female reproductive systems are summarized in Table 15-1.)

Still, many middle-aged people have concerns related to sexuality and reproductive functioning. Let's look at these.

menopause Cessation of menstruation and of ability to bear children, typically around age 50.

Menopause and Its Meanings

Menopause takes place when a woman permanently stops ovulating and menstruating and can no longer conceive a child; it is generally considered to have occurred one year after the last menstrual period. In four out of five women, this happens between ages 45 and 55; on average, at about 50 or 51 (Avis, 1999; Finch, 2001; Merrill & Verbrugge, 1999; Whitbourne, 2001).

perimenopause Period of several years during which a woman experiences physiological changes that bring on menopause; also called *climacteric*.

Beginning in her midthirties to midforties, a woman's production of mature ova begins to decline as the ovaries produce less of the female hormone estrogen. The period during which this slowing of hormone production and ovulation prior to menopause occurs is called **perimenopause,** also known as the *climacteric,* or "change of life." (Small amounts of estrogen continue to be secreted, in amounts that vary among individuals, by the adrenal and other glands.) Menstruation becomes irregular, with less flow than before and a longer time between menstrual periods, before it ceases altogether (Finch, 2001; Whitbourne, 2001). In women who have hysterectomies, however, menopause comes on abruptly, without preparation.

Table 15-1 Changes in Human Reproductive Systems During Middle Age

	Female	Male
Hormonal change	Drop in estrogen and progesterone	Drop in testosterone
Symptoms	Hot flashes, vaginal dryness, urinary dysfunction	Undetermined
Sexual changes	Less intense arousal, less frequent and quicker orgasms	Loss of psychological arousal, less frequent erections, slower orgasms, longer recovery between ejaculations, increased risk of erectile dysfunction
Reproductive capacity	Ends	Continues; some decrease in fertility may occur

Attitudes Toward Menopause At one time, in rural Ireland, women who no longer menstruated would retire to their beds and stay there, often for years, until they died (U.S. Office of Technology Assessment, 1992). This traditional custom may seem extreme, but the attitude it expressed—that a woman's usefulness ends with her ability to reproduce—was typical in western societies until fairly recently (Avis, 1999; Crowley, 1994). During the early nineteenth century, the term *climacteric* came to mean the "period of life . . . at which the vital forces begin to decline" (Lock, 1998, p. 48). Menopause was seen as a disease, a failure of the ovaries to perform their natural function (Lock, 1998).

By contrast, in some cultures, such as that of the southwestern Papago Indians, menopause seems to be virtually ignored. In other cultures, such as those found in India and South Asia, it is a welcome event; women's status and freedom of movement increase once they are free of taboos connected with menstruation and fertility (Avis, 1999; Lock, 1994).

In the United States today, most women who have gone through menopause view it positively (Avis, 1999). For many women, menopause is a sign of a transition into the second half of adult life—a time of role changes, greater independence, and personal growth. How a woman views menopause may depend on the value she places on being young and attractive, her attitudes toward women's roles, and her own circumstances. A childless woman may see menopause as closing off the possibility of motherhood; a woman who has had and raised children may see it as an opportunity for greater sexual freedom and enjoyment (Avis, 1999).

Symptoms and Myths Most women experience little or no physical discomfort during perimenopause (National Institute on Aging [NIA], 1993). Most common are "hot flashes," sudden sensations of heat that flash through the body due to hormones that affect the temperature control centers in the brain; but many women never have them, while others have them continually (Avis, 1999; Whitbourne, 2001). Administration of artificial estrogen, discussed later in this chapter, can alleviate hot flashes but carries risks.

Other possible physical symptoms include vaginal dryness, burning, and itching; vaginal and urinary infections; and urinary dysfunction caused by tissue shrinkage (Whitbourne, 2001). Since the hormones most directly linked to sexual desire in both men and women are the androgens (such as testosterone), declining estrogen levels in midlife do not seem to affect sexual desire in most women, as long as intercourse remains comfortable and there are no health-related problems that interfere with a healthy sex life (American Medical Association, 1998). Still, some women do not become sexually aroused as readily as before, and some find intercourse painful because of thinning vaginal tissues and inadequate lubrication. Small doses of testosterone may solve the first problem, and use of water-soluble gels can prevent or relieve the second (Katchadourian, 1987; King, 1996; M. E. Spence, 1989; Williams, 1995).

Such psychological problems as irritability, nervousness, anxiety, depression, memory loss, and even insanity have been blamed on the climacteric, but research shows no reason to attribute mental disturbances to this normal biological change (Whitbourne, 2001). The myth that menopause produces depression may derive from the fact that women at this time are undergoing changes in roles, relationships, and responsibilities. These changes may be stressful, and the way a woman perceives them can affect her view of menopause (Avis, 1999).

Taken together, the research suggests that "so-called menopausal syndrome may be related more to personal characteristics or past experiences than to menopause per se" (Avis, 1999, p. 129), as well as to societal views of women and of aging (see Box 15-1 on page 534). In cultures in which women view menopause positively, or in which older women acquire social, religious, or political power after menopause, few problems are associated with this natural event (Aldwin & Levenson, 2001; Avis, 1999; Dan & Bernhard, 1989).

BOX 15-1

Window on the World

Japanese Women's Experience of Menopause

Many women accept hot flashes and night sweats as normal accompaniments of menopause. However, that apparently is not true everywhere.

Margaret Lock (1994) surveyed 1,316 Japanese women ages 45 to 55 and compared the results with data on 9,376 women in Massachusetts and Manitoba, Canada. Japanese women's experience of menopause turned out to be quite different from the experience of western women.

Fewer than 10 percent of Japanese women whose menstruation was becoming irregular reported having had hot flashes during the previous two weeks, compared with about 40 percent of the Canadian sample and 35 percent of the U.S. sample. In fact, fewer than 20 percent of Japanese women had *ever* experienced hot flashes, compared with 65 percent of Canadian women, and most of the Japanese women who had experienced hot flashes reported little or no physical or psychological discomfort. (Indeed, so little importance is given in Japan to what in western cultures is considered the chief symptom of menopause that there is no specific Japanese term for "hot flash," even though the Japanese language makes many subtle distinctions about body states.) Furthermore, only about 3 percent of the Japanese women said they experienced night sweats, and Japanese women were far less likely than western women to suffer from insomnia, depression, irritability, or lack of energy (Lock, 1994).

The Japanese women were more likely to report stiffness in the shoulders, headaches, lumbago, constipation, and other complaints that, in western eyes, do not appear directly related to the hormonal changes of menopause (Lock, 1994). Japanese physicians link such symptoms with the decline of the female reproductive cycle, which they believe is associated with changes in the autonomic nervous system (Lock, 1998).

The symptoms physicians noted were quite similar to those the women reported. Hot flashes were not at the

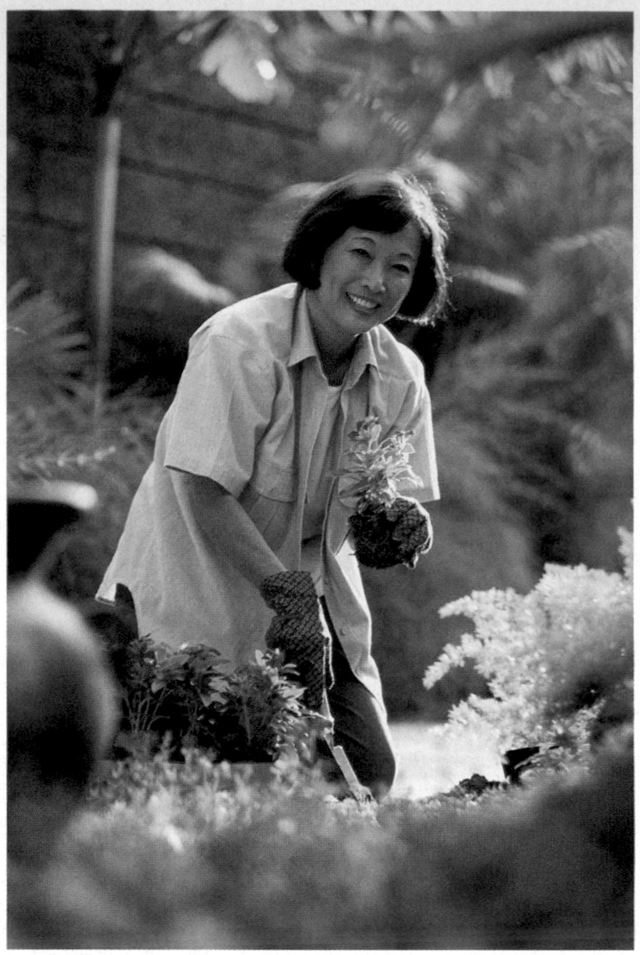

This middle-aged Japanese woman working in her garden seems the picture of health. Japanese women rarely experience hot flashes, discomfort, or other physical symptoms that some western women associate with menopause.

Changes in Male Sexuality Men have no experience comparable to menopause (Sternbach, 1998). They do not undergo a sudden drop in hormone production at midlife, as women do; but testosterone levels do tend to decrease slowly after age 60 in many men, a phenomenon that has been called "andropause" (Finch, 2001; Whitbourne, 2001).

The term *male climacteric* is sometimes used to refer to a period of physiological, emotional, and psychological change involving a man's reproductive system and other body systems. "Male menopause" is much more gradual than female menopause, and its severity varies widely (Rowe & Kahn, 1998). Symptoms supposedly associated with the climacteric include depression, anxiety, irritability, insomnia, fatigue, weakness, lower sexual drive, erectile failure, memory loss, and reduced muscle and bone mass top of the doctors' lists and in some cases did not appear at all. However, very few Japanese women consult doctors about menopause or its symptoms, and few physicians prescribe hormone therapy (Lock, 1994).

In Japan, menopause is regarded as a normal event in women's lives, not as a medical condition requiring treatment. The end of menstruation has far less significance than it does for western women; the closest term for it, *kônenki,* refers not specifically to what westerners call menopause, but to a considerably longer period comparable to the perimenopause or climacteric (Lock, 1994, 1998).

Aging in Japan is less feared than in the west. Not until old age can women and men alike escape the daily round of duty and do as they please. Aging brings not only respect for wisdom, but newfound freedom—as does menopause (Lock, 1998).

Cultural attitudes, then, may affect how women interpret their physical sensations, and these interpretations may be linked to their feelings about menopause. Hot flashes have been found to be rare or infrequent among Mayan women, North African women in Israel, Navajo women, and some Indonesian women (Beyene, 1986, 1989; Flint & Samil, 1990; Walfish, Antonovsky, & Maoz, 1984; Wright, 1983). For example, Mayan women, who are frequently pregnant or nursing babies, tend to regard childbearing as a burden and to look forward to its end (Beyene, 1986, 1989).

Do nutritional practices influence the experience of menopause? Some plants, such as soybeans—a staple of Far Eastern diets—contain relatively high amounts of compounds known as *phytoestrogens,* which have a weak estrogen-like effect. A diet high in foods made with these plants, such as tofu and soy flour, may influence hormone levels in the blood. This, it has been suggested, might help explain why middle-aged Japanese women do not experience the dramatic effects of a precipitous decline in estrogen levels, as many western women do. It also might explain Japanese women's low incidence of osteoporosis and of deaths from coronary heart disease (Margo N. Woods, M.D., Department of Family Medicine and Community Health, Tufts University School of Medicine, personal communication, November, 1996). In one small, prospective, randomized, controlled study, postmenopausal women who were not on hormone therapy experienced less severe hot flashes, night sweats, and vaginal dryness after six months of taking a placebo, but *not* after taking phytoestrogens (Balk, Whiteside, Naus, DeFerrari, & Roberts, 2002). On the other hand, in a placebo-controlled, double-blind study in Brazil, daily doses of soy isoflavene decreased hot flashes and other menopausal symptoms while decreasing total cholesterol and LDL, thus offering possible protection against heart disease (Han, Soares, Haidar, de Lima, & Baracat, 2002).

Further conclusions about the influence of diet on women's health during and after menopause must await the completion of additional controlled longitudinal studies. Meanwhile, the findings about Japanese women's experience of menopause show that even this universal biological event has major cultural variations, once again affirming the importance of cross-cultural research.

What's Your View?

What do you think might explain the differences between Japanese and western women's experience of menopause?

Check It Out:

For more information on this topic, go to http://www. mhhe.com/papaliah9.

and body hair (Henker, 1981; Sternbach, 1998; Weg, 1989), but it is not clear that these often vaguely defined complaints are related to testosterone levels. Men's psychological adjustments, like women's, may stem from such events as illness, worries about work, children's leaving home, or the death of parents, as well as from negative cultural attitudes toward aging (King, 1996).

There is no strong relationship between testosterone levels and sexual desire or performance (Finch, 2001). However, men often do experience some changes in sexual functioning related to changes in the circulatory and endocrine systems, as well as to stress, smoking, obesity, health problems such as diabetes, and social factors such as those just mentioned (Finch, 2001; Whitbourne, 2001). Although a man can continue to reproduce until quite late in life, his sperm count begins to decline in the late forties or fifties, making it less likely that he will father a child (Merrill & Verbrugge, 1999). Erections tend to become slower and less firm, orgasms less frequent, and ejaculations less forceful; and it takes longer to recover and ejaculate again (Bremner, Vitiello, & Prinz, 1983; Katchadourian, 1987; King, 1996; Masters & Johnson, 1966). Still, sexual excitation and sexual activity can remain a normal, vital part of life.

Although testosterone supplementation therapy is sometimes touted as a boost to sexual desire and a cure for other problems of aging, it is medically advisable only for men with clear hormonal deficiencies. Testosterone therapy can increase risks of cancer, enlarged prostate gland, higher cholesterol, infertility, and acne (Whitbourne, 2001).

Sexual Activity

"My parents don't have sex. They have other things to do" (King, 1996, p. 258).

Many children of middle-aged parents are vastly ignorant of their parents' sexual activity. Myths about sexuality in midlife—for example, the idea that satisfying sex ends at menopause—have been believed even by middle-aged people themselves and have sometimes become self-fulfilling prophecies. Now, advances in health care and more liberal attitudes toward sex are making people more aware that sex can be a vital part of life during these and even later years.

Surveys suggest that sexual activity tends to diminish only slightly and gradually during the forties and fifties (King, 1996). Often a decline in frequency has nonphysiological causes: monotony in a relationship, preoccupation with business or financial worries, mental or physical fatigue, depression, failure to make sex a high priority, fear of failure to attain an erection, or lack of a partner. Possible physical causes include chronic disease, surgery, medications, and too much food or alcohol (King, 1996; Masters & Johnson, 1966; Weg, 1989).

Freed from worries about pregnancy, and having more uninterrupted time to spend with their partners, many people find their sexual relationship better than it has been in years. Women that age may know their own sexual needs and desires better, feel freer to take the initiative, and have more interest in sex. Because of men's slowed response, middle-aged lovers may enjoy longer, more leisurely periods of sexual activity. Women may find their partner's longer period of arousal helpful in reaching their own orgasm—often by means other than intercourse. Couples who hold and caress each other, with or without genital sex, can experience heightened sexuality as part of an intimate relationship (Weg, 1989).

What's Your View?

- How often, and in what ways, do you imagine your parents express their sexuality? When you are their age, do you expect to be more or less sexually active than they seem to be?

Checkpoint

Can you . . .

- ✔ Tell the chief difference between men's and women's reproductive changes at midlife?
- ✔ Identify factors that can affect women's experience of menopause?
- ✔ Describe changes in sexual activity during middle age?

Sexual Dysfunction For a surprising proportion of adults, sex is not easy or enjoyable. **Sexual dysfunction** is a persistent disturbance in sexual desire or sexual response. It can take the form of lack of interest in or pleasure from sex, painful intercourse, difficulty in arousal, premature orgasm or ejaculation, inability to reach climax, or anxiety about sexual performance.

sexual dysfunction Persistent disturbance in sexual desire or sexual response.

In interviews with a nationally representative sample of 1,749 women and 1,410 men ages 18 to 59, 43 percent of the women and 31 percent of the men reported some form of sexual dysfunction (Laumann et al., 1999). Among women, sexual dysfunction decreases with age; for men, it is just the opposite. Women in their fifties are about half as likely as the youngest women to report nonpleasurable sex or sexual anxiety, and only one-third as likely to report pain during sex. On the contrary, men in their fifties are more than three times as likely to report erection problems and low desire as 18- to 29-year-old men (Laumann, Paik, & Rosen, 1999, 2000).

Sexual dysfunction appears to be a widespread, and largely unsuspected, public health problem. Unfortunately, according to this study, only 10 percent of men and 20 percent of women who have the problem seek medical treatment (Laumann et al., 1999).

The most severe form of sexual dysfunction in men is **erectile dysfunction** (popularly called *impotence*): persistent inability to achieve or maintain an erect enough

erectile dysfunction Inability of a man to achieve or maintain an erect penis sufficient for satisfactory sexual performance.

penis for satisfactory sexual performance. An estimated 39 percent of 40-year-old men and 67 percent of 70-year-old men experience erectile dysfunction at least sometimes (Feldman, Goldstein, Hatzichristou, Krane, & McKinlay, 1994; Goldstein et al., 1998). According to the Massachusetts Male Aging Study, about 5 percent of 40-year-old and 15 percent of 70-year-old men are completely impotent (Feldman et al., 1994). Diabetes, hypertension, high cholesterol, kidney failure, depression, neurological disorders, and many chronic diseases are associated with erectile dysfunction (Utiger, 1998). Alcohol, drugs, smoking, poor sexual techniques, lack of knowledge, unsatisfying relationships, anxiety, and stress can be contributing factors.

Some men suffering erectile dysfunction can be helped by treating the underlying causes or by adjusting medications ("Effective Solutions for Impotence," 1994; National Institutes of Health [NIH], 1992). Sildenafil (known as Viagra), taken in the form of pills, has been found safe and effective (Goldstein et al., 1998; Nurnberg et al., 2003; Utiger, 1998). Other treatments, each of which has both benefits and drawbacks, include a wraparound vacuum constrictive device, which draws blood into the penis; injections of prostaglandin E1 (a drug found in semen, which widens the arteries); and penile implant surgery. If there is no apparent physical problem, psychotherapy or sex therapy (with the support and involvement of the partner) may help (NIH, 1992).

Concern with Appearance and Attractiveness In a youth-oriented society such as the United States, middle-aged people spend a great deal of time, effort, and money trying to look young. However, research so far has not found an intervention that actually slows the rate of aging (Olshansky, Hayflick, & Carnes, 2002a).

More than 1.6 million people in 2001 had injections of Botox, a drug that has been found to temporarily smooth facial "worry wrinkles" and frown lines by paralyzing the muscles that cause them (American Society for Aesthetic Plastic Surgery, 2002). The drug wears off in a matter of months and needs to be repeated regularly.

Until recently, it was mostly women who fell prey to the relentless pursuit of youth. As long ago as medieval times, a mature man was considered wise, whereas a mature woman was considered "cold" and "dry" (Lock, 1998). A societal standard "that regards beauty as the exclusive preserve of the young . . . makes women especially vulnerable to the fear of aging. . . . The relentless social pressures to retain a slim 'girlish'

What's Your View?

- In your experience, do middle-aged women show more concern about appearance than middle-aged men? If so, in what ways, specifically?

Wrinkles and graying hair often imply that a woman is "over the hill" but that a man is "in the prime of life." This double standard of aging, which downgrades the attractiveness of middle-aged women but not of their partners, can affect a couple's sexual adjustment.

figure make women self-conscious about their bodies . . . [and] can be detrimental to the midlife woman's personal growth and sense of self-worth" (Lenz, 1993, pp. 26, 28).

Today the double standard of aging is waning (Gullette, 1998); men, too, suffer from the premium placed on youth. This is particularly true in the job market and the business world. It's no coincidence that "antiaging" treatments for men have boomed in an era of corporate downsizing (Spindler, 1996). Men now spend as much as women on cosmetic products (Gullette, 1998) and are turning to cosmetic surgery in greater numbers.

Self-esteem suffers when people devalue their physical being. On the other hand, an effort to maintain youth and vigor can be positive if it is not obsessive and reflects concern with health and fitness (Gallagher, 1993). Men and women who can stay as fit as possible while accepting realistically the changes taking place in themselves, and who can appreciate maturity as a positive achievement for both sexes, are better able to make the most of middle adulthood—a time when both physical and cognitive functioning are likely to be at an impressively high level.

Checkpoint

Can you . . .

- ✔ Discuss the prevalence of sexual dysfunction among men and women in relation to age?
- ✔ Give reasons for the "double standard of aging" and its recent decline?

Health

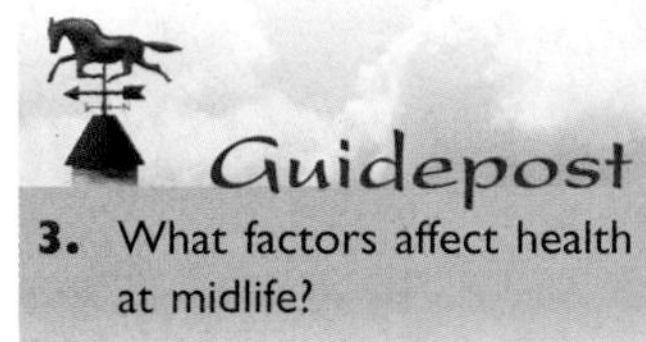

Guidepost

3. What factors affect health at midlife?

A century ago, most people did not live through what we now call middle age; the average American died in the midforties (Spiro, 2001). Today most middle-aged Americans—like middle-aged people in other industrialized countries—are quite healthy. All but 12 percent of 45- to 54-year-olds and 18 percent of 55- to 64-year-olds consider themselves in good or excellent health (NCHS, 2002b). However, 23 percent of 45- to 64-year-olds are limited in activities because of chronic conditions such as arthritis, back problems, and rheumatism, which increase with age (Merrill & Verbrugge, 1999; Summer, O'Neill, & Shirey, 1999).

Nutrition, smoking, alcohol and drug use, physical activity, and other influences discussed in Chapter 13 continue to affect health in middle age (see Table 15-2) and beyond. People who do not smoke, are not overweight, and exercise regularly at midlife not only live longer but have shorter periods of disability at the end of life (Vita, Terry, Hubert, & Fries, 1998). Middle-aged men and women who stop smoking reduce their risk of heart disease and stroke (AHA, 1995; Kawachi et al., 1993; Stamler et al., 1993; Wannamethee et al., 1995). Unfortunately, leisure-time physical activity diminishes rapidly with age, especially among people with low socioeconomic status (Schoenborn & Barnes, 2002).

Besides SES, other indirect influences, such as race or ethnicity and gender, continue to affect health. One important influence is stress, whose cumulative effects on both physical and mental health often begin to appear in middle age (Aldwin & Levenson, 2001). And, as we'll see, individual differences in personality and emotionality may affect how people physically weather the challenges of midlife.

Health Concerns

Despite their generally good health, many people in midlife are concerned about signs of potential decline. They may have less energy than in their youth and are likely to experience occasional or chronic pains and fatigue. They can no longer "burn the midnight oil" with ease, they are more likely to contract certain diseases, and they take longer to recover from illness or extreme exertion (Merrill & Verbrugge, 1999; Siegler, 1997).

hypertension Chronically high blood pressure.

Hypertension (chronically high blood pressure) is an increasingly important concern from midlife on. It is the most common chronic condition among 45- to 64-year-old men and second most common (after arthritis) in women in that age group (Spiro, 2001). Hypertension can lead to heart attack or stroke, or to cognitive impairment in late life (Launer, Masaki, Petrovitch, Foley, & Havlik, 1995). Blood

Table 15-2 Lifestyle Factors in Selected Diseases

Risk factor	Coronary Heart Disease	Stroke	Diabetes (non-insulin dependent)	Breast Cancer	Lung Cancer	Prostate Cancer	Colorectal Cancer	Melanoma (skin cancer)	Osteoporosis	Osteoarthritis
Cigarette smoking	×	×	×	×	×	×	×	×	×	×
Alcohol	?		?	?					×	
Dietary factors										
Cholesterol	×	×								
Calories			×							
Fat intake	×	×	?	?		×	?			
Salt intake		×								
Fiber			O							
Calcium									O	
Potassium	O									
Overweight	×	×	×						×	?
Physical inactivity	O	O	O						O	O
Exposure to toxins				×	×	×	×			
Exposure to ultraviolet rays								×		

Note: × = increases risk of disease; O = decreases risk of disease; ? = may increase risk of disease.
Source: Adapted from Merrill & Verbrugge, 1999, Table IV, p. 87.

pressure screening, low-salt diets, and medication have reduced the prevalence of hypertension, but it still affects about 34 percent of men and about 25 percent of women ages 45 to 54, and more than 40 percent of both men and women ages 55 to 64 (NCHS, 1998). People in the latter age group have a 90 percent risk of becoming hypertensive eventually (Vasan et al., 2002).

As life has lengthened, the leading causes of death have changed. In the early twentieth century people commonly died of infectious diseases and epidemics (Spiro, 2001). Today the two leading causes of death between ages 45 and 64 are diseases related to aging: cancer and heart disease (Anderson, 2002). However, death rates have declined sharply since the 1970s for people in this age bracket (Hoyert, Arias, Smith, Murphy, & Kochanek, 2001), in large part because of a decline in deaths from coronary heart disease (Siegler, 1997) due to improvements in treatment of heart attack patients (Rosamond et al., 1998).

About one-third of recorded cases of AIDS in adults are in people over 40 (NCHS, 1998), and 10 to 15 percent of cases occur in people over 50 (National Association on HIV Over Fifty, 2002; National Institute on Aging, 1999). Many patients in this age group contracted the disease through contaminated blood transfusions before routine screening began in 1985, and diagnosis often does not occur until a late stage of infection. The disease tends to be more severe and to progress more rapidly in middle-aged and older people, whose immune systems may be weakened (Collaborative Group on AIDS Incubation and HIV Survival, 2000; Levin, 2002; National Association on HIV Over Fifty, 2002).

Diabetes is the seventh-leading cause of death in middle age (Anderson, 2001a). The most common type, mature-onset (Type II) diabetes, typically develops after age 30 and becomes more prevalent with age (American Diabetes Association, 1992). Unlike juvenile-onset, or insulin-dependent, diabetes, in which the level of blood sugar rises because the body does not produce enough insulin, in mature-onset diabetes glucose levels rise because the cells lose their ability to use the insulin the body produces. As a result, the body may try to compensate by producing too much insulin (Spence, 1989). People with mature-onset diabetes often do not realize it until they develop such serious complications as heart disease, stroke, blindness, kidney disease, or loss of limbs (American Diabetes Association, 1992).

Preventive care can stave off or even prevent some diseases. For example, early treatment can lower elevated pressure in the eye and delay onset of glaucoma, a major cause of blindness (Heijl et al., 2002).

Indirect Influences on Health: Socioeconomic Status

People with lower socioeconomic status have lower life expectancy, more activity limitations due to chronic disease, lower well-being, and more restricted access to health care than people with higher SES (Spiro, 2001). In part, the reasons may be psychosocial: people with higher SES tend to have a greater sense of control over what happens to their bodies as they age, and they may choose healthier lifestyles (Whitbourne, 2001). Still, in an eight-year nationally representative study of more than 3,600 U.S. adults, people with lower and moderate incomes had higher mortality rates than those with higher incomes even when differences in age, sex, race, urban or rural residence, education, and health risk behaviors (such as smoking, use of alcohol, overweight, and activity levels) were controlled (Lantz et al., 1998).

One explanation is that many poor people lack insurance (NCHS, 2002a). In a prospective national study of 7,577 adults who were 51 to 61 years old in 1992, those without health insurance were 63 percent more likely to show a decline in health during the next four years and 23 percent more likely to develop problems in walking or climbing stairs (Baker, Sudano, Albert, Borawski, & Dor, 2001). But insurance is not the whole story. In a longitudinal study of 8,355 British civil servants ages 39 to 63, those in the lower ranks had poorer health than those in higher classifications, despite equal access to Britain's national health care system (Hemingway, Nicholson, Stafford, Roberts, & Marmot, 1997).

Indirect Influences on Health: Race/Ethnicity

As in young adulthood, death rates in middle age are higher for African Americans than for white, Hispanic, Asian, and Native Americans (Hoyert et al., 2001; Miniño et al., 2002). About one in three African American adults has hypertension, as compared with fewer than one in four white Americans (NCHS, 1998). Hypertension accounts for one in five deaths among black people—twice as many as among whites (Cooper, Rotimi, & Ward, 1999). One in ten African Americans has diabetes, and African Americans have higher rates of blindness, kidney failure, and amputation of limbs as a result (American Diabetes Association, 2000). African American women are four times as likely as white women to die of heart disease or stroke before age 60 (Mosca et al., 1998). While death rates from cancer have generally declined, this is not so among blacks, who continue to have high death rates from lung, colorectal, prostate, and breast cancer (CDC, 2002a). A review of the research found that this difference in cancer deaths is related mostly to differing treatment (Bach et al., 2002).

Some observers attribute the health gap between black and white Americans in part to stress and frustration caused by prejudice and discrimination (Chissell, 1989; Lawler, 1990, in Goleman, 1990; Whitbourne, 2001). In parts of the Caribbean, where race relations may be smoother than in the United States, blacks' average blood pressure is about the same as that of other ethnic groups (Cooper et al., 1999).

Probably the largest single underlying factor in African Americans' health problems is poverty, which is related to poor nutrition, substandard housing, and poor access to health care (Otten, Teutsch, Williamson, & Marks, 1990). Still, poverty cannot be the sole explanation, since the death rate for middle-aged Hispanic Americans, who also are disproportionately poor, is lower than that of white Americans (Hoyert et al., 2001).

Hispanic Americans are not a single homogeneous group; there are significant differences among various subgroups, and Puerto Ricans lag behind other Hispanics in several health status indicators. For example, about 21 percent of Puerto Ricans report activity limitations, as compared with about 15 percent of persons of Mexican, Cuban, or other Hispanic origin. Puerto Ricans also are more likely to report being in fair or poor health, to spend more days sick in bed, and to see physicians or go to a hospital (Hajat, Lucas, & Kington, 2000).

Racial and ethnic disparities have decreased since 1990, but substantial disparities persist. For example, blacks improved more than the general population in death rates from stroke and lung cancer, but not in breast cancer deaths; and the lung cancer death rate among American Indian or Alaska Natives increased by 28 percent. This group also did not benefit from overall declines in death rates from breast cancer and stroke (Keppel, Pearcy, & Wagener, 2002).

Checkpoint

Can you . . .

- ✔ Describe the typical health status in middle age, and identify health concerns that become more prevalent at this age?
- ✔ Discuss socioeconomic and ethnic factors in helath and mortality at middle age?

Women's Health After Menopause

Although women's health tends to be better overall than men's, with lower death rates (Miniño et al., 2002), women are at increased risk after menopause, particularly for heart disease and osteoporosis. With longer life spans, women in many developed countries now can expect to live half their adult lives after menopause. As a result, increasing attention is being paid to women's health issues at this time of life (Barrett-Connor et al., 2002).

Heart Disease After age 50, women's risk of heart disease begins to catch up with men's (Avis, 1999). This happens faster after a hysterectomy. For every ten years after menopause, heart disease risk increases about threefold (Barrett-Connor et al., 2002). Furthermore, women younger than 74 have less chance than men of surviving a heart attack (Vaccarino et al., 1999). Regular exercise or walking—as little as one hour each week—can lower the risk of coronary heart disease after age 45 (Lee, Rexrode, Cook, Manson, & Buring, 2001; Manson et al., 1999; Owens, Matthews, Wing, & Kuller, 1992). A diet high in fiber, especially from cereals, also reduces the risk (Wolk et al., 1999).

Bone Loss and Osteoporosis In women, bone loss rapidly accelerates in the first five to ten years after menopause (Avis, 1999; Barrett-Connor et al., 2002; Levinson & Altkorn, 1998). This is because estrogen plays an important role in helping the blood absorb calcium from food and helping the bones absorb calcium from blood. When estrogen levels fall after menopause, calcium absorption slows down (Stoppard, 1999).

Extreme bone loss may lead to **osteoporosis** ("porous bones"), a condition in which the bones become thin and brittle as a result of calcium depletion associated with loss of estrogen. Frequent signs of osteoporosis are marked loss in height and a "hunchbacked" posture that results from compression and collapse of weakened bones. In a national observational study of 200,160 postmenopausal women, almost half had previously undetected low bone mineral density, and 7 percent of these women had osteoporosis (Siris et al., 2001). Osteoporosis is a major cause of broken bones in old age and can greatly affect quality of life and even survival (Levinson & Altkorn,

osteoporosis Condition in which the bones become thin and brittle as a result of rapid calcium depletion.

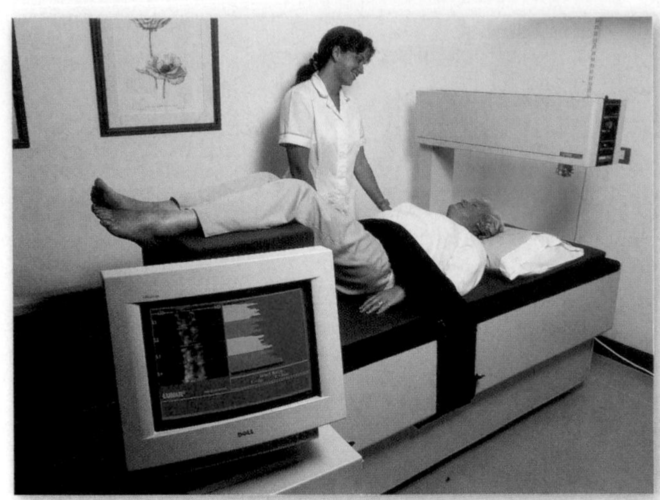

A bone density scan is a simple, painless X-ray procedure to measure bone density so as to determine whether osteoporosis is present. Osteoporosis, or thinning of the bones, is most common in women after menopause. The procedure is especially advisable for women with a family history of osteoporosis. Here, the monitor shows an image of this woman's spinal column.

1998; NIH Consensus Development Panel on Osteoporosis Prevention, Diagnosis, and Therapy, 2001; Siris et al., 2001). Almost three out of four cases of osteoporosis occur in white women, most often in those with fair skin, small frame, low weight and BMI, and a family history of the condition, and those whose ovaries were surgically removed before menopause (NIA, 1993; NIH Consensus Development Panel, 2001; "Should You Take," 1994; Siris et al., 2001). African American women, who have greater bone density, are less likely than white women to develop osteoporosis, whereas Hispanic and Asian women are more likely (Siris et al., 2001). Other risk factors, besides age, include smoking and lack of exercise (Siris et al., 2001). Since a predisposition to osteoporosis seems to have a genetic basis, measurement of bone density is an especially wise precaution for women with affected family members (Prockop, 1998; Uitterlinden et al., 1998).

Genetic factors may dictate peak bone mass, but good lifestyle habits make a significant difference, especially if started early in life (NIH Consensus Development Panel, 2001). However, bone loss, once started, can be slowed or even reversed with proper nutrition, weight-bearing exercise, and avoidance of smoking (Barrett-Connor et al., 2002; Eastell, 1998; Krall & Dawson-Hughes, 1994; NIA, 1993). High-intensity strength training and resistance training have proven particularly effective (Layne & Nelson, 1999; Nelson et al., 1994). Women over age 40 should get 1,000 to 1,500 milligrams of dietary calcium a day, along with recommended daily amounts of vitamin D, which helps the body absorb calcium (NIA, 1993). Studies have found value in calcium and vitamin D supplements (Dawson-Hughes, Harris, Krall, & Dallal, 1997; Eastell, 1998; NIH Consensus Development Panel, 2001).

Breast Cancer and Mammography One in eight American women and one in nine British women develop breast cancer at some point in their lives (American Cancer Society, 2001; Pearson, 2002). As with other cancers, the chance of developing breast cancer increases with age (Barrett-Connor et al., 2002). Overweight women, those who drink alcohol, those who experienced early menarche and late menopause, those with a family history of breast cancer, and those who bore children late and had fewer children have greater risk of breast cancer, while those who are physically active and eat low-fat, high-fiber diets are at less risk (Barrett-Connor et al., 2002; Clavel-Chapelton et al., 2002; U.S. Preventive Services Task Force, 2002). A study of 90,000 middle-aged French women found no link between miscarriage and the risk of breast cancer (Clavel-Chapelton et al., 2002).

Scientists have identified two genes, BRCA1 and BRCA2, that may be involved in a small percentage of breast cancers. Because women with the flawed genes have an estimated 85 percent chance of developing breast cancer someday, they may choose to have more frequent examinations and possibly even preventive mastectomy ("The Breast Cancer Genes," 1994).

Advances in diagnosis and treatment have dramatically improved prospects for breast cancer patients. More than 95 percent of women with breast cancer can survive at least five years if the cancer is caught before it spreads, and 50 percent can expect to survive at least fifteen years (American Cancer Society, 2001). Although benefits of **mammography,** diagnostic X-ray examination of the breasts, appear to be strongest for women over 50, a U.S. Preventive Services Task Force (2002) recommends screening every one or two years for all women beginning at age 40, especially those with a family history of breast cancer before menopause.

mammography Diagnostic X-ray examination of the breasts.

Hysterectomy Nearly one in three U.S. women has a **hysterectomy,** or surgical removal of the uterus, by age 60 (Farquhar & Steiner, 2002). The surgery is generally done to remove uterine fibroids (benign tumors), or because of abnormal uterine bleeding or endometriosis (Kjerulff, Langenberg, & Rhodes, 2000). Hysterectomy rates are second only to rates for cesarean section in surgery performed on U.S. women (Broder, Kanouse, Mittman, & Bernstein, 2000) and are three to four times higher than in Australia, New Zealand, and most European countries (Farquhar & Steiner, 2002).

hysterectomy Surgical removal of the uterus.

About two-thirds of these operations in the United States are abdominal hysterectomies. Nearly one-fourth are vaginal hysterectomies, which usually involve shorter hospital stays, lower costs, fewer complications, and better outcomes. A third type, laparoscopic hysterectomy, which requires only a few small incisions in the abdomen, is growing in popularity. Vaginal hysterectomy is much more popular in other countries, accounting for 40 to 50 percent of the procedures in France and Australia (Farquhar & Steiner, 2002).

Many experts believe that hysterectomy is overused. In a study of nine managed care organizations in Southern California, 76 percent of the recommended hysterectomies did not meet established criteria of the American College of Obstetricians and Gynecologists for this type of surgery, usually because of failure to first rule out other conditions or try alternative medical or surgical treatments (Broder et al., 2000). Painful or bleeding fibroids, for example, may be treated by myomectomy (cutting away only the fibroids and not the entire uterus), myolysis (electric current), or embolization (cutting off their blood supply) (Bren, 2001).

Hormone Replacement Therapy Since the most troublesome physical effects of menopause are linked to reduced levels of estrogen, **hormone replacement therapy (HRT)** in the form of artificial estrogen is often prescribed. As many as 38 percent of postmenopausal American women have used HRT (Keating, Cleary, Rossi, Zaslavsky, & Ayanian, 1999). Because estrogen taken alone increases the risk of uterine cancer, women whose uterus has not been surgically removed are usually given estrogen in combination with progestin, a form of the female hormone progesterone. Now, however, medical evidence has begun to challenge some of HRT's presumed benefits and bear out its suspected risks.

hormone replacement therapy (HRT) Treatment with artificial estrogen, sometimes in combination with the hormone progesterone, to relieve or prevent symptoms caused by decline in estrogen levels after menopause.

Besides relieving hot flashes, night sweats, and vaginal dryness, HRT is often used to prevent or stop bone loss after menopause (Barrett-Connor et al., 2002; Davidson, 1995; Eastell, 1998; Levinson & Altkorn, 1998). HRT is thought to be most effective, even in low doses, when started at menopause and continued for at least five years (Lindsay, Gallagher, Kleerekoper, & Pickar, 2002). However, an analysis of 22 studies by British researchers found no benefit in starting treatment after age 60 and also questioned the benefits for younger women (Grady & Cummings, 2002). Taking HRT for only five to ten years will not prevent future osteoporosis; bone loss resumes whenever HRT is stopped (Barrett-Connor et al., 2002).

Early correlational studies suggested that estrogen, alone or combined with progestin, dramatically cut the risk of heart disease (Davidson, 1995; Ettinger, Friedman, Bush, & Quesenberry, 1996; Grodstein, 1996). However, the validity of these findings was uncertain because estrogen users tend to have better health habits than nonusers (Avis, 1999; Manson & Martin, 2001). More recently, a large-scale randomized, controlled study found that, rather than protecting high-risk women (those who already have heart disease or related problems), hormone treatments either provide no benefit or actually *increase* the risks of heart attack, stroke, and gall bladder disease (Grady et al., 2002; Hulley et al., 2002; Pettiti, 2002). Other research found a greater risk of worsened coronary disease or death when HRT was combined with high doses of antioxidant vitamins (Waters et al., 2002). Then a randomized, controlled trial of estrogen plus progestin in healthy women was stopped after five years because the risks of breast cancer, heart attack, stroke, and blood clots exceeded any benefits (Writing Group for the Women's Health Initiative Investigators, 2002). The American Heart Association now advises *against* HRT (Mosca et al., 2001). Lifestyle changes such as losing weight and stopping smoking, and, if necessary, drugs to lower cholesterol and blood pressure may be wiser courses for many women (Manson & Martin, 2001).

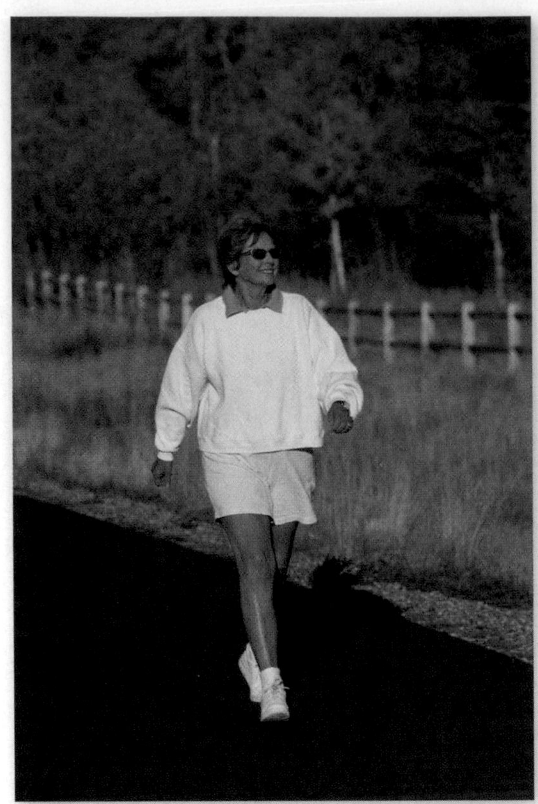

Lifestyle changes, such as getting more exercise and losing weight, are now recommended over hormone replacement therapy (HRT) for postmenopausal women. Recent studies have challenged the health benefits of HRT.

The effect of estrogen on breast cancer is still under study. One large-scale study found the risk of estrogen alone less than when it is combined with progestin (Schairer et al., 2000). Heightened risk of breast cancer seems to be mainly among current or recent estrogen users, and the risk increases with length of use (Chen, Weiss, Newcomb, Barlow, & White, 2002; Willett, Colditz, & Stampfer, 2000). Long-term estrogen use is also associated with increased risk of ovarian cancer (Rodriguez, Patel, Calle, Jacob, & Thun, 2001).

Some epidemiological studies of HRT have found that women who used estrogen were less likely to develop Alzheimer's disease (Baldereschi et al., 1998; Henderson, 2000; Mayeux, 1996; Paganini-Hill & Henderson, 1994, 1996; Tang et al., 1996), but only if they currently received HRT and had done so for more than ten years (Zandi et al., 2002). There is no clinical trial evidence that estrogen improves symptoms or delays the progression of the disease (Barrett-Connor et al., 2002). Estrogen also has been linked to improvements in cognitive functioning, particularly memory, in postmenopausal women; but this research has had conflicting results and has been criticized on methodological grounds (Avis, 1999; Foy, Henderson, Berger, & Thompson, 2000; LeBlanc, Janowsky, Chan, & Nelson, 2001; Shaywitz et al., 1999; Yaffe, Sawaya, Lieberburg, & Grady, 1998). Furthermore, in a randomized 3-year study of 16,608 postmenopausal women, HRT had no significant positive effects on quality of life (Hays et al., 2003).

Checkpoint

Can you . . .

✔ Discuss changes in women's health risks after menopause, and weigh the risks and benefits of hysterectomy and hormone replacement therapy?

With the safety and efficacy of long-term hormone treatment in question, many women no longer take hormones and other treatments are being tested. A new group of nonhormonal chemicals called *selective estrogen receptor modulators*, chiefly tamoxifen and raloxifene (sometimes called "designer estrogens"), seem to have favorable effects on bone density and possibly on cholesterol levels without increasing the risk of breast cancer and greatly reduce the risk of breast cancer in women with a genetic predisposition. However, tamoxifen also increases the risk of uterine cancer (Avis, 1999; Eastell, 1998; King et al., 2001). Raloxifene, a drug normally used for treatment of osteoporosis, seems to reduce the risk of genetic breast cancer, but without negative side effects (Barrett-Connor et al., 2002). However, the long-term effects of these drugs have yet to be documented.

Influence of Emotional States, Personality, and Stress

The ancient proverb of Solomon, "A merry heart doeth good like medicine" (Proverbs 17:22), is being borne out by contemporary research. Negative emotion, such as anxious or depressed mood, is often associated with poor physical and mental health, and positive emotion with good health (Salovey, Rothman, Detweiler, & Steward, 2000; Spiro, 2001). Negative moods seem to suppress immune functioning—increasing susceptibility to illness—whereas positive moods seem to enhance it. Furthermore, negative emotional states may lead people to think that they are more sick than they actually are and may impair their judgment about what can be done to improve their condition (Salovey et al., 2000).

The health consequences of negative emotionality depend on how well individuals are able to manage and repair their moods, and this may be a function of disposition (Salovey et al., 2000). It should not be surprising, then, that personality is related to health (Spiro, 2001). People rated as extraverted, agreeable, or conscientious are more likely to report excellent health than people high in the personality dimension called *neuroticism* (Siegler, 1997; refer back to Chapter 14).

An important aspect of the relationship between emotion, personality, and health is the way a person handles stress.

Stress: Causes and Effects The more stressful the changes that take place in a person's life, the greater the likelihood of illness within the next year or two. That was the finding of a classic study in which two psychiatrists, on the basis of interviews with 5,000 hospital patients, ranked the stressfulness of life events that had preceded illness (Holmes & Rahe, 1976; see Table 15-3). About half the people with between 150 and 300 "life change units" (LCUs) in a single year, and about 70 percent of those with 300 or more LCUs, became ill.

Change—even positive change—can be stressful, and some people react to stress by getting sick. The most frequently reported physical symptoms of stress are headaches, stomachaches, muscle aches or muscle tension, and fatigue. The most common psychological symptoms are nervousness, anxiety, tenseness, anger, irritability, and depression. There are different kinds of **stressors** (stress-producing experiences). Hassles of day-to-day living are associated with minor physical ills such as colds and may have a stronger effect on mental health than major life events or transitions, or chronic or long-lasting problems (Chiriboga, 1997).

stressors Stress-producing experiences.

The connection between stress and illness has long been observed, but only recently have we begun to understand more about how stress produces illness and why some people handle stress better than others. Intense or prolonged stress seems to weaken the immune system and increase susceptibility to illness (Harvard Medical School, 2002a; Kiecolt-Glaser & Glaser, 1995; Salovey et al., 2000). Research has found suppressed immune function in breast cancer patients (Compas & Luecken, 2002),

Table 15-3 Life Events in Order of Diminishing Stressfulness

Life Event	Value	Life Event	Value
Death of spouse	100	Son or daughter leaving home	29
Divorce	73	Trouble with in-laws	29
Marital separation	65	Outstanding personal achievement	28
Jail term	63	Wife beginning or stopping work	26
Death of close family member	63	Beginning or ending school	26
Personal injury or illness	53	Revision of habits	24
Marriage	50	Trouble with boss	23
Being fired at work	47	Change in work hours	20
Marital reconciliation	45	Change in residence	20
Retirement	45	Change in schools	20
Change in health of family	44	Change in recreation	19
Pregnancy	40	Change in social activity	18
Sex difficulties	39	Change in sleeping habits	16
Gain of new family member	39	Change in number of family get-togethers	15
Change in financial state	38	Change in eating habits	15
Death of close friend	37	Vacation	13
Change of work	36	Minor violations of law	11
Change in number of arguments with spouse	35		
Foreclosure of mortgage	30		
Change of responsibility at work	29		

Source: Adapted from Holmes & Rahe, 1976, p. 213.

abused women, hurricane survivors, and men with a history of post-traumatic stress disorder (PTSD) (Harvard Medical School, 2002a).

Stress also may harm health indirectly, through other lifestyle factors. People under stress may sleep less, smoke and drink more, eat poorly, and pay too little attention to their health. Conversely, regular exercise, good nutrition, at least seven hours of sleep a night, and frequent socializing are associated with lower stress (Baum, Cacioppo, Melamed, Gallant, & Travis, 1995). Some adults drink under economic, marital, or job stress. But while low doses of alcohol may reduce stress response and improve performance, higher doses may actually induce stress by stimulating release of adrenaline and other hormones (NIAAA, 1996a).

Stress is under increasing scrutiny as a factor in such diseases as hypertension, heart ailments, stroke, diabetes, osteoporosis, peptic ulcers, and cancer (Krieger, 1982; Levenstein, Ackerman, Kiecolt-Glaser, & Dubois, 1999; Light et al., 1999; Munck, Guyre, & Holbrook, 1984; Sapolsky, 1992). Stress seems to cause blockage of the arteries, which can lead to cardiovascular disease (Baum et al., 1995). Middle-aged men with high levels of anxiety or tension are more likely to develop high blood pressure later in life (Markovitz, Matthews, Kannel, Cobb, & D'Agostino, 1993) and are four to six times more likely than less anxious men to die of sudden heart failure (Kawachi, Colditz, et al., 1994; Kawachi, Sparrow, Vokonas, & Weiss, 1994). Female nurses who work rotating night shifts (which tend to upset the body's natural rhythms) for more than six years are more likely than coworkers to have heart attacks (Kawachi et al., 1995).

However, the role of stress in heart disease has been questioned. In a twenty-year longitudinal study of Scottish men, those who reported the most stress were *less* likely to show signs of heart disease or to die of heart attacks. These men tended to smoke more and exercise less than the other men in the sample, and they had higher socioeconomic status. Thus the benefits of high SES may have helped to offset unhealthy lifestyles and to moderate the effects of stress (Macleod et al., 2002).

Stress may lead to illness through loss of a sense of mastery or control. When expectations of control are violated, chronic stress-related problems tend to compound the physiological effects (Baum & Fleming, 1993).

Dramatic evidence of the power of stress comes from the reactions of New Yorkers to the September 11, 2001, terrorist attacks on the World Trade Center. A survey of 1,008 adult Manhattan residents found a substantial amount of acute PTSD and current depression five to eight weeks following the attacks, especially among those who lived near the site of the destruction and those who had suffered personal losses (Galea et al., 2002). One-third of the respondents—especially those who experienced PTSD or depression—reported using more alcohol, marijuana, or cigarettes since the attacks (Vlahov et al., 2002).

Managing Stress To some degree, stress is normal throughout adulthood (Siegler, 1997). Middle-aged people may experience different *kinds* of stressful events than younger adults, but consistent age differences in *numbers* of stressful life events have not been found (Aldwin & Levenson, 2001). On the other hand, health-related daily hassles, such as problems with parents, children, spouses, work, relatives, and money, tend to decrease with age (Chiriboga, 1997).

By middle age, people may tend to be more realistic in coping with stress. They have a better sense of what they can do to change stressful circumstances and may be better able to accept what cannot be changed. They also have learned more effective strategies for avoiding or minimizing stress. For example, instead of having to worry about running out of gas on a long trip, they are likely to check to make sure the gas tank is full before starting out (Aldwin & Levenson, 2001).

In the classic longitudinal Grant Study of Harvard men born around 1920 (introduced in Chapter 14), those who, between ages 20 and 60, experienced large

Months after the September 11, 2001, terrorist attacks, many Manhattan residents—especially those who lived near the World Trade Center site—experienced post-traumatic stress syndrome or depression.

numbers of severe life events were most likely to suffer major depression. However, depression did *not* occur among men who used the most *adaptive defenses*—who adapted to stress in ways that helped them make the best of bad situations. Similarly, use of adaptive defenses tended to protect World War II combat veterans from PTSD. In another longitudinal study, men who used adaptive defenses between ages 20 and 47 were more likely to see themselves as having good physical health and vigor at age 65—regardless of their actual physical condition (Vaillant, 2000).

Stress management workshops teach people to control their reactions through such techniques as relaxation, meditation, and biofeedback. Men infected with the AIDS virus who learn such techniques are slower to develop symptoms of the disease; and women with breast cancer who participate in group therapy live longer than those who do not participate (Sleek, 1995). Breast cancer patients who are taught stress management techniques and are given social support, with opportunities to face and express their feelings, tend to have the least psychological distress. By actively coping with their illness, they may gain a sense of personal control (Compas & Luecken, 2002).

Health tends to benefit when people can confront and process traumatic life events (Solovey et al., 2000). In one experiment, asthma and rheumatoid arthritis patients who wrote down their most stressful experiences improved their physical condition as compared with a control group of patients who wrote about emotionally neutral topics (Smyth, Stone, Hurewitz, & Kaell, 1999).

What's Your View?

- What are the main sources of stress in your life? How do you handle stress? What methods have you found most successful?

Occupational Stress The Japanese have a word for it: *karoshi,* "death from overwork." One survey found that 40 percent of Japanese workers are afraid of literally working themselves to death. Reported deaths from overwork increased from 21 in 1987 to 143 in 2001 (Associated Press, 2002a).

Occupational stress—stress that is work-related—has become a worldwide epidemic. Workplaces are generally designed for efficiency and profit, not for workers' well-being; but human costs can hurt the bottom line. When people feel they are in the wrong jobs, or when efforts to meet job demands are out of proportion to job satisfaction and other rewards, stress can result. And, as we have just seen, stress—intense, frequent, and prolonged—can play havoc with physical and mental health (Levi, 1990; Siegrist, 1996).

In the United States, many workers are working harder and longer than ever to maintain their standard of living. Telephone interviews with a representative national sample of 1,003 employed adults found that more than one-fourth often felt overworked or overwhelmed with work, and more than half sometimes felt that way (Galinsky, Kim, & Bond, 2001).

Employees who feel overworked, or who believe that their skills are not adequately recognized, or who do not have clear goals, tend to show high stress and low morale and productivity (Veninga, 1998). Overworked employees tend to make mistakes, to be angry at their employers, to have problems with health and family life, to neglect themselves and lose sleep, to have difficulty coping with everyday events, and eventually to look for new jobs (Galinksy et al., 2001).

A combination of high job demands with low autonomy or control and little pride in the product is a common stress-producing pattern (Galinsky et al., 2001; Johnson, Stewart, Hall, Fredlund, & Theorell, 1996; United Nations International Labor Organization [UNILO], 1993; G. Williams, 1991), which increases the risk of high blood pressure and heart disease (Schnall et al., 1990; Siegrist, 1996). Among 10,308 British civil servants ages 35 to 55, low job control and an imbalance between effort and reward were strongly associated with increased coronary risk during the next five years (Bosma, Peter, Siegrist, & Marmot, 1998). On the other hand, employees with a high degree of responsibility on the job who lack confidence in their ability to carry out their responsibilities are also under stress and tend to be vulnerable to respiratory infections (Schaubroeck, Jones, & Xie, 2001).

Not everyone reacts to stress in the same way. In a field study in Stockholm, Sweden, the heart rate, blood pressure, and self-rated mental strain of 46 bus drivers were measured immediately after they finished their routes and again after a ten-minute rest. The drivers also filled out checklists about the hassles they experienced on the job. Those who showed the strongest correlations between job hassles and mental and physiological reactions had higher blood pressure and mental strain ratings in the "unwinding" phase (Johansson, Evans, Rydstedt, & Carrere, 1998). Thus, the ability to leave job-related stresses behind may be as important to maintaining good health as the level of perceived stress on the job.

Many women, in addition to juggling work and family, are under special pressure in the workplace, especially in corporations, where their superiors often are men. Some women complain that an invisible but inflexible "glass ceiling" inhibits their advancement to the highest ranks (Federal Glass Ceiling Commission, 1995). Another frequent source of stress is *sexual harassment:* psychological pressure created by unwelcome sexual overtures, particularly from a superior, which create a hostile or abusive environment.

burnout Syndrome of emotional exhaustion and a sense that one can no longer accomplish anything on the job.

Burnout **Burnout** involves emotional exhaustion, a feeling of being unable to accomplish anything on the job, and a sense of helplessness and loss of control. It is especially common among people in the helping professions (such as teaching, medicine, therapy, social work, and police work) who feel frustrated by their inability to help people as much as they would like to. Burnout is usually a response to continual stress rather than to an immediate crisis. Its symptoms include fatigue, insomnia, headaches, persistent colds, stomach disorders, abuse of alcohol or drugs, and trouble getting along with people. A burned-out worker may quit suddenly, pull away from family and friends, and sink into depression (Briley, 1980; Maslach & Jackson, 1985).

Measures that seem to help burned-out workers include cutting down on working hours and taking breaks, including long weekends and vacations. Other standard stress-reducing techniques—exercise, music, and meditation—also may help. However, the most effective way to relieve stress and burnout may be to change the conditions that cause it by seeing that employees have opportunities to do work that is meaningful to them, uses their skills and knowledge, and gives them a sense of achievement and self-esteem (Knoop, 1994).

Unemployment Perhaps the greatest work-related stressor is the loss of a job. In 2001, 6.6 percent of U.S. families reported having a member out of work (Bureau of Labor Statistics, 2002a).

Corporate downsizing has added a substantial number of middle-aged middle management executives to the unemployment rolls. Since employers generally prefer to hire younger workers, whose skills they believe to be more transferable, many of these longtime employees are forced into early retirement or lower-paid jobs (Forteza & Prieto, 1994). Laid-off workers tend to feel resentful and alienated if they believe they were not treated fairly and sensitively (Murray, 2002).

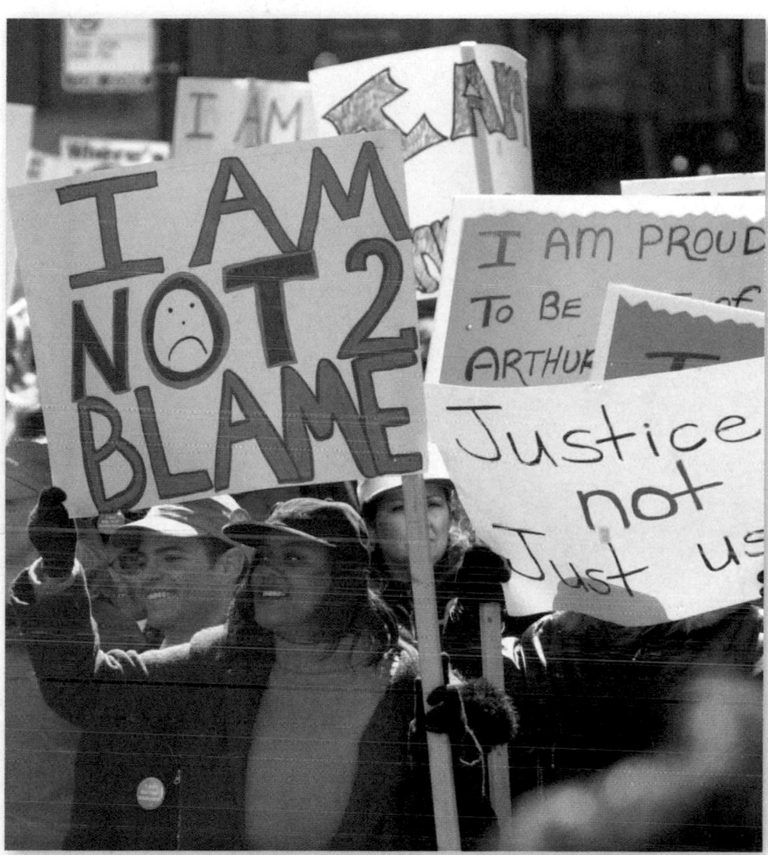

Corporate scandals at such companies as Arthur Andersen and Enron forced many innocent people out of work. People cope with unemployment better when they can draw on financial, psychological, and social resources and can see this forced change as an opportunity to do something new or as a challenge for growth.

Research on unemployment has linked it to headaches, stomach trouble, and high blood pressure; to physical and mental illness, including heart attack, stroke, anxiety, and depression; to marital and family problems; to health, psychological, and behavior problems in offspring; and to suicide, homicide, and other crimes (Brenner, 1991; Merva & Fowles, 1992; Perrucci, Perrucci, & Targ, 1988; Voydanoff, 1990).

Stress comes not only from loss of income and the resulting financial hardship, but also from declines in psychological well-being following job loss (Murphy & Athanasou, 1999; Winefield, 1995). Men who define manhood as supporting a family, and workers of both sexes who derive their identity from their work and define their worth in terms of its dollar value, lose more than their paychecks when they lose their jobs. They lose a piece of themselves and their self-esteem and feel less in control of their lives (Forteza & Prieto, 1994; Perrucci et al., 1988; Voydanoff, 1987, 1990). In a study of 248 unemployed men and women in Queensland, Australia, the most important psychological factor in diminution of well-being was loss of status, followed by the loss of a sense of collective purpose and of a way to structure time (Creed & Macintyre, 2001). In a study of 90 Canadian families that had undergone job loss, psychological problems were 55 to 75 percent greater among those who remained unemployed than among those who had found steady work (Veninga, 1998).

Those who cope best with unemployment have financial resources. Rather than blaming themselves or seeing themselves as failures, they assess their situation objectively. They have the support of understanding, adaptable families and friends (Voydanoff, 1990). A sense of control is important. Among 190 unemployed workers, those who believed they had some influence on their circumstances were less anxious

What's Your View?

- What would you do if you were told that the job you had been doing for ten years was obsolete or that you were being let go because of downsizing?

Checkpoint

Can you . . .

- ✔ Tell how emotions and stress can affect health?
- ✔ Identify sources of work stress and burnout?
- ✔ Summarize physical and psychological effects of losing a job?

and depressed, had fewer physical symptoms, and had higher self-esteem and life satisfaction than those who believed external forces were in control (Cvetanovski & Jex, 1994).

The psychological impact of unemployment is generally temporary; finding a new job can restore well-being. Motivation and a sense of mastery are key factors in finding work, but demographic factors also play a role. Older workers, women, and nonwhites tend to experience greater problems in job-hunting than younger, male, and white workers (Vinokur, Schul, Vuori, & Price, 2000).

COGNITIVE DEVELOPMENT

What happens to cognitive abilities in middle age? Do they improve or decline, or both? Do people develop distinctive ways of thinking at this time of life? How does age affect the ability to solve problems, to learn, to create, and to perform on the job?

Measuring Cognitive Abilities in Middle Age

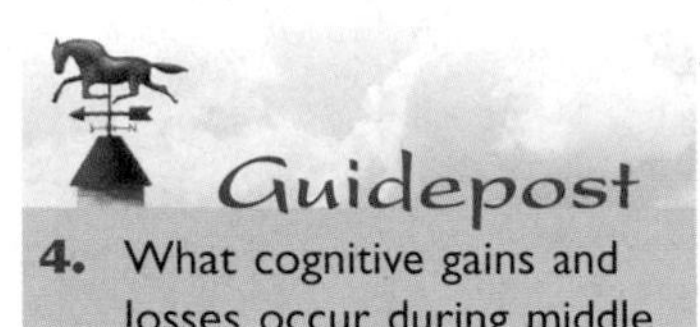

Guidepost

4. What cognitive gains and losses occur during middle age?

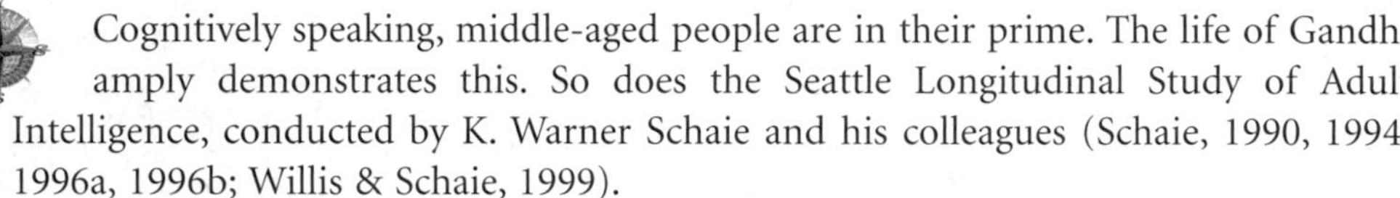

Cognitively speaking, middle-aged people are in their prime. The life of Gandhi amply demonstrates this. So does the Seattle Longitudinal Study of Adult Intelligence, conducted by K. Warner Schaie and his colleagues (Schaie, 1990, 1994, 1996a, 1996b; Willis & Schaie, 1999).

Although this ongoing study is called longitudinal, it uses sequential methods (refer back to Chapter 2). The study began in 1956 with 500 randomly chosen participants: 25 men and 25 women in each five-year age bracket from 22 to 67. Participants took timed tests of six primary mental abilities based on those identified by Thurstone (1938). (Table 15-4 gives definitions and sample tasks for each ability.) Every seven years, the original participants were retested and new participants were added. By 1994, about 5,000 people, forming a broadly diverse socioeconomic sample from young adulthood to old age, had been tested.

The researchers found "no uniform pattern of age-related changes . . . [for] all intellectual abilities" (Schaie, 1994, p. 306). Although perceptual speed declines steadily beginning at age 25, and numerical ability begins to decline around 40, peak performance in four of the six abilities, inductive reasoning, spatial orientation, vocabulary, and verbal memory—occurs about halfway through middle adulthood (see

Table 15-4 Tests of Primary Mental Abilities Given in Seattle Longitudinal Study of Adult Intelligence

Test	Ability Measured	Task	Type of Intelligence
Vocabulary	Recognition and understanding of words	Find synonym by matching stimulus word with another word from multiple-choice list	Crystallized
Verbal memory	Retrieving words from long-term memory	Think of as many words as possible beginning with a given letter, in a set time period	Part crystallized, part fluid
Number	Performing computations	Do simple addition problems	Crystallized
Spatial orientation	Manipulating objects mentally in two-dimensional space	Select rotated examples of figure to match stimulus figure	Fluid
Inductive reasoning	Identifying patterns and inferring principles and rules for solving logical problems	Complete a letter series	Fluid
Perceptual speed	Making quick, accurate discriminations between visual stimuli	Identify matching and nonmatching images flashed on a computer screen	Fluid

Sources: Schaie, 1989; Willis & Schaie, 1999.

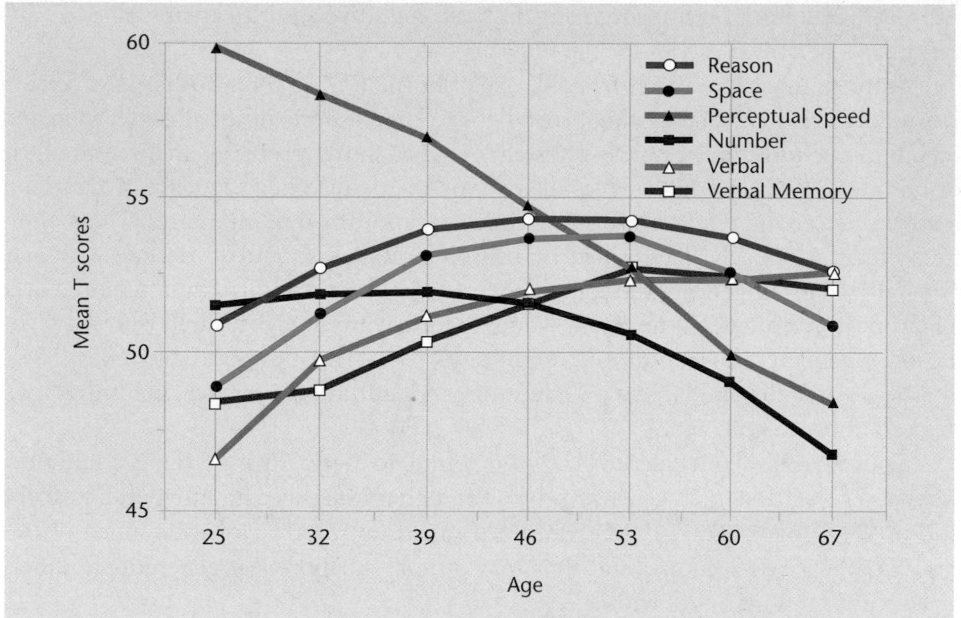

Figure 15-2
Longitudinal change in six basic mental abilities, ages 25 to 67.
(*Source:* Shaie, 1994; reprinted in Willis & Schaie, 1999, p. 237.)

Figure 15-2). In all four of these abilities, middle-aged people, especially women, score higher on average than they did at 25. Men's spatial orientation, vocabulary, and verbal memory peak in the fifties; women's, not until the early sixties. On the other hand, women's perceptual speed declines faster than men's (Willis & Schaie, 1999).

Despite wide individual differences, most participants in the Seattle study showed *no* significant reduction in most abilities until after age 60, and then not in all or even most areas. Virtually no one declined on all fronts, and many people improved in some areas (Schaie, 1994). Consistent with previous research, successive generations scored progressively higher at the same ages on reasoning, spatial orientation, and verbal abilities. However, among baby boomers currently in middle age, vocabulary showed less improvement than in previous cohorts, and numerical ability declined (Willis & Schaie, 1999; see Figure 15-3). These cohort trends suggest that U.S. society may be

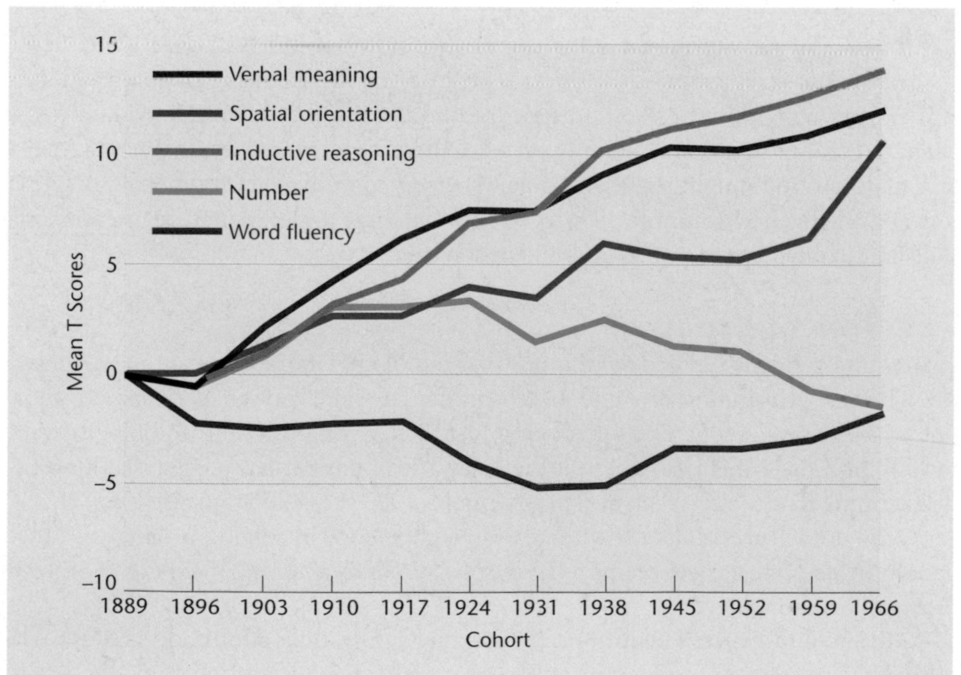

Figure 15-3
Cohort differences in scores on tests of basic mental abilities. In a group with mean birth years from 1889 to 1966, more recent cohorts scored higher on inductive reasoning, verbal meaning, and spatial orientation. Ability with numbers showed a decline.
(*Source:* Schaie, 1994.)

approaching a limit on improvements in basic cognitive abilities attributable to education and healthy lifestyles (Schaie, 1990).

Another line of research (Cattell, 1965; Horn, 1967, 1968, 1970, 1982a, 1982b; Horn & Hofer, 1992) has distinguished between two aspects of intelligence: *fluid* and *crystallized.* **Fluid intelligence** is the ability to solve novel problems that require little or no previous knowledge, such as discovering the pattern in a sequence of figures. It involves perceiving relations, forming concepts, and drawing inferences. These abilities, which are largely determined by neurological status, tend to decline with age. **Crystallized intelligence** is the ability to remember and use information acquired over a lifetime, for example, in finding a synonym for a word. It is measured by tests of vocabulary, general information, and responses to social situations and dilemmas. These abilities, which depend largely on education and cultural experience, hold their own or even improve with age.

fluid intelligence Type of intelligence, proposed by Horn and Cattell, which is applied to novel problems and is relatively independent of educational and cultural influences.

crystallized intelligence Type of intelligence, proposed by Horn and Cattell, involving the ability to remember and use learned information; it is largely dependent on education and cultural background.

Typically, fluid intelligence has been found to peak during young adulthood, whereas crystallized intelligence improves through middle age and often until near the end of life (Horn, 1982a, 1982b; Horn & Donaldson, 1980). However, much of this research was cross-sectional and thus may at least partly reflect generational differences rather than changes with age.

The Seattle study's sequential findings were somewhat different. Although fluid abilities did decline earlier than crystallized abilities, losses in such fluid abilities as inductive reasoning and spatial orientation did not set in until the midsixties, and in crystallized abilities, not until the seventies or eighties (Willis & Schaie, 1999).

One fluid ability that does peak quite early, beginning in the twenties, is perceptual speed. Middle-aged adults may make up for losses in this basic neurological ability by gains in areas affected by learning and experience—higher-order abilities necessary for independent, productive living. Improvements in these crystallized abilities may be related to career development and the exercise of family responsibilities. Advances in verbal memory during middle age are especially notable, since memory loss is a major worry of many people at midlife. Given the strong performance of most middle-agers in this area, objective evidence of substantial memory deficits in persons younger than 60 may indicate a neurological problem (Willis & Schaie, 1999).

Checkpoint

Can you . . .

- ✔ Summarize results of the Seattle Longitudinal Study concerning changes in basic mental abilities in middle age?
- ✔ Distinguish between fluid and crystallized intelligence and how they are affected by age?

The Distinctiveness of Adult Cognition

Guidepost

5. Do mature adults think differently than younger people do?

Instead of measuring the same cognitive abilities at different ages, some developmental scientists find distinctive qualities in the thinking of mature adults. Some, working within the psychometric tradition, claim that accumulated knowledge changes the way fluid intelligence operates. Others, as we noted in Chapter 13, maintain that mature thought represents a new stage of cognitive development—a "special form of intelligence" (Sinnott, 1996, p. 361), which may underlie mature interpersonal skills and contribute to practical problem solving.

The Role of Expertise

Two young resident physicians in a hospital radiology laboratory examine a chest X ray. They study an unusual white blotch on the left side. "Looks like a large tumor," one of them says finally. The other nods. Just then, a longtime staff radiologist walks by and looks over their shoulders at the X ray. "That patient has a collapsed lung and needs immediate surgery," he declares (Lesgold, 1983; Lesgold et al., 1988).

Why do mature adults show increasing competence in solving problems in their chosen fields? One answer seems to lie in specialized knowledge, or expertise—a form of crystallized intelligence.

Advances in expertise continue at least through middle adulthood and are relatively independent of general intelligence and of any declines in the brain's information-processing machinery. With experience, it has been suggested, information processing and fluid abilities become *encapsulated,* or dedicated to specific kinds of knowledge, making that knowledge easier to access, add to, and use. In other words, **encapsulation** "captures" fluid abilities for expert problem solving. Thus, although middle-aged people may take somewhat longer than younger people to process new information, in solving problems in their own fields they more than compensate with judgment developed from experience (Hoyer & Rybash, 1994; Rybash, Hoyer, & Roodin, 1986).

encapsulation In Hoyer's terminology, progressive dedication of information processing and fluid thinking to specific knowledge systems, making knowledge more readily accessible.

In one study (Ceci & Liker, 1986), researchers identified 30 middle-aged and older men who were avid horse racing fans. On the basis of skill in picking winners, the investigators divided the men into two groups: "expert" and "nonexpert." The experts used a more sophisticated method of reasoning, incorporating interpretations of much interrelated information, whereas nonexperts used simpler, less successful methods. Superior reasoning was not related to IQ; there was no significant difference in average measured intelligence between the two groups, and experts with low IQs used more complex reasoning than nonexperts with higher IQs. Similarly, on a much weightier plane, Gandhi, a man who claimed to have less than average intelligence, worked out an expert solution to the seemingly insoluble problem of empowering a powerless people to achieve independence.

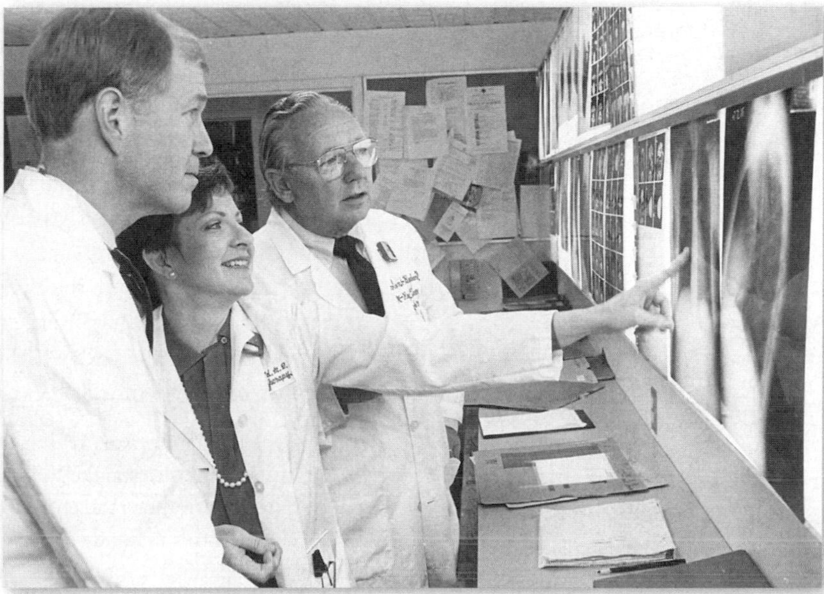

Expertise in interpreting X rays, as in many other fields, depends on accumulated, specialized knowledge, which continues to increase with age. Experts often appear to be guided by intuition and cannot explain how they arrive at conclusions.

Studies of such diverse occupations as chess players, street vendors, abacus counters, physics experts, hospitality workers, and airline counter workers illustrate how specific knowledge contributes to superior performance in a particular domain (Billet, 2001). Even *within* a field, expertise can be highly specialized; different knowledge and skills are needed to design and interpret an experiment in cognitive psychology than in social psychology (Schunn & Anderson, 1999).

What's Your View?

- If you needed surgery, would you rather go to a middle-aged doctor or one who is considerably older or younger? Why?

Experts notice different aspects of a situation than novices do, and they process information and solve problems differently. Their thinking is often more flexible and adaptable. They assimilate and interpret new knowledge more efficiently by referring to a rich, highly organized storehouse of mental representations of what they already know. They sort information on the basis of basic principles, rather than surface similarities and differences. And they are more aware of what they do *not* know (Charness & Schultetus, 1999; Goldman, Petrosino, & Cognition and Technology Group at Vanderbilt, 1999).

But cognitive performance is not the only ingredient of expertise. Problem solving occurs in a social context. Ability to make expert judgments depends on familiarity with the way things are done—with the expectations and demands of the job and the culture of the community or enterprise. Even concert pianists, who spend hours practicing in isolation, must adapt to various concert halls with different acoustics, to the musical conventions of the time and place, and to the musical tastes of their audiences (Billet, 2001).

Expert thinking often seems automatic and intuitive. Experts generally are not fully aware of the thought processes that lie behind their decisions (Charness & Schultetus, 1999; Dreyfus, 1993–1994; Rybash et al., 1986). They cannot readily explain how they arrive at a conclusion or where a nonexpert has gone wrong. (The experienced radiologist could not see why the residents would even consider diagnosing a collapsed lung as a tumor.) Such intuitive, experience-based thinking is characteristic of what has been called postformal thought.

Integrative Thought

Although not limited to any particular period of adulthood, postformal thought (introduced in Chapter 13) seems well suited to the complex tasks, multiple roles, and perplexing choices and challenges of midlife (Sinnott, 1998). An important feature of postformal thought is its *integrative* nature. Mature adults integrate logic with intuition and emotion; they integrate conflicting facts and ideas; and they integrate new information with what they already know. They interpret what they read, see, or hear in terms of its meaning for them. Instead of accepting something at face value, they filter it through their life experience and previous learning.

In one study (C. Adams, 1991), early and late adolescents and middle-aged and older adults were asked to summarize a Sufi teaching tale. In the story, a stream was unable to cross a desert until a voice told it to let the wind carry it; the stream was dubious but finally agreed and was blown across. Adolescents recalled more details of the story than adults did, but their summaries were largely limited to repeating the story line. Adults, especially women, gave summaries that were rich in interpretation, integrating what was in the text with its psychological and metaphorical meaning for them, as in this response of a 39-year-old:

> I believe what this story was trying to say was that there are times when everyone needs help and must sometimes make changes to reach their goals. Some people may resist change for a long time until they realize that certain things are beyond their control and they need assistance. When this is finally achieved and they can accept help and trust from someone, they can master things even as large as a desert. (p. 333)

Society benefits from this integrative feature of adult thought. Generally it is mature adults who, like Gandhi, become moral and spiritual leaders (see Box 15-2) and who translate their knowledge about the human condition into inspirational stories to which younger generations can turn for guidance. Postformal thought also may help in solving practical problems.

Practical Problem Solving

Does deciding what to do about a flooded basement take the same kind of intelligence as playing word games? Is the ability to solve practical problems affected by age? Much research on practical problem solving has *not* found the declines sometimes seen in measures of fluid intelligence, and some research has found marked improvement, at least through middle age (Berg & Klaczynski, 1996; Sternberg, Grigorenko, & Oh, 2001).

In a number of studies, the quality of practical decisions (such as what car to buy, what kind of treatment to get for breast cancer, how much money to put away in a pension plan, or how to compare insurance policies) bore only a modest relationship, if any, to performance on tasks like those on intelligence tests (M. M. S. Johnson, Schmitt, & Everard, 1994; Meyer, Russo, & Talbot, 1995) and, often, no relationship to age (Capon, Kuhn, & Carretero, 1989; M. M. S. Johnson, 1990; Meyer et al., 1995; Walsh & Hershey, 1993). In other studies, problem solving improved with age (Cornelius & Caspi, 1987; Perlmutter, Kaplan, & Nyquist, 1990).

In one study (Denney & Palmer, 1981), 84 adults ages 20 to 79 were given two kinds of problems. One kind was like the game Twenty Questions. Participants were shown pictures of common objects and were told to figure out which one the examiner was thinking of, by asking questions that could be answered "yes" or "no." The older the participants were, the worse they did on this part of the test. The second kind of

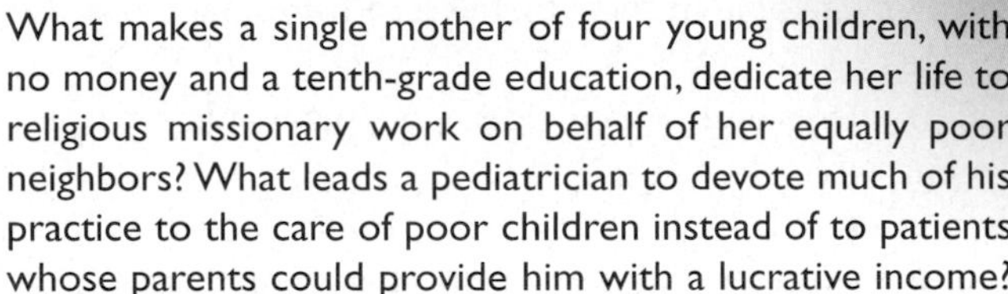

Digging Deeper

BOX 15–2

Moral Leadership in Middle and Late Adulthood

What makes a single mother of four young children, with no money and a tenth-grade education, dedicate her life to religious missionary work on behalf of her equally poor neighbors? What leads a pediatrician to devote much of his practice to the care of poor children instead of to patients whose parents could provide him with a lucrative income?

In the mid-1980s, two psychologists, Anne Colby and William Damon, sought answers to questions like these. They embarked on a two-year search for people who showed unusual moral excellence in their day-to-day lives. The researchers eventually identified 23 "moral exemplars," interviewed them in depth, and studied how they had become moral leaders (Colby & Damon, 1992).

To find moral exemplars, Colby and Damon worked with a panel of 22 "expert nominators," people who in their professional lives regularly think about moral ideas: philosophers, historians, religious thinkers, and so forth. The researchers drew up five criteria: sustained commitment to principles that show respect for humanity; behavior consistent with one's ideals; willingness to risk self-interest; inspiring others to moral action; and humility, or lack of concern for one's ego.

The chosen exemplars varied widely in age, education, occupation, and ethnicity. There were 10 men and 13 women, ages 35 to 86, of white, African American, and Hispanic backgrounds. Education ranged from eighth grade up through M.D.s, Ph.D.s, and law degrees; and occupations included religious callings, business, teaching, and social leadership. Areas of concern involved poverty, civil rights, education, ethics, the environment, peace, and religious freedom.

The research yielded a number of surprises, not least of which was this group's showing on Kohlberg's classic measure of moral judgment. Each exemplar was asked about "Heinz's dilemma" (refer back to Chapter 11) and about a follow-up question: how the man should be punished if he steals the drug. Of 22 exemplars (one response was not scorable), only half scored at the postconventional level; the other half scored at the conventional level. The major difference between the two groups was level of education: those with college and advanced degrees were much more likely to score at the higher level, and no one with only a high school diploma scored above the conventional level. Clearly, it is not necessary to score at Kohlberg's highest stages to live an exemplary moral life.

How does a person become morally committed? The 23 moral exemplars did not develop in isolation, but responded to social influences. Some of these influences, such as those of parents, were important from childhood on. Many other influences became significant in later years, helping these people evaluate their capacities, form moral goals, and develop strategies to achieve them.

These moral exemplars had a lifelong commitment to change: they focused their energy on changing society and people's lives for the better. But they remained stable in their moral commitments. At the same time, they kept growing throughout life, remained open to new ideas, and continued to learn from others.

The processes responsible for stability in moral commitments were gradual, taking many years to build up. They were also collaborative: leaders took advice from supporters, and people noted for independent judgment drew heavily on feedback from those close to them—both those people who shared their goals and those who had different perspectives.

Along with their enduring moral commitments, certain personality characteristics seemed to remain with the moral exemplars throughout middle and late adulthood: enjoyment of life, ability to make the best of a bad situation, solidarity with others, absorption in work, a sense of humor, and humility. They tended to believe that change was possible, and this optimism helped them battle what often seemed like overwhelming odds and to persist in the face of defeat.

While their actions often meant risk and hardship, these people did not see themselves as courageous. Nor did they agonize over decisions. Since their personal and moral goals coincided, they just did what they believed needed to be done, not calculating personal consequences to themselves or their families and not feeling that they were sacrificing or martyring themselves.

Of course, there is no "blueprint" for creating a moral giant, just as it does not seem possible to write directions to produce a genius in any field. What studying the lives of such people can bring is the knowledge that ordinary people can rise to greatness and that openness to change and new ideas can persist throughout adulthood.

What's Your View?

Think of someone you would consider a moral exemplar. How do that person's qualities compare to those found in this study?

Check It Out:

OLC

For more information on this topic, go to http://www.mhhe.com/papaliah9.

problem involved situations like the following: *Your basement is flooding,* or *You are stranded in a car during a blizzard,* or *Your 8-year-old child is $1\frac{1}{2}$ hours late coming home from school.* High scores were given for responses that showed self-reliance and recognition of a number of possible causes and solutions. According to these criteria, the best practical problem solvers were people in their forties and fifties, who based their answers on everyday experience.

A follow-up study posed problems with which elderly people would be especially familiar (concerning retirement, widowhood, and ill health), yet people in their forties still came up with better solutions (Denney & Pearce, 1989). However, in other studies in which problems were real rather than hypothetical and were brought up by the participants themselves, and in which solutions were rated by quality rather than quantity, practical problem-solving ability did *not* seem to decline after middle age (Camp, Doherty, Moody-Thomas, & Denney, 1989; Cornelius & Caspi, 1987).

What explains these inconsistencies? As we have seen, there are differences in the kinds of problems various researchers study, in the relevance of these problems to real life, and in the criteria used to rate the solutions. Also, individual differences—for example, in educational level—may affect how people perceive and solve problems (Berg & Klaczynski, 1996; Blanchard-Fields, Chen, & Norris, 1997).

Some studies focus on *instrumental* problems, or activities of daily living, such as reading a map. These abilities are highly related to fluid intelligence and show age-related decline (see Chapter 17). Declines may occur sooner in people with especially slow perceptual speed (Willis & Schaie, 1999; Willis et al., 1998).

Checkpoint

Can you . . .

- ✔ Discuss the relationship between expertise, knowledge, and intelligence?
- ✔ Give an example of integrative thinking?
- ✔ Identify two types of practical problem solving, and tell how they are affected by age?

By contrast, studies such as those just described deal mainly with *social* problems. These studies suggest that people of different ages interpret problems differently and see different kinds of solutions as effective. When problems are relevant to older adults' lives and feelings, the participants show more complex thought (Berg & Klaczynski, 1996) On this type of problem, both middle-aged and older adults tend to do better than younger ones; they have more extensive and varied repertoires of strategies to apply to different situations (Blanchard-Fields et al., 1997).

One thing seems clear: middle-aged people tend to be effective practical problem solvers. If the function of intelligence is to deal with real-life problems, as Gandhi did, the strengths of mature thought in midlife are plain.

Creativity

Guidepost

6. What accounts for creative achievement, and how does it change with age?

At about age 40, Frank Lloyd Wright designed Robie House in Chicago, Agnes deMille choreographed the Broadway musical *Carousel,* and Louis Pasteur developed the germ theory of disease. Charles Darwin was 50 when he presented his theory of evolution. Toni Morrison won the Pulitzer Prize for *Beloved,* a novel she wrote at about 55. But creativity is not limited to the Darwins and deMilles; we can see it in an inventor who comes up with a better mousetrap, or a promoter who finds an innovative way to sell it.

Creativity begins with talent, but talent is not enough. Children may show *creative potential;* but in adults, what counts is *creative performance:* what, and how much, a creative mind produces (Sternberg & Lubart, 1995). Creative performance is the product of a web of biological, personal, social, and cultural forces. It emerges from the dynamic interaction among the creator, the rules and techniques of the domain, and the colleagues who work in that domain (Gardner, 1986, 1988; Simonton, 2000b).

Exceptional talents are less born than made—they require systematic training and practice (Simonton, 2000b). Extraordinary creative achievement, according to one analysis (Keegan, 1996), results from deep, highly organized knowledge of a subject;

intrinsic motivation to work hard for the sake of the work, not for external rewards; and a strong emotional attachment to the work, which spurs the creator to persevere in the face of obstacles. What carries an Einstein "over the threshold from competent but ordinary thinker to extraordinary and creative thinker," says Keegan (p. 63), is the acquisition of expert knowledge. A person must first be thoroughly grounded in a field before she or he can see its limitations, envision radical departures, and develop a new and unique point of view.

Creativity begins with talent, but talent is not enough. The author Toni Morrison, 1993 winner of the Nobel Prize in Literature, worked long, hard hours throughout her prolific career. Her achievements are examples of the creative productivity possible in middle age. (Ulf Andersen/Gamma-Liaison)

However, the relationship between creativity and expertise is complex. In a study of the careers of 59 classical composers, creativity did not follow a straight upward course. Later compositions often were less aesthetically successful than earlier ones, and the amount of time spent in general musical training and composition was more predictive of aesthetic success in a particular genre, such as composing operas, than was the amount of time spent working in that genre. These findings suggest that overtraining in a particular genre may hamper creativity, and that versatility, not just expertise, may count (Simonton, 2000a).

Highly creative people are self-starters (Torrance, 1988) and risk takers; they tend to be independent, nonconformist, unconventional, and flexible, and they are open to new ideas and experiences (Simonton, 2000b). Their thinking processes are often unconscious, leading to sudden moments of illumination (Torrance, 1988). Like Gandhi, they look at a problem more deeply than other people do and come up with solutions that do not occur to others (Sternberg & Horvath, 1998).

Creativity develops over a lifetime in a social context, and not necessarily in nurturing environments. Instead, it seems to emerge from diverse experiences that weaken conventional constraints and from challenging experiences that strengthen the ability to persevere and overcome obstacles. The political and cultural environment can affect the flowering or inhibiting of creativity—as occurred, for example, in the former Soviet Union (Simonton, 2000b).

Creativity and Intelligence

General intelligence, as measured by standard IQ tests, has little relationship to creative performance (Simonton, 2000b). However, the three *aspects* of intelligence identified by Sternberg (see Chapters 9 and 13) may play a role (Sternberg & Lubart, 1995).

The *insightful* component helps to define a problem or to see it in a new light. Creative people show special insight in three ways: (1) they pick out information relevant to the problem—often information that no one else thought to consider; (2) they "put two and two together," seeing relationships between apparently unrelated pieces of information; and (3) they see analogies between a new problem and one they have already encountered. Again, these abilities become more efficient with experience and knowledge (Sternberg & Horvath, 1998).

The *analytic* component of intelligence can evaluate an idea and decide whether it is worth pursuing. James D. Watson, a molecular biologist who won the Nobel Prize for the discovery of the structure of DNA, was described by one of his graduate students at Harvard University as having "an uncanny instinct for the important problem, the thing that leads to big-time results. He seems to . . . pluck it out of thin air" (Edson, 1968, pp. 29–31).

The *practical* aspect of intelligence comes into play in "selling" an idea—getting it accepted. Thomas Edison held more than 1,000 patents for his inventions, created

What's Your View?

- Think of an adult you know who is a creative achiever. To what combination of personal qualities and environmental forces would you attribute her or his creative performance?

several companies to market them, and had a knack for getting his name and picture in the newspapers. This practical aspect may well be strongest in middle age.

Creativity and Age

Is there a relationship between creative performance and age? On psychometric tests of divergent thinking (refer back to Chapter 9), age differences consistently appear. Whether data are cross-sectional or longitudinal, scores peak, on average, around the late thirties. A similar age curve emerges when creativity is measured by variations in output (number of publications, paintings, or compositions). A person in the last decade of a creative career typically produces only about half as much as during the late thirties or early forties, though somewhat more than in the twenties (Simonton, 1990).

However, the age curve varies depending on the field. Poets, mathematicians, and theoretical physicists tend to be most prolific in their late twenties or early thirties. Research psychologists reach a peak around age 40, followed by a moderate decline. Novelists, historians, and philosophers become increasingly productive through their late forties or fifties and then level off. These patterns hold true across cultures and historical periods (Dixon & Hultsch, 1999; Simonton, 1990).

Of course, not everything a creator produces is equally notable; even a Picasso is bound to produce some minor material. The *quality ratio*—the proportion of major works to total output—bears no relationship to age. The periods in which a person creates the largest number of memorable works also tend to be the ones in which that same person produces the largest number of forgettable ones (Simonton, 1998). Thus, the likelihood that a *particular* work will be a masterpiece has nothing to do with age. Some of the composer Irving Berlin's top song hits were written in his fifties, sixties, seventies, and eighties; and they were no more or less likely to prove immortal than songs he wrote in his early twenties.

Sometimes losses in productivity are offset by gains in quality. Age-related analyses of themes of ancient Greek and Shakespearean plays show a shift from youthful preoccupation with love and romance to more spiritual concerns (Simonton, 1983, 1986). And a study of the "swan songs" of 172 composers found that their last works—usually fairly short and melodically simple—were among their richest, most important, and most successful (Simonton, 1989).

Checkpoint

Can you . . .

- ✔ Discuss prerequisites for creative achievement?
- ✔ Tell how Sternberg's three aspects of intelligence apply to creative performance?
- ✔ Summarize the relationship between creative performance and age?

Work and Education: Are Age-Based Roles Obsolete?

age-differentiated Life structure in which primary roles—learning, working, and leisure—are based on age; typical in industrialized societies.

The traditional life structure in industrialized societies is **age-differentiated:** roles are based on age (as in the left side of Figure 15-4). Young people are students; young and middle-aged adults are workers; older adults organize their lives around retirement and leisure. Yet, as the gerontologist Matilda White Riley (1994) has observed:

> . . . these structures fail to accommodate many of the changes in people's lives. After all, does it make sense to spend nearly one-third of adult lifetime in retirement? Or to crowd most work into the harried middle years? Or to label as "too old" those as young as 55 who want to work? Does it make sense to assume that . . . physically capable older people—an estimated 40 million of them in the next century—should expect greater support from society than they contribute to society? . . . Surely, something will have to change! (p. 445)

According to Riley, age-differentiated roles are a holdover from a time when life was shorter and social institutions less diverse. By devoting themselves to one aspect of life at a time, people do not enjoy each period as much as they might and may not prepare adequately for the next phase. By concentrating on work, adults may forget how to play; then, when they retire, they may not know what to do with a sudden

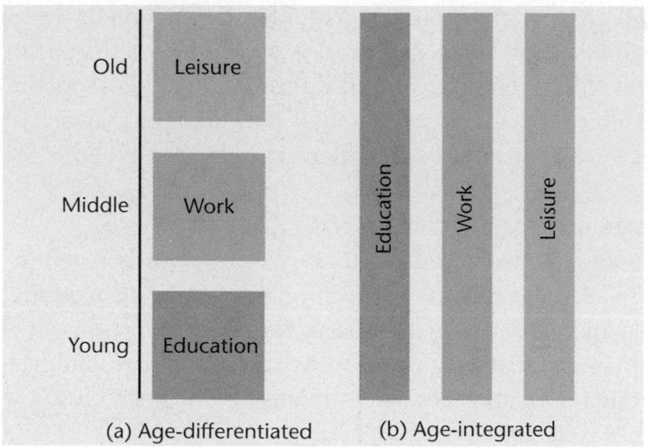

Figure 15-4
Contrasting social structures. (*a*) Traditional age-differentiated structure, typical of industrialized societies. Education, work, and leisure roles are largely "assigned" to different phases of life. (*b*) Age-integrated structure, which would spread all three kinds of roles throughout the adult life span and help break down social barriers between generations.
(*Source:* M. W. Riley, 1994, p. 445.)

abundance of leisure time. Increasing numbers of older adults (like Gandhi in his later years) are able to contribute to society, but opportunities to use and reward their abilities are inadequate.

In an **age-integrated** society (as in the right side of Figure 15-4), all kinds of roles—learning, working, and playing—would be open to adults of all ages (Riley, 1994). They could intersperse periods of education, work, and leisure throughout the life span. Things seem to be moving in that direction. College students take work-study programs or "stop out" for a while before resuming their education. Mature adults take evening classes or take time off work to pursue a special interest. A person may have several careers in succession, each requiring additional education or training. People retire earlier or later than in the past, or not at all. Retirees devote time to study or to a new line of work.

age-integrated Life structure in which primary roles—learning, working, and leisure—are open to adults of all ages and can be interspersed throughout the life span.

Much of the existing research on education, work, leisure, and retirement reflects the old, age-differentiated model of social roles and the cohorts whose lives it describes. As "age integration" emerges, future cohorts may have very different experiences and attitudes. With that reservation in mind, let's look at work and education in middle adulthood.

Checkpoint

Can you . . .

- ✔ Explain how an age-integrated society would differ from an age-differentiated society, and give examples?

Occupational Patterns and Paths

In a society undergoing dramatic change, career decisions are often open-ended. A theory that seeks to capture the dynamic character of vocational development is that of Eli Ginzberg (1972). After examining the occupational histories of women and men from a wide variety of backgrounds, Ginzberg concluded that career paths fall into one of two patterns: *stable* or *shifting*.

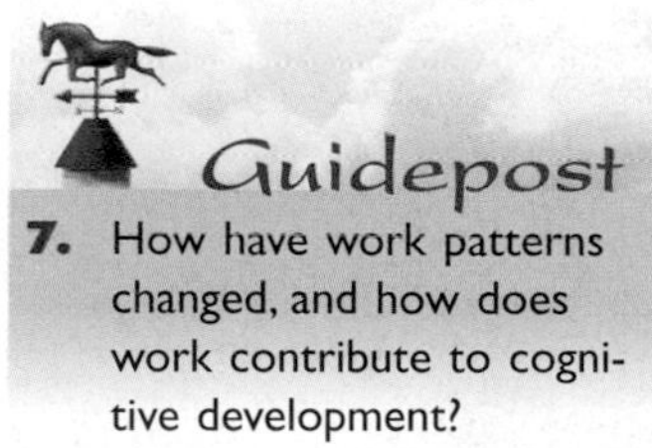

7. How have work patterns changed, and how does work contribute to cognitive development?

People with *stable* career patterns stay with a single vocation and, by midlife, often reach positions of power and responsibility. Middle-aged men with stable careers tend to be either "workaholics" or "mellowed" (Tamir, 1989). Workaholics work at a frenzied pace, either in a last-ditch effort to reach financial security before they retire or because they find it hard to relinquish authority. "Mellowed" people have come to terms with their level of achievement, even if they have not gone as far as they had hoped. The best adjusted among them have a sense of relaxation rather than failure. Although they want to do challenging work, they do not pin their emotional well-being on their jobs as they used to (Bray & Howard, 1983).

By contrast, people who follow the *shifting* pattern—rather than settle for their initial occupational choice—try to achieve a better match between what they can do, what they want and expect from their work, and what they are getting out of it. This reevaluation can lead to career change, as it did with Gandhi when he gave up a busy urban law practice for collective farming to prepare for moral and political leadership.

People may shift careers anytime during adulthood, but middle age, with its altered family responsibilities and financial needs, is a typical time to do it. Because fewer middle-aged and older women have worked throughout adulthood, they are less likely than men to exhibit the stable pattern; and, if they do, they may reach the traditional stages of career development later than men typically do (Avolio & Sosik, 1999).

Work versus Early Retirement

In the United States, 80 percent of 40- to 59-year-olds work. At 60 to 69, 61 percent work full time and 36 percent part time (National Academy on an Aging Society, 2000). Whereas 50-year-olds tend to work primarily for financial reasons, at 60 intrinsic values such as enjoyment of work, wanting to remain productive, and feeling valued and respected become more important determinants of whether a person will continue to work (Sterns & Huyck, 2001).

Public and private pension programs and other inducements to make way for younger workers, such as the availability of social security benefits (at a reduced level) at age 62, have contributed to a trend toward early retirement in the United States, as in many industrialized countries (Kinsella & Gist, 1995). However, many of today's middle-aged and older workers—caught between inadequate savings or pensions and a strained social security system, or simply unwilling to give up the stimulation of work—are choosing *not* to retire or to try a new line of work. Thus retirement is "increasingly a transition *within,* rather than *from* midlife" (Kim & Moen, 2001, p. 488). Furthermore, the transition has become fuzzier, "involving multiple transitions out of and into paid and unpaid 'work'" (p. 489).

The main predictors of retirement age are health, pension eligibility, and financial circumstances. Marital status also can make a difference, as decisions about timing of each spouse's retirement have to be negotiated by the couple (Moen, Kim, & Hofmeister, 2001). Married men, those who are members of younger cohorts, those with lower socioeconomic status, those with traditional career paths, those who are dissatisfied with their jobs, and those who have planned for retirement are most likely to retire early (Kim & Moen, 2001).

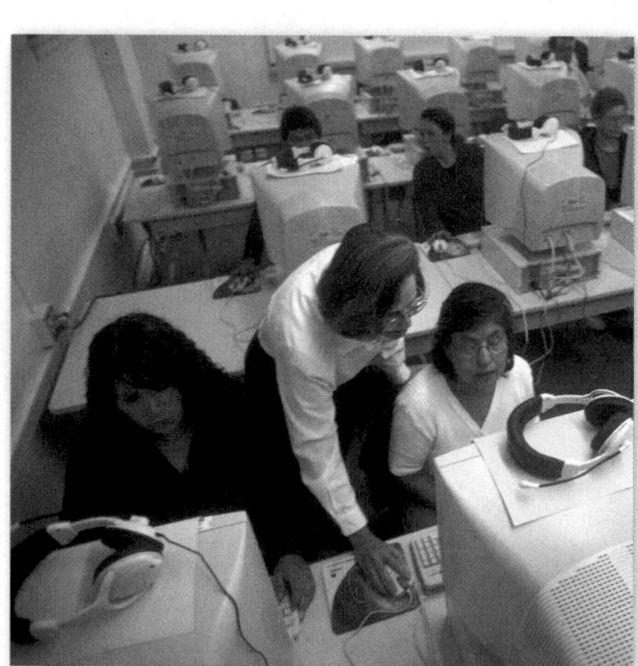

These adults improving their computer skills are among the 45 percent of middle-aged people in the United States who participate in continuing education. Most mature adults who take part-time classes do so for job-related reasons, and they tend to be more motivated than younger students.

Work and Cognitive Development

"Use it or lose it" applies to the mind as well as the body. Work can influence future cognitive functioning.

As we mentioned in Chapter 13, some research suggests that flexible thinkers tend to obtain substantively complex work—work requiring thought and independent judgment. This kind of work, in turn, stimulates more flexible thinking; and flexible thinking increases the ability to do complex work (Kohn, 1980). Thus, people who are deeply engaged in complex work tend to show stronger cognitive performance in comparison to their peers as they age (Avolio & Sosik, 1999; Kohn & Schooler, 1983; Schaie, 1984; Schooler, 1984, 1990). Indeed, it has been estimated that as much as one-third of the individual variance in changes in cognitive ability with age may be attributable to such factors as education, occupation, and socioeconomic status (Schaie, 1990). If work could be made more meaningful and challenging, more adults might retain or improve their cognitive abilities (Avolio & Sosik, 1999).

This seems to be happening already. The gains in most cognitive abilities found in recent middle-aged and older cohorts in the Seattle Longitudinal Study may well reflect workplace changes that emphasize self-managed, multifunctional teams and put a premium on adaptability, initiative, and decentralized decision making (Avolio & Sosik, 1999). Unfortunately, older workers are less likely than younger workers to be offered, or to volunteer for, training, education, and challenging job assignments, in the mistaken belief that older people cannot handle such opportunities. Yet the Seattle study found that declines in cognitive ability generally do not occur until very late in life, well after the working years. Indeed, work performance shows greater variability *within* age groups than between them (Avolio & Sosik, 1999).

Adults can actively affect their future cognitive development by the occupational choices they make. Those who constantly seek more stimulating opportunities are likely to remain mentally sharp (Avolio & Sosik, 1999).

Checkpoint

Can you . . .

- ✔ Summarize Ginzberg's theory of career development?
- ✔ Describe societal changes in career paths, and discuss trends in early retirement?
- ✔ Explain how work can affect cognitive functioning?

The Mature Learner

At 41, Margaret had worked in the travel department of a large international corporation for nearly twenty years when she lost her job as a result of downsizing and changes in the travel business. A married mother of three, she had been taking evening and weekend classes for almost ten years toward an undergraduate degree. After losing her job, Margaret made up her mind to gain more control of her work situation. She enrolled as a full-time student and earned her degree in less than two years.

Guidepost

8. What is the value of education for mature learners?

Changes in the workplace often entail a need for more training or education. Expanding technology and shifting job markets require a life-span approach to learning. For many adults, formal learning is a way to develop their cognitive potential and to keep up with the changing world of work. In 1999, close to one-fifth of college and university students and about one-third of those enrolled part time were 35 or older (Snyder & Hoffman, 2002).

To accommodate the practical needs of students of nontraditional age, some colleges grant credit for life experience and previous learning. They also offer part-time matriculation, Saturday and night classes, independent study, child care, financial aid, free or reduced-tuition courses, and distance learning via computers or closed-circuit broadcasts (refer back to Chapter 13).

What's Your View?

- From what you have seen, do students of nontraditional age seem to do better or worse in college than younger students? How would you explain your observation?

In 1999, about 45 percent of middle-aged people participated in continuing, or adult, education, most of them for job-related reasons or for personal development (Snyder & Hoffman, 2001). Some adults seek training to update their knowledge and skills. Some train for new occupations. Some want to move up the career ladder or to go into business for themselves. Some women who have devoted their young adult years to homemaking and parenting are taking the first steps toward reentering the job market. People close to retirement often want to expand their minds and skills to make more productive and interesting use of leisure. Some adults simply enjoy learning and want to keep doing it throughout life.

Unfortunately, some learning institutions are not structured to meet mature adults' educational and psychological needs or to take advantage of their cognitive strengths. Adult learners have their own motives, goals, developmental tasks, and experiences. They come with their own expertise and, often, with postformal thinking skills, and they need knowledge they can apply to specific problems. Cooperative study built around self-generated problems or projects is most appropriate to a mature adult (Sinnott, 1998).

Checkpoint

Can you . . .

- ✔ Give reasons why mature adults return to the classroom, and tell some ways in which educational institutions attempt to meet their needs?

Refocus

- How does Gandhi's story exemplify the significance of middle adulthood?
- How would you expect the regimen Gandhi adopted when he moved to the farm outside Durban to have influenced his health?
- In what ways do Gandhi's decisions and actions seem to show fluid and crystallized intelligence? Postformal thought? Practical problem solving? Creativity?
- Does Gandhi seem to fit the profile of the moral exemplars described in Box 15-2?
- Why do you think Gandhi undertook such major life changes in middle age?

Research about education and work—as well as about problem solving, creativity, and moral choices—shows that the mind continues to develop during adulthood. Such research also illustrates the links between the cognitive side of development and its social and emotional aspects, to which we turn again in Chapter 16.

SUMMARY AND KEY TERMS

Middle Age: A Cultural Construct

Guidepost 1. What are the distinguishing features of middle age?

- The concept of middle age is socially constructed. It came into use as an increasing life span led to new roles at midlife.
- Middle adulthood is a time of both gains and losses.
- The span of middle adulthood can be defined chronologically, contextually, or biologically.
- Most middle-aged people are in good physical, cognitive, and emotional condition. They have heavy responsibilities and multiple roles and feel competent to handle them.
- Middle age is a time for taking stock and making decisions about the remaining years.

PHYSICAL DEVELOPMENT

Physical Changes

Guidepost 2. What physical changes generally occur during the middle years, and what is their psychological impact?

- Although some physiological changes result from aging and genetic makeup, behavior and lifestyle can affect their timing and extent.
- Most middle-aged adults compensate well for gradual, minor declines in sensory and psychomotor abilities, including such age-related conditions as presbyopia and presbycusis, increases in myopia, and loss of endurance due to slowing of basal metabolism. Losses in bone density and vital capacity are common.
- Menopause occurs, on average, at about age 50 or 51, following the physiological changes of perimenopause. Attitudes toward menopause, and symptoms experienced, may depend on personal characteristics, past experiences, and cultural attitudes.
- Although men can continue to father children until late in life, many middle-aged men experience a decline in fertility and in frequency of orgasm.
- Sexual activity generally diminishes slightly and gradually, and the quality of sexual relations may improve.
- Among women, sexual dysfunction decreases with age; in men, it is just the opposite. A large proportion of middle-aged men experience erectile dysfunction. Sexual dysfunction can have physical causes but also may be related to health, lifestyle, and emotional well-being.
- The "double standard of aging" causes women to seem less desirable as they lose their youthful appearance. For both men and women, anxiety about getting older is heightened in a society that places a premium on youth.

presbyopia *(530)*
myopia *(530)*
presbycusis *(530)*
basal metabolism *(531)*
vital capacity *(532)*
menopause *(532)*
perimenopause *(532)*
sexual dysfunction *(536)*
erectile dysfunction *(536)*

Health

Guidepost 3. What factors affect health at midlife?

- Most middle-aged people are healthy and have no functional limitations.
- Diet, exercise, alcohol use, and smoking affect present and future health. Preventive care is important.
- Hypertension is a major health problem beginning in midlife. AIDS tends to be more severe in older people because of weakened immune functioning.

- Leading causes of death in middle age are cancer and heart disease. Diabetes also is a major cause of death.
- Low income is associated with poorer health, in part because of lack of insurance.
- Racial and ethnic disparities in health have decreased but still exist.
- Postmenopausal women become more susceptible to heart disease and bone loss leading to osteoporosis. Chances of developing breast cancer also increase with age, and routine mammography is recommended for women beginning at age 40.
- Nearly one in three U.S. women has a hysterectomy by age 60, usually because of uterine fibroids, abnormal uterine bleeding, or endometriosis. Many experts believe this procedure is overused.
- Hormone replacement therapy (HRT) is often prescribed for symptoms related to menopause, but there is mounting evidence that its risks may outweigh the benefits for long-term use. Alternative treatments are being tested.
- Personality and negative emotionality can affect health.
- Stress is related to a variety of physical and psychological problems. An accumulation of minor, everyday stressors can be more harmful than major life changes. Everyday hassles tend to decrease with age, perhaps because people learn strategies for managing stress.
- Causes of occupational stress include work overload, interpersonal conflict, sexual harassment, a combination of high pressure and low control, and inability to "unwind." Continual stress may lead to burnout.
- Unemployment creates psychological as well as financial stress. Physical and psychological effects may depend on coping resources.

hypertension *(538)*

osteoporosis *(541)*

mammography *(542)*

hysterectomy *(543)*

hormone replacement therapy (HRT) *(543)*

stressors *(545)*

burnout *(548)*

COGNITIVE DEVELOPMENT

Measuring Cognitive Abilities in Middle Age

Guidepost **4.** What cognitive gains and losses occur during middle age?

- The Seattle Longitudinal Study found that most basic mental abilities peak during middle age. Fluid intelligence declines earlier than crystallized intelligence.

fluid intelligence *(552)*

crystallized intelligence *(552)*

The Distinctiveness of Adult Cognition

Guidepost **5.** Do mature adults think differently than younger people do?

- Some theorists propose that cognition takes distinctive forms at midlife. Advances in expertise, or specialized knowledge, have been attributed to encapsulation of fluid abilities within a person's chosen field. Expertise also depends on the social context.
- Postformal thought seems especially useful in situations calling for integrative thinking.
- The ability to solve practical problems is strong, and may peak, at midlife.

encapsulation *(553)*

Creativity

Guidepost **6.** What accounts for creative achievement, and how does it change with age?

- Creative performance depends on personal attributes and environmental forces, as well as cognitive abilities.
- Creativity is not strongly related to intelligence. However, according to Sternberg, the insightful, analytic, and practical aspects of intelligence play a part in creative performance.
- An age-related decline appears in both psychometric tests of divergent thinking and actual creative output, but peak ages for output vary by occupation. Losses in productivity with age may be offset by gains in quality.

Work and Education: Are Age-Based Roles Obsolete?

Guidepost **7.** How have work patterns changed, and how does work contribute to cognitive development?

- A shift from age-differentiated to age-integrated roles appears to be occurring in response to longer life and social change.
- Ginzberg's theory, based on recent changes in work life, describes two basic career paths: stability and change.
- Complex work may improve cognitive flexibility. Changes in the workplace may make work more meaningful and cognitively challenging for many people.

age-differentiated *(558)*

age-integrated *(559)*

Guidepost **8.** What is the value of education for mature learners?

- Many adults go to college at a nontraditional age or participate in continuing education. Adults go to school chiefly to improve work-related skills and knowledge or to prepare for a change of career.
- Mature adults have special educational needs and strengths.

Chapter 16

Psychosocial Development in Middle Adulthood

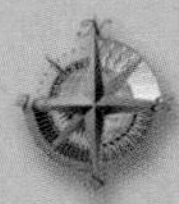

To accept all experience as raw material out of which the human spirits distill meanings and values is a part of the meaning of maturity.

—Howard Thurman, *Meditations of the Heart,* 1953

Focus: Madeleine Albright, Top-Ranking Diplomat

Madeleine Albright

On January 23, 1997, four months before her sixtieth birthday, Madeleine Korbel Albright* (b. 1937) was sworn in as secretary of state, the highest rank ever achieved by a woman in the U.S. government. It was a heady moment for a woman who had arrived at age 11 with her family as refugees from Communist Czechoslovakia.

Albright's life is the story of "someone who has again and again reinvented herself" (Heilbrunn, 1998, p. 12). First there was the journey from her childhood as the daughter of a diplomat in war-torn Europe to her adolescence as a scholarship student at a private school in Denver. Then came a scholarship to Wellesley College; and, three days after commencement, her "Cinderella marriage" to Joseph Medill Patterson Albright, heir to a prominent publishing family, followed by the birth of twin girls. Thirteen years and a third daughter later, she obtained a Ph.D. in political science at Columbia University.

As the women's movement gathered steam, President Jimmy Carter's national security adviser, Zbigniew Brzezinski, tapped Albright, his former student at Columbia, as congressional liaison for the National Security Council. Less than a year after the Carter presidency and Albright's White House stint ended, her husband of twenty-three years announced that he was in love with a younger woman. The divorce was a turning point in her life. At 45, she was a single mother of three (one still in high school), "aching to chart a new path" (Blackman, 1998, p. 187). She joined the faculty of Georgetown University's School of Foreign Service and became a "regular" on public television talk shows. The woman whom colleagues had seen as shy and self-effacing, whose self-esteem had been shattered by divorce, developed confidence and self-assurance as she honed her crisp, succinct speaking style.

Albright broke into the national limelight as foreign policy adviser to vice-presidential candidate Geraldine Ferraro in 1984 and to presidential candidate Michael Dukakis in 1988. It was in the Dukakis campaign that Albright, then

*Sources of biographical material about Madeleine Albright were Blackman (1998) and Blood (1997).

OUTLINE

over 50, met Bill Clinton, who, in 1992, as president-elect, appointed her ambassador to the United Nations and four years later chose her to head the State Department.

As her middle years came to an end, Albright's life was full and fulfilling. Her bonds with her married daughters, her grandchildren, and the many friends who have supported her throughout her career were strong.

One more twist in the "reinvention" of Madeleine Albright came as she was settling in at the State Department. Press reports revealed that Albright, who was raised Catholic, had been born Jewish and that several close relatives had perished in the Holocaust. Her now-deceased parents had never told her of her Jewish heritage. At 59, she had to come to a new understanding of her identity and her family history—an understanding brought home when she walked through the Old Jewish Cemetery in Prague and came face-to-face with the synagogue wall on which the names of her grandparents were inscribed along with nearly eighty thousand other victims of Naziism. As she stood there, silent, she thought about her parents and the "excruciating decision" they had made to cut off their roots by converting to Catholicism in order to save their children from "certain death" (Blackman, 1998, p. 293).

"I'm very proud of what my parents did for me and my brother and sister," Albright told the press. "I was very close to them. . . . I have always been very proud of my heritage. And as I find out more about it, I am even more proud" (Blood, 1997, p. 226).

Although the specifics of Madeleine Albright's story are unusual, its main thrust is similar to the adult experience of many other women her age: marriage and motherhood, followed by a midlife career, sometimes a midlife divorce, and a blossoming of possibilities that comes with the emptying of the nest.

One of Albright's greatest assets is adaptability. Again and again, she has adjusted to new environments, learned new languages, mastered new challenges, and reshaped her identity. As she did, she grew in personal strength. Much of that mastery and growth occurred during middle age. Her divorce represented a sharp break with her past: a trauma that forced her to rethink who she was and what she wanted to do.

Midlife is a special time. Middle-aged people are not only in the middle of the adult life span, in a position to look back and ahead in their own lives; they also bridge older and younger generations. Very often, they are the ones who hold families together and, like Madeleine Albright, make societal institutions and enterprises work. Much can happen during the twenty-five-year span we call *middle adulthood;* and these experiences affect the way people look, feel, and act as they enter old age.

In this chapter we look at theoretical perspectives and research on psychosocial issues and themes at midlife. We then focus on intimate relationships, which shape the occurrence and timing of life events. As we examine marriage and divorce, gay and lesbian relationships, and friendship, as well as relationships with maturing children, aging parents, siblings, and grandchildren, we see how richly textured are these middle years.

After you have read and studied this chapter, you should be able to answer each of the following Guidepost questions. Look for them again in the margins, where they point to important concepts throughout the chapter. To check your understanding of these Guideposts, review the end-of-chapter summary. Checkpoints located at periodic spots throughout the chapter will help you verify your understanding of what you have read.

Guideposts for Study

1. How do developmental scientists approach the study of psychosocial development in middle adulthood?
2. What do classic theorists have to say about psychosocial change in middle age?
3. What issues concerning the self come to the fore during middle adulthood?
4. What role do social relationships play in the lives of middle-aged people?
5. Do marriages typically become happier or unhappier during the middle years?
6. How common is divorce at this time of life?
7. How do midlife gay and lesbian relationships compare with heterosexual ones?
8. How do friendships fare during middle age?
9. How do parent-child relationships change as children approach and reach adulthood?
10. How do middle-aged people get along with parents and siblings?
11. How has grandparenthood changed, and what roles do grandparents play?

Looking at the Life Course in Middle Age

Developmental scientists view the course of midlife psychosocial development in several ways. *Objectively,* they look at trajectories or pathways, such as Madeleine Albright's evolution from a wife and mother with a passion for politics to the most powerful woman in the country. But continuities and changes in roles and relationships also have a *subjective* side: people actively construct their sense of self and the structure of their lives. Thus, it is important to consider how a person like Albright defines herself and how satisfied she is with her life (Moen & Wethington, 1999).

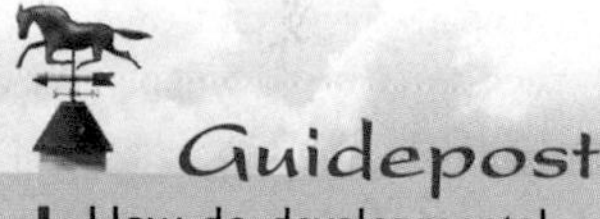

Guidepost

1. How do developmental scientists approach the study of psychosocial development in middle adulthood?

Change and continuity in middle age must be seen in the perspective of the entire life span. Albright's midlife career built on her childhood experiences and youthful strivings. But early patterns are not necessarily blueprints for later ones (Lachman & James, 1997); nor are the concerns of early middle age the same as those of late middle age (Helson, 1997; Staudinger & Bluck, 2001; Sterns & Huyck, 2001). Just think of the difference between Albright's life at 40 and her life at 60!

Furthermore, lives do not progress in isolation. Individual pathways intersect or collide with those of family members, friends and acquaintances, and strangers. Work and personal roles are interdependent, as exemplified by Albright's career change after her divorce; and those roles are affected by trends in the larger society, as Albright's opportunities were enhanced by the changing status of women (Moen & Wethington, 1999).

Checkpoint

Can you . . .

- Distinguish between objective and subjective views of the life course?
- Identify several factors that affect the life course at middle age?

Cohort, gender, ethnicity, culture, and socioeconomic status can profoundly affect the life course (Helson, 1997; Moen & Wethington, 1999; Staudinger & Bluck, 2001; Sterns & Huyck, 2001). Madeleine Albright's path was very different from that of her mother, who made her family her total life's work. Unusual as Albright was for her time, her course also was different from that of most educated women today, who embark on careers before marriage and motherhood. We can speculate on what Albright's expectations and trajectory would have been had she been a man, rather than a woman seeking to use her capabilities in a society based on male dominance. Albright's path also would have been different had she not married into a wealthy family, affording her the means to hire housekeepers while her children were young and she was working on her doctorate. All these factors, and more, enter into the study of psychosocial development in middle adulthood.

Change at Midlife: Classic Theoretical Approaches

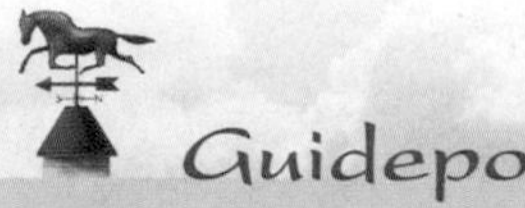

Guidepost

2. What do classic theorists have to say about psychosocial change in middle age?

In psychosocial terms, middle adulthood once was considered a relatively settled period (Whitbourne & Connolly, 1999). Freud (1906/1942) saw no point in psychotherapy for people over 50 because he believed personality is permanently formed by that age. Costa and McCrae (1994a), whose trait model we introduced in Chapter 14, also describe middle age as a time of essential stability in personality.

By contrast, humanistic theorists such as Abraham Maslow and Carl Rogers looked on middle age as an opportunity for positive change. According to Maslow (1968), *self-actualization* (full realization of human potential) can come only with maturity. Rogers (1961) held that full human functioning requires a constant, lifelong process of bringing the self in harmony with experience.

As we noted in Chapter 14, developmental research today has moved beyond the debate over stability versus change. A number of longitudinal studies show that psychosocial development involves both (Franz, 1997; Helson, 1997). The question is, what *kinds* of changes occur and what brings them about?

What's Your View?

- On the basis of your observations, do you believe that adults' personalities change significantly during middle age? If so, do such changes seem related to maturation, or do they accompany important events, such as divorce, occupational change, or grandparenthood?

Researchers study three types of psychosocial developmental change (Franz, 1997): change related to maturational needs or tasks that all human beings experience at particular times of life; change related to culturally endorsed roles or historical events that affect a particular population; and change related to unusual experiences or the unusual timing of life events. Classic theories that deal with these three types of change are normative-stage models and the timing-of-events model (both introduced in Chapter 14). Normative-stage theories generally propose maturational stages of development, but these stages may be limited to the particular cohorts and cultures the theorists studied. The timing-of-events model focuses on unusual, or nonnormative, change.

Normative-Stage Models

Two early normative-stage theorists whose work continues to provide a frame of reference for much developmental theory and research on middle adulthood are Carl G. Jung and Erik Erikson.

Carl G. Jung: Individuation and Transcendence Swiss psychologist Carl Jung (1933, 1953, 1969, 1971), the first major theorist about adult development, held that healthy midlife development calls for **individuation,** the emergence of the true self through balancing or integrating conflicting parts of the personality, including those parts that previously have been neglected. Until about age 40, said Jung, adults concentrate on obligations to family and society and develop those aspects of personality that will help them reach external goals. Women emphasize expressiveness and nurturance; men are primarily oriented toward achievement. At midlife, people shift their preoccupation to their inner, spiritual selves. Both men and women seek a "union of opposites" by expressing their previously "disowned" aspects.

individuation Jung's term for emergence of the true self through balancing or integration of conflicting parts of the personality.

Two necessary but difficult tasks of midlife are giving up the image of youth and acknowledging mortality. According to Jung (1966), the need to acknowledge mortality requires a search for meaning within the self. This inward turn may be unsettling; as people question their commitments, they may temporarily lose their moorings. But people who avoid this transition and do not reorient their lives appropriately miss the chance for psychological growth.

generativity versus stagnation Erikson's seventh stage of psychosocial development, in which the middle-aged adult develops a concern with establishing, guiding, and influencing the next generation or else experiences stagnation (a sense of inactivity or lifelessness).

generativity In Erikson's terminology, concern of mature adults for establishing, guiding, and influencing the next generation.

Erik Erikson: Generativity versus Stagnation In contrast to Jung, who saw midlife as a time of turning inward, Erikson described an outward turn. Erikson saw the years around age 40 as the time when people enter their seventh normative stage **generativity versus stagnation. Generativity,** as Erikson defined it, is the concern of mature adults for establishing and guiding the next generation, perpetuating oneself through one's influence on those to follow. Looking ahead to the waning of their lives, people feel a need to leave a legacy—to participate in life's continuation. People who do not find an outlet for generativity become self-absorbed, self-indulgent, or stagnant (inactive or lifeless). The "virtue" of this period is *care:* "a widening commitment to *take care of* the persons, the products, and the ideas one has learned *to care for*" (Erikson, 1985, p. 67).

Generativity can be expressed not only through parenting and grandparenting, but through teaching or mentorship, productivity or creativity, and "self-generation," or self-development. It can extend to the world of work, to politics, art, music, and other spheres—or as Erikson called it, "maintenance of the world." In *Gandhi's Truth,* Erikson (1969) pointed out how Gandhi—who was not a good father—emerged as "father of his country" at age 49, expressing generativity in his concern for the well-being of an entire nation.

A later theorist (Kotre, 1984) distinguished four specific forms of generativity: *biological* (conceiving and bearing children), *parental* (nurturing and raising children), *technical* (teaching skills to apprentices), and *cultural* (transmitting cultural values and institutions). Regardless of the form, Kotre said, generativity can be expressed in two different ways, or styles: *communal* (involving care and nurturance of others) or *agentic* (personal contributions to society—creative, scientific, or entrepreneurial).

How does generativity arise? According to one model (McAdams, 2001), inner desires for symbolic immortality or a need to be needed combine with external demands (in the form of increased expectations and responsibilities) to produce a conscious concern for the next generation. This, together with what Erikson called "belief in the species," leads to generative commitments and actions.

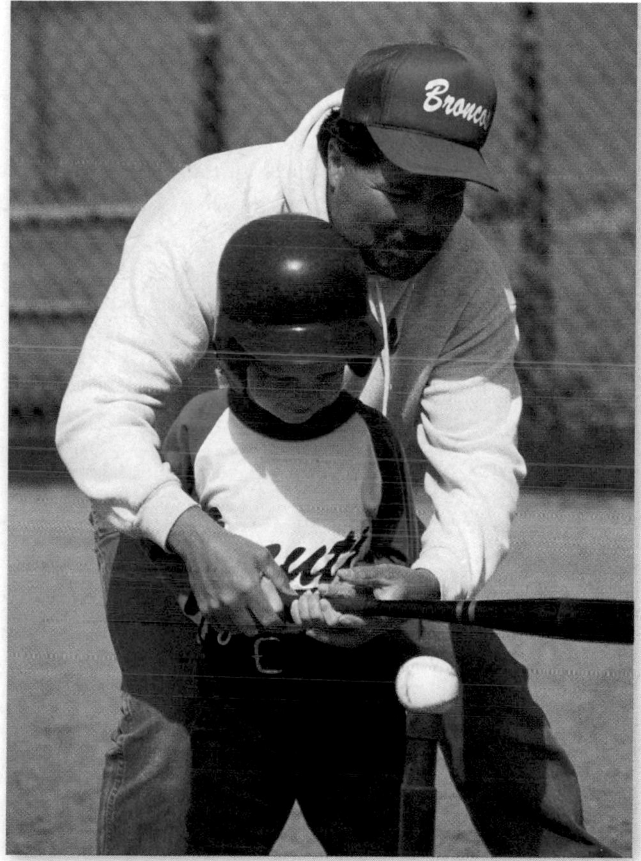

What Erikson called generativity*—a concern for guiding the younger generation—can be expressed through coaching or mentoring. Generativity may be a key to well-being at midlife.*

Jung's and Erikson's Legacy: Vaillant and Levinson Jung's and Erikson's ideas and observations inspired George Vaillant's (1977) and Daniel Levinson's (1978) longitudinal studies of men (introduced in Chapter 14). Both described major midlife shifts—from occupational striving in the thirties to reevaluation and often drastic restructuring of lives in the forties to mellowing and relative stability in the fifties.*

*Levinson's description of the fifties was only projected.

Vaillant, like Jung, reported a lessening of gender differentiation at midlife and a tendency for men to become more nurturant and expressive. Likewise, Levinson's men at midlife became less obsessed with personal achievement and more concerned with relationships; and they showed generativity by becoming mentors to younger men. As we discuss later in this chapter, Vaillant studied the relationship between generativity and mental health.

Vaillant also echoed Jung's concept of turning inward. In the forties, many of his sample of Harvard graduates abandoned the "compulsive, unreflective busywork of their occupational apprenticeships and once more [became] explorers of the world within" (1977, p. 220). Bernice Neugarten (1977) noted a similar introspective tendency at midlife, which she called **interiority.** For Levinson's men, the transition to middle adulthood was stressful enough to be called a "crisis."

interiority Neugarten's term for a concern with inner life (introversion or introspection), which usually appears in middle age.

As we pointed out in Chapter 14, these classic studies, insightful as they may have been, had serious weaknesses of sampling and methodology (Lachman & Bertrand, 2001). Despite Levinson's (1996) posthumous publication of a small study of women, his model and that of Vaillant were built on research on mostly middle-class or upper-middle-class men, whose experiences were taken as norms. Furthermore, their findings reflected the experiences of particular members of a particular cohort in a particular culture. They may not apply in a society in which masculinity and femininity no longer have such distinct meanings, and in which career development and life choices for both men and women have become more varied and more flexible. These findings also may not apply to people for whom economic survival is a pressing issue, or to cultures that have very different patterns of life course development (see Box 16-1).

Checkpoint

Can you . . .

- ✔ Identify three types of change that researchers study, and give an example of each?
- ✔ Summarize important changes that occur at midlife, according to Jung and Erikson, and tell how their ideas have influenced other research?

Finally, these studies dealt exclusively with heterosexuals, and the patterns may not apply to gays and lesbians (Kimmel & Sang, 1995). More recent research on midlife psychosocial development is more broadly based, uses more diverse samples and research designs, and covers more dimensions of personality and experience (Lachman & James, 1997).

Timing of Events: The Social Clock

According to the timing-of-events model introduced in Chapter 14, adult personality development hinges less on age than on important life events. Middle age often brings a restructuring of social roles: launching children, becoming grandparents, changing jobs or careers, and, eventually, retirement (Lachman, 2001). For the cohorts represented by the early normative-crisis studies, the occurrence and timing of such major events were fairly predictable. Today lifestyles are more diverse, people's "social clocks" tick at different rates, and a "fluid life cycle" has blurred the boundaries of middle adulthood (Neugarten & Neugarten, 1987).

When women's lives revolved around bearing and rearing children, the end of the reproductive years meant something different from what it means now, when so many middle-aged women (like Madeleine Albright) have entered the workforce. When occupational patterns were more stable and retirement at age 65 was almost universal, the meaning of work at midlife may have been different from its current meaning in a period of frequent job changes, downsizing, and early or delayed retirement. When people died earlier, middle-aged survivors felt old, realizing that they too were nearing the end of their lives. Many middle-aged people now find themselves busier and more involved than ever—some still raising young children while others redefine their roles as parents to adolescents and young adults and often as caregivers to aging parents. Yet despite the multiple challenges and variable events of midlife, most middle-aged adults seem well able to handle them (Lachman, 2001).

The social clock has not stopped altogether, at least in some societies. In one study done in Berlin, Germany (Krueger, Heckhausen, & Hundertmark, 1995), adults of all ages were asked their impressions of hypothetical 45-year-old adults of their own sex

Window on the World

BOX 16-1

A Society Without Middle Age

The universality of midlife personality change is questionable even in the United States. What, then, happens in non-western cultures, some of which do not even have a clear concept of middle age? One such culture is that of the Gusii, a rural society of more than 1 million people in south-western Kenya (Levine, 1980; LeVine & LeVine, 1998). The Gusii have a "life plan" with well-defined expectations for each stage, but this plan is very different from that in western societies. It is a hierarchy of stages based largely on the anticipation and achievement of reproductive capacity and its extension through the next generation (see table).

Gusii Life Stages

Female	Male
Infant	Infant
Uncircumcised girl	Uncircumcised boy
Circumcised girl	Circumcised man, warrior
Young married woman	
Female elder	Male elder

Source: Adapted from LeVine & LeVine, 1998, Table 2, p. 200.

The Gusii have no words for "adolescent," "young adult," or "middle-aged." A boy or girl is circumcised sometime between ages 9 and 11 and becomes an elder when his or her first child marries. Between these two events, a man is in the stage of *omomura,* or "warrior." The *omomura* stage may last anywhere from twenty-five to forty years, or even longer. Because of the greater importance of marriage in a woman's life, women have an additional stage: *omosubaati,* or "young married woman."

Childbearing is not confined to early adulthood. As in other preindustrial societies where many hands are needed to raise crops and death in infancy or early childhood is common, fertility is highly valued. Today, even though babies are much more likely to survive than in the past, people continue to reproduce as long as they are physiologically able. The average woman bears ten children. When a woman reaches menopause, her husband may take a younger wife and breed another family.

In Gusii society, then, transitions depend on life events. Status is linked to circumcision, marriage (for women), having children, and finally, becoming a parent of a married child and thus a prospective grandparent and respected elder. The Gusii have a "social clock," a set of expectations for the ages at which these events should normally occur. People who marry late or do not marry at all, men who become impotent or sterile, and women who fail to conceive, have their first child late, bear no sons, or have few children are ridiculed and ostracized and may undergo rituals to correct the situation.

Many Gusii in western Kenya become ritual practitioners after their children are grown, seeking spiritual powers to compensate for their waning physical strength. For women like the diviner shown here, ritual practice may be a way to wield power in a male-dominated society.

Although the Gusii have no recognized midlife transition, some of them do reassess their lives around the time they are old enough to be grandparents. Awareness of mortality and of waning physical powers, especially among women, may lead to a career as a ritual healer. The quest for spiritual powers has a generative purpose, too: elders are responsible for ritually protecting their children and grandchildren from death or illness. Many older women who become ritual practitioners or witches seek power either to help people or to harm them, perhaps to compensate for their lack of personal and economic power in a male-dominated society.

Gusii society has undergone change, particularly since the 1970s, as a result of British colonial rule and its aftermath. With infant mortality curtailed, rapid population growth is straining the supply of food and other resources; and a life plan organized around maximizing reproduction is no longer adaptive. Growing acceptance of birth limitation among younger Gusii suggest that "conceptions of adult maturity less centered on fertility will eventually become dominant in the Gusii culture" (LeVine & LeVine, 1998, p. 207).

What's Your View?

Given the current dramatic changes in Gusii society, would you expect shifts in the way the Gusii define life's stages? If so, in what direction?

Check It Out:

OLC

For more information on this topic, go to http://www. mhhe.com/papaliah9.

whose family or work situations violated normal expectations for that age. Participants, regardless of their own age, expressed surprise about these "off-time" conditions and called them atypical. Reactions were stronger and more negative when development seemed late (as, for example, when a 45-year-old woman was described as having a 1-year-old child). Reactions were positive when development seemed early or on time (as, for example, when a 45-year-old man was said to be branch director of a bank). Society, apparently, is not yet age-blind; "people are sensitive to social clocks and . . . use them to understand and judge others" (Kreuger et al., 1995, p. P91).

Checkpoint

Can you . . .

✔ Tell how historical and cultural changes have affected the social clock for middle age?

The Self at Midlife: Issues and Themes

Guidepost

3. What issues concerning the self come to the fore during middle adulthood?

"I'm a completely different person now from the one I was twenty years ago," said a 47-year-old architect as six friends, all in their forties and fifties, nodded vigorously in agreement. Many people feel and observe personality change occurring at midlife. Whether we look at middle-aged people objectively, in terms of their outward behavior, or subjectively, in terms of how they describe themselves, certain issues and themes emerge. Is there such a thing as a "midlife crisis"? How does identity develop in middle age? Do men and women change in different ways? What contributes to psychological well-being? All of these questions revolve around the self.

Is There a Midlife Crisis?

Changes in personality and lifestyle during the early to middle forties are often attributed to the **midlife crisis,** a supposedly stressful period triggered by review and reevaluation of one's life. The midlife crisis was conceptualized as a crisis of identity; indeed, it has been called a second adolescence. What brings it on, said Elliott Jacques (1967), the psychoanalyst who coined the term, is awareness of mortality. Many people now realize that they will not be able to fulfill the dreams of their youth, or that fulfillment of their dreams has not brought the satisfaction they expected. They know that if they want to change direction, they must act quickly. Levinson (1978, 1980, 1986, 1996) maintained that midlife turmoil is inevitable as people struggle with the need to restructure their lives.

midlife crisis In some normative-crisis models, stressful life period precipitated by the review and reevaluation of one's past, typically occurring in the early to middle forties.

However, the reality of the midlife crisis as a normative developmental experience is greatly in doubt today (Lachman & Bertrand, 2001). Although the concept is somewhat fuzzy and hard to test, extensive research—including findings in Hong Kong (Shek, 1996) as well as in western industrialized countries—fails to support its universality (Chiriboga, 1989, 1997; Costa et al., 1986; Klohnen, Vandewater, & Young, 1996; Rosenberg, Rosenberg, & Farrell, 1999), at least as a source of psychological disturbance (Helson, 1997). In fact, its occurrence seems to be fairly unusual (Aldwin & Levenson, 2001; Heckhausen, 2001; Lachman & Bertrand, 2001).

The onset of middle age may be stressful, but no more so than some events of young adulthood (Chiriboga, 1997). Apparently, midlife is just one of life's transitions, a transition typically involving an introspective review and reappraisal of values and priorities (Helson, 1997; Reid & Willis, 1999; Robinson, Rosenberg, & Farrell, 1999), the simultaneous managing of gains and losses, and recognition of the finitude of life (Heckhausen, 2001).

This **midlife review** can be a psychological turning point, a time of stocktaking yielding new insights into the self and spurring midcourse corrections in the design and trajectory of one's life (Clausen, 1990; Moen & Wethington, 1999; Stewart & Ostrove, 1998; Stewart & Vandewater, 1999). It may bring regret over failure to achieve a dream, or keener awareness of the social clock: the imminence of *developmental deadlines,* or time constraints on, say, the ability to have a child or find a new intimate partner (Heckhausen, 2001; Heckhausen, Wrosch, & Fleeson, 2001; Wrosch & Heckhausen, 1999).

midlife review Introspective examination that often occurs in middle age, leading to reappraisal and revision of values and priorities.

Table 16-1 Characteristics of Ego-Resilient Adults

Most Characteristic	Most Uncharacteristic
Has insight into own motives and behavior	Has brittle ego-defense; maladaptive under stress
Has warmth; capacity for close relationships	Is self-defeating
Has social poise and presence	Is uncomfortable with uncertainty and complexities
Is productive; gets things done	Overreacts to minor frustrations; is irritable
Is calm, relaxed in manner	Denies unpleasant thoughts and experiences
Is skilled in social techniques of imaginary play	Does not vary roles; relates to all in same way
Is socially perceptive of interpersonal cues	Is basically anxious
Can see to the heart of important problems	Gives up and withdraws from frustration or adversity
Is genuinely dependable and responsible	Is emotionally bland
Responds to humor	Is vulnerable to real or fancied threat; fearful
Values own independence and autonomy	Tends to ruminate and have preoccupying thoughts
Tends to arouse liking and acceptance	Feels cheated and victimized by life
Initiates humor	Feels a lack of personal meaning in life

Note: These items are used as criteria for rating ego-resiliency, using the California Adult Q-Set.
Source: Adapted from Block, 1991, as reprinted in Klohnen, 1996.

Whether a transition turns into a crisis may depend less on age than on individual circumstances and personal resources. People with *ego-resiliency*—the ability to adapt flexibly and resourcefully to potential sources of stress—are more likely to navigate the midlife crossing successfully (Heckhausen, 2001; Klohnen et al., 1996). (Table 16-1 outlines qualities considered most and least characteristic of ego-resilient adults.) For people with resilient personalities, like Madeleine Albright, even negative events, such as an unwanted divorce, can become springboards for positive growth (Klohnen et al., 1996; Moen & Wethington, 1999).

What's Your View?

- As far as you know, did one or both of your parents go through what appeared to be a midlife crisis? If you are middle-aged, did you go through such a crisis? If so, what issues made it a crisis? Did it seem more serious than transitions at other times of life?

Identity Development

Although Erikson defined identity formation as the main concern of adolescence, he noted that identity continues to develop. Indeed, some developmental scientists view the process of identity formation as the central issue of adulthood (McAdams & de St. Aubin, 1992). Identity may consist, not just of one self, but of multiple "possible selves," including the self a person hopes to become and the self a person is afraid of becoming (Markus & Nurius, 1986). Turning points such as the midlife transition often involve changes in the way people see themselves.

As Erikson observed, identity is closely tied to social roles and commitments ("I am a mother," "I am a teacher," "I am a citizen"). Because midlife is a time of stock-taking with regard to roles and relationships, it may bring to the surface unresolved identity issues. Changing roles and relationships for men and women at this time may affect gender identity.

Susan Krauss Whitbourne: Identity as a Process The **identity process model** of Susan Krauss Whitbourne (1987, 1996; Whitbourne & Connolly, 1999) seeks to describe how identity changes, drawing on Erikson, Marcia, and Piaget. Whitbourne views identity as "an organizing schema through which the individual's experiences are interpreted" (Whitbourne & Connolly, 1999, p. 28). Identity is made up of

identity process model Whitbourne's model of identity development based on processes of assimilation and accommodation.

accumulated perceptions of the self, both conscious and unconscious. Perceived personality traits ("I am sensitive" or "I am stubborn"), physical characteristics, and cognitive abilities are incorporated into the identity schema. These self-perceptions are continually confirmed or revised in response to incoming information, which can come from intimate relationships, work-related situations, community activities, and other experiences.

identity assimilation Whitbourne's term for effort to fit new experience into an existing self-concept.

identity accommodation Whitbourne's term for adjusting the self-concept to fit new experience.

People interpret their interactions with the environment by means of two ongoing processes, similar to those Piaget described for children's cognitive development (refer back to Chapter 2): *identity assimilation* and *identity accommodation.* **Identity assimilation** is an attempt to fit new experience into an existing schema; **identity accommodation** is adjustment of the schema to fit the new experience. Identity assimilation tends to maintain continuity of the self; identity accommodation tends to bring about needed change. Most people use both processes to some extent. Madeleine Albright, when confronted with proof of her Jewish birth, accommodated her identity schema to include her Jewishness but also assimilated her new knowledge to her image of herself as the daughter of loving parents who had done their utmost to protect her. People often resist accommodation (as Albright apparently did for a while) until events (in this case, the imminence of press reports) force them to recognize the need.

identity style Whitbourne's term for characteristic ways of confronting, interpreting, and responding to experience.

The equilibrium a person customarily reaches between assimilation and accommodation determines his or her **identity style.** A person who uses assimilation more than accommodation has an *assimilative identity style.* A person who uses accommodation more has an *accommodative identity style.* Overuse of either assimilation or accommodation is unhealthy, says Whitbourne. People who constantly *assimilate* are inflexible and do not learn from experience; they see only what they are looking for. They may go to great lengths to avoid recognizing their inadequacies. People who constantly *accommodate* are weak, easily swayed, and highly vulnerable to criticism; their identity is easily undermined. Most healthy is a *balanced identity style,* in which "identity is flexible enough to change when warranted but not unstructured to the point that every new experience causes the person to question fundamental assumptions about the self" (Whitbourne & Connolly, 1999, p. 29). Whitbourne sees identity styles as related to Marcia's identity statuses (refer back to Chapter 12); for example, a person who has achieved identity would be expected to have a balanced identity style, whereas a person in foreclosure would most likely have an assimilative style.

According to Whitbourne, people deal with physical, mental, and emotional changes associated with the onset of aging much as they deal with other experiences that challenge the identity schema. Assimilative people seek to maintain a youthful self-image at all costs. Accommodative people may see themselves—perhaps prematurely—as old and may become preoccupied with symptoms of aging and disease. People with a balanced style realistically recognize changes that are occurring and seek to control what can be controlled and accept what cannot. However, identity styles can shift in the face of highly unsettling events, such as loss of a longtime job to a younger person. Thus, a midlife crisis may be "an extreme accommodative reaction to a set of experiences that no longer can be processed through identity assimilation" (Whitbourne & Connolly, 1999, p. 30).

With or without the presence of a crisis, Whitbourne's model is a comprehensive attempt to account for both stability and change in the self. However, it is in need of longitudinal research support (Lachman & Bertrand, 2001).

Checkpoint

Can you . . .

- ✔ Explain the concept of the midlife crisis and discuss its prevalence?
- ✔ State typical concerns of the midlife transition and factors that affect how successfully people come through it?
- ✔ Summarize Whitbourne's model of identity, and describe how people with each of the three identity styles might deal with signs of aging?

Generativity, Identity, and Age Erikson saw generativity as an aspect of identity formation. As he wrote, "I am what survives me" (1968, p. 141). Research supports this connection. In a study of 40 middle-class female bank employees in their early forties, who were mothers of school-age children (DeHaan & MacDermid, 1994),

The increasing popularity of Botox injections to temporarily smoothe lines and wrinkles may express what Susan Krauss Whitbourne calls an accommodative identity style. *Accommodative people tend to be preoccupied with signs of aging.*

women who had achieved identity by Marcia's criteria were the most psychologically healthy. They also expressed the greatest degree of generativity, bearing out Erikson's view that successful achievement of identity paves the way for other tasks.

Instruments—behavioral checklists, Q-sorts, and self-reports (see Table 16-2)—have been devised to measure and refine the meaning of generativity. Using such techniques, researchers have found that while the age at which individuals achieve generativity varies, middle-aged people tend to score higher on generativity than younger and

Table 16-2 A Self-Report Test for Generativity

- I try to pass along the knowledge I have gained through my experiences.
- I do not feel that other people need me.
- I think I would like the work of a teacher.
- I feel as though I have made a difference to many people.
- I do not volunteer to work for a charity.
- I have made and created things that have had an impact on other people.
- I try to be creative in most things that I do.
- I think that I will be remembered for a long time after I die.
- I believe that society cannot be responsible for providing food and shelter for all homeless people.
- Others would say that I have made unique contributions to society.
- If I were unable to have children of my own, I would like to adopt children.
- I have important skills that I try to teach others.
- I feel that I have done nothing that will survive after I die.
- In general, my actions do not have a positive effect on others.
- I feel as though I have done nothing of worth to contribute to others.
- I have made many commitments to many different kinds of people, groups, and activities in my life.
- Other people say that I am a very productive person.
- I have a responsibility to improve the neighborhood in which I live.
- People come to me for advice.
- I feel as though my contributions will exist after I die.

Source: Loyola Generativity Scale. Reprinted from McAdams & de St. Aubin, 1992.

older ones (McAdams, de St. Aubin, & Logan, 1993; Keyes & Ryff, 1998; Stewart & Vandewater, 1998).

In a large national random survey of adults ages 25 to 74, middle-aged and older adults reported providing more assistance and emotional support to others than did younger adults. They also expressed higher levels of civic responsibility, but younger adults felt more direct generative obligations to their families and others. This suggests that a lessening of primary family responsibilities may free middle-aged and older adults to express generativity on a broader scale. By almost all measures, women (especially educated women) reported higher levels of generativity than men; but in old age, men's and women's generative concerns were equal (Keyes & Ryff, 1998).

These studies were cross-sectional and so cannot with certainty trace a connection between generativity and age. However, the few longitudinal studies of generativity also support this connection (Stewart & Vandewater, 1998). As the men in Vaillant's (1993) Grant Study approached and moved through middle age, an increasing proportion were rated as having achieved generativity: 50 percent at age 40 and 83 percent at 60. An analysis of two longitudinal studies of women from the 1964 class of Radcliffe College and the 1967 class of University of Michigan suggests that, while the *desire* for generativity tends to arise in young adulthood, its accomplishment, and the sense of capacity for generativity, tends to come in middle age (Stewart & Vandewater, 1998).

However, such findings may be class- and cohort-based and also may disguise individual differences. Instead of defining generativity as a midlife stage in development, some investigators argue for a *life-course perspective on generativity.* Generativity at any point in time may be affected by social expectations, social roles (work, marital, parenting, civic, and the like) and their timing and sequence, as well as by gender, education, race, ethnicity, and cohort (McAdams, 2001; Cohler, Hostetler, & Boxer, 1998). Generativity may express itself differently, or with different timing, in gays and lesbians, who may develop intimate relationships or become parents later than heterosexuals typically do, or never have these experiences (refer back to Chapter 14). Many gays and lesbians have expressed generativity through activism for gay rights or other causes (Cohler et al., 1998).

Narrative Psychology: Identity as a Life Story The relatively new field of *narrative psychology* views the development of the self as a continuous process of constructing one's own life story—a dramatic narrative to help make sense of one's life. Indeed, some narrative psychologists view identity itself as this internalized story, or "script." People follow the "script" they have created as they act out their identity (McAdams, Diamond, de St. Aubin, & Mansfield, 1997). Midlife often is a time for revision of the life story (McAdams, 1993) or for a break in the continuity and coherence of the story line (Rosenberg et al., 1999).

The themes of identity narratives reflect culture and cohort. In in-depth interviews with 20 New England men who came of age during the 1940s and 1950s, a critical break in their stories tended to occur in their fifties in conjunction with loss of an active fathering role. For these men, whose formative years had been focused on family and security, the "organizing axis of their . . . narrative identities" was suddenly gone (Rosenberg et al., 1999, p. 61).

A younger group of men who came of age during the Vietnam era told very different narratives. Many of these baby boomers had been skeptics or rebels from adolescence on, alienated from traditional roles. Their midlife shift was toward a search for meaning and fulfillment and more stable families and careers. Their break with the past reflected a belated quest for an adult identity (Rosenberg et al., 1999).

As people grow older, generativity may become an important theme of the life story. A *generativity script* can give the life story a happy ending. It is built on the conviction that generative acts make a difference and that the results of one's life can outlive the self (McAdams, 2001; McAdams & de St. Aubin, 1992).

Highly generative adults often tell a *commitment story* (McAdams et al., 1997). Typically, such people have enjoyed privileged lives and want to alleviate the suffering of others. They dedicate their lives to social improvement and do not swerve from that mission despite grievous obstacles, which eventually have positive outcomes. Moral exemplars organize their lives around such commitment stories (Colby & Damon, 1992; refer back to Box 15-2 in Chapter 15).

Gender Identity In many studies during the 1960s, 1970s, and 1980s, middle-aged men were more open about feelings, more interested in intimate relationships, and more nurturing (characteristics traditionally labeled as feminine) than at earlier ages, whereas middle-aged women were more assertive, self-confident, and achievement-oriented (characteristics traditionally labeled as masculine) (Cooper & Gutmann, 1987; Cytrynbaum et al., 1980; Helson & Moane, 1987; Huyck, 1990, 1999; Neugarten, 1968). Some social scientists attributed this development to hormonal changes at midlife (Rossi, 1980). Jung saw it as part of the process of individuation, or balancing the personality. Psychologist David Gutmann (1975, 1977, 1985, 1987) offers an explanation that goes further than Jung's.

Traditional gender roles, according to Gutmann, evolved to ensure the security and well-being of growing children. The mother must be the caregiver, the father the provider. Once active parenting is over, there is not just a balancing but a reversal of roles—a **gender crossover.** Men, now free to explore their previously repressed "feminine" side, become more passive; women become more dominant and independent.

gender crossover Gutmann's term for reversal of gender roles after the end of active parenting.

These changes may have been normative in the preliterate agricultural societies Gutmann studied, which had very distinct gender roles, but they are not necessarily universal (Franz, 1997). In U.S. society today, men's and women's roles are becoming less distinct (Verbrugge, Gruber-Baldini, & Fozard, 1996). In an era in which most young women combine employment with child rearing, when many men take an active part in parenting, and when childbearing may not even begin until midlife, gender crossover in middle age seems less likely. Indeed, the very use of the terms "masculine" and "feminine" to describe personality traits such as "dominant" and "submissive" has become questionable (Antonucci & Akiyama, 1997; James & Lewkowicz, 1997).

In studies that have found increasing "masculinization" of women and "feminization" of men across adulthood, the amount and pattern of change varies. One factor seems to be methodology. Some studies (including Gutmann's) have used instruments that measure values, goals, interests, or motivations (for example, the relative priority men and women give to career and family). Other studies have measured personality traits, such as competitiveness ("masculine") and compliance ("feminine"). Some studies are longitudinal and others are cross-sectional. Most do not take possible cohort differences into account (Parker & Aldwin, 1997).

What's Your View?

- From what you have observed, do men and women face similar or different kinds of challenges at midlife?

A sequential analysis of data from two longitudinal studies that together followed 20-, 30-, and 40-year-old, mostly well-educated men and women for more than two decades was designed to deal with these methodological issues (Parker & Aldwin, 1997). The studies used both personality measures and values-oriented measures.

The personality measures did show age-related change: both men and women became increasingly "masculine" (or decreasingly "feminine") during their twenties. However, this trend leveled off by the forties. Contrary to Gutmann's model, there was *no* gender crossover. Nor was there evidence of increasing *androgyny* (integration of both "masculine" and "feminine" traits) in successive cohorts. Regardless of age or cohort, men remained more "masculine" than women.

The values-oriented measures showed what at first appeared to be change but turned out to be cohort differences. For example, men and women in one cohort became less family-oriented and more career-oriented between their twenties and thirties (in the 1970s) and then more family-oriented between their thirties and forties (the 1980s). However, this could not have been a developmental change, because a younger cohort who were in their twenties during the second time period followed the same career-to-family shift during that time as the older cohort did, but at an earlier age. Thus, the shift in values was probably due to sociocultural or historical influences affecting both cohorts at the same time.

One personality-oriented study that did show opposite changes in men and women was the Mills longitudinal study (introduced in Chapter 14). Between the beginning and the end of active parenting, the Mills women increased more than their male partners in competence, confidence, and independence, while the men increased more in affiliative traits. The women changed more dramatically than the men, perhaps because women's lives in the United States changed more than men's between the 1970s and the 1990s, when these couples' children were growing up (Helson, 1997). However, these changes did not amount to a gender crossover. Indeed, in line with Jung's view, the highest quality of life for women in their fifties was associated with a *balance* between autonomy and involvement in an intimate relationship (Helson, 1993).

Checkpoint

Can you . . .

- ✔ Explain the connection between generativity and identity and discuss research on generativity and age?
- ✔ Explain the concept of identity as a life story, and how it applies to the midlife transition and to generativity?
- ✔ Compare Jung's and Gutmann's concepts of changes in gender identity at midlife, and assess their research support?

Further research undoubtedly will sharpen our understanding of change and continuity in men's and women's personalities and attitudes at midlife. Two things seem clear: (1) development of gender identity during adulthood is far more complex than a simple gender crossover; and (2) influences of cohort and culture and of the individual life course need to be factored in.

Psychological Well-Being and Positive Mental Health

Mental health is not just the absence of mental illness. *Positive* mental health involves a sense of psychological well-being, which goes hand in hand with a healthy sense of self (Ryff & Singer, 1998). This subjective sense of well-being, or happiness, is a person's evaluation of his or her own life (Diener, 2000).

In numerous surveys worldwide, using various techniques for assessing subjective well-being, most people of all ages, both sexes, and all races report being happy and satisfied with their lives; no particular time of life is the most satisfying (Myers, 2000; Myers & Diener, 1995, 1996). Even after distressing events, people soon adapt, and subjective well-being returns to its previous level (Diener, 2000). Except among the very poor, wealth seems to make little difference in happiness, but social support—friends and spouses—and religiosity do. So do certain personality traits, such as extraversion, and the quality of a person's work and leisure experiences (Csikszenmihalyi, 1999; Diener, 2000; Myers, 2000).

Yet—in contrast with these findings of emotional stability throughout life—when adults of various ages reported their emotional state many times a day for a week, negative feelings diminished through midlife. Emotions also became more complex, or bittersweet—perhaps, the authors of this research suggested, because middle-agers have learned to accept what comes (Carstensen, Pasupathi, Mayr, & Nesselroade, 2000).

How can we reconcile these findings? What factors affect well-being at midlife?

Carol Ryff: Multiple Dimensions of Well-Being Well-being has many facets, and different researchers have used different criteria to measure it, making it difficult to compare results. Now Carol Ryff and her colleagues (Keyes & Ryff, 1999; Ryff, 1995; Ryff & Singer, 1998), drawing on a range of theorists from Erikson to Maslow, have developed a multifaceted model that includes six dimensions of well-being and a self-report scale to measure them. The six dimensions are *self-acceptance, positive relations* *with others, autonomy, environmental mastery, purpose in life,* and *personal growth* (see Table 16-3). According to Ryff, psychologically healthy people have positive attitudes toward themselves and others. They make their own decisions and regulate their own behavior, and they choose or shape environments compatible with their needs. They have goals that make their lives meaningful, and they strive to explore and develop themselves as fully as possible.

A series of cross-sectional studies based on Ryff's scale show midlife to be a period of generally positive mental health (Ryff & Singer, 1998). Middle-aged people expressed greater well-being than older and younger adults in some areas but not in others. They were more autonomous than younger adults but somewhat less purposeful and less focused on personal growth—future-oriented dimensions that declined even more sharply in late adulthood. Environmental mastery, on the other hand, increased between middle and late adulthood. Self-acceptance was relatively stable for all age groups. Of course, since this research was cross-sectional, we do not know whether the differences were due to maturation, aging, or cohort factors. Overall, men's and

Table 16-3 Dimensions of Well-Being Used in Ryff's Scale

Self-Acceptance

High scorer: possesses a positive attitude toward the self, acknowledges and accepts multiple aspects of self including good and bad qualities: feels positive about past life.

Low scorer: feels dissatisfied with self; is disappointed with what has occurred in past life; is troubled about certain personal qualities; wishes to be different [from] what he or she is.

Positive Relations with Others

High scorer: has warm, satisfying, trusting relationships with others; is concerned about the welfare of others; [is] capable of strong empathy, affection, and intimacy; understands give and take of human relationships.

Low scorer: has few close, trusting relationships with others; finds it difficult to be warm, open, and concerned about others; is isolated and frustrated in interpersonal relationships; [is] not willing to make compromises to sustain important ties with others.

Autonomy

High scorer: is self-determining and independent; [is] able to resist social pressures to think and act in certain ways; regulates behavior from within; evaluates self by personal standards.

Low scorer: is concerned about the expectations and evaluations of others; relies on judgments of others to make important decisions; conforms to social pressures to think and act in certain ways.

Environmental Mastery

High scorer: has a sense of mastery and competence in managing the environment; controls complex array of external activities; makes effective use of surrounding opportunities; [is] able to choose or create contexts suitable to personal needs and values.

Low scorer: has difficulty managing everyday affairs; feels unable to change or improve surrounding context; is unaware of surrounding opportunities; lacks sense of control over external world.

Purpose in Life

High scorer: has goals in life and a sense of directedness; feels there is meaning to present and past life; holds beliefs that give life purpose; has aims and objectives for living.

Low scorer: lacks a sense of meaning in life; has few goals or aims, lacks sense of direction; does not see purpose in past life; has no outlooks or beliefs that give life meaning.

Personal Growth

High scorer: has a feeling of continued development; sees self as growing and expanding; is open to new experiences; has sense of realizing his or her potential; sees improvement in self and behavior over time; is changing in ways that reflect more self-knowledge and effectiveness.

Low scorer: has a sense of personal stagnation; lacks sense of improvement or expansion over time; feels bored [with] and uninterested [in] life; feels unable to develop new attitudes or behaviors.

Source: Adapted from Keyes & Ryff, 1999, Table 1, p. 163.

women's well-being was quite similar, but women had more positive social relationships. Well-being was greater for men and women with more education and better jobs (Ryff & Singer, 1998).

Indeed, paid work—long seen as central to men's well-being—is today being recognized as an important source of well-being for women as well, providing a sense of independence and competence apart from family duties. Despite the potential for stress, many middle-aged women seem to flourish in multiple roles (Antonucci & Akiyama, 1997; Barnett, 1997).

Generativity as a Factor in Psychosocial Adjustment Generativity, according to Erikson, is "a sign of both psychological maturity and psychological health" (McAdams, 2001, p. 425). Generativity emerges as the defining feature of psychosocial adjustment at midlife because the roles and challenges of this period—the demands of work and family—call for generative responses. Research has generally supported and expanded on Erikson's view.

In their fifties, the best-adjusted men in Vaillant's (1989) sample of Harvard alumni were the most generative, as measured by their responsibility for other people at work, their gifts to charity, and the accomplishments of their children, and also were most likely to use mature ways of coping, such as altruism and humor. Similarly, in a longitudinal study of 306 inner-city men, those who at age 47 used mature coping techniques had the best health and psychosocial functioning (Soldz & Vaillant, 1998).

In other research on generativity and mental health, a 32-year longitudinal study followed 87 young men who were students at George Williams College, a training institution for social service work. In their fifties, according to Erikson's and Vaillant's criteria, more than half of the group had achieved generativity, defined as the highest stage of positive mental health. They had been successful in their work, taken responsibility for others, and achieved intimacy, typically through a longtime happy marriage (Westermeyer, 1998, 1999).

Generativity, then, may derive from involvement in multiple roles—as heads of families and leaders in organizations and communities (Staudinger & Bluck, 2001). Such involvement has been linked to well-being and satisfaction both in midlife (McAdams, 2001) and in later life (Vandewater, Ostrove, & Stewart, 1997), perhaps through the sense of having contributed meaningfully to society. However, because these findings are correlational, we cannot be sure that generativity causes well-being; it may be that people who are happy with their lives are more likely to be generative (McAdams, 2001). Generativity is not necessarily across-the-board; a person may be generative as a parent but less so as a worker or spouse, or vice versa, and generativity in each of these roles may affect well-being differently (MacDermid, Heilbrun, & DeHaan, 1997).

Women in their early fifties are in what Ravenna Helson and her colleagues call "the prime of life"—young enough to be healthy and active but old enough to have launched their children and to have the time and resources for enjoying friends and fun. Women this age tend to be comfortable with themselves and no longer concerned about meeting social expectations.

Is Middle Age a Woman's Prime of Life? For many women, like Madeleine Albright, late middle age may be the prime of life. Among a cross-sectional sample of nearly 700 Mills College alumnae ages 26 to 80, women in their early fifties most often described their lives as "first-rate" (Mitchell & Helson, 1990). They were young enough to be in good health and old enough to have launched their children and to be financially secure. Life at home was simpler; the energy that had gone into child rearing was redirected to partners, work, community, or themselves. They tended to be caring for others, showing generativity. They had developed greater confidence, involvement, security, and breadth of personality.

Table 16-4 Selected Feelings about Life Reported by Women in Their Early Fifties

	More True Now Than in Early Forties	Less True Now Than in Early Forties
Identity questioning and turmoil:		
Excitement, turmoil about my impulses and potential	21	56
Searching for a sense of who I am	28	47
Anxious that I won't live up to my potential	25	47
Coming near the end of one road and not finding another	27	45
Assurance of status:		
Feeling established	78	11
Influence in my community or field of interest	63	24
A new level of productivity	70	11
Feeling selective in what I do	91	2
A sense of being my own person	90	3
Cognitive breadth and complexity:		
Bringing both feeling and rationality into decisions	76	1
Realizing larger patterns of meaning and relationship	72	7
Appreciating my complexity	69	10
Discovering new parts of myself	72	11
Present rather than future orientation:		
Focus on reality—meeting the needs of the day and not being too emotional about them	76	6
More satisfied with what I have; less worried about what I won't get	76	11
Feeling the importance of time's passing	76	10
Adjustment and relational smoothness:		
Feeling secure and committed	71	12
Feeling my life is moving well	74	15
Feeling optimistic about the future	58	20
A new level of intimacy	53	30
Doing things for others and then feeling exploited	14	56
Feeling very much alone	26	45
Feelings of competition with other women	7	63
Feeling angry at men and masculinity	14	52
Awareness of aging and reduced vitality:		
Looking old	70	15
Being treated as an older person	64	14
Reducing the intensity of my achievement efforts	44	26
Liking an active social life	27	52
Being very interested in sex	19	64

Note: The women judged whether each item was more applicable to them now than in their early forties, less applicable now than then, or about the same.

Source: Helson & Wink, 1992.

Similarly, most of the Mills graduates found their early forties their time of greatest turmoil but by the early fifties rated their quality of life as high. They were more self-confident, independent, decisive, dominant, and self-affirming and less self-critical than they had been earlier in life. They became more comfortable with themselves, partly because they were adhering to their own standards (Helson & Wink, 1992; see Table 16-4). Whereas in their early forties these women had been keenly aware of the social clock, by the early fifties they were no longer concerned about meeting outside expectations (Helson, 1997; Helson & McCabe, 1993).

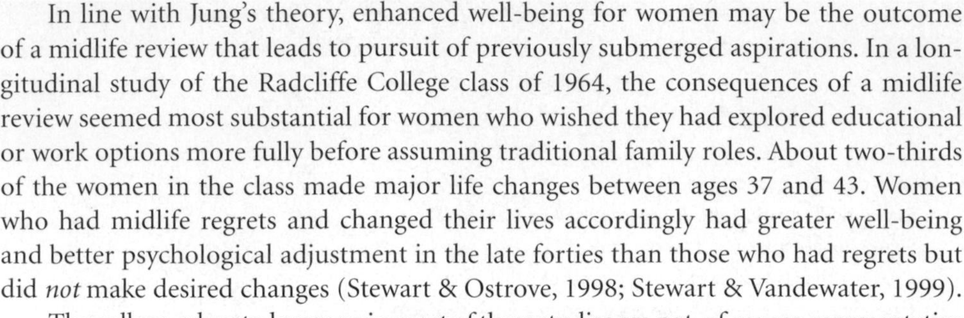

In line with Jung's theory, enhanced well-being for women may be the outcome of a midlife review that leads to pursuit of previously submerged aspirations. In a longitudinal study of the Radcliffe College class of 1964, the consequences of a midlife review seemed most substantial for women who wished they had explored educational or work options more fully before assuming traditional family roles. About two-thirds of the women in the class made major life changes between ages 37 and 43. Women who had midlife regrets and changed their lives accordingly had greater well-being and better psychological adjustment in the late forties than those who had regrets but did *not* make desired changes (Stewart & Ostrove, 1998; Stewart & Vandewater, 1999).

Checkpoint

Can you . . .

- ✔ Discuss the relationship between generativity, mental health, and well-being?
- ✔ Explain the importance of a multifaceted measure of well-being, and name and describe the six dimensions in Ryff's model?
- ✔ Explain how a midlife review can affect well-being?
- ✔ Discuss influences on women's well-being at midlife?

The college-educated women in most of these studies are not, of course, representative of the whole population; and the changes they went through are not necessarily maturational changes, which would occur regardless of class, cohort, and culture. The women in these studies were members of the first generation of American middle-class women to experience a shift between traditional and nontraditional female roles. Socialized to be homemakers and mothers, they matured at a time when large numbers of women began to take advantage of expanding educational and vocational opportunities. Their midlife pattern was not characteristic of their mothers' generation, who generally accepted the traditional woman's role. Nor may this pattern apply to more recent cohorts who have started careers earlier and put off motherhood longer, or to women of other socioeconomic groups (Stewart & Ostrove, 1998; Stewart & Vandewater, 1999).

Changes in Relationships at Midlife

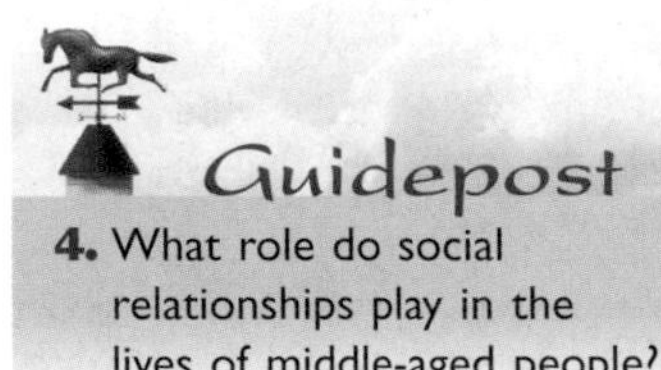

Guidepost

4. What role do social relationships play in the lives of middle-aged people?

It is hard to generalize about the meaning of relationships in middle age today. Not only does that period cover a quarter-century of development; it also embraces a greater multiplicity of life paths than ever before. One 45-year-old may be happily married and raising children; another may be contemplating marriage or, like Madeleine Albright, on the brink of divorce. One 60-year-old may have a large network of friends, relatives, and colleagues; another may have no known living relatives and only a few intimate friendships. For most middle-aged people, however, relationships with others are very important—perhaps in a different way than earlier in life.

Theories of Social Contact

social convoy theory Theory, proposed by Kahn and Antonucci, that people move through life surrounded by concentric circles of intimate relationships of varying degrees of closeness, on which they rely for assistance, well-being, and social support.

According to **social convoy theory,** people move through life surrounded by *social convoys:* circles of close friends and family members of varying degrees of closeness, on whom they can rely for assistance, well-being, and social support, and to whom they in turn also offer care, concern, and support (Antonucci & Akiyama, 1997; Kahn & Antonucci, 1980). Characteristics of the person (gender, race, religion, age, education, and marital status), together with characteristics of that person's situation (role expectations, life events, financial stress, daily hassles, demands, and resources), influence the size and composition of the convoy, or support network; the amount and kind of social support a person receives; and the satisfaction derived from this support. All of these factors contribute to health and well-being (Antonucci, Akiyama, & Merline, 2001).

Although convoys usually show long-term stability, their composition can change. At one time, bonds with siblings may be more significant; at another time, ties with friends (Paul, 1997). Middle-aged people in industrialized countries tend to have the largest convoys because they are likely to be married, to have children, to have living parents, and to be in the workforce unless they have retired early (Antonucci et al., 2001). Women's convoys, particularly the inner circle, tend to be larger than men's (Antonucci & Akiyama, 1997).

socioemotional selectivity theory Theory, proposed by Carstensen, that people select social contacts on the basis of the changing relative importance of social interaction as a source of information, as an aid in developing and maintaining a self-concept, and as a source of emotional well-being.

Laura Carstensen's (1991, 1995, 1996; Carstensen, Isaacowitz, & Charles, 1999) **socioemotional selectivity theory** offers a life-span perspective on how people choose with whom to spend their time. According to Carstensen, social interaction has three

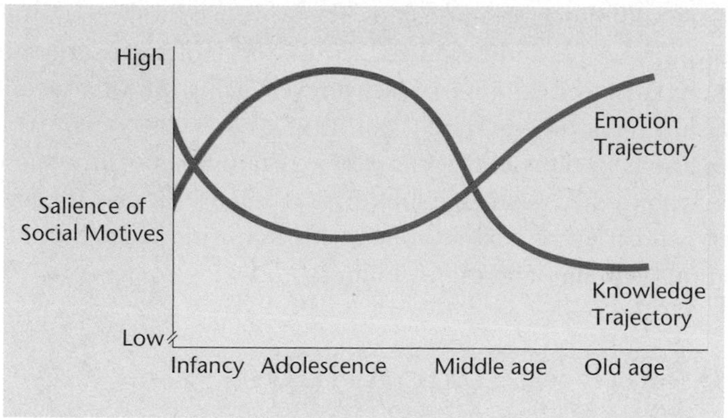

Figure 16-1
How motives for social contact change across the life span. According to socioemotional selectivity theory, infants seek social contact primarily for emotional comfort. In adolescence and young adulthood, people tend to be most interested in seeking information from others. From middle age on, emotional needs increasingly predominate. *(Source:* Carstensen, Gross, & Fung, 1997. Copyright 1997 by Springer Publishing Company. Reprinted with permission.)

main goals: (1) it is a source of information; (2) it helps people develop and maintain a sense of self; and (3) it is a source of pleasure and comfort, or emotional well-being. In infancy, the third goal, the need for emotional support, is paramount. From childhood through young adulthood, information-seeking comes to the fore. As young people strive to learn about their society and their place in it, strangers may well be the best sources of knowledge. By middle age, although information-seeking remains important (Fung, Carstensen, & Lang, 2001), the original, emotion-regulating function of social contacts begins to reassert itself. In other words, middle-aged people increasingly seek out others who make them feel good (see Figure 16-1). In research testing the theory, middle-aged and older adults placed greater emphasis than young adults on emotional affinity in choosing hypothetical social partners (Carstensen et al., 1999).

What's Your View?

- Does either the social convoy model or socioemotional selectivity theory fit your own experience and observations?

Relationships and Quality of Life

Most middle-aged and older adults are optimistic about the quality of their lives as they age, according to a mail survey of 1,384 adults ages 45 and older (NFO Research, Inc., 1999). Although they consider satisfying sexual relationships important to that quality of life, social relationships are even more important. About nine out of ten men and women say a good relationship with a spouse or partner is important to their quality of life, and so are close ties to friends and family.

As in young adulthood, relationships seem to be good for physical as well as mental health. In a longitudinal study of 32,624 healthy U.S. men between ages 42 and 77, socially isolated men—those who were not married, had fewer than six friends and relatives, and did not belong to religious or community groups—were more likely to die of cardiovascular disease, accidents, or suicide during the next four years than men with larger social networks (Kawachi et al., 1996).

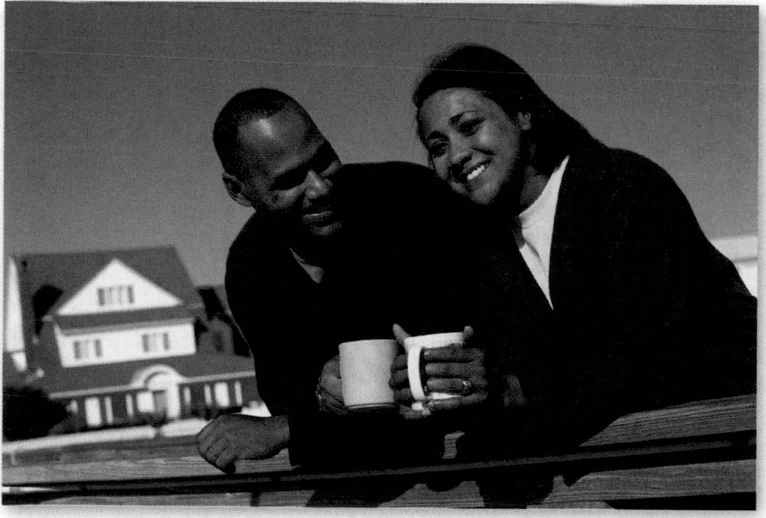

This couple, glowing with health and enjoyment, seem to typify the connection between relationships and quality of life.

On the other hand, midlife relationships also present demands that can be stressful and restrictive. These demands, and their psychological repercussions, tend to fall most heavily on women. A sense of responsibility and concern for others may impair a woman's well-being when problems or misfortunes beset her mate, children, parents, friends, or coworkers. This "vicarious stress" may help explain why middle-aged women are especially susceptible to depression and other mental health problems and why they tend to be unhappier with their marriages than men (Antonucci & Akiyama, 1997; Thomas, 1997).

Checkpoint

Can you . . .

- Summarize two theoretical models of the selection of social contacts?
- Discuss how relationships can affect quality of life in middle adulthood?

In studying midlife social relationships, then, we need to keep in mind that their effects can be both positive and negative. "More" does not necessarily mean "better"; the quality of a relationship and its impact on well-being are what counts, and these attributes can shift from time to time (Paul, 1997).

In the remaining sections of this chapter, we examine how intimate relationships develop during the middle years. We look first at relationships with spouses, homosexual partners, and friends; next at bonds with maturing children; and then at ties with aging parents, siblings, and grandchildren.

Consensual Relationships

Marriages, homosexual unions, and friendships typically involve two people of the same generation and involve mutual choice. How do these relationships fare in middle age?

Marriage

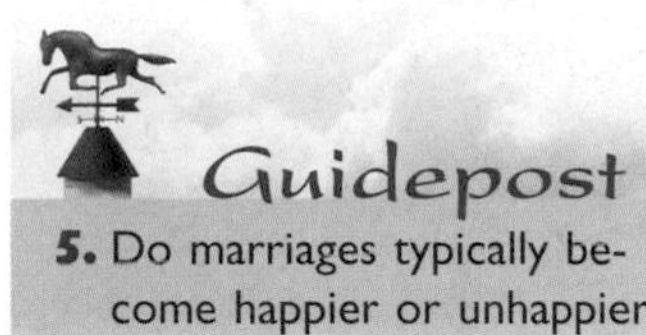

Guidepost

5. Do marriages typically become happier or unhappier during the middle years?

Midlife marriage today is very different from what it used to be. When life expectancies were shorter, couples who remained together for twenty-five, thirty, or forty years were rare. The most common pattern was for marriages to be broken by death and for survivors to remarry. People had many children and expected them to live at home until they married. It was unusual for a middle-aged husband and wife to be alone together. Today, more marriages end in divorce, but couples who stay together can often look forward to twenty or more years of married life after the last child leaves home.

What happens to the quality of a longtime marriage? Marital satisfaction, in almost all studies, follows a U-shaped curve: after the first few years of marriage, satisfaction appears to decline and then, sometime in middle age, to rise again through the first part of late adulthood (S. A. Anderson, Russell, & Schumm, 1983; Gilford, 1984; Glenn, 1991; Gruber & Schaie, 1986; Hiedemann, Suhomlinova, & O'Rand, 1998; Lavee, Sharlin, & Katz, 1996; Orbuch, House, Mero, & Webster, 1996).

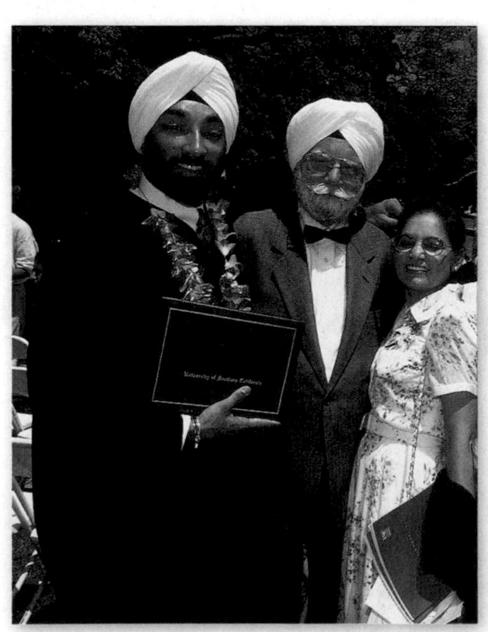

The launching of a son or daughter may give a midlife marriage a new lease on life. Marital satisfaction generally improves when children are grown.

Although the U-shaped pattern is well established, the research has been criticized for its methodology. Many of the early studies dealt with only the husband's or wife's satisfaction, not with both. Also, most studies are cross-sectional: they show differences among couples of different cohorts rather than changes in the *same* couples, and they focus on age, not length of marriage. Furthermore, reports of rising marital satisfaction in late life may in part reflect the fact that older samples do not include couples who have divorced along the way (Blieszner, 1986; Lavee et al., 1996).

An analysis of data from two surveys of individuals in first marriages, conducted in 1986 and 1987–1988 (Orbuch et al., 1996), sought to ascertain just when the dip and rise in satisfaction occur, and why. The samples were, of necessity, cross-sectional (there are no comparable longitudinal data covering the entire span of adulthood); but they were large (a total of 8,929), and one was nationally representative. Both women and men were included, and marital satisfaction was measured against the duration of a marriage. To control for any skewing of data due to termination of unsatisfactory marriages, statistical techniques simulated the inclusion of such couples, attributing to them low marital quality.

The picture that emerged is a clear affirmation of the U-shaped pattern. During the first twenty to twenty-four years of marriage, the longer a couple have been married, the less satisfied they tend to be. Then the association between marital satisfaction and length of marriage begins to turn positive. At thirty-five to forty-four years of marriage, a couple tend to be even more satisfied than during the first four years.

The years of marital decline are those in which parental and work responsibilities tend to be greatest (Orbuch et al., 1996). Two important factors in the demands on parents are family finances and the number of children still at home. The pressure of too little income and too many mouths to feed burdens a relationship, especially if the burdens are not equally shared (Lavee et al., 1996).

The U-shaped curve generally hits bottom early in middle age, when many couples have teenage children and are heavily involved in careers. Satisfaction usually reaches a height when children are grown; many people are entering or are in retirement, and a lifetime accumulation of assets helps ease financial worries (Orbuch et al., 1996). On the other hand, these changes may produce new pressures and challenges (Antonucci et al., 2001).

Researchers today are recognizing that measuring marital satisfaction is more complex than simply asking people to rate how they feel about their marriages. Research on marital quality needs to include more complex and nuanced measures, including observation of interpersonal processes between the spouses (Bradbury, Fincham, & Beech, 2000). For example, an observational study of a representative sample of couples in their forties and sixties found that the older couples showed less negative emotion in resolving conflicts than the younger ones (Carstensen, Gottman, & Levenson, 1995). Future research on marital satisfaction also must take into consideration the many contextual factors that affect a marriage, such as the partners' backgrounds and characteristics, the presence or absence of children, life stressors and transitions, and such larger environmental factors as neighborhood socioeconomic status, mobility, ethnicity, and religiosity (Bradbury et al., 2000).

What's Your View?

- How many longtime happily married couples do you know? Are the qualities that seem to characterize these marriages similar to those mentioned in the text?

Midlife Divorce

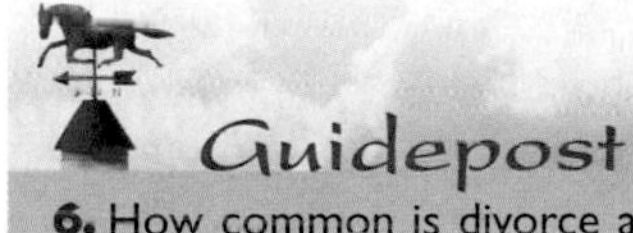

Guidepost

6. How common is divorce at this time of life?

Divorce in midlife is relatively rare (Aldwin & Levenson, 2001); most divorces occur during the first ten years of marriage (Clarke, 1995; Bramlett & Mosher, 2002). Thus, for people who, like Madeleine Albright, go through a divorce at midlife when they may have assumed their lives were settled, the breakup can be traumatic, especially for women, who are more negatively affected by divorce at any age than men are (Marks & Lambert, 1998). Middle-aged people who divorce and do not remarry tend to have less financial security than those who remain married. Again, this is particularly true for women (Wilmoth & Koso, 2002), who may have to go to work, perhaps for the first time (Huyck, 1999). On the positive side, as with Albright, the stress of divorce may lead to personal growth (Aldwin & Levenson, 2001; Helson & Roberts, 1994). And the sense of violated expectations may be diminishing as midlife divorce becomes more common (Marks & Lambert, 1998; Norton & Moorman, 1987). This change appears to be due largely to women's growing economic independence (Hiedemann et al., 1998).

Long-standing marriages may be less likely to break up than more recent ones because as couples stay together they build up **marital capital,** financial and emotional benefits of marriage that become difficult to give up (Becker, 1991; Jones, Tepperman, & Wilson, 1995). College education decreases the risk of separation or divorce after the first decade of marriage, perhaps because college-educated women and their husbands tend to have accumulated more marital assets and may have more to lose financially from divorce than less-educated couples (Hiedemann et al., 1998).

marital capital Financial and emotional benefits built up during a long-standing marriage, which tend to hold a couple together.

The effects of the **empty nest**—the transition that occurs when the youngest child leaves home—depend on the quality and length of the marriage. In a good marriage, the departure of grown children may usher in a second honeymoon (Robinson & Blanton, 1993). In a shaky marriage, if a couple have stayed together for the sake of the children, they may now see no reason to prolong the bond.

empty nest Transitional phase of parenting following the last child's leaving the parents' home.

Divorce rates among aging baby boomers now in their fifties, many of whom married later and had fewer children than in previous generations, are projected to continue to rise (Hiedemann et al., 1998; Uhlenberg, Cooney, & Boyd, 1990). Even in long marriages, the increasing number of years that people can expect to live in good health after child rearing ends may make the dissolution of a marginal marriage and the prospect of possible remarriage a more practical and attractive option (Hiedemann et al., 1998).

Furthermore, divorce today may be *less* a threat to well-being in middle age than in young adulthood. That conclusion comes from a five-year longitudinal study that compared the reactions of 6,948 young and middle-aged adults taken from a nationally representative sample. The researchers used Ryff's six-dimensional measure of psychological well-being, as well as other criteria. In almost all respects, middle-aged people showed more adaptability than younger people in the face of separation or divorce, despite their more limited prospects for remarriage. Their greater maturity and expertise in handling life's problems may have given them an advantage in coping with the loss of a spouse. Middle-aged women in that position reported better social relations and greater personal mastery than younger women, as well as less depression and hostility. After remaining separated or divorced for five years, they also had a greater sense of autonomy. Middle-aged men facing termination of marriage were more self-accepting than younger men. Those who remained separated or divorced for five years reported less depression and hostility, but also less personal growth (Marks & Lambert, 1998).

Checkpoint

Can you . . .

- ✔ Describe the U-shaped curve of marital satisfaction, and cite factors than may help explain it?
- ✔ Give reasons for the tendency for divorce to occur early in a marriage, and cite factors that may increase the risk of divorce in midlife?

Gay and Lesbian Relationships

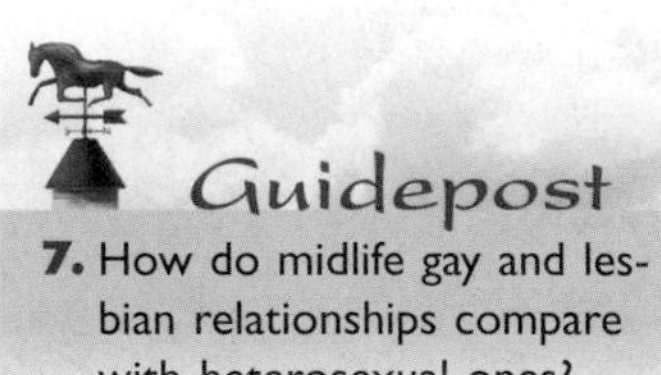

Guidepost

7. How do midlife gay and lesbian relationships compare with heterosexual ones?

Gays and lesbians now in middle age grew up at a time when homosexuality was considered a mental illness, and homosexuals tended to be isolated not only from the larger community but from each other. Today this pioneer generation is just beginning to explore the opportunities inherent in the growing acceptance of homosexuality.*

Since many homosexuals still do not come out until well into adulthood, the timing of this crucial event can affect other aspects of development. Middle-aged gays and lesbians may be associating openly for the first time and establishing relationships. Many are still working out conflicts with parents and other family members (sometimes including spouses) or hiding their homosexuality from them.

Many middle-aged lesbians who did not come out until well into adulthood are openly forming relationships for the first time.

Because of the secrecy and stigma that have surrounded homosexuality, studies of gays and lesbians tend to have sampling problems. What little research exists on gay men has focused mostly on urban white men with above-average income and education. Lesbians studied so far also tend to be mostly white, professional, and middle or upper class. In one study, more than 25 percent of middle-aged lesbians lived alone, even if they were in intimate relationships (Bradford & Ryan, 1991). This may in part be a cohort effect; lesbians who grew up in the 1950s may be uncomfortable about living openly with a partner, as many younger lesbians do now.

Gay men who do not come out until midlife often go through a prolonged search for identity, marked by guilt, secrecy, heterosexual marriage,

*Unless otherwise referenced, this discussion is based on Kimmel & Sang (1995).

and conflicted relationships with both sexes. By contrast, those who recognize and accept their sexual orientation early in life often cross racial, socioeconomic, and age barriers within the gay community. Some move to cities with large gay populations, where they can more easily seek out and form relationships.

For the most part, the principles that apply to sustaining a heterosexual marriage also apply to maintaining gay and lesbian partnerships. Gay and lesbian relationships tend to be stronger if known as such to family and friends, and if the couple seek out supportive gay and lesbian environments (Haas & Stafford, 1998). Coming out to parents is often difficult but need not necessarily have an adverse impact on the couple's relationship (LaSala, 1998). When family and friends are supportive and validate the relationship, its quality tends to be higher (R. B. Smith & Brown, 1997).

Gay and lesbian couples tend to be more egalitarian than heterosexual couples, but, as with many heterosexual couples, balancing commitments to careers and relationship can be difficult. Gay couples in which one partner is less career-oriented than the other have an easier time, but couples in which both partners are relationship-centered tend to be happiest.

Friendships

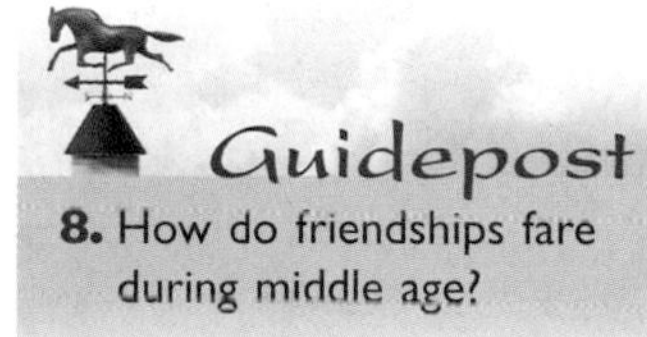

8. How do friendships fare during middle age?

As Carstensen's theory predicts, social networks tend to become smaller and more intimate at midlife. As compared with younger people, many middle-aged people have little time and energy to devote to friends; they are too busy with family and work and with building up security for retirement. Still, friendships do persist and, as with Madeleine Albright, are a strong source of emotional support and well being, especially for women (Adams & Allan, 1998; Antonucci et al., 2001). Friendships often revolve around work and parenting; others are based on neighborhood contacts or on association in volunteer organizations (Antonucci et al., 2001; Hartup & Stevens, 1999).

The quality of midlife friendships often makes up for what they lack in quantity of time spent. Especially during a crisis, such as a divorce or a problem with an aging parent, adults turn to friends for emotional support, practical guidance, comfort, companionship, and talk (Antonucci & Akiyama, 1997; Hartup & Stevens, 1999; Suitor & Pillemer, 1993). Conflicts with friends often center on differences in values, beliefs, and lifestyles; friends usually can "talk out" these conflicts while maintaining mutual dignity and respect (Hartup & Stevens, 1999).

The importance of friendships can vary from time to time. In a longitudinal study of 155 mostly white men and women from middle- and lower-class backgrounds, friends were more important to women's well-being in early middle age, but to men's well-being in late middle age (Paul, 1997).

Friendships often have a special importance for homosexuals. Lesbians are more likely to get emotional support from lesbian friends, lovers, and even ex-lovers than from relatives. Gay men, too, rely on friendship networks, which they actively create and maintain. Friendship networks provide solidarity and contact with younger people, which middle-aged heterosexuals normally get through family. Loss of friends to the scourge of AIDS has been traumatic for many gay men (Kimmel & Sang, 1995).

Checkpoint

Can you . . .

- ✔ Compare the formation and maintenance of homosexual relationships and heterosexual ones?
- ✔ Discuss the quantity, quality, and importance of friendships at midlife?

Relationships with Maturing Children

Parenthood is a process of letting go. This process usually reaches its climax during the parents' middle age. It is true that, with modern trends toward delaying marriage and parenthood, an increasing number of middle-aged people now face such issues as finding a good day care or preschool program and screening the content of Saturday morning cartoons. Still, most parents in the early part of middle age must cope with a different set of issues, which arise from living with children who will soon be leaving the nest. Once children become adults and have their own children, the

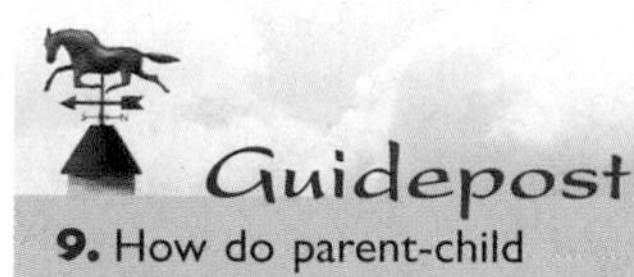

9. How do parent-child relationships change as children approach and reach adulthood?

intergenerational family multiplies in number and in connections. It is middle-aged parents, usually women, who tend to be the family "kinkeepers," maintaining ties among the various branches of the extended family (Putney & Bengtson, 2001).

Families today are diverse and complex. Increasingly, middle-aged parents have to deal with such nonnormative events as an adult child's continuing to live in the family home, or leaving it only to return. But one thing has not changed: parents' well-being tends to hinge on how their children turn out (Allen, Blieszner, & Roberto, 2000).

Adolescent Children: Issues for Parents

It is ironic that the people at the two times of life popularly linked with emotional crises—adolescence and midlife—often live in the same household. It is usually middle-aged adults who are the parents of adolescent children. While dealing with their own special concerns, parents have to cope daily with young people who are undergoing great physical, emotional, and social changes.

Although research contradicts the stereotype of adolescence as a time of inevitable turmoil and rebellion (refer back to Chapter 12), some rejection of parental authority is necessary. An important task for parents is to accept maturing children as they are, not as what the parents had hoped they would be.

Theorists from a variety of perspectives have described this period as one of questioning, reappraisal, or diminished well-being for parents. However, this too is not inevitable, according to a questionnaire survey of 129 two-parent, intact, mostly white, socioeconomically diverse families with a firstborn son or daughter between ages 10 and 15. Most vulnerable were mothers who were not heavily invested in paid work; apparently work can bolster a parent's self-worth despite the challenges of having a teenage child. For some other parents, especially white-collar and professional men with sons, their children's adolescence brought increased satisfaction, well-being, and even pride. For most parents, the normative changes of adolescence elicited a mixture of positive and negative emotions. This was particularly true of mothers with early adolescent daughters, whose relationships generally tend to be both close and conflict-filled (Silverberg, 1996).

When Children Leave: The Empty Nest

Research is also challenging popular ideas about the empty nest, a supposedly difficult transition, especially for women. Although some women, heavily invested in mothering, do have problems at this time, they are far outnumbered by those who, like Madeleine Albright, find the departure liberating (Antonucci et al., 2001; Antonucci & Akiyama, 1997; Barnett, 1985; Chiriboga, 1997; Helson, 1997; Mitchell & Helson, 1990). Today, the refilling of the nest by grown children returning home (discussed in an upcoming section) is far more stressful (Thomas, 1997).

The empty nest does not signal the end of parenthood. It is a transition to a new stage: the relationship between parents and adult children. For many women, this transition brings relief from what Gutmann called the "chronic emergency of parenthood" (Cooper & Gutmann, 1987, p. 347). They can now pursue their own interests as they bask in their grown children's accomplishments. The empty nest may be harder on couples whose identity is dependent on the parental role, or who now must face marital problems they had previously pushed aside under the press of parental responsibilities (Antonucci et al., 2001).

In a longitudinal study of employed married women with multiple roles, the empty nest had *no* effect on psychological health, but cutting back on employment *increased* distress, whereas going to work full-time *decreased* it (Wethington & Kessler, 1989). On the other hand, in a comparison of stress at various stages of life, men in the empty nest stage were most likely to report health-related stress (Chiriboga, 1997).

Parenting Grown Children

Elliott Roosevelt, a son of President Franklin Delano Roosevelt, used to tell this story about his mother, Eleanor Roosevelt: at a state dinner, Eleanor, who was seated next to him, leaned over and whispered in his ear. A friend later asked Elliott, then in his forties, what she had said. "She told me to eat my peas," he answered.

Even after the years of active parenting are over and children have left home for good, parents are still parents. The midlife role of parent to young adults raises new issues and calls for new attitudes and behaviors on the part of both generations. In middle-class families, at least, middle-aged parents generally give their children more support than they get from them as the young adults establish careers and families (Antonucci et al., 2001). Some parents have difficulty treating their offspring as adults, and many young adults have difficulty accepting their parents' continuing concern about them. In a warm, supportive family environment, such conflicts can be managed by an open airing of feelings (Putney & Bengtson, 2001).

Most young adults and their middle-aged parents enjoy each other's company and get along well. However, intergenerational families do not all fit one mold. It has been estimated that about 25 percent of intergenerational families are *tight-knit,* both geographically and emotionally; they have frequent contact with mutual help and support. Another 25 percent are *sociable,* but with less emotional affinity or commitment. About 16 percent have *obligatory* relationships, with much interaction but little emotional attachment; and 17 percent are *detached,* both emotionally and geographically. An in-between category consists of those who are *intimate but distant* (16 percent), spending little time together but retaining warm feelings that might lead to a renewal of contact and exchange. Adult children tend to be closer to their mothers than to their fathers (Bengtson, 2001; Silverstein & Bengtson, 1997).

Parents of grown children generally express satisfaction with their parenting role and with the way their children turned out (Umberson, 1992). Parents who believe that their children have turned out well tend to feel good about themselves. In one study, researchers interviewed 215 mothers and fathers (average age, about 54) on their grown children's attainments and personal and social adjustment. Parents who saw their children as successful and, especially, as well adjusted scored higher on all dimensions of well-being (except autonomy) than those who did not.

Prolonged Parenting: The "Cluttered Nest"

What happens if the nest does not empty when it normally should, or unexpectedly refills? Since the 1980s, in most western nations, more and more adult children have delayed leaving home. Furthermore, the **revolving door syndrome** (sometimes called the *boomerang phenomenon*) has become more common, as increasing numbers of young adults, especially men, return to their parents' home, sometimes more than once, and sometimes with their own families. The family home can be a convenient, supportive, and affordable haven while young adults are getting on their feet or regaining their balance in times of financial, marital, or other trouble (Aquilino, 1996; Putney & Bengtson, 2001).

revolving door syndrome Tendency for young adults to return to their parents' home while getting on their feet or in times of financial, marital, or other trouble.

In the United States, in the year 2000—a time of economic decline—10.5 percent of 25- to 34-year-olds were living in the family home (Grieder, 2001). This "nonnormative" experience is becoming less so, especially for parents with more than one child. Rather than an abrupt leave-taking, the empty nest transition may be seen as a more prolonged process of separation, often lasting several years. Most likely to come home are single, divorced, or separated children and those who end a cohabiting relationship (Aquilino, 1996; Putney & Bengtson, 2001).

What's Your View?

- Do you think it is a good idea for adult children to live with their parents? If so, under what circumstances? What "house rules" do you think should apply?

Prolonged parenting contradicts traditional expectations (Putney & Bengtson, 2001). As children move from adolescence to young adulthood, parents normally

Checkpoint

Can you . . .

- Discuss the changes parents of adolescent children tend to go through?
- Tell how most women and men respond to the empty nest?
- Describe typical features of relationships between parents and grown children?
- Give reasons for the prolonged parenting phenomenon, and discuss how families deal with it?

expect them to become independent, and they themselves normally expect to do so. An adult child's autonomy is a sign of parental success. As the timing-of-events model would predict, then, a grown child's delaying departure from the nest, or returning to it, may lead to tension. Serious conflicts or open hostility may arise when a young adult child is unemployed and financially dependent or has returned after the failure of a marriage. Relations are smoother when the parents see the adult child moving toward autonomy, for example by enrolling in college (Antonucci et al., 2001; Aquilino, 1996).

Adult children tend to be less satisfied with having to live in their parents' home than the parents are with having them there (Putney & Bengtson, 2001). Disagreements may center on household responsibilities and the adult child's lifestyle. The young adult is likely to feel isolated from peers, while the parents may feel hampered in renewing their intimacy, exploring personal interests, and resolving marital issues (Aquilino & Supple, 1991). The return of an adult child works best when parents and child negotiate roles and responsibilities, acknowledging the child's adult status and the parents' right to privacy (Aquilino, 1996).

Other Kinship Ties

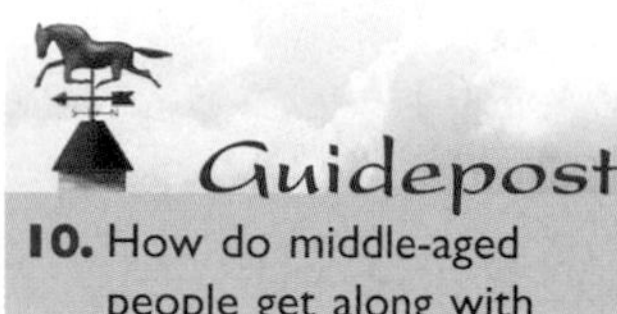

Guidepost

10. How do middle-aged people get along with parents and siblings?

Except in times of need, ties with the family of origin—parents and siblings—tend to recede in importance during young adulthood, when work, spouses or partners, and children take precedence. At midlife, these earliest kinship ties may reassert themselves in a new way, as the responsibility for care and support of aging parents may begin to shift to their middle-aged children. In addition, a new relationship typically begins at this time of life: grandparenthood.

Relationships with Aging Parents

In 1900, a middle-aged couple had only a 10 percent chance of having at least two parents alive (Cutler & Devlin, 1996). Today, with dramatically increased life expectancy (see Chapter 17), seven out of ten people enter middle age with two living parents. Most leave middle age with none (Bumpass & Aquilino, 1993). The years in between may bring dramatic, though gradual, changes in filial relationships. Many middle-aged people look at their parents more objectively than before, seeing them as individuals with both strengths and weaknesses. Something else may happen during these years: one day a middle-aged adult may look at a mother or father and see an old person, who may need a daughter's or son's care (Troll & Fingerman, 1996).

Contact and Mutual Help The bond between middle-aged children and their elderly parents is strong, growing out of earlier attachment and continuing as long as both generations live (Bengtson, 2001; Cicirelli, 1980, 1989b; Rossi & Rossi, 1990). Most middle-aged adults and their parents have close, affectionate relationships based on frequent contact and mutual help (Antonucci & Akiyama, 1997; Bengtson, 2001). Many live near each other and see each other frequently (Lin & Rogerson, 1995; Umberson, 1992). Relations with older mothers are especially likely to be tightly knit (Bengtson, 2001).

Mostly, help and assistance continue to flow from parents to child, especially in times of crisis (Bengtson, 2001). But while most older adults are physically fit, vigorous, and independent, some seek their children's assistance in making decisions and may depend on them for daily tasks and financial help. There may even be a role reversal; the parent now becomes the one who needs help from the child (Antonucci et al., 2001).

filial maturity Stage of life, proposed by Marcoen and others, in which middle-aged children, as the outcome of a filial crisis, learn to accept and meet their parents' need to depend on them.

With the lengthening of the life span, some developmental scientists have proposed a new life stage called **filial maturity,** when middle-aged children "learn to accept and

This middle-aged daughter is beginning to realize that her mother is no longer a tower of strength but instead is beginning to lean on her. With filial maturity, *middle-aged children learn to accept and meet their parents' dependency needs with a combination of love and a sense of duty, while letting the parents retain as much autonomy as possible.*

to meet their parents' dependency needs" (Marcoen, 1995, p. 125). This normative development is seen as the healthy outcome of a **filial crisis,** in which adults learn to balance love and duty to their parents with autonomy within a two-way relationship. Most middle-aged people willingly accept their obligations to their parents (Antonucci et al., 2001) and often expect more of themselves than the parents do of them (Hamon & Blieszner, 1990).

filial crisis In Marcoen's terminology, normative development of middle age, in which adults learn to balance love and duty to their parents with autonomy within a two-way relationship.

Becoming a Caregiver for Aging Parents Given the high cost of nursing homes and most older people's reluctance to enter and stay in them (see Chapter 18), many dependent elders receive long-term care in their own home or in a caregiver's. The chances of becoming a caregiver to an aging parent increase through middle age. Often the need arises when a mother is widowed, or when a woman divorced years before can no longer manage alone. Longer life, especially in developed countries, means more risk of chronic diseases and disabilities; and families are smaller than in the past, with fewer siblings to share in a parent's care (Kinsella & Velkiff, 2001).

Cultural assumptions that caregiving is a female function make it most likely that a daughter will assume the role (Antonucci et al., 2001; Matthews, 1995). Also, perhaps because of the intimate nature of the contact and the strength of the mother-daughter bond, mothers may prefer a daughter's care (Lee, Dwyer, & Coward, 1993). Sons do contribute, more than is often recognized, but they are less likely to provide primary, personal care (Marks, 1996; Matthews, 1995). The world over, caregiving is mostly a female function (Kinsella & Velkoff, 2001).

The generations typically get along best while parents are healthy and vigorous. When older people become infirm—especially if they undergo mental deterioration or personality changes—the burden of caring for them may strain the relationship (Antonucci et al., 2001; Marcoen, 1995). Many caregivers find the task a physical, emotional, and financial burden, especially if they work full time, have limited financial resources, or lack support and assistance (Lund, 1993a).

It is hard for women who work outside the home to assume an added caregiving role (Marks, 1996). About one-third of family caregivers in the United States work for pay, and more than one-fourth have had to quit jobs to meet caregiving obligations (Noelker & Whitlatch, 1995). (Flexible work schedules and family and medical leave can help alleviate this problem.) On the other hand, the need to care for aging parents may come at a time when a middle-aged child is preparing to retire and can ill afford the additional costs of caring for a frail older person, or the adult child may have health problems of his or her own (Kinsella & Velkoff, 2001).

Caring for a person with physical impairments is hard. It can be even harder to care for someone with dementia, who, in addition to being unable to carry on basic functions of daily living, may be incontinent, suspicious, agitated, subject to hallucinations, likely to wander about at night, dangerous to self and others, and in need of constant supervision (Biegel, 1995). Sometimes the strains created by incessant, heavy demands are so great as to lead to abuse, neglect, or even abandonment of the dependent elderly person (see Chapter 18).

Emotional strain may come not only from caregiving itself but from the need to balance it with other aspects of a caregiver's life, such as a marital relationship (Lund, 1993a), work responsibilities (Antonucci et al., 2001), personal interests, social activities, and travel plans (Mui, 1992). The dependence of elderly parents may come at a time when middle-aged adults are trying to launch their own children or, if parenthood was delayed, to raise them. Members of this "generation in the middle," sometimes called the **sandwich generation,** may be caught in a squeeze between these competing needs and their limited resources of time, money, and energy. The result of these strains may be **caregiver burnout,** a physical, mental, and emotional exhaustion that affects adults who care for aged relatives (Barnhart, 1992). (Box 16-2 discusses sources of assistance to help prevent caregiver burnout.)

sandwich generation Middle-aged adults squeezed by competing needs to raise or launch children and to care for elderly parents.

caregiver burnout Condition of physical, mental, and emotional exhaustion affecting adults who care for aged persons.

For some adults, it is argued, the needs of aging parents represent nonnormative, unanticipated demands. Adults expect to assume the physical, financial, and emotional care of their children. Most do *not* expect to have to care for their parents. When parents' dependency becomes undeniable, many adult children may find it hard to cope (Barnhart, 1992). Still, 95 percent of caregivers accept their filial responsibility; they do not abandon their parents (Noelker & Whitlatch, 1995).

Practically Speaking

BOX 16-2

Preventing Caregiver Burnout

Even the most patient, loving caregiver may become frustrated, anxious, or resentful under the constant strain of meeting an older person's seemingly endless needs. Often families and friends fail to recognize that caregivers have a right to feel discouraged, frustrated, and put upon. Caregivers need a life of their own, beyond the loved one's disability or disease (J. Evans, 1994).

Community support programs can reduce the strains and burdens of caregiving, prevent burnout, and postpone the need for institutionalization of the dependent person. Support services may include meals and housekeeping; transportation and escort services; and adult day care centers, which provide supervised activities and care while caregivers work or attend to personal needs. *Respite care* (substitute supervised care by visiting nurses or home health aides) gives regular caregivers some time off, whether for a few hours, a day, a weekend, or a week. Temporary admission to a nursing home is another alternative.

Although there is some dispute about their effectiveness, some research suggests that such programs do improve caregivers' morale and reduce stress (Gallagher-Thompson, 1995). In one longitudinal study, caregivers with adequate community support reported many dimensions of personal growth. Some had become more empathic, caring, understanding, patient, and compassionate, closer to the person they were caring for, and more appreciative of their own good health. Others felt good about having fulfilled their responsibilities. Some had "learned to value life more and to take one day at a time," and a few had learned to "laugh at situations and events" (Lund, 1993a).

Behavioral training and psychotherapy can help caregivers deal with a patient's difficult behavior and their own tendency toward depression (Gallagher-Thompson, 1995). One behavioral training program at the University of Chicago had considerable success in getting patients to handle some self-care and to be more sociable and less verbally abusive. Caregivers learned such techniques as contingency contracting ("If you do this, the consequence will be . . .), modeling desired behaviors, rehearsal, and giving feedback (Gallagher-Thompson, 1995).

Through counseling, support, and self-help groups, caregivers can share problems, gain information about community resources, and improve skills. One such program helped daughters recognize the limits of their ability to meet their mothers' needs, and the value of encouraging their mothers' self-reliance. This understanding lightened the daughters' burden and improved their relationship with their mothers; as a result, the mothers became less lonely (Scharlach, 1987).

A "Caregiver's Bill of Rights" (Home, 1985) can help caregivers keep a positive perspective and remind them that their needs count, too.

A Caregiver's Bill of Rights

I have the right

- to take care of myself. This is not an act of selfishness. It will give me the capability of taking better care of my relative.
- to seek help from others even though my relative may object. I recognize the limits of my own endurance and strength.
- to maintain facets of my own life that do not include the person I care for, just as I would if he or she were healthy. I know that I do everything that I reasonably can for this person, and I have the right to do some things just for myself.
- to get angry, be depressed, and express other difficult feelings occasionally.
- to reject any attempt by my relative (either conscious or unconscious) to manipulate me through guilt, anger, or depression.
- to receive consideration, affection, forgiveness, and acceptance for what I do from my loved ones for as long as I offer these qualities in return.
- to take pride in what I am accomplishing and to applaud the courage it has sometimes taken to meet the needs of my relative.
- to protect my individuality and my right to make a life for myself that will sustain me in the time when my relative no longer needs my full-time help.
- to expect and demand that as new strides are made in finding resources to aid physically and mentally impaired older persons in our country, similar strides will be made toward aiding and supporting caregivers.
- to *(add your own statements of rights to this list. Read this list to yourself every day).*

What's Your View?

What more could be done to ease caregivers' burdens?

Check It Out:

OLC

For more information on this topic, go to http://www. mhhe.com/papaliah9.

Recent research has challenged the prevalence of the sandwich generation (Kinsella & Velkoff, 2001; Putney & Bengtson, 2001; Staudinger & Bluck, 2001). Studies in the United States, Europe, and Canada have found relatively few middle-aged adults sandwiched between caregiving, work, and dependent children (Hagestad, 2000; Marks, 1998; Penning, 1998; Rosenthal, Martin-Andrews, & Matthews, 1996), as children generally have left the nest before the need for caregiving arises. Furthermore, while role conflicts undeniably can bring severe stress, that is not necessarily the case. Some caregivers flourish in multiple roles. Particular circumstances and contexts make a difference, as do the attitudes individuals bring to the task (Bengtson, 2001). Caregiving can be an opportunity for growth if a caregiver feels deeply about a parent and about family solidarity, looks at caregiving as a challenge, and has adequate personal, family, and community resources to meet that challenge (Bengtson, 2001; Bengtson, Rosenthal, & Burton, 1996; Biegel, 1995; Lund, 1993a).

What's Your View?

- What would you do if one or both of your parents required long-term care? To what extent should children or other relatives be responsible for such care? To what extent, and in what ways, should society help?

Relationships with Siblings

Relationships with siblings are the longest-lasting in most people's lives (Antonucci et al., 2001). About 85 percent of middle-aged Americans, like Madeleine Albright, have at least one living sibling, and most siblings remain in contact. Sisters, especially, stay in touch and stand ready to help each other (Cicirelli, 1980, 1995; H. G. Ross, Dalton, & Milgram, 1980; Scott & Roberto, 1981). Step- and half-siblings are also likely to maintain contact, depending on how long they lived together during childhood; but they do not see each other as often as full siblings do, and they may provide less help. These differences may diminish as stepfamilies become more common (Antonucci et al., 2001).

In some cross-sectional research, sibling relationships over the life span appear to take the form of an hourglass, with the most contact at the two ends—childhood and middle to late adulthood—and the least contact during the childraising years. After establishing careers and families, siblings may renew ties (Bedford, 1995; Cicirelli, 1995; Putney & Bengtson, 2001). Other studies indicate a decline in frequency of contact throughout adulthood. Sibling conflict tends to diminish with age—perhaps because siblings who do *not* get along see each other less (Putney & Bengtson, 2001).

Relationships with siblings who remain in contact are important to psychological well-being in midlife (Antonucci et al., 2001), though their importance relative to other relationships, such as friendships, may rise and fall from time to time. Sibling relationships seem to serve somewhat different purposes for men and women. For women, positive feelings toward siblings are linked with a favorable self-concept; for men, with high morale. The more contact both men and women have with their siblings, the less likely they are to show symptoms of psychological problems (Paul, 1997).

Dealing with the care of aging parents brings some siblings closer together but causes resentment and conflict among others (Antonucci et al., 2001; Bedford, 1995; Bengtson et al., 1996). The quality of a sibling relationship during the early years—cooperative or conflictual—may affect the way adult siblings handle such issues (Bedford, 1995). Disagreements may arise over the division of care (Lerner, Somers, Reid, Chiriboga, & Tierney, 1991; Strawbridge & Wallhagen, 1991) or over an inheritance, especially if the sibling relationship has not been good. Among 95 married daughters caring for parents with dementia, siblings were a strong source of support, but also the most important source of interpersonal stress (Suitor & Pillemer, 1993).

Checkpoint

Can you . . .

- ✔ Describe the change in the balance of filial relationships that often occurs between middle-aged children and elderly parents?
- ✔ Cite sources of potential strain on caregivers for elderly parents?
- ✔ Discuss the nature and importance of sibling relationships in middle age as compared with other parts of the life span?

Grandparenthood

In some African communities, grandparents are called "noble." In Japan, grandmothers have traditionally worn red as a sign of their status (Kornhaber, 1986). In western societies, too, becoming a grandparent is an important event in a person's life; but its timing and meaning vary.

Guidepost

11. How has grandparenthood changed, and what roles do grandparents play?

In Japan, grandmothers like this one traditionally wear red as a sign of their noble status. Grandparenthood is an important milestone in western societies as well.

Often grandparenthood begins before the end of active parenting. Adults in the United States become grandparents at an average age of 48, according to a telephone survey of 1,500 grandparents belonging to the American Association of Retired Persons (AARP) (Davies & Williams, 2002). With today's lengthening life spans, many adults spend several decades as grandparents. Since women tend to live longer than men, grandmothers typically live to see at least the oldest grandchild become an adult and to become great-grandmothers (Szinovacz, 1998).

Grandparenthood today is different in other ways from grandparenthood in the past. The average U.S. grandparent has six grandchildren (Davies & Williams, 2002), compared with twelve to fifteen around the turn of the century (Szinovacz, 1998; Uhlenberg, 1988). With the rising incidence of midlife divorce, about one in five grandparents is divorced, widowed, or separated (Davies & Williams, 2002), and many children have stepgrandparents. Grandmothers of younger children are more likely to be in the workforce (and thus less available to help out). On the other hand, trends toward early retirement free more grandparents to spend time with older grandchildren. Many grandparents still have living parents, whose care they must balance with grandchildren's needs. And many grandparents in both developed and developing countries provide part-time or primary care for grandchildren (Kinsella & Velkoff, 2001; Szinovacz, 1998).

The Grandparent's Role In many developing societies, such as those in Latin America and Asia, extended-family households predominate, and grandparents play an integral role in child raising and family decisions. In such Asian countries as Thailand and Taiwan, about 40 percent of the population ages 50 and over live in the same household with a minor grandchild, and half of those with grandchildren ages 10 or younger—usually grandmothers—provide care for the child (Kinsella & Velkoff, 2001).

In the United States, the extended family household is common in some minority communities, but the dominant household pattern is the nuclear family. When children

Grandparents, like this grandmother teaching her granddaughter to make a quilt, can have an important influence on their grandchildren's development. Grandmothers tend to have closer, warmer relationships with their grandchildren than grandfathers.

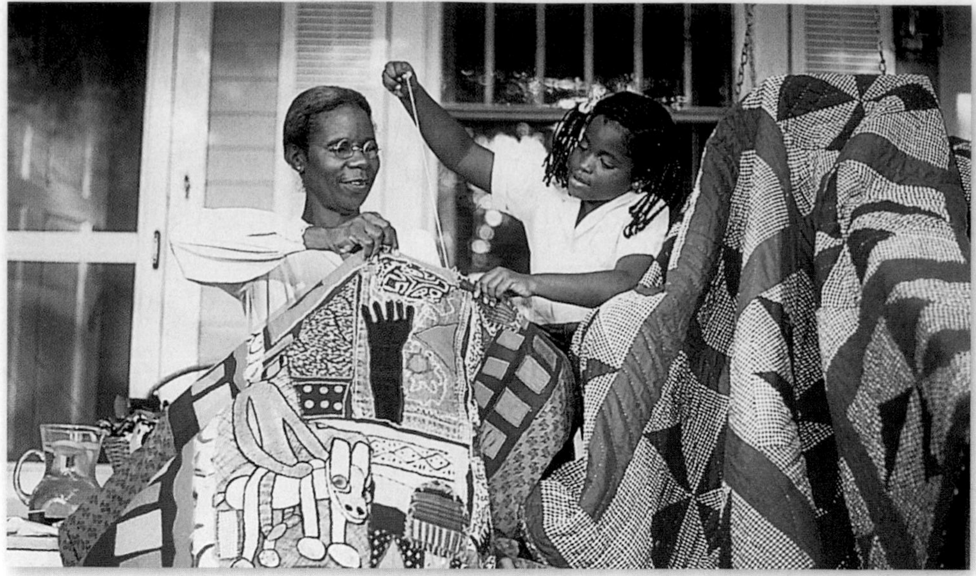

What's Your View?

- Have you had a close relationship with a grandmother or grandfather? If so, in what specific ways did that relationship influence your development?

grow up, they typically leave home and establish new, autonomous nuclear families wherever their inclinations, aspirations, and job hunts take them. Although 68 percent of the grandparents in the AARP survey see at least one grandchild every one to two weeks, 45 percent live too far away to see their grandchildren regularly (Davies & Williams, 2002). However, distance does not necessarily affect the quality of relationships with grandchildren (Kivett, 1991, 1993, 1996).

Grandparents frequently walk a tightrope between reluctance to interfere in adult children's family lives and obligation to provide help and support, and their level of involvement is often up to the parents (Silverstein, Giarrusso, & Bengtson, 1998). A major study of a nationally representative three-generation sample found that "grandparents play a limited but important role in family dynamics," and many have strong emotional ties to their grandchildren (Cherlin & Furstenberg, 1986a, p. 26).

Grandmothers tend to be kinkeepers; they are the ones who keep in touch with the grandchildren. In general, grandmothers have closer, warmer, more affectionate relationships with their grandchildren (especially granddaughters) than grandfathers do, and see them more (Putney & Bengtson, 2001).

The most frequent activities grandparents in the AARP sample do with their grandchildren are having dinner together, watching television, going shopping, and reading to them; more than half exercise or play sports with their grandchildren. More than half spend money on their grandchildren's educational needs, and about 45 percent say they help pay grandchildren's living expenses. About 15 percent of these grandparents provide child care while the parents work (Davies & Williams, 2002). Indeed, as we reported in Chapter 6, grandparents are now the nation's number one child care providers; 21 percent of all preschoolers and 15 percent of grade-school-age children stay with grandparents while their mothers work (Smith, 2002). A similar trend exists in some other developed countries (Kinsella & Velkoff, 2001).

Checkpoint

Can you . . .

- ✔ Tell how grandparenthood has changed in recent generations?
- ✔ Describe the roles grandparents play in family life?

As grandchildren grow older, contact tends to diminish, but affection grows. The decline in contact is more rapid among younger cohorts of grandparents, who tend to have better health, more money, and busier lives (Silverstein & Long, 1998).

Grandparenting After Divorce and Remarriage One result of the rise in divorce and remarriage is a growing number of grandparents and grandchildren whose relationships are endangered or severed. Another result is the creation of large numbers of stepgrandparents.

After a divorce, since the mother usually has custody, her parents tend to have more contact and stronger relationships with their grandchildren, and the paternal grandparents tend to have less (Cherlin & Furstenberg, 1986b; Myers & Perrin, 1993). A divorced mother's remarriage typically reduces her need for support from her parents, but not their contact with their grandchildren. For paternal grandparents, however, the new marriage increases the likelihood that they will be displaced or that the family will move away, making contact more difficult (Cherlin & Furstenberg, 1986b).

Because ties with grandparents are important to children's development, every state in the Union has given grandparents (and in some states, great-grandparents, siblings, and others) the right to visitation after a divorce or the death of a parent, if a judge finds it in the best interests of the child. However, a few state courts have struck down such laws, and some legislatures have restricted grandparents' visitation rights. The Supreme Court in June 2000 invalidated Washington State's "grandparents' rights" law as too broad an intrusion on parental rights (Greenhouse, 2000a).

The remarriage of either parent often brings a new set of grandparents into the picture, and often stepgrandchildren as well. Stepgrandparents may find it hard to become close to their new stepgrandchildren, especially older children and those who do not live with the grandparent's adult child (Cherlin & Furstenberg, 1986b; Longino & Earle, 1996; Myers & Perrin, 1993). Such issues as birthday and Christmas presents for a "real" grandchild's half- or stepsiblings, or which grandparents are visited or included at holidays, can generate tension. Creating new family traditions; including *all* the grandchildren, step and otherwise, in trips, outings, and other activities; offering a safe haven for the children when they are unhappy or upset; and being understanding and supportive of all members of the new stepfamily are ways in which stepgrandparents can build bridges, not walls (T. S. Kaufman, 1993; Visher & Visher, 1991).

Raising Grandchildren Many grandparents are their grandchildren's sole or primary caregivers. One reason, in developing countries, is the migration of rural parents to urban areas to find work. These "skip-generation" families exist in all regions of the world, particularly in Afro-Caribbean countries. In sub-Saharan Africa, the AIDS epidemic has left many orphans whose grandparents step into the parents' place (Kinsella & Velkoff, 2001).

In the United States, an increasing number of grandparents (and even great-grandparents) are serving as "parents by default" for children whose parents are unable to care for them—often as a result of teenage pregnancy or substance abuse, or of illness, divorce, or death (Allen et al., 2000). In 2000, more than 4.5 million children lived in 2.4 million grandparent-headed households—a 30 percent increase since 1990 (AARP, 2002). In the AARP survey mentioned earlier, 6 percent of grandparents had grandchildren living with them, and in more than 43 percent of those homes, no parent was present (Davies & Williams, 2001). Many of these caregiver-grandparents are divorced or widowed and live on fixed incomes (Hudnall, 2001), and many are in dire financial straits (Casper & Bryson, 1998).

Unplanned surrogate parenthood can be a physical, emotional, and financial drain on middle-aged or older adults. They may have to quit their jobs, shelve their retirement plans, drastically reduce their leisure pursuits and social life, and endanger their health (Burton, 1992; Chalfie, 1994; Minkler & Roe, 1992, 1996). Most grandparents do not have as much energy, patience, or stamina as they once had and may not be up on current educational and social trends (Hudnall, 2001).

Most grandparents who take on the responsibility to raise their grandchildren do it because they love the children and do not want them placed in a stranger's foster home. However, the age difference can become a barrier, and both generations may feel cheated out of their traditional roles. At the same time, grandparents often have to deal not only with a sense of guilt because the adult children they raised have failed

kinship care Care of children living without parents in the home of grandparents or other relatives, with or without a change of legal custody.

Checkpoint

Can you . . .

- ✔ Tell how parents' divorce and remarriage can affect grandparents' relationships with grandchildren?
- ✔ Discuss the challenges involved in raising grandchildren?

their own children, but with the rancor they feel toward this adult child. For some caregiver couples, the strains produce tension in their own relationship. If one or both parents later resume their normal roles, it may be emotionally wrenching to return the child (Crowley, 1993; Larsen, 1990–1991).

Grandparents providing **kinship care** who do not become foster parents or gain custody have no legal status and no more rights than unpaid baby-sitters. They may face many practical problems, from enrolling the child in school and gaining access to academic records to obtaining medical insurance for the child. Grandchildren are usually not eligible for coverage under employer-provided health insurance even if the grandparent has custody (Chalfie, 1994; Simon-Rusinowitz, Krach, Marks, Piktialis, & Wilson, 1996). Like working parents, working grandparents need good, affordable child care and family-friendly workplace policies, such as time off to care for a sick child (Simon-Rusinowitz et al., 1996). The federal Family and Medical Leave Act of 1993 does cover grandparents who are raising grandchildren, but many do not realize it.

Refocus

- In what ways did Madeleine Albright's life course in middle age reflect the points discussed in this chapter?
- How would each of the theories discussed in this chapter describe and explain the changes Albright went through in her middle years?
- Did Albright show the changes in gender identity described by either Jung or Gutmann or in the Mills Longitudinal Study?
- How do you think Albright would score herself on Ryff's six dimensions of well-being?
- What aspects of the discussions on changing relationships at midlife seem to apply to Albright?

Grandparents can be sources of guidance, companions in play, links to the past, and symbols of family continuity. They express generativity, a longing to transcend mortality by investing themselves in the lives of future generations. Men and women who do not become grandparents may fulfill generative needs by becoming foster grandparents or volunteering in schools or hospitals (Porcino, 1983, 1991). By finding ways to develop what Erikson called the "virtue" of care, adults prepare themselves to enter the culminating period of adult development, which we discuss in Part Eight.

SUMMARY AND KEY TERMS

Looking at the Life Course in Middle Age

Guidepost 1. How do developmental scientists approach the study of psychosocial development in middle adulthood?

- Developmental scientists view midlife psychosocial development both objectively, in terms of trajectories or pathways, and subjectively, in terms of people's sense of self and the way they actively construct their lives.
- Change and continuity must be seen in context and in terms of the whole life span.

Change at Midlife: Classic Theoretical Approaches

Guidepost 2. What do classic theorists have to say about psychosocial change in middle age?

- Although some theorists hold that personality is essentially formed by midlife, there is a growing consensus that midlife development shows change as well as stability. Change can be maturational (normative) or nonnormative.
- Humanistic theorists such as Maslow and Rogers saw middle age as an opportunity for positive change.
- Carl Jung held that men and women at midlife express previously suppressed aspects of personality. Two necessary tasks are giving up the image of youth and acknowledging mortality.
- Erikson's seventh psychosocial stage is generativity versus stagnation. Generativity can be expressed through parenting and grandparenting, teaching or mentorship, productivity or creativity, self-development, and "maintenance of the world." The "virtue" of this period is care.
- Vaillant and Levinson found major midlife shifts. Their findings echo Jung's and Erikson's theories.
- Despite the greater fluidity of the life cycle today, people still tend to expect and assess important events in their lives by a "social clock."

individuation *(568)*

generativity versus stagnation *(569)*

generativity *(569)*

interiority *(570)*

The Self at Midlife: Issues and Themes

Guidepost 3. What issues concerning the self come to the fore during middle adulthood?

- Key psychosocial issues and themes during middle adulthood concern the existence of a midlife crisis, identity development (including gender identity), and psychological well-being.
- Research does not support a normative midlife crisis. It is more accurate to refer to a transition that often involves a midlife review, which may be a psychological turning point.
- According to Whitbourne's model, identity development is a process in which people continually confirm or revise their self-perceptions based on experience and feedback from others. Identity style can predict adaptation to the onset of aging.
- Generativity is an aspect of identity development. Current research on generativity finds it most prevalent at middle age but not universally so. Generativity may be affected by social roles and expectations and by individual characteristics.
- Narrative psychology describes identity development as a continuous process of constructing a life story.
- Research has found increasing "masculinization" of women and "feminization" of men at midlife, but this may be largely a cohort effect and may reflect the types of measures used. Research generally does *not* support Gutmann's proposed gender crossover.
- Research based on Ryff's six-dimensional scale has found that midlife is generally a period of positive mental health and well-being, though socioeconomic status is a factor.
- Generativity is related to psychological well-being in middle age. It may derive from involvement in multiple roles, but not necessarily in all roles equally.
- Much research suggests that for women the fifties are a "prime time" of life.

midlife crisis *(572)*

midlife review *(572)*

identity process model *(573)*

identity assimilation *(574)*

identity accommodation *(574)*

identity style *(574)*

gender crossover *(577)*

Changes in Relationships at Midlife

Guidepost 4. What role do social relationships play in the lives of middle-aged people?

- Two theories of the changing importance of relationships are Kahn and Antonucci's social convoy theory and Laura Carstensen's socioemotional selectivity theory. According to both theories, social-emotional support is an important element in social interaction at midlife and beyond.
- Relationships at midlife are important to physical and mental health but also can present stressful demands.

social convoy theory *(582)*

socioemotional selectivity theory *(582)*

Consensual Relationships

Guidepost 5. Do marriages typically become happier or unhappier during the middle years?

- Research on the quality of marriage suggests a dip in marital satisfaction during the years of child rearing, followed by an improved relationship after the children leave home.

Guidepost 6. How common is divorce at this time of life?

- Divorce at midlife is relatively uncommon but is increasing. Marital capital, socioeconomic status, and the timing and effects of the empty nest may play a part.
- Divorce today may be less threatening to well-being in middle age than in young adulthood.

marital capital *(585)*

empty nest *(585)*

Guidepost 7. How do midlife gay and lesbian relationships compare with heterosexual ones?

- Because many homosexuals delay coming out, at midlife they are often just establishing intimate relationships.

- Gay and lesbian couples tend to be more egalitarian than heterosexual couples but experience similar problems in balancing family and career commitments.

Guidepost 8. How do friendships fare during middle age?

- Middle-aged people tend to invest less time and energy in friendships than younger adults do, but depend on friends for emotional support and practical guidance.
- Friendships may have special importance for homosexuals.

Relationships with Maturing Children

Guidepost 9. How do parent-child relationships change as children approach and reach adulthood?

- Parents of adolescents have to come to terms with a loss of control over their children's lives, and some parents do this more easily than others.
- The "emptying of the nest" is liberating for most women but may be stressful for couples whose identity is dependent on the parental role or those who now must face previously submerged marital problems.
- Today, more young adults are delaying departure from their childhood home or are returning to it, sometimes with their own families. This situation can be disturbing to both sides; adjustment tends to be smoother if the parents see the adult child as moving toward autonomy and if parents and child negotiate roles and responsibilities.
- Middle-aged parents tend to remain involved with their adult children, and most are generally happy with the way their children turned out. Conflict may arise over grown children's need to be treated as adults and parents' continuing concern about them.

revolving door syndrome *(589)*

Other Kinship Ties

Guidepost 10. How do middle-aged people get along with parents and siblings?

- Relationships between middle-aged adults and their parents are usually characterized by a strong bond of affection. The two generations generally maintain frequent contact and offer and receive assistance. Aid usually flows from parents to children.
- As life lengthens, more and more aging parents become dependent for care on their middle-aged children. Acceptance of these dependency needs is the mark of filial maturity and may be the outcome of a filial crisis.
- The chances of becoming a caregiver to an aging parent increase through middle age, especially for women.
- Caregiving can be a source of considerable stress but also of satisfaction. Community support programs can help prevent caregiver burnout.
- Although siblings tend to have less contact at midlife than before and after, most middle-aged siblings remain in touch, and their relationships are important to well-being.

Guidepost 11. How has grandparenthood changed, and what roles do grandparents play?

- Most U.S. adults become grandparents in middle age and have an average of six grandchildren.
- Although most American grandparents today are less intimately involved in grandchildren's lives than in the past (often because of geographic separation), they can play an important role.
- Grandmothers tend to be more involved in "kinkeeping" than grandfathers.
- Divorce and remarriage of an adult child can affect grandparent-grandchild relationships and create new stepgrandparenting roles.
- An increasing number of grandparents are raising grandchildren whose parents are unable to care for them. Raising grandchildren can create physical, emotional, and financial strains.

filial maturity *(590)*
filial crisis *(591)*
sandwich generation *(592)*
caregiver burnout *(592)*
kinship care *(598)*

PART 8

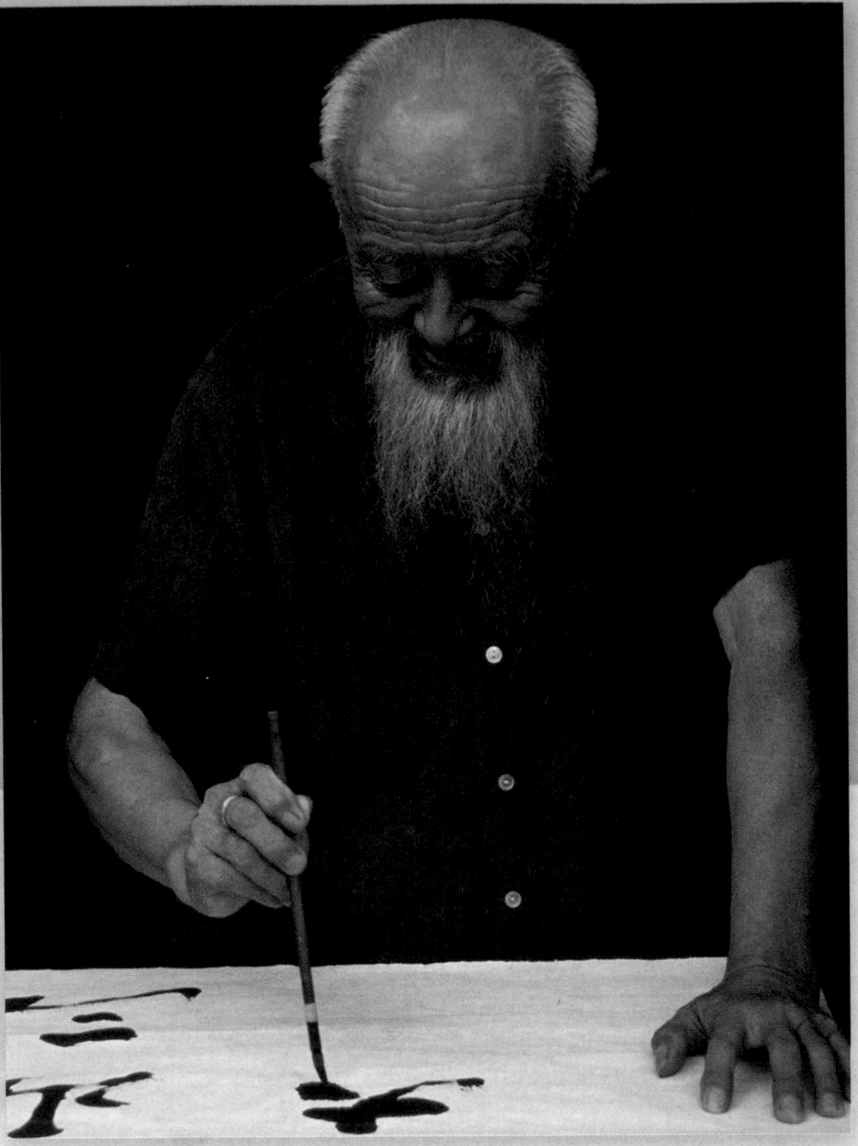

Linkups to look for

- Comprehension of health-related information can affect access to appropriate care.
- Exercise may improve mental alertness and morale.
- Blood flow to the brain can affect cognitive performance.
- Confidence, interest, and motivation can influence performance on intelligence tests.
- Conscientiousness and marital stability tend to predict long life.
- Cognitive appraisal of emotion-laden problems may help people develop coping strategies.
- Men who continue to work after age 65 tend to be in better health and better educated than those who retire, and they are more likely to view paid work as necessary to self-fulfillment.
- Physical limitations and cultural patterns affect older people's choice of living arrangements.
- People who can confide in friends tend to live longer.

Age 65 is the traditional entrance point for late adulthood, the last phase of life. Yet many adults at 65—or even 75 or 85—do not feel or act "old."

Individual differences become more pronounced in the later years, and "use it or lose it" becomes an urgent mandate. Most older adults enjoy good physical and mental health; people who keep physically and intellectually active can hold their own in most respects and even grow in competence. Physical and cognitive functioning in turn have psychosocial effects, often determining an older person's emotional state and whether she or he can live independently. ▸

Late Adulthood

PREVIEW

CHAPTER 17

Physical and Cognitive Development in Late Adulthood

Most people are healthy and active, although health and physical abilities decline somewhat.

Slowing of processing time affects some aspects of functioning.

Most people are mentally alert.

Although intelligence and memory may deteriorate in some areas, most people find ways to compensate.

CHAPTER 18

Psychosocial Development in Late Adulthood

Retirement may offer new options for exploration of interests and activities.

People need to cope with personal losses and impending death as they seek to understand the meaning and purpose of their lives.

Relationships with family and close friends can provide important support.

Search for meaning in life assumes central importance.

Chapter 17

Physical and Cognitive Development in Late Adulthood

Why not look at these new years of life in terms of continued or new roles in society, another stage in personal or even spiritual growth and development?

—**Betty Friedan, *The Fountain of Age*, 1993**

Focus: John Glenn, Space Pioneer

John Glenn

When John H. Glenn, Jr.* (b. 1921) blasted off from the Kennedy Space Center at Cape Canaveral on October 29, 1998, as a payload specialist on the shuttle *Discovery*, he became a space pioneer for the second time. In 1962, at the age of 40, Glenn had been the first American to orbit the earth. What made him a pioneer in 1998, when he next donned the orange jumpsuit, was that he was 77 years old—the oldest person ever to go into outer space.

Throughout his adult life, Glenn has won medals and set records. As a fighter pilot during the Korean War, he earned five Distinguished Flying Crosses. In 1957 he made the first cross-country supersonic jet flight. In 1962, when his *Friendship 7* one-man space capsule circled the globe three times in less than five hours, he instantly became a national hero.

Glenn was elected a U.S. senator from Ohio in 1974 and served four terms. As a member of the Senate Special Committee on Aging, his interest in the subject of aging prompted him to offer himself as a human guinea pig on the nine-day *Discovery* mission.

As Glenn discovered while browsing through a medical textbook, the zero gravity conditions of space flight mimic at accelerated speed what normally happens to the body as it ages. Thus, Glenn reasoned, sending an older man into space might give scientists a thumbnail glimpse of processes of aging. By studying how weightlessness affected Glenn's bones, muscles, blood pressure, heart rates, balance, immune system, and sleep cycles, as well as his ability to bounce back after the flight as compared with younger astronauts, medical researchers could obtain information that might ultimately have broader applications. The data would not, of course, provide conclusive findings but, as in any good case study, could generate hypotheses to be tested by further research with larger groups of participants. The flight also would have an important side effect: to demolish common stereotypes about aging.

*Sources of information about John Glenn were Cutler (1998), Eastman (1965), and articles from *The New York Times* and other newspapers.

OUTLINE

Space travel is a challenge even for the youngest and most physically fit adults. Not everyone can be an astronaut; candidates have to pass stringent physical and mental tests. Because of his age, Glenn was held to even tougher physical standards. An avid weight lifter and power walker, he was in superb physical condition. He passed the examinations with flying colors and then spent nearly 500 hours in training.

It was a clear, cloudless October day when, after two suspenseful delays, the shuttle *Discovery* lifted off with what the countdown commentator called "a crew of six astronaut heroes and one American legend." Three hours and ten minutes later, 342 miles above Hawaii, a beaming Glenn repeated his own historic words broadcast thirty-six years before: "Zero G, and I feel fine." On November 7, *Discovery* touched down at Cape Canaveral, and John Glenn, though weak and wobbly, walked out of the shuttle on his own two feet. Within four days he had fully recovered his balance and was completely back to normal.

Glenn's achievement proved that, at 77, he still had "the right stuff." His heroic exploit captured public imagination around the world. As Stephen J. Cutler, president of the Gerontological Society of America, put it, ". . . it's hard to imagine a better demonstration of the capabilities of older persons and of the productive contributions they can make" (1998, p. 1).

John Glenn epitomizes a new view of aging, challenging the formerly pervasive picture of old age as a time of inevitable physical and mental decline. On the whole, people today are living longer and better than at any time in history. In the United States, older adults as a group are healthier, more numerous, and younger at heart than ever before. With improved health habits and medical care, it is becoming harder to draw the line between the end of middle adulthood and the beginning of late adulthood. Many 70-year-olds act, think, and feel much as 50-year-olds did a decade or two ago.

Of course, not all older adults are models of vigor and zest. Indeed, Glenn's achievement is impressive precisely because it is unusual. As we will see in this chapter and the next, older adults vary greatly in health, education, income, occupation, and living arrangements. Like people of all ages, they are individuals with differing needs, desires, abilities, lifestyles, and cultural backgrounds.

In this chapter we begin by sketching demographic trends among today's older population. We look at the increasing length and quality of life in late adulthood and at theories and research on causes of biological aging. We examine physical changes and health. We then turn to cognitive development: changes in intelligence and memory, the emergence of wisdom, and the prevalence of continuing education in late life. In Chapter 18, we look at adjustment to aging and at changes in lifestyles and relationships. What emerges is a picture not of "the elderly" but of individual human beings—some needy and frail, but most of them independent, healthy, and involved.

After you have read and studied this chapter, you should be able to answer each of the following Guidepost questions. Look for them again in the margins, where they point to important concepts throughout the chapter. To check your understanding of these Guideposts, review the end-of-chapter summary. Checkpoints located at periodic spots throughout the chapter will help you verify your understanding of what you have read.

Guideposts for Study

1. How is today's older population changing?
2. How has life expectancy changed, and how does it vary?
3. What theories have been advanced for causes of aging, and what does research suggest about possibilities for extending the life span?
4. What physical changes occur during old age, and how do these changes vary among individuals?
5. What health problems are common in late adulthood, and what factors influence health at that time?
6. What mental and behavioral disorders do some older people experience?
7. What gains and losses in cognitive abilities tend to occur in late adulthood, and are there ways to improve older people's cognitive performance?
8. What educational opportunities can older adults pursue?

Old Age Today

In Japan, old age is a mark of status. There, for example, travelers checking into hotels are often asked their age to ensure that they will receive proper deference.

In the United States, by contrast, aging is generally seen as undesirable. The media "bombard us with advertising for cosmetic surgery, hair coloring, anti-wrinkle creams, pills, potions, tonics and diet programs that, they assure us, will make it possible to maintain our youthful attractiveness forever" (Lenz, 1993, p. 26).

Today, efforts to combat **ageism**—prejudice or discrimination (usually against older persons) based on age—are making headway, thanks to the growing visibility of active, healthy older adults such as John Glenn. Articles with such titles as "Achievers After the Age of 90" (Wallechinsky & Wallace, 1993) appear in newspapers and magazines. On television, older people are less often portrayed as "comical, stubborn, eccentric, and foolish" and more often as "powerful, affluent, healthy, active, admired, and sexy" (Bell, 1992, p. 305).

We need to look beyond distorted images of age to its true, multifaceted reality. What does today's older population look like?

What's Your View?

- What stereotypes about aging have you heard in the media and in everyday life?

ageism Prejudice or discrimination against a person (most commonly an older person) based on age.

The Graying of the Population

The global population is aging. During 2000, the world's elderly population grew by more than 795,000 each month (Kinsella & Velkoff, 2001), and it is expected to more than double by 2025. By then, there will be more than 800 million people over 65, two-thirds of them in developing countries (U.S. Bureau of the Census, 1999c; see Figure 17-1 on page 608).

People today are living longer, especially in developed countries, due to economic growth, better nutrition, healthier lifestyles, improved control of infectious disease, and better access to safe water, sanitation facilities, and medical care (Kinsella & Velkoff, 2001). In the United States, the graying of the population has several specific causes,

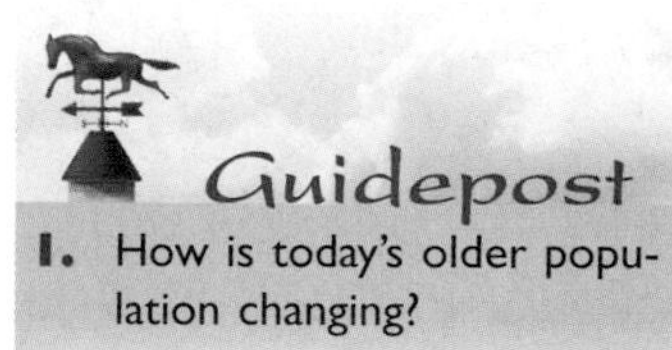

Guidepost

1. How is today's older population changing?

Figure 17-1
Population aging in developed and developing countries. The 65-and-over population is growing fastest, on average, in developing countries; but even in developed countries, there is a marked contrast between the growth of this age group and the gradual decline in total population. Growth rates of the elderly population will peak around 2020, as the baby-boom generation reaches old age, and then will decline. (*Source:* Kinsella & Velkoff, 2001, Figure 2.2, p. 9.)

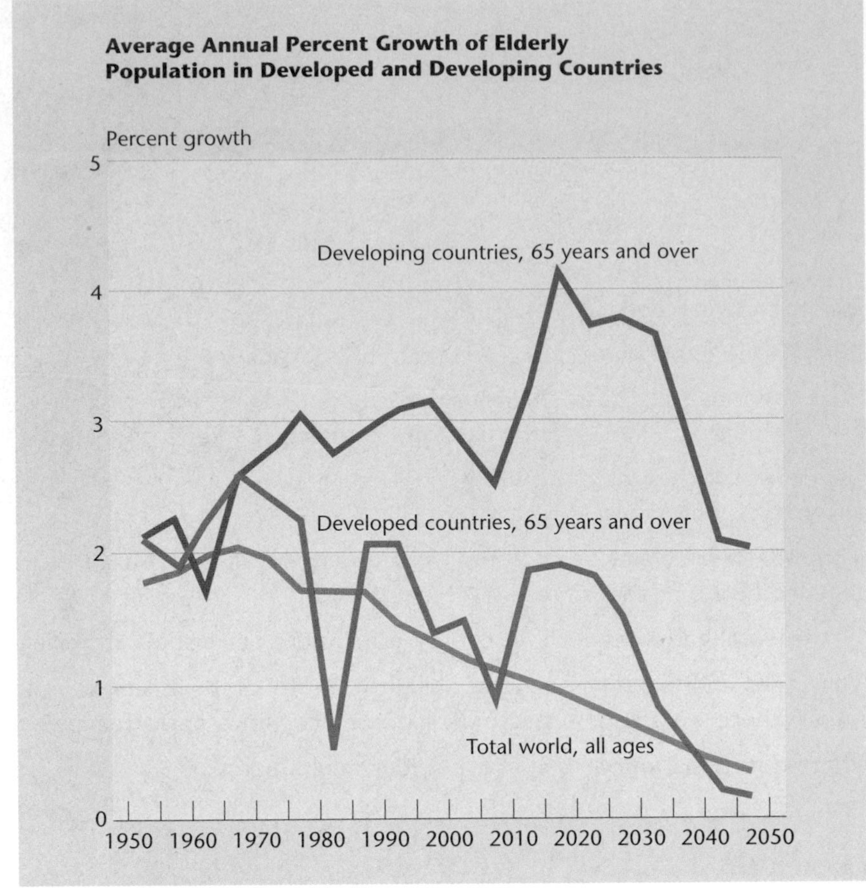

among them high birthrates and high immigration rates during the early to mid-twentieth century and a trend toward smaller families, which has reduced the relative size of younger age groups.

Since 1900 the proportion of Americans who are 65 and over has more than tripled, from 4.1 to 12.4 percent, still relatively low compared with most developed countries. By 2030, fully 20 percent of Americans are likely to be 65 and over (Administration on Aging, 2001; Kinsella & Velkoff, 2001; see Figure 17-2). Ethnic

Figure 17-2
United States population age 65 and over, 1950–2030 (projected). (*Source:* Kramarow et al., 1999, Figure 1, p. 23.)

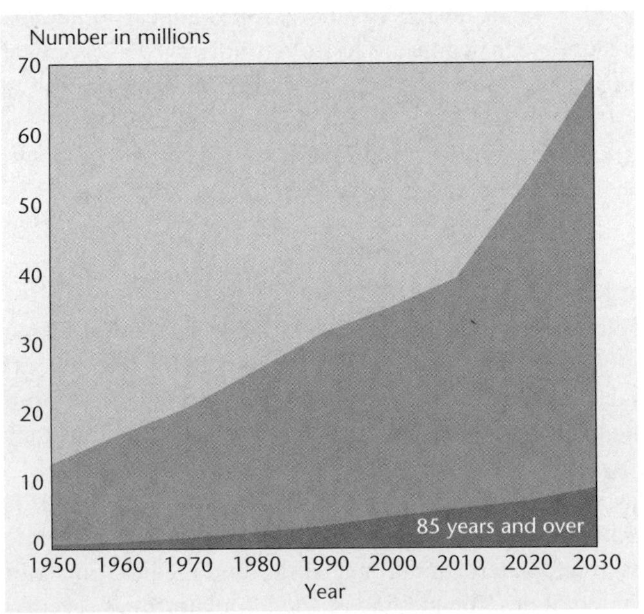

diversity among older adults is increasing. In 2000, 16.4 percent of older Americans were members of minority groups; by 2030, more than 25 percent will be (Administration on Aging, 2001).

The aged population itself is aging. Its fastest-growing segment in the United States and worldwide consists of people in their eighties and older. In 2000, this age group constituted 17 percent of the world's elderly (Administration on Aging, 2001; Kinsella & Velkoff, 2001; U.S. Census Bureau, 2001).

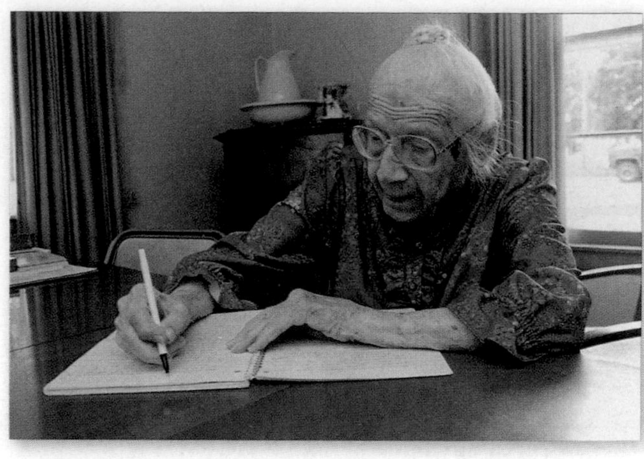

At 104, Anna Grupe of Sherburn, Minnesota, continued to write stories about her life and her family. The United States may have the largest proportion of centenarians among developed countries. Most are women, and a surprising number are healthy and active.

The 2000 U.S. census counted 50,545 centenarians—people past their one-hundredth birthdays (Administration on Aging, 2001), up from virtually none at the beginning of the twentieth century. During the 1990s the number of centenarians nearly doubled in the United States and Europe, as it has each decade since 1950 (Kinsella & Velkoff, 2001). Since women tend to live longer than men, four out of five U.S. centenarians are women, and most are widows (Krach & Velkoff, 1999).

Centenarians tend to run in families; if one sibling is a centenarian, the other probably is as well (Perls et al., 2002). Centenarians tend to be relatively free of genes linked to age-related fatal diseases and premature death. A gene on chromosome 4 has been linked to exceptionally long life (Perls, Kunkel, & Puca, 2002a, 2002b; Puca et al., 2001).

"Young Old," "Old Old," and "Oldest Old"

The economic impact of a graying population depends on the proportion of that population which is healthy and able-bodied. In this regard, the trend is encouraging. Many problems that used to be considered part of old age are now understood to be due, not to aging itself, but to lifestyle factors or diseases.

Primary aging is a gradual, inevitable process of bodily deterioration that begins early in life and continues through the years, irrespective of what people do to stave it off. **Secondary aging** consists of results of disease, abuse, and disuse—factors that are often avoidable and within people's control (Busse, 1987; J. C. Horn & Meer, 1987). By eating sensibly and keeping physically fit throughout adulthood, many people can and do stave off secondary effects of aging.

primary aging Gradual, inevitable process of bodily deterioration throughout the life span.

secondary aging Aging processes that result from disease and bodily abuse and disuse and are often preventable.

Health and longevity are closely linked to education and other aspects of socioeconomic status (Kinsella & Velkoff, 2001). In a 60-year longitudinal study of 237 Harvard students and 332 disadvantaged urban youth, the disadvantaged men's health deteriorated faster—unless they had finished college. Some predictors of physical and mental health and length of life were beyond the individual's control: parents' social class, cohesion of the childhood family, ancestral longevity, and childhood temperament. But other predictors, in addition to higher education, were at least partly controllable: alcohol abuse, smoking, body mass index, exercise, marital stability, and coping mechanisms.

functional age Measure of a person's ability to function effectively in his or her physical and social environment in comparison with others of the same chronological age.

Today, social scientists who specialize in the study of aging refer to three groups of older adults: the "young old," "old old," and "oldest old." Chronologically, *young old* generally refers to people ages 65 to 74, who are usually active, vital, and vigorous. The *old old,* ages 75 to 84, and the *oldest old,* ages 85 and above, are more likely to be frail and infirm and to have difficulty managing activities of daily living.

Checkpoint

Can you . . .

- ✔ Discuss the causes and impact of the aging population?
- ✔ State two criteria for differentiating among the young old, old old, and oldest old?

A more meaningful classification, though, is by **functional age:** how well a person functions in a physical and social environment in comparison with others of the same chronological age. A person of 90 who is still in good health may be functionally younger than a person of 65 who is not. Thus, we can use the term *young old* for

gerontology Study of the aged and the process of aging.

geriatrics Branch of medicine concerned with processes of aging and age-related medical conditions.

the healthy, active majority of older adults (such as John Glenn), and *old old* for the frail, infirm minority, regardless of chronological age (Neugarten & Neugarten, 1987). Research in **gerontology,** the study of the aged and aging processes, and **geriatrics,** the branch of medicine concerned with aging, has underlined the need for support services, especially for the oldest old, many of whom have outlived their savings and cannot pay for their own care.

PHYSICAL DEVELOPMENT

Longevity and Aging

life expectancy Age to which a person in a particular cohort is statistically likely to live (given his or her current age and health status), on the basis of average longevity of a population.

longevity Length of an individual's life.

life span The longest period that members of a species can live.

How long will you live? Why do you have to grow old? Would you want to live forever? Human beings have been wondering about these questions for thousands of years.

The first question involves several related concepts. **Life expectancy** is the age to which a person born at a certain time and place is statistically likely to live, given his or her current age and health status. **Longevity** is how long a person actually does live. Life expectancy is based on the average longevity of members of a population. The human **life span** is the longest period that members of our species can live.

The second question expresses an age-old theme: a yearning for a fountain or potion of youth. Behind this yearning is a fear, not so much of chronological age as of biological aging: loss of health and physical powers. The third question expresses a concern not just with length but with quality of life.

Trends and Factors in Life Expectancy

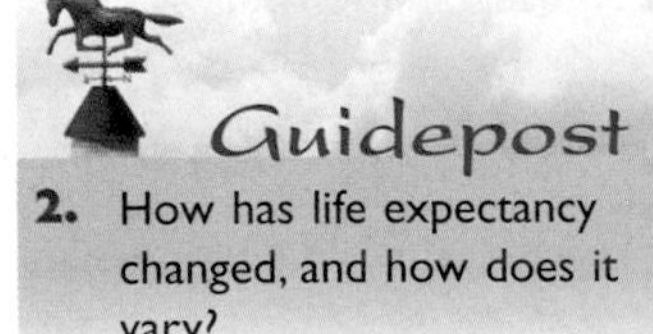

Guidepost

2. How has life expectancy changed, and how does it vary?

Underlying the graying of the population is a rapid rise in life expectancy. A baby born in the United States in 2000 could expect to live 76.9 years, about 29 years longer than a baby born in 1900 (Miniño et al., 2002; NCHS, 2002b) and three times as long as at the dawn of human history (Wilmoth, 2000). Worldwide, average life expectancy has risen 37 percent since 1955, from 48 years to 66 years, and is projected to reach 73 years by 2025 (WHO, 1998). Based on past and present demographic trends, one researcher has predicted that life expectancy at birth in industrialized countries will reach 85 to 87 by the middle of the twenty-first century (Wilmoth, 2000).

Such long life is unprecedented in the history of humankind (see Figure 17-3). In fact, of all the people who have ever lived to be 65 or older, half are alive today (Rowe & Kahn, 1998).

The longer people live, the longer they are likely to live. An American woman who survives to age 65 can expect to reach 84, and a man to reach 81 (Sahyoun, Lentzner, Hoyert, & Robinson, 2001).

Gains in life expectancy since the 1970s have come mainly from reductions in diseases that mainly affect older people, such as heart disease, cancer, and stroke (Wilmoth, 2000). Even if these diseases could be eliminated, some gerontologists say, life expectancy might rise into the upper nineties (Olshansky, Carnes, & Cassel, 1990), but other maladies would replace them, and body systems would continue to decline (Olshansky, Hayflick, & Carnes, 2002a). Life expectancy is unlikely to rise much higher than that unless scientists find ways to modify the basic processes of aging on a widespread scale (International Longevity Center, 2002; Olshansky, Carnes, & Desesquelles, 2001).

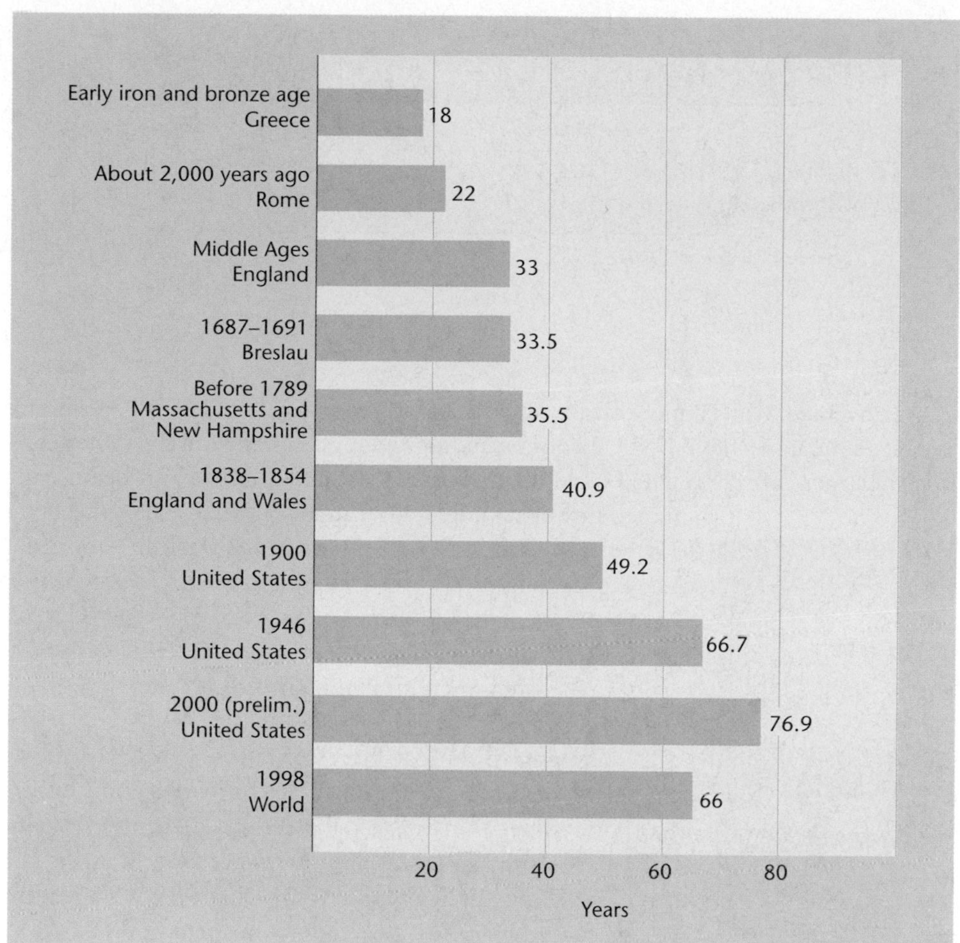

Figure 17-3
Changes in life expectancy from ancient to modern times. (*Source:* Adapted from Katchadourian, 1987; 1998 world data from WHO, 1998; 2000 U.S. data from Miniño et al., 2002.)

Regional and Ethnic Differences On average, a person born in a developed country can expect to live thirteen years longer than a person born in a developing country. But life expectancy varies more widely in certain countries. In the African nations of Zimbabwe and Malawi, a child born in 2000 could expect to live less than 38 years. In Japan, in the same year, life expectancy was 80.7 years, the highest in the world (Kinsella & Verloff, 2001).

The most dramatic improvements in developing regions have occurred in East Asia, where life expectancy grew from less than 45 years in 1950 to more than 72 years in 2000. In some places, though, life expectancy has *decreased.* Between 1987 and 1994 life expectancy for Russian men dropped by 7.3 years (Kinsella & Verloff, 2001), due largely to economic and social instability, high rates of alcohol and tobacco use, poor nutrition, depression, and deterioration of the health care system (Notzon et al., 1998). In parts of Africa hard hit by the scourge of AIDS, life expectancy may be at least 30 years lower by 2010 than otherwise expected (Kinsella & Verloff, 2001).

Wide disparities also exist within the United States. Death rates among the elderly are highest in small towns and rural areas (NCHS, 2001). American Indian men in South Dakota have a life expectancy of only 56.5 years, and African American men in Washington, D. C., can expect to live only to about 58. Meanwhile, Asian American men in affluent regions of New York and Massachusetts survive to nearly 90 (Murray, Michaud, McKenna, & Marks, 1998). These radical disparities may be due in part to differences in income, education, and lifestyle and possibly to genetic factors as well.

Table 17-1 Life Expectancy at Birth in Years, by Sex and Race, 2000, in the United States

	All Races	White	Black
Males	74.1	74.8	68.2
Females	79.5	80.0	74.9

Source: Miniño et al., 2002.

On average, white Americans live nearly six years longer than African Americans (NCHS, 2002b; see Table 17-1). As discussed in previous chapters, African Americans, especially men, are more vulnerable than white Americans to illness and death from infancy through middle adulthood. However, the gap begins to close in older adulthood, and by age 85 African Americans can expect slightly more remaining years than whites (Kramarow, Lentzner, Rooks, Weeks, & Saydah, 1999; Treas, 1995). The difference between black and white life expectancies has narrowed; men and women of both races are living longer than ever before (NCHS, 2002b).

This elderly Japanese woman doing tai chi *is a picture of health and serenity. Japan has the longest life expectancy among industrialized countries.*

A new way to look at life expectancy is in terms of the number of years a person can expect to live in good health, free of disabilities (Kinsella & Velkoff, 2001). Among 191 countries, Japan has the longest *healthy* life expectancy at birth, 74.5 years. The United States ranks twenty-fourth, with a healthy life expectancy of 70 to 72.6 years for women and 67.5 years for men. Reasons for this relatively poor showing as compared with other industrialized nations include ill health among the urban poor and some ethnic groups; a relatively large proportion of HIV-related death and disability in young and middle adulthood; high rates of lung disease and coronary heart disease; and fairly high levels of violence (WHO, 2000).

Gender Differences Nearly all over the world, women typically live longer than men, though there are exceptions in developing countries where girls and women face severe discrimination (Kinsella & Velkoff, 2001). Women's longer life has been attributed to several factors: their greater tendency to take care of themselves and to seek medical care; the higher level of social support they enjoy; and the greater biological vulnerability of males throughout life.

Women in the United States benefited more than men from the gains in life expectancy during the twentieth century, particularly the reduction in deaths from childbirth. In 1900, there was only a two-year gender difference in life expectancy. The gap widened to nearly eight years in 1979; since then it has narrowed to about five and one-third years, two years less than the world average, largely because more men are surviving heart attacks than before (Miniño et al., 2002; NCHS, 2002b; Kinsella & Velkoff, 2001; Treas, 1995; refer back to Table 17-1).

Because of the difference in life expectancy, older women outnumber older men by nearly 3 to 2, and this disparity increases with advancing age. By age 85, the ratio of women to men is $2\frac{1}{2}$ to 1 (Administration on Aging, 2001). Similar gender ratios exist internationally (Kinsella & Velkoff, 2001).

Checkpoint

Can you . . .

✔ Summarize trends in life expectancy, including regional, ethnic and gender differences?

Table 17-2 Theories of Biological Aging

Genetic-Programming Theories	Variable-Rate Theories
Programmed senescence theory. Aging is the result of the sequential switching on and off of certain genes. Senescence is the time when the resulting age-associated deficits become evident.	*Wear-and-tear theory.* Cells and tissues have vital parts that wear out.
Endocrine theory. Biological clocks act through hormones to control the pace of aging.	*Free-radical theory.* Accumulated damage from oxygen radicals causes cells and eventually organs to stop functioning.
Immunological theory. A programmed decline in immune system functions leads to increased vulnerability to infectious disease and thus to aging and death.	*Rate-of-living theory.* The greater an organism's rate of metabolism, the shorter its life span.
	Autoimmune theory. Immune system becomes confused and attacks its own body cells.

Source: Adapted from NIH/NIA, 1993, p. 2.

Why People Age

Hope of further lengthening healthy life expectancy depends on our growing knowledge of what happens to the human body with the passage of time. Early in adulthood, physical losses are typically so small and so gradual as to be barely noticed. With age, individual differences increase. One 80-year-old man can hear every word of a whispered conversation; another cannot hear the doorbell. One 70-year-old woman runs marathons; another cannot walk around the block. The onset of **senescence**—a period marked by obvious declines in body functioning sometimes associated with aging—varies greatly. Why? For that matter, why do people age at all?

Guidepost

3. What theories have been advanced for causes of aging, and what does research suggest about possibilities for extending the life span?

senescence Period of the life span marked by changes in physical functioning sometimes associated with aging; begins at different ages for different people.

genetic-programming theories Theories that explain biological aging as resulting from a genetically determined developmental timetable.

Hayflick limit Genetically controlled limit, proposed by Hayflick, on the number of times cells can divide in members of a species.

Most theories about biological aging fall into two categories (summarized in Table 17-2): *genetic-programming theories* and *variable-rate theories.**

Genetic-Programming Theories

Genetic-programming theories hold that bodies age according to a normal developmental timetable built into the genes. Such a timetable may imply a genetically decreed maximum life span.

As we described in Chapter 3, cells in the body are constantly multiplying through cell division; this process is essential to balance the programmed death of useless or potentially dangerous cells and to keep organs and systems functioning properly (Golstein, 1998; Raff, 1998). Leonard Hayflick (1974) found that human cells will divide in the laboratory no more than fifty times; this is called the **Hayflick limit,** and it has been shown to be genetically controlled (Schneider, 1992). If, as Hayflick (1981) suggested at one point, cells go through the same aging process in the body as in a laboratory culture, there might be a biological limit to the life span of human cells, and therefore of human life—a limit Hayflick then estimated at 110 years.

Failure might come through *programmed senescence:* specific genes "switching off" before age-related losses (for example, in vision, hearing, and motor control) become evident. Or the biological clock might act through genes that control *hormonal changes* or cause problems in the *immune system,* leaving the body vulnerable to infectious disease. There is evidence that some age-related physical changes, such as loss of muscle strength, accumulation of fat, and atrophy of organs, may be related to declines in hormonal activity (Lamberts, van den Beld, & van der Lely, 1997; Rudman et al., 1990).

*This summary is indebted largely to NIH/NIA (1993).

We also know that the efficiency of the immune system declines with age (Kiecolt-Glaser & Glaser, 2001). Levels of immune cell production can predict two-year survival rates among the oldest old (R. A. Miller, 1996).

Another hypothesis is that the biological clock is regulated by a gradual shortening of the *telomeres,* the protective tips of chromosomes, each time cells divide. This programmed erosion may eventually progress to the point where cell division stops (de Lange, 1998). Supporting evidence came from a laboratory study in which the gene for *telomerase*—an enzyme that enables sex chromosomes to repair their telomeres—was injected and activated in human cells. The cells continued to divide well beyond their normal life span without apparent abnormalities (Bodnar et al., 1998), raising hopes for a cure for diseases and disabilities of old age. A study of 143 normal, unrelated adults ages 60 and up found a link between shorter telomeres in blood DNA and early death, particularly from heart disease and infectious diseases (Cawthon, Smith, O'Brien, Sivatchenko, & Kerber, 2003).

Hayflick and his colleagues recently have challenged the existence of a specific, predetermined, and rigidly timed genetic program for aging and death. Instead, they say, genes that influence aging do so indirectly, as a by-product of complex processes involved in normal growth and development (Olshansky, Hayflick, & Carnes, 2002a). Even if genes do "exert strong controls on life-span and patterns of aging" (Finch & Tanzi, 1997, p. 407), genetic programming alone cannot be the whole story. Otherwise all human beings would die at the same age. Environmental and experiential factors must interact with genetic ones (Finch & Tanzi, 1997).

variable-rate theories Theories that explain biological aging as a result of processes that vary from person to person and are influenced by both the internal and the external environment; sometimes called *error theories.*

metabolism Conversion of food and oxygen into energy.

free radicals Unstable, highly reactive atoms or molecules, formed during metabolism, which can cause internal bodily damage.

Variable-Rate Theories **Variable-rate theories,** sometimes called *error theories,* view aging as a result of processes that vary from person to person and may be influenced by both internal and external factors. In most variable-rate theories, aging involves damage due to chance errors in, or environmental assaults on, biological systems. Other variable-rate theories focus on internal processes such as **metabolism** (the process by which the body turns food and oxygen into energy), which may directly and continuously influence the rate of aging (NIA, 1993; Schneider, 1992).

Wear-and-tear theory holds that the body ages as a result of accumulated damage to the system beyond the body's ability to repair it. As cells grow older, they are believed to be less able to repair or replace damaged components. Internal and external stressors (including the accumulation of harmful materials, such as chemical by-products of metabolism) may aggravate the wearing-down process.

Free-radical theory focuses on harmful effects of **free radicals:** highly unstable oxygen atoms or molecules, formed during metabolism, which react with and can damage cell membranes, cell proteins, fats, carbohydrates, and even DNA. Damage from free radicals accumulates with age; it has been associated with arthritis, muscular dystrophy, cataracts, cancer, late-onset diabetes, and neurological disorders such as Parkinson's disease (Stadtman, 1992; Wallace, 1992).

Support for free-radical theory comes from research in which fruit flies, given extra copies of genes that eliminate free radicals, lived as much as one-third longer than usual (Orr & Sohal, 1994). Conversely, a strain of mice bred without a gene called *MsrA* that normally protects against free radicals had shorter-than-normal life spans (Moskovitz et al., 2001). There also is evidence that mutations in the DNA of aging *mitochondria,* which generate energy in human cells, cause them to produce free radicals (Michikawa, Mazzucchelli, Bresolin, Scarlato, & Attardi, 1999). Although research on the reputed effects of antioxidant supplements in counteracting free radical activity is generally inconclusive (International Longevity Center, 2002), in one study high intake of vitamin C and of vegetables high in beta-carotene did seem to protect against early death, particularly from heart disease (Sahyoun, Jacques, & Russell, 1996).

Rate-of-living theory suggests that the body can do just so much work, and that's all; the faster it works, the faster it wears out. Thus, speed of metabolism determines length of life. Fish whose metabolism is lowered by putting them in cooler water live longer than they would in warm water (Schneider, 1992). (We present other evidence for rate-of-living theory in the next section.)

Autoimmune theory suggests that an aging immune system can become "confused" and release antibodies that attack the body's own cells. This malfunction, called **autoimmunity,** is thought to be responsible for some aging-related diseases. A part of the picture seems to be how cell death is regulated. Normally this process is genetically programmed. However, when mechanisms for destruction of unneeded cells malfunction, a breakdown in cell clean-out can lead to stroke damage, Alzheimer's disease, cancer, or autoimmune disease. Sometimes malfunction is triggered by exposure to environmental "insults," such as exposure to ultraviolet rays, X rays, and chemotherapy (Miller & Marx, 1998). On the other hand, problems may be caused by the death of *needed* cells. The growing receptivity of T cells—white cells that destroy invading substances—to signals to self-destruct may help account for the weakening of the aging immune system (Aggarwal, Gollapudi, & Gupta, 1999).

autoimmunity Tendency of an aging body to mistake its own tissues for foreign invaders and to attack and destroy them.

Genetic-programming and variable-rate theories have practical consequences. If human beings are programmed to age at a certain rate, they can do little to retard the process except to try to alter the appropriate genes. To that end, scientists have begun to identify alleles that occur with unusual frequency in centenarians. Laboratory research on genetic modifications in animals (discussed in the next section) also holds promise. If, on the other hand, aging is variable, then sound lifestyle and health practices (like John Glenn's exercise regimen) may influence it. However, there is *no* evidence to support the profusion of commercial "anti-aging" remedies now on the market (International Longevity Center, 2002; Olshansky, Hayflick, & Carnes, 2002a, 2002b; see Box 17-1 on page 616).

It seems likely that each of these theoretical perspectives offers part of the truth. Controllable environmental and lifestyle factors may interact with genetic factors to determine how long a person lives and in what condition.

How Far Can the Life Span Be Extended?

When Jeanne Calment of France died in 1997 at the age of 122, hers was the longest well-documented human life span. Is it possible for human beings to live even longer?

Until recently, **survival curves**—percentages of people or animals who live to various ages—supported the idea of a biological limit to the life span, with more and more members of a species dying each year as they approach it. Although many people were living longer than in the past, the curves still ended around age 100; this suggested that, regardless of health and fitness, the maximum life span is not much higher.

survival curves Curves, plotted on a graph, showing percentages of a population that survive at each age level.

However, it now appears that the pattern changes at very old ages. The rate of increase in mortality slows down after age 80 (Kinsella & Velkoff, 2001), and mortality rates begin to *decrease* after 100. People at 110 are no more likely to die in a given year than people in their eighties (Vaupel et al., 1998). In Sweden, for example, the maximum life span increased from about 101 years in the 1860s to 108 years in the 1990s, mainly due to reductions in death rates after age 70 (Wilmoth, Deegan, Lundstrom, & Horiuchi, 2000). From this and other demographic evidence, at least one researcher concludes that there is no evidence of a fixed limit on the human life span (Wilmoth, 2000).

BOX 17–1

Digging Deeper
Do "Anti-Aging" Remedies Work?

Throughout much of human history people have sought elixirs to stop or reverse the aging process. In 1889 Charles Edouard Brown-Sequard claimed that old men could regain strength and vigor by drinking an extract of dog's testicles. The explorer Ponce de León's search for the legendary Fountain of Youth ended in failure. Today, hucksters on the Internet and elsewhere tout anti-aging products and therapies—from yogurt cures to glandular extracts and hormone injections—that claim to have proven results.

Unfortunately, such claims have no scientific basis, according to a position paper issued by 51 top scientists in the field of aging (Olshansky, Hayflick, & Carnes, 2002b). An accompanying report of the International Longevity Center (2002, p. 1) states: "there is as yet no convincing evidence that administration of any specific compound, natural or artificial, can globally slow aging in people, or even in mice or rats. Claims to the contrary . . . are . . . misleading . . . and these substances should not be administered or used."

One reason it is difficult to test the efficacy of anti-aging products is that there are no clear biomarkers of aging—that is, no measurable biological changes that apply to everyone at a given age. Thus, there is no objective way to assess claims that a particular remedy can set back the biological clock (International Longevity Center, 2002; Olshansky et al., 2002a).

Although, as reported in this chapter, antioxidants such as vitamins C and E in the diet may help combat certain diseases, supplements containing these substances have *not* been shown to have similar effects. Furthermore, some of the products being hyped are not necessarily harmless, scientists say. Dietary supplements carry "no guarantees of purity or potency, no established guidelines on dosage, and often no warnings" of possible interaction effects with other medications. Growth hormone treatments can have negative side effects, such as excessive bone growth and carpal tunnel syndrome (Olshansky et al., 2002a, p. 94).

What about "brain boosters" and "memory cocktails"? The herbal extract ginkgo biloba, vitamin E, and other nonprescription supplements have been promoted as having positive effects on memory and cognition. Most studies have not been scientifically adequate; samples are small and methodology questionable or not replicable. Preliminary controlled studies on some of these substances have been mildly promising, but more rigorous research needs to be done on healthy older adults before sound conclusions can be reached (McDaniel, Maier, & Einstein, 2002).

With regard to ginkgo biloba in particular, a review of the research found no basis for either conclusively supporting or refuting its reputed effects (Gold, Cahill, & Wenk, 2002). More recently, a six-week randomized placebo-controlled trial of more than 200 men and women ages 60 and up found no measurable benefits to memory or cognitive functioning in healthy adults (Solomon, Adams, Silver, Zimmer, & DeVeaux, 2002).

The search for anti-aging remedies has the negative connotation that something is wrong with aging, whereas it is actually a natural part of life. Rather than looking for anti-aging remedies, gerontologists and other scientists who study aging have been making progress in "longevity medicine"—seeking ways to combat specific diseases and prolong life (International Longevity Center, 2002; Olshansky et al., 2002a).

What's Your View?

Have you, or has someone you know, ever taken gingko biloba or another remedy claimed to improve memory or combat other effects of aging? If so, what, if any, were the effects? How do you know?

Check It Out:

For more information on this topic, go to http://www.mhhe.com/papaliah9.

Animal research, too, is challenging the idea of an unalterable biological limit for each species. Scientists have extended the healthy life spans of worms, fruit flies, and mice through slight genetic mutations (Ishii et al., 1998; T. E. Johnson, 1990; Kolata, 1999; Lin, Seroude, & Benzer, 1998; Parkes et al., 1998; Pennisi, 1998). In human beings, however, genetic control of a biological process may be far more complex. Since no single gene or process seems responsible for senescence and the end of life, we are unlikely to find genetic "quick fixes" for aging (Olshansky et al., 2002a).

One promising line of research is on dietary restriction (International Longevity Center, 2002). Rats fed 35 to 40 percent fewer calories than usual, but with all neces-

Jeanne Calment of Arles, France, is one of the only two human beings known to have lived to age 120, believed by some scientists to be the limit of the human life span. (The other was Shigechiyo Izumi of Japan, who died in 1986.) Calment is shown here shortly before her 120th birthday in March 1995, holding up her family photo album open to a picture of herself at age 40.

sary nutrients, live as much as 50 percent longer than other laboratory rodents—about 1,500 days as compared with 1,000 days. Caloric restriction also has been found to extend life in worms and fish—in fact, in virtually all species on which it has been tried (Weindruch & Walford, 1988).

These findings support rate-of-living theories that view the speed of metabolism, or energy use, as the crucial determinant of aging (Masoro, 1985, 1988, 1992; Sohal & Weindruch, 1996). A gene that makes it more difficult to use the calories in food has been found to nearly double the average life spans of fruit flies, from 37 to 71 days (Rogina, Reenan, Nilsen, & Helfand, 2000). Caloric restriction also seems to reduce production of free radicals, facilitate DNA repair, and preserve the immune system's ability to fight disease (Walford, quoted in Couzin, 1998).

Systematic dietary restriction studies have not yet been done on human beings, and it is doubtful that most people would willingly subject themselves to such a spartan diet. However, more modest caloric reduction—as little as 10 percent—was found to increase rodent survival by about 24 percent (Duffy et al., 2001), making this strategy potentially practical for humans (Masoro, 2001). But is it caloric reduction that causes long life, or some related factor? Among 700 healthy men with normal diets, those who lived longest showed three physiological markers associated with long-term caloric restriction in monkeys: low body temperature, low blood insulin levels, and high blood levels of dehydroepiandrosterone sulfate (DHEAS), a steroid hormone that diminishes during normal aging. This suggests that there might be other ways to achieve the same results that caloric restriction does, through treatments that would affect these markers directly (Roth et al., 2002).

Will human beings soon realize the age-old dream of a "fountain of youth"? If so, some gerontologists fear a rise in age-related diseases and disabling infirmities (Banks & Fossel, 1997; Cassel, 1992; Treas, 1995). However, life-extension studies in animals and research on human centenarians, many of whom are still healthy and functioning independently, suggest that such fears may be unwarranted and that fatal diseases would come very near the end of a longer life (International Longevity Center, 2002).

What's Your View?

- If you could live as long as you wanted to, how long would you choose to live? What factors would affect your answer?
- Which would you rather do: live a long life, or live a shorter time with a higher quality of life?

Checkpoint

Can you . . .

- ✔ Compare two kinds of theories of biological aging, their implications and supporting evidence?
- ✔ Describe two lines of research on extension of life and discuss the import of their findings?

Physical Changes

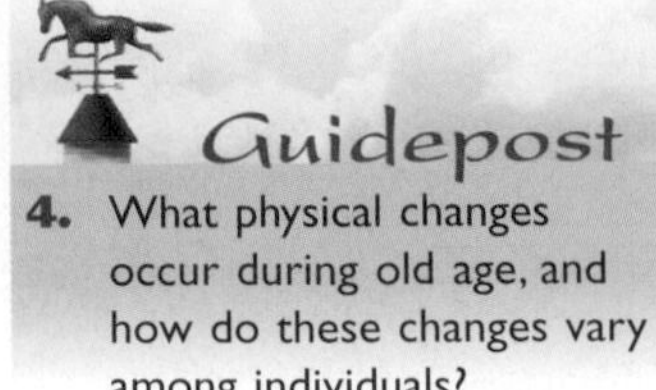

Guidepost

4. What physical changes occur during old age, and how do these changes vary among individuals?

How does aging affect physical functioning? John Glenn's *Discovery* space mission was intended to shed light on this question.

Some physical changes typically associated with aging are obvious to a casual observer. Older skin tends to become paler, splotchier, and less elastic; and, as fat and muscle shrink, the skin may wrinkle. Varicose veins of the legs become more common. The hair on the head turns white and becomes thinner, and body hair becomes sparser.

Older adults become shorter as the disks between their spinal vertebrae atrophy, and stooped posture may make them look even smaller. Thinning of the bones may cause a "dowager's hump" at the back of the neck, especially in women with osteoporosis. In addition, the chemical composition of the bones changes, creating a greater risk of fractures.

Less visible changes affect internal organs and body systems; the brain; and sensory, motor, and sexual functioning.

Organic and Systemic Changes

Changes in organic and systemic functioning are highly variable, both among and within individuals. Some body systems decline rapidly, others hardly at all (see Figure 17-4). Aging, together with chronic stress, can depress immune function, making older people more susceptible to colds, pneumonia, and other respiratory infections (Kiecolt-Glaser & Glaser, 2001) and less likely to ward them off (Koivula, Sten, & Makela, 1999). The digestive system, on the other hand, remains relatively efficient. Among the more serious changes are those affecting the heart. Its rhythm tends to become slower and more irregular, deposits of fat accumulate around it and may interfere with functioning, and blood pressure often rises.

reserve capacity Ability of body organs and systems to put forth four to ten times as much effort as usual under stress; also called *organ reserve*.

Another important change that may affect health is a decline in **reserve capacity** (or *organ reserve*), a backup capacity that helps body systems function to their utmost limits in times of stress. With age, reserve levels tend to drop, and many older people cannot respond to extra physical demands as quickly or efficiently as before. A person who used to be able to shovel snow and then go skiing afterward may now exhaust the heart's capacity just by shoveling.

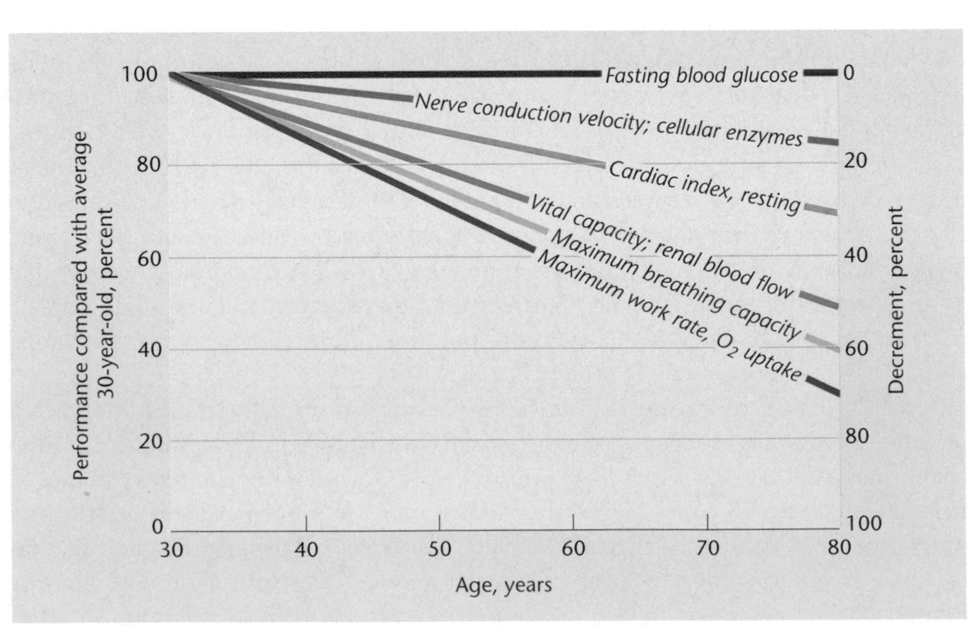

Figure 17-4
Declines in organ functioning. Differences in functional efficiency of various internal body systems are typically very slight in young adulthood but widen by old age. (*Source:* Katchadourian, 1987.)

Still, many normal, healthy older adults like John Glenn barely notice changes in systemic functioning. Many activities do not require peak performance to be enjoyable and productive. By pacing themselves, most older adults can do just about anything they need and want to do.

The Aging Brain

In normal, healthy older people, changes in the brain are generally modest and make little difference in functioning (Kemper, 1994). After age 30, the brain loses weight, at first slightly, then more rapidly, until, by age 90, it may have lost up to 10 percent of its weight. This weight loss has been attributed to a loss of *neurons* (nerve cells) in the *cerebral cortex,* the part of the brain that handles most cognitive tasks. Newer research suggests that the cause is not a widespread reduction in the number of neurons, but rather a shrinkage in neuronal size due to loss of connective tissue: *axons, dendrites,* and *synapses* (refer back to Chapter 4). This shrinkage seems to begin earliest and to advance most rapidly in the frontal cortex, which is important to memory and high-level cognitive functioning (West, 1996; Wickelgren, 1996). Formation of lesions in the white matter of axons can affect cognitive performance (Deary, Leaper, Marray, Staff, & Whalley, 2003).

Changes in the brain vary considerably from one person to another (Deary et al., 2003; Selkoe, 1991, 1992). Certain brain structures, including the cerebral cortex, shrink more rapidly in men than in women (Coffey et al., 1998). Cortical atrophy also occurs more rapidly in less-educated people (Coffey, Saxton, Ratcliff, Bryan, & Lucke, 1999). It has been suggested that education (or related factors, such as high income or decreased likelihood of disability) may increase the brain's reserve capacity—its ability to tolerate potentially injurious effects of aging (Friedland, 1993; Satz, 1993). Aerobic exercise can slow brain tissue loss (Colcombe et al., 2003). In rats, a diet heavy in fruits and vegetables can retard or reverse age-related declines in brain function (Galli, Shukitt-Hale, Youdim, & Joseph, 2002).

Along with loss of brain matter may come a gradual slowing of responses, beginning in middle age. As we discuss later in this chapter, a slowdown of the central nervous system may affect not only physical coordination, but cognition as well.

Not all changes in the brain are destructive. Researchers have discovered that older brains can grow new nerve cells—something once thought impossible. Evidence has been found of cell division in a section of the hippocampus, a portion of the brain involved in learning and memory (Eriksson et al., 1998). In adult mice, such newly generated hippocampal cells matured into functional neurons (Van Praag et al., 2002). These discoveries raise hope that scientists may eventually find ways to use the brain's own restorative potential to cure disorders such as Alzheimer's disease.

Checkpoint

Can you . . .

- ✔ Summarize common changes and variations in systemic functioning during late life?
- ✔ Identify a likely source of loss of brain weight, and explain the importance of regenerative changes in the brain?

Sensory and Psychomotor Functioning

While some older people experience sharp declines in sensory and psychomotor functioning, others find their daily lives virtually unchanged. Impairments tend to be more severe among the old old. Visual and hearing problems may deprive them of activities, social relationships, and independence (Desai, Pratt, Lentzner, & Robinson, 2001; O'Neill, Summer, & Shirey, 1999), and motor impairments may limit everyday activities. New technologies, such as corrective surgery for cataracts and improved hearing aids or cochlear implants to correct hearing loss, help many older adults avoid sensory limitations. And inventors are redesigning the physical environment to meet the needs of an aging population (see Box 17-2 on page 620).

Vision Many older people have trouble perceiving depth or color or doing such daily activities as reading, sewing, shopping, and cooking. Losses in visual contrast sensitivity can cause difficulty reading very small or very light print (Akutsu, Legge,

BOX 17-2

Practically Speaking

New Environments for an Aging Population

The "aging avalanche" is changing the physical, social, economic, and political environment as the older population becomes more influential at the polls and in the marketplace. Engineering psychologists are applying knowledge of age-related differences in perception, mobility, and information processing to the design of safer, more convenient products and services for older adults (Fisk & Rogers, 2002). As the population continues to age, we can expect further changes in our physical environment and in the products we use.

One study found that more than half of the problems older adults encounter in everyday activities could be solved through redesigning products or systems, age-tailored training, or both (Rogers, Meyer, Walker, & Fisk, 1998). Examples of age-friendly changes might include lowering steps on buses, improving chair design, developing more usable tools for grasping or scrubbing, enlarging the letter size on labels, and simplifying the operation and instructions for use of ATM machines, automated phone menu systems, home computers, and home medical devices, such as blood pressure gauges and blood glucose meters (Azar, 2002b; Rogers et al., 1998).

Here are more examples of innovations along this line—some already in place, some still on the drawing boards. (Unless otherwise referenced, these examples come from Dychtwald & Flower, 1990.)

Aids to Vision Signals now given visually will be spoken as well. There will be talking exit signs, talking clocks, talking appliances that tell you when they get hot, talking cameras that warn you when the light is too low, and talking automobiles that caution you when you're about to collide with something. Windshields will adjust their tint automatically to varying weather and light conditions and will be equipped with large, liquid-crystal displays of speed and other information (so that older drivers need not take their eyes off the road and readjust their focus). Reading lights will be brighter, and books will have larger print. Floors will be carpeted or textured, not waxed to a smooth, glaring gloss.

Aids to Hearing Public address systems and recordings will be engineered to an older adult's auditory range. Park benches and couches will be replaced by angled or clustered seating so that older adults can communicate face-to-face.

Aids to Manual Dexterity To compensate for stiff, aging joints, it will become increasingly common to find such items as comb and brush extenders, stretchable shoelaces, Velcro tabs instead of buttons, lightweight motorized pot-and-pan scrubbers and garden tools, tap turners on faucets, foot mops that eliminate bending, voice-activated telephone

Ross, & Schuebel, 1991; Kline & Scialfa, 1996). Vision problems can cause accidents and falls (Desai et al., 2001).

Traffic injuries and deaths involving older Americans have increased since 1990 and are most frequent among men and among those ages 75 and older. Older eyes need more light to see, are more sensitive to glare, and may have trouble locating and reading signs; thus, driving may become hazardous, especially at night (Kline et al., 1992; Kline & Scialfa, 1996). Older drivers' higher collision risk may be related not so much to loss of visual acuity (sharpness of vision) as to impaired visual attentiveness, slowed reaction time, less efficient coordination, and slowed visual processing (Owsley et al., 1998; Wiseman & Souder, 1996). Declines in cognitive and motor skills may be contributing factors (National Center for Injury Prevention and Control [NCIPC], 2001).

Moderate visual problems often can be helped by corrective lenses, medical or surgical treatment, or changes in the environment. However, nearly one in five adults ages 70 and older has visual losses that cannot be corrected by glasses or contact lenses. Approximately 1.8 million community-dwelling older adults report difficulty with bathing, dressing, and walking around the house, in part because they are visually impaired (Desai et al., 2001).

Most visual impairments (including blindness) are caused by cataracts, age-related macular degeneration, glaucoma, or diabetic retinopathy (a complication of diabetes not related to age). More than half of people over 65 develop **cataracts,** cloudy or opaque areas in the lens of the eye that eventually cause blurred vision. Surgery to remove cataracts is usually successful and is one of the most common operations among

cataracts Cloudy or opaque areas in the lens of the eye, which cause blurred vision.

Practically Speaking

—continued

BOX 17-2

dialers, long-handled easy-grip zippers, and contoured eating utensils. Already, pain relievers, previously packaged in childproof bottles that stymied arthritic adults, are being repackaged in easier-to-open containers.

Aids to Mobility and Safety in the Home Ramps will become more common, levers will replace knobs, street lights will change more slowly, and traffic islands will let slow walkers pause and rest. Closet shelves and bus platforms will be lower, as will windows, for people who sit a lot. Regulators will keep tap water from scalding. "Soft tubs" will prevent slips, add comfort, and keep bath water from cooling too fast. Sensors can monitor the movements of an older person living alone and alert friends or relatives to any unusual pattern. Such devices could help older adults stay in their homes rather than go to nursing homes (Eisenberg, 2001).

Aids to Safety on the Road The increasing number of older drivers on the roads have led highway engineers to think about ways to accommodate the needs of those drivers—for example, by making road signs and pavement markings more clearly visible (Staplin, Lococo, Byington, & Harkey, 2001a, 2001b). Automobiles will be programmed to operate windows, radio, heater, lights, wipers, and even the ignition by verbal commands.

Temperature Adjustments Because older bodies take longer to adjust to temperature changes and many have more trouble keeping warm, homes and hotels will have heated furniture and thermostats in each room. Some people will wear heated clothing and eat heat-producing foods.

Such innovations will make life easier and more convenient for everyone. An environment designed for older rather than younger adults can be more user-friendly for all age groups.

What's Your View?

Can you think of ways to make to make everyday living safer and easier for older adults?

Check It Out:

For more information on this topic, go to http://www. mhhe.com/papaliah9, where you will find links to websites that contain ideas for making a new or remodeled home more user-friendly for all ages, sizes, and abilities, as well as ideas on enhancing the ability of older residents to live independently in their own homes.

older Americans. **Age-related macular degeneration,** in which the center of the retina gradually loses the ability to sharply distinguish fine details, is the leading cause of irreversible visual impairment in older adults. **Glaucoma** is irreversible damage to the optic nerve caused by increased pressure in the eye; if left untreated it can cause blindness. In 1995, 8 percent of the elderly population reported having glaucoma, but many more may be unaware they have it. Elderly African Americans are twice as likely to develop glaucoma as elderly white people (Desai et al., 2001).

age-related macular degeneration Condition in which the center of the retina gradually loses its ability to discern fine details; leading cause of irreversible visual impairment in older adults.

glaucoma Irreversible damage to the optic nerve caused by increased pressure in the eye.

Hearing Forty-three percent of older adults have hearing loss, often caused by *presbycusis,* an age-related reduction in ability to hear high-pitched sounds (O'Neill et al., 1999). Presbycusis makes it hard to hear what other people are saying, especially when there is competing noise from radio or television or several people talking at once. Other causes of hearing loss are extreme or chronic exposure to loud noise, smoking, a history of middle ear infections, and long exposure to certain chemicals (Desai et al., 2001). Hearing loss may contribute to a false perception of older people as distractible, absentminded, and irritable.

Hearing impairments increase with age. About 17 percent of persons 85 and older are totally deaf (Desai et al., 2001). Men are more likely than women to have hearing problems, and whites are more likely than blacks (Desai et al., 2001; O'Neill et al., 1999). Hearing aids can help but can be hard to adjust to, since they tend to magnify background noises as well as the sounds a person wants to hear. Another device for assisting hearing is a built-in telephone amplifier (Desai et al., 2001).

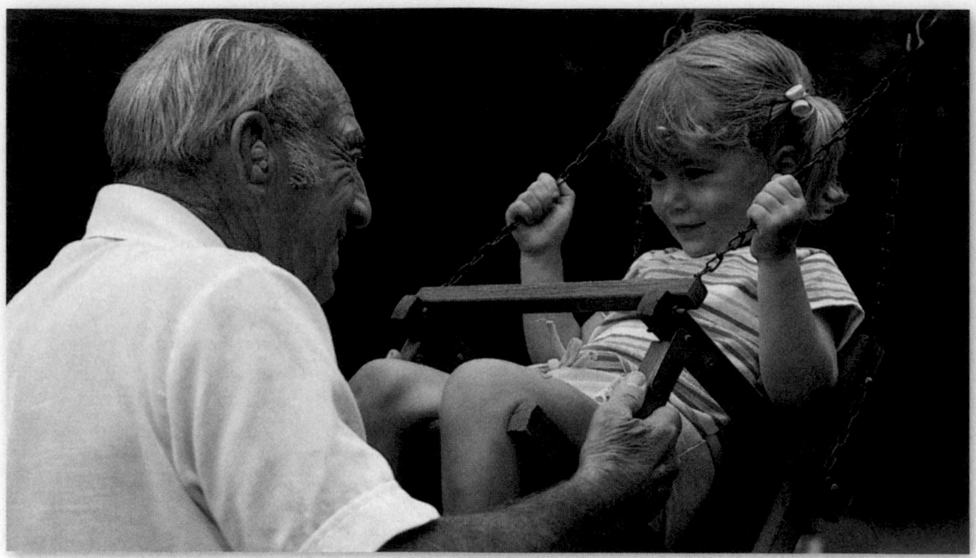

The hearing aid in this man's ear makes it easier for him to understand his young granddaughter's high-pitched speech. About one-third of 65- to 74-year-olds and one-half of those 85 and older have some degree of hearing loss that interferes with everyday activities, but only about one in five has a hearing aid, and many of those who do own one do not use it regularly.

Taste and Smell What you taste often depends on what you can smell. Losses in both these senses can be a normal part of aging, but also may be caused by a wide variety of diseases and medications, by surgery, or by exposure to noxious substances in the environment.

When older people complain that their food does not taste good anymore, it may be because they have fewer taste buds in the tongue, or because the taste receptors are not working properly. It also may be because the olfactory bulb—the organ in the brain that is responsible for the sense of smell—or other related brain structures are damaged (Schiffman, 1997). Sensitivity to sour, salty, and bitter flavors may be affected more than sensitivity to sweetness (Spitzer, 1988). Women seem to retain the senses of taste and smell better than men do (Ship & Weiffenbach, 1993).

Strength, Endurance, Balance, and Reaction Time Older people have less strength than they once had and are limited in activities requiring endurance or the ability to carry heavy loads. Adults generally lose about 10 to 20 percent of their strength up to age 70, especially in the muscles of the lower body, and more after that. Walking endurance declines more consistently with age, especially among women, than some other aspects of fitness, such as flexibility (Van Heuvelen, Kempen, Ormel, & Rispens, 1998).

These losses may be largely reversible, however. In controlled studies with people in their sixties to nineties, weight training, power training, or resistance training programs lasting eight weeks to two years increased muscle strength, size, and mobility; speed, endurance, and leg muscle power; and spontaneous physical activity (Ades, Ballor, Ashikaga, Utton, & Nair, 1996; Fiatarone et al., 1990, 1994; Fiatarone, O'Neill, & Ryan, 1994; Foldvari et al., 2000; McCartney, Hicks, Martin, & Webber, 1996). Even low-impact, moderate-intensity aerobic dance and exercise training can increase peak oxygen uptake, leg muscle strength, and vigor (Engels, Drouin, Zhu, & Kazmierski, 1998).

This evidence of *plasticity,* or modifiability of performance, is especially important because people whose muscles have atrophied are more likely to suffer falls and fractures and to need help with tasks of day-to-day living. One reason for older adults' susceptibility to falls is reduced sensitivity of the receptor cells that give the brain in-

Table 17-3 Safety Checklist for Preventing Falls in the Home	
Stairways, hallways, and pathways	Free of clutter
	Good lighting, especially at top of stairs
	Light switches at top and bottom of stairs
	Tightly fastened handrails on both sides and full length of stairs
	Carpets firmly attached and not frayed; rough-textured or abrasive strips to secure footing
Bathrooms	Grab bars conveniently located inside and outside of tubs and showers and near toilets
	Nonskid mats, abrasive strips, or carpet on all surfaces that may get wet
	Night lights
Bedrooms	Telephones and night lights or light switches within easy reach of beds
All living areas	Electrical cords and telephone wires out of walking paths
	Rugs and carpets well secured to floor
	Inspect for hazards, such as exposed nails and loose threshold trim
	Furniture and other objects in familiar places and not in the way; rounded or padded table edges
	Couches and chairs proper height to get into and out of easily

Source: Adapted from NIA, 1993.

formation about the body's position in space—information needed to maintain balance. Slower reflexes and impaired depth perception also contribute to loss of balance (Agency for Healthcare Research and Quality and CDC, 2002; Neporent, 1999). Older adults may find it harder than younger adults to recover when they lose their balance (L. A. Brown, Shumway-Cook, & Wollacott, 1999), much as John Glenn was a bit slower than younger crewmates to recover his "sea legs" after floating weightless for nine days.

Many falls and fractures are preventable by boosting muscle strength, balance, and gait speed (Agency for Healthcare Research and Quality and CDC, 2002) and by eliminating hazards commonly found in the home (Gill, Williams, Robison, & Tinetti, 1999; NIH Consensus Development Panel, 2001). (Table 17-3 is a checklist for eliminating home hazards.)

Exercises designed to improve balance can restore body control and postural stability. The traditional Chinese practice of *tai chi* is especially effective in maintaining balance, strength, and aerobic capacity (Baer, 1997; Kutner, Barnhart, Wolf, McNeely, & Xu, 1997; Lai, Lan, Wong, & Teng, 1995; Wolf et al., 1996; Wolfson et al., 1996). Response time, which is generally related to neurological changes, also can improve with training. Older people who played video games for eleven weeks, using "joy sticks" and "trigger buttons," had faster reaction times than a sedentary control group (Dustman, Emmerson, Steinhaus, Shearer, & Dustman, 1992).

Sexual Functioning

The most important factor in maintaining sexual functioning is consistent sexual activity over the years. A healthy man who has been sexually active normally can continue some form of active sexual expression into his seventies or eighties. Women are physiologically able to be sexually active as long as they live; their main barrier to a fulfilling sexual life is likely to be lack of a partner (Masters & Johnson, 1966, 1981; NIA, 1994; NFO Research Inc., 1999).

Sex is different in late adulthood from what it was earlier. Men typically take longer to develop an erection and to ejaculate, may need more manual stimulation, and may experience longer intervals between erections. Erectile dysfunction may increase, but it is often treatable (Bremner, Vitiello, & Prinz, 1983; NIA, 1994; refer back to Chapter 15). Women's breast engorgement and other signs of sexual arousal are less intense than before. The vagina may become less flexible and may need artificial lubrication.

Checkpoint

Can you . . .

- ✔ Describe typical changes in sensory and motor functioning, and tell how they can affect everyday living?
- ✔ Summarize changes in sexual functioning and attitudes toward sexual activity in late life?

Still, most older men and women can enjoy sexual expression (Bortz, Wallace, & Wiley, 1999). In a mail survey of a national sample of 1,384 middle-aged and older adults, two-thirds of those with sexual partners said they were satisfied with their sex lives (NFO Research, Inc., 1999).

Sexual expression can be more satisfying for older people if both young and old recognize it as normal and healthy. Housing arrangements and care providers should consider the sexual needs of elderly people. Physicians should avoid prescribing drugs that interfere with sexual functioning and, when such a drug must be taken, should alert the patient to its effects.

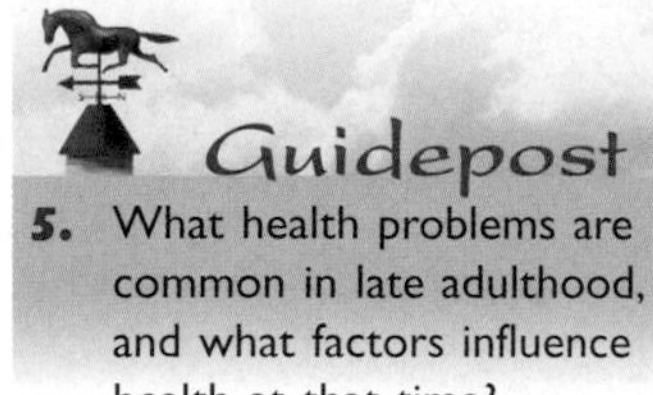

Guidepost

5. What health problems are common in late adulthood, and what factors influence health at that time?

Physical and Mental Health

Most older adults in the United States are in good general health, though not as good, on average, as younger and middle-aged adults. The chances of being healthy and fit in late life often depend on lifestyle, especially exercise and diet.

Health Status and Health Care

In 2001, more than 38 percent of Americans ages 65 and older considered themselves in excellent or very good health, as compared with about 68 percent of 18- to 64-year-olds (NCHS, 2002c). The proportion in fair or poor health increases with age and is greater for most minorities than for whites and Asians (NCHS, 2002b). Poverty is strongly related to poor health and to limited access to, and use of, health care (NCHS, 2001, 2002b).

As people get older they tend to experience more persistent and potentially incapacitating health problems. In the presence of chronic conditions and loss of reserve capacity, even a minor illness or injury may have serious repercussions.

In 1999, older Americans spent 11 percent of their budgets on health care, more than twice the proportion (5 percent) spent by the general population (Administration on Aging, 2001). Even with Medicare benefits and supplements, people who are 75 or older, disabled, in poor or fair health, or severely limited in activities of daily living, or who lack drug coverage, spend an average of 21 to 30 percent of their income on health care, and 4 to 7 percent on drugs alone (Gibson, Brangan, Gross, & Caplan, 1999).

Chronic Conditions and Disabilities Most older people have one or more chronic physical conditions or disabilities. Such conditions become more frequent with age (Administration on Aging, 2001; NCHS, 2002c); but when a condition is not severe, it can usually be managed so that it does not interfere with daily life.

Nearly half of older Americans have arthritis, more than one-third have hypertension, more than one-fourth have heart disease, nearly one-fifth have orthopedic impairments, and one-tenth have diabetes. About 29 percent of 65- to 74-year-olds and 50 percent of those 75 and older limit their activities because of chronic conditions (Administration on Aging, 2001).

arthritis Group of disorders affecting the joints, causing pain and loss of movement.

Arthritis—a group of disorders that cause pain and loss of movement, most often involving inflammation of the joints—is the most common chronic health problem of older adults (Administration on Aging, 2001). Its chief forms are *osteoarthritis,* or degenerative joint disease, which most often affects weight-bearing joints, such as the hips and knees, and *rheumatoid arthritis,* a crippling disease that progressively destroys joint tissue.

Treatment usually involves a combination of anti-inflammatory drugs, rest, physical therapy, application of heat or cold, protecting the joints from stress, and sometimes replacing a joint, especially the hip. Withdrawal of fluid that may form in the joint cavity can relieve osteoarthritis. So can cortisone injections (especially in the knee). Dietary supplements containing glucosamine and chondroitin sulfate, which stimulate cartilage formation, have had good anecdotal results, and controlled studies have found that they are moderately effective (McAlindon, LaValley, Gulin, & Felson, 2000; Phoon & Manolios, 2002). Aerobic or resistance exercise can help prevent disabilities due to osteoarthritis of the knee (Penninx et al., 2001).

The proportion of older adults with physical disabilities has declined since the mid-1980s (Kramarow et al., 1999). Only about 14 percent have difficulty carrying out activities of daily living, such as eating, dressing, bathing, and getting around the house. Disabilities increase sharply with age; almost three-fourths of those ages 80 and up report at least one disability, and more than one-third need assistance because of disabilities (Administration on Aging, 2001).

Influences on Health

Physical activity, nutrition, and other lifestyle factors influence health and disease. Obesity, for example, affects the circulatory system, the kidneys, and sugar metabolism; contributes to degenerative disorders; and tends to shorten life. Healthier lifestyles may enable an increasing number of today's young and middle-aged adults to maintain a high level of physical functioning well into old age.

Physical Activity A lifelong program of exercise, such as John Glenn engaged in, may prevent many physical changes formerly associated with "normal aging." Regular exercise can strengthen the heart and lungs and decrease stress. It can protect against hypertension, hardening of the arteries, heart disease, osteoporosis, and diabetes. It helps maintain speed, stamina, strength, and endurance, and such basic functions as circulation and breathing. It reduces the chance of injuries by making joints and muscles stronger and more flexible, and it helps prevent or relieve lower-back pain and symptoms of arthritis. It may improve mental alertness and cognitive performance, may help relieve anxiety and mild depression, and often improves morale. It can help people with such conditions as lung disease and arthritis to remain independent (Agency for Healthcare Research and Quality and CDC, 2002; Blumenthal et al., 1991; Butler, Davis, Lewis, Nelson, & Strauss, 1998a, 1998b; Kramer et al., 1999; Mazzeo et al.,

What's Your View?

- Do you engage regularly in physical exercise? How many of the older people you know do so? What kinds of physical activity do you think you will be able to maintain as you get older?

These enthusiastic cross-country skiers are deriving the benefits of regular physical exercise in old age, along with having fun. Exercise may well help them extend their lives and avoid some of the physical changes commonly—and apparently mistakenly—associated with "normal aging."

1998; NIA, 1995b; NIH Consensus Development Panel, 2001; Rall, Meydani, Kehayias, Dawson-Hughes, & Roubenoff, 1996). *In*activity contributes to such major chronic diseases as heart disease, diabetes, colon cancer, and high blood pressure, as well as to obesity (Agency for Healthcare Research and Quality and CDC, 2002).

Unfortunately, the older U.S. adults get, the less they exercise (Schoenhorn & Barnes, 2002). About 31 percent of 65- to 74-year-olds exercise moderately for twenty minutes at least three times a week, and 16 percent exercise moderately for thirty minutes five times a week. Only 13 percent in this age group exercise vigorously three times a week. Activity levels are even lower for those 75 and over. About 28 to 34 percent of 65- to 74-year-olds and 35 to 44 percent of those 75 and older engage in no meaningful leisure-time physical activity at all (Agency for Healthcare Research and Quality and CDC, 2002).

Nutrition Many older people do not eat as well as they should, whether because of diminished senses of taste and smell, dental problems, difficulty in shopping and preparing food, or inadequate income. Many live by themselves and may not feel like fixing nourishing meals for one. Studies have found evidence of malnutrition or specific dietary deficiencies in the diets of many elderly people (Lamy, 1994; Ryan, Craig, & Finn, 1992), especially lack of zinc, vitamin E, magnesium, and calcium and overconsumption of fats (Voelker, 1997).

More older Americans are keeping their natural teeth than ever before, but there are marked differences by race and socioeconomic status (Vargas, Kramarow, & Yellowitz, 2001). Loss of teeth due to decay or *periodontitis* (gum disease), often attributable to infrequent dental care (NCHS, 1998), can have serious implications for nutrition.

Nutrition plays a part in susceptibility to such chronic illnesses as atherosclerosis, heart disease, and diabetes (Mohs, 1994). Eating fruits and vegetables—especially those rich in vitamin C, citrus fruits and juices, green leafy vegetables, broccoli, cabbage, cauliflower, and brussels sprouts—lowers the risk of stroke (Joshipura et al., 1999). Vitamin D deficiency increases the risk of hip fracture (LeBoff et al., 1999).

Checkpoint

Can you . . .

- ✔ Summarize the health status of older adults, and identify several common chronic conditions in late life?
- ✔ Give evidence of the influences of exercise and nutrition on health?

Mental and Behavioral Problems

Contrary to common belief, decline in mental health is *not* typical in late life (Wilson, Beckett, et al., 2002). However, mental and behavioral disturbances that do occur in older adults can be devastating. **Dementia** is the general term for physiologically caused cognitive and behavioral decline sufficient to affect daily life (American Psychiatric Association [APA], 1994). Most dementias are irreversible, but some can be reversed with early diagnosis and treatment.

Guidepost

6. What mental and behavioral disorders do some older people experience?

About two-thirds of cases of dementia may be caused by **Alzheimer's disease (AD),** a progressive, degenerative brain disorder, discussed in the next section (Small et al., 1997). **Parkinson's disease,** the second most common disorder involving progressive neurological degeneration, is characterized by tremor, stiffness, slowed movement, and unstable posture (Nussbaum, 1998). Medications that replenish the brain's supply of the chemical neurotransmitter *dopamine* can alleviate Parkinson's symptoms (Alzheimer's Association, 1998b). These two diseases, together with *multi-infarct dementia (MD),* which is caused by a series of small strokes, account for at least eight out of ten cases of dementia, all irreversible.

dementia Deterioration in cognitive and behavioral functioning due to physiological causes.

Alzheimer's disease Progressive, irreversible degenerative brain disorder characterized by cognitive deterioration and loss of control of bodily functions, leading to death.

Parkinson's disease Progressive, irreversible degenerative neurological disorder, characterized by tremor, stiffness, slowed movement, and unstable posture.

Alzheimer's Disease Alzheimer's disease (AD) is one of the most common and most feared terminal illnesses among aging persons in the industrialized world. It gradually robs patients of intelligence, awareness, and even the ability to control their bodily functions—and finally kills them. An estimated 4 million people in the United States have it, and nearly 400,000 new cases are diagnosed each year ("Alzheimer's

Disease, Part I," 2001). Alzheimer's disease generally begins after age 60, and the risk rises dramatically with age ("Alzheimer's Disease, Part I," 2001).

neurofibrillary tangles Twisted masses of protein fibers found in brains of persons with Alzheimer's disease.

amyloid plaque Waxy chunks of insoluble tissue found in brains of persons with Alzheimer's disease.

Symptoms and Diagnosis So far, the only sure diagnosis of Alzheimer's disease depends on analysis of brain tissue ("Early Detection," 2002). The brain of a person with Alzheimer's disease shows excessive amounts of **neurofibrillary tangles** (twisted masses of collapsed protein fibers) and large waxy chunks of **amyloid plaque** (nonfunctioning tissue formed in the spaces between neurons by an abnormal variant of a protein called *beta amyloid*). Because these plaques are insoluble, the brain cannot clear them away. They may become dense, spread, and destroy surrounding neurons. These changes probably occur to some extent in all aging brains but are more pronounced in people with AD (Haroutunian et al., 1999; "Alzheimer's Disease, Part II," 2001).

Doctors usually diagnose Alzheimer's disease in a living person through physical, neurological, and memory tests, as well as detailed interviews with patients and caregivers or close family members. Diagnoses made in this way can be about 85 percent accurate (Alzheimer's Association, 1998a; "Alzheimer's Disease, Part I," 1998; Cullum & Rosenberg, 1998).

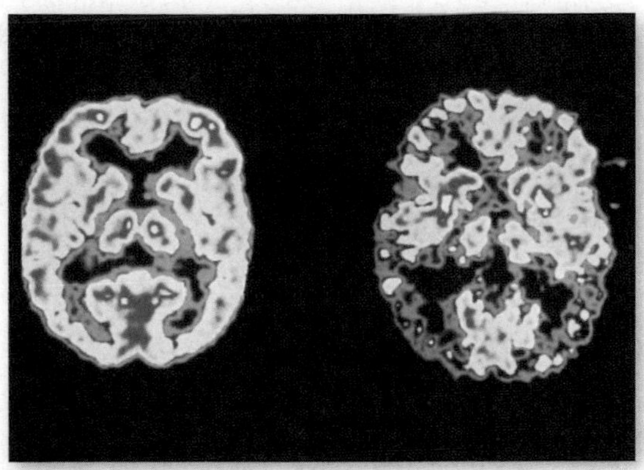

These PET (positron emission tomography) scans show dramatic deterioration in the brain of an Alzheimer's patient (right) as compared with a normal brain (left). The red and yellow areas represent high brain activity; the blue and black areas, low activity. The scan on the right shows reduction of both function and blood flow in both sides of the brain, a change often seen in Alzheimer's disease. To obtain the PET scans, a radioactive tracer is injected into the blood to reveal metabolic activity in the brain.

Mild cognitive impairment, not yet severe enough to interfere with activities of daily life, can be an early sign of AD ("Alzheimer's Disease, Part I," 2001; "Early Detection," 2002). The most prominent early symptom is inability to recall recent events or take in new information. A person may repeat questions that were just answered or leave an everyday task unfinished. These early signs may be overlooked because they look like ordinary forgetfulness or may be interpreted as signs of normal aging. (Table 17-4 compares early warning signs of Alzheimer's disease with normal mental lapses.)

More symptoms follow: irritability, anxiety, depression, and, later, delusions, delirium, and wandering. Long-term memory, judgment, concentration, orientation, and speech all become impaired, and patients have trouble handling activities of daily life. Skills are lost in about the same order they were originally acquired; by the end, the patient, like an infant, cannot understand or use language, does not recognize family members, cannot eat without help, cannot control the bowels and

Table 17-4 Alzheimer's Disease versus Normal Behavior

Normal Behavior	Symptoms of Disease
Temporarily forgetting things	Permanently forgetting recent events; asking the same questions repeatedly
Inability to do some challenging tasks	Inability to do routine tasks with many steps, such as making and serving a meal
Forgetting unusual or complex words	Forgetting simple words
Getting lost in a strange city	Getting lost on one's own block
Becoming momentarily distracted and failing to watch a child	Forgetting that a child is in one's care and leaving the house
Making mistakes in balancing a checkbook	Forgetting what the numbers in a checkbook mean and what to do with them
Misplacing everyday items	Putting things in inappropriate places where one cannot usefully retrieve them (e.g., a wristwatch in a fishbowl)
Occasional mood changes	Rapid, dramatic mood swings and personality changes; loss of initiative

Source: Adapted from Alzheimer's Association (undated).

bladder, and loses the ability to walk, sit up, and swallow solid food. Death usually comes within eight to ten years but may occur as long as twenty years after symptoms appear ("Alzheimer's Disease, Part I," 1998; Hoyert & Rosenberg, 1999; Small et al., 1997).

Researchers are developing tools for early diagnosis or prediction of AD. Neurocognitive screening tests can make reliable initial distinctions between patients experiencing cognitive changes related to normal aging and those in early stages of dementia ("Early Detection," 2002; Solomon et al., 1998). In a study at the Mayo Clinic, 12 percent of older people diagnosed with mild cognitive impairment through a Clinical Dementia Rating Scale developed AD within one year, 40 percent in four years, and 80 percent within six years ("Early Detection," 2002). In another study at the University of California, San Diego, performance on paper-and-pencil cognitive tests predicted which participants would develop AD within a year or two (Jacobson, Delis, Bondi, & Salmon, 2002).

Persons diagnosed with mild cognitive impairment may be tested again after several months to reveal any significant declines. The tests may be followed by brain imaging to measure changes in the size of structures associated with preliminary stages of the disease, primarily the hippocampus (Bobinski et al., 1999; Jack et al., 1998, 1999); brain scans that can show atrophy and diminished rates of blood flow and energy consumption; or analysis of beta amyloid levels in cerebrospinal fluid (Andreasen et al., 1999). For the first time, researchers at the University of California, Los Angeles, have used a brain scanning technique combined with a chemical marker to actually see brain lesions indicative of AD in a living patient (Shoghi-Jadid et al., 2002).

These diagnostic procedures are not yet considered reliable enough, but researchers are improving them ("Early Detection," 2002). Accurate diagnosis is important, not only for persons with AD, but for those with depression or reversible dementias, which are sometimes misdiagnosed as AD (Small et al., 1997).

Causes and Risk Factors Alzheimer's disease is strongly heritable. The concordance rate among identical twins is nearly 90 percent. Siblings and children of a person with AD have at least a 50 percent risk of having it by age 90 ("Alzheimer's Disease, Part I," 2001). At least four alleles that increase production or reduce clearance of beta amyloid have been linked to AD ("Alzheimer's Disease, Part II," 1998).

An early-onset form of the disease, which appears in middle age, is related to dominant genetic mutations on chromosomes 1, 14, and 21 (Corliss, 1996; "Alzheimer's Disease, Part I," 2001; Karlinsky, Lennox, & Rossor, 1994; Post et al., 1997; Schellenberg et al., 1992; Small et al., 1997). *ApoE-4,* a variant of a gene on chromosome 19 carried by about 30 percent of the U.S. population, is an important risk factor for the late-onset type, which appears after age 65 and accounts for 95 percent of cases ("Alzheimer's Disease, Part I," 2001; Bondi, Salmon, Galasko, Thomas, & Thal, 1999; Corder et al., 1993; Farrer et al., 1997; Lennox et al., 1994; Reiman et al., 1996; Roses, 1994; Small et al., 1997). Healthy, middle-aged people without apparent symptoms who have the ApoE-4 gene have been found to have deficits in spatial attention and working memory similar to those seen in AD (Parasuraman, Greenwood, & Sunderland, 2002). However, late-onset AD probably involves a complex interaction of many genes, possibly different in different people. Unknown environmental factors also may play a part ("Alzheimer's Disease, Part I," 2001).

Thus, while genetic testing for the mutations on chromosomes 1, 14, and 21 is highly predictive of the relatively rare early-onset form, the presence of the ApoE-4 gene alone does not conclusively predict or diagnose late-onset AD. Still, it may be useful in combination with cognitive tests, brain scans, and clinical evidence of symptoms ("Alzheimer's Disease, Part I," 2001; Mayeux et al., 1998; Post et al., 1997).

Diet, exercise, and other lifestyle factors also may play a part. African Americans in Indiana are two to three times more likely to develop AD than genetically similar Nigerians. Nigerians have lower risk factors for stroke, such as hypertension and high cholesterol (Hendrie et al., 2001), which often accompany AD (Snowdon et al., 1996, 1997). Education and cognitively stimulating activities are associated with reduced risk of AD ("Alzheimer's Disease, Part II," 1998; Launer et al., 1999; Small et al., 1997; Wilson, Mendes de Leon, et al., 2002), and smoking with increased risk (Launer et al., 1999; Ott et al., 1998). Other possible risk factors under investigation include sleep apnea and head injuries earlier in life ("Alzheimer's Disease, Part III," 2001).

Treatment and Prevention The outlook for people with AD is brighter than before. Although no cure has been found, early diagnosis and treatment can slow the progress of the disease and improve quality of life.

Cholinesterase inhibitors, such as donepezil (commercially known as Aricept), can slow or stabilize symptoms for at least six months to a year in one-third to one-half of patients ("Alzheimer's Disease, Part I," 2001) but do not stop the underlying deterioration ("Alzheimer's Disease, Part II," 1998; Small et al., 1997). Behavioral therapies can slow the deterioration in capabilities, improve communication, and reduce disruptive behavior (Barinaga, 1998). Drugs can relieve agitation, lighten depression, and help patients sleep. Proper nourishment and fluid intake, together with exercise, physical therapy, and social interaction may be helpful. In the early stages, memory training and memory aids may improve cognitive functioning (Camp et al., 1993; Camp & McKitrick, 1992; McKitrick, Camp, & Black, 1992).

Researchers are investigating new ways to diagnose AD and to understand the brain changes involved, and are developing new preventive or ameliorative treatments ("Alzheimer's Disease, Part II," 2001). Blood tests that measure levels of the amino acid homocysteine (Seshadri et al., 2002) and of amyloid precursor proteins (Padovani et al., 2002) may predict or diagnose AD or other forms of dementia in the early stages. The discovery of a brain enzyme believed to be responsible for formation of amyloid plaque may make it possible to block the enzyme's action and prevent or slow the disease (Vassar et al., 1999).

Studies of rats and mice suggest that small clumps of misfolded amyloid beta protein may trigger the changes involved in AD (Bucciantini et al., 2002; Walsh et al., 2002). Drugs could be developed that would block the formation of these clumps. One drug now being tested in humans shrank the amyloid plaques in mice (Pepys et al., 2002).

Also being tested for effectiveness in protecting against Alzheimer's or slowing its progress are anti-inflammatory drugs, the herbal remedy gingko biloba, and dietary intake of antioxidants, such as selenium ("Early Detection," 2002) and vitamins C and E (Foley & White, 2002; Morris, Evans, Bienias, Tangney, & Wilson, 2002).

Reversible Conditions: Depression Many older people and their families mistakenly believe that they can do nothing about mental and behavioral problems, even though close to 100 such conditions, including about 10 percent of dementia cases, can be cured or alleviated. Sometimes apparent dementia turns out to be a side effect of drug intoxication. Because physicians do not always ask what other medicines a patient is taking, they may prescribe drugs that interact harmfully. Also, because of age-related changes in the body's metabolism, a dosage that would be right for a 40-year-old may be an overdose for an 80-year-old. Besides drug intoxication, other common reversible conditions include delirium, metabolic or infectious disorders, malnutrition, anemia, low thyroid functioning, minor head injuries, alcoholism, and depression (NIA, 1980, 1993; Wykle & Musil, 1993).

Symptoms of depression are common in older adults but are often overlooked because they are wrongly thought to be a natural accompaniment of aging. Some older people become depressed as a result of physical and emotional losses, and some apparent "brain disorders" are actually due to depression. But depression often can be relieved if older people seek help.

Nearly 2 million older Americans—about 6 percent—are known to suffer from some form of depression, but the illness often goes unrecognized and untreated (NIMH, 1999b). Contrary to popular belief, depression is diagnosed less often in late life, even though *symptoms* of depression are *more* common among older adults than among younger ones. Why is this so? Depression may be mistaken for dementia, or it may be wrongly seen as a natural accompaniment of aging ("Alzheimer's Disease, Part I," 1998; American Association for Geriatric Psychiatry [AAGP], 1996; George, 1993; Jefferson & Greist, 1993). It may be masked by physical illness. Or older people simply may be less likely to *say* they feel depressed—perhaps because of a belief that depression is a sign of weakness or that it will lift by itself (Gallo, Anthony, & Muthen, 1994; Wolfe et al., 1996). One indication that depression is often overlooked in older adults is the high prevalence of suicide in this age group (NIMH, 1999b; see Chapter 19). Since depression can speed physical declines of aging, accurate diagnosis, prevention, and treatment could help many older people live longer and remain more active (Penninx et al., 1998).

Vulnerability to depression seems to result from the influence of multiple genes interacting with environmental factors (NIMH, 1999b), such as lack of exercise. Stressful events, loneliness, or the use of certain medications may trigger it (Jefferson & Greist, 1993; "Listening to Depression," 1995). Brain imaging of depressed patients revealed a chemical imbalance of critical neurotransmitters and a malfunctioning of neural circuits that regulate moods, thinking, sleep, appetite, and behavior (NIMH, 1999b).

A strong network of family and friends can help older people ward off depression or cope with it. Cognitive-behavioral psychotherapy and interpersonal therapy have had good results. Antidepressant drugs can restore the chemical balance in the brain; *selective serotonin reuptake inhibitors (SSRIs),* such as Prozac, have fewer side effects than older drugs. More than eight out of ten people with depression improve when given appropriate treatment with medication, psychotherapy, or both; the combination treatment also can reduce recurrence (NIMH, 1999b). Electroconvulsive therapy (ECT), also called shock therapy, may be administered in severe cases.

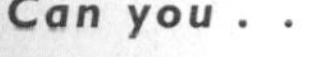

Checkpoint

Can you . . .

- ✔ Name the three main causes of dementia in older adults?
- ✔ Summarize what is known about the prevalence, symptoms, diagnosis, causes, risk factors, treatment, and prevention of Alzheimer's disease?
- ✔ Tell why late-life depression may be more common than is generally realized?

COGNITIVE DEVELOPMENT

Aspects of Cognitive Development

Guidepost

7. What gains and losses in cognitive abilities tend to occur in late adulthood, and are there ways to improve older people's cognitive performance?

Old age "adds as it takes away," said the poet William Carlos Williams in one of three books of verse written between his first stroke at the age of 68 and his death at 79. This comment seems to sum up current findings about cognitive functioning in late adulthood. As Baltes's life-span developmental approach suggests, age brings gains as well as losses. Let's look first at intelligence and processing abilities, then at memory, and then at wisdom, which is popularly associated with the later years.

Intelligence and Processing Abilities

Does intelligence diminish in late adulthood? The answer depends on what abilities are being measured, and how. Some abilities, such as speed of mental processes and abstract reasoning, may decline in later years, but aspects of practical and integrative thinking tend to improve throughout most of adult life (Sternberg, Grigorenko, & Oh, 2001). And, although changes in processing abilities may reflect neurological deterioration, there is much individual variation, suggesting that declines in functioning are not inevitable and may be preventable.

Measuring Older Adults' Intelligence Measuring older adults' intelligence is complicated. A number of physical and psychological factors may lower their test scores and lead to underestimation of their intelligence. Older adults, like younger ones, test best when they are physically fit and well rested. Neurophysiological problems, high blood pressure, or other cardiovascular disorders, which can affect blood flow to the brain, can interfere with cognitive performance (Sands & Meredith, 1992; Schaie, 1990). Vision and hearing losses may make understanding test instructions difficult. The time limits on most intelligence tests are particularly hard on older people. Since both physical and psychological processes, including perceptual abilities, tend to slow with age, older adults do better when they are allowed as much time as they need (Hertzog, 1989; Schaie & Hertzog, 1983).

Test anxiety is common among older adults. They may expect to do poorly, and this expectation may become a self-fulfilling prophecy (Schaie, 1996b). They may lack interest and motivation unless they are taking the test to qualify for a job or for some other important purpose.

To measure the intelligence of older adults, researchers often use the **Wechsler Adult Intelligence Scale (WAIS).** Scores on the WAIS subtests yield a verbal IQ, a performance IQ, and, finally, a total IQ.

Wechsler Adult Intelligence Scale (WAIS) Intelligence test for adults, which yields verbal and performance scores as well as a combined score.

Older adults, as a group, do not perform as well as younger adults on the WAIS, but the difference is primarily in nonverbal performance. On the five subtests in the performance scale (such as identifying the missing part of a picture, copying a design, and mastering a maze), scores drop with age; but on the six tests making up the verbal scale—particularly tests of vocabulary, information, and comprehension—scores fall only slightly and very gradually (see Figure 17-5). This is called the *classic aging pattern* (Botwinick, 1984).

What might account for this pattern? For one thing, the verbal items that hold up with age are based on knowledge; unlike the performance tests, they do not require the test taker to figure out or do anything new. The performance tasks, which involve the processing of new information, require perceptual speed and motor skills, which can reflect muscular and neurological slowing.

Another line of research, introduced in Chapter 15, has made a similar distinction between *fluid* and *crystallized* abilities, the former depending largely on neurological status and the latter on accumulated knowledge. As in the classic aging pattern

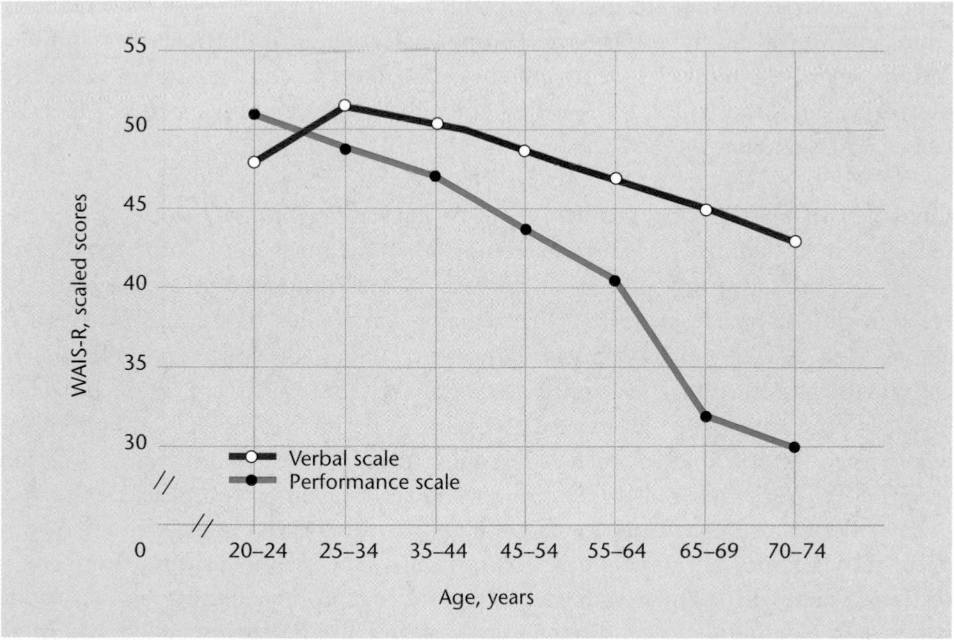

Figure 17-5
Classic aging pattern on the revised version of the Wechsler Adult Intelligence Scale (WAIS-R). Scores on the performance subtests decline far more rapidly with age than scores on the verbal subtests. (*Source:* Botwinick, 1984.)

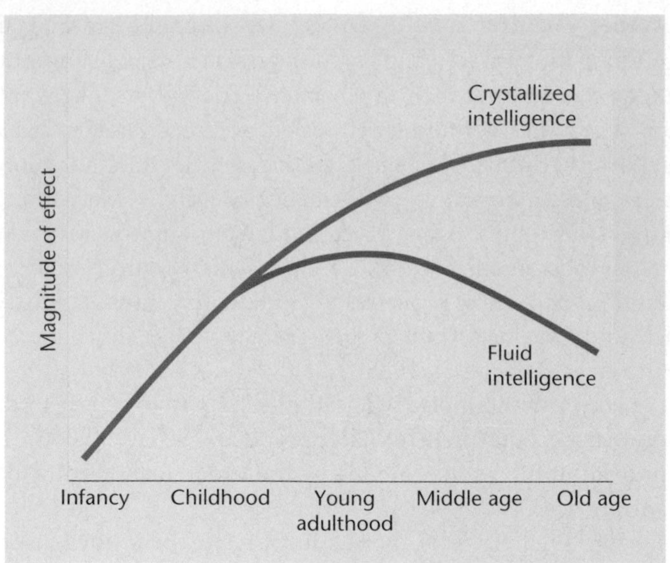

Figure 17-6
Changes in fluid intelligence and crystallized intelligence across the life span. According to classic studies by Horn and Cattell, fluid abilities (largely biologically determined) decline after young adulthood, but crystallized abilities (largely culturally influenced) increase until late adulthood. More recently, the Seattle Longitudinal Study found a more complex pattern, with some fluid abilities holding their own until late middle age (refer back to Figure 15-2 in Chapter 15). *(Source:* J. L. Horn & Donaldson, 1980.)

on the WAIS, these two kinds of intelligence follow different paths. In the classic aging pattern, however, the trend in both verbal and performance scores is downward throughout most of adulthood; the difference, though substantial, is one of degree. Far more encouraging is the pattern of crystallized intelligence, which improves until fairly late in life, even though fluid intelligence declines earlier (see Figure 17-6). Indeed, it has been argued that the importance of crystallized intelligence increases in later life, outweighing any decline in fluid abilities (Sternberg et al., 2001).

dual-process model Model of cognitive functioning proposed by Baltes, which identifies and seeks to measure two dimensions of intelligence: mechanics and pragmatics.

mechanics of intelligence In Baltes's dual-process model, the abilities to process information and solve problems, irrespective of content; the area of cognition in which there is often an age-related decline.

pragmatics of intelligence In Baltes's dual-process model, the dimension of intelligence that tends to grow with age and includes practical thinking, application of accumulated knowledge and skills, specialized expertise, professional productivity, and wisdom.

selective optimization with compensation In Baltes's dual-process model, strategy for maintaining or enhancing overall cognitive functioning by using stronger abilities to compensate for those that have weakened.

Baltes and his colleagues have proposed a **dual-process model,** which identifies and seeks to measure aspects of intelligence that may continue to advance as well as aspects that are more likely to deteriorate. In this model, **mechanics of intelligence** consist of information-processing and problem-solving functions independent of any particular content. This dimension, like fluid intelligence, is physiologically based and often declines with age. **Pragmatics of intelligence** include such potential growth areas as practical thinking, application of accumulated knowledge and skills, specialized expertise, professional productivity, and wisdom (discussed later in this chapter). This domain, which often continues to develop in late adulthood, is similar to, but broader than, crystallized intelligence and includes information and know-how garnered from education, work, and life experience. Through **selective optimization with compensation,** older people may use their pragmatic strengths to compensate for weakened mechanical abilities (Baltes, 1993; Baltes, Lindenberger, & Staudinger, 1998; Marsiske, Lange, Baltes, & Baltes, 1995).

Changes in Processing Abilities Just what happens to the "mechanics" of intelligence in late adulthood? How does aging affect the machinery of the mind?

A general slowdown in central nervous system functioning, as measured by reaction time, is widely believed to be a major contributor to changes in cognitive abilities and efficiency of information processing. Older adults do tend to decline in abilities used for learning and acquiring new skills (Craik & Salthouse, 2000). But while losses in processing speed are related to cognitive performance, they do not tell the whole story. Certain abilities, such as reasoning, spatial abilities, and memory, do not seem to decline as rapidly as processing speed (Verhaeghen & Salthouse, 1997).

Furthermore, the evidence for the role of processing speed in cognitive performance—like the evidence for cognitive decline itself—comes almost entirely from cross-sectional studies, which may confound cohort with age. Younger adults may have done better than older adults because they were healthier and better nourished, had more or better schooling, had gained more information from the media, had jobs that depended on thinking rather than on physical labor, or had more—and more recent—experience taking tests.

Longitudinal studies, by contrast, do *not* tend to show the marked declines in cognitive performance reported in cross-sectional studies. However, the longitudinal design may favor an older sample because of attrition and practice effects. People who score poorly are more likely to drop out of a study, and those who remain benefit from having taken the tests before.

One study designed to resolve the discrepancy between the cross-sectional and longitudinal findings measured links between age, speed, and cognition longitudinally as well as cross-sectionally among 302 adults ranging in age from 66 to 92 when the study began. Speed of processing accounted for most of the cross-sectional age differences in cognitive abilities, but these effects were reduced or eliminated by controlling for individual differences in longitudinal decline. Thus "changes in speed are not nearly as strong a determinant of within-person, age-related decline as cross-sectional analyses would suggest" (Sliwinski & Buschke, 1999, p. 32).

Until recently the prevalent view had been that all components of processing slow equally. Now cognitive neuroscientists have challenged that view by observing the complex steps in stimulus-and-response processing that enter into reaction time.

Event-related potentials (ERPs) are fluctuations in the direction of the brain's electrical activity that can be measured with electrodes attached to the scalp (Ridderinkhof & Bashore, 1995). In one study, researchers measured ERPs in young and older adults in three versions of a reaction-time task. Participants were to press a button when they located a particular word amid a jumbled mass of characters. The older adults were slower only in the final step of processing, the pressing of the button. This finding suggests that the brain's slowing is *not* global, but specific to certain tasks and operations (Bashore, Ridderinkhof, & van der Molen, 1998).

One ability that appears to slow with age is ease in switching from one task or function to another (Salthouse, Fristoe, McGuthry, & Hambrick, 1998). This may help explain, for example, why older adults tend to have difficulties driving a car, which requires rapid switching among such skills as watching other vehicles and pedestrians, reading signs, and ignoring irrelevant information, as well as the specific skills required to operate the vehicle.

Checkpoint

Can you . . .

- ✔ Give several reasons why older adults' intelligence tends to be underestimated?
- ✔ Compare the classic aging pattern on the WAIS with the trajectories of fluid and crystallized intelligence?
- ✔ Discuss findings on the slowdown in neural processing and its relationship to cognitive decline?

The Seattle Longitudinal Study In the Seattle Longitudinal Study of Adult Intelligence, introduced in Chapter 15, researchers measured six primary mental abilities: verbal meaning (vocabulary), verbal memory, number (computational ability), spatial orientation, inductive reasoning, and perceptual speed.

An encouraging finding is that cognitive decline is slow and not across-the-board. If they live long enough, most people's functioning will flag at some point; but very few weaken in all or even most abilities, and many improve in some areas. Most fairly healthy older adults show only small losses until the seventies. Not until the eighties do they fall below the average performance of younger adults (Schaie, 1996b).

The most striking feature of the Seattle findings is the tremendous variation among individuals. Some participants showed declines during their thirties or forties, but a few maintained full functioning very late in life. Even in their late eighties, virtually all retained their competence in one or more of the abilities tested (Schaie, 1996b). Some people remained relatively strong in one area, others in another.

What accounts for these differences? Genetic endowment undoubtedly plays a part. So do physical and neurological status and environmental opportunities. People with higher scores tended to be healthier and better educated and to have higher incomes. High scorers also were more likely to have stable marriages, intelligent spouses, cognitively complex occupations, and active, stimulating lives. When measured in midlife, they tended to have flexible personality styles and to be relatively satisfied with their accomplishments (Gruber-Baldini, 1991; Schaie, 1990, 1994, 1996b; Schaie & Willis, 1996).

engagement hypothesis Proposal that an active, engaged lifestyle that challenges cognitive skills predicts retention or growth of those skills in later life.

According to the **engagement hypothesis** (similar to Kohn's substantive complexity hypothesis, introduced in Chapter 13), people who show high intellectual ability early in life and receive favorable educational and environmental opportunities tend, as adults, to have an "engaged" lifestyle marked by complex, intellectually demanding occupational and social activities. Engaging in activities that challenge cognitive skills in turn promotes the retention or growth of those skills (Schaie, 1983).

Several longitudinal studies seem to offer partial support for this "use-it-or-lose-it" hypothesis. A forty-five-year study of 132 Canadian World War II army veterans (Arbuckle, Maag, Pushkar, & Chaikelson, 1998; Gold et al., 1995) found considerable stability in individual differences in intelligence from young adulthood to late middle and old age. Participants with higher intelligence, education, and childhood socioeconomic status tended to have more engaged adult lifestyles. High engagement, in turn, predicted better maintenance of verbal (but not nonverbal) intelligence.

However, a six-year study of 250 middle-aged and older adults by Hultsch and his colleagues (Hultsch, Hertzog, Small, & Dixon, 1999) gave questionable support to the engagement hypothesis. Intellectually engaging activities—but not social or physical ones—were related to cognitive change, suggesting that intellectual activities may act as buffers against cognitive decline. On the other hand, the findings could support an alternative hypothesis: that "high-ability individuals lead intellectually active lives until cognitive decline sets in" (Hultsch et al., 1999, p. 245). In other words, decline might occur regardless of what people do.

A six-year longitudinal study of 2,076 55- to 85-year-olds in Amsterdam sought to resolve the issue of causation raised in the Hultsch study. Do certain types of everyday activities affect cognitive functioning, or does the level of cognitive functioning affect the activities people choose to engage in? These researchers found little evidence of *either* effect when age, gender, education, and health were controlled. They suggested that, rather than specific activities, general lifestyles and living conditions associated with the activities may account for their relationship with cognitive functioning (Aartsen, Smits, van Tilburg, Knipscheer, & Deeg, 2002).

Competence in Everyday Tasks and Problem Solving The purpose of intelligence, of course, is not to take tests but to deal with the challenges of daily life. Research has found a strong relationship between fluid intelligence and certain practical skills that tend to decline with age, such as the ability to read a map or a newspaper or to perform everyday tasks (Diehl, Willis, & Schaie, 1994; Schaie, 1996a; Willis & Schaie, 1986a).

instrumental activities of daily living (IADLs) Everyday activities, competence in which is considered a measure of the ability to live independently.

As people get older, an important test of cognitive competence is the ability to live independently, as measured by seven **instrumental activities of daily living (IADLs):** managing finances, shopping for necessities, using the telephone, obtaining transportation, preparing meals, taking medication, and housekeeping. Schaie and his colleagues gave older adults tasks in each of these areas: for example, filling out a Medicare form; filling out a mail-order catalog form; looking up an emergency telephone number; figuring out a bus schedule; reading a nutrition label on a food package; reading a medicine bottle label; and reading instructions for using a household appliance. Fluid intelligence and, to a lesser extent, crystallized intelligence accounted for more than half of the variance in performance. Health and educational background affected the results through their effects on cognitive ability. This relationship may be bidirectional. Not only may poor health and lack of education limit cognition, but people with higher cognitive ability tend to get better educations and take care of their health (Schaie & Willis, 1996).

Although IADLs, which depend heavily on information-processing skills, generally decline with age, that is not necessarily true of the ability to solve interpersonal problems, which tend to have strong emotional overtones and solutions that are less cut and dried. The effectiveness of older adults' responses to such problems often depends on how meaningful the problem is to them (Blanchard-Fields, Chen, & Norris, 1997).

In one study, when presented with consumer or home management problems, for which they could draw on a great deal of accumulated experience, older adults tended to use cognitive analysis of the situation and direct action, whereas adolescents and younger adults tended to avoid or deny the problem or depend on others to solve it. When a problem involved an emotionally charged situation, such as conflict with friends, older adults tended to call on a wider repertoire of strategies than younger ones, including both action and withdrawal (Blanchard-Fields et al., 1997).

Can Older People Improve Their Cognitive Performance? Can cognitive performance be improved with training and practice? Plasticity is a key feature of Baltes's life-span developmental approach, and he and his colleagues have been in the forefront of research on effects of training. Several of these studies have been based on the Adult Development and Enrichment Project (ADEPT), originated at Pennsylvania State University (Baltes & Willis, 1982; Blieszner, Willis, & Baltes, 1981; Plemons, Willis, & Baltes, 1978; Willis, Blieszner, & Baltes, 1981). In one study based on ADEPT, adults with an average age of 70 who received training in figural relations (rules for determining the next figure in a series), a measure of fluid intelligence, improved more than a control group who received no training. A third group who worked with the same training materials and problems without formal instruction also did better than the control group, and this self-taught group maintained their gains better after one month (Blackburn, Papalia-Finlay, Foye, & Serlin, 1988). Apparently the opportunity to work out their own solutions fostered more lasting learning.

In training connected with the Seattle Longitudinal Study (Schaie, 1990, 1994, 1996b; Schaie & Willis, 1986; Willis & Schaie, 1986b), older people who already had

Young people are not the only ones becoming computer-literate these days. Many older people are joining the computer age and learning useful new skills. Research has found that older adults can expand their cognitive performance with training and practice.

shown declines in intelligence gained significantly in two fluid abilities: spatial orientation and, especially, inductive reasoning. In fact, about four out of ten participants regained levels of proficiency they had shown fourteen years earlier. Gains measured in the laboratory showed substantial correlations with objective measures of everyday functioning (Schaie, 1994; Willis, Jay, Diehl, & Marsiske, 1992).

In both the ADEPT and Seattle studies, trained participants retained an edge over an untrained control group, even after seven years (Schaie, 1994, 1996a, 1996b; Willis, 1990; Willis & Nesselroade, 1990). Longitudinal findings suggest that training may enable older adults not only to recover lost competence but even to surpass their previous attainments (Schaie & Willis, 1996). (In the next section, we discuss results of memory training.)

Cognitive deterioration, then, often may be related to disuse (Schaie, 1994, 1996b). Much as many aging athletes can call on physical reserves, older people who get training, practice, and social support seem to be able to draw on mental reserves. Adults may be able to maintain or expand this reserve capacity and avoid cognitive decline by engaging in a lifelong program of mental exercise (Dixon & Baltes, 1986).

Checkpoint

Can you . . .

- ✔ Summarize findings of the Seattle Longitudinal Study with regard to cognitive changes in old age?
- ✔ Compare how older adults deal with instrumental and social problems?
- ✔ Cite evidence for the plasticity of cognitive abilities in late adulthood?

Memory: How Does It Change?

Failing memory is often considered a sign of aging. The man who always kept his schedule in his head now has to write it in a calendar; the woman who takes several medicines now measures out each day's dosages and puts them where she is sure to see them. Yet in memory, as in other cognitive abilities, older people's functioning varies greatly. To understand why, we need to recall how memory works, as described in Chapters 7 and 9.

Short-Term Memory Researchers assess short-term memory by asking a person to repeat a sequence of numbers, either in the order in which they were presented (*digit span forward*) or in reverse order (*digit span backward*). Digit span forward ability holds up well with advancing age (Craik & Jennings, 1992; Poon, 1985; Wingfield & Stine, 1989), but digit span backward performance does not (Craik & Jennings, 1992; Lovelace, 1990). Why? A widely accepted explanation is that immediate forward repetition requires only **sensory memory,** which retains efficiency throughout life, whereas backward repetition requires the manipulation of information in **working memory,** which gradually shrinks in capacity after about age 45 (Swanson, 1999). It is also harder for working memory to handle more than one task at a time (Smith et al., 2001).

sensory memory Initial, brief, temporary storage of sensory information.

working memory Short-term storage of information being actively processed.

A key factor is the complexity of the task (Kausler, 1990; Wingfield & Stine, 1989). Tasks that require only *rehearsal,* or repetition, show very little decline. Tasks that require *reorganization* or *elaboration* show greater falloff (Craik & Jennings, 1992). If you are asked to verbally rearrange a series of items (such as "Band-Aid, elephant, newspaper") in order of increasing size ("Band-Aid, newspaper, elephant"), you must call to mind your previous knowledge of Band-Aids, newspapers, and elephants (Cherry & Park, 1993). More mental effort is needed to keep this additional information in mind, using more of the limited capacity of working memory.

Long-Term Memory Information-processing researchers divide long-term memory into three main components: *episodic memory, semantic memory,* and *procedural memory.*

Do you remember what you had for breakfast this morning? Did you lock your car when you parked it? Such information is stored in **episodic memory** (refer back to Chapter 7), the component of long-term memory most likely to deteriorate with age. The ability to recall newly encountered information, especially, seems to drop off (Poon, 1985; A. D. Smith & Earles, 1996).

episodic memory Long-term memory of specific experiences or events, linked to time and place.

Because episodic memory is linked to specific events, you retrieve an item from this mental "diary" by reconstructing the original experience in your mind. Older adults are less able than younger people to do this, perhaps because they focus less on context (where something happened, who was there) and so have fewer connections to jog their memory (Kausler, 1990; Lovelace, 1990). Also, older people have had many similar experiences that tend to run together. When older people perceive an event as distinctive, they can remember it as well as younger ones (Camp, 1989; Cavanaugh, Kramer, Sinnott, Camp, & Markley, 1985; Kausler, 1990).

Semantic memory is like a mental encyclopedia; it holds stored knowledge of historical facts, geographic locations, social customs, meanings of words, and the like. Semantic memory does not depend on remembering when and where something was learned, and it shows little decline with age (Camp, 1989; Horn, 1982b; Lachman & Lachman, 1980). In fact, vocabulary and knowledge of rules of language may even increase (Camp, 1989; Horn, 1982b). On a test that calls for definitions of words, older adults often do better than younger ones, but they have more trouble coming up with a word when given its meaning (A. D. Smith & Earles, 1996). Such "tip-of-the-tongue" experiences may relate to problems in working memory (Heller & Dobbs, 1993; Light, 1990; Schonfield, 1974; Schonfield & Robertson, 1960, cited in Horn, 1982b).

semantic memory Long-term memory of general factual knowledge, social customs, and language.

Remembering how to ride a bicycle is an example of **procedural memory,** sometimes called *implicit memory* (Squire, 1992, 1994; see Chapter 7). This includes motor skills, habits, and ways of doing things that often can be recalled without conscious effort.

procedural memory Long-term memory of motor skills, habits, and ways of doing things, which often can be recalled without conscious effort; sometimes called *implicit memory.*

A special use of unconscious memory that holds up with age is **priming,** an increase in ability to solve a problem, answer a question, or do a task that a person has previously encountered (A. D. Smith & Earles, 1996). Much as priming a surface prepares it for paint, priming the memory prepares a person to answer a test question by first seeing it on a list for review, or to do a math problem involving the same process as one done in class. Priming can improve all three types of long-term memory. It explains why older adults are about as likely as younger ones to identify a familiar picture or recall a familiar word association (for example, *dragon* and *fire,* but not *dragon* and *fudge*).

priming Increase in ease of doing a task or remembering information as a result of a previous encounter with the task or information.

Why Do Some Aspects of Memory Decline? What explains older adults' losses, especially in working memory and episodic memory? Investigators have offered several hypotheses. One approach focuses on problems with the three steps required to process information in memory: *encoding, storage,* and *retrieval* (refer back to Chapter 9). Another approach focuses on the biological structures that make memory work.

Problems in Encoding, Storage, and Retrieval Older adults tend to be less efficient and precise than younger ones in *encoding* new information to make it easier to remember—for example, by arranging material alphabetically or creating mental associations (Craik & Byrd, 1982). Most studies have found that older and younger adults are about equally knowledgeable as to effective encoding strategies (Salthouse, 1991). Yet in laboratory experiments, older adults are less likely to *use* such strategies unless trained—or at least prompted or reminded—to do so (Craik & Jennings, 1992; Salthouse, 1991).

When younger and older adults were briefly instructed in an effective memory strategy (visual imagery) for recalling associated word pairs (such as *king* and *crown*), age differences in frequency of use of the strategy were fairly small and did not adequately account for age differences in recall. Thus, even when older adults use the same strategy as younger adults, they may use it less effectively (Dunlosky & Hertzog, 1998).

Another hypothesis is that material in *storage* may deteriorate to the point where retrieval becomes difficult or impossible. Some research suggests that a small increase in "storage failure" may occur with age (Camp & McKitrick, 1989; Giambra & Arenberg, 1993). However, since traces of decayed memories are likely to remain, it may be possible to reconstruct them, or at least to relearn the material speedily (Camp & McKitrick, 1989; Chafetz, 1992).

Older adults have more trouble with recall than younger adults but do about as well with recognition, which puts fewer demands on the *retrieval* system (Hultsch, 1971; Lovelace, 1990). Even in recognition tasks, however, it takes older people longer than younger ones to search their memories (Lovelace, 1990).

Of course, we must keep in mind that most research on encoding, storage, and retrieval has been done in the laboratory. Those functions may operate somewhat differently in the real world.

Neurological Change The decline in processing speed described earlier, which reflects a general slowdown in central nervous system functioning, seems to be a fundamental contributor to age-related memory loss (Luszcz & Bryan, 1999; Hartley, Speer, Jonides, Reuter-Lorenz, & Smith, 2001). In a number of studies, controlling for perceptual speed eliminated virtually the entire age-related drop in memory performance (A. D. Smith & Earles, 1996).

The *hippocampus,* which seems critical to the ability to store new information in long-term memory (Squire, 1992), loses an estimated 20 percent of its nerve cells with advancing age (Ivy, MacLeod, Petit, & Markus, 1992). Unconscious learning—apparently independent of the hippocampus—is less affected (Moscovitch & Winocur, 1992). So is recall of prior learning, which may even improve as a result of the growing complexity of neural connections in the cortex (Squire, 1992).

Atrophy in the *corpus callosum* may affect tasks that involve sensorimotor coordination between the hemispheres—for example, the left hand's responding to a light coming from the right. Older adults tend to be slower than younger ones in such tasks, but the attentional functions of the corpus callosum, which tend to hold their own with age, may compensate (Reuter-Lorenz & Stanczak, 2000).

Early decline in the *prefrontal cortex* may underlie such common memory problems of late adulthood as forgetting to keep appointments and thinking that imagined events actually happened (West, 1996), which may have to do with a failure of *source monitoring* (awareness of where a memory originated). A particular region of the left prefrontal cortex seems to be involved in older adults' vulnerability to false recall and recognition—for example, "remembering" that a familiar item was on a list when it was not (Jonides et al., 2000).

The likelihood that neurological deterioration underlies the weakening of certain abilities does *not* mean that nothing can be done. Older adults can improve source judgments by paying attention to factual, rather than emotional, aspects of a situation (who? what? when? where? how?) and by being more careful and critical in evaluating where a "memory" came from (Henkel, Johnson, & De Leonardis, 1998).

The brain often compensates for age-related declines in specialized regions by tapping other regions to help. In one study, researchers used positron-emission tomography (PET) to compare brain activity of college students with that of older adults during two memory tasks. When asked to remember sets of letters on a computer screen, the students used only the left hemisphere; when asked to remember the location of points on the screen, they used only the right hemisphere. The older adults, who did just as well as the students, used *both* the right and left frontal lobes for both tasks (Reuter-Lorenz, Stanczak, & Miller, 1999; Reuter-Lorenz et al., 2000). The brain's ability to compensate in this way may help explain why symptoms of Alzheimer's disease often do not appear until the disease is well advanced, and previously unaffected regions of the brain, which have taken over for impaired regions, also lose working capacity ("Alzheimer's Disease, Part I," 1998).

Metamemory: The View from Within

"I'm less efficient at remembering things now than I used to be."
"I have little control over my memory."
"I am just as good at remembering as I ever was."

These items come from **Metamemory in Adulthood (MIA),** a questionnaire designed to measure *metamemory,* beliefs or knowledge about how memory works.

Metamemory in Adulthood (MIA) Questionnaire designed to measure various aspects of adults' metamemory, including beliefs about their own memory and the selection and use of strategies for remembering.

Older adults taking the MIA report more perceived change in memory, less memory capacity, and less control over their memory than young adults do (Dixon, Hultsch, & Hertzog, 1988). However, these perceptions may, at least in part, reflect stereotyped expectations of memory loss in old age (Hertzog, Dixon, & Hultsch, 1990; Poon, 1985). When asked for a blanket assessment of their own memory, older adults are likely to claim that it has deteriorated; but when it comes to specific items or tasks, older adults are about as accurate as younger adults in judging their "feeling of knowing" or estimating how well they have done (Hertzog & Dixon, 1994; Hertzog, Saylor, Fleece, & Dixon, 1994; Salthouse, 1991).

This and other research suggests that older adults' complaints about their memory may be unrelated to their objective performance. However, this conclusion does not consider individual differences. An older person who once had an outstanding memory may well be aware of a loss not detectable by comparison with the norm. A study that did take account of this factor found a modest link between memory complaints and objective performance (Levy-Cushman & Abeles, 1998).

Improving Memory in Older Adults Some investigators have offered training programs in *mnemonics* (refer back to Chapter 9): techniques designed to help people remember, such as visualizing a list of items, making associations between a face and a name, or transforming the elements in a story into mental images. An analysis of thirty-three studies found that older people do benefit from mnemonic training. The particular kind of mnemonic made little difference (Verhaeghen, Marcoen, & Goossens, 1992). Memory training programs also may include training in attention and relaxation, as well as information about memory and aging, including effects of mood on memory (Levy-Cushman & Abeles, 1998).

An experiment with mice has raised hopes that genetic manipulation may eventually be able to counteract memory loss. The gene involved controls a unit of a neural signal receptor that normally becomes less active with age. A strain of mice bred with extra copies of this gene performed better than normal mice on a series of memory tests (Tang et al., 1999). In another experiment with rats, diets high in antioxidant fruits and vegetables, such as blueberries and spinach, retarded or even reversed age-related declines in brain function and in cognitive and motor performance (Galli et al., 2002). On the other hand, there is little evidence that highly touted memory-enhancing drugs such as ginkgo biloba have much, if any, effect (refer back to Box 17-1).

Checkpoint

Can you . . .

- ✔ Identify two aspects of memory that tend to decline with age, and give reasons for this decline?
- ✔ Explain how problems in encoding, storage, and retrieval may affect memory in late adulthood?
- ✔ Point out several neurological changes related to memory?
- ✔ Discuss how well older adults judge their memory capacities, and cite ways in which their memory can be improved?

Wisdom

With the graying of the planet, wisdom has become an important topic of psychological research. Erikson (as we'll see in Chapter 18) viewed wisdom as an aspect of late-life personality development. Other investigators define wisdom as an extension of postformal thought, a synthesis of reason and emotion. Some say that wisdom is seeing through illusions (McKee & Barber, 1999) or the loss of what Jung called the "false self" (Aldwin & Levenson, 2001). Another approach, rooted in eastern philosophy, focuses on the spiritual domain.

Robert Sternberg classifies wisdom as a *cognitive* ability that can be studied and tested. According to Sternberg (1998), wisdom is a special form of practical intelligence with a moral aspect. It draws on *tacit knowledge* (refer back to Chapter 13) and is aimed at achieving a common good through the balancing of multiple, often conflicting interests. Unlike other forms of intelligence, which can be used for any purpose, wisdom involves value judgments about what ends are good and how best to reach them. An example might be John Glenn's decision to return to space, which balanced the potential benefits to medical science and his own sense of fulfillment against his bodily danger and his family's anxiety.

The most extensive research on wisdom has been done by Baltes and his colleagues (Baltes, 1993; Baltes & Staudinger, 2000; Pasupathi, Staudinger, & Baltes, 2001). They define wisdom as expertise concerning the *fundamental pragmatics of life*—that is, knowledge and judgment about life's conduct and meaning. Although wisdom is related to crystallized intelligence, creativity, a judicious style of thinking, and such personality dimensions as openness to experience and interest in psychological needs and motives, research suggests that it is a separate, unique quality (Staudinger, Lopez, & Baltes, 1997). Favorable conditions for its growth may include learning and practice in the requisite skills and motivation to strive for excellence. Guidance from mentors and the mastery of critical life experiences may prepare the way (Baltes & Staudinger, 2000; Pasupathi et al., 2001).

In a series of studies, Baltes and his associates have asked adults of various ages and occupations to think aloud about hypothetical dilemmas. Responses were rated according to criteria drawn up by the researchers. The basic criteria for wisdom were expert factual and procedural knowledge about the human condition and about strategies for life planning, life management, and solving life problems. Other criteria included awareness that life is unpredictable, that circumstances vary greatly, and that people differ in values, goals, and priorities, so that no one solution is best for everyone (Baltes & Staudinger, 2000; Pasupathi et al., 2001).

In one of these studies (J. Smith & Baltes, 1990), 60 well-educated German professionals ages 25 to 81 were given four dilemmas involving such issues as weighing career against family needs and deciding whether to accept early retirement. Of 240 solutions, only 5 percent were rated wise according to the criteria just listed, and these responses were distributed nearly evenly among young, middle-aged, and older adults. Participants showed more wisdom about decisions applicable to their own stage of life. For example, the oldest group gave its best answers to the problem of a 60-year-old widow who, having just started her own business, learns that her son has been left with two young children and wants her to help care for them.

In another study, the researchers assembled 14 middle-aged and older adults (average age, 67) who were named by others as wise. When presented with two dilemmas—the one about the 60-year-old widow and another about a phone call from a friend who intends to commit suicide—these "wisdom nominees" equaled the performance of elderly clinical psychologists (the best performers in the previous study), who were trained to deal with the kinds of problems presented. Both of these "expert" groups gave wiser answers than control groups of older and younger adults with similar education and professional standing (Baltes, Staudinger, Maercker, & Smith, 1995).

Wisdom has an interactive aspect. In one experiment, both younger and older adults gave wiser responses to hypothetical dilemmas when told to think about what someone whose opinion they valued would say. When given extra time to think about a problem after discussing it with a spouse, domestic partner, relative, or friend, older adults gave wiser answers than younger ones (Staudinger & Baltes, 1996).

All in all, wisdom seems to be a highly individual thing, not subject to generalizations about normative development, and not gender-related. Such qualities as openness to experience, creativity, reflective thinking, and sophisticated moral reasoning seem to contribute to it (Pasupathi et al., 2001).

Perhaps the most significant contribution of this line of research to the study of wisdom is the attempt to measure it systematically and scientifically. The key developmental finding is that wisdom, though not exclusively the province of old age, is one area in which older people, especially those who have had certain kinds of experiences, can hold their own or better.

What's Your View?

- In what ways do your observations of older adults' cognitive functioning agree or differ with the research reported in this chapter?
- What are some ways to sustain a high level of intellectual activity in late life? Do you think you need to develop new or broader interests that you will want to pursue as you age?
- Think of the wisest person you know. Do the criteria that either Sternberg or Baltes and his colleagues established for wisdom seem to describe this person? If not, how would you define and measure wisdom?

Checkpoint

Can you . . .

- ✔ Contrast several approaches to the study of wisdom?
- ✔ Summarize findings from Baltes's studies of wisdom?

Lifelong Learning

Qian Likun, a star student who walks to his classes on health care and ancient Chinese poetry, took part in a 2.3-mile footrace. This might not seem unusual until you learn that Qian is 102 years old, one of thousands of students in China's network of "universities for the aged." More than 800 of these schools have been founded since the 1980s, showing China's commitment to its elderly population and demonstrating older people's willingness and ability to learn (Kristof, 1990). China's program exemplifies a trend toward **lifelong learning:** organized, sustained study by adults of all ages.

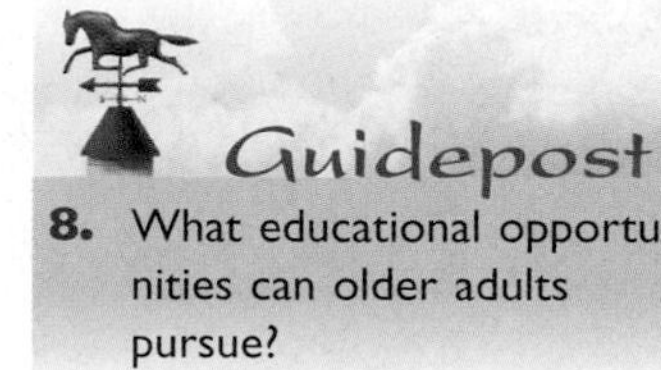

8. What educational opportunities can older adults pursue?

lifelong learning Organized, sustained study by adults of all ages.

Many older people in rural areas of developing countries have low literacy levels, having grown up when education was not widespread. By contrast, in many developed countries older adults are better educated than their predecessors, and this trend will continue as younger cohorts age. In 1970, about 27 percent of older Americans had finished high school; by 1998 fully two-thirds had done so (Kinsella & Velkoff, 2001).

In today's complex society, the need for education is never over. Educational programs specifically designed for mature adults are booming. In one category are free or low-cost classes, taught by professionals or volunteers, at neighborhood senior centers, community centers, religious institutions, or storefronts. These classes generally have a practical or social focus (Moskow-McKenzie & Manheimer, 1994). In Japan, for example, *kominkans* (community educational centers) offer classes in child care, health, traditional arts and crafts, hobbies, exercise, and sports (Nojima, 1994). A second category consists of college- and university-based programs with education as the primary goal (Moskow-McKenzie & Manheimer, 1994). Elderhostel is an international not-for-profit network of 2,300 educational and cultural institutions, which offers low-cost, noncredit residential courses and outdoor learning adventures for adults ages 55 and over and their spouses. In 2001, nearly 25,000 people in more than 100 countries took part ("Elderhostel," 2002).

In the United States, continuing education courses for older people have mushroomed since the mid-1970s (Moskow McKenzie & Manheimer, 1994). Many regional community colleges and state universities, as well as a few private universities, offer special programs for the elderly. Some vocational programs give special attention to the needs of older women who have never worked for pay but now must do so.

Older people learn best when the materials and methods take into account physiological, psychological, and cognitive changes they may be experiencing (Fisk & Rogers, 2002). For example, in learning to calibrate a blood glucose meter, older adults performed more poorly than younger ones when using a manual but did just as well as the younger learners, and retained their learning, when taught by a user-friendly video demonstration (Mykityshyn, Fisk, & Rogers, in press).

Checkpoint

Can you . . .

- ✔ Differentiate between two types of educational programs for older adults?
- ✔ Identify conditions conducive to older adults' learning?

Refocus

- How did John Glenn's *Discovery* voyage help shatter ageist stereotypes?
- How does Glenn exemplify the distinction between "young old" and "old old"?
- Which of the theories and research findings presented in this chapter seem to best explain Glenn's physical and cognitive condition in late adulthood?

The trend toward continuing education in late life illustrates how each stage of life could be made more satisfying by restructuring the course of life. Today, young adults usually plunge into education and careers, middle-aged people use most of their energy earning money, and some older people who have retired from work cast about for ways to fill time. If people wove work, leisure, and study into their lives in a more balanced way at all ages, young adults would feel less pressure to establish themselves early, middle-aged people would feel less burdened, and older people would be more stimulated and would feel—and be—more useful. Such a pattern might make an important contribution to emotional well-being in late adulthood, as we discuss in Chapter 18.

SUMMARY AND KEY TERMS

Old Age Today

Guidepost 1. How is today's older population changing?

- Efforts to combat ageism are making headway, thanks to the visibility of a growing number of active, healthy older adults.
- The proportion of older people in the United States and world populations is greater than ever before and is expected to continue to grow. People over 80 are the fastest-growing age group.
- Today, many older people are healthy, vigorous, and active. Although effects of primary aging may be beyond people's control, they often can avoid effects of secondary aging.
- Specialists in the study of aging sometimes refer to people between ages 65 and 74 as the *young old,* those over 75 as the *old old,* and those over 85 as the *oldest old.* However, these terms may be more useful when used to refer to functional age.

ageism *(607)*
primary aging *(609)*
secondary aging *(609)*
functional age *(609)*
gerontology *(610)*
geriatrics *(610)*

PHYSICAL DEVELOPMENT

Longevity and Aging

Guidepost 2. How has life expectancy changed, and how does it vary?

- Life expectancy has increased dramatically. The longer people live, the longer they are likely to live.
- In general, life expectancy is greater in developed countries than in developing countries, among white Americans than among African Americans, and among women as compared with men.
- Recent gains in life expectancy come largely from progress toward reducing death rates from diseases affecting older people. Further large improvements in life expectancy may depend on whether scientists can learn to modify basic processes of aging.

life expectancy *(610)*
longevity *(610)*
life span *(610)*

Guidepost 3. What theories have been advanced for causes of aging, and what does research suggest about possibilities for extending the life span?

- Senescence begins at different ages for different people.
- Theories of biological aging fall into two categories: genetic-programming theories and variable-rate, or error theories.
- Research on extension of the life span through genetic manipulation or caloric restriction has challenged the idea of a biological limit to the life span.

senescence *(613)*
genetic-programming theories *(613)*
Hayflick limit *(613)*
variable-rate theories *(614)*
metabolism *(614)*
free radicals *(614)*
autoimmunity *(615)*
survival curves *(615)*

Physical Changes

Guidepost 4. What physical changes occur during old age, and how do these changes vary among individuals?

- Changes in body systems and organs are highly variable and may be results of disease, which in turn may be affected by lifestyle.
- Most body systems generally continue to function fairly well, but the heart becomes more susceptible to disease. Reserve capacity declines.
- Although the brain changes with age, the changes are usually modest. They include loss or shrinkage of nerve cells and a general slowing of responses. However, the brain also seems able to grow new neurons and build new connections late in life.
- Visual and hearing problems may interfere with daily life but often can be corrected. Irreversible damage may result from age-related macular degeneration or glaucoma. Losses in taste and smell may lead to poor nutrition. Training can improve muscular strength, balance, and reaction time. Older adults tend to be susceptible to accidents and falls.

- Many older people are sexually active, though the frequency and intensity of sexual experience are generally lower than for younger adults.

reserve capacity *(618)*

cataracts *(620)*

age-related macular degeneration *(621)*

glaucoma *(621)*

Physical and Mental Health

Guidepost 5. What health problems are common in late adulthood, and what factors influence health at that time?

- Most older people are reasonably healthy, especially if they follow a healthy lifestyle. Most do have chronic conditions, but these usually do not greatly limit activities or interfere with daily life. The proportion of older adults with physical disabilities has declined. Still, older adults do need more medical care than younger ones.
- Exercise and diet are important influences on health. Loss of teeth can seriously affect nutrition.

arthritis *(624)*

Guidepost 6. What mental and behavioral disorders do some older people experience?

- Most older people are in good mental health. Depression, alcoholism, and many other conditions can be reversed with treatment; a few, such as Alzheimer's disease, are irreversible.
- Alzheimer's disease becomes more prevalent with age. It is highly heritable, but diet, exercise, and other lifestyle factors may play a part. Behavioral and drug therapies can slow deterioration. Mild cognitive impairment can be an early sign of the disease, and researchers are attempting to develop tools for early diagnosis.
- Major depressive disorder tends to be underdiagnosed in older adults.

dementia *(626)*

Alzheimer's disease *(626)*

Parkinson's disease *(626)*

neurofibrillary tangles *(627)*

amyloid plaque *(627)*

COGNITIVE DEVELOPMENT

Aspects of Cognitive Development

Guidepost 7. What gains and losses in cognitive abilities tend to occur in late adulthood, and are there ways to improve older people's cognitive performance?

- Physical and psychological factors that influence older people's performance on intelligence tests may lead to underestimation of their intelligence. Cross-sectional research showing declines in intelligence may reflect cohort differences.
- Measures of fluid and crystallized intelligence show a more encouraging pattern, with crystallized abilities increasing into old age.
- In Baltes's dual-process model, the mechanics of intelligence often decline, but the pragmatics of intelligence may continue to grow.
- A general slowdown in central nervous system functioning may affect the speed of information processing. However, this slowdown may be limited to certain processing tasks and may vary among individuals.
- The Seattle Longitudinal Study found that cognitive functioning in late adulthood is highly variable. Few people decline in all or most areas, and many people improve in some. The engagement hypothesis seeks to explain these differences.
- Although the ability to perform instrumental activities of daily living (IADLs) generally declines with age, ability to solve interpersonal or emotionally charged problems does not.
- Older people show considerable plasticity in cognitive performance and can benefit from training.
- Some aspects of memory, such as sensory memory, semantic and procedural memory, and priming appear nearly as efficient in older adults as in younger people. Other aspects, mainly the capacity of working memory and the ability to recall specific events or recently learned information, are often less efficient.
- Neurological changes, as well as declines in perceptual speed, may account for much of the decline in memory functioning in older adults. However, the brain can compensate for some age-related declines.
- According to studies of metamemory, some older adults may overestimate their memory loss, perhaps because of stereotypes about aging.
- According to Baltes's studies, wisdom is not age-related, but people of all ages give wiser responses to problems affecting their own age group.

Wechsler Adult Intelligence Scale (WAIS) *(631)*

dual-process model *(632)*

mechanics of intelligence *(632)*

pragmatics of intelligence *(632)*

selective optimization with compensation *(632)*

engagement hypothesis *(634)*

instrumental activities of daily living (IADLs) *(634)*

sensory memory *(636)*

working memory *(636)*

episodic memory *(636)*

semantic memory *(637)*

procedural memory *(637)*

priming *(637)*

Metamemory in Adulthood (MIA) *(639)*

Lifelong Learning

Guidepost 8. What educational opportunities can older adults pursue?

- Lifelong learning can keep older people mentally alert.
- Educational programs for older adults are proliferating. Most of these programs have either a practical-social focus or a more serious educational one.
- Older adults learn better when material and methods are geared to the needs of this age group.

lifelong learning *(641)*

Psychosocial Development in Late Adulthood

Chapter 18

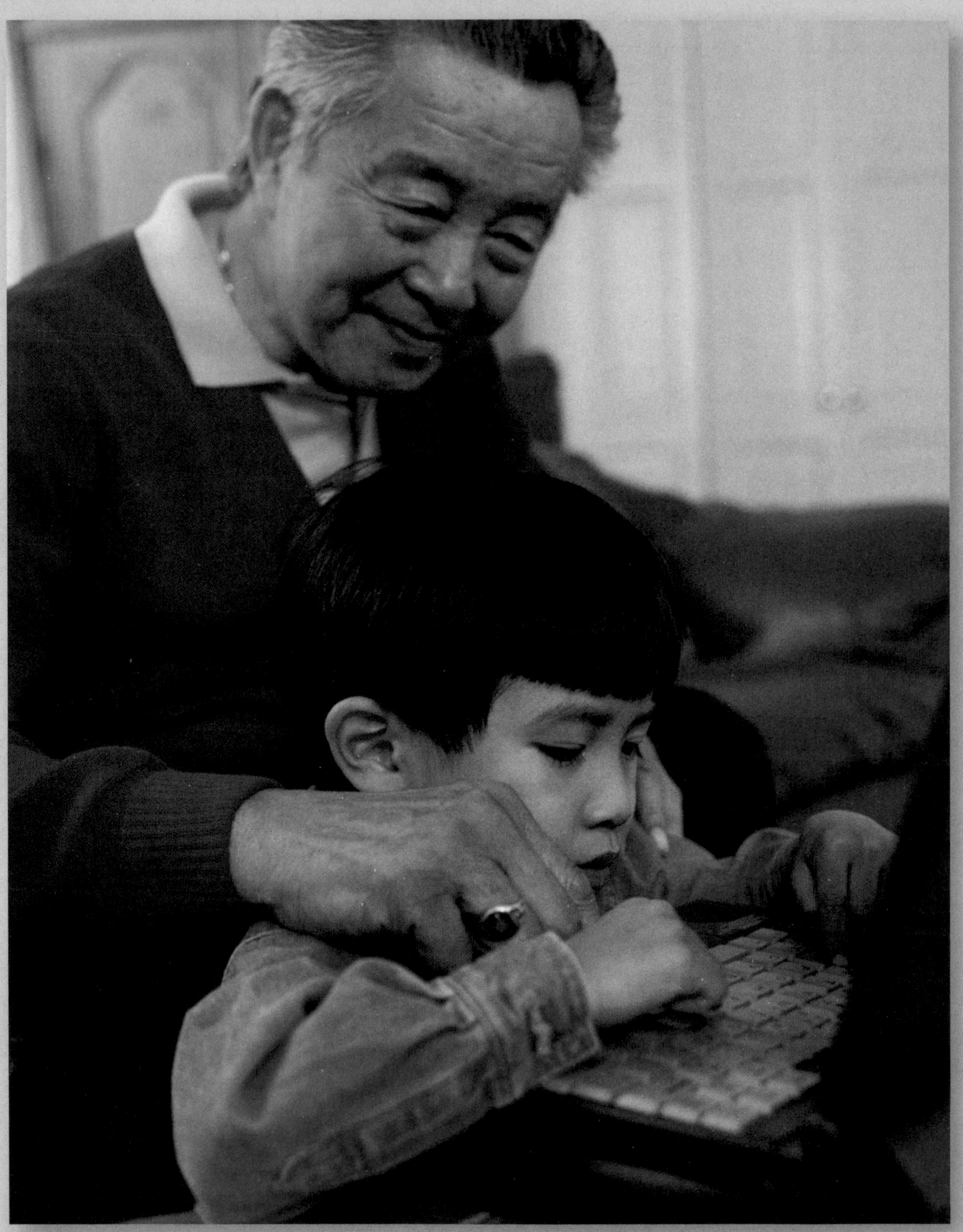

There is still today
And tomorrow fresh with dreams:
Life never grows old

Rita Duskin, "Haiku," *Sound and Light,* 1987

OUTLINE

Focus: Jimmy Carter, "Retired" President

Jimmy Carter

James Earl ("Jimmy") Carter, Jr. (b. 1924)* was one of the most unpopular presidents of the United States in the twentieth century. Yet more than two decades after having been turned out of office, he is one of the most active and admired ex-presidents in American history, "pursuing lost and neglected causes with a missionary's zeal"—and amazing success (Nelson, 1994).

In 1976, in the wake of the Watergate scandal, Carter, a peanut farmer who had completed a term as governor of Georgia, became the first southerner in the twentieth century to be elected president. His appeal was as an outsider who would clean up government and restore a moral tone. But despite such historic achievements as peace between Israel and Egypt, he became bogged down in the interminable Iranian hostage crisis and was blamed for high fuel prices and a sagging economy. After a devastating defeat in 1980, he retired from political life at the age of 56.

Carter and his wife and longtime helpmate, Rosalynn, faced a devastating crisis. His farm and warehouse business were deeply in debt, and he had no immediate prospects for work. "We thought the best of our life was over," he recalls. "And we went through a very difficult time with each other" (Beyette, 1998, p. 6A). Finally, determined to take charge of the remaining part of their lives, they asked themselves what experiences they could build on, what interests they had had too little time to pursue, and what talents they had not been able to fully develop.

What has Carter done since then? He is a professor at Emory University and teaches in a Baptist Sunday school. He helps build houses for low-income families through Habitat for Humanity. He established the Carter Center, which sponsors international programs in human rights, education, preventive health care, agricultural techniques, and conflict resolution and has secured the release of hundreds of political prisoners. As a roving peacemaker and guardian of

*Sources of biographical information on Jimmy Carter were Beyette (1998), Bird (1990), Carter (1975, 1998), Carter Center (1995), J. Nelson (1994), Spalding (1977), Wooten (1995), and various news articles.

freedom, Carter oversaw the Nicaraguan elections that ousted the Sandanistas. He brokered a cease-fire between Bosnian Muslims and Serbs. He pressed China to release political prisoners. He has helped set up or observed fair elections in Indonesia, China, Nigeria, Mozambique, and several other developing countries. He was the first former U.S. president to visit Communist Cuba. For these acts of courage, idealism, and service, he received the Presidential Medal of Freedom and the first United Nations Human Rights Prize. In 2002, at 78, he won the Nobel Peace Prize.

It has been said that Carter "used his presidency as a stepping stone to higher things" (Bird, 1990, p. 564). Freed from the pressures of politics, he has risen to the role of elder statesman.

Carter has written fourteen books, most recently *The Virtues of Aging.* In it, he talks about how he and Rosalynn have learned to "give each other some space"; how becoming grandparents deepened their relationship; how the active lives of close friends and acquaintances have served as examples and inspiration; how he handled the loss of his mother, brother, and two sisters; and how his religious faith helps him face the prospect of his own death without fear.

What does Carter see as the virtues of aging? "We have an unprecedented degree of freedom to choose what we want to do. . . . We have a chance to heal wounds. . . . We have an opportunity to expand the ties of understanding with the people we love most." And there are still new worlds to conquer. "Our primary purpose" says Carter, "is not just to stay alive . . . but to savor every opportunity for pleasure, excitement, adventure and fulfillment" (Beyette, 1998, pp. 6A–7A).

Although few adults have the resources and opportunities of an ex-president, Jimmy Carter is far from unique in using his retirement years productively. He is one of many older adults whose activism is creating a new view of life in old age.

In the early 1980s, shortly after Carter left office, the writer Betty Friedan was asked to organize a seminar at Harvard University on "Growth in Aging." The distinguished behaviorist B. F. Skinner declined to participate. Age and growth, he said, were "a contradiction in terms" (Friedan, 1993, p. 23). Skinner was far from alone in that belief. Yet two decades later, late adulthood is increasingly recognized as a time of potential growth.

Today, such terms as *successful aging* and *optimal aging* appear frequently in the theoretical and research literature. These terms are controversial because they seem to imply that there is a "right" or "best" way to age. Still, some older adults, like the Carters, do seem to get more out of life than others. "Growth in aging" *is* possible; and many older adults who feel healthy, competent, and in control of their lives experience this last stage of life as a positive one.

In this chapter, we look at theory and research on psychosocial development in late adulthood. We discuss such late-life options as work, retirement, and living arrangements, and their impact on society's ability to support an aging population and to care for the frail and infirm. Finally, we look at relationships with families and friends, which greatly affect the quality of these last years.

After you have read and studied this chapter, you should be able to answer each of the following Guidepost questions. Look for them again in the margins, where they point to important concepts throughout the chapter. To check your understanding of these Guideposts, review the end-of-chapter summary. Checkpoints located at periodic spots throughout the chapter will help you verify your understanding of what you have read.

Guideposts for Study

1. What happens to personality in old age?
2. What special issues or tasks do older people need to deal with?
3. How do older adults cope?
4. What is successful aging and how can it be measured?
5. What are some issues regarding work and retirement in late life, and how do older adults handle time and money?
6. What options for living arrangements do older adults have?
7. How do personal relationships change in old age, and what is their effect on well-being?
8. What are the characteristics of long-term marriages in late life, and what impact do divorce, remarriage, and widowhood have at this time?
9. How do unmarried older people and those in gay and lesbian relationships fare?
10. How does friendship change in old age?
11. How do older adults get along with—or without—grown children and with siblings, and how do they adjust to great-grandparenthood?

Theory and Research on Psychosocial Development

How much does personality change in late life? Not much, according to some research. Still, the experience of such people as Jimmy Carter leads some theorists to view late adulthood as a developmental stage with its own special issues and tasks. Many older people reexamine their lives, complete unfinished business, and decide how best to channel their energies and spend their remaining days, months, or years. Acutely aware of the passage of time, some wish to leave a legacy to their children or to the world, pass on the fruits of their experience, and validate the meaning of their lives. Others simply want to take this last chance to enjoy favorite pastimes or to do things they never had enough time for when they were younger.

Let's see what theory and research on psychosocial development can tell us about this final phase of the life span, about ways older people cope with stress and loss, and what constitutes "successful," or "optimal" aging.

Stability of Personality Traits

Although some research has found late-life change in certain of the "Big Five" personality dimensions, such as increases in agreeableness and decreases in extraversion (D. Field & Millsap, 1991), Costa and McCrae's (1994a, 1994b, 1996) work has made an impressive case for the essential stability of personality traits (refer back to Chapter 14). Hostile people are unlikely to mellow much with age, unless they get psychotherapeutic treatment; and optimistic people are likely to remain their hopeful

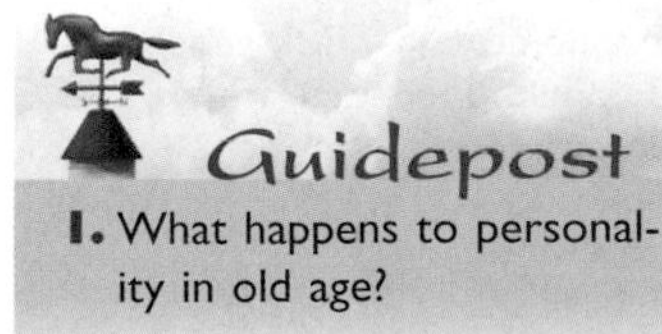

Guidepost

1. What happens to personality in old age?

selves. Certain persistent trait patterns contribute to adaptation to aging and may even predict health and longevity (Baltes, Lindenberger, & Staudinger, 1998; see Box 18-1).

Contrary to the common belief that older adults tend to be depressed, they actually tend to grow more content and satisfied with life. In a longitudinal study that followed four generations for twenty-three years, self-reported *negative* emotions such as restlessness, boredom, loneliness, unhappiness, and depression decreased with age (though the *rate* of decrease slowed after 60). At the same time, *positive* emotionality—excitement, interest, pride, and a sense of accomplishment—tended to remain stable until late life and then declined only slightly and gradually (Charles, Reynolds, & Gatz, 2001).

A possible explanation for this generally positive picture comes from socioemotional selectivity theory (introduced in Chapter 16): as people get older, they tend to seek out activities and people that give them emotional gratification. In addiition, older adults' ability to regulate their emotions may help explain why they tend to be happier and more cheerful than younger adults (Mroczek & Kolarz, 1998) and to experience negative emotions less often and more fleetingly (Carstensen, 1999).

However, two of the Big Five personality traits tend to modify the pattern just described. People with *extraverted* personalities (outgoing and socially oriented) tend to report especially high levels of positive emotion initially and are more likely than others to retain their positivity throughout life. People with *neurotic* personalities (moody, touchy, anxious, and restless) are more likely to report negative, and not positive, emotions, and they tend to become even less positive, and no less negative, over time (Charles et al., 2001). Neuroticism is a far more powerful predictor of moods and mood disorders than age, race, gender, income, education, and marital status (Costa & McCrae, 1996).

Does personality become more rigid in old age? Early cross-sectional research seemed to support that view. However, McCrae and Costa (1994), in large longitudinal studies using a variety of samples and measures, have shown that this is *not* true for most people. Likewise, personality tests of 3,442 participants in the Seattle Longitudinal Study, discussed in Chapters 15 and 17, found only modest longitudinal declines in flexibility between ages 60 and 81 but much larger cohort differences (Schaie & Willis, 1991).

As a group, people in more recent cohorts seem to be more flexible (that is, less rigid) than previous cohorts. These findings suggest that "increases" in rigidity found in early cross-sectional studies may actually have been tied, not to age, but to the culturally influenced "baggage" of life experience that a particular generation carries throughout adulthood. If flexibility is becoming more characteristic of today's young adults, and if they carry that flexibility into late life, then future generations of older adults may be able to adapt more readily than their predecessors to the challenges of aging (Schaie & Willis, 1991).

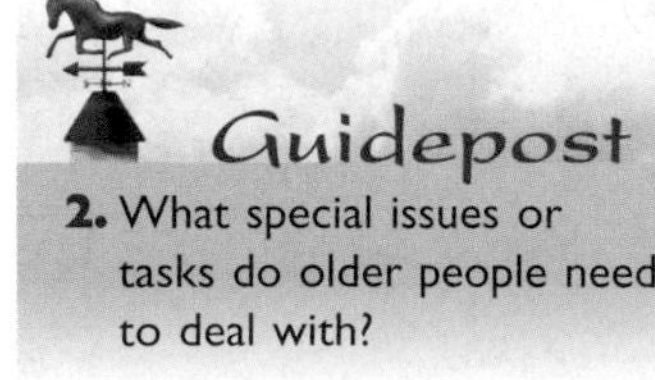

ego integrity versus despair According to Erikson, the eighth and final stage of psychosocial development, in which people in late adulthood either achieve a sense of integrity of the self by accepting the lives they have lived, and thus accept death, or yield to despair that their lives cannot be relived.

Normative Issues and Tasks

Whereas trait models emphasize the fundamental stability of the personality structure, other models, such as Baltes's life-span developmental approach, look at factors that may contribute to personal growth. According to normative-stage theorists, growth depends on carrying out the psychological tasks of each stage of life in an emotionally healthy way.

For Erikson, the crowning achievement of late adulthood is a sense of *ego integrity,* or integrity of the self, an achievement based on reflection about one's life. In the eighth and final stage of the life span, **ego integrity versus despair,** older adults need to evaluate, sum up, and accept their lives so as to accept the approach of death. Building on the outcomes of the seven previous stages, they struggle to achieve a sense of coherence and wholeness, rather than give way to despair over their inability to relive the past differently (Erikson, Erikson, & Kivnick, 1986). People who succeed in

Digging Deeper

BOX 18–1

Does Personality Predict Health and Longevity?

In the Terman study of gifted children, childhood personality characteristics and family environment played an important part in adult success. Now it appears that such factors may influence how long people live.

Most of the approximately 1,500 California schoolchildren chosen for the study at about age 11 on the basis of high IQ have been followed periodically since 1921. Between 1986 and 1991, when the survivors were approaching age 80, a group of researchers (Friedman et al., 1993; Friedman, Tucker, Schwartz, Martin et al., 1995; Friedman, Tucker, Schwartz, Tomlinson-Keasey et al., 1995; Tucker & Friedman, 1996) decided to find out how many had died and at what ages, so as to spot predictors of longevity. Since the "Termites" as a group were bright and well educated, the results were not likely to be confounded by poor nutrition, poverty, or inadequate medical care.

Surprisingly, neither childhood self-confidence, energy, nor sociability turned out to be related to longevity. Nor was optimism or a sense of humor in childhood associated with long life. In fact, the reverse was true: cheerful children were more likely to die young. What *did* strongly predict longevity was the personality dimension called *conscientiousness,* or dependability—sometimes described as orderliness, prudence, or self-control.

What might explain these findings?

One possibility is that while a carefree, optimistic approach to life may be helpful in coping with short-term situations, such as recovery from illness, in the long run it may be unhealthy if it leads a person to ignore warnings and engage in risky behaviors. Just as optimistic people may be inclined to be risk takers, conscientious people may be less so. They may be less likely to smoke, to drink, to be injured, and to overeat and become obese. Conscientious people may be more likely to cultivate good health habits, follow sound advice, and cooperate with doctors. They may avoid stress by thinking ahead, steeling themselves for the worst that might happen, staying out of situations they can't handle, and preparing for contingencies—for example, by carrying extra car keys and plenty of insurance. Then too, their qualities may enable them to achieve career success and to have greater financial, informational, and social resources to deal with medical and other problems. They also may be more likely to have stable marriages and reliable, supportive friendship networks.

Conscientiousness (but not cheerfulness) was related to a variety of variables that have positive influences on longevity. By midlife, conscientious children tended to have finished more years of education than less conscientious children and were less likely to have shown mental problems. They also were less likely to have been divorced or to have experienced parental divorce in their childhood.

This older couple seem comfortable with, and supportive of, each other. According to the Terman study, conscientiousness *(dependability) and marital stability are related to long life.*

Apparently it is not marriage itself but marital *stability* that can lead to long life. Termites who, at age 40, were in their first marriages tended to live significantly longer than those who had been divorced, whether or not the latter had remarried. By contrast, Termites who had *never* married had only slightly increased risk of early death.

Marital instability in the childhood home also was a threat to longevity. People who, before the age of 21, had experienced the divorce of their parents—13 percent of the sample—lived, on average, four years less than those whose parents had stayed together. Early death of a parent, on the other hand, made little difference.

The findings about marital stability and personality are interrelated. Children rated as impulsive were more likely to grow into adults with unstable marital histories and were more likely to die young. Also, children of divorce were more likely to go through divorce themselves—explaining part of the influence of parental divorce on longevity.

It seems, then, that people who are dependable, trustworthy, and diligent both in taking good care of themselves and in preserving their marriages—and who are fortunate enough to have had parents who stayed married—may be rewarded with more years of life.

What's Your View?

Think of someone you know who lived a very long life. Did that person have a conscientious personality? A stable marriage?

Check It Out:

For more information on this topic, go to http://www.mhhe.com/papaliah9.

this final, integrative task gain a sense of the order and meaning of their lives within the larger social order, past, present, and future. The "virtue" that may develop during this stage is *wisdom,* an "informed and detached concern with life itself in the face of death itself" (Erikson, 1985, p. 61).

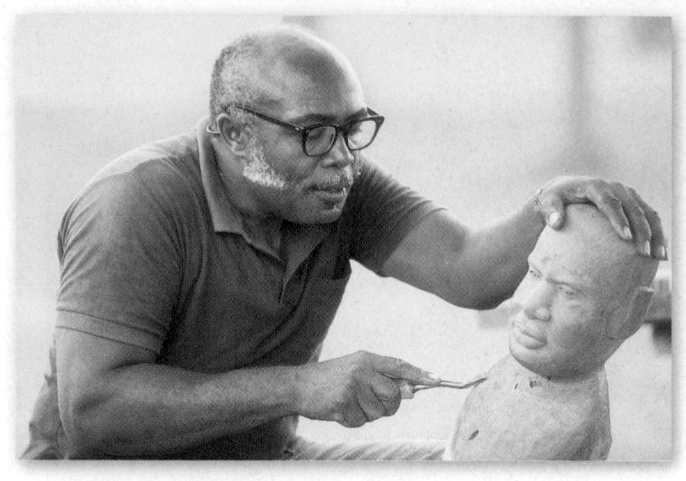

According to Erikson, ego integrity in late adulthood requires continuing stimulation and challenge, which, for this elderly sculptor, come from creative work. Sources of ego integrity vary widely, from political activity to fitness programs to building relationships with grandchildren.

Wisdom, said Erikson, means accepting the life one has lived, without major regrets: without dwelling on "should-have-dones" or "might-have-beens." It involves accepting one's parents as people who did the best they could and thus deserve love, even though they were not perfect. It implies accepting one's death as the inevitable end of a life lived as well as one knew how to live it. In sum, it means accepting imperfection in the self, in parents, and in life. (This definition of *wisdom* as an important psychological resource differs from the largely cognitive definitions explored in Chapter 17.)

People who do not achieve acceptance are overwhelmed by despair, realizing that time is too short to seek other roads to ego integrity. Although integrity must outweigh despair if this stage is to be resolved successfully, Erikson maintained that some despair is inevitable. People need to mourn—not only for their own misfortunes and lost chances but for the vulnerability and transience of the human condition.

Checkpoint

Can you . . .

- Summarize what is known about stability of personality traits and emotionality in old age?
- Describe Erikson's stage of ego integrity versus despair, and tell what Erikson meant by *wisdom?*

Yet, Erikson believed, even as the body's functions weaken, people must maintain a "vital involvement" in society. On the basis of studies of life histories of people in their eighties, he concluded that ego integrity comes not just from reflecting on the past but, as with Jimmy Carter, from continued stimulation and challenge—whether through political activity, fitness programs, creative work, or relationships with grandchildren (Erikson et al., 1986). Research inspired by Erikson's theory supports the importance men and women place on striving for ego integrity in late adulthood (Ryff, 1982; Ryff & Baltes, 1976; Ryff & Heincke, 1983).

Models of Coping

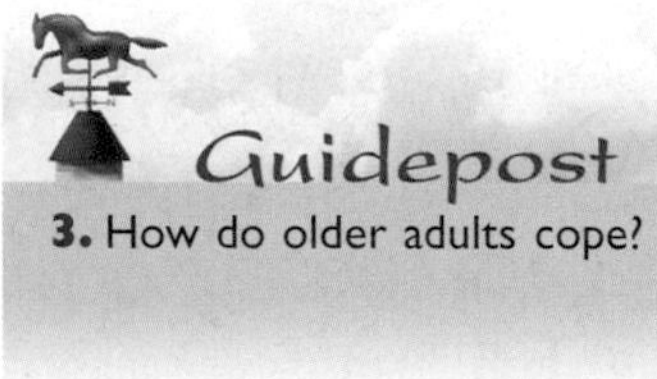

Guidepost

3. How do older adults cope?

Their health may not be what it was, they've lost old friends and family members—often spouses—and they probably don't earn the money they once did. Their lives keep changing in countless stressful ways. Yet in general, older adults have fewer mental disorders and are more satisfied with life than younger ones (Mroczek & Kolarz, 1998; Wykle & Musil, 1993). What accounts for this remarkable ability to cope?

coping Adaptive thinking or behavior aimed at reducing or relieving stress that arises from harmful, threatening, or challenging conditions.

Coping is adaptive thinking or behavior aimed at reducing or relieving stress that arises from harmful, threatening, or challenging conditions. It is an important aspect of mental health. Do older adults cope better or less well than younger ones? Do they use different coping strategies? Findings vary, depending in part on methodology (Aldwin & Levenson, 2001). Let's examine two theoretical approaches to the study of coping: adaptive defenses and the cognitive-appraisal model. Then we'll look at a support system to which many older adults turn: religion.

George Vaillant: Factors in Emotional Health What makes for positive mental health in late life? According to three 50-year prospective studies of lives, an important predictive factor is the use of mature *adaptive defenses* in coping with problems.

Vaillant (2000) looked at the survivors of his own Grant Study of Harvard men born around 1920 (refer back to Chapters 14–16), as well as his study of inner-city men born around 1930 (refer back to Chapter 15) and a subsample of women from

Terman's study of gifted California schoolchildren born about 1910 (refer back to Chapter 9). In all three groups, those who, in old age, showed the best psychosocial adjustment, had the highest incomes and the strongest social supports, and reported the highest marital satisfaction and joy in living were those who, earlier in adulthood, had used such mature adaptive defenses as altruism, humor, suppression (keeping a stiff upper lip), anticipation (planning for the future), and sublimation (turning lemons into lemonade). Use of adaptive defenses was relatively independent of IQ, education, and parents' social class.

How do adaptive defenses work? According to Vaillant (2000), they can change people's perceptions of realities they are powerless to change. For example, in the studies just described, the use of adaptive defenses predicted *subjective* physical functioning even though it did *not* predict objective physical health as measured by physicians. Among World War II combat veterans, those who used adaptive defenses were less likely to suffer post-traumatic stress disorder.

Adaptive defenses may be unconscious or intuitive. By contrast, the cognitive-appraisal model, to which we turn now, emphasizes consciously chosen coping strategies.

Checkpoint

Can you . . .

✔ Identify five mature adaptive mechanisms identified by Vaillant, and discuss how they work?

Cognitive-Appraisal Model In the **cognitive-appraisal model** (Lazarus & Folkman, 1984), people consciously choose coping strategies on the basis of the way they perceive and analyze a situation. Coping occurs when a person perceives a situation as taxing or exceeding his or her resources and thus demanding unusual effort. Coping includes anything an individual thinks or does in trying to adapt to stress, regardless of how well it works. Because the situation is constantly changing, coping is a dynamic, evolving process; choosing the most appropriate strategy requires continuous reappraisal of the relationship between person and environment (see Figure 18-1).

cognitive-appraisal model Model of coping, proposed by Lazarus and Folkman, which holds that, on the basis of continuous appraisal of their relationship with the environment, people choose appropriate coping strategies to deal with situations that tax their normal resources.

Coping strategies may be either *problem-focused* or *emotion-focused.* **Problem-focused coping** aims at eliminating, managing, or improving a stressful condition. It generally predominates when a person sees a realistic chance of changing the situation, as Jimmy Carter and his wife did when together they looked at their options after

problem-focused coping In the cognitive-appraisal model, coping strategy directed toward eliminating, managing, or improving a stressful situation.

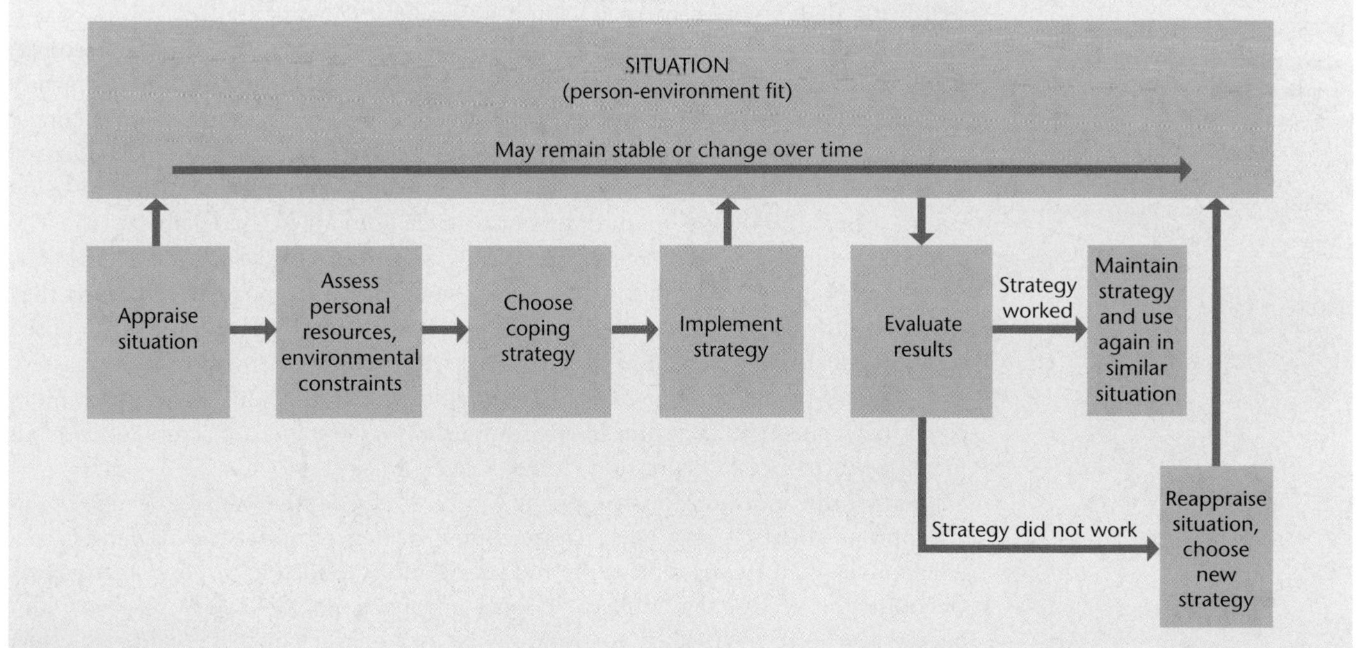

Figure 18-1
Cognitive-appraisal model of coping. (*Source:* Based on Lazarus & Folkman, 1984.)

emotion-focused coping In the cognitive-appraisal model, coping strategy directed toward managing the emotional response to a stressful situation so as to lessen its physical or psychological impact; sometimes called *palliative coping*.

he lost his reelection bid. **Emotion-focused coping,** sometimes called *palliative coping,* is directed toward "feeling better": managing, or regulating, the emotional response to a stressful situation to relieve its physical or psychological impact. This form of coping is likely to predominate when a person concludes that little or nothing can be done about the situation itself. One emotion-focused strategy is to divert attention away from a problem; another is to give in; still another is to deny that the problem exists. Problem-focused responses to a series of harsh reprimands from an employer might be to work harder, seek ways to improve one's work skills, or look for another job. Emotion-focused responses might be to refuse to think about the reprimands or to convince oneself that the boss didn't really mean to be so critical.

In general, older adults do more emotion-focused coping than younger people (Folkman, Lazarus, Pimley, & Novacek, 1987; Prohaska, Leventhal, Leventhal, & Keller, 1985). Is that because they are less able to focus on problems, or because they are better able to control their emotions?

In one study (Blanchard-Fields, Jahnke, & Camp, 1995), 70 adolescents, 69 young adults, 74 middle-aged adults, and 74 older adults wrote essays on how to handle each of fifteen problems. The participants, regardless of age, most often picked problem-focused strategies (either direct action or analyzing the problem so as to understand it better). This was especially true in situations that were *not* highly emotional, such as what to do about defective merchandise. The largest age differences appeared in problems with highly emotional implications, such as that of a divorced man who is allowed to see his child only on weekends but wants to see the child more often. Both young and old were more likely to use emotion regulation in such situations, but older adults chose emotion-regulating strategies (such as doing nothing, waiting until the child is older, or trying not to worry about it) more often than younger adults did.

Apparently, with age, people develop a more flexible repertoire of coping strategies. Older people *can* do problem-focused coping, but they also may be more able than younger people to use emotion regulation when a situation seems to call for it—when problem-focused action might be futile or counterproductive (Blanchard-Fields & Camp, 1990; Blanchard-Fields, Chen, & Norris, 1997; Blanchard-Fields & Irion, 1987; Folkman & Lazarus, 1980; Labouvie-Vief, Hakim-Larson, & Hobart, 1987).

What's Your View?

- Which kind of coping do you tend to use more: problem-focused or emotion-focused? Which kind do your parents use more? your grandparents? In what kinds of situations does each type of coping seem most effective?

Problem-focused coping tends to have a more positive effect on older people's well-being than emotion-focused coping, according to a comparative analysis of two longitudinal studies involving 449 women with an average age of about 70. The women in one study were moving from their longtime homes to an independent living facility for older adults. The women in the other study were long-term caregivers for mentally retarded adult children. The women in the first group reported more problem-focused coping and, eight months after the move, showed more improvement in well-being (as measured by Ryff's multidimensional scale, described in Chapter 16). The caregivers, who were followed for nine years, were more likely to choose emotion-focused coping to deal with a situation that most of them apparently believed they could do little about. However, among the caregivers who did use problem-focused coping, that strategy was more closely linked with a sense of environmental mastery and purpose in life; for those who used emotion-focused coping, its use was more clearly associated with a decline in environmental mastery and self-acceptance and an increased incidence of depression (Kling, Seltzer, & Ryff, 1997).

Sometimes emotion-focused coping can be quite adaptive, and its flexible use in appropriate situations can be a mature coping strategy. In one study (Diehl, Coyle, & Labouvie-Vief, 1996), adolescents and young adults tended to respond aggressively to conflict, whereas older adults were less confrontational and less impulsive. Older people also were more likely to withdraw from a conflict or to see its bright side. Emotion-focused coping can be especially useful in coping with what the family therapist Pauline Boss (1999) calls **ambiguous loss** (see Box 19-1 in Chapter 19). Boss

ambiguous loss A loss that is not clearly defined or does not bring closure.

applies that term to losses that are not clearly defined or do not bring closure, such as the loss of a still-living loved one to Alzheimer's disease or the loss of a homeland, which elderly immigrants may feel as long as they live. In such situations, experience may teach people to accept what they cannot change—a lesson often reinforced by religion.

Religion and Well-Being in Late Life Religion seems to play a supportive role for many elderly people, such as Jimmy Carter. Possible explanations include social support, encouragement of healthy lifestyles, the perception of a measure of control over life through prayer, fostering of positive emotional states, reduction of stress, and faith in God as a way of interpreting misfortunes (Seybold & Hill, 2001). But does religion actually improve health and well-being?

A review of the literature dealing with presumed effects of religion on two measures of health—cardiovascular disease and high blood pressure—found few relevant studies, and many of those had methodological flaws. The investigators concluded that there is little empirical basis for assertions of health benefits from religious involvement (Sloan & Bagiella, 2002).

However, other studies, less limited in scope, have found that religious involvement seems to have a mostly positive impact on physical and mental health and longevity (Ellison & Levin, 1998; Koenig, George, & Peterson, 1998; McFadden & Levin, 1996; Mitka, 1998; Seybold & Hill, 2001). A review of this research found positive associations between religiosity or spirituality and well-being, marital satisfaction, and psychological functioning; and negative associations with suicide, delinquency, criminality, and drug and alcohol use (Seybold & Hill, 2001).

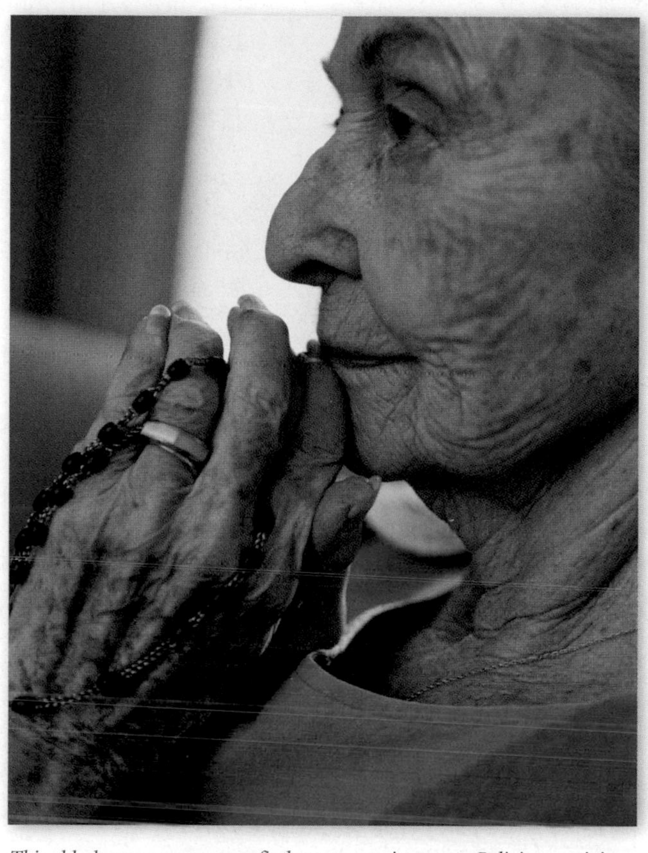

This elderly woman seems to find sustenance in prayer. Religious activity helps many people cope with the stresses and losses of late life.

Elderly African Americans are more involved in religious activity than elderly white people, and black women are more involved than black men (Coke & Twaite, 1995; Levin & Taylor, 1993; Levin, Taylor, & Chatters, 1994). For elderly black people, religion is closely related to life satisfaction and well-being (Coke, 1992; Coke & Thwaite, 1995; Walls & Zarit, 1991). However, among black men the most significant factor in satisfaction is self-rated religiosity, whereas for black women the significant factor is the number of hours spent on church work (Coke & Thwaite, 1995).

People with the most *or the least* religious commitment tend to have the highest self-esteem (Krause, 1995). It may be, as Fowler (1981) suggested (refer back to Chapter 13), that the emotional benefits nonreligious people derive from strong commitment to secular values are similar to the benefits religious people derive from a strong faith in God. Or it may be that people's self-esteem is highest when their behavior is consistent with their beliefs, whatever those beliefs may be.

Checkpoint

Can you . . .

- ✔ Describe the cognitive-appraisal model of coping, and discuss the relationship between age and choice of coping strategies?
- ✔ Discuss how religiosity relates to well-being in late life?

Models of "Successful" or "Optimal" Aging

Theorists and researchers disagree on how to define and measure *successful,* or *optimal, aging.* Some investigators focus on such criteria as cardiovascular functioning, cognitive performance, and mental health, about which there is consensus as to desirable outcomes. However, the whole may not be the same as the sum of its parts: a strong heart, a large vocabulary, and absence of depression do not necessarily add up to

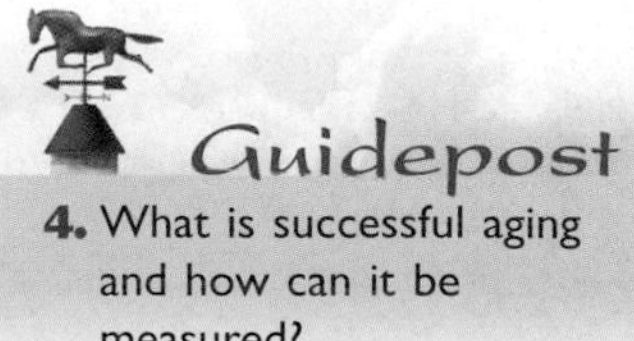

Guidepost

4. What is successful aging and how can it be measured?

success in living. Other researchers view productivity, economic or otherwise, as an important criterion for a meaningful or healthful life. Still others look at longevity, which can be a sign of physical and mental health.

Another approach is to examine subjective experience: how well individuals attain their goals and how satisfied they are with their lives. One model, for example, emphasizes the degree of control people retain: their ability to shape their lives to fit their needs and optimize their development (Schulz & Heckhausen, 1996). In one study, people reported greater feelings of control over their work, finances, and marriages as they aged, but less control over their sex lives and relationships with children (Lachman & Weaver, 1998). Another study found that people tend to live longer if they have a sense of control over the role (such as spouse, parent, provider, or friend) that is most important to them (Krause & Shaw, 2000).

All definitions of successful, or optimal, aging are value-laden—unavoidably so. Keeping this in mind, let's look at some classic and current theories and research about aging well.

disengagement theory Theory of aging, proposed by Cumming and Henry, which holds that successful aging is characterized by mutual withdrawal between the older person and society.

activity theory Theory of aging, proposed by Neugarten and others, which holds that in order to age successfully a person must remain as active as possible.

Disengagement Theory versus Activity Theory Who is making a healthier adjustment: a person who tranquilly watches the world go by from a rocking chair or one who keeps busy from morning till night? According to **disengagement theory,** aging normally brings a gradual reduction in social involvement and greater preoccupation with the self. According to **activity theory,** the more active people remain, the better they age.

Disengagement theory was one of the first influential theories in gerontology. Its proponents (Cumming & Henry, 1961) saw disengagement as a universal condition of aging. They maintained that declines in physical functioning and awareness of the approach of death result in a gradual, inevitable withdrawal from social roles (worker, spouse, parent); and, since society stops providing useful roles for the older adult, the disengagement is mutual. Disengagement is thought to be accompanied (as Jung suggested) by introspection and a quieting of the emotions.

The author Betty Friedan, whose 1963 book, The Feminine Mystique, *is credited with launching the women's movement in the United States, exemplifies successful aging as described by activity theory. At age 60, she went on the first Outward Bound survival expedition for people over 55. In her seventies she was teaching at universities in California and New York and, in 1993, published another best-seller,* The Fountain of Age.

After nearly four decades, disengagement theory has received little independent research support and has "largely disappeared from the empirical literature" (Achenbaum & Bengtson, 1994, p. 756). David Gutmann (1974, 1977, 1992) has argued that what *looks* like disengagement in traditional cultures is only a transition between the active roles of middle age and the more passive, spiritual roles of late adulthood, and that true disengagement occurs only in societies in which elderly people have no established roles appropriate to their stage of life. The result may be less-than-optimal satisfaction with life and underuse of human potential.

According to *activity theory,* an adult's roles are major sources of satisfaction; the greater the loss of roles through retirement, widowhood, distance from children, or infirmity, the less satisfied a person will be. People who are aging well keep up as many activities as possible and find substitutes for lost roles (Neugarten, Havighurst, & Tobin, 1968). For some older adults, even such a mundane activity as mall walking can serve as a substitute for the sense of purpose, belonging, social contact, and self-discipline previously derived from paid work (Duncan, Travis, & McAuley, 1995). Research on the *engagement hypothesis* (refer back to Chapter 17) suggests that involvement in challenging activities and social roles promotes retention of cognitive abilities and may have positive effects on health and social adjustment as well.

Activity theory has been influential, but, at least as originally framed, it is generally regarded as oversimplistic. In early research (Neugarten et al., 1968), activity generally was associated with satisfaction. However, some disengaged people also were well adjusted. This finding suggests that while activity may work best for most people, disengagement may be appropriate for some, and that generalizations about a particular pattern of "successful aging" may be risky. For some people, in some circumstances, accumulated roles can enhance health and well-being; for others, the result may be role strain and ill health (Moen, Dempster-McClain, & Williams, 1992; Musick, Herzog, & House, 1999).

Furthermore, most of the research on activity theory has been, of necessity, correlational. If a relationship between activity levels and successful aging were found, it would not reveal whether people age well because they are active or whether people remain active because they are aging well (Musick et al., 1999).

Much research has found that healthy older people *do* tend to cut down on social contacts and that activity in and of itself bears little relationship to psychological well-being or satisfaction with life (Carstensen, 1995, 1996; Lemon, Bengtson, & Peterson, 1972). However, activity theory has not, so far, been discarded. A new view is that activities do affect well-being—not so much through social roles as through their impact on the sense of self-efficacy, mastery, and control (Herzog, Franks, Markus, & Holmberg, 1998). Some gerontologists have sought to refine activity theory by comparing past and present activity levels. Others maintain that the type or content of the activity makes a difference.

Continuity Theory **Continuity theory,** as described by the gerontologist Robert Atchley (1989), emphasizes people's need to maintain a connection between past and present. In this view, activity is important not for its own sake, but to the extent that it represents the continuation of a lifestyle. For older adults who always have been active and involved, it may be important to continue a high level of activity. Many retired people are happiest pursuing work or leisure activities similar to those they have enjoyed in the past (J. R. Kelly, 1994). Women who have been involved in multiple roles (such as wife, mother, worker, and volunteer) tend to continue to have multiple roles, and to reap the benefits, as they age (Moen et al., 1992). On the other hand, people who have been less active may do better in the proverbial rocking chair.

continuity theory Theory of aging, described by Atchley, which holds that in order to age successfully people must maintain a balance of continuity and change in both the internal and external structures of their lives.

When aging brings marked physical or cognitive changes, a person may become dependent on caregivers or may have to make new living arrangements. Support from family, friends, or community services can help minimize discontinuity. Continuity theory, then, offers a reason to keep older adults out of institutions and in the community, and to help them live as independently as possible.

The Role of Productivity Some researchers focus on productive activity, either paid or unpaid, as a key to aging well. One study (Glass, Seeman, Herzog, Kahn, & Berkman, 1995) compared nearly 1,200 men and women ages 70 to 79, who showed high physical and cognitive functioning ("successful agers"), with 162 medium- and low-functioning adults in the same age group ("usual agers"). Nearly all successful agers and more than 9 out of 10 usual agers engaged in some form of productive activity, but successful agers were far more productive. On average, they did one-third more housework than usual agers, more than twice as much yard work, more than three times as much paid work, and almost four times as much volunteer work.

Three years later, when interviewed again, 15 percent of the successful agers had become less productive, but 13 percent had become more so. People who originally had been more satisfied with their lives were more likely to have increased in productivity; so were people who showed gains in personal mastery. This research supports the idea that productive activity plays an important part in successful aging, and that older people not only can continue to be productive but can become even more so.

On the other hand, frequent participation in *leisure* activities can be as beneficial to health and well-being as frequent participation in productive ones. It may be that *any* regular activity that expresses and enhances some aspect of the self can contribute to successful aging (Herzog et al., 1998).

What's Your View?

- Are you satisfied with any of the definitions of successful (or optimal) aging presented in this section? Why or why not?

Selective Optimization with Compensation According to Baltes and his colleagues (Marsiske et al., 1995), successful aging depends on having goals to guide development and resources that make those goals potentially achievable. In old age—indeed, throughout life, say these investigators—this occurs through *selective optimization with compensation.*

According to this concept, introduced in Chapter 17, the aging brain compensates for losses in certain areas by selectively "optimizing," or making the most of, other abilities. For example, the celebrated concert pianist Arthur Rubinstein, who gave his farewell concert at 89, compensated for memory and motor losses by keeping up a smaller repertoire, practicing longer each day, and playing more slowly before fast movements (which he could no longer play at top speed) to heighten the contrast (Baltes & Baltes, 1990).

The same principle applies to psychosocial development. As we have seen, older adults often can be more flexible than younger ones in selecting coping strategies, and thus can optimize well-being in the face of overwhelming, intractable problems. Their greater ability to avail themselves of emotion-focusing strategies may compensate for loss of control over certain areas of their lives. Also, as Carstensen's (1991, 1995, 1996) socioemotional selectivity theory suggests, people become more selective about social contacts as they age, maintaining contact with people who can best meet their current needs for emotional satisfaction. Such meaningful contacts may help older people compensate for the narrowing of possibilities in their lives. As in cognitive-appraisal theory, assessment of available resources is important to these and other adaptations (Baltes et al., 1998).

Checkpoint

Can you . . .

- ✔ Compare disengagement theory, activity theory, continuity theory, and productive aging?
- ✔ Give examples of how Baltes's concept of selective optimization with compensation applies to successful aging in the psychosocial realm?

The argument about what constitutes successful, or optimal, aging is far from settled, and may never be. One thing is clear: people differ greatly in the ways they can and do live—and want to live—the later years of life.

Lifestyle and Social Issues Related to Aging

Guidepost

5. What are some issues regarding work and retirement in late life, and how do older adults handle time and money?

"I—will—never—retire!" wrote the comedian George Burns (1983, p. 138) at age 87. Burns, who continued performing until two years before his death at the age of 100, was one of many late-life achievers who have kept their minds and bodies active doing the work they love.

Whether and when to retire are among the most crucial lifestyle decisions people make as they approach late adulthood. These decisions affect their financial situation and emotional state, as well as the ways they spend their waking hours and the ways they relate to family and friends. The problem of providing financial support for large numbers of retired older people also has serious implications for society, especially as the baby-boom generation nears old age. A related problem is the need for appropriate living arrangements and care for older people who can no longer manage on their own. (Box 18-2 reports on issues related to support of the aging in Japan.)

Work, Retirement, and Leisure

Retirement is a relatively new idea; it took hold in many industrialized countries during the late nineteenth and early twentieth centuries as life expectancy increased. In the United States, the economic depression of the 1930s was the impetus for the social security system, which, together with company-sponsored pension plans negotiated by labor unions, made it possible for many older workers to retire with financial security. Eventually, mandatory retirement at age 65 became almost universal.

Window on the World

BOX 18–2

Aging in Japan

Since the 1940s Asia has been the most successful region of the world in reducing fertility. At the same time, higher standards of living, better sanitation, and immunization programs have extended the adult life span (Kinsella & Velkoff, 2001; Martin, 1988). The result: fewer young people to care for the old.

In Japan, nearly one person in six is now older than 65 (Kinsella & Velkoff, 2001), accounting for close to half of the nation's total government-sponsored health care spending. By 2025 Japan will have twice as many older adults as children, and nearly 40 percent of them will be at least 80 years old. Pension reserves will likely be exhausted, and the social welfare burden—largely for retirement and health care costs for the elderly—may consume nearly three-fourths of the national income (Kinsella & Velkoff, 2001; WuDunn, 1997).

The Japanese pension system is a pay-as-you-go plan like social security in the United States, and it has similar problems. Everyone is required to join and to pay a basic minimum into the fund. But many self-employed people do not make their required contributions because they no longer trust the system. Many people also belong to supplementary corporate plans, but with the stock market collapse in the early 1990s, many of those plans went bankrupt or were underfunded. Today's retirees, many of whom joined pension plans late in their working lives but collect full benefits, are doing well. The crunch will come when younger workers, who now are subsidizing the elderly, are ready to retire. As in the United States, the Japanese government plans to gradually raise the retirement age (now 60 in Japan). There also is talk of cutting benefits by one-fifth. Middle-aged workers worry that they cannot count on adequate pensions when they retire (WuDunn, 1997).

Throughout Asia, a large proportion of older people live with their children, but as financial and health status improve, this pattern is less common than it used to be. In Japan, only about 55 percent of the aged lived with relatives in 1995 as compared with more than 80 percent in 1960, while the proportions who live alone or with spouses only have increased (Kinsella & Velkoff, 2001). Along with the shifting balance between old and young, such trends as urbanization, migration, and a larger proportion of women in the workforce make home care of elderly relatives less feasible. To halt the erosion in family care, Japan has made it a legal obligation to care for elderly relatives and has provided tax relief to those who give older relatives financial help (Martin, 1988; Oshima, 1996).

Multigenerational households like this one are becoming less common in Japan. There, as in the west, migration to cities and the movement of women into the workforce make home care of elderly relatives more difficult than in the past.

Institutionalization is seen as a last resort for those who are destitute or without families. But eventually Japan's exploding older population will outgrow family-based care. Six percent of the elderly were in residential care in the early to mid-1990s; such facilities were virtually nonexistent in 1960 (Kinsella & Velkoff, 2001).

Most Japanese, like most other Asians, want to help elderly people remain independent and productive as long as possible and, when they do need assistance, to help their families care for them. Meeting these goals is a difficult challenge.

What's Your View?

In what ways is aging in Japan becoming similar to what happens in the United States?

Check It Out:

For more information on this topic, go to http://www. mhhe.com/papaliah9.

Since the 1950s compulsory retirement has been virtually outlawed in the United States as a form of age discrimination, and the line between work and retirement is not as clear as it used to be. There are no longer norms concerning the timing of retirement, how to plan for it, and what to do afterward. Adults have many choices,

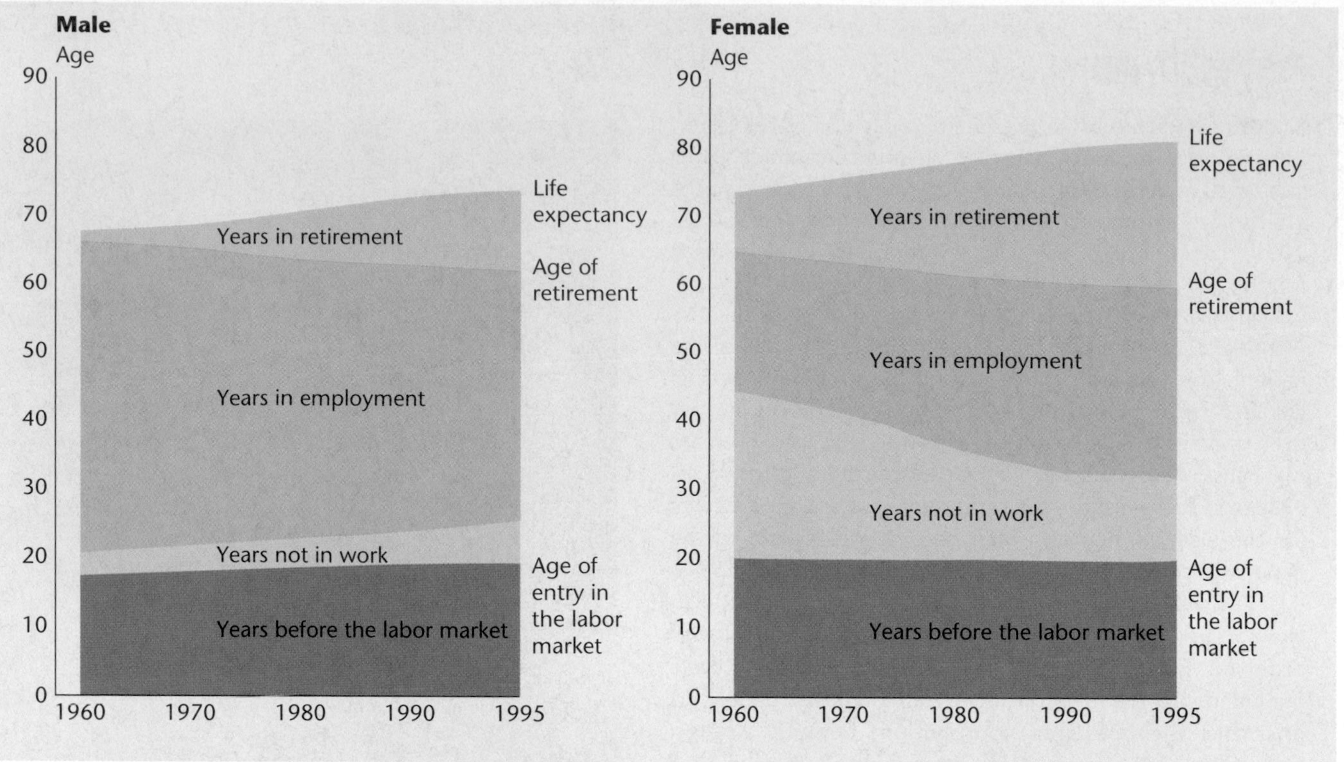

Figure 18-2

Changes in average number of years spent in and out of the workforce in 15 industrialized countries, 1960–1995. With increasing life expectancy, the number of years spent in retirement has increased, especially for women. Although women (unlike men) spend more years in employment than in the past, they also tend to retire earlier than before. (*Source:* Kinsella & Velkoff, 2001, Figure 10-13, p.111, from Organization for Economic Co-Operation and Development, 1998.)

among them early retirement (refer back to Chapter 15), retiring from one career or job to start another, working part time to keep busy or to supplement income, going back to school, doing volunteer work, pursuing other leisure interests—or not retiring at all. The biggest factors in the decision are usually health and financial considerations (Kim & Moen, 2001).

Trends in Late-Life Work and Retirement Most adults who *can* retire *do* retire; and, with increasing longevity, they spend more time in retirement than in the past (Kim & Moen, 2001; Kinsella & Velkoff, 2001; see Figure 18-2). In all countries, elderly people are a small proportion of the workforce, and the percentage decreases with age. Older men are more likely to work than older women—though women's economic activity, especially in developing countries, may include occupations that are hard to document, such as subsistence farming and taking in laundry. Women in developed countries are more likely than men to work part time (Kinsella & Velkoff, 2001).

Whether older adults can afford to retire generally depends on whether a country is rich or poor. In industrialized countries, workforce participation rates for men ages 65 and over range from less than 3 percent in Belgium to more than 35 percent in Japan, but most countries have participation rates less than 10 percent. In the United States, about 17 percent of older men and 9 percent of older women were in the workforce in the late 1990s—the men, mostly in managerial, professional, technical, or production occupations, and the women mostly in clerical or service jobs. The pattern is quite different in most of the developing world, where large proportions of older people continue to work, mostly on farms (Kinsella & Velkoff, 2001).

Public and private pension programs and other inducements to make way for younger workers, such as the availability of social security benefits (at a reduced level) at age 62, have contributed to a trend toward early retirement in many developed countries. However, this trend appears to have stopped or leveled off (Kinsella & Velkoff, 2001). In the United States, the number of people 55 and older in the workforce rose by more than 8 percent between June 2001 and June 2002, a much larger increase than in previous years (Bureau of Labor Statistics, 2002b), possibly because the drop in the stock market curtailed retirement plans. Men are more likely to retire early than women (Kim & Moen, 2001). Older black men are less likely to remain in the workforce than older white men, often because of health problems that force them to stop working before normal retirement age. Those who do remain healthy tend to continue working longer than white men (Gendell & Siegel, 1996; Hayward, Friedman, & Chen, 1996).

For many Americans, retirement is a "phased phenomenon, involving multiple transitions out of and into paid and unpaid 'work'" (Kim & Moen, 2001, p. 489). Some retire into "bridge jobs," new part-time or full-time jobs that may serve as bridges to eventual complete retirement. Some are semiretired; they keep doing what they were doing before but cut down on their hours and responsibilities. A poll of 803 men and women ages 50 to 75 found that 40 percent were working for pay in retirement or planned to do so (Peter D. Hart Research Associates, 1999).

People who continue to work after age 65 or 70 usually like their work and do not find it unduly stressful (Kiefer, Summer, & Shirey, 2001; Kim & Moen, 2001). They tend to be better educated than those who retire and are more likely to be in good health (Kim & Moen, 2001; Parnes & Sommers, 1994). More than half (54 percent) of older workers say they are in very good or excellent health, as compared with 32 percent of nonworkers the same age, and the workers are almost three times as likely to say they expect to live another ten years. They also tend to be more active during their leisure time than retirees (Kiefer et al., 2001).

What's Your View?

- At what age, if ever, do you expect to retire? Why? How would you like to spend your time if and when you retire?

How Does Age Affect Job Performance and Attitudes Toward Work? Older workers are often more productive than younger workers. Although they may work more slowly than younger people, they are more accurate (Czaja & Sharit, 1998; Salthouse & Maurer, 1996; Treas, 1995). Older workers tend to be more dependable, careful, responsible, and frugal with time and materials than younger workers; and their suggestions are more likely to be accepted. While work requiring quick responses is likely to be done better by a young person, work that depends on precision, a steady pace, and mature judgment may be better handled by an older person (Forteza & Prieto, 1994; Warr, 1994). A key factor may be experience rather than age: when older people perform better, it may be because they have been on a job, or have done similar work, longer (Warr, 1994).

Older adults tend to be more satisfied with their work than younger ones (Salthouse & Maurer, 1996). They are more involved, more committed to their employers, better paid, and less likely to change jobs than young adults, who may have higher goals and expectations and are still establishing careers (Forteza & Prieto, 1994; Rhodes, 1983; Warr, 1994). As usual, though, we need to be careful about drawing conclusions from cross-sectional studies. For example, older people's commitment to the "work ethic"—the idea that hard work develops character—may reflect a difference between cohorts, not how long a person has lived (Warr, 1994).

In the United States, the Age Discrimination in Employment Act (ADEA), which applies to firms with twenty or more employees, protects workers ages 40 and older from being denied a job, fired, paid less, or forced to retire because of age. Still, many employers exert subtle pressures on older employees (Landy, 1994).

Powerful ammunition for older workers fighting age stereotypes came from a comprehensive study by an interdisciplinary task force commissioned by the United States

Congress (Landy, 1992, 1994). The chief findings were that (1) physical fitness and mental abilities vary increasingly with age and differ more within age groups than between age groups, and (2) tests of specific psychological, physical, and perceptual-motor abilities can predict job performance far better than age can.

How Do Older Adults Fare Financially? Even Jimmy and Rosalynn Carter had to face financial issues after retirement. So do most older adults.

Nine out of ten older Americans receive social security benefits, and nearly two out of three report income from assets. Other sources of income include pensions, earnings from work, and public assistance (Administration on Aging, 2001; see Figure 18-3). For Americans born after 1937, the age of eligibility for full social security benefits is scheduled to rise gradually from 65 to 67. This change was predicated on the rise in life expectancy, decreases in mortality, and improvements in health among older adults (Crimmins, Reynolds, & Saito, 1999).

Social security and other government programs, such as Medicare, which covers basic health insurance for people on social security, have enabled today's older adults, as a group, to be about as well off financially as younger and middle-aged adults, and their median net worth is well above the national average (AARP, 1995, 1999). Between 1959 and 2000, the proportion of older Americans living in poverty dropped from 35 percent to 10.2 percent. Older women—especially if they are single, widowed, or divorced—are more likely than older men to live in poverty, and older African Americans and Hispanic Americans are more than twice as likely as older white Americans to do so (Administration on Aging, 2001; Kinsella & Gist, 1995; Kramarow et al., 1999; Treas, 1995).

Although fewer older people live in poverty today, an estimated 30 percent of 60-year-olds will spend at least a year below the poverty line (Rank & Hirschl, 1999). Once poor, older adults are likely to stay poor (Treas, 1995). They may no longer be able to work, and inflation may have eroded their savings and pensions. Infirm or disabled people often outlive their savings at a time when their medical bills are soaring.

How will today's middle-aged adults fare financially during retirement? With a growing elderly population and proportionately fewer workers contributing to the social security system, it seems likely that benefits (in real dollars) will not continue to rise and may even decline. As for private pensions, a shift from defined benefit plans that guarantee a fixed retirement income to riskier defined contribution plans, in which benefits depend on returns from invested funds, is making the financial future less certain for many workers (Rix, 1994; Treas, 1995).

Still, among a nationally representative sample of 2,001 men and women ages 33 to 52 (AARP, 2000), about 60 percent—chiefly those with higher current income—

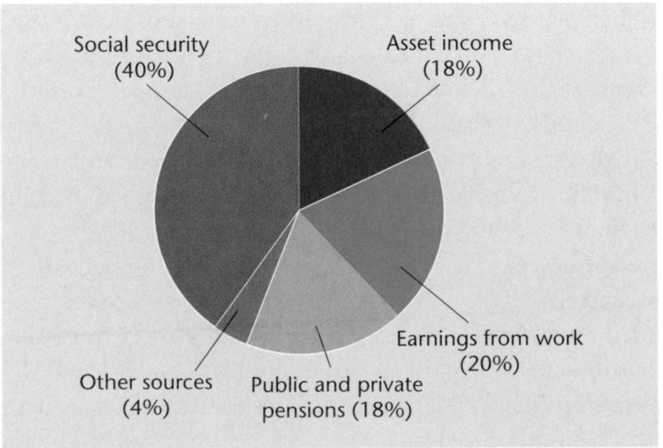

Figure 18-3
Sources of income of Americans ages 65 and older. (*Source:* Based on data from Administration on Aging, 2001.)

expressed confidence in their ability to prepare financially for the future. Fewer than half (48 percent) were counting on social security as a source of retirement income. About 60 percent were depending on savings and investments, and 68 percent on self-directed retirement plans, such as IRAs and 401(k)s. The vast majority (84 percent) planned to work at least part time.

Life After Retirement People who retire may feel the loss of a role that is central to their identity; or they may enjoy the loss of the strains that go with that role (Kim & Moen, 2002). Retirement may bring other role adjustments. It not only alters household income but also can change the division of household work, marital quality, and distribution of power and decision making. There may be more time for contact with extended family and friends and for caring for grandchildren. Unexpected illness or disability, or marital troubles of adult children, can affect the retirement experience (Szinovacz & Ekerdt, 1995).

Retirement is not a single event but an ongoing process, and its impact must be assessed in context. Personal resources (health, SES, and personality), economic resources, and social-relational resources, such as support from a partner and friends, can affect how well retirees weather this transition (Kim & Moen, 2001, 2002). So can a person's morale *before* retirement. In a two-year longitudinal study of 458 married white, relatively healthy men and women, ages 50 to 72, men whose morale had been low tended to enjoy a boost during the "honeymoon period" immediately following retirement. On the other hand, *continuous* retirement was associated with an increase in depressive symptoms—especially among men who had experienced such symptoms before. Women's well-being was less influenced by retirement—their own or their husbands'—than men's; their morale was less affected by changes in income level, and more by marital quality. A sense of personal control was a key predictor of morale in both men and women (Kim & Moen, 2002). In other research, people who had a strong sense of competence and self-esteem during their working lives were more likely to have positive feelings about retirement (Mutran, Reitzes, & Fernandez, 1997).

During the first few years after retirement, people may have a special need for emotional support to make them feel they are still valued and to cope with the changes in their lives. In one longitudinal study, the most powerful predictor of satisfaction with retirement was the size of a retiree's social support network (Tarnowski & Antonucci, 1998).

Continuity theory suggests that people who maintain their earlier activities and lifestyles adjust most successfully. Socioeconomic status may affect the way retired people use their time. One common pattern, the **family-focused lifestyle,** consists largely of accessible, low-cost activities that revolve around family, home, and companions: conversation, watching television, visiting with family and friends, informal entertaining, playing cards, or just doing "what comes along." A second pattern, **balanced investment,** is typical of more educated people, who allocate their time more equally among family, work, and leisure (J. R. Kelly, 1987, 1994). These patterns may change with age. In one study, younger retirees who were most satisfied with their quality of life were those who traveled regularly and went to cultural events; but after age 75, family- and home-based activity yielded the most satisfaction (J. R. Kelly, Steinkamp, & Kelly, 1986).

family-focused lifestyle Pattern of retirement activity that revolves around family, home, and companions.

balanced investment Pattern of retirement activity allocated among family, work, and leisure.

Sunday painters, amateur carpenters, and others who have made the effort to master a craft or pursue an intense interest often make that passion central to their lives during retirement (Mannell, 1993). This third lifestyle pattern, **serious leisure,** is dominated by activity that "demands skill, attention, and commitment" (J. R. Kelly, 1994, p. 502). Retirees who engage in this pattern tend to be extraordinarily satisfied with their lives.

serious leisure Leisure activity requiring skill, attention, and commitment.

By using his leisure time to work as a volunteer tutoring a community college student, this retiree is helping not only the young man and the community but also himself. The self-esteem gained from using hard-won skills and from continuing to be a useful, contributing member of society is a valuable by-product of volunteer service.

Checkpoint

Can you . . .

- ✔ Describe current trends in late-life work and retirement?
- ✔ Cite findings on the relationship between aging and work skills and attitudes?
- ✔ Discuss the economic status of older adults?
- ✔ Discuss how retirement can affect well-being, and describe three common lifestyle patterns after retirement?

Since the late 1960s the proportion of older adults doing volunteer work (like Jimmy and Rosalynn Carter) has increased greatly (Chambre, 1993). In one poll, 57 percent of retirees said they had done volunteer or community service work during the past year (Peter D. Hart Research Associates, 1999). Volunteer work is closely tied to well-being during retirement; it may "help replace the social capital lost when an individual exits the world of work" (Kim & Moen, 2001, p. 510).

The many paths to a meaningful, enjoyable retirement have two things in common: doing satisfying things and having satisfying relationships. For most older people, both "are an extension of histories that have developed throughout the life course" (J. R. Kelly, 1994, p. 501).

Living Arrangements

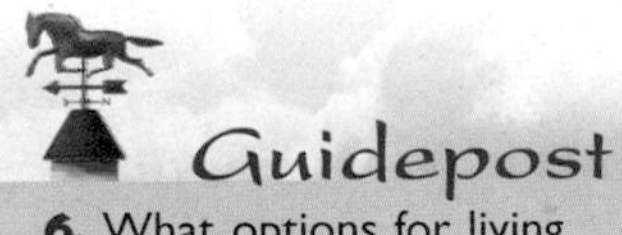

Guidepost

6. What options for living arrangements do older adults have?

Many factors affect older people's living arrangements: marital status, finances, health, and family size. Decisions about where and with whom to live also are affected by broader societal influences: cultural traditions and values, availability of social services, and the types of housing available (Kinsella & Velkoff, 2001).

In developing countries, both elderly men and women typically live with adult children and grandchildren in multigenerational households. In developed countries, such as the United States, Canada (see Figure 18-4), and most European nations, the minority of older adults living alone has increased greatly since the 1960s. Also, with increases in survival, the main person many older people in both developed and developing countries depend on for care and support is their spouse (Kinsella & Velkoff, 2001).

In the United States, in 2000, 95.5 percent of persons ages 65 and older lived in the community, more than half (55 percent) with a spouse. About 30 percent lived alone, and this proportion increased with age (Administration on Aging, 2001; see Figure 18-5 for a breakdown by gender). Minority elders, in keeping with their traditions, are more likely than white elders to live in extended-family households.

Living arrangements alone do not tell us much about older adults' well-being. For example, living alone does not necessarily imply lack of family cohesion and support;

Elderly Living Alone in Canada: 1961 to 1996

Thousands

800

600

400

200

0

Female

Male

1961 1966 1971 1976 1981 1986 1991 1996

Figure 18-4

Elderly Canadians living alone, 1961 to 1996. (*Source:* Kinsella & Velkoff, 2001, Figure 7-2, p. 66.)

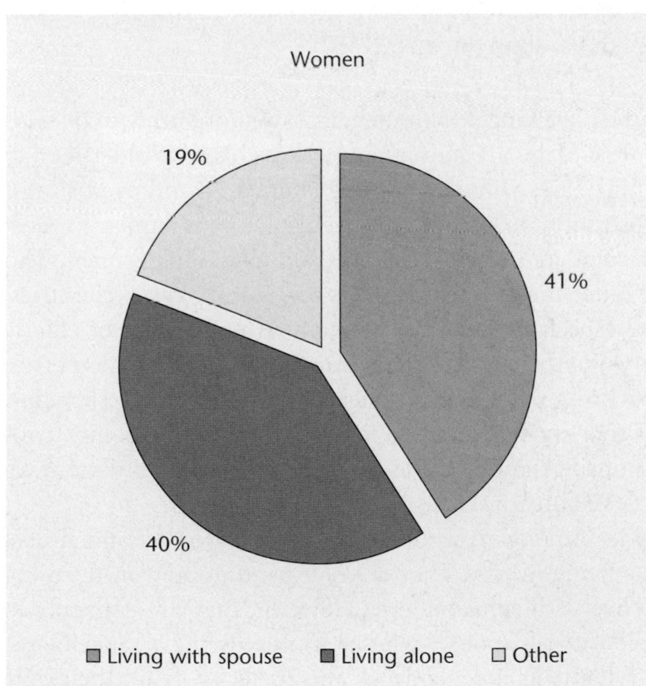

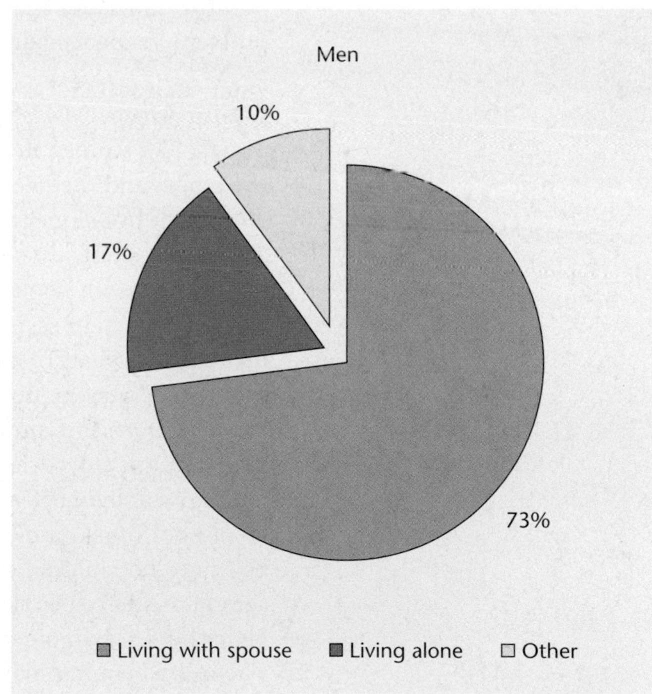

Figure 18-5

Living arrangements of noninstitutionalized men and women ages 65 and over, United States, 2000. In part because of women's longer life expectancy, women are more likely to live alone (especially as they get older), while men are more likely to live with a spouse. (*Source:* Administration on Aging, 2001; based on data from U.S. Bureau of the Census).

instead, it may reflect an older person's good health, economic self-sufficiency, and desire for independence. By the same token, living with adult children tells us nothing about the quality of relationships in the household (Kinsella & Velkoff, 2001).

Aging in Place—and Other Options About eight out of ten elderly heads of households own their homes, and most prefer to stay there; many, even after being widowed (Administration on Aging, 2001; Treas, 1995).

"Aging in place" may make sense for those who can manage on their own or with minimal help, have an adequate income or a paid-up mortgage, can handle the upkeep, are happy in the neighborhood, and want to be independent, to have privacy, and to be near friends, adult children, or grandchildren (Gonyea, Hudson, & Seltzer, 1990). For older people with impairments that make it hard to get along entirely on their own, minor support—such as meals, transportation, and home health aides—often can help them stay put. So can ramps, grab bars, and other modifications within the home. Older adults who cannot or do not want to maintain a house, do not have family nearby, prefer a different locale or climate, or want to travel may move into low-maintenance or maintenance-free townhouses, condominiums, cooperative or rental apartments, or mobile homes.

Most older people do not need much help; and those who do can often remain in the community if they have at least one person to depend on. The single most important factor keeping people out of institutions is being married. As long as a couple are in relatively good health, they can usually live fairly independently and care for each other. The issue of living arrangements becomes more pressing when one or both become frail, infirm, or disabled, or when one spouse dies. People who are not living with a spouse most often get help from a child, usually a daughter. Those who cannot call on a spouse or child usually turn to friends (Chappell, 1991).

Let's look more closely at the two most common living arrangements for older adults without spouses—living alone and living with adult children—and then at living in institutions and alternative forms of group housing. Finally, we'll discuss a serious problem for dependent older adults: abuse by caregivers.

Living Alone Because women live longer than men and are more likely to be widowed, older women in the United States are more than twice as likely as older men to live alone, and the likelihood increases with age. Among women 75 and over, almost 50 percent live alone (Administration on Aging, 2001). The picture is similar in most developed countries: older women are more likely to live alone than older men, who usually live with spouses or other family members. In the Scandinavian countries, where home help services are especially common, as many as one-fourth of elderly men and one-half of elderly women live alone. The growth of elderly single-person households may be due in part to governmental policies: increased old age benefits, "reverse mortgage" programs that enable people to live off their homes' equity, construction of elder-friendly housing, and long-term care policies that discourage institutional living (Kinsella & Velkoff, 2001).

About four out of five older Americans who live alone are widowed, and almost half have no children or none living nearby. They are older and poorer on the average than elderly people who live with someone else. However, they are generally in better health than older people without spouses who have other living arrangements. The overwhelming majority value their independence and prefer to be on their own (Commonwealth Fund, 1986; Kramarow et al., 1999; U.S. Bureau of the Census, 1992).

It may seem that older people who live alone, particularly the oldest old, would be lonely. However, other factors, such as personality, cognitive abilities, physical health, and a depleted social network may play a more significant role in vulnerability to loneliness (P. Martin, Hagberg, & Poon, 1997). Social activities, such as going to church or temple or a senior center, or doing volunteer work, can help an older person stay connected to the community (Steinbach, 1992).

Living with Adult Children Older people in many African, Asian, and Latin American societies can expect to live and be cared for in their children's or grandchildren's homes; in Singapore, for example, about nine out of ten elders live with their children (Kinsella & Velkoff, 2001). Most older people in the United States, even those in difficult circumstances, do not wish to do so. They are reluctant to burden their families and to give up their own freedom. It can be inconvenient to absorb an extra person into a household, and everyone's privacy—and relationships—may suffer. The elderly parent may feel useless, bored, and isolated from friends. If the adult child is married and parent and spouse do not get along well, or caregiving duties become too burdensome, the marriage may be threatened (Lund, 1993a; Shapiro, 1994). (Caregiving of elderly parents is discussed in Chapter 16.)

Despite these concerns, many older Americans, with advancing age, do live with adult children. The success of such an arrangement depends largely on the quality of the relationship that has existed in the past and on the ability of both generations to communicate fully and frankly. The decision to move a parent into an adult child's home should be mutual and needs to be thought through carefully and thoroughly. Parents and children need to respect each other's dignity and autonomy and accept their differences (Shapiro, 1994).

What's Your View?

- Were you surprised to read that a large number of older adults like living alone, and that few want to live with their children? Why do you think this is so?

Living in Institutions The use of nonfamily institutions for care of the frail elderly varies greatly around the world. Institutionalization is very rare in developing regions but is becoming less rare in Southeast Asia, where declines in fertility have resulted in a rapidly aging population and a shortage of family caregivers. In developed countries the percentage of elderly people in residential care in the 1990s ranged from 2 percent in Portugal to nearly 9 percent in the Netherlands and Sweden (Kinsella & Velkoff, 2001). Comprehensive geriatric home visitation programs in some countries, such as the United Kingdom, Denmark, and Australia have been effective in preventing functional decline and holding down nursing home admissions (Stuck, Egger, Hammer, Minder, & Beck, 2002).

In the United States in 2000, 4.5 percent of older adults were in institutions, as compared with 5.1 percent in 1990 (U.S. Census Bureau, 2001). But the lifetime probability of spending time in a nursing home is higher, especially for women, who live longer than men. About half of the women and one-third of the men who were 60 years old in 1990 will eventually stay in a nursing home at least once (AARP, 1999; Center on Elderly People Living Alone, 1995a; Treas, 1995). In all countries, the likelihood of living in a nursing home increases with age (Kinsella & Velkoff, 2001)—in the United States, from about 1 percent at ages 65 to 74 to 18 percent at ages 85 and over (Administration on Aging, 2001).

At highest risk of institutionalization are those living alone, those who do not take part in social activities, those whose daily activities are limited by poor health or disability, and those whose caregivers are overburdened (McFall & Miller, 1992; Steinbach, 1992). Three-fourths of nursing home residents are women (Kinsella & Velkoff, 2001), mostly white widows in their eighties. A large minority of residents are incontinent. Many have visual and hearing problems. A little over half are cognitively impaired. On average, they need help with four to five of six basic activities of daily living: bathing, eating, dressing, getting into a chair, toileting, and walking (Sahyoun, Pratt, Lentzner, Dey, & Robinson, 2001).

A good nursing home has an experienced professional staff, an adequate government insurance program, and a coordinated structure that can provide various levels of care. It offers stimulating activities and opportunities to spend time with people of both sexes and all ages. It provides privacy—among other reasons, so that residents can be sexually active and so they can visit undisturbed with family members. A good nursing home also offers a full range of social, therapeutic, and rehabilitative services.

An essential element of good care is the opportunity for residents to make decisions and exert some control over their lives. Among 129 intermediate-care nursing home residents, those who had higher self-esteem, less depression, and a greater sense of satisfaction and meaning in life were less likely to die within four years—perhaps because their psychological adjustment motivated them to want to live and to take better care of themselves (O'Connor & Vallerand, 1998).

Federal law (the Omnibus Budget Reconciliation Act of 1987 and 1990) sets tough requirements for nursing homes and gives residents the right to choose their own doctors, to be fully informed about their care and treatment, and to be free from physical or mental abuse, corporal punishment, involuntary seclusion, and physical or chemical restraints. Some states train volunteer ombudsmen to act as advocates for nursing home residents, to explain their rights, and to resolve their complaints about such matters as privacy, treatment, food, and financial issues.

As the baby-boom generation born after World War II ages, and if current nursing home usage rates continue, it is projected that the number of residents will double by 2030 (Sahyoun, Pratt, et al., 2001). However, with liberalization of Medicare coverage and the emergence of widespread private long-term care insurance, there is a shift toward less expensive home health care services and group housing alternatives. Home health services are most prevalent in Scandinavia and the United Kingdom (Kinsella & Velkoff, 2001).

Alternative Housing Options Today an emerging array of group housing options (see Table 18-1), together with modern medical aids and home health programs, make it possible for many older people with health problems to remain in the community longer and to obtain needed services or care without sacrificing independence and dignity (Laquatra & Chi, 1998; Porcino, 1993; Sahyoun, Pratt, et al., 2001).

One popular option is *assisted living,* the fastest-growing form of housing for the elderly in the United States. Assisted-living facilities enable tenants to maintain privacy, dignity, autonomy, and a sense of control over their own homelike space, while giving them easy access to needed personal and health care services (Citro & Hermanson, 1999).

Assisted living in a homelike facility with easy access to medical and personal care is an increasingly popular alternative to nursing homes. These residents in an assisted-living facility can maintain a large degree of autonomy, as well as dignity, privacy, and companionship.

Table 18-1 Group Living Arrangements for Older Adults

Facility	Description
Retirement hotel	Hotel or apartment building remodeled to meet the needs of independent older adults. Typical hotel services (switchboard, maid service, message center) are provided.
Retirement community	Large, self-contained development with owned or rental units or both. Support services and recreational facilities are often available.
Shared housing	Housing can be shared informally by adult parents and children or by friends. Sometimes social agencies match people who need a place to live with people who have houses or apartments with extra rooms. The older person usually has a private room but shares living, eating, and cooking areas and may exchange services such as light housekeeping for rent.
Accessory apartment or ECHO (elder cottage housing opportunity) housing	An independent unit created so that an older person can live in a remodeled single-family home or in a portable unit on the grounds of a single-family home—often, but not necessarily, that of an adult child. Units offer privacy, proximity to caregivers, and security.
Congregate housing	Private or government-subsidized rental apartment complexes or mobile home parks designed for older adults provide meals, housekeeping, transportation, social and recreational activities, and sometimes health care. One type of congregate housing is called a group home. A social agency that owns or rents a house brings together a small number of elderly residents and hires helpers to shop, cook, do heavy cleaning, drive, and give counseling. Residents take care of their own personal needs and take some responsibility for day-to-day tasks.
Assisted-living facility	Semi-independent living in one's own room or apartment. Similar to congregate housing, but residents receive personal care (bathing, dressing, and grooming) and protective supervision according to their needs and desires. Board-and-care homes are similar but smaller and offer more personal care and supervision.
Foster-care home	Owners of a single-family residence take in an unrelated older adult and provide meals, housekeeping, and personal care.
Continuing care retirement community	Long-term housing planned to provide a full range of accommodations and services for affluent elderly people as their needs change. A resident may start out in an independent apartment; then move into congregate housing with such services as cleaning, laundry, and meals: then into an assisted-living facility; and finally into a nursing home. Life-care communities are similar but guarantee housing and medical or nursing care for a specified period or for life; they require a substantial entry fee in addition to monthly payments.

Source: Laquatra & Chi, 1998; Porcino, 1993.

Currently less than 1 percent of older adults live in group housing, but if more such residences were available, up to 50 percent of people who would otherwise go into nursing homes might be able to stay in the community at lower cost (Laquatra & Chi, 1998).

What's Your View?

- As you become older and possibly incapacitated, what type of living arrangement would you prefer?

Mistreatment of the Elderly

A middle-aged woman drives up to a hospital emergency room in a middle-sized American city. She lifts a frail, elderly woman (who appears somewhat confused) out of the car and into a wheelchair, wheels her into the emergency room, and quietly walks out and drives away, leaving no identification (Barnhart, 1992).

"Granny dumping" is one form of **elder abuse:** maltreatment or neglect of dependent older persons or violation of their personal rights. Mistreatment of the elderly may fall under any of four categories: (1) *physical violence* intended to cause injury; (2) *psychological or emotional abuse,* which may include insults and threats (such as the threat of abandonment or institutionalization); (3) *material exploitation,* or misappropriation of money or property; and (4) *neglect*—intentional or unintentional failure to meet a dependent older person's needs (Lachs & Pillemer, 1995). Physical violence may be less common than is generally believed; financial exploitation is probably more so (Bengtson, Rosenthal, & Burton, 1996). The American Medical Association (1992) has added a fifth category: *violating personal rights,* for example, the older person's right to privacy and to make her or his own personal and health decisions.

elder abuse Maltreatment or neglect of dependent older persons, or violation of their personal rights.

Contrary to popular belief, most elder abuse does *not* occur in institutions, where there are laws and regulations to prevent it. It most often happens to frail or demented elderly people living with spouses or children. The abuser is more likely to be a spouse, since more older people live with spouses (Lachs & Pillemer, 1995; Paveza et al., 1992; Pillemer & Finkelhor, 1988). Often, abuse of an elderly wife is a continuation of abuse that went on throughout the marriage (Bengtson et al., 1996). Neglect by family caregivers is usually unintentional; many don't know how to give proper care or are in poor health themselves.

Checkpoint

Can you . . .

- ✔ Compare various kinds of living arrangements for older adults, their relative prevalence, and their advantages and disadvantages?
- ✔ Identify five types of elder abuse, give examples of each, and tell where and by whom abuse is most likely to occur?

Elder abuse should be recognized as a type of domestic violence. Most physical abuse can be resolved by counseling or other services (AARP, 1993a). Abusers need treatment to recognize what they are doing and assistance to reduce the stress of caregiving. Self-help groups may help victims acknowledge what is happening, recognize that they do not have to put up with mistreatment, and find out how to stop it or get away from it.

Because the needs and human rights of older adults have become an international concern, the United Nations General Assembly in 1991 adopted a set of Principles for Older Persons. They cover rights to independence, participation in society, care, and opportunities for self-fulfillment (see Table 18-2).

Personal Relationships in Late Life

Guidepost

7. How do personal relationships change in old age, and what is their effect on well-being?

Most older people's lives are enriched by the presence of longtime friends and family members. Although older adults may see people less often, personal relationships continue to be important—perhaps even more so than before (Antonucci & Akiyama, 1995; Carstensen, 1995; C. L. Johnson & Troll, 1992).

Social Contact

As people age, they tend to spend less time with others (Carstensen, 1996). Work is often a convenient source of social contact; thus, longtime retirees have fewer social contacts than more recent retirees or those who continue to work. For some older adults, infirmities make it harder to get out and see people. Studies also show that older people often bypass opportunities for increased social contact and are more likely than younger adults to be satisfied with smaller social networks. Yet the social contacts older adults *do* have are more important to their well-being than ever (Lansford, Sherman, & Antonucci, 1998).

Why is this? According to *social convoy theory* (introduced in Chapter 16), changes in social contact typically affect only a person's outer, less intimate social circles. After retirement, as coworkers and other casual friends drop away, most older adults retain a stable inner circle of social convoys: close friends and family members on whom they can rely for continued social support and who strongly affect their well-being for better or worse (Antonucci & Akiyama, 1995; Kahn & Antonucci, 1980).

According to *socioemotional selectivity theory* (Carstensen, 1991, 1995, 1996), older adults become increasingly selective about the people with whom they spend their time. When people perceive their remaining time as short, immediate emotional needs take precedence over long-range goals. A college student may be willing to put up with a disliked teacher for the sake of gaining knowledge to get into graduate school; an older adult may be less willing to spend precious time with a friend who gets on her nerves. Young adults with a free half hour and no urgent commitments may choose to spend the time with someone they would like to get to know better; older adults tend to choose someone they know well.

Table 18-2 United Nations Principles for Older Persons

Independence	Participation
Older persons should have access to adequate food, water, shelter, clothing, and health care through the provision of income, family and community support, and self-help. Older persons should have the opportunity to work or to have access to other income-generating opportunities. Older persons should be able to participate in determining when and at what pace withdrawal from the labor force takes place. Older persons should have access to appropriate educational and training programs. Older persons should be able to live in environments that are safe and adaptable to personal preferences and changing capacities. Older persons should be able to reside at home for as long as possible.	Older persons should remain integrated in society, participate actively in the formulation and implementation of policies that directly affect their well-being, and share their knowledge and skills with younger generations. Older persons should be able to seek and develop opportunities for service to the community and to serve as volunteers in positions appropriate to their interests and capabilities. Older persons should be able to form movements or associations of older persons.
Care	**Self-fulfilment**
Older persons should benefit from family and community care and protection in accordance with each society's system of cultural values. Older persons should have access to health care to help them to maintain or regain the optimum level of physical, mental, and emotional well-being and to prevent or delay the onset of illness. Older persons should have access to social and legal services to enhance their autonomy, protection, and care. Older persons should be able to utilize appropriate levels of institutional care providing protection, rehabilitation, and social and mental stimulation in a humane and secure environment. Older persons should be able to enjoy human rights and fundamental freedoms when residing in any shelter, care, or treatment facility, including full respect for their dignity, beliefs, needs, and privacy and for the right to make decisions about their care and the quality of their lives.	Older persons should be able to pursue opportunities for the full development of their potential. Older persons should have access to the educational, cultural, spiritual, and recreational resources of society. **Dignity** Older persons should be able to live in dignity and security and be free of exploitation and physical or mental abuse. Older persons should be treated fairly regardless of age, gender, racial or ethnic background, disability or other status, and be valued independently of their economic contribution.

Even though older people may have fewer close relationships than younger people do, they tend to be more satisfied with those they have (Antonucci & Akiyama, 1995). While the size of the social network and the frequency of contacts declines, the quality of social support apparently does not (Bosse, Aldwin, Levenson, Spiro, & Mroczek, 1993).

Relationships and Health As is true earlier in life, social relationships and health go hand in hand (Bosworth & Schaie, 1997). When Vaillant and his colleagues looked at 223 aging men from the Grant Study, social support during the previous twenty years—from friends more than from spouses and children—was a powerful predictor of physical health at age 70. However, the effect was much weaker when the researchers controlled for prior alcohol abuse, smoking, and depression—all of which can undermine both social relationships and health (Vaillant, Meyer, Mukamal, & Soldz, 1998).

Social interaction seems to prolong life. Among 2,575 men and women ages 65 to 102 in rural Iowa, those who reported regular contact with no more than two people during a three-year period were much more likely to die during the next eight years than those with larger social networks. This was true regardless of age, education, smoking history, symptoms of depression, or changes in physical health (Cerhan & Wallace, 1997). In a ten-year longitudinal study of 28,369 men, the most socially isolated men were 53 percent more likely than the most socially connected men to die from cardiovascular disease and more than twice as likely to die from accidents or suicide (Eng, Rimm, Fitzmaurice, & Kawachi, 2002).

Throughout the developed world, married people are healthier and live longer than unmarried people (Kinsella & Velkoff, 2001). But the relationship between marriage and health may be different for husbands than for wives. Whereas being married *itself* seems to have health benefits for older men, older women's health seems to be linked to the *quality* of the marriage (Carstensen, Graff, Levenson, & Gottman, 1996).

The Multigenerational Family The late-life family has special characteristics (Brubaker, 1983, 1990; C. L. Johnson, 1995). Historically, even when and where the multigenerational family was prevalent, the years people spent in such a family were few, and the family rarely spanned more than three generations. Today, many families in developed countries include four or even five generations (with fewer members in each generation), making it possible for a person to be both a grandparent and a grandchild at the same time (Kinsella & Velkoff, 2001).

The presence of so many family members can be enriching but also can create special pressures. Increasing numbers of families are likely to have at least one member who has lived long enough to have several chronic illnesses and whose care may be physically and emotionally draining (C. L. Johnson, 1995). Now that the fastest-growing group in the population is age 85 and over, many people in their late sixties or beyond, whose own health and energy may be faltering, find themselves serving as caregivers. Indeed, many women spend more of their lives caring for parents than for children (Abel, 1991).

The ways families deal with these issues often have cultural roots. The nuclear family, and the desire of older adults to live apart from their children whenever possible, reflect American values of individualism, autonomy, and self-reliance. Hispanic and Asian American cultures traditionally emphasize *lineal,* or intergenerational obligations, with power and authority lodged in the older generation. However, this pattern is being modified through assimilation into the dominant U.S. culture. African Americans and Irish Americans, whose cultures have been heavily impacted by poverty, stress *collateral,* egalitarian relationships. Household structures may be highly flexible, often taking in siblings, aunts, uncles, cousins, or friends who need a place to stay. These varied cultural patterns affect family relationships and responsibilities toward the older generation (C. L. Johnson, 1995).

In the rest of this chapter we'll look more closely at older people's relationships with family and friends. We'll also examine the lives of older adults who are divorced, remarried or widowed, those who have never married, and those who are childless. (We discuss widowhood more fully in Chapter 19.) Finally we'll consider the importance of a new role: that of great-grandparent.

What's Your View?

- Have you ever lived in a multigenerational household? Do you think you ever might? What aspects of this lifestyle do or do not appear to you?

Checkpoint

Can you . . .

- ✔ Tell how social contact changes in late life, and discuss theoretical explanations of this change?
- ✔ Cite evidence for a relationship between social interaction and health?
- ✔ Discuss characteristics of the new multigenerational family?

Consensual Relationships

Unlike other family relationships, marriage—at least in contemporary western cultures—is generally formed by mutual consent. Thus, in its effect on well-being, it has characteristics of both friendship and kinship ties (Antonucci & Akiyama, 1995). It can provide both the highest emotional highs and the lowest lows a person experiences (Carstensen et al., 1996). What happens to marital satisfaction in late life?

Guidepost

8. What are the characteristics of long-term marriages in late life, and what impact do divorce, remarriage, and widowhood have at this time?

Long-Term Marriage

The long-term marriage is a relatively new phenomenon. Most marriages, like most people, used to have a shorter life span. Today, about one marriage in five, like Jimmy and Rosalynn Carter's, lasts fifty or more years (Brubaker, 1983, 1993). Because women usually marry older men and outlive them, and because men are more likely to remarry after divorce or widowhood, in most countries many more men than women are married in late life (Administration on Aging, 2001; Kinsella & Velkoff, 2001; see Figure 18-6).

Married couples who are still together in late adulthood are more likely than middle-aged couples to report their marriage as satisfying, and many say it has improved (Carstensen et al., 1996; Gilford, 1986). Since divorce has been easier to obtain for some years, spouses who are still together late in life are likely to have worked out their differences and to have arrived at mutually satisfying accommodations (Huyck, 1995). With the end of child rearing, children tend to become a source of shared pleasure and pride instead of a source of conflict (Carstensen et al., 1996).

How couples resolve conflicts is a key to marital satisfaction throughout adulthood. Patterns of conflict resolution tend to remain fairly constant throughout a marriage, but older couples' greater ability to regulate their emotions may make their conflicts less severe (Carstensen et al., 1996).

Late-life marriage can be severely tested by advancing age and physical ills. Spouses who must care for disabled partners may feel isolated, angry, and frustrated, especially when they are in poor health themselves. Such couples may be caught in a "vicious cycle": the illness puts strains on the marriage, and these strains may aggravate the illness, stretching coping capacity to the breaking point (Karney & Bradbury, 1995)

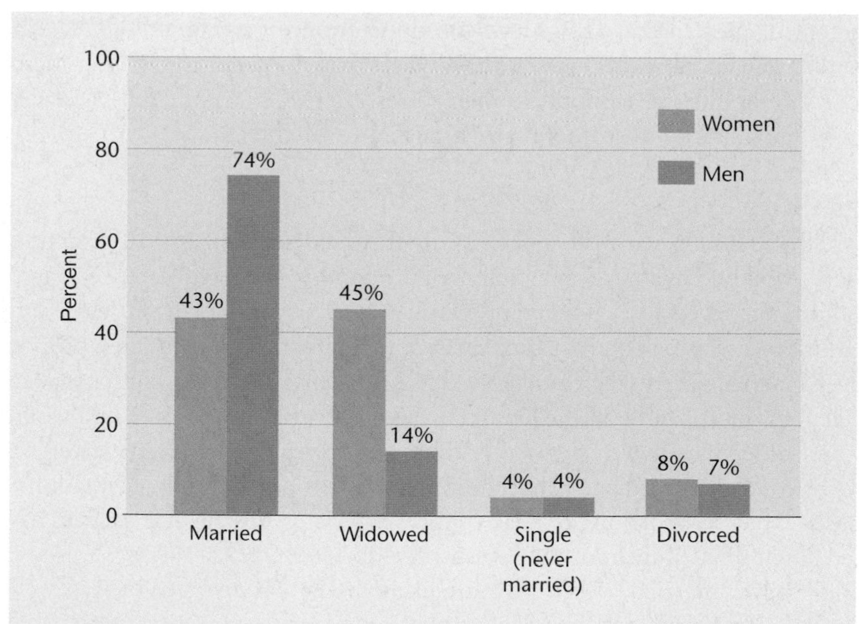

Figure 18-6
Marital status of persons age 65 and over, 2000. (*Source:* Administration on Aging, 2001; based on data from U.S. Bureau of the Census.)

Many couples who are still together late in life, especially in the middle to late sixties, say that they are happier in marriage now than they were in their younger years. Important benefits of marriage, which may help older couples face the ups and downs of late life, include intimacy, sharing, and a sense of belonging to one another. Romance, fun, and sensuality have their place, too, as this couple in a hot tub demonstrate.

and putting the caregiver's life at heightened risk (Kiecolt-Glaser & Glaser, 1999; Schulz & Beach, 1999). Caregiving spouses who are optimistic and well adjusted to begin with, and who stay in touch with friends, usually cope best (Hooker, Monahan, Shifren, & Hutchinson, 1992; Skaff & Pearlin, 1992).

Divorce and Remarriage

Divorce in late life is rare; couples who take this step usually do it much earlier. Only 8 percent of women and 7 percent of men age 65 and over are divorced and not remarried (refer back to Figure 18-6). However, since 1990 these numbers have increased significantly and probably will continue to increase as younger cohorts with larger proportions of divorced people reach late adulthood (Administration on Aging, 2001; Kinsella & Velkoff, 2001).

Remarriage in late life may have a special character. Among 125 well-educated, fairly affluent men and women, those in late-life remarriages seemed more trusting and accepting, and less in need of deep sharing of personal feelings. Men, but not women, tended to be more satisfied in late-life remarriages than in midlife ones (Bograd & Spilka, 1996).

Remarriage has societal benefits, since older married people are less likely than those living alone to need help from the community. Remarriage could be encouraged by letting people keep pension and social security benefits derived from a previous marriage and by greater availability of shared living quarters, such as group housing.

Checkpoint

Can you . . .

- ✔ Explain the difference in marital satisfaction between middle and late adulthood?
- ✔ Tell how remarriage differs in earlier and late adulthood?
- ✔ Summarize gender differences in the prevalence of widowhood?

Widowhood

Just as older men are more likely than women to be married, older women are much more likely than men to be widowed, and for similar reasons. Women tend to outlive their husbands and are less likely than men to marry again. In most countries, more than half of older women are widows (Kinsella & Velkoff, 2001). In the United States in 2000, 45 percent of women ages 65 and older were widowed, as compared with only 14 percent of men in that age group (Administration on Aging, 2001). However, as the gender gap in life expectancy narrows, as it has done since 1990, an increasing number of elderly men will outlive their wives (Hetzel & Smith, 2001). Issues concerning adjustment to widowhood are discussed in Chapter 19.

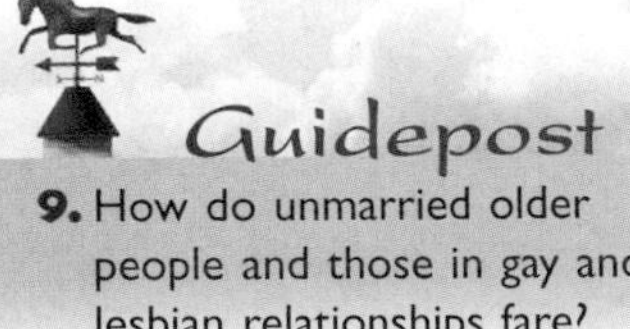

Guidepost

9. How do unmarried older people and those in gay and lesbian relationships fare?

Single Life

In more than half of the world, 5 percent or less of elderly men and 10 percent or less of elderly women have never married. In Europe, this gender difference may reflect the toll on marriageable men taken by World War II, when the current elderly cohort were of marrying age. In some Latin American and Caribbean countries, proportions of never-marrieds are higher, probably due to the prevalence of consensual unions (Kinsella & Velkoff, 2001). In the United States, only 4 percent of men and women 65 years and older have never married (Administration on Aging, 2001; refer back to Figure 18-6). This percentage is likely to increase as today's middle-aged adults grow old, since larger proportions of that cohort, especially African Americans, have remained single (U.S. Bureau of the Census, 1991a, 1991b, 1992, 1993).

Older never-married people are more likely than older divorced or widowed people to prefer single life and less likely to be lonely (Dykstra, 1995). Never-married, childless women in one study rated three kinds of roles or relationships as important: bonds with blood relatives, such as siblings and aunts; parent-surrogate ties with younger people; and same-generation, same-sex friendships (Rubinstein, Alexander, Goodman, & Luborsky, 1991).

Previously married older men are much more likely to date than older women, probably because of the greater availability of women in this age group. Most elderly daters are sexually active but do not expect to marry. Among both whites and African Americans, men are more interested in romantic involvement than women, who may fear getting "locked into" traditional gender roles (K. Bulcroft & O'Conner, 1986; R. A. Bulcroft & Bulcroft, 1991; Tucker, Taylor, & Mitchell-Kernan, 1993).

As black women age, they are increasingly less likely than black men to be married, romantically involved, or interested in a romantic relationship—perhaps for practical reasons, as unmarried black women tend to be better off financially than married ones (Tucker et al., 1993). Yet a single state entails risk: a black woman living alone in late life is three times as likely to be poor as a white woman in that situation (U.S. Bureau of the Census, 1991b).

Gay and Lesbian Relationships

There is little research on homosexual relationships in old age. This is largely because the current cohort of older adults grew up at a time when living openly as a homosexual was rare (Huyck, 1995). An important distinction is between elderly homosexuals who recognized themselves as gay or lesbian before the rise of the gay liberation movement in the late 1960s and those who did not do so until that movement (and the shift in public discourse it brought about) was in full swing. Whereas the self-concept of the first group was shaped by the prevailing stigma against homosexuality, the second group tend to view their homosexuality simply as a *status:* a characteristic of the self, like any other (Rosenfeld, 1999).

Intimacy is important to older lesbians and gays, as it is to older heterosexual adults. Contrary to stereotype, homosexual relationships in late life are generally strong and supportive.

Older homosexual adults, like older heterosexual adults, have strong needs for intimacy, social contact, and generativity. Gays' and lesbians' relationships in late life tend to be strong, supportive, and diverse. Many homosexuals have children from earlier marriages; others have adopted children. Friendship networks or support groups may substitute for the traditional family (Reid, 1995).

Many gays and lesbians, especially those who have maintained close relationships and strong involvement in the homosexual community, adapt to aging with relative ease. Coming out—whenever it occurs—is an important developmental transition, which can enhance mental health, life satisfaction, self-acceptance, and self-respect and smooth the adjustment to aging (Friend, 1991; Reid, 1995).

The main problems of many older gays and lesbians grow out of societal attitudes: strained relationships with the family of origin, discrimination, lack of medical or social services and social support, insensitive policies of social agencies, and dealing with health care providers or bereavement and inheritance issues when a partner falls ill or dies (Berger & Kelly, 1986; Kimmel, 1990; Reid, 1995).

Friendships

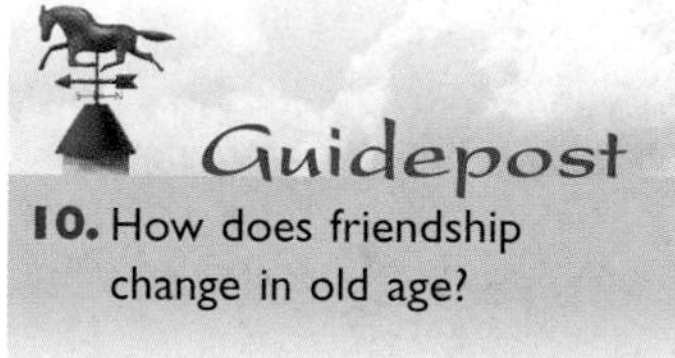

The meaning of friendship—a relationship involving mutual give-and-take—changes little over the life span, but its context and content change. Among older adults, friendships typically are no longer linked to work and parenting, as in earlier periods of adulthood. Instead, they focus on companionship and support (Hartup & Stevens, 1999).

Most older people have close friends, and those with an active circle of friends are healthier and happier (Antonucci & Akiyama, 1995; Babchuk, 1978–1979; Lemon et al., 1972; Steinbach, 1992). Friends soften the impact of stress on physical and mental health (Cutrona, Russell, & Rose, 1986). People who can confide their feelings and thoughts and can talk about their worries and pain with friends deal better with the changes and crises of aging (Genevay, 1986; Lowenthal & Haven, 1968). They also tend to live longer (Steinbach, 1992).

Older people often enjoy the time they spend with friends more than the time they spend with family members. The openness and excitement of relationships between friends help them rise above worries and problems. Intimate friendships give older people a sense of being valued and wanted and help them deal with the changes and crises of aging.

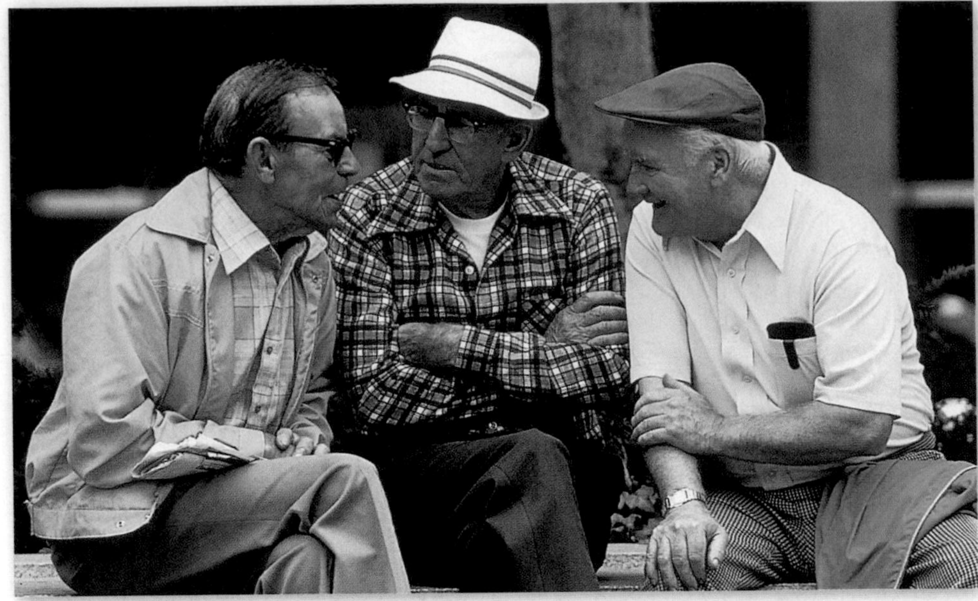

The element of choice in friendship may be especially important to older people, who may feel their control over their lives slipping away (R. G. Adams, 1986). Intimacy is another important benefit of friendship for older adults, who need to know that they are still valued and wanted despite physical and other losses (Essex & Nam, 1987). It may be that women's greater comfort with self-disclosure and expression of feelings contributes to their greater life expectancy (Weg, 1987).

Older people enjoy time spent with their friends more than time spent with their families. As earlier in life, friendships revolve around pleasure and leisure, whereas family relationships tend to involve everyday needs and tasks (Antonucci & Akiyama, 1995; Larson, Mannell, & Zuzanek, 1986). Still, spending time with friends does *not* result in higher overall life satisfaction, whereas spending more time with a spouse does. It may be the very brevity and infrequency of the time spent with friends that give it its special flavor. Friends are a powerful source of *immediate* enjoyment; the family provides greater emotional security and support. Thus, friendships have the greatest positive effect on older people's well-being; but when family relationships are poor or absent, the negative effects can be profound (Antonucci & Akiyama, 1995).

People usually rely on neighbors in emergencies and on relatives for long-term commitments, such as caregiving; but friends may, on occasion, fulfill both these functions. Friends and neighbors often take the place of family members who are far away. And, although friends cannot replace a spouse or partner, they can help compensate for the lack of one (Hartup & Stevens, 1999). Among 131 older adults in the Netherlands who were never married or were divorced or widowed, those who received high levels of emotional and practical support from friends were less likely to be lonely (Dykstra, 1995).

In line with social convoy and socioemotional selectivity theories, casual friends may fall by the wayside, but longtime friendships often persist into very old age (Hartup & Stevens, 1999). Sometimes, however, relocation, illness, or disability make it hard to keep up with old friends. Although many older people do make new friends, even after age 85 (C. L. Johnson & Troll, 1994), older adults are more likely than younger ones to attribute the benefits of friendship (such as affection and loyalty) to specific individuals, who cannot easily be replaced if they die, go into a nursing home, or move away (de Vries, 1996).

Checkpoint

Can you . . .

- ✔ Discuss differences between never-married and previously married singles in late life?
- ✔ Give reasons for the diversity of gay and lesbian relationships in late life and identify factors that influence homosexuals' adaption to aging?
- ✔ Cite special benefits of friendship in old age and tell in what ways friendships tend to change?

Nonmarital Kinship Ties

Some of the most lasting and important relationships in late life are the ones that come, not from mutual choice (as marriages, homosexual partnerships, and friendships do), but from kinship bonds. Let's look at these.

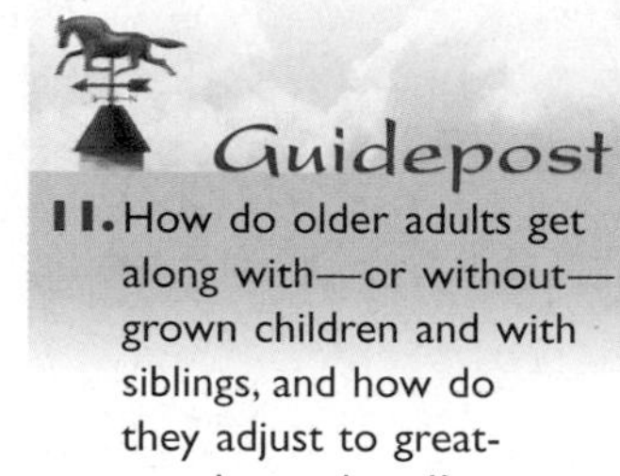

Guidepost

11. How do older adults get along with—or without—grown children and with siblings, and how do they adjust to great-grandparenthood?

Relationships with Adult Children—or Their Absence

As socioemotional selectivity theory predicts, aging adults seek to spend more of their time with the people who mean the most to them, such as their children (Troll & Fingerman, 1996). Four out of five older adults have living children, six out of ten see their children at least once a week, and three out of four talk on the phone that often (AARP, 1995). Most older people live within ten miles of at least one adult child, and (if they have more than one child) within thirty miles of another (Lin & Rogerson, 1995).

Children provide a link with other family members—especially, of course, with grandchildren. In one group of 150 "old-old" people in diverse socioeconomic circumstances, those who were parents were more actively in touch with other relatives than were childless people (C. L. Johnson & Troll, 1992). Older people in better health have more contact with their families than those in poorer health and report feeling closer to them (Field, Minkler, Falk, & Leino, 1993).

The balance of mutual aid that flows between parents and their adult children tends to shift as parents age, with children providing a greater share of support (Bengtson, Rosenthal, & Burton, 1990; 1996). This is especially true in developing countries. Even there, however, older adults make important contributions to family well-being—for example, through housekeeping and child care (Kinsella & Velkoff, 2001).

In the United States and other developed countries, institutional supports such as social security and Medicare have lifted some responsibilities for the elderly from family members; but many adult children do provide significant assistance and care to aged parents (refer back to Chapter 16). Still, elderly parents in North America are more likely to provide financial support than to receive it (Kinsella & Velkoff, 2001). An exception are immigrants who arrive as older adults; they are more likely to live with adult children and to be dependent on them (Glick & Van Hook, 2002).

Older adults are likely to be depressed if they need help from their children. In a society in which both generations value their independence, the prospect of dependency can be demoralizing. Parents do not want to be a burden on their children or to deplete their children's resources. Yet parents also may be depressed if they fear that their children will *not* take care of them (G. R. Lee, Netzer, & Coward, 1995).

Older parents continue to show strong concern about their children, think about them often, and help them when needed (Bengtson et al., 1996). Elderly parents tend to be distressed or become depressed if their children have serious problems, for example, with drugs or financial dependency; parents may consider such problems a sign of their own failure (G. R. Lee et al., 1995; Pillemer & Suitor, 1991; Suitor, Pillemer, Keeton, & Robison, 1995; Troll & Fingerman, 1996).

Many elderly people whose adult children are mentally ill, retarded, physically disabled, or stricken with serious illnesses serve as primary caregivers for as long as both parent and child live (Brabant, 1994; Greenberg & Becker, 1988; Ryff & Seltzer, 1995). And a growing number of grandparents, and even great-grandparents, particularly African Americans, raise or help raise children.

As we discussed in Chapter 16, nonnormative caregivers, who are pressed into active parenting at a time when such a role is unexpected, frequently feel strain. This may be even more true of elderly caregivers than of middle-aged ones. Often ill-prepared physically, emotionally, and financially for the task, they may not know where to turn for help and support. They worry about who will take over for them when they become sick or die—as well as who will take care of *them* (Abramson, 1995).

What about the increasing number of older adults without living children? In 1998, one out of five women in the United States had no children (Kinsella & Velkoff, 2001). How will childlessness affect them as they age? Early studies suggested that childless people are no lonelier, no more negative about their lives, and no more afraid of death than those with children (C. L. Johnson & Catalano, 1981; Keith, 1983; Rempel, 1985). However, some older women who never had children expressed regret, and that feeling became more intense the older they got (Alexander, Rubinstein, Goodman, & Luborsky, 1992).

Widows without grown children may lack an important source of solace (O'Bryant, 1988; Suitor et al., 1995). Childless people also may lack a ready source of care and support if they become infirm. In Canada, where 5 to 10 percent of older adults are unmarried and childless, three-fourths of this group report a lack of support, especially emotional support (Wu & Pollard, 1998).

Relationships with Siblings

When Elizabeth ("Bessie") Delany was 102 and her sister Sarah ("Sadie") was 104, they published a best-selling book, *Having Our Say: The Delany Sisters' First 100 Years* (Delany, Delany, & Hearth, 1993). The daughters of a freed slave, Bessie overcame racial and gender discrimination to become a dentist, and Sadie a high school teacher. The sisters never married; for three decades they lived together in Mount Vernon, New York. Although their personalities were as different as sugar and spice, the two women were best friends, sharing a sense of fun and the values their parents had instilled in them.

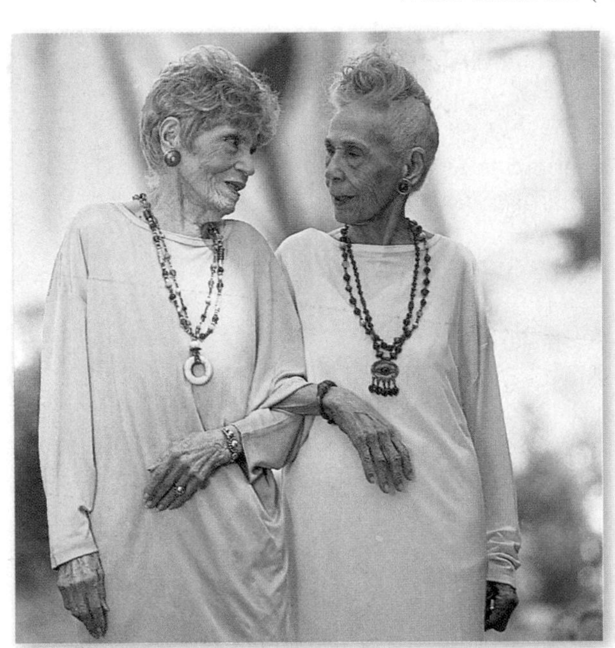

Bessie and Sadie Delany, daughters of a freed slave, were best friends all their lives—more than 100 years—and wrote two books together about the values they grew up with and the story of their long, active lives. Elderly siblings are an important part of each other's support network, and sisters are especially vital in maintaining family relationships.

More than three out of four Americans age 60 and older have at least one living sibling, and those in the "young-old" bracket average two or three (Cicirelli, 1995). Brothers and sisters play important roles in the support networks of older people. Siblings, more than other family members, provide companionship, as friends do; but siblings, more than friends, also provide emotional support (Bedford, 1995). Conflict and overt rivalry generally decrease by old age, and some siblings try to resolve earlier conflicts. However, underlying feelings of rivalry may remain, especially between brothers (Cicirelli, 1995).

Most older adult siblings say they stand ready to provide tangible help and would turn to a sibling for such help if needed, but relatively few actually do so except in emergencies such as illness (when they may become caregivers) or the death of a spouse (Cicirelli, 1995). Siblings in developing countries are more likely to furnish economic aid (Bedford, 1995). Regardless of how much help they actually give, siblings' *readiness* to help is a source of comfort and security in late life (Cicirelli, 1995). For people who are unmarried or have only one or two children, or none, relationships with siblings and their children in late life may become increasingly significant (Bedford, 1995; Rubinstein et al., 1991).

The nearer older people live to their siblings and the more siblings they have, the more likely they are to confide in them (Connidis & Davies, 1992). Reminiscing about shared early experiences becomes more frequent in old age; it may help in reviewing a life and putting the significance of family relationships into perspective (Cicirelli, 1995).

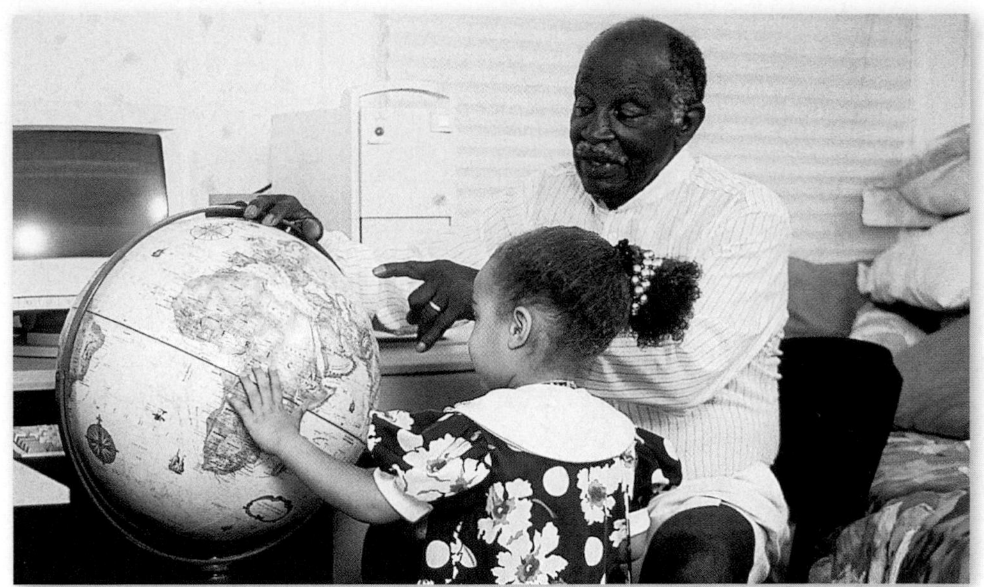

Grandparents and great-grandparents are an important source of wisdom and companionship, a link to the past, and a symbol of the continuity of family life. This African American great-grandfather points out to his great-granddaughter where her ancestors came from.

Sisters are especially vital in maintaining family relationships and well-being, perhaps because of women's emotional expressiveness and traditional role as nurturers (Bedford, 1995; Cicirelli, 1989a, 1995). Older people who are close to their sisters feel better about life and worry less about aging than those without sisters, or without close ties to them (Cicirelli, 1977, 1989a). Among a national sample of bereaved adults in the Netherlands, those coping with the death of a sister experienced more difficulty than those who had lost a spouse or a parent (Cleiren, Diekstra, Kerkhof, & van der Wal, 1994).

The death of a sibling in old age may be understood as a normative part of that stage of life, but still, survivors may grieve intensely and become lonely or depressed. The loss of a sibling represents not only a loss of someone to lean on and a shift in the family constellation, but perhaps even a partial loss of identity. To mourn for a sibling is to mourn for the lost completeness of the original family within which one came to know oneself. It also can bring home one's own nearness to death (Cicirelli, 1995).

Becoming Great-Grandparents

As grandchildren grow up, grandparents generally see them less often (see the discussion of grandparenthood in Chapter 16). Then, when grandchildren become parents, grandparents move into a new role: great-grandparenthood.

Because of age, declining health, and the scattering of families, great-grandparents tend to be less involved than grandparents in a child's life. And because four- or five-generation families are relatively new, there are few generally accepted guidelines for what great-grandparents are supposed to do (Cherlin & Furstenberg, 1986b). Still, most great-grandparents find the role fulfilling (Pruchno & Johnson, 1996). Great-grandparenthood offers a sense of personal and family renewal, a source of diversion, and a mark of longevity. When 40 great-grandfathers and great-grandmothers, ages 71 to 90, were interviewed, 93 percent made such comments as "Life is starting again in my family," "Seeing them grow keeps me young," and "I never thought I'd live to see it" (Doka & Mertz, 1988, pp. 193–194). More than one-third of the sample (mostly women) were close to their great-grandchildren. The ones with the most intimate connections were likely to live nearby and to be close to the children's parents and grandparents as well, often helping out with loans, gifts, and baby-sitting.

Checkpoint

Can you . . .

- ✔ Tell how contact and mutual aid between parents and grown children changes during late adulthood, and how childlessness can affect older people?
- ✔ Discuss the importance of sibling relationships in late life?
- ✔ Identify several values great-grandparents find in their role?

What's Your View?

- Which theories of psychosocial development in late life seem best supported by the information in this chapter on work, retirement, living arrangements, and relationships? Why?

Refocus

- How did Jimmy and Rosalynn Carter resolve Erikson's stage of ego integrity versus despair?
- What techniques of coping did they use?
- Which model of successful aging do they best illustrate?
- Which pattern of use of time after retirement do they follow?
- Does their pattern of late-life relationships seem to illustrate either social convoy theory or socioemotional selectivity theory?
- What do you think might account for the success of their long-term marriage?

Grandparents and great-grandparents are important to their families. They are sources of wisdom, companions in play, links to the past, and symbols of the continuity of family life. They are engaged in the ultimate generative function: expressing the human longing to transcend mortality by investing themselves in the lives of future generations.

SUMMARY AND KEY TERMS

Theory and Research on Psychosocial Development

Guidepost 1. What happens to personality in old age?

- Personality traits tend to remain stable in late adulthood, but cohort differences have been found.
- Emotionality tends to become more positive and less negative in old age, but personality traits can modify this pattern.

Guidepost 2. What special issues or tasks do older people need to deal with?

- Erik Erikson's final stage, ego integrity versus despair, culminates in the "virtue" of *wisdom*, or acceptance of one's life and impending death.

ego integrity versus despair *(648)*

Guidepost 3. How do older adults cope?

- George Vaillant found that the use of mature adaptive mechanisms earlier in adulthood predicts psychosocial adjustment in late life.
- In the cognitive-appraisal model, adults of all ages generally prefer problem-focused coping, but older adults do more emotion-focused coping than younger adults when the situation calls for it.
- Religion is an important source of emotion-focused coping for many older adults. Older African Americans are more involved in religious activity than elderly white people, and black women are more involved than black men.

coping *(650)*
cognitive-appraisal model *(651)*
problem-focused coping *(651)*
emotion-focused coping *(652)*
ambiguous loss *(652)*

Guidepost 4. What is successful aging and how can it be measured?

- Two contrasting early models of "successful," or "optimal," aging are disengagement theory and activity theory. Disengagement theory has little support, and findings on activity theory are mixed. Newer refinements of activity theory are continuity theory and a distinction between productive and leisure activity.
- Baltes and his colleagues suggest that successful aging may depend on selective optimization with compensation, in the psychosocial as well as the cognitive realm.

disengagement theory *(654)*
activity theory *(654)*
continuity theory *(655)*

Lifestyle and Social Issues Related to Aging

Guidepost 5. What are some issues regarding work and retirement in late life, and how do older adults handle time and money?

- Some older people continue to work for pay, but most are retired. However, many retired people start new careers or do part-time paid or volunteer work. Often retirement is a phased phenomenon.
- Age has both positive and negative effects on job performance, and individual differences are more significant than age differences. Older adults tend to be more satisfied with their work and more committed to it than younger ones.

- The financial situation of older people has improved, but still a large proportion can expect to live in poverty at some point. For many of today's middle-aged adults, retirement funding is shaky.
- Retirement is an ongoing process, and its emotional impact must be assessed in context. Personal, economic, and social resources, as well as the length of time a person has been retired, may affect morale.
- Common lifestyle patterns after retirement include a family-focused lifestyle, balanced investment, and serious leisure.

  family-focused lifestyle *(661)*

  balanced investment *(661)*

  serious leisure *(661)*

Guidepost 6. What options for living arrangements do older adults have?

- In developing countries, the elderly often live with children or grandchildren. In developed countries, most older people live with a spouse, and a growing minority live alone. Minority elders are more likely than white elders to live with extended family members.
- Most older Americans prefer to "age in place." Most can remain in the community if they can depend on a spouse or child for help.
- Older women are more likely than older men to live alone. Most Americans who live alone are widowed.
- Institutionalization is rare in developing countries. Its extent varies in developed countries. In the United States, only about 4.5 percent of the older population are institutionalized at a given time, but the proportion increases greatly with age. Most nursing home residents are older widows.
- Fast-growing alternatives to institutionalization include assisted-living facilities and other kinds of group housing.
- Elder abuse is most often suffered by a frail or demented older person living with a spouse or child.

  elder abuse *(667)*

Personal Relationships in Late Life

Guidepost 7. How do personal relationships change in old age, and what is their effect on well-being?

- Relationships are very important to older people, even though frequency of social contact declines in old age.
- According to social convoy theory, reductions or changes in social contact in late life do not impair well-being because a stable inner circle of social support is maintained.
- According to socioemotional selectivity theory, older people prefer to spend time with people who enhance their emotional well-being.
- Social support is associated with good health, and isolation is a risk factor for mortality.
- The way multigenerational late-life families function often has cultural roots.

Consensual Relationships

Guidepost 8. What are the characteristics of long-term marriages in late life, and what impact do divorce, remarriage, and widowhood have at this time?

- As life expectancy increases, so does the potential longevity of marriage. More men than women are married in late life. Marriages that last into late adulthood tend to be relatively satisfying.
- Divorce is relatively uncommon among older people, and most older adults who have been divorced are remarried. Divorce can be especially difficult for older people. Remarriages may be more relaxed in late life.
- Although a growing proportion of men are widowed, women tend to outlive their husbands and are less likely to marry again.

Guidepost 9. How do unmarried older people and those in gay and lesbian relationships fare?

- A small but increasing percentage of adults reach old age without marrying. Never-married adults are less likely to be lonely than divorced or widowed ones.
- Older homosexuals, like heterosexuals, have needs for intimacy, social contact, and generativity. Many gays and lesbians adapt to aging with relative ease. Adjustment may be influenced by coming-out status.

Guidepost 10. How does friendship change in old age?

- Friendships in old age focus on companionship and support, not on work and parenting. Most older adults have close friends, and those who do are healthier and happier.
- Older people enjoy time spent with friends more than with family, but the family is the main source of emotional support.

Nonmarital Kinship Ties

Guidepost 11. How do older adults get along with—or without—grown children and with siblings, and how do they adjust to great-grandparenthood?

- Elderly parents and their adult children frequently see or contact each other, are concerned about each other, and offer each other assistance. An increasing number of elderly parents are caregivers for adult children, grandchildren, or great-grandchildren.
- In some respects, childlessness does not seem to be an important disadvantage in old age, but providing care for infirm elderly people without children can be a problem.
- Often siblings offer each other emotional support, and sometimes more tangible support as well. Sisters in particular maintain sibling ties.
- Great-grandparents are less involved in children's lives than grandparents, but most find the role fulfilling.

PART 9

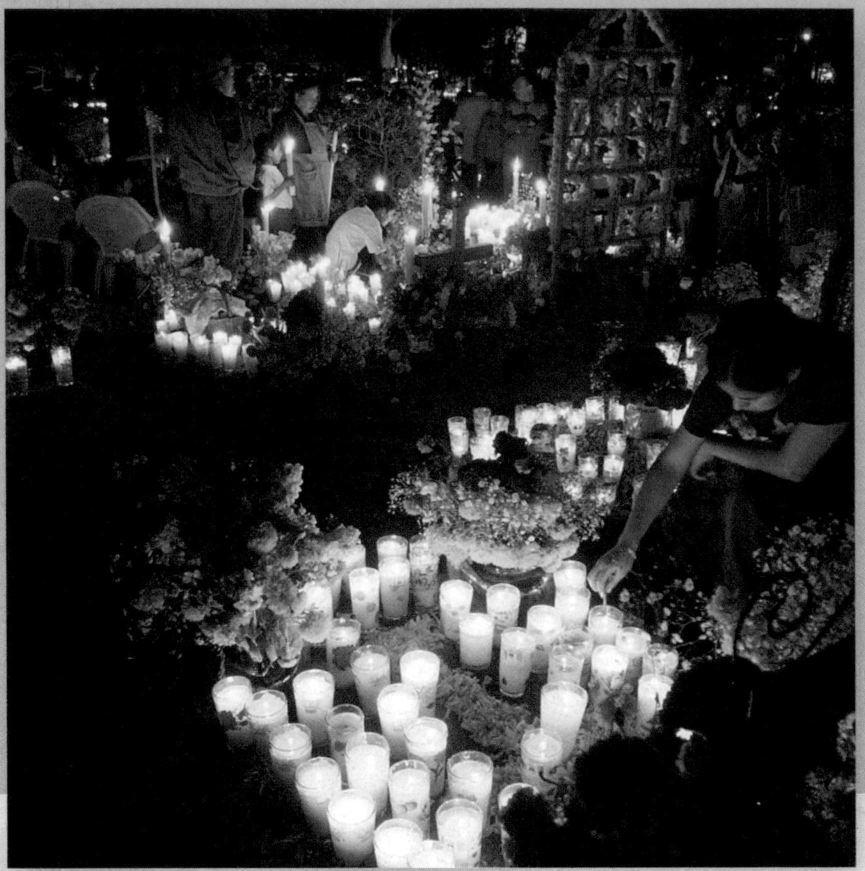

Linkups to look for

- Death has biological, psychological, social, and cultural aspects.
- People approaching death often suffer cognitive declines.
- Mourning customs reflect a society's understanding of what death is and what happens afterward.
- Immediately following a death, survivors often experience intense physical as well as emotional reactions.
- Children and adolescents at different ages show grief in special ways, depending on cognitive and emotional development.
- It is not unusual for a widowed person to die soon after the spouse.
- The issue of aid in dying involves deep-seated emotions, moral and ethical rights and principles, societal attitudes, and medical techniques for relief of pain.

Human beings are individuals; they undergo different experiences and react to them in different ways. Yet one unavoidable part of everyone's life is its end. Death is an integral element of the life span. The better we understand this inevitable event and the more wisely we approach it, the more fully we can live until it comes.

In facing death and bereavement, as in all other aspects of life, physical, cognitive, and psychosocial elements intertwine. The psychological experience surrounding the biological fact of death depends on our understanding of its meaning. That understanding reflects the way a society defines death and the customs that have evolved around it. ▸

The End of Life

PREVIEW

CHAPTER 19

Dealing with Death and Bereavement

Cultures have varying customs related to death.

Individuals differ in their ways of facing death and patterns of grieving.

Attitudes toward death and bereavement change across the life span.

Current issues concerning the "right to die" include euthanasia and assisted suicide.

Facing death honestly can help give meaning and purpose to life.

Dealing with Death and Bereavement

Chapter 19

The key to the question of death unlocks the door of life.

—Elisabeth Kübler-Ross *Death: The Final Stage of Growth,* 1975

All the while I thought I was learning how to live, I have been learning how to die.

—Notebooks of Leonardo da Vinci

Focus:
Louisa May Alcott, Devoted Sister

Louisa May Alcott

One of the most moving parts of the classic nineteenth-century novel *Little Women* by Louisa May Alcott (1832–1888) is the chapter recounting the last year in the life of gentle, home-loving Beth, the third of the March sisters (the others being Meg, Jo, and Amy). Beth's life and her death at age 18 are based on those of Alcott's own sister Elizabeth (Lizzie), who wasted away and died at 23.* Alcott's fictionalized account of her family's growing intimacy in the face of tragedy has struck an empathic chord in generations of readers and in viewers of the four film versions of the book, many of whom have never actually seen a person die.

In the novel, realizing that Beth's illness was terminal, "the family accepted the inevitable, and tried to bear it cheerfully. . . . They put away their grief, and each did his or her part toward making that last year a happy one.

"The pleasantest room in the house was set apart for Beth, and in it was gathered everything that she most loved. . . . Father's best books found their way there, mother's easy chair, Jo's desk, Amy's finest sketches; and every day Meg brought her babies on a loving pilgrimage, to make sunshine for Aunty Beth. . . .

"Here, cherished like a household saint in its shrine, sat Beth, tranquil and busy as ever. . . . The feeble fingers were never idle, and one of her pleasures was to make little things for the school-children daily passing to and fro . . ." (Alcott, 1929, pp. 533–534).

As Beth's illness progressed, the increasingly frail invalid put down the sewing needle that had become "so heavy." Now "talking wearied her, faces troubled her, pain claimed her for its own, and her tranquil spirit was sorrowfully perturbed by the ills that vexed her feeble flesh." But with "the wreck

*This comparison of the real and fictional accounts of Louisa May Alcott's sister Elizabeth's death is based on Alcott (1929); Elbert (1984); MacDonald (1983); Myerson, Shealy, and Stern (1987); and Stern (1950).

OUTLINE

of her frail body, Beth's soul grew strong." Jo stayed with Beth constantly (as Alcott herself stayed with her sister Lizzie), sleeping on a couch by her side and "waking often to renew the fire, to feed, lift, or wait upon the patient creature" (pp. 534–535). Beth finally drew her last quiet breath "on the bosom where she had drawn her first"; and "mother and sisters made her ready for the long sleep that pain would never mar again" (p. 540).

The sequence of events described in *Little Women* is strikingly close to reality, as outlined by one of Alcott's biographers: "In February, Lizzie began to fail rapidly from what Dr. Geist labeled consumption. With aching heart Louisa watched while her sister sewed or read or lay looking at the fire. . . . Anna [Alcott's older sister] did the housekeeping so that Mother and Louisa could devote themselves to Lizzie. The sad, quiet days stretched on in her room, and during endless nights Louisa kindled the fire and watched her sister" (Stern, 1950, pp. 85–86).

Alcott herself wrote after her sister's death, "Our Lizzie is well at last, not in this world but another where I hope she will find nothing but rest from her long suffering. . . . Last Friday night after suffering much all day, she asked to lie in Father's arms & called us all about her holding our hands & smiling at us as she silently seemed to bid us good bye. . . . At midnight she said 'Now I'm comfortable & so happy,' & soon after became unconscious. We sat beside her while she quietly breathed her life away, opening her eyes to give us one beautiful look before they closed forever" (Myerson, Shealy, & Stern, 1987, pp. 32–33).

In Louisa May Alcott's time, death was a frequent, normal, expected event, sometimes welcomed as a peaceful end to suffering. Caring for a dying person at home, as the Alcott family did, was a common experience (as it still is in many contemporary rural cultures). Looking death in the eye, bit by bit, day by day, Alcott and her family absorbed an important truth: that dying is part of living. Its meaning and impact are profoundly influenced by what people feel and do, and people's feelings and behavior are shaped by the time and place in which they live.

In this chapter, we look at the many interwoven aspects of death (the state) and dying (the process), including societal views and customs surrounding death and mourning. We examine how people of different ages think and feel about dying. We describe various forms grief can take and how people deal with the loss of a spouse, parent, or child. We discuss suicide and controversial issues that revolve around a "right to die." Finally, we see how confronting death can give deeper meaning and purpose to life.

After you have read and studied this chapter, you should be able to answer each of the following Guidepost questions. Look for them again in the margins, where they point to important concepts throughout the chapter. To check your understanding of these Guideposts, review the end-of-chapter summary. Checkpoints located at periodic spots throughout the chapter will help you verify your understanding of what you have read.

Guideposts for Study

1. How do attitudes and customs concerning death differ across cultures?
2. What are the implications of the "mortality revolution," and how does it affect care of the dying?
3. How do people change as they confront their own death?
4. Is there a normal pattern of grieving?
5. How do attitudes and understandings about death and bereavement differ across the life span?
6. What special challenges are involved in surviving a spouse, a parent, or a child, or in mourning a miscarriage?
7. How common is suicide?
8. Why are attitudes toward euthanasia ("mercy killing") and assisted suicide changing, and what concerns do these practices raise?
9. How can people overcome fear of dying and come to terms with death?

The Many Faces of Death

Death is a *biological* fact; but it also has *social, cultural, historical, religious, legal, psychological, developmental, medical,* and *ethical* aspects, and often these are closely intertwined.

Although death and loss are universal experiences, they have a cultural context. Cultural and religious attitudes toward death and dying affect psychological and developmental aspects of death: how people of various ages face their own death and the deaths of those close to them. Death may mean one thing to an elderly Japanese Buddhist, imbued with teachings of accepting the inevitable, and another to a third-generation Japanese American youth who has grown up with a belief in directing one's own destiny.

Death is generally considered to be the cessation of bodily processes. However, criteria for death have become more complex with the development of medical apparatus that can prolong basic signs of life. These medical developments have raised questions about whether or when life supports may be withheld or removed and whose judgment should prevail. In some places, the claim of a "right to die" has led to laws either permitting or forbidding physicians to help a terminally ill person end a life that has become a burden.

We explore all these issues in this chapter. First let's look at death and mourning in their cultural and historical context.

The Cultural Context

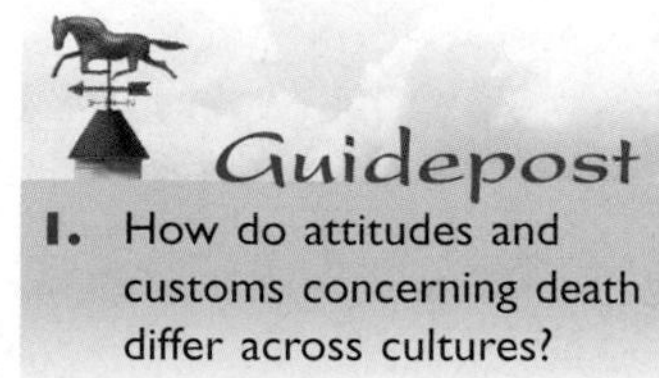

Guidepost

1. How do attitudes and customs concerning death differ across cultures?

Customs concerning disposal and remembrance of the dead, transfer of possessions, and even expression of grief vary greatly from culture to culture and often are governed by religious or legal prescriptions that reflect a society's view of what death is and what

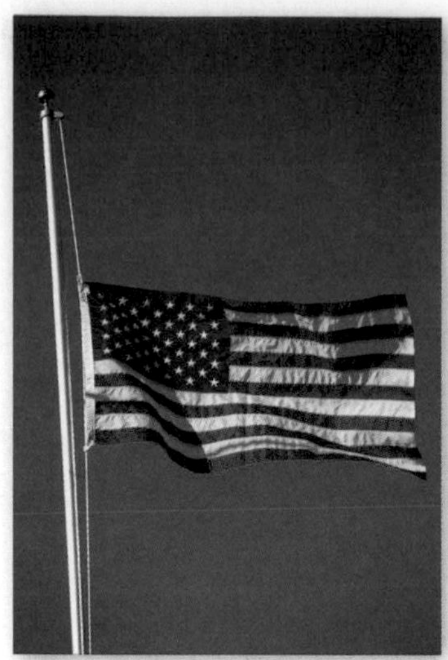

Flying the flag at half-mast is a way that Americans officially show grief over the death of an important public figure. Customary expressions of grief vary from one culture to another.

happens afterward. Cultural aspects of death include care of and behavior toward the dying and the dead, the setting where death usually takes place, and mourning customs and rituals—from the all-night Irish wake, at which friends and family toast the memory of the dead person, to the week-long Jewish *shiva,* at which mourners vent their feelings and share memories of the deceased. Some cultural conventions, such as flying a flag at half-mast after the death of a public figure, are codified in law.

In Malayan society, as in many other preliterate societies, death was seen as a gradual transition. A body was at first given only provisional burial. Survivors continued to perform mourning rites until the body decayed to the point where the soul was believed to have left it and to have been admitted into the spiritual realm. In ancient Romania, warriors went laughing to their graves in the expectation of meeting Zalmoxis, their supreme god.

In ancient Greece, bodies of heroes were publicly burned as a sign of honor. Public cremation still is practiced by Hindus in India and Nepal. By contrast, cremation is prohibited under Orthodox Jewish law in the belief that the dead will rise again for a Last Judgment and the chance for eternal life (Ausubel, 1964).

In Japan, religious rituals encourage survivors to maintain contact with the deceased. Families keep an altar in the home dedicated to their ancestors; they talk to their dead loved ones and offer them food or cigars. In Gambia the dead are considered part of the community; among Native Americans, the Hopi fear the spirits of the dead and try to forget a deceased person as quickly as possible. Muslims in Egypt show grief through expressions of deep sorrow; Muslims in Bali are encouraged to suppress sadness, to laugh, and to be joyful (Stroebe, Gergen, Gergen, & Stroebe, 1992). All these varied customs and practices help people deal with death and bereavement through well-understood cultural meanings that provide a stable anchor amid the turbulence of loss.

Checkpoint

Can you . . .

✔ Give examples of cross-cultural differences in customs and attitudes related to death?

Some modern social customs have evolved from ancient ones. Embalming goes back to a practice common in ancient Egypt and China: *mummification,* preserving a body so the soul can return to it. A traditional Jewish custom is never to leave a dying person alone. Anthropologists suggest that the original reason for this may have been a belief that evil spirits hover around, trying to enter the dying body (Ausubel, 1964). Such rituals give people facing a loss something predictable and important to do at a time when they otherwise might feel confused and helpless.

The Mortality Revolution

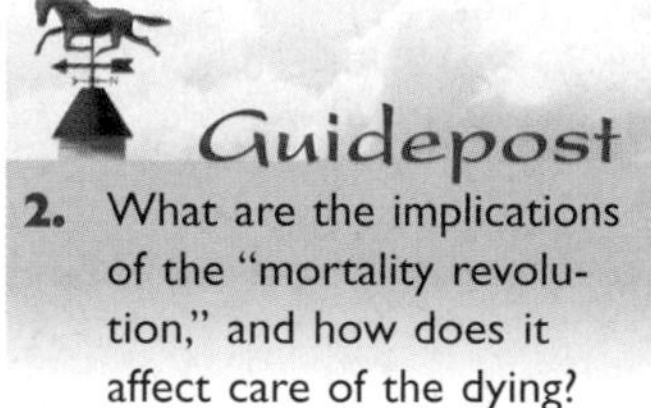

Guidepost

2. What are the implications of the "mortality revolution," and how does it affect care of the dying?

Reading *Little Women* is a vivid reminder of the great historical changes regarding death and dying that have taken place since the late nineteenth century. Especially in developed countries, advances in medicine and sanitation, new treatments for many once-fatal illnesses, and a better-educated, more health-conscious population have brought about a "mortality revolution." Women today are less likely to die in childbirth, infants are more likely to survive their first year, children are more likely to grow to adulthood, young adults like Alcott's sister Lizzie are more likely to reach old age, and older people often can overcome illnesses they grew up regarding as fatal.

The top causes of death in the United States in the 1900s were diseases that most often affected children and young people: pneumonia and influenza, tuberculosis, diarrhea, and enteritis. Today three-quarters of all deaths in the United States occur among people ages 65 and over (NCHS, 2001), and 60 percent of all deaths are from heart disease, cancer, and stroke, the three leading causes of death in late adulthood (Sahyoun, Lentzner, Hoyert, & Robinson, 2001). Mortality rates for older adults have decreased sharply in recent years, especially among men, mainly due to a declining rate of deaths from heart disease in the United States (Sahyoun et al., 2001) and other developed countries (Kinsella & Velkoff, 2001). Death rates from some cancers also have fallen (Sahyoun et al., 2001). Even with further reductions in cancer death rates, the incidence and burden of cancer will most likely increase as the population continues to age (Edwards et al., 2002).

As death increasingly became a phenomenon of late adulthood, it became "invisible and abstract" (Fulton & Owen, 1987–1988, p. 380). Many older people lived and died in retirement communities. Care of the dying and the dead became largely a task for professionals. Such social conventions as placing the dying person in a hospital or nursing home and refusing to openly discuss his or her condition reflected and perpetuated attitudes of avoidance and denial of death. Death—even of the very old—came to be regarded as a failure of medical treatment rather than as a natural end to life (McCue, 1995).

Today, this picture is changing. Violence, drug abuse, poverty, and the spread of AIDS make it harder to deny the reality of death. **Thanatology,** the study of death and dying, is arousing interest, and educational programs have been established to help people deal with death. Because of the prohibitive cost of extended hospital care that cannot save the terminally ill, many more deaths are occurring at home (Techner, 1994).

thanatology Study of death and dying.

Care of the Dying

Along with the growing tendency to face death more honestly, movements have arisen to make dying more humane. These include hospice care and self-help support groups for dying people and their families.

Hospice care is personal, patient- and family-centered care for the terminally ill. Its focus is on **palliative care:** relief of pain and suffering, control of symptoms, maintaining a satisfactory quality of life, and allowing the patient to die in peace and dignity. Hospice care usually takes place at home; but such care can be given in a hospital or another institution, at a hospice center, or through a combination of home and institutional care. Family members often take an active part. In 2001 about 3,200 hospice programs in the United States provided care to an estimated 775,000 patients (National Hospice and Palliative Care Organization, 2002).

hospice care Warm, personal patient- and family-centered care for a person with a terminal illness.

palliative care Care aimed at relieving pain and suffering and allowing the terminally ill to die in peace, comfort, and dignity.

What does it mean to preserve the dignity of dying patients? One research team decided to ask patients themselves. From interviews with fifty Canadian patients with advanced terminal cancer, the researchers developed a list of dignity-related questions, concerns, and treatment guidelines (Chochinov, Hack, McClement, Harlos, & Kristjanson, 2002; see Table 19-1). Above all, the researchers concluded, dignity-

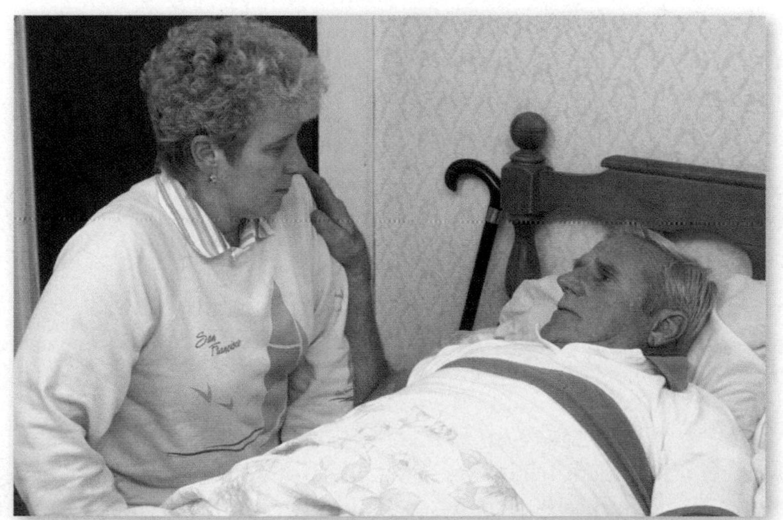

Many terminally ill people are able to remain in their own homes, with family members involved in their care, under the guidance and support of hospice workers. Hospice care seeks to ease patients' pain and treat their symptoms, to keep them as comfortable and alert as possible, to show interest and kindness to them and their families, and to help families deal with illness and death.

Table 19-1 Dignity-Conserving Interventions for Patients Nearing Death

Factors/Subthemes	Dignity-Related Questions	Therapeutic Interventions
Illness-Related Concerns		
Symptom distress		
Physical distress	"How comfortable are you?" "Is there anything we can do to make you more comfortable?"	Vigilance to symptom management. Frequent assessment. Application of comfort care.
Psychological distress	"How are you coping with what is happening to you?"	Assume a supportive stance. Empathetic listening. Referral to counseling.
Medical uncertainty	"Is there anything further about your illness that you would like to know?" "Are you getting all the information you feel you need?"	Upon request, provide accurate, understandable information and strategies to deal with possible future crises.
Death anxiety	"Are there things about the later stages of your illness that you would like to discuss?"	
Level of independence		
Independence	"Has your illness made you more dependent on others?"	Have patients participate in decision making, regarding both medical and personal issues.
Cognitive acuity	"Are you having any difficulty with your thinking?"	Treat delirium. When possible, avoid sedating medication.
Functional capacity	"How much are you able to do for yourself?"	Use orthotics, physiotherapy, and occupational therapy.
Dignity-Conserving Repertoire		
Dignity-conserving perspectives		
Continuity of self	"Are there things about you that this disease does not affect?"	Acknowledge and take interest in those aspects of the patient's life that he/she most values. See the patient as worthy of honor, respect, and esteem.
Role preservation	"What things did you do before you were sick that were most important to you?"	
Maintenance of pride	"What about yourself or your life are you most proud of?"	
Hopefulness	"What is still possible?"	Encourage and enable the patient to participate in meaningful or purposeful activities.

(Continued)

Checkpoint

Can you . . .

- ✔ Explain how death became increasingly "invisible and abstract" and how attitudes are changing today?
- ✔ Tell the chief goals of hospice care?

conserving care depends not only on how patients are treated, but on how they are viewed: "When dying patients are seen, and know that they are seen, as being worthy of honor and esteem by those who care for them, dignity is more likely to be maintained" (Chochinov, 2002, p. 2259).

Palliative care is not only for the very old. Hospitals and medical professionals around the country are developing protocols for pain-free treatment of dying newborns whose lives cannot be saved (Catlin & Carter, 2002).

Facing Death and Loss: Psychological Issues

What changes do people undergo shortly before death? How do they come to terms with its imminence? How do people deal with grief? The answers may differ for different people.

Guidepost

3. How do people change as they confront their own death?

Confronting One's Own Death

In the absence of any identifiable illness, people around the age of 100—close to the present limit of the human life span—usually suffer cognitive and other functional

Autonomy/control	"How in control do you feel?"	Involve patient in treatment and care decisions.
Generativity/legacy	"How do you want to be remembered?"	Life project (e.g., making audio/videotapes, writing letters, journaling). Dignity psychotherapy.
Acceptance	"How at peace are you with what is happening to you?"	Support the patient in his/her outlook. Encourage doing things that enhance his/her sense of well-being (e.g., meditation, light exercise, listening to music, prayer).
Resilience/fighting spirit	"What part of you is strongest right now?"	
Dignity-conserving practices		
Living in the moment	"Are there things that take your mind away from illness, and offer you comfort?"	Allow the patient to participate in normal routines, or take comfort in momentary distractions (e.g., daily outings, light exercise, listening to music).
Maintaining normalcy	"Are there things you still enjoy doing on a regular basis?"	
Finding spiritual comfort	"Is there a religious or spiritual community that you are, or would like to be, connected with?"	Make referrals to chaplain or spiritual leader. Enable the patient to participate in particular spiritual and/or culturally based practices.
Social Dignity Inventory		
Privacy boundaries	"What about your privacy or your body is important to you?"	Ask permission to examine patient. Proper draping to safeguard and respect privacy.
Social support	"Who are the people that are most important to you?" "Who is your closest confidante?"	Liberal policies about visitation, rooming in. Enlist involvement of a wide support network.
Care tenor	"Is there anything in the way you are treated that is undermining your sense of dignity?"	Treat the patient as worthy of honor, esteem, and respect; adopt a stance conveying this.
Burden to others	"Do you worry about being a burden to others?" "If so, to whom and in what ways?"	Encourage explicit discussion about these concerns with those they fear they are burdening.
Aftermath concerns	"What are your biggest concerns for the people you will leave behind?"	Encourage the setting of affairs, preparation of an advanced directive, making a will, funeral planning.

Source: Adapted from Chochinov, 2002, p. 2255.

declines, lose interest in eating and drinking, and die a natural death (McCue, 1995). Such changes also have been noted in younger people whose death is near. Some people who have come close to death have had "near-death" experiences, often involving a sense of being out of the body and visions of bright lights or mystical encounters. These are sometimes interpreted as resulting from physiological changes that accompany the process of dying or psychological responses to the perceived threat of death.

The psychiatrist Elisabeth Kübler-Ross, in her work with dying people, found that most of them welcomed an opportunity to speak openly about their condition and were aware of being close to death, even when they had not been told. After speaking with some 500 terminally ill patients, Kübler-Ross (1969, 1970) outlined five stages in coming to terms with death: (1) *denial* (refusal to accept the reality of what is happening); (2) *anger;* (3) *bargaining for extra time;* (4) *depression;* and ultimately (5) *acceptance.* She also proposed a similar progression in the feelings of people facing imminent bereavement (Kübler-Ross, 1975).

Kübler-Ross's model has been criticized and modified by other professionals who work with dying patients. Although the emotions she described are common, not everyone goes through all five stages, and not necessarily in the same sequence. A person may go back and forth between anger and depression, for example, or may feel both at once. Unfortunately, some health professionals assume that these stages are inevitable and universal, and others feel that they have failed if they cannot bring a patient to the final stage of acceptance.

Dying, like living, is an individual experience. For some people, denial or anger may be a healthier way to face death than the calm acceptance that Beth seemed to exemplify in *Little Women.* Kübler-Ross's description, useful as it may be in helping us understand the feelings of those who are facing the end of life, should not be considered a model or a criterion for a "good death."

Patterns of Grieving

Guidepost

4. Is there a normal pattern of grieving?

bereavement Loss, due to death, of someone to whom one feels close and the process of adjustment to the loss.

grief Emotional response experienced in the early phases of bereavement.

grief work Pattern of working out of psychological issues connected with grief.

Bereavement—the loss of someone to whom a person feels close and the process of adjusting to it—can affect practically all aspects of a survivor's life. Bereavement often brings a change in status and role (for example, from a wife to a widow or from a son or daughter to an orphan). It may have social and economic consequences—a loss of friends and sometimes of income. But first there is **grief**—the emotional response experienced in the early phases of bereavement.

Grief, like dying, is a highly personal experience. Today research has challenged earlier notions of a single, "normal" pattern of grieving and a "normal" timetable for recovery. A widow talking to her late husband might once have been considered emotionally disturbed; now this is recognized as a common and helpful behavior (Lund, 1993b). Although some people recover fairly quickly after bereavement, others never do.

Perhaps the most widely studied pattern of grief is a three-stage one, in which the bereaved person accepts the painful reality of the loss, gradually lets go of the bond with the dead person, and readjusts to life by developing new interests and relationships. This process of **grief work,** the working out of psychological issues connected with grief, generally takes the following path—though, as with Kübler-Ross's stages, it may vary (J. T. Brown & Stoudemire, 1983; R. Schulz, 1978).

1. *Shock and disbelief.* Immediately following a death, survivors often feel lost and confused. As awareness of the loss sinks in, the initial numbness gives way to overwhelming feelings of sadness and frequent crying. This first stage may last several weeks, especially after a sudden or unexpected death.
2. *Preoccupation with the memory of the dead person.* In the second stage, which may last six months or longer, the survivor tries to come to terms with the death but cannot yet accept it. A widow may relive her husband's death and their entire relationship. From time to time, she may be seized by a feeling that her dead husband is present. These experiences diminish with time, though they may recur—perhaps for years—on such occasions as the anniversary of the marriage or of the death.
3. *Resolution.* The final stage has arrived when the bereaved person renews interest in everyday activities. Memories of the dead person bring fond feelings mingled with sadness, rather than sharp pain and longing.

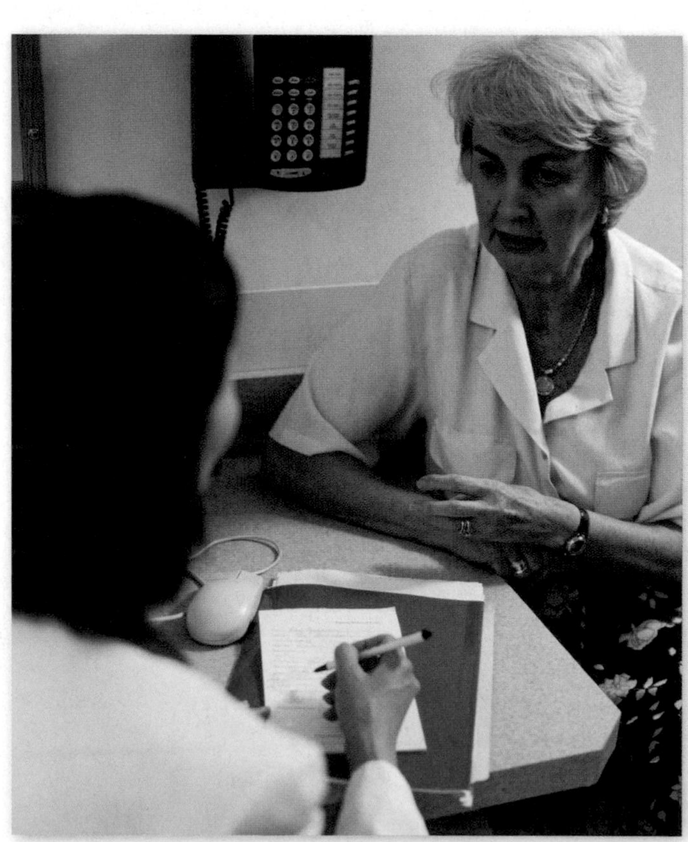

Grief therapy can help a bereaved person express her feelings, review her relationship with the deceased, and go on with her life.

Although the pattern of grief work just described is common, grieving does not necessarily follow a straight line from shock to resolution. One team of psychologists (Wortman & Silver, 1989) reviewed studies of reactions to major losses: the death of a loved one or the loss of mobility due to spinal injury. These researchers found some common assumptions to be more myth than fact.

First, depression is far from universal. From three weeks to two years after their loss, only 15 to 35 percent of widows, widowers, and victims of spinal cord injury showed signs of depression. *Second,* failure to show distress at the outset does not necessarily lead to problems; the people who were most upset immediately after a loss or injury were likely to be most troubled up to two years later. *Third,* not everyone needs to "work through" a loss or will benefit from doing so; some of the people who did the most intense grief work had more problems later. *Fourth,* not everyone returns to normal quickly. More than 40 percent of widows and widowers show moderate to severe anxiety up to four years after the spouse's death, especially if it was sudden. *Fifth,* people cannot always resolve their grief and accept their loss. Parents and spouses of people who die in car accidents often have painful memories of the loved one even after many years (Wortman & Silver, 1989). Acceptance may be particularly difficult when a loss is *ambiguous,* as when a loved one is missing and presumed dead (see Box 19-1 on page 692).

Rather than a single three-stage pattern, this research found three main patterns of grieving. In the generally expected pattern, the mourner goes from high to low distress. In a second pattern, the mourner does not experience intense distress immediately or later. In a third pattern, the mourner remains distressed for a long time (Wortman & Silver, 1989).

The finding that grief takes varied forms and patterns has important implications for helping people deal with loss. It may be unnecessary and even harmful to urge or lead mourners to "work through" a loss, or to expect them to follow a set pattern of emotional reactions—just as it may be unnecessary and harmful to expect all dying patients to experience Kübler-Ross's stages. Respect for different ways of showing grief can help the bereaved deal with loss without making them feel that their reactions are abnormal.

Most bereaved people eventually are able, often with the help of family and friends, to come to terms with their loss and resume normal lives. For some, however, **grief therapy**—treatment to help the bereaved cope with their loss—is indicated. Professional grief therapists help survivors express sorrow, guilt, hostility, and anger. They encourage clients to review the relationship with the deceased and to integrate the fact of the death into their lives. In helping people handle grief, counselors need to take into account ethnic and family traditions and individual differences.

grief therapy Treatment to help the bereaved cope with loss.

Checkpoint

Can you . . .

- ✔ Name Kübler-Ross's five stages of confronting death and tell why her work is controversial?
- ✔ Describe the three stages of what is usually called *grief work,* and cite five common, mistaken assumptions about the grieving process?

Death and Bereavement Across the Life Span

There is no single way of viewing death at any age; people's attitudes toward it reflect their personality and experience, as well as how close they believe they are to dying. Still, broad developmental differences apply. As the timing-of-events model suggests, death probably does not mean the same thing to an 85-year-old man with excruciatingly painful arthritis, a 56-year-old woman at the height of a brilliant legal career who discovers she has breast cancer, and a 15-year-old who dies of an overdose of drugs. Typical changes in attitudes toward death across the life span depend both on cognitive development and on the normative or nonnormative timing of the event.

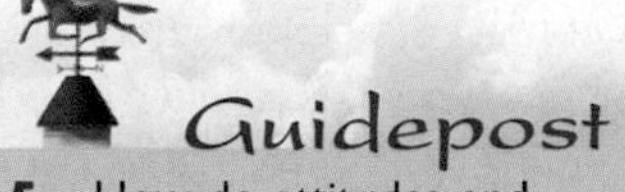

Guidepost

5. How do attitudes and understandings about death and bereavement differ across the life span?

Childhood and Adolescence

Not until sometime between the ages of 5 and 7 do most children understand that death is *irreversible*—that a dead person, animal, or flower cannot come to life again. At about the same age, children realize two other important concepts about death: first, that it is *universal* (all living things die) and therefore *inevitable;* and second, that

BOX 19–1

Digging Deeper
Ambiguous Loss

A woman whose husband was in the World Trade Center at the time of the terrorist attack on September 11, 2001, did not believe he was dead until months later, when clean-up workers turned up a shard of his bone. Middle-aged women and men fly to Southeast Asia to search for the remains of husbands and fathers whose planes were shot down decades ago. A woman whose father committed suicide and who did not see him buried in a different state has recurring dreams that he is still alive.

Dealing with the death of a loved one is difficult enough under normal circumstances. But when there is no body—no clear evidence of death—it can be harder to face the finality of loss. This is especially true in U.S. culture, with its media-fed tendency to deny the reality of death. "People yearn for a body," says family therapist Pauline Boss (2002, p. 15), "because, paradoxically, *having* the body enables them to let go of it." Viewing the body "provides cognitive certainty of death" and thus enables the bereaved to begin mourning. Boss tells of a woman whose husband was missing in the World Trade Center, who wished for just a part of him to bury—even a fingernail.

Boss (1999, 2002) applies the term *ambiguous loss* (introduced in Chapter 18) to situations in which loss is not clearly defined and therefore is confusing and difficult to resolve. Ambiguous loss can be especially stressful, and waiting and wondering for clear answers can be tormenting. "If the environment remains ambiguous, uncertain, and incomprehensible," Boss explains, "cognition is blocked, emotions are frozen, and continued individual and family functioning is severely hampered" (Boss, 2002, p. 15). When a loss is uncertain, people are denied the ritual closure that a funeral provides and tend to be immobilized—unable to go on with the necessary task of reorganizing family roles and relationships. The loss goes on and on, creating physical and emotional exhaustion, and the support of friends and family may drop away.

In New York, after the September 11 attack, thousands of families had to cope with this kind of loss. Giving the situation a name seems to alleviate the anguish of the bereaved, who otherwise may blame themselves for feeling confused, helpless, anxious, and unable to grieve normally. Boss also has applied the concept of ambiguous loss to sitations in which the loved one is physically present but psychologically absent, as in Alzheimer's disease, drug addiction, and other chronic mental illnesses.

People who can best tolerate ambiguous loss tend to have certain characteristics: (1) they are deeply spiritual and do not expect to understand what happens in the world—they have faith and trust in the unknown; (2) they are optimistic by nature; (3) they can hold two opposite ideas at one time ("My son is gone but is also here with me") and thus can live with uncertainty; and (4) often they grew up in a family or culture where mastery, control, and finding answers to questions was less important than learning to live with what is.

Some Native American cultures provide rituals, ceremonies, and symbols to mark ambiguous loss. An Anishinabe woman in northern Minnesota, who was taking care of her demented mother, held a "funeral" for her "because the woman that I knew was just not there anymore" (Boss, 1999, p. 17). In New York, Mayor Rudolph Guiliani offered official certificates of presumed death and an urn of ashes from Ground Zero. Some people accepted these tokens as evidence of death, allowing themselves to begin the grieving process, but others chose to wait for more solid proof. Different families, different cultures, and different people within a family may have different ways of coping.

Therapy can help people to "understand, cope, and move on after the loss, even if it remains unclear" (1999, p. 7). But therapists working with people suffering from ambiguous loss need to be able to tolerate ambiguity themselves. They must recognize that the loss is ambiguous and that the classic stages of grief work do not apply. Pressing for closure will only bring resistance. Families can learn to manage the stress of ambiguous loss at their own pace and in their own way.

Source: Boss (1999, 2002).

What's Your View?

Have you ever experienced an ambiguous loss, or do you know someone who has? If so, what coping strategies seemed most effective?

Check It Out:

For more information related to this topic, go to http://www.mhhe.com/papaliah9.

a dead person is *nonfunctional* (all life functions end at death). Before then, children may believe that certain groups of people (say, teachers, parents, and children) do not die, that a person who is smart enough or lucky enough can avoid death, and that they themselves will be able to live forever. They also may believe that a dead person still can think and feel. The concepts of irreversibility, universality, and cessation of

Table 19-2 Manifestations of Grief in Children

Under 3 years	3 to 5 years	School-Age Children	Adolescents
Regression	Increased activity	Deterioration of school performance caused by loss of concentration, lack of interest, lack of motivation, failure to complete assignments, and daydreaming in class	Depression
Sadness	Constipation	Resistance to attending school	Somatic complaints
Fearfulness	Soiling	Crying spells	Delinquent behavior
Loss of appetite	Bed-wetting	Lying	Promiscuity
Failure to thrive	Anger and temper tantrums	Stealing	Suicide attempts
Sleep disturbance	"Out-of-control" behavior	Nervousness	Dropping out of school
Social withdrawal	Nightmares	Abdominal pain	
Developmental delay	Crying spells	Headaches	
Irritability		Listlessness	
Excessive crying		Fatigue	
Increased dependency			
Loss of speech			

Source: Adapted from AAP Committee on Psychosocial Aspects of Child and Family Health, 1992.

functions usually develop at the time when, according to Piaget, children move from preoperational to concrete operational thinking (Speece & Brent, 1984). During this period concepts of causation also become more sophisticated.

Children can be helped to understand death if they are introduced to the concept at an early age and are encouraged to talk about it. The death of a pet may provide a natural opportunity. If another child dies, teachers and parents need to try to allay the surviving children's anxieties.

The way children show grief depends on cognitive and emotional development (see Table 19-2). Children sometimes express grief through anger, acting out, or refusal to acknowledge a death, as if the pretense that a person is still alive will make it so. They may be confused by adults' euphemisms: that someone "expired" or that the family "lost" someone or that someone is "asleep" and will never awaken. A loss is more difficult if the child had a troubled relationship with the person who died; if a troubled surviving parent depends too much on the child; if the death was unexpected, especially if it was a murder or suicide; if the child has had previous behavioral or emotional problems; or if family and community support are lacking (AAP Committee on Psychosocial Aspects of Child and Family Health, 1992).

Parents and other adults can help children deal with bereavement by helping them understand that death is final and inevitable and that they did not cause the death by their misbehavior or thoughts. Children need reassurance that they will continue to receive care from loving adults. It is usually helpful to make as few changes as possible in a child's environment, relationships, and daily activities; to answer questions simply and honestly; and to encourage the child to talk about the person who died and about their feelings (AAP Committee on Psychosocial Aspects of Child & Family Health, 2000).

Death is not something adolescents normally think much about unless they are faced with it, as the March sisters were in *Little Women.* Still, in many communities in which adolescents (and even younger children) live, violence and the threat of death are inescapable facts of daily life. Many adolescents take heedless risks. They hitchhike, drive recklessly, and experiment with drugs and sex—often with tragic results. In their urge to discover and express their identity, they may be more concerned with *how* they live than with how *long* they will live.

Adulthood

Young adults who have finished their education and have embarked on careers, marriage, or parenthood are generally eager to live the lives they have been preparing for. If they are suddenly struck by a potentially fatal illness or injury, they are likely to be extremely frustrated. Frustration may turn to rage, which can make them difficult hospital patients.

Today, many people who develop AIDS in their twenties or thirties—often gay men—must face issues of death and dying at an age when they normally would be dealing with such issues of young adulthood as establishing an intimate relationship. Rather than having a long lifetime of losses as gradual preparation for the final loss of life, "the gay man may find his own health, the health of his friends, and the fabric of his community all collapsing at once" (Cadwell, 1994, p. 4).

In middle age, most people realize more keenly than before that they are indeed going to die. Their bodies send them signals that they are not as young, agile, and hearty as they once were. More and more they think about how many years they may have left and of how to make the most of those years (Neugarten, 1967). Often—especially after the death of both parents—there is a new awareness of being the older generation next in line to die (Scharlach & Fredriksen, 1993).

Older adults may have mixed feelings about the prospect of dying. Physical losses and other problems and losses of old age may diminish their pleasure in living and their will to live (McCue, 1995). On the other hand, when 414 hospitalized patients in their eighties and nineties were asked how much time they would be willing to trade for excellent health, about two out of three were unwilling to give up more than one month of life (Tsevat et al., 1998).

According to Erikson, older adults who resolve the final critical alternative of *integrity versus despair* (refer back to Chapter 18) achieve acceptance both of what they have done with their lives and of their impending death. One way to accomplish this resolution is through a *life review,* discussed later in this chapter. People who feel that their lives have been meaningful and who have adjusted to their losses may be better able to face death.

What's Your View?

- Try to imagine that you are terminally ill. What do you imagine your feelings would be? Would they be similar to or different from those described in the text with reference to your age group?

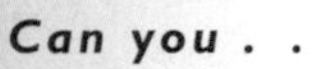

Checkpoint

Can you . . .

✔ Discuss how people of different ages cope with death and bereavement?

Special Losses

Especially difficult losses that may occur during adulthood are the deaths of a spouse, a parent, and a child. Less publicly noted is the loss of a potential offspring through miscarriage or stillbirth.

Guidepost

6. What special challenges are involved in surviving a spouse, a parent, or a child, or in mourning a miscarriage?

Surviving a Spouse

Widowhood is one of the greatest emotional challenges that can face a human being. As we mentioned in Chapter 18, because women tend to live longer than men and to be younger than their husbands, they are more likely to be widowed. Women also tend to be widowed younger than men. One-third of women lose their husbands by age 65, but it is not until 75 that an equal proportion of men lose their wives (Atchley, 1997).

Effects of widowhood differ for men and women. Women may show their distress more openly, but men also may feel that they have lost their moorings (Aldwin & Levenson, 2001). Friends and family usually rally to the mourner's side immediately after the death but then may go back to their own lives (Brubaker, 1990). Older widows are more likely than older widowers to stay in touch with friends from whom they receive social support (Kinsella & Velkoff, 2001). On the other hand, widows whose husbands were chief breadwinners may experience economic hardship and may fall into poverty (Hungerford, 2001). Even when both spouses have been employed, the

Widowhood can be one of the most wrenching challenges to face a human being. Widowed women tend to express their distress more openly than widowed men, but they also are more likely to become depressed.

Friendship is often a source of support and satisfaction for elderly widows.

loss of one income can be a blow. When a husband is widowed, he has to buy many of the household services his wife provided.

The survivor of a long marriage is likely to face many emotional and practical problems. A good marriage can leave a gaping emotional void. Even if the marriage was a troubled one, the bereaved spouse is likely to feel a loss. This loss may be especially hard for a woman who has structured her life and her identity around caring for her husband. Widowed women have elevated rates of depression, at least during the first five years after the death (Marks & Lambert, 1998).

There is a strong likelihood that a widowed person, especially a man, will soon follow a spouse to the grave. In a large-scale Finnish study, men who lost their wives within a five-year period were 21 percent more likely to die within the same period than married men who did not become widowed. The "excess mortality" figure for widowed women was 10 percent. The risk was greatest for young adults and for those whose loss was still fresh (Martikainen & Valkonen, 1996).

Many studies have found older adults to adjust better to widowhood than younger adults (DiGiulio, 1992). In general, though, age is not a major factor in the grieving process; coping skills are. People who have had practice in coping with loss and have developed effective coping resources—self-esteem and competence in meeting the demands of everyday life—are better able to deal with bereavement (Lund, 1993b).

Although it takes time for the pain to heal, most bereaved spouses eventually rebuild their lives. Loneliness, sadness, and depression give way to confidence in the ability to manage on their own. People who adjust best are those who keep busy, take on new roles (such as new paid or volunteer work), or become more deeply involved in ongoing activities. They see friends often, and they may join support or self-help groups (Lund, 1989, 1993b). Adult children can be an important source of assistance and emotional support (Suitor et al., 1995). The ability to talk openly about their experience can help some people find meaning and coherence in the transition to widowhood (van den Hoonard, 1999).

For women, especially, the distress of loss can be a catalyst for introspection and growth—for discovering submerged aspects of themselves and learning to stand on their own feet. More acutely aware of their own mortality, they may reevaluate their lives in a search for personal meaning. In the process, they may look back at their marriages more realistically. Some return to school or find new jobs (Lieberman, 1996).

With available women greatly outnumbering available men, elderly widowers are four times as likely to remarry as elderly widows (Carstensen & Pasupathi, 1993), typically within a year (Aldwin & Levenson, 2001). The need for intimacy may be a factor. If a husband has a confidant, it is likely to be his wife, whereas wives (who generally have more intimate friendships) are more likely to confide in someone outside the marriage (Tower & Kasl, 1996). Many widows are not interested in remarriage (Talbott, 1998). Women usually can handle their household needs and may be reluctant to give up survivors' pension benefits or the freedom of living alone, or to face the prospect of caring for an infirm husband, perhaps for the second time.

Losing a Parent in Adulthood

Little attention has been paid to the impact of a parent's death on an adult child. Today, with longer life expectancies, this loss normally occurs in middle age (Aldwin & Levenson, 2001).

In-depth interviews with 83 volunteers ages 35 to 60 found a majority of bereaved adult children still experiencing emotional distress—ranging from sadness and crying to depression and thoughts of suicide—after one to five years, especially following loss of a mother (Scharlach & Fredriksen, 1993). Still, the death of a parent can be a maturing experience. It can push adults into resolving important developmental issues: achieving a stronger sense of self and a more pressing, realistic awareness of their own mortality, along with a greater sense of responsibility, commitment, and attachment to others (M. S. Moss & Moss, 1989; Scharlach & Fredriksen, 1993; see Table 19-3).

The death of a parent often brings changes in other relationships. A bereaved adult child may assume more responsibility for the surviving parent and for keeping the family together (Aldwin & Levenson, 2001). The intense emotions of bereavement may draw siblings closer, or they may become alienated over differences that arose during the parent's final illness. A parent's death may free an adult child to spend more time and energy on relationships that were temporarily neglected to meet demands of caregiving. Or the death may free an adult child to shed a relationship that was being maintained to meet the parent's expectations (M. S. Moss & Moss, 1989; Scharlach & Fredriksen, 1993).

The death of a second parent can have especially great impact. The adult child may feel a sharpened sense of mortality now that the buffer of the older generation is gone (Aldwin & Levenson, 2001). This awareness can be an opportunity for growth, leading to a more mature outlook on life and a greater appreciation of the value of personal relationships (Scharlach & Fredriksen, 1993). Recognition of the finality of death and of the impossibility of saying anything more to the deceased parent motivates some people to resolve disturbances in their ties to the living while there is still time. Some people are moved to reconcile with their own adult children. Sometimes estranged siblings, realizing that the parent who provided a link between them is no longer there, try to mend the rift.

Table 19-3 Self-reported Psychological Impacts of a Parent's Death

Impacts	Death of Mother (Percent)	Death of Father (Percent)
Self-concept		
More "adult"	29	43
More self-confident	19	20
More responsible	11	4
Less mature	14	3
Other	8	17
No impact	19	12
Feelings about mortality		
Increased awareness of own mortality	30	29
More accepting of own death	19	10
Made concrete plans regarding own death	10	4
Increased fear of own death	10	18
Other	14	16
No impact	17	23
Religiosity		
More religious	26	29
Less religious	11	2
Other	3	10
No impact	60	59
Personal priorities		
Personal relationships more important	35	28
Simple pleasures more important	16	13
Personal happiness more important	10	7
Material possessions less important	5	8
Other	20	8
No impact	14	36
Work or career plans		
Left job	29	16
Adjusted goals	15	10
Changed plans due to family needs	5	6
Moved	4	10
Other	13	19
No impact	34	39

Source: Scharlach & Fredriksen, 1993, table 1, p. 311.

Losing a Child

In earlier times, it was not unusual for a parent to bury a child, as Louisa May Alcott's mother did. Today, with medical advances and the increase in life expectancy in industrialized countries, infant mortality has reached record lows, and a child who survives the first year of life is far more likely to live to old age.

A parent is rarely prepared emotionally for the death of a child. Such a death, no matter at what age, comes as a cruel, unnatural shock, an untimely event that, in the normal course of things, should not have happened. The parents may feel they have failed, no matter how much they loved and cared for the child, and they may find it hard to let go.

If a marriage is strong, the couple may draw closer together, supporting each other in their shared loss. But in other cases, the loss weakens and eventually destroys the marriage (Brandt, 1989). The stress of losing a child may even hasten a parent's death (Li, Precht, Mortensen, & Olsen, 2003).

What's Your View?

- Have you lost a parent? a sibling? a spouse? a child? a friend? If not, which of these losses do you imagine would be hardest to bear, and why? If you have experienced more than one of these kinds of loss, how did your reactions differ?
- What advice would you give a friend about what to say—and what *not* to say—to a person in mourning?

Checkpoint

Can you . . .

- ✔ Describe specific challenges involved in losing a spouse?
- ✔ Tell ways in which an adult's loss of a spouse or parent can be a maturing experience?
- ✔ Explain why parents are rarely prepared emotionally for the death of a child?
- ✔ Discuss ways to help expectant parents cope with the loss of a pregnancy?

Although each bereaved parent must cope with grief in his or her own way, some have found that plunging into work, interests, and other relationships or joining a support group eases the pain. The Chilean writer Isabel Allende wrote a family memoir while sitting at the bedside of her comatose, dying daughter (refer back to Chapter 8 Focus vignette). Some well-meaning friends tell parents not to dwell on their loss; but remembering the child in a meaningful way may be exactly what they need to do.

Mourning a Miscarriage

At a Buddhist temple in Tokyo, small statues of infants accompanied by toys and gifts are left as offerings to Jizo, an enlightened being who is believed to watch over miscarried and aborted fetuses and eventually, through reincarnation, to guide them into a new life. The ritual of *mizuko kuyo,* a rite of apology and remembrance, is observed as a means of making amends to the aborted life (Orenstein, 2002).

The Japanese word *mizuko* means "water child." Japanese Buddhists believe that life flows into an organism gradually, like water, and a mizuko is somewhere on the continuum between life and death (Orenstein, 2002). In English, by contrast, there is no word for a miscarried or aborted fetus, nor any ritual of mourning. Families, friends, and health professionals tend to avoid talking about such losses, because they are often considered insignificant compared with the loss of a living child (Van, 2001).

Because each person's (or couple's) experience of loss is unique, it is hard to generalize about the way people deal with these losses. They tend to rely on inner, instinctive strategies and resources (Van, 2001). Differences in the ways men and women grieve may be a source of tension and divisiveness in the couple's relationship (Caelli, Downie, & Letendre, 2002). In one small study, 11 men whose child had died in utero reported being overcome with frustration and helplessness during and after the delivery, but several found relief in supporting their partners (Samuelsson, Radestad, & Segesten, 2001). In another study, grieving parents perceived their spouses and extended families as most helpful and their doctors as least helpful. Some bereaved parents benefited from a support group, and some not (DiMarco, Menke, & McNamara, 2001). Couples who have gone through the loss of a baby may need extra-compassionate care during a later pregnancy—though again, responses are diverse (Caelli et al., 2002).

Medical, Legal, and Ethical Issues: The "Right to Die"

Do people have a right to die? If so, under what circumstances? Should a terminally ill person who wants to commit suicide be allowed or helped to do so? Should a doctor prescribe medicine that will relieve pain but may shorten the patient's life? What about giving a lethal injection to end a patient's suffering? Who decides that a life is not worth prolonging? These are some of the thorny moral, ethical, and legal questions that face individuals, families, physicians, and society—questions involving the quality of life and the nature and circumstances of death.

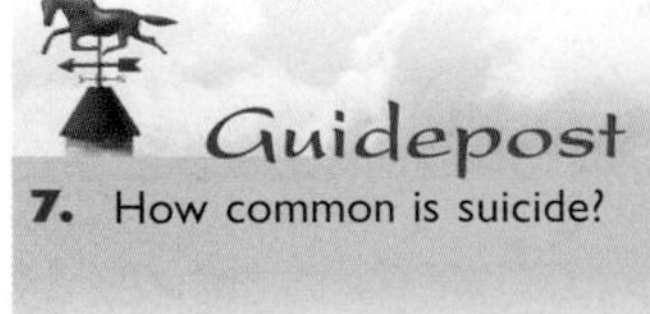

Guidepost

7. How common is suicide?

Suicide

Although suicide is no longer a crime in modern societies, there is still a stigma against it, based in part on religious prohibitions and on society's interest in preserving life. A person who expresses suicidal thoughts may be considered—often with good reason—mentally ill. On the other hand, as longevity increases and, with it, the risk of long-term degenerative illness, a growing number of people consider a mature adult's deliberate choice of a time to end his or her life a rational decision and a right to be defended.

Suicide rates in the United States began declining in the late 1990s after a 25 percent rise from 1981 to 1997 (Sahyoun, Lentzner, et al., 2001). Still, more than 29,000 people took their own lives in 2000, making suicide the eleventh leading cause of death and the third-leading cause among 15- to 24-year-olds (Anderson, 2002; CDC, 2002b; Miniño et al., 2002). The suicide rate in the United States—10.7 deaths per 100,000 population (Miniño et al., 2002)—is lower than that in many other industrialized countries (Kinsella & Velkoff, 2001).

Statistics probably understate the number of suicides, since many go unreported and some (such as traffic "accidents" and "accidental" medicinal overdoses) are not recognized as such. Also, the figures on suicides often do not include suicide *attempts;* an estimated 10 to 40 percent of people who commit suicide have tried before (Meehan, 1990; "Suicide—Part II," 1996). A national study found that 60 percent of nonfatal self-inflicted injuries treated in U.S. hospital emergency rooms, especially among teenage girls and young women, are probable suicide attempts and 10 percent are possible attempts (Ikeda et al., 2002). (Teenage suicide is discussed in more depth in Chapter 11.)

In most nations, suicide rates rise with age and are higher among men than among women (Kinsella & Velkoff, 2001). In the United States, although more women than men attempt suicide, men are four times as likely to succeed. That is because they tend to use more reliable methods, such as firearms, whereas women are equally likely to choose poisoning (CDC, 2002b; NCHS, 2001). Native Americans have the highest suicide rates, followed by non-Hispanic white persons. Members of these two groups are approximately twice as likely to commit suicide as Asian Americans, African Americans, and Hispanic Americans (NCHS, 2001). Suicide rates are higher in the western states and lower in the eastern and midwestern states (CDC, 2002b).

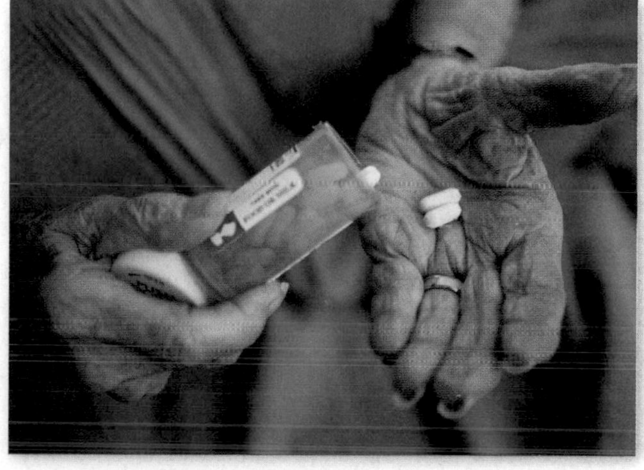

Many "accidental" overdoses of medication are actually suicides. Suicide is a leading cause of death in the United States.

By far the highest rate of suicide is among elderly white men, particularly those 85 and older who are divorced or widowed (CDC, 2002b; NCHS, 1998a; NIMH, 1999b; Sahyoun, Lentzner, et al., 2001). Older people are more likely than younger people to be depressed and socially isolated, and if they try to commit suicide, they are more likely to succeed the first time (CDC, 2002b). Older African Americans are much less likely to commit suicide than older white people, perhaps in part because of religious commitment and in part because they may be accustomed to coping with hard knocks (NCHS, 1998a; NIMH, 1999a).

Although some people intent on suicide carefully conceal their plans, there often are warning signs. These may include withdrawing from family or friends; talking about death, the hereafter, or suicide; giving away prized possessions; abusing drugs or alcohol; and personality changes, such as unusual anger, boredom, or apathy. People who are about to kill themselves may neglect their appearance, stay away from work or other customary activities, complain of physical problems when nothing is organically wrong, or sleep or eat much more or much less than usual. They often show signs of depression, such as unusual difficulty concentrating, loss of self-esteem, and feelings of helplessness, hopelessness, extreme anxiety, or panic. Nine out of ten people who kill themselves have depression or another mental or substance use disorder (NIMH, 1999a).

What's Your View?

- In your opinion, is the intentional ending of one's own life ever justified? Would you ever consider this option? If so, under what circumstances?

Aid in Dying

In Evanston, Illinois, a 70-year-old man visited his 66-year-old wife, who was suffering from cancer and two strokes, in the hospital. Firing through a pillow to muffle the sound, he shot her in the heart to end her pain, then turned the handgun on himself. He left a long note explaining that they had planned their deaths together. "It appears to have been euthanasia," a hospital spokesman said (Wisby, 2001).

Guidepost

8. Why are attitudes toward euthanasia ("mercy killing") and assisted suicide changing, and what concerns do these practices raise?

active euthanasia Deliberate action taken to shorten the life of a terminally ill person in order to end suffering or to allow death with dignity; also called *mercy killing*.

passive euthanasia Deliberate withholding or discontinuation of life-prolonging treatment of a terminally ill person in order to end suffering or allow death with dignity.

assisted suicide Suicide in which a physician or someone else helps a person take his or her own life.

Euthanasia means "good death." This husband's act was an example of **active euthanasia** (sometimes called *mercy killing*), action taken deliberately to shorten a life in order to end suffering or allow a terminally ill person to die with dignity. **Passive euthanasia** is deliberately withholding or discontinuing treatment that might extend the life of a terminally ill patient, such as medication, life-support systems, or feeding tubes. Active euthanasia is generally illegal; passive euthanasia, in some circumstances, is not. An important question regarding either form of euthanasia is whether it is *voluntary;* that is, whether it is done at the direct request, or to carry out the expressed wishes, of the person whose death results.

Assisted suicide—in which a physician or someone else helps a person bring about a self-inflicted death by, for example, prescribing or obtaining drugs or enabling a patient to inhale a deadly gas—is illegal in most places but recently has come to the forefront of public debate. Assisted suicide is similar in principle to voluntary active euthanasia, in which, for example, a patient asks for, and receives, a lethal injection. The main difference is that in assisted suicide the person who wants to die performs the actual deed. All of these are varying forms of what is sometimes called *aid in dying.*

Advance Directives In Louisa May Alcott's time and place, the idea of helping a suffering loved one hasten death was virtually unheard of. Changing attitudes toward aid in dying can be attributed largely to revulsion against technologies that keep patients alive against their will despite intense suffering, and sometimes even after the brain has, for all practical purposes, stopped functioning.

The United States Supreme Court has held that a person whose wishes are clearly known has a constitutional right to refuse or discontinue life-sustaining treatment (*Cruzan v. Director, Missouri Department of Health,* 1990; Gostin, 1997)—in other words, to request passive euthanasia. A mentally competent person's wishes can be spelled out in advance in a document called an **advance directive,** or *living will.* The living will may contain specific provisions with regard to relief of pain, cardiac resuscitation, mechanical respiration, antibiotics, and artificial nutrition and hydration. A person also may specify, through use of a donor card, that his or her organs be donated to someone in need of an organ transplant (see Box 19-2).

advance directive (living will) Document specifying the type of care wanted by the maker in the event of terminal illness.

Some "living will" legislation applies only to terminally ill patients, not to those who are incapacitated by illness or injury but may live many years in severe pain. Nor do advance directives help many patients in comas or in a *persistent vegetative state,* in which, while technically alive, they have no awareness and only rudimentary brain functioning. Such situations can be covered by a **durable power of attorney,** which appoints another person to make decisions if the maker of the document becomes incompetent to do so. A number of states have adopted a simple form known as a *medical durable power of attorney,* expressly for decisions about health care.

durable power of attorney Legal instrument that appoints an individual to make decisions in the event of another person's incapacitation.

Even with advance directives, many people die in pain after protracted, fruitless treatment. Concern about peer review, the press of a perceived medical emergency, or a philosophical commitment to sustaining life may lead physicians and nurses to continue "heroic" measures despite patients' wishes (M. Solomon, 1993).

In a five-year study of some 9,000 critically ill patients at five U.S. teaching hospitals, doctors were frequently unaware of patients' request not to be resuscitated in the event of cardiac arrest (The SUPPORT Principal Investigators, 1995). According to family members of patients who died, one in ten of these patients disagreed with the care they received. Clear doctor-patient communication about preferences and prognoses was uncommon (Lynn et al., 1997).

Such findings have led the American Medical Association to form a Task Force on Quality Care at the End of Life. Many hospitals now have ethics committees that create guidelines, review cases, and help doctors, patients, and their families with decisions about end-of-life care (Simpson, 1996).

Window on the World

BOX 19-2

Organ Donation: The Gift of Life

Snowboarder Chris Klug won a bronze medal in the Men's Parallel Giant Slalom event at the winter Olympics in Salt Lake City in February 2002—just eighteen months after receiving a lifesaving liver transplant.

In 2001, a total of 12,522 persons in the United States donated organs and tissue, such as skin and bone marrow, an increase of 7 percent from the previous year. The increase was largely due to a rise in Hispanic and African American donors and in "living donation"—donation of a kidney or a portion of a liver or lung by a living person. The growing use of living donations is partly due to a shortage of deceased (or brain-dead) donors and partly to medical advances that make donation safer and more likely to succeed (USDHHS, 2002a).

Despite the increasing acceptance of organ donation, there is a worldwide shortage of organs (West & Burr, 2002). In the United States about 16 people die every day—6,000 each year—while waiting for transplants. More than 79,000 are currently on the waiting list. Organs are less likely to be rejected by the body of the recipient if they come from a donor of the same race or ethnicity; and some diseases of the kidney, heart, lung, pancreas, and liver are more common among certain racial and ethnic minorities than among the general population (USDHHS, 2002a).

A major factor is the refusal of families of potential donors to give consent. The decision to be a donor, or to allow a deceased loved one to be a donor, is not always an easy one. When one man collapsed and died of a brain aneurysm, his 16-year-old daughter initially opposed the idea but changed her mind when she thought about the possibility that another girl's father might be helped. Ultimately five people received transplants and a chance for life as a result of that one man's death (USDHHS, 2002a).

Among the factors influencing denial of consent are misunderstanding of brain death, the timing and setting of the request, and the approach of the person making the request. Cultural attitudes also play a part (West & Burr, 2002). For example, the waiting list for African Americans is about twice as long as for other ethnic groups. Among African American women in the rural south, objections to donation seem related to religious beliefs and kinship ties (Wittig, 2001). In the United Kingdom, where the shortage of organs is particularly acute among Asian immigrants, Asians in the Glasgow, Scotland, region were generally unsympathetic to organ transplantation, especially after death, even when they understood the issues (Baines, Joseph, & Jindal, 2002). In India, most of the transplants that are done come from living donors—again, because of moral, religious, and emotional constraints against donating organs of a brain-dead person (Chandra & Singh, 2001).

Culturally sensitive education may make a difference. An educational program among American Indian communities in the southwestern United States showed the need to change not only the attitudes of potential donors but also the stereotypes about Native Americans commonly held by health care providers who ask for the donations (Thomas, 2002). Interviews with Japanese, Korean, and Indian immigrants to the United States found vastly different views, not only about organ donation, but about broader aspects of the medical experience, such as when to seek such assistance, the roles of doctors and nurses, how to talk with medical specialists, issues of privacy and disclosure, and end-of-life care (Andresen, 2001).

The National Organ Transplant Act regulates the procurement, distribution, and transplantation of scarce organs in the United States. Any healthy person of any age can be an organ donor—even a newborn baby. Donors under age 18 need parental consent. Adults who wish to be donors after death can express that wish by so indicating on their driver's licenses, filling out and carrying an organ donor card, and informing their families, who may need to sign a consent form at the time of donation. The family does not pay the cost; it is paid by the recipient, usually through insurance or Medicare. Sale of human organs and tissues is illegal (USDHHS, 2002a).

What's Your View?

Would you donate an organ to a friend or family member who needed it? To a stranger? Upon your death? Why or why not?

Check It Out:

OLC

For more information on this topic, go to http://www.mhhe.com/papaliah9, where you will find links to facts and statistics about organ donation.

Attitudes Toward Euthanasia and Assisted Suicide Some ethicists advocate legalizing all forms of voluntary euthanasia and assisted suicide, with safeguards against involuntary euthanasia. They argue that the key issue is not how death occurs but who makes the decision; that there is no difference in principle between pulling the plug on a respirator and giving a lethal injection or prescribing an overdose of pills; and that a mentally competent person should have the right to control his or her own life and death. They maintain that aid in dying, if openly available, would reduce fear and helplessness by enabling patients to control their fate (Brock, 1992; R. A. Epstein, 1989; Orentlicher, 1996).

Opponents maintain a distinction between passive euthanasia, in which nature is allowed to take its course, and directly causing a death. They contend that physician-assisted suicide would inevitably lead to voluntary active euthanasia, since self-administered pills do not always work (Groenewoud et al., 2000). The next step on the "slippery slope," they warn, would be involuntary euthanasia, especially for patients unable to express their wishes. They claim that people who want to die are often temporarily depressed and might change their minds with treatment or palliative care (Butler, 1996; Hendin, 1994; Latimer, 1992; Quill, Lo, & Brock, 1997; Simpson, 1996; Singer, 1988; Singer & Siegler, 1990).

In the United States, assisted suicide is illegal in almost all states. However, such activity often goes on covertly, without regulation. The American Medical Association opposes physician aid in dying as contrary to a practitioner's oath to "do no harm." But doctors can give drugs that may shorten a life if the purpose is to relieve pain (Gostin, 1997; Quill et al., 1997).

With national polls among laypeople favoring aid in dying by as much as three to one, some physicians are acceding to patients' requests for it (Castaneda, 1996; Lee et al., 1996; Quill, 1991; "Suicide—Part II," 1996; Taylor, 1995). A nationwide survey of 1,902 physicians whose specialties involve care of dying patients found that, of those who had received requests for help with suicide (18 percent) or lethal injections (11 percent), about 7 percent had complied at least once (Meier et al., 1998). In a poll of 352 doctors, nearly three out of four said they should be allowed to help terminally ill patients die with dignity; 37 percent approved of providing the means for suicide, and nearly 13 percent said they would administer a lethal medication (Larson, 1995–1996). In a survey in the United Kingdom, 80 percent of geriatric physicians—but only 52 percent of intensive care physicians—considered active voluntary euthanasia to be *never* ethically justified (Dickinson, Lancaster, Clark, Ahmedzai, & Noble, 2002).

Efforts to Legalize Physician Aid in Dying In September 1996, a 66-year-old Australian man with advanced prostate cancer was the first person to die legally by assisted suicide. Under a law passed in the Northern Territory, he pressed a computer key that administered a lethal dose of barbiturates. In 1997 the law was repealed ("Australian Man," 1996; Voluntary Euthanasia Society, 2002).

Since 1997, when a unanimous U.S. Supreme Court left regulation of physician aid in dying up to the states, measures to legalize assisted suicide for the terminally ill have been introduced in several states. So far Oregon is the only state to pass such a law. In 1994, Oregonians voted to let mentally competent patients who have been told by two doctors that they have less than six months to live request a lethal prescription, with strong safeguards to make sure that the request is serious and voluntary and that all other alternatives have been considered. The Oregon Death with Dignity Act survived a court challenge and a repeal referendum in 1997; and in 2002 a federal district court overruled U.S. Attorney General John Ashcroft's attempt to countermand it. The case may well end up in the Supreme Court.

What has been the experience under the Oregon law? In its first two years of operation, only 43 terminally ill patients were reported to state health officials to have taken their lives under the act (Sullivan, Hedberg, & Fleming, 2000). Physicians reported granting about one-sixth of the 221 requests for lethal prescriptions, but nearly half of these patients changed their minds and did not take the medications. Patients who received palliative interventions, such as control of pain or referral to a hospice program, were more likely to change their minds (Ganzini et al., 2000). Patients who requested and used lethal prescriptions tended to be more concerned about loss of autonomy or control of bodily functions than about fear of pain or financial loss (Chin, Hedberg, Higginson, & Fleming, 1999; Sullivan et al., 2000).

Active euthanasia remains far more controversial in the United States and is not permitted even in Oregon. In the Netherlands, both assisted suicide and active euthanasia have been technically illegal, but during the past thirty years physicians who engaged in them could avoid prosecution under strict conditions (Simons, 1993). Now the Dutch parliament has voted to legalize euthanasia for patients in a state of continuous, unbearable, and incurable suffering (Johnston, 2001; Osborn, 2002). Belgium followed suit ("Belgium Legalises Euthanasia," 2002). In 1995, 2.5 percent of deaths in the Netherlands resulted from euthanasia or assisted suicide (Van der Maas et al., 1996).

What's Your View?

- Do you think assisted suicide should be legalized? If so, who should be permitted to participate—physicians only, or others as well? What safeguards should be provided? Would your answers be the same or different for voluntary active euthanasia? Do you see an ethical distinction between euthanasia and terminal sedation?

End-of-Life Options One salutary result of the aid-in-dying controversy has been to call attention to the need for better palliative care and closer attention to patients' motivation and state of mind. A request for aid in dying can provide an opening to explore the reasons behind it. When doctors talk openly with patients about their physical and mental symptoms, their expectations, their fears and goals, their options for end-of-life care, their family concerns, and their need for meaning and quality of life, ways may be found to diminish these concerns without physician-assisted suicide (Bascom & Tolle, 2002). Sometimes a psychiatric consultation may discover an underlying disturbance masked by a seemingly rational request (Muskin, 1998). In terminally ill patients, the will to live can fluctuate greatly, so it is essential to ensure that such a request is not just a passing one (Chochinov, Tataryn, Clinch, & Dudgeon, 1999). If lethal measures *are* taken, it is important that a physician be present to ensure that the death is as merciful and pain-free as possible (Nuland, 2000).

The issue of aid in dying will become more pressing as the population ages. Much of the debate turns on whether it is possible to write laws permitting some forms of aid with adequate protections against abuse (Baron et al., 1996; Callahan & White, 1996). In years to come, both the courts and the public will be forced to come to terms with that question, as increasing numbers of people claim a right to die with dignity and with help.

Checkpoint

Can you . . .

- ✔ Explain why suicides are sometimes not recognized, and list some warning signs?
- ✔ Discuss the ethical, practical, and legal issues involved in advance directives, euthanasia, and assisted suicide?

Finding Meaning and Purpose in Life and Death

The central character in Leo Tolstoy's "The Death of Ivan Ilyich" is wracked by a fatal illness. Even greater than his physical suffering is his mental torment. He asks himself over and over what meaning there is to his agony, and he becomes convinced that his life has been without purpose and his death will be equally pointless. At the last minute, though, he experiences a spiritual revelation, a concern for his wife and son, which gives him a final moment of integrity and enables him to conquer his terror.

Guidepost

9. How can people overcome fear of dying and come to terms with death?

What Tolstoy dramatized in literature is being confirmed by research. In one study of 39 women whose average age was 76, those who saw the most purpose in life had the least fear of death (Durlak, 1973). Conversely, according to Kübler-Ross (1975), facing the reality of death is a key to living a meaningful life:

> It is the denial of death that is partially responsible for [people's] living empty, purposeless lives; for when you live as if you'll live forever, it becomes too easy to postpone the things you know that you must do. In contrast, when you fully understand that each day you awaken could be the last you have, you take the time that day to grow, to become more of who you really are, to reach out to other human beings. (p. 164)

Reviewing a Life

In Charles Dickens's *A Christmas Carol,* Scrooge changes his greedy, heartless ways after seeing ghostly visions of his past, his present, and his future death. In Akira Kurosawa's film *Ikiru* (*To Live*), a petty bureaucrat who discovers that he is dying of cancer looks back over the emptiness of his life and, in a final burst of energy, creates a meaningful legacy by pushing through a project for a children's park, which he has previously blocked. These fictional characters make their remaining time more purposeful through **life review,** a process of reminiscence that enables a person to see the significance of his or her life.

life review Reminiscence about one's life in order to see its significance.

Life review can, of course, occur at any time. However, it may have special meaning in old age, when it can foster ego integrity—according to Erikson, the final critical task of the life span. As the end of their journey approaches, people may look back over their accomplishments and failures and ask themselves what their lives have meant. Awareness of mortality may be an impetus for reexamining values and seeing one's experiences and actions in a new light. Some people find the will to complete unfinished tasks, such as reconciling with estranged family members or friends, and thus to achieve a satisfying sense of closure.

Sharing memories evoked by a family photo album is one way to review a life. Life review can help people see important events in a new light and can motivate them to seek a sense of closure by rebuilding damaged relationships or completing unfinished tasks.

Not all memories are equally conducive to mental health and growth. Older people who use reminiscence for self-understanding show the strongest ego integrity, while those who entertain only pleasurable memories show less. Most poorly adjusted are those who keep recalling negative events and are obsessed with regret, hopelessness, and fear of death; their ego integrity has given way to despair (Sherman, 1993; Walasky, Whitbourne, & Nehrke, 1983–1984).

Life-review therapy can help focus the natural process of life review and make it more conscious, purposeful, and efficient (Butler, 1961; M. I. Lewis & Butler, 1974). Methods often used for uncovering memories in life-review therapy (which also may be used by individuals on their own) include writing or taping one's autobiography; constructing a family tree; talking about scrapbooks, photo albums, old letters, and other memorabilia; making a trip back to scenes of childhood and young adulthood; reunions with former classmates or colleagues or distant family members; describing ethnic traditions; and summing up one's life's work.

Checkpoint

Can you . . .

- ✔ Explain why life review can be especially helpful in old age and how it can help overcome fear of death?
- ✔ Tell what types of memories are most conducive to a life review?
- ✔ List several activities used in life-review therapy?
- ✔ Tell how dying can be a developmental experience?

Development: A Lifelong Process

In his late seventies, the artist Pierre-Auguste Renoir had crippling arthritis and chronic bronchitis and had lost his wife. He spent his days in a wheelchair, and his pain was so great that he could not sleep through the night. He was unable to hold a palette or grip a brush: his brush had to be tied to his right hand. Yet he continued to produce brilliant paintings, full of color and vibrant life. Finally, stricken by pneumonia, he lay in bed, gazing at some anemones his attendant had picked. He gathered enough strength to sketch the form of these beautiful flowers, and then—just before he died—lay back and whispered, "I think I am beginning to understand something about it" (L. Hanson, 1968).

Even dying can be a developmental experience. As one health practitioner put it, ". . . there are things to be gained, accomplished in dying. Time with and for those whom we are close to, achieving a final and enduring sense of self-worth, and a readiness to let go are priceless elements of a good death" (Weinberger, 1999)—the kind of death Louisa May Alcott described in *Little Women.*

Refocus

- How does Louisa May Alcott's description of the process of her sister Lizzie's ("Beth's") dying illustrate attitudes and customs of her time and place?
- Did Beth seem to follow Kübler-Ross's stages of dying?
- How did her family deal with their grief?
- How did Beth and her family find meaning in her last months and days?

Within a limited life span, no person can realize all capabilities, gratify all desires, explore all interests, or experience all the richness that life has to offer. The tension between possibilities for growth and a finite time in which to do the growing defines human life. By choosing which possibilities to pursue and by continuing to follow them as far as possible, even up to the very end, each person contributes to the unfinished story of human development.

SUMMARY AND KEY TERMS

The Many Faces of Death

- Death has biological, social, cultural, historical, religious, legal, psychological, developmental, and ethical aspects.

Guidepost 1. How do attitudes and customs concerning death differ across cultures?

- Customs surrounding death and mourning vary greatly from one culture to another, depending on the society's view of the nature and consequences of death. Some modern customs have evolved from ancient beliefs and practices.

Guidepost 2. What are the implications of the "mortality revolution," and how does it affect care of the dying?

- Death rates dropped drastically during the twentieth century, especially in developed countries.
- Today three-quarters of deaths in the United States occur among the elderly, and the top causes of death are diseases that primarily affect older adults.
- As death became primarily a phenomenon of late adulthood, it became largely "invisible," and care of the dying took place in isolation, by professionals.
- There is now an upsurge of interest in understanding and dealing realistically and compassionately with death. Examples of this tendency are a growing interest in thanatology and increasing emphasis on hospice care and palliative care.

thanatology *(687)*

hospice care *(687)*

palliative care *(687)*

Facing Death and Loss: Psychological Issues

Guidepost 3. How do people change as they confront their own death?

- People often undergo cognitive and functional declines shortly before death.
- Some people who come close to dying have "near-death" experiences.
- Elisabeth Kübler-Ross proposed five stages in coming to terms with dying: denial, anger, bargaining, depression, and acceptance. These stages, and their sequence, are not universal.

Guidepost 4. Is there a normal pattern of grieving?

- There is no universal pattern of grief.
- The most widely studied pattern of grief work moves from shock and disbelief to preoccupation with the memory of the dead person and finally to resolution. Research has found several variations, including high to low distress, no intense distress, and prolonged distress.

- For some people who have great difficulty adjusting to a loss, grief therapy may be indicated.

bereavement *(690)*

grief *(690)*

grief work *(690)*

grief therapy *(691)*

Death and Bereavement Across the Life Span

Guidepost 5. How do attitudes and understandings about death and bereavement differ across the life span?

- Before ages 5 to 7, children do not understand that death is irreversible, universal, inevitable, and nonfunctional. Young children can better understand death if it is part of their own experience. Although children experience grief, as adults do, there are age-related reactions based on cognitive and emotional development.
- Although adolescents generally do not think much about death, violence and the threat of death are part of some adolescents' daily life. Adolescents tend to take needless risks.
- Realization and acceptance of the inevitability of death increases throughout adulthood.

Special Losses

Guidepost 6. What special challenges are involved in surviving a spouse, a parent, or a child, or in mourning a miscarriage?

- Women are more likely to be widowed, and widowed younger, than men, and may experience widowhood somewhat differently. Coping skills are more important than age in determining how widowed persons adjust. For some people, widowhood can ultimately become a positive developmental experience.
- Today, loss of parents often occurs in middle age. Death of a parent can precipitate changes in the self and in relationships with others.
- The loss of a child can be especially difficult because it is no longer normative. Often such a loss weakens or destroys the parents' marriage.
- Miscarriage is not generally considered a significant loss in U.S. society. People are left to deal with a miscarriage in their own way.

Medical, Legal, and Ethical Issues: The "Right to Die"

Guidepost 7. How common is suicide?

- Although suicide is no longer illegal in modern societies, there is still a stigma attached to it. Some people maintain a "right to die," especially for people with long-term degenerative illness.
- Suicide is the eleventh leading cause of death in the United States, lower than in many other countries. The number of suicides is probably underestimated.
- Suicide rates tend to rise with age and are more common among men than among women, though women are more likely to attempt suicide. The highest rate of suicide in the United States is among elderly white men. It is often related to depression, isolation, and debilitating ailments.

Guidepost 8. Why are attitudes toward euthanasia ("mercy killing") and assisted suicide changing, and what concerns do these practices raise?

- Euthanasia and assisted suicide involve controversial issues concerning the "right to die," protection from abuse, and medical ethics.
- To avoid unnecessary suffering through artificial prolongation of life, passive euthanasia is generally permitted with the patient's consent or with advance directives. However, such directives are not consistently followed. Most hospitals now have ethics committees to deal with decisions about end-of-life care.
- Active euthanasia and assisted suicide are generally illegal, but public support for physician aid in dying has increased. The state of Oregon has a law permitting physician-assisted suicide for the terminally ill. The Netherlands and Belgium have legalized both euthanasia and assisted suicide.
- The aid-in-dying controversy has focused more attention on the need for better palliative care and understanding of patients' state of mind.

active euthanasia *(700)*

passive euthanasia *(700)*

assisted suicide *(700)*

advance directive (living will) *(700)*

durable power of attorney *(700)*

Finding Meaning and Purpose in Life and Death

Guidepost 9. How can people overcome fear of dying and come to terms with death?

- The more meaning and purpose people find in their lives, the less they tend to fear death.
- Life review can help people prepare for death and give them a last chance to complete unfinished tasks.
- Even dying can be a developmental experience.

life review *(704)*

Glossary

A, not-B error Tendency for 8- to 12-month-old infants to search for a hidden object in a place where they previously found it, rather than in the place where they most recently saw it being hidden.

acceleration Approach to educating the gifted, which moves them through the curriculum at an unusually rapid pace.

accommodation Piaget's term for changes in a cognitive structure to include new information.

achieving stage Second of Schaie's seven cognitive stages, in which young adults use knowledge to gain competence and independence.

acquired immune deficiency syndrome (AIDS) Viral disease that undermines effective functioning of the immune system.

acquisitive stage First of Schaie's seven cognitive stages, in which children and adolescents learn information and skills largely for their own sake or as preparation for participation in society.

active engagement Involvement in schooling.

active euthanasia Deliberate action taken to shorten the life of a terminally ill person in order to end suffering or to allow death with dignity; also called *mercy killing*.

activity theory Theory of aging, proposed by Neugarten and others, which holds that in order to age successfully a person must remain as active as possible.

acute medical conditions Illnesses that last a short time.

adaptation Piaget's term for adjustment to new information about the environment.

adaptive mechanisms Vaillant's term to describe four characteristic ways people adapt to life circumstances: mature, immature, psychotic, and neurotic.

adolescent growth spurt Sharp increase in height and weight that precedes sexual maturity.

adolescent rebellion Pattern of emotional turmoil, characteristic of a minority of adolescents, which may involve conflict with family, alienation from adult society, reckless behavior, and rejection of adult values.

advance directive (living will) Document specifying the type of care wanted by the maker in the event of terminal illness.

age-differentiated Life structure in which primary roles—learning, working, and leisure—are based on age; typical in industrialized societies.

age-integrated Life structure in which primary roles—learning, working, and leisure—are open to adults of all ages and can be interspersed throughout the life span.

ageism Prejudice or discrimination against a person (most commonly an older person) based on age.

age-related macular degeneration Condition in which the center of the retina gradually loses its ability to discern fine details; leading cause of irreversible visual impairment in older adults.

alcoholism Chronic disease involving dependence on use of alcohol, causing interference with normal functioning and fulfillment of obligations.

alleles Paired genes (alike or different) that affect a trait.

allocentric In Piaget's terminology, able to objectively consider relationships among objects or people.

altruism Behavior intended to help others out of inner concern and without expectation of external reward; may involve self-denial or self-sacrifice.

Alzheimer's disease Progressive, irreversible degenerative brain disorder characterized by cognitive deterioration and loss of control of bodily functions, leading to death.

ambiguous loss A loss that is not clearly defined or does not bring closure.

ambivalent (resistant) attachment Pattern in which an infant becomes anxious before the primary caregiver leaves, is extremely upset during his or her absence, and both seeks and resists contact on his or her return.

amyloid plaque Waxy chunks of insoluble tissue found in brains of persons with Alzheimer's disease.

animism Tendency to attribute life to objects that are not alive.

anorexia nervosa Eating disorder characterized by self-starvation.

art therapy Therapeutic approach that allows a child to express troubled feelings without words, using a variety of art materials and media.

arthritis Group of disorders affecting the joints, causing pain and loss of movement.

assimilation Piaget's term for incorporation of new information into an existing cognitive structure.

assisted suicide Suicide in which a physician or someone else helps a person take his or her own life.

asthma A chronic respiratory disease characterized by sudden attacks of coughing, wheezing, and difficulty in breathing.

attachment Reciprocal, enduring tie between infant and caregiver, each of whom contributes to the quality of the relationship.

attention-deficit/hyperactivity disorder (ADHD) Syndrome characterized by persistent inattention and distractibility, impulsivity, low tolerance for frustration, and inappropriate overactivity.

authoritarian In Baumrind's terminology, parenting style emphasizing control and obedience.

authoritative In Baumrind's terminology, parenting style blending respect for a child's individuality with an effort to instill social values.

autism Pervasive developmental disorder of the brain, characterized by lack of normal social interaction, impaired communication and imagination, and a highly restricted range of abilities and interests.

autobiographical memory Memory of specific events in one's own life.

autoimmunity Tendency of an aging body to mistake its own tissues for foreign invaders and to attack and destroy them.

autonomy versus shame and doubt Erikson's second stage in psychosocial development, in which children achieve a balance between self-determination and control by others.

autosomes The 22 pairs of chromosomes not related to sexual expression.

avoidant attachment Pattern in which an infant rarely cries when separated from the primary caregiver and avoids contact upon his or her return.

balanced investment Pattern of retirement activity allocated among family, work, and leisure.

basal metabolism Use of energy to maintain vital functions.

basic trust versus basic mistrust Erikson's first stage in psychosocial development, in which infants develop a sense of the reliability of people and objects.

Bayley Scales of Infant Development Standardized test of infants' mental, motor, and behavioral development.

behavior therapy Therapeutic approach using principles of learning theory to encourage desired behaviors or eliminate undesired ones; also called behavior modification.

behavioral genetics Quantitative study of relative hereditary and environmental influences.

behaviorism Learning theory that emphasizes the predictable role of environment in causing observable behavior.

behaviorist approach Approach to the study of cognitive development that is concerned with basic mechanics of learning.

bereavement Loss, due to death, of someone to whom one feels close and the process of adjustment to the loss.

bilingual Fluent in two languages.

bilingual education System of teaching non-English-speaking children in their native language while they learn English, and later switching to all-English instruction.

bioecological theory Bronfenbrenner's approach to understanding processes and contexts of development.

body image Descriptive and evaluative beliefs about one's appearance.

bulimia nervosa Eating disorder in which a person regularly eats huge quantities of food and then purges the body by laxatives, induced vomiting, fasting, or excessive exercise.

bullying Aggression deliberately and persistently directed against a particular target, or victim, typically one who is weak, vulnerable, and defenseless.

burnout Syndrome of emotional exhaustion and a sense that one can no longer accomplish anything on the job.

canalization Limitation on variance of expression of certain inherited characteristics.

caregiver burnout Condition of physical, mental, and emotional exhaustion affecting adults who care for aged persons.

case study Study of an individual.

cataracts Cloudy or opaque areas in the lens of the eye, which cause blurred vision.

central executive In Baddeley's model, element of working memory that controls the processing of information.

centration In Piaget's theory, tendency of preoperational children to focus on one aspect of a situation and neglect others.

cephalocaudal principle Principle that development proceeds in a head-to-tail direction; that is, that upper parts of the body develop before lower parts.

child-directed speech (CDS) Form of speech often used in talking to babies or toddlers; includes slow, simplified speech, a high-pitched tone, exaggerated vowel sounds, short words and sentences, and much repetition. Also called *parentese.*

childhood depression Mood disorder characterized by such symptoms as a prolonged sense of friendlessness, inability to have fun or concentrate, fatigue, extreme activity or apathy, feelings of worthlessness, weight change, physical complaints, and thoughts of death or suicide.

chromosomes Coils of DNA that carry the genes.

chronic medical conditions Illnesses or impairments that persist for at least three months.

chronosystem Bronfenbrenner's term for effects of time on other developmental systems.

circular reactions Piaget's term for processes by which an infant learns to reproduce desired occurrences originally discovered by chance.

class inclusion Understanding of the relationship between a whole and its parts.

classical conditioning Learning based on association of a stimulus that does not ordinarily elicit a response with another stimulus that does elicit the response.

clone (verb) To make a genetic copy of an individual; (noun) a genetic copy of an individual.

code mixing Use of elements of two languages, sometimes in the same utterance, by young children in households where both languages are spoken.

code switching Changing one's speech to match the situation, as in people who are bilingual.

cognitive development Change or stability in mental abilities, such as learning, attention, memory, language, thinking, reasoning, and creativity.

cognitive neuroscience approach Approach to the study of cognitive development that links brain processes with cognitive ones.

cognitive perspective View that thought processes are central to development.

cognitive-appraisal model Model of coping, proposed by Lazarus and Folkman, which holds that, on the basis of continuous appraisal of their relationship with the environment, people choose appropriate coping strategies to deal with situations that tax their normal resources.

cohabitation Status of an unmarried couple who live together and maintain a sexual relationship.

cohort Group of people growing up at about the same time.

coming out Process of openly disclosing one's homosexual orientation.

commitment Marcia's term for personal investment in an occupation or system of beliefs.

committed compliance Kochanska's term for wholehearted obedience of a parent's orders without reminders or lapses.

componential element Sternberg's term for the analytic aspect of intelligence.

concordant Term describing twins who share the same trait or disorder.

concrete operations Third stage of Piagetian cognitive development (approximately from ages 7 to 12), during which children develop logical but not abstract thinking.

conduct disorder (CD) Repetitive, persistent pattern of aggressive, antisocial behavior violating societal norms or the rights of others.

conscience Internal standards of behavior, which usually control one's conduct and produce emotional discomfort when violated.

conservation Piaget's term for awareness that two objects that are equal according to a certain measure remain equal in the face of perceptual alteration so long as nothing has been added to or taken away from either object.

constructive play Play involving use of objects or materials to make something.

contextual element Sternberg's term for the practical aspect of intelligence.

contextual perspective View of development that sees the individual as inseparable from the social context.

continuity theory Theory of aging, described by Atchley, which holds that in order to age successfully people must maintain a balance of continuity and change in both the internal and external structures of their lives.

control group In an experiment, a group of people, similar to those in the experimental group, who do not receive the treatment whose effects are to be measured.

conventional morality Second level of Kohlberg's theory of moral reasoning, in which standards of authority figures are internalized.

convergent thinking Thinking aimed at finding the one right answer to a problem.

coping Adaptive thinking or behavior aimed at reducing or relieving stress that arises from harmful, threatening, or challenging conditions.

coregulation Transitional stage in the control of behavior in which parents exercise general supervision and children exercise moment-to-moment self-regulation.

corporal punishment Use of physical force with the intention of causing pain, but not injury, to correct or control behavior.

correlational study Research design intended to discover whether a statistical relationship between variables exists.

creativity Ability to see situations in a new way, to produce innovations, or to discern previously unidentified problems and find novel solutions.

crisis Marcia's term for a period of conscious decision making related to identity formation.

critical period Specific time when a given event, or its absence, has a specific impact on development.

cross-modal transfer Ability to use information gained by one sense to guide another.

cross-sectional study Study design in which people of different ages are assessed on one occasion.

crystallized intelligence Type of intelligence, proposed by Horn and Cattell, involving the ability to remember and use learned information; it is largely dependent on education and cultural background.

cultural bias Tendency of intelligence tests to include items calling for knowledge or skills more familiar or meaningful to some cultural groups than to others.

culture A society's or group's total way of life, including customs, traditions, beliefs, values, language, and physical products—all learned behavior passed on from parents to children.

culture-fair Describing an intelligence test that deals with experiences common to various cultures, in an attempt to avoid cultural bias.

culture-free Describing an intelligence test that, if it were possible to design, would have no culturally linked content.

decenter In Piaget's terminology, to think simultaneously about several aspects of a situation.

deductive reasoning Type of logical reasoning that moves from a general premise about a class to a conclusion about a particular member or members of the class.

deferred imitation Piaget's term for reproduction of an observed behavior after the passage of time.

dementia Deterioration in cognitive and behavioral functioning due to physiological causes.

deoxyribonucleic acid (DNA) Chemical that carries inherited instructions for the formation and function of body cells.

dependent variable In an experiment, the condition that may or may not change as a result of changes in the independent variable.

developmental priming mechanisms Aspects of the home environment that seem necessary for normal cognitive and psychosocial development.

"difficult" children Children with irritable temperament, irregular biological rhythms, and intense emotional responses.

discipline Methods of molding children's character and of teaching them to exercise self-control and engage in acceptable behavior.

disengagement theory Theory of aging, proposed by Cumming and Henry, which holds that successful aging is characterized by mutual withdrawal between the older person and society.

dishabituation Increase in responsiveness after presentation of a new stimulus.

disorganized-disoriented attachment Pattern in which an infant, after separation from the primary caregiver, shows contradictory behaviors upon his or her return.

divergent thinking Thinking that produces a variety of fresh, diverse possibilities.

dizygotic (two-egg) twins Twins conceived by the union of two different ova (or a single ovum that has split) with two sperm cells; also called *fraternal twins.*

dominant inheritance Pattern of inheritance in which, when a child receives contradictory alleles, only the dominant one is expressed.

Down syndrome Chromosomal disorder characterized by moderate-to-severe mental retardation and by such physical signs as a downward-sloping skin fold at the inner corners of the eyes.

drug therapy Administration of drugs to treat emotional disorders.

dual representation hypothesis Proposal that children under the age of 3 have difficulty grasping spatial relationships because of the need to keep more than one mental representation in mind at the same time.

dual-process model Model of cognitive functioning, proposed by Baltes, which identifies and seeks to measure two dimensions of intelligence: mechanics and pragmatics.

durable power of attorney Legal instrument that appoints an individual to make decisions in the event of another person's incapacitation.

dyslexia Developmental disorder in which reading achievement is substantially lower than predicted by IQ or age.

early intervention Systematic process of providing services to help families meet young children's developmental needs.

"easy" children Children with a generally happy temperament, regular biological rhythms, and readiness to accept new experiences.

ego integrity versus despair According to Erikson, the eighth and final stage of psychosocial development, in which people in late adulthood either achieve a sense of integrity of the self by accepting the lives they have lived, and thus accept death, or yield to despair that their lives cannot be relived.

egocentric In Piaget's terminology, unable to consider any point of view other than one's own; a characteristic of young children's thought.

egocentrism Piaget's term for inability to consider another person's point of view.

ego-control Self-control.

ego-resiliency Adaptability under potential sources of stress.

elaboration Mnemonic strategy of making mental associations involving items to be remembered.

elder abuse Maltreatment or neglect of dependent older persons, or violation of their personal rights.

embryonic stage Second stage of gestation (2 to 8 weeks), characterized by rapid growth and development of major body systems and organs.

emergent literacy Preschoolers' development of skills, knowledge, and attitudes that underlie reading and writing.

emotional intelligence Salovey and Mayer's term for ability to understand and regulate emotions; an important component of effective, intelligent behavior.

emotional maltreatment Action or inaction that may cause behavioral, cognitive, emotional, or mental disorders.

emotion-focused coping In the cognitive-appraisal model, coping strategy directed toward managing the emotional response to a stressful situation so as to lessen its physical or psychological impact; sometimes called *palliative coping.*

emotions Subjective reactions to experience that are associated with physiological and behavioral changes.

empathy Ability to put oneself in another person's place and feel what the other person feels.

empty nest Transitional phase of parenting following the last child's leaving the parents' home.

encapsulation In Hoyer's terminology, progressive dedication of information processing and fluid thinking to specific knowledge systems, making knowledge more readily accessible.

encoding Process by which information is prepared for long-term storage and later retrieval.

engagement hypothesis Proposal that an active, engaged lifestyle that challenges cognitive skills predicts retention or growth of those skills in later life.

English-immersion Approach to teaching English as a second language in which instruction is presented only in English.

enrichment Approach to educating the gifted, which broadens and deepens knowledge and skills through extra activities, projects, field trips, or mentoring.

enuresis Repeated urination in clothing or in bed.

environment Totality of nonhereditary, or experiential, influences on development.

episodic memory Long-term memory of specific experiences or events, linked to time and place.

equilibration Piaget's term for the tendency to seek a stable balance among cognitive elements.

erectile dysfunction Inability of a man to achieve or maintain an erect penis sufficient for satisfactory sexual performance.

ethnic group Group united by ancestry, race, religion, language, and/or national origins, which contribute to a sense of shared identity.

ethnographic study In-depth study of a culture, which uses a combination of methods including participant observation.

ethology Study of distinctive adaptive behaviors of species of animals that have evolved to increase survival of the species.

evolutionary psychology Application of Darwinian principles of natural selection and survival of the fittest to individual behavior.

executive stage Fourth of Schaie's seven cognitive stages, in which middle-aged people responsible for societal systems deal with complex relationships on several levels.

exosystem Bronfenbrenner's term for linkages between two or more settings, one of which does not contain the child.

experiential element Sternberg's term for the insightful or creative aspect of intelligence.

experiment Rigorously controlled, replicable procedure in which the researcher manipulates variables to assess the effect of one on the other.

experimental group In an experiment, the group receiving the treatment under study.

explicit memory Intentional and conscious memory, generally of facts, names, and events.

extended family Kinship network of parents, children, and other relatives, sometimes living together in an extended-family household.

external memory aids Mnemonic strategies using something outside the person.

family therapy Psychological treatment in which a therapist sees the whole family together to analyze patterns of family functioning.

family-focused lifestyle Pattern of retirement activity that revolves around family, home, and companions.

fast mapping Process by which a child absorbs the meaning of a new word after hearing it once or twice in conversation.

fertilization Union of sperm and ovum fuse to produce a zygote; also called *conception.*

fetal alcohol syndrome (FAS) Combination of mental, motor, and developmental abnormalities affecting the offspring of some women who drink heavily during pregnancy.

fetal stage Final stage of gestation (from 8 weeks to birth), characterized by increased detail of body parts and greatly enlarged body size.

filial crisis In Marcoen's terminology, normative development of middle age, in which adults learn to balance love and duty to their parents with autonomy within a two-way relationship.

filial maturity Stage of life, proposed by Marcoen and others, in which middle-aged children, as the outcome of a filial crisis, learn to accept and meet their parents' need to depend on them.

fine motor skills Physical skills that involve the small muscles and eye-hand coordination.

five-factor model Theoretical model, developed and tested by Costa and McCrae, based on the "Big Five" factors underlying clusters of related personality traits: neuroticism, extraversion, openness to experience, conscientiousness, and agreeableness.

fluid intelligence Type of intelligence, proposed by Horn and Cattell, which is applied to novel problems and is relatively independent of educational and cultural influences.

foreclosure Identity status, described by Marcia, in which a person who has not spent time considering alternatives (that is, has not been in crisis) is committed to other people's plans for his or her life.

formal operations Piaget's final stage of cognitive development, characterized by the ability to think abstractly.

free radicals Unstable, highly reactive atoms or molecules, formed during metabolism, which can cause internal bodily damage.

functional age Measure of a person's ability to function effectively in his or her physical and social environment in comparison with others of the same chronological age.

functional play Play involving repetitive muscular movements.

gateway drugs Drugs such as alcohol, tobacco, and marijuana, the use of which may lead to use of more addictive drugs.

gender Significance of being male or female.

gender constancy Awareness that one will always be male or female. Also called *sex-category constancy.*

gender crossover Gutmann's term for reversal of gender roles after the end of active parenting.

gender identity Awareness, developed in early childhood, that one is male or female.

gender roles Behaviors, interests, attitudes, skills, and traits that a culture considers appropriate for males or for females.

gender stereotypes Preconceived generalizations about male or female role behavior.

gender-schema theory Theory, proposed by Bem, that children socialize themselves in their gender roles by developing a mentally organized network of information about what it means to be male or female in a particular culture.

gender-typing Socialization process by which children, at an early age, learn appropriate gender roles.

generalized anxiety disorder Anxiety not focused on any single target.

generativity versus stagnation Erikson's seventh stage of psychosocial development, in which the middle-aged adult develops a concern with establishing, guiding, and influencing the next generation or else experiences stagnation (a sense of inactivity or lifelessness).

generativity In Erikson's terminology, concern of mature adults for establishing, guiding, and influencing the next generation.

generic memory Memory that produces scripts of familiar routines to guide behavior.

genes Small segments of DNA located in definite positions on particular chromosomes.

genetic code Sequence of base pairs within DNA, which determine inherited characteristics.

genetic counseling Clinical service that advises couples of their probable risk of having children with hereditary defects.

genetic-programming theories Theories that explain biological aging as resulting from a genetically determined developmental timetable.

genotype Genetic makeup of a person, containing both expressed and unexpressed characteristics.

genotype-environment correlation Tendency of certain genetic and environmental influences to reinforce each other; may be passive, reactive (evocative), or active. Also called *genotype-environment covariance.*

genotype-environment interaction The portion of phenotypic variation that results from the reactions of genetically different individuals to similar environmental conditions.

geriatrics Branch of medicine concerned with processes of aging and age-related medical conditions.

germinal stage First 2 weeks of prenatal development, characterized by rapid cell division, increasing complexity and differentiation, and implantation in the wall of the uterus.

gerontology Study of the aged and the process of aging.

glaucoma Irreversible damage to the optic nerve caused by increased pressure in the eye.

goodness of fit Appropriateness of environmental demands and constraints to a child's temperament.

grief Emotional response experienced in the early phases of bereavement.

grief therapy Treatment to help the bereaved cope with loss.

grief work Working out of psychological issues connected with grief.

gross motor skills Physical skills that involve the large muscles.

guided participation Participation of an adult in a child's activity in a manner that helps to structure the activity and to bring the child's understanding of it closer to that of the adult.

habituation Simple type of learning in which familiarity with a stimulus reduces, slows, or stops a response.

handedness Preference for using a particular hand.

Hayflick limit Genetically controlled limit, proposed by Hayflick, on the number of times cells can divide in members of a species.

heredity Inborn characteristics inherited from the biological parents at conception.

heritability Statistical estimate of contribution of heredity to individual differences in a specific trait within a given population.

heterozygous Possessing differing alleles for a trait.

holophrase Single word that conveys a complete thought.

Home Observation for Measurement of the Environment (HOME) Checklist to measure the influence of the home environment on children's cognitive growth.

homozygous Possessing two identical alleles for a trait.

horizontal dècalage Piaget's term for inability to transfer learning about one type of conservation to other types, which causes a child to master different types of conservation tasks at different ages.

hormone replacement therapy (HRT) Treatment with artificial estrogen, sometimes in combination with the hormone progesterone, to relieve or prevent symptoms caused by decline in estrogen levels after menopause.

hospice care Warm, personal patient- and family-centered care for a person with a terminal illness.

hostile aggression Aggressive behavior intended to hurt another person.

human development Scientific study of processes of change and stability throughout the human life span.

human genome Complete sequence or mapping of genes in the human body and their locations.

hypertension Chronically high blood pressure.

hypotheses Possible explanations for phenomena, used to predict the outcome of research.

hypothetical-deductive reasoning Ability, believed by Piaget to accompany the stage of formal operations, to develop, consider, and test hypotheses.

hysterectomy Surgical removal of the uterus.

ideal self The self one would like to be.

identification In Freudian theory, the process by which a young child adopts characteristics, beliefs, attitudes, values, and behaviors of the parent of the same sex.

identity According to Erikson, a coherent conception of the self, made up of goals, values, and beliefs to which a person is solidly committed.

identity accommodation Whitbourne's term for adjusting the self-concept to fit new experience.

identity achievement Identity status, described by Marcia, that is characterized by commitment to choices made following a crisis, a period spent in exploring alternatives.

identity assimilation Whitbourne's term for effort to fit new experience into an existing self-concept.

identity diffusion Identity status, described by Marcia, that is characterized by absence of commitment and lack of serious consideration of alternatives.

identity process model Whitbourne's model of identity development based on processes of assimilation and accommodation.

identity statuses Marcia's term for states of ego development that depend on the presence or absence of crisis and commitment.

identity style Whitbourne's term for characteristic ways of confronting, interpreting, and responding to experience.

identity versus identity confusion Erikson's fifth stage of psychosocial development, in which an adolescent seeks to develop a coherent sense of self, including the role she or he is to play in society. Also called *identity versus role confusion.*

imaginary audience Elkind's term for an observer who exists only in an adolescent's mind and is as concerned with the adolescent's thoughts and actions as the adolescent is.

implicit memory Unconscious recall, generally of habits and skills; sometimes called *procedural memory.*

imprinting Instinctive form of learning in which, during a critical period in early development, a young animal forms an attachment to the first moving object it sees, usually the mother.

incomplete dominance Partial expression of a trait.

independent variable In an experiment, the condition over which the experimenter has direct control.

individual differences Differences in characteristics, influences, or developmental outcomes.

individual psychotherapy Psychological treatment in which a therapist sees a troubled person one-on-one.

individuation Jung's term for emergence of the true self through balancing or integration of conflicting parts of the personality.

inductive reasoning Type of logical reasoning that moves from particular observations about members of a class to a general conclusion about that class.

inductive techniques Disciplinary techniques designed to induce desirable behavior by appealing to a child's sense of reason and fairness.

industry versus inferiority Erikson's fourth stage of psychosocial development, in which children must learn the productive skills their culture requires or else face feelings of inferiority.

infertility Inability to conceive after twelve months of trying.

information-processing approach Approach to the study of cognitive development by observing and analyzing the mental processes involved in perceiving and handling information.

inhibitory control Conscious, effortful holding back of impulses.

initiative versus guilt Erikson's third stage in psychosocial development, in which children balance the urge to pursue goals with moral reservations that may prevent carrying them out.

instrumental activities of daily living (IADLs) Everyday activities, competence in which is considered a measure of the ability to live independently.

instrumental aggression Aggressive behavior used as a means of achieving a goal.

intelligent behavior Behavior that is goal-oriented and adaptive to circumstances and conditions of life.

interiority Neugarten's term for a concern with inner life (introversion or introspection), which usually appears in middle age.

internalization Process by which children accept societal standards of conduct as their own; fundamental to socialization.

intimacy versus isolation Erikson's sixth stage of psychosocial development, in which young adults either make commitments to others or face a possible sense of isolation and self-absorption.

invisible imitation Imitation with parts of one's body that one cannot see.

IQ (intelligence quotient) tests Psychometric tests that seek to measure intelligence by comparing a test-taker's performance with standardized norms.

irreversibility Piaget's term for a preoperational child's failure to understand that an operation can go in two or more directions.

I-self James's term for the subjective entity that seeks to know about itself.

Kaufman Assessment Battery for Children (K-ABC) Nontraditional individual intelligence test designed to provide fair assessments of minority children and children with disabilities.

kinship care Care of children living without parents in the home of grandparents or other relatives, with or without a change of legal custody.

laboratory observation Research method in which all participants are observed under the same controlled conditions.

language Communication system based on words and grammar.

language acquisition device (LAD) In Chomsky's terminology, an inborn mechanism that enables children to infer linguistic rules from the language they hear.

learning disabilities (LDs) Disorders that interfere with specific aspects of learning and school achievement.

learning perspective View of development that holds that changes in behavior result from experience, or adaptation to the environment.

legacy-creating stage Seventh of Schaie's seven cognitive stages, in which very old people prepare for death by recording their life stories, distributing possessions, and the like.

life expectancy Age to which a person in a particular cohort is statistically likely to live (given his or her current age and health status), on the basis of average longevity of a population.

life review Reminiscence about one's life in order to see its significance.

life span The longest period that members of a species can live.

life structure In Levinson's theory, the underlying pattern of a person's life at a given time, built on whatever aspects of life the person finds most important.

lifelong learning Organized, sustained study by adults of all ages.

life-span development Concept of development as a lifelong process, which can be studied scientifically.

linguistic speech Verbal expression designed to convey meaning.

literacy (1) Ability to read and write. (2) In an adult, ability to use printed and written information to function in society, achieve goals, and develop knowledge and potential.

longevity Length of an individual's life.

longitudinal study Study designed to assess changes in a sample over time.

long-term memory Storage of virtually unlimited capacity, which holds information for very long periods.

macrosystem Bronfenbrenner's term for a society's overall cultural patterns.

mammography Diagnostic X-ray examination of the breasts.

marital capital Financial and emotional benefits built up during a long-standing marriage, which tend to hold a couple together.

maturation Unfolding of a natural sequence of physical and behavioral changes, including readiness to master new abilities.

mechanics of intelligence In Baltes's dual-process model, the abilities to process information and solve problems, irrespective of content; the area of cognition in which there is often an age-related decline.

mechanistic model Model that views development as a passive, predictable response to stimuli.

menarche Girl's first menstruation.

menopause Cessation of menstruation and of ability to bear children, typically around age 50.

mental retardation Significantly subnormal cognitive functioning.

Me-self James's term for what a person objectively knows about himself or herself. Also called *self-concept.*

mesosystem Bronfenbrenner's term for linkages between two or more microsystems.

metabolism Conversion of food and oxygen into energy.

metacognition Awareness of a person's own mental processes.

Metamemory in Adulthood (MIA) Questionnaire designed to measure various aspects of adults' metamemory, including beliefs about their own memory and the selection and use of strategies for remembering.

metamemory Understanding of processes of memory.

microgenetic study Study design that allows researchers to directly observe change by repeated testing over a short time.

microsystem Bronfenbrenner's term for a setting in which a child interacts with others on an everyday, face-to-face basis.

midlife crisis In some normative-crisis models, stressful life period precipitated by the review and reevaluation of one's past, typically occurring in the early to middle forties.

midlife review Introspective examination that often occurs in middle age, leading to reappraisal and revision of values and priorities.

mnemonic strategies Techniques to aid memory.

monozygotic (one-egg) twins Twins resulting from the division of a single zygote after fertilization; also called *identical twins.*

moratorium Identity status, described by Marcia, in which a person is currently considering alternatives (in crisis) and seems headed for commitment.

multifactorial transmission Combination of genetic and environmental factors to produce certain complex traits.

mutations Permanent alterations in genes or chromosomes that may produce harmful characteristics.

mutual regulation Process by which infant and caregiver communicate emotional states to each other and respond appropriately.

myopia Nearsightedness.

nativism Theory that human beings have an inborn capacity for language acquisition.

naturalistic observation Research method in which behavior is studied in natural settings without intervention or manipulation.

neglect Failure to meet a child's basic needs.

neurofibrillary tangles Twisted masses of protein fibers found in brains of persons with Alzheimer's disease.

niche-picking Tendency of a person, especially after early childhood, to seek out environments compatible with his or her genotype.

nonnormative Characteristic of an unusual event that happens to a particular person, or a typical event that happens at an unusual time of life.

nonshared environmental effects The unique environment in which each child grows up, consisting of distinctive influences or influences that affect one child differently than another.

normative Characteristic of an event that occurs in a similar way for most people in a group.

normative life events In the timing-of-events model, commonly expected life experiences that occur at customary times.

normative-stage models Theoretical models that describe psychosocial development in terms of a definite sequence of age-related changes.

nuclear family Kinship and household unit made up of one or two parents and their natural, adopted, or stepchildren.

obesity (1) Extreme overweight in relation to age, sex, height, and body type; defined in childhood as having a body mass index (weight-for-height) at or above the 95th percentile of growth curves for children of the same age and sex. (2) Extreme overweight, often measured in adults by a body mass index of 30 or more, or by more than 25 percent body fat in men and more than 30 percent in women.

object permanence Piaget's term for the understanding that a person or object still exists when out of sight.

observational learning Learning through watching the behavior of others.

obsessive-compulsive disorder Anxiety aroused by repetitive, intrusive thoughts, images, or impulses, often leading to compulsive ritual behaviors.

open adoption Adoption in which the birth parents and the adoptive parents know each other's identities and share information or have direct contact.

operant conditioning Learning based on reinforcement or punishment.

operational definitions Definitions stated solely in terms of the operations or procedures used to produce or measure a phenomenon.

oppositional defiant disorder (ODD) Pattern of behavior, persisting into middle childhood, marked by negativity, hostility, and defiance.

organismic model Model that views development as internally initiated by an active organism, and as occurring in a sequence of qualitatively different stages.

organization (1) Piaget's term for integration of knowledge into systems. (2) Mnemonic strategy of categorizing material to be remembered.

osteoporosis Condition in which the bones become thin and brittle as a result of rapid calcium depletion.

Otis-Lennon School Ability Test Group intelligence test for kindergarten through twelfth grade.

overt aggression Aggression that is openly directed at its target.

palliative care Care aimed at relieving pain and suffering and allowing the terminally ill to die in peace, comfort, and dignity.

Parkinson's disease Progressive, irreversible degenerative neurological disorder, characterized by tremor, stiffness, slowed movement, and unstable posture.

participant observation Research method in which the observer lives with the people or participates in the activity being observed.

passive euthanasia Deliberate withholding or discontinuation of life-prolonging treatment of a terminally ill person in order to end suffering or allow death with dignity.

perimenopause Period of several years during which a woman experiences physiological changes that bring on menopause; also called *climacteric.*

permissive In Baumrind's terminology, parenting style emphasizing self-expression and self-regulation.

personal fable Elkind's term for the conviction that one is special, unique, and not subject to the rules that govern the rest of the world.

phenotype Observable characteristics of a person.

phonetic, or code emphasis approach Approach to teaching reading that emphasizes decoding of unfamiliar words.

physical abuse Infliction of bodily injury on a child.

physical development Growth of body and brain and change or stability in sensory capacities, motor skills, and health.

Piagetian approach Approach to the study of cognitive development that describes qualitative stages in cognitive functioning.

plasticity (1) Modifiability of performance. (2) Modifiability, or "molding" of the brain through experience.

play therapy Therapeutic approach in which a child plays freely while a therapist observes and occasionally comments, asks questions, or makes suggestions.

polygenic inheritance Pattern of inheritance in which multiple genes affect a complex trait.

postconventional morality Third level of Kohlberg's theory of moral reasoning, in which people follow internally held moral principles and can decide among conflicting moral standards.

postformal thought Mature type of thinking, which relies on subjective experience and intuition as well as logic and is useful in dealing with ambiguity, uncertainty, inconsistency, contradiction, imperfection, and compromise.

power assertion Disciplinary strategy designed to discourage undesirable behavior through physical or verbal enforcement of parental control.

pragmatics (1) Set of linguistic rules that govern the use of language for communication. (2) The practical knowledge needed to use language for communicative purposes.

pragmatics of intelligence In Baltes's dual-process model, the dimension of intelligence that tends to grow with age and includes practical thinking, application of accumulated knowledge and skills, specialized expertise, professional productivity, and wisdom.

preconventional morality First level of Kohlberg's theory of moral reasoning, in which control is external.

prejudice Unfavorable attitude toward members of certain groups outside one's own, especially racial or ethnic groups.

prelinguistic speech Forerunner of linguistic speech; utterance of sounds that are not words. Includes crying, cooing, babbling, and accidental and deliberate imitation of sounds without understanding their meaning.

premenstrual syndrome (PMS) Disorder producing symptoms of physical discomfort and emotional tension during the one to two weeks before a menstrual period.

preoperational stage In Piaget's theory, the second major stage of cognitive development, in which children become more sophisticated in their use of symbolic thought but are not yet able to use logic.

presbycusis Gradual loss of hearing, which accelerates after age 55, especially with regard to sounds at the upper frequencies.

presbyopia Farsightedness associated with aging, resulting when the lens of the eye becomes less elastic.

pretend play Play involving imaginary people or situations; also called fantasy play, dramatic play, or imaginative play.

primary aging Gradual, inevitable process of bodily deterioration throughout the life span.

primary sex characteristics Organs directly related to reproduction, which enlarge and mature during adolescence.

priming Increase in ease of doing a task or remembering information as a result of a previous encounter with the task or information.

private speech Talking aloud to oneself with no intent to communicate.

problem-focused coping In the cognitive-appraisal model, coping strategy directed toward eliminating, managing, or improving a stressful situation.

procedural memory Long-term memory of motor skills, habits, and ways of doing things, which often can be recalled without conscious effort; sometimes called *implicit memory.*

prosocial behavior Any voluntary behavior intended to help others.

prospective memory Remembering to perform future actions.

protective factors Influences that reduce the impact of early stress and tend to predict positive outcomes.

proximodistal principle Principle that development proceeds from within to without; that is, that parts of the body near the center develop before the extremities.

psychoanalytic perspective View of development as shaped by unconscious forces.

psychometric approach Approach to the study of cognitive development that seeks to measure the quantity of intelligence a person possesses.

psychosexual development In Freudian theory, an unvarying sequence of stages of personality development during infancy, childhood, and adolescence, in which gratification shifts from the mouth to the anus and then to the genitals.

psychosocial development (1) Change and stability in emotions, personality, and social relationships. (2) In Erikson's eight-stage theory, the socially and culturally influenced process of development of the ego, or self.

puberty Process by which a person attains sexual maturity and the ability to reproduce.

punishment In operant conditioning, a stimulus that discourages repetition of a behavior.

qualitative change Change in kind, structure, or organization, such as the change from nonverbal to verbal communication.

qualitative research Research that focuses on "soft" data, such as subjective experiences, feelings, or beliefs.

quantitative change Change in number or amount, such as in height, weight, or size of vocabulary.

quantitative research Research that focuses on "hard" data and numerical or statistical measures.

reaction range Potential variability, depending on environmental conditions, in the expression of a hereditary trait.

real self The self one actually is.

recall Ability to reproduce material from memory.

recessive inheritance Pattern of inheritance in which a child receives identical recessive alleles, resulting in expression of a nondominant trait.

recognition Ability to identify a previously encountered stimulus.

rehearsal Mnemonic strategy to keep an item in working memory through conscious repetition.

reinforcement In operant conditioning, a stimulus that encourages repetition of a desired behavior.

reintegrative stage Sixth of Schaie's seven cognitive stages, in which older adults choose to focus limited energy on tasks that have meaning to them.

relational aggression Aggression aimed at damaging or interfering with another person's relationships, reputation, or psychological well-being; also called *covert, indirect,* or *psychological aggression.*

reorganizational stage Fifth of Schaie's seven cognitive stages, in which adults entering retirement reorganize their lives around nonwork-related activities.

representational ability Piaget's term for capacity to store mental images or symbols of objects and experiences.

representational mappings In neo-Piagetian terminology, second stage in development of self-definition, in which a child makes logical connections between aspects of the self but still sees these characteristics in all-or-nothing terms.

representational systems In neo-Piagetian terminology, the third stage in development of self-definition, characterized by breadth, balance, and the integration and assessment of various aspects of the self.

reserve capacity Ability of body organs and systems to put forth four to ten times as much effort as usual under stress; also called *organ reserve.*

resilient children Children who weather adverse circumstances, function well despite challenges or threats, or bounce back from traumatic events.

responsible stage Third of Schaie's seven cognitive stages, in which middle-aged people are concerned with long-range goals and practical problems related to their responsibility for others.

retrieval Process by which information is accessed or recalled from memory storage.

revolving door syndrome Tendency for young adults to return to their parents' home while getting on their feet or in times of financial, marital, or other trouble.

risk factors Conditions that increase the likelihood of a negative developmental outcome.

rough-and-tumble play Vigorous play involving wrestling, hitting, and chasing, often accompanied by laughing and screaming.

sample Group of participants chosen to represent the entire population under study.

sandwich generation Middle-aged adults squeezed by competing needs to raise or launch children and to care for elderly parents.

scaffolding Temporary support to help a child master a task.

schemes Piaget's term for organized patterns of behavior used in different situations.

schizophrenia Mental disorder marked by loss of contact with reality; symptoms include hallucinations and delusions.

school phobia Unrealistic fear of going to school; may be a form of separation anxiety disorder or social phobia.

scientific method System of established principles and processes of scientific inquiry.

script General remembered outline of a familiar, repeated event, used to guide behavior.

secondary aging Aging processes that result from disease and bodily abuse and disuse and are often preventable.

secondary sex characteristics Physiological signs of sexual maturation (such as breast development and growth of body hair) that do not involve the sex organs.

secular trend Trend that can be seen only by observing several generations, such as the trend toward earlier attainment of adult height and sexual maturity, which began a century ago.

secure attachment Pattern in which an infant cries or protests when the primary caregiver leaves and actively seeks out the caregiver upon his or her return.

secure base Infant's use of a parent or other familiar caregiver as a departure point for exploration and a safe place to return periodically for emotional support.

selective optimization with compensation In Baltes's dual-process model, strategy for maintaining or enhancing overall cognitive functioning by using stronger abilities to compensate for those that have weakened.

self-awareness Realization that one's existence and functioning are separate from those of other people and things.

self-concept Sense of self; descriptive and evaluative mental picture of one's abilities and traits.

self-conscious emotions Emotions, such as embarrassment, empathy, and envy, that depend on self-awareness.

self-definition Cluster of characteristics used to describe oneself.

self-efficacy Sense of capability to master challenges and achieve goals.

self-esteem The judgment a person makes about his or her self-worth.

self-evaluative emotions Emotions, such as pride, shame, and guilt, which depend on both self-awareness and knowledge of socially accepted standards of behavior.

self-fulfilling prophecy Expectation or prediction of behavior that tends to come true because it leads people to act as if it already were true.

self-regulation Child's independent control of behavior to conform to understood social expectations.

semantic memory Long-term memory of general factual knowledge, social customs, and language.

senescence Period of the life span marked by changes in physical functioning sometimes associated with aging; begins at different ages for different people.

sensitive periods Times in development when a person is particularly responsive to certain kinds of experiences.

sensorimotor stage In Piaget's theory, the first stage in cognitive development, during which infants learn through senses and motor activity.

sensory memory Initial, brief, temporary storage of sensory information.

separation anxiety Distress shown by an infant when a familiar caregiver leaves.

separation anxiety disorder Condition involving excessive, prolonged anxiety concerning separation from home or from people to whom a child is attached.

sequential study Study design that combines cross-sectional and longitudinal techniques.

seriation Ability to order items along a dimension.

serious leisure Leisure activity requiring skill, attention, and commitment.

sex chromosomes Pair of chromosomes that determines sex: XX in the normal female, XY in the normal male.

sex-linked inheritance Pattern of inheritance in which certain characteristics carried on the X chromosome inherited from the mother are transmitted differently to her male and female offspring.

sexual abuse Sexual activity involving a child and an older person.

sexual dysfunction Persistent disturbance in sexual desire or sexual response.

sexual orientation Focus of consistent sexual, romantic, and affectionate interest, either heterosexual, homosexual, or bisexual.

sexually transmitted diseases (STDs) Diseases spread by sexual contact.

single representations In neo-Piagetian terminology, first stage in development of self-definition, in which children describe themselves in terms of individual, unconnected characteristics and in all-or-nothing terms.

situational compliance Kochanska's term for obedience of a parent's orders only in the presence of signs of ongoing parental control.

"slow-to-warm-up" children Children whose temperament is generally mild but who are hesitant about accepting new experiences.

social capital Family and community resources on which a child can draw.

social clock Set of cultural norms or expectations for the times of life when certain important events, such as marriage, parenthood, entry into work, and retirement, should occur.

social cognition Ability to understand that other people have mental states and to gauge their feelings and intentions.

social cognitive neuroscience An emerging interdisciplinary field that draws on cognitive neuroscience, information processing, and social psychology.

social cognitive theory Albert Bandura's expansion of social learning theory; holds that children learn gender roles through socialization.

social construction Concept about the nature of reality, based on societally shared perceptions or assumptions.

social convoy theory Theory proposed by Kahn and Antonucci that people move through life surrounded by concentric circles of intimate relationships on which they rely for assistance, well-being, and social support.

social learning theory Theory that behaviors are learned by observing and imitating models. Also called *social cognitive theory*.

social phobia Extreme fear and/or avoidance of social situations.
social promotion Policy of automatically promoting children even if they do not meet academic standards.
social referencing Understanding an ambiguous situation by seeking out another person's perception of it.
social speech Speech intended to be understood by a listener.
social-contextual approach Approach to the study of cognitive development by focusing on environmental influences, particularly parents and other caregivers.
socialization Development of habits, skills, values, and motives shared by responsible, productive members of a society.
sociobiological perspective View of development that focuses on biological bases of social behavior.
sociocultural theory Vygotsky's theory of how contextual factors affect children's development.
socioeconomic status (SES) Combination of economic and social factors describing an individual or family, including income, education, and occupation.
socioemotional selectivity theory Theory, proposed by Carstensen, that people select social contacts on the basis of the changing relative importance of social interaction as a source of information, as an aid in developing and maintaining a self-concept, and as a source of emotional well-being.
spermarche Boy's first ejaculation.
spillover hypothesis Hypothesis that there is a positive correlation between intellectuality of work and of leisure activities because of a carryover of cognitive gains from work to leisure.
spontaneous abortion Natural expulsion from the uterus of a conceptus that cannot survive outside the womb; also called *miscarriage.*
Stanford-Binet Intelligence Scale Individual intelligence test used to measure memory, spatial orientation, and practical judgment.
Sternberg Triarchic Abilities Test (STAT) Test that seeks to measure componential, experiential, and contextual intelligence.
"still-face" paradigm Research method used to measure mutual regulation in infants 2 to 9 months old.
storage Retention of memories for future use.
Strange Situation Laboratory technique used to study attachment.
stranger anxiety Wariness of strange people and places, shown by some infants during the second half of the first year.
stress Response to physical or psychological demands.
stressors Stress-producing experiences.
substantive complexity Degree to which a person's work requires thought and independent judgment.
survival curves Curves, plotted on a graph, showing percentages of a population that survive at each age level.
symbolic function Piaget's term for ability to use mental representations (words, numbers, or images) to which a child has attached meaning.
syntax Rules for forming sentences in a particular language.
systems of action Increasingly complex combinations of skills, which permit a wider or more precise range of movement and more control of the environment.

tacit knowledge Sternberg's term for information that is not formally taught or openly expressed but is necessary to get ahead.
telegraphic speech Early form of sentence consisting of only a few essential words.
temperament Characteristic disposition, or style of approaching and reacting to situations.
teratogenic Capable of causing birth defects.
thanatology Study of death and dying.
theory Coherent set of logically related concepts that seeks to organize, explain, and predict data.
theory of mind Awareness and understanding of mental processes.
theory of multiple intelligences Gardner's theory that each person has several distinct forms of intelligence.
timing-of-events model Theoretical model that describes adult psychosocial development as a response to the expected or unexpected occurrence and timing of important life events.
trait models Theoretical models that focus on mental, emotional, temperamental, and behavioral traits, or attributes.
transduction Piaget's term for a preoperational child's tendency to mentally link particular phenomena, whether or not there is logically a causal relationship.
transitive inference Understanding of the relationship between two objects by knowing the relationship of each to a third object.
triangular theory of love Sternberg's theory that patterns of love hinge on the balance among three elements: intimacy, passion, and commitment.
triarchic theory of intelligence Sternberg's theory describing three types of intelligence: componential, experiential, and contextual.
two-way (dual-language) learning Approach to second-language education in which English speakers and non-English speakers learn together in their own and each other's languages.
typological models Theoretical models that identify broad personality types, or styles.

ultrasound Prenatal medical procedure using high-frequency sound waves to detect the outline of a fetus and its movements, so as to determine whether a pregnancy is progressing normally.

variable-rate theories Theories that explain biological aging as a result of processes that vary from person to person and are influenced by both the internal and the external environment; sometimes called *error theories.*
violation-of-expectations Research method in which dishabituation to a stimulus that conflicts with experience is taken as evidence that an infant finds the new stimulus surprising.
visible imitation Imitation with parts of one's body that one can see.
visual preference Tendency of infants to spend more time looking at one sight than another.
visual recognition memory Ability to distinguish a familiar visual stimulus from an unfamiliar one when shown both at the same time.
vital capacity Amount of air that can be drawn in with a deep breath and expelled.

Wechsler Adult Intelligence Scale (WAIS) Intelligence test for adults, which yields verbal and performance scores as well as a combined score.
Wechsler Intelligence Scale for Children (WISC-III) Individual intelligence test for schoolchildren, which yields verbal and performance scores as well as a combined score.
Wechsler Preschool and Primary Scale of Intelligence, Revised (WPPSI-R) Individual intelligence test for children ages 3 to 7, which yields verbal and performance scores as well as a combined score.

whole-language approach Approach to teaching reading that emphasizes visual retrieval and use of contextual clues.

withdrawal of love Disciplinary strategy that may involve ignoring, isolating, or showing dislike for a child.

working memory Short-term storage of information being actively processed.

zone of proximal development (ZPD) Vygotsky's term for the difference between what a child can do alone and with help.

zygote One-celled organism resulting from fertilization.

Bibliography

Aaron, V., Parker, K. D., Ortega, S., & Calhoun, T. (1999). The extended family as a source of support among African Americans. Challenge: A Journal of Research on African American Men, 10(2), 23–36.

Aartsen, M. J., Smits, C. H. M., van Tilburg, T, Knipscheer, K. C. P. M., & Deeg, D. J. H. (2002). Activity in older adults: Cause or consequence of cognitive functioning? A longitudinal study on everyday activities and cognitive performance in older adults. *Journal of Gerontology: Psychological Sciences, 57B,* P153–P162.

Abbey, A., Andrews, F. M., & Halman, J. (1992). Infertility and subjective well-being: The mediating roles of self-esteem, internal control, and interpersonal conflict. *Journal of Marriage and the Family, 54,* 408–417.

Abel, E. K. (1991). *Who cares for the elderly?* Philadelphia: Temple University Press.

Abma, J. C., & Sonenstein, F. L. (2001). Sexual activity and contraceptive practices among teenagers in the United States, 1988 and 1995. *Vital and Health Statistics,* Series 23, No. 21.

Abma, J. C., Chandra, A., Mosher, W. D., Peterson, L., & Piccinino, L. (1997). Fertility, family planning, and women's health: New data from the 1995 National Survey of Family Growth. *Vital Health Statistics, 23*(19). Washington, DC: National Center for Health Statistics.

Abramovitch, R., Corter, C., & Lando, B. (1979). Sibling interaction in the home. *Child Development, 50,* 997–1003.

Abramovitch, R., Corter, C., Pepler, D., & Stanhope, L. (1986). Sibling and peer interactions: A final follow-up and comparison. *Child Development, 57,* 217–229.

Abramovitch, R., Pepler, D., & Corter, C. (1982). Patterns of sibling interaction among preschool-age children. In M. E. Lamb (Ed.), *Sibling relationships: Their nature and significance across the lifespan.* Hillsdale, NJ: Erlbaum.

Abrams, B., & Parker, J. D. (1990). Maternal weight gain in women with good pregnancy outcome. *Obstetrics and Gynecology, 76*(1), 1–7.

Abramson, T. A. (1995, Fall). From nonnormative to normative caregiving. *Dimensions: Newsletter of American Society on Aging,* pp. 1–2.

Achenbach, T. M., & Howell, C. T. (1993). Are American children's problems getting worse? A 13-year comparison. *Journal of the American Academy of Child and Adolescent Psychiatry, 32,* 1145–1154.

Achenbaum, W. A., & Bengtson, V. L. (1994). Re-engaging the disengagement theory of aging: On the history and assessment of theory development in gerontology. *The Gerontologist, 34,* 756–763.

Ackerman, B. P., Kogos, J., Youngstrom, E., Schoff, K., & Izard, C. (1999). Family instability and the problem behaviors of children from economically disadvantaged families. *Developmental Psychology, 35*(1), 258–268.

Ackerman, M. J., Siu, B. L., Sturner, W. Q., Tester D. J., Valdivia, C. R., Makielski, J. C., & Towbin, J. A. (2001). Postmortem molecular analysis of SCN5A defects in sudden infant death syndrome. *Journal of The American Medical Association, 286,* 2264–2269.

Adams, C. (1991). Qualitative age differences in memory for text: A life-span developmental perspective. *Psychology and Aging, 6,* 323–336.

Adams, R., & Laursen, B. (2001). The organization and dynamics of adolescent conflict with parents and friends. *Journal of Marriage and the Family, 63,* 97–110.

Adams, R. G. (1986). Friendship and aging. *Generations, 10*(4), 40–43.

Adams, R. G., & Allan, G. (1998). *Placing friendship in context.* Cambridge, MA: Cambridge University Press.

Ades, P. A., Ballor, D. L., Ashikaga, T., Utton, J. L., & Nair, K. S. (1996). Weight training improves walking endurance in healthy elderly persons. *Annals of Internal Medicine, 124,* 568–572.

Adler, N. E., & Newman, K. (2002). Socioeconomic disparities in health: Pathways and policies. *Health Affairs, 21,* 60–76.

Administration on Aging. (2001). *A profile of older Americans: 2001.* Washington, DC: Author.

Agency for Healthcare Research and Quality and the Centers for Disease Control. (2002). *Physical activity and older Americans: Benefits and strategies.* [On-line]. Available: http://www.ahrq.gov/ppip/activity.htm

Aggarwal, S., Gollapudi, S., & Gupta, S. (1999). Increased TNF-alpha-induced apoptosis in lymphocytes from aged humans: Changes in TNF-alpha receptor expression and activation of caspases. *Journal of Immunology, 162,* 2154–2161.

Agoda, L. (1995). Minorities and ESRD. Review: African American study of kidney disease and hypertension clinical trials. *Nephrology News & Issues, 9,* 18–19.

Agosin, M. (1999). Pirate, conjurer, feminist. In J. Rodden (Ed.), *Conversations with Isabel Allende* (pp. 35–47). Austin: University of Texas Press.

Ainsworth, M. D. S. (1967). *Infancy in Uganda: Infant care and the growth of love.* Baltimore: Johns Hopkins University Press.

Ainsworth, M. D. S. (1969). Object relations, dependency, and attachment: A theoretical review of the infant-mother relationship. *Child Development, 40,* 969–1025.

Ainsworth, M. D. S., Blehar, M. C., Waters, E., & Wall, S. (1978). *Patterns of attachment: A psychological study of the strange situation.* Hillsdale, NJ: Erlbaum.

Akhtar, N., Jipson, J., & Callanan, M. A. (2001). Learning words through overhearing. *Child Development, 72*(2), 416–430.

Akutsu, H., Legge, G. E., Ross, J. A., & Schuebel, K. J. (1991). Psychophysics of reading: Effects of age-related changes in vision. *Journal of Gerontology: Psychological Sciences, 46*(6), P325–331.

Alaimo, K., Olson, C. M., & Frongillo, E. A. (2001). Food insufficiency and American school-aged children's cognitive, academic, and psychosocial development. *Pediatrics, 108,* 44–53.

Alan Guttmacher Institute (AGI). (1994). *Sex & America's teenagers.* New York: Author.

Alan Guttmacher Institute (AGI). (1999a). Facts in brief: Teen sex and pregnancy. [Online] Available: http://www.agi_usa.org/pubs/fb_teen _sex.html#sfd. Access date: January 31, 2000.

Alan Guttmacher Institute (AGI). (1999b). Occasional report: Why is teenage pregnancy declining? The roles of abstinence, sexual activity and contraceptive use. [Online]. Available: http://www.agi_usa.org/pubs/or _teen_preg_decline.html. Access date: January 31, 2000.

Albanese, A., & Stanhope, R. (1993). Growth and metabolic data following growth hormone treatment of children with intrauterine growth retardation. *Hormone Research, 39,* 8–12.

Alcott, L. M. (1929). *Little women.* New York: Saalfield. (Original work published 1868)

Aldwin, C. M., & Levenson, M. R. (2001). Stress, coping, and health at midlife: A developmental perspective. In M. E. Lachman (Ed.), *Handbook of midlife development* (pp. 188–214). New York: Wiley.

Aldwin, C. M., Sutton, K. J., Chiara, G., & Spiro, A., III. (1996). Age differences in stress, coping, and appraisal: Findings from the Normative Aging Study. *Journal of Gerontology: Psychological Sciences, 51B,* P178–P188.

Alexander, B. B., Rubinstein, R. L., Goodman, M., & Luborsky, M. (1992). A path not taken: A cultural analysis of regrets and childlessness in the lives of older women. *The Gerontologist, 32*(5), 618–626.

Alexander, G. R., Tompkins, M. E., Allen, M. C., & Hulsey, T. C. (2000). Trends and racial differences in birth weight and related survival. *Maternal and Child Health Journal, 3,* 71–79.

Alexander, K. L., Entwisle, D. R., & Dauber, S. L. (1993). First-grade classroom behavior: Its short- and long-term consequences for school performance. *Child Development, 64,* 801–814.

Aligne, C. A., & Stoddard, J. J. (1997). Tobacco and children: An economic evaluation of the medical effects of parental smoking. *Archives of Pediatric and Adolescent Medicine, 151,* 648–653.

Allen, G. L., & Ondracek, P. J. (1995). Age-sensitive cognitive abilities related to children's acquisition of spatial knowledge. *Developmental Psychology, 31,* 934–945.

Allen, J. P., Philliber, S., Herrling, S., & Kuperminc, G. P. (1997). Preventing teen pregnancy and academic failure: Experimental evaluation of a developmentally based approach. *Child Development, 64,* 729–742.

Allen, K. R., Blieszner, R., & Roberto, K. A. (2000). Families in the middle and later years: A review and critique of research in the 1990s. *Journal of Marriage and the Family, 62,* 911–926.

Allende, I. (1995). *Paula.* (M. S. Peden, Trans.) New York: HarperCollins.

Allison, D., Fontaine, K., Manson, J., & Stevens, J., & Vanltallie, T. (1999). Annual deaths attributable to obesity in the United States. *Journal of the American Medical Association, 282,* 1530–1538.

Almeida, D. M., & McDonald, D. (1998). Weekly rhythms of parents' work stress, home stress, and parent-adolescent tension. In A. Crouter & R. Larson (Eds.), *Temporal rhythms in adolescence: Clocks, calendars, and the coordination of daily life* (pp. 69–82). [*New Directions in Child and Adolescent Development,* No. 82]. San Francisco: Jossey-Bass.

Almeida, D. M., Maggs, J. L., & Galambos, N. L. (1993). Wives' employment hours and spousal participation in family work. *Journal of Family Psychology, 7,* 233–244.

Altman, L. K. (1992, July 21). Women worldwide nearing higher rate for AIDS than men. *The New York Times,* pp. C1, C3.

Alvidrez J., & Weinstein, R. S. (1999). Early teacher perceptions and later student academic achievement. *Journal of Educational Psychology, 91,* 731–746.

Alzheimer's disease: Recent progress and prospects. Part I. (2001, October). *The Harvard Mental Health Letter, 18*(4), pp. 1–4.

Alzheimer's disease: Recent progress and prospects. Part II. (2001, November). *The Harvard Mental Health Letter, 18*(5), pp. 1–3.

Alzheimer's disease: Recent progress and prospects. Part III. (2001, December). *The Harvard Mental Health Letter, 18*(6), pp. 1–4.

Alzheimer's Association. (1998a, Fall). New avenues for diagnosis and treatment. *Advances: Progress in Alzheimer Research and Care,* pp. 1, 4.

Alzheimer's Association. (1998b, Fall). When the diagnosis isn't Alzheimer's. *Advances: Progress in Alzheimer Research and Care,* pp. 2–3.

Alzheimer's Association. (undated). *Is it Alzheimer's? Warning signs you should know.* Chicago: Author.

Alzheimer's Disease: The search for causes and treatments—Part I. (1998, August). *The Harvard Mental Health Letter, 15*(2).

Alzheimer's Disease: The search for causes and treatments—Part II. (1998, September). *The Harvard Mental Health Letter, 15*(3).

Amabile, T. M. (1983). *The social psychology of creativity.* New York: Springer-Verlag.

Amato, P. R. (1987). Family processes in one-parent, stepparent, and intact families: The child's point of view. *Journal of Marriage and the Family, 49,* 327–337.

Amato, P. R. (2000). The consequences of divorce for adults and children. *Journal of Marriage and the Family, 62,* 1269–1287.

Amato, P. R., & Booth, A. (1997). *A generation at risk: Growing up in an era of family upheaval.* Cambridge, MA: Harvard University Press.

Amato, P. R., & Gilbreth, J. G. (1999). Nonresident fathers and children's wellbeing: A meta-analysis. *Journal of Marriage and the Family, 61,* 557–573.

Amato, P. R., & Keith, B. (1991). Parental divorce and the well-being of children: A meta-analysis. *Psychological Bulletin, 110,* 26–46.

Amato, P. R., Kurdek, L. A., Demo, D. H., & Allen, K. R. (1993). Children's adjustment to divorce: Theories, hypotheses, and empirical support. *Journal of Marriage and the Family, 55,* 23–54.

American Academy of Child and Adolescent Psychiatry (AACAP). (1997). *Children's sleep problems.* [Fact sheet] No. 34.

American Academy of Pediatrics (AAP) and Canadian Paediatric Society. (2000). Prevention and management of pain and stress in the neonate. *Pediatrics, 105*(2), 454–461.

American Academy of Pediatrics (AAP) Committee on Accident and Poison Prevention. (1988). Snowmobile statement. *Pediatrics, 82,* 798–799.

American Academy of Pediatrics (AAP) Committee on Adolescence and Committee on Early Childhood, Adoption, and Dependent Care. (2001). Care of adolescent parents and their children. *Pediatrics, 107,* 429–434.

American Academy of Pediatrics (AAP) Committee on Adolescence. (1994). Sexually transmitted diseases. *Pediatrics, 94,* 568–572.

American Academy of Pediatrics (AAP) Committee on Adolescence. (1999). Adolescent pregnancy—Current trends and issues: 1998. *Pediatrics, 103,* 516–520.

American Academy of Pediatrics (AAP) Committee on Adolescence. (2000). Suicide and suicide attempts in adolescents. *Pediatrics, 105*(4), 871–874.

American Academy of Pediatrics Committee on Adolescence. (2003). Policy statement: Identifying and treating eating disorders. *Pediatrics, 111,* 204–211.

American Academy of Pediatrics Committee on Bioethics. (1992, July). Ethical issues in surrogate motherhood. *AAP News,* pp. 14–15.

American Academy of Pediatrics (AAP) Committee on Bioethics. (2001). Ethical issues with genetic testing in pediatrics. *Pediatrics, 107*(6), 1451–1455.

American Academy of Pediatrics (AAP) Committee on Child Abuse and Neglect. (1999). Guidelines for the evaluation of sexual abuse in children: Subject review. *Pediatrics, 103,* 186–191.

American Academy of Pediatrics (AAP) Committee on Children with Disabilities and Committee on Drugs. (1996). Medication for children with attentional disorders. *Pediatrics, 98,* 301–304.

American Academy of Pediatrics (AAP) Committee on Children with Disabilities and Committee on Psychosocial Aspects of Child and Family Health. (1993). Psychosocial risks of chronic health conditions in childhood and adolescence. *Pediatrics, 92,* 876–877.

American Academy of Pediatrics (AAP) Committee on Children with Disabilities. (2001). The pediatrician's role in the diagnosis and management of autistic spectrum disorder in children. *Pediatrics, 107*(5), 1221–1226.

American Academy of Pediatrics (AAP) Committee on Communications. (1995). Sexuality, contraception, and the media. *Pediatrics, 95,* 298–300.

American Academy of Pediatrics (AAP) Committee on Community Health Services. (1996). Health needs of homeless children and families. *Pediatrics, 88,* 789–791.

American Academy of Pediatrics (AAP) Committee on Drugs and Committee on Bioethics. (1997). Considerations related to the use of recombinant human growth hormone in children, *Pediatrics, 99,* 122–128.

American Academy of Pediatrics (AAP) Committee on Drugs. (1994). The transfer of drugs and other chemicals into human milk. *Pediatrics, 93,* 137–150.

American Academy of Pediatrics (AAP) Committee on Environmental Health. (1997). Environmental tobacco smoke: A hazard to children. *Pediatrics, 99,* 639–642.

American Academy of Pediatrics (AAP) Committee on Environmental Health. (1998). Screening for elevated blood lead levels. *Pediatrics, 101,* 1072–1078.

American Academy of Pediatrics (AAP) Committee on Fetus and Newborn and American College of Obstetricians and Gynecologists Committee on Obstetric Practice. (1996). Use and abuse of the Apgar score. *Pediatrics, 98,* 141–142.

American Academy of Pediatrics (AAP) Committee on Genetics. (1996). Newborn screening fact sheet. *Pediatrics, 98,* 1–29.

American Academy of Pediatrics (AAP) Committee on Genetics. (1999). Folic acid for the prevention of neural tube defects. *Pediatrics, 104,* 325–327.

American Academy of Pediatrics (AAP) Committee on Infectious Diseases. (1994). *Red book* (23rd ed.). Elk Grove Village, IL: Author.

American Academy of Pediatrics (AAP) Committee on Infectious Diseases. (2000). Recommended childhood immunization schedule—United States, January–December, 2000, 105, 148.

American Academy of Pediatrics (AAP) Committee on Injury and Poison Prevention and Committee on Sports Medicine and Fitness. (1999). Policy statement: Trampolines at home, school, and recreational centers. *Pediatrics, 103,* 1053–1056.

American Academy of Pediatrics (AAP) Committee on Injury and Poison Prevention. (2000). Firearm-related injuries affecting the pediatric population. *Pediatrics, 105*(4), 888–895.

American Academy of Pediatrics (AAP) Committee on Nutrition. (1992a). Statement on cholesterol. *Pediatrics, 90,* 469–473.

American Academy of Pediatrics (AAP) Committee on Nutrition. (1992b). The use of whole cow's milk in infancy. *Pediatrics, 89,* 1105–1109.

American Academy of Pediatrics (AAP) Committee on Pediatric AIDS and Committee on Infectious Diseases. (1999). Issues related to human immunodeficiency virus transmission in schools, child care, medical settings, the home, and community. *Pediatrics, 104,* 318–324.

American Academy of Pediatrics (AAP) Committee on Pediatric AIDS. (2000). Education of children with human immunodeficiency virus infection. *Pediatrics, 105,* 1358–1360.

American Academy of Pediatrics (AAP) Committee on Psychosocial Aspects of Child and Family Health. (1992). The pediatrician and childhood bereavement. *Pediatrics, 89*(3), 516–518.

American Academy of Pediatrics (AAP) Committee on Psychosocial Aspects of Child and Family Health. (1998). Guidance for effective discipline. *Pediatrics, 101,* 723–728.

American Academy of Pediatrics Committee on Psychosocial Aspects of Child and Family Health. (2000). The pediatrician and childhood bereavement. *Pediatrics, 105,* 445–447.

American Academy of Pediatrics Committee on Psychosocial Aspects of Child and Family Health. (2002). Coparent or second-parent adoption by same-sex parents. *Pediatrics, 109,* 339–340.

American Academy of Pediatrics (AAP) Committee on Sports Medicine and Committee on School Health. (1989). Organized athletics for preadolescent children. *Pediatrics, 84,* 583–584.

American Academy of Pediatrics (AAP) Committee on Sports Medicine and Fitness. (1992). Fitness, activity, and sports participation in the preschool child. *Pediatrics, 90,* 1002–1004.

American Academy of Pediatrics (AAP) Committee on Sports Medicine and Fitness. (1997). Participation in boxing by children, adolescents, and young adults. *Pediatrics, 99,* 134–135.

American Academy of Pediatrics (AAP) Committee on Sports Medicine and Fitness. (1999). Human immunodeficiency virus and other blood-borne viral pathogens in the athletic setting. *Pediatrics, 104*(6), 1400–1403.

American Academy of Pediatrics (AAP) Committee on Sports Medicine and Fitness. (2000). Injuries in youth soccer: A subject review. *Pediatrics, 105*(3), 659–660.

American Academy of Pediatrics (AAP) Committee on Substance Abuse and Committee on Children with Disabilities. (1993). Fetal alcohol syndrome and fetal alcohol effects. *Pediatrics, 91,* 1004–1006.

American Academy of Pediatrics (AAP) Newborn Screening Task Force. (2000). Serving the family from birth to the medical home. A report from the Newborn Screening Task Force convened in Washington, DC, May 10–11, 1999. *Pediatrics, 106*(2), Part 2 of 3.

American Academy of Pediatrics (AAP) Task Force on Infant Positioning and SIDS. (1997). Does bed sharing affect the risk of SIDS? *Pediatrics, 100,* 272.

American Academy of Pediatrics (AAP) Task Force on Infant Sleep Position and Sudden Infant Death Syndrome. (2000). Changing concepts of sudden infant death syndrome: Implications for infant sleeping environment and sleep position. *Pediatrics, 105*(3), 650–656.

American Academy of Pediatrics (AAP) Work Group on Breastfeeding. (1997). Breastfeeding and the use of human milk. *Pediatrics, 100,* 1035–1039.

American Academy of Pediatrics (AAP). (1986). *Positive approaches to day care dilemmas: How to make it work.* Elk Grove Village, IL: Author.

American Academy of Pediatrics (AAP). (1989a, November). *The facts on breast feeding* [Fact sheet]. Elk Grove Village, IL: Author.

American Academy of Pediatrics (AAP). (1989b). Follow-up on weaning formulas. *Pediatrics, 83,* 1067.

American Academy of Pediatrics (AAP). (1996, October). *Where we stand* [On-line]. Available: http://www.aap.org/advocacy/wwestand.htm.

American Academy of Pediatrics (AAP). (1998). Policy statement on female genital mutilation. *Pediatrics, 102,* 153–156.

American Academy of Pediatrics Committee on Adolescence. (2001). Condom use by adolescents. *Pediatrics, 107*(6), 1463–1469.

American Academy of Pediatrics Committee on Drugs. (2000). Use of psychoactive medication during pregnancy and possible effects on the fetus and newborn. *Pediatrics, 105,* 880–887.

American Academy of Pediatrics Committee on Injury and Poison Prevention. (2001a). Bicycle helmets. *Pediatrics, 108*(4), 1030–1032.

American Academy of Pediatrics Committee on Injury and Poison Prevention. (2001b). Injuries associated with infant walkers. *Pediatrics, 108*(3), 790–792.

American Academy of Pediatrics Committee on Native American Child Health and Committee on Infectious Diseases. (1999). Immunizations for Native American children. *Pediatrics, 104,* 564–567.

American Academy of Pediatrics Committee on Pediatric Research. (2000). Race/ethnicity, gender, socioeconomic status—Research exploring their effects on child health: A subject review. *Pediatrics, 105,* 1349–1351.

American Academy of Pediatrics Committee on Psychosocial Aspects of Child and Family Health. (2002). Coparent or second-parent adoption by same-sex parents. *Pediatrics, 109*(2), 339–340.

American Academy of Pediatrics Committee on Psychosocial Aspects of Child and Family Health and Committee on Adolescence. (2001). Sexuality education for children and adolescence. *Pediatrics, 108*(2), 498–502.

American Academy of Pediatrics Committee on Psychosocial Aspects of Child and Family Health. (2002). Coparent or second-parent adoption by same-sex parents. *Pediatrics, 109,* 339–340.

American Academy of Pediatrics Committee on Quality Improvement. (2002). Making Advances Against Jaundice in Infant Care (MAJIC). [Online]. Available: http://www/aap.org/visit/majic.htm. Access date: October 25, 2002.

American Academy of Pediatrics Committee on Sports Medicine and Fitness. (2001). Risk of injury from baseball and softball in children. *Pediatrics, 107*(4), 782–784.

American Academy of Pediatrics Committee on Substance Abuse. (2001). Tobacco's toll: Implications for the pediatrician. *Pediatrics, 107,* 794–798.

American Association for Geriatric Psychiatry (AAGP). (1996). *Brief fact sheet on late-life depression.* Bethesda, MD: Author.

American Association of Retired Persons (AARP). (1993a). *Abused elders or battered women?* Washington, DC: Author.

American Association of Retired Persons (AARP). (1995). *A profile of older Americans.* Washington, DC: Author.

American Association of Retired Persons (AARP). (1999). *A profile of older Americans. 1998.* Washington, DC: Author.

American Association of Retired Persons (AARP). (2000). *Baby boomers envision their retirement: An AARP segmentation analysis.* Washington, DC: Author.

American Association of Retired Persons (AARP). (2002). Facts about grandparents raising grandchildren. [Online]. Available: http://www.aarp.org/confacts/grandparents/grandfacts.html. Access date: December 18, 2002.

American Association of University Women (AAUW) Educational Foundation. (1992). *The AAUW report: How schools shortchange girls.* Washington, DC: Author.

American Association of University Women (AAUW) Educational Foundation. (1998a, October 14). *Gender gaps fact sheets* [On-line]. Available: http://www.aauw.org/2000/ggfs.html

American Association of University Women (AAUW) Educational Foundation. (1998b, October 14). *Technology gender gap develops while gaps in math and science narrow, AAUW Foundation report shows.* [On-line, Press release]. Available: http://www.aauw.org/2000/ggpr.html

American Cancer Society. (2001). *Cancer facts and figures.* Atlanta: Author.

American College of Obstetrics and Gynecology. (1994). *Exercise during pregnancy and the postpartum pregnancy* (Technical Bulletin No. 189). Washington, DC: Author.

American Diabetes Association. (1992). *Diabetes facts.* Alexandria, VA: Author.

American Diabetes Association. (2000). *Diabetes facts.* Alexandria, VA: Author.

American Heart Association (AHA). (1995). *Silent epidemic: The truth about women and heart disease.* Dallas: Author.

American Medical Association (AMA). (1992). *Diagnosis and treatment guidelines on elder abuse and neglect.* Chicago: Author.

American Medical Association. (1998). *Essential guide to menopause.* New York: Simon & Schuster.

American Psychiatric Association (APA). (1994). *Diagnostic and statistical manual of mental disorders* (4th ed.). Washington, DC: Author.

American Psychological Association. (1992). Ethical principles of psychologists and code of conduct. *American Psychologist, 47,* 1597–1611.

American Psychological Association. (undated). *Answers to your questions about sexual orientation and homosexuality* [Brochure]. Washington, DC: Author.

American Psychological Association and American Academy of Pediatrics. (1996). *Raising children to resist violence: What you can do* [On-line, Brochure]. Available: http:/www.apa.org/pubinfo/apaaap.html

American Psychological Association Commission on Violence and Youth. (1994). *Reason to hope.* Washington, DC: Author.

American Society for Aesthetic Plastic Surgery. (2002, May 23). Botox parties not just fun and games, advises the American Society for Aesthetic Plastic Surgery. (News release). [Online]. Available: http://surgery.org/news_releases/may2303btx.html. Access date: October 22, 2002.

Americans on Values Follow-Up Survey, 1998. (1999). Washington, DC: Kaiser Family Foundation/Washington Post/Harvard University.

Ames, E. W. (1997). *The development of Romanian orphanage children adopted to Canada: Final report* (National Welfare Grants Program, Human Resources Development, Canada). Burnaby, BC, Canada: Simon Fraser University, Psychology Department.

Ammenheuser, M. M., Berenson, A. B., Babiak, A. E., Singleton, C. R., & Whorton, E. B. (1998). Frequencies of hprt mutant lymphocytes in marijuana-smoking. *Mutation Research, 403,* 55–64.

Amsel, E., Goodman, G., Savoie, D., & Clark, M. (1996). The development of reasoning about causal and noncausal influences on levers. *Child Development, 67,* 1624–1646.

Anastasi, A. (1988). *Psychological testing* (6th ed.). New York: Macmillan.

Anastasi, A., & Schaefer, C. E. (1971). Note on concepts of creativity and intelligence. *Journal of Creative Behavior, 3,* 113–116.

Anastasi, A., & Urbina, S. (1997). *Psychological testing* (7th ed.). Upper Saddle River, NJ: Prentice-Hall.

Andersen, A. E. (1995). Eating disorders in males. In K. D. Brownell & C. G. Fairburn (Eds.), *Eating disorders and obesity: A comprehensive handbook* (pp. 177–187). New York: Guilford.

Andersen, R. E., Crespo, C. J., Bartlett, S. J., Cheskin, L. J., & Pratt, M. (1998). Relationship of physical activity and television watching with body weight and level of fatness among children: Results from the Third National Health and Nutrition Examination Survey. *Journal of the American Medical Association, 279,* 938–942.

Andersen, R. E., Wadden, T. A., Bartlett, S. J., Zemel, B., Verde, T. J., & Franckowiak, S. C. (1999). Effects of lifestyle activity vs. structured aerobic exercise in obese women: A randomized trial. *Journal of the American Medical Association, 281,* 335–340.

Anderson, A. H., Clark, A., & Mullin, J. (1994). Interactive communication between children: Learning how to make language work in dialog. *Journal of Child Language, 21,* 439–463.

Anderson, M. (1992). *My Lord, what a morning.* Madison: University of Wisconsin Press.

Anderson, M., Kaufman, J., Simon, T. R., Barrios, L., Paulozzi, L., Ryan, G., Hammond, R., Modzeleski, W., Feucht, T., Potter, L., & the School-Associated Violent Deaths Study Group. (2001). School-associated violent deaths in the United States, 1994–1999. *Journal of the American Medical Association, 286*(21), 2695–2702.

Anderson, R. N. (2001a). Deaths: Leading causes for 1999. *National Vital Statistics Reports, 49*(11).

Anderson, R. N. (2001b). United States Life Tables, 1998. *National Vital Statistics Reports, 48*(18). Hyattsville, MD: National Center for Health Statistics.

Anderson, R. N. (2002). Deaths: Leading causes for 2000. *National Vital Statistics Reports, 50* (16). Hyattsville, MD: National Center for Health Statistics.

Anderson, S. A., Russell, C. S., & Schumm, W. R. (1983). Perceived marital quality and family life-cycle categories: A further analysis. *Journal of Marriage and the Family, 45,* 127–139.

Anderson, W. F. (1998). Human gene therapy. *Nature, 392*(Suppl.), 25–30.

Anderssen N., Amlie, C., & Ytteroy, E. A. (2002). Outcomes for children with lesbian or gay parents: A review of studies from 1978 to 2000. *Scandinavian Journal of Psychology, 43,* 335–351.

Andreasen, N., Hesse, C., Davidsson, P., Minthon, L., Wallin, A., Winblad, B., Vanderstichele, H., Vanmechelen, E., & Blennow, K. (1999). Cerebrospinal fluid B-amyloid(1-42) in Alzheimer disease: Differences between early- and late-onset Alzheimer disease and stability during the course of disease. *Archives of Neurology, 56,* 673–680.

Andresen, J. (2001). Cultural competence and health care: Japanese, Korean, and Indian patients in the United States. *Journal of Cultural Diversity, 8,* 109–121.

Angelsen, N. K., Vik, T., Jacobsen, G., & Bakketeig, L. S. (2001). Breast feeding and cognitive development at age 1 and 5 years. *Archives of Disease in Childhood, 85,* 183–188.

Anisfeld, M. (1996). Only tongue protrusion modeling is matched by neonates. *Developmental Review, 16,* 149–161.

Ann Bancroft (1955–), explorer. (1999). Women in American history by Encyclopedia Britannica. [Online]. Available: http://www.britannica.com/women/articles/Bancroft_Ann.html. Access date: April 4, 2002.

Ann Bancroft, 1955–. (1998). National Women's Hall of Fame. [Online]. Available: http://www.jerseycity.k12.nj.us/womenshistory/ bancroft.htm. Access date: April 4, 2002.

Ann Bancroft, explorer. (undated). [Online]. http://www.people/memphis.edu/~cbburr/gold/bancroft.htm. Access date: April 4, 2002.

Antonarakis, S. E., & Down Syndrome Collaborative Group. (1991). Parental origin of the extra chromosome in trisomy 21 as indicated by analysis of DNA polymorphisms. *New England Journal of Medicine, 324,* 872–876.

Antonucci, T., & Akiyama, H. (1997). Concern with others at midlife: Care, comfort, or compromise? In M. E. Lachman & J. B. James (Eds.), *Multiple paths of midlife development* (pp. 145–169). Chicago: University of Chicago Press.

Antonucci, T. C., & Akiyama, H. (1995). Convoys of social relations: family and friendships within a life span context. In R. Blieszner & V. Hilkevitch (Eds.), *Handbook of aging and the family* (pp. 355–371). Westport, CT: Greenwood Press.

Antonucci, T. C., Akiyama, H., & Merline, A. (2001). Dynamics of social relationships in midlife. In M. E. Lachman (Ed.), *Handbook of midlife development* (pp. 571–598). New York: Wiley.

Apgar, V. (1953). A proposal for a new method of evaluation of the newborn infant. *Current Research in Anesthesia and Analgesia, 32,* 260–267.

Applbaum, K. D. (1995). Marriage with the proper stranger: Arranged marriage in metropolitan Japan. *Ethnology, 34,* 37–51.

Aquilino, W. S. (1996). The returning adult child and parental experience at midlife. In C. Ryff & M. M. Seltzer (Eds.), *The parental experience in midlife* (pp. 423–458). Chicago: University of Chicago Press.

Aquilino, W. S., & Supple, K. R. (1991). Parent-child relations and parent's satisfaction with living arrangements when adult children live at home. *Journal of Marriage and the Family, 53,* 13–27.

Arbuckle, T. Y., Maag, U., Pushkar, D., & Chaikelson, J. S. (1998). Individual differences in trajectory of intellectual development over 45 years of adulthood. *Psychology and Aging, 13,* 663–675.

Archer, S. L. (1993). Identity in relational contexts: A methodological proposal. In J. Kroger (Ed.), *Discussions on ego identity* (pp. 75–99). Hillsdale, NJ: Erlbaum.

Arcus, D., & Kagan, J. (1995). Temperament and craniofacial variation in the first two years. *Child Development, 66,* 1529–1540.

Aries, P. (1962). *Centuries of childhood.* New York: Vintage.

Arlin, P. K. (1984). Adolescent and adult thought: A structural interpretation. In M. L. Commons, F. A. Richards, & C. Armon (Eds.),

Beyond formal operations (pp. 258–271). New York: Praeger.

Armistead, L., Summers, P., Forehand, R., Morse, P. S., Morse, E., & Clark, L. (1999). Understanding of HIV/AIDS among children of HIV-infected mothers: Implications for prevention, disclosure, and bereavement. *Children's Health Care, 28,* 277–295.

Arnett, J. J. (1999). Adolescent storm and stress, reconsidered. *American Psychologist, 54,* 317–326.

Arnold, D. S., & Whitehurst, G. J. (1994). Accelerating language development through picture book reading: A summary of dialogic reading and its effects. In D. K. Dickinson (Ed.), *Bridges to literacy: Children, families, and schools* (pp. 103–128). Oxford: Blackwell.

Ashe, A., & Rampersad, A. (1993). *Days of grace: A memoir.* New York: Ballantine.

Aslin, R. N. (1987). Visual and auditory development in infancy. In J. D. Osofsky (Ed.), *Handbook of infant development* (2nd ed.). New York: Wiley.

Associated Press. (2002a, May 26). Dedicated Japanese are dying from overwork. *Minneapolis Star-Tribune,* p. A13.

Associated Press. (2002b, July 15). Fewer children lack health insurance. Washington, DC: Author.

Astington, J. W. (1993). *The child's discovery of the mind.* Cambridge, MA: Harvard University Press.

Astington, J. W., & Jenkins, J. M. (1999). A longitudinal study of the relation between language and theory-of-mind development. *Developmental Psychology, 35,* 1311–1320.

Atchley, R. C. (1989). A continuity theory of normal aging. *The Gerontologist, 29,* 183–190.

Atchley, R. C. (1997). *Social forces and aging: An introduction to social gerontology* (8th ed.). Belmont, CA: Wadsworth.

Athansiou, M. S. (2001). Using consultation with a grandmother as an adjunct to play therapy. *Family Journal—Consulting and Therapy for Couples and Families, 9,* 445–449.

Austin, E. W., Pinkleton, B. E., & Fujioka, Y. (2000). The role of interpretation processes and parental discussion in the media's effects on adolescents' use of alcohol. *Pediatrics, 105*(2), 343–349.

Australian man first in world to die with legal euthanasia. (1996, September 26). *The New York Times* (International Ed.), p. A5.

Austrom, D., & Hanel, K. (1985). Psychological issues of single life in Canada: An exploratory study. *International Journal of Women's Studies, 8,* 12–23.

Ausubel, N. (1964). *The book of Jewish knowledge.* New York: Crown.

Autism-Part I. (2001, June). *The Harvard Mental Health Letter, 17*(12), pp. 1–4.

Autism-Part II. (2001, July). *The Harvard Mental Health Letter, 18*(1), pp. 1–4.

Avis, N. E. (1999). Women's health at midlife. In S. L. Willis & J. D. Reid (Eds.), *Life in the middle: Psychological and social development in middle age* (pp. 105–146). San Diego: Academic Press.

Avolio, B. J., & Sosik, J. J. (1999). A life-span framework for assessing the impact of work on white-collar workers. In S. L. Willis & J. D. Reid (Eds.), *Life in the middle: Psychological and social development in middle age.* San Diego: Academic Press.

Aylward, G. P., Pfeiffer, S. I., Wright, A., & Verhulst, S. J. (1989). Outcome studies of low birth weight infants published in the last decade: A meta-analysis. *Journal of Pediatrics, 115,* 515–520.

Azar, B. (2002a, January). At the frontier of science. *Monitor on Psychology,* pp. 40–41.

Azar, B. (2002b, March). Helping older adults get on the technology bandwagon. *Monitor on Psychology, 33*(3), [Online]. Available http://www.apa.org/monitor/mar02/helpin gold.html. Access date: April 15, 2002.

Azuma, H. (1994). Two modes of cognitive socialization in Japan and the United States. In P. M. Greenfield & R. R. Cocking (Eds.), *Cross-cultural roots of minority child development* (pp. 275–284). Hillsdale, NJ: Erlbaum.

Babchuk, N. (1978–1979). Aging and primary relations. *International Journal of Aging and Human Development, 9*(2), 137–151.

Babu, A., & Hirschhorn, K. (1992). *A guide to human chromosome defects* (Birth Defects: Original Article Series, 28[2]). White Plains, NY: March of Dimes Birth Defects Foundation.

Bach, P. B., Schrag, D., Brawley, O. W., Galaznik, A., Yakren, S., & Begg, C. B. (2002). Survival of blacks and whites after a cancer diagnosis. *Journal of the American Medical Association, 287,* 2106–2113.

Bachman, J. G., & Schulenberg, J. (1993). How part-time work intensity relates to drug use, problem behavior, time use, and satisfaction among high school seniors: Are these consequences or merely correlates? *Developmental Psychology, 29,* 220–235.

Bachman, R. (1994, January). *Violence against women: A national crime victimization report* (NCJ-145325). Washington, DC: Bureau of Justice Statistics Clearinghouse.

Bachu, A., & O'Connell, M. (2001). Fertility of American women: June 2000. *Current Population Reports,* P20–543RV. Washington, DC: U.S. Census Bureau.

Baddeley, A. D. (1981). The concept of working memory: A view of its current state and probable future development. *Cognition, 10,* 17–23.

Baddeley, A. D. (1986). *Working memory.* London: Oxford University Press.

Baer, K. (1997, July). A movement toward t'ai chi. *Harvard Health Letter, 22*(9), 6–7.

Bagwell, C. L., Newcomb, A. F., & Bukowski, W. M. (1998). Preadolescent friendship and peer rejection as predictors of adult adjustment. *Child Development, 69,* 140–153.

Bailey, A., Le Couteur, A., Gottesman, I., & Bolton, P. (1995). Autism as a strongly genetic disorder: Evidence from a British twin study. *Psychological Medicine, 25,* 63–77.

Bailey, D. B., Jr., & Symons, F. J. (2001). Critical periods: Reflections and future directions. In D. B. Bailey, Jr., J. T. Bruer, F. J. Symons, & J. W. Lichtman (Eds.), *Critical thinking about critical periods: A series from the National Center for Early Development and Learning* (pp. 289–292). Baltimore: Paul H. Brookes.

Bailey, J. M., Bobrow, D., Wolfe, M., & Mikach, S. (1995). Sexual orientation of adult sons of gay fathers. *Developmental Psychology, 31,* 124–129.

Baillargeon, R. (1994a). How do infants learn about the physical world? *Current Directions in Psychological Science, 3,* 133–140.

Baillargeon, R. (1994b). Physical reasoning in young infants: Seeking explanations for impossible events. *British Journal of Developmental Psychology, 12,* 9–33.

Baillargeon, R. (1999). Young infants' expectations about hidden objects. *Developmental Science, 2,* 115–132.

Baillargeon, R., & DeVos, J. (1991). Object permanence in young infants: Further evidence. *Child Development, 62,* 1227–1246.

Baines, L. S., Joseph, J. T., & Jindal, R. M. (2002). A public forum to promote organ donation amongst Asians: The Scottish initiative. *Transplant International, 15,* 124–131.

Baker, D. W., Sudano, J. J., Albert, J. M., Borawski, E. A., & Dor, A. (2001). Lack of health insurance and decline in overall health in late middle age. *New England Journal of Medicine, 345,* 1106–1112.

Baldereschi, M., Di Carlo, A., Lepore, V., Bracco, L., Maggi, S., Grigoletto, F., Scarlato, G., & Amaducci, L. (1998). Estrogen-replacement therapy and Alzheimer's disease in the Italian Longitudinal Study on Aging. *Neurology, 50,* 996–1002.

Baldwin, D. A., & Moses, L. J. (1996). The ontogeny of social information gathering. *Child Development, 67,* 1915–1939.

Balk, J. L., Whiteside, D. A., Naus, G., DeFerrari, E., & Roberts, J. M. (2002). A pilot study of the effects of phytoestrogen supplementation on postmenopausal endometrium. *Journal of the Society of Gynecologic Investigation, 9,* 238–242.

Baltes, P. B. (1987). Theoretical propositions of life-span development psychology: On the dynamics between growth and decline. *Developmental Psychology, 23*(5), 611–626.

Baltes, P. B. (1993). The aging mind: Potential and limits. *The Gerontologist, 33,* 580–594.

Baltes, P. B., & Baltes, M. M. (1990). Psychological perspectives on successful aging: The model of selective optimization with compensation. In P. B. Baltes & M. M. Baltes (Eds.), *Successful aging: Perspectives from the behavioral sciences* (pp. 1–34). New York: Cambridge University Press.

Baltes, P. B., & Staudinger, U. M. (2000). Wisdom: A metaheuristic (pragmatic) to orchestrate mind and virtue toward excellence. *American Psychologist, 55,* 122–136.

Baltes, P. B., & Willis, S. L. (1982). Enhancement (plasticity) of intellectual functioning in old age: Penn State's Adult Development and Enrichment Project (ADEPT). In F. I. M. Craik

& S. Trehub (Eds.), *Aging and cognitive processes* (pp. 353–389). New York: Plenum.

Baltes, P. B., Lindenberger, U., & Staudinger, U. M. (1998). Life-span theory in developmental psychology. In R. M. Lerner (Ed.), *Handbook of child psychology: Vol. 1. Theoretical models of human development* (pp. 1029–1143). New York: Wiley.

Baltes, P. B., Reese, H. W., & Lipsitt, L. (1980). Life-span developmental psychology. *Annual Review of Psychology, 31,* 65–110.

Baltes, P. B., Staudinger, U. M., Maercker, A., & Smith, J. (1995). People nominated as wise: A comparative study of wisdom-related knowledge. *Psychology and Aging, 10,* 155–166.

Bandura, A. (1977). *Social learning theory.* Englewood Cliffs, NJ: Prentice-Hall.

Bandura, A. (1986). *Social foundations of thought and action: A social cognitive theory.* Englewood Cliffs, NJ: Prentice-Hall.

Bandura, A. (1989). Social cognitive theory. In R. Vasta (Ed.), *Annals of child development.* Greenwich, CT: JAI.

Bandura, A. (1994). Self-efficacy. In V. S. Ramachaudran (Ed.), *Encyclopedia of human behavior* (Vol. 4, pp. 71–81). New York: Academic Press.

Bandura, A., Barbaranelli, C., Caprara, G. V., & Pastorelli, C. (1996). Multifaceted impact of self-efficacy beliefs on academic functioning. *Child Development, 67,* 1206–1222.

Bandura, A., Barbaranelli, C., Caprara, G. V., & Pastorelli, C. (2001). Self-efficacy beliefs as shapers of children's aspirations and career trajectories. *Child Development, 72*(1), 187–206.

Bandura, A., Ross, D., & Ross, S. A. (1961). Transmission of aggression through imitation of aggressive models. *Journal of Abnormal and Social Psychology, 63,* 575–582.

Bandura, A., Ross, D., & Ross, S. A. (1963). Imitation of film-mediated aggressive models. *Journal of Abnormal and Social Psychology, 66,* 3–11.

Banks, D. A., & Fossel, M. (1997). Telomeres, cancer, and aging: Altering the human life span. *Journal of the American Medical Association, 278,* 1345–1348.

Banks, E. (1989). Temperament and individuality: A study of Malay children. *American Journal of Orthopsychiatry, 59,* 390–397.

Barber, B. K. (1994). Cultural, family, and personal contexts of parent-adolescent conflict. *Journal of Marriage and the Family, 56,* 375–386.

Barber, B. L., & Eccles, J. S. (1992). Long-term influence of divorce and single parenting on adolescent family- and work-related values, behaviors, and aspirations. *Psychological Bulletin, 111*(1), 108–126.

Barinaga, M. (1998). Alzheimer's treatments that work now. *Science, 282,* 1030–1032.

Barkley, R. A. (1998a, February). How should attention deficit disorder be described? *Harvard Mental Health Letter,* p. 8.

Barkley, R. A. (1998b, September). Attention-deficit hyperactivity disorder. *Scientific American,* pp. 66–71.

Barkley, R. A., Murphy, K. R., & Kwasnik, D. (1996). Motor vehicle competencies and risks in teens and young adults with attention deficit hyperactivity disorder. *Pediatrics, 98,* 1089–1095.

Barlow, S. E., & Dietz, W. H. (1998). Obesity evaluation and treatment: Expert committee recommendations [On-line]. *Pediatrics, 102*(3), e29. Available: http://www.pediatrics.org/cgi/content/full/102/3/e29

Barnett, R. (1985, March). *We've come a long way—but where are we and what are the rewards?* Paper presented at the conference on Women in Transition, New York University School of Continuing Education, Center for Career and Life Planning, New York, NY.

Barnett, R. C. (1997). Gender, employment, and psychological well-being: Historical and life-course perspectives. In M. E. Lachman & J. B. James (Eds.), *Multiple paths of midlife development* (pp. 325–343). Chicago: University of Chicago Press.

Barnett, R. C., & Hyde, J. S. (2001). Women, men, work, and family. *American Psychologist, 56,* 781–796.

Barnhart, M. A. (1992, Fall). Coping with the Methuselah syndrome. *Free Inquiry,* pp. 19–22.

Baron, C. H., Bergstresser, C., Brock, D. W., Cole, G. F., Dorfman, N. S., Johnson, J. A., Schnipper, L. E., Vorenberg, J., & Wanzer, S. (1996). A model state act to authorize and regulate physician-assisted suicide. *Harvard Journal on Legislation, 33*(1), 1–34.

Barrett-Connor, E., Hendrix, S., Ettinger, B., Wenger, N. K., Paoletti, R., Lenfant, C. J. M., & Pinn, V. W. (2002). Best clinical practices: Chapter 13. *International position paper on women's health and menopause: A comprehensive approach.* Washington, DC: National Heart, Lung, and Blood Institute.

Bartecchi, C. E., MacKenzie, T. D., & Schrier, R. W. (1995, May). The global tobacco epidemic. *Scientific American,* pp. 44–51.

Bartoshuk, L. M., & Beauchamp, G. K. (1994). Chemical senses. *Annual Review of Psychology, 45,* 419–449.

Bascom, P. B., & Tolle, S. W. (2002). Responding to requests for physician-assisted suicide: "These are uncharted waters for both of us. . . ." *Journal of the American Medical Association, 288,* 91–98.

Bashore, T. R., Ridderinkhof, F., & van der Molen, M. W. (1998). The decline of cognitive processing speed in old age. *Current Directions in Psychological Science, 6,* 163–169.

Bassuk, E. L. (1991). Homeless families. *Scientific American, 265*(6), 66–74.

Bassuk, E. L., Weinreb, L. F., Dawson, R., Perloff, J. N., & Buckner, J. C. (1997). Determinants of behavior in homeless and low-income housed preschooler children. *Pediatrics, 100,* 92–100.

Bates, E., Bretherton, I., & Snyder, L. (1988). *From first words to grammar: Individual differences and dissociable mechanisms.* New York: Cambridge University Press.

Bates, E., O'Connell, B., & Shore, C. (1987). Language and communication in infancy. In J. D. Osofsky (Ed.), *Handbook of infant development* (2nd ed.). New York: Wiley.

Bateson, M. C. (1984). *With a daughter's eye: A memoir of Margaret Mead and Gregory Bateson.* New York: William Morrow & Co.

Baum, A., & Fleming, I. (1993). Implications of psychological research on stress and technological accidents. *American Psychologist, 48,* 665–672.

Baum, A., Cacioppo, J. T., Melamed, B. G., Gallant, S. J., & Travis, C. (1995). *Doing the right thing: A research plan for healthy living.* Washington, DC: American Psychological Association Science Directorate.

Baumeister, R. F., & Leary, M. R. (1995). The need to belong: Desire for interpersonal attachments as a fundamental human motivation. *Psychological Bulletin, 117*(3), 497–529.

Baumer, E. P., & South, S. J. (2001). Community effects on youth sexual activity. *Journal of Marriage and the Family, 63,* 540–554.

Baumrind, D. (1971). Harmonious parents and their preschool children. *Developmental Psychology, 41,* 92–102.

Baumrind, D. (1989). Rearing competent children. In W. Damon (Ed.), *Child development today and tomorrow* (pp. 349–378). San Francisco: Jossey-Bass.

Baumrind, D. (1991). Parenting styles and adolescent development. In J. Brooks-Gunn, R. Lerner, & A. C. Peterson (Eds.), *The encyclopedia of adolescence* (pp. 746–758). New York: Garland.

Baumrind, D. (1995). Commentary on sexual orientation: Research and social policy implications. *Developmental Psychology, 31,* 130–136.

Baumrind, D. (1996a). A blanket injunction against disciplinary use of spanking is not warranted by the data. *Pediatrics, 88,* 828–831.

Baumrind, D. (1996b). The discipline controversy revisited. *Family Relations, 45,* 405–414.

Baumrind, D., & Black, A. E. (1967). Socialization practices associated with dimensions of competence in preschool boys and girls. *Child Development, 38,* 291–327.

Bauserman, R. (2002). Child adjustment in joint-custody versus sole-custody arrangements: A meta-analytic review. *Journal of Family Psychology, 16,* 91–102.

Bayley, N. (1969). *Bayley Scales of Infant Development.* New York: Psychological Corporation.

Bayley, N. (1993). *Bayley Scales of Infant Development: II.* New York: Psychological Corporation.

Beal, C. R. (1994). *Boys and girls: The development of gender roles.* New York: McGraw-Hill.

Beall, A. E., & Sternberg, R. J. (1995). The social construction of love. *Journal of Social and Personal Relationships, 12*(3), 417–438.

Becker, A. E., Grinspoon, S. K., Klibanski, A., & Herzog, D. B. (1999). Eating disorders. *New England Journal of Medicine, 340,* 1092–1098.

Becker, G. S. (1991). *A treatise on the family* (enlarged ed.). Cambridge, MA: Harvard University Press.

Becker, P. E., & Moen, P. (1999). Scaling back: Dual-earner couples' work-family strategies. *Journal of Marriage and the Family, 61,* 995–1007.

Beckwith, L., Cohen, S. E., & Hamilton, C. E. (1999). Maternal sensitivity during infancy and subsequent life events relate to attachment representation at early adulthood. *Developmental Psychology, 35,* 693–700.

Bedford, V. H. (1995). Sibling relationships in middle and old age. In R. Blieszner & V. Hilkevitch (Eds.), *Handbook of aging and the family* (pp. 201–222). Westport, CT: Greenwood Press.

Bedford, V. H. (1998). Sibling relationship troubles and well-being in middle and old age. *Family Relations, 47,* 369–376.

Behrman, R. E. (1992). *Nelson textbook of pediatrics* (13th ed.). Philadelphia: Saunders.

Beidel, D. C., & Turner, S. M. (1998). *Shy children, phobic adults: Nature and treatment of social phobia.* Washington, DC: American Psychological Association.

Beilin, H. (1994). Jean Piaget's enduring contribution to developmental psychology. In R. D. Parke, P. A. Ornstein, J. J. Rieser, & C. Zahn-Wexler (Eds.), *A century of developmental psychology* (pp. 257–290). Washington, DC: American Psychological Association.

Belbin, R. M. (1967). Middle age: What happens to ability? In R. Owen (Ed.), *Middle age.* London: BBC.

Belgium legalises euthanasia. (May 16, 2002). BBC-News online. Available: http://www.nvve.nl [website of the Dutch Voluntary Euthanasia Society].

Belizzi, M. (2002, May). *Obesity in children—What kind of future are we creating?* Presentation at the Fifty-Fifth World Health Assembly Technical Briefing, Geneva.

Bell, J. (1992). In search of a discourse on aging: The elderly on television. *The Gerontologist, 32*(3), 305–311.

Bell, M. A., & Fox, N. A. (1992). The relations between frontal brain electrical activity and cognitive development during infancy. *Child Development, 63,* 1142–1163.

Bell, R., Wechsler, H., & Johnston, L. D. (1997). Correlates of college student marijuana use: Results of a U.S. national survey. *Addiction, 92,* 571–581.

Bellinger, D., Leviton, A., Watermaux, C., Needleman, H., & Rabinowitz, M. (1987). Longitudinal analyses of prenatal and postnatal lead exposure and early cognitive development. *New England Journal of Medicine, 316*(17), 1037–1043.

Belsky, J. (1984). Two waves of day care research: Developmental effects and conditions of quality. In R. Ainslie (Ed.), *The child and the day care setting.* New York: Praeger.

Belsky, J. (1993). Etiology of child maltreatment: A developmental-ecological analysis. *Psychological Bulletin, 114,* 413–434.

Belsky, J., & Rovine, M. (1990). Patterns of marital change across the transition to parenthood: Pregnancy to three years postpartum. *Journal of Marriage and the Family, 52,* 5–19.

Belsky, J., Fish, M., & Isabella, R. (1991). Continuity and discontinuity in infant negative and positive emotionality: Family antecedents and attachment consequences. *Developmental Psychology, 27,* 421–431.

Bem, S. L. (1983). Gender schema theory and its implications for child development: Raising gender-aschematic children in a gender-schematic society. *Signs, 8,* 598–616.

Bem, S. L. (1985). Androgyny and gender schema theory: A conceptual and empirical integration. In T. B. Sondregger (Ed.), *Nebraska Symposium on Motivation, 1984: Psychology and gender.* Lincoln: University of Nebraska Press.

Bem, S. L. (1993). *The lenses of gender: Transforming the debate on sexual inequality.* New Haven, CT: Yale University Press.

Benenson, J. F. (1993). Greater preference among females than males for dyadic interaction in early childhood. *Child Development, 64,* 544–555.

Benes, F. M., Turtle, M., Khan, Y., & Farol, P. (1994). Myelination of a key relay zone in the hippocampal formation occurs in the human brain during childhood, adolescence, and adulthood. *Archives of General Psychiatry, 51,* 447–484.

Bengtson, V. L. (2001). Beyond the nuclear family: The increasing importance of multigenerational bonds. *Journal of Marriage and Family, 63,* 1–16.

Bengtson, V. L., Rosenthal, C. J., & Burton, L. M. (1990). Families and aging: Diversity and heterogeneity. In R. Binstock & L. George (Eds.), *Handbook of aging and the social sciences* (pp. 263–287). San Diego: Academic Press.

Bengtson, V. L., Rosenthal, C., & Burton, L. (1996). Paradoxes of families and aging. In R. H. Binstock & L. K. George (Eds.), *Handbook of aging and the social sciences* (pp. 253–282). San Diego: Academic Press.

Benson, J. B., & Uzgiris, I. C. (1985). Effect of self-inflicted locomotion on infant search activity. *Developmental Psychology, 21,* 923–931.

Ben-Ze'ev A. (1997). Emotions and morality. *Journal of Value Inquiry, 31,* 195–212.

Berg, C. A., & Klaczynski, P. A. (1996). Practical intelligence and problem solving: Search for perspectives. In F. Blanchard-Fields & T. M. Hess (Eds.), *Perspectives on cognitive change in adulthood and aging* (pp. 323–357). New York: McGraw-Hill.

Bergeman, C. S., & Plomin, R. (1989). Genotype-environment interaction. In M. Bornstein & J. Bruner (Eds.), *Interaction in human development* (pp. 157–171). Hillsdale, NJ: Erlbaum.

Bergen, D., Reid, R., & Torelli, L. (2000). *Educating and caring for very young children: The infant-toddler curriculum.* Washington, DC: National Association for the Education of Young Children.

Berger, R. M., & Kelly, J. J. (1986). Working with homosexuals of the older population. *Social Casework, 67,* 203–210.

Bergman, I., & Burgess, A. (1980). *Ingrid Bergman: My story.* New York: Delacorte.

Berk, L. E. (1986a). Development of private speech among preschool children. *Early Child Development and Care, 24,* 113–136.

Berk, L. E. (1986b). Private speech: Learning out loud. *Psychology Today, 20*(5), 34–42.

Berk, L. E. (1992). Children's private speech: An overview of theory and the status of research. In R. M. Diaz & L. E. Berk (Eds.), *Private speech: From social interaction to self-regulation* (pp. 17–53). Hillsdale, NJ: Erlbaum.

Berk, L. E., & Garvin, R. A. (1984). Development of private speech among low-income Appalachian children. *Developmental Psychology, 20,* 271–286.

Berkowitz, G. S., Skovron, M. L., Lapinski, R. H., & Berkowitz, R. L. (1990). Delayed childbearing and the outcome of pregnancy. *New England Journal of Medicine, 322,* 659–664.

Bernard, B. P. (Ed.). (1997). *Musculoskeletal disorders and workplace factors: A critical review of epidemiologic evidence for work-related musculoskeletal disorders of the neck, upper extremity, and low back.* Cincinnati, OH: National Institute for Occupational Safety and Health.

Berndt, T. J. (1982). The features and effects of friendship in early adolescence. *Child Development, 53,* 1447–1460.

Berndt, T. J., & Perry, T. B. (1990). Distinctive features and effects of early adolescent friendships. In R. Montemayor, G. R. Adams, & T. P. Gullotta (Eds.), *From childhood to adolescence: A transitional period?* Newbury Park, CA: Sage.

Bernhardt, P. C. (1997). Influences of serotonin and testosterone in aggression and dominance: Convergence with social psychology. *Current Directions in Psychological Science, 6,* 44–48.

Bernstein, G. A., & Garfinkel, B. D. (1988). Pedigrees, functioning, and psychopathology in families of school phobic children. *American Journal of Psychiatry, 145,* 70–74.

Berrueta-Clement, J. R., Schweinhart, L. J., Barnett, W. S., & Weikart, D. P. (1987). The effects of early educational intervention on crime and delinquency in adolescence and early adulthood. In J. D. Burchard & S. N. Burchard (Eds.), *Primary prevention of psychopathology: Vol. 10. Prevention of delinquent behavior* (pp. 220–240). Newbury Park, CA: Sage.

Berrueta-Clement, J. R., Schweinhart, L. J., Barnett, W. S., Epstein, A. S., & Weikart, D. P. (1985). *Changed lives: The effects of the Perry Preschool Program on youths through age 19.* Ypsilanti, MI: High/Scope.

Berry, M., Dylla, D. J., Barth, R. P., & Needell, B. (1998). The role of open adoption in the adjustment of adopted children and their families. *Children and Youth Services Review, 20,* 151–171.

Berry, R. J., Li, Z., Erickson, J. D., Li, S., Moore, C. A., Wang, H., Mulinare, J., Zhao, P., Wong, L.-Y. C., Gindler, J., Hong, S.-X., & Correa, A. for the China-U.S. Collaborative Project for Neural Tube Defect Prevention. (1999). Prevention of neural-tube defects with folic acid in China. *New England Journal of Medicine, 341,* 1485–1490.

Bertenthal, B. I., & Campos, J. J. (1987). New directions in the study of early experience. *Child Development, 58,* 560–567.

Bertenthal, B. I., & Clifton, R. K. (1998). Perception and action. In W. Damon (Ed.-in-Chief) & D. Kuhn & R. S. Siegler (Vol. Eds.), *Handbook of child psychology, Vol. 2: Cognition, perception, and language* (pp. 51–102). New York: Wiley.

Bertenthal, B. I., Campos, J. J., & Barrett, K. C. (1984). Self-produced locomotion: An organizer of emotional, cognitive, and social development in infancy. In R. N. Emde & R. J. Harmon (Eds.), *Continuities and discontinuities in development.* New York: Plenum.

Bertenthal, B. I., Campos, J. J., & Kermoian, R. (1994). An epigenetic perspective on the development of self-produced locomotion and its consequences. *Current Directions in Psychological Science, 3*(5), 140–145.

Beumont, P. J. V., Russell, J. D., & Touyz, S. W. (1993). Treatment of anorexia nervosa. *The Lancet, 341,* 1635–1640.

Beversdorf, D. Q., Manning, S. E., Anderson, S. L., Nordgren, R. E., Walters, S. E., Cooley, W. C., Gaelic, S. E., & Bauman, M. L., (2001, November 10–15). *Timing of prenatal stressors and autism.* Presentation at the 31st Annual Meeting of the Society for Neuroscience, San Diego.

Beyene, Y. (1986). Cultural significance and physiological manifestations of menopause: A biocultural analysis. *Culture, Medicine, and Psychiatry, 10,* 47–71.

Beyene, Y. (1989). *From menarche to menopause: Reproductive lives of peasant women in two cultures.* Albany: State University of New York Press.

Beyette, B. (1998, November 29). Carter keeps zest for life. *Chicago Sun-Times,* pp. A6-A7.

Bianchi, S. M. (1995). The changing demographic and socioeconomic characteristics of single parent families. *Marriage and Family Review, 20*(1–2), 71–97.

Bianchi, S. M., & Spain, D. (1986). *American women in transition.* New York: Russell Sage Foundation.

Biegel, D. E. (1995). Caregiver burden. In G. E. Maddox (Ed.), *The encyclopedia of aging* (2nd ed., pp. 138–141). New York: Springer.

Bielby, D., & Papalia, D. (1975). Moral development and perceptual role-taking egocentrism: Their development and interrelationship across the lifespan. *International Journal of Aging and Human Development, 6*(4), 293–308.

Bierman, K. L., Smoot, D. L., & Aumiller, K. (1993). Characteristics of aggressive-rejected, aggressive (non-rejected), and rejected (non-aggressive) boys. *Child Development, 64,* 139–151.

Billet, S. (2001). Knowing in practice: Re-conceptualising vocational expertise. *Learning & Instruction, 11,* 431–452.

Binkley, M., Matheson, N., & Williams, T. (1997). *Adult literacy: An international perspective* (Working Paper No. 97–33). Washington, DC: National Center for Education Statistics.

Bird, K. (1990, November 12). The very model of an ex-president. *The Nation,* pp. 545, 560–564.

Birmaher, B. (1998). Should we use antidepressant medications for children and adolescents with depressive disorders? *Psychopharmacology Bulletin, 34,* 35–39.

Birmaher, B., Ryan, N. D., Williamson, D. E., Brent, D. A., Kaufman, J., Dahl, R. E., Perel, J., & Nelson, B. (1996). Childhood and adolescent depression: A review of the past 10 years. *Journal of the American Academy of Child, 35,* 1427–1440.

Birren, J. E., Woods, A. M., & Williams, M. V. (1980). Behavioral slowing with age: Causes, organization, and consequences. In L. W. Poon (Ed.), *Aging in the 1980s.* Washington, DC: American Psychological Association.

Bjorklund, D. F. (1997). The role of immaturity in human development. *Psychological Bulletin, 122,* 153–169.

Bjorklund, D. F., & Harnishfeger, K. K. (1990). The resources construct in cognitive development: Diverse sources of evidence and a theory of inefficient inhibition. *Developmental Review, 10,* 48–71.

Bjorklund, D. F., & Pellegrini, A. D. (2002). The Origins of Human Nature: Evolutionary developmental psychology.

Bjorklund, D. F., and Pellegrini, A. D. (2000). Child development and evolutionary psychology. *Child Development, 71*(6), 1687–1708.

Black, J. E. (1998). How a child builds its brain: Some lessons from animal studies of neural plasticity. *Preventive Medicine, 27,* 168–171.

Black, M. M., & Krishnakumar, A. (1998). Children in low-income, urban settings: Interventions to promote mental health and well-being. *American Psychologist, 53,* 636–646.

Black, M. M., Dubowitz, H., and Starr, R. H. (1999). African American fathers in low income, urban families: Development, behavior, and home environment of their three-year-old children. *Child Development, 70,* 967–978.

Blackburn, J. A., Papalia-Finlay, D., Foye, B. F., & Serlin, R. C. (1988). Modifiability of figural relations performance among elderly adults. *Journal of Gerontology: Psychological Sciences, 43*(3), P87–89.

Blackman, A. (1998). *The seasons of her life: A biography of Madeleine Korbel Albright.* New York: Scribner.

Blagrove, M., Alexander, C., & Horne, J. A. (1995). The effects of chronic sleep reducation on the performance of cognitive tasks sensitive to sleep deprivation. *Applied Cognitive Psychology, 9,* 21–40.

Blakeslee, S. (1997, April 17). Studies show talking with infants shapes basis of ability to think. *The New York Times,* p. D21.

Blanchard-Fields, F. (1986). Reasoning on social dilemmas varying in emotional saliency: An adult developmental perspective. *Psychology and Aging, 1,* 325–333.

Blanchard-Fields, F., & Camp, C. J. (1990). Affect, individual differences, and real world problem solving across the adult life span. In T. Hess (Ed.), *Aging and cognition: Knowledge organization and utilization* (pp. 461–498). Amsterdam: North-Holland, Elsevier.

Blanchard-Fields, F., & Irion, J. (1987). Coping strategies from the perspective of two developmental markers: Age and social reasoning. *Journal of Genetic Psychology, 149,* 141–151.

Blanchard-Fields, F., & Norris, L. (1994). Causal attributions from adolescence through adulthood: Age differences, ego level, and generalized response style. *Aging and Cognition, 1,* 67–86.

Blanchard-Fields, F., Chen, Y., & Norris, L. (1997). Everyday problem solving across the adult life span: Influence of domain specificity and cognitive appraisal. *Psychology and Aging, 12,* 684–693.

Blanchard-Fields, F., Jahnke, H. C., & Camp, C. J. (1995). Age differences in problem solving style: The role of emotional salience. *Psychology and Aging, 10,* 173–180.

Blieszner, R. (1986). Trends in family gerontology research. *Family Relations, 35,* 555–562.

Blieszner, R., Willis, S. L., & Baltes, P. B. (1981). Training research on induction ability: A short-term longitudinal study. *Journal of Applied Developmental Psychology, 2,* 247–265.

Block, J. (1971). *Lives through time.* Berkeley, CA: Bancroft.

Block, J. (1991). *Prototypes for the California Adult Q-Set.* Berkeley: University of California, Department of Psychology.

Block, J. (1995a). A contrarian view of the Five-Factor approach to personality description. *Psychological Bulletin, 117,* 187–215.

Block, J. (1995b). Going beyond the five factors given: Rejoinder to Costa and McCrae (1995) and Goldberg and Saucier (1995). *Psychological Bulletin, 117,* 226–229.

Blood, T. (1997). *Madam secretary: A biography of Madeleine Albright.* New York: St. Martin's.

Bloom, B., & Tonthat, L. (2002). Summary health statistics for U.S. children: National Health Interview Survey, 1997. *Vital and Health Statistics, 10,* 203.

Bloom, B. S. (1985). *Developing talent in young people.* New York: Ballantine.

Bloom, H. (Ed.). (1999). *A scholarly look at The Diary of Anne Frank.* Philadelphia: Chelsea.

Blumenthal, J. A., Emery, C. F., Madden, D. J., Schniebolk, S., Walsh-Riddle, M., George, L. K., McKee, D. C., Higginbotham, M. B., Cobb, F. R., & Coleman, R. E. (1991). Long-term effects of exercise on psychological functioning in older men and women. *Journal of Gerontology, 46*(6), P352–361.

Blyth, D. A., & Foster-Clark, F. S. (1987). Gender differences in perceived intimacy with different members of adolescents' social networks. *Sex Roles, 17,* 689–718.

Board of Education of the City of New York. (2002, May 6). Effects of the World Trade Center attack on NYC public school students. [Online]. Available: www.nycenet.edu. Access date: May 8, 2002.

Boatman, D., Freeman, J., Vining, E., Pulsifer, M., Miglioretti, D., Minahan, R., Carson, B., & Brandt, J., & McKhann, G. (1999). Language recovery after left hemispherectomy in children with late-onset seizures. *Annals of Neurology, 46*(4), 579–586.

Bobinski, M., De Leon, M. H., Convit, A., De Santi, S., Wegiel, J., Tarshish, C. Y., Saint Louis, L. A., & Wisniewski, H. M. (1999). MRI of entorhinal cortex in mild Alzheimer's disease. *Lancet, 353,* 38–40.

Bodnar, A. G., Ouellette, M., Frolkis, M., Holt, S. E., Chiu, C., Morin, G. B., Harley, C. B., Shay, J. W., Lichtsteiner, S., & Wright, W. E. (1998). Extension of life-span by introduction of telomerase into normal human cells. *Science, 279,* 349–352.

Bodrova, E., & Leong, D. J. (1998). Adult influences on play: The Vygotskian approach. In D. P. Fromberg & D. Bergen (Eds.), *Play from birth to twelve and beyond: Contexts, perspectives, and meanings* (pp. 277–282). New York: Garland.

Bograd, R., & Spilka, B. (1996). Self-disclosure and marital satisfaction in mid-life and late-life remarriages. *International Journal of Aging and Human Development, 42*(3), 161–172.

Bolger, K. E., Patterson, C. J., Thompson, W. W., & Kupersmidt, J. B. (1995). Psychosocial adjustment among children experiencing persistent and intermittent family economic hardship. *Child Development, 66,* 1107–1129.

Bolla, K. I., Cadet, J. L., & London, E. D. (1998). The neuropsychiatry of chronic cocaine abuse. *Journal of Neuropsychiatry and Clinical Neuroscience, 10,* 280–289.

Bolla, K. I., Rothman, R., & Cadet, J. L. (1999). Dose-related neurobehavioral effects of chronic cocaine use. *Journal of Neuropsychiatry & Clinical Neurosciences, 11,* 361–369.

Bond, C. A. (1989, September). A child prodigy from China wields a magical brush. *Smithsonian,* pp. 70–79.

Bond, J. T., & Galinsky, E. (1998). *1997 National Study of the Changing Workforce.* New York: Families and Work Institute.

Bondi, M. W., Salmon, D. P., Galasko, D., Thomas, R. G., & Thal, L. J. (1999). Neuropsychological function and apolipoprotein E genotype in the preclinical detection of Alzheimer's disease. *Psychology and Aging, 14,* 295–303.

Booth, A., & Edwards, J. N. (1992). Starting over: Why remarriages are more unstable. *Journal of Family Issues, 13,* 179–194.

Booth, J. R., Perfetti, C. A., & MacWhinney, B. (1999). Quick, automatic, and general activation of orthographic and phonological representations in young readers. *Developmental Psychology, 35,* 3–19.

Booth-Kewley, S., Minagawa, R. Y., Shaffer, R. A., & Brodine, S. K. (2002). A behavioral intervention to prevent sexually transmitted diseases/human immunodeficiency virus in a Marine Corps sample. *Military Medicine, 167,* 145–150.

Borman G., Boulay, M., Kaplan, J., Rachuba, L., & Hewes, G. (1999, December 13). *Evaluating the long-term impact of multiple summer interventions on the reading skills of low-income, early-elementary students.* Preliminary report, Year 1.

Bornstein, M. H., & Sigman, M. D. (1986). Continuity in mental development from infancy. *Child Development, 57,* 251–274.

Bornstein, M. H., & Tamis-LeMonda, C. S. (1994). Antecedents of information processing skills in infants: Habituation, novelty responsiveness, and cross-modal transfer. *Infant Behavior and Development, 17,* 371–380.

Bornstein, M. H., Tamis-LeMonda, C. S., & Haynes, O. M. (1999). First words in the second year: Continuity, stability, and models of concurrent and predictive correspondence in vocabulary and verbal responsiveness across age and context. *Infant Behavior and Development, 22,* 65–85.

Borowsky, I. A., Ireland, M., & Resnick, M. D. (2001). Adolescent suicide attempts: Risks and protectors. *Pediatrics, 107*(3), 485–493.

Bortz, W. M., II, & Wallace, D. H., & Wiley, D. (1999). Sexual function in 1,202 aging males: Differentiating aspects. *The Journals of Gerontology: Series A. Biological Sciences and Medical Sciences, 54,* M237-M241.

Bosma, H., Peter, R., Siegrist, J., & Marmot, M. (1998). Two alternative job stress models and the risk of coronary heart disease. *American Journal of Public Health, 88,* 68–74.

Boss, P. (1999). *Ambiguous loss:* Learning to live with unresolved grief. Cambridge, MA: Harvard University Press.

Boss, P. G. (2002). Ambiguous loss: Working with families of the missing. *Family Processes, 41,* 14–17.

Bossé, R., Aldwin, C. M., Levenson, M. R., Spiro, A., & Mroczek, D. K. (1993). Change in social support after retirement: Longitudinal findings from the normative aging study. *Journal of Gerontology: Psychological Sciences, 48,* P210–217.

Bosworth, H. B., & Schaie, K. W. (1997). The relationship of social environment, social networks, and health outcomes in the Seattle Longitudinal Study: Two analytical approaches. *Journals of Gerontology: Psychological Sciences, 52B,* P197–P205.

Botto, L. D., Moore, C. A., Khoury, M. J., & Erickson, J. D. (1999). Neural-tube defects. *New England Journal of Medicine, 341,* 1509–1519.

Botwinick, J. (1984). *Aging and behavior* (3rd ed.). New York: Springer.

Bouchard, T. J. (1994). Genes, environment, and personality. *Science, 264,* 1700–1701.

Bouchard, T. J., & Loehlin, J. C. (2001). Genes, evolution, and personality. *Behavior Genetics, 31*(3), 243–273.

Boulé, N. G., Haddad, E., Kenny, G. P., Wells, G. A., & Sigal, R. J. (2001). Effects of exercise on glycemic control and body mass in type 2 diabetes mellitus: A meta-analysis of controlled clinical trials. *Journal of the American Medical Association, 286,* 1218–1227.

Boulton, M. J. (1995). Playground behaviour and peer interaction patterns of primary school boys classified as bullies, victims and not involved. *British Journal of Educational Psychology, 65,* 165–177.

Boulton, M. J., & Smith, P. K. (1994). Bully/victim problems in middle-school children: Stability, self-perceived competence, peer perception, and peer acceptance. *British Journal of Developmental Psychology, 12,* 315–329.

Bouza, A. V. (1990). *The police mystique: An insider's look at cops, crime, and the criminal justice system.* New York: Plenum.

Bower, B. (1993). A child's theory of mind. *Science News, 144,* 40–42.

Bowlby, J. (1951). Maternal care and mental health. *Bulletin of the World Health Organization, 3,* 355–534.

Boyum, L. A., & Parke, R. D. (1995). The role of family emotional expressiveness in the development of children's social competence. *Journal of Marriage and the Family, 57,* 593–608.

Brabant, S. (1994). An overlooked AIDS affected population: The elderly parent as caregiver. *Journal of Gerontological Social Work, 22,* 131–145.

Bracher, G., & Santow, M. (1999). Explaining trends in teenage childbearing in Sweden. *Studies in Family Planning, 30,* 169–182.

Brackbill, Y., & Broman, S. H. (1979). *Obstetrical medication and development in the first year of life.* Unpublished manuscript.

Bradbury, T. N., Fincham, F. D., & Beach, S. R. H. (2000). Research on the nature and determinants of marital satisfaction: A decade in review. *Journal of Marriage and the Family, 62,* 964–980.

Bradford, J., & Ryan, C. (1991). Who are we: Health concerns of middle-aged lesbians. In J. W. B. Sang & A. Smith (Eds.), *Lesbians at midlife: The creative transition* (pp. 147–163). San Francisco: Spinsters.

Bradley, R. H. (1989). Home measurement of maternal responsiveness. In M. H. Bornstein (Ed.), *Maternal responsiveness: Characteristics and consequences* (New Directions for Child Development No. 43). San Francisco: Jossey-Bass.

Bradley, R. H., Caldwell, B. M., Rock, S. L., Ramey, C. T., Barnard, K. E., Gray, C., Hammond, M. A., Mitchell, S., Gottfried, A. W., Siegel, L., & Johnson, D. L. (1989). Home environment and cognitive development in the first 3 years of life: A collaborative study involving six sites and three ethnic groups in North America. *Developmental Psychology, 25,* 217–235.

Bradley, R. H., Corwyn, R. F., Burchinal, M., McAdoo, H. P., & Coll, C. G. (2001). The home environment of children in the United States: Part II: Relations with behavioral development through age thirteen. *Child Development, 72*(6), 1868–1886.

Bradley, R. H., Corwyn, R. F., McAdoo, H. P., & Coll, C. G. (2001). The home environment of children in the United States: Part I: Variation by age, ethnicity, and poverty status. *Child Development, 72*(6), 1844–1867.

Bradley, R., & Caldwell, B. (1982). The consistency of the home environment and its relation to child development. *International Journal of Behavioral Development, 5,* 445–465.

Bradley, R., Caldwell, B., & Rock, S. (1988). Home environment and school performance: A ten-year follow-up and examination of three models of environmental action. *Child Development, 59,* 852–867.

Braine, M. (1976). Children's first word combinations. *Monographs of the Society for Research in Child Development, 41*(1, Serial No. 164).

Bramlett, M. D., & Mosher, W. D. (2001). *First marriage dissolution, divorce, and remarriage: United States.* (Advance data from vital and health statistics, no. 323). Hyattsville, MD: National Center for Health Statistics.

Bramlett, M. D., & Mosher, W. D. (2002). Cohabitation, marriage, divorce, and remarriage in the United States. *Vital Health Statistics, 23*(22). Hyattsville, MD: National Center for Health Statistics.

Brandt, B. (1989). A place for her death. *Humanistic Judaism, 17*(3), 83–85.

Brass, L. M., Isaacsohn, J. L., Merikangas, K. R., & Robinette, C. D. (1992). A study of twins and stroke. *Stroke, 23*(2), 221–223.

Bratton, S. C., & Ray, D. (2002). Humanistic play therapy. In D. J. Cain (Ed.), *Humanistic psychotherapies: Handbook of research and practice* (pp. 369–402). Washington, DC: American Psychological Association.

Braungart, J. M., Fulker, D. W., & Plomin, R. (1992). Genetic mediation of the home environment during infancy: A sibling adoption study of the HOME. *Developmental Psychology, 28,* 1048–1055.

Braungart, J. M., Plomin, R., DeFries, J. C., & Fulker, D. W. (1992). Genetic influence on tester-rated infant temperament as assessed by Bayley's Infant Behavior Record: Nonadoptive and adoptive siblings and twins. *Developmental Psychology, 28,* 40–47.

Braungart-Rieker, J., Garwood, M. M., Powers, B. P., & Notaro, P. C. (1998). Infant affect and affect regulation during the still-face paradigm with mothers and fathers: The role of infant characteristics and parental sensitivity. *Developmental Psychology, 34*(6), 1428–1437.

Braungart-Rieker, J. M., Garwood, M. M., Powers, B. P., & Wang, X. (2001). Parental sensitivity, infant affect, and affect regulation: Predictors of later attachment. *Child Development, 72,* 252–270.

Braver, S. L., & O'Connell, D. (1998). *Divorced dads: Shattering the myths.* New York: Tarcher/Putnam.

Bray, D. W., & Howard, A. (1983). The AT&T longitudinal study of managers. In K. W. Schaie (Ed.), *Longitudinal studies of adult psychological development* (pp. 266–312). New York: Guilford.

Bray, J. H. (1991). Psychosocial factors affecting custodial and visitation arrangements. *Behavioral Sciences and the Law, 9,* 419–437.

Bray, J. H., & Hetherington, E. M. (1993). Families in transition: Introduction and overview. *Journal of Family Psychology, 7,* 3–8.

Brazelton, T. B. (1973). *Neonatal behavioral assessment scale.* Philadelphia: Lippincott.

Brazelton, T. B. (1984). *Neonatal Behavioral Assessment Scale.* Philadelphia: Lippincott.

Brazelton, T. B., & Nugent, J. K. (1995). *Neonatal Behavioral Assessment Scale, 3rd edition.* Cambridge, England: Cambridge University Press.

Bremner, W. J., Vitiello, M. V., & Prinz, P. N. (1983). Loss of circadian rhythmicity in blood testosterone levels with aging in normal men. *Journal of Clinical Endocrinology and Metabolism, 56,* 1278–1281.

Bren, L. (2001, November/December). Alternatives to hysterectomy: New technologies, more options. *FDA Consumer Magazine.* [Online]. Available: http://www.fda.gov/fdac/features/2001/601_tech.html. Access date December 2, 2002.

Brener, N. D., Simon, T. R., Krug, E. G., & Lowry, R. (1999). Recent trends in violence-related behaviors among high school students in the United States. *Journal of the American Medical Association, 282,* 440–446.

Brenneman, K., Massey, C., Machado, S. F., & Gelman, R. (1996). Young children's plans differ for writing and drawing. *Cognitive Development, 11,* 397–419.

Brenner, M. H. (1991). Health, productivity, and the economic environment: Dynamic role of socio-economic status. In G. Green & F. Baker (Eds.), *Work, health, and productivity* (pp. 241–255). New York: Oxford University Press.

Brenner, R. A., Simons-Morton, B. G., Bhaskar, B., Revenis, M., Das, A., & Clemens, J. D. (2003). Infant-parent bed sharing in an inner-city population. *Archives of Pediatrics and Adolescent Medicine, 57,* 33–39.

Breslow, L., & Breslow, N. (1993). Health practices and disability: Some evidence from Alameda County. *Preventive Medicine, 22*(1), 86–95.

Bretherton, I. (1990). Communication patterns, internal working models, and the intergenerational transmission of attachment relationships. *Infant Mental Health Journal, 11*(3), 237–252.

Bretherton, I. (Ed.). (1984). *Symbolic play: The development of social understanding.* Orlando, FL: Academic.

Brezina, T. (1999). Teenage violence toward parents as an adaptation to family strain: Evidence from a national survey of male adolescents. *Youth & Society, 30,* 416–444.

Briley, M. (1980, July–August). Burnout stress and the human energy crisis. *Dynamic Years,* pp. 36–39.

Briss, P. A., Sacks, J. J., Addiss, D. G., Kresnow, M., & O'Neil, J. (1994). A nationwide study of the risk of injury associated with day care center attendance. *Pediatrics, 93,* 364–368.

Brock, D. W. (1992, March–April). Voluntary active euthanasia. *Hastings Center Report,* pp. 10–22.

Broder, M. S., Kanouse, D. E., Mittman, B. S., & Bernstein, S. J. (2000). The appropriateness of recommendations for hysterectomy. *Obstetrics & Gynecology, 95,* 199–205.

Brody, G. H. (1998). Sibling relationship quality: Its causes and consequences. *Annual Review of Psychology, 49,* 1–24.

Brody, G. H., & Flor, D. L. (1998). Maternal resources, parenting practices, and child competence in rural, single-parent African American families. *Child Development, 69,* 803–816.

Brody, G. H., Flor, D. L., & Gibson, N. M. (1999). Linking maternal efficacy beliefs, developmental goals, parenting practices, and child competence in rural single-parent African American families. *Child Development, 70*(5), 1197–1208.

Brody, G. H., Ge, X., Conger, R., Gibbons, F. X., Murry, V. M., Gerrard, M., and Simons, R. L. (2001). The influence of neighborhood disadvantage, collective socialization, and parenting on African American children's affiliation with deviant peers. *Child Development, 72*(4), 1231–1246.

Brody, G. H., Stoneman, Z., & Flor, D. (1995). Linking family processes and academic competence among rural African American youths. *Journal of Marriage and the Family, 57,* 567–579.

Brody, G. H., Stoneman, Z., & Gauger, K. (1996). Parent-child relationships, family problem-solving behavior, and sibling relationship quality: The moderating role of sibling temperaments. *Child Development, 67,* 1289–1300.

Brody, G. H., Stoneman, Z., Flor, D., McCrary, C., Hastings, L., & Conyers, O. (1994). Financial resources, parent psychological functioning, parent co-caregiving, and early adolescent competence in rural two-parent African-American families. *Child Development, 65,* 590–605.

Brody, J. E. (1995, June 28). Preventing birth defects even before pregnancy. *The New York Times,* p. C10.

Brody, L. R., Zelazo, P. R., & Chaika, H. (1984). Habituation-dishabituation to speech in the neonate. *Developmental Psychology, 20,* 114–119.

Brodzinsky, D. (1997). Infertility and adoption adjustment: Considerations and clinical issues. In S. R. Leiblum (Ed.), *Infertility: Psychological issues and counseling strategies* (pp. 246–262). New York: Wiley.

Bronfenbrenner, U. (1979). *The ecology of human development.* Cambridge, MA: Harvard University Press.

Bronfenbrenner, U. (1986). Ecology of the family as a context for human development: Research perspectives. *Developmental Psychology, 22,* 723–742.

Bronfenbrenner, U. (1994). Ecological models of human development. In T. Husen & T. N. Postlethwaite (Eds.), *International encyclopedia of education* (2nd ed., Vol. 3). Oxford: Pergamon Press/Elsevier Science.

Bronfenbrenner, U., & Crouter, A. (1982). Work and family through time and space. In S. B. Kamerman & C. D. Hayes (Eds.), *Families that work: Children in a changing world.* Washington, DC: National Academy of Science.

Bronfenbrenner, U., & Morris, P. A. (1998). The ecology of developmental processes. In W. Damon (Series Ed.) & R. Lerner (Vol. Ed.), *Handbook of child psychology: Vol. 1. Theoretical models of human development* (5th ed., pp. 993–1028). New York: Wiley.

Bronner, E. (1999, January 22). Social promotion is bad; repeating a grade may be worse. *The New York Times* [On-line]. Available: http://search.nytimes.com/search/daily/bin/fastweb?getdoc+site+site+13235+0+wAAA+social%7Epromotion

Bronstein, P. (1988). Father-child interaction: Implications for gender role socialization. In P. Bronstein & C. P. Cowan (Eds.), *Fatherhood today: Men's changing role in the family.* New York: Wiley.

Bronstein, P., Clauson, J., Stoll, M. F., & Abrams, C. L. (1993). Parenting behavior and children's social, psychological, and academic adjustment in diverse family structures. *Family Relations, 42,* 268–276.

Brooks, P. J., Tomasello, M., Dodson, K., and Lewis, L. B. (1999). Young children's overgeneralizations with fixed transitivity verbs. *Child Development, 70,* 1325–1337.

Brooks-Gunn, J., & Duncan, G. J. (1997). The effects of poverty on children. *The Future of Children, 7,* 55–71.

Brooks-Gunn, J., Britto, P. R., & Brady, C. (1998). Struggling to make ends meet: Poverty and child development. In M. E. Lamb (Ed.), *Parenting and child development in "non-traditional" families* (pp. 279–304). Mahwah, NJ: Erlbaum.

Brooks-Gunn, J., Duncan, G. J., Leventhal, T., & Aber, J. L. (1997). Lessons learned and future directions for research on the neighborhoods in which children live. In J. Brooks-Gunn, G. J. Duncan, & J. L. Aber (Eds.), *Neighborhood poverty: Context and consequences for children* (Vol. 1, pp. 279–297). New York: Russell Sage Foundation.

Brooks-Gunn, J., Han, W.-J., & Waldfogel, J. (2002). Maternal employment and child cognitive outcomes in the first three years of life: The NICHD study of early child care. *Child Development, 73,* 1052–1072.

Brooks-Gunn, J., Klebanov, P. K., & Duncan, G. J. (1996). Ethnic differences in children's intelligence test scores: Role of economic deprivation, home environment, and maternal characteristics. *Child Development, 67,* 396–408.

Brooks-Gunn, J., Klebanov, P. K., Liaw, F., & Spiker, D. (1993). Enhancing the development of low-birthweight, premature infants: Changes in cognition and behavior over the first three years. *Child Development, 64,* 736–753.

Brooks-Gunn, J., McCarton, C. M., Casey, P. H., et al. (1994). Early intervention in low-birthweight premature infants: Results through age 5 years from the Infant Health Development Program. *Journal of the American Medical Association, 272,* 1257–1262.

Broude, G. J. (1994). *Marriage, family, and relationships: A cross-cultural encyclopedia.* Santa Barbara, CA: ABC-CLIO.

Broude, G. J. (1995). *Growing up: A cross-cultural encyclopedia.* Santa Barbara, CA: ABC-CLIO.

Brown, A. L., Metz, K. E., & Campione, J. C. (1996). Social interaction and individual understanding in a community of learners: The influence of Piaget and Vygotsky. In A. Tryphon & J. Voneche (Eds), *Piaget-Vygotsky: The social genesis of thought* (pp. 145–170). Hove, England: Psychology/Erlbaum (UK) Taylor & Francis.

Brown, B. (1999). Optimizing expression of the common human genome for child development. *Current Directions in Psychological Science, 8*(2), 37–41.

Brown, B. B., Mounts, N., Lamborn, S. D., & Steinberg, L. (1993). Parenting practices and peer group affiliation in adolescence. *Child Development, 64,* 467–482.

Brown, J. L. (1987). Hunger in the U.S. *Scientific American, 256*(2), 37–41.

Brown, J. M. (1989). *Gandhi: Prisoner of hope.* New Haven: Yale University Press.

Brown, J. R., & Dunn, J. (1996). Continuities in emotion understanding from three to six years. *Child Development, 67,* 789–802.

Brown, J. T., & Stoudemire, A. (1983). Normal and pathological grief. *Journal of the American Medical Association, 250,* 378–382.

Brown, L. A., Shumway-Cook, A., & Wollacott, M. H. (1999). Attentional demands and postural recovery: The effects of aging. *Journals of Gerontology: Series A. Biological Sciences & Medical Sciences, 54A,* M165–M171.

Brown, L. J., Wall, T. P., & Lazar, V. (2000). Trends in untreated caries in primary teeth of children 2 to 10 years old. *Journal of the American Dental Association, 131,* 93–100.

Brown, L. M., & Gilligan, C. (1990, April). *The psychology of women and the development of girls.* Paper presented at the Laurel-Harvard Conference on the Psychology of Women and the Education of Girls, Cleveland, OH.

Brown, N. M. (1990). Age and children in the Kalahari. *Health and Human Development Research, 1,* 26–30.

Brown, P. (1993, April 17). Motherhood past midnight. *New Scientist,* pp. 4–8.

Brown, R., & Pressley, M. (1994). Self-regulated reading and getting meaning from text: The transactional strategies instruction model and its ongoing validation. In D. Schunk & B. Zimmerman (Eds.), *Self-regulation of learning and performance: Issues and educational applications* (pp. 155–179). Hillsdale, NJ: Erlbaum.

Brown, R., Pressley, M., Schuder, T., & Van Meter, P. (1994) *A quasi-experimental validation of transactional strategies instruction with previously low-achieving grade-2 readers.* Buffalo and Albany: State University of New York.

Brown, S. S. (1985). Can low birth weight be prevented? *Family Planning Perspectives, 17*(3), 112–118.

Browne, A., & Finkelhor, D. (1986). Impact of child sexual abuse: A review of research. *Psychological Bulletin, 99*(1), 66–77.

Brownell, K. (1998, July/August). The pressure to eat: Why we're getting fatter. *Nutrition Action Health Letter* [On-line]. Available: http://www.cspinet.org/nah/7_98eat.htm

Brubaker, T. H. (1983). Introduction. In T. H. Brubaker (Ed.), *Family relationships in later life.* Beverly Hills, CA: Sage.

Brubaker, T. H. (1990). Families in later life: A burgeoning research area. *Journal of Marriage and the Family, 52,* 959–981.

Brubaker, T. H. (Ed.). (1993). *Family relationships: Current and future directions.* Newbury Park, CA: Sage.

Bruce, J., Lloyd, C. B., & Leonard, A. (1995). *Families in focus: New perspectives on mothers, fathers, and children.* New York: Population Council.

Bruck, M., & Ceci, S. J. (1997). The suggestibility of young children. *Current Directions in Psychological Science, 6,* 75–79.

Bruck, M., Ceci, S. J., & Hembrooke, H. (1998). Reliability and credibility of young children's reports: From research to policy and practice. *American Psychologist, 53,* 136–151.

Bruer, J. T. (2001). A critical and sensitive period primer. In D. B. Bailey, J. T. Bruer, F. J. Symons, & J. W. Lichtman (Eds.). *Critical thinking about critical periods: A series from the National Center for Early Development and Learning* (pp. 289–292). Baltimore, MD: Paul Brooks Publishing.

Bruner, A. B., Joffe, A., Duggan, A. K., Casella, J. F., & Brandt, J. (1996). Randomised study of cognitive effects of iron supplementation in non-anaemic iron-deficient adolescent girls. *Lancet, 348,* 992–996.

Brunner, E., White, I., Thorogood, M., Bristow, A., Curle, D., & Marmot, M. (1997). Can dietary interventions change diet and cardiovascular risk factors? A meta-analysis of randomized controlled trials. *American Journal of Public Health, 87,* 1415–1422.

Bryant, B. K. (1987). Mental health, temperament, family, and friends: Perspectives on children's empathy and social perspective taking. In N. Eisenberg & J. Strayer (Eds.), *Empathy and its development* (pp. 245–270). Cambridge, UK: Cambridge University Press.

Bucciantini, M., Giannoni, E., Chiti, F., Baroni, F., Formigli, L., Zurdo, J., Taddei, N., Ramponi, G., Dobson, C. M., & Stefani, M. (2002). Inherent toxicity of aggregates implies a common mechanism for protein misfolding diseases. *Nature, 416,* 507–511.

Buchanan, C. M., Eccles, J. S., & Becker, J. B. (1992). Are adolescents the victims of raging hormones?: Evidence for activational effects of hormones on moods and behavior at adolescence. *Psychological Bulletin, 111,* 62–107.

Buckner, J. C., Bassuk, E. L., Weinreb, L. F., & Brooks, M. G. (1999). Homelessness and its relation to the mental health and behavior of low-income school-age children. *Developmental Psychology, 35*(1), 246–257.

Buckner, J. P., & Fivush, R. (1998). Gender and self in children's autobiographical narratives. *Applied Cognitive Psychology, 12,* 407–429.

Buell, J. (2000). *The end of homework: How homework disrupts families, overburdens children, and limits learning.* Boston: Bristol.

Buhrmester, D. (1990). Intimacy of friendship, interpersonal competence, and adjustment during preadolescence and adolescence. *Child Development, 61,* 1101–1111.

Buhrmester, D. (1996). Need fulfillment, interpersonal competence, and the developmental contexts of early adolescent friendship. In W. M. Bukowski, A. F. Newcomb, & W. W. Hartup (Eds.), *The company they keep: Friendship in childhood and adolescence* (pp. 158–185). New York: Cambridge University Press.

Buhrmester, D., & Furman, W. (1990). Perceptions of sibling relationships during middle childhood and adolescence. *Child Development, 61,* 138–139.

Buhs, E. S., & Ladd, G. W. (2001). Peer rejection as an antecedent of young children's school adjustment: An examination of mediating processes. *Developmental Psychology, 37*(4), 550–560.

Bukowski, W. M., & Kramer, T. L. (1986). Judgments of the features of friendship among early adolescent boys and girls. *Journal of Early Adolescence, 6,* 331–338.

Bulcroft, K., & O'Conner, M. (1986). The importance of dating relationships on quality of life for older persons. *Family Relations, 35,* 397–401.

Bulcroft, R. A., & Bulcroft, K. A. (1991). The nature and function of dating in later life. *Research on Aging, 13,* 244–260.

Bumpass, L. L., & Lu, H.-H. (2000). Trends in cohabitation and implications for children's family contexts in the United States. *Population Studies, 54,* 29–41.

Bumpass, L., & Aquilino, W. (1993). *Mapping the social terrain of midlife in the U.S.* Unpublished manuscript, University of Wisconsin.

Bunikowski, R., Grimmer, I., Heiser, A., Metze, B., Schafer, A., & Obladen, M. (1998). Neurodevelopmental outcome after prenatal exposure to opiates. *European Journal of Pediatrics, 157,* 724–730.

Burchinal, M. R., Campbell, F. A., Bryant, D. M., Wasik, B. H., & Ramey, C. T. (1997). Early intervention and mediating processes in cognitive performance of children of low-income African American families. *Child Development, 68,* 935–954.

Burchinal, M. R., Roberts, J. E., Nabors, L. A., & Bryant, D. M. (1996). Quality of center child care and infant cognitive and language development. *Child Development, 67,* 606–620.

Bureau of Labor Standards. (2000, Fall). Fastest growing occupations usually requiring a bachelor's degree or more education, projected 1998–2008. *Occupational Outlook Quarterly.* [Online]. Available: http:/www.bls.gov/opub/ooq.htm

Bureau of Labor Standards. (2000–2001, Winter). High-paying jobs requiring on-the-job training. *Occupational Outlook Quarterly.* [Online]. Available: http:/www.bls.gov/opub/ooq.htm

Bureau of Labor Standards. (2001, Fall). Highest paying occupations usually requiring at least a bachelor's degree. *Occupational Outlook Quarterly.* [Online]. Available: http:/www.bls.gov/opub/ooq.htm

Bureau of Labor Standards. (2002, Spring). Education pays. *Occupational Outlook Quarterly 46*(1). [Online]. Available: http:/www.bls.gov/opub/ooq.htm

Bureau of Labor Statistics. (1998). *Workers on flexible and shift schedules in 1997* (Suppl. to May 1997 Current Population Survey) [Online]. Available: http://www.bls.gov/news.release/flex.nws.htm

Bureau of Labor Statistics. (1999a). *Employment characteristics of families in 1998* [Online]. Available: http://www.bls.gov/news.release/famee.nws.htm

Bureau of Labor Statistics. (1999b, April). *Highlights of women's earnings in 1998* (Report No. 928) [On-line]. Available: http://www.bls.gov/cps.wom98.htm

Bureau of Labor Statistics. (1999c, July 2). *The employment situation: June 1999* [On-line]. Available: http://www.bls.gov/news.release/empsit.htm

Bureau of Labor Statistics. (2000, June 23). Employment characteristics of families in 1999 [news release] USDL 00–172. Washington, DC: U.S. Department of Labor.

Bureau of Labor Statistics. (2001a). *Highlights of women's earnings in 2000. Report 952.* Washington, DC: U.S. Department of Labor.

Bureau of Labor Statistics. (2001b). Industry at a glance. [Online] Available: http://www.bls.gov/iag/iaghome.htm

Bureau of Labor Statistics. (2002a). Employment Characteristics of Families, 2001. *Current Population Survey* (USDL 02–175). Washington, DC: U. S. Department of Labor.

Bureau of Labor Statistics. (2002b). Table D-6: Employed persons by age and sex, seasonally adjusted. [Online]. Available: ftp://ftp.bls.gov/pub/suppl/empsit.cpspeed6.txt. Access date: December 20, 2002.

Burhans, K. K., & Dweck, C. S. (1995). Helplessness in early childhood: The role of contingent worth. *Child Development, 66,* 1719–1738.

Burns, A. (1992). Mother-headed families: An international perspective and the case of Australia. *Social Policy Report of the Society for Research in Child Development, 6*(1).

Burns, G. (1983). *How to live to be 100—or more: The ultimate diet, sex, and exercise book.* New York: Putnam.

Burns, J. F. (1994, August 27). India fights abortion of female fetuses. *The New York Times,* p. A5.

Burt, M. R., Aron, L. Y., Douglas, T., Valente, J., Lee, E., & Iwen, B. (1999). *Homelessness: Programs and the people they serve: Summary report.* Washington, DC: Urban Institute.

Burton, L. M. (1992). Black grandparents rearing children of drug-addicted parents: Stressors, outcomes, and social service needs. *The Gerontologist, 32,* 744–751.

Bushnell, E. W., & Boudreau, J. P. (1993). Motor development and the mind: The potential role of motor abilities as a determinant of aspects of perceptual development. *Child Development, 64,* 1005–1021.

Busse, E. W. (1987). Primary and secondary aging. In G. L. Maddox (Ed.), *The encyclopedia of aging* (p. 534). New York: Springer.

Bussey, K., & Bandura, A. (1992). Self-regulatory mechanisms governing gender development. *Child Development, 63,* 1236–1250.

Bussey, K., & Bandura, A. (1999). Social cognitive theory of gender development and differentiation. *Psychological Review, 106,* 676–713.

Butler, R. (1961). Re-awakening interests. *Nursing Homes: Journal of the American Nursing Home Association, 10,* 8–19.

Butler, R. (1996). The dangers of physician-assisted suicide. *Geriatrics, 51,* 7.

Butler, R. N., Davis, R., Lewis, C. B., Nelson, M. E., & Strauss, E. (1998a). Physical fitness: Benefits of exercise for the older patient. 2. *Geriatrics 53,* 46, 49–52, 61–62.

Butler, R. N., Davis, R., Lewis, C. B., Nelson, M. E., & Strauss, E. (1998b). Physical fitness: How to help older patients live stronger and longer. 1. *Geriatrics, 53,* 26–28, 31–32, 39–40.

Butterworth, G., & Jarrett, N. (1991). What minds have in common is space: Spatial mechanisms serving joint visual attention in infancy. *British Journal of Developmental Psychology, 9,* 55–72.

Byrnes, J. P., & Fox, N. A. (1998). The educational relevance of research in cognitive neuroscience. *Educational Psychology Review, 10,* 297–342.

Cabrera, N. J., Tamis-LeMonda, C. S., Bradley, R. H., Hofferth, S., & Lamb, M. E. (2000). Fatherhood in the twenty-first century. *Child Development, 71,* 127–136.

Cadman, C., Brewer, J. (2001). Emotional intelligence: A vital prerequisite for recruitment in nursing. *Journal of Nursing Management, 9,* 321–324.

Cadwell, S. (1994, August). The psychological impact of HIV on gay men. *The Menninger Letter,* pp. 4–5.

Caelli, K., Downie, J., & Letendre, A. (2002). Parents' experiences of midwife-managed care following the loss of a baby in a previous pregnancy. *Journal of Advanced Nursing, 39,* 127–136.

Cain, W. S., Reid, F., & Stevens, J. C. (1990). Missing ingredients: Aging and the discrimination of flavor. *Journal of Nutrition for the Elderly, 9,* 3–15.

Caldwell, B. M., & Bradley, R. H. (1984). *Home Observation for Measurement of the Environment.* Unpublished manuscript, University of Arkansas at Little Rock.

Calkins, S. D., & Fox, N. A. (1992). The relations among infant temperament, security of attachment, and behavioral inhibition at twenty-four months. *Child Development, 63,* 1456–1472.

Call, K. T., Mortimer, J. T., & Shanahan, M. (1995). Helpfulness and the development of competence in adolescence. *Child Development, 66,* 129–138.

Call, V., Sprecher, S., & Schwartz, P. (1995). The incidence and frequency of marital sex in a national sample. *Journal of Marriage and the Family, 57,* 639–652.

Callahan, D., & White, M. (1996). The legalization of physician-assisted suicide: Creating a regulatory Potemkin village.

University of Richmond Law Review, 30(1), 1–83.

Callan, V. (1986). The impact of the first birth: Married and single women preferring childlessness, one child, or two children. *Journal of Marriage and the Family, 48,* 261–269.

Calle, E. E., Thun, M. J., Petrelli, J. M., Rodriguez, C., & Heath, Jr., C. W. (1999). Body-mass index and mortality in a prospective cohort of U.S. adults. *New England Journal of Medicine, 341,* 1097–1105.

Camp, C. J. (1989). World-knowledge systems. In L. W. Poon, D. C. Rubin, & B. A. Wilson (Eds.), *Everyday cognition in adulthood and late life.* Cambridge, England: Cambridge University Press.

Camp, C. J., & McKitrick, L. A. (1989). The dialectics of remembering and forgetting across the adult lifespan. In D. Kramer & M. Bopp (Eds.), *Dialectics and contextualism in clinical and developmental psychology: Change, transformation, and the social context* (pp. 169–187). New York: Springer.

Camp, C. J., & McKitrick, L. A. (1992). Memory interventions in Alzheimer's-type dementia populations: Methodological and theoretical issues. In R. L. West & J. D. Sinnott (Eds.), *Everyday memory and aging: Current research and methodology* (pp. 155–172). New York: Springer-Verlag.

Camp, C. J., Doherty, K., Moody-Thomas, S., & Denney, N. W. (1989). Practical problem solving in adults: A comparison of problem types and scoring methods. In J. D. Sinnott (Ed.), *Everyday problem solving: Theory and applications* (pp. 211–228). New York: Praeger.

Camp, C. J., Foss, J. W., Stevens, A. B., Reichard, C. C., McKitrick, L. A., & O'Hanlon, A. M. (1993). Memory training in normal and demented populations: The E-I-E-I-O model. *Experimental Aging Research, 19,* 277–290.

Campbell, J., & Moyers, W. (1988). *The power of myth with Bill Moyers.* New York: Doubleday.

Campbell, F. A., Pungello, E. P., Miller-Johnson, S., Burchinal, M., & Ramey, C. T. (2001). The development of cognitive and academic abilities: Growth curves from an early childhood education experiment. *Developmental Psychology, 37*(2), 231–242.

Campbell, S. B., Cohn, J. F., & Meyers, T. (1995). Depression in first-time mothers: Mother-infant interaction and depression chronicity. *Developmental Psychology, 31,* 349–357.

Campfield, L. A., Smith, F. J., & Burn, P. (1998, May 29). Strategies and potential molecular targets for obesity treatment. *Science, 280,* 1383–1387.

Campfield, L. A., Smith, F. J., Guisez, Y., Devos, R., & Burn, P. (1995). Recombinant mouse OB protein: Evidence for a peripheral signal linking adiposity and central neural networks. *Science, 269,* 546–549.

Campos, J., Bertenthal, B., & Benson, N. (1980, April). *Self-produced locomotion and the extraction of form invariance.* Paper presented at the meeting of the International Conference on Infant Studies, New Haven, CT.

Camras, L. A., Oster, H., Campos, J., Campos, R., Vjiie, T., Miyake, K., Wang, L., & Meng, Z. (1998). Production of emotional facial expressions in European American, Japanese, and Chinese infants. *Developmental Psychology, 34*(4), 616–628.

Cantor, J. (1994). Confronting children's fright responses to mass media. In D. Zillman, J. Bryant, & A. C. Huston (Eds.), *Media, children, and the family: Social scientific, psychoanalytic, and clinical perspectives.* Hillsdale, NJ: Erlbaum.

Cao, A., Saba, L., Galanello, R., & Rosatelli, M. C. (1997). Molecular diagnosis and carrier screening for β thalassemia. *Journal of the American Medical Association, 278,* 1273–1277.

Cao, X.-Y., Jiang, X.-M., Dou, Z.-H., Rakeman, M. A., Zhang, M.-L., O'Donnell, K., Ma, T., Amette, K., DeLong, N., & DeLong, G. R. (1994). Timing of vulnerability of the brain to iodine deficiency in endemic cretinism. *New England Journal of Medicine, 331,* 1739–1744.

Capaldi, D. M., Stoolmiller, M., Clark, S., & Owen, L. D. (2002). Heterosexual risk behaviors in at-risk young men from early adolescence to young adulthood: Prevalence, prediction, and association with STD contraction. *Developmental Psychology, 38,* 394–406.

Caplan, M., Vespo, J., Pedersen, J., & Hay, D. F. (1991). Conflict and its resolution in small groups of one- and two-year olds. *Child Development, 62,* 1513–1524.

Capon, N., Kuhn, D., & Carretero, M. (1989). Consumer reasoning. In J. D. Sinnott (Ed.), *Everyday problem solving: Theory and application* (pp. 153–174). New York: Praeger.

Capute, A. J., Shapiro, B. K., & Palmer, F. B. (1987). Marking the milestones of language development. *Contemporary Pediatrics, 4*(4), 24.

Caraballo, R. S., Giovino, G. A., Pechacek, T. F., Mowery, P. D., Richter, P. A., Strauss, W. J., Sharp, D. J., Eriksen, M. P., Pirkle, J. L., & Maurer, K. R. (1998). Racial and ethnic differences in serum cotinine levels of cigarette smokers. *Journal of the American Medical Association, 280,* 135–139.

Carbery, J., & Buhrmester, D. (1998). Friendship and need fulfillment during three phases of young adulthood. *Journal of Social & Personal Relationships, 15,* 393–409.

Cargan, L. (1981). Singles: An examination of two stereotypes. *Family Relations, 30,* 377–385.

Carlson, E. A. (1998). A prospective longitudinal study of attachment disorganization/disorientation. *Child Development, 69*(4), 1107–1128.

Carlson, S. M., Moses, L. J., & Hix, H. R. (1998). The role of inhibitory processes in young children's difficulties with deception and false belief. *Child Development, 69*(3), 672–691.

Carpenter, M., Akhtar, N., & Tomasello, M. (1998). Fourteen- through 18-month-old infants differentially imitate intentional and accidental actions. *Infant Behavior and Development, 21,* 315–330.

Carpenter, M. W., Sady, S. P., Hoegsberg, B., Sady, M. A., Haydon, B., Cullinane, E. M., Coustan, D. R., & Thompson, P. D. (1988). Fetal heart rate response to maternal exertion. *Journal of the American Medical Association, 259*(20), 3006–3009.

Carroll-Pankhurst, C., & Mortimer, E. A. (2001). Sudden infant death syndrome, bed sharing, parental weight, and age at death. *Pediatrics, 107*(3), 530–536.

Carskadon, M. A., Acebo, C., Richardson, G. S., Tate, B. A., & Seifer, R. (1997). Long nights protocol: Access to circadian parameters in adolescents. *Journal of Biological Rhythms, 12,* 278–289.

Carstensen, L. L. (1991). Selectivity theory: Social activity in life-span context. In *Annual review of gerontology and geriatrics* (Vol. 11, pp. 195–217). New York: Springer.

Carstensen, L. L. (1995). Evidence for a life-span theory of socioemotional selectivity. *Current Directions in Psychological Science, 4,* 150–156.

Carstensen, L. L. (1996). Socioemotional selectivity: A life span developmental account of social behavior. In M. R. Merrens & G. G. Brannigan (Eds.), *The developmental psychologists: Research adventures across the life span* (pp. 251–272). New York: McGraw-Hill.

Carstensen, L. L. (1999). Elderly show their emotional know how. (Cited in *Science News, 155,* p. 374). Paper presented at the meeting of the American Psychological Society, Denver, CO.

Carstensen, L. L., & Pasupathi, M. (1993). Women of a certain age. In S. Matteo (Ed.), *Critical issues facing women in the '90s* (pp. 66–78). Boston: Northeastern University Press.

Carstensen, L. L., Gottman, J. M., & Levenson, R. W. (1995). Emotional behavior in long-term marriage. *Psychology and Aging, 10,* 140–149.

Carstensen, L. L., Graff, J., Levenson, R. W., & Gottman, J. M. (1996). Affect in intimate relationships: The development course of marriage. In C. Magai & S. H. McFadden (Eds.), *Handbook of emotion, adult development, and aging* (pp. 227–247). San Diego: Academic Press.

Carstensen, L. L., Gross, J., & Fung, H. (1997). The social context of emotion. *Annual Review of Geriatrics and Gerontology, 17,* 331.

Carstensen, L. L., Isaacowitz, D. M., & Charles, S. T. (1999). Taking time seriously: A theory of socioemotional selectivity. *American Psychologist, 54,* 165–181.

Carstensen, L. L., Pasupathi, M., Mayr, U., & Nesselroade, J. (2000). Emotional experience in everyday life across the adult life span. *Journal of Personality and Social Psychology, 79,* 644–655.

Carter Center. (1995, Winter). *Carter Center News,* pp. 1, 3, 4–6, 9.

Carter, J. (1975). *Why not the best?* Nashville, TN: Broadman.

Carter, J. (1998). *The virtues of aging.* New York: Ballantine.

Casaer, P. (1993). Old and new facts about perinatal brain development. *Journal of Child Psychology and Psychiatry, 34*(1), 101–109.

Case, R. (1985). *Intellectual development: Birth to adulthood.* Orlando, FL: Academic Press.

Case, R. (1992). Neo-Piagetian theories of child development. In R. Sternberg & C. Berg (Eds.), *Intellectual development.* New York: Cambridge University Press.

Case, R. (1999). Conceptual development. In M. Bennett (Ed.), *Developmental psychology: Achievements and prospects* (pp. 36–54). Philadelphia: Psychology/Taylor & Francis.

Case, R., & Okamoto, Y. (1996). The role of central conceptual structures in the development of children's thought. *Monographs of the Society for Research in Child Development, 61*(1–2, Serial No. 246).

Case, R., Demetriou, A., Platsidou, M., & Kazi, S. (2001). Integrating concepts and tests of intelligence from the differential and developmental traditions. *Intelligence, 29,* 307–336.

Casey, B. M., McIntire, D. D., & Leveno, K. J. (2001). The continuing value of the Apgar score for the assessment of newborn infants. *New England Journal of Medicine, 344,* 467–471.

Casper, L. M. (1997). My daddy takes care of me: Fathers as care providers. *Current Population Reports* (P70–59). Washington, DC: U. S. Bureau of the Census.

Casper, L. M. (1998). Who's minding our preschoolers? (Fall 1994 update, PPL 81). *Current Population Reports: Household Economic Studies* (detailed tables for P70-62). [Online]. Available: http://www.census.gov/population/www/ socdemo/child/childcare98.html. CITATION.)

Casper, L. M., & Bryson, K. R. (1998). *Co-resident grandparents and their grandchildren: grandparent maintained families* (Population Division Working Paper No. 26). Washington, DC: U.S. Bureau of the Census.

Caspi, A. (1998). Personality development across the life course. In W. Damon (Series Ed.) & N. Eisenberg (Vol. Ed.), *Handbook of child psychology: Vol. 3. Social, emotional, and personality development* (5th ed., pp. 311–388). New York: Wiley.

Caspi, A. (2000). The child is father of the man: Personality continuity from childhood to adulthood. *Journal of Personality and Social Psychology, 78,* 158–172.

Caspi, A., & Silva, P. (1995). Temperamental qualities at age 3 predict personality traits in young adulthood: Longitudinal evidence from a birth cohort. *Child Development, 66,* 486–498.

Cassel, C. (1992). Ethics and the future of aging research: Promises and problems. *Generations, 16*(4), 61–65.

Cassidy, J. (1988). Child-mother attachment and the self in six-year-olds. *Child Development, 59,* 121–134.

Cassidy, J., & Hossler, A. (1992). State and federal definitions of the gifted: An update. *Gifted Child Quarterly, 15,* 46–53.

Castaneda, C. J. (1996, June 16). Right-to-die debate rages on. *Chicago Sun-Times,* p. 57.

Catlin, A., & Carter, B. (2002). Creation of a neonatal end-of-life palliative care protocol. *Journal of Perinatology, 22,* 184–195.

Cattell, R. B. (1965). *The scientific analysis of personality.* Baltimore: Penguin.

Cavanaugh, J. C., Kramer, D. A., Sinnott, J. D., Camp, C. J., & Markley, R. P. (1985). On missing links and such: Interfaces between cognitive research and everyday problem solving. *Human Development, 28,* 146–168.

Cavazanna-Calvo, M., Hacein-Bey, S., de Saint Basile, G., Gross, F., Yvon, E., Nusbaum, P., Selz, F., Hue, C., Certain, S., Casanova, J. L., Bousso, P., Deist, F. L., & Fischer, A. (2000). Gene therapy of humar severe combined immunodeficiency (SCID)-X1 disease. *Science, 288,* 669–672.

Cawthon, R. M., Smith, K. R., O'Brien, E., Sivatchenko, A., & Kerber, R. A. (2003). Association between telomere length in blook and mortality in people aged 60 years or older. *The Lancet, 361,* 393–394.

Ceballo, R., & McLoyd, V. C. (2002). Social support and parenting in poor, dangerous neighborhoods. *Child Development, 73,* 1310–1321.

Ceci, S. J. (1991). How much does schooling influence general intelligence and its cognitive components? A reassessment of the evidence. *Developmental Psychology, 27,* 703–722.

Ceci, S. J., & Bruck, M. (1993). Child witnesses: Translating research into policy. *Social Policy Report of the Society for Research in Child Development, 7*(3).

Ceci, S. J., & Williams, W. M. (1997). Schooling, intelligence, and income. *American Psychologist, 52*(10), 1105–1058.

Ceci, S., & Liker, J. (1986). A day at the races: A study of IQ, expertise, and cognitive complexity. *Journal of Experimental Psychology: General, 114,* 255–266.

Center on Addiction and Substance Abuse at Columbia University (CASA). (1996, June). *Substance abuse and the American woman.* New York: Author.

Center on Elderly People Living Alone. (1995a, January). *Nursing homes* (Public Policy Institute Fact Sheet FS10R). Washington, DC: American Association of Retired Persons.

Centers for Disease Control and Prevention (CDC). (undated). Patterns of prescription drug use in the United States, 1988–1994. National Health and Nutrition Examination Survey.

Centers for Disease Control and Prevention (CDC). (1997, April 25). Alcohol consumption among pregnant and childbearing-aged women—United States, 1991 and 1995. *Morbidity and Mortality Weekly Report, 46*(16), 346–350.

Centers for Disease Control and Prevention (CDC). (1999). Motor vehicle safety—a 20th century public health achievement. *Morbidity and Mortality Weekly Report, 48,* 369–374.

Centers for Disease Control and Prevention (CDC). (2000a). *CDC's guidelines for school and community programs: Promoting lifelong physical activity.* [Online]. Available: http://www.cdc.gov/nccdphp/dash/phactaag.htm. Access date: May 26, 2000.

Centers for Disease Control and Prevention (CDC). (2000b). National, state, and urban area vaccination coverage levels among children aged 19–35 months—United States, 1999. *49*(26), 585–589.

Centers for Disease Control and Prevention (CDC). (2000c). *Tracking the hidden epidemic: Trends in STDs in the U.S., 2000.* Washington, DC: Author.

Centers for Disease Control and Prevention (CDC). (2001a). *Assisted reproductive technology success rates: National summary and fertility clinic reports.* Atlanta, GA: Author.

Centers for Disease Control and Prevention (CDC). (2001b). *HIV/AIDS surveillance report, 13*(1).

Centers for Disease Control and Prevention (CDC). (2001c). HIV testing among racial/ethnic minorities—United States, 1999. *Morbidity and Mortality Weekly Report, 50,* 1054–1058.

Centers for Disease Control and Prevention (CDC). (2002a). Recent trends in mortality rates for four major cancers, by sex and race/ethnicity—United States, 1990–1998. *Morbidity and Mortality Weekly Report, 51,* 49–53.

Centers for Disease Control and Prevention (CDC) (2002b). Suicide in the United States. [On-line]. Available: http://www.cdc.gov/ncipc/factsheets/suifacts.htm

Centers for Disease Control and Prevention (CDC). (2002c). Use of assisted reproductive technology—United States, 1996 and 1998. *MMWR Weekly, 51,* 97–101.

Cerhan, J. R., & Wallace, R. B. (1997). Change in social ties and subsequent mortality in rural elders. *Epidemiology, 8,* 475–481.

Chafetz, M. D. (1992). *Smart for life.* New York: Penguin.

Chalfie, D. (1994). *Going it alone: A closer look at grandparents parenting grandchildren.* Washington, DC: AARP Women's Initiative.

Chambre, S. M. (1993). Volunteerism by elders: Past trends and future prospects. *The Gerontologist, 33,* 221–227.

Chan, R. W., Raboy, B., & Patterson, C. J. (1998). Psychosocial adjustment among children conceived via donor insemination by lesbian and heterosexual mothers. *Child Development, 69,* 443–457.

Chandra, A., Abma, J., Maza, P., & Bachrach, C. (1999). *Adoption, adoption seeking, and relinquishment for adoption in the United States* (Advance Data from Vital and Health Statistics No. 306). Hyattsville, MD: National Center for Health Statistics.

Chandra, H., & Singh, P. (2001). Organ transplantation: Present scenario and future strategies for transplant programme (specially cadaveric) in India: Socioadministrative respects. *Journal of the Indian Medical Association, 99,* 374–377.

Chao, R. (1996). Chinese and European American mothers' beliefs about the role of parenting in children's school success. *Journal of Cross-Cultural Psychology, 27,* 403–423.

Chao, R. K. (1994). Beyond parental control and authoritarian parenting style: Understanding Chinese parenting through the cultural notion of training. *Child Development, 65,* 1111–1119.

Chao, R. K. (2000). Cultural explanations for the role of parenting in the school success of Asian-American children. In R. D. Taylor & M. C. Wang (Eds.), *Resilience across contexts: Family, work, culture, and community,* (pp. 333–364). Mahwah, NJ: Erlbaum.

Chao, R. K. (2001). Extending research on the consequences of parenting style for Chinese

Americans and European Americans. *Child Development, 72,* 1832–1843.

Chapman, A. R., & Frankel, M. S. (2000). *Human inheritable genetic modifications: Assessing scientific, ethical, religious, and policy issues.* American Association for the Advancement of Science. [Online]. 73 pages. Available: http://www/aaas/org/spp/dspp/sfri/germline/main.htm. Access date: September 25, 2000.

Chapman, M., & Lindenberger, U. (1988). Functions, operations, and décalage in the development of transitivity. *Developmental Psychology, 24,* 542–551.

Chappell, N. L. (1991). Living arrangements and sources of caregiving. *Journal of Gerontology: Social Sciences, 46*(1), S1–8.

Charles, S. T., Reynolds, C. A., & Gatz, M. (2001). Age-related differences and change in positive and negative affect over 23 years. *Journal of Personality and Social Psychology, 80,* 136–151.

Charness, N., & Schultetus, R. S. (1999). Knowledge and expertise. In F. T. Durso, (Ed.), *Handbook of applied cognition* (pp. 57–81). Chichester, England: Wiley.

Chase-Lansdale, P. L., Cherlin, A. J., & Kiernan, K. E. (1995). The long-term effects of parental divorce on the mental health of young adults: A developmental perspective. *Child Development, 66,* 1614–1634.

Chehab, F. F., Mounzih, K., Lu, R., & Lim, M. E. (1997, January 3). Early onset of reproductive function in normal female mice treated with leptin. *Science, 275,* 88–90.

Chen, C. L., Weiss, N. S., Newcomb, P., Barlow, W., & White, E. (2002). Hormone replacement therapy in relation to breast cancer. *Journal of the American Medical Association, 287,* 734–741.

Chen, C., & Stevenson, H. W. (1989). Homework: A cross-cultural examination. *Child Development, 60,* 551–561.

Chen, C., & Stevenson, H. W. (1995). Motivation and mathematics achievement: A comparative study of Asian-American, Caucasian-American, and East Asian high school students. *Child Development, 66,* 1215–1234.

Chen, E., Matthews, K. A., & Boyce, W. T. (2002). Socioeconomic differences in children's health: How and why do these relationships change with age? *Psychological Bulletin, 128,* 295–329.

Chen, L., Baker S. P., Braver, E. R., & Li, G. (2000). Carrying passengers as a risk factor for crashes fatal to 16- and 17-year-old drivers. *Journal of the American Medical Association, 283*(12), 1578–1582.

Chen, X., Hastings, P. D., Rubin, K. H., Chen, H., Cen, G., & Stewart, S. L. (1998). Child-rearing attitudes and behavioral inhibition in Chinese and Canadian toddlers: A cross-cultural study. *Developmental Psychology, 34*(4), 677–686.

Chen, X., Rubin, K. H., & Li, D. (1997). Relation between academic achievement and social adjustment: Evidence from Chinese children. *Developmental Psychology, 33,* 518–525.

Chen, X., Rubin, K. H., & Li, Z. (1995). Social functioning and adjustment in Chinese children: A longitudinal study. *Developmental Psychology, 31,* 531–539.

Chen, X., Rubin, K. H., & Sun, Y. (1992). Social reputation and peer relationships in Chinese and Canadian children: A cross-cultural study. *Child Development, 63,* 1336–1343.

Cheng, T. L., Fields, C. B., Brenner, R. A., Wright, J. L., Lomax, T., Scheidt, P. C., & the District of Columbia Child/Adolescent Injury Research Network. (2000). Sports injuries; An important cause of morbidity in urban youth. *Pediatrics, 105*(3). Electronic abstracts. http://www.pediatrics.org/cgi/content/full/105/3/e32

Cherlin, A., & Furstenberg, F. F. (1986a). Grandparents and family crisis. *Generations, 10*(4), 26–28.

Cherlin, A., & Furstenberg, F. F. (1986b). *The new American grandparent.* New York: Basic Books.

Cherniss, C. (2002). Emotional intelligence and the good community. *American Journal of Community Psychology, 30,* 1–11.

Cherniss, C., & Adler, M. (2000). *Promoting emotional intelligence in organizations.* Alexandria, VA: American Society for Training & Development (ASTD).

Cherry, K. E., & Park, D. C. (1993). Individual differences and contextual variables influence spatial memory in younger and older adults. *Psychology and Aging, 8,* 517–526.

Chervenak, F. A., Isaacson, G., & Mahoney, M. J. (1986). Advances in the diagnosis of fetal defects. *New England Journal of Medicine, 315*(5), 305–307.

Cheung, M. C., Goldberg, J. D., & Kan, Y. W. (1996). Prenatal diagnosis of sickle cell anaemia and thalassaemia by analysis of fetal cells in maternal blood. *Nature Genetics, 14,* 264–268.

Children's Defense Fund. (1998). *The state of America's children yearbook, 1998.* Washington, DC: Author.

Children's Defense Fund. (2000). *The state of America's children yearbook, 2000.* Washington, DC: Author.

Children's Defense Fund. (2001). *The state of America's children yearbook 2001.* Washington, DC: Author.

Children's Defense Fund. (2002a). Frequently asked questions about child poverty. Available: www.childrensdefense.org. (Access date: March 26, 2002.)

Children's Defense Fund. (2002b). The state of children in America's union: A 2002 guide to "Leave No Child Behind," [Online]. Available: http://www.childrensdefense.org/pdf/minigreenbook.pdf. Access date: October 10, 2002.

Chin, A. E., Hedberg, K., Higginson, G. K., & Fleming, D. W. (1999). Legalized physician-assisted suicide in Oregon: the first year's experience. *New England Journal of Medicine, 340,* 577–583.

Chiriboga, C. A., Brust, J. C. M., Bateman, D., & Hauser, W. A. (1999). Dose-response effect of fetal cocaine exposure on newborn neurologic function. *Pediatrics, 103,* 79–85.

Chiriboga, D. (1989). Mental health at the midpoint: Crisis, challenge, or relief? In S. Hunter & M. Sundel (Eds.), *Midlife myths.* Newbury Park, CA: Sage.

Chiriboga, D. A. (1997). Crisis, challenge, and stability in the middle years. In M. E. Lachman & J. B. James (Eds.), *Multiple paths of midlife development* (pp. 293–322). Chicago: University of Chicago Press.

Chissell, J. T. (1989, July). Paper presented at symposium on race, racism, and health at the 94th annual convention of the National Medical Association, Orlando, FL.

Chochinov, H. M. (2002). Dignity-conserving care: A new model for palliative care: Helping the patient feel valued. *Journal of the American Medical Association, 287,* 2253–2260.

Chochinov, H. M., Hack, T., McClement, S., Harlos, M., & Kristjanson, L. (2002). Dignity in the terminally ill: A developing empirical model. *Social Science Medicine, 54,* 433–443.

Chochinov, H. M., Tataryn, D., Clinch, J. J., & Dudgeon, D. (1999). Will to live in the terminally ill. *Lancet, 354,* 816–819.

Choi, K.-H., Catania, J. A., & Dolcini, M. M. (1994). Extramarital sex and HIV risk behavior among US adults: Results from the national AIDS behavior survey. *American Journal of Public Health, 84,* 2003–2007.

Chomitz, V. R., Cheung, L. W. Y., & Lieberman, E. (1995). The role of lifestyle in preventing low birth weight. *The Future of Children, 5*(1), 121–138.

Chomsky, C. S. (1969). *The acquisition of syntax in children from five to ten.* Cambridge, MA: MIT Press.

Chomsky, N. (1957). *Syntactic structures.* The Hague: Mouton.

Chomsky, N. (1972). *Language and mind* (2nd ed.). New York: Harcourt Brace Jovanovich.

Chomsky, N. (1995). *The minimalist program.* Cambridge, MA: MIT Press.

Chorpita, B. P., & Barlow, D. H. (1998). The development of anxiety: The role of control in the early environment. *Psychological Bulletin, 124,* 3–21.

Christian, M. S., & Brent, R. L. (2001). Teratogen update: evaluation of the reproductive and developmental risks of caffeine. *Teratology, 64*(1), 51–78.

Christie, J. F. (1991). *Psychological research on play: Connections with early literacy development.* Albany: State University of New York Press.

Christie, J. F. (1998). Play as a medium for literacy development. In D. P. Fromberg & D. Bergen (Eds.), *Play from birth to twelve and beyond: Contexts, perspectives, and meanings* (pp. 50–55). New York: Garland.

Chubb, N. H., Fertman, C. I., & Ross, J. L. (1997). Adolescent self-esteem and locus of control: A longitudinal study of gender and age differences. *Adolescence, 32,* 113–129.

Chugani, H. T. (1998). A critical period of brain development: Studies of cerebral glucose utilization with PET. *Preventive Medicine, 27,* 184–187.

Chugani, H. T., Behen, M. E., Muzik, O., Juhasz, C., Nagy, F., & Chugani, D. C. (2001). Local brain functional activity following early deprivation: A study of postinstitutionalized Romanian orphans. *NeuroImage, 14,* 1290–1301.

Chumlea, W. C., Schubert, C. M., Roche, A. F., Kulin, H. E., Lee, P. A., Himes, J. H., & Sun, S. S. (2003). Age at menarche and racial comparisons in US girls. *Pediatrics, 111,* 110–113.

Cibelli. J., Lanza, R. P., & West, M. D., with Carol Ezell. (2002). The first human cloned embryo. *Scientific American,* January, pp. 44–51.

Cicchetti, D., & Toth, S. L. (1998). The development of depression in children and adolescents. *American Psychologist, 53,* 221–241.

Cicero, S., Curcio, P., Papageorghiou, A., Sonek, J., & Nicolaides, K. (2001). Absence of nasal bone in fetuses with trisomy 21 at 11–14 weeks of gestation: An observational study. *Lancet, 358,* 1665–1667.

Cicirelli, V. G. (1976). Family structure and interaction: Sibling effects on socialization. In M. F. McMillan & S. Henao (Eds.), *Child psychiatry: Treatment and research.* New York: Brunner/Mazel.

Cicirelli, V. G. (1977). Relationship of siblings to the elderly person's feelings and concerns. *Journal of Gerontology, 12*(3), 317–322.

Cicirelli, V. G. (1980, December). *Adult children's views on providing services for elderly parents.* Report to the Andrus Foundation.

Cicirelli, V. G. (1989a). Feelings of attachment to siblings and well-being in later life. *Psychology and Aging, 4*(2), 211–216.

Cicirelli, V. G. (1989b). Helping relationships in later life: A reexamination. In J. A. Mancini (Ed.), *Aging parents and adult children.* Lexington, MA: Heath.

Cicirelli, V. G. (1994a). Sibling relationships in cross-cultural perspective. *Journal of Marriage and the Family, 56,* 7–20.

Cicirelli, V. G. (1994b, November). *Sibling relationships over the life course.* Paper presented at the 49th Annual Scientific Meeting of the Gerontological Society of America, Atlanta, GA.

Cicirelli, V. G. (1995). *Sibling relationships across the life span.* New York: Plenum Press.

Citro, J., & Hermanson, S. (1999, March). *Assisted living in the United States* [On-line]. Available: http://www.research.aarp.org/il/fs62r_assisted.html

Clarke, S. C. (1995, March 22). Advance report of final divorce statistics, 1989 and 1990 (*Monthly Vital Statistics Report, 43*[9, Suppl.]). Hyattsville, MD: National Center for Health Statistics.

Clarke-Stewart, K. A. (1987). Predicting child development from day care forms and features: The Chicago study. In D. A. Phillips (Ed.), *Quality in child care: What does the research tell us?* (Research Monographs of the National Association for the Education of Young Children). Washington, DC: National Association for the Education of Young Children.

Clark-Plaskie, M., & Lachman, M. E. (1999). The sense of control in midlife. In S. L. Willis & J. D. Reid (Eds.), *Life in the middle* (pp. 181–208). San Diego: Academic Press.

Clausen, J. (1990). *Turning point as a life course concept.* Paper presented at the annual meeting of the American Sociological Association, Washington, D.C.

Clausen, J. A. (1993). *American lives.* New York: Free Press.

Clavel-Chapelon, G., and the E3N-EPIC Group. (2002). Differential effects of reproductive factors on the risk of pre- and postmenopausal breast cancer: Results from a large cohort of French women. *British Journal of Cancer,* DOI 10.1038/sj/bjc/6600124.

Clay, R. A. (1998, July). Many managers frown on use of flexible work options [On-line]. *APA Monitor, 29*(7). Available: http://www.apa.org/monitor/jul98/flex.html

Clayton, R., & Heard, D. (Eds.). (1994). *Elvis up close: In the words of those who knew him best.* Atlanta, GA: Turner.

Clément, K., Vaisse, C., Lahlou, N., Cabrol, S., Pelloux, V., Cassuto, D., Gourmelen, M., Dina, C., Chambaz, J., Lacorte, J.-M., Basdevant, A., Bougnères, P., Lebouc, Y., Froguel, P., & Guy-Grand, B. (1998). A mutation in the human leptin receptor gene causes obesity and pituitary dysfunction. *Nature, 392,* 398–401.

Clearfield, M. W., & Mix, K. S. (1999). Number versus contour length in infants' discrimination of small visual sets. *Current Directions in Psychological Science, 10,* 408–411.

Cleiren, M. P., Diekstra, R. F., Kerkhof, A. D., & van der Wal, J. (1994). Mode of death and kinship in bereavement: Focusing on "who" rather than "how." *Crisis, 14,* 22–36.

Clifton, R. K., Muir, D. W., Ashmead, D. H., & Clarkson, M. G. (1993). Is visually guided reaching in early infancy a myth? *Child Development, 64,* 1099–1110.

Cnattingius, S., Bergstrom, R., Lipworth, L., & Kramer, M. S. (1998). Prepregnancy weight and the risk of adverse pregnancy outcomes. *New England Journal of Medicine, 338,* 147–152.

Cobrinick, P., Hood, R., & Chused, E. (1959). Effects of maternal narcotic addiction on the newborn infant. *Pediatrics, 24,* 288–290.

Cochran, S. D. (2001). Emerging issues in research on lesbians' and gay men's mental health: Does sexual orientation really matter? *American Psychologist, 56,* 931–947.

Coffey, C. E., Lucke, J. F., Saxton, J. A., Ratcliff, G., Unitas, L. J., Billig, B., & Bryan, N. (1998). Sex differences in brain aging: A quantitative magnetic resonance imaging study. *Archives of Neurology, 55,* 169–179.

Coffey, C. E., Saxton, J. A., Ratcliff, G., Bryan, R. N., & Lucke, J. F. (1999). Relation of education to brain size in normal aging: Implications for the reserve hypothesis. *Neurology, 53,* 189–196.

Cohan, C. L., & Cole, S. W. (2002). Life course transitions and natural disaster: Marriage, birth, and divorce following Hurricane Hugo. *Journal of Family Psychology, 16,* 14–25.

Cohan, C. L., & Kleinbaum, S. (2002). Toward a greater understanding of the cohabitation effect: Premarital cohabitation and marital communication. *Journal of Marriage and Family, 64,* 180–192.

Cohen, D. A., Nsuami, M., Martin, D. H., & Farley, T. A. (1999). Repeated school-based screening for sexually transmitted diseases: A feasible strategy for reaching adolescents. *Pediatrics, 104*(6), 1281–1285.

Cohen, L. B., & Amsel, L. B. (1998). Precursors to infants' perception of the causality of a simple event. *Infant Behavior and Development, 21,* 713–732.

Cohen, L. B., & Oakes, L. M. (1993). How infants perceive a simple causal event. *Developmental Psychology, 29,* 421–433.

Cohen, L. B., Rundell, L. J., Spellman, B. A., & Cashon, C. H. (1999). Infants' perception of causal chains. *Current Directions in Psychological Science, 10,* 412–418.

Cohler, B. J., Hostetler, A. J., & Boxer, A. M. (1998). Generativity, social context, and lived experience: Narratives of gay men in middle adulthood. In D. P. McAdams & E. de St. Aubin (Eds.), *Generativity and adult development* (pp. 265–309). Washington, DC: American Psychological Association.

Cohn, J. F., & Tronick, E. Z. (1983). Three-month-old infants' reaction to simulated maternal depression. *Child Development, 54,* 185–193.

Coie, J. D., & Dodge, K. A. (1998). Aggression and antisocial behavior. In W. Damon (Series Ed.) & N. Eisenberg (Vol. Ed.), *Handbook of child psychology: Vol. 3. Social, emotional, and personality development* (5th ed., pp. 780–862). New York: Wiley.

Coke, M. M. (1992). Correlates of life satisfaction among elderly African-Americans. *Journal of Gerontology: Psychological Sciences, 47*(5), P316–320.

Coke, M. M., & Twaite, J. A. (1995). *The black elderly: Satisfaction and quality of later life.* New York: Haworth.

Colby, A., & Damon, W. (1992). *Some do care: Contemporary lives of moral commitment.* New York: Free Press.

Colby, A., Kohlberg, L., Gibbs, J., & Lieberman, M. (1983). A longitudinal study of moral development. *Monographs of the Society for Research in Child Development, 48*(1–2, Serial No. 200).

Colcombe, S. J., Erickson, K. I., Raz, N., Webb, A. G., Cohen, N. J., Mcauley, E., & Kramer, A. F. (2003). Aerobic fitness reduces brain tissue loss in aging humans *Journal of Gerontology: Medical Sciences, 58,* M176–M180.

Cole, M., & Cole, S. R. (1989). *The development of children.* New York: Freeman.

Cole, P. M., Barrett, K. C., & Zahn-Waxler, C. (1992). Emotion displays in two-year-olds during mishaps. *Child Development, 63,* 314–324.

Cole, P. M., Bruschi, C. J., & Tamang, B. L. (2002). Cultural differences in children's emotional reactions to difficult situations. *Child Development, 73,* 983–996.

Cole, T. B. (1999). Ebbing epidemic: Youth homicide rate at a 14-year low. *Journal of the American Medical Association, 281,* 25–26.

Coleman, J. S. (1988). Social capital in the creation of human capital. *American Journal of Sociology, 94*(Suppl. 95), S95–S120.

Coleman, M., Ganong, L., & Fine, M. (2000). Reinvestigating marriage: Another decade of progress. *Journal of Marriage & the Family, 62,* 1288–1307.

Coley, R. L. (1998). Children's socialization experiences and functioning in single-mother households: The importance of fathers and other men. *Child Development, 69,* 219–230.

Coley, R. L. (2001). (In)visible men: Emerging research on low-income, unmarried, and minority fathers. *American Psychologist, 56,* 743–753.

Collaborative Group on AIDS Incubation and HIV Survival. (2000). Time from HIV-1 seroconversion to AIDS and death before widespread use of highly-active retroviral therapy: A collaborative re-analysis. *Lancet, 355,* 1131–1137.

Collier, V. P. (1995). Acquiring a second language for school. *Directions in Language and Education, 1*(4), 1–11.

Collins, N. L., & Miller, L. C. (1994). Self-disclosure and liking: A meta-analytic review. *Psychological Bulletin, 116,* 457–475.

Collins, R. C., & Deloria, D. (1983). Head Start research: A new chapter. *Children Today, 12*(4), 15–19.

Collins, W. A. (1990). Parent-child relationships in transition to adolescence: Continuity and change in interaction, affect, and cognition. In R. Montemayor, G. R. Adams, & T. P. Gullotta (Eds.), *From childhood to adolescence: A transitional period?* Newbury Park, CA: Sage.

Collins, W. A., Maccoby, E. E., Steinberg, L., Hetherington, E. M., & Bornstein, M. H. (2000). Contemporary research in parenting: The case for nature and nurture. *American Psychologist, 55,* 218–232.

Colombo, J. (1993). *Infant cognition: Predicting later intellectual functioning.* Thousand Oaks, CA: Sage.

Colombo, J., & Janowsky, J. S. (1998). A cognitive neuroscience approach to individual differences in infant cognition. In J. E. Richards (Ed.), *Cognitive neuroscience of attention* (pp. 363–391). Mahwah, NJ: Erlbaum.

Colón, J. M. (1997). Assisted reproductive technologies. In M. L. Sipski, & C. J. Alexander (Eds.), *Sexual function in people with disability and chronic illness: A health professional's guide* (pp. 557–575). Gaithersburg, MD: Aspen.

Coltrane, S., & Adams, M. (1997). Work-family imagery and gender stereotypes: Television and the reproduction of difference. *Journal of Vocational Behavior, 50,* 323–347.

Comings, D. E., Muhleman, D., Johnson, J. P., & MacMurray, J. P. (2002). Parent-daughter transmission of the androgen receptor gene as an explanation of the effect of father absence on age of menarche. *Child Development, 73,* 1046–1051.

Commissioner's Office of Research and Evaluation and Head Start Bureau, Department of Health and Human Services. (2001). *Building their futures: How Early Head Start programs are enhancing the lives of infants and toddlers in low-income families. Summary report.* Washington, DC: Author.

Committee on Obstetric Practice. (2002). ACOG committee opinion: Exercise during pregnancy and the postpartum period. *International Journal of Gynaecology & Obstetrics, 77*(1), 79–81.

Commonwealth Fund Commission on Elderly People Living Alone. (1986). *Problems facing elderly Americans living alone.* New York: Harris & Associates.

Compas, B. E., & Luecken, L. (2002). Psychological adjustment to breast cancer. *Current Directions in Psychological Science, 11,* 111–114.

Comuzzie, A. G., & Allison, D. B. (1998). The search for human obesity genes. *Science, 280,* 1374–1377.

Condon pleased that crack baby decision is reaffirmed. (1997, October 27). South Carolina Attorney General's Office. [Online]. Available: http://scattorneygeneral.org. Access date: June 26, 1998.

Conel, J. L. (1959). *The postnatal development of the human cerebral cortex.* Cambridge, MA: Harvard University Press.

Conference Board. (1999, June 25). *Workplace education programs are benefiting U.S. corporations and workers* [On-line, Press release]. Available: http://www.newswise.com/articles/1999/6/WEP.TCB.html

Conger, J. J. (1988). Hostages to fortune: Youth, values, and the public interest. *American Psychologist, 43*(4), 291–300.

Conger, R. C., Ge, X., Elder, G. H., Lorenz, F. O., & Simons, R. L. (1994). Economic stress, coercive family processes, and developmental problems of adolescents. *Child Development, 65,* 541–561.

Conger, R. D., & Elder, G. H., Jr. (1994). *Families in troubled times: Adapting to change in rural America.* New York: Aldine de Gruyter.

Conger, R. D., Conger, K. J., Elder, G. H., Jr., Lorenz, F. O., Simons, R. L., & Whitbeck, L. B. (1993). Family economic stress and adjustment of early adolescent girls. *Developmental Psychology, 29,* 206–219.

Conger, R. D., Rueter, M. A., & Elder, G. H., Jr. (1999). Couple resilience to economic pressure. *Journal of Personality and Social Psychology, 76,* 54–71.

Connidis, I. A., & Davies, L. (1992). Confidants and companions: Choices in later life. *Journal of Gerontology: Social Sciences, 47*(30), S115–122.

Cook, E. H., Courchesne, R., Lord, C., Cox, N. J., Yan, S., Lincoln, A., Haas, R., Courchesne, E., & Leventhal, B. L. (1997). Evidence of linkage between the serotonin transporter and autistic disorder. *Molecular Psychiatry, 2,* 247–250.

Cook, P. J., & Laub, J. H. (1998). The unprecedented epidemic of youth violence. In M. Tonry & M. H. Moore (Eds.), *Youth violence. Crime and justice: A review of research* (Vol. 24, pp. 27–64). Chicago: University of Chicago Press.

Coon, H., Fulker, D. W., DeFries, J. C., & Plomin, R. (1990). Home environment and cognitive ability of 7-year-old children in the Colorado Adoption Project: Genetic and environmental etiologies. *Developmental Psychology, 26,* 459–468.

Cooper, H. (1989, November). Synthesis of research on homework. *Educational Leadership,* 85–91.

Cooper, H., Lindsay, J. J., Nye, B., & Greathouse, S. (1998). Relationships among attitudes about homework, amount of homework assigned and completed, and student achievement. *Journal of Educational Psychology, 90,* 70–83.

Cooper, H., Valentine, J. C., Nye, B., & Lindsay, J. J. (1999). Relationships between five after-school activities and academic achievement. *Journal of Educational Psychology, 91*(2), 369–378.

Cooper, K. L., & Gutmann, D. L. (1987). Gender identity and ego mastery style in middle-aged, pre- and post-empty nest women. *The Gerontologist, 27*(3), 347–352.

Cooper, R. P., & Aslin, R. N. (1990). Preference for infant-directed speech in the first month after birth. *Child Development, 61,* 1584–1595.

Cooper, R. S, Rotimi, C. N., & Ward, R. (1999, February). The puzzle of hypertension in African-Americans. *Scientific American,* pp. 56–63.

Coplan, R. J., Gavinski-Molina, M., Lagacé-Séguin, D. G., & Wichman, C. (2001). When girls versus boys play alone: Nonsocial play and adjusted in kindergarten. *Developmental Psychology, 37*(4), 464–474.

Corbet, A., Long, W., Schumacher, R., Gerdes, J., Cotton, R., & the American Exosurf Neonatal Study Group 1. (1995). Double-blind developmental evaluation at 1-year corrected age of 597 premature infants with birth weights from 500 to 1350 grams enrolled in three placebo-controlled trials of prophylactic synthetic surfactant. *Journal of Pediatrics, 126,* S5–S12.

Corbin, C. (1973). *A textbook of motor development.* Dubuque, IA: Brown.

Corder, E. H., Saunders, A. M., Strittmatter, W. J., Schmechel, D. E., Gaskell, P. C., Small, G. M., Roses, A. D., Haines, J. L., & Pericak-Vance, M. A. (1993). Gene dose of apolipoprotein E type 4 allele and the risk of Alzheimer's disease in late onset families. *Science, 261,* 921–923.

Corliss, J. (1996, October 29). Alzheimer's in the news. *HealthNews,* pp. 1–2.

Cornelius, S. W., & Caspi, A. (1987). Everyday problem solving in adulthood and old age. *Psychology and Aging, 2,* 144–153.

Costa, P. T., Jr., & McCrae, R. R. (1980). Still stable after all these years: Personality as a key to some issues in adulthood and old age. In P. B. Baltes, Jr., & O. G. Brim (Eds.), *Life-span development and behavior* (Vol. 3, pp. 65–102). New York: Academic Press.

Costa, P. T., Jr., & McCrae, R. R. (1988). Personality in adulthood: A six-year longitudinal study of self-reports and spouse ratings on the NEO Personality Inventory. *Journal of Personality and Social Psychology, 54,* 853–863.

Costa, P. T., Jr., & McCrae, R. R. (1994a). Set like plaster? Evidence for the stability of adult personality. In T. F. Heatherton & J. L. Weinberger (Eds.), *Can personality change?* (pp. 21–41). Washington, DC: American Psychological Association.

Costa, P. T., Jr., & McCrae, R. R. (1994b). Stability and change in personality from adolescence through adulthood. In C. F. Halverson, G. A. Kohnstamm, & R. P. Martin (Eds.), *The developing structure of temperament and personality from infancy to adulthood.* Hillsdale, NJ: Erlbaum.

Costa, P. T., Jr., & McCrae, R. R. (1995). Solid ground in the wetlands of personality: A reply to Block. *Psychological Bulletin, 117,* 216–220.

Costa, P. T., Jr., & McCrae, R. R. (1996). Mood and personality in adulthood. In C. Magai & S. H. McFadden (Eds.), *Handbook of emotion, adult development, and aging* (pp. 369–383). San Diego: Academic Press.

Costa, P. T., Jr., McCrae, R. R., Zonderman, A. B., Barbano, H. E., Lebowitz, B., & Larson, D. M. (1986). Cross-sectional studies of personality in a national sample: 2. Stability in neuroticism, extraversion, and openness. *Psychology and Aging, 1,* 144–149.

Costello, S. (1990, December). Yani's monkeys: Lessons in form and freedom. *School Arts,* pp. 10–11.

Coster, W. J., Gersten, M. S., Beeghly, M., & Cicchetti, D. (1989). Communicative functioning in maltreated toddlers. *Developmental Psychology, 25,* 1020–1029.

Council on Scientific Affairs, American Medical Association. (1995). Female genital mutilation. *Journal of the American Medical Association, 274*(21), 1714–1716.

Couzin, J. (1998). Low-calorie diets may slow monkeys' aging. *Science, 282,* 1018.

Cowan, N., Nugent, L. D., Elliott, E. M., Ponomarev, I., & Saults, J. S. (1999). The role of attention in the development of short-term memory: Age differences in the verbal span of apprehension. *Child Development, 70,* 1082–1097.

Cox, J., Daniel, N., & Boston, B. O. (1985). *Educating able learners: Programs and promising practices.* Austin: University of Texas Press.

Coyle, J. T. (2000). Psychotropic drug use in very young children. *Journal of the American Medical Association, 283*(8), 1059–1060.

Coyle, T. R., & Bjorklund, D. F. (1997). Age differences in, and consequences of, multiple- and variable-strategy use on a multitrial sort-recall task. *Developmental Psychology, 33,* 372–380.

Craik, F. I. M., & Byrd, M. (1982). Aging and cognitive deficits: The role of attentional resources. In F. I. M. Craik & S. Trehub (Eds.), *Aging and cognitive processes* (pp. 191–221). New York: Plenum.

Craik, F. I. M., & Jennings, J. M. (1992). Human memory. In F. I. M. Craik & T. A. Salthouse (Eds.), *Handbook of aging and cognition* (pp. 51–110). Hillsdale, NJ: Erlbaum.

Craik, F. I. M., & Salthouse, T. A. (Eds.). (2000). *The handbook of aging and cognition* (2nd ed.). Mahwah, NJ: Erlbaum.

Crain-Thoreson, C., & Dale, P. S. (1992). Do early talkers become early readers? Linguistic precocity, preschool language, and emergent literacy. *Developmental Psychology, 28,* 421–429.

Crane, D. R., Soderquist, J. N, & Gardner, M. D. (1995). Gender differences in cognitive and behavioral steps toward divorce. *American Journal of Family Therapy, 23*(2), 99–105.

Cratty, B. J. (1986). *Perceptual and motor development in infants and children* (3rd ed.). Englewood Cliffs, NJ: Prentice-Hall.

Creed, P. A., & Macintyre, S. R. (2001). The relative effects of deprivation of the latent and manifest benefits of employment on the well being of unemployed people. *Journal of Occupational Health Psychology, 6,* 324–331.

Crick, N. R., & Dodge, K. A. (1994). A review and reformulation of social information-processing mechanisms in children's social adjustment. *Psychological Bulletin, 115,* 74–101.

Crick, N. R., & Dodge, K. A. (1996). Social information-processing mechanisms in reactive and proactive aggression. *Child Development, 67,* 993–1002.

Crick, N. R., & Grotpeter, J. K. (1995). Relational aggression, gender, and social-psychological adjustment. *Child Development, 66,* 710–722.

Crick, N. R., Bigbee, M. A., & Howes, C. (1996). Gender differences in children's normative beliefs about aggression: How do I hurt thee? Let me count the ways. *Child Development, 67,* 1003–1014.

Crick, N. R., Casas, J. F., & Nelson, D. A. (2002). Toward a more comprehensive understanding of peer maltreatment: Studies of relational victimization. *Current Directions in Psychological Science, 11*(3), 98–101.

Crick, N. R., Werner. N. E., Casas, J. F., O'Brian, K. M., Nelson, D. A., Grotpeter, J. K., & Markon, K. (1999). Childhood aggression and gender: A new look at an old problem. In D. Bernstein (Ed.), *The Nebraska Symposium on Motivation* (Vol. 45). Lincoln: University of Nebraska Press.

Crijnen, A. A. M., Achenbach, T. M., & Verhulst, F. C. (1999). Problems reported by parents of children in multiple cultures: The Child Behavior Checklist syndrome constructs. *American Journal of Psychiatry, 156,* 569–574.

Crimmins, E. M., Reynolds, S. L., & Saito, Y. (1999). Trends in health and ability to work among the older working-age population. *Journal of Gerontology: Psychological Sciences, 54B,* S31–S40.

Crittenden, P. M. (1993). Comparison of two systems for assessing quality of attachment in the preschool years. In P. M. Crittenden (Chair), *Quality of attachment in the preschool years. Symposium conducted at the Ninth Biennial Meeting of the International Conference on Infant Studies,* Paris.

Crockenberg, S., & Lourie, A. (1996). Parents' conflict strategies with children and children's conflict strategies with peers. *Merrill-Palmer Quarterly, 42,* 495–518.

Cromwell, J., Bartosch, W. J., Fiore, M. C., Hasselblad, V., & Baker, T. (1997). Cost-effectiveness of the clinical practice recommendations in the AHCPR guidelines for smoking cessation. *Journal of the American Medical Association, 278,* 1759–1766.

Crouter, A., & Larson, R. (Eds.). (1998). *Temporal rhythms in adolescence: Clocks, calendars, and the coordination of daily life* (New Directions in Child and Adolescent Development, No. 82). San Francisco: Jossey-Bass.

Crouter A. C., Bumpus, M. F., Maguire, M. C., & McHale, S. M. (1999). Linking parents' work pressure and adolescents' well-being: Insights into dynamics in dual-earner families. *Developmental Psychology, 35*(6), 1453–1461.

Crouter, A. C., & Maguire, M. C. (1998). Seasonal and weekly rhythms: Windows into variability in family socialization experiences in early adolescence. In A. C. Crouter & R. Larson (Eds.), *Temporal rhythms in adolescence: Clocks, calendars, and the coordination of daily life* (New Directions for Child and Adolescent Development, No. 82). San Francisco: Jossey-Bass.

Crouter, A. C., & Manke, B. (1994). The changing American workplace: Implications for individuals and families. *Family Relations, 43,* 117–124.

Crouter, A. C., & McHale, S. M. (1993). Temporal rhythms in family life: Seasonal variation and the relation between parental work and family processes. *Developmental Psychology, 29,* 198–205.

Crouter, A. C., Helms-Erikson, H., Updegraff, K., & McHale, S. M. (1999). Conditions underlying parents' knowledge about children's daily lives in middle childhood: Between- and within-family comparisons. *Child Development, 70,* 246–259.

Crow, J. F. (1999). The odds of losing at genetic roulette. *Nature, 397,* 293–294.

Crowley, S. L. (1993, October). Grandparents to the rescue. *AARP Bulletin,* pp. 1, 16–17.

Crowley, S. L. (1994, May). Much ado about menopause: Plenty of information but precious few answers. *AARP Bulletin,* pp. 2, 7.

***Cruzan v. Director, Missouri Department of Health,* 110 S. Ct. 2841 (1990).**

Csikszentmihalyi, M. (1999). If we are so rich, why aren't we happy? *American Psychologist, 54,* 821–827.

Cullum, C. M., & Rosenberg, R. N. (1998). Memory loss—when is it Alzheimer Disease? *Journal of the American Medical Association, 279,* 1689–1690.

Cumming, E., & Henry, W. (1961). *Growing old.* New York: Basic Books.

Cummings, E. M. (1994). Marital conflict and children's functioning. *Social Development, 3,* 16–36.

Cummings, E. M., Iannotti, R. J., & Zahn-Waxler, C. (1989). Aggression between peers in early childhood: Individual continuity and developmental change. *Child Development, 60,* 887–895.

Cunningham, A. S., Jelliffe, D. B., & Jelliffe, E. F. P. (1991). Breastfeeding and health in the 1980s: A global epidemiological review. *Journal of Pediatrics, 118,* 659–666.

Cunningham, F. G., & Leveno, K. J. (1995). Childbearing among older women—The message is cautiously optimistic. *New England Journal of Medicine, 333,* 1002–1004.

Curtin, S. C., & Park, M. M. (1999). Trends in the attendant, place, and timing of births, and in the use of obstetric interventions: United States, 1989–97 (*National Vital Statistics*

Reports, 47[27]). Hyattsville, MD: National Center for Health Statistics.

Curtiss, S. (1977). *Genie.* New York: Academic Press.

Cutler, N. E., & Devlin, S. J. (1996). A framework for understanding financial responsibility among generations. *Generations, 20*(1), 24–28.

Cutler, S. J. (1998, December). Senator/astronaut John Glenn shows what older persons can do. *Gerontology News,* p. 1.

Cutrona, C., Russell, D., & Rose, J. (1986). Social support and adaptation to stress by the elderly. *Psychology and Aging, 1*(1), 47–54.

Cutting, A. L., & Dunn, J. (1999). Theory of mind, emotion understanding, language, and family background: Individual differences and interrelations. *Child Development, 70,* 853–865.

Cutz, E., Perrin, D. G., Hackman, R., & Czegledy-Nagy, E. N. (1996). Maternal smoking and pulmonary neuroendocrine cells in sudden infant death syndrome. *Pediatrics, 88,* 668–672.

Cvetanovski, J., & Jex, S. (1994). Locus of control of unemployed people and its relationship to psychological and physical well-being. *Work and Stress, 8*(1), 60–67.

Cytrynbaum, S., Bluum, L., Patrick, R., Stein, J., Wadner, D., & Wilk, C. (1980). Midlife development: A personality and social systems perspective. In L. Poon (Ed.), *Aging in the 1980s.* Washington, DC: American Psychological Association.

Czaja, A. J., & Sharit, J. (1998). Ability-performance relationships as a function of age and task experience for a data entry task. *Journal of Experimental Psychology-Applied, 4,* 332–351.

Dale, P. S., Crain-Thoreson, C., Notari-Syverson, A., & Cole, K. (1996). Parent-child book reading as an intervention technique for young children with language delays. *Topics in Early Childhood Special Education, 16,* 213–235.

D'Alton, M. E., & DeCherney, A. H. (1993). Prenatal diagnosis. *New England Journal of Medicine, 32*(2), 114–120.

Damewood, M. D. (2001). Ethical implications of a new application of preimplantation diagnosis. *Journal of the American Medical Association, 285,* 3143–3144.

Dan, A. J., & Bernhard, L. A. (1989). Menopause and other health issues for midlife women. In S. Hunter & M. Sundel (Eds.), *Midlife myths.* Newbury Park, CA: Sage.

Danesi, M. (1994). *Cool: The signs and meanings of adolescence.* Toronto: University of Toronto Press.

Daniel, M. H. (1997). Intelligence testing: Status and trends. *American Psychologist, 52,* 1038–1045.

Darling, N., & Steinberg, L. (1993). Parenting style as context: An integrative model. *Psychological Bulletin, 113,* 487–496.

Darroch, J. E., Singh, S., Frost, J. J., & the Study Team. (2001). Differences in teenage pregnancy rates among five developed countries: The roles of sexual activity and contraceptive use. *Family Planning Perspectives, 33,* 244–250, 281.

David, R. J., & Collins, J. W., Jr. (1997). Differing birth weight among infants of U.S.-born blacks, African-born blacks, and U.S.-born whites. *New England Journal of Medicine, 337,* 1209–1214.

Davidson, J. I. F. (1998). Language and play: Natural partners. In D. P. Fromberg & D. Bergen (Eds.), *Play from birth to twelve and beyond: Contexts, perspectives, and meanings* (pp. 175–183). New York: Garland.

Davidson, N. E. (1995). Hormone-replacement therapy—Breast versus heart versus bone. *New England Journal of Medicine, 332,* 1638–1639.

Davidson, R. J., & Fox, N. A. (1989). Frontal brain asymmetry predicts infants' response to maternal separation. *Journal of Abnormal Psychology, 948*(2), 58–64.

Davies, C., & Williams, D. (2002). *The grandparent study 2002 report.* Washington, DC: AARP.

Davies, M., Stankov, L., Roberts, R. D. (1998). Emotional intelligence: In search of an elusive construct. *Journal of Personality and Social Psychology, 75,* 989–1015.

Davies, P. T., & Cummings, E. M. (1998). Exploring children's emotional security as a mediator of the link between marital relations and child adjustment. *Child Development, 69,* 124–139.

Davis, D. L., Gottlieb, M. B., & Stampnitzky, J. R. (1998). Reduced ratio of male to female births in several industrial countries. *Journal of the American Medical Association, 279,* 1018–1023.

Davis, M., & Emory, E. (1995). Sex differences in neonatal stress reactivity. *Child Development, 66,* 14–27.

Davis-Kean, P. E., & Sandler, H. M. (2001). A meta-analysis of measures of self-esteem for young children: A framework for future measures. *Child Development, 72,* 887–906.

Davison, K. K., & Birch, L. L. (2001). Weight status, parent reaction, and self-concept in five-year-old girls. *Pediatrics, 107,* 46–53.

Dawson, D. A. (1991). Family structure and children's health and well-being: Data from the 1988 National Health Interview Survey on child health. *Journal of Marriage and the Family, 53,* 573–584.

Dawson, G., Frey, K., Panagiotides, H., Osterling, J., & Hessl, D. (1997). Infants of depressed mothers exhibit atypical frontal brain activity: A replication and extension of previous findings. *Journal of Child Psychology & Allied Disciplines, 38,* 179–186.

Dawson, G., Frey, K., Panagiotides, H., Yamada, E., Hessl, D., & Osterling, J. (1999). Infants of depressd mothers exhibit atypical frontal electrical brain activity during interactions with mother and with a familiar nondepressed adult. *Child Development, 70,* 1058–1066.

Dawson, G., Klinger, L. G., Panagiotides, H., Hill, D., & Spieker, S. (1992). Frontal lobe activity and affective behavior of infants of mothers with depressive symptoms. *Child Development, 63,* 725–737.

Dawson-Hughes, B., Harris, S. S., Krall, E. A., & Dallal, G. E. (1997). Effect of calcium and vitamin D supplementation on bone density in men and women 65 years of age and older. *New England Journal of Medicine, 337,* 670–676.

Day, J. C., & Newburger, E. C. (2002). The big payoff: Educational attainment and synthetic estimates of work-life earnings. *Current Population Reports* (P23–210). Washington, DC: U.S. Census Bureau.

Day, N.L., Leech, S.L., Richardson, G. A., Cornelius, M. D., Robles, N., & Larkby, C. (2002). Prenatal alcohol exposure predicts continued deficits in offspring size at 14 years of age. *Alcoholism: Clinical and Experimental Research, 26,* 1584–1591.

Day, S. (1993, May). Why genes have a gender. *New Scientist, 138*(1874), 34–38.

de Castro, B. O., Veerman, J. W., Koops, W., Bosch, J. D., & Monshouwer, H. J. (2002). Hostile attribution of intent and aggressive behavior: A meta-analysis. *Child Development, 73,* 916–934.

de Lange, T. (1998). Telomeres and senescence: Ending the debate. *Science, 279,* 334–335.

de Vaus, D. (2002). Marriage and mental health: Does marriage improve the mental health of men at the expense of women? *Family Matters, 62,* 26–32.

de Vries, B. (1996). The understanding of friendship: An adult life course perspective. In C. Magai & S. H. McFadden (Eds.), *Handbook of emotion, adult development, and aging* (pp. 249–269). San Diego: Academic Press.

De Wolff, M. S., & van IJzendoorn, M. H. (1997). Sensitivity and attachment: A meta-analysis on parental antecedents of infant attachment. *Child Development, 68,* 571–591.

Deary, I. J., Leaper, S. A., Murray, A. D., Staff, R. T., & Whalley, L. J. (2003). Cerebral white matter abnormalities and lifetime cognitive change: A 67 year follow up of the Scottish Mental Survey or 1932. *Psychology and Aging, 188,* 140–148.

DeCasper, A. J., & Fifer, W. P. (1980). Of human bonding: Newborns prefer their mothers' voices. *Science, 208,* 1174–1176.

DeCasper, A. J., & Spence, M. J. (1986). Prenatal maternal speech influences newborns' perceptions of speech sounds. *Infant Behavior and Development, 9,* 133–150.

DeCasper, A. J., Lecanuet, J. P., Busnel, M. C., Granier-Deferre, C., & Maugeais, R. (1994) Fetal reactions to recurrent maternal speech. *Infant Behavior and Development, 17,* 159–164.

DeGarmo, D. S., Forgatch, M. S., & Martinez, C. R. (1999). Parenting of divorced mothers as a link between social status and boys' academic outcomes: Unpacking the effects of socioeconomic status. *Child Development, 70*(5), 1231–1245.

DeHaan, L. G., & MacDermid, S. M. (1994). Is women's identity achievement associated with the expression of generativity? Examining identity and generativity in multiple roles. *Journal of Adult Development, 1,* 235–247.

Dekovic, M., & Janssens, J. M. A. M. (1992). Parents' child-rearing style and child's sociometric status. *Developmental Psychology, 28,* 925–932.

Del Carmen, R. D., Pedersen, F. A., Huffman, L. C., & Bryan, Y. E. (1993). Dyadic distress management predicts subsequent security of attachment. *Infant Behavior and Development, 16,* 131–147.

Delany, E., Delany, S., & Hearth, A. H. (1993). *The Delany sisters' first 100 years.* New York: Kodansha America.

DeLoache, J. (1995). The use of dolls in interviewing young children. In M. S. Zaragoza, J. R. Graham, G. C. N. Hall, & Y. S. Ben-Porath, (Eds.), *Memory and testimony in the child witness* (Vol. 1, pp. 160–178). Thousand Oaks, CA: Sage.

DeLoache, J. S., Miller, K. F., & Pierroutsakos, S. L. (1998). Reasoning and problem solving. In D. Kuhn & R. S. Siegler (Eds.), *Handbook of Child Psychology: Vol. 2. Cognition, perception, and language* (5th ed., pp. 801–850). New York: Wiley.

DeLoache, J. S., Miller, K. F., & Rosengren, K. S. (1997). The credible shrinking room: Very young children's performance with symbolic and nonsymbolic relations. *Psychological Science, 8,* 308–313.

DeLoache, J. S., Pierroutsakos, S. L., Uttal, D. H., Rosengren, K. S., & Gottleib, A. (1998). Grasping the nature of pictures. *Psychological Science, 9,* 205–210.

DeLoache, J., & Gottlieb, A. (2000). If Dr. Spock were born in Bali: Raising a world of babies. In J. DeLoache & A. Gottlieb (Eds.), *A world of babies: Imagined childcare guides for seven societies* (pp. 1–27). New York: Cambridge University Press.

Demo, D. H. (1991). A sociological perspective on parent-adolescent disagreements. In R. L. Paikoff (Ed.), *Shared views in the family during adolescence* (New Directions for Child Development, No. 51, pp. 111–118). San Francisco: Jossey-Bass.

Denney, N. W., & Palmer, A. M. (1981). Adult age differences on traditional and practical problem-solving measures. *Journal of Gerontology, 36*(3), 323–328.

Denney, N. W., & Pearce, K. A. (1989). A developmental study of practical problem solving in adults. *Psychology and Aging, 4*(4), 438–442.

Dennis, W. (1936). A bibliography of baby biographies. *Child Development, 7,* 71–73.

Denny, F. W., & Clyde, W. A. (1983). Acute respiratory tract infections: An overview [Monograph]. *Pediatric Research, 17,* 1026–1029.

Denton, K., & Zarbatany, L. (1996). Age differences in support in conversations between friends. *Child Development, 67,* 1360–1373.

Department of Commerce. (2002). *A nation online: How Americans are expanding their use of the Internet.* Washington, DC: Author.

Depression during pregnancy and after. (2002, September). *Harvard Mental Health Letter,* pp. 6–8.

Desai, M., Pratt, L. A., Lentzner, H., & Robinson, K. N. (2001). Trends in vision and hearing among older Americans. *Aging Trends,* No. 2. Hyattsville, MD: National Center for Health Statistics.

Deutsch, F. M. (2001). Equally shared parenting. *Current Directions in Psychological Science, 10,* 25–28.

Devaney, B., Johnson, A., Maynard, R., & Trenholm, C. (2002). *The evaluation of abstinence education programs funded under Title V, Section 510: Interim report.* Washington, DC: U.S. Department of Health and Human Services.

Devlin, B., Daniels, M., & Roeder, K. (1997). The heritability of IQ. *Nature, 388,* 468–471.

Dewey, K. G., Heinig, M. J., & Nommsen-Rivers, L. A. (1995). Differences in morbidity between breast-fed and formula-fed infants. *Journal of Pediatrics, 126,* 696–702.

Deykin, E. Y., Alpert, J. J., & McNamara, J. J. (1985). A pilot study of the effect of exposure to child abuse or neglect on adolescent suicidal behavior. *American Journal of Psychiatry, 142*(11), 1299–1303.

Diamond, A. (1991). Neuropsychological insights into the meaning of object concept development. In S. Carey & R. Gelman (Eds.), *Epigenesis of mind* (pp. 67–110). Hillsdale, NJ: Erlbaum.

Diamond, A., Cruttenden, L., & Neiderman, D. (1994). AB with multiple wells: 1. Why are multiple wells sometimes easier than two wells? 2. Memory or memory + inhibition? *Developmental Psychology, 30,* 192–205.

Diamond, L. M. (2000). Sexual identity, attractions, and behavior among young sexual-minority women over a 2-year period. *Developmental Psychology, 36,* 241–250.

Diamond, M. C. (1988). *Enriching heredity.* New York: Free Press.

Diamond, M., & Sigmundson, H. K. (1997). Sex reassignment at birth: Long-term review and clinical implications. *Archives of Pediatric and Adolescent Medicine, 151,* 298–304.

Diaz, R. M. (1983). Thought and two languages: The impact of bilingualism on cognitive development. *Review of Research in Education, 10,* 23–54.

Dickinson, G. E., Lancaster, C. J., Clark, D., Ahmedzai, S. H., & Noble, W. (2002). U.K. physicians' attitudes toward active voluntary euthanasia and physician-assisted suicide. *Death Studies, 26,* 479–490.

DiClemente, R. J., Wingood, G. M., Crosby, R., Sionean, C., Cobb, B. K., Harrington, K., Davies, S., Hook, E. W., & Oh, M. K. (2001). Parental monitoring: Association with adolescents' risk behaviors. *Pediatrics, 107,* 1363–1368.

Diehl, M., Coyle, N., & Labouvie-Vief, G. (1996). Age and sex differences in strategies of coping and defense across the life span. *Psychology and Aging, 11*(1), 127–139.

Diehl, M., Willis, S. L., & Schaie, K. W. (1994). *Practical problem solving in older adults: Observational assessment and cognitive correlates.* Unpublished manuscript, Wayne State University, Detroit.

Dien, D. S. F. (1982). A Chinese perspective on Kohlberg's theory of moral development. *Developmental Review, 2,* 331–341.

Diener, E. (2000). Subjective well-being: The science of happiness and a proposal for a national index. *American Psychologist, 55,* 34–43.

Dietz, W. H. (2001). Breastfeeding may help prevent childhood overweight. *Journal of the American Association, 285*(19), 2506–2507.

DiFranza, J. R., & Lew, R. A. (1995, April). Effect of maternal cigarette smoking on pregnancy complications and sudden infant death syndrome. *Journal of Family Practice, 40,* 385–394.

DiGiulio, J. F. (1992). Early widowhood: An atypical transition. *Journal of Mental Health Counseling, 14,* 97–109.

Dimant, R. J., & Bearison, D. J. (1991). Development of formal reasoning during successive peer interactions. *Developmental Psychology, 27,* 277–284.

DiMarco, M. A., Menke, E. M., & McNamara, T. (2001). Evaluating a support group for perinatal loss. *MCN American Journal of Maternal and Child Nursing, 26,* 135–140.

Ding, Y-C., Chi, H-C., Grady, D. L., Morishima, A., Kidd, J. R., Kidd, K. K., Flodman, P., Spence, M. A., Schuck, S., Swanson, J. M., Zhang, Y-P., & Moyzis, R. K. (2002). Evidence of positive selection acting at the human dopamine receptor D4 gene locus. *Proceedings of the National Academy of Science, 99,* 309–314.

DiPietro, J. A., Hodgson, D. M., Costigan, K. A., Hilton, S. C., & Johnson, T. R. B. (1996). Fetal neurobehavioral development. *Child Development, 67,* 2553–2567.

Dishion, T. J., McCord, J., & Poulin, F. (1999). When intervention harms. *American Psychologist, 54,* 755–764.

Dixon, R. A., & Baltes, P. B. (1986). Toward life-span research on the functions and pragmatics of intelligence. In R. J. Sternberg & R. K. Wagner (Eds.), *Practical intelligence: Nature and origins of competence in the everyday world* (pp. 203–235). New York: Cambridge University Press.

Dixon, R. A., & Hultsch, D. F. (1999). Intelligence and cognitive potential in late Life. In J. C. Cavanaugh & S. K. Whitbourne (Eds.), *Gerontology: An interdisciplinary perspective.* New York: Oxford University Press.

Dixon, R. A., Hultsch, D. F., & Herzog, C. (1988). The metamemory in adulthood (MIA) questionnaire. *Psychopharmacology Bulletin, 24,* 671–688.

Dlugosz, L., Belanger, K., Helienbrand, K., Holfard, T. R., Leaderer, B., & Bracken, M. B. (1996). Maternal caffeine consumption and spontaneous abortion: A prospective cohort study. *Epidemiology, 7,* 250–255.

Dodge, K. A., Bates, J. E., & Pettit, G. S. (1990). Mechanisms in the cycle of violence. *Science, 250,* 1678–1683.

Dodge, K. A., Coie, J. D., Pettit, G. S., & Price, J. M. (1990). Peer status and aggression in boys' groups: Developmental and contextual analysis. *Child Development, 61,* 1289–1309.

Dodge, K. A., Pettit, G. S., & Bates, J. E. (1994). Socialization mediators of the relation between socioeconomic status and child conduct problems. *Child Development, 65,* 649–665.

Dodge, K. A., Pettit, G. S., & Bates, J. E. (1997). How the experience of early physical abuse leads children to become chronically aggressive. In D. Cicchetti & S. L. Toth (Eds.), *Rochester symposium on developmental psychopathology. Vol. 8: Developmental perspectives on trauma* (pp. 263–288). Rochester, NY: University of Rochester Press.

Doherty, W. J., Kouneski, E. F., & Erickson, M. F. (1998). Responsible fathering: An overview and conceptual framework. *Journal of Marriage and the Family, 60,* 277–292.

Doka, K. J., & Mertz, M. E. (1988). The meaning and significance of greatgrandparenthood. *The Gerontologist, 28*(2), 192–197.

Dolan, M. A., & Hoffman, C. D. (1998). Determinants of divorce among women: A reexamination of critical influences. *Journal of Divorce & Remarriage, 28,* 97–106.

Donovan, W. L., Leavitt, L. A., & Walsh, R. O. (1998). Conflict and depression predict maternal sensitivity to infant cries. *Infant Behavior and Development, 21,* 505–517.

Dornbusch, S. M., Ritter, P. L., Leiderman, P. H., Roberts, D. F., & Fraleigh, M. J. (1987). The relation of parenting style to adolescent school performance. *Child Development, 58,* 1244–1257.

Dorris, M. (1989). *The broken cord.* New York: Harper & Row.

Dougherty, D. M. (1993). Adolescent health. *American Psychologist, 48*(2), 193–201.

Dougherty, T. M., & Haith, M. M. (1997). Infant expectations and reaction time as predictors of childhood speed of processing and IQ. *Developmental Psychology, 33,* 146–155.

Dozier, M., Stovall, K. C., Albus, K. E., & Bates, B. (2001). Attachment for infants in foster care: The role of caregiver state of mind. *Child Development, 72,* 1467–1477.

Dreher, M. C., Nugent, K., & Hudgins, R. (1994). Prenatal marijuana exposure and neonatal outcomes in Jamaica: An ethnographic study. *Pediatrics, 93,* 254–260.

Dreyfus, H. L. (1993–1994, Winter). What computers still can't do. *Key Reporter,* pp. 4–9.

Drummond, S. P. A., Brown, G. G., Gillin, J. C., Stricker, J. L., Wong, E. C., & Buxton, R. B. (2000). Altered brain response to verbal learning following sleep deprivation. *Nature, 403,* 655–657.

Drummond, S. P., Gillin, J. C., & Brown, G. G. (2001). Increased cerebral response during a divided attention task following sleep deprivation. *Journal of Sleep Research, 10,* 85–92.

Dubé, E. M., & Savin-Williams, R. C. (1999). Sexual identity development among ethnic sexual-minority youths. *Developmental Psychology, 35*(6), 1389–1398.

Dubowitz, H. (1999). The families of neglected children. In M. E. Lamb (Ed.), *Parenting and child development in "nontraditional" families* (pp. 327–345). Mahwah, NJ: Erlbaum.

Duffy, P. H., Seng, J. E., Lewis, S. M., Mayhugh, M. A., Aidoo, A., Hattan, D. G., Casciano, D. A., & Feuers, R. J. (2001). The effects of different levels of dietary restriction on aging and survival in the Sprague-Dawley rat: Implications for chronic studies. *Aging, 13,* 263–272.

Duncan, G. J., & Brooks-Gunn, J. (1997). Income effects across the life span: Integration and interpretation. In G. J. Duncan & J. Brooks-Gunn (Eds.), *Consequences of growing up poor* (pp. 596–610). New York: Russell Sage Foundation.

Duncan, H. H., Travis, S. S., & McAuley, W. J. (1995). An emergent theoretical model for interventions encouraging physical activity (mall walking) among older adults. *The Journal of Applied Gerontology, 14,* 64–77.

Dundy, E. (1985). *Elvis and Gladys.* New York: Dell.

Dunham, P. J., Dunham, F., & Curwin, A. (1993). Joint-attentional states and lexical acquisition at 18 months. *Developmental Psychology, 29,* 827–831.

Dunlosky, J., & Hertzog, C. (1998). Aging and deficits in associative memory: What is the role of strategy production? *Psychology and Aging, 13,* 597–607.

Dunn, A. L., Marcus, B. H., Kampert, J. B., Garcia, M. E., Kohl, H. W., III, & Blair, S. N. (1999). Comparison of lifestyle and structured interventions to increase physical activity and cardiorespiratory fitness: A randomized trial. *Journal of the American Medical Association, 281,* 327–334.

Dunn, J. (1996). Sibling relationships and perceived self-competence: Patterns of stability between childhood and early adolescence. In A. J. Sameroff & M. M. Haith (Eds.), *The five to seven year shift: The age of reason and responsibility* (pp. 253–269). Chicago: University of Chicago Press.

Dunn, J., & Hughes, C. (2001). "I got some swords and you're dead!": Violent fantasy, antisocial behavior, friendship, and moral sensibility in young children. *Child Development, 72,* 491–505.

Dunn, J., & Munn, P. (1985). Becoming a family member: Family conflict and the development of social understanding in the second year. *Child Development, 56,* 480–492.

Dunson, D. (2002). Late breaking research session. Increasing infertility with increasing age: good news and bad news for older couples. Paper presented at 18th Annual Meeting of the European Society of Human Reproduction and Embryology, Vienna.

Dunson, D. B., Colombo, B., & Baird, D. D. (2002). Changes with age in the level and duration of fertility in the menstrual cycle. *Human Reproduction, 17,* 1399–1403.

DuPont, R. L. (1983). Phobias in children. *Journal of Pediatrics, 102,* 999–1002.

Durand, A. M. (1992). The safety of home birth: The Farm study. *American Journal of Public Health, 82,* 450–452.

DuRant, R. H., Rich, M., Emans, S. J., Rome, E. S., Allred, E., & Woods, E. R. (1997). Violence and weapon carrying in music videos: A content analysis. *Archives of Pediatric and Adolescent Medicine, 151,* 443–448.

Durkin, K., & Bradley, N. (1998). Kindergarten children's gender-role expectations for television actors. *Sex Roles, 38,* 387–402.

Durlak, J. A. (1973). Relationship between attitudes toward life and death among elderly women. *Developmental Psychology, 8*(1), 146.

Dustman, R. E., Emmerson, R. Y., Steinhaus, L. A., Shearer, D. E., & Dustman, T. J. (1992). The effects of videogame playing on neuropsychological performance of elderly individuals. *Journal of Gerontology: Psychological Sciences, 47*(3), P168–171.

Dwyer, T., Ponsonby, A. L., Blizzard, L., Newman, N. M., & Cochrane, J. A. (1995). The contribution of changes in the prevalence of prone sleeping position to the decline in sudden infant death syndrome in Tasmania. *Journal of the American Medical Association, 273,* 783–789.

Dychtwald, K., & Flower, J. (1990). *Age wave: How the most important trend of our time will change your future.* New York: Bantam.

Dykstra, P. A. (1995). Loneliness among the never and formerly married: The importance of supportive friendships and a desire for independence. *Journal of Gerontology: Social Sciences, 50B,* S321–329.

Early detection of Alzheimer's disease. (2002, August). *Harvard Mental Health Letter,* pp. 3–5.

Eastell, R. (1998). Treatment of postmenopausal osteoporosis. *New England Journal of Medicine, 338,* 736–746.

Eastman, F. (1965). John H. Glenn. In *The world book encyclopedia* (Vol. 8, pp. 214–214d). Chicago: Field Enterprises Educational Corporation.

Eating disorders—Part I. (1997, October). *The Harvard Mental Health Letter,* pp. 1–5.

Eating disorders—Part II. (1997, November). *The Harvard Mental Health Letter,* pp. 1–5.

Eaton, W. O., & Enns, L. R. (1986). Sex differences in human motor activity level. *Psychological Bulletin, 100,* 19–28.

Echeland, Y., Epstein, D. J., St-Jacques, B., Shen, L., Mohler, J., McMahon, J. A., & McMahon, A. P. (1993). Sonic hedgehog, a member of a family of putative signality molecules, is implicated in the regulation of CNS polarity. *Cell, 75,* 1417–1430.

Eckenrode, J., Laird, M., & Doris, J. (1993). School performance and disciplinary problems among abused and neglected children. *Developmental Psychology, 29,* 53–62.

Eckerman, C. O., & Stein, M. R. (1982). The toddler's emerging interactive skills. In K. H. Rubin & H. S. Ross (Eds.), *Peer relationships and social skills in childhood.* New York: Springer-Verlag.

Eckerman, C. O., Davis, C. C., & Didow, S. M. (1989). Toddlers' emerging ways of achieving social coordination with a peer. *Child Development, 60,* 440–453.

Edson, L. (1968, August 18). To hell with being discovered when you're dead. *The New York Times Magazine,* pp. 26–27, 29–31, 34–36, 41, 44–46.

Edwards, C. P. (1981). The comparative study of the development of moral judgment and reasoning. In R. Monroe, R. Monroe, & B. B. Whiting (Eds.), *Handbook of cross-cultural human development.* New York: Garland.

Edwards, K. I. (1993). Obesity, anorexia, and bulimia. *Clinical Nutrition, 77,* 899–909.

Effective solutions for impotence. (1994, October). *Johns Hopkins Medical Letter: Health after 50,* pp. 2–3.

Egan, S. K., & Perry, D. G. (2001). Gender identity: A multi-dimensional analysis with implications for psychosocial adjustment. *Developmental Psychology, 37,* 451–463.

Egbuono, L., & Starfield, B. (1982). Child health and social status. *Pediatrics, 69,* 550–557.

Egeland, B., & Sroufe, L. A. (1981). Attachment and early maltreatment. *Child Development, 52,* 44–52.

Egeland, B., Jacobvitz, D., & Sroufe, L. A. (1988). Breaking the cycle of abuse. *Child Development, 59,* 1080–1088.

Egeland, B., Sroufe, L. A., & Erickson, M. (1993). The developmental consequences of different patterns of maltreatment. *Child Abuse & Neglect, 7,* 459–469.

Eggebeen, D. J., & Knoester, C. (2001). Does fatherhood matter for men? *Journal of Marriage and Family, 63,* 381–393.

Eiberg, H. (1995). Nocturnal enuresis is linked to a specific gene. *Scandinavian Journal of Urology and Nephrology, 173* (Supplement), 15–17.

Eiberg, H., Berendt, I., & Mohr, J. (1995). Assignment of dominant inherited nocturnal enuresis (ENUR1) to chromosome 13q. *Nature Genetics, 10,* 354–356.

Eiger, M. S., & Olds, S. W. (1999). *The complete book of breastfeeding* (3rd ed.). New York: Workman.

Eimas, P. (1985). The perception of speech in early infancy. *Scientific American, 252*(1), 46–52.

Eimas, P., Siqueland, E., Jusczyk, P., & Vigorito, J. (1971). Speech perception in infants. *Science, 171,* 303–306.

Eisen, M., & Zellman, G. L. (1987). Changes in incidence of sexual intercourse of unmarried teenagers following a community-based sex education program. *Journal of Sex Research, 23*(4), 527–544.

Eisenberg, A. (April 5, 2001). A "smart" home, to avoid the nursing home. *The New York Times,* pp. G1, G6.

Eisenberg, A. R. (1996). The conflict talk of mothers and children: Patterns related to culture, SES, and gender of child. *Merrill-Palmer Quarterly, 42,* 438–452.

Eisenberg, L. (1995, Spring). Is the family obsolete? *Key Reporter,* pp. 1–5.

Eisenberg, N. (1992). *The caring child.* Cambridge, MA: Harvard University Press.

Eisenberg, N. (2000). Emotion, regulation, and moral development. *Annual Review of Psychology, 51,* 665–697.

Eisenberg, N., & Fabes, R. A. (1998). Prosocial development. In W. Damon (Series Ed.) & N. Eisenberg (Vol. Ed.), *Handbook of child psychology: Vol. 3. Social, emotional, and personality development* (5th ed., pp. 701–778). New York: Wiley.

Eisenberg, A., Murkoff, H. E., & Hathaway, S. E. (1989). *What to expect in the first year.* New York: Workman.

Eisenberg, N., Fabes, R. A., & Murphy, B. C. (1996). Parents' reactions to children's negative emotions: Relations to children's social competence and comforting behavior. *Child Development, 67,* 2227–2247.

Eisenberg, N., Fabes, R. A., Guthrie, I. K., & Reiser, M. (2000). Dispositional emotionality and regulation: Their role in predicting quality of social functioning. *Journal of Personality and Social Psychology, 78,* 136–157.

Eisenberg, N., Fabes, R. A., Nyman, M., Bernzweig, J., & Pinuelas, A. (1994). The relations of emotionality and regulation to children's anger-related reactions. *Child Development, 65,* 109–128.

Eisenberg, N., Fabes, R. A., Schaller, M., & Miller, P. A. (1989). Sympathy and personal distress: Development, gender differences, and interrelations of indexes. In N. Eisenberg (Ed.), *Empathy and related emotional responses* (New Directions for Child Development No. 44). San Francisco: Jossey-Bass.

Eisenberg, N., Fabes, R. A., Shepard, S. A., Guthrie, I. K., Murphy, B. C., & Reiser, M. (1999). Parental reactions to children's negative emotions: Longitudinal relations to quality of children's social functioning. *Child Development, 70*(2), 513–534.

Eisenberg, N., Guthrie, I. K., Fabes, R. A., Reiser, M., Murphy, B. C., Holgren, R., Maszk, P., & Losoya, S. (1997). The relations of regulation and emotionality to resiliency and competent social functioning in elementary school children. *Child Development, 68,* 295–311.

Eisenberg, N., Guthrie, I. K., Murphy, B. C., Shepard, S. A., Cumberland, A., & Carlo, G. (1999). Consistency and development of prosocial dispositions: A longitudinal study. *Child Development, 70*(6), 1360–1372.

Elbert, S. E. (1984). *A hunger for home: Louisa May Alcott and "Little Women."* Philadelphia: Temple University Press.

Elder, G. H., Jr. (1974). *Children of the Great Depression: Social change in life experience.* Chicago: University of Chicago Press.

Elder, G. H., Jr. (1998). The life course and human development. In W. Damon (Series Ed.). & R. M. Lerner (Vol. Ed.), *Handbook of child psychology: Vol. 1. Theoretical models of human development* (5th ed., pp. 939–992). New York: Wiley.

Elder, G. H., Jr., & Caspi, A. (1990). Studying lives in a changing society: Sociological and personological explorations. In A. I. Rabin, R. A. Zucker, R. Emmons, & S. Franks (Eds.), *Studying persons and lives.* New York: Springer.

Elderhostel: Adventures in lifelong learning. (2002). [Online]. Available: http://www.elderhostel.org/. Access date: July 13, 2002.

Elia, J., Ambrosini, P. J., & Rapoport, J. L. (1999). Treatment of attention-deficit-hyperactivity disorder. *New England Journal of Medicine, 340,* 780–788.

Elicker, J., Englund, M., & Sroufe, L. A. (1992). Predicting peer competence and peer relationships in childhood from early parent-child relationships. In R. Parke & G. Ladd (Eds.), *Family-peer relationships: Modes of linkage* (pp. 77–106). Hillsdale, NJ: Erlbaum.

Elkind, D. (1981). *The hurried child.* Reading, MA: Addison-Wesley.

Elkind, D. (1984). *All grown up and no place to go.* Reading, MA: Addison-Wesley.

Elkind, D. (1986). *The miseducation of children: Superkids at risk.* New York: Knopf.

Elkind, D. (1997). *Reinventing childhood: Raising and educating children in a changing world.* Rosemont, NJ: Modern Learning Press.

Elkind, D. (1998). *All grown up and no place to go.* Reading, MA: Perseus Books.

Elliott, D. S. (1993). Health enhancing and health compromising lifestyles. In S. G. Millstein, A. C. Petersen, & E. O. Nightingale (Eds.), *Promoting the health of adolescents: New directions for the twenty-first century.* New York: Oxford University Press.

Ellis, B. J., & Garber, J. (2000). Psychosocial antecedents of variation in girls' pubertal timing: Maternal depression, stepfather presence, and marital family stress. *Child Development, 71*(2), 485–501.

Ellis, B. J., McFadyen-Ketchum, S., Dodge, K. A., Pettit, G. S., & Bates, J. E. (1999). Quality of early family relationships and individual differences in the timing of pubertal maturation in girls: A longitudinal test of an evolutionary model. *Journal of Personality and Social Psychology, 77,* 387–401.

Ellis, K. J., Abrams, S. A., & Wong, W. W. (1997). Body composition of a young, multiethnic female population. *American Journal of Clinical Nutrition, 65,* 724–731.

Ellis, L., & Ames, M. A. (1987). Neuro-hormonal functioning and sexual orientation: A theory of homosexuality-heterosexuality. *Psychological Bulletin, 101*(2), 233–258.

Ellison, C. G., & Levin, J. S. (1998). The religion-health connection: Evidence, theory, and future directions. *Health Education & Behavior, 25,* 700–720.

Emde, R. N. (1992). Individual meaning and increasing complexity: Contributions of Sigmund Freud and René Spitz to developmental psychology. *Developmental Psychology, 28,* 347–359.

Emde, R. N., Plomin, R., Robinson, J., Corley, R., DeFries, J., Fulker, D. W., Reznick, J. S., Campos, J., Kagan, J., & Zahn-Waxler, C. (1992). Temperament, emotion, and cognition at 14 months: The MacArthur longitudinal twin study. *Child Development, 63,* 1437–1455.

Emery, R. E. (1988). *Marriage, divorce, and children's adjustment.* Newbury Park, CA: Sage.

Eng, P. M., Rimm, E. B., Fitzmaurice, G., & Kawachi, I. (2002). Social ties and change in social ties in relation to subsequent total and cause-specific mortality and coronary heart disease incidence in men. *American Journal of Epidemiology, 155,* 700–709.

Engels, H., Drouin, J., Zhu, W., & Kazmierski, J. F. (1998). Effects of low-impact, moderate-intensity exercise training with and without wrist weights on functional capacities and mood states in older adults. *Gerontology, 44,* 239–244.

Engle, P. L., & Breaux, C. (1998). Fathers' involvement with children: Perspectives from developing countries. *Social Policy Report, 12*(1), 1–21.

Enloe, C. F. (1980). How alcohol affects the developing fetus. *Nutrition Today, 15*(5), 12–15.

Entwisle, D. R., & Alexander, K. L. (1998). Facilitating the transition to first grade: The nature of transition and research on factors affecting it. *The Elementary School Journal, 98,* 351–364.

Eppler, M. A., Adolph, K. E., & Weiner, T. (1996). The developmental relationship between infants' exploration and action on sloping surfaces. *Infant Behavior and Development, 19,* 259–264.

Epstein, E., & Gutmann, R. (1984). Mate selection in man: Evidence, theory, and outcome. *Social Biology, 31,* 243–278.

Epstein, R. A. (1989, Spring). Voluntary euthanasia. *Law School Record* (University of Chicago), pp. 8–13.

Erdley, C. A., Cain, K. M., Loomis, C. C., Dumas-Hines, F., & Dweck, C. S. (1997). Relations among children's social goals, implicit personality theories, and responses to social failure. *Developmental Psychology, 33,* 263–272.

Erikson, E. (1969). *Gandhi's Truth: On the origins of militant nonviolence.* New York: Norton.

Erikson, E. H. (1950). *Childhood and society.* New York: Norton.

Erikson, E. H. (1968). *Identity: Youth and crisis.* New York: Norton.

Erikson, E. H. (1982). *The life cycle completed.* New York: Norton.

Erikson, E. H. (1985). *The life cycle completed* (paperback reprint ed.). New York: Norton.

Erikson, E. H., Erikson, J. M., & Kivnick, H. Q. (1986). *Vital involvement in old age: The experience of old age in our time.* New York: Norton.

Eriksson, P. S., Perfilieva, E., Björk-Eriksson, T., Alborn, A., Nordborg, C., Peterson, D. A., & Gage, F. H. (1998). Neurogenesis in the adult human hippocampus. *Nature Medicine, 4,* 1313–1317.

Eron, L. D. (1980). Prescription for reduction of aggression. *American Psychologist, 35,* 244–252.

Eron, L. D. (1982). Parent-child interaction, television violence, and aggression in children. *American Psychologist, 37,* 197–211.

Eron, L. D., & Huesmann, L. R. (1986). The role of television in the development of prosocial and antisocial behavior. In D. Olweus, J. Block, & M. Radke-Yarrow (Eds.), *The development of antisocial and prosocial behavior: Research, theories, and issues.* New York: Academic.

Ertem, I. O., Votto, N., & Leventhal, J. M. (2001). The timing and predictors of the early termination of breastfeeding. *Pediatrics, 107*(3), 543–548.

Essex, M. J., & Nam, S. (1987). Marital status and loneliness among older women: The differential importance of close family and friends. *Journal of Marriage and the Family, 49,* 93–106.

Ettinger, B., Friedman, G. D., Bush, T., & Quesenberry, C. P. (1996). Reduced mortality associated with long-term postmenopausal estrogen therapy. *Obstetrics & Gynecology, 87,* 6–12.

Evans, G. (1976). The older the sperm . . . *Ms., 4*(7), 48–49.

Evans, G. W., & English, K. (2002). The environment of poverty: Multiple stressor exposure, psychophysiological stress, and socioemotional adjustment. *Child Development, 73,* 1238–1248.

Evans, J. (1994). *Caring for the caregiver: Body, mind and spirit.* New York: American Parkinson Disease Association.

Evans, J. (1998, November). "Princesses are not into war 'n things, they always scream and run off": Exploring gender stereotypes in picture books. *Reading,* pp. 5–11.

Eyre-Walker, A., & Keightley, P. D. (1999). High genomic deleterious rates in hominids. *Nature, 397,* 344–347.

Fabes, R. A., & Eisenberg, N. (1992). Young children's coping with interpersonal anger. *Child Development, 63,* 116–128.

Fabes, R. A., & Eisenberg, N. (1996). *An examination of age and sex differences in prosocial behavior and empathy.* Unpublished data, Arizona State University.

Fabes, R. A., Eisenberg, N., Smith, M. C., & Murphy, B. C. (1996). Getting angry at peers: Associations with liking of the provocateur. *Child Development, 67,* 942–956.

Fabes, R. A., Leonard, S. A., Kupanoff, K., & Martin, C. L. (2001). Parental coping with children's negative emotions: Relations with children's emotional and social responding. *Child Development, 72,* 907–920.

Fagot, B. I. (1997). Attachment, parenting, and peer interactions of toddler children. *Developmental Psychology, 33,* 489–499.

Fagot, B. I., & Gauvain, M. (1997). Mother-child problem solving: Continuity through the early childhood years. *Developmental Psychology, 33,* 480–488.

Fagot, B. I., & Leinbach, M. D. (1995). Gender knowledge in egalitarian and traditional families. *Sex Roles, 32,* 513–526.

Fagot, B. I., & Leve, L. (1998). Gender identity and play. In D. P. Fromberg & D. Bergen (Eds.), *Play from birth to twelve and beyond: Contexts, perspectives, and meanings* (pp. 187–192). New York: Garland.

Faison, S. (1997, August 17). Chinese happily break the "one child" rule. *The New York Times,* pp. 1, 10.

Faith, M. S., Berman, N., Heo, M., Pietrobelli, A., Gallagher, D., Epstein, L. H., Eiden, M. T., & Allison, D. B. (2001). Effects of contingent television on physical activity and television viewing in obese children. *Pediatrics, 107,* 1043–1048.

Falbo, T., & Polit, D. F. (1986). Quantitative review of the only child literature: Research evidence and theory development. *Psychological Bulletin, 100*(2), 176–189.

Falbo, T., & Poston, D. L. (1993). The academic, personality, and physical outcomes of only children in China. *Child Development, 64,* 18–35.

Falkner, D. (1995). *Great time coming: The life of Jackie Robinson, from baseball to Birmingham.* New York: Simon & Schuster.

Fantz, R. L. (1963). Pattern vision in newborn infants. *Science, 140,* 296–297.

Fantz, R. L. (1964). Visual experience in infants: Decreased attention to familiar patterns relative to novel ones. *Science, 146,* 668–670.

Fantz, R. L. (1965). Visual perception from birth as shown by pattern selectivity. In H. E. Whipple (Ed.), *New issues in infant development. Annals of the New York Academy of Science, 118,* 793–814.

Fantz, R. L., & Nevis, S. (1967). Pattern preferences and perceptual-cognitive development in early infancy. *Merrill-Palmer Quarterly, 13,* 77–108.

Fantz, R. L., Fagen, J., & Miranda, S. B. (1975). Early visual selectivity. In L. Cohen & P. Salapatek (Eds.), *Infant perception: From sensation to cognition: Vol. 1. Basic visual processes* (pp. 249–341). New York: Academic Press.

Farquhar, C. M., & Steiner, C. A. (2002). Hysterectomy rates in the United States 1990–1997. *Obstetrics & Gynecology, 99,* 229–234.

Farrer, L. A., Cupples, L. A., Haines, J. L., Hyman, B., Kukull, W. A., Mayeux, R., Myers, R. H., Pericak-Vance, M. A., Risch, N., & van Duijn, C. M. (1997). Effects of age, sex, and ethnicity on the association between apolipoprotein E genotype and Alzheimer disease. *Journal of the American Medical Association, 278,* 1349–1356.

Farver, J. A. M., Kim, Y. K., & Lee, Y. (1995). Cultural differences in Korean- and Anglo-American preschoolers' social interaction and play behavior. *Child Development, 66,* 1088–1099.

Fawcett, G. M., Heise, L. L., Isita-Espejel, L., & Pick, S. (1999). Change community responses to wife abuse: A research and demonstration project in Iztacalco, Mexico. *American Psychologist, 54,* 41–49.

Feagans, L. (1983). A current view of learning disabilities. *Journal of Pediatrics, 102*(4), 487–493.

Federal Glass Ceiling Commission. (1995). *Good for business: Making full use of the nation's human capital: The environmental scam.* Washington, DC: U.S. Department of Labor.

Feingold, A., & Mazzella, R. (1998). Gender differences in body image are increasing. *Psychological Science, 9*(3), 190–195.

Feinleib, J. A., & Michael, R. T. (2000). Reported changes in sexual behavior in response to AIDS in the United States. In Laumann, E. O., & Michael, R. T. (Eds.), *Sex, love, and health in America: Private choices and public policies* (pp. 302–326). Chicago: University of Chicago Press.

Feldhusen, J. F. (1992). *Talent identification and development in education (TIDE).* Sarasota, FL: Center for Creative Learning.

Feldhusen, J. F., & Moon, S. M. (1992). Grouping gifted students: Issues and concerns. *Gifted Child Quarterly, 36*(2), 63–67.

Feldman, H. A., Goldstein, I., Hatzichristou, D. G., Krane, R. J., & McKinlay, J. B. (1994). Impotence and its medical and psychosocial correlates: Results of the Massachusetts Male Aging Study. *Journal of Urology, 151,* 54–61.

Feldman, R. D. (1985, October). The pyramid project: Do we have the answer for the gifted? *Instructor,* pp. 62–71.

Feldman, R. D. (1986, April). What are thinking skills? *Instructor,* pp. 62–71.

Feldman, R., Greenbaum, C. W., & Yirmiya, N. (1999). Mother-infant affect synchrony as an antecedent of the emergence of self-control. *Developmental Psychology, 35*(5), 223–231.

Felner, R. D., Brand, S., DuBois, D. L., Adan, A. M., Mulhall, P. F., & Evans, E. G. (1995). Socioeconomic disadvantage, proximal environmental experiences, and socioemotional and academic adjustment in early adolescence: Investigation of a mediated effect. *Child Development, 66,* 774–792.

Fernald, A., & O'Neill, D. K. (1993). Peekaboo across cultures: How mothers and infants play with voices, faces, and expectations. In K. MacDonald (Ed.), *Parent-child play* (pp. 259–285). Albany: State University of New York Press.

Fernald, A., Pinto, J. P., Swingley, D., Weinberg, A., & McRoberts, G. W. (1998). Rapid gains in speed of verbal processing by infants in the 2nd year. *Psychological Science, 9*(3), 228–231.

Fernald, A., Swingley, D., and Pinto, J. P. (2001). When half a word is enough: Infants can recognize spoken words using partial phonetic information. *Child Development, 72*(4), 1003–1015.

Feskanich, D., Ziegler, R. G., Michaud, D. S., Giovannucci, E. L., Speizer, F. E., Willett, W. C., & Colditz, G. A. (2000). Prospective study of fruit and vegetable consumption and risk of lung cancer among men and women. *Journal of the National Institute of Cancer, 92,* 1812–1823.

Fiatarone, M. A., Marks, E. C., Ryan, N. D., Meredith, C. N., Lipsitz, L. A., & Evans, W. J. (1990). High-intensity strength training in nonagenarians: Effects on skeletal muscles. *Journal of the American Medical Association, 263,* 3029–3034.

Fiatarone, M. A., O'Neill, E. F., Ryan, N. D., Clements, K. M., Solares, G. R., Nelson, M. E., Roberts, S. B., Kehayias, J. J., Lipsitz, L. A., & Evans, W. J. (1994). Exercise training and nutritional supplementation for physical frailty in very elderly people. *New England Journal of Medicine, 330,* 1769–1775.

Fiatarone, M. A., O'Neill, E. F., & Ryan, N. D. (1994). Exercise training and nutritional supplementation for physical frailty in very elderly people. *New England Journal of Medicine, 330,* 1769–1775.

Field, A. E., Camargo, C. A., Taylor, B., Berkey, C. S., Roberts, S. B., & Colditz, G. A. (2001). Peer, parent, and media influence on the development of weight concerns and frequent dieting among preadolescent and adolescent girls and boys. *Pediatrics, 107*(1), 54–60.

Field, D., & Millsap, R. E. (1991). Personality in advanced old age: Continuity or change? *Journal of Gerontology: Psychological Sciences, 46,* P299–308.

Field, D., Minkler, M., Falk, R. F., & Leino, E. V. (1993). The influence of health on family contacts and family functioning in advanced old age: A longitudinal study. *Journal of Gerontology: Psychological Sciences, 48*(1), P18–28.

Field, T. (1995). Infants of depressed mothers. *Infant Behavior and Development, 18,* 1–13.

Field, T. (1998a). Emotional care of the at-risk infant: Early interventions for infants of depressed mothers. *Pediatrics, 102,* 1305–1310.

Field, T. (1998b). Massage therapy effects. *American Psychologist, 53,* 1270–1281.

Field, T. (1998c). Maternal depression effects on infants and early intervention. *Preventive Medicine, 27,* 200–203.

Field, T., Fox, N. A., Pickens, J., Nawrocki, T., & Soutollo, D. (1995). Right frontal EEG activation in 3- to 6-month-old infants of depressed mothers. *Developmental Psychology, 31,* 358–363.

Field, T., Grizzle, N., Scafidi, F., Abrams, S., Richardson, S., Kuhn, C., & Schanberg, S. (1996). Massage therapy for infants of depressed mothers. *Infant Behavior and Development, 19,* 107–112.

Field, T. M. (1978). Interaction behaviors of primary versus secondary caretaker fathers. *Developmental Psychology, 14,* 183–184.

Field, T. M. (1986). Interventions for premature infants. *Journal of Pediatrics, 109*(1), 183–190.

Field, T. M. (1987). Interaction and attachment in normal and atypical infants. *Journal of Consulting and Clinical Psychology, 55*(6), 853–859.

Field, T. M., & Roopnarine, J. L. (1982). Infant-peer interaction. In T. M. Field, A. Huston, H. C. Quay, L. Troll, & G. Finley (Eds.), *Review of human development.* New York: Wiley.

Field, T. M., Sandberg, D., Garcia, R., Vega-Lahr, N., Goldstein, S., & Guy, L. (1985). Pregnancy problems, postpartum depression, and early infant-mother interactions. *Developmental Psychology, 21,* 1152–1156.

Fielden, M. R., Halgren, R. G., Fong, C. J., Staub, C., Johnson, L., Chou, K., & Zacharewski, T. R. (2002). Gestational and lactational exposure of male mice to diethylstilbestrol causes long-term effects on the testis, sperm fertilizing ability in vitro, and testicular gene expression. *Endocrinology, 143,* 3044–3059.

Fields, J., & Casper, L. (2001). *America's families and living arrangements: March 2000.* (Current Population Reports, P20–537). Washington, DC: U.S. Census Bureau.

Fields, J. M., & Smith, K. E. (1998, April). *Poverty, family structure, and child well-being: Indicators from the SIPP* (Population Division Working Paper No. 23, U.S. Bureau of the Census). Paper presented at the Annual Meeting of the Population Association of America, Chicago, IL.

Fifer, W. P., & Moon, C. M. (1995). The effects of fetal experience with sound. In J. P. Lecanuet, W. P. Fifer, N. A. Krasnegor, & W. P. Smotherman (Eds.), *Fetal development: A psychobiological perspective* (pp. 351–366). Hillsdale, NJ: Erlbaum.

Finch, C. E. (2001). Toward a biology of middle age. In M. E. Lachman (Ed.), *Handbook of midlife development* (pp. 77–108). New York: Wiley.

Finch, C. E., & Tanzi, R. E. (1997). Genetics of aging. *Science, 278,* 407–411.

Finch, M. D., Shanahan, M. J., Mortimer, J. T., & Ryu, S. (1991). Work experience and control orientation in adolescence. *American Sociological Review, 56,* 597–611.

Fine, M. A., & Kurdek, L. A. (1995). Relation between marital quality and (step) parent-child relationship quality for parents and stepparents in stepfamilies. *Journal of Family Psychology, 9,* 216–223.

Finn, J. D., & Rock, D. A. (1997). Academic success among students at risk for dropout. *Journal of Applied Psychology, 82,* 221–234.

Finn, R. (1993, February 8). Arthur Ashe, tennis champion, dies of AIDS. *The New York Times,* pp. B1, B43.

First woman to both poles—Ann Bancroft. (1997). [Online]. Available: http://www.zplace.com/rhonda/abancroft/. Access date: April 4, 2002.

Fiscella, K., Kitzman, H. J., Cole, R. E., Sidora, K. J., & Olds, D. (1998). Does child abuse predict adolescent pregnancy? *Pediatrics, 101,* 620–624.

Fischer, K. (1980). A theory of cognitive development: The control and construction of hierarchies of skills. *Psychological Review, 87,* 477–531.

Fischer, K. W., & Rose, S. P. (1994). Dynamic development of cordination of components in brain and behavior: A framework for theory and research. In G. Dawson & K. W. Fischer (Eds.), *Human behavior and the developing brain* (pp. 3–66). New York: Guilford.

Fischer, K. W., & Rose, S. P. (1995, Fall). Concurrent cycles in the dynamic development of brain and behavior. *SRCD Newsletter,* pp. 3–4, 15–16.

Fisher, R. L., & Fisher, S. (1996). Antidepressants for children: Is scientific support necessary? *Journal of Nervous Mental Disorders (United States), 184,* 99–102.

Fisk, A. D., & Rogers, W. A. (2002). Psychology and aging: Enhancing the lives of an aging population. *Current Directions in Psychological Science, 11,* 107–110.

Fivush, R., & Schwarzmeuller, A. (1998). Children remember childhood: Implications for childhood amnesia. *Applied Cognitive Psychology, 12,* 455–473.

Fivush, R., Hudson, J., & Nelson, K. (1983). Children's long-term memory for a novel event: An exploratory study. *Merrill-Palmer Quarterly, 30,* 303–316.

Flake, A. W., Roncarolo, M. G., Puck, J. M., Almeida-Porada, G., Evans, M. I., Johnson, M. P., Abella, E. M., Harrison, D. D., & Zanjani, E. D. (1996). Treatment of X-linked severe combined immunodeficiency by in utero transplantation of paternal bone marrow. *New England Journal of Medicine, 335,* 1806–1810.

Flavell, J. (1963). *The developmental psychology of Jean Piaget.* New York: Van Nostrand.

Flavell, J. H. (1970). Developmental studies of mediated memory. In H. W. Reese & L. P. Lipsitt (Eds.), *Advances in child development and behavior* (Vol. 5, pp. 181–211). New York: Academic.

Flavell, J. H. (1992). Cognitive development: Past, present, and future. *Developmental Psychology, 28,* 998–1005.

Flavell, J. H. (1993). Young children's understanding of thinking and consciousness. *Current Directions in Psychological Science, 2,* 40–43.

Flavell, J. H., Beach, D., & Chinsky, J. (1966). Spontaneous verbal rehearsal in a memory task as a function of age. *Child Development, 37,* 283–299.

Flavell, J. H., Flavell, E. R., Green, F. L., & Korfmacher, J. E. (1990). Do young children think of television images as pictures, or as real objects? *Journal of Broadcasting and Electronic Media, 34,* 399–419.

Flavell, J. H., Green, F. L., & Flavell, E. R. (1986). Development of knowledge about the appearance-reality dinstinction. *Monographs of the Society for Research in Child Development, 51* (1, Serial No. 212).

Flavell, J. H., Green, F. L., & Flavell, E. R. (1995). Young children's knowledge about thinking. *Monographs of the Society for Research in Child Development, 60*(1, Serial No. 243).

Flavell, J. H., Green, F. L., Flavell, E. R., & Grossman, J. B. (1997). The development of children's knowledge about inner speech. *Child Development, 68,* 39–47.

Flavell, J. H., Green, F. L., Flavell, E. R., & Lin, N. T. (1999). Development of children's knowledge about unconsciousness. *Child Development, 70,* 396–412.

Flavell, J. H., Miller, P. H., & Miller, S. A. (1993). *Cognitive development.* Englewood Cliffs, NJ: Prentice-Hall.

Flavell, J. H., Miller, P. H., & Miller, S. A. (2002). *Cognitive development.* Englewood Cliffs, NJ: Prentice-Hall.

Flegal, K. M., Carroll, M. D., Ogden, C. L., & Johnson, C. L. (2002). Prevalence and trends in obesity among US adults, 1999–2000. *Journal of the American Medical Association, 288,* 1723–1727.

Flieller, A. (1999). Comparison of the development of formal thought in adolescent cohorts aged 10 to 15 years (1967–1996 and 1972–1993). *Developmental Psychology, 35,* 1048–1058.

Flint, M., & Samil, R. S. (1990). Cultural and subcultural meanings of the menopause. In M. Flint, F. Kronenberg, & W. Utian (Eds.), *Multidisciplinary perspectives on menopause* (pp. 134–148). New York: Annals of the New York Academy of Sciences.

Flores, G., Fuentes-Afflick, E., Barbot, O., Carter-Pokras, O., Claudio, L., Lara, M., McLaurin, J. A., Pachter, L., Gomez, F. R., Mendoza, F., Valdez, R. B., Villarruel, A. M., Zambrana, R. E., Greenberg, R., & Weitzman, M. (2002). The health of Latino children: Urgent priorities, unanswered questions, and a research agenda. *Journal of the American Medical Association, 288,* 82–90.

Fluoxetine-Bulimia Collaborative Study Group. (1992). Fluoxetine in the treatment of bulimia nervosa: A multicenter placebo-controlled, double-blind trial. *Archives of General Psychiatry, 49,* 139–147.

Foldvari, M., Clark, M., Laviolette, L. C., Bernstein, M. A., Kaliton, D., Castaneda, C., Pu, C. T., Hausdorff, J. M., Fielding, R. A., & Singh, M. A. (2000). Association of muscle power with functional status in community-dwelling elderly women. *Journal of Gerontology: Biological and Medical Sciences, 55,* M192–199.

Foley, D. J., & White, L. (2002). Dietary intake of antioxidants and risk of Alzheimer disease: Food for thought. *Journal of the American Medical Association, 287,* 3261–3263.

Folkman, S., & Lazarus, R. S. (1980). An analysis of coping in a middle-aged community sample. *Journal of Health and Social Behavior, 21,* 219–239.

Folkman, S., Lazarus, R. S., Pimley, S., & Novacek, J. (1987). Age differences in stress and coping processes. *Psychology and Aging, 2,* 171–184.

Fombonne, E. (2001). Is there an epidemic of autism? *Pediatrics, 107,* 411–412.

Fombonne, E. (2003). The prevalence of autism. *Journal of the American Medical Association, 289,* 87–89.

Ford, C. A., Bearman, P. S., & Moody, J. (1999). Foregone health care among adolescents. *Journal of the American Medical Association, 282*(23), 2227–2234.

Ford, D. Y., & Harris, J. J., III. (1996). Perceptions and attitudes of black students toward school, achievement, and other educational variables. *Child Development, 67,* 1141–1152.

Ford, P. (April 10, 2002). In Europe, marriage is back. *Christian Science Monitor,* p. 1.

Ford, R. P., Schluter, P. J., Mitchell, E. A., Taylor, B. J., Scragg, R., & Stewart, A. W. (1998). Heavy caffeine intake in pregnancy and sudden infant death syndrome (New Zealand Cot Death Study Group). *Archives of Disease in Childhood, 78*(1), 9–13.

Forgatch, M. S., & DeGarmo, D. S. (1999). Parenting through change: An effective prevention program for single mothers. *Journal of Consulting and Clinical Psychology, 67,* 711–724.

Forteza, J. A., & Prieto, J. M. (1994). Aging and work behavior. In H. C. Triandis, M. D. Dunnette, & L. M. Hough (Eds.), *Handbook of industrial and organizational psychology* (pp. 447–483). Palo Alto, CA: Consulting Psychologists Press.

Foster, D. (1999). Isabel Allende unveiled. In J. Rodden (Ed.), *Conversations with Isabel Allende* (pp. 105–113). Austin: University of Texas Press.

Fowler, J. (1981). *Stages of faith: The psychology of human development and the quest for meaning.* New York: Harper & Row.

Fowler, J. W. (1989). Strength for the journey: Early childhood development in selfhood and faith. In D. A. Blazer, J. W. Fowler, K. J. Swick, A. S. Honig, P. J. Boone, B. M. Caldwell, R. A. Boone, & L. W. Barber (Eds.), *Faith development in early childhood* (pp. 1–63). New York: Sheed & Ward.

Fowler, M. G., Simpson, G. A., & Schoendorf, K. C. (1993). Families on the move and children's health care. *Pediatrics, 91,* 934–940.

Fox, N. A., Henderson, H. A., Rubin, K. H., Calkins, S. D., & Schmidt, L. A. (2001). Continuity and discontinuity of behavioral inhibition and exuberance: Psychophysiological and behavioral influences across the first four years of life. *Child Development, 72,* 1–21.

Fox, N. A., Kimmerly, N. L., & Schafer, W. D. (1991). Attachment to mother/attachment to father: A meta-analysis. *Child Development, 62,* 210–225.

Foy, M. R., Henderson, V. W., Berger, T. W., & Thompson, R. F. (2000). Estrogen and neural plasticity. *Current Directions in Psychological Science, 9,* 148–152.

Fraga, C. G., Motchnik, P. A., Shigenaga, M. K., Helbock, H. J., Jacob, R. A., & Ames, B. N. (1991). Ascorbic acid protects against endogenous oxidative DNA damage in human sperm. *Proceedings of the National Academy of Sciences of the United States, 88,* 11003–11006.

Frank, A. (1958). *The diary of a young girl* (B. M. Mooyaart-Doubleday, Trans.). New York: Pocket.

Frank, A. (1995). *The diary of a young girl: The definitive edition* (O. H. Frank & M. Pressler, Eds.; S. Massotty, Trans.). New York: Doubleday.

Frank, D. A., Augustyn, M., Knight, W. G., Pell, T., & Zuckerman, B. (2001). Growth, development, and behavior in early childhood following prenatal cocaine exposure. *Journal of the American Medical Association, 285,* 1613–1625.

Frankenburg, W. K., Dodds, J., Archer, P., Bresnick, B., Maschka, P., Edelman, N., & Shapiro, H. (1992). *Denver II training manual.* Denver: Denver Developmental Materials.

Frankenburg, W. K., Dodds, J. B., Fandal, A. W., Kazuk, E., & Cohrs, M. (1975). *The Denver Developmental Screening Test: Reference manual.* Denver: University of Colorado Medical Center.

Franz, C. E. (1997). Stability and change in the transition to midlife: A longitudinal study of midlife adults. In M. E. Lachman & J. B. James (Eds.), *Multiple paths of midlife development* (pp. 45–66). Chicago: University of Chicago Press.

Fraser, A. M., Brockert, J. F., & Ward, R. H. (1995). Association of young maternal age with adverse reproductive outcomes. *New England Journal of Medicine, 332*(17), 1113–1117.

Frazier, J. A., & Morrison, F. J. (1998). The influence of extended-year schooling on growth of achievement and perceived competence in early elementary school. *Child Development, 69,* 495–517.

Freedman, D. S., Srinivasan, S. R., Valdez, R. A., Williamson, D. F., & Berenson, G. S. (1997). Secular increases in relative weight and adiposity among children over two decades:

The Bogalusa Heart Study. *Pediatrics, 88,* 420–426.

Freeman, D. (1983). *Margaret Mead and Samoa: The making and unmaking of an anthropological myth.* Cambridge, MA: Harvard University Press.

Freeman, E., Rickels, K., Sondheimer, S. J., & Polansky, M. (1990). Ineffectiveness of progesterone suppository treatment for premenstrual syndrome. *Journal of the American Medical Association, 264,* 349–353.

Freeman, E. W., Rickels, K., Sondheimer, S. J., & Polansky, M. (1995). A double-blind trial of oral progesterone, alprazolam, and placebo in treatment of severe premenstrual syndrome. *Journal of the American Medical Association, 274,* 51–57.

French, D. C., Jansen, E. A., & Pidada, S. (2002). United States and Indonesian children's and adolescents' reports of relational aggression by disliked peers. *Child Development, 73,* 1143–1150.

Freud, A. (1946). *The ego and the mechanisms of defense.* New York: International Universities Press.

Freud, S. (1942). On psychotherapy. In E. Jones (Ed.), *Collected papers.* London: Hogarth. (Original work published 1906)

Freud, S. (1953). *A general introduction to psychoanalysis* (J. Riviere, Trans.). New York: Perma-books. (Original work published 1935)

Freud, S. (1964a). New introductory lectures on psycho-analysis. In J. Strachey (Ed. & Trans.), *The standard edition of the complete psychological works of Sigmund Freud* (Vol. 22). London: Hogarth. (Original work published 1933)

Freud, S. (1964b). An outline of psycho-analysis. In J. Strachey (Ed. & Trans.), *The standard edition of the complete psychological works of Sigmund Freud* (Vol. 23). London: Hogarth. (Original work published 1940)

Fried, P. A., Watkinson, B., & Willan, A. (1984). Marijuana use during pregnancy and decreased length of gestation. *American Journal of Obstetrics and Gynecology, 150,* 23–27.

Friedan, B. (1993). *The fountain of age.* New York: Simon & Schuster.

Friedland, R. P. (1993). Epidemiology, education, and the ecology of Alzheimer's disease. *Neurology, 43,* 246–249.

Friedman, H. S., Tucker, J. S., Schwartz, J. E., Martin, L. R., Tomlinson-Keasey, C., Wingard, D. L., & Criqui, M. H. (1995). Childhood conscientiousness and longevity: Health behaviors and cause of death. *Journal of Personality and Social Psychology, 68,* 696–703.

Friedman, H. S., Tucker, J. S., Schwartz, J. E., Tomlinson-Keasey, C., Martin, L. R., Wingard, D. L., & Criqui, M. H. (1995). Psychosocial and behavioral predictors of longevity. *American Psychologist, 50,* 69–78.

Friedman, H. S., Tucker, J. S., Tomlinson-Keasey, C., Schwartz, J. E., Martin, L. R., Wingard, D. L., & Criqui, M. H. (1993). Does childhood personality predict longevity? *Journal of Personality and Social Psychology, 65,* 176–185.

Friedman, J. M., & Halaas, J. L. (1998). Leptin and the regulation of body weight in mammals. *Nature, 395,* 763–770.

Friedmann, P. D., Saitz, R., & Samet, J. H. (1998). Management of adults recovering from alcohol or other drug problems. *Journal of the American Medical Association, 279,* 1227–1231.

Friend, M., & Davis, T. L. (1993). Appearance-reality distinction: Children's understanding of the physical and affective domains. *Developmental Psychology, 29,* 907–914.

Friend, R. A. (1991). Older lesbian and gay people: A theory of successful aging. In J. A. Lee (Ed.), *Gay midlife and maturity* (pp. 99–118). New York: Haworth.

Frith, U. (1989). *Autism: Explaining the enigma.* Oxford: Basil Blackwell.

Fromkin, V., Krashen, S., Curtiss, S., Rigler, D., & Rigler, M. (1974). The development of language in Genie: Acquisition beyond the "critical period." *Brain and Language, 15*(9), 28–34.

Frone, M. R., Russell, M., & Barnes, G. M. (1996). Work-family conflict, gender, and health-related outcomes: A study of employed parents in two community samples. *Journal of Occupational Health Psychology, 1*(1), 57–69.

Fuchs, C. S., Stampfer, M. J., Colditz, G. A., Giovannucci, E. L., Manson, J. E., Kawachi, I., Hunter, D. J., Hankinson, S. E., Hennekens, C. H., Rosner, B., Speizer, F. E., & Willett, W. C. (1995). Alcohol consumption and mortality among women. *New England Journal of Medicine, 332,* 1245–1250.

Fuligni, A. J. (1997). The academic achievement of adolescents from immigrant families: The roles of family background, attitudes, and behavior. *Child Development, 68,* 351–363.

Fuligni, A. J., & Eccles, J. S. (1993). Perceived parent-child relationships and early adolescents' orientation toward peers. *Developmental Psychology, 29,* 622–632.

Fuligni, A. J., & Stevenson, H. W. (1995). Time use and mathematics achievement among American, Chinese, and Japanese high school students. *Child Development, 66,* 830–842.

Fuligni, A. J., Eccles, J. S., Barber, B. L., & Clements, P. (2001). Early adolescent peer orientation and adjustment during high school. *Developmental Psychology, 37*(1), 28–36.

Fuligni, A. J., Yip, T., & Tseng, V. (2002). The impact of family obligation on the daily activities and psychological well-being of Chinese American adolescents. *Child Development, 73*(1), 302–314.

Fulton, R., & Owen, G. (1987–1988). Death and society in twentieth-century America: Special issue—Research in thanatology. *Omega: Journal of Death and Dying, 18,* 379–395.

Fung, H. H., Carstensen, L. L., & Lang, F. R. (2001). Age-related patterns in social networks among European-Americans and African-Americans: Implications for socioemotional selectivity across the life span. *International Journal of Aging and Human Development, 52,* 185–206.

Furman, W. (1982). Children's friendships. In T. M. Field, A. Huston, H. C. Quay, L. Troll, & G. E. Finley (Eds.), *Review of human development.* New York: Wiley.

Furman, W., & Bierman, K. L. (1983). Developmental changes in young children's conception of friendship. *Child Development, 54,* 549–556.

Furman, W., & Buhrmester, D. (1985). Children's perceptions of the personal relationships in their social networks. *Developmental Psychology, 21,* 1016–1024.

Furnival, R. A., Street, K. A., & Schunk, J. E. (1999). Trampoline injuries triple among children. Pediatrics, 103, e57. [Online]. Available: http://www.pediatrics.org/egi/content/full/103/5/e57. Access date: May 21, 1999.

Furrow, D. (1984). Social and private speech at two years. *Child Development, 55,* 355–362.

Furstenberg, F. F., & Hughes, M. E. (1995). Social capital in successful development. *Journal of Marriage and the Family, 57,* 580–592.

Furstenberg, F. F., Levine, J. A., & Brooks-Gunn, J. (1990). The children of teenage mothers: Patterns of early child bearing in two generations. *Family Planning Perspectives, 22*(2), 54–61.

Furstenberg, F. F., and Kiernan, K. E. (2001). Delayed parental divorce: How much do children benefit? *Journal of Marriage and the Family, 63,* 446–457.

Furth, H. G., & Kane, S. R. (1992). Children constructing society: A new perspective on children at play. In H. McGurk (Ed.), *Childhood social development: Contemporary perspectives.* Hove: Erlbaum.

Fuson, K. C., & Kwon, Y. (1992). Korean children's understanding of multidigit addition and subtraction. *Child Development, 63,* 491–506.

Gabbard, C. P. (1996). *Lifelong motor development* (2nd ed.). Madison, WI: Brown and Benchmark.

Gabhainn, S., & François, Y. (2000). Substance use. In C. Currie, K. Hurrelmann, W. Settertobulte, R. Smith, & J. Todd (Eds.), *Health behaviour in school-aged children: a WHO cross-national study (HBSC) international report* (pp. 97–114). WHO Policy Series: Healthy Policy for Children and Adolescents, Series No. 1.

Gabriel, T. (1996, January 7). High-tech pregnancies test hope's limit. *The New York Times,* pp. 1, 18–19.

Gaddis, A., & Brooks-Gunn, J. (1985). The male experience of pubertal change. *Journal of Youth and Adolescence, 14,* 61–69.

Gaertner, S. L., Mann, J., Murrell, A., & Dovidio, J. F. (1989). Reducing inter-group bias: The benefits of recategorization. *Journal of Personality and Social Psychology, 57,* 239–249.

Galambos, N. L., Petersen, A. C., & Lenerz, K. (1988). Maternal employment and sex typing in early adolescence: Contemporaneous and longitudinal relations. In A. D. Gottfried & A. W. Gottfried (Eds.), *Maternal employment and children's development: Longitudinal research.* New York: Plenum.

Galambos, N. L., Sears, H. A., Almeida, D. M., & Kolaric, G. C. (1995). Parents' work overload and problem behavior in young adolescents. *Journal of Research on Adolescence, 5*(2), 201–223.

Gale, J. L., Thapa, P. B., Wassilak, S. G., Bobo, J. K., Mendelman, P. M., & Foy, H. M. (1994). Risk of serious acute neurological illness after immunization with diptheria-tetanus-pertussis vaccine: A population-based case-control study. *Journal of the American Medical Association, 271,* 37–41.

Galea, S., Ahern, J., Resnick, H., Kilpatrick, D., Bucuvalas, M., Gold, J., & Vlahov, D. (2002). Psychological sequel of the September 11 terrorist attacks in New York City. *New England Journal of Medicine, 346,* 982–987.

Galen, B. R., & Underwood, M. K. (1997). A developmental investigation of social aggression among children. *Developmental Psychology, 33,* 589–600.

Galinsky, E., Kim, S. S., & Bond, J. T. (2001). *Feeling overworked: When work becomes too much.* New York: Families and Work Institute.

Gallagher, W. (1993, May). Midlife myths. *The Atlantic Monthly,* pp. 51–68.

Gallagher-Thompson, D. (1995). Caregivers of chronically ill elders. In G. E. Maddox (Ed.), *The encyclopedia of aging* (pp. 141–144). New York: Springer.

Galli, R. L., Shukitt-Hale, B., Youdim, K. A., & Joseph, J. A. (2002). Fruit polyphenolics and brain aging: nutritional interventions targeting age-related neuronal and behavioral deficits. *Annals of the New York Academy of Science, 959,* 128–132.

Gallo, J. J., Anthony, J. C., & Muthen, B. O. (1994). Age differences in the symptoms of depression: A latent trace analysis. *Journal of Gerontology: Psychological Sciences, 49,* P251–264.

Galotti, K. M., Komatsu, L. K., & Voelz, S. (1997). Children's differential performance on deductive and inductive syllogisms. *Developmental Psychology, 33,* 70–78.

Gandhi, M. (1948). *Autobiography: The story of my experiments with truth.* New York: Dover.

Gannon, P. J., Holloway, R. L., Broadfield, D. C., & Braun, A. R. (1998). Asymmetry of chimpanzee planum temporale: Humanlike pattern of Wernicke's brain language homlog. *Science, 279,* 22–222.

Gans, J. E. (1990). *America's adolescents: How healthy are they?* Chicago: American Medical Association.

Garasky, S., & Meyer, D. R. (1996). Reconsidering the increase in father-only families. *Demography, 33,* 385–393.

Garbarino, J., & Kostelny, K. (1993). Neighborhood and community influences on parenting. In T. Luster & L. Okagaki (Eds.), *Parenting: An ecological perspective* (pp. 203–226). Hillsdale, NJ: Erlbaum.

Garbarino, J., Dubrow, N., Kostelny, K., & Pardo, C. (1992). *Children in danger: Coping with the consequences of community violence.* San Francisco: Jossey-Bass.

Garbarino, J., Dubrow, N., Kostelny, K., & Pardo, C. (1998). *Children in danger: Coping with the consequences of community violence.* San Francisco: Jossey-Bass.

Garcia, M. M., Shaw, D. S., Winslow, E. B., & Yaggi, K. E. (2000). Destructive sibling conflict and the development of conduct problems in young boys. *Developmental Psychology, 36*(1), 44–53.

Gardiner, H. W., Mutter, J. D., & Kosmitzki, C. (1998). *Lives across cultures: Cross-cultural human development.* Boston: Allyn and Bacon.

Gardner, H. (1986, Summer). Freud in three frames. *Daedalus,* 105–134.

Gardner, H. (1988). Creative lives and creative works: A synthetic scientific approach. In R. J. Sternberg (Ed.), *The nature of creativity: Contemporary psychological perspectives* (pp. 298–321). Cambridge, UK: Cambridge University Press.

Gardner, H. (1993). *Frames of mind: The theory of multiple intelligences.* New York: Basic. (Original work published 1983)

Gardner, H. (1995). Reflections on multiple intelligences: Myths and messages. *Phi Delta Kappan,* pp. 200–209.

Gardner, H. (1997). *Extraordinary minds: Portraits of exceptional individuals and an examination of our extraordinariness.* New York: Basic Books.

Gardner, H. (1998). Are there additional intelligences? In J. Kane (Ed.), *Education, information, and transformation: Essays on learning and thinking.* Englewood Cliffs, NJ: Prentice-Hall.

Gardner, M. (2002, Aug. 1). Meet the nanny—'Granny': Grandparents, says census, are nation's leading child-care providers. *Christian Science Monitor.* [Online]. Available: csmonitor.com

Garland, A. F., & Zigler, E. (1993). Adolescent suicide prevention: Current research and social policy implications. *American Psychologist, 48*(2), 169–182.

Garland, J. B. (1982, March). *Social referencing and self-produced locomotion.* Paper presented at the meeting of the International Conference on International Studies, Austin, TX.

Garmezy, N., Masten, A., & Tellegen, A. (1984). The study of stress and competence in children. A building block for developmental psychopathology. *Child Development, 55,* 97–111.

Garmon, L. C., Basinger, K. S., Gregg, V. R., & Gibbs, J. C. (1996). Gender differences in stage and expression of moral judgment. *Merrill-Palmer Quarterly, 42,* 418–437.

Garner, B. P. (1998). Play development from birth to age four. In D. P. Fromberg & D. Bergen (Eds.), *Play from birth to twelve and beyond: Contexts, perspectives, and meanings* (pp. 137–145). New York: Garland.

Garner, D. M. (1993). Pathogenesis of anorexia nervosa. *The Lancet, 341,* 1631–1635.

Garner, P. W., & Power, T. G. (1996). Preschoolers' emotional control in the disappointment paradigm and its relation to temperament, emotional knowledge, and family expressiveness. *Child Development, 67,* 1406–1419.

Garofalo, R., Wolf, R. C., Kessel, S., Palfrey, J., & DuRant, R. H. (1998). The association between health risk behaviors and sexual orientation among a school-based sample of adolescents. *Pediatrics, 101,* 895–902.

Gates, G. J., & Sonenstein, F. L. (2000). Heterosexual genital sexual activity among adolescent males: 1988 and 1995. *Family Planning Perspectives, 32,* 295–297.

Gauvain, M. (1993). The development of spatial thinking in everyday activity. *Developmental Review, 13,* 92–121.

Gazzaniga, M. S. (Ed.). (2000). The new cognitive neurosciences (2nd ed.). Cambridge, MA, US: The MIT Press.

Ge, X., Conger, R. D., & Elder, G. H. (2001). Pubertal transition, stressful life events, and the emergence of gender differences in adolescent depressive symptoms. *Developmental Psychology, 37*(3), 404–417.

Geary, D. C. (1993). Mathematical disabilities: Cognitive, neuropsychological, and genetic components. *Psychological Bulletin, 114,* 345–362.

Geary, D. C. (1999). Evolution and developmental sex differences. *Current Directions in Psychological Science, 8*(4), 115–120.

Geary, D. C., Bow-Thomas, C. C., Liu, F., & Siegler, R. S. (1996). Development of arithmetical competencies in Chinese and American children: Influence of age, language, and schooling. *Child Development, 67,* 2022–2044.

Gecas, V., & Seff, M. A. (1990). Families and adolescents: A review of the 1980s. *Journal of Marriage and the Family, 52,* 941–958.

Geen, R. G. (1994). Television and aggression: Recent developments in research and theory. In D. Zillman, J. Bryant, & A. C. Huston (Eds.), *Media, children, and the family: Social scientific, psychoanalytic, and clinical perspectives.* Hillsdale, NJ: Erlbaum.

Geiger, B. (1996). *Fathers as primary caregivers.* Westport, CT: Greenwood.

Gelfand, D. M., & Teti, D. M. (1995, November). How does maternal depression affect children? *The Harvard Mental Health Letter,* p. 8.

Gélis, J. (1991). *History of childbirth: Fertility, pregnancy, and birth in early modern Europe.* Boston: Northeastern University Press.

Geller, J. A. (1992). *Breaking destructive patterns: Multiple strategies for treating partner abuse.* New York: Free Press.

Gelles, R. J., & Maynard, P. E. (1987). A structural family systems approach to intervention in cases of family violence. *Family Relations, 36,* 270–275.

Gelman, R., & Gallistel, C. R. (1978). *The child's understanding of number.* Cambridge, MA: Harvard University Press.

Gelman, R., Spelke, E. S., & Meck, E. (1983). What preschoolers know about animate and inanimate objects. In D. R. Rogers & J. S. Sloboda (Eds.), *The acquisition of symbolic skills* (pp. 297–326). New York: Plenum.

Gendell, M., & Siegel, J. S. (1996). Trends in retirement age in the U.S., 1955–1993, by sex and race. *Journal of Gerontology: Social Sciences, 51B,* S132–139.

Genesee, F., Nicoladis, E., & Paradis, J. (1995). Language differentiation in early bilingual development. *Journal of Child Language, 22,* 611–631.

Genevay, B. (1986). Intimacy as we age. *Generations, 10*(4), 12–15.

George, C., Kaplan, N., & Main, M. (1985). *The Berkeley Adult Attachment Interview.* Unpublished protocol, Department of Psychology, University of California, Berkeley, CA.

George, L. K. (1993). Depressive disorders and symptoms in later life. *Generations, 17*(1), 35–38.

George, T. P., & Hartmann, D. P. (1996). Friendship networks of unpopular, average, and popular children. *Child Development, 67,* 2301–2316.

Gerbner, G., & Ozyegin, N. (1997, March 20). Alcohol, tobacco, and illicit drugs in entertainment television, commercials, news, "reality shows," movies, and music channels. *Report from the Robert Wood Johnson Foundation.* Princeton, NJ.

Gershoff, E. T. (2002). Corporal punishment by parents and associated child behaviors and experiences: A meta-analytic and theoretical review. *Psychological Bulletin, 128,* 539–579.

Gertner, B. L., Rice, M. L., & Hadley, P. A. (1994). Influence of communicative competence on peer preferences in a preschool classroom. *Journal of Speech and Hearing Research, 37,* 913–923.

Getzels, J. W. (1964). Creative thinking, problem-solving, and instruction. In *Yearbook of the National Society for the Study of Education* (Pt. 1, pp. 240–267). Chicago: University of Chicago Press.

Getzels, J. W. (1984, March). *Problem-finding in creativity in higher education* [The Fifth Rev. Charles F. Donovan, S. J., Lecture]. Boston College, School of Education, Boston, MA.

Getzels, J. W., & Jackson, P. W. (1962). *Creativity and intelligence: Explorations with gifted students.* New York: Wiley.

Getzels, J. W., & Jackson, P. W. (1963). The highly intelligent and the highly creative adolescent: A summary of some research findings. In C. W. Taylor & F. Baron (Eds.), *Scientific creativity: Its recognition and development* (pp. 161–172). New York: Wiley.

Giambra, L. M., & Arenberg, D. (1993). Adult age differences in forgetting sentences. *Psychology and Aging, 8,* 451–462.

Gibbs, J. C. (1991). Toward an integration of Kohlberg's and Hoffman's theories of moral development. In W. M. Kurtines & J. L. Gewirtz (Eds.), *Handbook of moral behavior and development: Advances in theory, research, and application,* Vol. 1. Hillsdale, N. J.: Erlbaum.

Gibbs, J. C., & Schnell, S. V. (1985). Moral development "versus" socialization. *American Psychologist, 40*(10), 1071–1080.

Gibbs, J. C., Arnold, K. O., Ahlborn, H. H., & Cheesman, F. L. (1984). Facilitation of sociomoral reasoning in adolescents. *Journal of Clinical and Consulting Psychology, 52,* 37–45.

Gibbs, N. (1995, October 2). The EQ factor. *Time,* pp. 60–68.

Gibson, E. J. (1969). *Principles of perceptual learning and development.* New York: Appleton-Century-Crofts.

Gibson, E. J., & Pick, A. D. (2000). *An ecological approach to perceptual learning and development.* New York: Oxford University Press.

Gibson, E. J., & Walker, A. S. (1984). Development of knowledge of visual-tactual affordances of substance. *Child Development, 55,* 453–460.

Gibson, J. J. (1979). *The ecological approach to visual perception.* Boston: Houghton-Mifflin.

Gibson, M. J., Brangan, N., Gross, D., & Caplan, C. (1999). *How much are Medicare beneficiaries paying out-of-pocket for prescription drugs?* [Executive Summary]. Washington, DC: AARP Public Policy Institute.

Gidycz, C. A., Hanson, K., & Layman, M. J. (1995). A prospective analysis of the relationships among sexual assault experiences: An extension of previous findings. *Psychology of Women Quarterly, 19,* 5–29.

Gielen, U., & Kelly, D. (1983, February). *Buddhist Ladakh: Psychological portrait of a nonviolent culture.* Paper presented at the Annual Meeting of the Society for Cross-Cultural Research: Washington, DC.

Gilbert, L. A. (1994). Current perspectives in dual-career families. *Current Directions in Psychological Science, 3,* 101–105.

Gilford, R. (1984). Contrasts in marital satisfaction throughout old age: An exchange theory analysis. *Journal of Gerontology, 39,* 325–333.

Gilford, R. (1986). Marriages in later life. *Generations, 10*(4), 16–20.

Gill, B., & Schlossman, S. (1996). "A sin against childhood": Progressive education and the crusade to abolish homework, 1897–1941. *American Journal of Education, 105,* 27–66.

Gill, T. M., Williams, C. S., Robison, J. T., & Tinetti, M. E. (1999). A population-based study of environmental hazards in the homes of older persons. *American Journal of Public Health, 89,* 553–556.

Gilligan, C. (1982). *In a different voice: Psychological theory and women's development.* Cambridge, MA: Harvard University Press.

Gilligan, C. (1987a). Adolescent development reconsidered. In E. E. Irwin (Ed.), *Adolescent social behavior and health.* San Francisco: Jossey-Bass.

Gilligan, C. (1987b). Moral orientation and moral development. In E. F. Kittay & D. T. Meyers (Eds.), *Women and moral theory* (pp. 19–33). Totowa, NJ: Rowman & Littlefield.

Gilligan, C., Murphy, J. M., & Tappan, M. B. (1990). Moral development beyond adolescence. In C. N. Alexander & E. J. Langer (Eds.), *Higher stages of human development* (pp. 208–228). New York: Oxford University Press.

Gillman, M. W., Cupples, L. A., Gagnon, D., Posner, B. M., Ellison, R. C., Castelli, W. P., & Wolf, P. A. (1995). Protective effects of fruit and vegetables on development of stroke in men. *Journal of the American Medical Association, 273,* 1113–1117.

Gillman, M. W., Rifas-Shiman, S. L., Camargo, C. A., Berkey, C. S., Frazier, A. L., Rockett, H. R. H., Field, A. E., & Colditz, G. A. (2001). Risk of overweight among adolescence who were breastfed as infants. *Journal of the American Medical Association, 285*(19), 2461–2467.

Ginsburg, G. S., & Bronstein, P. (1993). Family factors related to children's intrinsic/extrinsic motivational orientation and academic performance. *Child Development, 64,* 1461–1474.

Ginsburg, H. P. (1997). Mathematics learning disabilities: A view from developmental psychology. *Journal of Learning Disabilities, 30,* 20–33.

Ginsburg, H., & Opper, S. (1979). *Piaget's theory of intellectual development* (2nd ed.). Englewood Cliffs, NJ: Prentice-Hall.

Ginzberg, E. (1972). Toward a theory of occupational choice: A restatement. *Vocational Guidance Quarterly, 20,* 169–176.

Giordano, P. C., Cernkovich, S. A., & DeMaris, A. (1993). The family and peer relations of black adolescents. *Journal of Marriage and the Family, 55,* 277–287.

Giovannucci, E., Rimm, E. B., Colditz, G. A., Stampfer, M. J., Ascherio, A., Chute, C. C., & Willett, W. C. (1993). A prospective study of dietary fat and risk of prostate cancer. *Journal of the National Cancer Institute, 85,* 1571–1579.

Giovannucci, E., Rimm, E. B., Liu, Y., & Stampfer, M. J. (2002). A tomato-rich diet helps reduce risk of prostate cancer. *Journal of the National Cancer Institute, 94*(5), 391–398.

Giusti, R. M., Iwamoto, K., & Hatch, E. E. (1995). Diethylstibestrol revisited: A review of the long-term health effects. *Annals of Internal Medicine, 122,* 778–788.

Gladue, B. A. (1994). The biopsychology of sexual orientation. *Current Directions in Psychological Science, 3,* 150–154.

Glasgow, K. L., Dornbusch, S. M., Troyer, L., Steinberg, L., & Ritter, P. L. (1997). Parenting styles, adolescents' attributions, and educational outcomes in nine heterogeneous high schools. *Child Development, 68,* 507–529.

Glass, T. A., Seeman, T. E., Herzog, A. R., Kahn, R., & Berkman, L. F. (1995). Change in productive activity in late adulthood: MacArthur studies of successful aging. *Journal of Gerontology: Social Sciences, 50B,* S65–66.

Gleason, T. R., Sebanc, A. M., & Hartup, W. W. (2000). Imaginary companions of preschool children. *Developmental Psychology, 36,* 419–428.

Gleitman, L. R., Newport, E. L., & Gleitman, H. (1984). The current status of the motherese hypothesis. *Journal of Child Language, 11,* 43–79.

Glenn, N. D. (1991). The recent trend in marital success in the United States. *Journal of Marriage and the Family, 53,* 261–270.

Glick, J. E., & Van Hook, J. (2002). Parents' coresidence with adult children: Can immigration explain racial and ethnic variation? *Journal of Marriage and Family, 64,* 240–253.

Gold, D. P., Andres, D., Etezadi, J., Arbuckle, T. Y., Schwartzman, A. E., & Chaikelson, J. (1995).

Structural equation model of intellectual change and continuity and predictors of intelligence in older men. *Psychology and Aging, 10,* 294–303.

Gold, P. E., Cahill, L., & Wenk, G. L. (2002). Ginkgo biloba: A cognitive enhancer? *Psychological Science in the Public Interest, 3* (1), 3–11.

Goldberg, W. A., Greenberger, E., & Nagel, S. K. (1996). Employment and achievement: Mothers' work involvement in relation to children's achievement behaviors and mothers' parenting behaviors. *Child Development, 67,* 1512–1527.

Goldenberg, R. L., & Rouse, D. J. (1998). Prevention of premature labor. *New England Journal of Medicine, 339,* 313–320.

Goldenberg, R. L., Tamura, T., Neggers, Y., Copper, R. L., Johnston, K. E., DuBard, M. B., & Hauth, J. C. (1995). The effect of zinc supplementation on pregnancy outcome. *Journal of the American Medical Association, 274,* 463–468.

Goldin-Meadow, S., & Mylander, C. (1998). Spontaneous sign systems created by deaf children in two cultures. *Nature, 391,* 279–281.

Goldman, A. (1981). *Elvis.* New York: McGraw-Hill.

Goldman, S. R., Petrosino, A. J., & Cognition and Technology Group at Vanderbilt. (1999). Design principles for instruction in content domains: Lessons from research on expertise and learning. In F. T. Durso, (Ed.), *Handbook of applied cognition* (pp. 595–627). Chichester, England: Wiley.

Goldstein, A. O., Sobel, R. A., & Newman, G. R. (1999). Tobacco and alcohol use in G-rated children's animated films. *Journal of the American Medical Association, 281,* 1131–1136.

Goldstein, I., Padma-Nathan, H., Rosen, R. C., Steers, W. D., & Wicker, P. A., for the Sildenafil Study group. (1998). Oral sildenafil in the treatment of erectile dysfunction. *New England Journal of Medicine, 338,* 1397–1404.

Goleman, D. (1990, April 24). Anger over racism is seen as a cause of blacks' high blood pressure. *The New York Times,* p. C3.

Goleman, D. (1992, November 24). Anthropology goes looking in all the old places. *The New York Times,* p. B1.

Goleman, D. (1993, June 11). Studies reveal suggestibility of very young as witnesses. *The New York Times,* pp. A1, A23.

Goleman, D. (1995a). *Emotional intelligence: Why it can matter more than IQ.* New York: Bantam.

Goleman, D. (1995b, July 1). A genetic clue to bed-wetting is located: Researchers say discovery shows the problem is not emotions! *The New York Times,* p. 8.

Goleman, D. (1998). *Working with emotional intelligence.* New York: Bantam.

Goleman, D. (2001). An EI-based theory of performance. In C. Cherniss & D. Goleman (Eds.), *The emotionally intelligent workplace: How to select for, measure, and improve emotional intelligence in individuals, groups, and organizations* (pp. 27–44). San Francisco: Jossey-Bass.

Golinkoff, R. M., Jacquet, R. C., Hirsh-Pasek, K., & Nandakumar, R. (1996). Lexical principles may underlie the learning of verbs. *Child Development, 67,* 3101–3119.

Golomb, C., & Galasso, L. (1995). Make believe and reality: Explorations of the imaginary realm. *Developmental Psychology, 31,* 800–810.

Golombok, S., & Tasker, F. (1996). Do parents influence the sexual orientation of their children? Findings from a longitudinal study of lesbian families. *Developmental Psychology, 32,* 3–11.

Golombok, S., MacCallum, F., & Goodman, E. (2001). The "test-tube" generation: Parent-child relationships and the psychological well-being of in vitro fertilization children at adolescence. *Child Development, 72,* 599–608.

Golombok, S., MacCallum, F., Goodman, E., & Rutter, M. (2002). Families with children conceived by donor insemination: A follow-up at age twelve. *Child Development, 73,* 952–968.

Golstein, P. (1998). Cell death in us and others. *Science, 281,* 1283.

Gonyea, J. G., Hudson, R. B., & Seltzer, G. B. (1990). Housing preferences of vulnerable elders in suburbia. *Journal of Housing for the Elderly, 7,* 79–95.

Goode, E. (1999, February 16). New study finds middle age is prime of life. *The New York Times,* p. F6.

Goodman, G. S., Emery, R. E., & Haugaard, J. J. (1998). Developmental psychology and law: Divorce, child maltreatment, foster care, and adoption. In W. Damon (Series Ed.), I. E. Sigel, & K. A. Renninger (Vol. Eds.), *Handbook of child psychology* (Vol. 4, pp. 775–874). New York: Wiley.

Goodwyn, S. W., & Acredolo, L. P. (1998). Encouraging symbolic gestures: A new perspective on the relationship between gesture and speech. In J. M Iverson & S. Goldin-Meadow (Eds.), *The nature and functions of gesture in children's communication* (pp. 61–73). San Francisco: Jossey-Bass.

Gopnik, A., Sobel, D. M., Schulz, L. E., & Glymour, C. (2001). Causal learning mechanisms in very young children: Two-, three-, and four-year-olds infer causal relations from patterns of variation and covariation. *Developmental Psychology, 37*(5), 620–629.

Gordon, I., Lask, B., Bryantwaugh, R., Christie, D., & Timini, S. (1997). Childhood onset anorexia nervosa: Towards identifying a biological substrate. *International Journal of Eating Disorders, 22*(2), 159–165.

Gorin, S. S., & Jacobson, J. (2001). Diet and breast cancer surveillance behaviors among Harlem women. *Annals of the New York Academy of Science, 952,* 153–160.

Gorman, K. S., & Pollitt, E. (1996). Does schooling buffer the effects of early risk? *Child Development, 67,* 314–326.

Gorman, M. (1993). Help and self-help for older adults in developing countries. *Generations, 17*(4), 73–76.

Gortmaker, S. L., Hughes, M., Cervia, J., Brady, M., Johnson, G. M., Seage, G. R., Song, L. Y., Dankner, W. M., & Oleske, J. M. for the Pediatric AIDS clinical trial group protocol 219 team. (2001). Effect of combination therapy including protease inhibitors on mortality among children and adolescents infected with HIV-1. *New England Journal of Medicine, 345*(21), 1522–1528.

Gortmaker, S. L., Must, A., Perrin, J. M., Sobol, A. M., & Dietz, W. H. (1993). Social and economic consequences of overweight in adolescence and young adulthood. *New England Journal of Medicine, 329,* 1008–1012.

Gostin, L. O. (1997). Deciding life and death in the courtroom: From Quinlan to Cruzan, Glucksberg, and Vacco—A brief history and analysis of constitutional protection of the "right to die." *Journal of the American Medical Association, 278,* 1523–1528.

Goswami, U., & Brown, A. L. (1989). Melting chocolate and melting snowmen: Analogical reasoning and causal relations. *Cognition, 35,* 69–95.

Gottfried, A. E., Fleming, J. S., & Gottfried, A. W. (1998). Role of cognitively stimulating home environment in children's academic intrinsic motivation: A longitudinal study. *Child Development, 69,* 1448–1460.

Gottlieb, G. (1991). Experiential canalization of behavioral development theory. *Developmental Psychology, 27*(1), 4–13.

Gottman, J. M., & Krokoff, L. J. (1989). Marital interaction and satisfaction: A longitudinal view. *Journal of Consulting and Clinical Psychology, 57,* 47–52.

Gottman, J. M., & Notarius, C. I. (2000). Decade review: Observing marital interaction. *Journal of Marriage and the Family, 62,* 927–947.

Goubet, N. & Clifton, R. K. (1998). Object and event representation in 6 1/2-month-old infants. *Developmental Psychology, 34,* 63–76.

Gould, E., Reeves, A. J., Graziano, M. S. A., & Gross, C. G. (1999). Neurogenesis in the neocortex of adult primates. *Science, 286,* 548–552.

Graber, J. A., Brooks-Gunn, J., & Warren, M. P. (1995). The antecedents of menarcheal age: Heredity, family environment, and stressful life events. *Child Development, 66,* 346–359.

Grady, D., & Cummings, S. R. (2002). Postmenopausal hormone therapy for prevention of fractures: How good is the evidence? *Journal of the American Medical Association, 285,* 2909–2910.

Grady, D., Herrington, D., Bittner, V., Blumenthal, R., Davidson, M., Hlatky, M., Hsia, J., Hulley, S., Herd, Al., Khan, S., Newby, L. K., Waters, D., Vittinghoff, E., & Wenger, N. (2002). Cardiovascular disease outcomes during 6.8 years of hormone therapy: Heart and Estrogen/Progestin Replacement Study follow-up (HERS II). *Journal of the American Medical Association, 288,* 49–57.

Grantham-McGregor, S., Powell, C., Walker, S., Chang, S., & Fletcher, P. (1994). The long-term follow-up of severely malnourished children who participated in an intervention program. *Child Development, 65,* 428–439.

Gray, M. R., & Steinberg, L. (1999). Unpacking authoritative parenting: Reassessing a multidimensional construct. *Journal of Marriage and the Family, 61,* 574–587.

Greenberg, J., & Becker, M. (1988). Aging parents as family resources. *The Gerontologist, 28*(6), 786–790.

Greenberger, E., & Chen, C. (1996). Perceived family relationships and depressed mood in early and late adolescence: A comparison of European and Asian Americans. *Developmental Psychology, 32,* 707–716.

Greenberger, E., & Steinberg, L. (1986). *When teenagers work.* New York: Basic Books.

Greene, M. F. (2002). Outcomes of very low birthweight in young adults. *New England Journal of Medicine, 346*(3), 146–148.

Greenhoot, A. F. (2000). Remembering and understanding: The effects of changes in underlying knowledge on children's recollections. *Child Development, 71,* 1309–1328.

Greenhouse, L. (2000a, June 6). Justices reject visiting rights in divided case: Ruling favors mother over grandparents. *The New York Times* (national edition), pp. A1, A15.

Greenhouse, L. (2000b, February 29). Program of drug-testing pregnant women draws review by the Supreme Court. *The New York Times,* p. A12.

Greenhouse, L. (2000c, September 9). Should a fetus's well-being override a mother's rights? *The New York Times,* pp. B9–B11.

Greenough, W. T., Black, J. E., & Wallace, C. S. (1987). Experience and brain development. *Child Development, 58,* 539–559.

Greenstein, T. N. (1995). Gender ideology, marital disruption, and the employment of married women. *Journal of Marriage and the Family, 57,* 31–42.

Gregg, V., Gibbs, J. C., & Basinger, K. S. (1994). Patterns of developmental delay in moral judgment by male and female delinquents. *Merrill-Palmer Quarterly, 40,* 538–553.

Greider, L. (2001, December). Hard times drive adult kids "home": Parents grapple with rules for "boomerangers." *AARP Bulletin,* pp. 3, 14.

Grigorinko, E. L., & Sternberg, R. J. (1998). Dynamic testing. *Psych Bulletin, 124,* 75–111.

Grodstein, F. (1996). Postmenopausal estrogen and progestin use and the risk of cardiovascular disease. *New England Journal of Medicine, 335,* 453.

Grotevant, H. D., McRoy, R. G., Elde, C. L., & Fravel, D. L. (1994). Adoptive family system dynamics: Variations by level of openness in the adoption. *Family Process, 33*(2), 125–146.

Gruber, A., & Schaie, K. W. (1986, November 21). *Longitudinal-sequential studies of marital assortativity.* Paper presented at the annual meeting of the Gerontological Society of America, Chicago, IL.

Gruber, H. (1998). The social construction of extraordinary selves: Collaboration among unique creative people. In R. C. Friedman & K. B. Rogers (Eds.), *Talent in context: Historical and social perspectives on giftedness* (pp. 127–147). Washington, DC: American Psychological Association.

Gruber-Baldini, A. L. (1991). *The impact of health and disease on cognitive ability in adulthood and old age in the Seattle Longitudinal Study.* Unpublished doctoral dissertation, Pennsylvania State University.

Grunberg, J. A. (Ed. Dir.), Kann, L., Kinchen, S. A., Williams, B., Ross, J. G., Lowry, R., & Kolbe, L. (2002, June 28). Youth risk behavior surveillance—United States, 2001. *MMWR Surveillance Summaries, 51*(SS04), 1–64.

Grusec, J. E., & Goodnow, J. J. (1994). Impact of parental discipline methods on the child's internalization of values: A reconceptualization of current points of view. *Developmental Psychology, 30,* 4–19.

Grusec, J. E., Goodnow, J. J., & Kuczynski, L. (2000). New directions in analyses of parenting contributions to children's acquisition of values. *Child Development, 71,* 205–211.

Guerrero, L. (2001, April 25). Almost third of kids bullied or bullies: Health officials concerned either could lead to more aggressive behavior. *Chicago Sun-Times,* p. 28.

Guilford, J. P. (1956). Structure of intellect. *Psychological Bulletin, 53,* 267–293.

Guilford, J. P. (1959). Three faces of intellect. *American Psychologist, 14,* 469–479.

Guilford, J. P. (1960). Basic conceptual problems of the psychology of thinking. *Proceedings of the New York Academy of Sciences, 91,* 6–21.

Guilford, J. P. (1967). *The nature of human intelligence.* New York: McGraw-Hill.

Guilford, J. P. (1986). *Creative talents: Their nature, uses and development.* Buffalo, NY: Bearly.

Guilleminault, C., Palombini, L., Pelayo, R., & Chervin, R. D. (2003). Sleeping and sleep terrors in prepubertal children: What triggers them? *Pediatrics, 111,* pp. e17–e25.

Gullette, M. M. (1998). Midlife discourse in the twentieth-century United States: An essay on the sexuality, ideology, and politics of "middle-ageism." In R. A. Shweder (Ed.), *Welcome to middle age (and other cultural fictions)* (pp. 5–44). Chicago: University of Chicago Press.

Gullone, E. (2000). The development of normal fear: A century of research. *Clinical Psychology Review, 20,* 429–451.

Gunnar, M. R., Larson, M. C., Hertsgaard, L., Harris, M. L., & Brodersen, L. (1992). The stressfulness of separation among nine-month-old infants: Effects of social context variables and infant temperament. *Child Development, 63,* 290–303.

Gunnoe, M. L., & Mariner, C. L. (1997). Toward a developmental-contextual model of the effects of parental spanking on children's aggression. *Archives of Pediatric and Adolescent Medicine, 151,* 768–775.

Gunter, B., & Harrison, J. (1997). Violence in children's programmes on British television. *Children & Society, 11,* 143–156.

Guntheroth, W. G., & Spiers, P. S. (2001). Thermal stress in sudden infant death: Is there an ambiguity with the rebreathing hypothesis? *Pediatrics, 107,* 693–698.

Guralnick, P. (1994). *Last train to Memphis: The rise of Elvis Presley.* Boston: Little, Brown.

Gutmann, D. (1975). Parenting: A key to the comparative study of the life cycle. In N. Datan & L. H. Ginsberg (Eds.), *Life-span developmental psychology: Normative life crises.* New York: Academic Press.

Gutmann, D. (1977). The cross-cultural perspective: Notes toward a comparative psychology of aging. In J. E. Birren & K. W. Schaie (Eds.), *Handbook of the psychology of aging* (pp. 302–326). New York: Van Nostrand Reinhold.

Gutmann, D. (1985). The parental imperative revisited. In J. Meacham (Ed.), *Family and individual development.* Basel, Switzerland: Karger.

Gutmann, D. (1992). Culture and mental health in later life. In J. E. Birren, R. Sloane, & G. D. Cohen (Eds.), *Handbook of mental health and aging* (pp. 75–96). New York: Academic Press.

Gutmann, D. L. (1974). Alternatives to disengagement: Aging among the highland Druze. In R. LeVine (Ed.), *Culture and personality: Contemporary readings* (pp. 232–245). Chicago: Aldine.

Gutmann, D. L. (1987). *Reclaimed powers: Toward a new psychology of men and women in later life.* New York: Basic Books.

Guyer, B., Hoyert, D. L., Martin, J. A., Ventura, S. J., MacDorman, M. F., & Strobino, D. M. (1999). Annual summary of vital statistics—1998. *Pediatrics, 104,* 1229–1246.

Guyer, B., Strobino, D. M., Ventura, S. J., & Singh, G. K. (1995). Annual summary of vital statistics—1994. *Pediatrics, 96,* 1029–1039.

Guzick, D. S., Carson, S. A., Coutifaris, C., Overstreet, J. W., Factor-Litvak, P., Steinkampf, M. P., Hill, J. A., Mastroianni, L., Buster, J. E., Nakajima, S. T., Vogel, D. L., & Canfield, R. E. (1999). Efficacy of superovulation and intrauterine insemination in the treatment of infertility. *New England Journal of Medicine, 340,* 177–183.

Haas, S. M., & Stafford, L. (1998). An initial examination of maintenance behaviors in gay and lesbian relationships. *Journal of Social and Personal Relationships, 15,* 846–855.

Hack, M., Flannery, D. J., Schluchter, M., Cartar, L., Borawski, E., & Klein, N. (2002). Outcomes in young adulthood for very-low-birth-weight infants. *NEJM, 346*(3), 149–157.

Hack, M., Friedman, H., & Fanaroff, A. A. (1996). Outcomes of extremely low birth weight infants. *Pediatrics, 98,* 931–937.

Haddow, J. E., Palomaki, G. E., Allan, W. C., Williams, J. R., Knight, G. J., Gagnon, J., O'Heir, C. E., Mitchell, M. L., Hermos, R. J., Waisbren, S. E., Faix, J. D., & Klein, R. Z. (1999). Maternal thyroid deficiency during pregnancy and subsequent neuropsychological development of the child. *New England Journal of Medicine, 341,* 549–555.

Haddow, J. E., Palomaki, G. E., Knight, G. J., Williams, J., Polkkiner, A., Canick, J. A., Saller, D. N., & Bowers, G. B. (1992). Prenatal screening for Down's syndrome with use of maternal serum markers. *New England Journal of Medicine, 327,* 588–593.

Haden, C. A., & Fivush, F. (1996). Contextual variation in maternal conversational styles. *Merrill-Palmer Quarterly, 42,* 200–227.

Haden, C. A., Ornstein, P. A., Eckerman, C. O., & Didow, S. M. (2001). Mother-child conversational interactions as events unfold: Linkages to subsequent remembering. *Child Development, 72*(4), 1016–1031.

Hagestad, G. O. (2000). *Intergenerational relations.* Paper prepared for the United Nations Economic Commission for Europe Conference on Generations and Gender, Geneva, July 3–5.

Haight, W. L., Wang, X., Fung, H. H., Williams, K., & Mintz, J. (1999). Universal, developmental, and variable aspects of young children's play: A cross-cultural comparison of pretending at home. *Child Development, 70*(6), 1477–1488.

Haith, M. M. (1986). Sensory and perceptual processes in early infancy. *Journal of Pediatrics, 109*(1), 158–171.

Haith, M. M. (1998). Who put the cog in infant cognition? Is rich interpretation too costly? *Infant behavior and Development, 21*(2), 167–179.

Haith, M. M., & Benson, J. B. (1998). Infant cognition. In D. Kuhn & R. S. Siegler (Eds.), *Handbook of Child Psycholog: Vol. 2. Cognition, perception, and language* (5th ed., pp. 199–254). New York: Wiley.

Hajat, A., Lucas, J. B., & Kington, R. (2000). *Health outcomes among Hispanic subgroups: Data from National Health Interview Survey, 1992–1995. Advance Data No. 310.* (PHS) 2000-1250. Hyattsville, MD: National Center for Health Statistics.

Hala, S., & Chandler, M. (1996). The role of strategic planning in accessing false-belief understanding. *Child Development, 67,* 2948–2966.

Halaas, J. L., Gajiwala, K. S., Maffei, M., Cohen, S. L., Chait, B. T., Rabinowitz, D., Lallone, R. L., Burley, S. K., & Friedman, J. M. (1995). Weight reducing effects of the plasma protein encoded by the obese gene. *Science, 269,* 543–546.

Hale, S., Bronik, M. D., & Fry, A. F. (1997). Verbal and spatial working memory in school-age children: Developmental differences in susceptibility to interference. *Developmental Psychology, 33,* 364–371.

Hall, D. G., & Graham, S. A. (1999). Lexical form class information guides word-to-object mapping in preschoolers. *Child Development, 70,* 78–91.

Hall, D. R., & Zhao, J. Z. (1995). Cohabitation in Canada: Testing the selectivity hypothesis. *Journal of Marriage and the Family, 57,* 421–427.

Hall, E. (1983). A conversation with Erik Erikson. *Psychology Today, 17*(6), 22–30.

Hall, G. S. (1916). *Adolescence.* New York: Appleton. (Original work published 1904)

Halpern, D. F. (1997). Sex differences in intelligence: Implications for education. *American Psychologist, 52*(10), 1091–1102.

Halpern, S. H., Leighton, B. L., Ohlsson, A., Barrett, J. F. R., & Rice, A. (1998). Effect of epidural vs. parenteral opioid analgesia on the progress of labor. *Journal of the American Medical Association, 280,* 2105–2110.

Halterman, J. S., Aligne, A., Auinger, P., McBride, J. T., & Szilagyi, P. G. (2000). Inadequate therapy for asthma among children in the United States. *Pediatrics, 105*(1), 272–276.

Halterman, J. S., Kaczorowski, J. M., Aligne, A., Auinger, P., and Szilagyi, P. G. (2001). Iron deficiency and cognitive achievement among school-aged children and adolescence in the United States. *Pediatrics, 107*(6), 1381–1386.

Hamer, D. H., Hu, S., Magnuson, V. L., Hu, N., & Pattatucci, A. M. L. (1993). A linkage between DNA markers on the X chromosome and male sexual orientation. *Science, 261,* 321–327.

Hamm, J. V. (2000). Do birds of a feather flock together? The variable bases for African American, Asian American, and European American adolescents' selection of similar friends. *Developmental Psychology, 36*(2), 209–219.

Hamon, R. R., & Blieszner, R. (1990). Filial responsibility expectations among adult child–older parent pairs. *Journal of Gerontology: Psychological Sciences, 45*(3), P110–112.

Han, K. K., Soares, J. M., Jr., Haidar, M. A., de Lima, G. R., & Baracat, E. C. (2002). Benefits of soy isoflavene therapeutic regimen on menopausal symptoms. *Obstetrics & Gynecology, 99,* 389–394.

Hansen, M., Kurinczuk, J. J., Bower, C., & Webb, S. (2002). The risk of major birth defects after intracytoplasmic sperm injection and in vitro fertilization. *New England Journal of Medicine, 346,* 725–730.

Hanson, L. (1968). *Renoir: The man, the painter, and his world.* New York: Dodd, Mead.

Hardy-Brown, K., & Plomin, R. (1985). Infant communicative development: Evidence from adoptive and biological families for genetic and environmental influences on rate differences. *Developmental Psychology, 21,* 378–385.

Hardy-Brown, K., Plomin, R., & DeFries, J. C. (1981). Genetic and environmental influences on rate of communicative development in the first year of life. *Developmental Psychology, 17,* 704–717.

Harley, K., & Reese, E. (1999). Origins of autobiographical memory. *Developmental Psychology, 35,* 1338–1348.

Harlow, H. F., & Harlow, M. K. (1962). The effect of rearing conditions on behavior. *Bulletin of the Menninger Clinic, 26,* 213–224.

Harlow, H. F., & Zimmerman, R. R. (1959). Affectional responses in the infant monkey. *Science, 130,* 421–432.

Harnishfeger, K. K., & Bjorklund, D. F. (1993). The ontogeny of inhibition mechanisms: A renewed approach to cognitive development. In M. L. Howe & R. P. Pasnak (Eds.), *Emerging themes in cognitive development* (Vol. 1, pp. 28–49). New York: Springer-Verlag.

Harnishfeger, K. K., & Pope, R. S. (1996). Intending to forget: The development of cognitive inhibition in directed forgetting. *Journal of Experimental Psychology, 62,* 292–315.

Haroutunian, V., Purohit, D. P., Perl, D. P., Marin, D., Khan, K., Lantz, M., Davis, K. L., & Mohs, R. C. (1999). Neurofibrillary tangles in nondemented elderly subjects and mild Alzheimer disease. *Archives of Neurology, 56,* 713–718.

Harrell, J. S., Gansky, S. A., Bradley, C. B., & McMurray, R. G. (1997). Leisure time activities of elementary school children. *Nursing Research, 46,* 246–253.

Harris, P. L., Brown, E., Marriott, C., Whittall, S., & Harmer, S. (1991). Monsters, ghosts, and witches: Testing the limits of the fantasy-reality distinction in young children. In G. E. Butterworth, P. L. Harris, A. M. Leslie, & H. M. Wellman (Eds.), *Perspective on the child's theory of mind.* Oxford: Oxford University Press.

Harris, P. L., Olthof, T., Meerum Terwogt, M., & Hardman, C. (1987). Children's knowledge of situations that provoke emotion. *International Journal of Behavioral Development, 10,* 319–343.

Harrison, A. O., Wilson, M. N., Pine, C. J., Chan, S. Q., & Buriel, R. (1990). Family ecologies of ethnic minority children. *Child Development, 61,* 347–362.

Harrison, Y., & Horne, J. A. (1997). Sleep deprivation affects speech. *Sleep, 20,* 871–877.

Harrison, Y., & Horne, J. A. (2000a). Impact of sleep deprivation on decision making: A review. *Journal of Experimental Psychology, 6,* 236–249.

Harrison, Y., & Horne, J. A. (2000b). Sleep loss and temporal memory. *Quarterly Journal of Experimental Psychology: Human Experimental Psychology, 53A,* 271–279.

Harrison, Y., Horne, J. A., & Rothwell, A. (2000). Prefrontal neuropsychological effects of sleep deprivation in young adults—a model for healthy aging? *Sleep, 23,* 1067–1073.

Harrist, A. W., Zain, A. F., Bates, J. E., Dodge, K. A., & Pettit, G. S. (1997). Subtypes of social withdrawal in early childhood: Sociometric status and social-cognitive differences across four years. *Child Development, 68,* 278–294.

Hart, A. J., Whalen, P. J., Shin, L. M., McInerney, S. C., Fischer, H., & Rauch, S. L. (2000). Differential response in the human amygdala to racial outgroup vs. ingroup face stimuli. *Neuroreport, 11,* 2351–2355.

Hart, B., & Risley, T. (1996, August). *Individual differences in early intellectual experience of typical American children: Beyond SES, race, and IQ.* Address at the annual convention of the American Psychological Association, Toronto, Canada.

Hart, B., & Risley, T. R. (1989). The longitudinal study of interactive systems. *Education and Treatment of Children, 12,* 347–358.

Hart, B., & Risley, T. R. (1992). American parenting of language-learning children: Persisting differences in family-child interactions observed in natural home environments. *Developmental Psychology, 28,* 1096–1105.

Hart, C. H., DeWolf, M., Wozniak, P., & Burts, D. C. (1992). Maternal and paternal disciplinary styles: Relations with preschoolers' playground behavioral orientation and peer status. *Child Development, 63,* 879–892.

Hart, C. H., Ladd, G. W., & Burleson, B. R. (1990). Children's expectations of the outcome of social strategies: Relations with sociometric status and maternal disciplinary style. *Child Development, 61,* 127–137.

Hart, D., Hofmann, V., Edelstein, W., & Keller, M. (1997). The relation of childhood personality types to adolescent behavior and development: A longitudinal study of Icelandic children. *Developmental Psychology, 33,* 195–205.

Hart, S. N., & Brassard, M. R. (1987). A major threat to children's mental health: Psychological maltreatment. *American Psychologist, 42*(2), 160–165.

Hart, S., Field, T., del Valle, C., & Pelaez-Nogueras, M. (1998). Depressed mothers' interactions with their one-year-old infants. *Infant Behavior and Development, 21,* 519–525.

Harter, S. (1985a). Competence as a dimension of self-worth. In R. Leahy (Ed.), *The development of the self.* New York: Academic Press.

Harter, S. (1985b). *Manual for the Self-Perception Profile for Children.* Denver, CO: University of Denver.

Harter, S. (1990). Causes, correlates, and the functional role of global self-worth: A life-span perspective. In J. Kolligan & R. Sternberg (Eds.), *Competence considered: Perceptions of competence and incompetence across the life-span* (pp. 67–97). New Haven: Yale University Press.

Harter, S. (1993). Developmental changes in self-understanding across the 5 to 7 shift. In A. Sameroff & M. Haith (Eds.), *Reason and responsibility: The passage through childhood.* Chicago: University of Chicago Press.

Harter, S. (1996). Developmental changes in self-understanding across the 5 to 7 shift. In A. J. Sameroff & M. M. Haith (Eds.), *The five to seven year shift: The age of reason and responsibility* (pp. 207–235). Chicago: University of Chicago Press.

Harter, S. (1998). The development of self-representations. In W. Damon (Series Ed.) & N. Eisenberg (Vol. Ed.), *Handbook of child psychology: Vol. 3. Social, emotional, and personality development* (5th ed., pp. 553–617). New York: Wiley.

Hartley, A. A., Speer, N. K., Jonides, J., Reuter-Lorenz, P. A., & Smith, E. E. (2001). Is the dissociability of working memory systems for name identity, visual-object identity, and spatial location maintained in old age? *Neuropsychology, 15,* 3–17.

Hartshorn, K., Rovee-Collier, C., Gerhardstein, P., Bhatt, R. S., Wondoloski, R. L., Klein, P., Gilch, J., Wurtzel, N., & Campos-de-Carvalho, M. (1998). The ontogeny of long-term memory over the first year-and-a-half of life. *Developmental Psychobiology, 32,* 69–89.

Hartup, W. W. (1989). Social relationships and their developmental significance. *American Psychologist, 44,* 120–126.

Hartup, W. W. (1992). Peer relations in early and middle childhood. In V. B. Van Hasselt & M. Hersen (Eds.), *Handbook of social development: A lifespan perspective* (pp. 257–281). New York: Plenum.

Hartup, W. W. (1996a). The company they keep: Friendships and their developmental significance. *Child Development, 67,* 1–13.

Hartup, W. W. (1996b). Cooperation, close relationships, and cognitive development. In W. M. Bukowski, A. F. Newcomb, & W. W. Hartup (Eds.), *The company they keep: Friendship in childhood and adolescence* (pp. 213–237). New York: Cambridge University Press.

Hartup, W. W., & Stevens, N. (1999). Friendships and adaptation across the life span. *Current Directions in Psychological Science, 8,* 76–79.

Harvard Medical School. (2002a). The mind and the immune system—Part I. *The Harvard Mental Health Letter, 18*(10), pp. 1–3.

Harvard Medical School. (2002b, July). Treatment of bulimia and binge eating. *Harvard Mental Health Letter, 19*(1), pp. 1–4.

Harvey, E. (1999). Short-term and long-term effects of early parental employment on children of the National Longitudinal Survey of Youth. *Developmental Psychology, 35*(2), 445–459.

Harvey, J. H., & Omarzu, J. (1997). Minding the close relationship. *Personality and Psychology Review, 1,* 224–240.

Harvey, J. H., & Pauwels, B. G. (1999). Recent developments in close-relationships theory. *Current Directions in Psychological Science, 8*(3), 93–95.

Haskett, M. E., & Kistner, J. A. (1991). Social interaction and peer perceptions of young physically abused children. *Child Development, 62,* 979–990.

Haswell, K., Hock, E., & Wenar, C. (1981). Oppositional behavior of preschool children: Theory and prevention. *Family Relations, 30,* 440–446.

Hatano, G., Siegler, R. S., Richards, D. D., Inagaki, K., Stavy, R., & Wax, N. (1993). The development of biological knowledge: A multi-national study. *Cognitive Development, 8,* 47–62.

Hatcher, P. J., Hulme, C., & Ellis, A. W. (1994). Ameliorating early reading failure by integrating the teaching of reading and phonological skills: The phonological linkage hypothesis. *Child Development, 65,* 41–57.

Hatzichristou, C., & Hopf, D. (1996). A multiperspective comparison of peer sociometric status groups in childhood and adolescence. *Child Development, 67,* 1085–1102.

Hauck, F. R., Moore C. M., Herman, S. M., Donovan, M., Kalelkar, M., Christoffel, K. K., Hoffman, H. J., & Rowley, D. (2002). The contribution of prone sleeping position to the racial disparity in sudden infant death syndrome: The Chicago Infant Mortality Study. *Pediatrics, 110,* 772–780.

Haugaard, J. J. (1998). Is adoption a risk factor for the development of adjustment problems? *Clinical Psychology Review, 18,* 47–69.

Haugh, S., Hoffman, C., & Cowan, G. (1980). The eye of the very young beholder: Sex typing of infants by young children. *Child Development, 51,* 598–600.

Haupt, B. J. (1998). *Characteristics of hospice care users: Data from the 1996 National Home and Hospice Care Survey* (Advance data from vital and health statistics, No. 299). Hyattsville, MD: National Center for Health Statistics.

Hawkins, J. (1999). Trends in anesthesiology during childbirth. *Anesthesiology, 91,* A1060.

Hawkins, J. D., Catalano, R. F., & Miller, J. Y. (1992). Risk and protective factors for alcohol and other drug problems in adolescence and early adulthood: Implications for substance abuse programs. *Psychological Bulletin, 112*(1), 64–105.

Hawkins, J. D., Catalano, R. F., Kosterman, R., Abbott, R., & Hill, K. G. (1999). Preventing adolescent health-risk behaviors by strengthening protection during childhood. *Archives of Pediatrics and Adolescent Medicine, 153,* 226–234.

Hay, D. F., Pedersen, J., & Nash, A. (1982). Dyadic interaction in the first year of life. In K. H. Rubin & H. S. Ross (Eds.), *Peer relationships and social skills in children.* New York: Springer.

Hayes, A., & Batshaw, M. L. (1993). Down syndrome. *Pediatric Clinics of North America, 40,* 523–535.

Hayflick, L. (1974). The strategy of senescence. *The Gerontologist, 14*(1), 37–45.

Hayflick, L. (1981). Intracellular determinants of aging. *Mechanisms of Aging and Development, 28,* 177.

Hays, J., Ockene, J. K., Brunner, R. L., Kotchen, J. M., Manson, J. A. E., Patterson, R. E., Aragaki, A. K., Schumaker, S. A., Brzyski, R. G., LaCroix, A. Z., Granek, I. A., & Valanis, B. B., for the Women's Health Initiative Investigation. (2003, March 17). Effects of estrogen plus progestin on health-related quality of life. *New England Journal of Medicine, 348,* [Online]. Available: http://www.nejm.org (10.1056/NEJMoa030311). Access date: March 20, 2003.

Hayward, M. D., Friedman, S., & Chen, H. (1996). Race inequalities in men's retirement. *Journal of Gerontology: Social Sciences, 51B,* S1–10.

He, J., Vupputuri, S., Allen, K., Prerost, M. R., Hughes, J., & Whelton, P. K. (1999). Passive smoking and the risk of coronary heart disease—a meta-analysis of epipdemiologic studies. *New England Journal of Medicine, 340,* 920–926.

Healy, B. (1991). The Yentl syndrome. *New England Journal of Medicine, 325*(4), 274–276.

Heath, D. T. (1994). The impact of delayed fatherhood on the father-child relationship. *Journal of Genetic Psychology, 155,* 511–530.

Heath, S. B. (1989). Oral and literate tradition among black Americans living in poverty. *American Psychologist, 44,* 367–373.

Hebert, J. R., Hurley, T. G., Olendzki, B. C., Teas, J., Ma, Y., & Hampl, J. S. (1998). Nutritional and socioeconomic factors in relation to prostate cancer mortality: A cross-national study. *Journal of the National Cancer Institute, 90,* 1637–1647.

Heckhausen, J. (2001). Adaptation and resilience in midlife. In M. E. Lachman (Ed.), *Handbook of midlife development* (pp. 345–394). New York: Wiley.

Heckhausen, J., Wrosch, C., & Fleeson, W. (2001). Developmental regulation before and after a developmental deadline: The sample case of biological clock for childbearing. *Psychology and Aging, 16,* 400–413.

Hediger, M. L., Overpeck, M. D., Kuczmarski, R. J., & Ruan, W. J. (2001). Association between infant breastfeeding and overweight in young children. *Journal of the American Medical Association, 285*(19), 2453–2460.

Heijl, A., Leske, M. C., Bengtsson, B., Hyman, L., Bengtsson, B., & Hussein, M., for the Early Manifest Glaucoma Trial Group. (2002). Reduction of intraocular pressure and glaucoma progression: Results from the Early Manifest Glaucoma Trial. *Archives of Ophthalmology, 120,* 1268–1279.

Heilbrunn, J. (1998, November 15). Frequent flier: A biography of Secretary of State Madeleine Albright. *The New York Times Book Review,* p. 12.

Heller, R. B., & Dobbs, A. R. (1993). Age differences in word finding in discourse and nondiscourse situations. *Psychology and Aging, 8,* 443–450.

Helms, J. E. (1992). Why is there no study of cultural equivalence in standardized cognitive ability testing? *American Psychologist, 47,* 1083–1101.

Helson, R. (1993). Comparing longitudinal studies of adult development: Toward a paradigm of tension between stability and change. In D. C. Funder, R. D. Parke, C. Tomlinson-Keasey, & K. Widaman (Eds.), *Studying lives through time: Personality and development* (pp. 93–120). Washington, DC: American Psychological Association.

Helson, R. (1997). The self in middle age. In M. E. Lachman & J. B. James (Eds.), *Multiple paths of midlife development* (pp. 21–43). Chicago: University of Chicago Press.

Helson, R., & McCabe, L. (1993). The social clock in middle age. In B. F. Turner & L. E. Troll (Eds.), *Women growing older* (pp. 68–93). Newbury Park, CA: Sage.

Helson, R., & Moane, G. (1987). Personality change in women from college to midlife. *Journal of Personality and Social Psychology, 53,* 176–186.

Helson, R., & Roberts, B. W. (1994). Ego development and personality change in adulthood. *Journal of Personality and Social Psychology, 66,* 911–920.

Helson, R., & Wink, P. (1992). Personality change in women from the early 40s to the early 50s. *Psychology and Aging, 7*(1), 46–55.

Helwig, C. C., & Jasiobedzka, U. (2001). The relation between law and morality: Children's reasoning about socially beneficial and unjust laws. *Child Development, 72,* 1382–1393.

Hemingway, H., Nicholson, A., Stafford, M., Roberts, R., & Marmot, M. (1997). The impact of socioeconomic status on health functioning as assessed by the SF-35 questionnaire: The Whitehall II Study. *American Journal of Public Health, 87,* 1484–1490.

Henderson, V. W. (2000). *Hormone therapy and the brain: A clinical perspective on the role of estrogen.* New York: Parthenon.

Hendin, H. (1994, December 16). Scared to death of dying. *The New York Times,* p. A39.

Hendrie, H. C., Ogunniyi, A., Hall, K. S., Baiyewu, O., Unverzagt, F. W., Gureje, O., Gao, S., Evans, R. M., Ogunseyinde, A. O., Adeyinka, A., Musick, B., & Hui, S. L. (2001). Incidence of dementia and Alzheimer disease in 2 communities: Yoruba residing in Ibadan, Nigeria, and African Americans residing in Indianapolis, Indiana. *Journal of the American Medical Association, 285,* 739–795.

Henkel, L. A., Johnson, M. K., De Leonardis, D. M. (1998). Aging and source monitoring: Cognitive processes and neuropsychological correlates. *Journal of Experimental Psychology: General, 127,* 251–268.

Henker, F. O. (1981). Male climacteric. In J. G. Howells (Ed.), *Modern perspectives in the psychiatry of middle age.* New York: Brunner/Mazel.

Henly, W. L., & Fitch, B. R. (1966). Newborn narcotic withdrawal associated with regional enteritis in pregnancy. *New York Journal of Medicine, 66,* 2565–2567.

Henrich, C. C., Brown, J. L., & Aber, J. L. (1999). Evaluating the effectiveness of school-based violence prevention: Developmental approaches. *Social Policy Report, SRCD, 13*(3).

Herbig, B., Büssing, A., & Ewert, T. (2001). The role of tacit knowledge in the work context of nursing. *Journal of Advanced Nursing, 34,* 687–695.

Herman-Giddens, M. E., Slora, E. J., Wasserman, R. C., Bourdony, C. J., Bhapkar, M. V., Koch, G. G., & Hasemeier, C. M. (1997). Secondary sexual characteristics and menses in young girls seen in office practice: A study from the Pediatric Research in Office Settings network. *Pediatrics, 99,* 505–512.

Hernandez, D. J. (1997). Child development and the social demography of childhood. *Child Development, 68,* 149–169.

Herrnstein, R. J., & Murray, C. (1994). *The bell curve: Intelligence and class structure in American life.* New York: Free Press.

Hertzog, C. (1989). Influences of cognitive slowing on age differences in intelligence. *Developmental Psychology, 25*(4), 636–651.

Hertzog, C., & Dixon, R. A. (1994). Metacognitive development in adulthood and old age. In J. Metcalfe & A. P. Shimamura (Eds.), *Metacognition: Knowing about knowing* (pp. 221–251). Cambridge, MA: MIT Press.

Hertzog, C., Dixon, R. A., & Hultsch, D. F. (1990). Relationships between metamemory, memory predictions, and memory task performance in adults. *Psychology and Aging, 5*(2), 215–227.

Hertzog, C., Saylor, L. L., Fleece, A. M., & Dixon, R. A. (1994). Metamemory and aging: Relations between predicted, actual, and perceived memory task performance. *Aging and Cognition, 1,* 203–237.

Hertz-Pannier, L., Chiron, C., Jambaque, I., Renaux-Kieffer, V., Van de Moortele, P., Delalande, O., Fohlen, M., Brunelle, F., & Le Bihan, D. (2002). Late plasticity for language in a child's non-dominant hemisphere: A pre- and post-surgery fMRI study. Brain, 125(2), 361–372.

Herzog, A. R., Franks, M. M., Markus, H. R., & Holmberg, D. (1998). Activities and well-being in older age: Effects of self-concept and educational attainment. *Psychology and Aging, 13*(2), 179–185.

Herzog, D. B., Dorer, D. J., Keel, P. K., Selwyn, S. E., Ekeblad, E. R., Flores, A. T., Greenwood, D. N., Burwell, R. A., & Keller, M. B. (1999). Recovery and relapse in anorexia and bulimia nervosa: A 7.5-year follow-up study. *Journal of the American Academy of Child and Adolescent Psychiatry, 38,* 829–837. Hetherington, E. M., Bridges, M., & Insabella, G. M. (1998). What matters? What does not? Five perspectives on the association between marital transitions and children's adjustment. *American Psychologist, 53,* 167–184.

Herzog, D. B., Keller, M. B., & Lavori, P. W. (1988). Outcome in anorexia nervosa and bulimia. *Journal of Nervous and Mental Disease, 176,* 131–143.

Hetherington, E. M. (1987). Family relations six years after divorce. In K. Pasley & M. Ihinger-Tallman (Eds.), *Remarriage and parenting today: Research and theory.* New York: Guilford.

Hetherington, E. M. (1989). Coping with family transitions: Winners, losers, and survivors. *Child Development, 60,* 1–14.

Hetherington, E. M., & Stanley-Hagan, M. (1999). The adjustment of children with divorced parents: A risk and resiliency perspective. *Journal of Child Psychology and Psychiatry, 40,* 129–140.

Hetherington, E. M., Bridges, M., & Insabella, G. M. (1998). What matters? What does not? Five perspectives on the association between marital transitions and children's adjustment. *American Psychologist, 53,* 167–184.

Hetherington, E. M., Stanley-Hagan, M., & Anderson, E. (1989). Marital transitions: A child's perspective. *American Psychologist, 44,* 303–312.

Hetzel, B. S. (1994). Iodine deficiency and fetal brain damage. *New England Journal of Medicine, 331,* 1770–1771.

Hetzel, L., & Smith, A. (2001). The 65 years and over population: 2000 (Census 2000 Brief C2KBR/01-10). Washington, DC: U.S. Census Bureau.

Hewlett, B. S. (1987). Intimate fathers: Patterns of paternal holding among Aka pygmies. In M. E. Lamb (Ed.), *The father's role: Cross-cultural perspectives* (pp. 295–330). Hillsdale, NJ: Erlbaum.

Hewlett, B. S. (1992). Husband-wife reciprocity and the father-infant relationship among Aka pygmies. In B. S. Hewlett (Ed.), *Father-child relations: Cultural and biosocial contexts* (pp. 153–176). New York: de Gruyter.

Hewlett, B. S., Lamb, M. E., Shannon, D., Leyendecker, B., & Schölmerich, A. (1998). Culture and early infancy among central

African foragers and farmers. *Developmental Psychology, 34*(4), 653–661.

Heyman, R. E., O'Leary, K. D., & Jouriles, E. N. (1995). Alcohol and aggressive personality styles: Potentiators of serious physical aggression against wives? *Journal of Family Psychology, 9*(1), 44–57.

Heyns, B., & Catsambis, S. (1986). Mother's employment and children's achievement: A critique. *Sociology of Education, 59,* 140–151.

Hibbard, D. R., & Buhrmester, D. (1998). The role of peers in the socialization of gender-related social interaction styles. *Sex Roles, 39,* 185–202.

Hickling, A. K., & Wellman, H. M. (2001). The emergence of children's causal explanations and theories: Evidence from everyday conversations. *Developmental Psychology, 37*(5), 668–683.

Hickman, M., Roberts, C., & de Matos, M. G. (2000). Exercise and leisure time activities. In C. Currie, K. Hurrelmann, W. Settertobulte, R. Smith, & J. Todd (Eds.), *Health and health behaviour among young people.* WHO Policy Series: Healthy Policy for Children and Adolescents, Series No. 1. (pp. 73–82).

Hiedemann, B., Suhomilinova, O., & O'Rand, A. M. (1998). Economic independence, economic status, and empty nest in midlife marital disruption. *Journal of Marriage and the Family, 60,* 219–231.

Hill, J. O., & Peters, J. C. (1998, May 29). Environmental contributions to the obesity epidemic. *Science, 280,* 1371–1374.

Hill, J. P. (1987). Research on adolescents and their families: Past and prospect. In E. E. Irwin (Ed.), *Adolescent social behavior and health.* San Francisco: Jossey-Bass.

Hinds, T. S., West, W. L., Knight, E. M., & Harland, B. F. (1996). The effect of caffeine on pregnancy outcome variables. *Nutrition Reviews, 54,* 203–207.

Hines, A. M. (1997). Divorce-related transitions, adolescent development, and the role of the parent-child relationship: A review of the literature. *Journal of Marriage and the Family, 59,* 375–388.

Hines, M., Chiu, L., McAdams, L. A., Bentler, M. P., & Lipcamon, J. (1992). Cognition and the corpus callosum: Verbal fluency, visuospatial ability, language lateralization related to midsagittal surface areas of the corpus callosum. *Behavioral Neuroscience, 106,* 3–14.

Hirsch, H. V., & Spinelli, D. N. (1970). Visual experience modifies distribution of horizontally and vertically oriented receptive fields in cats. *Science, 168,* 869–871.

Ho, C. S. -H., & Fuson, K. C. (1998). Children's knowledge of teen quantities as tens and ones: Comparisons of Chinese, British, and American kindergartners. *Journal of Educational Psychology, 90,* 536–544.

Ho, W. C. (1989). *Yani: The brush of innocence.* New York: Hudson Hills.

Hobson, J. A., & Silvestri, L. (1999, February). Parasomnias. *Harvard Mental Health Letter,* pp. 3–5.

Hodges, E. V. E., Boivin, M., Vitaro, F., & Bukowski, W. M. (1999). The power of friendship: Protection against an escalating cycle of peer victimization. *Developmental Psychology, 35,* 94–101.

Hofferth, S. L. (1998). *Healthy environments, healthy children: Children in families* (Report of the 1997 Panel Study of Income Dynamics, Child Development Supplement). Ann Arbor: University of Michigan Institute for Social Research.

Hofferth, S. L., & Jankuniene, Z. (2000, April 2). Children's after-school activities. Paper presented at biennial meeting of the Society for Research on Adolescence, Chicago.

Hofferth, S. L., & Sandberg, J. (1998). *Changes in American children's time, 1981–1997* (Report of the 1997 Panel Study of Income Dynamics, Child Development Supplement). Ann Arbor: University of Michigan Institute for Social Research.

Hoffman, H. J., & Hillman, L. S. (1992). Epidemiology of the sudden infant death syndrome: Maternal, neonatal, and postneonatal risk factors. *Clinics in Perinatology, 19,* 717–737.

Hoffman, M. L. (1970a). Conscience, personality, and socialization techniques. *Human Development, 13,* 90–126.

Hoffman, M. L. (1970b). Moral development. In P. H. Mussen (Ed.), *Carmichael's manual of child psychology* (Vol. 2, 3rd ed., pp. 261–360). New York: Wiley.

Hoffman, M. L. (1977). Sex differences in empathy and related behaviors. *Psychological Bulletin, 84,* 712–722.

Hoffman, M. L. (1998). Varieties of empathy-based guilt. In J. Bybee (Ed.), *Guilt and children* (pp. 91–112). San Diego: Academic.

Holloway, L. (2000, October 17). Immersion promoted as alternative to bilingual instruction. *The New York Times,* p. B1.

Holloway, S. D. (1999). Divergent cultural models of child rearing and pedagogy in Japanese preschools. *New Directions for Child and Adolescent Development, 83,* 61–75.

Holmes, L. D. (1987). *Quest for the real Samoa: The Mead-Freeman controversy and beyond.* South Hadley, MA: Bergin & Garvey.

Holmes, M. D., Hunter, D. J., Colditz, G. A., Stampfer, M. J., Hankinson, S. E., Speizer, F. E., Rosner, B., & Willett, W. C. (1999). Association of dietary intake of fat and fatty acids with risk of breast cancer. *Journal of the American Medical Association, 281,* 914–920.

Holmes, T. H., & Rahe, R. H. (1976). The social readjustment rating scale. *Journal of Psychosomatic Research, 11,* 213.

Holtzman, N. A., Murphy, P. D., Watson, M. S., & Barr, P. A. (1997). Predictive genetic testing: From basic research to clinical practice. *Science, 278,* 602–605.

Holtzworth-Munroe, A., & Stuart, G. L. (1994). Typologies of male batterers: Three subtypes and the differences among them. *Psychological Bulletin, 116*(3), 476–497.

Home, J. (1985). *Caregiving: Helping an aging loved one.* Washington, DC: AARP Books.

Honein, M. A., Paulozzi, L. J., Mathews, T. J., Erickson, J. D., & Wong, L.-Y. C. (2001). Impact of folic acid fortification of the U.S. food supply on the occurrence of neural tube defects. *Journal of the American Medical Association, 285,* 2981–2986.

Hooker, K., Monahan, D., Shifren, K., & Hutchinson, C. (1992). Mental and physical health of spouse caregivers: The role of personality. *Psychology and Aging, 7*(3), 367–375.

Hopfensperger, J. (1996, April 15). Germany's fast track to a career. *Minneapolis Star-Tribune,* pp. A1, A6.

Hopkins, B., & Westra, T. (1988). Maternal handling and motor development: An intracultural study. *Genetic, Social and General Psychology Monographs, 14,* 377–420.

Hopkins, B., & Westra, T. (1990). Motor development, maternal expectations and the role of handling. *Infant Behavior and Development, 13,* 117–122.

Hopper, J. L., & Seeman, E. (1994). The bone density of female twins discordant for tobacco use. *New England Journal of Medicine, 330,* 387–392.

Horbar, J. D., Wright, E. C., Onstad, L., & the Members of the National Institute of Child Health and Human Development Neonatal Research Network. (1993). Decreasing mortality associated with the introduction of surfactant therapy: An observational study of neonates weighing 601 to 1300 grams at birth. *Pediatrics, 92,* 191–196.

Horikawa, Y., Oda, N., Cox, N. J., Li, X., Orho-Melander, M., Hara, M., Hinokio, Y., Lindner, T. H., Mashima, H., Schwarz, P. E., del Bosque-Plata, L., Horikawa, Y., Oda, Y., Yoshiuchi, I., Colilla, S., Polonsky, K. S., Wei, S., Concannon, P., Iwasaki, N., Schulze, J., Baier, L. J., Bogardus, C., Groop, L., Boerwinkle, E., Hanis, C. L., & Bell, G. I. (2000). Genetic variation in the gene encoding calpain-10 is associated with type 2 diabetes mellitus. *Nature Genetics, 26,* 163–175.

Horn, J. C., & Meer, J. (1987, May). The vintage years. *Psychology Today,* pp. 76–90.

Horn, J. L. (1967). Intelligence—Why it grows, why it declines. *Transaction, 5*(1), 23–31.

Horn, J. L. (1968). Organization of abilities and the development of intelligence. *Psychological Review, 75,* 242–259.

Horn, J. L. (1970). Organization of data on life-span development of human abilities. In L. R. Goulet & P. B. Baltes (Eds.), *Life-span developmental psychology: Theory and research* (pp. 424–466). New York: Academic Press.

Horn, J. L. (1982a). The aging of human abilities. In B. B. Wolman (Ed.), *Handbook of developmental psychology* (pp. 847–870). Englewood Cliffs, NJ: Prentice-Hall.

Horn, J. L. (1982b). The theory of fluid and crystallized intelligence in relation to concepts of cognitive psychology and aging in adulthood. In F. I. M. Craik & S. Trehub (Eds.), *Aging and cognitive processes* (pp. 237–278). New York: Plenum.

Horn, J. L., & Donaldson, G. (1980). Cognitive development: 2. Adulthood development of human abilities. In O. G. Brim & J. Kagan (Eds.), *Constancy and change in human* *development.* Cambridge, MA: Harvard University Press.

Horn, J. L., & Hofer, S. M. (1992). Major abilities and development in the adult. In R. J. Sternberg & C. A. Berg (Eds.), *Intellectual development.* Cambridge, UK: Cambridge University Press.

Horne, J. (2000). Neuroscience: Images of lost sleep. *Nature, 403,* 605–606.

Horowitz, F. D. (2000). Child development and the PITS: Simple questions, complex answers, and developmental theory. *Child Development, 71*(1), 1–10.

Horvath, T. B., & Davis, K. L. (1990). Central nervous system disorders in aging. In E. L. Schneider & J. W. Rowe (Eds.), *The handbook of the biology of aging* (3rd ed., pp. 306–329). San Diego: Academic.

Horwitz, A. V., White, H. R., & Howell-White, S. (1996). Becoming married and mental health: A longitudinal study of a cohort of young adults. *Journal of Marriage and the Family, 58,* 895–907.

Horwitz, B., Rumsey, J. M., & Donohue, B. C. (1998). Functional connectivity of the angular gyrus in normal reading and dyslexia. *Proceedings of the National Academy of Sciences USA, 95,* 8939–8944.

Horwood, L. J., & Fergusson, D. M. (1998). Breastfeeding and child achievement. *Pediatrics* [On-line], *101*(1). Available: http://www.pediatrics.org/cgi/content/full/101/1/e9[1998, January 5]

House, S. J., Landis, K. R., & Umberson, D. (1988). Social relationships and health. *Science, 241,* 540–544.

Householder, J., Hatcher, R., Burns, W., & Chasnoff, I. (1982). Infants born to narcotics-addicted mothers. *Psychological Bulletin, 92,* 453–468.

How to raise HDL. (2001, December). *University of California, Berkeley Wellness Letter, 18*(3), p. 3.

Howes, C., & Matheson, C. C. (1992). Sequences in the development of competent play with peers: Social and social pretend play. *Developmental Psychology, 28,* 961–974.

Howes, C., Matheson, C. C., & Hamilton, C. E. (1994). Maternal, teacher, and child care history correlates of children's relationships with peers. *Child Development, 65,* 264–273.

Hoyer, W. J., & Rybash, J. M. (1994). Characterizing adult cognitive development. *Journal of Adult Development, 1*(1), 7–12.

Hoyert, D. L., Kochanek, K. D., & Murphy, S. L. (1999). Deaths: Final data for 1997 (*National Vital Statistics Reports, 47*[19]). Hyattsville, MD: National Center for Health Statistics.

Hoyert, D. L., & Rosenberg, H. M. (1999). Mortality from Alzheimer's Disease: An update (*National Vital Statistics Reports, 47*[20]). Hyattsville, MD: National Center for Health Statistics.

Hoyert, D. L., Arias, E., Smith, B. L., Murphy, S. L., & Kochanek, K. D. (2001). Deaths: Final data for 1999. *National Vital Statistics Reports, 49*(8). Hyattsville, MD: National Center for Health Statistics.

Hoyert, D. L., Freedman, M. A., Strobino, D. M., & Guyer, B. (2001). Annual summary of vital statistics: 2000. *Pediatrics, 108*(6), 1241–1255.

Hoyert, D. L., Kochanek, K. D., & Murphy, S. L. (1999). Deaths: Final data for 1997 (*National Vital Statistics Reports, 47*[19]). Hyattsville, MD: National Center for Health Statistics.

Hu, F. B., Manson, J. E., Stampfer, M. J., Colditz, G., Liu, S., Solomon, C. G., & Willett, W. C. (2001). Diet, lifestyle, and the risk of type 2 diabetes mellitus in women. *New England Journal of Medicine, 345,* 790–797.

Hu, S., Pattatucci, A. M. L., Patterson, C., Li, L., Fulker, D. W., Cherny, S. S., Kruglyak, L., & Hamer, D. H. (1995). Linkage between sexual orientation and chromosome Xq28 in males but not in females. *Nature Genetics, 11,* 248–256.

Huang, G. G. (1995). Self-reported biliteracy and self-esteem: A study of Mexican American 8th graders. *Applied Psycholinguistics, 16,* 271–291.

Hubbard, F. O. A., & van IJzendoorn, M. H. (1991). Maternal unresponsiveness and infant crying across the first 9 months: A naturalistic longitudinal study. *Infant Behavior and Development, 14,* 299–312.

Hudnall, C. E. (2001, November). "Grand" parents get help: Programs aid aging caregivers and youngsters. *AARP Bulletin,* pp. 9, 12–13.

Hudson, J. I., & Pope, H. G. (1990). Affective spectrum disorder: Does antidepressant response identify a family of disorders with a common pathophysiology? *American Journal of Psychiatry, 147*(5), 552–564.

Huesmann, L. R., & Eron, L. D. (1984). Cognitive processes and the persistence of aggressive behavior. *Aggressive Behavior, 10,* 243–251.

Huesmann, L. R. (1986). Psychological processes promoting the relation between exposure to media violence and aggressive behavior by the viewer. *Journal of Social Issues, 42,* 125–139.

Huesmann, L. R., & Eron, L. D. (1986). *Television and the aggressive child: A cross-national perspective.* Hillsdale, NJ: Erlbaum.

Hughes, C., & Cutting, A. L. (1999). Nature, nurture, and individual differences in early understanding of mind. *Psychological Science, 10,* 429–432.

Hughes, J. R., Goldstein, M. G., Hurt, R. D., & Shiffman, S. (1999). Recent advances in the pharmacotherapy of smoking. *Journal of the American Medical Association, 281,* 72–76.

Hughes, M. (1975). *Egocentrism in preschool children.* Unpublished doctoral dissertation, Edinburgh University, Edinburgh, Scotland.

Hulley, S., Furberg, C., Barrett-Connor, E., Cauley, J., Grady, D., Haskell, W., Knopp, R., Lowery, M., Satterfield, S., Schrott, H., Vittinghoff, E., & Hunninghake, D. (2002). Noncardiovascular disease outcomes during 6.8 years of hormone therapy. *Journal of the American Medical Association, 288,* 58–66.

Hultsch, D. F. (1971). Organization and memory in adulthood. *Human Development, 14,* 16–29.

Hultsch, D. F., Hertzog, C., Small, B. J., & Dixon, R. A. (1999). Use it or lose it: Engaged lifestyle as a buffer of cognitive decline in aging? *Psychology and Aging, 14,* 245–263.

Humphrey, L. L. (1986). Structural analysis of parent-child relationships in eating disorders. *Journal of Abnormal Psychology, 95*(4), 395–402.

Humphreys, A. P., & Smith, P. K. (1984). Rough-and-tumble in preschool and playground. In P. K. Smith (Ed.), *Play in animals and humans.* Oxford: Blackwell.

Humphreys, G. W. (2002). Cognitive neuroscience. In H. Pashler, & D. Medin, (Eds.), Steven's handbook of experimental psychology (3rd ed.), Vol. 2: Memory and cognitive processes. (pp. 77–112). New York, NY, US: John Wiley & Sons, Inc.

Hungerford, T. L. (2001). The economic consequences of widowhood on elderly women in the United States and Germany. *The Gerontologist, 41,* 103–110.

Hunsaker, S. L., & Callahan, C. M. (1995). Creativity and giftedness: Published instrument uses and abuses. *Gifted Child Quarterly, 39*(2), 110–114.

Hunt, C. E. (1996). Prone sleeping in healthy infants and victims of sudden infant death syndrome. *Journal of Pediatrics, 128,* 594–596.

Huntsinger, C. S., & Jose, P. E. (1995). Chinese American and Caucasian American family interaction patterns in spatial rotation puzzle solutions. *Merrill-Palmer Quarterly, 41,* 471–496.

Huntsinger, C. S., Jose, P. E., & Larson, S. L. (1998). Do parent practices to encourage academic competence influence the social adjustment of young European American and Chinese American children? *Developmental Psychology, 34*(4), 747–756.

Huston, A., Donnerstein, E., Fairchild, H., Feshbach, N. D., Katz, P. A., Murray, J. P., Rubenstein, E. A., Wilcox, B. L., & Zuckerman, D. (1992). *Big world, small screen: The role of television in American society.* Lincoln: University of Nebraska Press.

Huston, H. C., Duncan, G. J., Granger, R., Bos, J., McLoyd, V., Mistry, R., Crosby, D., Gibson, C., Magnuson, K., Romich, J., and Ventura, A. (2001). Work-based antipoverty programs for parents can enhance the performance and social behavior of children. *Child Development, 72*(1), 318–336.

Huttenlocher, J. (1998). Language input and language growth. *Preventive Medicine, 27,* 195–199.

Huttenlocher, J., Haight, W., Bryk, A., Seltzer, M., & Lyons, T. (1991). Early vocabulary growth: Relation to language input and gender. *Developmental Psychology, 27,* 236–248.

Huttenlocher, J., Levine, S., & Vevea, J. (1998). Environmental input and cognitive growth: A study using time-period comparisons. *Child Development, 69,* 1012–1029.

Huttenlocher, J., Newcombe, N., & Vasilyeva, M. (1999). Spatial scaling in young children. *Psychological Science, 10,* 393–398.

Huttenlocher, J., Vasilyeva, M., Cymerman, E., & Levine, S. (2002). Language input and child syntax. *Cognitive Psychology, 45,* 337–374.

Huyck, M. H. (1990). Gender differences in aging. In J. E. Birren & K. W. Schaie (Eds.), *Handbook of the psychology of aging* (3rd ed., pp. 124–132). San Diego: Academic Press.

Huyck, M. H. (1995). Marriage and close relationships of the marital kind. In R. Blieszner & V. Hilkevitch (Eds.), *Handbook of aging and the family* (pp. 181–200). Westport, CT: Greenwood Press.

Huyck, M. H. (1999). Gender roles and gender identity in midlife. In S. L. Willis & J. D. Reid (Eds.), *Life in the middle: Psychological and social development in middle age* (pp. 209–232). New York: Academic.

Hwang, S. J., Beaty, T. H., Panny, S. R., Street, N. A., Joseph, J. M., Gordon, S., McIntosh, I., & Francomano, C. A. (1995). Association study of transforming growth factor alpha (TGFa) TaqI polymorphism and oral clefts: Indication of gene-environment interaction in a population-based sample of infants with birth defects. *American Journal of Epidemiology, 141,* 629–636.

Hyman, S. L., Rodier, P. M., & Davidson, P. (2001). Pervasive developmental disorders in young children. *Journal of the American Medical Association, 285,* 3141–3142.

Ialongo, N. S., Edelsohn, G., & Kellam, S. G. (2001). A further look at the prognostic power of young children's reports of depressed mood and feelings. *Child Development, 72,* 736–747.

Iervolino, A. C., Pike, A., Manke, B., Reiss, D., Hetherington, E. M., & Plomin, R. (2002). Genetic and environmental influences in adolescent peer socialization: Evidence from two genetically sensitive designs. *Child Development, 73*(1), 162–174.

Iglowstein, I., Jenni, O. G., Molinari, L., & Largo, R. H. (2003). Sleep duration from infancy to adolescence: Reference values and generational trends. *Pediatrics, 111,* 302–307.

Ikeda, R., Mahendra, R., Saltzman, L., Crosby, A., Willis, L., Mercy, J., Holmgreen, P., & Annest, J. L. (2002). Nonfatal self-inflicted injuries treated in hospital departments, United States, 2000. *Morbidity and Mortality Weekly Report 51,* 436–438.

Impagnatiello, F., Guidotti, A. R., Pesold, C., Dwivedi, Y., Caruncho, H., Pisu, M. G., Uzonov, D. P., Smalheiser, N. R., Davis, J. M., Pandey, G. N., Pappas, G. D., Tueting, P., Sharma, R. P., & Costa, E. (1998). A decrease of reelin expression as a putative vulnerability factor in schizophrenia. *Proceedings of the National Academy of Science, 95,* 15718–15723.

Infant Health and Development Program (IHDP). (1990). Enhancing the outcomes of low-birth-weight, premature infants. *Journal of the American Medical Association, 263*(22), 3035–3042.

Infante-Rivard, C., Fernández, A., Gauthier, R., David, M., & Rivard, G. E. (1993). Fetal loss associated with caffeine intake before and during pregnancy. *Journal of the American Medical Association, 270,* 2940–2943.

Ingersoll, E. W., & Thoman, E. B. (1999). Sleep/wake states of preterm infants: Stability, developmental change, diurnal variation, and relation with caregiving activity. *Child Development, 70,* 1–10.

Ingoldsby, B. B. (1995). Mate selection and marriage. In B. B. Ingoldsby & S. Smith (Eds.), *Families in multicultural perspective* (pp.143–160). New York: Guilford.

Ingram, J. L., Stodgell, C. S., Hyman, S. L., Figlewicz, D. A., Weitkamp, L. R., & Rodier, P. M. (2000). Discovery of allelic variants of HOXA1 and HOXB1: Genetic susceptibility to autism spectrum disorders. *Teratology, 62,* 393–406.

Institute of Medicine (IOM) National Academy of Sciences. (1993, November). *Assessing genetic risks: Implications for health and social policy.* Washington, DC: National Academy of Sciences.

International Agency for Cancer Research. (2002). Second-hand smoke carcinogenic to humans. Monographs Programme of the International Agency for Research on Cancer. Lyon, France: World Health Organization.

International Longevity Center-USA. (2002). Is there an anti-aging medicine? ILC Workshop Report. On-line. Available at http://www.il cusa.org

International Perinatal HIV Group. (1999). The mode of delivery and the risk of vertical transmission of human immunodeficiency virus type 1: A meta-analysis of 15 prospective cohort studies. *New England Journal of Medicine, 340,* 977–987.

Isabella, R. A. (1993). Origins of attachment: Maternal interactive behavior across the first year. *Child Development, 64,* 605–621.

Ishii, N., Fujii, M., Hartman, P. S., Tsuda, M., Yasuda, K., Senoo-Matsuda, N., Yanase, S., Ayusawa, D., & Suzuki, K. (1998). A mutation in succinate dehydrogenase cytochrome b causes oxidative stress and ageing in nematodes. *Nature, 394,* 694–697.

Isley, S., O'Neil, R., & Parke, R. (1996). The relation of parental affect and control behaviors to children's classroom acceptance: A concurrent and predictive analysis. *Early Education and Development, 7,* 7–23.

Iverson, J. M., & Goldin-Meadow, S. (1998). Why people gesture when they speak. *Nature, 396,* 228.

Ivy, G. O., MacLeod, C. M., Petit, T. L., & Markus, E. J. (1992). A physiological framework for perceptual and cognitive changes in aging. In F. I. M. Craik & T. A. Salthouse (Eds.), *Handbook of aging and cognition* (pp. 273–314). Hillsdale, NJ: Erlbaum.

Izard, C. E., Huebner, R. R., Resser, D., McGinness, G. C., & Dougherty, L. M. (1980). The young infant's ability to produce discrete emotional expressions. *Developmental Psychology, 16,* 132–140.

Izard, C. E., Porges, S. W., Simons, R. F., Haynes, O. M., & Cohen, B. (1991). Infant cardiac activity: Developmental changes and relations with attachment. *Developmental Psychology, 27,* 432–439.

Jack, C. R., Jr., Petersen, R. C., Xu, Y. C., O'Brien, P. C., Smith, G. E., Ivnik, R. J., Boeve, B. F., Waring, S. C., Tangalos, E. G., Kokmen, E. (1999). Prediction of AD with MRI-based hippocampal volume in mild cognitive impairment. *Neurology, 22,* 1397–1403.

Jack, C. R., Jr., Petersen, R. C., Xu, Y., O'Brien, P. C., Smith, G. E., Ivnik, R. J., Tangalos, E. G., & Kokmen, E. (1998). Rate of medial temporal lobe atrophy in typical aging and Alzheimer's disease. *Neurology, 51,* 993–999.

Jackson, R. S., Creemers, J. W. M., Ohagi, S., Raffin-Sanson, M. L., Sanders, L., Montague, C. T., Hutton, J. C., & O'Rahilly, S. (1997). Obesity and impaired prohormone processing associated with mutations in the human prohormone convertase 1 gene. *Nature Genetics, 16,* 303–306.

Jacobsen, T., & Hofmann, V. (1997). Children's attachment representations: Longitudinal relations to school behavior and academic competency in middle childhood and adolescence. *Developmental Psychology, 33,* 703–710.

Jacobson, J. L., & Wille, D. E. (1986). The influence of attachment pattern on developmental changes in peer interaction from the toddler to the preschool period. *Child Development, 57,* 338–347.

Jacobson, M. W., Delis, D. C., Bondi, M. W., & Salmon, D. P. (2002). Do neuropsychological tests detect preclinical Alzheimer's disease?: Individual-test versus cognitive-discrepancy score analyses. *Neuropsychology, 16,* 132–139.

Jacobson, S. W., Chiodo, L. M., & Jacobson, J. L. (1999). Breast-feeding effects on intelligence quotient in 4- and 11-year-old children. 103, (5). [Online]. Available: http://www.pediatrics.org/cgi/content/full/103/s/e71

Jacques, E. (1967). The mid-life crisis. In R. Owen (Ed.), *Middle age.* London: BBC.

Jaffee, S., & Hyde, J. S. (2000). Gender differences in moral orientation: A meta-analysis. *Psychological Bulletin, 126,* 703–725.

Jagers, R. J., Bingham, K., & Hans, S. L. (1996). Socialization and social judgments among inner-city African-American kindergartners. *Child Development, 67,* 140–150.

Jain, A., Concato, J., & Leventhal, J. M. (2002). How good is the evidence linking breastfeeding and intelligence? *Pediatrics, 109,* 1044–1053.

James, J. B., & Lewkowicz, C. J. (1997). Themes of power and affiliation across time. In M. E. Lachman & J. B. James (Eds.), *Multiple paths of midlife development* (pp. 109–143). Chicago: University of Chicago Press.

James, W. (1950). *The principles of psychology* (2 vols.). New York: Dover. (Original work published 1890)

Jankowiak, W. (1992). Father-child relations in urban China. *Father-child relations: Cultural and bisocial contexts* (pp. 345–363). New York: de Gruyter.

Jankowski, J. J., Rose, S. A., & Feldman, J. F. (2001). Modifying the distribution of attention in infants. *Child Development, 72,* 339–351.

Janowsky, J. S., & Carper, R. (1996). Is there a neural basis for cognitive transitions in school-age children? In A. J. Sameroff & M. M. Haith (Eds.), *The five to seven year shift: The age of reason and responsibility* (pp. 33–56). Chicago: University of Chicago Press.

Jarrell, R. H. (1998). Play and its influence on the development of young children's mathematical thinking. In D. P. Fromberg & D. Bergen (Eds.), *Play from birth to twelve and beyond: Contexts, perspectives, and meanings* (pp. 56–67). New York: Garland.

Jaslow, C. K. (1982). *Teenage pregnancy* (ERIC/CAPS Fact Sheet). Ann Arbor, MI: Counseling and Personnel Services Clearing House.

Jefferson, J. W., & Greist, J. H. (1993). *Depression and older people: Recognizing hidden signs and taking steps toward recovery.* Madison, WI: Pratt Pharmaceuticals.

Jeffords, J. M., & Daschle, T. (2001). Political issues in the genome era. *Science, 291,* 1249–1251.

Jensen, A. R. (1969). How much can we boost IQ and scholastic achievement? *Harvard Educational Review, 39,* 1–123.

Jeynes, W. H., & Littell, S. W. (2000). A meta-analysis of studies examining the effect of whole language instruction on the literacy of low-SES students. *Elementary School Journal, 101,* 21–33.

Ji, B. T., Shu, X. O., Linet, M. S., Zheng, W., Wacholder, S., Gao, Y. T., Ying, D. M., & Jin, F. (1997). Paternal cigarette smoking and the risk of childhood cancer among offspring of nonsmoking mothers. *Journal of the National Cancer Institute, 89,* 238–244.

Jiao, S., Ji, G., & Jing, Q. (1996). Cognitive development of Chinese urban only children and children with siblings. *Child Development, 67,* 387–395.

Jimerson, S., Egeland, B., & Teo, A. (1999). A longitudinal study of achievement trajectories: Factors associated with change. *Journal of Educational Psychology, 91*(1), 116–126.

Jodl, K. M., Michael, A., Malanchuk, O., Eccles, J. S., & Sameroff, A. (2001). Parents' roles in shaping early adolescents' occupational aspirations. *Child Development, 72*(4), 1247–1265.

Johansson, G., Evans, G. W., Rydstedt, L. W., & Carrere, S. (1998). Job hassles and cardiovascular reaction patterns among urban bus drivers. *International Journal of Behavioral Medicine, 5,* 267–280.

Johnson, C. L. (1995). Cultural diversity in the late-life family. In R. Blieszner & V. Hilkevitch (Eds.), *Handbook of aging and the family* (pp. 307–331). Westport, CT: Greenwood Press.

Johnson, C. L., & Catalano, D. J. (1981). Childless elderly and their family supports. *The Gerontologist, 21*(6), 610–618.

Johnson, C. L., & Troll, L. (1992). Family-functioning in late late life. *Journal of Gerontology: Social Sciences, 47*(2), S66–72.

Johnson, C. L., & Troll, L. E. (1994). Constraints and facilitators to friendships in late late life. *The Gerontologist, 34,* 79–87.

Johnson, D. W., Johnson, R. T., & Tjosvold, D. (2000). Constructive controversy: The value of intellectual opposition. In M. Deutsch & P. T. Coleman (Eds.), *The handbook of conflict resolution: Theory and practice* (pp. 65–85). San Francisco: Jossey-Bass.

Johnson, J. E. (1998). Play development from ages four to eight. In D. P. Fromberg & D. Bergen (Eds.), *Play from birth to twelve and beyond: Contexts, perspectives, and meanings* (pp. 145–153). New York: Garland.

Johnson, J. G., Cohen, P., Smailes, E. M., Kasen, S., & Brook, J. S. (2002). Television viewing and aggressive behavior during adolescence and adulthood. *Science, 295,* 2468–2471.

Johnson, J., Stewart, W., Hall, E., Fredlund, P., & Theorell, T. (1996). Long-term psychosocial work environment and cardiovascular mortality among Swedish men. *American Journal of Public Health, 86,* 324–331.

Johnson, M. H. (1998). The neural basis of cognitive development. In D. Kuhn & R. S. Siegler (Eds.), *Handbook of child psychology: Vol. 2. Cognition, perception, and language* (5th ed., pp. 1–49). New York: Wiley.

Johnson, M. H. (1999). Developmental cognitive neuroscience. In M. Bennett, (Ed.), Developmental psychology: Achievements and prospects. (pp. 147–164). Philadelphia, PA., US: Psychology Press/Taylor & Francis.

Johnson, M. M. S. (1990). Age differences in decision making: A process methodology for examining strategic information processing. *Journal of Gerontology, Psychological Sciences, 45,* P75–78.

Johnson, M. M. S., Schmitt, F. A., & Everard, K. (1994). *Task driven strategies: The impact of age and information on decision-making performance.* Unpublished manuscript, University of Kentucky, Lexington.

Johnson, M. O. (1996). Television violence and its effect on children. *Journal of Pediatric Nursing, 11,* 94–98.

Johnson, M. H. (2001). Functional brain development during infancy. In G. Bremner, & A. Fogel, (Eds.), Handbooks of developmental psychology: Blackwell handbook of infant development. (pp. 169–190). Malden, MA, US: Blackwell Publishers.

Johnson, R. A., Hoffmann, J. P., & Gerstein, D. R. (1996). *The relationship between family structure and adolescent substance use* (DHHS Publication No. SMA 96–3086). Washington, DC: U.S. Department of Health and Human Services.

Johnson, S. J., & Rybash, J. M. (1993). A cognitive neuroscience perspective on age-related slowing: Developmental changes in the functional architecture. In J. Cerella, J. M. Rybash, W. J. Hoyer, & M. L. Commons (Eds.), *Adult information processing: Limits on loss* (pp. 143–175). San Diego: Academic Press.

Johnson, S. L. (2000). Improving preschoolers' self-regulation of energy intake. *Pediatrics, 106,* 1429–1435.

Johnson, S. L., & Birch, L. L. (1994). Parents' and children's adiposity and eating styles. *Pediatrics, 94,* 653–661.

Johnson, T. E. (1990). Age-1 mutants of Caenorhabditis elegans prolong life by modifying the Gompertz rate of aging. *Science, 229,* 908–912.

Johnston, J., & Ettema, J. S. (1982). *Positive images: Breaking stereotypes with children's television.* Newbury Park, CA: Sage.

Johnston, L. D., O'Malley, P. M., & Bachman, J. G. (2000). *Monitoring the future results on adolescent drug use. Overview of key findings 1999.* USDHSS, PHS, NIDA, NIH Publication number 00-490. Bethesda, MD: National Institute on Drug Abuse.

Johnston, L. D., O'Malley, P. M., & Bachman, J. G. (2001). Rise in ecstasy use among American teens begins to slow. University of Michigan News and Information Services: Ann Arbor, MI. [Online]. Available: www.monitoringthe future.org Access date: 12/19/01.

Johnston, L. D., O'Malley, P. M., & Bachman, J. G. (2002a, December 16). *Ecstasy use among American teens drops for the first time in recent years, and overall drug and alcohol use also decline in the year after 9/11.* Ann Arbor, MI: University of Michigan News and Information Services. [Online]. Available: http://www.monitoringthefuture.org. Access date December 20, 2002.

Johnston, L. D., O'Malley, P. M., & Bachman, J. G. (2002b). *Monitoring the future national results on adolescent drug use: Overview of key findings, 2001.* NIH Publication No. 02-5105. Bethesda MD: National Institute on Drug Abuse.

Johnston, P. (2001, April 10). Dutch make euthanasia legal. *Chicago Sun-Times,* p. 22.

Jones, C. L., Tepperman, L., & Wilson, S. J. (1995). *The future of the family.* Englewood Cliffs, NJ: Prentice-Hall.

Jones, D. C., Swift, D. J., & Johnson, M. A. (1988). Nondeliberate memory for a novel event among preschoolers. *Developmental Psychology, 24,* 641–645.

Jones, H. W., & Toner, J. P. (1993). The infertile couple. *New England Journal of Medicine, 329,* 1710–1715.

Jones, N. A., Field, T., Fox, N. A., Davalos, M., Lundy, B., & Hart, S. (1998). Newborns of mothers with depressive symptoms are physiologically less developed. *Infant Behavior & Development, 21*(3), 537–541.

Jones, N. A., Field, T., Fox, N. A., Lundy, B., & Davalos, M. (1997). *EEG activation in one-month-old infants of depressed mothers.* Unpublished manuscript, Touch Research Institute, University of Miami School of Medicine.

Jones, S. S. (1996). Imitation or exploration? Young infants' matching of adults' oral gestures. *Child Development, 67,* 1952–1969.

Jones, X., McGrattan, E., Manuelli, R. (2002, January). *Why are married women working so much?* Paper presented at the American Economic Association annual meeting in Atlanta.

Jonides, J., Marshuetz, C., Smith, E. E., Reuter-Lorenz, P. A., Koeppe, R. A., & Hartley, A. J. (2000). Age differences in behavior and PET activation reveal differences in interference resolution in verbal working memory. *Journal of Cognitive Neuroscience, 12,* 188–196.

Jonsson, P. (2001, July 2). Latest battle over the unborn: S. Carolina goes after pregnant drug users, *Chicago Sun-Times,* p. 4.

Jordan, B. (1993). *Birth in four cultures: A crosscultural investigation of childbirth in Yucatan, Holland, Sweden, and the United States* (4th ed.). Prospect Heights, IL: Waveland Press. (Original work published 1978)

Joshipura, K. J., Ascherio, A., Manson, J. E., Stampfer, M. H., Rim, E. B., Speizer, F. E., Hennekens, C. H., Spiegleman, D., & Willett, W. C. (1999). Fruit and vegetable intake in relation to risk of ischemic stroke. *Journal of the American Medical Association, 282,* 1233–1239.

Jouriles, E. N., & Norwood, W. D. (1995). Physical aggression toward boys and girls in families characterized by the battering of women. *Journal of Family Psychology, 9*(1), 69–78.

Jung, C. G. (1933). *Modern man in search of a soul.* New York: Harcourt Brace.

Jung, C. G. (1953). The stages of life. In H. Read, M. Fordham, & G. Adler (Eds.), *Collected works* (Vol. 2). Princeton, NJ: Princeton University Press. (Original work published 1931)

Jung, C. G. (1966). Two essays on analytic psychology. In *Collected works* (Vol. 7). Princeton, NJ: Princeton University Press.

Jung, C. G. (1969). *The structure and dynamics of the psyche.* Princeton, NJ: Princeton University Press.

Jung, C. G. (1971). Aion: Phenomenology of the self (the ego, the shadow, the syzgy:Anima/animus). In J. Campbell (Ed.), *The portable Jung.* New York: Viking Penguin.

Jusczyk, P. W. (2003). The role of speech perception capacities in early language acquisition. In M. T. Banich & M. Mack (Eds.), *Mind, brain, and language: Multidisciplinary perspectives.* Mahwah, NJ: Erlbaum.

Jusczyk, P. W., & Hohne, E. A. (1997). Infants' memory for spoken words. *Science, 277,* 1984–1986.

Jussim, L., Eccles, J., & Madon, S. (1996). Social perception, social stereotypes, and teacher expectations: Accuracy and the quest for the powerful self-fulfilling prophecy. In M. P. Zanna (Ed.), *Advances in experimental social psychology* (Vol. 28, pp. 281–388). San Diego: Academic.

Juul-Dam, N., Townsend, J. & Courchesne, E. (2001). Prenatal, perinatal, and neonatal factors in autism, pervasive developmental disorder-not otherwise specified, and the general population. *Pediatrics, 107*(4), p. e63.

Kaback, M., Lim-Steele, J., Dabholkar, D., Brown, D., Levy, N., & Zeiger, K., for the International TSD Data Collection Network. (1993). Tay-Sachs disease—Carrier screening, prenatal diagnosis, and the molecular era. *Journal of the American Medical Association, 270,* 2307–2315.

Kadlubar, F. F., et al. (2001, April). Kadlubar, F., Berkowitz, G., Delongchamp, R., Green, B., Wang, C., & Wolff, M. (2001). The putative high activity variant, CYP3A*1B, predicts the onset of puberty in young girls. *Proceedings of the American Association for Cancer Research, 12,* 2198.

Kagan, J. (1997). Temperament and the reactions to unfamiliarity. *Child Development, 68,* 139–143.

Kagan, J., & Snidman, N. (1991a). Infant predictors of inhibited and uninhibited behavioral profiles. *Psychological Science, 2,* 40–44.

Kagan, J., & Snidman, N. (1991b). Temperamental factors in human development. *American Psychologist, 46,* 856–862.

Kahana-Kalman, R., & Walker-Andrews, A. S. (2001). The role of person familiarity in young infants' perception of emotional expressions. *Child Development, 72,* 352–369.

Kahn, R. L., & Antonucci, T. C. (1980). Convoys over the life course: Attachment, roles, and social support. In P. B. Baltes & O. G. Brim, Jr. (Eds.), *Life-span development and behavior* (pp. 253–286). New York: Academic Press.

Kail, R. (1991). Processing time declines exponentially during childhood and adolescence. *Developmental Psychology, 27,* 259–266.

Kail, R. (1997). Processing time, imagery, and spatial memory. *Journal of Experimental Child Psychology, 64,* 67–78.

Kail, R., & Park, Y. (1994). Processing time, articulation time, and memory span. *Journal of Experimental Child Psychology, 57,* 281–291.

Kalish, C. W. (1998). Young children's predictions of illness: Failure to recognize probabilistic cause. *Developmental Psychology, 34*(5), 1046–1058.

Kalmuss, D. S., & Straus, M. A. (1982). Wife's marital dependency and wife abuse. *Journal of Marriage and the Family, 44,* 277–286.

Kamerman, S. B. (2000). Parental leave policies: An essential ingredient in early childhood education and care policies. *Social Policy Report, 14*(2), 3–15.

Kamin, L. J. (1974). *The science and politics of IQ.* Potomac, MD: Erlbaum.

Kamin, L. J. (1981). Commentary. In S. Scarr (Ed.), *Race, social class, and individual differences in I.Q.* Hillsdale, NJ: Erlbaum.

Kaplan, H., & Dove, H. (1987). Infant development among the Ache of East Paraguay. *Developmental Psychology, 23,* 190–198.

Kaplowitz, P. B. , Oberfield, S. E., & the Drug and Therapeutics and Executive Committees of the Lawson Wilkins Pediatric Endocrine Society. (1999). Reexamination of the age limit for defining when puberty is precocious in girls in the United States: Implications for evaluation and treatment. *Pediatrics, 104,* 936–941.

Kaplowitz, P. B., Slora, E. J., Wasserman, R. C., Pedlow, S. E., & Herman-Giddens, M. E. (2001). Earlier onset of puberty in girls: Relation to increased body mass index and race. *Pediatrics, 108*(2), 347–353.

Karlinsky, H., Lennox, A., & Rossor, M. (1994). Alzheimer's disease and genetic testing. *Alzheimer's Disease and Associated Disorders, 8*(2), 63–65.

Karney, B. R., & Bradbury, T. N. (1995). The longitudinal course of marital quality and stability: A review of theory, method, and research. *Psychological Bulletin, 118,* 3–34.

Katchadourian, H. (1987). *Fifty: Midlife in perspective.* New York: Freeman.

Katzman, R. (1993). Education and prevalence of Alzheimer's disease. *Neurology, 43,* 13–20.

Kaufman, A. S., & Kaufman, N. L. (1983). *Kaufman assessment battery for children: Administration and scoring manual.* Circle Pines, MN: American Guidance Service.

Kaufman, J., & Zigler, E. (1987). Do abused children become abusive parents? *American Journal of Orthopsychiatry, 57*(2), 186–192.

Kaufman, T. S. (1993). *The combined family: A guide to creating successful step-relationships.* New York: Plenum.

Kausler, D. H. (1990). Automaticity of encoding and episodic memory-processes. In E. A. Lovelace (Ed.), *Aging and cognition: Mental processes, self-awareness, and interventions* (pp. 29–67). Amsterdam: North-Holland, Elsevier.

Kawachi, I., Colditz, G. A., Ascherio, A., Rimm, E. B., Giovannucci, E., Stampfer, M. J., & Willett, W. C. (1994). Prospective study of phobic anxiety and risk of coronary heart disease in men. *Circulation, 89,* 1992–1997.

Kawachi, I., Colditz, G. A., Ascherio, A., Rimm, E. B., Giovannucci, E., Stampfer, M. J., & Willett, W. C. (1996). A prospective study of social networks in relation to total mortality and cardiovascular disease in men in the USA. *Journal of Epidemiology and Community Health, 50,* 245–251.

Kawachi, I., Colditz, G. A., Stampfer, M. J., Willett, W. C., Manson, J. E., Rosner, B., Speizer, F. E., & Hennekens, C. H. (1993). Smoking cessation and decreased risk of stroke in women. *Journal of the American Medical Association, 269,* 232–236.

Kawachi, I., Colditz, G. A., Stampfer, M. J., Willett, W. C., Manson, J. E., Speizer, F. E., & Hennekens, C. H. (1995). Prospective study of shift work and risk of coronary heart disease in women. *Circulation, 92,* 3178–3182.

Kawachi, I., Sparrow, D., Vokonas, P. S., & Weiss, S. T. (1994). Symptoms of anxiety and risk of coronary heart disease: The Normative Aging Study. *Circulation, 90,* 2225–2229.

Kaye, W. H., Weltzin, T. E., Hsu, L. K. G., & Bulik, C. M. (1991). An open trial of fluoxetine in patients with anorexia nervosa. *Journal of Clinical Psychiatry, 52,* 464–471.

Keating, N. L., Cleary, P. D., Rossi, A. S., Zaslavsky, A. M., & Ayanian, J. Z. (1999). Use of hormone replacement therapy by postmenopausal women in the United States. *Annals of Internal Medicine, 130,* 545–553.

Keegan, R. T. (1996). Creativity from childhood to adulthood: A difference of degree and not of kind. *New Directions for Child Development, 72,* 57–66.

Keegan, R. T., & Gruber, H. E. (1985). Charles Darwin's unpublished "Diary of an Infant": An early phase in his psychological work. In G. Eckardt, W. G. Bringmann, & L. Sprung (Eds.), *Contributions to a history of developmental psychology: International William T. Preyer Symposium* (pp. 127–145). Berlin, Germany: Walter de Gruyter.

Keel, P. K., & Mitchell, J. E. (1997). Outcome in bulimia nervosa. *American Journal of Psychiatry, 154,* 313–321.

Keenan, K., & Shaw, D. (1997). Developmental and social influences on young girls' early problem behavior. *Psychological Bulletin, 121*(1), 95–113.

Keeney, T. J., Canizzo, S. R., & Flavell, J. H. (1967). Spontaneous and induced verbal rehearsal in a recall task. *Child Development, 38,* 953–966.

Keightley, P. D., & Eyre-Walker, A. (2001). Response to Kondrashov. *Trends in Genetics, 17*(2), 77–78.

Keith, P. M. (1983). A comparison of the resources of parents and childless men and women in very old age. *Family Relations, 32,* 403–409.

Kelleher, K. J., Casey, P. H., Bradley, R. H., Pope, S. K., Whiteside, L., Barrett, K. W., Swanson, M. E., & Kirby, R. S. (1993). Risk factors and outcomes for failure to thrive in low birth weight preterm infants. *Pediatrics, 91,* 941–948.

Keller, A. (2000). *Marian Anderson: A singer's journey.* New York: Scribner.

Kelley, M. L., Smith, T. S., Green, A. P., Berndt, A. E., & Rogers, M. C. (1998). Importance of fathers' parenting to African-American toddler's social and cognitive development. *Infant Behavior & Development, 21,* 733–744.

Kellogg, R. (1970). Understanding children's art. In P. Cramer (Ed.), *Readings in developmental psychology today.* Delmar, CA: CRM.

Kelly, J. R. (1987). *Peoria winter: Styles and resources in later life.* Lexington, MA: Lexington.

Kelly, J. R. (1994). Recreation and leisure. In A. Monk (Ed.), *The Columbia retirement handbook* (pp. 489–508). New York: Columbia University Press.

Kelly, J. R., Steinkamp, M., & Kelly, J. (1986). Later life leisure: How they play in Peoria. *The Gerontologist, 26,* 531–537.

Kemp. J. S., Unger, B., Wilkins, D., Psara, R. M., Ledbetter, T. L., Graham, M. A., Case, M., & Thach, B. T. (2000). Unsafe sleep practices and an analysis of bedsharing among infants dying suddenly and unexpectedly: Results of a four-year, population-based, death-scene investigation study of sudden infant death and related syndromes. *Pediatrics, 106*(3), e41.

Kemper, T. L. (1994). Neuroanatomical and neuropathological changes during aging and dementia. In M. L. Albert & J. E. Knoefel (Eds.), *Clinical neurology of aging* (pp. 3–67). New York: Oxford University Press.

Kendall-Tackett, K. A. (1997, July 7). *Postpartum depression and the breastfeeding mother.* Paper presented to the 25th Annual Seminar for Physicians on Breastfeeding, sponsored by La Leche League International, the American Academy of Pediatrics, and the American College of Obstetricians and Gynecologists, Washington, DC.

Kendall-Tackett, K. A., Williams, L. M., & Finkelhor, D. (1993). Impact of sexual abuse on children: A review and synthesis of recent empirical studies. *Psychological Bulletin, 113*(1), 164–180.

Kendler, K. S., MacLean, C., Neale, M., Kessler, R., Heath, A., & Eaves, L. (1991). The genetic epidemiology of bulimia nervosa. *American Journal of Psychiatry, 148,* 1627–1637.

Kendler, K. S., Thornton, L. M., Gilman, S. E., & Kessler, R. C. (2000). Sexual orientation in a U.S. national sample of twin and nontwin sibling pairs. *American Journal of Psychiatry, 157,* 1843–1847.

Keppel, K. G., Pearcy, J. N., & Wagener, D. K. (2002). Trends in racial and ethnic-specific rates for the health status indicators: United States, 1990–1998. *Statistical Notes,* No. 23. Hyattsville, MD: National Center for Health Statistics.

Kernan, M. (1993, June). The object at hand. *Smithsonian,* pp. 14–16.

Kerns, K. A., Don, A., Mateer, C. A., & Streissguth, A. P. (1997). Cognitive deficits in nonretarded adults with fetal alcohol syndrome. *Journal of Learning Disabilities, 30,* 685–693.

Kestenbaum, R., & Gelman, S. A. (1995). Preschool children's identification and understanding of mixed emotions. *Cognitive Development, 10,* 443–458.

Keyes, C. L. M., & Ryff, C. D. (1998). Generativity in adult lives: Social structural contours and quality of life consequences. In D. P. McAdams & E. de St. Aubin (Eds.), *Generativity and adult development* (pp. 227–263). Washington, DC: American Psychological Association.

Keyes, C. L. M., & Ryff, C. D. (1999). Psychological well-being in midlife. In S. L. Willis & J. D. Reid (Eds.), *Life in the middle* (pp. 161–180). San Diego: Academic Press.

Khoury, M. J., McCabe, L. L., & McCabe, E. R. B. (2003). Population screening in the age of genomic medicine. *New England Journal of Medicine, 348,* 50–58.

Kiecolt-Glaser, J. K., & Glaser, R. (1995). Psychoneuroimmunology and health consequences: Data and shared mechanisms. *Psychosomatic Medicine, 57,* 269–274.

Kiecolt-Glaser, J. K., & Glaser, R. (1999). Chronic stress and mortality among older adults. *Journal of the American Medical Association, 282,* 2259–2260.

Kiecolt-Glaser, J. K., & Glaser, R. (2001). Stress and immunity: Age enhances the risks. *Current Directions in Psychological Science, 10,* 18–21.

Kiefe, C. I., Williams, O. D., Weissman, N. W., Schreiner, P. J., Sidney, S., & Wallace, D. D. (2000). Changes in US health care access in the 90s: Race and income differences from the CARDIA study. Coronary Artery Risk Development in Young Adults. *Ethnicity and Disease, 10,* 418–431.

Kiefer, K. M., Summer, L., & Shirey, L. (2001). What are the attitudes of young retirees and older workers? *Data Profiles: Young Retirees and Older Workers, 5.*

Kier, C., & Lewis, C. (1998). Preschool sibling interaction in separated and married families: Are same-sex pairs or older sisters more sociable? *Journal of Child Psychology and Psychiatry, 39,* 191–201.

Kim, J. E., & Moen, P. (2001). Moving into retirement: Preparation and transitions in late midlife. In M. E. Lachman (Ed.), *Handbook of midlife development* (pp. 487–527). New York: Wiley.

Kim, J. E., & Moen, P. (2002). Retirement transitions, gender, and psychological well-being: A life-course, ecological model. *Journal of Gerontology: Psychological Sciences, 57B,* P212–P222.

Kimball, M. M. (1986). Television and sex-role attitudes. In T. M. Williams (Ed.), *The impact of television: A natural experiment in three communities* (pp. 265–301). Orlando, FL: Academic Press.

Kimbrough, R. D., LeVois, M., & Webb, D. R. (1994). Management of children with slightly elevated blood lead levels. *Pediatrics, 93,* 188–191.

Kimmel, D. (1990). *Adulthood and aging: An interdisciplinary, developmental view.* New York: Wiley.

Kimmel, D. C., & Sang, B. E. (1995). Lesbians and gay men in midlife. In A. R. D'Augelli & C. J. Patterson (Eds.), *Lesbian, gay, and bisexual identities over the lifespan: Psychological perspectives* (pp. 190–214). New York: Oxford University Press.

King, B. M. (1996). *Human sexuality today.* Englewood Cliffs, NJ: Prentice-Hall.

King, C., Siegel, M., Celebucki, C., & Connolly, G. N. (1998). Adolescent exposure to cigarette advertising in magazines. *Journal of the American Medical Association, 279,* 1–520.

King, M., Wieand, S., Hale, K., Lee, M., Walsh, T., Owens, K., Tait, J., Ford, L., Dunn, B. K., Costantino, J., Wickerham, L., Wolmark, N., & Fisher, B. (2001). Tamoxifen and breast cancer incidence among women with inherited mutations in BRCA1 and BRCA2. *Journal of the American Medical Association, 286,* 2251–2256.

Kinney, H. C., Filiano, J. J., Sleeper, L. A., Mandell, F., Valdes-Dapena, M., & White, W. F. (1995). Decreased muscarinic receptor binding in the arcuate nucleus in Sudden Infant Death Syndrome. *Science, 269,* 1446–1450.

Kinsella, K., & Gist, Y. J. (1995). *Older workers, retirement, and pensions: A comparative international chartbook* (International Population Center Report IPC/95–2). Washington, DC: U.S. Bureau of the Census.

Kinsella, K., & Velkoff, V. A. (2001). *An aging world: 2001. U.S. Census Bureau, Series P95/01-1.* Washington, DC: U.S. Government Printing Office.

Kinsman, S., Romer, D., Furstenberg, F. F., & Schwarz, D. F. (1998). Early sexual initiation: The role of peer norms. *Pediatrics, 102,* 1185–1192.

Kirby, D. (1997). *No easy answers: Research findings on programs to reduce teen pregnancy.* Washington, DC: National Campaign to Prevent Teen Pregnancy.

Kirschenbaum, R. J. (1990, November-December). An interview with Howard Gardner. *Gifted Child Today,* pp. 26–32.

Kisilevsky, B. S., Hains, S. M. J., Lee, K., Muir, D. W., Xu, F., Fu, G., Zhao, Z. Y., & Yang, R. L. (1998). The still-face effect in Chinese and Canadian 3- to 6-month-old infants. *Developmental Psychology, 34*(4), 629–639.

Kisilevsky, B. S., Muir, D. W., & Low, J. A. (1992). Maturation of human fetal responses to vibroacoustic stimulation. *Child Development, 63,* 1497–1508.

Kistner, J., Eberstein, I. W., Quadagno, D., Sly, D., Sittig, L., Foster, K., Balthazor, M., Castro, R., & Osborne, M. (1997). Children's AIDS-related knowledge and attitudes: Variations by grade, race, gender, socioeconomic status, and size of community. *AIDS Education and Prevention, 9,* 285–298.

Kitson, G. C., & Morgan, L. A. (1990). The multiple consequences of divorce: A decade review. *Journal of Marriage and Family Therapy, 52,* 913–924.

Kivett, V. R. (1991). Centrality of the grandfather role among older rural black and white men. *Journal of Gerontology: Social Sciences, 46*(5), S250–258.

Kivett, V. R. (1993). Racial comparisons of the grandmother role: Implications for strengthening the family support system of older Black women. *Family Relations, 42,* 165–172.

Kivett, V. R. (1996). The saliency of the grandmother–granddaughter relationship: Predictors of association. *Journal of Women & Aging, 8,* 25–39.

Kjerulff, K. H., Langenberg, P. W., & Rhodes, J. C. (2000). Effectiveness outcome of hysterectomy. *Obstetrics & Gynecology, 95,* 319–326.

Kjos, S. L., & Buchanan, T. A. (1999). Gestational diabetes mellitus. *New England Journal of Medicine,* 341.

Klar, A. J. S. (1996). A single locus, RGHT, specifies preference for hand utilization in humans. In *Cold Spring Harbor Symposia on Quantitative Biology* (Vol. 61, pp. 59–65). Cold Spring Harbor, NY: Cold Spring Harbor Laboratory Press.

Klebanoff, M. A., Levine, R. J., DerSimonian, R., Clemens, J. D., & Wilkins, D. G. (1999). Maternal serum paraxanthine, a caffeine metabolite, and the risk of spontaneous abortion. *New England Journal of Medicine, 341,* 1639–1644.

Klebanov, P. K., Brooks-Gunn, J., & McCormick, M. C. (1994). Classroom behavior of very low birth weight elementary school children. *Pediatrics, 94,* 700–708.

Klebanov, P. K., Brooks-Gunn, J., & McCormick, M. C. (2001). Maternal coping strategies and emotional distress: Results of an early intervention program for low birth weight young children. *Developmental Psychology, 37*(5), 654–667.

Klebanov, P. K., Brooks-Gunn, J., McCarton, C., & McCormick, M. C. (1998). The contribution of neighborhood and family income to developmental test scores over the first three years of life. *Child Development, 69*(5), 1420–1436.

Kleinman, R. E., Murphy, J. M., Little, M., Pagano, M., Wehler, C. A., Regal, K., & Jellinek, M. S. (1998). Hunger in children in the United States: Potential behavioral and emotional correlates. *Pediatrics, 101*(1), e3.

Klesges, R. C., Klesges, L. M., Eck, L. H., & Shelton, M. L. (1995). A longitudinal analysis of accelerated weight gain in preschool children. *Pediatrics, 95,* 126–130.

Kline, D. W., & Scialfa, C. T. (1996). Visual and auditory aging. In J. E. Birren & K. W. Schaie (Eds.), *Handbook of the psychology of aging* (pp. 191–208). San Diego: Academic Press.

Kline, D. W., Kline, T. J. B., Fozard, J. L., Kosnik, W., Schieber, F., & Sekuler, R. (1992). Vision, aging, and driving: The problems of older drivers. *Journal of Gerontology: Psychological Sciences, 47*(1), P27–34.

Kling, K. C., Hyde, J. S., Showers, C. J., & Buswell, B. N. (1999). Gender differences in self-esteem: A meta-analysis. *Psychological Bulletin, 125,* 470–500.

Kling, K. C., Seltzer, M. M., & Ryff, C. D. (1997). Distinctive late-life challenges: Implications for coping and well-being. *Psychology and Aging, 12,* 288–295.

Klinnert M., Nelson, H. S., Price, M. R., Adinoff, A. D., Leung, D. Y. M., & Mrazek, D. A. (2001). Onset and persistence of childhood asthma: Predictors from infancy. *Pediatrics, 108*(4), e69.

Klohnen, E. C. (1996). Conceptual analysis and measurement of the construct of ego-resiliency. *Journal of Personality and Social Psychology, 70,* 1067–1079.

Klohnen, E. C., Vandewater, E., & Young, A. (1996). Negotiating the middle years: Ego-resiliency and successful midlife adjustment in women. *Psychology and Aging, 11,* 431–442.

Knoop, R. (1994). Relieving stress through value-rich work. *Journal of Social Psychology, 134,* 829–836.

Kochanek, K. D., Smith, B. L., & Anderson, R. N. (2001). Deaths: Preliminary data for 1999. *National Vital Statistics Reports, 49*(3). Hyattsville, MD: National Center for Health Statistics.

Kochanska, G. (1992). Children's interpersonal influence with mothers and peers. *Developmental Psychology, 28,* 491–499.

Kochanska, G. (1993). Toward a synthesis of parental socialization and child temperament in early development of conscience. *Child Development, 64,* 325–437.

Kochanska, G. (1995). Children's temperament, mothers' discipline, and security of attachment: Multiple pathways to emerging internalization. *Child Development, 66,* 597–615.

Kochanska, G. (1997a). Multiple pathways to conscience for children with different temperaments: From toddlerhood to age 5. *Developmental Psychology, 33,* 228–240.

Kochanska, G. (1997b). Mutually responsive orientation between mothers and their young children: Implications for early socialization. *Child Development, 68,* 94–112.

Kochanska, G. (1998). Mother-child relationship, child fearfulness, and emerging attachment: A short-term longitudinal study. *Developmental Psychology, 34,* 480–490.

Kochanska, G. (2001). Emotional development in children with different attachment histories: The first three years. *Child Development, 72,* 474–490.

Kochanska, G. Tjebkes, T. L., & Forman, D. R. (1998). Children's emerging regulation of conduct: Restraint, compliance, and internalization from infancy to the second year. *Child Development, 69*(5), 1378–1389.

Kochanska, G., & Aksan, N. (1995). Mother-child positive affect, the quality of child compliance to requests and prohibitions, and maternal control as correlates of early internalization. *Child Development, 66,* 236–254.

Kochanska, G., Murray, K., & Coy, K. C. (1997). Inhibitory control as a contributor to conscience in childhood: From toddler to early school age. *Child Development, 68,* 263–277.

Kochenderfer, B. H., & Ladd, G. W. (1996). Peer victimization: Cause or consequence of school maladjustment? *Child Development, 67,* 1305–1317.

Koechlin, E., Basso, G., Pietrini, P., Panzer, S., & Grafman, J. (1999). The role of the anterior prefrontal cortex in human cognition. *Nature, 399,* 148–151.

Koechlin, E., Dehaene, S., & Mehler, J. (1997). Numerical transformations in five month-old human infants. *Mathematical Cognition, 3,* 89–104.

Koenig, H. G. (1994). *Aging and God.* New York: Haworth.

Koenig, H. G., George, L. K., & Peterson, B. L. (1998). Religiosity and remission of depression in medically ill older patients. *American Journal of Psychiatry, 155,* 536–542.

Kogan, M. D., Alexander, G. R., Kotelchuck, M., MacDorman, M. F., Buekens, P., Martin, J. A., & Papiernik, E. (2000). Trends in twin birth outcomes and prenatal care utilization in the United States, 1981–1997. *Journal of the American Medical Association, 284,* 335–341.

Kogan, M. D., Martin, J. A., Alexander, G. R., Kotelchuck, M., Ventura, S. J., & Frigoletto, F. D. (1998). The changing pattern of prenatal care utilization in the United States, 1981–1995, using different prenatal care indices. *Journal of the American Medical Association, 279,* 1623–1628.

Kohlberg, L. (1966). A cognitive-developmental analysis of children's sex-role concepts and attitudes. In E. E. Maccoby (Ed.), *The development of sex differences.* Stanford, CA: Stanford University Press.

Kohlberg, L. (1969). Stage and sequence: The cognitive-developmental approach to socialization. In D. A. Goslin (Ed.), *Handbook of socialization theory and research.* Chicago: Rand McNally.

Kohlberg, L. (1973). Continuities in childhood and adult moral development revisited. In P. Baltes & K. W. Schaie (Eds.), *Life-span developmental psychology: Personality and socialization* (pp. 180–207). New York: Academic Press.

Kohlberg, L. (1981). *Essays on moral development.* San Francisco: Harper & Row.

Kohlberg, L., & Ryncarz, R. A. (1990). Beyond justice reasoning: Moral development and consideration of a seventh stage. In C. N. Alexander & E. J. Langer (Eds.), *Higher stages of human development* (pp. 191–207). New York: Oxford University Press.

Kohlberg, L., Yaeger, J., & Hjertholm, E. (1968). Private speech: Four studies and a review of theories. *Child Development, 39,* 691–736.

Kohn, M. L. (1980). Job complexity and adult personality. In N. J. Smelser & E. H. Erikson (Eds.), *Themes of work and love in adulthood.* Cambridge, MA: Harvard University Press.

Kohn, M. L., & Schooler, C. (1983). The cross-national universality of the interpretive model. In M. L. Kohn & C. Schooler (Eds.), *Work and personality: An inquiry into the impact of social stratification* (pp. 281–295). Norwood, NJ: Ablex.

Koivula, I., Sten, M., & Makela, P. H. (1999). Prognosis after community-acquired pneumonia in the elderly. *Archives of Internal Medicine, 159,* 1550–1555.

Kolata, G. (1988, March 29). Fetuses treated through umbilical cords. *The New York Times,* p. C3.

Kolata, G. (1999, March 9). Pushing limits of the human life span. *The New York Times* [Online]. Available: http://www.nytimes.com/library/national/science/030999sci-aging.html

Kolata, G. (2003, February 18). Using genetic tests, Ashkenazi Jews vanquish a disease. *The New York Times,* pp. D1, D6.

Kolbert, E. (1994, January 11). Canadians curbing TV violence. *The New York Times,* pp. C15, C19.

Kolder, V. E., Gallagher, J., & Parsons, M. T. (1987). Court-ordered obstetrical interventions. *New England Journal of Medicine, 316,* 1192–1196.

Kopka, T. L. C., Schantz, N. B., & Korb, R. A. (1998). *Adult education in the 1990s: A report on the 1991 National Household Education Survey* (Working Paper No. 98-03). Washington, DC: National Center for Education Statistics.

Kopp, C. B. (1982). Antecedents of self-regulation. *Developmental Psychology, 18,* 199–214.

Kopp, C. B., & Kaler, S. R. (1989). Risk in infancy: Origins and implications. *American Psychologist, 44*(2), 224–230.

Kopp, C. B., & McCall, R. B. (1982). Predicting later mental performance for normal, at-risk, and handicapped infants. In P. B. Baltes & O. G. Brim (Eds.), *Life-span development and behavior* (Vol. 4). New York: Academic Press.

Koren, G., Pastuszak, A., & Ito, S. (1998). Drugs in pregnancy. *New England Journal of Medicine, 338,* 1128–1137.

Korner, A. (1996). Reliable individual differences in preterm infants' excitation management. *Child Development, 67,* 1793–1805.

Korner, A. F., Zeanah, C. H., Linden, J., Berkowitz, R. I., Kraemer, H. C., & Agras, W. S. (1985). The relationship between neonatal and later activity and temperament. *Child Development, 56,* 38–42.

Kornhaber, A. (1986). *Between parents and grandparents.* New York: St. Martin's.

Korte, D., & Scaer, R. (1984). *A good birth, a safe birth.* New York: Bantam.

Kosnik, W., Winslow, L., Kline, D., Rasinski, K., & Sekuler, R. (1988). Visual changes in daily life throughout adulthood. *Journal of Gerontology: Psychological Sciences, 43*(3), P63–70.

Kosterman, R., Graham, J. W., Hawkins, J. D., Catalano, R. F., & Herrenkohl, T. I. (2001). Childhood risk factors for persistence of violence in the transition to adulthood: A social developmental perspective. *Violence & Victims. Special Issue: Perspectives on Violence and Victimization, 16,* 355–369.

Kotre, J. (1984). *Outliving the self: Generativity and the interpretation of lives.* Baltimore: Johns Hopkins University Press.

Kottak, C. P. (1994). *Cultural anthropology.* New York: McGraw-Hill.

Kozlowska, K., & Hanney, L. (1999). Family assessment and intervention using an interactive art exercise. *Australia and New Zealand Journal of Family Therapy, 20*(2), 61–69.

Kraaykamp, G. (2002). Trends and countertrends in sexual permissiveness: Three decades of attitude change in the Netherlands 1965–1995. *Journal of Marriage and Family, 64,* 225–239.

Krach, C. A., & Velkoff, V. A. (1999). Centenarians in the United States (*U.S. Bureau of the Census, Current Population Reports,* Series P23-1999RV). Washington, DC: U.S. Government Printing Office.

Kraemer, H. C., Korner, A., Anders, T., Jacklin, C. N., & Dimiceli, S. (1985). Obstetric drugs and infant behavior: A reevaluation. *Journal of Pediatric Psychology, 10,* 345–353.

Krall, E. A., & Dawson-Hughes, B. (1994). Walking is related to bone density and rates of bone loss. *American Journal of Medicine, 96,* 20–26.

Kralovec, E., & Buell, J. (2000). *The end of homework.* Boston: Beacon.

Kramarow, E., Lentzner, H., Rooks, R., Weeks, J., & Saydah, S. (1999). *Health and Aging Chartbook from Health, United States, 1999.* Hyattsville, MD: National Center for Health Statistics.

Kramer, A. F., Hahn, S., McAuley, E., Cohen, N. J., Banich, M. T., Harrison, C., Chason, J., Boileau, R. A., Bardell, L., Colcombe, A., & Vakil, E. (1999). Ageing, fitness and neurocognitive function. *Nature, 400,* 418–419.

Kramer, M. S., Chalmers, B., Hodnett, E. D., Sevkovskaya, Z., Dzikovich, I., Shapiro, S., Collet, J.-P., Vanilovich, I., Ducruet, T., Shishko, G., Zubovich, V., Mknuik, D., Gluchanina, E., Dombrovskiy, V., Ustinovich, N., Ovchinikova, L., & Helsing, E., for the PROBIT Study Group. (2001). Promotion of Breastfeeding Intervention Trial (PROBIT): A randomized trial in the republic of Belarus. *Journal of the American Medical Association, 285,* 413–420.

Kramer, M. S., Platt, R., Yang, H., Joseph, K. S., Wen, S. W., Morin, L., & Usher, R. H. (1998). Secular trends in preterm birth: A hospital-based cohort study. *Journal of the American Medical Association, 280,* 1849–1854.

Krause, N. (1995). Religiosity and self-esteem among older adults. *Journal of Gerontology: Psychological Sciences, 50B,* P236–246.

Krause, N., & Shaw, B. A. (2000). Role-specific feelings of control and mortality. *Psychology and Aging, 15,* 617– 626.

Krauss, S., Concordet, J. P., & Ingham, P. W. (1993). A functionally conserved homolog of the Drosophila segment polarity gene hh is expressed in tissues with polarizing activity in zebrafish embryos. *Cell, 75,* 1431–1444.

Kraut, R., Kiesler, S., Boneva, B., Cummings, J., Helgeson, V., & Crawford, A. (2002). Internet paradox revisited. *Journal of Social Issues, 58,* 49–74.

Kraut, R., Lundmark, V., Patterson, M., Kiesler, S., Mukopadhyay, R., & Scherlis, W. (1998). Internet paradox: A social technology that reduces social involvement and psychological well-being? *American Psychologist, 53,* 1017–1031.

Kravetz, J. D., & Federman, D. G. (2002). Cat-associated zoonoses. *Archives of Internal Medicine, 162,* 1945–1952.

Kreider, R. M., & Fields, J. M. (2002). Number, timing, and duration of marriages and divorces: Fall 1996. *Current Population Reports, P70–80.* Washington, DC: U.S. Census Bureau.

Kreutzer, M., Leonard, C., & Flavell, J. (1975). An interview study of children's knowledge about memory. *Monographs of the Society for Research in Child Development, 40*(1, Serial No. 159).

Krevans, J., & Gibbs, J. C. (1996). Parents' use of inductive discipline: Relations to children's empathy and prosocial behavior. *Child Development, 67,* 3263–3277.

Krieger, D. (1982). Cushing's syndrome. *Monographs in Endocrinology, 22,* 1–142.

Kristensen, P., Judge, M. E., Thim, L., Ribel, U., Christjansen, K. N., Wulff, B. S., Clausen, J. T., Jensen, P. B., Madsen, O. D., Vrang, N., Larsen, P. J., & Hastrup, S. (1998). Hypothalamic CART is a new anorectic peptide regulated by leptin. *Nature, 393,* 72–76.

Kristof, N. D. (1990, December 6). At 102, he's back in school, with many like him. *The New York Times,* p. A4.

Kristof, N. D. (1991, June 17). A mystery from China's census: Where have young girls gone? *The New York Times,* pp. A1, A8.

Kristof, N. D. (1993, July 21). Peasants of China discover new way to weed out girls. *The New York Times,* pp. A1, A6.

Kroenke, K., & Spitzer, R. L. (1998). Gender differences in the reporting of physical and somatoform symptoms. *Psychosomatic Medicine, 60,* 50–155.

Kroger, J. (1993). Ego identity: An overview. In J. Kroger (Ed.), *Discussions on ego identity.* Hillsdale, NJ: Erlbaum.

Kroger, J., & Haslett, S. J. (1991). A comparison of ego identity status transition pathways and change rates across five identity domains. *International Journal of Aging and Human Development, 32,* 303–330.

Krueger, J., Heckhausen, J., & Hundertmark, J. (1995). Perceiving middle-aged adults: Effects of stereotype-congruent and incongruent information. *Journal of Gerontology: Psychological Sciences, 50B.* P82–93.

Ku, L. C., Sonenstein, F. L., & Pleck, J. H. (1992). The association of AIDS education and sex education with sexual behavior and condom use among teenage men. *Family Planning Perspectives, 24,* 100–106.

Kübler-Ross, E. (1969). *On death and dying.* New York: Macmillan.

Kübler-Ross, E. (1970). *On death and dying* [Paperback]. New York: Macmillan.

Kübler-Ross, E. (Ed.). (1975). *Death: The final stage of growth.* Englewood Cliffs, NJ: Prentice-Hall.

Kuczmarski, R. J., Ogden, C. L., Grummer-Strawn, L. M., Flegal, K. M., Guo, S. S., Wei, R., Mei, Z., Curtin, L. R., Roche, A. F., & Johnson, C. L. (2000). CDC growth charts: United States. *Advance Data,* No. 314. Centers for Disease Control and Prevention, U.S. Department of Health and Human Services.

Kuczynski, L., & Kochanska, G. (1995). Function and content of maternal demands: Developmental significance of early demands for competent action. *Child Development, 66,* 616–628.

Kuhl, P. K., Andruski, J. E., Chistovich, I. A., Chistovich, L. A., Kozhevnikova, E. V., Ryskina, V. L., Stolyarova, E. I., Sundberg, U., & Lacerda, F. (1997). Cross-language analysis of phonetic units in language addressed to infants. *Science, 277,* 684–686.

Kuhl, P. K., Williams, K. A., Lacerda, F., Stevens, K. N., & Lindblom, B. (1992). Linguistic experience alters phonetic perception in infants by 6 months of age. *Science, 255,* 606–608.

Kuhn, D., Garcia-Mila, M., Zohar, A., & Andersen, C. (1995). Strategies of knowledge acquisition. *Monographs of the Society for Research in Child Development, 60*(4,Serial No. 245).

Kujala, U. M., Kaprio, J., Sarna, S., & Koskenvuo, M. (1998). Relationship of leisure-time physical activity and mortality: The Finnish Twin Cohort. *Journal of the American Medical Association, 279,* 440–444.

Kuklinski, M. R., & Weinstein, R. S. (2001). Classroom and developmental differences in a path model of teacher expectancy effects. *Child Development, 72*(5), 1554–1578.

Kumar, C., & Puri, M. (1983). *Mahatma Gandhi: His life and influence.* New York: Franklin Watts.

Kupersmidt, J. B., & Coie, J. D. (1990). Preadolescent peer status, aggression, and school adjustment as predictors of externalizing problems in adolescence. *Child Development, 61,* 1350–1362.

Kupfersmid, J., & Wonderly, D. (1980). Moral maturity and behavior: Failure to find a link. *Journal of Youth and Adolescence, 9*(3), 249–261.

Kurdek, L. A. (1995). Assessing multiple determinants of relationship commitment in cohabiting gay, cohabiting lesbian, dating heterosexual, and married heterosexual couples. *Family Relations, 44,* 261–266.

Kurdek, L. A. (1999). The nature and predictors of the trajectory of change in marital quality for husbands and wives over the first 10 years of marriage. *Developmental Psychology, 35,* 1283–1296.

Kurjak, A., Kupesic, S., Matijevic, R., Kos, M., & Marton, U. (1999). First trimester malformation screening. *European Journal of Obstetrics, Gynecology, and Reproductive Biology (E4L), 85,* 93–96.

Kutner, N. G., Barnhart, H., Wolf, S. L., McNeely, E., & Xu, T. (1997). Self-report benefits of tai chi practice by older adults. *Journal of Gerontology: Series B: Psychological Sciences & Social Sciences, 52B,* P242–P246.

Kvavilashvili, L., Messer, D. J., & Ebdon, P. (2001). Prospective memory in children: The effects of age and task interruption. *Developmental Psychology, 37,* 418–430.

Kye, C., & Ryan, N. (1995). Pharmacologic treatment of child and adolescent depression. *Child and Adolescent Psychiatric Clinics of North America, 4,* 261–281.

Kyriacou, D. N., Anglin, D., Taliaferro, E., Stone, S., Tubb, T., Linden, J. A., Muelleman, R., Barton, E., & Kraus, F. J. (1999). Risk factors for injury to women from domestic violence. *New England Journal of Medicine, 341,* 1892–1898.

La Sala, M. C. (1998). Coupled gay men, parents, and in-laws: Intergenerational disapproval and the need for a thick skin. *Families in Society, 79,* 585–595.

Labouvie-Vief, G. (1985). Intelligence and cognition. In J. E. Birren & K. W. Schaie (Eds.), *Handbook of the psychology of aging* (pp. 500–530). New York: Van Nostrand Reinhold.

Labouvie-Vief, G. (1990a). Modes of knowledge and the organization of development. In M. L. Commons, L. Kohlberg, F. Richards, & J. Sinnott (Eds.), *Beyond formal operations: 2. Models and methods in the study of adult and adolescent thought.* New York: Praeger.

Labouvie-Vief, G. (1990b). Wisdom as integrated thought: Historical and development perspectives. In R. J. Sternberg (Ed.), *Wisdom: Its nature, origins, and development* (pp. 52–83). Cambridge, England: Cambridge University Press.

Labouvie-Vief, G., & Hakim-Larson, J. (1989). Developmental shifts in adult thought. In S. Hunter & M. Sundel (Eds.), *Midlife myths.* Newbury Park, CA: Sage.

Labouvie-Vief, G., Adams, C., Hakim-Larson, J., Hayden, M., & DeVoe, M. (1987). *Modes of text processing from preadolescence to mature adulthood.* Unpublished manuscript, Wayne State University, Detroit, MI.

Labouvie-Vief, G., Hakim-Larson, J., & Hobart, C. J. (1987). Age, ego level, and the life-span development of coping and defense processes. *Psychology and Aging, 2,* 286–293.

Labov, T. (1992). Social and language boundaries among adolescents. *American Speech, 67,* 339–366.

Lachman, J. L., & Lachman, R. (1980). Age and the actualization of knowledge. In L. W. Poon, J. L. Fozard, L. S. Cermak, D. Arenberg, & L. W. Thompson (Eds.), *New directions in memory and aging* (pp. 313–343). Hillsdale, NJ: Erlbaum.

Lachman, M. E. (2001). Introduction. In M. E. Lachman (Ed.), *Handbook of midlife development.* New York: Wiley.

Lachman, M. E., & Bertrand, R. M. (2001). Personality and the self in midlife. In M. E. Lachman (Ed.), *Handbook of midlife development* (pp. 279–309). New York: Wiley.

Lachman, M. E., & James, J. B. (1997). Charting the course of midlife development: An overview. In M. E. Lachman & J. B. James (Eds.), *Multiple paths of midlife development* (pp. 1–17). Chicago: University of Chicago Press.

Lachman, M. E., & Weaver, S. L. (1998). Sociodemographic variations in the sense of control by domain: Findings from the MacArthur Studies of Midlife. *Psychology and Aging, 13,* 553–562.

Lachman, M. E., Lewkowicz, C., Marcus, A., & Peng, Y. (1994). Images of midlife development among young, middle-aged, and elderly adults. *Journal of Adult Development, 1,* 201–211.

Lachs, M. S., & Pillemer, K. (1995). Abuse and neglect of elderly persons. *New England Journal of Medicine, 332,* 437–443.

Lackmann, G. M., Salzberger, U., Tollner, U., Chen, M., Carmella, S. G., & Hecht, S. S. (1999). Metabolites of a tobacco-specific carcinogen in the urine of newborns. *Journal of the National Cancer Institute, 91,* 459–465.

Ladd, G. W. (1996). Shifting ecologies during the 5 to 7 year period: Predicting children's adjustment during the transition to grade school. In A. J. Sameroff & M. M. Haith (Eds.), *The five to seven year shift: The age of reason and responsibility* (pp. 363–386). Chicago: University of Chicago Press.

Ladd, G. W., & Hart, C. H. (1992). Creating informal play opportunities: Are parents' and preschoolers' initiations related to children's competence with peers? *Developmental Psychology, 28,* 1179–1187.

Ladd, G. W., Birch, S. H., & Buhs, E. S. (1999). Children's social and scholastic lives in kindergarten: Related spheres of influence? *Child Development, 70,* 1373–1400.

Ladd, G. W., Kochenderfer, B. J., & Coleman, C. C. (1996). Friendship quality as a predictor of young children's early school adjustment. *Child Development, 67,* 1103–1118.

Lagercrantz, H., & Slotkin, T. A. (1986). The "stress" of being born. *Scientific American, 254*(4), 100–107.

Lai, C. S. L., Fisher, S. E., Hurst, J. A., Vargha-Khadem, F., & Monaco, A.P. (2001). A forkhead-domain gene is mutated in a severe speech and language disorder. *Nature, 413,* 519–523.

Lai, J. S., Lan, C., Wong, M. K., & Teng, S. H. (1995). Two-year trends in cardiorespiratory function among older Tai Chi Chuan practitioners and sedentary subjects. *Journal of the American Geriatrics Society, 43,* 1222–1227.

Laible, D. J., & Thompson, R. A. (1998). Attachment and emotional understanding in preschool children. *Developmental Psychology, 34*(5), 1038–1045.

Laible, D. J., & Thompson, R. A. (2002). Mother-child conflict in the toddler years:

Lessons in emotion, morality, and relationships. *Child Development, 73,* 1187–1203.

Lalonde, C. E., & Werker, J. F. (1995). Cognitive influences on cross-language speech perception in infancy. *Infant Behavior and Development, 18,* 459–475.

Lamb, M. E. (1981). The development of father-infant relationships. In M. E. Lamb (Ed.), *The role of the father in child development* (2nd ed.). New York: Wiley.

Lamb, M. E. (1987). Predictive implications of individual differences in attachment. *Journal of Consulting and Clinical Psychology, 55*(6), 817–824.

Lamb, M. E., Frodi, A. M., Frodi, M., & Hwang, C. P. (1982). Characteristics of maternal and paternal behavior in traditional and non-traditional Swedish families. *International Journal of Behavior Development, 5,* 131–151.

Lamb, M. E., Pleck, J., Charnov, E. L., & Levine, J. A. (1985). Paternal behavior in humans. *American Zoologist, 25,* 883–894.

Lamberts, S. W. J., van den Beld, A. W., & van der Lely, A. (1997). The endocrinology of aging. *Science, 278,* 419–424.

Lambeth, G. S., & Hallett, M. (2002). Promoting healthy decision making in relationships: Developmental interventions with young adults on college and university campuses. In C. L. & D. R. Atkinson (Eds.), *Counseling across the lifespan: Prevention and treatment* (pp. 209–226). Thousand Oaks, CA: Sage.

Lamborn, S. D., Mounts, N. S., Steinberg, L., & Dornbusch, S. M. (1991). Patterns of competence and adjustment among adolescents from authoritative, authoritarian, indulgent, and neglectful families. *Child Development, 62,* 1049–1065.

Lamy, P. P. (1994). Drug-nutrient interactions in the aged. In R. R. Watson (Ed.), *Handbook of nutrition in the aged* (2nd ed., pp. 165–200). Boca Raton, FL: CRC Press.

Landesman-Dwyer, S., & Emanuel, I. (1979). Smoking during pregnancy. *Teratology, 19,* 119–126.

Landy, F. J. (1992, February). *Research on the use of fitness tests for police and fire fighting jobs.* Paper presented at the Second Annual Scientific Psychology Forum of the American Psychological Association, Washington, DC.

Landy, F. J. (1994, July–August). Mandatory retirement age: Serving the public welfare? *Psychological Science Agenda* (Science Directorate, American Psychological Association), pp. 10–11, 20.

Lane, H. (1976). *The wild boy of Aveyron.* Cambridge, MA: Harvard University Press.

Lange, G., MacKinnon, C. E., & Nida, R. E. (1989). Knowledge, strategy, and motivational contributions to preschool children's object recall. *Developmental Psychology, 25,* 772–779.

Lanphear, B. P., Aligne, C. A., Auinger, P., Weitzman, M., & Byrd, R. S. (2001). Residential exposure associated with asthma in US children. *Pediatrics, 107,* 505–511.

Lansford, J. E., & Parker, J. G. (1999). Children's interactions in triads: Behavioral profiles and effects of gender and patterns of friendships among members. *Developmental Psychology, 35,* 80–93.

Lansford, J. E., Sherman, A. M., & Antonucci, T. C. (1998). Satisfaction with social networks: An examination of socioemotional selectivity. *Psychology and Aging, 13*(4), 544–552.

Lanting, C. I., Fidler, V., Huisman, M., Touwen, B. C. L., & Boersma, E. R. (1994). Neurological differences between 9-year-old children fed breast-milk or formula-milk as babies. *The Lancet, 334,* 1319–1322.

Lantz, P. M., House, J. S., Lepkowski, J. M., Williams, D. R., Mero, R. P., & Chen, J. (1998). Socioeconomic factors, health behaviors, and mortality: Results from a nationally representative prospective study of U.S. adults. *Journal of the American Medical Association, 279,* 1703–1708.

Lapham, E. V., Kozma, C., & Weiss, J. O. (1996). Genetic discrimination: Perspectives of consumers. *Science, 274,* 621–624.

Laquatra, J., & Chi, P. S. K. (1998, September). *Housing for an aging-in-place society.* Paper presented at the European Network for Housing Research Conference, Cardiff, Wales.

Larivée, S., Normandeau, S., & Parent, S. (2000). The French connection: Some contributions of French-language research in the post-Piagetian era. *Child Development, 71,* 823–839.

Larsen D. (1990, December–1991, January). Unplanned parenthood. *Modern Maturity,* pp. 32–36.

Larson, R. (1998). Implications for policy and practice: Getting adolescents, families, and communities in sync. In A. Crouter & R. Larson (Eds.), *Temporal rhythms in adolescence: Clocks, calendars, and the coordination of daily life* (New Directions in Child and Adolescent Development, No. 82, pp. 83–88). San Francisco: Jossey-Bass.

Larson, R., Mannell, R., & Zuzanek, J. (1986). Daily well being of older adults with friends and family. *Psychology and Aging, 1*(2), 117–126.

Larson, R., & Richards, M. (1998). Waiting for the weekend: Friday and Saturday nights as the emotional climax of the week. In A. Crouter & R. Larson (Eds.), *Temporal rhythms in adolescence: Clocks, calendars, and the coordination of daily life (*New Directions in Child and Adolescent Development, No. 82, pp. 37–51). San Francisco: Jossey-Bass.

Larson, R., & Richards, M. H. (1991). Daily companionship in late childhood and early adolescence: Changing developmental contexts. *Child Development, 62,* 284–300.

Larson, R., & Richards, M. H. (1994). *Divergent realities: The emotional lives of mothers, fathers, and adolescents.* New York: Basic Books.

Larson, R. W. (1997). The emergence of solitude as a constructive domain of experience in early adolescence. *Child Development, 68,* 80–93.

Larson, R. W., & Verma, S. (1999). How children and adolescents spend time across the world: Work, play, and developmental opportunities. *Psychological Bulletin, 125,* 701–736.

Larson, R. W., Moneta, G., Richards, M. H., & Wilson, S. (2002). Continuity, stability, and change in daily emotional experience across adolescence. *Child Development, 73,* 1151–1165.

Larson, R. W., Richards, M. H., Moneta, G., Holmbeck, G., & Duckett, E. (1996). Changes in adolescents' daily interactions with their families from ages 10 to 18: Disengagement and transformation. *Developmental Psychology, 32,* 744–754.

Latimer, E. J. (1992, February). Euthanasia: A physician's reflections. *Ontario Medical Review,* pp. 21–29.

Laucht, M., Esser, G., & Schmidt, M. H. (1994). Contrasting infant predictors of later cognitive functioning. *Journal of Child Psychology and Psychiatry, 35,* 649–652.

Laumann, E. O., & Michael, R. T. (Eds.). (2000). *Sex, love, and health in America: Private choices and public policies.* Chicago: University of Chicago Press.

Laumann, E. O., Gagnon, J. H., Michael, R. T., & Michaels, S. (1994). *The social organization of sexuality: Sexual practices in the United States.* Chicago: University of Chicago Press.

Laumann, E. O., Paik, A., & Rosen, R. C. (1999). Sexual dysfunction in the United States. *Journal of the American Medical Association, 281,* 537–544.

Laumann, E. O., Paik, A., & Rosen, R. C. (2000). Sexual dysfunction in the United States: Prevalence and predictors. In E. O. Laumann, & R. T. Michael, (Eds.), *Sex, love, and health in America: Private choices and public policies* (pp. 352–376). Chicago: University of Chicago Press.

Launer, L. J., Andersen, K., Dewey, M. E., Letenneur, L., Ott, A., Amaducci, L. A., Brayne, C., Copeland, J. R. M., Dartigues, J.-F., Kragh-Sorensen, P., Lobo, A., Martinez-Lage, J. M., Stijnen, T., & Hofman, A. (1999). Rates and risk factors for dementia and Alzheimer's disease: Results from EURODEM pooled analyses. *Neurology, 52,* 78–84.

Launer, L. J., Masaki, K., Petrovitch, H., Foley, D., & Havlik, R. J. (1995). The association between midlife blood pressure levels and late-life cognitive function. *Journal of the American Medical Association, 274,* 1846–1851.

Laursen, B. (1996). Closeness and conflict in adolescent peer relationships: Interdependence with friends and romantic partners. In W. M. Bukowski, A. F. Newcomb, & W. W. Hartup (Eds.), *The company they keep: Friendship in childhood and adolescence* (pp. 186–210). New York: Cambridge University Press.

Laursen, B., Coy, K. C., & Collins, W. A. (1998). Reconsidering changes in parent-child conflict across adolescence: A meta-analysis. *Child Development, 69,* 817–832.

Laursen, B., Pulkkinen, L., & Adams, R. (2002). The antecedents and correlates of agreeableness in adulthood. *Developmental Psychology, 38,* 591–603.

Lavee, Y., Sharlin, S., & Katz, R. (1996). The effects of parenting stress on marital quality. *Journal of Family Issues, 17,* 114–135.

Lazarus, R. S., & Folkman, S. (1984). *Stress, appraisal, and coping.* New York: Springer.

Leaper, C., Anderson, K. J., & Sanders, P. (1998). Moderators of gender effects on parents' talk to their children: A meta-analysis. *Developmental Psychology, 34*(1), 3–27.

LeBlanc, E. S., Janowsky, J., Chan, B. K. S., & Nelson, H. D. (2001). Hormone replacement therapy and cognition: Systematic review and meta-analysis. *Journal of the American Medical Association, 285,* 1489–1499.

Leblanc, M., & Ritchie, M. (2001). A meta-analysis of play therapy outcomes. *Counseling Psychology Quarterly, 14,* 149–163.

LeBoff, M. S., Kohlmeier, L., Hurwitz, S., Franklin, J., Wright, J., & Glowacki, J. (1999). Occult vitamin D deficiency in postmenopausal US women with acute hip fracture. *Journal of the American Medical Association, 281,* 1505–1511.

Lecanuet, J. P., Granier-Deferre, C., & Busnel, M.-C. (1995). Human fetal auditory perception. In J. P. Lecanuet, W. P. Fifer, N. A. Krasnegor, & W. P. Smotherman (Eds.), *Fetal development: A psychobiological perspective* (pp. 239–262). Hillsdale, NJ: Erlbaum.

Lee, G. R., Dwyer, J. W., & Coward, R. T. (1993). Gender differences in parent care: Demographic factors and some gender preferences. *Journal of Gerontology: Social Sciences, 48,* S9–16.

Lee, G. R., Netzer, J. K., & Coward, R. T. (1995). Depression among older parents: The role of intergenerational exchange. *Journal of Marriage and the Family, 57,* 823–833.

Lee, I., Rexrode, K. M., Cook, N. R., Manson, J. E., & Buring, J. E. (2001). Physical activity and coronary heart disease in women: Is "no pain, no gain" passé? *Journal of the American Medical Association, 285,* 1447–1454.

Lee, I.-M., & Paffenbarger, R. S. (1992). Changes in body weight and longevity. *Journal of the American Medical Association, 268,* 2045–2049.

Lee, I.-M., Hsieh, C.-C., & Paffenbarger, R. S. (1995). Exercise intensity and longevity in men. *Journal of the American Medical Association, 273,* 1179–1184.

Lee, J. (1998). Children, teachers, and the internet. *Delta Kappa Gamma Bulletin, 64*(2), 5–9.

Lee, M. A., Nelson, H. D., Tilden, V. P., Ganzini, L., Schmidt, T. A., & Tolle, S. W. (1996). Legalizing assisted suicide—Views of physicians in Oregon. *New England Journal of Medicine, 334,* 310–315.

Legerstee, M., & Varghese, J. (2001). The role of maternal affect mirroring on social expectancies in three-month-old infants. *Child Development, 72,* 1301–1313.

Legro, R. S., Lin, H. M., Demers, L. M., & Lloyd, T. (2000). Rapid maturation of the reproductive axis during perimenarche independent of body composition. *Journal of Clinical Endocrinology and Metabolism, 85,* 1021–1025.

Lehman, D. R., & Nisbett, R. T. (1990). A longitudinal study of the effects of undergraduate training on reasoning. *Developmental Psychology, 26,* 952–960.

Leibel, R. L. (1997). And finally, genes for human obesity. *Nature Genetics, 16,* 218–220.

Leichtman, M. D., & Ceci, S. J. (1995). The effects of stereotypes and suggestions on preschoolers' reports. *Developmental Psychology, 31,* 568–578.

Leigh, B. C. (1999). Peril, chance, adventure: Concepts of risk, alcohol use, and risky behavior in young adults. *Addiction, 94*(3), 371–383.

Lemon, B., Bengtson, V., & Peterson, J. (1972). An exploration of the activity theory of aging: Activity types and life satisfaction among inmovers to a retirement community. *Journal of Gerontology, 27*(4), 511–523.

Lenneberg, E. H. (1967). *Biological functions of language.* New York: Wiley.

Lenneberg, E. H. (1969). On explaining language. *Science, 164* (3880), 635–643.

Lennox, A., Karlinsky, H., Meschino, J., Buchanan, J. A., Percy, M. E., & Berg, J. M. (1994). Molecular genetic predictive testing for Alzheimer's disease: Deliberations and preliminary recommendations. *Alzheimer Disease and Associated Disorders, 8,* 126–127.

Lenz, E. (1993, August–September). Mirror, mirror . . . : One woman's reflections on her changing image. *Modern Maturity,* pp. 24, 26–28, 80.

Lerman, C., Caporaso, N. E., Audrain, J., Main, D., Bowman, E. D., Lockshin, B., Boyd, N. R., & Shields, P. G. (1999). Evidence suggesting the role of specific genetic factors in cigarette smoking. *Health Psychology, 18,* 14–20.

Lerner, J. V., & Galambos, N. L. (1985). Maternal role satisfaction, mother-child interaction, and child temperament: A process model. *Child Development, 21,* 1157–1164.

Lerner, M. J., Somers, D. G., Reid, D., Chiriboga, D., & Tierney, M. (1991). Adult children as caregivers: Egocentric biases in judgments of sibling contributions. *The Gerontologist, 31*(6), 746–755.

Lesch, K. P., Bengel, D., Heils, A., Sabol, S. Z., Greenberg, B. D., Petri, S., Benjamin, J., Müller, C. R., Hamer, D. H., & Murphy, D. L. (1996). Association of anxiety-related traits with a polymorphism in the serotonin transporter gene regulatory region. *Science, 274,* 1527–1531.

Lesgold, A. M. (1983). *Expert systems.* Paper represented at the Cognitive Science Meetings, Rochester, NY.

Lesgold, A., Glaser, R., Rubinson, H., Klopfer, D., Feltovich, P., & Wang, Y. (1988). Expertise in a complex skill: Diagnosing x-ray pictures. In M. T. H. Chi, R. Glaser, & M. J. Farr (Eds.), *The Nature of Expertise* (pp. 311–342). Hillsdale, NJ: Erlbaum.

Leslie, A. M. (1982). The perception of causality in infants. *Perception, 11,* 173–186.

Leslie, A. M. (1994). ToMM, ToBy, and Agency: Core architecture and domain specificity. In S. A. Gelman & L. A. Hirschfeld (Eds.), *Mapping the mind: Domain specificity in cognition and culture* (pp. 119–148). New York: Cambridge University Press.

Leslie, A. M., & Polizzi, P. (1998). Inhibitory processing in the false belief task: Two conjectures. *Developmental Science, 1,* 247–254.

Lester, B. M., & Boukydis, C. F. Z. (1985). *Infant crying: Theoretical and research perspectives.* New York: Plenum.

Lester, B. M., & Dreher, M. (1989). Effects of marijuana use during pregnancy on newborn cry. *Child Development, 60,* 765–771.

LeVay, S. (1991). A difference in hypothalamic structure between heterosexual and homosexual men. *Science, 253,* 1034–1037.

Leve, L. D., & Fagot, B. I. (1997). Gender-role socialization and discipline processes in one- and two-parent families. *Sex Roles, 36,* 1–21.

Levenstein, S., Ackerman, S., Kiecolt-Glaser, J. K., & Dubois, A. (1999). Stress and peptic ulcer disease. *Journal of the American Medical Association, 281,* 10–11.

Leventhal, T., & Brooks-Gunn, J. (2000). The neighborhoods they live in: The effects of neighborhood residence on child and adolescent outcomes. *Psychological Bulletin, 126*(2), 309–337.

Levi, L. (1990). Occupational stress: Spice of life or kiss of death? *American Psychologist, 45,* 1142–1145.

Levin, J. (2002, Winter). HIV and age: Do older people fare as well as younger? *NAHOF Connection,* pp. 5–6.

Levin, J. S., & Taylor, R. J. (1993). Gender and age differences in religiosity among black Americans. *The Gerontologist, 33*(1), 16–23.

Levin, J. S., Taylor, R. J., & Chatters, L. M. (1994). Race and gender differences in religiosity among older adults: Findings from four national surveys. *Journal of Gerontology: Social Sciences, 49,* S137–145.

Levine, R. (1980). Adulthood among the Gusii of Kenya. In N. J. Smelser & E. H. Erikson (Eds.), *Themes of work and love in adulthood* (pp. 77–104). Cambridge, MA: Harvard University Press.

LeVine, R. A. (1974). Parental goals: A cross-cultural view. *Teacher College Record, 76,* 226–239.

LeVine, R. A. (1989). Human parental care: Universal goals, cultural strategies, individual behavior. In R. A. LeVine, P. M. Miller, & M. M. West (Eds.), *Parental behavior in diverse societies* (pp. 3–12). San Francisco: Jossey-Bass.

LeVine, R. A. (1994). *Child care and culture: Lessons from Africa.* Cambridge, England: Cambridge University Press.

LeVine, R. A., & LeVine, S. (1998). Fertility and maturity in Africa: Gusii parents in middle adulthood. In R. A. Schweder (Ed.), *Welcome to middle age! (and other cultural fictions).* Chicago: University of Chicago Press.

LeVine, R. A., Dixon, S., LeVine, S., Richman, A., Leiderman, P. H., Keefer, C. H., & Brazelton, T. B. (1994). *Child care and culture: Lessons from Africa.* New York: Cambridge University Press.

Levine, S. C., Huttenlocher, J., Taylor, A., & Langrock, A. (1999). Early sex differences in spatial skill. *Developmental Psychology, 35*(4), 940–949.

Levinson, D. (1978). *The seasons of a man's life.* New York: Knopf.

Levinson, D. (1980). Toward a conception of the adult life course. In N. J. Smelser &

E. H. Erikson (Eds.), *Themes of work and love in adulthood* (pp. 265–290). Cambridge, MA: Harvard University Press.

Levinson, D. (1986). A conception of adult development. *American Psychologist, 41,* 3–13.

Levinson, D. (1996). *The seasons of a woman's life.* New York: Knopf.

Levinson, D. J. (1977). The mid-life transition. *Psychiatry, 40,* 99–112.

Levinson, W., & Altkorn, D. (1998). Primary prevention of postmenopausal osteoporosis. *Journal of the American Medical Association, 280,* 1821–1822.

Leviton, A., & Cowan, L. (2002). A review of the literature relating caffeine consumption by women to their risk of reproductive hazards. *Food & Chemical Toxicology, 40*(9), 1271–1310.

Levitt, M. J., Guacci-Franco, N., & Levitt, J. L. (1993). Convoys of social support in childhood and early adolescence: Structure and function. *Developmental Psychology, 29,* 811–818.

Levron, J., Aviram, A., Madgar, I., Livshits, A., Raviv, G., Bider, D., Hourwitz, A., Barkai, G., Goldman, B., & Mashiach, S. (1998, October). *High rate of chromosomal aneupoloidies in testicular spermatozoa retrieved from azoospermic patients undergoing testicular sperm extraction for in vitro fertilization.* Paper presented at the 16th World Congress on Fertility and Sterility and the 54th annual meeting of the American Society for Reproductive Medicine, San Francisco, CA.

Levy, G. D., & Carter, D. B. (1989). Gender schema, gender constancy, and gender-role knowledge: The roles of cognitive factors in preschoolers' gender-role stereotype attributions. *Developmental Psychology, 25,* 444–449.

Levy-Cushman, J., & Abeles, N. (1998). Memory complaints in the able elderly. *Clinical Gerontologist, 19,* 3–24.

Levy-Shiff, R. (1994). Individual and contextual correlates of marital change across the transition to parenthood. *Developmental Psychology, 30,* 591–601.

Levy-Shiff, R., Zoran, N., & Shulman, S. (1997). International and domestic adoption: Child, parents, and family adjustment. *International Journal of Behavioral Development, 20,* 109–129.

Lewin, T. (1997, April 23). Detention of pregnant women for drug use is struck down. *The New York Times,* p. A-16.

Lewinsohn, P. M., Gotlib, I. H., Lewinsohn, M., Seeley, J. R., & Allen, N. B. (1998). Gender differences in anxiety disorders and anxiety symptoms in adolescents. *Journal of Abnormal Psychology, 107,* 109–117.

Lewis, M. (1995). Self-conscious emotions. *American Scientist, 83,* 68–78.

Lewis, M. (1997). The self in self-conscious emotions. In S. G. Snodgrass & R. L. Thompson (Eds.), *The self across psychology: Self-recognition, self-awareness, and the self-concept* (Vol. 818). New York: The New York Academy of Sciences, Annals of the New York Academy of Sciences.

Lewis, M. (1998). Emotional competence and development. In D. Pushkar, W. Bukowski, A. E. Schwartzman, D. M. Stack, & D. R. White (Eds.), *Improving competence across the lifespan* (pp. 27–36). New York: Plenum.

Lewis, M. I., & Butler, R. N. (1974). Life-review therapy: Putting memories to work in individual and group psychotherapy. *Geriatrics, 29,* 165–173.

Lewis, M., & Brooks, J. (1974). Self, other, and fear: Infants' reaction to people. In H. Lewis & L. Rosenblum (Eds.), *The origins of fear: The origins of behavior* (Vol. 2). New York: Wiley.

Lewis, M., Worobey, J., Ramsay, D. S., & McCormack, M. K. (1992). Prenatal exposure to heavy metals: Effect on childhood cognitive skills and health status. *Pediatrics, 89,* 1010–1015.

Li, J., Precht, D. H., Mortensen, P. B., & Olsen, J. (2003). Mortality in parents after death of a child in Denmark: A nationwide follow-up study. *The Lancet, 361,* 363–367.

Liaw, F., & Brooks-Gunn, J. (1993). Patterns of low-birth-weight children's cognitive development. *Developmental Psychology, 29,* 1024–1035.

Liberman, I. Y., & Liberman, A. M. (1990). Whole language vs. code emphasis: Underlying assumptions and their implications for reading instruction. *Annals of Dyslexia, 40,* 51–76.

Lickona, T. (Ed.). (1976). *Moral development and behavior.* New York: Holt.

Lie, R. T., Wilcox, A. J., & Skjaerven, R. (2001). Survival and reproduction among males with birth defects and risk of recurrence in their children. *Journal of the American Medical Association, 285,* 755–760.

Lieberman, M. (1996). *Doors close, doors open: Widows, grieving and growing.* New York: Putnam.

Liebman, B. (1995a, June). A meat & potatoes man. *Nutrition Action Health Letter, 22*(5), 6–7.

Light, K. C., Girdler, S. S., Sherwood, A., Bragdon, E. E., Brownley, K. A., West, S. G., & Hinderliter, A. L. (1999). High stress responsivity predicts later blood pressure only in combination with positive family history and high life stress. *Hypertension, 33,* 1458–1464.

Light, L. L. (1990). Interactions between memory and language in old age. In J. E. Birren & K. W. Schaie (Eds.), *Handbook of the psychology of aging* (pp. 275–290). San Diego: Academic Press.

Lillard, A. S. (1998). Ethnopsychologies: Cultural variations in theory of mind. *Psychological Bulletin, 123,* 3–33.

Lillard, A., & Curenton, S. (1999). Do young children understand what others feel, want, and know? *Young Children, 54*(5), 52–57.

Lin, G., & Rogerson, P. A. (1995). Elderly parents and their geographic availability to their adult children. *Research on Aging, 17,* 303–331.

Lin, S., Hwang, S. A., Marshall, E. G., & Marion, D. (1998). Does paternal occupational lead exposure increase the risks of low birth weight or prematurity? *American Journal of Epidemiology, 148,* 173–181.

Lin, Y., Seroude, L., & Benzer, S. (1998). Extended life-span and stress resistance in the Drosophila mutant methuselah. *Science, 282,* 943–946.

Lindegren, M. L., Byers, R. H., Jr., Thomas, P., Davis, S. F., Caldwell, B., Rogers, M., Gwinn, M., Ward, J. W., & Fleming, P. L. (1999). Trends in perinatal transmission of HIV/AIDS in the United States. *Journal of the American Medical Association, 282,* 531–538.

Linder, K. (1990). *Functional literacy projects and project proposals: Selected examples.* Paris: United Nations Educational, Scientific, and Cultural Organization.

Lindsay, R., Gallagher, J. C., Kleerekoper, M., & Pickar, J. H. (2002). Effect of lower doses of conjugated equine estrogens with and without medroxyprogesterone acetate on bone in early postmenopausal women. *Journal of the American Medical Association, 287,* 2668–2676.

Lindsey, E. W., & Mize, J. (2001). Contextual differences in parent-child play: Implications for children's gender role development. *Sex Roles, 44,* 155–176.

Lindwer, W. (1991). *The last seven months of Anne Frank* (A. Meersschaert, Trans.). New York: Pantheon.

Linney, J. A., & Seidman, E. (1989). The future of schooling. *American Psychologist, 44*(2), 336–340.

Lino, M. (2001). *Expenditures on children by families, 2000 annual report* (Misc. Publication No. 1528-2000). Washington, DC: U.S. Department of Agriculture, Center for Nutrition Policy and Promotion.

Lipid Research Clinics Program. (1984a). The lipid research clinic coronary primary prevention trial results: I. Reduction in incidence of coronary heart disease. *Journal of the American Medical Association, 251,* 351–364.

Lipid Research Clinics Program. (1984b). The lipid research clinic coronary primary prevention trial results: II. The relationship of reduction in incidence of coronary heart disease to cholesterol lowering. *Journal of the American Medical Association, 251,* 365–374.

Listening to depression: The new medicines. (1995, January). *Johns Hopkins Medical Letter: Health after 50,* pp. 4–5.

Litovitz, T. L., Klein-Schwartz, W., Caravati, E. M., Youniss, J., Crouch, B., & Lee, S. (1999). Annual report of the American Association of Poison Control Centers Toxic Exposure Surveillance System. *American Journal of Emergency Medicine, 17,* 435–487.

Liu, S., Manson, J. E., Lee, I. M., Cole, S. R., Hennekens, C. H., Willett, W. C., & Buring, J. E. (2000). Fruit and vegetable intake and risk of cardiovascular disease: The Women's Health Study. *American Journal of Clinical Nutrition, 72,* 922–928.

Lloyd, T., Andon, M. B., Rollings, N., Martel, J. K., Landis, J. R., Demers, L. M., Eggli, D. F., Kieselhorst, K., & Kulin, H. E. (1993). Calcium supplementation and bone mineral density in adolescent girls. *Journal of the American Medical Association, 270,* 841–844.

Lock, A., Young, A., Service, V., & Chandler, P. (1990). Some observations on the origin of the pointing gesture. In V. Volterra & C. J. Erting

(Eds.), *From gesture to language in hearing and deaf children.* New York: Springer.

Lock, M. (1994). Menopause in cultural context. *Experimental Gerontology, 29,* 307–317.

Lock, M. (1998). Deconstructing the change: Female maturation in Japan and North America. In R. A. Shweder (Ed.), *Welcome to middle age (and other cultural fictions)* (pp. 45–74). Chicago: University of Chicago Press.

Loewen, N., & Bancroft, A. (2001). *Four to the Pole: The American Women's Expedition to Antartica, 1992–1993.* North Haven, CT: Shoestring Press.

Lonczak, H. S., Abbott, R. D., Hawkins, J. D., Kosterman, R., & Catalano, R. F. (2002). Effects of the Seattle Social Development Project on sexual behavior, pregnancy, birth, and sexually transmitted disease. *Archives of Pediatric and Adolescent Medicine, 156,* 438–447.

Longino, C. F., & Earle, J. R. (1996). Who are the grandparents at century's end? *Generations, 20*(1), 13–16.

Longmore, M. A., Manning, W. D., & Giordano, P. C. (2001). Preadolescent parenting strategies and teens' dating and sexual initiation: A longitudinal analysis. *Journal of Marriage and the Family, 63,* 322–335.

Longnecker, M. P., Klebanoff, M. A., Zhou, H., & Brock, J. W. Association between maternal serum concentration of the DDT metabolite DDE and preterm and small-for-gestational-age babies at birth. *Lancet, 358,* 110–114.

Lonigan, C. J., Burgess, S. R., & Anthony, J. L. (2000). Development of emergent literacy and early reading skills in preschool children: Evidence from a latent-variable longitudinal study. *Developmental Psychology, 36,* 593–613.

Lonigan, C. J., Fischel, J. E., Whitehurst, G. J., Arnold, D. S., & Valdez-Menchaca, M. C. (1992). The role of otitis media in the development of expressive language disorder. *Developmental Psychology, 28,* 430–440.

Looft, W. R. (1973). Socialization and personality: Contemporary psychological approaches. In P. B . Baltes & K. W. Schaie (Eds.), *Life-span developmental psychology.* New York: Academic Press.

Lorenz, K. (1957). Comparative study of behavior. In C. H. Schiller (Ed.), *Instinctive behavior.* New York: International Universities Press.

Lorsbach, T. C., & Reimer, J. F. (1997). Developmental changes in the inhibition of previously relevant information. *Journal of Experimental Child Psychology, 64,* 317–342.

Louis Harris & Associates. (1986). *American teens speak: Sex, myths, TV and birth control: The Planned Parenthood poll.* New York: Planned Parenthood Federation of America.

Louis Harris & Associates. (1995). *Women's issues* (Survey conducted for Families and Work Institute and the Whirlpool Foundation). New York: Author.

Lourenco, O., & Machado, A. (1996). In defense of Piaget's theory: A reply to 10 common criticisms. *Psychological Review, 103*(1), 143–164.

Lovelace, E. A. (1990). Basic concepts in cognition and aging. In E. A. Lovelace (Ed.), *Aging and cognition: Mental processes, self-awareness, and interventions* (pp. 1–28). Amsterdam: North-Holland, Elsevier.

Lowenthal, M., & Haven, C. (1968). Interaction and adaptation: Intimacy as a critical variable. *American Sociological Review, 33,* 20–30.

Lozoff, B., Wolf, A., & Davis, N. S. (1985). Sleep problems seen in pediatric practice. *Pediatrics, 75,* 477–483.

Luecke-Aleksa, D., Anderson, D. R., Collins, P. A., & Schmitt, K. L. (1995). Gender constancy and television viewing. *Developmental Psychology, 31,* 773–780.

Luke, B., Mamelle, N., Keith, L., Munoz, F., Minogue, J., Papiernik, E., Johnson, T. R., & Timothy, R. B. (1995). The association between occupational factors and preterm birth: A United States nurses' study. *American Journal of Obstetrics and Gynecology, 173,* 849–862.

Lund, D. A. (1993a). Caregiving. In R. Kastenbaum (Ed.), *Encyclopedia of adult development* (pp. 57–63). Phoenix: Oryx.

Lund, D. A. (1993b). Widowhood: The coping response. In R. Kastenbaum (Ed.), *Encyclopedia of adult development* (pp. 537–541). Phoenix: Oryx.

Lund, D. A. (Ed.). (1989). *Older bereaved spouses: Research with practical applications.* Washington, DC: Hemisphere.

Lundy, B. L., Jones, N. A., Field, T., Nearing, G., Davalos, M., Pietro, P. A., Schanberg, S., & Kuhn, C. (1999). Prenatal depression effects on neonates. *Infant Behavior and Development, 22,* 119–129.

Lundy, B., Field, T., & Pickens, J. (1996). Newborns of mothers with depressive symptoms are less expressive. *Infant Behavior and Development, 19,* 419–424.

Luster, T., & Small, S. A. (1994). Factors associated with sexual risk-taking among adolescents. *Journal of Marriage and the Family, 56,* 622–632.

Luszcz, M.A., & Bryan, J. (1999). Toward understanding age-related memory loss in late adulthood. *Gerontology, 45,* 2–9.

Lydon-Rochelle, M., Holt, V. L., Easterling, T. R., & Martin, D. P. (2001). Risk of uterine rupture during labor among women with a prior cesarean delivery. *New England Journal of Medicine, 345,* 3–8.

Lyman, R. (1997, April 15). Michael Dorris dies at 52: Wrote of his son's suffering. *The New York Times,* p. C24.

Lynn, J., Teno, J. M., Phillips, R. S., Wu, A. W., Desbiens, N., Harrold, J., Claessens, M. T., Wenger, N., Kreling, B., & Connors, A. F., Jr., for the SUPPORT Investigators. (1997). Perceptions by family members of the dying experience of older and seriously ill patients. *Annals of Internal Medicine, 126,* 97–106.

Lynskey, M. T., Heath, A. C., Bucholz, K. K., Slutske, W. S., Madden, P. A. F., Nelson, E. C., Statham, D. J., & Martin, N. G. (2003). Escalation of drug use in early-onset cannabis users versus co-twin controls. *Journal of the American Medical Association, 289,* 427–433.

Lyon, T. D., & Saywitz, K. J. (1999). Young maltreated children's competence to take the oath. *Applied Developmental Science, 3*(1), 16–27.

Lyons-Ruth, K., Alpern, L., & Repacholi, B. (1993). Disorganized infant attachment classification and maternal psychosocial problems as predictors of hostile-aggressive behavior in the preschool classroom. *Child Development, 64,* 572–585.

Lytton, H., & Romney, D. M. (1991). Parents' differential socialization of boys and girls: A meta-analysis. *Psychological Bulletin, 109*(2), 267–296.

Maccoby, E. (1980). *Social development.* New York: Harcourt Brace Jovanovich.

Maccoby, E. E. (1984). Middle childhood in the context of the family. In W. A. Collins (Ed.), *Development during middle childhood.* Washington, DC: National Academy.

Maccoby, E. E. (1988). Gender as a social category. *Developmental Psychology, 24,* 755–765.

Maccoby, E. E. (1990). Gender and relationships: A developmental account. *American Psychologist, 45*(11), 513–520.

Maccoby, E. E. (1992). The role of parents in the socialization of children: An historical overview. *Developmental Psychology, 28,* 1006–1017.

Maccoby, E. E. (1994). Commentary: Gender segregation in childhood. In C. Leaper (Ed.), *Childhood gender segregation: Causes and consequences* (New Directions for Child Development No. 65, pp. 87–97). San Francisco: Jossey-Bass.

Maccoby, E. E., & Martin, J. A. (1983). Socialization in the context of the family: Parent-child interaction. In P. H. Mussen (Series Ed.) & E. M. Hetherington (Vol. Ed.), *Handbook of child psychology: Vol. 4. Socialization, personality, and social development* (pp. 1–101). New York: Wiley.

MacDermid, S. M., Heilbrun, G., & DeHaan, L. G. (1997). The generativity of employed mothers in multiple roles: 1979 and 1991. In M. E. Lachman & J. B. James (Eds.), *Multiple paths of midlife development* (pp. 207–240). Chicago: University of Chicago Press.

MacDonald, R. K. (1983). *Louisa May Alcott.* Boston: Twayne.

MacDonald, W. L., & DeMaris, A. (1996). Parenting stepchildren and biological children. *Journal of Family Issues, 17,* 5–25.

Macfarlane, A. (1975). Olfaction in the development of social preferences in the human neonate. In *Parent-infant interaction* (CIBA Foundation Symposium No. 33). Amsterdam: Elsevier.

MacKinnon-Lewis, C., Starnes, R., Volling, B., & Johnson, S. (1997). Perceptions of parenting as predictors of boys' sibling and peer relations. *Developmental Psychology, 33,* 1024–1031.

Macklin, R. (2000). Ethical dilemmas in pediatric endocrinology: Growth hormone for short normal children. *Journal of Pediatric Endocrinology, 13,* 1349–1352.

Macleod, J., Smith, G. D., Heslop, P., Metcalfe, C., Carroll, D., & Hart, C. (2002). Psychological stress and cardiovascular disease: empirical demonstration of bias in a prospective observational study of Scottish men. British Medical Journal, 324, 1247–1251.

Macmillan, C., Magder, L. S., Brouwers, P., Chase, C., Hittelman, J., Lasky, T., Malee, K., Mellins, C. A., & Velez-Borras, J. (2001). Head growth and neurodevelopment of infants born to HIV-1-infected drug-using women. *Neurology, 57,* 1402–1411.

MacMillan, H. M., Boyle, M. H., Wong, M. Y.-Y., Duku, E. K., Fleming, J. E., & Walsh, C. A. (1999). Slapping and spanking in childhood and its association with lifetime prevalence of psychiatric disorders in a general population sample. *Canadian Medical Association Journal, 161,* 805–809.

Mahoney, J. L. (2000). School extracurricular activity participation as a moderator in the development of antisocial patterns. *Child Development, 71*(2), 502–516.

Main, M. (1983). Exploration, play, and cognitive functioning related to infant-mother attachment. *Infant Behavior and Development, 6,* 167–174.

Main, M. (1995). Recent studies in attachment: Overview, with selected implications for clinical work. In S. Goldberg, R. Muir, & J. Kerr (Eds.), *Attachment theory: Social, developmental, and clinical perspectives* (pp. 407–470). Hillsdale, NJ: Analytic Press.

Main, M., & Solomon, J. (1986). Discovery of an insecure, disorganized/disoriented attachment pattern: Procedures, findings, and implications for the classification of behavior. In M. Yogman & T. B. Brazelton (Eds.), *Affective development in infancy.* Norwood, NJ: Ablex.

Main, M., Kaplan, N., & Cassidy, J. (1985). Security in infancy, childhood and adulthood: A move to the level of representation. In I. Bretherton & E. Waters (Eds.), Growing points in attachment. *Monographs of the Society for Research in Child Development, 50*(1–20), 66–104.

Mainemer, H., Gilman, L. C., & Ames, E. W. (1998). Parenting stress in families adopting children from Romanian orphanages. *Journal of Family Issues, 19,* 164–180.

Makrides, M., Neumann, M., Simmer, K., Pater, J., & Gibson, R. (1995). Are long-chain polyunsaturated fatty acids essential nutrients in infancy? *The Lancet, 345,* 1463–1468.

Malaspina, D., Harlap, S., Fennig, S., Heiman, D., Nahon, D., Feldman, D., & Susser, E. S. (2001). Advancing paternal age and the risk of schizophrenia. *Archives of General Psychiatry, 58,* 361–371.

Mandel, D. R., Jusczyk, P. W., & Pisoni, D. B. (1995). Infants' recognition of the sound patterns of their own names. *Psychological Science, 6*(5), 314–317.

Mandler, J. (1998). The rise and fall of semantic memory. In M. A. Conway, S. E. Gathercole, & C. Cornoldi (Eds.), *Theories of memory* (Vol. 2). East Sussex, England: Psychology Press.

Mandler, J. M., & McDonough, L. (1993). Concept formation in infancy. *Cognitive Development, 8,* 291–318.

Mandler, J. M., & McDonough, L. (1996). Drinking and driving don't mix: inductive generalization in infancy. *Cognition, 59,* 307–335.

Mandler, J. M., & McDonough, L. (1998). Cognition across the life span: On developing a knowledge base in infancy. *Developmental Psychology. 34,* 1274–1288.

Mannell, R. (1993). High investment activity and life satisfaction: Commitment, serious leisure, and flow in the daily lives of older adults. In J. Kelly (Ed.), *Activity and aging.* Newbury Park, CA: Sage.

Mansfield, R. S., & Busse, T. V. (1981). *The psychology of creativity and discovery: Scientists and their work.* Chicago: Nelson-Hall.

Manson, J. E., & Martin, K. A. (2001). Postmenopausal hormone-replacement therapy. *New England Journal of Medicine, 345,* 34–40.

Manson, J. E., Hu, F. B., Rich-Edwards, J. W., Colditz, G. A., Stampfer, M. J., Willett, W. C., Speizer, F. E., & Hennekens, C. H. (1999). A prospective study of walking as compared with vigorous exercise in the prevention of coronary heart disease in women. *New England Journal of Medicine, 341,* 650–658.

March of Dimes Birth Defects Foundation. (1987). *Genetic counseling: A public health information booklet* (Rev. ed.). White Plains, NY: Author.

March of Dimes Foundation. (2002). Toxoplasmosis. (Fact Sheet). Wilkes-Barre, PA: Author.

Marcia, J. E. (1966). Development and validation of ego identity status. *Journal of Personality and Social Psychology, 3*(5), 551–558.

Marcia, J. E. (1979, June). *Identity status in late adolescence: Description and some clinical implications.* Address given at symposium on identity development, Rijksuniversitat Groningen, Netherlands.

Marcia, J. E. (1980). Identity in adolescence. In J. Adelson (Ed.), *Handbook of adolescent psychology.* New York: Wiley.

Marcia, J. E. (1993). The relational roots of identity. In J. Kroger (Ed.), *Discussions on ego identity* (pp. 101–120). Hillsdale, NJ: Erlbaum.

Marcia, J. E. (2002). Identity and psychosocial development in adulthood. *Identity, 2*(1), 7–28.

Marcoen, A. (1995). Filial maturity of middle-aged adult children in the context of parent care: Model and measures. *Journal of Adult Development, 2,* 125–136.

Marcon, R. A. (1999). Differential impact of preschool models on development and early learning of inner-city children: A three-cohort study. *Developmental Psychology, 35*(2), 358–375.

Marcovitch, S., & Zelazo, P. D. (1999). The A-Not-B error: Results from a logistic meta-analysis. *Child Development, 70,* 1297–1313.

Marcus, G. F., Vijayan, S., Rao, S. B., & Vishton, P. M. (1999). Rule learning by seven-month-old infants. *Science, 283,* 77–80.

Margolis, L. H., Foss, R. D., & Tolbert, W. G. (2000). Alcohol and motor vehicle-related deaths of children as passengers, pedestrians, and bicyclists. *Journal of the American Medical Association, 283*(17), 2245–2248.

Mariani, M. (Summer 2001). Distance learning in postsecondary education: Learning whenever, wherever. *Occupational Outlook Quarterly,* 1–10.

Markman, H. J., Renick, M. J., Floyd, F. J., Stanley, S. M., & Clements, M. (1993). Preventing marital distress through communication and conflict management training: A 4- and 5-year follow-up. *Journal of Consulting and Clinical Psychology, 61,* 70–77.

Markoff, J. (1992, October 12). Miscarriages tied to chip factories. *The New York Times,* pp. A1, D2.

Markovitz, J. H., Matthews, K. A., Kannel, W. B., Cobb, J. L., & D'Agostino, R. B. (1993). Psychological predictors of hypertension in the Framingham study. *Journal of the American Medical Association, 270,* 2439–2443.

Marks, N. (1998). Does it hurt to care? Caregiving, work-family conflict, and midlife well-being. *Journal of Marriage and the Family, 60,* 951–956.

Marks, N. F. (1996). Caregiving across the lifespan: National prevalence and predictors. *Family Relations, 45,* 27–36.

Marks, N. F., & Lambert, J. D. (1998). Marital status continuity and change among young and midlife adults. *Journal of Family Issues, 19,* 652–686.

Markus, H., & Nurius, P. (1986). Possible selves. *American Psychologist, 41,* 954–969.

Marling, K. A. (1996). *Graceland: Going home with Elvis.* Cambridge, MA: Harvard University Press.

Marsiske, M., Lange, F. R., Baltes, P. B., & Baltes, M. M. (1995). Selective optimization with compensation: Life-span perspectives on successful human development. In R. A. Dixon & L. Backman (Eds.), *Compensating for psychological deficits and declines: Managing losses and promoting gains* (pp. 35–79). Mahwah, NJ: Erlbaum.

Martikainen, P., & Valkonen, T. (1996). Mortality after the death of a spouse: Rates and causes of death in a large Finnish cohort. *American Journal of Public Health, 86,* 1087–1093.

Martin, C. L., & Halverson, C. F. (1981). A schematic processing model of sex typing and stereotyping in children. *Child Development, 52,* 1119–1134.

Martin, C. L., Eisenbud, L., & Rose, H. (1995). Children's gender-based reasoning about toys. *Child Development, 66,* 1453–1471.

Martin, J. A., Hamilton, B. E., & Ventura, S. J. (2001). Births: Preliminary data for 2000. *National Vital Statistics Reports, 49*(5). Hyattsville, MD: National Center for Health Statistics.

Martin, J. A., Hamilton, B. E., Ventura, S. J., Menacker, F., & Park, M. M. (2002). Births: Final Data for 2000. *National Vital Statistics Reports, 50*(5). Hyattsville, MD: National Center for Health Statistics.

Martin, J. A., Park, M. M., & Sutton, P. D. (2002). Births: Preliminary data for 2001. *National Vital Statistics Reports, 50*(10). Hyattsville, MD: National Center for Health Statistics.

Martin, L. G. (1988). The aging of Asia. *Journal of Gerontology: Social Sciences, 43*(4), S99–113.

Martin, P., Hagberg, B., & Poon, L. W. (1997). Predictors of loneliness in centenarians: A parallel study. *Journal of Cross-Cultural Gerontology, 12,* 203–224.

Martin, S. L., Mackie, L., Kupper, L. L., Buescher, P. A., & Moracco, K. E. (2001). Physical abuse of women before, during, and after pregnancy. *Journal of the American Medical Association, 285,* 1581–1584.

Martínez-González, M. A., Gual, P., Lahortiga, F., Alonso, Y., de Irala-Estévez, J., & Cervera, S. (2003). Parental factors, mass media influences, and the onset of eating disorders in a prospective population-based cohort. *Pediatrics, 111,* 315–320.

Marwick, C. (1997). Health care leaders from drug policy group. *Journal of the American Medical Association, 278,* 378.

Marwick, C. (1998). Physician leadership on national drug policy finds addiction treatment works. *Journal of the American Medical Association, 279,* 1149–1150.

Masataka, N. (1996). Perception of motherese in a signed language by 6-month-old deaf infants. *Developmental Psychology, 32,* 874–879.

Masataka, N. (1998). Perception of motherese in Japanese sign language by 6-month-old hearing infants. *Developmental Psychology, 34*(2), 241–246.

Maslach, C., & Jackson, S. E. (1985). Burnout in health professions: A social psychological analysis. In G. Sanders & J. Suls (Eds.), *Social psychology of health and illness.* Hillsdale, NJ: Erlbaum.

Masoro, E. J. (1985). Metabolism. In C. E. Finch & E. L. Schneider (Eds.), *Handbook of the biology of aging* (pp. 540–563). New York: Van Nostrand Reinhold.

Masoro, E. J. (1988). Minireview: Food-restriction in rodents: An evaluation of its role in the study of aging. *Journal of Gerontology: Social Sciences, 43*(3), S59–64.

Masoro, E. J. (1992). The role of animal models in meeting the gerontologic challenge of the 21st century. *The Gerontologist, 32*(5), 627–633.

Masoro, E. J. (2001). Dietary restriction: Current status. *Aging Clinical & Experimental Research, 13,* 261–262.

Masse, L. C., & Tremblay, R. E. (1997). Behavior of boys in kindergarten and the onset of substance use during adolescence. *Archives of General Psychiatry, 54,* 62–68.

Masten, A. S. (2001). Ordinary magic: Resilience processes in development. *American Psychologist, 56,* 227–238.

Masten, A., Best, K., & Garmezy, N. (1990). Resilience and development: Contributions from the study of children who overcome adversity. *Development and Psychopathology, 2,* 425–444.

Masten, A. S., & Coatsworth, J. D. (1998). The development of competence in favorable and unfavorable environments: Lessons from research on successful children. *American Psychologist, 53,* 205–220.

Masters, W. H., & Johnson, V. E. (1966). *Human sexual response.* Boston: Little, Brown.

Masters, W. H., & Johnson, V. E. (1981). Sex and the aging process. *Journal of the American Geriatrics Society, 29,* 385–390.

Mathews, T. J., & Ventura, S. J. (1997). *Birth and fertility rates by educational attainment: United States, 1994* (Monthly Vital Statistics Report, 45[10, Suppl.], DHHS Publication No. PHS 97–1120). Hyattsville, MD: National Center for Health Statistics.

Mathews, T. J., Curtin, S. C., & MacDorman, M. F. (2000). Infant mortality statistics from the 1998 period linked birth/infant death data set. *National Vital Statistics Reports,* Vol. 48, No. 12. Hyattsville, MD: National Center for Health Statistics.

Mathias, R. (1999). Tracking trends in teen drug abuse over the years. *NIDA Notes* (National Institute on Drug Abuse), *14*(1), p. S8.

Matthews, K. A., Shumaker, S. A., Bowen, D. J., Langer, R. D., Hunt, J. R., Kaplan, R. M., Klesges, R. C., & Ritenbaugh, C. (1997). Women's health initiative: Why now? What is it? What's new? *American Psychologist, 52*(2), 101–116.

Matthews, S. H. (1995). Gender and the division of filial responsibility between lone sisters and their brothers. *Journal of Gerontology: Social Sciences, 50B,* S312–320.

Maughan, B., & Rutter, M. (2001). Antisocial children grown up. In J. Hill & B. Maughan (Eds.), *Conduct disorders in childhood and adolescence,* (pp. 507–552). Cambridge, UK: Cambridge University Press.

Maurer, D., Stager, C. L., & Mondloch, C. J. (1999). Cross-modal transfer of shape is difficult to demonstrate in one-month-olds. *Child Development,* 70, 1047–1057.

Mayeux, R. (1996). Development of a national prospective study of Alzheimer disease. *Alzheimer Disease and Associated Disorders, 10*(Suppl. 1), 38–44.

Mayeux, R., Saunders, A. M., Shea, S., Mirra, S., Evans, D., Roses, A. D., Hyman, B. T., Crain, B., Tang, M., & Phelps, C. H. (1998). Utility of the apolipoprotein E genotype in the diagnosis of Alzheimer's Disease. *New England Journal of Medicine, 338,* 506–511.

Maynard, A. E. (2002). Cultural teaching: The development of teaching skills in Maya sibling interactions. *Child Development, 73,* 969–982.

Mazzeo, R. S., Cavanaugh, P., Evans, W. J., Fiatarone, M., Hagberg, J., McAuley, E., & Startzell, J. (1998). ACSM position stand on exercise and physical activity for older adults. *Medicine & Science in Sports & Exercise, 30,* 992–1008.

McAdams, D. (1993). *The stories we live by.* New York: Morrow.

McAdams, D. P. (2001). Generativity in midlife. In M. E. Lachman (Ed.), *Handbook of midlife development* (pp. 395–443). New York: Wiley.

McAdams, D. P., & de St. Aubin, E. (1992). A theory of generativity and its assessment through self-report, behavioral acts, and narrative themes in autobiography. *Journal of Personality and Social Psychology, 62,* 1003–1015.

McAdams, D. P., de St. Aubin, E., & Logan, R. L. (1993). Generativity among young, midlife, and older adults. *Psychology and Aging, 8,* 221–230.

McAdams, D. P., Diamond, A., de St. Aubin, E., & Mansfield, E. (1997). Stories of commitment: The psychosocial construction of generative lives. *Journal of Personality and Social Psychology, 72,* 678–694.

McAlindon, T. E., LaValley, M. P., Gulin, J. P., & Felson, D. T. (2000). Glucosamine and chondroitin for treatment of osteoarthritis: A systematic quality assessment and meta-analysis. *Journal of the American Medical Association, 283,* 1469–1475.

McCall, R. B., & Carriger, M. S. (1993). A meta-analysis of infant habituation and recognition memory performance as predictors of later IQ. *Child Development, 64,* 57–79.

McCartney, N., Hicks, A. L., Martin, J., & Webber, C. E. (1996). A longitudinal trial of weight training in the elderly: Continued improvements in year 2. *The Journals of Gerontology: Series A: Biological Sciences and Medical Sciences, 51,* B425-B433.

McCarton, C. M., Brooks-Gunn, J., Wallace, I. F., Bauer, C. R., Bennett, F. C., Bernbaum, J. C., Broyles, S., Casey, P. H., McCormick, M. C., Scott, D. T., Tyson, J., Tonascia, J., & Meinert, C. L., for the Infant Health and Development Program Research Group. (1997). Results at age 8 years of early intervention for low-birth-weight premature infants. *Journal of the American Medical Association, 277,* 126–132.

McCarton, C. M., Wallace, I. F., Divon, M., & Vaughan, H. G. (1996). Cognitive and neurologic development of the preterm, small for gestational age infant through age 6: Comparison by birth weight and gestational age. *Pediatrics, 98,* 1167–1178.

McCarty, M. E., Clifton, R. K., Ashmead, D. H., Lee, P., & Goubet, N. (2001). How infants use vision for grasping objects. *Child Development, 72,* 973–987.

McClearn, G. E., Johansson, B., Berg, S., Pedersen, N. L., Ahern, F., Petrill, S. A., & Plomin, R. (1997). Substantial genetic influence on cognitive abilities in twins 80 or more years old. *Science, 276,* 1560–1563.

McCord, J. (1996). Unintended consequences of punishment. *Pediatrics, 88,* 832–834.

McCormick, M. C., McCarton, C., Brooks-Gunn, J., Belt, P., & Gross, R. T. (1998). The infant health and development program: Interim summary. *Journal of Developmental and Behavioral Pediatrics, 19,* 359–371.

McCoy, A. R., & Reynolds, A. J. (1999). Grade retention and school performance: An extended investigation. *Journal of School Psychology, 37,* 273–298.

McCrae, R. R., & Costa, P. T. (1994). The stability of personality: Observations and evaluations. *Current Directions in Psychological Science, 3*(6), 173–175.

McCrae, R. R., & Costa, P. T., Jr. (1984). *Emerging lives, enduring dispositions.* Boston: Little, Brown.

McCrae, R. R., Costa, P. T., Jr., & Busch, C. M. (1986). Evaluating comprehensiveness in personality systems: The California Q-set and the five factor model. *Journal of Personality, 54,* 430–446.

McCue, J. D. (1995). The naturalness of dying. *Journal of the American Medical Association, 273,* 1039–1043.

McDaniel, M. A., Maier, S. F., & Einstein, G. O. (2002). "Brain-specific" nutrients: A memory cure? *Psychological Science in the Public Interest, 3*(1), 12–38.

McEnany, G., & Lee, K. A. (2000). Owls, larks and the significance of morningness/eveningness rhythm propensity in psychiatric-mental health nursing. *Issues in Mental Health Nursing, 21,* 203–216.

McFadden, S. H., & Levin, J. S. (1996). Religion, emotions, and health. In C. Magai, & S. H. McFadden (Eds.), *Handbook of emotion, adult development, and aging* (pp. 349–365). San Diego: Academic Press.

McFall, S., & Miller, B. H. (1992). Caregiver burden and nursing home admission of frail elderly patients. *Journal of Gerontology: Social Sciences, 47,* S73–79.

McFarland, R. A., Tune, G. B., & Welford, A. (1964). On the driving of automobiles by older people. *Journal of Gerontology, 19,* 190–197.

McGauhey, P. J., Starfield, B., Alexander, C., & Ensminget, M. E. (1991). Social environment and vulnerability of low birth weight children: A social-epidemiological perspective. *Pediatrics, 88,* 943–953.

McGee, R., Partridge, F., Williams, S., & Silva, P. A. (1991). A twelve-year follow-up of preschool hyperactive children. *Journal of the American Academy of Child and Adolescent Psychiatry, 30,* 224–232.

McGrath, M. M., Sullivan, M. C., Lester, B. M., and Oh., W. (2000). Longitudinal neurologic follow-up in neonatal intensive care unit survivors with various neonatal morbidities. *Pediatrics, 106*(6), 1397–1405.

McGue, M. (1993). From proteins to cognitions: The behavioral genetics of alcoholism. In R. P. Plomin & G. E. McClearn (Eds.), *Nature, nurture, and psychology.* Washington, DC: American Psychological Association.

McGue, M. (1997). The democracy of the genes. *Nature, 388,* 417–418.

McGue, M., Bouchard, T. J., Jr., Iacono, W. G., & Lykken, D. T. (1993). Behavioral genetics of cognitive ability: A life-span perspective. In R. Plomin & G. E. McClearn (Eds.), *Nature, nurture, and psychology* (pp. 59–76). Washington, DC: American Psychological Association.

McGuffin, P., Owen, M. J., & Farmer, A. E. (1995). Genetic basis of schizophrenia. *The Lancet, 346,* 678–682.

McGuffin, P., Riley, B., & Plomin, R. (2001). Toward behavioral genomics. *Science, 291,* 1232, 1249.

McGuire, P. A. (1998, July). Wanted: Workers with flexibility for 21st century jobs [On-line]. *APA Monitor Online, 29*(7). Available: http://www.apa.org/monitor/jul98/factor.html

McHale, S. M., Updegraff, K. A., Helms-Erikson, H., & Crouter, A. C. (2001). Sibling influences on gender development in middle childhood and early adolescence: A longitudinal study. *Developmental Psychology, 37,* 115–125.

McIntire, D. D., Bloom, S. L., Casey, B. M., & Leveno, K. J. (1999). Birth weight in relation to morbidity and mortality among newborn infants. *New England Journal of Medicine, 340,* 1234–1238.

McKay, N. Y. (1992). Introduction. In M. Anderson, *My Lord, what a morning* (pp. ix–xxxiii). Madison: University of Wisconsin Press.

McKee, P., & Barber, C. (1999). On defining wisdom. *International Journal of Aging and Human Development, 249,* 149–164.

McKenna, J. J., & Mosko, S. (1993). Evolution and infant sleep: An experimental study of infant-parent co-sleeping and its implications for SIDS. *Acta Paediatrica, 389*(Suppl.), 31–36.

McKenna, J. J., Mosko, S. S., & Richard, C. A. (1997). Bedsharing promotes breastfeeding. *Pediatrics, 100,* 214–219.

McKenry, P. C., Julian, T. W., & Gavazzi, S. M. (1995). Toward a biopsychosocial model of domestic violence. *Journal of Marriage and the Family, 57,* 307–320.

McKinney, K. (1987, March). *A look at Japanese education today* (Research in Brief No. IS 87–107 RIB). Washington, DC: U.S. Department of Education, Office of Educational Research and Improvement.

McKitrick, L. A., Camp, C. J., & Black, F. W. (1992). Prospective memory intervention in Alzheimer's disease. *Journal of Gerontology: Psychological Sciences, 47*(5), P337–343.

McKusick, V. A. (2001). The anatomy of the human genome. *Journal of the American Medical Association, 286*(18), 2289–2295.

McLanahan, S., & Sandefur, G. (1994). *Growing up with a single parent.* Cambridge, MA: Harvard University Press.

McLaughlin, I. G., Leonard, K. E., & Senchak, M. (1992). Prevalence and distribution of premarital aggression among couples applying for a marriage license. *Journal of Family Violence, 7*(4), 309–319.

McLeskey, J., Lancaster, M., & Grizzle, K. L. (1995). Learning disabilities and grade retention: A review of issues with recommendations for practice. *Learning Disabilities Research & Practice, 10,* 120–128.

McLoyd, V. C. (1990). The impact of economic hardship on black families and children: Psychological distress, parenting, and socioemotional development. *Child Development, 61,* 311–346.

McLoyd, V. C. (1998). Socioeconomic disadvantage and child development. *American Psychologist, 53,* 185–204.

McLoyd, V. C., Jayaratne, T. E., Ceballo, R., & Borquez, J. (1994). Unemployment and work interruption among African American single mothers: Effects on parenting and adolescent socioemotional functioning. *Child Development, 65,* 562–589.

McMahon, M. J., Luther, E. R., Bowes, W. A., & Olshan, A. F. (1996). Comparison of a trial of labor with an elective second cesarean section. *New England Journal of Medicine, 335,* 689–695.

McNeilly-Choque, M. K., Hart, C. H., Robinson, C. C., Nelson, L. J., & Olsen, S. F. (1996). Overt and relational aggression on the playground: Correspondence among different informants. *Journal of Research in Childhood Education, 11,* 47–67.

Mead, M. (1928). *Coming of age in Samoa.* New York: Morrow.

Mead, M. (1930). *Growing up in New Guinea.* New York: Blue Ribbon.

Mead, M. (1935). *Sex and temperament in three primitive societies.* New York: Morrow.

Mead, M. (1972). *Blackberry winter: My earlier years.* New York: Morrow.

Measelle, J. R., Ablow, J. C., Cowan, P. A., & Cowan, C. P. (1998). Assessing young children's view of their academic, social, and emotional lives: An evaluation of the self-perception scales of the Berkeley Puppet Interview. *Child Development, 69,* 1556–1576.

Mednick, S. C., Nakayama, K., Cantero, J. L., Atienza, M., Levin, A. A., Pathak, N., & Stickgold, R. (2002). The restorative effect of naps on perceptual deterioration. *Nature Neuroscience, 5,* 677–681.

Meehan, P. J. (1990). Prevention: The endpoint of suicidology. *Mayo Clinic Proceedings, 65,* 115–118.

Meier, D. (1995). *The power of their ideas.* Boston: Beacon.

Meier, D. E., Emmons, C.-A., Wallenstein, S., Quill, T., Morrison, R. S., & Cassel, C. (1998). A national survey of physician-assisted suicide and euthanasia in the United States. *New England Journal of Medicine, 338,* 1193–1201.

Meier, R. (1991, January-February). Language acquisition by deaf children. *American Scientist, 79,* 60–70.

Meins, E. (1998). The effects of security of attachment and maternal attribution of meaning on children's linguistic acquisitional style. *Infant Behavior and Development, 21,* 237–252.

Meisels, S. J., & Atkins-Burnett, S. (2000). The elements of early childhood assessment. In J. P. Shonkoff & S. J. Meisels (Eds.), *Handbook of early childhood intervention* (2nd ed., 231–257). New York: Cambridge University Press.

Meltzoff, A. N. (1995). What infant memory tells us about infantile amnesia: Long-term recall and deferred imitation. *Journal of Experimental Child Psychology, 59,* 497–515.

Meltzoff, A. N., & Moore, M. K. (1983). Newborn infants imitate adult facial gestures. *Child Development, 54,* 702–709.

Meltzoff, A. N., & Moore, M. K. (1989). Imitation in newborn infants: Exploring the range of gestures imitated and the underlying mechanisms. *Developmental Psychology, 25,* 954–962.

Meltzoff, A. N., & Moore, M. K. (1994). Imitation, memory, and the representation of persons. *Infant Behavior and Development, 17,* 83–99.

Meltzoff, A. N., & Moore, M. K. (1998). Object representation, identity, and the paradox of early permanence: Steps toward a new framework. *Infant Behavior & Development, 21,* 201–235.

Mendelsohn, A. L., Dreyer, B. P., Fierman, A. H., Rosen, C. M., Legano, L. A., Kruger, H. A., Lim, S. W., & Courtlandt., C. D. (1998). Low-level lead exposure and behavior in early childhood. *Pediatrics, 101,* e10.

Mennella, J. A., & Beauchamp, G. K. (1996a). The early development of human flavor preferences. In E. D. Capaldi (Ed.), *Why we eat what we eat: The psychology of eating* (pp. 83–112). Washington, DC: American Psychological Association.

Mennella, J. A., & Beauchamp, G. K. (1996b). The human infants' response to vanilla flavors in mother's milk and formula. *Infant Behavior and Development, 19,* 13–19.

Menon, U. (2001). Middle adulthood in cultural perspective: The imagined and the experienced in three cultures. In M. E. Lachman (Ed.), *Handbook of midlife development* (pp. 40–74). New York: Wiley.

Ment, L. R., Vohr, B., Allan, W., Katz, K. H., Schneider, K. C., Westerveld, M., Duncan, C. C., & Makuch, R. W. (2003). Changes in cognitive function over time in very low-birth-weight infants. *Journal of the American Medical Association, 289,* 705–711.

Merrill, S. S., & Verbrugge, L. M. (1999). Health and disease in midlife. In S. L. Willis & J. D. Reid (Eds.), *Life in the middle: Psychological and social development in middle age* (pp. 78–103). San Diego: Academic Press.

Merva, M., & Fowles, R. (1992). *Effects of diminished economic opportunities on social stress: Heart attacks, strokes, and crime* [Briefing paper]. Washington, DC: Economic Policy Institute.

Meyer, B. J. F., Russo, C., & Talbot, A. (1995). Discourse comprehension and problem solving: Decisions about the treatment of breast cancer by women across the life-span. *Psychology in Aging, 10,* 84–103.

Meyer, D. R., & Garasky, S. (1993). Custodial fathers: Myths, realities, and child support policy. *Journal of Marriage and the Family, 55,* 73–89.

Michael, R. T., Gagnon, J. H., Laumann, E. O., & Kolata, G. (1994). *Sex in America: A definitive survey.* Boston: Little, Brown.

Michaud, D. S., Feskanich, D., Rimm, E. B., Colditz, G. A., Speizer, F. E., Willett, W. C., & Giovannucci, E. (2000). Intake of specific carotenoids and risk of lung cancer in 2 prospective U.S. cohorts. *American Journal of Clinical Nutrition, 72,* 990–997.

Michelmore, P. (1962). *Einstein: Profile of the man.* London: Frederick Muller, Ltd.

Michels, K. B., Giovannucci, E., Joshipura, K. J., Rosner, B. A., Stampfer, M. J., Fuchs, C. S., Colditz, G. A., Speizer, F. E., & Willett, W. C. (2000). Prospective study of fruit and vegetable consumption and incidence of colon and rectal cancers. *Journal of the National Cancer Institute, 92,* 1740–1752.

Michelson, D., Faries, D., Wernicke, J., Kelsey, D., Kendrick, K., Sallee, F. R., Spencer, T., & the Atomoxetine ADHD Study Group from the Lilly Research Laboratories and Indiana University School of Medicine, University of Cincinnati, and Massachusetts General Hospital. (2001). Atomoxetine in the treatment of children and adolescents with attention-deficit/hyperactivity disorder: A randomized, placebo-controlled, dose-response study. *Pediatrics, 108,* e83.

Michikawa, Y., Mazzucchelli, F., Bresolin, N., Scarlato, G., & Attardi, G. (1999). Aging-dependent large accumulation of point mutations in the human mtDNA control region for replication. *Science, 286,* 774–779.

Miedzian, M. (1991). *Boys will be boys: Breaking the link between masculinity and violence.* New York: Doubleday.

Milberger, S., Biederman, J., Faraone, S. V., Chen, L., & Jones, J. (1996). Is maternal smoking during pregnancy a risk factor for attention hyperactivity disorder in children? *American Journal of Psychiatry, 153,* 1138–1142.

Milkie, M. A, & Peltola, P. (1999). Playing all the roles: Gender and the work-family balancing act. *Journal of Marriage and the Family, 61,* 476–490.

Miller, B. C., & Moore, K. A. (1990). Adolescent sexual behavior, pregnancy, and parenting: Research through the 1980s. *Journal of Marriage and the Family, 52,* 1025–1044.

Miller, K. F., Smith, C. M., Zhu, J., & Zhang, H. (1995). Preschool origins of cross-national differences in mathematical competence: The role of number-naming systems. *Psychological Science, 6,* 56–60.

Miller, K., & Kohn, M. (1983). The reciprocal effects of job condition and the intellectuality of leisure-time activities. In M. L. Kohn & C. Schooler (Eds.), *Work and personality: An inquiry into the impact of social stratification* (pp. 217–241). Norwood, NJ: Ablex.

Miller, L. J., & Marx, J. (1998). Apoptosis. *Science, 281,* 1301.

Miller, M. W., Astley, S. J., & Clarren, S. K. (1999). Number of axons in the corpus callosum of the mature macaca nemestrina: Increases caused by prenatal exposure to ethanol. *Journal of Comparative Neurology, 412,* 123–131.

Miller, R. A. (1996, July 5). The aging immune system: Primer and prospectus. *Science,* pp. 70–74.

Miller-Jones, D. (1989). Culture and testing. *American Psychologist, 44*(2), 360–366.

Mills, D. L., Cofley-Corina, S. A., & Neville, H. J. (1997). Language comprehension and cerebral specialization from 13 to 20 months. *Developmental Neuropsychology, 13,* 397–445.

Mills, J. L., & England, L. (2001). Food fortification to prevent neural tube defects: Is it working? *Journal of the American Medical Association, 285,* 3022–3033.

Mills, J. L., Holmes, L. B., Aarons, I. H., Simpson, J. L., Brown, Z. A., Jovanovic-Peterson, L. G., Conley, M. R., Graubard, B. I., Knopp, R. H., & Metzger, B. E. (1993). Moderate caffeine use and the risk of spontaneous abortion and intrauterine growth retardation. *Journal of the American Medical Association, 269,* 593–597.

Millstein, S. G., Irwin, C. E., Adler, N. E., Cohn, L. D., Kegeles, S. M., & Dolcini, M. M. (1992). Health-risk behaviors and health concerns among young adolescents. *Pediatrics, 89,* 422–428.

Milunsky, A. (1992). *Heredity and your family's health.* Baltimore: Johns Hopkins University Press.

Miniño, A. M., & Smith, B. L. (2001). *Deaths: Preliminary data for 2000, 49(12)* (PHS) 2001-1120. Hyattsville, MD: National Center-for Health Statistics.

Miniño, A. M., Arias, E., Kochanek, K. D., Murphy, S. L., & Smith, B. L. (2002). Deaths: Final data for 2000. *National Vital Statistics Reports, 50*(15). Hyattsville, MD: National Center for Health Statistics.

Minkler, H., & Roe, K. (1992). *Forgotten caregivers: Grandmothers raising the children of the crack cocaine epidemic.* Newbury Park, CA: Sage.

Minkler, M., & Roe, K. M. (1996). Grandparents as surrogate parents. *Generations, 20*(1), 34–38.

Minnesota explorer Ann Bancroft. (2002). Minnesota Public Radio. [Online]. http://news.mpr.org/programs/midmorning/. Access date: February 20, 2002.

Miotti, P. G., Taha, T. E. T., Kumwenda, N. I., Broadhead, R., Mtimavalye, L. A. R., Van der Hoeven, L., Chiphangwi, J. D., Liomba, G., & Biggar, R. J. (1999). HIV transmission through breastfeeding: A study in Malawi. *Journal of the American Medical Association, 282,* 744–749.

Miserandino, M. (1996). Children who do well in school: Individual differences in perceived competence and autonomy in above-average children. *Journal of Educational Psychology, 88*(2), 203–214.

Misra, D. P., & Guyer, B. (1998). Benefits and limitations of prenatal care: From counting visits to measuring content. *Journal of the American Medical Association, 279,* 1661–1662.

Mistry, R. S., Vandewater, E. A., Huston, A. C., & McLoyd, V. (2002). Economic well-being and children's social adjustment: The role of family process in an ethnically diverse low-income sample. *Child Development, 73,* 935–951.

Mitchell, B. A., Wister, A. V., & Burch, T. K. (1989). The family environment and leaving the parental home. *Journal of Marriage and the Family, 51,* 605–613.

Mitchell, V., & Helson, R. (1990). Women's prime of life: Is it the 50s? *Psychology of Women Quarterly, 16,* 331–347.

Mitka, M. (1998). Getting religion seen as help in being well. *Journal of the American Medical Association, 280,* 1896–1897.

Mittendorf, R. (1995). Teratogen update: Carcinogenesis and teratogenesis associated with exposure to diethylstilbestrol (DES) in utero. *Teratology, 51,* 435–445.

Mix, K. S., Huttenlocher, J., & Levine, S. C. (2002). Multiple cues for quantification in infancy: Is number one of them? *Psychological Bulletin, 128,* 278–294.

Miyake, K., Chen, S., & Campos, J. (1985). Infants' temperament, mothers' mode of interaction and attachment in Japan: An interim report. In I. Bretherton & E. Waters (Eds.), Growing points of attachment theory and research. *Monographs of the Society for Research in Child Development, 50*(1–2, Serial No. 109), 276–297.

Mlot, C. (1998). Probing the biology of emotion. *Science, 280,* 1005–1007.

Modell, J. (1989). *Into one's own: From youth to adulthood in the United States, 1920–1975.* Berkeley: University of California Press.

Moen, P., & Wethington, E. (1999). Midlife development in a life course context. In S. L. Willis & J. D. Reid (Eds.), *Life in the middle: Psychological and social development in middle age* (pp. 1–23). San Diego: Academic Press.

Moen, P., Dempster-McClain, D., & Williams, R. M., Jr. (1992). Successful aging. A life-course perspective on women's multiple roles and health. *American Journal of Sociology, 97,* 1612–1638.

Moen, P., Kim, J. E., & Hofmeister, H. (2001). Couples' work/retirement transitions, gender, and marital quality. *Social Psychology Quarterly, 64,* 55–71.

Moffitt, T. E. (1993). Adolescent-limited and life-course persistent antisocial behavior: A developmental taxonomy. *Psychological Review, 100,* 674–701.

Moffitt, T. E., Caspi, A., Belsky, J., & Silva, P. A. (1992). Childhood experience and the onset of menarche: A test of a sociobiological model. *Child Development, 63,* 47–58.

Mohs, M. E. (1994). Assessment of nutritional status in the aged. In R. R. Watson (Ed.), *Handbook of nutrition in the aged* (2nd ed., pp. 145–164). Boca Raton, FL: CRC Press.

Mokdad, A. H., Bowman, B. A., Ford, E. S., Vinicor, F., Marks, J. S., & Koplan, J. P. (2001). The continuing epidemics of obesity and diabetes in the United States. *Journal of the American Medical Association, 286,* 1195–1200.

Mokdad, A. H., Ford, E. S., Bowman, B. A., Dietz, W. H., Vinicor, F., Bales, V. S., & Marks, J. S. (2003). Prevalence of obesity, diabetes, and obesity-related health risk factors, 2001. *Journal of the American Medical Association, 289,* 76–79.

Molina, B. S. G., & Chassin, L. (1996). The parent-adolescent relationship at puberty: Hispanic ethnicity and parent alcoholism as moderators. *Developmental Psychology, 32,* 675–686.

Money, J., & Ehrhardt, A. A. (1972). *Man and woman/Boy and girl.* Baltimore: Johns Hopkins University Press.

Money, J., Hampson, J. G., & Hampson, J. L. (1955). Hermaphroditism: Recommendations concerning assignment of sex, change of sex, and psychologic management. *Bulletin of Johns Hopkins Hospital, 97,* 284–300.

Monk, T. H. (2000). What can the chronobiologist do to help the shift worker? *Journal of Biological Rhythms, 15,* 86–94.

Montague, C. T., Farooqi, I. S., Whitehead, J. P., Soos, M. A., Rau, H., Wareham, N. J., Sewter, C. P., Digby, J. E., Mohammed, S. N., Hurst, J. A., Cheetham, C. H., Earley, A. R., Barnett, A. H., Prins, J. B., & Orahilly, S. (1997). Congenital leptin deficiency is associated with severe early onset obesity in humans. *Nature, 387,* 903–908.

Montague, D. P. F., & Walker-Andrews, A. S. (2001). Peekaboo: A new look at infants' perception of emotion expressions. *Developmental Psychology, 37,* 826–838.

Montgomery, L. E., Kiely, J. L., & Pappas, G. (1996). The effects of poverty, race, and family structure on U.S. children's health: Data from the NHIS, 1978 through 1980 and 1989 through 1991. *American Journal of Public Health, 86,* 1401–1405.

Moon, C., & Fifer, W. P. (1990, April). *Newborns prefer a prenatal version of mother's voice.* Paper presented at the biannual meeting of the International Society of Infant Studies, Montreal, Canada.

Moon, C., Cooper, R. P., & Fifer, W. P. (1993). Two-day-olds prefer their native language. *Infant Behavior and Development, 16,* 495–500.

Mooney-Somers, J., & Golombok, S, (2000). Children of lesbian mothers: From the 1970s to the new millenium. *Sexual & Relationship Therapy, 15,* 121–126.

Moore, G. A., Cohn, J. F., & Campbell, S. B. (2001). Infant affective responses to mother's still face at 6 months differentially predict externalizing and internalizing behaviors at 18 months. *Developmental Psychology, 37,* 706–714.

Moore, S. E., Cole, T. J., Poskitt, E. M. E., Sonko, B. J., Whitehead, R. G., McGregor, I. A., & Prentice, A. M. (1997). Season of birth predicts mortality in rural Gambia. *Nature, 388,* 434.

Morelli, G. A., Rogoff, B., Oppenheim, D., & Goldsmith, D. (1992). Cultural variation in infants' sleeping arrangements: Questions of independence. *Developmental Psychology, 28,* 604–613.

Morihisa, J. M. (Ed.). (2001). Review of psychiatry: Vol. 20, no. 4. Advances in brain imaging. Washington, DC, US: American Psychiatric Association.

Morison, P., & Masten, A. S. (1991). Peer reputation in middle childhood as a predictor of adaptation in adolescence: A seven-year follow-up. *Child Development, 62,* 991–1007.

Morison, S. J., & Ellwood, A.-L. (2000). Resiliency in the aftermath of deprivation: A second look at the development of Romanian orphanage children. *Merrill-Palmer Quarterly, 46,* 717–737.

Morison, S. J., Ames, E. W., & Chisholm, K. (1995). The development of children adopted from Romanian orphanages. *Merrill-Palmer Quarterly Journal of Developmental Psychology, 41,* 411–430.

Morissette, P., Ricard, M., & Decarie, T. G. (1995). Joint visual attention and pointing in infancy: A longitudinal study of comprehension. *British Journal of Developmental Psychology, 13,* 163–175.

Morris, M. C., Evans, D. A., Bienias, J. L., Tangney, C. C., & Wilson, R. S. (2002). Vitamin E and cognitive decline in older persons. *Archives of Neurology, 59,* 1125–1132.

Morris, R., & Kratochwill, T. (1983). *Treating children's fears and phobias: A behavioral approach.* Elmsford, NY: Pergamon.

Morris, R. D., Stuebing, K. K., Fletcher, J. M., Shaywitz, S. E., Lyon, G. R., Shankweiler, D. P., Katz, L., Francis, D. J., & Shaywitz, B. A. (1998). Subtypes of reading disability: Variability around a phonological core. *Journal of Educational Psychology, 90,* 347–373.

Morrison, D. R., & Cherlin, A. J. (1995). The divorce process and young children's well-being: A prospective analysis. *Journal of Marriage and the Family, 57,* 800–812.

Morse, J. M., & Field, P. A. (1995). *Qualitative research methods for health professionals.* Thousand Oaks, CA: Sage.

Mortensen, E. L., Michaelson, K. F., Sanders, S. A., & Reinisch, J. M. (2002). The association between duration of breastfeeding and adult intelligence. *Journal of the American Medical Association, 287,* 2365–2371.

Mortensen, P. B., Pedersen, C. B., Westergaard, T., Wohlfahrt, J., Ewald, H., Mors, O., Andersen, P. K., & Melbye, M. (1999). Effects of family history and place and season of birth on the risk of schizophrenia. *New England Journal of Medicine, 340,* 603–608.

Mortimer, J. (2003). *Working and growing up in America.* Cambridge, MA: Harvard University Press.

Mortimer, J. T., & Shanahan, M. J. (1991). *Adolescent work experience and relations with peers.* Paper presented at the American Sociological Association Annual Meeting, Cincinnati, OH.

Mortimer, J. T., Finch, M. D., Ryu, S., Shanahan, M. J., & Call, K. T. (1996). The effects of work intensity on adolescent mental health, achievement, and behavioral adjustment: New evidence from a prospective study. *Child Development, 67,* 1243–1261.

Morton, K. R., Worthley, J. S., Nitch, S. R., Lamberton, H. H., Loo, L. K., & Testerman, J. K. (2000). Integration of cognition and emotion: A postformal operations model of physician-patient interaction. *Journal of Adult Development, 7,* 151–160.

Mosca, L., Barrett-Connor, E., D'Agostino, R. B., Hames, C., Hawthorne, V., Kannel, W. B., Kiel, J., Mitchell, B., Sutherland, S. E., Tyroler, H. A., Szklo, M., & Higgens, M. (1998). Race and risk of premature death in the Women's Pooling Project. *Circulation, 17,* 1–97.

Mosca, L., Collins, P., Harrington, D. M., Mendelsohn, M. E., Pasternak, R. C., Robertson, R. M., Schen K-Gustafsson, K., Smith, S. C., Jr., Taubert, K. A., & Wenger, N. K., (2001). Hormone therapy and cardiovascular disease: A statement for healthcare professionals from the American Heart Association. *Circulation, 104,* 499–503.

Moses, L. J., Baldwin, D. A., Rosicky, J. G., & Tidball, G. (2001). Evidence for referential understanding in the emotions domain at twelve and eighteen months. *Child Development, 72,* 718–735.

Moshman, D. (1998). Cognitive development in childhood. In W. Damon (Series Ed.), D. Kuhn, & R. S. Siegler (Vol. Eds.), *Handbook of child psychology: Vol 2. Cognition, perception, and language* (5th ed., pp. 947–978). New York: Wiley.

Moskovitz, J., Bar-Noy, S., Williams, W. M., Requena, J., Berlett, B. S., & Stadtman, E. R. (2001). Methionine sulfoxide reductase (MsrA) is a regulator of antioxidant defense and lifespan in mammals. *Proceedings of the National Academy of Sciences, 98,* 12920–12925.

Moskow-McKenzie, D., & Manheimer, R. J. (1994). *A planning guide to organize educational programs for older adults.* Asheville, NC: University Publications, UNCA.

Moss, E., & St-Laurent, D. (2001). Attachment at school age and academic performance. *Developmental Psychology, 37,* 863–874.

Moss, M. S., & Moss, S. Z. (1989). The death of a parent. In R. A. Kalish (Ed.), *Midlife loss: Coping strategies.* Newbury Park, CA: Sage.

Mounts, N. S., & Steinberg, L. (1995). An ecological analysis of peer influence on adolescent grade point average and drug use. *Developmental Psychology, 31,* 915–922.

Mroczek, D. K., & Kolarz, C. M. (1998). The effect of age on positive and negative affect: A developmental perspective on happiness. *Journal of Personality and Social Psychology, 75*(5), 1333–1349.

MTA Cooperative Group. (1999). A 14-month randomized clinical trial of treatment strategies for attention-deficit/hyperactivity disorder. *Archives of General Psychiatry, 56,* 1073–1986.

Müller, M. (1998). *Anne Frank: The biography.* New York: Holt.

Mui, A. C. (1992). Caregiver strain among black and white daughter caregivers: A role theory perspective. *The Gerontologist, 32*(2), 203, 212.

Mullan, D., & Currie, C. (2000). Socioeconomic equalities in adolescent health. In C. Currie, K. Hurrelmann, W. Settertobulte, R. Smith, & J. Todd (Eds.), *Health and health behaviour among young people: a WHO cross-national study (HBSC) international report* (pp. 65–72). WHO Policy Series: Healthy Policy for Children and Adolescents, Series No. 1.

Mullis, I. V. S., Martin, M. O., Beaton, A. E., Gonzalez, E. J., Kelly, D. L., & Smith, T. A. (1997). *Mathematics achievement in the primary school years: IEA's Third International Mathematics and Science Study (TIMSS).* Chestnut Hill, MA: TIMSS International Study Center, Boston College.

Mumme, D. L., & Fernald, A. (2003). The infant as onlooker: Learning from emotional reactions observed in a television scenario *Child Development, 74,* 221–237.

Muñoz, K. A., Krebs-Smith, S. M., Ballard-Barbash, R., & Cleveland, L. E. (1997). Food intakes of U.S. children and adolescents compared with recommendations. *Pediatrics, 100,* 323–329.

Munakata, Y. (2001). Task-dependency in infant behavior: Toward an understanding of the processes underlying cognitive development. In F. Lacerda, C. von Hofsten, & M. Heimann (Eds.), *Emerging cognitive abilities in early infancy.* Hillsdale, NJ: Erlbaum.

Munakata, Y., McClelland, J. L., Johnson, M. J., & Siegler, R. S. (1997). Rethinking infant knowledge: Toward an adaptive process account of successes and failures in object permanence tasks. *Psychological Review, 104,* 686–714.

Munck, A., Guyre, P., & Holbrook, N. (1984). Physiological functions of glucocorticoids in stress and their relation to pharmacological actions. *Endocrine Reviews, 5,* 25–44.

Murachver, T., Pipe, M., Gordon, R., Owens, J. L., & Fivush, R. (1996). Do, show, and tell: Children's event memories acquired through direct experience, observation, and stories. *Child Development, 67,* 3029–3044.

Murchison, C., & Langer, S. (1927). Tiedemann's observations on the development of the mental facilities of children. *Journal of Genetic Psychology, 34,* 205–230.

Muris, P., Merckelbach, H., & Collaris, R. (1997). Common childhood fears and their origins. *Behaviour Research and Therapy, 35,* 929–937.

Murphy, C. M., & Bootzin, R. R. (1973). Active and passive participation in the contact desensitization of snake fear in children. *Behavior Therapy, 4,* 203–211.

Murphy, G. C., & Athanasou, J. (1999). The effect of unemployment on mental health. *Journal of Occupational and Organizational Psychology, 72,* 83–99.

Murray, A. D., Dolby, R. M., Nation, R. L., & Thomas, D. B. (1981). Effects of epidural anesthesia on newborns and their mothers. *Child Development, 52,* 71–82.

Murray, B. (1998, July 29). Does "emotional intelligence" matter in the workplace? [On-line]. *APA Monitor Online.* Available: http://www.apa.org/monitor/jul98/emot.html

Murray, B. (April 2002). Psychologists help companies traverse the minefields of layoffs. *Monitor on Psychology,* pp. 50–51.

Murray, C. J. L., Michaud, C. M., McKenna, M., & Marks, J. (1998). *U.S. county patterns of mortality by race, 1965–1994.* Cambridge, MA: Harvard Center for Population and Development Studies.

Murstein, B. I. (1980). Mate selection in the 1970s. *Journal of Marriage and the Family, 42,* 777–792.

Musick, M. A., Herzog, A. R., & House, J. S. (1999). Volunteering and mortality among older adults: Findings from a national sample. *Journal of Gerontology: Psychological Sciences, 54B,* S173-S180.

Muskin, P. R. (1998). The request to die. Role for a psychodynamic perspective on physician-assisted suicide. *Journal of the American Medical Association, 279,* 323–328.

Must, A., Jacques, P. F., Dallal, G. E., Bajema, C. J., & Dietz, W. H. (1992). Long-term morbidity and mortality of overweight adolescents: A follow-up of the Harvard Growth Study of 1922 to 1935. *New England Journal of Medicine, 327*(19), 1350–1355.

Mutran, E. J., Reitzes, D. C., & Fernandez, M. E. (1997). Factors that influence attitudes toward retirement. *Research on Aging, 19,* 251–273.

Myers, D. G. (2000). The funds, friends, and faith of happy people. *American Psychologist, 55,* 56–67.

Myers, D. G., & Diener, E. (1996). The pursuit of happiness. *Scientific American, 274,* 54–56.

Myers, D., & Diener, E. (1995). Who is happy? *Psychological Science, 6,* 10–19.

Myers, J. E., & Perrin, N. (1993). Grandparents affected by parental divorce: A population at risk? *Journal of Counseling and Development, 72,* 62–66.

Myerson, J., Shealy, D., & Stern, M. B. (Eds.). (1987). *The selected letters of Louisa May Alcott.* Boston: Little, Brown.

Mykityshyn, A. L., Fisk, A. D., & Rogers, W. A. (in press). Learning to use a home medical device: Mediating age-related differences with training. *Human Factors.*

Naeye, R. L., & Peters, E. C. (1984). Mental development of children whose mothers smoked during pregnancy. *Obstetrics and Gynecology, 64,* 601.

Naito, M., & Miura, H. (2001). Japanese children's numerical competencies: Age- and schooling-related influences on the development of number concepts and addition skills. *Developmental Psychology, 37,* 217–230.

Nakonezny, P. A., Shull, R. D., & Rodgers, J. L. (1995). The effect of no-fault divorce rate across the 50 states and its relation to income, education, and religiosity. *Journal of Marriage and the Family, 57,* 477–488.

Nansel, T. R., Overpeck, M., Pilla, R. S., Ruan, W. J., Simons-Morton, B., & Scheidt, P. (2001). Bullying behaviors among U.S. youth: Prevalence and association with psychosocial adjustment. *Journal of the American Medical Association, 285,* 2094–2100.

Nash, J. M. (1997, February 3). Fertile minds. *Time,* pp. 49–56.

Nathanielsz, P. W. (1995). The role of basic science in preventing low birth weight. *The Future of Our Children, 5*(1), 57–70.

National Academy on an Aging Society. (2000). *Data profiles: Young retirees and older workers* (No. 1). Washington, DC: Author.

National Association on HIV Over Fifty [NAHOF]. (2002). *Educational tip sheet: HIV/AIDS and older adults.* [Online]. Available: http://www.hivoverfifty.org/

National Center for Biotechnology Information. (2002). Genes and disease. [Online] Available: http://www.ncbi.nlm.nih.gov/disease

National Center for Education Statistics (NCES). (1985). *The relationship of parental involvement to high school grades* (Publication

No. NCES-85–205b). Washington, DC: U.S. Government Printing Office.

National Center for Education Statistics (NCES). (1987). *Who drops out of high school? From high school and beyond.* Washington, DC: U.S. Department of Education, Office of Educational Research and Improvement.

National Center for Education Statistics (NCES). (1996). *Education indicators: An international perspective* (NCES 96–003). Washington, DC: U.S. Department of Education.

National Center for Education Statistics (NCES). (1997). *The condition of education 1997: Women in mathematics and science* (NCES 97–982). Washington, DC: Author.

National Center for Education Statistics (NCES). (1998, June). *Nonresident fathers can make a difference in children's school performance* (Issue Brief, NCES 98–117). Washington, DC: U.S. Department of Education, Office of Educational Research and Improvement.

National Center for Education Statistics (NCES). (1999). *The condition of education, 1999* (NCES 1999-022). Washington, DC: U.S. Government Printing Office.

National Center for Education Statistics (NCES). (2001). *The condition of education 2001* (NCES 2001-072). Washington, DC: U.S. Government Printing Office.

National Center for Health Statistics (NCHS). (1993). *Health, United States, 1992 and prevention profile.* Washington, DC: U.S. Public Health Service.

National Center for Health Statistics (NCHS). (1994a). Advance report of final natality statistics, 1992 (*Monthly Vital Statistics Report, 43*[5, Suppl.]). Hyattsville, MD: U.S. Public Health Service.

National Center for Health Statistics (NCHS). (1994b). *Health, United States, 1993.* Hyattsville, MD: U.S. Public Health Service.

National Center for Health Statistics (NCHS). (1998). *Health, United States, 1998 with socioeconomic status and health chartbook.* Hyattsville, MD: Author.

National Center for Health Statistics (NCHS). (2001). *Health, United States, 2001 With Urban and Rural Health Chartbook.* (PHS) 2001-1232. Hyattsville, MD: Author.

National Center for Health Statistics (NCHS). (2002a). Early release of selected estimates from the National Health Interview Survey (NHIS).

National Center for Health Statistics (NCHS). (2002b). *Health, United States, 2002.* Hyattsville, MD: Author.

National Center for Health Statistics (NCHS). (2002c, May). *Vital and Health Statistics, 10*(205). Hyattsville, MD: Author.

National Center for Injury Prevention and Control. (2001). Motor vehicle-related deaths among older Americans fact sheet. [Online]. Available http://www.cdc.gov/nccdphp/aging/index.html

National Center for Learning Disabilities. (2001). *LD fast facts.* [Online]. Available: http://www.ncld.org/info/fastfacts.cfm. (Access date: 2001, December 29).

National Child Abuse and Neglect Data System (NCANDS). (2001). *Child maltreatment 1999.* [Online]. Available: http://www.calib.com/nccanch/pubs.factsheets/canstats.cfm. Access date: April 8, 2002.

National Commission for the Protection of Human Subjects of Biomedical and Behavioral Research. (1978). *Report.* Washington, DC: Author.

National Commission on Youth. (1980). *The transition to adulthood: A bridge too long.* New York: Westview.

National Committee for Citizens in Education (NCCE). (1986, Winter Holiday). Don't be afraid to start a suicide prevention program in your school. *Network for Public Schools,* pp. 1, 4.

National Enuresis Society. (1995). Enuresis. [Fact sheet].

National Hospice and Palliative Care Organization. (2002). *NHPCO Facts and Figures.* Alexandria, VA: Author.

National Institute of Child Health and Development (NICHD). (1997; updated 1/12/00). [Fact sheet] Sudden Infant Death Syndrome. [Online]. Available: http://www.nichd.nih.gov/sids/sids_fact.htm Access date: January 30, 2001.

National Institute of Mental Health (NIMH). (1982). *Television and behavior: Ten years of scientific progress and implications for the eighties: Vol. 1. Summary report* (DHHS Publication No. ADM 82–1195). Washington, DC: U.S. Government Printing Office.

National Institute of Mental Health (NIMH). (1999a, April). *Suicide facts* [On-line]. Washington, DC: Author. Available: http://www.nimh.nih.gov/research/suifact.htm

National Institute of Mental Health (NIMH). (1999b, June 1). *Older adults: Depression and suicide facts* [On line]. Washington, DC: Author. Available: http:www.nimh.hin.gov/publicat/elderlydepsuicide.htm

National Institute of Neurological Disorders and Stroke. (1999, November 10). *Autism* [Fact sheet]. (NIH Publication No. 96–1877.) Bethesda, MD: National Institutes of Health.

National Institute on Aging (NIA). (1980). *Senility: Myth or madness.* Washington, DC: U.S. Government Printing Office.

National Institute on Aging (NIA). (1993). *Bound for good health: A collection of Age Pages.* Washington, DC: U.S. Government Printing Office.

National Institute on Aging (NIA). (1994). *Age page: Sexuality in later life.* Washington, DC: U.S. Government Printing Office.

National Institute on Aging (NIA). (1995b). *Don't take it easy—exercise.* Washington, DC: U.S. Government Printing Office.

National Institute on Aging (NIA). (1999). *AgePage: HIV, AIDS, and older people.* Gaithersburg, MD: Author.

National Institute on Alcohol Abuse and Alcoholism (NIAAA). (1996a, April). *Alcohol alert* (No. 32–1996 [PH 363]). Bethesda, MD: Author.

National Institute on Alcohol Abuse and Alcoholism (NIAAA). (1996b, July). *Alcohol alert* (No. 33–1996 [PH 366]). Bethesda, MD: Author.

National Institute on Alcohol Abuse and Alcoholism (NIAAA). (1998, January). *Alcohol Alert,* No. 39-1998. Rockville, MD: Author.

National Institute on Alcohol Abuse and Alcoholism (NIAAA). (2002). *A call to action: Changing the culture of drinking at U.S. colleges.* Washington, DC: Author.

National Institute on Drug Abuse (NIDA). (1996). *Monitoring the future.* Washington, DC: National Institutes of Health.

National Institutes of Health (NIH) Consensus Development Panel on Physical Activity and Cardiovascular Health. (1996). Physical activity and cardiovascular health. *Journal of the American Medical Association, 276,* 241–246.

National Institutes of Health (NIH). (1992, December 7–9). Impotence (*NIH Consensus Statement, 10*[4]). Washington, DC: U.S. Government Printing Office.

National Institutes of Health (NIH). (1993). Early identification of hearing impairment in infants and young children. *NIH Consensus Statement, 11*(1), 1–24.

National Institutes of Health (NIH). (1998). Diagnosis and treatment of attention deficit hyperactivity disorder (ADHD). *NIH Consensus Statement, 16*(2), 1–37.

National Institutes of Health Consensus Development Panel. (2001). National Institutes of Health Consensus Development conference statement: Phenylketonuria screening and management. October 16–18, 2000. *Pediatrics, 108*(4), 972–982.

National Institutes of Health/National Institute on Aging (NIH/NIA). (1993, May). *In search of the secrets of aging* (NIH Publication No. 93-2756). Washington, DC: National Institutes of Health.

National Parents' Resource Institute for Drug Education. (1999, September 8). *PRIDE surveys, 1998–99 national summary: Grades 6–12.* Bowling Green, KY: Author.

National Reading Panel. (2000). *Report of the National Reading Panel: Teaching children to read: An evidence-based assessment of the scientific research literature on reading and its implications for reading instruction: Reports of the subgroups.* Washington, DC: National Institute of Child Health and Human Development.

National Research Council (NRC). (1993a). *Losing generations: Adolescents in high-risk settings.* Washington, DC: National Academy Press.

National Research Council (NRC). (1993b). *Understanding child abuse and neglect.* Washington, DC: National Academy Press.

National Research Council (NRC). (1998). *Work-related musculoskeletal disorders: A review of the evidence.* Washington, DC: National Academy Press.

National Research Council (NRC). (2001). *Musculoskeletal disorders and the workplace: Low back and upper extremities.* Washington, DC: National Academy Press.

National Sleep Foundation. (2001). *2001 Sleep in America poll.* [Online]. Available:

http://www.sleepfoundation.org/publications/2001poll.html. Access date: October 18, 2002.

National Task Force on the Prevention and Treatment of Obesity. (1993). Very low-calorie diets. *Journal of the American Medical Association, 270,* 967–974.

National Television Violence Study. (1995). *Scientific Papers: 1994–1995.* Studio City, CA: Mediascope.

National Television Violence Study: Key findings and recommendations. (1996, March). *Young Children, 51*(3), 54–55.

NCES Digest of Education Statistics (2001). [Online] Available: http://nces.ed.gov/pubsearch/pubsinfo.asp?pubid=2002130.

Nduati, R., John, G., Mbori-Ngacha, D., Richardson, B.,Overbaugh, J., Mwatha, A., Ndinya-Achola, J., Bwayo, J., Onyango, F. E., Hughes, J., & Kreiss, J. (2000). Effect of breastfeeding and formula feeding on transmission of HIV-i. A randomized clinical trial. *Journal of the American Medical Association, 283*(9), 1167–1174.

Needleman, H. L., & Gatsonis, C. A. (1990). Low-level lead exposure and the IQ of children: A meta-analysis of modern studies. *Journal of the American Medical Association, 263,* 673–678.

Needleman, H. L., Riess, J. A., Tobin, M. J., Biesecker, G. E., & Greenhouse, J. B. (1996). Bone lead levels and delinquent behavior. *Journal of the American Medical Association, 275,* 363–369.

Neiderhiser, J. M., Reiss, D., Hetherington, E. M., & Plomin, R. (1999). Relationships between parenting and adolescent adjustment over time: Genetic and environmental contributions. *Developmental Psychology, 35*(3), 680–692.

Neisser, U. (1976). General, academic, and artificial intelligence. In L. Resnick (Ed.), *Human intelligence: Perspectives on its theory and measurement* (pp. 179–189). Norwood, NJ: Ablex.

Neisser, U., Boodoo, G., Bouchard, T. J., Jr., Boykin, A. W., Brody, N., Ceci, S. J., Halpern, D. F., Loehlin, J. C., Perloff, R., Sternberg, R. J., & Urbina, S. (1996). Intelligence: Knowns and unknowns. *American Psychologist, 51*(2), 77–101.

Nelson, C. A. (1995). The ontogeny of human memory: A cognitive neuroscience perspective. *Developmental Psychology, 31,* 723–738.

Nelson, C. A., Monk, C. S., Lin, J., Carver, L. J., Thomas, K. M., & Truwit, C. L. (2000). Functional neuroanatomy of spatial working memory in children. *Developmental Psychology, 36,* 109–116.

Nelson, J. (1994, December 18). Motive behind Carter's missions spark debate. *Chicago Sun-Times,* p. 40.

Nelson, K. (1992). Emergence of autobiographical memory at age 4. *Human Development, 35,* 172–177.

Nelson, K. (1993b). The psychological and social origins of autobiographical memory. *Psychological Science, 47,* 7–14.

Nelson, K. B., Dambrosia, J. M., Ting, T. Y., & Grether, J. K. (1996). Uncertain value of electronic fetal monitoring in predicting cerebral palsy. *New England Journal of Medicine, 334,* 613–618.

Nelson, L. J., & Marshall, M. F. (1998). *Ethical and legal analyses of three coercive policies aimed at substance abuse by pregnant women.* Report published by the Robert Wood Johnson Substance Abuse Policy Research Foundation.

Nelson, M. E., Fiatarone, M. A., Morganti, C. M., Trice, I., Greenberg, R. A., & Evans, W. J. (1994). Effects of high-intensity strength training on multiple risk factors for osteoporotic fractures: A randomized controlled trial. *Journal of the American Medical Association, 272,* 1909–1914.

Neporent, L. (1999, January 12). Balancing exercises keep injuries at bay. *The New York Times,* p. D8.

Neppl, T. K., & Murray, A. D. (1997). Social dominance and play patterns among preschoolers: Gender comparisons. *Sex Roles, 36,* 381–393.

Netherlands State Institute for War Documentation. (1989). *The diary of Anne Frank: The critical edition* (D. Barnouw & G. van der Stroom, Eds.; A. J. Pomerans & B. M. Mooyaart-Doubleday, Trans.). New York: Doubleday.

Neugarten, B. L. (1967). The awareness of middle age. In R. Owen (Ed.), *Middle age.* London: BBC.

Neugarten, B. L. (1968). Adult personality: Toward a psychology of the life cycle. In B. Neugarten (Ed.), *Middle age and aging.* Chicago: University of Chicago Press.

Neugarten, B. L. (1977). Personality and aging. In J. E. Birren & K. W. Schaie (Eds.), *Handbook of the psychology of aging and the social sciences.* New York: Van Nostrand Reinhold.

Neugarten, B. L., & Neugarten, D. A. (1987, May). The changing meanings of age. *Psychology Today,* pp. 29–33.

Neugarten, B. L., Havighurst, R., & Tobin, S. (1968). Personality and patterns of aging. In B. Neugarten (Ed.), *Middle age and aging.* Chicago: University of Chicago Press.

Neugarten, B. L., Moore, J. W., & Lowe, J. C. (1965). Age norms, age constraints, and adult socialization. *American Journal of Sociology, 70,* 710–717.

Neugebauer, R., Hoek, H. W., & Susser, E. (1999). Prenatal exposure to wartime famine and development of antisocial personality disorder in early adulthood. *Journal of the American Medical Association, 282,* 455–462.

Neville, H. J., & Bavelier, D. (1998). Neural organization and plasticity of language. Current Opinion in Neurobiology, 8(2), 254–258.

Newacheck, P. W., & Halfon, N. (2000). Prevalence, impact, and trends in childhood disability due to asthma. *Archives of Pediatrics and Adolescent Medicine, 154,* 287–293.

Newacheck, P. W., Stoddard, J. J., & McManus, M. (1993). Ethnocultural variations in the prevalence and impact of childhood chronic conditions. *Pediatrics, 91,* 1031–1047.

Newacheck, P. W., Strickland, B., Shonkoff, J. P., Perrin, J. M., McPherson, M., McManus, M., Lauver, C., Fox, H., & Arango, P. (1998). An epidemiologic profile of children with special health care needs. *Pediatrics, 102,* 117–123.

Newcomb, A. F., & Bagwell, C. L. (1995). Children's friendship relations: A meta-analytic review. *Psychological Bulletin, 117*(2), 306–347.

Newcomb, A. F., Bukowski, W. M., & Pattee, L. (1993). Children's peer relations: A meta-analytic review of popular, rejected, neglected, controversial, and average sociometric status. *Psychological Bulletin, 113,* 99–128.

Newman, A. J., Bavelier, D., Corina, D., Jezzard, P., & Neville, H. J. (2002). A critical period for right hemisphere recruitment in American Sign Language processing. *Nature Neuroscience, 5*(1), 76–80.

Newman, D. L., Caspi, A., Moffitt, T. E., & Silva, P. A. (1997). Antecedents of adult interpersonal functioning: Effects of individual differences in age 3 temperament. *Developmental Psychology, 33,* 206–217.

Newman, J. (1995). How breast milk protects newborns. *Scientific American, 273,* 76–79.

Newport, E., & Meier, R. (1985). The acquisition of American Sign Language. In D. Slobin (Ed.), *The crosslinguistic study of language acquisition* (Vol. 1, pp. 881–938). Hillsdale, NJ: Erlbaum.

Newport, E. L. (1991). Contrasting conceptions of the critical period for language. In S. Carey & R. Gelman (Eds.), *The epigenesis of mind: Essays on biology and cognition.* Hillsdale, NJ: Erlbaum.

Newport, E. L., & Supalla, T. (2000). Sign language research at the millennium. In K. Emmorey, & H. Lane, Harlan (Eds.). The signs of language revisited: An anthology to honor Ursula Bellugi and Edward Klima. (pp. 103–114). Mahwah, NJ, US: Lawrence Erlbaum.

Newport, E. L., Bavelier, D., & Neville, H. J. (2001). Critical thinking about critical periods: Perspectives on a critical period for language acquisition. In E. Dupoux, Emmanuel (Ed.), Language, brain, and cognitive development: Essays in honor of Jacques Mehler. (pp. 481–502). Cambridge, MA, US: The MIT Press.

Newsweek Poll. (2000). *Post super Tuesday/gays and lesbians (United States).* Storrs, CT: Roper Center for Public Opinion Research.

NFO Research, Inc. (1999). AARP/Modern Maturity *Sexuality survey: Summary of findings.* [On-line]. Available: http://research.aarp.org/health/mmsexsurvey 1.html

NICHD Early Child Care Research Network. (1996). Characteristics of infant child care: Factors contributing to positive caregiving. *Early Childhood Research Quarterly, 11,* 269–306.

NICHD Early Child Care Research Network. (1997a). The effects of infant child care on infant-mother attachment security: Results of the NICHD study of early child care. *Child Development, 68,* 860–879.

NICHD Early Child Care Research Network. (1997b). Familial factors associated with the characteristics of nonmaternal care for infants.

Journal of Marriage and the Family, 59, 389–408.

NICHD Early Child Care Research Network. (1998a). Early child care and self-control, compliance and problem behavior at twenty-four and thirty-six months. *Child Development, 69,* 1145–1170.

NICHD Early Child Care Research Network. (1998b). Relations between family predictors and child outcomes: Are they weaker for children in child care? *Developmental Psychology, 34,* 1119–1128.

NICHD Early Child Care Research Network. (1998c, November). *When childcare classrooms meet recommended guidelines for quality.* Paper presented at the meeting of the National Association for the Education of Young People.

NICHD Early Child Care Research Network. (1999a). Child outcomes when child care center classes meet recommended standards for quality. *American Journal of Public Health, 89,* 1072–1077.

NICHD Early Child Care Research Network. (1999b). Chronicity of maternal depressive symptoms, maternal sensitivity, and child functioning at 36 months. *Developmental Psychology, 35,* 1297–1310.

NICHD Early Child Care Research Network. (2000). The relation of child care to cognitive and language development. *Child Development, 71,* 960–980.

NICHD Early Child Care Research Network. (2001a). Child care and children's peer interaction at 24 and 36 months: The NICHD Study of Early Child Care. *Child Development, 72,* 1478–1500.

NICHD Early Child Care Research Network. (2001b). Child care and family predictors of preschool attachment and stability from infancy. *Developmental Psychology, 37,* 847–862.

NICHD Early Child Care Research Network. (2002). Child-care structure → process → outcome: Direct and indirect effects of child-care quality on young children's development. *Psychological Science, 13,* 199–206.

NIH Consensus Development Panel on Osteoporosis Prevention, Diagnosis, and Therapy. (2001). Osteoporosis prevention, diagnosis, and therapy. *Journal of the American Medical Association, 285,* 785–794.

NIH Consensus Development Panel on Physical Activity and Cardiovascular Health. (1996). Physical activity and cardiovascular health. *Journal of the American Medical Association, 276,* 241–246.

Nisan, M., & Kohlberg, L. (1982). Universality and variation in moral judgment: A longitudinal and cross-sectional study in Turkey. *Child Development, 53,* 865–876.

Nishimura, H., Hashikawa, K., Doi, K., Iwaki, T., Watanabe, Y., Kusuoka, H., Nishimura, T., & Kubo, T. (1999). Sign language 'heard' in the auditory cortex. *Nature, 397,* 116.

Niskar, A. S., Kieszak, S. M., Holmes, A., Esteban, E., Rubin, C., & Brody D. J. (1998). Prevalence of hearing loss among children 6 to 19 years of age: The third National Health and Nutrition Examination Survey. *Journal of the American Medical Association, 279,* 1071–1075.

Nix, R. L., Pinderhughes, E. E., Dodge, K. A., Bates, J. E., Pettit, G. S., & McFadyen-Ketchum, S. A. (1999). The relation between mothers' hostile attribution tendencies and children's externalizing behavior problems: The mediating role of mothers' harsh discipline practices. *Child Development, 70*(4), 896–909.

Nobre, A. C., & Plunkett, K. (1997). The neural system of language: Structure and development. *Current Opinion in Neurobiology, 7,* 262–268.

Nock, S. L. (1995). Commitment and dependency in marriage. *Journal of Marriage and the Family, 57,* 503–514.

Noelker, L. S., & Whitlatch, C. J. (1995). Caregiving. In G. E. Maddox (Ed.), *The encyclopedia of aging* (pp. 144–146). New York: Springer.

Nojima, M. (1994). Japan's approach to continuing education for senior citizens. *Educational Gerontology, 20,* 463–471.

Noone, K. (2000). Ann Bancroft, polar explorer. *MyPrimeTime.* [Online]. Available: http://www.myprimetime.com/misc/bae_abpro/index.shtml. Access date: April 4, 2002.

Norton, A. J., & Moorman, J. E. (1987). Current trends in marriage and divorce among American women. *Journal of Marriage and the Family, 49*(1), 3–14.

Norwitz, E. R., Schust, D. J., and Fisher, S. J. (2001). Implantation and the survival of early pregnancy. *New England Journal of Medicine, 345*(19), 1400–1408.

Notzon, F. C. (1990). International differences in the use of obstetric interventions. *Journal of the American Medical Association, 263*(24), 3286–3291.

Notzon, F. C., Komarov, Y. M., Ermakov, S. P., Sempos, C. T., Marks, J. S., & Sempos, E. V. (1998). Causes of declining life expectancy in Russia. *Journal of the American Medical Association, 279,* 793–800.

Nourot, P. M. (1998). Sociodramatic play: Pretending together. In D. P. Fromberg & D. Bergen (Eds.), *Play from birth to twelve and beyond: Contexts, perspectives, and meanings* (pp. 378–391). New York: Garland.

NOW Legal Defense and Education Fund & Chernow-O'Leary, R. (1987). *The state-by-state-guide to women's legal rights.* New York: McGraw-Hill.

Nsamenang, A. B. (1987). A West African perspective. In M. E. Lamb (Ed.), *The father's role: Cross-cultural perspectives* (pp. 273–293). Hillsdale, NJ: Erlbaum.

Nsamenang, A. B. (1992a). *Human development in a third world context.* Newbury Park: Sage.

Nsamenang, A. B. (1992b). Perceptions of parenting among the Nso of Cameroon. *Father-child relations: Cultural and biosocial contexts* (pp. 321–344). New York: de Gruyter.

Nugent, J. K., Lester, B. M., Greene, S. M., Wieczorek-Deering, D., & O'Mahony, P. (1996). The effects of maternal alcohol consumption and cigarette smoking during pregnancy on acoustic cry analysis. *Child Development, 67,* 1806–1815.

Nugent, T. (1999, September). At risk: 4 million students with asthma: Quick access to rescue inhalers critical for schoolchildren. *AAP News,* pp. 1, 10.

Nuland, S. B. (2000). Physician-assisted suicide and euthanasia in practice. *New England Journal of Medicine, 342,* 583–584.

Nurnberg, H. G., Hensley, P. L., Gelenberg, A. J., Fava, M., Lauriello, J., & Paine, S. (2003). Treatment of antidepressant-associated sexual dysfunction with sildenafil. *Journal of the American Medical Association, 289,* 56–64.

Nurnberger, J. I., Foroud, T., Flury, L., Su, J., Meyer, E. T., Hu, K., Crowe, R., Edenberg, H., Goate, A., Bierut, L., Reich, T., Schuckit, M., & Reich, W. (2001). Evidence for a locus on chromosome 1 that influences vulnerability to alcoholism and affective disorder. American *Journal of Psychiatry, 158,* 718–724.

Nussbaum, R. L. (1998). Putting the parkin into Parkinson's. *Nature, 392,* 544–545.

Nyström, L., Andersson, I., Bjurstam, N., Frisell, J., Nordenskjöld, B., & Rutqvist, L. E. (2002). Long-term effects of mammography screening: updated overview of the Swedish randomised trials. *Lancet, 359,* 909–919.

O'Brien, C. M., & Jeffery, H. E. (2002). Sleep deprivation, disorganization and fragmentation during opiate withdrawal in newborns. *Paediatric Child Health, 38,* 66–71.

O'Connor, B. P., & Vallerand, R. J. (1998). Psychological adjustment variables as predictors of mortality among nursing home residents. *Psychology and Aging, 13*(3), 368–374.

O'Connor, T. G., & Croft, C. M. (2001). A twin study of attachment in preschool children. *Child Development, 72,* 1501–1511.

O'Connor, T. G., Caspi, A., DeFries, J. C., & Plomin, R. (2000). Are associations between parental divorce and children's adjustment genetically mediated? An adoption study. *Developmental Psychology, 36*(4), 429–437.

O'Neill, G., Summer, L, & Shirey, L. (1999). Hearing loss: A growing problem that affects quality of life. Washington, DC: National Academy on an Aging Society.

Oakes, L. M. (1994). Development of infants' use of continuity cues in their perception of causality. *Developmental Psychology, 30,* 869–879.

O'Bryant, S. L. (1988). Sibling support and older widows' well-being. *Journal of Marriage and the Family, 50,* 173–183.

Ochsner, K. N., & Lieberman, M. D. (2001). The emergence of social cognitive neuroscience. *American Psychologist, 56,* 717–734.

Offer, D. (1987). In defense of adolescents. *Journal of the American Medical Association, 257,* 3407–3408.

Offer, D., & Church, R. B. (1991). Generation gap. In R. M. Lerner, A. C. Petersen, & J. Brooks-Gunn (Eds.), *Encyclopedia of adolescence* (pp. 397–399). New York: Garland.

Offer, D., & Schonert-Reichl, K. A. (1992). Debunking the myths of adolescence: Findings from recent research. *Journal of the American Academy of Child and Adolescent Psychiatry, 31,* 1003–1014.

Offer, D., Ostrov, E., & Howard, K. I. (1989). Adolescence: What is normal? *American Journal of Diseases of Children, 143,* 731–736.

Offer, D., Ostrov, E., Howard, K. I., & Atkinson, R. (1988). *The teenage world: Adolescents' self-image in ten countries.* New York: Plenum.

Ogden, C. L., Flegal, K. M., Carroll, M. D., & Johnson, C. L. (2002). Prevalence and trends in overweight among US children and adolescents, 1999–2000. *Journal of the American Medical Association, 288,* 1728–1732.

Ogden, C. L., Troiano, R. P., Briefel, R. R., Kuczmarski, R. J., Flegal, K. M., & Johnson, C. L. (1997). Prevalence of overweight among preschool children in the United States, 1971 through 1994 [On-line]. *Pediatrics, 99.* Available: http://www.pediatrics.org/cgi/content/ full/99/4/e1

Olds, D. L., Henderson, C. R., & Tatelbaum, R. (1994a). Intellectual impairment in children of women who smoke cigarettes during pregnancy. *Pediatrics, 93,* 221–227.

Olds, D. L., Henderson, C. R., & Tatelbaum, R. (1994b). Prevention of intellectual impairment in children of women who smoke cigarettes during pregnancy. *Pediatrics, 93,* 228–233.

Olds, S. W. (1989). *The working parents' survival guide.* Rocklin, CA: Prima.

O'Leary, K. D., Barling, J., Arias, I., Rosenbaum, A., Malone, J., & Tyree, A. (1989). Prevalence and stability of physical aggression between spouses: A longitudinal analysis. *Journal of Consulting and Clinical Psychology, 57*(2), 263–268.

Oliver, M. B., & Hyde, J. S. (1993). Gender differences in sexuality: A meta-analysis. *Psychological Bulletin, 114,* 29–51.

Ollendick, T. H., Yang, B., King, N. J., Dong, Q., & Akande, A. (1996). Fears in American, Australian, Chinese, and Nigerian children and adolescents: A crosscultural study. *Journal of Child Psychology and Psychiatry, 37,* 213–220.

Olmsted, P. P., & Weikart, D. P. (Eds.). (1994). *Family speak: Early childhood care and education in eleven countries.* Ypsilanti, MI: High/Scope.

Olshansky, S. J., Carnes, B. A., & Cassel, C. (1990). In search of Methuselah: Estimating the upper limits to human longevity. *Science, 250,* 634–640.

Olshansky, S. J., Carnes, B. A., & Desesquelles, A. (2001). Prospects for human longevity. *Science, 291*(5508), 1491–1492.

Olshansky, S. J. Hayflick, L., & Carnes, B. A. (2002a). No truth to the fountain of youth. *Scientific American, 286,* 92–95.

Olshansky, S. J., Hayflick, L., & Carnes, B. A. (2002b). The truth about human aging. *Scientific American.* [Online]. Available: http://www.sciam.com/explorations/ 2002/ 051302aging/. Access date: August 23, 2002.

Olthof, T., Schouten, A., Kuiper, H., Stegge, H., & Jennekens-Schinkel, A. (2000). Shame and guilt in children: Differential situational antecedents and experiential correlates. *British Journal of Developmental Psychology, 18,* 51–64.

Olweus, D. (1995). Bullying or peer abuse at school: Facts and intervention. *Current Directions in Psychological Science, 4,* 196–200.

O'Rahilly, S. (1998). Life without leptin. *Nature, 392,* 330–331.

Orbuch, T. L., & Eyster, S. L. (1997). Division of household labor among black couples and white couples. *Social Forces, 76,* 301–332.

Orbuch, T. L., House, J. S., Mero, R. P., & Webster, P. S. (1996). Marital quality over the life course. *Social Psychology Quarterly, 59,* 162–171.

Orenstein, P. (2002, April 21). Mourning my miscarriage. *NYTimes.com.*

Orentlicher, D. (1996). The legalization of physician-assisted suicide. *New England Journal of Medicine, 335,* 663–667.

Organization for Economic Co-Operation and Development. (1998). *Maintaining prosperity in an ageing society.* Paris: Author.

Orr, D. P., & Ingersoll, G. M. (1995). The contribution of level of cognitive complexity and pubertal timing to behavioral risk in young adolescents. *Pediatrics, 95*(4), 528–533.

Orr, W. C., & Sohal, R. S. (1994). Extension of life-span by overexpression of superoxide dimutase and catylase in drosphila melanogaster. *Science, 263,* 1128–1130.

Osborn, A. (2002, April 1). Mercy killing now legal in Netherlands. *The Guardian.* [Online]. Available: http://www.nvve.ni/english/info/euth.legal_guardian01-04-02.htm. Access date: July 31, 2002.

Oshima, S. (1996, July 5). Japan: Feeling the strains of an aging population. *Science,* pp. 44–45.

Oshima-Takane, Y., Goodz, E., & Derevensky, J. L. (1996). Birth order effects on early language development: Do secondborn children learn from overheard speech? *Child Development, 67,* 621–634.

Ostrea, E. M., & Chavez, C. J. (1979). Perinatal problems (excluding neonatal withdrawal) in maternal drug addiction: A study of 830 cases. *Journal of Pediatrics, 94*(2), 292–295.

O'Sullivan, J. T., Howe, M. L., & Marche, T. A. (1996). Children's beliefs about long-term retention. *Child Development, 67,* 2989–3009.

Otsuka, R., Watanabe, H., Hirata, K., Tokai, K., Muro, T., Yoshiyama, M., Takeuchi, K., & Yoshikawa, J. (2001). Acute effects of passive smoking on the coronary circulation in healthy young adults. *Journal of the American Medical Association, 286,* 436–441.

Ott, A., Slooter, A. J. C., Hofman, A., Van Harskamp, F., Witteman, J. C. M., Van Broeckhoven, C., Van Duijn, C. M., & Breteler, M. M. B. (1998). Smoking and risk of dementia and Alzheimer's disease in a population-based cohort study. *Lancet, 351,* 1840–1843.

Otten, M. W., Teutsch, S. M., Williamson, D. F., & Marks, J. S. (1990). The effect of known risk factors on the excess mortality of black adults in the United States. *Journal of the American Medical Association, 263*(6), 845–850.

Owens, J. F., Matthews, K. A., Wing, R., & Kuller, L. H. (1992). Can physical activity mitigate the effects of aging in middle-aged women? *Circulation, 85*(3), 1265–1270.

Owens, R. E. (1996). *Language development* (4th ed.). Boston: Allyn and Bacon.

Owsley, C., Ball, K., McGwin, G., Jr., Sloane, M. E., Roenker, D. L., White, M. F., & Overley, E. T. (1998). Visual processing impairment and crash risk among older adults. *Journal of the American Medical Association, 279,* 1083–1088.

Padden, C. A. (1996). Early bilingual lives of deaf children. In I. Parasnis (Ed.), *Cultural and language diversity and the deaf experience* (pp. 99–116). New York: Cambridge University Press.

Paden, S. L., & Buehler, C. (1995). Coping with the dual-income lifestyle. *Journal of Marriage and the Family, 57,* 101–110.

Padilla, A. M., Lindholm, K. J., Chen, A., Durán, R., Hakuta, K., Lambert, W., & Tucker, G. R. (1991). The English-only movement: Myths, reality, and implications for psychology. *American Psychologist, 46*(2), 120–130.

Padovani, A., Borroni, B., Colciaghi, F., Pettenati, C., Cottini, E., Agosti, C., Lenzi, G. L., Caltagirone C, Trabucchi M, Cattabeni F, & Di Luca M. (2002). Abnormalities in the pattern of platelet amyloid precursor protein forms in patients with mild cognitive impairment and Alzheimer disease. *Archives of Neurology, 59,* 71–75.

Paganini-Hill, A., & Henderson, V. W. (1996). Estrogen replacement therapy and risk of Alzheimer's disease. *Archives of Internal Medicine, 156,* 2213–2217.

Palaniappan, L., Anthony, M. N., Mahesh, C., Elliott, M., Killeen, A., Giacherio, D., & Rubenfire, M. (2002). Cardiovascular risk factors in ethnic minority women aged less-than-or-equal 30 years. *American Journal of Cardiology, 89,* 524–529.

Pally, R. (1997). How brain development is shaped by genetic and environmental factors. *International Journal of Psycho-Analysis, 78,* 587–593.

Pamuk, E., Makuc, D., Heck, K., Reuben, C., & Lochner, K. (1998). Socioeconomic status and health chartbook. In *Health, United States, 1998.* Hyattsville, MD: National Center for Health Statistics.

Panigrahy, A., Filiano, J., Sleeper, L. A., Mandell, F., Vales-Dapena, M., Krous, H. F., Rava, L. A., Foley, E., White, W. F., & Kinney, H. C. (2000). Decreased serotonergic receptor binding in rhombic lip-derived regions of the medulla oblongata in the sudden infant death syndrome. *Journal of Neuropathology and Experimental Neurology, 59,* 377–384.

Papernow, P. (1993). *Becoming a stepfamily: Patterns of development in remarried families.* San Francisco: Jossey-Bass.

Parasuraman, R., Greenwood, P. M., & Sunderland, T. (2002). The Apolilpoprotein E gene, attention, and brain function. *Neuropsychology, 16,* 254–274.

Parikh, F., Naik, N., Gada, S., Bhartiya, D., Athalye, A., & Madon, P. (2001). Preimplantation genetic diagnosis for the better management of couples during assisted reproduction. *International Journal of Human Genetics, 1,* 117–121.

Parish, S., Collins, R., Peto, R., Youngman, L., Barton, J., Jayne, K., Clarke, R., Appleby, P., Lyon, V., Cederholm-Williams, S., Marshall, J., & Sleight, P. for the International Studies of Infarct Survival (ISIS). (1995). Cigarette smoking, tar yields, and non-fatal myocardial infarction: 14,000 cases and 32,000 controls in the United Kingdom. *British Medical Journal, 311,* 471–477.

Park, S., Belsky, J., Putnam, S., & Crnic, K. (1997). Infant emotionality, parenting, and 3-year inhibition: Exploring stability and lawful discontinuity in a male sample. *Developmental Psychology, 33,* 218–227.

Parke, R. D., & Buriel, R. (1998). Socialization in the family: Ethnic and ecological perspectives. In W. Damon (Series Ed.) & N. Eisenberg (Vol. Ed.), *Handbook of child psychology: Vol. 3. Social, emotional, and personality development* (5th ed., pp. 463–552). New York: Wiley.

Parke, R. D., Grossman, K., & Tinsley, R. (1981). Father-mother-infant interaction in the newborn period: A German-American comparison. In T. M. Field, A. M. Sostek, P. Viete, & P. H. Leideman (Eds.), *Culture and early interaction.* Hillsdale, NJ: Erlbaum.

Parke, R. D., Ornstein, P. A., Rieser, J. J., & Zahn-Waxler, C. (1994). The past as prologue: An overview of a century of developmental psychology. In R. D. Parke, P. A. Ornstein, J. J. Rieser, & C. Zahn-Waxler (Eds.), *A century of developmental psychology* (pp. 1–70). Washington, DC: American Psychological Association.

Parker, J. G., & Asher, S. R. (1987). Peer relations and later personal adjustment: Are low-accepted children at risk? *Psychological Bulletin, 102,* 357–389.

Parker, L., Pearce, M. S., Dickinson, H. O., Aitkin, M., & Craft, A. W. (1999). Stillbirths among offspring of male radiation workers at Sellafield nuclear reprocessing plant. *Lancet, 354,* 1407–1414.

Parker, R. A., & Aldwin, C. M. (1997). Do aspects of gender identity change from early to middle adulthood? Disentangling age, cohort, and period effects. In M. E. Lachman & J. B. James (Eds.), *Multiple paths of midlife development* (pp. 67–107). Chicago: University of Chicago Press.

Parkes, T. L., Elia, A. J., Dickinson, D., Hilliker, A. J., Phillips, J. P., & Boulianne, G. L. (1998). Extension of Drosophila lifespan by overexpression of human SOD1 in motorneurons. *Nature Genetics, 19,* 171–174.

Parmelee, A. H., Wenner, W. H., & Schulz, H. R. (1964). Infant sleep patterns: From birth to 16 weeks of age. *Journal of Pediatrics, 65,* 576.

Parnes, H. S., & Sommers, D. G. (1994). Shunning retirement: Work experience of men in their seventies and early eighties. *Journal of Gerontology: Social Sciences, 49,* S117–124.

Parrish, K. M., Holt, V. L., Easterling, T. R., Connell, F. A., & LeGerfo, J. P. (1994). Effect of changes in maternal age, parity, and birth weight distribution on primary cesarean delivery rates. *Journal of the American Medical Association, 271,* 443–447.

Parten, M. B. (1932). Social play among preschool children. Journal of Abnormal and Social *Psychology, 27,* 243–269.

Pascarella, E. T., Edison, M. I., Nora, A., Hagedorn, L. S., & Terenzini, P. T. (1998). Does work inhibit cognitive development during college? *Educational Evaluation and Policy Analysis, 20,* 75–93.

Pastor, P. N., Makuc, D. M., Reuben, C., & Xia, H. (2002). Chartbook on trends in the health of Americans. In *Health, United States, 2002.* Hyattsville, MD: National Center for Health Statistics.

Pasupathi, M., Staudinger U. M., & Baltes, P. B. (2001). Seeds of wisdom: Adolescents' knowledge and judgment about difficult life problems. *Developmental Psychology, 37*(3), 351–361.

Pate, R. R., Pratt, M., Blair, S. N., Haskell, W. L., & Macera, C. A. (1995). Physical activity and public health. *Journal of the American Medical Association, 273,* 402–407.

Patenaude, A. F., Guttmacher, A. E., & Collins, F. S. (2002). Genetic testing and psychology: New roles, new responsibilities. *American Psychologist, 57,* 271–282.

Patterson, C. J. (1992). Children of lesbian and gay parents. *Child Development, 63,* 1025–1042.

Patterson, C. J. (1995a). Lesbian mothers, gay fathers, and their children. In A. R. D'Augelli & C. J. Patterson (Eds.), *Lesbian, gay, and bisexual identities over the lifespan: Psychological perspectives* (pp. 293–320). New York: Oxford University Press.

Patterson, C. J. (1995b). Sexual orientation and human development: An overview. *Developmental Psychology, 31,* 3–11.

Patterson, C. J. (1997). Children of gay and lesbian parents. In T. H. Ollendick & R. J. Prinz (Eds.), *Advances in clinical child psychology* (Vol. 19, pp. 235–282). New York: Plenum.

Patterson, G. R. (1995). Coercion—A basis for early age of onset for arrest. In J. McCord (Ed.), *Coercion and punishment in long-term perspective* (pp. 81–105). New York: Cambridge University Press.

Patterson, G. R., DeBaryshe, B. D., & Ramsey, E. (1989). A developmental perspective on antisocial behavior. *American Psychologist, 44*(2), 329–335.

Patterson, G. R., Reid, J. B., & Dishion, T. J. (1992). *Antisocial boys.* Eugene, OR: Castalia.

Pauen, S. (2002). Evidence for knowledge-based category discrimination in infancy. *Child Development, 73,* 1016–1033.

Paul, E. L. (1997). A longitudinal analysis of midlife interpersonal relationships and well-being. In M. E. Lachman & J. B. James (Eds.), *Multiple paths of midlife development* (pp. 171–206). Chicago: University of Chicago Press.

Paveza, G. J., Cohen, D., Eisdorfer, C., Freels, S., Semla, T., Ashford, J. W., Gorelick, P., Hirschman, R., Luchins, -D., & Levy, P. (1992). Severe family violence and Alzheimer's disease: Prevalence and risk factors. *The Gerontologist, 32*(4), 493–497.

Peeters, A., Barendregt, J. J., Willekens, F., Mackenbach, J. P., Al Mamun, A., & Bonneux, L., for NEDCOM, the Netherlands Epidemiology and Demography Compression of Morbidity Research Group (2003). Obesity in adulthood and its consequences for life expectancy. *Annals of Internal Medicine, 138,* 24–32.

Pérez-Stable, E. J., Herrera, B., Jacob, P., III, & Benowitz, N. L. (1998). Nicotine metabolism and intake in black and white smokers. *Journal of the American Medical Association, 280,* 152–156.

Pérusse, L., Chagnon, Y. C., Weisnagel, J., & Bouchard, C. (1999). The human obesity gene map: The 1998 update. *Obesity Research, 7,* 111–129.

Pearson, H. (2002, February 12). Study refines breast cancer risks. *Nature Science Update.* [Online]. Available: http://www.nature.com/nsu/020211/020211–8. html. Access date: February 19, 2002.

Pearson, J. D., Morell, C. H., Gordon-Salant, S., Brant, L. J., Metter, E. J., Klein, L., & Fozard, J. L. (1995). Gender differences in a longitudinal study of age-associated hearing loss. *Journal of the Acoustical Society of America, 97,* 1196–1205.

Peisner-Feinberg, E. S., Burchinal, M. R., Clifford, R. M., Culkin, M. L., Howes, C., Kagan, S. L., & Yazejian, N. (2001). The relation of preschool child-care quality to children's cognitive and social developmental trajectories through second grade. *Child Development, 72,* 1534–1553.

Pellegrini, A. D. (1998). Rough-and-tumble play from childhood through adolescence. In D. P. Fromberg & D. Bergen (Eds.), *Play from birth to twelve and beyond: Contexts, perspectives, and meanings* (pp. 401–408). New York: Garland.

Pellegrini, A. D., & Smith, P. K. (1998). Physical activity play: The nature and function of a neglected aspect of play. *Child Development, 69,* 577–598.

Pelletier, A. R., Quinlan, K. P., Sacks, J. J., Van Gilder, T. J., Gilchrist, J., & Ahluwalia, H. K. (2000). Injury prevention practices as depicted in G-rated and PG-rated movies. *Archives of Pediatrics and Adolescent Medicine, 154,* 283–286.

Pelleymounter, N. A., Cullen, M. J., Baker, M. B., Hecht, R., Winters, D., Boone, T., & Collins, F. (1995). Effects of the obese gene product on body regulation in ob/ob mice. *Science, 269,* 540–543.

Penning, M. J. (1998). In the middle: Parental caregiving in the context of other roles. *Journal of Gerontology: Social Sciences, 53B,* S188–S197.

Penninx, B. W. J. H., Guralnik, J. M., Ferrucci, L., Simonsick, E. M., Deeg, D. J. H., & Wallace, R. B. (1998). Depressive symptoms and physical decline in community-dwelling older persons. *Journal of the American Medical Association, 279,* 1720–1726.

Penninx, B. W., Messier, S. P., Rejeski, W. J., Williamson, J. D., DiBari, M., Cavazzini, C., Applegate, W. B., & Pahor, M. (2001). Physical exercise and the prevention of disability in activities of daily living in older persons with osteoarthritis. *Archives of Internal Medicine, 161,* 2309–2316.

Pennisi, E. (1998). Single gene controls fruit fly life-span. *Science, 282,* 856.

Pepper, S. C. (1942). *World hypotheses.* Berkeley: University of California Press.

Pepper, S. C. (1961). *World hypotheses.* Berkeley: University of California Press.

Pepys, M. B., Herbert, J., Hutchinson, W. L., Tennent, G. A., Lachmann, H. J., Gallimore, J. R., Lovat, I. B., Bartfai, T., Alanine, A., Hertel, C., Hoffmann, T., Jakob-Roetne, R., Norcross, R. D., Kemp, J. A., Yamamura, K., Suzuki, M., Taylor, G. W., Murray, S., Thompson, D., Purvis, A., Kolstoe, S., Wood, S. P., & Hawkins, P. N. (2002). Targeted pharmacological depletion of serum amyloid P component for treatment of human amyloidosis. *Nature, 417,* 254–259.

Perera, V. (1995). Surviving affliction. [Online.] Available: http://www.metroactive.com/papers/metro/12.14.95/allende-9550.html. Access date: April 1, 2002.

Perex, L. (1994). The households of children of immigrants in south Florida: An exploratory study of extended family arrangements. International Migration Review, 28(4), 736–47.

Perlmutter, M., Kaplan, M., & Nyquist, L. (1990). Development of adaptive competence in adulthood. *Human Development, 33,* 185–197.

Perls, T., Kunkel, L. M., & Puca, A. (2002a). The genetics of aging. *Current Opinion in Genetics and Development, 12,* 362–369.

Perls, T., Kunkel, L. M., & Puca, A. A. (2002b). The genetics of exceptional human longevity. *Journal of the American Geriatric Society, 50,* 359–368.

Perls, T. T., Wilmoth, J., Levenson, R., Drinkwater, M., Cohen, M., Bogan, H., Joyce, E., Brewster, S., Kunkel, L., & Puca, A. (2002). Life-long sustained mortality advantage of siblings of centenarians. *Proceedings of the National Academy of Sciences, 99,* 8442–8447.

Perozynski, L., & Kramer, L. (1999). Parental beliefs about managing sibling conflict. *Developmental Psychology, 35,* 489–499.

Perrin, E. C. and the Committee on Psychosocial Aspects of Child and Family Health. (2002). Technical report: Coparent or second-parent adoption by same-sex parents. *Pediatrics, 109*(2), 341–344.

Perrucci, C. C., Perrucci, R., & Targ, D. B. (1988). *Plant closings.* New York: Aldine.

Perry, W. G. (1970). *Forms of intellectual and ethical development in the college years.* New York: Holt.

Peter D. Hart Research Associates. (1999). *The new face of retirement.* Washington, DC: Author.

Peters, R. D., Kloeppel, A. E., Fox, E., Thomas, M. L., Thorne, D. R., Sing, H. C., & Balwinski, S. M. (1994). *Effects of partial and total sleep deprivation on driving performance.* Washington, DC: Federal Highway Administration.

Petersen, A. C. (1993). Presidential address: Creating adolescents: The role of context and process in developmental transitions. *Journal of Research on Adolescents, 3*(1), 1–18.

Petersen, A. C., Compas, B. E., Brooks-Gunn, J., Stemmler, M., Ey, S., & Grant, K. E. (1993). Depression in adolescence. *American Psychologist, 48*(2), 155–168.

Peterson, C. C. (1996). The ticking of the social clock: Adults' beliefs about the timing of transition events. *International Journal of Aging and Human Development, 42*(3), 189–203.

Peterson, C. C. (1999). Children's memory for medical emergencies: 2 years later. *Developmental Psychology, 35,* 1493–1506.

Peterson, J. L., Moore, K. A., & Furstenberg, F. F., Jr. (1991). Television viewing and early initiation of sexual intercourse: Is there a link? *Journal of Homosexuality, 21,* 93–118.

Peterson, J. T., (1993). Generalized Extended Family Exchange: A Case from the Philippines. Journal of Marriage and the Family, 55(3), 570–84.

Peth-Pierce, R. (1998). *The NICHD study of early child care* [On-line]. Available: http://www.nih.gov/nichd/html/news/early-child/Early_Child_ Care.htm

Petitti, D. B. (2002). Hormone replacement therapy for prevention: More evidence, more pessimism. *Journal of the American Medical Association, 288,* 99–101.

Petitto, L. A., & Marentette, P. F. (1991). Babbling in the manual mode: Evidence for the ontogeny of language. *Science, 251,* 1493–1495.

Pettit, G. S., Bates, J. E., & Dodge, K. A. (1997). Supportive parenting, ecological context, and children's adjustment: A seven-year longitudinal study. *Child Development, 68,* 908–923.

Pharaoh, P. D. P., Antoniou, A., Bobrow, M., Zimmern, R. L., Easton, D. F., & Ponder, B. A. J. (2002). Polygenic susceptibility to breast cancer and implications for prevention. *Nature Genetics, 31,* 33–36.

Phelps, E. A., O'Connor, K. J., Cunningham, W. A., Funayama, E. S., Gatenby, J. C., Gore, J. C., & Banaji, M. (2000). Performance on indirect measures of race evaluation predicts amygdala activation. *Journal of Cognitive Neuroscience, 12,* 729–738.

Phelps, J. A., Davis, J. O., & Schartz, K. M. (1997). Nature, nurture, and twin research strategies. *Current Directions in Psychological Science, 6*(5), 117–121.

Philipp, B. L., Merewood, A., Miller, L. W., Chawla, N., Murphy-Smith, M. M., Gomes, J. S., Cimo, S., & Cook, J. T. (2001). Baby-friendly hospital initiative improves breastfeeding initiation rates in a U.S. hospital setting. *Pediatrics, 108*(3), 677–681.

Phillips, D. F. (1998). Reproductive medicine experts till an increasingly fertile field. *Journal of the American Medical Association, 280,* 1893–1895.

Phillips, S., & Sandstrom, K. L. (1990). Parental attitudes towards youth work. *Youth and Society, 22,* 160–183.

Phinney, J. S. (1998). Stages of ethnic identity development in minority group adolescents. In R. E. Muuss & H. D. Porton (Eds.), *Adolescent behavior and society: A book of readings* (pp. 271–280). Boston: McGraw-Hill.

Phoon, S., & Manolios, N. (2002). *Australian Family Physician, 31,* 539–541.

Piaget, J. (1929). *The child's conception of the world.* New York: Harcourt Brace.

Piaget, J. (1932). *The moral judgment of the child.* New York: Harcourt Brace.

Piaget, J. (1951). *Play, dreams, and imitation* (C. Gattegno & F. M. Hodgson, Trans.). New York: Norton.

Piaget, J. (1952). *The origins of intelligence in children.* New York: International Universities Press. (Original work published 1936)

Piaget, J. (1954). *The construction of reality in the child.* New York: Basic.

Piaget, J. (1962). *The language and thought of the child* (M. Gabain, Trans.). Cleveland, OH: Meridian. (Original work published 1923)

Piaget, J. (1969). *The child's conception of time* (A. J. Pomerans, Trans.). London: Routledge & Kegan Paul.

Piaget, J. (1972). Intellectual evolution from adolescence to adulthood. *Human Development, 15,* 1–12.

Piaget, J., & Inhelder, B. (1967). *The child's conception of space.* New York: Norton.

Piaget. J., & Inhelder, B. (1969). *The psychology of the child.* New York: Basic Books.

Pianezza, M. L., Sellers, E. M., & Tyndale, R. F. (1998). Nicotine metabolism defect reduces smoking. *Nature, 393,* 750.

Pick, H. L., Jr. (1992). Eleanor J. Gibson: Learning to perceive and perceiving to learn. *Developmental Psychology, 28,* 787–794.

Pierce, K. M., Hamm, J. V., & Vandell, D. L. (1999). Experiences in after-school programs and children's adjustment in first-grade classrooms. *Child Development, 70*(3), 756–767.

Pillemer, K., & Finkelhor, D. (1988). The prevalence of elder abuse: A random sample survey. *The Gerontologist, 28*(1), 51–57.

Pillemer, K., & Suitor, J. J. (1991). "Will I ever escape my child's problems?" Effects of adult children's problems on elderly parents. *Journal of Marriage and the Family, 53,* 585–594.

Pillow, B. H., & Henrichon, A. J. (1996). There's more to the picture than meets the eye: Young children's difficulty understanding biased interpretation. *Child Development, 67,* 803–819.

Piña, J. A. (1999). The "uncontrollable" rebel. In J. Rodden (Ed.), *Conversations with Isabel Allende* (pp. 167–200). Austin: University of Texas Press.

Pines, M. (1981). The civilizing of Genie. *Psychology Today, 15*(9), 28–34.

Pinzone-Glover, H. A., Gidycz, C. A., & Jacobs, C. D. (1998). An acquaintance rape prevention program: Effects on attitudes toward women, rape-related attitudes, and perceptions of rape scenarios. *Psychology of Women Quarterly, 22,* 605–621.

Pirkle, J. L., Brody, D. J., Gunter, E. W., Kramer, R. A., Raschal, D. C., Flegal, K. M., & Matte, T. D. (1994). The decline in blood lead levels in the United States. *Journal of the American Medical Association, 272,* 284–291.

Pleck, J. H. (1997). Paternal involvement: Levels, sources, and consequences. In M. E. Lamb et al. (Eds.), *The role of the father in child development* (3rd ed., pp. 66–103). New York: Wiley.

Plemons, J., Willis, S., & Baltes, P. (1978). Modifiability of fluid intelligence in aging: A short-term longitudinal training approach. *Journal of Gerontology, 33*(2), 224–231.

Plomin, R. (1989). Environment and genes: Determinants of behavior. *American Psychologist, 44*(2), 105–111.

Plomin, R. (1990). The role of inheritance in behavior. *Science, 248,* 183–188.

Plomin, R. (1995). Molecular genetics and psychology. *Current Directions in Psychological Science, 4*(4), 114–117.

Plomin, R. (1996). Nature and nurture. In M. R. Merrens & G. G. Brannigan (Eds.), *The developmental psychologist: Research adventures across the life span* (pp. 3–19). New York: McGraw-Hill.

Plomin, R. (2001). Genetic factors contributing to learning and language delays and disabilities. *Child & Adolescent Psychiatric Clinics of North America, 10*(2), 259–277.

Plomin, R., & Crabbe, J. (2000). DNA. *Psychological Bulletin, 126*(6), 806–828.

Plomin, R., & Daniels, D. (1987). Why are children in the same family so different from one another? *Behavioral and Brain Sciences, 10,* 1–16.

Plomin, R., & DeFries, J. C. (1999). The genetics of cognitive abilities and disabilities. In S. J. Ceci & W. M. Williams (Eds.), *The nature nurture debate: The essential readings* (pp. 178–195). Malden, MA: Blackwell.

Plomin, R., & Rutter, M. (1998). Child development, molecular genetics, and what to do with genes once they are found. *Child Development, 69*(4), 1223–1242.

Plomin, R., Dale, P., Simonoff, E., Eley, T., Oliver, B., Price, T., Purcell, S., Bishop, D., & Stevenson, J. (1998). Genetic influence on language delay in two-year-old children. *Nature Neuroscience, 1,* 324–328.

Plomin, R., Owen, M. J., & McGuffin, P. (1994). The genetic bases of behavior. *Science, 264,* 1733–1739.

Plotkin, S. A., Katz, M., & Cordero, J. F. (1999). The eradication of rubella. *Journal* specialization? *Child Development, 72,* 691–695.

Plumert, J. M., Pick, H. L., Jr., Marks, R. A., Kintsch, A. S., & Wegesin, D. (1994). Locating objects and communicating about locations: Organizational differences in children's searching and direction-giving. *Developmental Psychology, 30,* 443–453.

Plumert, J., & Nichols-Whitehead, P. (1996). Parental scaffolding of young children's spatial communication. *Developmental Psychology, 32,* 523–532.

PMS: It's real. (1994, July). *Harvard Women's Health Watch,* pp. 2–3.

Polit, D. F., & Falbo, T. (1987). Only children and personality development: A quantitative review. *Journal of Marriage and the Family, 49,* 309–325.

Pollock, L. A. (1983). *Forgotten children.* Cambridge, England: Cambridge University Press.

Pomerantz, E. M., & Saxon, J. L. (2001). Conceptions of ability as stable and self-evaluative processes: A longitudinal examination. *Child Development, 72,* 152–173.

Pong, S. L. (1997). Family structure, school context, and eighth-grade math and reading achievement. *Journal of Marriage and the Family, 59,* 734–746.

Poon, L. W. (1985). Differences in human memory with aging: Nature, causes, and clinical implications. In J. E. Birren & K. W. Schaie (Eds.), *Handbook of the psychology of aging* (pp. 427–462). New York: Van Nostrand Reinhold.

Pope, A. W., Bierman, K. L., & Mumma, G. H. (1991). Aggression, hyperactivity, and inattention-immaturity: Behavior dimensions associated with peer rejection in elementary school boys. *Developmental Psychology, 27,* 663–671.

Popenoe, D., & Whitehead, B. D. (1999). *Should we live together? What young adults need to know about cohabitation before marriage.* New Brunswick: National Marriage Project Rutgers, State University of New Jersey.

Porcino, J. (1983). *Growing older, getting better: A handbook for women in the second half of life.* Reading, MA: Addison-Wesley.

Porcino, J. (1991). *Living longer, living better: Adventures in community housing for the second half of life.* New York: Continuum.

Porcino, J. (1993, April–May). Designs for living. *Modern Maturity,* pp. 24–33.

Portwood, S. G., & Repucci, N. D. (1996). Adults' impact on the suggestibility of preschoolers' recollections. *Journal of Applied Developmental Psychology, 17,* 175–198.

Posada, G., Gao, Y., Wu, F., Posada, R., Tascon, M., Schoelmerich, A., Sagi, A., Kondo Ikemura, K., Haaland, W., & Synnevaag, B. (1995). The secure-base phenomenon across cultures: Children's behavior, mothers' preferences, and experts' concepts. In E. Waters, B. E. Vaughn, G. Posada, & K. Kondo-Ikemura (Eds.), Caregiving, cultural, and cognitive perspectives on secure-base behavior and working models: New growing points of attachment theory and research (pp. 27–48). *Monographs of the Society for Research in Child Development, 60*(2–3, Serial No. 244).

Posada, G., Jacobs, A., Richmond, M. K., Carbonell, O. A., Alzate, G., Bustamante, M. R., & Quiceno, J. (2002). Maternal caregiving and infant security in two cultures. *Developmental Psychology, 38*(1), 67–78.

Posner, J. K., & Vandell, D. L. (1999). After-school activities and the development of low-income urban children: A longitudinal study. *Developmental Psychology, 35*(3), 868–879.

Posner, M. L., & DiGirolamo, G. J. (2000). Cognitive neuroscience: Origins and promise. Psychological Bulletin, 126(6), 873–889.

Post, S. G. (1994). Ethical commentary: Genetic testing for Alzheimer's disease. *Alzheimer Disease and Associated Disorders, 8,* 66–67.

Post, S. G., Whitehouse, P. J., Binstock, R. H., Bird, T. D., Eckert, S. K., Farrer, L. A., Fleck, L. M., Gaines, A. D., Juengst, E. T., Karlinsky, H., Miles, S., Murray, T. H., Wuaid, K. A., Relkin, N. R., Roses, A. D., St. George-Hyslop, P. H., Sachs, G. A., Steinbock, B., Truschke, E. F., & Zinn, A. B. (1997). The clinical introduction of genetic testing for Alzheimer Disease: An ethical perspective. *Journal of the American Medical Association, 277,* 832–836.

Povinelli, D. J., & Giambrone, S. (2001). Reasoning about beliefs: A human specialization? *Child Development, 72,* 691–695.

Powell, M. B., & Thomson, D. M. (1996). Children's memory of an occurrence of a repeated event: Effects of age, repetition, and retention interval across three question types. *Child Development, 67,* 1988–2004.

Power, T. G., & Chapieski, M. L. (1986). Childrearing and impulse control in toddlers: A naturalistic investigation. *Developmental Psychology, 22,* 271–275.

Pratt, M. (1999). Benefits of lifestyle activity vs. structured exercise. *Journal of the American Medical Association, 281,* 375–376.

Prechtl, H. F. R., & Beintema, D. J. (1964). The neurological examination of the full-term newborn infant. *Clinics in Developmental Medicine* (No. 12). London: Heinemann.

Price, J. M. (1996). Friendships of maltreated children and adolescents: Contexts for expressing and modifying relationship history. In W. M. Bukowski, A. F. Newcomb, & W. W. Hartup (Eds.), *The company they keep: Friendship in childhood and adolescence* (pp. 262–285). New York: Cambridge University Press.

Price, T. S., Simonoff, E., Waldman, I., Asherson, P., & Plomin, R. (2001). Hyperactivity in preschool children is highly heritable. *Journal of the American Academy of Child & Adolescent Psychiatry, 40*(12), 1362–1364.

Price-Williams, D. R., Gordon, W., & Ramirez, M., III. (1969). Skills and conservation: A study of pottery-making children. *Developmental Psychology, 1,* 769.

Princeton Survey Research Associates. (1996). *The 1996 Kaiser Family Foundation Survey on Teens and Sex: What they say teens today need to know, and who they listen to.* Menlo Park, CA: Kaiser Family Foundation.

Prockop, D. J. (1998). The genetic trail of osteoporosis. *New England Journal of Medicine, 338,* 1061–1062.

Prohaska, T. R., Leventhal, E. A., Leventhal, H., & Keller, M. L. (1985). Health practices and illness cognition in young, middle-aged, and elderly adults. *Journal of Gerontology, 40,* 569–578.

Pruchno, R., & Johnson, K. W. (1996). Research on grandparenting: Current studies and future needs. *Generations, 20*(1), 65–70.

Puca, A. A., Daly, M. J., Brewster, S. J., Matise, T. C., Barrett, J., SheapDrinkwater, M., Kang, S., Joyce, E., Nicoli, J., Benson, E., Kunkel, L. M., & Perls, T. (2001). A genomewide scan for linkage to human exceptional longevity identifieds a locus on chromosome 4.

Proceedings of the National Academy of Science, 28, 10505–10508.

Pulkkinen, L. (1996). Female and male personality styles: A typological and developmental analysis. *Journal of Personality and Social Psychology, 70,* 1288–1306.

Pungello, E. P., Kupersmidt, J. B., Burchinal, M. R., & Patterson, C. J. (1996). Environmental risk factors and children's achievement from middle childhood to early adolescence. *Developmental Psychology, 32,* 755–767.

Purcell, J. H. (1995). Gifted education at a crossroads: The program status study. *Gifted Child Quarterly, 39*(2), 57–65.

Putney, N. M., & Bengtson, V. L. (2001). Families, intergenerational relationships, and kinkeeping in midlife. In M. E. Lachman (Ed.), *Handbook of midlife development* (pp. 528–570). New York: Wiley.

Quadrel, M. J., Fischoff, B., & Davis, W. (1993). Adolescent (in)vulnerability. *American Psychologist, 48,* 102–116.

Quill, T. E. (1991). Death and dignity: A case of individualized decision making. *New England Journal of Medicine, 324,* 691–694.

Quill, T. E., Lo, B., & Brock, D. W. (1997). Palliative options of the last resort. *Journal of the American Medical Association, 278,* 2099–2104.

Quinlan, K. P., Brewer, R. D., Sleet, D. A., & Dellinger, A. M. (2000). Characteristics of child passenger deaths and injuries involving drinking drivers. *Journal of the American Medical Association, 283,* 2249–2252.

Quinn, P. C., Eimas, P. D., & Rosenkrantz, S. L. (1993). Evidence for representations of perceptually similar natural categories by 3-month-old and 4-month-old infants. *Perception, 22,* 463–475.

Quintero, R. A., Abuhamad, A., Hobbins, J. C., & Mahoney, M. J. (1993). Transabdominal thin-gauge embryofetoscopy: A technique for early prenatal diagnosis and its use in the diagnosis of a case of Meckel-Gruber syndrome. *American Journal of Obstetrics and Gynecology, 168,* 1552–1557.

Rabiner, D., & Coie, J. (1989). Effect of expectancy induction on rejected peers' acceptance by unfamiliar peers. *Developmental Psychology, 25,* 450–457.

Raff, M. (1998). Cell suicide for beginners. *Nature, 396,* 119–122.

Rafferty, Y., & Shinn, M. (1991). Impact of homelessness on children. *American Psychologist, 46*(11), 1170–1179.

Ragozin, A. S., Basham, R. B., Crnic, K. A., Greenberg, M. T., & Robinson, N. M. (1982). Effects of maternal age on parenting role. *Developmental Psychology, 18*(4), 627–634.

Rall, L. C., Meydani, S. N., Kehayias, B. D.-H., Dawson-Hughes, B., & Roubenoff, R. (1996). The effect of progressive resistance training in rheumatoid arthritis. *Arthritis and Rheumatism, 39,* 415–426.

Ram, A., & Ross, H. S. (2001). Problem solving, contention, and struggle: How siblings resolve a conflict of interests. *Child Development, 72,* 1710–1722.

Ramey, C. T., & Campbell, F. A. (1991). Poverty, early childhood education, and academic competence. In A. Huston (Ed.), *Children reared in poverty* (pp. 190–221). Cambridge, England: Cambridge University Press.

Ramey, C. T., & Ramey, S. L. (1998a). Early intervention and early experience. *American Psychologist, 53,* 109–120.

Ramey, C. T., & Ramey, S. L. (1998b). Prevention of intellectual disabilities: Early interventions to improve cognitive development. *Preventive Medicine, 21,* 224–232.

Ramey, C. T., Campbell, F. A., Burchinal, M., Skinner, M. L., Gardner, D. M., & Ramey, S. L. (2000). Persistent effects of early childhood education on high-risk children and their mothers. *Applied Developmental Science, 4*(1), 2–14.

Ramey, S. L. (1999). Head Start and preschool education: Toward continued improvement. *American Psychologist, 54,* 344–346.

Ramey, S. L., & Ramey, C. T. (1992). Early educational intervention with disadvantaged children—To what effect? *Applied and Preventive Psychology, 1,* 131–140.

Rampersad, A. (1997). *Jackie Robinson: A biography.* New York: Knopf.

Ramsey, P. G., & Lasquade, C. (1996). Preschool children's entry attempts. *Journal of Applied Developmental Psychology, 17,* 135–150.

Rand, C. S. W., Kellner, K. R., Reval-Lutz, R., & Massey, J. K. (1998). Parental behavior after perinatal death: Twelve years of observations. *Journal of Psychosomatic Obstetrics and Gynecology, 19,* 44–48.

Rank, M. R., & Hirschl, T. A. (1999). Estimating the proportion of Americans ever experiencing poverty during their elderly years. *Journal of Gerontology: Psychological Sciences, 54B,* S184–S193.

Rantanen, T, Guralnik, J. M., Foley, D., Masak, K., Leveille, S., Curb, J. D., & White, L. (1999). Midlife hand grip strength as a predictor of old age disability. *Journal of the American Medical Association, 281,* 558–560.

Rapin, I. (1997). Autism. *New England Journal of Medicine, 337,* 97–104.

Rask-Nissilä, L., Jokinen, E., Terho, P., Tammi, A., Lapinleimu, H., Ronnemaa, T., Viikari, J., Seppanen, R., Korhonen, T., Tuominen, J., Valimaki, I., & Simell, O. (2000). Neurological development of 5-year-old children receiving a low-saturated fat, low-cholesterol diet since infancy. *Journal of the American Medical Association, 284*(8), 993–1000.

Ratner, H. H., & Foley, M. A. (1997, April). *Children's collaborative learning: Reconstructions of the other in the self.* Paper presented at the meeting of the Society for Research in Child Development, Washington, DC.

Redding, R. E., Harmon, R. J., & Morgan, G. A. (1990). Maternal depression and infants' mastery behaviors. *Infant Behavior and Development, 113,* 391–396.

Reese, E. (1995). Predicting children's literacy from mother-child conversations. *Cognitive Development, 10,* 381–405.

Reese, E., & Cox, A. (1999). Quality of adult book reading affects children's emergent literacy. *Developmental Psychology, 35,* 20–28.

Reese, E., & Fivush, R. (1993). Parental styles of talking about the past. *Developmental Psychology, 29,* 596–606.

Reese, E., Haden, C., & Fivush, R. (1993). Mother-child conversations about the past: Relationships of style and memory over time. *Cognitive Development, 8,* 403–430.

Reid, J. D. (1995). Development in late life: Older lesbian and gay life. In A. R. D'Augelli & C. J. Patterson (Eds.), *Lesbian, gay, and bisexual identities over the lifespan: Psychological perspectives* (pp. 215–240). New York: Oxford University Press.

Reid, J. D., & Willis, S. K. (1999). Middle age: New thoughts, new directions. In S. L. Willis & J. D. Reid (Eds.), *Life in the middle* (pp. 272–289). San Diego: Academic Press.

Reid, J. R., Patterson, G. R., & Loeber, R. (1982). The abused child: Victim, instigator, or innocent bystander? In D. J. Berstein (Ed.), *Response structure and organization.* Lincoln: University of Nebraska Press.

Reid, R. L., & Yen, S. S. C. (1981). Premenstrual syndrome. *American Journal of Obstetrics and Gynecology, 139*(1), 85–104.

Reijo, R., Alagappan, R. K., Patrizio, P., & Page, D. C. (1996). Severe oligozoospermia resulting from deletions of azoospermia factor gene on Y chromosome. *The Lancet, 347,* 1290–1293.

Reiman, E. M., Caselli, R. J., Yun, L. S., Chen, K., Bandy, D., Minoshima, S., Thibodeau, S. N., & Osborne, D. (1996). Preclinical evidence of Alzheimer's disease. *New England Journal of Medicine, 334*(12), 752–758.

Reiner, W. (2000, May 12). Cloacal exstrophy: A happenstance model for androgen imprinting. Presentation at the meeting of the Pediatric Endocrine Society, Boston.

Reis, H. T., & Patrick, B. C. (1996). Attachment and intimacy: Component processes. In E. T. Higgins & A. Kruglanski (Eds.), *Social psychology: Handbook of basic principles* (pp. 523–563). New York: Guilford.

Reis, S. M. (1989). Reflections on policy affecting the education of gifted and talented students: Past and future perspectives. *American Psychologist, 44,* 399–408.

Reiss, A. J., Jr., & Roth, J. A. (Eds.). (1994). *Understanding and preventing violence.* Washington, DC: National Academy Press.

Reiss, A. L., Abrams, M. T., Singer, H. S., Ross, J. L., & Denckla, M. B. (1996). Brain development, gender and IQ in children: A volumetric imaging study. *Brain, 119,* 1763–1774.

Remafedi, G., French, S., Story, M., Resnick, M. D., & Blum, R. (1998). The relationship between suicide risk and sexual orientation: Results of a population-based study. *American Journal of Public Health, 88,* 57–60.

Remafedi, G., Resnick, M., Blum, R., & Harris, L. (1992). Demography of sexual orientation in adolescents. *Pediatrics, 89,* 714–721.

Remez, L. (2000). Oral sex among adolescents: Is it sex or is it abstinence? *Family Planning Perspectives, 32,* 298–304.

Rempel, J. (1985). Childless elderly: What are they missing? *Journal of Marriage and the Family, 47*(2), 343–348.

Rennie, J. (1994, June). Grading the gene tests. *Scientific American*, pp. 86–97.

Renzulli, J. S., & McGreevy, A. M. (1984). *A study of twins included and not included in gifted programs.* Storrs: University of Connecticut, School of Education.

Repacholi, B. M., & Gopnik, A. (1997). Early reasoning about desires: Evidence from 14- and 18-month-olds. *Developmental Psychology, 33,* 12–21.

Rescorla, L. (1991). Early academics: Introduction to the debate. In L. Rescorla, M. C. Hyson, & K. Hirsh-Pasek (Eds.), *Academic instruction in early childhood: Challenge or pressure?* (New Directions for Child Development No. 53, pp. 5–11). San Francisco: Jossey-Bass.

Research Unit on Pediatric Pharmacology Anxiety Study Group. (2001). Fluvoxamine for the treatment of anxiety disorder in children and adolescents. *New England Journal of Medicine, 344,* 1279–1285.

Resnick, L. B. (1989). Developing mathematical knowledge. *American Psychologist, 44,* 162–169.

Resnick, M. D., Bearman, P. S., Blum, R. W., Bauman, K. E., Harris, K. M., Jones, J., Tabor, J., Beuhring, T., Sieving, R. E., Shew, M., Ireland, M., Bearinger, L. H., & Udry, J. R. (1997). Protecting adolescents from harm: Findings from the National Longitudinal Study on Adolescent Health. *Journal of the American Medical Association, 278,* 823–832.

Restak, R. (1984). *The brain.* New York: Bantam.

Reuter-Lorenz, P. A., & Stanczak, L. (2000). Differential effects of aging on the functions of the corpus callosum. *Developmental Neuropsychology, 18,* 113–137.

Reuter-Lorenz, P. A., Stanczak, L., & Miller, A. (1999). Neural recruitment and cognitive aging: Two hemispheres are better than one especially as you age. *Psychological Science, 10,* 494–500.

Reynolds, A. J. (1994). Effects of a preschool plus follow-on intervention for children at risk. *Developmental Psychology, 30,* 787–804.

Reynolds, A. J., & Temple, J. A. (1998). Extended early childhood intervention and school achievement: Age thirteen findings from the Chicago Longitudinal Study. *Child Development, 69,* 231–246.

Reynolds, A. J., Temple, J. A., Robertson, D. L., & Mann, E. A. (2001). Long-term effects of an early childhood intervention on educational achievement and juvenile arrest. *Journal of the American Medical Association, 285,* 2339–2346.

Reznick, J. S., Chawarska, K., & Betts, S. (2000). The development of visual expectations in the first year. *Child Development, 71,* 1191–1204.

Rheingold, H. L. (1985). Development as the acquisition of familiarity. *Annual Review of Psychology, 36,* 1–17.

Rhodes, S. R. (1983). Age-related differences in work attitudes and behaviors: A review and conceptual analysis. *Psychological Bulletin, 93*(2), 328–367.

Rice, C., Koinis, D., Sullivan, K., Tager-Flusberg, H., & Winner, E. (1997). When 3-year-olds pass the appearance-reality test. *Developmental Psychology, 33,* 54–61.

Rice, G. , Anderson, C., Risch, N., & Ebers, G. (1999). Male homosexuality: Absence of linkage to microsatellite markers at Xq28. *Science, 284,* 665–667.

Rice, M. L. (1982). Child language: What children know and how. In T. M. Field, A. Huston, H. C. Quay, L. Troll, & G. E. Finley (Eds.), *Review of human development research.* New York: Wiley.

Rice, M. L. (1989). Children's language acquisition. *American Psychologist, 44*(2), 149–156.

Rice, M. L., Hadley, P. A., & Alexander, A. L. (1993). Social biases toward children with speech and language impairments: A correlative causal model of language limitations. *Applied Psycholinguistics, 14,* 445–471.

Rice, M. L., Huston, A. C., Truglio, R., & Wright, J. (1990). Words from "Sesame Street": Learning vocabulary while viewing. *Developmental Psychology, 26,* 421–428.

Rice, M. R., Alvanos, L., & Kenney, B. (2000). Snowmobile injuries and deaths in children: A review of national injury data and state legislation. *Pediatrics, 105*(3), 615–619.

Rice, M., Oetting, J. B., Marquis, J., Bode, J., & Pae, S. (1994). Frequency of input effects on SLI children's word comprehension. *Journal of Speech and Hearing Research, 37,* 106–122.

Richards, M. H., Boxer, A. M., Petersen, A. C., & Albrecht, R. (1990). Relation of weight to body image in pubertal girls and boys from two communities. *Developmental Psychology, 26,* 313–321.

Richards, T. L., Dager, S. R., Corina, D., Serafini, S., Heide, A. C., Steury, K., Strauss, W., Hayes, C. E., Abbott, R. D., Craft, S., Shaw, D., Posse, S., & Berninger, V. W. (1999). Dyslexic children have abnormal brain lactate response to reading-related language tasks. *American Journal of Neuroradiology, 20,* 1393–1398.

Richardson, J. (1995). *Achieving gender equality in families: The role of males* (Innocenti Global Seminar, Summary Report). Florence, Italy: UNICEF International Child Development Centre, Spedale degli Innocenti.

Richardson, J. L., Radziszewska, B., Dent, C. W., & Flay, B. R. (1993). Relationship between after-school care of adolescents and substance use, risk-taking, depressed mood, and academic achievement. *Pediatrics, 92,* 32–38.

Ridderinkhof, K. R., & Bashore, T. R. (1995). Using event-related brain potentials to draw inferences about human information processing. In P. A. Allen & T. R. Bashore (Eds.), *Age differences in word and language processing* (pp. 294–313). Amsterdam: North-Holland.

Riddle, R. D., Johnson, R. L., Laufer, E., & Tabin, C. (1993). Sonic hedgehog mediates the polarizing activity of the ZPA. *Cell, 75,* 1401–1416.

Riemann, M. K., & Kanstrup Hansen, I. L. (2000). Effects on the fetus of exercise in pregnancy. *Scandinavian Journal of Medicine & Science in Sports. 10*(1), 12–19.

Rifkin, J. (1998, May 5). Creating the "perfect" human. *Chicago Sun-Times*, p. 29.

Riley, M. W. (1994). Aging and society: Past, present, and future. *The Gerontologist, 34,* 436–446.

Rimm, E. B., Ascherio, A., Giovannucci, E., Spiegelman, D., Stampfer, M. J., & Willett, W. C. (1996). Vegetable, fruit, and cereal fiber intake and risk of coronary heart disease among men. *Journal of the American Medical Association, 275,* 447–451.

Ripple, C. H., Gilliam, W. S., Chanana, N., & Zigler, E. (1999). Will fifty cooks spoil the broth? The debate over entrusting Head Start to the states. *American Psychologist, 54,* 327–343.

Ritter, J. (1999, November 23). Scientists close in on DNA code. *Chicago Sun-Times*, p. 7.

Rivara, F. P. (1999). Pediatric injury control in 1999: Where do we go from here? *Pediatrics, 103*(4), 883–888.

Rivara, F. P., & Grossman, D. C. (1996). Prevention of traumatic deaths to children in the United States: How far have we come and where do we need to go? *Pediatrics, 97,* 791–798.

Rivera, S. M., Wakely, A., & Langer, J. (1999). The drawbridge phenomenon: Representational reasoning or perceptual preference? *Developmental Psychology, 35*(2), 427–435.

Rix, S. E. (1994). *Older workers: How do they measure up?* (Pub. No. 9412). Washington, DC: AARP Public Policy Institute.

Rizzo, J. A., Abbott, T. A., & Berger, M. L. (1998). The labor productivity effects of chronic backache in the United States. *Medical Care, 36,* 1471–1488.

Rizzo, T. A., Metzger, B. E., Dooley, S. L., & Cho, N. H. (1997). Early malnutrition and child neurobehavioral development: Insights from the study of children of diabetic mothers. *Child Development, 68,* 26–38.

Roberts, G. C., Block, J. H., & Block, J. (1984). Continuity and change in parents' child-rearing practices. *Child Development, 55,* 586–597.

Roberts, P., Papalia-Finlay, D., Davis, E. S., Blackburn, J., & Dellman, M. (1982). "No two fields ever grow grass the same way": Assessment of conservation abilities in the elderly. *International Journal of Aging and Human Development, 15,* 185–195.

Robin, D. J., Berthier, N. E., & Clifton, R. K. (1996). Infants' predictive reaching for moving objects in the dark. *Developmental Psychology, 32,* 824–835.

Robins, R. W., John, O. P., Caspi, A., Moffitt, T. E., & Stouthamer-Loeber, M. (1996). Resilient, overcontrolled, and undercontrolled boys: Three replicable personality types. *Journal of Personality and Social Psychology, 70,* 157–171.

Robinson, J. (as told to A. Duckett). (1995). *I never had it made.* Hopewell, NJ: Ecco.

Robinson, L. C., & Blanton, P. W. (1993). Marital strengths in enduring marriages. *Family Relations, 42,* 38–45.

Robinson, S. (1996). *Stealing home.* New York: HarperCollins.

Robinson, S. D., Rosenberg, H. J., & Farrell, M. P. (1999). The midlife crisis revisited. In S. L.

Willis & J. D. Reid (Eds.), *Life in the middle: Psychological and social development in middle age* (pp. 47–77). San Diego, CA: Academic.

Robinson, T. N., Wilde, M. L., Navracruz, L. C., Haydel, K. F., and Varady, A. (2001). Effects of reducing children's television and video game use on aggressive behavior: A randomized controlled trial. *Archives of Pediatric and Adolescent Medicine, 155,* 17–23.

Rochat, P., & Striano, T. (2002). Who's in the mirror? Self-other discrimination in specular images by four- and nine-month-old infants. *Child Development, 73,* 35–46.

Rochat, P., Querido, J. G., & Striano, T. (1999). Emerging sensitivity to the timing and structure of proto conversations in early infancy. *Developmental Psychology, 35,* 950–957.

Rodden, J. (Ed.). (1999). *Conversations with Isabel Allende.* Austin: University of Texas Press.

Rodin, J., & Ickovics, J. (1990). Women's health: Review and research agenda as we approach the 21st century. *American Psychologist, 45,* 1018–1034.

Rodkin, P. C., Farmer, T. W., Pearl, R., & Van Acker, R. (2000). Heterogeneity of popular boys: Antisocial and prosocial configurations. *Developmental Psychology, 36*(1), 14–24.

Rodrigues, D. (1999, April 26). Ensuring safe and effective psychotropic medications for children [News release]. Washington, DC: National Institute of Mental Health.

Rodriguez, C., Patel, A. V., Calle, E. E., Jacob, E. J., & Thun, M. J. (2001). Estrogen replacement therapy and ovarian cancer mortality in a large prospective study of US women. *Journal of the American Medical Association, 285,* 1460–1465.

Rogers, R. G. (1995). Marriage, sex and mortality. *Journal of Marriage and the Family, 57,* 515–526.

Rogers, W. A., Meyer, B., Walker, N., & Fisk, A. D. (1998). Functional limitations to daily living tasks in the aged: A focus group analysis. *Human Factors, 40,* 111–125.

Rogina, B., Reenan, R. A., Nilsen, S. P., & Helfand, S. L. (2000). Extended life-span conferred by cotransporter gene mutations in Drosophila. *Science, 290,* 2137–2140.

Rogoff, B. (1990). *Apprenticeship in thinking: Cognitive development in social context.* New York: Oxford University Press.

Rogoff, B. (1998). Cognition as a collaborative process. In W. Damon (Ed.), D. Kuhn, & R. S. Siegler (Vol. Eds.), *Handbook of child psychology: Vol. 2. Cognition, perception, and language* (5th ed., pp. 679–744). New York: Wiley.

Rogoff, B., & Morelli, G. (1989). Perspectives on children's development from cultural psychology. *American Psychologist, 44,* 343–348.

Rogoff, B., Mistry, J., Göncü, A., & Mosier, C. (1993). Guided participation in cultural activity by toddlers and caregivers. *Monographs of the Society for Research in Child Development, 58*(8, Serial No. 236).

Rolls, B. J., Engell, D., & Birch, L. L. (2000). Serving portion size influences 5-year-old but not 3-year-old children's food intake. *Journal of the American Dietetic Association, 100,* 232–234.

Rome-Flanders, T., Cronk, C., & Gourde, C. (1995). Maternal scaffolding in mother-infant games and its relationship to language development: A longitudinal study. *First Language, 15,* 339–355.

Ronca, A. E., & Alberts, J. R. (1995). Maternal contributions to fetal experience and the transition from prenatal to postnatal life. In J. P. Lecanuet, W. P. Fifer, N. A. Krasnegor, & W. P. Smotherman (Eds.), *Fetal development: A psychobiological perspective* (pp. 331–350). Hillsdale, NJ: Erlbaum.

Roopnarine, J. L., Hooper, F. H., Ahmeduzzaman, M., & Pollack, B. (1993). Gentle play partners: Mother-child and father-child play in New Delhi, India. In K. MacDonald (Ed.), *Parent-child play* (pp. 287–304). Albany: State University of New York Press.

Roopnarine, J. L., Talokder, E., Jain, D., Josh, P., & Srivastav, P. (1992). Personal well-being, kinship ties, and mother-infant and father-infant interactions in single-wage and dual-wage families in New Delhi, India. *Journal of Marriage and the Family, 54,* 293–301.

Roopnarine, J., & Honig, A. S. (1985, September). The unpopular child. *Young Children,* pp. 59–64.

Rosamond, W. D., Chambless, L. E., Folsom, A. R., Cooper, L. S., Conwill, D. E., Clegg, L., Wang, C.-H., & Heiss, G. (1998). Trends in the incidence of myocardial infarction and in mortality due to coronary heart disease, 1987 to 1994. *New England Journal of Medicine, 339,* 861–867.

Rose, S. A. (1994). Relation between physical growth and information processing in infants born in India. *Child Development, 65,* 889–902.

Rose, S. A., & Feldman, J. F. (1995). Prediction of IQ and specific cognitive abilities at 11 years from infancy measures. *Developmental Psychology, 31,* 685–696.

Rose, S. A., & Feldman, J. F. (1997). Memory and speed: Their role in the relation of infant information processing to later IQ. *Child Development, 68,* 630–641.

Rose, S. A., Feldman, J. F., & Jankowski, J. J. (2001). Attention and recognition memory in the 1st year of life: A longitudinal study of preterm and full-term infants. *Developmental Psychology, 37,* 135–151.

Rosenberg, L., Palmer, J. R., & Shapiro, S. (1990). Decline in the risk of myocardial infarction among women who stop smoking. *New England Journal of Medicine, 322,* 213–217.

Rosenberg, S. D., Rosenberg, H. J., & Farrell, M. P. (1999). The midlife crisis revisited. In S. L. Willis & J. D. Reid (Eds.), *Life in the middle* (pp. 47–73). San Diego: Academic Press.

Rosenblatt, P. C. (1999). Multiracial families. In M. E. Lamb (Ed.), *Parenting and child development in "nontraditional" families* (pp. 263–278). Mahwah, NJ: Lawrence Erlbaum Associates.

Rosenblum, G. D., & Lewis, M. (1999). The relations among body image, physical attractiveness, and body mass in adolescence. *Child Development, 70,* 50–64.

Rosenblum, K. L., McDonough, S., Muzik, M., Miller, A., & Sameroff, A. (2002). Maternal representations of the infant: Associations with infant response to the still face. *Child Development, 73,* 999–1015.

Rosenbluth, S. C., & Steil, J. M. (1995). Predictors of intimacy for women in heterosexual and homosexual couples. *Journal of Social and Personal Relationships, 12*(2), 163–175.

Rosenfeld, D. (1999). Identity work among lesbian and gay elderly. *Journal of Aging Studies, 13,* 121–144.

Rosengren, K. S., Gelman, S. A., Kalish, C. W., & McCormick, M. (1991). As time goes by: Children's early understanding of growth in animals. *Child Development, 62,* 1302–1320.

Rosenthal, C. J., Martin-Matthews, A., & Matthews, S. H. (1996). Caught in the middle? Occupancy in multiple roles and help to parents in a national probability sample of Canadian adults. *Journal of Gerontology: Social Sciences, 51B,* S274–S283.

Rosenthal, E. (1998, November 1). For one-child policy, China rethinks iron hand. *The New York Times,* pp. 1, 20.

Rosenthal, R., & Jacobson, L. (1968). *Pygmalion in the classroom.* New York: Holt.

Rosenthal, R., & Vandell, D. L. (1996). Quality of care at school-aged child-care programs: Regulatable features, observed experiences, child perspectives, and parent perspectives. *Child Development, 67,* 2434–2445.

Roses, A. D. (1994, September). *Apolipoprotein E affects Alzheimer's disease expression.* Paper presented at the annual meeting of the Gerontological Society of America, San Diego, CA.

Ross, C. (1995). Reconceptualizing marital status as a continuum of social attachment. *Journal of Marriage and the Family, 57,* 129–140.

Ross, C. E., & Mirowsky, J. (1999). Parental divorce, life-course disruption and adult depression. *Journal of Marriage and the Family, 61,* 1034–1045.

Ross, C. E., Mirowsky, J., & Goldsteen, K. (1990). The impact of the family on health: A decade in review. *Journal of Marriage and the Family, 52,* 1059–1078.

Ross, G., Lipper, E. G., & Auld, P. A. M. (1991). Educational status and school-related abilities of very low birth weight premature children. *Pediatrics, 8,* 1125–1134.

Ross, H. G., Dalton, M. J., & Milgram, J. I. (1980, November). *Older adults' perceptions of closeness in sibling relationships.* Paper presented at the annual meeting of the Gerontological Society of America, San Diego, CA.

Ross, H. S. (1996). Negotiating principles of entitlement in sibling property disputes. *Developmental Psychology, 32,* 90–101.

Ross Products Division of Abbott Laboratories. (2002). Breastfeeding trends through 2000. Data from the Ross Mothers Survey. Columbus, OH: Author.

Rossel, C., & Ross, J. M. (1986). *The social science evidence on bilingual education.* Boston: Boston University Press.

Rossi, A. S. (1980). Aging and parenthood in the middle years. In P. B. Baltes & O. G. Brim (Eds.), *Life-span development and behavior.* New York: Academic Press.

Rossi, A. S., & Rossi, P. H. (1990). *Of human bonding: Parent-child relations across the life course.* New York: Aldine de Gruyter.

Rossi, R. (1996, August 30). Small schools under microscope. *Chicago Sun-Times,* p. 24.

Rotenberg, K. J., & Eisenberg, N. (1997). Developmental differences in the understanding of and reaction to others' inhibition of emotional expression. *Developmental Psychology, 33,* 526–537.

Roth, G. S., Lane, M. A., Ingram, D. K., Mattison, J. A., Elahi, D., Tobin, J. D., Muller, D., & Metter, E. J. (2002). Biomarkers of caloric restriction may predict longevity in humans. *Science, 297,* 811.

Rothbart, M. K., Ahadi, S. A., & Evans, D. E. (2000). Temperament and personality: Origins and outcomes. *Journal of Personality and Social Psychology, 78,* 122–135.

Rothbart, M. K., Ahadi, S. A., Hershey, K. L., & Fisher, P. (2001). Investigations of temperament at three to seven years: The Children's Behavior Questionnaire. *Child Development, 72,* 1394–1408.

Rotheram-Borus, M. J., & Futterman, D. (2000). Promoting early detection of human immunodeficiency virus infection among adolescents. *Archives of Pediatric and Adolescent Medicine, 154,* 435–439.

Roush, W. (1995). Arguing over why Johnny can't read. *Science, 267,* 1896–1898.

Rovee-Collier, C. (1996). Shifting the focus from what to why. *Infant Behavior and Development, 19,* 385–400.

Rovee-Collier, C. (1999). The development of infant memory. *Current Directions in Psychological Science, 8,* 80–85.

Rovee-Collier, C., & Boller, K. (1995). Current theory and research on infant learning and memory: Application to early intervention. *Infants and Young Children, 7*(3), 1–12.

Rowe, J. W., & Kahn, R. L. (1998). *Successful aging.* New York: Random House.

Rowland, A. S., Umbach, D. M., Stallone, L., Naftel, J., Bohlig, E. M., & Sandler, D. P. (2002). Prevalence of medication treatment for attention-deficit hyperactivity disorder among elementary school children in Johnston County, North Carolina. *American Journal of Public Health, 92,* 231–234.

Rubin, D. H., Erickson, C. J., San Agustin, M., Cleary, S. D., Allen, J. K., & Cohen, P. (1996). Cognitive and academic functioning of homeless children compared with housed children. *Pediatrics, 97,* 289–294.

Rubin, D. H., Krasilnikoff, P. A., Leventhal, J. M., Weile, B., & Berget, A. (1986, August 23). Effect of passive smoking on birth-weight. *The Lancet,* pp. 415–417.

Rubin, K. (1982). Nonsocial play in preschoolers: Necessary evil? *Child Development, 53,* 651–657.

Rubin, K. H., Bukowski, W., & Parker, J. G. (1998). Peer interactions, relationships, and groups. In W. Damon (Series Ed.) & N. Eisenberg (Vol. Ed.), *Handbook of child psychology: Vol. 3. Social, emotional, and personality development* (5th ed., pp. 619–700). New York: Wiley.

Rubin, K. H., Fein, G. G., & Vandenberg, B. (1983). Play. In P. H. Mussen (Series Ed.) & E. M. Hetherington (Vol. Ed.), *Handbook of child psychology: Vol. 4. Socialization, personality, and social development* (pp. 694–774). New York: Wiley.

Rubinstein, R. L., Alexander, B. B., Goodman, M., & Luborsky, M. (1991). Key relationships of never married, childless older women: A cultural analysis. *Journal of Gerontology: Social Sciences, 46,* S270–277.

Ruble, D. N., & Dweck, C. S. (1995). Self-conceptions, person conceptions, and their development. In N. Eisenberg, (Ed.), *Social development: Review of personality and social psychology* (pp. 109–139). Thousand Oaks, CA: Sage.

Ruble, D. N., & Martin, C. L. (1998). Gender development. In W. Damon (Series Ed.) & N. Eisenberg (Vol. Ed.), *Handbook of child psychology: Vol. 3. Social, emotional, and personality development* (5th ed., pp. 933–1016). New York: Wiley.

Rudman, D., Axel, G. F., Hoskote, S. N., Gergans, G. A., Lalitha, P. Y., Goldberg, A. F., Schlenker, R. A., Cohn, L., Rudman, I. W., & Mattson, D. E. (1990). Effects of human growth hormone in men over 60 years old. *New England Journal of Medicine, 323*(1), 1–6.

Rudolph, K. D., Lambert, S. F., Clark, A. G., & Kurlakowsky, K. D. (2001). Negotiating the transition to middle school: The role of self-regulatory processes. *Child Development, 72*(3), 929–946.

Rueter, M. A., & Conger, R. D. (1995). Antecedents of parent-adolescent disagreements. *Journal of Marriage and the Family, 57,* 435–448.

Ruff, H. A., Bijur, P. E., Markowitz, M., Ma, Y. C., & Rosen, J. F. (1993). Declining blood lead levels and cognitive changes in moderately lead-poisoned children. *Journal of the American Medical Association, 269,* 1641–1646.

Ruffman, T., Slade, L., & Crowe, E. (2002). The relation between children's and mothers' mental state language and theory-of-mind understanding. *Child Development, 73,* 734–751.

Ruitenberg, A., van Swieten, J. C., Witteman, J. C., Mehta, K. M., van Duijn, C. M., Hofman, A., & Breteler, M. M. (2002). Alcohol consumption and risk of dementia: The Rotterdam Study. *Lancet, 359,* 281–286.

Rushton, J. L., Clark, S. J., & Freed, G. L. (May 1999). *Newest depression medications widely prescribed for children.* Paper presented at the Pediatric Academic Societies Annual Meeting, San Francisco, CA.

Rutland, A. F., & Campbell, R. N. (1996). The relevance of Vygotsky's theory of the "zone of proximal development" to the assessment of children with intellectual disabilities. *Journal of Intellectual Disability Research, 40,* 151–158.

Rutter, M. (1987). Continuities and discontinuities from infancy. In J. Osofsky (Ed.), *Handbook of infant development.* New York: Wiley.

Rutter, M. (2002). Nature, nurture, and development: From evangelism through science toward policy and practice. *Child Development, 73,* 1–21.

Ryan, A. (2001). The peer group as a context for the development of young adolescent motivation and achievement. *Child Development, 72*(4), 1135–1150.

Ryan, A. S., Craig, L. D., & Finn, S. C. (1992). Nutrient intakes in dietary patterns of older Americans: A national study. *Journal of Gerontology: Medical Sciences, 47*(5), M145–150.

Ryan, V., & Needham, C. (2001). Nondirective play therapy with children experiencing psychic trauma. *Clinical Child Psychology and Psychiatry* (special issue), *6,* 437–453.

Rybash, J. M., Hoyer, W. J., & Roodin, P. A. (1986). *Adult cognition and aging: Developmental changes in processing, knowing, and thinking.* New York: Pergamon.

Ryff, C. D. (1982). Self-perceived personality change in adulthood and aging. *Journal of Personality and Social Psychology, 42*(1), 108–115.

Ryff, C. D. (1995). Psychological well-being in adult life. *Current Directions in Psychological Science, 4,* 99–104.

Ryff, C. D., & Baltes, P. B. (1976). Value transition and adult development in women: The instrumentality-terminality sequence hypothesis. *Developmental Psychology, 12*(6), 567–568.

Ryff, C. D., & Heincke, S. G. (1983). Subjective organization of personality in adulthood and aging. *Journal of Personality and Social Psychology, 44*(4), 807–816.

Ryff, C. D., & Seltzer, M. M. (1995). Family relations and individual development in adulthood and aging. In R. Blieszner & V. Hilkevitch (Eds.), *Handbook of aging and the family* (pp. 95–113). Westport, CT: Greenwood Press.

Ryff, C. D., & Singer, B. (1998). Middle age and well-being. *Encyclopedia of Mental Health, 2,* 707–719.

Rymer, R. (1993). *An abused child: Flight from silence.* New York: HarperCollins.

Saarni, C., Mumme, D. L., & Campos, J. J. (1998). Emotional development: Action, communication, and understanding. In W. Damon (Series Ed.) & N. Eisenberg (Vol. Ed.), *Handbook of child psychology: Vol. 3. Social, emotional, and personality development* (5th ed., pp. 237–309). New York: Wiley.

Sabbagh, M. A., & Baldwin, D. A. (2001). Learning words from knowledgeable versus ignorant speakers: Links between preschoolers' theory of mind and semantic development. *Child Development, 72*(4), 1054–1070.

Sabbagh, M. A., & Taylor, M. (2000). Neural correlates of theory-of-mind reasoning: An event-related potential study. *Psychological Science, 11*(1), 46–50.

Sabol, S. Z., Nelson, M. L., Fisher, C., Gunzerath, L., Brody, C. L., Hu, S., Sirota, L. A., Marcus, S. E., Greenberg, B. D., Lucas, F. R., IV, Benjamin, J., Murphy, D. L., & Hamer, D. H. (1999). A genetic association for cigarette smoking behavior. *Health Psychology, 18,* 7–13.

Sachs, B. P., Kobelin, C., Castro, M. A., & Frigoletto, F. (1999). The risks of lowering the cesarean-delivery rate. *New England Journal of Medicine, 340,* 54–57.

Sadeh, A., Raviv, A., & Gruber, R. (2000). Sleep patterns and sleep disruptions in school age children. *Developmental Psychology, 36*(3), 291–301.

Sahyoun, N. R., Jacques, P. F., & Russell, R. M. (1996). Carotenoids, vitamins C and E, and mortality in an elderly population. *American Journal of Epidemiology, 144,* 501–511.

Sahyoun, N. R., Lentzner, H., Hoyert, D., & Robinson, K. N. (2001). Trends in causes of death among the elderly. *Aging Trends, No. 1.* Hyattsville, MD: National Center for Health Statistics.

Sahyoun, N. R., Pratt, L. A., Lentzner, H., Dey, A., & Robinson, K. N. (2001). The changing profile of nursing home residents: 1985–1997. *Aging Trends,* No. 4.

Saigal, S., Hoult, L. A., Streiner, D. L., Stoskopf, B. L., & Rosenbaum, P. L. (2000). School difficulties at adolescence in a regional cohort of children who were extremely low birth weigth. *Pediatrics, 105,* 325–331.

Saigal, S., Stoskopf, B. L., Streiner, D. L., & Burrows, E. (2001). Physical growth and current health status of infants who were of extremely low birth weight and controls at adolescence. *Pediatrics, 108*(2), 407–415.

Salovey, P., Rothman, A. J., Detweiler, J. B., & Steward, W. T. (2000). Emotional states and physical health. *American Psychologist, 55,* 110–121.

Salthouse, T. A. (1984). Effects of age and typing skill. *Journal of Experimental Psychology: General, 113,* 345–371.

Salthouse, T. A. (1991). *Theoretical perspectives on cognitive aging.* Hillsdale, NJ: Erlbaum.

Salthouse, T. A., & Maurer, T. J. (1996). Aging, job performance, and career development. In J. E. Birren & K. W. Schaie (Eds.), *Handbook of the psychology of aging* (pp. 353–364). San Diego: Academic Press.

Salthouse, T. A., Fristoe, N., McGuthry, K. E., & Hambrick, D. Z. (1998). Relation of task switching to speed, age, and fluid intelligence. *Psychology and Aging, 13,* 445–461.

Salzinger, S., Feldman, R. S., Hammer, M., & Rosario, M. (1993). Effects of physical abuse on children's social relations. *Child Development, 64,* 169–187.

Samad, A. (1996, August). Understanding a controversial rite of passage: Afterword. *Natural History,* p. 52.

Samdal, O., & Dür, W. (2000). The school environment and the health of adolescents. In C. Currie, K. Hurrelmann, W. Settertobulte, R. Smith, & J. Todd (Eds.), *Health and health behaviour among young people: a WHO cross-national study (HBSC) international report* (pp. 49–64). WHO Policy Series: Healthy Policy for Children and Adolescents, Series No. 1.

Sameroff, A. J., Seifer, R., Baldwin, A., & Baldwin, C. (1993). Stability of intelligence from preschool to adolescence: The influence of social and family risk factors. *Child Development, 64,* 80–97.

Samuelsson, M., Radestad, I., & Segesten, K. (2001). A waste of life: Fathers' experience of losing a child before birth. *Birth, 28,* 124–130.

Sandler, D. P., Everson, R. B., Wilcox, A. J., & Browder, J. P. (1985). Cancer risk in adulthood from early life exposure to parents' smoking. *American Journal of Public Health, 75,* 487–492.

Sandnabba, H. K., & Ahlberg, C. (1999). Parents' attitudes and expectations about children's cross-gender behavior. *Sex Roles, 40,* 249–263.

Sands, L. P., & Meredith, W. (1992). Blood pressure and intellectual functioning in late midlife. *Journal of Gerontology: Psychological Sciences, 47*(2), P81–84.

Sandstrom, M. J., & Coie, J. D. (1999). A developmental perspective on peer rejection: Mechanisms of stability and change. *Child Development, 70*(4), 955–966.

Santer, L. J., & Stocking, C. B. (1991). Safety practices and living conditions of low-income urban families. *Pediatrics, 88,* 111–118.

Santos, I. S., Victora, C. G., Huttly, S., & Carvalhal, J. B. (1998). Caffeine intake and low birthweight: A population-based case-control study. *American Journal of Epidemiology, 147,* 620–627.

Sapienza, C. (1990, October). Parental imprinting of genes. *Scientific American,* pp. 52–60.

Sapolsky, R. M. (1992). Stress and neuroendocrine changes during aging. *Generations, 16*(4), 35–38.

Sapp, F., Lee, K., & Muir, D. (2000). Three-year-olds' difficulty with the appearance-reality distinction: Is it real or apparent? *Developmental Psychology, 36,* 547–560.

Sargent, J. D., & Dalton, M. (2001). Does parental disapproval of smoking prevent adolescents from becoming established smokers? *Pediatrics, 108*(6), 1256–1262.

Satcher, D. (2001). *Women and smoking: A report of the Surgeon General.* Washington, DC: Department of Health and Human Services.

Satz, P. (1993). Brain reserve capacity on symptom onset after brain injury: A formulation and review of evidence for threshold theory. *Neuropsychology, 7,* 273–295.

Saucier, G., & Ostendorf, F. (1999). Hierarchical subcomponents of the Big Five personality factors: A cross-language replication. *Journal of Personality and Social Psychology, 76,* 613–627.

Saunders, K., Spensley, J., Munro, J., & Halasz, G. (1996). Growth and physical outcome of children conceived by in vitro fertilization. *Pediatrics, 97,* 688–692.

Savage, S. L., & Au, T. K. (1996). What word learners do when input contradicts the mutual exclusivity assumption. *Child Development, 67,* 3120–3134.

Saxe, G. B., Guberman, S. R., & Gearhart, M. (1987). Social processes in early number development. *Monographs of the Society for Research in Child Development, 52*(216).

Scandinavian Simvastatin Survival Study Group. (1994). Randomized trial of cholesterol lowering in 4444 patients with coronary heart disease: The Scandinavian Simvastatin Survival Study (4S). *The Lancet, 344,* 1383–1389.

Scarborough, H. S. (1990). Very early language deficits in dyslexic children. *Child Development, 61,* 1728–1743.

Scariati, P. D., Grummer-Strawn, L. M., & Fein, S. B. (1997). A longitudinal analysis of infant morbidity and the extent of breastfeeding in the United States. *Pediatrics, 99,* e5.

Scarr, S. (1992). Developmental theories for the 1990s: Development and individual differences. *Child Development, 63,* 1–19.

Scarr, S. (1997a). Behavior-genetics and socialization theories of intelligence: Truce and reconciliation. In R. J. Sternberg & E. Grigorenko (Eds.), *Intelligence, heredity, and environment* (pp. 3–41). Cambridge, England: Cambridge University Press.

Scarr, S. (1998). American child care today. *American Psychologist, 53,* 95–108.

Scarr, S., & McCartney, K. (1983). How people make their own environments: A theory of genotype → environment effects. *Child Development, 54,* 424–435.

Schacter, D. L. (1999). The seven sins of memory: Insights from psychology and cognitive neuroscience. *American Psychologist, 54,* 182–203.

Schaie, K. W. (1977–1978). Toward a stage theory of adult cognitive development. *Journal of Aging and Human Development, 8*(2), 129–138.

Schaie, K. W. (1983). The Seattle Longitudinal Study: A twenty-one-year investigation of psychometric intelligence. In K. W. Schaie (Ed.), *Longitudinal studies of adult personality development* (pp. 64–155). New York: Guilford.

Schaie, K. W. (1984). Midlife influences upon intellectual functioning in old age. *International Journal of Behavioral Development, 7,* 463–478.

Schaie, K. W. (1989). The hazards of cognitive aging. *The Gerontologist, 29*(4), 484–493.

Schaie, K. W. (1990). Intellectual development in adulthood. In J. E. Birren & K. W. Schaie (Eds.), *Handbook of the psychology of aging* (pp. 291–309). San Diego: Academic Press.

Schaie, K. W. (1994). The course of adult intellectual development. *American Psychologist, 49*(4), 304–313.

Schaie, K. W. (1996a). Intellectual development in adulthood. In J. E. Birren & K. W. Schaie (Eds.), *Handbook of the psychology of aging* (4th ed., pp. 266–286). San Diego: Academic Press.

Schaie, K. W. (1996b). *Intellectual development in adulthood: The Seattle Longitudinal Study.*

Cambridge, England: Cambridge University Press.

Schaie, K. W., & Hertzog, C. (1983). Fourteen-year cohort sequential analyses of adult intellectual development. *Developmental Psychology, 19*(4), 531–543.

Schaie, K. W., & Willis, S. L. (1986). Can decline in adult intellectual functioning be reversed? *Developmental Psychology, 22,* 223–232.

Schaie, K. W., & Willis, S. L. (1991). Adult personality and psychomotor performance: Cross-sectional and longitudinal analysis. *Journal of Gerontology, 46*(6), P275–284.

Schaie, K. W., & Willis, S. L. (1996). Psychometric intelligence and aging. In F. Blanchard-Fields & T. M. Hess (Eds.), *Perspectives on cognitive change in adulthood and aging* (pp. 293–322). New York: McGraw-Hill.

Schaie, K. W., & Willis, S. L. (2000). A stage theory model of adult cognitive development revisited. In B. Rubinstein, M. Moss, & M. Kleban (Eds.). *The many dimensions of aging: Essays in honor of M. Powell Lawton* (pp. 173–191). New York: Springer.

Schairer, C., Lubin, J., Troisi, R., Sturgeon, S., Brinton, L., & Hoover, R. (2000). Menopausal estrogen and estrogen-progestin replacement therapy and breast cancer risk. *Journal of the American Medical Association, 283,* 485–491.

Schanberg, S. M., & Field, T. M. (1987). Sensory deprivation illness and supplemental stimulation in the rat pup and preterm human neonate. *Child Development, 58,* 1431–1447.

Schardt, D. (1995, June). For men only. *Nutrition Action Health Letter, 22*(5), 4–7.

Scharlach, A. E. (1987). Relieving feelings of strain among women with elderly mothers. *Psychology and Aging, 2*(1), 9–13.

Scharlach, A. E., & Fredriksen, K. I. (1993). Reactions to the death of a parent during midlife. *Omega, 27,* 307–319.

Schauble, L. (1996). The development of scientific reasoning in knowledge-rich contexts. *Developmental Psychology, 32,* 102–119.

Schaubroeck, J., Jones, J. R., & Xie, J. L. (2001). Individual differences in utilizing control to cope with job demands: Effects on susceptibility to infectious disease. *Journal of Applied Psychology, 86,* 265–278.

Scheidt, P., Overpeck, M. D., Wyatt, W., & Aszmann, A. (2000). In C. Currie, K. Hurrelmann, W. Settertobulte, R. Smith, & J. Todd (Eds.), *Health and health behaviour among young people: a WHO cross-national study (HBSC) international report* (pp. 24–38). WHO Policy Series: Healthy Policy for Children and Adolescents, Series No. 1.

Schellenberg, G. D., Bird, T. D., Wijsman, E. M., Orr, H. T., Anderson, L., Nemens, E., White, J. A., Bonnycastle, L., Weber, J. L., Alonso, M. E., Potter, H., Heston, L. L., & Martin, G. M. (1992). Genetic linkage evidence for a familial Alzheimer's disease locus on chromosome 14. *Science, 258,* 668–671.

Scher, M. S., Richardson, G. A., & Day, N. L., (2000). Effects of prenatal crack/cocaine and other drug exposure on electroencephalographic sleep studies at birth and one year. *Pediatrics, 105,* 39–48.

Scherer, M. (1985, January). How many ways is a child intelligent? *Instructor,* pp. 32–35.

Schieve, L. A., Meikle, S. F., Ferre, C., Peterson, H. B., Jeng, G., & Wilcox, L. S. (2002). Low and very low birth weight in infants conceived with use of assisted reproductive technology. *New England Journal of Medicine, 346,* 731–737.

Schiffman, S. S. (1997). Taste and smell losses in normal aging and disease. *Journal of the American Medical Association, 278,* 1357–1362.

Schlegel, A., & Barry, H. (1991). *Adolescence: An anthropological inquiry.* New York: Free Press.

Schmidt, P. J., Nieman, L. K., Danaceau, M. A., Adams, L. F., & Rubinow, D. R. (1998). Differential behavioral effects of gonadal steroids in women with and in those without premenstrual syndrome. *New England Journal of Medicine, 338,* 209–216.

Schmitt, B. D. (1997). Nocturnal enuresis. *Pediatrics in Review, 18,* 183–190.

Schmitz, S., Saudino, K. J., Plomin, R., Fulker, D. W., & DeFries, J. C. (1996). Genetic and environmental influences on temperament in middle childhood: Analyses of teacher and tester ratings. *Child Development, 67,* 409–422.

Schmuckler, M. A., & Fairhall, J. L. (2001). Visual-proprioceptive intermodal perception using point light displays. *Child Development, 72,* 949–962.

Schnall, P. L., Pieper, C., Schwartz, J. E., Karasek, R. A., Schlussel, Y., Devereaux, R. B., Ganau, A., Alderman, M., Warren, K., & Pickering, T. G. (1990). The relationship between "job strain," workplace diastolic blood pressure, and left ventricular mass index: Results of a case-control study. *Journal of the American Medical Association, 263,* 1929–1935.

Schneider, B. H., Atkinson, L., & Tardif, C. (2001). Child-parent attachment and children's peer relations: A quantitative review. *Developmental Psychology, 37,* 86–100.

Schneider, E. L. (1992). Biological theories of aging. *Generations, 16*(4), 7–10.

Schoen, R. (1992). First unions and the stability of first marriages. *Journal of Marriage and the Family, 54,* 281–284.

Schoenborn, C. A., & Barnes, P. M. (2002). Leisure-time physical activity among adults: United States, 1997–1998. *Advance Data from Vital and Health Statistics, No. 325.* Hyattsville, MD: National Center for Health Statistics.

Scholer, S. J., Mitchel, E. F., & Ray, W. A. (1997). Predictors of injury mortality in early childhood. *Pediatrics, 100,* 342–347.

Scholl, B. J., & Leslie, A. M. (2001). Minds, modules, and meta-analysis. *Child Development, 72,* 696–701.

Schonfeld, D. J., Johnson, S. R., Perrin, E. C., O'Hare, L. L., & Cicchetti, D. V. (1993). Understanding of acquired immunodeficiency syndrome by elementary school children—A developmental survey. *Pediatrics, 92,* 389–395.

Schonfield, D. (1974). Translations in gerontology—From lab to life: Utilizing information. *American Psychologist, 29,* 228–236.

Schooler, C. (1984). Psychological effects of complex environments during the life-span: A review and theory. *Intelligence, 8,* 259–281.

Schooler, C. (1990). Psychosocial factors and effective cognitive functioning in adulthood. In J. E. Burren & K. W. Schaie (Eds.), *The handbook of aging* (pp. 347–358). San Diego: Academic Press.

Schore, A. N. (1994). *Affect regulation and the origin of the self: The neurobiology of emotional development.* Hillsdale, NJ: Erlbaum.

Schreiber, J. B., Robins, M., Striegel-Moore, R., Obarzanek, E., Morrison, J. A., & Wright, D. J. (1996). Weight modification efforts reported by preadolescent girls. *Pediatrics, 96,* 63–70.

Schulz, R. (1978). *A psychology of death, dying, and bereavement.* Reading, MA: Addison-Wesley.

Schulz, R., & Beach, S. R. (1999). Caregiving as a risk factor for mortality: The Caregiver Health Effects Study. *Journal of the American Medical Association, 282,* 2215–2219.

Schulz, R., & Heckhausen, J. (1996). A life span model of successful aging. *American Psychologist, 51,* 702–714.

Schumann, J. (1997). The view from elsewhere: Why there can be no best method for teaching a second language. *The Clarion: Magazine of the European Second Language Acquisition, 3*(1), 23–24.

Schunn, C. D., & Anderson, J. R. (1999). The generality/specificity of expertise in scientific reasoning. *Cognitive Science, 23,* 337–370.

Schwartz, D., Chang, L., & Farver, J. M. (2001). Correlates of victimization in Chinese children's peer groups. *Developmental Psychology, 37*(4), 520–532.

Schwartz, D., Dodge, K. A., Pettit, G. S., & Bates, J. E. The Conduct Problems Prevention Research Group (2000). Friendship as a moderating factor in the pathway between early harsh home environment and later victimization in the peer group. *Developmental Psychology, 36*(5), 646–662.

Schwartz, D., McFadyen-Ketchum, S. A., Dodge, K. A., Pettit, G. S., & Bates, J. E. (1998). Peer group victimization as a predictor of children's behavior problems at home and in school. *Development and Psychopathology, 10,* 87–99.

Schwebel, D. C., & Plumert, J. M. (1999). Longitudinal and concurrent relations among temperament, ability estimation, and injury proneness. *Child Development, 70,* 700–712.

Schweinhart, L. J., Barnes, H. V., & Weikart, D. P. (1993). *Significant benefits: The High/Scope Perry Preschool Study through age 27* (Monographs of the High/Scope Educational Research Foundation No. 10). Ypsilanti, MI: High/Scope.

Scott, J. (1998). Changing attitudes to sexual morality: A cross-national comparison. *Sociology, 32,* 815–845.

Scott, J. P., & Roberto, K. A. (1981, October). *Sibling relationships in late life.* Paper presented at the annual meeting of the National Council on Family Relations, Milwaukee, WI.

Seccombe, K. (1991). Assessing the costs and benefits of children: Gender comparisons among childfree husbands and wives. *Journal of Marriage and the Family, 53,* 191–202.

Sedlak, A. J., & Broadhurst, D. D. (1996). *Executive summary of the third national incidence study of child abuse and neglect* (NIS-3). Washington, DC: U.S. Department of Health and Human Services.

Seftor, N. S., & Turner, S. E. (2002). Back to school: Federal student aid policy and adult college enrollment. *Journal of Human Resources, 37,* 336–352.

Sege, R., & Dietz, W. (1994). Television viewing and violence in children: The pediatrician as agent for change. *Pediatrics, 94,* 600–607.

Seifer, R., Schiller, M., Sameroff, A. J., Resnick, S., & Riordan, K. (1996). Attachment, maternal sensitivity, and infant temperament during the first year of life. *Developmental Psychology, 32,* 12–25.

Seiner, S. H., & Gelfand, D. M. (1995). Effects of mother's simulated withdrawal and depressed affect on mother-toddler interactions. *Child Development, 60,* 1519–1528.

Seitz, V. (1990). Intervention programs for impoverished children: A comparison of educational and family support models. *Annals of Child Development, 7,* 73–103.

Selkoe, D. J. (1991). The molecular pathology of Alzheimer's disease. *Neuron, 6*(4), 487–498.

Selkoe, D. J. (1992). Aging brain, aging mind. *Scientific American, 267,* 135–142.

Sellers, E. M. (1998). Pharmacogenetics and ethnoracial differences in smoking. *Journal of the American Medical Association, 280,* 179–180.

Selman, R. L. (1980). *The growth of interpersonal understanding: Developmental and clinical analyses.* New York: Academic.

Selman, R. L., & Selman, A. P. (1979, April). Children's ideas about friendship: A new theory. *Psychology Today,* pp. 71–80.

Seltzer, J. A. (1998). Father by law: Effects of joint legal custody on nonresident fathers' involvement with children. *Demography, 35,* 135–146.

Seltzer, J. A. (2000). Families formed outside of marriage. *Journal of Marriage and the Family, 62,* 1247–1268.

Senghas, A., & Coppola, M. (2001). Children creating language: How Nicaraguan sign language acquired a spatial grammar. *Psychological Science, 12,* 323–328.

Serbin, L. A., Moller, L. C., Gulko, J., Powlishta, K. K., & Colburne, K. A. (1994). The emergence of gender segregation in toddler playgroups. In C. Leaper (Ed.), *Childhood gender segregation: Causes and consequences* (New Directions for Child Development No. 65, pp. 7–17). San Francisco: Jossey-Bass.

Seshadri, S., Beiser, A., Selhub, J., Jacques, P. F., Rosenberg, I. H., D'Agostino, R. B., Wilson, P. W., & Wolf, P. A. (2002). Plasma homocysteine as a risk factor for dementia and Alzheimer's disease. *New England Journal of Medicine, 346,* 476–483.

Sethi, A., Mischel, W., Aber, J. L., Shoda, Y., & Rodriguez, M. L. (2000). The role of strategic attention deployment in development of self-regulation: Predicting preschoolers' delay of gratification from mother-toddler interactions. *Developmental Psychology, 36,* 767–777.

Seybold, K. S., & Hill, P. C. (2001). The role of religion and spirituality in mental and physical health. *Current Directions in Psychological Science, 10,* 21–24.

Shanahan, M. J., & Flaherty, B. P. (2001). Dynamic patterns of time use in adolescence. *Child Development, 72*(2), 385–401.

Shanahan, M. J., Finch, M. D., Mortimer, J. T., & Ryu, S. (1991). Adolescent work experience and depressive affect. *Social Psychology Quarterly,* 54, 299–317.

Shannon, L. W. (1982). *Assessing the relationship of adult criminal careers to juvenile careers.* Iowa City: University of Iowa, Iowa Urban Community Research Center.

Shannon, M. (2000). Ingestion of toxic substances by children. *New England Journal of Medicine, 342,* 186–191.

Shapiro, P. (1994, November). My house is your house: Advanced planning can ease the way when parents move in with adult kids. *AARP Bulletin,* p. 2.

Sharma, A. R., McGue, M. K., & Benson, P. L. (1996a). The emotional and behavioral adjustment of United States adopted adolescents, Part I: An overview. *Children and Youth Services Review, 18,* 83–100.

Sharma, A. R., McGue, M. K., & Benson, P. L. (1996b). The emotional and behavioral adjustment of United States adopted adolescents, Part II: Age at adoption. *Children and Youth Services Review, 18,* 101–114.

Shatz, M., & Gelman, R. (1973). The development of communication skills: Modifications in the speech of young children as a function of listener. *Monographs of the Society for Research in Child Development, 38*(5, Serial No. 152).

Shaw, D. S., Winslow, E. B., & Flanagan, C. (1999). Prospective study of marital status and young children's adjustment. *Child Development, 70,* 742–755.

Shaywitz, B. A., Sullivan, C. M., Anderson, G. M., Gillespie, S. M., Sullivan, B., & Shaywitz, S. E. (1994). Aspartame, behavior, and cognitive function in children with attention deficit disorder. *Pediatrics, 93,* 70–75.

Shaywitz, S. E. (1998). Current concepts: Dyslexia. *New England Journal of Medicine, 338,* 307–312.

Shaywitz, S. E., Shaywitz, B. A., Pugh, K. R., Fulbright, R. K., Skudlarski, P., Mencl, W. E., Constable, R. T., Naftolin, F., Palter, S. F., Marchione, K. E., Katz, L., Shankweiler, D. P., Fletcher, J. M., Lacadie, C., Keltz, M., & Gore, J. C. (1999). Effects of estrogen on brain activation patterns in postmenopausal women during working memory tasks. *Journal of the American Medical Association, 281,* 1197–1202.

Shaywitz, S. E., Shaywitz, B. A., Pugh, K. R., Fulbright, R. K., Constable, R. T., Mencl, W. E., Shankweiler, D. P., Liberman, A. M., Skudlarski, P., Fletcher, J. M., Katz, L., Marchione, K. E., Lacadie, C., Gatenby, C., & Gore, J. C. (1998). Functional disruption in the organization of the brain for reading in dyslexia. *Proceedings of the National Academy of Sciences of the United States of America, 95,* 2636–2641.

Shea, K. M., Little, R. E., & the ALSPAC Study Team (1997). Is there an association between preconceptual paternal x-ray exposure and birth outcome? *American Journal of Epidemiology, 145,* 546–551.

Shea, S., Basch, C. E., Stein, A. D., Contento, I. R., Irigoyen, M., & Zybert, P. (1993). Is there a relationship between dietary fat and stature or growth in children three to five years of age? *Pediatrics, 92,* 579–586.

Shek, D. T. L. (1996). Midlife crisis in Chinese men and women. *Journal of Psychology, 130,* 109–119.

Shepherd, J., Cobbe, S. M., Ford, I., Isles, C. G., Lorimer, A. R., MacFarlane, P. W., McKillop, J. H., & Packard, C. J. (1995). Prevention of coronary heart disease with pravastatin in men with hypercholesterolemia. *New England Journal of Medicine, 333,* 1301–1307.

Sherman, A. (1997). *Poverty matters: The cost of child poverty in America.* Washington, DC: Children's Defense Fund.

Sherman, E. (1993). Mental health and successful adaptation in late life. *Generations, 17*(1), 43–46.

Sherman, L. W., & Berk, R. A. (1984, April). The Minneapolis domestic violence experiment. *Police Foundation Reports,* pp. 1–8.

Sherman, L. W., & Cohn, E. G. (1989). The impact of research on legal policy: The Minneapolis domestic violence experiment. *Law and Society Review, 23*(1), 118–144.

Shifflett, K., & Cummings, M. (1999). A program for educating parents about the effects of divorce and conflict on children: An initial evaluation. *Family Relations, 48*(1), 79–89.

Shiono, P. H., & Behrman, R. E. (1995). Low birth weight: Analysis and recommendations. *The Future of Children, 5*(1), 4–18.

Ship, J. A., & Weiffenbach, J. M. (1993). Age, gender, medical treatment, and medication effects on smell identification. *Journal of Gerontology: Medical Sciences, 48*(1), M26–32.

Shoghi-Jadid, K., Small, G. W., Agdeppa, E. D., Kepe, V., Ercoli, L. M., Siddarth, P., Read, S., Satyamurthy, N., Petric, A., Huang, S. C., & Barrio, J. R. (2002). Localization of neurofibrillary tangles and beta-amyloid plaques in the brains of living patients with Alzheimer disease. *American Journal of Geriatric Psychiatry, 10,* 24–35.

Shonk, S. M., & Cicchetti, D. (2001). Maltreatment, competency deficits, and risk for academic and behavioral maladjustment. *Developmental Psychology, 37,* 3–17.

Should you take estrogen to prevent osteoporosis? (1994, August). *Johns Hopkins Medical Letter: Health after 50,* pp. 4–5.

Shulik, R. N. (1988). Faith development in older adults. *Educational Gerontology, 14,* 291–301.

Shulman, S., Scharf, M., Lumer, D., & Maurer, O. (2001). Parental divorce and young adult children's romantic relationships: Resolution of the divorce experience. *American Journal of Orthopsychiatry, 71,* 473–478.

Shurkin, J. N. (1992). *Terman's kids: The groundbreaking study of how the gifted grow up.* Boston: Little, Brown.

Shwe, H. I., & Markman, E. M. (1997). Young children's appreciation of the mental impact of their communicative signals. *Developmental Psychology, 33*(4), 630–636.

Siegal, M., & Peterson, C. C. (1998). Preschoolers' understanding of lies and innocent and negligent mistakes. *Developmental Psychology, 34*(2), 332–341.

Siegel, A. C., & Burton, R. V. (1999). Effects of baby walkers on motor and mental development in human infants. *Journal of Developmental and Behavioral Pediatrics, 20,* 355–361.

Siegler, I. C. (1997). Promoting health and minimizing stress in midlife. In M. E. Lachman & J. B. James (Eds.), *Multiple paths of midlife development* (pp. 241–255). Chicago: University of Chicago Press.

Siegler, R. S. (1998). *Children's thinking* (3rd ed.). Upper Saddle River, NJ: Prentice-Hall.

Siegler, R. S., & Richards, D. (1982). The development of intelligence. In R. Sternberg (Ed.), *Handbook of human intelligence.* London: Cambridge University Press.

Siegrist, J. (1996). Adverse health effects of high-effort/low-reward conditions. *Journal of Occupational Health Psychology, 1*(1), 27–41.

Sigelman, C., Alfeld-Liro, C., Derenowski, E., Durazo, O., Woods, T., Maddock, A., & Mukai, T. (1996). Mexican-American and Anglo-American children's responsiveness to a theory-centered AIDS education program. *Child Development, 67,* 253–266.

Sigman, M., Cohen, S. E., & Beckwith, L. (1997). Why does infant attention predict adolescent intelligence? *Infant Behavior and Development, 20,* 133–140.

Signorello, L. B., Nordmark, A., Granath, F., Blot, W. J., McLaughlin, J. K., Anneren, G., Lundgren, S., Ekbom, A., Rane, A., & Cnattingius, S. (2001). Caffeine metabolism and the risk of spontaneous abortion of normal karyotype fetuses. *Obstetrics & Gynecology, 98*(6), 1059–1066.

Sikora, A. C., & Carroll, C. D. (2002). A profile of participation in distance education: 1999–2000. *Postsecondary Education Descriptive Analysis Reports,* NCES 2003-154. Washington, DC: National Center for Education Statistics.

Silverberg, S. B. (1996). Parents' well-being as their children transition to adolescence. In C. Ryff & M. M. Seltzer (Eds.), *The parental experience in midlife* (pp. 215–254). Chicago: University of Chicago Press.

Silverman, J. G., Raj, A., Mucci, L. A., & Hathaway, J. E. (2001). Dating violence against adolescent girls and associated substance use, unhealthy weight control, sexual risk behavior, pregnancy, and suicidality. *Journal of the American Medical Association, 286,* 572–579.

Silverman, W. K., La Greca, A. M., & Wasserstein, S. (1995). What do children worry about? Worries and their relation to anxiety. *Child Development, 66,* 671–686.

Silvern, S. B. (1998). Educational implications of play with computers. In D. P. Fromberg & D. Bergen (Eds.), *Play from birth to twelve and beyond: Contexts, perspectives, and meanings* (pp. 530–536). New York: Garland.

Silverstein, M., & Bengtson, V. L. (1997). Intergenerational solidarity and the structure of adult child-parent relationships in American families. *American Journal of Sociology, 103,* 429–460.

Silverstein, M., & Long, J. D. (1998). Trajectories of grandparents' perceived solidarity with adult grandchildren: A growth curve analysis over 23 years. *Journal of Marriage and the Family, 60,* 912–923.

Silverstein, M., Giarrusso, R., & Bengtson, V. L. (1998). Intergenerational solidarity and the grandparent role. In M. Szinovacz (Ed.), *Handbook on grandparenthood* (pp. 144–158). Westport, CT: Greenwood.

Simmons, R. G., Blyth, D. A., & McKinney, K. L. (1983). The social and psychological effect of puberty on white females. In J. Brooks-Gunn & A. C. Petersen (Eds.), *Girls at puberty: Biological and psychological perspectives.* New York: Plenum.

Simon, T. J., Hespos, S. J., & Rochat, P. (1995). Do infants understand simple arithmetic: A replication of Wynn (1992). *Cognitive Development, 10,* 253–269.

Simon-Rusinowitz, L., Krach, C. A., Marks, L. N., Piktialis, D., & Wilson, L. B. (1996). Grandparents in the workplace: The effects of economic and labor trends. *Generations, 20*(1), 41–44.

Simons, M. (1993, February 10). Dutch parliament approves law permitting euthanasia. *The New York Times,* p. A10.

Simons, R. L., Chao, W., Conger, R. D., & Elder, G. H. (2001). Quality of parenting as mediator of the effect of childhood defiance on adolescent friendship choices and delinquency: A growth curve analysis. *Journal of Marriage and the Family, 63,* 63–79.

Simons, R. L., Lin, K.-H., & Gordon, L. C. (1998). Socialization in the family of origin and male dating violence: A prospective study. *Journal of Marriage and the Family, 60,* 467–478.

Simonton, D. K. (1983). Dramatic greatness and content: A quantitative analysis of 82 Athenian and Shakespearean plays. *Empirical Studies of the Arts, 1,* 109–123.

Simonton, D. K. (1986). Popularity, content, and context in 37 Shakespearean plays. *Poetics, 15,* 493–510.

Simonton, D. K. (1989). The swan-song phenomenon: Last-works effects for 172 classical composers. *Psychology and Aging, 4,* 42–47.

Simonton, D. K. (1990). Creativity and wisdom in aging. In J. E. Birren & K. W. Schaie (Eds.), *Handbook of the psychology of aging* (pp. 320–329). New York: Academic Press.

Simonton, D. K. (1998). Career paths and creative lives: A theoretical perspective on late life potential. In C. E. Adams-Price (Ed)., *Creativity and successful aging.* New York: Springer.

Simonton, D. K. (2000a). Creative development as acquired expertise: Theoretical issues and an empirical test. *Developmental Review, 20,* 283–318.

Simonton, D. K. (2000b). Creativity: Cognitive, personal, developmental, and social aspects. *American Psychologist, 55,* 151–158.

Simpson, G. A., & Fowler, M. G. (1994). Geographic mobility and children's emotional/behavioral adjustment and school functioning. *Pediatrics, 93,* 303–309.

Simpson, G. B., & Foster, M. R. (1986). Lexical ambiguity and children's word recognition. *Developmental Psychology, 22,* 147–154.

Simpson, G. B., & Lorsbach, T. C. (1983). The development of automatic and conscious components of contextual facilitation. *Child Development, 54,* 760–772.

Simpson, J. L., & Elias, S. (1993). Isolating fetal cells from maternal blood: Advances in prenatal diagnosis through molecular technology. *Journal of the American Medical Association, 270,* 2357–2361.

Simpson, K. H. (1996). Alternatives to physician-assisted suicide. *Humanistic Judaism, 24*(4), 21–23.

Singer, D. G., & Singer, J. L. (1990). *The house of make-believe: Play and the developing imagination.* Cambridge, MA: Harvard University Press.

Singer, J. L., & Singer, D. G. (1981). *Television, imagination, and aggression: A study of preschoolers.* Hillsdale, NJ: Erlbaum.

Singer, J. L., & Singer, D. G. (1998). *Barney & Friends* as entertainment and education: Evaluating the quality and effectiveness of a television series for preschool children. In J. K. Asamen & G. L. Berry (Eds.), *Research paradigms, television, and social behavior* (pp. 305–367). Thousand Oaks, CA: Sage.

Singer, M. I., Slovak, K., Frierson, T., & York, P. (1998). Viewing preferences, symptoms of psychological trauma, and violent behaviors among children who watch television. *Journal of the American Academy of Child and Adolescent Psychiatry, 37*(10), 1041–1048.

Singer, P. A. (1988, June 1). Should doctors kill patients? *Canadian Medical Association Journal, 138,* 1000–1001.

Singer, P. A., & Siegler, M. (1990). Euthanasia—A critique. *New England Journal of Medicine, 322,* 1881–1883.

Singh, S., Wulf, D., Samara, R., & Cuca, Y. P. (2000). Gender differences in the timing of first intercourse: Data from 14 countries. *International Family Planning Perspectives, Part 1, 26,* 21–28.

Singletary, K. W., & Gapstur, S. M. (2001). Alcohol and breast cancer: Review of epidemiologic and experimental evidence and potential mechanisms. *Journal of the American Medical Association, 286,* 2143–2151.

Sinnott, J. (1996). The developmental approach: Postformal thought as adaptive intelligence. In F. Blanchard-Fields & T. M. Hess (Eds.), *Perspectives on cognitive change in adulthood and aging* (pp. 358–386). New York: McGraw-Hill.

Sinnott, J. D. (1984). Postformal reasoning: The relativistic stage. In M. L. Commons, F. A. Richards, & C. Armon (Eds.), *Beyond formal* *operations: Late adolescence and adult cognitive development* (pp. 357–380). New York: Praeger.

Sinnott, J. D. (1989a). A model for solution of ill-structured problems: Implications for everyday and abstract problem-solving. In J. D. Sinnott (Ed.), *Everyday problem solving: Theory and applications* (pp. 72–99). New York: Praeger.

Sinnott, J. D. (1989b). Life-span relativistic postformal thought: Methodology and data from everyday problem–solving studies. In M. L. Commons, J. D. Sinnott, F. A. Richards, & C. Armon (Eds.), *Adult development: Vol. 1. Comparison and application of developmental models* (pp. 239–278). New York: Praeger.

Sinnott, J. D. (1991). Limits to problem solving: Emotion, intention, goal clarity, health and other factors in postformal thought. In J. D. Sinnott & J. C. Cavanaugh (Eds.), *Bridging paradigms: Positive development in adulthood and cognitive aging* (pp. 169–202). New York: Praeger.

Sinnott, J. D. (1998). *The development of logic in adulthood: Postformal thought and its applications.* New York: Plenum.

Siris, E. S., Miller, P. D., Barrett-Connor, E., Faulkner, K. G., Wehren, L. E., Abbott, T. A., Berger, M. L., Santora, A. C., & Sherwood, L. M. (2001). Identification and fracture outcomes of undiagnosed low bone mineral density in postmenopausal women: Results from the National Osteoporosis Risk Assessment. *Journal of the American Medical Association, 286,* 2815–2822.

Skadberg, B. T., Morild, I., & Markestad, T. (1998). Abandoning prone sleeping: Effects on the risk of sudden infant death syndrome. *Journal of Pediatrics, 132,* 234–239.

Skaff, M. M., & Pearlin, L. I. (1992). Caregiving: Role engulfment and the loss of self. *The Gerontologist, 32*(5), 656–664.

Skinner, B. F. (1938). *The behavior of organisms: An experimental approach.* New York: Appleton-Century.

Skinner, B. F. (1957). *Verbal behavior.* New York: Appleton-Century-Crofts.

Skinner, D. (1989). The socialization of gender identity: Observations from Nepal. In J. Valsiner (Ed.), *Child development in cultural context* (pp. 181–192). Toronto: Hogrefe & Huber.

Skjaerven, R., Wilcox, A. J., & Lie, R. T. (1999). A population-based study of survival and childbearing among female subjects with birth defects and the risk of recurrence in their children. *New England Journal of Medicine, 340,* 1057–1062.

Skoe, E. E., & Diessner, R. E. (1994). Ethic of care, justice, identity, and gender: An extension and replication. *Merrill-Palmer Quarterly, 40,* 272–289.

Skoe, E. E., & Gooden, A. (1993). Ethics of care and real-life moral dilemma content in male and female early adolescents. *Journal of Early Adolescence, 13*(2), 154–167.

Skuse, D. H., James, R. S., Bishop, D. V. M., Coppin, B., Dalton, P., Aamodt-Leeper, G., Bacarese-Hamilton, M., Creswell, C., McGurk, R., & Jacobs, P. A. (1997). Evidence from Turner's syndrome of an imprinted X-linked locus affecting cognitive function. *Nature, 387,* 705–708.

Slade, A., Belsky, J., Aber, J. L., & Phelps, J. L. (1999). Mothers' representation of their relationships with their toddlers: Links to adult attachment and observed mothering. *Developmental Psychology, 35,* 611–619.

Slap, G. B., Vorters, D. F., Chaudhuri, S., & Centor, R. M. (1989). Risk factors for attempted suicide during adolescence. *Pediatrics, 84,* 762–772.

Slattery, M. L. (2001). Does an apple a day keep breast cancer away? *Journal of the American Medical Association, 285,* 799–801.

Sleek, S. (1995, December). Rallying the troops inside our bodies. *APA Monitor,* pp. 1, 24–25.

Slemenda, C. W. (1994). Cigarettes and the skeleton. *New England Journal of Medicine, 330,* 430–431.

Sliwinski, M., & Buschke, H. (1999). Cross-sectional and longitudinal relationships among age, cognition, and processing speed. *Psychology and Aging, 14,* 18–33.

Sloan, R. P., & Bagiella, E. (2002). Claims about religious involvement and health outcomes. *Annals of Behavioral Medicine, 24,* 14–21.

Slobin, D. (1971). Universals of grammatical development in children. In W. Levett & G. B. Flores d'Arcais (Eds.), *Advances in psycholinguistic research.* Amsterdam: New Holland.

Slobin, D. (1973). Cognitive prerequisites for the acquisition of language. In C. Ferguson & D. Slobin (Eds.), *Studies of child language development.* New York: Holt, Rinehart, & Winston.

Slobin, D. (1983). Universal and particular in the acquisition of grammar. In E. Wanner & L. Gleitman (Eds.), *Language acquisition: The state of the art.* Cambridge, England: Cambridge University Press.

Sly, R. M. (2000). Decreases in asthma mortality in the United States. *Annals of Allergy, Asthma, and Immunology, 85,* 121–127.

Small, G. W., Rabins, P. V., Barry, P. P., Buckholtz, N. S., DeKosky, S. T., Ferris, S. H., Finkel, S. I., Gwyther, L. P., Khachaturian, Z. S., Lebowitz, B. D., McRae, T. D., Morris, J. C., Oakley, F., Schneider, L. S., Streim, J. E., Sunderland, T., Teri, L. A., & Tune, L. E. (1997). Diagnosis and treatment of Alzheimer Disease and related disorders: Consensus statement of the American Association for Geriatric Psychiatry, the Alzheimer's Association, and the American Geriatrics Society. *Journal of the American Medical Society, 278,* 1363–1371.

Small, M. Y. (1990). *Cognitive development.* New York: Harcourt Brace.

Smedley, B. D., Stith, A. Y., & Nelson, A. R. (Eds.). (2002). *Unequal treatment: Confronting racial and ethnic disparities in health care.* Washington, DC: National Academy Press.

Smilansky, S. (1968). *The effects of sociodramatic play on disadvantaged preschool children.* New York: Wiley.

Smith, A. C., & Smith, D. I. (2001). Emergency and transitional shelter population: 2000. *Census 2000 Special Reports,* Series CENSR/01–2. Washington, DC: U.S. Government Printing Office.

Smith, A. D., & Earles, J. L. (1996). Memory changes in normal aging. In F. Blanchard-Fields & T. M. Hess (Eds.), *Perspectives on cognitive change in adulthood and aging* (pp. 165–191). New York: McGraw-Hill.

Smith, B. A., & Blass, E. M. (1996). Taste-mediated calming in premature, preterm, and full-term human infants. *Developmental Psychology, 32,* 1084–1089.

Smith, D. J., (1997). Indigenous peoples' extended family relationships: A source for classroom structure. McGill Journal of Education, 32(2), 125-138.

Smith, E. A. (2001). The role of tacit and explicit knowledge in the workplace. *Journal of Knowledge Management, 5,* 311–321.

Smith, E. E., Geva, A., Jonides, J., Miller, A., Reuter-Lorenz, P., & Koeppe, R. A. (2001). The neural basis of task-switching in working memory: effects of performance and aging. *Proceedings of the National Academy of Science USA, 98,* 2095-2100.

Smith, G. A., & Shields, B. J. (1998). Trampoline-related injuries to children. *Archives of Pediatrics and Adolescent Medicine, 152,* 694–699.

Smith, G. C. S., Pell, J. P., Cameron, A. D., & Dobbie, R. (2002). Risk of perinatal death associated with labor after previous cesarean delivery in uncomplicated term pregnancies. *Journal of the American Medical Association, 287,* 2684–2690.

Smith, J., & Baltes, P. B. (1990). Wisdom-related knowledge: Age/cohort differences in response to life planning problems. *Developmental Psychology, 26*(3), 494–505.

Smith, K. (2002). Who's minding the kids? Child care arrangements: Spring 1997. *Current Population Reports,* P70–86. Washington, DC: U.S. Census Bureau.

Smith, K. A., Fairburn, C. G., & Cowen, P. J. (1999). Symptomatic release in bulimia nervosa following acute tryptophan depletion. *Archives of General Psychiatry (72C), 56*(2), 171–176.

Smith, K. E., & Bachu, A. (1999). *Women's labor force attachment patterns and maternity leave: A review of the literature. Population Division Working Paper No. 32.* Washington, DC: U.S. Census Bureau.

Smith, M. E. (1993). Television violence and behavior: A research summary [On-line]. *ERIC/IT Digest* (ED366 329). Available:http://npin.org/respar/texts/media/viole397.html

Smith, P. K., & Levan, S. (1995). Perceptions and experiences of bullying in younger pupils. *British Journal of Educational Psychology, 65,* 489–500.

Smith, R. (1999, March). The timing of birth. *Scientific American,* pp. 68–75.

Smith, R. B., & Brown, R. A. (1997). The impact of social support on gay male couples. *Journal of Homosexuality, 33,* 39–61.

Smith, T. (1999). *The emerging 21st-century American family.* Chicago: National Opinion Research Center, University of Chicago.

Smith, T. W. (1994). *The demography of sexual behavior.* Menlo Park, CA: Henry J. Kaiser Family Foundation.

Smith-Warner, S. A., Spiegelman, D., Yaun, S., Adami, H., Beeson, W. L., van den Brandt, P. A., Folsom, A. R., Fraser, G. E., Freudenheim, J. L., Goldbohm, R. A., Graham, S., Miller, A. B., Potter, J. D., Rohan, T. E., Speizer, F. E., Toniolo, P., Willett, W. C., Wolk, A., Zeleniuch-Jacquotte, A., & Hunter, D. J. (2001). Intake of fruits and vegetables and risk of breast cancer: A pooled analysis of cohort studies. *Journal of the American Medical Association, 285,* 769–776.

Smith-Warner, S. A., Spiegelman, D., Yaun, S., van den Brandt, P. A., Folsom, A. R., Goldbohm, A., Graham, S., Holmberg, L., Howe, G. R., Marshall, J. R., Miller, A. B., Potter, M. D., Speizer, F. E., Willett, W. C., Wolk, A., & Hunter, D. J. (1998). Alcohol and breast cancer in women: A pooled analysis of cohort studies. *Journal of the American Medical Association, 279,* 535–540.

Smotherman, W. P., & Robinson, S. R. (1995). Tracing developmental trajectories into the prenatal period. In J. P. Lecanuet, W. P. Fifer, N. A. Krasnegor, & W. P. Smotherman (Eds.), *Fetal development: A psychobiological perspective* (pp. 15–32). Hillsdale, NJ: Erlbaum.

Smotherman, W. P., & Robinson, S. R. (1996). The development of behavior before birth. *Developmental Psychology, 32,* 425–434.

Smyth, J. M., Stone, A. A., Hurewitz, A., & Kaell, A. (1999). Effects of writing about stressful experiences on symptom reduction in patients with asthma or rheumatoid arthritis. *Journal of the American Medical Association, 281,* 1304–1309.

Snarey, J. R. (1985). Cross-cultural universality of social-moral development: A critical review of Kohlbergian research. *Psychological Bulletin, 97,* 202–232.

Snow, C. E. (1990). The development of definitional skill. *Journal of Child Language, 17,* 697–710.

Snow, C. E. (1993). Families as social contexts for literacy development. In C. Daiute (Ed.), *The development of literacy through social interaction* (New Directions for Child Development No. 61, pp. 11–24). San Francisco: Jossey-Bass.

Snow, M. E., Jacklin, C. N., & Maccoby, E. E. (1983). Sex-of-child differences in father-child interaction at one year of age. *Child Development, 54,* 227–232.

Snowdon, D. A., Greiner, L. H., Mortimer, J. A., Riley, K. P., Greiner, P. A., & Markesbery, W. R. (1997). Brain infarction and the clinical expression of Alzheimer Disease: The Nun Study. *Journal of the American Medical Association, 277,* 813–817.

Snowdon, D. A., Kemper, S. J., Mortimer, J. A., Greiner, L. H., Wekstein, D. R., & Markesbery, W. R. (1996). Linguistic ability in early life and cognitive function and Alzheimer's disease in late life: Findings from the Nun Study. *Journal of the American Medical Association, 275,* 528–532.

Snyder, H. N. (2000). *Special analyses of FBI serious violent crimes data.* Pittsburgh, PA: National Center for Juvenile Justice.

Snyder, J., West, L., Stockemer, V., Gibbons, S., & Almquist-Parks, L. (1996). A social learning model of peer choice in the natural environment. *Journal of Applied Developmental Psychology, 17,* 215–237.

Snyder, T. D., & Hoffman, C. M. (2001). *Digest of Education Statistics, 2000.* NCES 2001-034. Washington, DC: National Center for Education Statistics.

Snyder, T. D., & Hoffman, C. M. (2002). *Digest of Education Statistics 2001.* Washington, DC: National Center for Education Statistics.

Society for Assisted Reproductive Technology and the American Society for Reproductive Medicine. (2002). Assisted reproductive technology in the United States: 1998 results generated from the American Society for Reproductive Medicine/Society for Assisted Reproductive Technology Registry. *Fertility & Sterility, 77*(1), 18–31.

Society for Assisted Reproductive Technology, The American Fertility Society. (1993). Assisted reproductive technology in the United States and Canada: 1991 results from the Society for Assisted Reproductive Technology generated from The American Fertility Society Registry. *Fertility and Sterility, 59,* 956–962.

Society for Research in Child Development. (1996). Ethical standards for research with children. In *Directory of members* (pp. 337–339). Ann Arbor, MI: Author.

Sohal, R. S., & Weindruch, R. (1996). Oxidative stress, caloric restriction, and aging. *Science, 273,* 59–63.

Soldz, S., & Vaillant, G. E. (1998). A 50-year longitudinal study of defense use among inner city men: A validation of the DSM-IV defense axis. *Journal of Nervous and Mental Disease, 186,* 104–111.

Solomon, M. (1993). Report of survey of doctors and nurses about treatment of terminally ill patients. *American Journal of Public Health, 83*(1), 23–25.

Solomon, P. R., Adams, F., Silver, A., Zimmer, J., & DeVeaux, R. (2002). Ginkgo for memory enhancement: A randomized controlled trial. *Journal of the American Medical Association, 288,* 835–840.

Solomon, P. R., Hirschoff, A., Kelly, B., Relin, M., Brush, M., DeVeaux, R. D., & Pendlebury, W. W. (1998). A 7-minute neurocognitive screening battery highly sensitive to Alzheimer's disease. *Archives of Neurology, 55,* 349–355.

Solowij, N., Stephens, R. S., Roffman, R. A., Babor, T., Kadden, R. Miller, M., Christiansen, K., McRee, B., & Vendetti, J. for the Marijuana Treatment Research Group. (2002). Cognitive functioning of long-term heavy cannabis users seeking treatment. *Journal of the American Medical Association, 287,* 1123–1131.

Sommers-Flanagan, J., & Sommers-Flanagan, R. (1996). Efficacy of antidepressant medication with depressed youth: What psychologists should know. *Professional Psychology: Research & Practice, 27,* 145–153.

Sondergaard, C., Henriksen, T. B., Obel, C., & Wisborg, K. (2001). Smoking during pregnancy and infantile colic. *Pediatrics, 108*(2), 342–346.

Sonenstein, F. L., Pleck, J. H., & Ku, L. C. (1991). Levels of sexual activity among adolescent males in the United States. *Family Planning Perspectives, 23*(4), 162–167.

Song, M., & Ginsburg, H. P. (1987). The development of informal and formal mathematical thinking in Korean and U.S. children. *Child Development, 58,* 1286–1296.

Sood, B., Delaney-Black, V., Covington, C., Nordstrom-Klee, B., Ager, J., Templin, T., Janisse, J., Martier, S., & Sokol, R. J. (2001). Prenatal alcohol exposure and childhood behavior at age 6 to 7 years: I. Dose-response effect. *Pediatrics, 108*(8), e461–462.

Sophian, C. (1988). Early developments in children's understanding of numbers: Inferences about numerosity and one-to-one correspondence. *Child Development, 59,* 1397–1414.

Sophian, C., Wood, A., & Vong, K. I. (1995). Making numbers count: The early development of numerical inferences. *Developmental Psychology, 31,* 263–273.

Sorce, J. F., Emde, R. N., Campos, J., & Klinnert, M. D. (1985). Maternal emotional signalling: Its effect on the visual cliff behavior of 1-year-olds. *Developmental Psychology, 21,* 195–200.

Sorensen, T., Nielsen, G., Andersen, P., & Teasdale, T. (1988). Genetic and environmental influence of premature death in adult adoptees. *New England Journal of Medicine, 318,* 727–732.

Sorrentino, C. (1990). The changing family in international perspective. *Monthly Labor Review, 113*(3), 41–58.

Spalding, J. J. (1977). Carter, James Earl, Jr. In W. H. Nault (Ed.), *The 1977 World Book Yearbook* (pp. 542–547). Chicago: Field Enterprises Educational Corporation.

Speece, M. W., & Brent, S. B. (1984). Children's understanding of death: A review of three components of a death concept. *Child Development, 55,* 1671–1686.

Spelke, E. (1994). Initial knowledge: Six suggestions. *Cognition, 50,* 431–445.

Spelke, E. S. (1998). Nativism, empiricism, and the origins of knowledge. *Infant Behavior and Development, 21*(2), 181–200.

Spence, A. P. (1989). *Biology of human aging.* Englewood Cliffs, NJ: Prentice-Hall.

Spencer, J. M., Zimet, G. D., Aalsma, M. C., & Orr, D. P. (2002). Self-esteem as a predictor of initiation of coitus in early adolescents. *Pediatrics, 109,* 581–584.

Spencer, J. P., Smith, L. B., & Thelen, E. (2001). Tests of a dynamic systems account of the A-not-B error: The influence of prior experience on the spatial memory abilities of two-year-olds. *Child Development, 72,* 1327–1346.

Spencer, L. M., Jr., & Spencer, S. (1993). *Competence at work: Models for superior performance.* New York: Wiley.

Spencer, M. B., & Dornbusch, S. M. (1998). Challenges in studying minority youth. In R. E. Muuss & H. D. Porton (Eds.), *Adolescent behavior and society: A book of readings* (pp. 316–330). Boston: McGraw-Hill.

Spindler, A. M. (1996, June 9). It's a face-lifted, tummy-tucked jungle out there: Fearing the axe, men choose the scalpel. *The New York Times,* pp. 1, 8–9.

Spirduso, W. W., & MacRae, P. G. (1990). Motor performance and aging. In J. E. Birren & K. W. Schaie (Eds.), *Psychology of aging* (3rd ed., pp. 183–200). New York: Academic Press.

Spiro, A., III (2001). Health in midlife: Toward a life-span view. In M. E. Lachman (Ed.), *Handbook of midlife development* (pp. 156–187). New York: Wiley.

Spitz, R. A. (1945). Hospitalism: An inquiry into the genesis of psychiatric conditioning in early childhood. In D. Fenschel et al. (Eds.), *Psychoanalytic studies of the child* (Vol. 1, pp. 53–74). New York: International Universities Press.

Spitz, R. A. (1946). Hospitalism: A follow-up report. In D. Fenschel et al. (Eds.), *Psychoanalytic studies of the child* (Vol. 1, pp. 113–117). New York: International Universities Press.

Spitzer, M. E. (1988). Taste acuity in institutionalized and noninstitutionalized elderly men. *Journal of Gerontology, 43*(3), 71–74.

Spohr, H. L., Willms, J., & Steinhausen, H.-C. (1993). Prenatal alcohol exposure and long-term developmental consequences. *The Lancet, 341,* 907–910.

Spoto, D. (1997). *Notorious: The life of Ingrid Bergman.* New York: HarperCollins.

Spurlock, J. (1990). Single women. In J. Spurlock & C. B. Robinowitz (Eds.), *Women's progress: Promises and problems* (pp. 23–33). Washington, DC: American Psychiatric Association.

Squire, L. R. (1992). Memory and the hippocampus: A synthesis of findings with rats, monkeys, and humans. *Psychological Review, 99,* 195–231.

Squire, L. R. (1994). Declarative and nondeclarative memory: Multiple brain systems supporting learning and memory. In D. L. Schacter & E. Tulving (Eds.), *Memory systems 1994* (pp. 203–232). Cambridge, MA: MIT Press.

Sroufe, L. A. (1979). Socioemotional development. In J. Osofsky (Ed.), *Handbook of infant development.* New York: Wiley.

Sroufe, L. A. (1997). *Emotional development.* Cambridge, England: Cambridge University Press.

Sroufe, L. A., Bennett, C., Englund, M., Urban, J., & Shulman, S. (1993). The significance of gender boundaries in preadolescence: Contemporary correlates and antecedents of boundary violation and maintenance. *Child Development, 64,* 455–466.

Sroufe, L. A., Carlson, E., & Shulman, S. (1993). Individuals in relationships: Development from infancy through adolescence. In D. C. Funder, R. D. Parke, C. Tomlinson-Keasey, & K. Widaman (Eds.), *Studying lives through time: Personality and development* (pp. 315–342). Washington, DC: American Psychological Association.

Stadtman, E. R. (1992). Protein oxidation and aging. *Science, 257,* 1220–1224.

Stahl, S. A., & Miller, P. D. (1989). Whole language and language experience approaches for beginning reading: A quantitative research synthesis. *Review of Educational Research, 59,* 87–116.

Stahl, S. A., McKenna, M. C., & Pagnucco, J. R. (1994). The effects of whole-language instruction: An update and a reappraisal. *Educational Psychologist, 29,* 175–185.

Stamler, J., Dyer, A. R., Shekelle, R. B., Neaton, J., & Stamler, R. (1993). Relationship of baseline major risk factors to coronary and all-cause mortality, and to longevity: Findings from long-term follow-up of Chicago cohorts. *Cardiology, 82*(2–3), 191–222.

Stapleton, S. (1998, May 11). Asthma rates hit epidemic numbers; experts wonder why [On-line]. *American Medical News, 41*(18). Available: http://www.ama-assn.org/special/asthma/newsline/special/epidem.htm

Staplin, L., Lococo, K., Byington, S., & Harkey, D. (2001a). *Guidelines and recommendations to accommodate older drivers and pedestrians.* McLean, VA: Office of Safety and Traffic Operations, Federal Highway Administration.

Staplin, L., Lococo, K., Byington, S., & Harkey, D. (2001b). *Highway design handbook for older drivers and pedestrians.* McLean, VA: Office of Safety and Traffic Operations, Federal Highway Administration.

Starfield, B. (1991). Childhood morbidity: Comparisons, clusters, and trends. *Pediatrics, 88,* 519–526.

Starfield, B., Katz, H., Gabriel, A., Livingston, G., Benson, P., Hankin, J., Horn, S., & Steinwachs, D. (1984). Morbidity in childhood—a longitudinal view. *New England Journal of Medicine, 310,* 824–829.

Stark, M. J., Tesselaar, H. M., O'Connell, A. A., Person, B., Galavotti, C., Cohen, A., & Walls, C. (1998). Psychosocial factors associated with the stages of change for condom use among women at risk for HIV and STDs: Implications for intervention development. *Journal of Consulting and Clinical Psychology, 66,* 967–978.

Starr, J. M., Deary, I. J., Lemmon, H., & Whalley L. J. (2000). Mental ability age 11 years and health status age 77 years. *Age and Ageing, 29,* 523–528.

States look to detention for pregnant drug users. (1998, May 2). *Minneapolis Star-Tribune,* p. A15.

Statistics Canada. (1996). *1996 Census* Nation *tables* [On-line]. Available: http://www.statcan.ca/english/Pgdb/People/Families/famil5a.htm

Statistics Canada. (1997). *Average hours per week of television viewing, Fall 1997* (Catalogue no. 87F0006XPB) [On-line]. Available: http://www.statcan.ca/cgi-bin/search.cgi?

Staub, E. (1996). Cultural-societal roots of violence: The examples of genocidal violence and of contemporary youth violence in the United States. *American Psychologist, 51,* 117–132.

Stauder, J. E. A., Molenaar, P. C. M., & Van der Molen, M. W. (1993). Scalp topography of event-related brain potentials and cognitive transition during childhood. *Child Development, 64,* 769–788.

Staudinger, U. M., & Baltes, P. B. (1996). Interactive minds: A facilitative setting for wisdom-related performance? *Journal of Personality and Social Psychology, 71,* 746–762.

Staudinger, U. M., & Bluck, S. (2001). A view of midlife development from life-span theory. In M. E. Lachman (Ed.), *Handbook of midlife development* (pp. 3–39). New York: Wiley.

Staudinger, U. M., Fleeson, W., & Baltes, P. B. (1999). Predictors of subjective physical health and global well-being: Similarities and differences between the United States and Germany. *Journal of Personality and Social Psychology, 76,* 305–319.

Staudinger, U. M., Lopez, D. F., & Baltes, P. B. (1997). The psychometric location of wisdom-related performance: Intelligence, personality, or more? *Personality and Social Psychology Bulletin, 23,* 1200–1214.

Steel, L. (1991). Early work experience among white and non-white youths: Implications for subsequent enrollment and employment. *Youth and Society, 22,* 419–447.

Steinbach, U. (1992). Social networks, institutionalization, and mortality among elderly people in the United States. *Journal of Gerontology: Social Sciences, 47*(4), S183–190.

Steinberg, L. (1981). Transformations in family relations at puberty. *Developmental Psychology, 17,* 833–840.

Steinberg, L. (1987). Impact of puberty on family relations: Effect of pubertal status and pubertal timing. *Developmental Psychology, 23,* 451–460.

Steinberg, L. (1988). Reciprocal relation between parent-child distance and pubertal maturation. *Developmental Psychology, 24,* 122–128.

Steinberg, L., & Darling, N. (1994). The broader context of social influence in adolescence. In R. Silberstein & E. Todt (Eds.), *Adolescence in context.* New York: Springer.

Steinberg, L., Dornbusch, S. M., & Brown, B. B. (1992). Ethnic differences in adolescent achievement: An ecological perspective. *American Psychologist, 47,* 723–729.

Steinberg, L., Fegley, S., & Dornbusch, S. M. (1993). Negative impact of part-time work on adolescent adjustment: Evidence from a longitudinal study. *Developmental Psychology, 29,* 171–180.

Stennies, G., Ikeda, R., Leadbetter, S., Houston, B., & Sacks, J. (1999). Firearm storage practices and children in the home, United States, 1994. *Archives of Pediatrics and Adolescent Medicine, 153,* 586–590.

**Stephens, J. C., Schneider, J. A., Tanguay, D. A., Choi, J., Acharya, T., Stanley, S. E., Jiang, R., Messer, C. J., Chew, A., Han, J.-H., Duan, J., Carr., J. L., Lee, M. S., Koshy, B., Madan Kumar, A., Zhang, G., Newell, W. R., Windemuth, A., Xu, C., Kalbfleisch, T. S.,

Shaner, S. L., Arnold, K., Schulz, V., Drysdale, C. M., Nandabalan, K., Judson, R. S., Ruano, G., & Vovis, G. F. (2001). Haplotype variation and linkage disequilibrium in 313 human genes. *Science, 293,* 489–493.

Stern, M. B. (1950). *Louisa May Alcott.* Norman: University of Oklahoma Press.

Sternbach, H. (1998). Age-associated testosterone decline in men: Clinical issues for psychiatry. *American Journal of Psychiatry, 155,* 1310–1318.

Sternberg, R. J. (1984, September). How can we teach intelligence? *Educational Leadership,* pp. 38–50.

Sternberg, R. J. (1985a). *Beyond IQ: A triarchic theory of human intelligence.* New York: Cambridge University Press.

Sternberg, R. J. (1986). A triangular theory of love. *Psychological Review, 93,* 119–135.

Sternberg, R. J. (1985b, November). Teaching critical thinking, Part I: Are we making critical mistakes? *Phi Delta Kappan,* pp. 194–198.

Sternberg, R. J. (1987, September 23). The use and misuse of intelligence testing: Misunderstanding meaning, users over-rely on scores. *Education Week,* pp. 22, 28.

Sternberg, R. J. (1993). *Sternberg Triarchic Abilities Test.* Unpublished manuscript.

Sternberg, R. J. (1995). Love as a story. *Journal of Social and Personal Relationships, 12*(4), 541–546.

Sternberg, R. J. (1997). The concept of intelligence and its role in lifelong learning and success. *American Psychologist, 52,* 1030–1037.

Sternberg, R. J. (1998). A balance theory of wisdom. *Review of General Psychology, 2,* 347–365.

Sternberg, R. J., & Barnes, M. L. (1985). Real and ideal other in romantic relationships: Is four a crowd? *Journal of Personality and Social Psychology, 49,* 1586–1608.

Sternberg, R. J., & Clinkenbeard, P. (1995). A triarchic view of identifying, teaching, and assessing gifted children. *Roeper Review, 17,* 255–260.

Sternberg, R. J., & Grajek, S. (1984). The nature of love. *Journal of Personality and Social Psychology, 47,* 312–329.

Sternberg, R. J., & Horvath, J. A. (1998). Cognitive conceptions of expertise and their relations to giftedness. In R. C. Friedman & K. B. Rogers (Eds.), *Talent in context: Historical and social perspectives on giftedness* (pp. 177–191). Washington, DC: American Psychological Association.

Sternberg, R. J., & Lubart, T. I. (1995). *Defying the crowd: Cultivating creativity in a culture of conformity.* NY: Free Press.

Sternberg, R. J., & Wagner, R. K. (1989). Individual differences in practical knowledge, and its acquisition. In P. L. Ackerman, R. J. Sternberg, & R. Glaser (Eds.), *Learning and individual differences* (pp. 255–278). New York: Freeman.

Sternberg, R. J., & Wagner, R. K. (1993). The *g*-ocentric view of intelligence and job performance is wrong. *Current Directions in Psychological Science, 2*(1), 1–4.

Sternberg, R. J., Forsythe, G. B., Hedlund, J., Horvath, J. A., Wagner, R. K., Williams, W. M., Snook, S. A., & Grigorenko, E. L. (2000). *Practical intelligence in everyday life.* New York: Cambridge University Press.

Sternberg, R. J., Grigorenko, E. L., & Oh, S. (2001). The development of intelligence at midlife. In M. E. Lachman (Ed.), *Handbook of midlife development* (pp. 217–247). New York: Wiley.

Sternberg, R. J., Torff, B., & Grigorenko, E. L. (1998). Teaching triarchically improves school achievement. *Journal of Educational Psychology, 90*(3), 374–384.

Sternberg, R. J., Wagner, R. K., Williams, W. M., & Horvath, J. A. (1995). Testing common sense. *American Psychologist, 50,* 912–927.

Sterns, H. L., & Huyck, M. H. (2001). The role of work in midlife. In M. E. Lachman (Ed.), *Handbook of midlife development* (pp. 447–486). New York: Wiley.

Stevens, J. A., Hasbrouck, I., Durant, T. M., Dellinger, A. M., Batabyal, P. K., Crosby, A. E., Valluru, B. R., Kresnow, M., Guerrero, J. L. (1999). Surveillance for injuries and violence among older adults. *CDC Surveillance Summaries, MMWR, 48*(No. SS-8), 27–50. This update describes (1) falls among older adults and (2) motor vehicle-related injuries among older adults.

Stevens, J. C., Cain, W. S., Demarque, A., & Ruthruff, A. M. (1991). On the discrimination of missing ingredients: Aging and salt flavor. *Appetite, 16,* 129–140.

Stevens, J. C., Cruz, L. A., Hoffman, J. M., & Patterson, M. Q. (1995). Taste sensitivity and aging: High incidence of decline revealed by repeated threshold measures. *Chemical Senses, 20,* 451–459.

Stevens, J. H., & Bakeman, R. (1985). A factor analytic study of the HOME scale for infants. *Developmental Psychology, 21,* 1106–1203.

Stevenson, H. W. (1995). Mathematics achievement of American students: First in the world by the year 2000? In C. A. Nelson (Ed.), *The Minnesota Symposia on Child Psychology: Vol. 28. Basic and applied perspectives on learning, cognition, and development* (pp. 131–149). Mahwah, NJ: Erlbaum.

Stevenson, H. W., Chen, C., & Lee, S. Y. (1993). Mathematics achievement of Chinese, Japanese, and American children: Ten years later. *Science, 258* (5081), 53–58.

Stevenson, H. W., Lee, S. Y., Chen, C., Stigler, J. W., Hsu, C. C., & Kitamura, S. (1990). Contexts of achievement: A study of American, Chinese, and Japanese children. *Monographs of the Society for Research in Child Development, 55*(1–2, Serial No. 221).

Stevenson, H. W., Lee, S., Chen, C., & Lummis, M. (1990). Mathematics achievement of children in China and the United States. *Child Development, 61,* 1053–1066.

Stevenson-Hinde, J., & Shouldice, A. (1996). Fearfulness: Developmental consistency. In A. J. Sameroff & M. M. Haith (Eds.), *The five to seven year shift: The age of reason and responsibility* (pp. 237–252). Chicago: University of Chicago Press.

Steward, M. S., & Steward, D. S. (1996). Interviewing young children about body touch and handling. *Monographs of the Society for Research in Child Development, 61*(4–5, Serial No. 248).

Stewart, A. J., & Ostrove, J. M. (1998). Women's personality in middle age: Gender, history, and midcourse correction. *American Psychologist, 53,* 1185–1194.

Stewart, A. J., & Vandewater, E. A. (1998). The course of generativity. In D. P. McAdams & D. de St. Aubin (Eds.), *Generativity and adult development: How and why we care for the next generation.* Washington, DC: American Psychological Association.

Stewart, A. J., & Vandewater, E. A. (1999). "If I had to do it over again . . . ": Midlife review, midlife corrections, and women's well-being in midlife. *Journal of Personality and Social Psychology, 76,* 270–283.

Stewart, I. C. (1994, January 29). Two-part message [Letter to the editor]. *The New York Times,* p. A18.

Stice, E., & Bearman, K. (2001). Body-image and eating disturbances prospectively predict increases in depressive symptoms in adolescent girls: A growth curve analysis. *Developmental Psychology, 37*(5), 597–607.

Stice, E., Presnell, K., & Bearman, S. K. (2001). Relation of early menarche to depression, eating disorders, substance abuse, and comorbid psychopathology among adolescent girls. *Developmental Psychology, 37,* 608–619.

Stick, S. M., Burton, P. R., Gurrin, L., Sly, P. D., & LeSouëf, P. N. (1996). Effects of maternal smoking during pregnancy and a family history of asthma on respiratory function in newborn infants. *The Lancet, 348,* 1060–1064.

Stifter, C. A., Coulehan, C. M., & Fish, M. (1993). Linking employment to attachment: The mediating effects of maternal separation anxiety and interactive behavior. *Child Development, 64,* 1451–1460.

Stigler, J. W., Lee, S., & Stevenson, H. W. (1987). Mathematics classrooms in Japan, Taiwan, and the United States. *Child Development, 58,* 1272–1285.

Stipek, D. J., Gralinski, H., & Kopp, C. B. (1990). Self-concept development in the toddler years. *Developmental Psychology, 26,* 972–977.

Stoecker, J. J., Colombo, J., Frick, J. E., & Allen, J. R. (1998). Long- and short-looking infants' recognition of symmetrica and asymmetrical forms. *Journal of Experimental Child Psychology, 71,* 63–78.

Stolberg, S. G. (2000, January 27). Teenager's death is shaking up field of human gene-therapy experiments. *The New York Times,* p. A20.

Stones, M. J., & Kozma, A. (1996). Activity, exercise, and behavior. In J. E. Birren & K. W. Schaie (Eds.), *Handbook of the psychology of aging* (4th ed., pp. 338–352). San Diego: Academic Press.

Stoppard, M. (1999). HRT: Hormone Replacement Therapy. New York: DK Publishing, Inc.

Strasburger, V. C., & Donnerstein, E. (1999). Children, adolescents, and the media: Issues and solutions. *Pediatrics, 103,* 129–139.

Strassberg, Z., Dodge, K. A., Pettit, G. S., & Bates, J. E. (1994). Spanking in the home and children's subsequent aggression toward kindergarten peers. *Development and Psychopathology, 6,* 445–461.

Straus, M. A. (1994a). *Beating the devil out of them: Corporal punishment in American families.* San Francisco, CA: Jossey-Bass.

Straus, M. A. (1994b). Should the use of corporal punishment by parents be considered child abuse? In M. A. Mason & E. Gambrill (Eds.), *Debating children's lives: Current controversies on children and adolescents* (pp. 196–222). Newbury Park, CA: Sage.

Straus, M. A. (1999). The benefits of avoiding corporal punishment: New and more definitive evidence. Submitted for publication in K. C. Blaine (Ed.), *Raising America's Children.*

Straus, M. A., & Paschall, M. J. (1999, July). *Corporal punishment by mothers and children's cognitive development: A longitudinal study of two age cohorts.* Paper presented at the Sixth International Family Violence Research Conference, University of New Hampshire, Durham, NH.

Straus, M. A., & Stewart, J. H. (1999). Corporal punishment by American parents: National data on prevalence, chronicity, severity, and duration, in relation to child and family characteristics. *Clinical Child and Family Psychology Review, 2*(2), 55–70.

Straus, M. A., Sugarman, D. B., & Giles-Sims, J. (1997). Spanking by parents and subsequent antisocial behavior of children. *Archives of Pediatric and Adolescent Medicine, 151,* 761–767.

Strauss, M., Lessen-Firestone, J., Starr, R., & Ostrea, E. (1975). Behavior of narcotics-addicted newborns. *Child Development, 46,* 887–893.

Strauss, R. S. (2000). Adult functional outcome of those born small for gestational age: Twenty-six-year follow-up of the 1970 British Birth Cohort. *Journal of the American Medical Association, 283,* 625–632.

Strawbridge, W. J., & Wallhagen, M. I. (1991). Impact of family conflict on adult child caregivers. *The Gerontologist, 31*(6), 770–777.

Streissguth, A. P., Aase, J. M., Clarren, S. K., Randels, S. P., LaDue, R. A., & Smith, D. F. (1991). Fetal alcohol syndrome in adolescents and adults. *Journal of the American Medical Association, 265,* 1961–1967.

Streissguth, A. P., Martin, D. C., Barr, H. M., Sandman, B. M., Kirchner, G. L., & Darby, B. L. (1984). Intrauterine alcohol and nicotine exposure: Attention and reaction time in 4-year-old children. *Developmental Psychology, 20,* 533–541.

Strömland, K., & Hellström, A. (1996). Fetal alcohol syndrome—An ophthalmological and socioeducational prospective study. *Pediatrics, 97,* 845–850.

Strobel, A., Camoin, T. I. L., Ozata, M., & Strosberg, A. D. (1998). A leptin missense mutation associated with hypogonadism and morbid obesity. *Nature Genetics, 18,* 213–215.

Stroebe, M., Gergen, M. M., Gergen, K. J., & Stroebe, W. (1992). Broken hearts or broken bonds: Love and death in historical perspective. *American Psychologist, 47*(10), 1205–1212.

Strube, M. J., & Barbour, L. S. (1984). Factors related to the decision to leave an abusive relationship. *Journal of Marriage and the Family, 46,* 837–844.

Stuart, J. (1991). Introduction. In Z. Zhensun & A. Low, *A young painter: The life and paintings of Wang Yani–China's extraordinary young artist* (pp. 6–7). New York: Scholastic.

Stuck, A. E., Egger, M., Hammer, A., Minder, C. E., & Beck, J. C. (2002). Home visits to prevent nursing home admission and functional decline in elderly people: Systematic review and meta-regression analysis. *Journal of the American Medical Association, 287,* 1022–1028.

Sturges, J. W., & Sturges, L. V. (1998). In vivo systematic desensitization in a single-session treatment of an 11-year-old girl's elevator phobia. *Child & Family Behavior Therapy, 20,* 55–62.

Sturm, R. (2002). The effects of obesity, smoking, and drinking on medical problems and costs. *Health Affairs, 21,* 245–253.

Subar, A. F., Krebs-Smith, S. M., Cook, A., & Kahle, L. L. (1998). Dietary sources of nutrients among US children, 1989–1991. *Pediatrics, 102,* 913–923.

Subramanian, G., Adams, M. D., Venter, J. C., & Broder, S. (2001). Implications of the human genome for understanding human biology and medicine. *Journal of the American Medical Association, 26*(18), 2296–2307.

Substance Abuse and Mental Health Services Administration (SAMHSA). (1998). *Preliminary results from the 1997 National Household Survey on Drug Abuse.* Washington, DC: Author.

Substance Abuse and Mental Health Services Administration (SAMHSA). (2001). *Summary of findings from the 2000 National Household Survey on Drug Abuse.* NHSDA Series H-13, DHHS Publication No. (SMA) 01-3549. Rockville, MD: Office of Applied Studies.

Sue, S., & Okazaki, S. (1990). Asian-American educational achievements: A phenomenon in search of an explanation. *American Psychologist, 45*(8), 913–920.

Sugarman, J. (1999). Ethical considerations in leaping from bench to bedside. *Science, 285,* 2071–2072.

Suicide—Part I. (1996, November). *The Harvard Mental Health Letter,* pp. 1–5.

Suicide—Part II. (1996, December). *The Harvard Mental Health Letter,* pp. 1–5.

Suitor, J. J., & Pillemer, K. (1993). Support and interpersonal stress in the social networks of married daughters caring for parents with dementia. *Journal of Gerontology: Social Sciences, 41*(1), S1–8.

Suitor, J. J., Pillemer, K., Keeton, S., & Robison, J. (1995). Aged parents and aging children: Determinants of relationship quality. In R. Blieszner & V. Hilkevitch (Eds.), *Handbook of aging and the family* (pp. 223–242). Westport, CT: Greenwood Press.

Sullivan, A. D., Hedberg, K., & Fleming, D. W. (2000). Legalized physician-assisted suicide in Oregon: the second year. *New England Journal of Medicine, 342,* 598–604.

Sullivan, P. F., Bulik, C. M., Fear, J. L., & Pickering, A. (1998). Outcome of anorexia nervosa: A case-control study. *American Journal of Psychiatry, 155,* 939–946.

Sullivan-Bolyai, J., Hull, H. F., Wilson, C., & Corey, L. (1983). Neonatal herpes simplex virus infection in King County, Washington. *Journal of the American Medical Association, 250,* 3059–3062.

Sum, A., Kirsch, I., & Taggart, R. (2002). *The twin challenges of mediocrity and inequality: Literacy in the U.S. from an international perspective.* Princeton, NJ: Policy Information Center, Educational Testing Service.

Summer, L., O'Neill, G., & Shirey, L. (1999). *Chronic conditions: A challenge for the 21st century.* Washington, DC: National Academy on an Aging Society.

Summers, T., Kates, J., & Murphy, G. (2002). The tip of the iceberg: The global impact of HIV/AIDS on youth. Menlo Park, CA: Henry J. Kaiser Family Foundation.

Sun, Y. (2001). Family environment and adolescents' well-being before and after parents' marital disruption. *Journal of Marriage and the Family, 63,* 697–713.

Suomi, S., & Harlow, H. (1972). Social rehabilitation of isolate-reared monkeys. *Developmental Psychology, 6,* 487–496.

Supreme Court ruling a victory for South Carolina's children. (1998, May 26). South Carolina Attorney General's Office. [Online]. 3 paragraphs. Available: http://scattorneygeneral.org. Access date: June 26, 1998.

Susman-Stillman, A., Kalkoske, M., Egeland, B., & Waldman, I. (1996). Infant temperament and maternal sensitivity as predictors of attachment security. *Infant Behavior and Development, 19,* 33–47.

Suzuki, L. A., & Valencia, R. R. (1997). Race-ethnicity and measured intelligence: Educational implications. *American Psychologist, 52,* 1103–1114.

Swain, I. U., Zelazo, P. R., & Clifton, R. K. (1993). Newborn infants' memory for speech sounds retained over 24 hours. *Developmental Psychology, 29,* 312–323.

Swan, S. H. (2000). Intrauterine exposure to diethylstilbestrol: Long-term effects in humans. *APMIS, 108,* 793–804.

Swanson, H. L. (1999). What develops in working memory? *Developmental Psychology, 35,* 986–1000.

Swarr, A. E., & Richards, M. H. (1996). Longitudinal effects of adolescent girls' pubertal development, perceptions of pubertal timing, and parental relations on eating problems. *Developmental Psychology, 32,* 636–646.

Swedo, S., Rettew, D. C., Kuppenheimer, M., Lum, D., Dolan, S., & Goldberger, E. (1991). Can adolescent suicide attemptors be distinguished from at-risk adolescents? *Pediatrics, 88*(3), 620–629.

Symons, D. (1978). *Play and aggression: A study of rhesus monkeys.* New York: Columbia University Press.

Szatmari, P. (1999). Heterogeneity and the genetics of autism. *Journal of Psychiatry and Neuroscience, 24,* 159–165.

Szinovacz, M. E. (1998). Grandparents today: A demographic profile. *The Gerontologist, 38,* 37–52.

Szinovacz, M., & Ekerdt, D. J. (1995). Families and retirement. In R. Blieszner & V. Hilkevitch (Eds.), *Handbook of aging and the family* (pp. 375–400). Westport, CT: Greenwood Press.

Szkrybalo, J., & Ruble, D. N. (1999). "God made me a girl": Sex category constancy judgments and explanations revisited. *Developmental Psychology, 35,* 392–403.

Takanishi, R. (1993). The opportunities of adolescence—Research, interventions, and policy. *American Psychologist, 48,* 85–87.

Talbott, M. M. (1998). Older widows' attitudes towards men and remarriage. *Journal of Aging Studies, 12,* 429–449.

Tamir, L. M. (1989). Modern myths about men at midlife: An assessment. In S. Hunter & M. Sundel (Eds.), *Midlife myths.* Newbury Park, CA: Sage.

Tamis-LeMonda, C. S., Bornstein, M. H., & Baumwell, L. (2001). Maternal responsiveness and children's achievement of language milestones. *Child Development, 72*(3), 748–767.

Tang, M., Jacobs, C., Stern, Y., Marder, K., Schofield, P., Gurland, B., Andrews, H., & Mayeux, R. (1996). Effect of estrogen during menopause on risk and age at onset of Alzheimer's disease. *The Lancet, 348,* 429–433.

Tang, Y.-P., Shimizu, E., Dube, G. R., Rampon, C., Kerchner, G. A., Zhuo, M., Liu, G., & Tsien, J. Z. (1999). Genetic enhancement of learning and memory in mice. *Nature, 401*(6748), 63–68.

Taniguchi, H. (1999). The timing of childbearing and women's wages. *Journal of Marriage and the Family, 61,* 1008–1019.

Tao, K.-T. (1998). An overview of only child family mental health in China. *Psychiatry and Clinical Neurosciences, 52*(Suppl.), S206–S211.

Tarnowski, A. C., & Antonucci, T. C. (1998, June 21). Adjustment to retirement: The influence of social relations. Paper presented at the SPSSI Convention, Ann Arbor, MI.

Taubes, G. (1998, May 29). As obesity rates rise, experts struggle to explain why. *Science, 280,* 1367–1368.

Taylor, H. (1995, January 30). *Doctor-assisted suicide: Support for Doctor Kevorkian remains strong, and 2-to-1 majority approves Oregon-style assisted suicide bill.* New York: Harris & Associates.

Taylor, H. G., Klein, N., Minich, N. M., & Hack, M. (2001). Middle-school-age outcomes in children with very low birthweight. *Child Development, 71*(6), 1495–1511.

Taylor, H. S., Arici, A., Olive, D., & Igarashi, P. (1998). HOXA10 is expressed in response to sex steroids at the time of implantation in the human endometrium. *Journal of Clinical Investigation, 101,* 1379–1384.

Taylor, J. A., Krieger, J. W., Reay, D. T., Davis, R. L., Harruff, R., & Cheney, L. K. (1996). Prone sleep position and the sudden infant death syndrome in King's County, Washington: A case-control study. *Journal of Pediatrics, 128,* 626–630.

Taylor, J. H., & Walker, L. J. (1997). Moral climate and the development of moral reasoning: The effects of dyadic discussions between young offenders. *Journal of Moral Education, 26*(1), 21–43.

Taylor, M. (1997). The role of creative control and culture in children's fantasy/reality judgments. *Child Development, 68,* 1015–1017.

Taylor, M. G. (1996). The development of children's beliefs about social and biological aspects of gender differences. *Child Development, 67,* 1555–1571.

Taylor, M., & Carlson, S. M. (1997). The relation between individual differences in fantasy and theory of mind. *Child Development, 68,* 436–455.

Taylor, M., Cartwright, B. S., & Carlson, S. M. (1993). A developmental investigation of children's imaginary companions. *Developmental Psychology, 28,* 276–285.

Taylor, R. D., & Roberts, D. (1995). Kinship support in maternal and adolescent well-being in economically disadvantaged African-American families. *Child Development, 66,* 1585–1597.

Teachman, J. D., Paasch, K., & Carver, K. (1996). Social capital and dropping out of school early. *Journal of Marriage and the Family, 58,* 773–783.

Teachman, J. D., Tedrow, L. M., & Crowder, K. D. (2000). The changing demography of America's families. *Journal of Marriage and Family, 62,* 1234–1246.

Techner, D. (1994, February 6). *Death and dying.* Seminar presentation for candidates in Leadership Program, International Institute for Secular Humanistic Judaism, Farmington Hills, MI.

Temple, J. A., Reynolds, A. J., & Miedel, W. T. (2000). Can early intervention prevent high school dropout? Evidence from the Chicago Child-Parent Centers. *Urban Education, 35*(1), 31–57.

Tercyak, K. P., Goldman, P., Smith, A., & Audrain, J. (2002). Interacting effects of depression and tobacco advertising receptivity on adolescent smoking. *Journal of Pediatric Psychology, 27,* 145–154.

Terman, L. M., & Oden, M. H. (1959). *Genetic studies of genius: Vol. 5. The gifted group at mid-life.* Stanford, CA: Stanford University Press.

Termine, N. T., & Izard, C. E. (1988). Infants' responses to their mothers' expressions of joy and sadness. *Developmental Psychology, 24,* 223–229.

Terry, D. (1996, August 17). In Wisconsin, a rarity of a fetal-harm case: Attempted-murder charges for alcoholic, *The New York Times,* p. 6.

Terry, P., Giovannucci, E., Michels, K. B., Bergkvist, L., Hansen, H., Holmberg, L., & Wolk, A. (2001). Fruit, vegetables, dietary fiber, and risk of colorectal cancer. *Journal of the National Cancer Institute, 93,* 525–533.

Tesman, J. R., & Hills, A. (1994). Developmental effects of lead exposure in children. *Social Policy Report of the Society for Research in Child Development, 8*(3), 1–16.

Teti, D. M., & Ablard, K. E. (1989). Security of attachment and infant-sibling relationships: A laboratory study. *Child Development, 60,* 1519–1528.

Teti, D. M., Gelfand, D. M., Messinger, D. S., & Isabella, R. (1995). Maternal depression and the quality of early attachment: An examination of infants, preschoolers, and their mothers. *Developmental Psychology, 31,* 364–376.

Thabes, V. (1997). A survey analysis of women's long-term, postdivorce adjustment. *Journal of Divorce & Remarriage, 27,* 163–175.

Thacker, S. B., Addiss, D. G., Goodman, R. A., Holloway, B. R., & Spencer, H. C. (1992). Infectious diseases and injuries in child day care: Opportunities for healthier children. *Journal of the American Medical Association, 268,* 1720–1726.

Thal, D., Tobias, S., & Morrison, D. (1991). Language and gesture in late talkers: A one-year follow-up. *Journal of Speech and Hearing Research, 34,* 604–612.

The breast cancer genes. (1994, December). *Harvard Women's Health Watch,* p. 1.

The SUPPORT Principal Investigators. (1995). A controlled trial to improve care for seriously ill hospitalized patients: The Study to Understand Prognoses and Preferences for Outcomes and Risks of Treatments (SUPPORT). *Journal of the American Medical Association, 274,* 1591–1598.

Thelen, E. (1994). Three month-old infants can learn task-specific patterns of interlimb coordination. *Psychological Science, 5,* 280–285.

Thelen, E. (1995). Motor development: A new synthesis. *American Psychologist, 50*(2), 79–95.

Thelen, E., & Fisher, D. M. (1982). Newborn stepping: An explanation for a "disappearing" reflex. *Developmental Psychology, 18,* 760–775.

Thelen E., & Fisher, D. M. (1983). The organization of spontaneous leg movements in newborn infants. *Journal of Motor Behavior, 15,* 353–377.

Thomas, A., & Chess, S. (1977). *Temperament and development.* New York: Brunner/Mazel.

Thomas, A., & Chess, S. (1984). Genesis and evolution of behavioral disorders: From infancy to early adult life. *American Journal of Orthopsychiatry, 141*(1), 1–9.

Thomas, A., Chess, S., & Birch, H. G. (1968). *Temperament and behavior disorders in children.* New York: New York University Press.

Thomas, C. (2002). Development of a culturally sensitive, locality-based program to increase kidney donation. *Advances in Renal Replacement Therapy, 9,* 54–56.

Thomas, C. R., Holzer, C. E., & Wall, J. (2002). The Island Youth Programs: Community interventions for reducing youth violence and delinquency. In L. T. Flaherty (Ed.), *Adolescent psychiatry: Developmental and clinical studies,*

Vol. 26. Annals of the American Society for Adolescent Psychiatry (pp. 125–143). Hillsdale, NJ: Analytic Press.

Thomas, R. M. (1996). *Comparing theories of child development* (4th ed.). Pacific Grove, CA: Brooks-Cole.

Thomas, S. P. (1997). Psychosocial correlates of women's self-rated physical health in middle adulthood. In M. E. Lachman & J. B. James (Eds.), *Multiple paths of midlife development* (pp. 257–291). Chicago: University of Chicago Press.

Thomas, W. P., & Collier, V. P. (1997). *School effectiveness for language minority students.* Washington, DC: National Clearinghouse for Bilingual Education.

Thomas, W. P., & Collier, V. P. (1998). Two languages are better than one. *Educational Leadership, 55*(4), 23–28.

Thomas, W. P., & Collier, V. P. (1999, April). Accelerated schooling for English language learners. *Educational Leadership,* pp. 46–49.

Thompson, L., & Walker, A. J. (1989). Gender in families: Women and men in marriage, work, and parenthood. *Journal of Marriage and the Family, 51,* 845–871.

Thompson, P. M., Cannon, T. D., Narr, K. L. K., van Erp, T., Poutanen, V.-P., Huttunen, M., Lñqvist, J., Standertskjöld-Nordenstam, C.-G., Kaprio, J., Khaledy, M., Dail, R., Zoumalan, C. I., & Toga, A. W. (2001). Genetic influences on brain structure. *Nature Neuroscience 4,* 1253–1258.

Thompson, R. A. (1991). Emotional regulation and emotional development. *Educational Psychology Review, 3,* 269–307.

Thompson, R. A. (1998). Early sociopersonality development. In W. Damon (Series Ed.) & N. Eisenberg (Vol. Ed.), *Handbook of child psychology: Vol. 3. Social, emotional, and personality development* (4th ed., pp. 25–104). New York: Wiley.

Thompson, S. L. (2001). The social skills of previously institutionalized children adopted from Romania, *Dissertation Abstracts International: Section B: The Sciences & Engineering, 61*(7-B), 3906.

Thomson, E., Mosley, J., Hanson, T. L., & McLanahan, S. S. (2001). Remarriage, cohabitation, and changes in mothering behavior. *Journal of Marriage and Family, 63,* 370–380.

Thorne, A., & Michaelieu, Q. (1996). Situating adolescent gender and self-esteem with personal memories. *Child Development, 67,* 1374–1390.

Thurstone, L. L. (1938). Primary mental abilities. *Psychometric Monographs,* No. 1.

Tiedemann, D. (1897). *Beobachtungen über die entwickelung der seelenfähigkeiten bei kindern [Record of an infant's life].* Altenburg, Germany: Oscar Bonde. (Original work published 1787)

Tincoff, R., & Jusczyk, P. W. (1999). Some beginnings of word comprehension in 6-month-olds. *Psychological Science, 10,* 172–177.

Tisdale, S. (1988). The mother. *Hippocrates, 2*(3), 64–72.

Tong, S., Baghurst, P. A., Sawyer, M. G., Burns, J., & McMichael, A. J. (1998). Declining blood lead levels and changes in cognitive function during childhood: The Port Pirie Cohort Study. *Journal of the American Medical Association, 280,* 1915–1919.

Torrance, E. P. (1966). *The Torrance Tests of Creative Thinking: Technical-norms manual (Research ed.).* Princeton, NJ: Personnel Press.

Torrance, E. P. (1972a). Career patterns and peak creative experiences of creative high school students 12 years later. *Gifted Child Quarterly, 16,* 75–88.

Torrance, E. P. (1972b). Predictive validity of the Torrance Test of Creative Thinking. *Journal of Creative Behavior, 6,* 236–252.

Torrance, E. P. (1974). *The Torrance Tests of Creative Thinking: Technical-norms manual.* Bensonville, IL: Scholastic Testing Service.

Torrance, E. P. (1981). Predicting the creativity of elementary school children (1958–1980)—and the teacher who made a "difference." *Gifted Child Quarterly, 25,* 55–62.

Torrance, E. P. (1988). The nature of creativity as manifest in its testing. In R. J. Sternberg (Ed.), *The nature of creativity: Contemporary psychological perspectives* (pp. 43–75). Cambridge, UK: Cambridge University Press.

Torrance, E. P., & Ball, O. E. (1984). *Torrance Tests of Creative Thinking: Streamlined (revised) manual, Figural A and B.* Bensonville, IL: Scholastic Testing Service.

Tower, R. B., & Kasl, S. V. (1996). Gender, marital closeness, and depressive symptoms in elderly couples. *Journal of Gerontology: Psychological Sciences, 51B,* P115–129.

Townsend, N. W. (1997). Men, migration, and households in Botswana: An exploration of connections over time and space. *Journal of Southern African Studies, Vol. 23,* 405–420.

Tramontana, M. G., Hooper, S. R., & Selzer, S. C. (1988). Research on the preschool prediction of later academic achievement: A review. *Developmental Review, 8,* 89–146.

Travis, J. (1996, January 6). Obesity researchers feast on two scoops. *Science News,* p. 6.

Treas, J. (1995, May). Older Americans in the 1990s and beyond. *Population Bulletin, 50*(2). Washington, DC: Population Reference Bureau.

Treffers, P. E., Hanselaar, A. G., Helmerhorst, T. J., Koster, M. E., & van Leeuwen, F. E. (2001). [Consequences of diethylstilbestrol during pregnancy; 50 years later still a significant problem.] *Ned Tijdschr Geneeskd, 145,* 675–680.

Troll, L. E. (1985). *Early and middle adulthood* (2nd ed.). Monterey, CA: Brooks/Cole.

Troll, L. E., & Fingerman, K. L. (1996). Connections between parents and their adult children. In C. Magai & S. H. McFadden (Eds.), *Handbook of emotion, adult development, and aging* (pp. 185–205). San Diego: Academic Press.

Tronick, E. (1972). Stimulus control and the growth of the infant's visual field. Perception and *Psychophysics, 11,* 373–375.

Tronick, E. Z. (1980). On the primacy of social skills. In D. B. Sawin, L. O. Walker, & J. H. Penticuff (Eds.), *The exceptional infant: Psychosocial risk in infant environment transactions.* New York: Brunner/Mazel.

Tronick, E. Z. (1989). Emotions and emotional communication in infants. *American Psychologist, 44*(2), 112–119.

Tronick, E. Z., Morelli, G. A., & Ivey, P. (1992). The Efe forager infant and toddler's pattern of social relationships: Multiple and simultaneous. *Developmental Psychology, 28,* 568–577.

Tronick, E., Als, H., Adamson, L., Wise, S., & Brazelton, T. B. (1978). The infant's response to entrapment between contradictory messages in face-to-face interaction. *American Academy of Child Psychiatry, 17,* 1–13.

Troseth, G. L., & DeLoache, J. S. (1998). The medium can obscure the message: Young children's understanding of video. *Child Development, 69,* 950–965.

Trotter, R. J. (1986, August). Profile: Robert J. Sternberg: Three heads are better than one. *Psychology Today,* pp. 56–62.

Trottier, G., Srivastava, L., & Walker, C. (1999). Etiology of infantile autism: A review of recent advances in genetic and neurobiological research. *Journal of Psychiatry and Neuroscience, 24,* 103–115.

True, M. M., Pisani, L., & Oumar, F. (2001). Infant-mother attachment among the Dogon of Mali. *Child Development, 72,* 1451–1466.

Trueheart, C. (1999, October 14). France gives right to unwed couples. *Boston Globe,* p. A4.

Tschann, J., Johnston, J. R., & Wallerstein, J. S. (1989). Resources, stressors, and attachment as predictors of adult adjustment after divorce: A longitudinal study. *Journal of Marriage and Family Therapy, 51,* 1033–1046.

Tsevat, J., Dawson, N. V.,Wu, A. W., Lynn, J., Soukup, J. R., Cook, E. F., Vidaillet, H., Phillips, R. S. (1998). Health values of hospitalized patients 80 years or older. *Journal of the American Medical Association, 279,* 371–375.

Tucker, J. S., & Friedman, H. S. (1996). Emotion, personality, and health. In C. Magai, & S. H. McFadden (Eds.), *Handbook of emotion, adult development, and aging* (pp. 307–326). San Diego: Academic Press.

Tucker, M. B., & Mitchell-Kernan, C. (1998). Psychological well-being and perceived marital opportunity among single African American, Latina and White women. *Journal of Comparative Family Studies, 29,* 57–72.

Tucker, M. B., Taylor, R. J., & Mitchell-Kernan, C. (1993). Marriage and romantic involvement among aged African Americans. *Journal of Gerontology: Social Sciences, 48,* S123–132.

Turiel, E. (1998). The development of morality. In W. Damon (Series Ed.) & N. Eisenberg (Vol. Ed.), *Handbook of child psychology: Vol. 3. Social, emotional, and personality development* (4th ed., pp. 863–932). New York: Wiley.

Turner, C. F., Ku, L., Rogers, S. M., Lindberg, L. D., Pleck, J. H., & Sonenstein, F. L. (1998). Adolescent sexual behavior, drug use, and violence: Increased reporting with computer survey technology. *Science, 280,* 867–873.

Turner, P. J., & Gervai, J. (1995). A multidimensional study of gender typing in preschool children and their parents: Personality, attitudes, preferences, behavior, and cultural differences. *Developmental Psychology, 31,* 759–772.

Turrisi, R., Wiersman, K. A., & Hughes, K. K. (2000). Binge-drinking-related consequences in college students: Role of drinking beliefs and mother-teen communication. *Psychology of Addictive Behaviors, 14*(4), 342–345.

Tuulio-Henriksson, A., Haukka, J., Partonen, T., Varilo, T., Paunio, T., Ekelund, J., Cannon, T. D., Meyer, J. M., & Lonnqvist, J. (2002). Heritability and number of quantitative trait loci of neurocognitive functions in families with schizophrenia. *American Journal of Medical Genetics, 114*(5), 483–490.

Twenge, J. M. (2000). The age of anxiety? Birth cohort change in anxiety and neuroticism, 1952–1993. *Journal of Personality and Social Psychology, 79,* 1007–1021.

Tygiel, J. (1983). Baseball's great experiment: Jackie Robinson and his legacy. New York: Oxford University Press.

Tygiel, J. (Ed.). (1997). *The Jackie Robinson reader.* New York: Dutton.

U.S. Bureau of Justice Statistics. (1994, November). *Selected findings: Violence between intimates.* Washington, DC: U.S. Government Printing Office.

U.S. Bureau of the Census. (1991a). *Household and family characteristics, March 1991* (Publication No. AP 20–458). Washington, DC: U.S. Government Printing Office.

U.S. Bureau of the Census. (1991b). *1990 census of population and housing.* Washington, DC: Data User Service Division.

U.S. Bureau of the Census. (1992). *Marital status and living arrangements: March 1991* (Current Population Reports, Series P-20–461). Washington, DC: U.S. Government Printing Office.

U.S. Bureau of the Census. (1993). *Sixty-five plus in America.* Washington, DC: U.S. Government Printing Office.

U.S. Bureau of the Census. (1995). *Sixty-five plus in the United States.* Washington, DC: U.S. Government Printing Office.

U.S. Bureau of the Census. (1998). *Household and family characteristics: March 1998 (Update)* (Current Population Reports, P20–514). Washington, DC: U.S. Government Printing Office.

U.S. Bureau of the Census. (1999). *World population profile: 1998—Highlights.* [Online]. Available://www.census.gov/ipc/www/wp98001.html

U.S. Bureau of the Census. (2002). *Statistical abstract of the United States: 2001.* Washington, DC: U.S. Government Printing Office.

U.S. Census Bureau. (2001). *The 65 years and over population: 2000.* Washington, DC: Author.

U.S. Department of Agriculture. (1999). *Household food security in the United States 1995–1998.* Washington, DC: Author.

U.S. Department of Education. (1992). *Dropout rates in the U.S., 1991* (Publication No. NCES 92–129). Washington, DC: U.S. Government Printing Office.

U.S. Department of Education. (1996). *National Center for Education Statistics: Schools and staffing in the United States: A statistical profile, 1993–94* (NCES 96–124). Washington, DC: Author.

U.S. Department of Education. (2000, February). *Vocational education in the United States: Toward the year 2000.* [Online]. Available: http://nces.ed.gov/pubs2000/2000029.pdf

U.S. Department of Health and Human Services (USDHHS). (1992). *Health, United States, 1991, and Prevention Profile* (DHHS Publication No. PHS 92–1232). Washington, DC: U.S. Government Printing Office.

U.S. Department of Health and Human Services (USDHHS). (1996a). *Health, United States, 1995* (DHHS Publication No. PHS 96–1232). Washington, DC: U.S. Government Printing Office.

U.S. Department of Health and Human Services (USDHHS). (1996b). *HHS releases study of relationship between family structure and adolescent substance abuse* [Press release, online]. Available: http://www.hhs.gov

U.S. Department of Health and Human Services (USDHHS). (1999a). *Blending perspectives and building common ground: A report to Congress on substance abuse and child protection.* Washington, DC: U.S. Government Printing Office.

U.S. Department of Health and Human Services (USDHHS). (1999b). *Healthy People 2000 Review* (PHS 99–1256). Washington, DC: Author.

U.S. Department of Health and Human Services (USDHHS). (1999c). *Mental health: A report of the Surgeon General*—Rickville, MD: U.S. Department of Health and Human Services, Substance Abuse and Mental Health Services Administration, National Institutes of Health, National Institute of Mental Health.

U.S. Department of Health and Human Services (USDHHS). (2000a). *HHS Blueprint for Action on Breastfeeding.* Washington, DC; Author.

U.S. Department of Health and Human Services (USDHHS). (2000b, December 6). *Statistics on child care help* (HHS Press Release). [Online] 10 paragraphs. Available: http://www.hhs.gov/search/press.html. Access date: December 6, 2000.

U.S. Department of Health and Human Services (USDHHS). (2002a). "Gift of life" donation initiative fact sheet. [Online]. Available: http://www.organdonor.gov

U.S. Department of Health and Human Services (USDHHS). (2002b). Physical activity fundamental to preventing disease. [Online]. Available: http://aspe.hhs.gov/health/reports/physicalactivity/

U.S. Environmental Protection Agency. (1994). *Setting the record straight: Secondhand smoke is a preventable health risk* (EPA Publication No. 402-F-94-005). Washington, DC: U.S. Government Printing Office.

U.S. Office of Technology Assessment. (1992). *The menopause, hormone therapy, and women's health.* Washington, DC: U.S. Government Printing Office.

U.S. Preventive Services Task Force. (2002). *Screening for breast cancer: Recommendations and rationale.* Rockville, MD: Agency for Healthcare Research and Quality. [Online]. Available: http://www.ahrq.gov/clinic/3rduspstf/breastcancer/brcanrr.htm

Uhlenberg, P. (1988). Aging and the social significance of cohorts. In J. E. Birren & V. L. Bengtson (Eds.), *Emergent theories of aging* (pp. 405–425). New York: Springer.

Uhlenberg, P., Cooney, T., & Boyd, R. (1990). Divorce for women after midlife. *Journal of Gerontology, 45*(1), 53–61.

Uitterlinden, A. G., Burger, H., Huang, Q., Yue, F., McGuigan, F. E. A., Grant, S. F. A., van Leeuwen, J. P. T., Pols, H. A. P., & Ralston, S. H. (1998). Relation of alleles of the collagen type Ia1 gene to bone density and the risk of osteoporitic fractures in postmenopausal women. *New England Journal of Medicine, 33,* 1016–1021.

Uller, C., Carey, S., Huntley-Fenner, G., & Klatt, L. (1999). What representations might underlie infant numerical knowledge? *Cognitive Development, 14,* 1–36.

Umberson, D. (1992). Relationships between adult children and their parents: Psychological consequences for both generations. *Journal of Marriage and the Family, 54,* 664–674.

Underwood, M. K., Schockner, A. E., & Hurley, J. C. (2001). Children's responses to same- and other-gender peers: An experimental investigation with 8-, 10-, and 12-year-olds. *Developmental Psychology, 37,* 362–372.

UNESCO. (1998). *UNESCO statistical yearbook.* Lanham, MD: Bernan Press.

UNICEF. (1996). *State of the world's children.* New York: Oxford University Press.

UNICEF. (2002). Official summary of The State of the World's Children 2002. [Online]. Available: http://www.unicef.org/pubsgen/sowc02summary/index.html. Access date: September 19, 2002.

United Nations International Labor Organization (UNILO). (1993). *Job stress: The 20th-century disease.* New York: United Nations.

Utiger, R. D. (1998). A pill for impotence. *New England Journal of Medicine, 338,* 1458–1459.

Vaccarino, V., Parsons, L., Every, N. R., Barron, H. V., & Krumholz, H. M., for the National Registry of Myocardial Infarction 2 Participants. (1999). Sex-based differences in early mortality after myocardial infarction. *New England Journal of Medicine, 341,* 217–225.

Vaillant, G. E. (1977). *Adaptation to life.* Boston: Little, Brown.

Vaillant, G. E. (1989). The evolution of defense mechanisms during the middle years. In J. M.

Oldman & R. S. Liebert (Eds.), *The middle years.* New Haven: Yale University Press.

Vaillant, G. E. (1993). *The wisdom of the ego.* Cambridge, MA: Harvard University Press.

Vaillant, G. E. (2000). Adaptive mental mechanisms: Their role in a positive psychology. *American Psychologist, 55,* 89–98.

Vaillant, G. E., Meyer, S. E., Mukamal, K., & Soldz, S. (1998). Are social supports in late midlife a cause or a result of successful physical aging? *Psychological Medicine, 28*(5), 1159–1168.

Vainio, S., Heikkiia, M., Kispert, A., Chin, N., & McMahon, A. P. (1999). Female development in mammals is regulated by Wnt-4 signalling. *Nature, 397,* 405–409.

Valeski, T. N., & Stipek, D. J. (2001). Young children's feelings about school. *Child Development, 72*(4), 1198–1213.

Van den Boom, D. C. (1989). Neonatal irritability and the development of attachment. In G. A. Kohnstamm, J. E. Bates, & M. K. Rothbart (Eds.), *Temperament in childhood* (pp. 299–318). Chichester, England: Wiley.

Van den Boom, D. C. (1994). The influence of temperament and mothering on attachment and exploration: An experimental manipulation of sensitive responsiveness among lower-class mothers with irritable infants. *Child Development, 65,* 1457–1477.

van den Hoonaard, D. K. (1999). No regrets: Widows' stories about the last days of their husbands' lives. *Journal of Aging Studies, 13,* 59–72.

Van der Maas, P. J., Van der Wal, G., Haverkate, I., De Graeff, C. L. M., Kester, J. G. C., Onwuteaka-Philipsen, B. D., Van der Heide, A., Bosma, J. M., & Willems, D. L. (1996). Euthanasia, physician-assisted suicide, and other medical practices involving the end of life in the Netherlands, 1990–1995. *New England Journal of Medicine, 335,* 1699–1705.

Van Dongen, H. P. A., Maislin, G., Mullington, J. M., & Dinges, D. F. (2003). The cumulative cost of additional wakefulness: Dose-response effects on neurobehavioral functions and sleep physiology from chronic sleep restriction and total sleep deprivation. *Sleep, 26,* 117–126.

Van Heuvelen, M. J., Kempen, G. I., Ormel, J., & Rispens, P. (1998). Physical fitness related to age and physical activity in older persons. *Medicine & Science in Sports and Exercise, 30,* 434–441.

van IJzendoorn, M. H. (1995). Adult attachment representations, parental responsiveness, and infant attachment: A meta-analysis on the predictive validity of the Adult Attachment Interview. *Psychological Bulletin, 117*(3), 387–403.

van IJzendoorn, M. H., & Kroonenberg, P. M. (1988). Cross-cultural patterns of attachment: A meta-analysis of the strange situation. *Child Development, 59,* 147–156.

van IJzendoorn, M. H., & Sagi, A. (1997). Cross-cultural patterns of attachment: Universal and contextual dimensions. In J. Cassidy & P. Shaver (Eds.), *Handbook on attachment theory and research.* New York: Guilford Press.

van IJzendoorn, M. H., & Sagi, A. (1999). Cross-cultural patterns of attachment: Universal and contextual dimensions. In J. Cassidy & P. R. Shaver (Eds.), *Handbook of attachment: Theory, research, and clinical applications* (pp. 713–734). New York: Guilford.

van Lieshout, C. F. M., Haselager, G. J. T., Riksen-Walraven, J. M., & van Aken, M. A. G. (1995, April). Personality development in middle childhood. In D. Hart (Chair), *The contribution of childhood personality to adolescent competence: Insights from longitudinal studies from three societies.* Symposium conducted at the Biennial Meeting of the Society for Research in Child Development, Indianapolis, IN.

van Noord-Zaadstra, B. M., Looman, C. W., Alsbach, H., Habbema, J. D., te Velde, E. R., & Karbaat, J. (1991). Delayed childbearing: Effect of age on fecundity and outcome of pregnancy. *British Medical Journal, 302,* 1361–1365.

Van Praag, H., Schinder, A. F., Christie, B. R., Toni, N., Palmer, T. D., & Gage, F. H. (2002). Functional neurogenesis in the adult hippocampus. *Nature, 415,* 1030–1034.

Van, P. (2001). Breaking the silence of African American women: Healing after pregnancy loss. *Health Care Women International, 22,* 229–243.

Vance, M. L., & Mauras, N. (1999). Growth hormone therapy in adults and children. *New England Journal of Medicine, 341*(16), 1206–1216.

Vandell, D. L. (2000). Parents, peer groups, and other socializing influences. *Developmental Psychology, 36,* 699–710.

Vandell, D. L., & Bailey, M. D. (1992). Conflicts between siblings. In C. U. Shantz & W. W. Hartup (Eds.), *Conflict in child and adolescent development* (pp. 242–269). New York: Cambridge University Press.

Vandell, D. L., & Ramanan, J. (1992). Effects of early and recent maternal employment on children from low-income families. *Child Development, 63,* 938–949.

Vandewater, E. A., Ostrove, J. M., & Stewart, A. J. (1997). Predicting women's well-being in midlife: The importance of personality development and social role involvements. *Journal of Personality and Social Psychology, 72,* 1147–1160.

Vargas, C. M., Kramarow, F. A., & Yellowitz, J. A. (2001). The oral health of older Americans. *Aging Trends,* No. 3. Hyattsville, MD: National Center for Health Statistics.

Vargha-Khadem, F., Gadian, D. G., Watkins, K. E., Connelly, A., Van Paesschen, W., & Mishkin, M. (1997). Differential effects of early hippocampal pathology on episodic and semantic memory. *Science, 277,* 376–380.

Vartanian, L. R., & Powlishta, K. K. (1996). A longitudinal examination of the social-cognitive foundations of adolescent egocentrism. *Journal of Early Adolescence, 16,* 157–178.

Vasan, R. S., Beiser, A., Seshadri, S., Larson, M. G., Kannel, W. B., D' Agostino, R. B., & Levy, D. (2002). Residual lifetime risk for developing hypertension in middle-aged women and men. *Journal of the American Medical Association, 287,* 1003–1010.

Vassar, R., Bennett, B. D., Babu-Khan, S., Kahn, S., Mendiaz, E. A., Denis, P., Teplow, D. B., Ross, S., Amarante, P., Loeloff, R., Luo, Y., Fisher, S., Fuller, J., Edenson, S., Lile, J., Jaronsinski, M. A., Biere, A. L., Curran, E., Burgess, R., Louis, J., Collins, F., Treanor, J., Rogers, G., & Citron, M. (1999). B-secretase cleavage of Alzheimer's amyloid precursor protein by the transmembrane aspartic protease BACE. *Science, 286,* 735–741.

Vaswani, M., & Kapur, S. (2001). Genetic basis of schizophrenia: trinucleotide repeats. *An update Progress in Neuro-Psychopharmacology & Biological Psychiatry, 25*(6), 1187–1201.

Vaughn, B. E., Stevenson-Hinde, J., Waters, E., Kotsaftis, A., Lefever, G. B., Shouldice, A., Trudel, M., & Belsky, J. (1992). Attachment security and temperament in infancy and early childhood: Some conceptual clarifications. *Developmental Psychology, 28,* 463–473.

Vaupel, J. W., Carey, J. R., Christensen, K., Johnson, T. E., Yashin, A. I., Holm, N. V., Iachine, I. A., Kannisto, V., Khazaeli, A. A., Liedo, P., Longo, V. D., Zeng, Y., Manton, K. G., & Curtsinger, J. W. (1998). Biodemographic trajectories of longevity. *Science, 280,* 855–860.

Veninga, R. L. (1998, January 15). Stress in the workplace: How to create a productive and healthy work environment. *Vital Speeches, 64,* 217–219.

Ventura, S. J., Martin, J. A., Curtin, S. C., & Mathews, T. J. (1998). Report of final natality statistics, 1996 (*Monthly Vital Statistics Report, 46*[11, Suppl.]). Hyattsville, MD: National Center for Health Statistics.

Ventura, S. J., Martin, J. A., Curtin, S. C., & Mathews, T. J. (1999). Births: Final data for 1997 (*National Vital Statistics Reports, 47*[18]). Hyattsville, MD: National Center for Health Statistics.

Ventura, S. J., Martin, J. A., Curtin, S. C., Menacker, F., & Hamilton, B. E. (2001). Births: Final data for 1999. *National Vital Statistics Reports, 49*(1). Hyattsville, MD: National Center for Health Statistics.

Ventura, S. J., Mathews, T. J., & Curtin, S. C. (1998). Declines in teenage birth rates, 1991–97: National and state patterns. *National Vital Statistics Reports, 47,* 1–17. Hyattsville, MD: National Center for Health Statistics.

Ventura, S. J., Mathews, T. J., & Hamilton, B. E. (2001). Births to teenagers in the United States, 1940–2000. *National Vital Statistics Reports, 49*(10). Hyattsville, MD: National Center for Health Statistics.

Verbrugge, L. M., Gruber-Baldini, A. L., & Fozard, J. L. (1996). Age differences and age changes in activities: Baltimore Longitudinal Study of Aging. *Journal of Gerontology: Social Sciences, 51B,* S30–41.

Vercruyssen, M. (1997). Movement control and speed of behavior. In A. D. Fisk & W. A. Rogers (Eds.), *Handbook of human factors and the older adult* (pp. 55–86). San Diego: Academic Press, Inc.

Vereecken, C., & Maes, L. (2000). Eating habits, dental care and dieting. In C. Currie, K. Hurrelmann, W. Settertobulte, R. Smith, & J. Todd (Eds.), *Health and health behaviour among young people: a WHO cross-national study (HBSC) international report* (pp. 83–96). WHO Policy Series: Healthy Policy for Children and Adolescents, Series No. 1.

Verhaeghen, P., & Salthouse, T. A. (1997). Meta-analyses of age-cognition relations in adulthood: Estimates of linear and nonlinear age effects and structural models. *Psychological Bulletin, 122,* 231–249.

Verhaeghen, P., Marcoen, A., & Goossens, L. (1992). Improving memory performance in the aged through mnemonic training: A meta-analytic study. *Psychology and Aging, 7*(2), 242–251.

Verschueren, K., & Marcoen, A. (1999). Representation of self and socioemotional competence in kindergartners: Differential and combined effects of attachment to mother and to father. *Child Development, 70,* 183–201.

Verschueren, K., Buyck, P., & Marcoen, A. (2001). Self-representations and socioemotional competence in young children: A 3-year longitudinal study. *Developmental Psychology, 37,* 126–134.

Verschueren, K., Marcoen, A., & Schoefs, V. (1996). The internal working model of the self, attachment, and competence in five-year-olds. *Child Development, 67,* 2493–2511.

Verschuren, W. M. M., Jacobs, D. R., Bloemberg, B. P. M., Kromhout, D., Menotti, A., Aravanis, C., Blackburn, H., Buzina, R., Dontas, A. S., Fidanza, F., Karvonen, M. J., Nedeljkovic, S., Nissinen, A., & Toshima, H. (1995). Serum total cholesterol and long-term coronary heart disease mortality in different cultures. *Journal of the American Medical Association, 274,* 131–136.

Vgontzas, A. N., & Kales, A. (1999). Sleep and its disorders. *Annual Review of Medicine, 50,* 387–400.

Vigorito, A. J., & Curry, T. J. (1998). Marketing masculinity: Gender identity and popular magazines. *Sex Roles, 39,* 135–152.

Vink, T., Hinney, A., van Elburg, A. A., van Goozen, S. H. M., Sandkuijl, L. A., Sinke, R. J., Herpertz-Dahlmann, B.-M., Hebebrand, J., Remschmidt, H., van Engeland, H., & Adan, R. A. H. (2001). Association between an agouti-related protein gene polymorphism and anorexia nervosa. *Molecular Psychiatry, 6, 325–328.*

Vinokur, A. D., Schul, Y., Vuori, J., & Price, R. H. (2000). Two years after a job loss: Long-term impact of the JOBS program on reemployment and mental health. *Journal of Occupational Health Psychology, 5,* 32–47.

Visher, E. B., & Visher, J. S. (1991). *How to win as a step-family* (2nd ed.). New York: Brunner/Mazel.

Vita, A. J., Terry, R. B., Hubert, H. B., & Fries, J. F. (1998). Aging, health risk, and cumulative disability. *New England Journal of Medicine, 338,* 1035–1041.

Vitaro, F., Tremblay, R. E., Kerr, M., Pagani, L., & Bukowski, W. M. (1997). Disruptiveness, friends' characteristics, and delinquency in early adolescence: A test of two competing models of development. *Child Development, 68,* 676–689.

Vitaterna, M. H., Takahashi, J. S., & Turek, F. W. (2001). Overview of circadian rhythms. *Alcohol Research & Health, 25,* 85–93.

Vlahov, D., Galea, S., Resnick, H., Ahern, J., Boscarino, J. A., Bucuvalas, M., Gold, J., & Kilpatrick, D. (2002). Increased use of cigarettes, alcohol, and marijuana among Manhattan, New York, residents after the September 11th terrorist attacks. *American Journal of Epidemiology, 155,* 988–996.

Voelker, R. (1997). Federal program nourishes poor elderly. *Journal of the American Medical Association, 278,* 1301.

Voluntary Euthanasia Society. (2002). In depth: Factsheets. Australia. [Online]. Available: http://www.ves.org.uk/DpFS_Aust.html

von Kries, R., Koletzko, B., Saurewald, T., von Mutius, E., Barnert, T., Grunert, V., & von Voss, H. (1999). Breast feeding and obesity: Cross-sectional study. *British Medical Journal, 319,* 147–150.

Vosniadou, S. (1987). Children and metaphors. *Child Development, 58,* 870–885.

Voydanoff, P. (1987). *Work and family life.* Newbury Park, CA: Sage.

Voydanoff, P. (1990). Economic distress and family relations: A review of the eighties. *Journal of Marriage and the Family, 52,* 1099–1115.

Vuchinich, S., Angelelli, J., & Gatherum, A. (1996). Context and development in family problem solving with preadolescent children. *Child Development, 67,* 1276–1288.

Vuori, L., Christiansen, N., Clement, J., Mora, J., Wagner, M., & Herrera, M. (1979). Nutritional supplementation and the outcome of pregnancy: 2. Visual habitation at 15 days. *Journal of Clinical Nutrition, 32,* 463–469.

Vygotsky, L. S. (1956). *Selected psychological investigations.* Moscow: Izdstel'sto Akademii Pedagogicheskikh Nauk USSR.

Vygotsky, L. S. (1962). *Thought and language.* Cambridge, MA: MIT Press. (Original work published 1934)

Vygotsky, L. S. (1978). *Mind in society: The development of higher psychological processes.* Cambridge, MA: Harvard University Press.

Wade, N. (2001 Aug. 24). Human genome now appears more complicated after all. *The New York Times,* p. A13.

Wagner, C. L., Katikaneni, L. D., Cox, T. H., & Ryan, R. M. (1998). The impact of prenatal drug exposure on the neonate. *Obstetrics and Gynecology Clinics of North America, 25,* 169–194.

Wagner, R. K., & Sternberg, R. J. (1985). Practical intelligence in real-world pursuits: The role of tacit knowledge. *Journal of Personality and Social Psychology, 49,* 436–458.

Wagner, R. K., & Sternberg, R. J. (1986). Tacit knowledge and intelligence in the everyday world. In R. J. Sternberg & R. K. Wagner (Eds.), *Practical intelligence: Nature and origins of competence in the everyday world.* Cambridge, UK: Cambridge University Press.

Wahlbeck, K., Forsen, T., Osmond, C., Barker, D. J. P., & Erikkson, J. G. (2001). Association of schizophrenia with low maternal body mass index, small size at birth, and thinness during childhood. *Archives of General Psychiatry, 58,* 48–55.

Waite, L. J., & Joyner, K. (2000). Emotional and physical satisfaction with sex in married, cohabiting, and dating sexual unions: Do men and women differ? In Laumann, E. O., & Michael, R. T. (Eds.), *Sex, love, and health in America: Private choices and public policies* (pp. 239–269). Chicago: University of Chicago Press.

Wakeley, A., Rivera, S., & Langer, J. (2000a). Can young infants add and subtract? *Child Development, 71,* 1525–1534.

Wakeley, A., Rivera, S., & Langer, J. (2000b). Not proved: Reply to Wynn. *Child Development, 71,* 1537–1539.

Wakschlag, L. S., Lahey, B. B., Loeber, R., Green, S. M., Gordon, R. A., & Leventhal, B. L. (1997). Maternal smoking during pregnancy and the risk of conduct disorder in boys. *Archives of General Psychiatry, 54,* 670–676.

Walasky, M., Whitbourne, S. K., & Nehrke, M. F. (1983–1984). Construction and validation of an ego-integrity status interview. *International Journal of Aging and Human Development, 81,* 61–72.

Waldfogel, J., Han, W., & Brooks-Gunn, J. (2002). The effects of early maternal employment on child cognitive development. *Demography, 39,* 369–392.

Waldman, I. D. (1996). Aggressive boys' hostile perceptual and response biases: The role of attention and impulsivity. *Child Development, 67,* 1015–1033.

Walfish, S., Antonovsky, A., & Maoz, B. (1984). Relationship between biological changes and symptoms and health and behavior during the climacteric. *Maturitas, 6,* 9–17.

Walk, R. D., & Gibson, E. J. (1961). A comparative and analytical study of visual depth perception. *Psychology Monographs, 75*(15).

Walker, D., Greenwood, C., Hart, B., & Carta, J. (1994). Prediction of school outcomes based on early language production and socioeconomic factors. *Child Development, 65,* 606–621.

Walker, L. (1995). Sexism in Kohlberg's moral psychology? In W. M. Kurtines & J. L. Gewirtz (Eds.), *Moral development: An introduction* (pp. 83–107). Boston: Allyn and Bacon.

Walker, L. E. (1999). Psychology and domestic violence around the world. *American Psychologist, 54,* 21–29.

Walker, L. J. (1984). Sex differences in the development of moral reasoning: A critical review. *Child Development, 55,* 677–691.

Walker, L. J., & Hennig, K. H. (1997). Parent/child relationships in single-parent families. *Canadian Journal of Behavioural Science, 29,* 63–75.

Walker, L. J., & Taylor, J. H. (1991). Family interactions and the development of moral reasoning. *Child Development, 62,* 264–283.

Walker, M. P., Brakefield, T., Morgan, A., Hobson, J. A., & Stickgold, R. (2002). Practice with sleep makes perfect: Sleep-dependent motor skill learning. *Neuron, 35,* 205–211.

Wallace, D. C. (1992). Mitochondrial genetics: A paradigm for aging and degenerative diseases? *Science, 256,* 628–632.

Wallach, M. A., & Kogan, M. (1965). *Modes of thinking in young children: A study of the creativity-intelligence distinction.* New York: Holt.

Wallechinsky, D., & Wallace, I. (1993, September 26). Achievers after the age of 90. *Parade,* p. 17.

Wallerstein, J. S., & Blakeslee, S. (1995). *The good marriage: How and why love lasts.* Boston & New York: Houghton Mifflin.

Wallerstein, J. S., & Lewis, J. (1998). The long-term impact of divorce on children: A first report from a 25-year study. *Family and Conciliation Courts Review, 36,* 363–383.

Wallerstein, J., & Corbin, S. B. (1999). The child and the vicissitudes of divorce. In R. M. Galatzer-Levy & L. Kraus (Eds.), *The scientific basis of child custody decisions* (pp. 73–95). New York: Wiley.

Wallhagen, M. I., Strawbridge, W. J., Cohen, R. D., & Kaplan, G. A. (1997). An increasing prevalence of hearing impairment and associated risk factors over three decades of the Alameda County Study. *American Journal of Public Health, 87,* 440–442.

Walls, C., & Zarit, S. (1991). Informal support from black churches and well-being of elderly blacks. *The Gerontologist, 31,* 490–495.

Walsh, D. A., & Hershey, D. A. (1993). Mental models and the maintenance of complex problem solving skills into old age. In J. Cerella & W. Hoyer (Eds.), *Adult information processing: Limits on loss* (pp. 553–584). New York: Academic Press.

Walsh, D. M., Klyubin, I., Fadeeva, J. V., Cullen, W. K., Anwyl, R., Wolfe, M. S., Rowan, M. J., & Selkoe, D. J. (2002). Naturally secreted oligomers of amyloid beta protein potently inhibit hippocampal long-term potentiation in vivo. *Nature, 416,* 535–539.

Wannamethee, S. G., Shaper, A. G., Whincup, P. H., & Walker, M. (1995). Smoking cessation and the risk of stroke in middle-aged men. *Journal of the American Medical Association, 274,* 155–160.

Ward, L. M., & Rivadeneyra, R. (1999). Contributions of entertainment television to adolescents' sexual attitudes and expectations: The roles of viewing amount versus viewer involvement. *Journal of Sex Research, 36,* 237–249.

Warr, P. (1994). Age and employment. In H. C. Triandis, M. D. Dunnette, & L. M. Hough (Eds.), *Handbook of industrial and organizational psychology* (Vol. 4, pp. 485–550). Palo Alto, CA: Consulting Psychologists Press.

Warren, J. A., & Johnson, P. J. (1995). The impact of workplace support on work-family role strain. *Family Relations, 44,* 163–169.

Washington, DC: American Psychological Association.

Wasik, B. H., Ramey, C. T., Bryant, D. M., & Sparling, J. J. (1990). A longitudinal study of two early intervention strategies: Project CARE. *Child Development, 61,* 1682–1696.

Waters, D. D., Alderman, E. L., Hsia, J., Howard, B. V., Cobb, F. R., Rogers, W. J., Ouyang, P., Thompson, P., Tardif, J. C., Higginson, L., Bittner, V., Steffes, M., Gordon, D. J., Proschan, M., Younes, N., & Verter, J. I. (2002). Effects of hormone replacement therapy and antioxidant vitamin supplements on coronary atherosclerosis in postmenopausal women. *Journal of the American Medical Association, 288,* 2432–2440.

Waters, E., & Deane, K. E. (1985). Defining and assessing individual differences in attachment relationships: Q-methodology and the organization of behavior in infancy and early childhood. *Monographs of the Society for Research in Child Development, 50,* 41–65.

Waters, K. A., Gonzalez, A., Jean, C., Morielli, A., & Brouillette, R. T. (1996). Face-straight-down and face-near-straight-down positions in healthy prone-sleeping infants. *Journal of Pediatrics, 128,* 616–625.

Watson, A. C., Nixon, C. L., Wilson, A., & Capage, L. (1999). Social interaction skills and theory of mind in young children. *Developmental Psychology, 35*(2), 386–391.

Watson, J. B., & Rayner, R. (1920). Conditioned emotional reactions. *Journal of Experimental Psychology, 3,* 1–14.

Wechsler, H., Dowdall, G., Davenport, A., & Castillo, S. (1995). Correlates of college student binge drinking. *American Journal of Public Health, 85,* 921–926.

Weg, R. B. (1987). Intimacy and the later years. In G. Lesnoff-Caravaglia (Ed.), *Handbook of applied gerontology.* New York: Human Sciences Press.

Weg, R. B. (1989). Sensuality/sexuality of the middle years. In S. Hunter & M. Sundel (Eds.), *Midlife myths.* Newbury Park, CA: Sage.

Wegman, M. E. (1992). Annual summary of vital statistics—1991. *Pediatrics, 90,* 835–845.

Wegman, M. E. (1994). Annual summary of vital statistics—1993. *Pediatrics, 94,* 792–803.

Wegman, M. E. (1999). Foreign aid, international organizations, and the world's children. *Pediatrics, 103*(3), 646–654.

Weinberg, M. K., & Tronick, E. Z. (1996). Infant affective reactions to the resumption of maternal interaction after still face. *Child Development, 67,* 905–914.

Weinberg, M. K., Tronick, E. Z., Cohn, J. F., & Olson, K. L. (1999). Gender differences in emotional expressivity and self-regulation during early infancy. *Developmental Psychology, 35*(1), 175–188.

Weinberg, R. A. (1989). Intelligence and IQ: Landmark issues and great debates. *American Psychologist, 44*(2), 98–104.

Weinberger, B., Anwar, M., Hegyi, T., Hiatt, M., Koons, A., & Paneth, N. (2000). Antecedents and neonatal consequences of low Apgar scores in preterm newborns. *Archives of Pediatric and Adolescent Medicine, 154,* 294–300.

Weinberger, D. R. (2001, March 10). A brain too young for good judgment. *The New York Times.* [Online]. Available: http://www.nytimes.com/2001/03/10/opinion/10WEIN.html?ex=985250309&ei=1&en=995bc03f7a8c7207

Weinberger, J. (1999, May 18). Enlightening conversation [Letter to the editor]. *The New York Times,* p. F3.

Weindruch, R., & Walford, R. L. (1988). *The retardation of aging and disease by dietary restriction.* Springfield, IL: Thomas.

Weinman, J. (1998). Do public schools shortchange girls on educational opportunities? *Insight, 14*(46), 24–26.

Weisner, T. S. (1993). Ethnographic and ecocultural perspectives on sibling relationships. In Z. Stoneman & P. W. Berman (Eds.), *The effects of mental retardation, visibility, and illness on sibling relationships* (pp. 51–83). Baltimore, MD: Brooks.

Weiss, B., Dodge, K. A., Bates, J. E., & Pettit, G. S. (1992). Some consequences of early harsh discipline: Child aggression and a maladaptive social information processing style. *Child Development, 63,* 1321–1335.

Weissman, M. M., Warner, V., Wickramaratne, P. J., & Kandel, D. B. (1999). Maternal smoking during pregnancy and psychopathology in offspring followed to adulthood. *Journal of the American Academy of Child and Adolescent Psychiatry, 38,* 892–899.

Weisz, J. R., Weiss, B., Han, S. S., Granger, D. A., & Morton, T. (1995). Effects of psychotherapy with children and adolescents revisited: A meta-analysis of treatment outcome studies. *Psychological Bulletin, 117*(3), 450–468.

Weitzman, M., Gortmaker, S., & Sobol, A. (1992). Maternal smoking and behavior problems of children. *Pediatrics, 90,* 342–349.

Welch-Ross, M. K., & Schmidt, C. R. (1996). Gender-schema development and children's story memory: Evidence for a developmental model. *Child Development, 67,* 820–835.

Wellman, H. M., & Cross, D. (2001). Theory of mind and conceptual change. *Child Development, 72,* 702–707.

Wellman, H. M., & Gelman, S. A. (1998). Knowledge acquisition in foundational domains. In W. Damon (Series Ed.), D. Kuhn, & R. S. Siegler (Vol. Eds.), *Handbook of child psychology: Vol. 2. Cognition, perception, and language* (5th ed., pp. 523–573). New York: Wiley.

Wellman, H. M., & Woolley, J. D. (1990). From simple desires to ordinary beliefs: The early development of everyday psychology. *Cognition, 35,* 245–275.

Wellman, H. M., Cross, D., & Bartsch, K. (1986). Infant search and object permanence: A meta-analysis of the A-not-B error. *Monographs of the Society for Research in Child Development, 51*(3, Serial No. 214).

Wellman, H. M., Cross, D., & Watson, J. (2001). Meta-analysis of theory-of-mind development: The truth about false belief. *Child Development, 72,* 655–684.

Wells, G. (1985). Preschool literacy-related activities and success in school. In D. R. Olson, N. Torrence, & A. Hilyard (Eds.), *Literacy, language, and learning* (pp. 229–255). New York: Cambridge University Press.

Wender, P. H. (1995). *Attention-deficit hyperactivity disorder in adults.* New York: Oxford University Press.

Wentworth, N., Benson, J. B., & Haith, M. M. (2000). The development of infants' reaches for stationary and moving targets. *Child Development, 71,* 576–601.

Wentzel, K. R. (2002). Are effective teachers like good parents? Teaching styles and student adjustment in early adolescence. *Child Development, 73*(1), 287–301.

Wenzel, D. (1990). *Ann Bancroft: On top of the world.* Minneapolis: Dillon.

Werker, J. F. (1989). Becoming a native listener. *American Scientist, 77,* 54–59.

Werker, J. F., Pegg, J. E., & McLeod, P. J. (1994). A cross-language investigation of infant preference for infant-directed communication. *Infant Behavior and Development, 17,* 323–333.

Werner, E. E. (1985). Stress and protective factors in children's lives. In A. R. Nichol (Ed.), *Longitudinal studies in child psychology and psychiatry.* New York: Wiley.

Werner, E. E. (1987, July 15). *Vulnerability and resiliency: A longitudinal study of Asian Americans from birth to age 30.* Invited address at the Ninth Biennial Meeting of the International Society for the Study of Behavioral Development, Tokyo, Japan.

Werner, E. E. (1989). Children of the garden island. *Scientific American, 260*(4), 106–111.

Werner, E. E. (1993). Risk and resilience in individuals with learning disabilities: Lessons learned from the Kauai longitudinal study. *Learning Disabilities Research and Practice, 8,* 28–34.

Werner, E. E. (1995). Resilience in development. *Current Directions in Psychological Science, 4*(3), 81–85.

Werner, E., & Smith, R. S. (2001). *Journeys from childhood to midlife.* Ithaca: Cornell University Press.

Werner, E., Bierman, L. , French, F. E., Simonian, K., Conner, A., Smith, R., & Campbell, M. (1968). Reproductive and environmental casualties: A report on the 10-year follow-up of the children of the Kauai pregnancy study. *Pediatrics, 42,* 112–127.

West, R. L. (1996). An application of prefrontal cortex function theory to cognitive aging. *Psychological Bulletin, 120,* 272–292.

West, R., & Burr, G. (2002). Why families deny consent to organ donation. *Australian Critical Care, 15,* 27–32.

Westen, D. (1998). The scientific legacy of Sigmund Freud: Toward a psychodynamically informed psychological science. *Psychological Bulletin, 124,* 333–371.

Westermeyer, J. (1999, May). *Mentally healthy men at midlife.* Paper presented at the meeting of the American Psychiatric Association, Washington, DC.

Westermeyer, J. F. (1998). Predictors and characteristics of mental health among men at midlife: A 32-year longitudinal study. *American Journal of Orthopsychiatry, 68,* 265–273.

Wethington, E., & Kessler, R. C. (1989). Employment, parental responsibility, and psychological distress: A longitudinal study of married women. *Journal of Family Issues, 10,* 527–546.

Whalley, L. J., & Deary, I. J. (2001). Longitudinal cohort study of childhood IQ and survival up to age 76. *British Medical Journal, 322,* 819.

Whalley, L. J., Starr, J. M., Athawes, R., Hunter, D., Pattie, A., & Deary, I. J. (2000). Childhood mental ability and dementia. *Neurology, 55,* 1455–1459.

Whitaker, R. C., Wright, J. A., Pepe, M. S., Seidel, K. D., & Dietz, W. H. (1997). Predicting obesity in young adulthood from childhood and parental obesity. *New England Journal of Medicine, 337,* 869–873.

Whitbourne, S. K. (1987). Personality development in adulthood and old age: Relationships among identity style, health, and well-being. In K. W. Schaie (Ed.), *Annual review of gerontology and geriatrics* (pp. 189–216). New York: Springer.

Whitbourne, S. K. (1996). *The aging individual: Physical and psychological perspectives.* New York: Springer.

Whitbourne, S. K. (1999). Physical changes. In J. C. Cavanaugh & S. K. Whitbourne (Eds.), *Gerontology: An interdisciplinary perspective* (pp. 91–122). New York: Oxford University Press.

Whitbourne, S. K. (2001). The physical aging process in midlife: Interactions with psychological and sociocultural factors. In M. E. Lachman (Ed.), *Handbook of midlife development* (pp. 109–155). New York: Wiley.

Whitbourne, S. K., & Connolly, L. A. (1999). The developing self in midlife. In S. L. Willis & J. D. Reid (Eds.), *Life in the middle: Psychological and social development in middle age* (pp. 25–45). San Diego: Academic Press.

White, B. L. (1971, October). *Fundamental early environmental influences on the development of competence.* Paper presented at the Third Western Symposium on Learning: Cognitive Learning, Western Washington State College, Bellingham, WA.

White, B. L., Kaban, B., & Attanucci, J. (1979). *The origins of human competence.* Lexington, MA: Heath.

White, L. K. (1990). Determinants of divorce: A review of research in the eighties. *Journal of Marriage and the Family, 52,* 904–912.

Whitehurst, G. J., & Lonigan, C. J. (1998). Child development and emergent literacy. *Child Development, 69,* 848–872.

Whitehurst, G. J., Falco, F. L., Lonigan, C. J., Fischel, J. E., DeBaryshe, B. D., Valdez-Menchaca, M. D., & Caufield, M. (1988). Accelerating language development through picture book reading. *Developmental Psychology, 24,* 552–559.

WHO/UNICEF Constitution on HIV Transmission and Breastfeeding. (1992). Consensus statement from the WHO/UNICEF Constitution on HIV Transmission and Breastfeeding, Geneva. *Weekly Epidemiological Record, 67,* 177–184.

Wickelgren, I. (1996, July 5). For the cortex, neuron loss may be less than thought. *Science,* pp. 48–50.

Wickelgren, I. (1998, May 29). Obesity: How big a problem? *Science, 280,* 1364–1367.

Widom, C. S. (1989). The cycle of violence. *Science, 244,* 160–166.

Wiggins, S., Whyte, P., Higgins, M., Adams, S., et al. (1992). The psychological consequences of predictive testing for Huntington's disease. *New England Journal of Medicine, 327,* 1401–1405.

Wilcox, A. J., Baird, D. D., Weinberg, C. R., Hornsby, P. P., & Herbst, A. L. (1995). Fertility in men exposed prenatally to diethylstilbestrol. *New England Journal of Medicine, 332,* 1411–1416.

Wilcox, A. J., Weinberg, C. R., & Baird, D. D. (1995). Timing of sexual intercourse in relation to ovulation: Effects on the probability of conception, survival of the pregnancy, and sex of the baby. *New England Journal of Medicine, 333,* 1563–1565.

Willett, W. C. (1994). Diet and health: What should we eat? *Science, 264,* 532–537.

Willett, W. C., Colditz, G., & Stampfer, M. (2000). Postmenopausal estrogens–opposed, unopposed, or none of the above. *Journal of the American Medical Association, 283,* 534–535.

Willett, W. C., Hunter, D. J., Stampfer, M. J., Colditz, G., Manson, J. E., Spiegelman, D., Rosner, B., Hennekens, C. H., & Spiezer, F. E. (1992). Dietary fat and fiber in relation to risk of breast cancer. *Journal of the American Medical Association, 268,* 2037–2044.

Willett, W. C., Stampfer, M. J., Colditz, G. A., Rosner, B. A., & Speizer, F. E. (1990). Relation of meat, fat, and fiber intake to the risk of colon cancer in a prospective study among women. *New England Journal of Medicine, 323,* 1664–1672.

Williams, G. (1991, October–November). Flaming out on the job: How to recognize when it's all too much. *Modern Maturity,* pp. 26–29.

Williams, G. J. (2001). The clinical significance of visual-verbal processing in evaluating children with potential learning-related visual problems. Journal of Optometric Vision Development, 32(2), 107–110.

Williams, J. E., & Best, D. L. (1982). *Measuring sex stereotypes: A thirty-nation study.* Beverly Hills, CA: Sage.

Williams, M. E. (1995). *The American Geriatric Society's complete guide to aging and health.* New York: Harmony.

Williams, W. M., & Sternberg, R. J. (in press). *Success acts for managers.* Orlando, FL: Harcourt Brace.

Willinger, M., Hoffman, H. T., & Hartford, R. B. (1994). Infant sleep position and risk for sudden infant death syndrome: Report of meeting held January 13 and 14, 1994. *Pediatrics, 93,* 814–819.

Willis, S. L. (1990). Current issues in cognitive training research. In E. A. Lovelace (Ed.), *Aging and cognition: Mental processes, self-awareness, and intervention* (pp. 263–280). Amsterdam: North-Holland, Elsevier.

Willis, S. L., & Nesselroade, C. S. (1990). Long-term effects of fluid ability training in old-old age. *Developmental Psychology, 26,* 905–910.

Willis, S. L., & Reid, J. D. (1999). *Life in the middle.* San Diego: Academic Press.

Willis, S. L., & Schaie, K. W. (1986a). Practical intelligence in later adulthood. In R. J. Sternberg & R. K. Wagner (Eds.), *Practical intelligence: Nature and origins of competence in the everyday world* (pp. 236–268). New York: Cambridge University Press.

Willis, S. L., & Schaie, K. W. (1986b). Training the elderly on the ability factors of spatial orientation and inductive reasoning. *Psychology and Aging, 2,* 239–247.

Willis, S. L., & Schaie, K. W. (1999). Intellectual functioning in midlife. In S. L. Willis & J. D. Reid (Eds.), *Life in the middle: Psychological and social development in middle age* (pp. 233–247). San Diego: Academic Press.

Willis, S. L., Blieszner, R., & Baltes, P. B. (1981). Intellectual training research in aging: Modification of performance on the fluid ability of figural relations. *Journal of Educational Psychology, 73,* 41–50.

Willis, S. L., Jay, G. M., Diehl, M., & Marsiske, M. (1992). Longitudinal change and prediction of everyday task competence in the elderly. *Research on Aging, 14,* 68–91.

Willis, S. L., Schaie, K. W., Yanling, Z., Kennett, J., Intrieri, B., & Persaud, A. (1998). *Longitudinal studies of practical intelligence.* University Park: Pennsylvania State University.

Wilmoth, J. R. (2000). Demography of longevity: Past, present, and future trends. *Experimental Gerontology, 35,* 1111–1129.

Wilmoth, J. R., Deegan, L. J., Lundstrom, H., & Horiuchi, S. (2000). Increase of maximum life-span in Sweden, 1861–1999. *Science, 289,* 2366–2368.

Wilmoth, J., & Koso, G. (2002). Does marital history matter? Marital status and wealth outcomes among preretirement adults. *Journal of Marriage and Family, 64,* 254–268.

Wilson, E. O. (1975). *Sociobiology: The new synthesis.* Cambridge, MA: Belknap Press of Harvard University Press.

Wilson, G., McCreary, R., Kean, J., & Baxter, J. (1979). The development of preschool children of heroin-addicted mothers: A controlled study. *Pediatrics, 63,* 135–141.

Wilson, K., & Ryan, V. (2001). Helping parents by working with their children in individual child therapy. *Child and Family Social Work* (special issue), *6,* 209–217.

Wilson, R. S., Beckett, L. A., Barnes, L. L., Schneider, J. A., Bach, J., Evans, D. A., & Bennett, D. A. (2002). Individual differences in rates of change in cognitive abilities of older persons. *Psychology and Aging, 17,* 179–193.

Wilson, R. S., Mendes De Leon, C. F., Barnes, L. L., Schneider, J. A., Bienias, J. L., Evans, D. A., & Bennett, D. A. (2002). Participation in cognitively stimulating activities and risk of incident Alzheimer disease. *Journal of the American Medical Association, 287,* 742–748.

Winefield, A. H. (1995). Unemployment: Its psychological costs. In C. L. Cooper & I. T. Robertson (Eds.), *International review of industrial and organizational psychology* (pp. 169–212). Chichester, England: Wiley.

Winerip, M. (1999, January 3). Homework bound. *Education Life supplement to New York Times,* pp. 28–31, 40.

Wingfield, A., & Stine, E. A. L. (1989). Modeling memory processes: Research and theory on memory and aging. In G. C. Gilmore, P. J. Whitehouse, & M. L. Wykle (Eds.), *Memory, aging, and dementia: Theory, assessment, and treatment* (pp. 4–40). New York: Springer.

Wingo, P. A., Ries, L. A. G., Giovino, G. A., Miller, D. S., Rosenberg, H. M., Shopland, D. R., Thun, M. J., & Edwards, B. K. (1999). Annual report to the nation on the status of cancer, 1973–1996. *Journal of the National Cancer Institute, 91,* 675–690.

Wink, P. (1991). Self- and object-directedness in adult women. *Journal of Personality, 59,* 769–791.

Wink, P. (1992). Three types of narcissism in women from college to midlife. *Journal of Personality, 60,* 7–30.

Winkleby, M. A., Robinson, T. N., Sundquist, J., & Kraemer, H. C. (1999). Ethnic variation in cardiovascular disease risk factors among children and young adults: Findings from the Third National Health and Nutrition Examination Survey, 1988–1994. *Journal of the American Medical Association, 281,* 1006–1013.

Winkler, A. E. (1998). Earnings of husbands and wives in dual-earner families. *Monthly Labor Review, 121,* 42–48.

Winner, E. (1997). Exceptionally high intelligence and schooling. *American Psychologist, 52*(10), 1070–1081.

Winsler, A., Díaz, R. M., Espinosa, L., & Rodríguez, J. L. (1999). When learning a second language does not mean losing the first: Bilingual language development in low-income, Spanish-speaking children attending bilingual preschool. *Child Development, 70*(2), 349–362.

Wisby, G. (2001, Sept. 27). Husband kills wife, himself in hospital. *Chicago Sun-Times,* p. 18.

Wiseman, E. J., & Souder, E. (1996). The older driver: A handy tool to assess competence behind the wheel. *Geriatrics, 51*(7), 36–43.

Witteman, P. A. (1993, February 15). A man of fire and grace: Arthur Ashe, 1943–1993. *Time,* p. 70.

Wittig, D. R. (2001). Organ donation beliefs of African American women residing in a small southern community. *Journal of Transcultural Nursing, 12,* 203–210.

Wittrock, M. C. (1980). Learning and the brain. In M. C. Wittrock (Ed.), *The brain and psychology.* New York: Academic Press.

Wolchik, S. A., Sandler, I. N., Millsap, R. E., Plummer, B. A., Greene, S. M., Anderson, E. R., Dawson-McClure, S. R., Hipke, K., & Haine, R. A. (2002). Six-year follow-up of preventive interventions for children of divorce: A randomized controlled trial. *Journal of the American Medical Association, 288,* 1874–1881.

Wolf, M. (1968). *The house of Lim.* Englewood Cliffs, NJ: Prentice-Hall.

Wolf, S. L., Barnhart, H. X., Kutner, N. G., McNeely, E., Coogler, C., Xa, T., & the Atlanta FICSIT Group. (1996). Reducing frailty and falls in older persons: An investigation of Tai Chi and computerized balance training. *Journal of the American Geriatrics Society, 44,* 489–497.

Wolfe, D. A. (1985). Child-abusive parents: An empirical review and analysis. *Psychological Bulletin, 97*(3), 462–482.

Wolff, P. H. (1963). Observations on the early development of smiling. In B. M. Foss (Ed.), *Determinants of infant behavior* (Vol. 2). London: Methuen.

Wolff, P. H. (1966). The causes, controls, and organizations of behavior in the newborn. *Psychological Issues, 5*(1, Whole No. 17), 1–105.

Wolff, P. H. (1969). The natural history of crying and other vocalizations in early infancy. In B. M. Foss (Ed.), *Determinants of infant behavior* (Vol. 4). London: Methuen.

Wolff, R. (1993). *Good sports: The concerned parent's guide to Little League and other competitive youth sports.* New York: Dell.

Wolfinger, N. H. (1999, August 10). *Coupling and uncoupling: Changing marriage patterns and the intergenerational transmission of divorce.* Paper presented at the annual meeting of the American Sociological Association, Chicago, IL.

Wolfson, A. R., & Carskadon, M. A. (1998). Sleep schedules and daytime functioning in adolescents. *Child Development, 69,* 875–887.

Wolfson, L., Whipple, R., Derby, C., Judge, J., King, M., Amerman, P., Schmidt, J., & Smyers, D. (1996). Balance and strength training in older adults: Intervention gains and Tai Chi maintenance. *Journal of the American Geriatrics Society, 44,* 498–506.

Wolk, A., Manson, J. E., Stampfer, M. J., Colditz, G. A., Hu, F. B., Speizer, F. E., Hennekens, C. H., & Willett, W. C. (1999). Long-term intake of dietary fiber and decreased risk of coronary heart disease among women. *Journal of the American Medical Association, 281,* 1998–2004.

Woman delivers a baby boy after refusing a caesarean. (1993, December 30). *The New York Times,* p. A12.

Wood, D. (1980). Teaching the young child: Some relationships between social interaction, language, and thought. In D. Olson (Ed.), *The social foundations of language and thought.* New York: Norton.

Wood, D., Bruner, J., & Ross, G. (1976). The role of tutoring in problem solving. *Journal of Child Psychiatry and Psychology, 17,* 89–100.

Wood, R. M., & Gustafson, G. E. (2001). Infant crying and adults' anticipated caregiving responses: Acoustic and contextual influences. *Child Development, 72,* 1287–1300.

Woodward, A. L., Markman, E. M., & Fitzsimmons, C. M. (1994). Rapid word learning in 13- and 18-month olds. *Developmental Psychology, 30,* 553–566.

Woodward, E. H., & Gridina, N. (2000). Media in the home 2000: The fifth annual survey of parents and children. The Annenberg Public Policy Center of the University of Pennsylvania. Survey Series Number 7.

Woodward, S. A., McManis, M. H., Kagan, J., Deldin, P., Snidman, N., Lewis, M., & Kahn, V. (2001). Infant temperament and the brainstem auditory evoked response in later childhood. *Developmental Psychology, 37,* 533–538.

Woolley, J. D. (1997). Thinking about fantasy: Are children fundamentally different thinkers and believers from adults? *Child Development, 68*(6), 991–1011.

Woolley, J. D., & Boerger, E. A. (2002). Development of beliefs about the origins and controlability of dreams. *Developmental Psychology, 38*(1), 24–41.

Woolley, J. D., & Bruell, M. J. (1996). Young children's awareness of the origins of their mental representations. *Developmental Psychology, 32,* 335–346.

Woolley, J. D., Phelps, K. E., Davis, D. L., & Mandell, D. J. (1999). Where theories of mind meet magic: The development of children's beliefs about wishing. *Child Development, 70,* 571–587.

Wooten, J. (1995, January 29). The conciliator. *The New York Times Magazine,* pp. 28–33.

World Cancer Research Fund and the American Institute for Cancer Research. (1997). *Food, nutrition and the prevention of cancer: A global perspective.* Washington, DC: Author.

World Health Organization (WHO). (1996, May). *WHO Fact Sheet, 119,* pp. 1–3.

World Health Organization (WHO). (1998). *Obesity: Preventing and managing the global epidemic.* Geneva: Author.

World Health Organization (WHO). (2000, June 4). WHO issues new healthy life expectancy rankings: Japan number one in new "healthy life" system. (Press release). Washington, DC: Author.

World Health Organization (WHO). (2001). AIDS epidemic update, December 2001.

World Health Organization (WHO). (2002a). *Move for Health.* Geneva: Author.

World Health Organization (WHO). (2002b). *Toward health with justice: Litigation and public inquiries as tools for tobacco control.* Geneva: World Health Organization.

Wortman, C. B., & Silver, R. C. (1989). The myths of coping with loss. *Journal of Consulting and Clinical Psychology, 57*(3), 349–357.

Wright, A. L. (1983). A cross-cultural comparison of menopausal symptoms. *Medical Anthropology, 7,* 20–35.

Wright, A. L., Holberg, C. J., Taussig, L. M., & Martinez, F. D. (1995). Relationship of infant feeding to recurrent wheezing at age 6 years. *Archives of Pediatric Adolescent Medicine, 149,* 758–763.

Wright, J. C., Huston, A. C., Murphy, K. C., St. Peters, M., Pinon, M., Scantlin, R., & Kotler, J. (2001). The relations of early television viewing to school readiness and vocabulary of children from low-income families: The Early Window Project. *Child Development, 72*(5), 1347–1366.

Wright, J. T., Waterson, E. J., Barrison, I. G., Toplis, P. J., Lewis, I. G., Gordon, M. G., MacRae, K. D., Morris, N. F., & Murray Lyon, I. M. (1983, March 26). Alcohol consumption, pregnancy, and low birth weight. *The Lancet,* pp. 663–665.

Writing Group for the Women's Health Initiative Investigators. (2002). Risks and benefits of estrogen plus progestin in healthy postmenopausal women. *Journal of the American Medical Association, 288,* 321–333.

Wrosch, C., & Heckhausen, J. (1999). Control processes before and after passing a developmental deadline: Activation and deactivation of intimate relationship goals. *Journal of Personality and Social Psychology, 77,* 415–427.

Wu, Z. (1999). Premarital cohabitation and the timing of first marriage. *Canadian Review of Sociology and Anthropology, 36,* 109–127.

Wu, Z., & Pollard, M. S. (1998). Social support among unmarried childless elderly persons. *Journal of Gerontology: Social Sciences, 53B*(6), S324–S335.

WuDunn, S. (1996, March 23). Japan's single mothers face discrimination. *Cleveland Plain Dealer,* p. 5E.

WuDunn, S. (1997, January 14). Korean women still feel demands to bear a son. *The New York Times* (International Ed.), p. A3.

Wykle, M. L., & Musil, C. M. (1993). Mental health of older persons: Social and cultural factors. *Generations, 17*(1), 7–12.

Wynn, K. (1990). Children's understanding of counting. *Cognition, 36,* 155–193.

Wynn, K. (1992). Evidence against empiricist accounts of the origins of numerical knowledge. *Mind and Language, 7,* 315–332.

Wynn, K. (1996). Infants' individuation and enumeration of actions. *Psychological Science, 7,* 164–169.

Wynn, K. (2000). Findings of addition and subtraction in infants are robust and consistent: Reply to Wakeley, Rivera, and Langer. *Child Development, 71,* 1535–1536.

Yaffe, K., Sawaya, G., Lieberburg, I., & Grady, D. (1998). Estrogen therapy in postmenopausal women: Effects on cognitive functioning and dementia. *Journal of the American Medical Association, 279,* 688–695.

Yamazaki, J. N., & Schull, W. J. (1990). Perinatal loss and neurological abnormalities among children of the atomic bomb. *Journal of the American Medical Association, 264,* 605–609.

Yang, B., Ollendick, T. H., Dong, Q., Xia, Y., & Lin, L. (1995). Only children and children with siblings in the People's Republic of China: Levels of fear, anxiety, and depression. *Child Development, 66,* 1301–1311.

Yau, J., & Smetana, J. G. (1996). Adolescent-parent conflict among Chinese adolescents in Hong Kong. *Child Development, 67,* 1262–1275.

Yazigi, R. A., Odem, R. R., & Polakoski, K. L. (1991). Demonstration of specific binding of cocaine to human spermatozoa. *Journal of the American Medical Association, 266,* 1956–1959.

Yeargin-Allsopp, M., Rice, C., Karapurkar, T., Doernberg, N., Boyle, C., & Murphy, C. (2003). Prevalence of autism in a US metropolitan area. *Journal of the American Medical Association, 289,* 49–55.

Yeung, W. J., Sandberg, J. F., Davis-Kean, P. E., & Hofferth, S. L. (2001). Children's time with fathers in intact families. *Journal of Marriage and Family, 63,* 136–154.

Yingling, C. D. (2001). Neural mechanisms of unconscious cognitive processing. Clinical Neurophysiology, 112(1), 157–158.

Yllo, K. (1984). The status of women, marital equality, and violence against women: A contextual analysis. *Journal of Family Issues, 5,* 307–320.

Yllo, K. A. (1993). Through a feminist lens: Gender, power, and violence. In R. J. Gelles & D. R. Loseke (Eds.), *Current controversies on family violence* (pp. 47–62). Newbury Park, CA: Sage.

Yoshikawa, H. (1994). Prevention as cumulative protection: Effects of early family support and education on chronic delinquency and its risks. *Psychological Bulletin, 115*(1), 28–54.

Young, B. A. (2002). *Public high school dropouts and completes from the common core of data: School years 1998–99 and 1999–2000* (NCES 2002-382). Washington, DC: National Center for Education Statistics.

Young, L. R., & Nestle, M. (2002). The contribution of expanding portion sizes to the US obesity epidemic. *American Journal of Public Health, 92,* 246–249.

Youngblade, L. M., & Belsky, J. (1992). Parent-child antecedents of 5-year-olds' close friendships: A longitudinal analysis. *Developmental Psychology, 28,* 700–713.

Younger, B. (1990). Infants' detection of correlations among feature categories. *Child Development, 61,* 614–620.

Youth violence: A report of the Surgeon General. (2001, January). [Online]. Available: http://www.surgeongeneral.gov/library/youthviolence/default.htm

Zahn-Waxler, C., Friedman, R. J., Cole, P. M., Mizuta, I., & Hiruma, N. (1996). Japanese and U.S. preschool children's responses to conflict and distress. *Child Development, 67,* 2462–2477.

Zahn-Waxler, C., Radke-Yarrow, M., Wagner, E., & Chapman, M. (1992). Development of concern for others. *Developmental Psychology, 28,* 126–136.

Zametkin, A. J. (1995). Attention-deficit disorder: Born to be hyperactive. *Journal of the American Medical Association, 273*(23), 1871–1874.

Zametkin, A. J., & Ernst, M. (1999). Problems in the management of Attention-Deficit-Hyperactivity Disorder. *New England Journal of Medicine, 340,* 40–46.

Zandhi, P. P., Carlson, M. C., Plassman, B. L., Welsh-Bohmer. K. A., Mayer, L. S., Steffens, D. C., & Breitner, J. C. S., for the Cache County Memory Study Investigators. (2002). Hormone replacement therapy and incidence of Alzheimer disease in older women: The Cache County Study. *Journal of the American Medical Association, 288,* 2123–2129.

Zelazo, P. D., Reznick, J. S., & Spinazzola, J. (1998). Representational flexibility and response control in a multistep, multilocation search task. *Developmental Psychology, 34,* 203–214.

Zelazo, P. R., Kearsley, R. B., & Stack, D. M. (1995). Mental representations for visual sequences: Increased speed of central processing from 22 to 32 months. *Intelligence, 20,* 41–63.

Zhang, J., Meikle, S., Grainger, D. A., & Trumble, A. (2002). Multifetal pregnancy in older women and perinatal outcomes. *Fertility and Sterility, 78,* 562–568.

Zhang, Y., Proenca, R., Maffei, M., Barone, M., Leopold, L., & Friedman, J. M., (1994). Positional cloning of the mouse obese gene in its human homologue. *Nature, 372,* 425–431.

Zhao, Y. (2002, May 29). Cultural divide over parental discipline. *The New York Times.* [Online]. Available: http://www.nytimes.com/2002/05/29/nyregion/29DISC.html?ex=1023674535&ei=1&en=5eeaee8e940eee1a.

Zhensun, Z., & Low, A. (1991). *A young painter: The life and paintings of Wang Yani—China's extraordinary young artist.* New York: Scholastic.

Zhu, B.-P., Rolfs, R. T., Nangle, B. E., & Horan, J. M. (1999). Effect of the interval between pregnancies on perinatal outcomes. *New England Journal of Medicine, 340,* 589–594.

Zigler, E. (1998). School should begin at age 3 years for American children. *Journal of Developmental and Behavioral Pediatrics, 19,* 37–38.

Zigler, E. F. (1987). Formal schooling for four-year-olds? *North American Psychologist, 42*(3), 254–260.

Zigler, E., & Styfco, S. J. (1993). Using research and theory to justify and inform Head Start expansion. *Social Policy Report of the Society for Research in Child Development, 7*(2).

Zigler, E., & Styfco, S. J. (1994). Head Start: Criticisms in a constructive context. American *Psychologist, 49*(2), 127–132.

Zigler, E., & Styfco, S. J. (2001). Extended childhood intervention prepares children for school and beyond. *Journal of the American Medical Association, 285,* 2378.

Zigler, E., Taussig, C., & Black, K. (1992). Early childhood intervention: A promising preventative for juvenile delinquency. *American Psychologist, 47,* 997–1006.

Zimiles, H., & Lee, V. E. (1991). Adolescent family structure and educational progress. *Developmental Psychology, 27,* 314–320.

Zimmerman, B. J., Bandura, A., & Martinez-Pons, M. (1992). Self-motivation for academic attainment: The role of self-efficacy beliefs and personal goal setting. *American Educational Research Journal, 29,* 663–676.

Zimmerman, M. A., Salem, D. A., & Maton, K. I. (1995). Family structure and psychosocial correlates among urban African-American adolescent males. *Child Development, 66,* 1598–1613.

Zimrin, H. (1986). A profile of survival. *Child Abuse and Neglect, 10,* 339–349.

Zito, J. M., Safer, D. J., dosReis, S., Gardner, J. F., Boles, M., & Lynch, F. (2000). Trends in the prescribing of psychotropic medications to preschoolers. *Journal of the American Medical Association, 283*(8), 1025–1030.

Zito, J. M., Safer, D. J., dosReis, S., Gardner. J. F., Magder, L., Soeken, K., Boles, M., Lynch, F., & Riddle, M. A. (2003). Psychotropic practice patterns for youth: A 10-year perspective. *Archives of Pediatrics and Adolescent Medicine, 57,* 17–25.

Zizza, C., Siega-Riz, A. M., & Popkin, B. M. (2001). Significant increase in young adults' snacking between 1977–1978 and 1994–1996 represents a cause for concern! *Preventive Medicine, 32,* 303–310.

Zuckerman, B. S., & Beardslee, W. R. (1987). Maternal depression: A concern for pediatricians. *Pediatrics, 79,* 110–117.

Zuckerman, M. (1994). Impulsive unsocialized sensation seeking: The biological foundation of a basic dimension of personality. In J. E. Bates & T. D. Wachs (Eds.), *Temperament: Individual differences at the interface of biology and behavior* (pp. 219–255). Washington, DC: American Psychological Association.

Acknowledgments

Textual Credits

Chapter 3

Table 3-2: From *Choices, Not Chances* by Aubrey Milunsky, M.D, table 32, p. 122. Copyright © 1977, 1989 by Aubrey Milunsky, M.D. By permission of Little, Brown and Company, (Inc.)

Figure 3-7: From *A Child's World*, 8th Edition by Diane E. Papalia, Sally Wendkos Olds, Ruth Duskin Feldman. Copyright © 1998 McGraw-Hill. Reproduced by permission of The McGraw-Hill Companies.

Figure 3-9: From J. Brody, "Preventing birth defects even before pregnancy," *The New York Times*, June 28, 1995, p. C10. Copyright © 1995 by The New York Times Co. Reprinted by permission.

Chapter 4

Figure 4-1: From H. Lagercrantz and T.A. Slotkin, "The 'stress' of being born," *Scientific-American*, 254(4), 1986, pp. 100-107. Reprinted by permission of Patricia J. Wynne.

Table 4-2: Adapted from V. Apgar, "A proposal for a new method of evaluation of the newborn infant," pp. 260-267, *Current Research in Anesthesia and Analgesia*, 32, 1953. Reprinted by permission of Williams & Wilkins.

Table 4-3: From *A Child's World*, 9th Edition by Diane E. Papalia, Sally Wendkos Olds, Ruth Duskin Feldman. Copyright © 2000 McGraw-Hill. Reproduced by permission of The McGraw-Hill Companies.

Figure 4-2: From *A Child's World*, 9th Edition by Diane E. Papalia, Sally Wendkos Olds, Ruth Duskin Feldman. Copyright © 2000 McGraw-Hill. Reproduced by permission of The McGraw-Hill Companies.

Figure 4-5: From *The Brain* by Richard Restak, M.D. Copyright © 1984 by Educational Broadcasting Corporation and Richard M. Restak, M.D. Used by permission of Bantam Books, a division of Random House, Inc.

Figure 4-6: From J. Lach, "Cultivating the mind," *Newsweek* Special Issue, Spring/Summer 1997, pp. 38-39. Copyright © 1997 Newsweek, Inc. All rights reserved. Reprinted by permission.

Figure 4-7: Reprinted by permission of the publisher from The Postnatal Development of *The Human Cerebral Cortex*, Vols. I-VIII by Jesse LeRoy Conel, Cambridge, Mass.: Harvard University Press. Copyright © 1939, 1975 by the President and Fellows of Harvard College.

Figure 4-8(a-d): From "Fertile Lands" by J. M. Nash, *Time*, February 3, 1997. Copyright © 1997 Time Inc. Reprinted by permission.

Chapter 5

Figure 5-2: From C. Rovee-Collier-Collier & K. Boller, "Current theory and research on infant learning and memory: Application to early intervention" in *Infants and Young Children*, Vol. 7, No. 3, p. 7. Copyright © 1995 Aspen Publishers, Inc. Reprinted with permission by Lippincott Williams & Wilkins.

Table 5-4: From *A Child's World*, 9th Edition by Diane E. Papalia, Sally Wendkos Olds, Ruth Duskin Feldman, p. 157. Copyright © 2000 McGraw-Hill. Reproduced by permission of The McGraw-Hill Companies.

Figure 5-4: From R. Baillargeon and J. DeVos, "Object permanence in young infants: Further evidence," *Child Development*, Vol. 62, 1991, pp. 1227-1246. Reprinted by permission of the Society for Research in Child Development.

Figure 5-5: From R. Baillargeon, "How do infants learn about the physical world?" in *Current Directions in Psychological Science*, Vol. 3, No. 5, 1994, pp. 133-139. Reprinted by permission of Blackwell Publishers.

Chapter 6

P. 187: From J. Hartford, "Life Prayer." Copyright © 1968 by Ensign Music Corporation.

Table 6-1: From L.A. Sroufe, "Socioemotional development" in *Handbook of Infant Development* by J. Osotsky, John Wiley & Sons, Inc., 1979. This material is used by permission of John Wiley & Sons, Inc.

Figure 6-1: From *A Child's World*, 9th Edition by Diane E. Papalia, Sally Wendkos Olds, Ruth Duskin Feldman, p. 182. Copyright © 2000 McGraw-Hill. Reproduced by permission of The McGraw-Hill Companies.

Table 6-2: From *A Child's World*, 9th Edition by Diane E. Papalia, Sally Wendkos Olds, Ruth Duskin Feldman, p. 184. Copyright © 2000 McGraw-Hill. Reproduced by permission of The McGraw-Hill Companies.

Table 6-5: From *A Child's World*, 9th Edition by Diane E. Papalia, Sally Wendkos Olds, Ruth Duskin Feldman, p. 206. Copyright © 2000 McGraw-Hill. Reproduced by permission of The McGraw-Hill Companies.

Table 6-6: From *A Child's World*, 9th Edition by Diane E. Papalia, Sally Wendkos Olds, Ruth Duskin Feldman, p. 207. Copyright © 2000 McGraw-Hill. Reproduced by permission of The McGraw-Hill Companies.

Chapter 7

Table 7-1: From *A Child's World*, 9th Edition by Diane E. Papalia, Sally Wendkos Olds, Ruth Duskin Feldman, p. 213. Copyright © 2000 McGraw-Hill. Reproduced by permission of The McGraw-Hill Companies.

Table 7-2: From *A Child's World*, 9th Edition by Diane E. Papalia, Sally Wendkos Olds, Ruth Duskin Feldman, p. 218. Copyright © 2000 McGraw-Hill. Reproduced by permission of The McGraw-Hill Companies.

Figure 7-1: From *Analyzing Children's Art* by Rhoda Kellogg, Mayfield Publishing Company, 1969, 1970. Copyright © 1969, 1970 by Rhoda Kellogg. Reprinted by permission of The McGraw-Hill Companies.

Table 7-4: From *A Child's World*, 9th Edition by Diane E. Papalia, Sally Wendkos Olds, Ruth Duskin Feldman, p. 237. Copyright © 2000 McGraw-Hill. Reproduced by permission of The McGraw-Hill Companies.

Table 7-5: From *A Child's World*, 9th Edition by Diane E. Papalia, Sally Wendkos Olds, Ruth Duskin Feldman, p. 241. Copyright © 2000 McGraw-Hill. Reproduced by permission of The McGraw-Hill Companies.

Chapter 8

Table 8-2: Adapted from M.B. Parten, "Social play among preschool children," *Journal of Abnormal and Social Psychology*, 27, 1943, pp. 3243-269.

Table 8-3: From R.J. Morris and T.R. Kratochwill, "Childhood Fears" in *Treating Children's Fears and Phobias: A Behavioral Approach*. Published by Allyn and Bacon, Boston, MA. Copyright © 1983 by Pearson Education. Reprinted by permission of the publisher.

Table 8-4: From K.A. Kendall-Tackett, L.M. Williams and D. Finkelhor, "Impact of sexual abuse on children: A review and synthesis of recent empirical studies," *Psychological Bulletin*, 113, 1993, pp. 164-180. Copyright © 1993 by the American Psychological Association. Reprinted with permission of American Psychological Association and the author.

Chapter 9

Table 9-1: From Bryant J. Cratty in *Perceptual and Motor Development in Infants and Children*, 3rd Edition. Copyright © 1986 by Allyn & Bacon. Adapted with permission.

Table 9-3: From M.L. Hoffman, "Moral development" in *Carmichael's Manual of Child Psychology*, Vol. 2, edited by P.H. Mussen, John Wiley & Sons, Inc., 1970, pp. 261-380. This material is used by permission of John Wiley & Sons, Inc.

Table 9-5: From *A Child's World*, 9th Edition by Diane E. Papalia, Sally Wendkos Olds, Ruth Duskin Feldman, p. 333. Copyright © 2000 McGraw-Hill. Reproduced by permission of The McGraw-Hill Companies.

Chapter 10

Table 10-3: From Masten & Coatsworth, "Characteristics of Resilient Children and Adolescents" in *American Psychologist*, 53, 212. Copyright © 1998 by the American Psychological Association. Reprinted with permission of American Psychological Association and the author.

Chapter 11

Table 11-1: From *A Child's World*, 9th Edition by Diane E. Papalia, Sally Wendkos Olds, Ruth Duskin Feldman, p. 333. Copyright © 2000 McGraw-Hill. Reproduced by permission of The McGraw-Hill Companies.

Table 11-2: From L. Kohlberg, "Stage and sequence: The cognitive-development approach to socialization," in *Handbook of Socialization Theory and Research* by David A. Goslin, Rand McNally, 1969. Reprinted by permission of David A. Goslin.

Figure 11-1: From *Promoting the Health of Adolescents: New Directions for the Twenty-First Century*, edited by Susan G. Millstein, et al. Copyright © 1994 by Oxford University Press Inc. Used by permission of Oxford University Press, Inc.

Figure 11-3: From *Cognitive Development* by Melinda Y. Small and Jerome Kagan. Copyright ©1990 by Harcourt, Inc. Reprinted by permission of Thomson Learning.

Chapter 12

P. 423: From *A Sky Full of Poems* by Eve Merriam. Copyright © 1964, 1970, 1973 by Eve Merriam. Used by permission of Marian Reiner.

Table 12-1: From J.E. Marcia, "Development and validation of ego identity status," *Journal of Personality and Social Psychology*, 3(5), 1966, pp. 551-558. Copyright © 1966 by the American Psychological Association. Adapted by permission

Table 12-2: From J. Kroger, "Ego identity: An overview," in *Discussions on Ego and Identity*, edited by J. Kroger, 1993. Reprinted by permission of Lawrence Erlbaum Associates Inc. and Dr. Jane Kroger.

Chapter 13

Table 13-1: Reprinted and adapted by permission of the publisher from *In A Different Voice: Psychological Theory and Women's Development* by Carol Gilligan, Cambridge, Mass.: Harvard University Press. Copyright © 1982, 1993 by Carol Gilligan.

Chapter 14

Figure 14-1: Reprinted from P.T. Costa, Jr. and R.R. McCraie, "Still stable after all these years: Personality as a key to some issues in adulthood and old age," *Life-Span Development and Behavior*, Vol. 3, edited by P.B. Baltes, Jr. and O.G. Brim, pp. 65-102. Copyright © 1980 by Academic Press. With permission from Elsevier Science.

Chapter 15

Table 15-2: Reprinted from Merrill and Verbrugge, "Health & Disease in Midlife," in S.L. Willis & J.D. Reid, eds., *Life in the Middle: Psychological & Social Development in Middle Age*, p. 87. Copyright © 1999 by Academic Press. With permission from Elsevier Science.

Table 15-3: Reprinted from Holmes and Rahe, "The Social Readjustment Rating Scale," *Journal of Psychosomatic Research*, Vol. 11. Copyright ©1967 by Elsevier Science. With permission from Elsevier Science.

Figure 15-1: From E. Goode "New study finds middle age is prime of life," *The New York Times*, Feb. 16, 1999. Copyright © 1999 by The New York Times Co. Reprinted by permission.

Figures 15-2, 15-3: From K.W. Schaie, "The course of adult intellectual development," *American Psychologist*, 49(4), 1994, pp. 303-313. Copyright © 1994 by the American Psychological Association. Reprinted with permission of American Psychological Association and the author.

Figure 15-4: Republished with permission of The Gerontologist, from M.W. Riley, "Aging and Society: Past, Present, and Future," pp. 436-445, *The Gerontologist*, 34, 1994. Permission conveyed through Copyright Clearance Center, Inc.

Chapter 16

Figure 16-1: From L.L. Carstensen, J. Gross, & H. Fung, "The Social Context of Emotion" in *Annual Review of Geriatrics and Gerontology*, 17, p. 331. Copyright © 1997 by Springer Publishing Company, Inc., New York 10012. Used by permission.

Table 16-1: From Klohnen, Vandewater & Young, "Negotiating the middle years: Ego resilience and successful midlife adjustment in women", *Psychology & Aging*, 11, pp. 431-442, 1996. Copyright © 1996 by the American Psychological Association. Reprinted with permission of American Psychological Association and the author.

Table 16-2: From McAdams and de St. Aubin, "Loyola Generativity Scale", *Journal of Personality & Social Psychology*, 62, 1003-1015, 1992. Copyright © 1992 by the American Psychological Association. Reprinted with permission of American Psychological Association and the author.

Table 16-3: Reprinted from Keyes & Ryff, "Psychological Well Being in Mid-life", in S.L. Willis & J.D. Reid, eds., *Life in the Middle: Psychological & Social Development in Middle Age*, p. 87. Copyright © 1999 by Academic Press. With permission from Elsevier Science.

Table 16-4: From R. Helson and P. Wink, "Personality change in women from the early 40s to the early 50s," *Psychology and Aging*, 7(1), 1992, pp. 46-55. Copyright © 1992 by the American Psychological Association. Reprinted with permission of American Psychological Association and the author.

Chapter 17

Table 17-4: From *Is It Alzheimer's? Warning Signs You Should Know*, 1993. Adapted with permission from the Alzheimer's Association.

Figure 17-4: From *Fifty: Midlife In Perspective* by H. Katchadourian Copyright © 1987 by W.H. Freeman and Company. Reprinted with permission from Henry Holt Inc.

Figure 17-5: From J. Botwinick in *Aging and Behavior*, 3rd Edition. Copyright © 1984 by Springer-Verlag. Reprinted with permission of Springer-Verlag GmbH & Co. KG.

Figure 17-6: Reprinted by permission of the publisher from *Constancy and Change in Human Development*, edited by Orville G. Brim, Jr. and Jerome Kagan, Cambridge, Mass.: Harvard University Press, Copyright © 1980 by the President and Fellows of Harvard College.

Chapter 18

Figure 18-2: From K. Kinsella & V.A. Velkoff in *An Aging World: 2001, U.S. Census Bureau Series* P95/01-1, figure 10-13, p. 111. Washington, DC: U.S. Government Printing Office. Graphs used by permission of OECD–Organization for Economic Cooperation and Development.

Chapter 19

Table 19-1: Adapted from H.M. Chochinov, "Dignity-conserving care: A new model of palliative care: Helping the patient feel valued," *Journal of the American Medical Association*, 287, 2002, p. 2255. Reprinted by permission of American Medical Association.

Table 19-2: From "The Pediatrician and Childhood Bereavement," *Pediatrics*, 2000; 105:446. Used with permission from the American Academy of Pediatrics, Committee on Psychosocial Aspects of Child and Family Health.

Table 19-3: Reprinted from A.E. Scharlach & K.I. Frederiksen, "Reactions to the death of a parent during midlife," *Omega*, Vol. 27, table 1, p. 311. Copyright © 1993 Elsevier. With permission from Elsevier Science.

Photo Credits

Chapter 1

p. 2: ©Walter Hodges/Corbis Images; **p. 3** (left): ©Richard Hutching/PhotoEdit; **p. 3** (right): ©Bob Daemmrich/Image Works; **p. 4:** ©Richard Hutching/PhotoEdit; **p. 5:** ©By permission of the British Library; **p. 10:** ©Zhang Yanhui/Sovfoto/Eastfoto/PictureQuest; **p. 14:** ©Blair Seitz/Photo Researchers; **p. 18** (top): ©John Vachon/Library of Congress; **p. 17:** ©Erika Stone; **p. 18 (bottom):** ©Nina Leen/TimePix; **p. 20:** Figure from "chapter title" in Genie: A Psycholinguitic Study of a Modern Day "Wild Child," by Susan Curtiss, copyright 1977, Elsevier Science (USA), reproduced with permission of the publisher.

Chapter 2

p. 24: ©Bob Daemmrich/Image Works; **p. 25:** ©Bettmann/Corbis Images; **p. 28:** ©Adam Butler/Topham/Image Works; **p. 31:** ©Mary Evans Picture Library/Sigmund Freud Copyrights; **p. 33:** ©Bettmann/Corbis Images, Los Angeles; **p. 35:** Courtesy, Dr. Albert Bandura; **p. 36:** ©Bill Anderson/Photo Researchers; **p. 40:** ©Richard Hutchings/Photo Researchers; **p. 42:** A.R. Luria/Dr. Michael Cole, Laboratory of Human Cognition, University of California, San Diego; **p. 47:** ©Laura Dwight/PhotoEdit; **p. 51:** ©James Wilson/Woodfin Camp

Chapter 3

p. 58: ©Bob Krist/Corbis Images; **p. 59 (Left):** ©Barbara Peacock/Getty Images; **p. 59 (center**

left): ©Camille Tokerud/Getty Images; **p. 59 (center right):** ©PhotoDisc; **p. 59 (right):** ©David Young-Wolff /PhotoEdit; **p. 60:** ©Barbara Peacock/Getty Images; **p. 64:** ©Petit Format/SPL/Photo Researchers; **p. 69:** ©David Young-Wolff/PhotoEdit; **p. 73:** ©Ellen Senisi/Image Works; **p. 78:** ©T.K. Wanstal/Image Works; **p. 81:** ©Anthony Jalandoni; **p. 85:** ©Daniel Hulshizer/AP/Wide World Photos; **p. 88 (1 month):** ©Petit Format/Nestle/Science Source/Photo Researchers; **p. 88 (7 weeks):** ©Petit Format/Nestle/Science Source/Photo Researchers; **p. 88 (3 months):** ©Lennart Nilsson/Albert Bonniers Forlag AB,A CHILD IS BORN, Dell Publishing Company; **p. 88 (4 months):** ©J.S. Allen/Daily Telegraph/International Stock; **p. 88 (5 months):** ©James Stevenson/Photo Researchers; **p. 89 (6 months):** ©Lennart Nilsson, from BEING BORN; **p. 89 (7 months):** ©Petit Format/Nestle/Science Source/Photo Researchers; **p. 89 (8 months):** ©Petit Format/Nestle/Science Source/Photo Researchers; **p. 89 (9 months):** ©Ronn Maratea/International Stock; **p. 94:** ©George Steinmetz; **p. 98:** ©Fred R. Conrad/New York Times Pictures; **p. 100:** ©Billy E. Barnes/PhotoEdit

Chapter 4

p. 106: ©Camille Tokerud/Getty Images; **p. 107:** ©Bettmann/Corbis Images, Los Angeles; **p. 111:** ©David & Peter Turnley/Corbis Images; **p. 113:** ©Mark Richards/PhotoEdit; **p. 114:** ©Joseph Nettis/Stock Boston; p. 120: ©Chuck Savage/Corbis Images; **p. 122:** ©Mike Teruya/Free Spirit Photography; **p. 127:** ©Myrleen Ferguson Cate/PhotoEdit; **p. 135 (top left):** ©Astier/Photo Researchers; **p. 135 (top center):** ©Lew Merrim; **p. 135 (top right, bottom left):** ©Laura Dwight; **p. 135 (bottom center, right):** ©Elizabeth Crews; **p. 138 (top left):** ©Erika Stone; **p. 138 (top right):** ©Elizabeth Crews; **p. 138 (bottom):** ©Jennie Woodcock/Corbis Images; **p. 142:** ©Innervisions; **p. 143:** ©Steve Maines/Stock Boston

Chapter 5

p. 146: ©PhotoDisc; **p. 147:** ©Courtesy Department Library Services, American Museum of Natural History, Neg. No. 32799; **p. 150:** ©Mary Ellen Mark; **p. 182:** ©Digital Vision; **p. 151:** Courtesy, Carolyn Rovee-Collier; **p. 154:** ©PhotoDisc; **p. 160:** ©Brand X Pictures; **p. 163:** ©Enrico Ferorelli; **p. 165:** ©James Kilkelly; **p. 168:** ©Doug Goodman; **p. 169:** ©Peter Southwick/Stock Boston; **p. 174:** ©PhotoDisc; **p. 178:** ©Jose L. Pelaez/Corbis Stock Market; **p. 181:** ©Rubberball

Chapter 6

p. 186: ©David Young-Wolff /PhotoEdit; **p. 187:** ©Ken Heyman/Woodfin Camp; **p. 191:** ©Digital Stock; **p. 192:** ©Laura Dwight; **p. 195:** ©Ruth Duskin Feldman; **p. 199:** Harlow Primate Laboratory, University of Wisconsin; **p. 201:** ©Brand X Pictures; **p. 202:** ©Corbis; **p. 205:** ©Jonathan Finlay; **p. 208:** ©PhotoDisc; **p. 209:** ©Michael Newman/PhotoEdit; **p. 213:** Courtesy, Dr. Michael Lewis; **p. 214:** ©PhotoDisc; **p. 217:** ©Eastcott/Image Works; **p. 218:** ©Paul Conklin/PhotoDisc

Chapter 7

p. 224: ©Stephen Simpson/Getty Images; **p. 225 (left):** ©Bob Daemmrich/Stock Boston; **p. 225 (right):** ©CLEO Photo/Index Stock Imagery; **p. 226:** ©Bob Daemmrich/Stock Boston; **p. 227:** ©Cynthia Johnson/Getty Images News Services; **p. 231:** ©David Young-Wolff/PhotoEdit; **p. 233 (left):** ©Laura Dwight; **p. 233 (center):** ©PhotoDisc; **p. 233 (right):** ©Miro Vintoni/Stock Boston; **p. 235:** ©Elliot Varner-Smith/International Stock; **p. 237:** ©Tony Freeman/PhotoEdit; **p. 240:** ©Erika Stone; **p. 247:** ©AP/Wide World Photos; **p. 250:** ©Newman Brown; **p. 255:** ©Creatas/Creatas/PictureQuest; **p. 259:** ©Erika Stone; **p. 260:** ©David Young-Wolff/PhotoEdit

Chapter 8

p. 266: ©CLEO Photo/Index Stock Imagery; **p. 267:** ©AP/Wide World Photos; **p. 270:** ©Laura Dwight/PhotoEdit; **p. 272:** ©Nancy Richmond/Image Works; **p. 274:** ©Leanna Rathkelly/Getty Images; **p. 276:** Courtesy, HarperCollins Publishers; **p. 277 (both):** ©Sandra Lipsitz Bem; **p. 279:** ©Stephen McBrady/PhotoEdit; **p. 281:** ©David Young-Wolff/PhotoEdit; **p. 286:** ©Myrleen Ferguson Cate/PhotoEdit; **p. 290:** ©Margaret Miller/Photo Researchers; **p. 291:** ©Sybil Shackman; **p. 297:** ©Janet Fries; **p. 299:** ©Nita Winter

Chapter 9

p. 304: ©Bill Bachmann/Photo Network/PictureQuest; **p. 305 (left):** ©Brand X Pictures; **p. 305 (right):** ©Digital Vision; **p. 306:** ©Brand X Pictures; **p. 307:** ©AP/Wide World Photos; **p. 310:** ©Digital Vision; **p. 311:** ©AP/Wide World Photos; **p. 315:** ©PhotoDisc; **p. 316:** ©Bob Daemmrich/Stock Boston; **p. 319:** ©Laura Dwight; **p. 322:** ©David Lassman/Image Works; **p. 327, p. 332:** ©PhotoDisc; **p. 333:** ©Laura Dwight/PhotoEdit; **p. 337:** ©Peter Dublin/Stock Boston; **p. 339:** ©Bob Daemmrich/Image Works; **p. 340:** ©Richard Orton ; **p. 343:** ©Ken Kerbs

Chapter 10

p. 348: ©Digital Vision; **p. 349:** ©Bettmann/Corbis Images, Los Angeles; **p. 352:** ©Michael Justice/Image Works; **p. 355:** ©Laura Dwight/PhotoEdit; **p. 359:** ©Chuck Pefley/Stock Boston/PictureQuest; **p. 360:** ©C. Boretz/Image Works; **p. 364:** ©Amy Etra/PhotoEdit; **p. 365:** ©James R. Holland/Stock Boston; **p. 366:** ©Mindy E. Klarman/Photo Researchers
p. 369: ©Dallas & John Heaton/Stock Boston; **p. 370:** ©Erika Stone; **p. 371:** ©Bob Daemmrich/Image Works; **p. 373:** ©David Young-Wolff/PhotoEdit; **p. 376:** ©Mike Siluk /Image Works

Chapter 11

p. 382: ©Bob Daemmrich/Image Works; **p. 383 (left):** ©Lori Adamski Peek/Getty Images; **p. 383 (right):** ©Arthur Tilley/Getty Images; **p. 384:** ©Lori Adamski Peek/Getty Images; **p. 385:** ©Culver Pictures; **p. 388:** ©AP/Wide World Photos; **p. 391:** ©Mary Kate Denny/PhotoEdit; **p. 392:** ©Robert Brenner/PhotoEdit; **p. 395:** ©David Young-Wolff/PhotoEdit; **p. 397:** ©Richard Nowitz/Photo Researchers; **p. 399, p. 400:** ©PhotoDisc; **p. 402:** ©Laura Dwight; **p. 412:** ©EyeWire; **p. 414:** ©Erika Stone; **p. 417:** ©David Young-Wolff/PhotoEdit

Chapter 12

p. 422: ©Arthur Tilley/Getty Images; **p. 423:** ©AP/Wide World Photos; **p. 426:** ©Miro Vintoniv/Stock Boston; **p. 429:** ©Bob Daemmrich/Image Works; **p. 432:** ©Ellen Skye; **p. 436:** Courtesy, The Children's Defense Fund; **p. 439:** ©Tim Greenway/AP/Wide World Photos; **p. 441:** ©Digital Vision; **p. 443:** ©Ruth Duskin Feldman; **p. 446:** ©Tom McCarthy/PhotoEdit; **p. 450:** ©Laura Rauch/AP/Wide World Photos

Chapter 13

p. 454: ©L. Koolvoord/Image Works; **p. 455 (left):** ©Bob Daemmrich/Image Works; **p. 455 (right):** ©AP/Wide World Photos; **p. 456:** ©Bob Daemmrich/Image Works; **p. 457:** ©Rob Straus/Woodfin Camp; **p. 459, p. 462, p. 463, p. 464:** ©PhotoDisc; **p. 466:** ©Lester Sloan/Getty Images News Services; **p. 468:** ©Corbis; **p. 471:** ©Mehau Kulyk/SPL/Photo Researchers; **p. 477:** ©David Young-Wolf/PhotoEdit; **p. 480:** ©Keith Carter Photography; **p. 484:** ©Charles Gupton/Stock Boston

Chapter 14

p. 490, p. 491: ©AP/Wide World Photos; **p. 494:** ©Corbis; **p. 496:** ©AP/Wide World Photos; **p. 498:** ©PhotoDisc; **p. 501:** ©Michael Dwyer/Stock Boston; **p. 505:** ©Ron Chapple/Getty Images; **p. 506 (both):** ©PhotoDisc; **p. 508:** ©AP/Wide World Photos; **p. 510, p. 513:** ©PhotoDisc

Chapter 15

p. 522: ©Paul Chesley/Getty Images; **p. 523 (left):** ©USDA/Science Source/Photo Researchers; **p. 523 (right):** ©PhotoDisc; **p. 524:** ©USDA/Science Source/Photo Researchers; **p. 525:** ©Kanu Ghandi/Library of Congress; **p. 528:** ©AP/Wide World Photos; **p. 530:** ©PhotoDisc; **p. 534:** ©Ron Chapple/Getty Images; **p. 537:** ©Brian Yarvin/Image Works; **p. 542:** ©Science Photo Library/Photo Researchers; **p. 544:** ©PhotoDisc; **p. 547, p. 549:** ©AP/Wide World Photos; **p. 553:** ©Tim Davis/Photo Researchers; **p. 557:** ©Ulf Andersen/Gamma; **p. 560:** ©Spencer Grant/PhotoEdit

Chapter 16

p. 564: ©PhotoDisc; **p. 565:** ©AP/Wide World Photos; **p. 569:** ©PhotoDisc; **p. 570:**

©Levine/Anthro-Photo; **p. 575:** ©AP/Wide World Photos; **p. 580:** ©PhotoDisc; **p. 583:** ©Corbis; **p. 584:** ©A. Ramey/Woodfin Camp; **p. 586:** ©PhotoDisc; **p. 591:** ©Chuck Savage/Corbis Images; **p. 595:** ©Cameramann/Image Works; **p. 596:** ©Tom McCarthy/Index Stock Imagery

Chapter 17

p. 602: ©Keren Su/Getty Images; **p. 603 (left):** ©David Young-Wolff/PhotoEdit; **p. 603 (right):** ©PhotoDisc; **p. 604:** ©David Young-Wolff/PhotoEdit; **p. 605:** ©NASA; **p. 609:** ©AP/Wide World Photos; **p. 612:** ©Digital Vision ; **p. 617:** ©Robert Ricci/Gamma; **p. 622:** ©Barbara Kirk/Corbis Stock Market; **p. 625:** ©Boiffin-Vivierre/Explorer/Photo Researchers; **p. 627:** ©Dr. Robert Friedland/Science Photo Library; **p. 630:** ©Oscar Burriel/Latin Stock/SPL/Photo Researchers; **p. 635:** ©Joe Carini/Image Works

Chapter 18

p. 644: ©PhotoDisc; **p. 645:** ©Evan Agostini/Getty Images News Services; **p. 648:** ©Corbis; **p. 650:** ©Skip O'Rourke/Image Works; **p. 653:** ©PhotoDisc; **p. 654:** ©Shelley Gazin/Corbis Impages; **p. 657:** ©Dave Bartriff/Image Works; **p. 662:** ©Spencer Grant/Stock Boston; **p. 666:** ©Blair Seitz/Photo Researchers; **p. 672:** ©Paul Fusco/Magnum Photos; **p. 673:** ©Bill Aron/PhotoEdit; **p. 674:** ©Cary Wolinsky/Stock Boston; **p. 676:** ©Matthew Jordan Smith/LVA Represents; **p. 677:** ©CLEO Photo/Index Stock Imagery

Chapter 19

p. 680: ©AP/Wide World Photos; **p. 681, 682:** ©Bob Daemmrich/Stock Boston; **p. 683:** ©AP/Orchard House/Wide World Photos; **p. 686:** ©Corbis; **p. 687:** ©Richard Pasley/Stock Boston; **p. 690, p. 695 (both), p. 699:** ©PhotoDisc; **p. 704:** ©Image100.

Name Index

Subject Index

boldface terms indicate key terms; **boldface** page references indicate pages on which they are defined.